*The*

AMERICAN HERITAGE®

# DICTIONARY OF IDIOMS

## FOR STUDENTS OF ENGLISH

HOUGHTON MIFFLIN COMPANY
BOSTON • NEW YORK

Director, World Languages: Marketing and ESL Publishing Susan Maguire
Senior Associate Editor Kathy Sands Boehmer
Editorial Assistant Manuel Muñoz
Development Editor Angela Castro
Project Editor Tracy Patruno
Senior Manufacturing Coordinator Priscilla J. Bailey
Marketing Manager Jay Hu
Marketing Assistant Claudia Martínez

Writers Linda Butler, Julia Penelope
Adapted from *The American Heritage® Dictionary of Idioms* by Christine Ammer

Cover design Rebecca Fagan



Printed in the U.S.A.

*Library of Congress Cataloging-in-Publication Data*

The American heritage dictionary of idioms for students of English.
p. cm.
ISBN 0-395-97619-7 (cloth)—ISBN 0-395-97620-0 (paper)
1. English language—United States—Idioms—Dictionaries. 2. English language—United States—Terms and phrases. 3. English language—Textbooks for foreign speakers. 4. English language—Idioms—Dictionaries. 5. Americanisms—Dictionaries. I. Houghton Mifflin Company.

PE2839.A46 2000
423'.1—dc21 00-040732

Hardcover ISBN: 0-395-97619-7
Paperback ISBN: 0-395-97620-0

3456789-DOC-04

As part of Houghton Mifflin's ongoing
commitment to the environment, this text
has been printed on recycled paper.

# GUIDE TO USING THIS BOOK

*The American Heritage® Dictionary of Idioms for Students of English* provides intermediate and advanced learners of English with an up-to-date collection of the idioms, set phrases, proverbs, and two-part verbs (phrasal verbs) they are likely to hear in the media and in daily conversations, and their most common meanings. Such idioms and phrases occur frequently in informal English and, because the meaning of idioms cannot be determined from the literal senses of words, students learning English may often have difficulty interpreting them. For example, if a person is described as "having ants in his (or her) pants," it should not be understood to mean that someone actually has live ants crawling around in his or her clothing. Rather, it describes an individual who behaves in a restless, impatient, or nervous manner.

The entries in the dictionary also provide readers with information about the context in which an idiom is most commonly used, or explain the origin of a particular usage. The diagram of the idiom **all over** illustrates the kinds of information readers can find in each entry and where it will be found.

## Entries

Each entry begins with the idiom in boldface type, for example, **abide by** and **about to.** Idioms that are always used with a specific verb have a comma followed by that verb, for

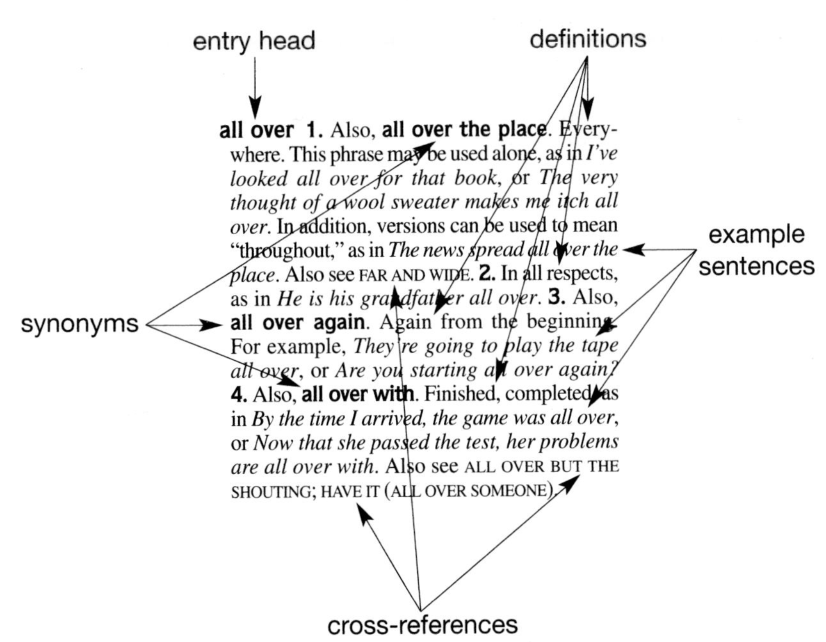
entry head
definitions
example sentences
synonyms
cross-references
**all over 1.** Also, **all over the place**. Everywhere. This phrase may be used alone, as in *I've looked all over for that book,* or *The very thought of a wool sweater makes me itch all over.* In addition, versions can be used to mean "throughout," as in *The news spread all over the place.* Also see FAR AND WIDE. **2.** In all respects, as in *He is his grandfather all over.* **3.** Also, **all over again**. Again from the beginning. For example, *They're going to play the tape all over,* or *Are you starting all over again?* **4.** Also, **all over with**. Finished, completed, as in *By the time I arrived, the game was all over,* or *Now that she passed the test, her problems are all over with.* Also see ALL OVER BUT THE SHOUTING; HAVE IT (ALL OVER SOMEONE).

example, **all in, be** and **ants in one's pants, have,** also in boldface. If a determiner such as *a/an* or *the* must be used with an idiom, that information is also shown in boldface following a comma, for example, **accident waiting to happen, an**. In addition, variations of idioms that have the same meaning are shown in boldface type before the definition. For example, **all kidding aside** has exactly the same meaning as **all joking aside,** the main entry; **on the lines of** means the same thing as **along the lines of** (main entry); and **at first sight** is a variation of **at first glance** (main entry). Also set in boldface type, but set off by parentheses, are parts of proverbs that speakers now often omit because the entire proverb is well known to them. For example, at the entry for **all work and no play,** the part of the proverb that is often omitted, **makes Jack a dull boy,** is provided within parentheses.

Students will also find related or similar expressions in boldface type within the text of an entry. For example, the entry for **above suspicion** also discusses the idiom **above the law,** which is similar to *above suspicion* but means something different. Phrases and idioms that have more than one meaning have numbered definitions, with the definitions usually given in the order of frequency of use. The entry for **at home**, for example, has five definitions and begins with "In one's own residence. . .," the most commonly used meaning. The entry ends with "In team sports, playing on one's own field or in one's own town. . .," the idiom's least common (or more specialized) meaning.

Example sentences appear in italic type and cross-references in small capitals.

## Alphabetization and Cross-References

Entries in the dictionary are arranged in alphabetical order, letter by letter up to the comma in those entries that have required or sometimes omitted elements. For example, **all things being equal** comes before **all things considered,** and **all things considered** is followed by **all things to all people, be** (a required element).

To find the entry for a particular idiom, readers may sometimes be unsure about which word has been chosen for its main entry. Is *beat around (about) the bush* under *beat, around,* or *about*? Is *accidentally on purpose* at *accidentally, on,* or *purpose*? To help sort out these problems, entries listing cross-references for key words appear alphabetically among the main entries. At **about,** for example, readers are told that,

> In addition to the idioms beginning with ABOUT, also see AT ABOUT; BEAT AROUND (ABOUT) THE BUSH; BRING ABOUT; CAST ABOUT; . . .

If readers look up *of one's own accord* at *accord*, they will find a cross-reference to *of one's own accord,* where the definition will be found. If they search for *aboveboard* at *aboveboard,* a cross-reference will tell them that the main entry is *open and aboveboard.* If, however, a cross-referenced entry would immediately follow the main entry in which it is mentioned, the entry has been omitted. For example, because the idiom **after-hours club** would immediately follow the entry **after hours,** it has been omitted as a main entry. In contrast, **after a sort,** a synonym for **after a fashion,** does have a main entry where readers are told to go back and read the entry

**after a fashion,** because two entries separate **after a sort** and **after a fashion.**

By checking these key-word entries, readers can locate every phrase treated as an entry in this book. The reader who does not find *as luck would have it* under *as* can look under the entries beginning with the next word, *luck.* If more help is needed, the entry for the word *luck* itself lists all the idioms containing that word that appear elsewhere in the dictionary.

Both synonyms (phrases that mean the same thing as an expression) and antonyms (phrases that have the opposite meaning of an expression) are also provided in cross-references. At the end of the entry **about time, it's,** for example, readers are told that they can also read the entry for its synonym, *high time.* Similarly, at the end of the entry for **at best,** readers are told that an antonym can be found at *at worst.* Variants or related expressions that are covered under other entry words appear in parentheses in the cross-references. Thus, at the entry **soft** the reader is referred to **hard (soft) sell**, which means that the entry **hard sell** also treats the phrase *soft sell.* Note, however, that words in parentheses are *not* considered part of the alphabetical order, so one should look for *hard sell,* not *hard soft sell.*

## Variable Pronouns

Many idioms can be used with different pronouns, as, for example, *clean up his act, clean up her act, clean up my act.* Consequently, the pronouns *one* and *someone* are used in entry words and variants to indicate that the object or possessive pronoun in the idiom may vary according to context. *One* or *one's* means that the antecedent of the pronoun must be the subject of the clause, or in some cases an inanimate noun or gerund must be the subject. For example, the idiom *hit one's stride* can appear in a sentence such as *She finally hit her stride,* or the idiom *serve one right* can be used in a sentence such as *It serves him right to be thrown off the team.* But note that sentences like *She finally hit his stride* are not possible.

The use of *someone* or *someone's* in the idiom means that the pronoun can be replaced only by a noun or pronoun that does *not* refer to the grammatical subject of the clause. In other words, the action of the verb is directed from one person to another (the "someone"). For example, the idiom *call someone's bluff* implies that you (or he or she or they) can only call someone else's bluff, never your (or his or her or their) own.

## Labels

In general, most idioms are used only in ordinary speech and informal writing but not in more formal contexts. For this reason, the label *colloquial* (or *informal*) has not been provided in this dictionary. However, some labels are provided to guide learners in the use of idioms that might be considered rude, insulting, or offensive. These are provided at the end of an entry or definition in single quotation marks. *Slang* indicates that a phrase or idiom is appropriate only to very informal contexts or is used to suggest that the speaker is critical of what is generally held to be true. *Vulgar slang* indicates that a phrase is considered offensive by most speakers. The absence of such a label indicates that a term is considered standard English and so is acceptable in formal situations.

Many entries also provide some information about the idiom's origin and development. At the phrasal verb **ace it,** for example, readers will find that the expression has developed from the verb *ace*, used in tennis to refer to a serve that an opponent cannot return, and, with the addition of the object *it,* became a slang term used by students for getting an "A" on a test or in a course. Now the idiom is used to describe any successful activity.

The idioms in a language can tell us much about the people who use it and the worldview of the dominant culture. *The American Heritage Dictionary of Idioms for Students of English* will provide students of English with useful information about the language and the people who use it.

# Aa

**A** see FROM SOUP TO NUTS (A TO Z).

**aback** see TAKE ONE ABACK.

**abide** In addition to the idiom beginning with ABIDE, also see CAN'T STAND (ABIDE).

**abide by** Accept and follow a decision or set of rules; also, remain faithful to something. For example, *All members must agree to abide by the club regulations*, or *A trustworthy person abides by his or her word.*

**a bit** **1.** A small amount of anything; also, a short period of time. For example, *Here's a bit of meat*, or *I'll be ready in a bit*, or *Just wait a bit.* **2.** Somewhat or rather, as in *It stings a bit*, or *Will you have a bit more to eat?* Also see BIT BY BIT; NOT A BIT.

**about** In addition to the idioms beginning with ABOUT, also see AT ABOUT; BEAT AROUND (ABOUT) THE BUSH; BRING ABOUT; CAST ABOUT; COME ABOUT; DO AN ABOUT-FACE; GET ABOUT; GO ABOUT (ONE'S BUSINESS); HOW ABOUT; HOW ABOUT THAT; JUST ABOUT; KNOCK ABOUT; LAY ABOUT ONE; MAN ABOUT TOWN; NOSE ABOUT; NO TWO WAYS ABOUT IT; ORDER SOMEONE ABOUT; OUT AND ABOUT; SEE ABOUT; SEND SOMEONE ABOUT SOMEONE'S BUSINESS; SET ABOUT; THAT'S ABOUT THE SIZE OF IT; UP AND ABOUT; WHAT ABOUT SOMEONE (SOMETHING).

**about time, it's** **1.** Long past the right time, as in *It's about time you got here.* **2.** Approximately the right time, as in *It's about time you went to bed.* For a synonym, see HIGH TIME.

**about to** **1.** Ready to or almost ready to do something, as in *I was about to leave when it began to rain*, or *He hasn't finished yet, but he's about to.* **2. not about to**. Having no intention of doing something, as in *She was not about to call her friend*, or *Are you staying longer? No, I'm not about to.*

**above** In addition to the idioms beginning with ABOVE, also see ALL (NONE) OF THE ABOVE; CUT ABOVE; HEAD AND SHOULDERS ABOVE; OVER AND ABOVE.

**above all** More than anything else, as in *Above all, you should be careful driving at night.* Also see FIRST AND LAST.

**above and beyond** More than is required, as in *She went above and beyond.* This somewhat redundant expression—*above* and *beyond* here both express excess—often precedes **the call of duty**; the resulting phrase means doing more than a particular job requires. Thus, *Working overtime without pay is above and beyond the call of duty.* Also see OVER AND ABOVE.

**aboveboard** see OPEN AND ABOVEBOARD.

**above suspicion** So trustworthy as never to be suspected of doing wrong, as in *Whatever you do, your motives must be above suspicion.* A similar phrase using *above* in the sense of "beyond" is **above the law**, which usually describes an individual or a business behaving as though exempt from rules or laws that apply to others.

**above the law** see under ABOVE SUSPICION.

**absence** In addition to the idiom beginning with ABSENCE, also see CONSPICUOUS BY ITS ABSENCE.

**absence makes the heart grow fonder** Separation makes love stronger, as in *After a year in another country, she accepted his proposal; I guess absence makes the heart grow fonder.* The opposite sentiment is expressed by FAMILIARITY BREEDS CONTEMPT.

**absent without leave** Away without permission or explanation, as in *Her daughter went to the mall but got in trouble for being absent without leave.* The term and its acronym, **AWOL**, originated in the U.S. military during World War I for soldiers absent from duty without permission (leave). It later was transferred to civilian situations, as in *John didn't just cut his Tuesday classes; he went AWOL.*

**accidentally on purpose** see ON PURPOSE, def. 2.

**accident waiting to happen, an** A person or an object that will probably cause an unpleasant or dangerous situation. For example, *He drives when he's drunk, so he's an accident waiting to happen*, or *That unstable pile of books on the table is an accident waiting to happen.* Also see RECIPE FOR DISASTER; SPELL DISASTER.

**accord** see OF ONE'S OWN ACCORD.

**according to all accounts** see BY ALL ACCOUNTS.

**account** In addition to the idiom beginning with ACCOUNT, also see ALL PRESENT AND ACCOUNTED FOR; BY ALL ACCOUNTS; GIVE A GOOD ACCOUNT; NO ACCOUNTING FOR TASTES; ON ACCOUNT OF; ON NO ACCOUNT; ON ONE'S OWN ACCOUNT; TAKE ACCOUNT OF; TAKE INTO ACCOUNT.

**account for** **1.** Be the determining factor in something; cause. For example, *The heat*

*accounts for the high power use*, or *Icy roads account for the increase in accidents.* **2.** Explain or justify something, as in *They were upset because their son couldn't account for the three hours between his last class and his arrival at home.* Both of these related usages are derived from the literal meaning of the phrase, that is, "make a reckoning of an account."

**accustomed to** Used to something or someone; having the habit of doing something. For example, *In Spain we gave up our usual schedule and became accustomed to eating dinner at 10 o'clock at night.*

**ace** In addition to the idioms beginning with ACE, also see HOLD ALL THE ACES.

**ace in the hole** A hidden advantage or resource kept in reserve until needed, as in *The prosecutor had an ace in the hole: an eyewitness.* The term comes from stud poker, a card game in which each player is dealt one card face down—the hole card—and the rest face up. If the hole card is an ace, the player has a hidden advantage. *Hole* here simply means "a hiding place."

**ace it** Do something successfully, as in *I'm sure she'll ace it when she takes that bar exam.* The verb *ace* originated in tennis with the meaning "hit an unreturnable serve against an opponent." The idiom **ace it**, however, originated as student slang for getting an "A" on an exam or in a course, but it soon was extended to other successful accomplishments.

**Achilles' heel** A major weakness, a weak area, as in *This division, which is rarely profitable, is the company's Achilles' heel.* The term refers to the Greek legend about the heroic warrior Achilles, whose mother tried to make him immortal by holding the infant by his heel and dipping him into the River Styx. Eventually he was killed by an arrow shot into his undipped heel.

**acid test** A decisive trial to determine worth or quality, as in *Her first time defending a client will be her acid test as a lawyer.* This term was originally used to refer to a chemical test for distinguishing gold from other metals.

**acquaintance** see NODDING ACQUAINTANCE.

**acquired taste, an** Something one learns to like over time rather than immediately. For example, *Because it is so salty, caviar is an acquired taste*, or *With its decorative detail, this furniture is definitely an acquired taste.*

**across** In addition to the idiom beginning with ACROSS, also see COME ACROSS; CUT ACROSS; GET ACROSS; PUT ACROSS; RUN ACROSS.

**across the board** Applying to all the individuals in a group, as in *The governor promised a tax cut across the board*, that is, one applying to all taxpayers, regardless of income. The phrase can also be used as an adjective, as in *The new law would guarantee across-the-board savings for every taxpayer.* This expression comes from horseracing and refers to a bet that covers all possible ways of winning money on a race: win (first), place (second), or show (third). The *board* here is the notice board on which the races and betting odds are listed.

**act** In addition to the idioms beginning with ACT, also see CATCH SOMEONE RED-HANDED (IN THE ACT); CLEAN UP (ONE'S ACT); DO A DISAPPEARING ACT; GET INTO THE ACT; GET ONE'S ACT TOGETHER; HARD (TOUGH) ACT TO FOLLOW; HIGH-WIRE ACT; IN THE ACT; PUT ON AN ACT.

**action** In addition to the idiom beginning with ACTION, also see ALL TALK (AND NO ACTION); PIECE OF THE ACTION; SWING INTO ACTION.

**actions speak louder than words** What one does is more important than what one says, as in *Politicians need to be reminded that actions speak louder than words.* Also see ALL TALK (AND NO ACTION); DO AS I SAY, NOT AS I DO.

**active** In addition to the idiom beginning with ACTIVE, also see HAVE AN ACTIVE FANTASY LIFE.

**active duty** Full-time service, as in *Mr. Smith is 81, but he still comes to the office every day and is very much on active duty.* This term comes from the military. It is the opposite of *reserve*, which refers to troops still in the military but not actively engaged. It is occasionally used in a nonmilitary sense, as in the example.

**act of faith** Behavior that shows or tests a person's religious or other beliefs, as in *Rock climbing with a new, inexperienced partner was a real act of faith.* The term is a translation of the Portuguese *auto da fé,* which referred to the sentencing and execution of nonbelievers during the Inquisition. In modern times it is used for less serious reasons.

**act of God** An unforeseen and uncontrollable natural event, such as a hurricane, fire, or flood. For example, *The publisher shall publish the work within twelve months except in case of delay caused by acts of God such as fires or floods or other circumstances beyond its control.* This phrase often appears in legal contracts.

**act on** Also, **act upon**. Behave in a certain way as a result of information received or as a result of another action, as in *I will act on my lawyer's advice*, or *The manager refused to act upon the hotel guest's complaints.*

**act one's age** Behave more maturely. The phrase often is used to ask children to act in a more grown-up fashion, as in *Only babies suck their thumbs; act your age.* It also may refer to an adult who is acting much younger than might be considered appropriate, as in

*You're almost 40. When will you start acting your age?*

**act out 1.** Perform or play something or someone, as in *As she read to the class, the teacher had each child act out a different character in the story.* **2.** Express feelings through one's behavior, without being aware of it. For example, *Is he really angry at you, or is he just acting out a childhood frustration?* This term is sometimes used without an object to mean "misbehave," as in *The child is acting out in class.* In both usages, *out* means "openly" or "publicly."

**act up 1.** Misbehave. For example, *With an inexperienced rider, this horse always acts up.* **2.** Fail to work properly, as in *I'm not sure what's wrong with my car, but it is acting up.* In both usages, *up* means "abnormally."

**act upon** see ACT ON.

**Adam** see NOT KNOW FROM ADAM; OLD AS THE HILLS (ADAM).

**add fuel to the fire** Also, **add fuel to the flames.** Make a bad situation worse, often by increasing anger, hostility, or passion, as in *She was upset, and your making fun of her just added fuel to the fire.* Also see ADD INSULT TO INJURY; FAN THE FLAMES.

**add insult to injury** Hurt a person's feelings after doing him or her harm; also, make a bad situation worse. For example, *Not only did the company fire him, but it published a list of the fired workers—that's adding insult to injury,* or *The nearest parking space was half a mile away, and then, to add insult to injury, it began to rain.*

**addition** see IN ADDITION.

**add up 1.** Amount to an expected or a correct total, as in *These figures don't add up,* that is, they are not correct. **2.** Be consistent, make sense, as in *I'm not sure that all this testimony will add up.* Both senses are often used in a negative way, as in the first example. Also see ADD UP TO.

**add up to** Amount to something, mean, as in *The smooth airline connections, luxury hotel, and fine weather added up to the best vacation we'd ever had.* Also see ADD UP.

**ad hoc** For the special purpose at hand; also, improvised. The term is Latin for "to this," and it is most often used for committees established for a specific purpose, as in *The committee was formed ad hoc to address health insurance problems.* The term is also used as an adjective, as in *An ad hoc committee was formed.*

**admiration** see MUTUAL ADMIRATION SOCIETY.

**ad nauseam** To ridiculous excess, to a sickening degree. For example, *I wish he'd drop the subject; we have heard about budget cuts ad nauseam.* The term is Latin for "to 'the point of' nausea."

**a drag** An uninteresting experience, a bore, as in *After several thousand times, signing your autograph can be a drag.* This expression probably uses *drag* in the sense of something that prevents movement or progress.

**advance** see IN ADVANCE; MAKE ADVANCES.

**advantage** see GET THE ADVANTAGE OF; SHOW TO ADVANTAGE; TAKE ADVANTAGE OF; TO ADVANTAGE.

**advocate** see DEVIL'S ADVOCATE.

**a far cry** see FAR CRY FROM.

**a few** A small number of people or things. This phrase differs from *few* used without the article *a,* which means "not many." For example, *The party was supposed to end at eight o'clock, but a few guests stayed until midnight* means that a small number of guests remained, but *The party began at eight, and few people attended* means that not many guests came. Also see QUITE A BIT (FEW).

**afoul of** see RUN AFOUL OF.

**afraid of one's own shadow** Very timid and fearful, as in *He constantly worries about security; he's afraid of his own shadow.*

**after** In addition to the idioms beginning with AFTER, also see DAY AFTER DAY; GET AFTER; GO AFTER; INQUIRE AFTER; KEEP AFTER; LIVE HAPPILY EVER AFTER; LOOK AFTER; MORNING AFTER; NAME AFTER; RUN AFTER; SEE AFTER; SOUGHT AFTER; TAKE AFTER; THROW GOOD MONEY AFTER BAD; TIME AFTER TIME.

**after a fashion** Also, **after a sort.** Somehow or other; not very well, as in *I can read music, after a fashion,* or *We managed to paint the house, after a sort.* In the first phrase *fashion* means "a manner of doing something." Also see IN A WAY; (SOMEHOW) OR OTHER.

**after all 1.** In spite of everything, nevertheless, as in *The plane took off half an hour late but landed on time after all.* **2.** After everything else has been considered, finally, as in *She has final approval of the guest list; after all, it's her wedding.* The two usages are pronounced differently, the first giving stress to the word *after* and the second to the word *all.* Also see WHEN ALL'S SAID AND DONE.

**after all's said and done** see WHEN ALL'S SAID AND DONE.

**after a sort** see AFTER A FASHION.

**after a while** see IN A WHILE.

**after hours** After normal working hours, after closing time; also, after legal or established opening hours. For example, *I don't have time while I'm working, but I can see you after hours,* or *The restaurant employees sometimes stayed for a meal after hours.* This term originally referred to laws governing business hours. It also led to the term **after-hours club**, for a drinking club that remained open later than similar establishments.

A

**after one's own heart** To one's own personal liking, as in *He's very patient with the students; he's a teacher after my own heart.*

**after the fact** After an actual event, especially after a crime. For example, *I know the roof should have been repaired, but that doesn't help much after the fact.*

**again** In addition to the idiom beginning with AGAIN, also see COME AGAIN; DO SOMETHING OVER AGAIN; EVERY NOW AND AGAIN; HERE GOES (SOMEONE GOES AGAIN); NOW AND AGAIN; OFF AND ON (OFF AGAIN, ON AGAIN); OVER AGAIN; SOMETHING ELSE AGAIN; TIME AFTER TIME (TIME AND AGAIN); YET AGAIN; YOU CAN SAY THAT AGAIN.

**again and again** Repeatedly, often, as in *I've told you again and again, don't turn up the heat.* This idiom uses repetition for the purpose of emphasis, as does its synonym, OVER AND OVER.

**against** In addition to the idioms beginning with AGAINST, also see BEAT ONE'S HEAD AGAINST THE WALL; CARDS ARE STACKED AGAINST; COME UP AGAINST; COUNT AGAINST; DEAD SET AGAINST; HAVE SOMETHING AGAINST; HOLD SOMETHING AGAINST; LIFT A HAND AGAINST; PIT SOMEONE AGAINST; RUN AGAINST; SET SOMEONE AGAINST; SWIM AGAINST; TURN ONE AGAINST; TWO STRIKES AGAINST; UP AGAINST.

**against all odds** In spite of seeming very unlikely, as in *Against all odds we had a snowstorm in early May*, or *Against all odds the slower team won.*

**against one's better judgment** In spite of one's serious concerns or objections, as in *Against my better judgment, I told her to come whenever she pleased.*

**against one's will** Without one's consent, forcibly, as in *The defendant knew he could not be made to testify against his will.* Originally one meaning of *will* was "consent," but this sense survives only in this idiom, which today nearly always suggests some use of force.

**against the clock** Also, **against time**. In a great hurry, as fast as possible, as in *With her term paper due on Monday, she was racing against the clock to finish it*, or *They were working against time to stay on schedule.* The term comes from sports in which the contestants do not directly compete against each other but instead are timed individually, the winner being the one who is fastest.

**against the grain** Opposed to one's wishes or preference, as in *We followed the new supervisor's advice, though it went against the grain.* This term refers to the natural direction of the fibers in a piece of wood, called its *grain*; when sawed "against the grain," the wood tends to splinter. For a synonym, see RUB THE WRONG WAY.

**against the tide** see SWIM AGAINST THE TIDE.

**against time** see AGAINST THE CLOCK.

**age** see ACT ONE'S AGE; COON'S AGE; GOLDEN AGE; IN THIS DAY AND AGE; OF AGE; RIPE OLD AGE; UNDER AGE.

**agenda** see HIDDEN AGENDA.

**a goner** Something or someone that is dead, doomed, or ruined, as in *If this new drug doesn't work, he's a goner*, or *Without a new engine, my car's a goner.*

**a good deal** Also, **a great deal**. See under GOOD DEAL.

**agree to differ** Accept a difference of opinion, as in *We agreed to differ about whose parents were strangest.*

**ahead** In addition to the idioms beginning with AHEAD, also see COME OUT AHEAD; DEAD AHEAD; FULL SPEED AHEAD; GET AHEAD; GO AHEAD; ONE JUMP AHEAD; QUIT WHILE ONE'S AHEAD.

**ahead of one's time** In advance of current ideas, customs, or methods, as in *His treatment of light showed this painter to be well ahead of his time*, or *Wearing pants and smoking cigars marked Amy Lowell as a woman ahead of her time.* This idiom uses *time* in the sense of "era" or "generation." The phrase is usually but not always used to express approval.

**ahead of the game** In a position of advantage, especially financially; succeeding or winning. For example, *If we can sell 2,000 units of this product by next month, we'll be well ahead of the game.* This idiom uses *ahead of* in the sense of "in advance of," and transfers success in gambling (*the game*) to winning in other areas. Also see COME OUT AHEAD.

**ahead of time** Earlier, sooner, as in *The meeting was scheduled for three o'clock, but most people arrived ahead of time.*

**aim** In addition to the idiom beginning with AIM, also see TAKE AIM.

**aim to** Try or intend to do something, as in *We aim to please*, or *She aims to fly to California.* This term comes from *aim* in the sense of "direct the course of something," such as an arrow or a bullet.

**air** In addition to the idiom beginning with AIR, also see BREATH OF FRESH AIR; CASTLES IN THE AIR; CLEAR THE AIR; HOT AIR; IN THE AIR; INTO (OUT OF) THIN AIR; NOSE IN THE AIR; OFF THE AIR; PUT ON AIRS; UP IN THE AIR; WALK ON AIR; WASH (AIR) ONE'S DIRTY LINEN.

**air one's grievances** Complain publicly, as in *Jane was afraid to complain at work but freely aired her grievances at home.*

**à la** Like, in the manner of, as in *He hoped to break all records, à la Babe Ruth.* This expression is an abbreviation of the French phrase *à la mode de,* meaning "in the manner of."

**alarm** see FALSE ALARM.

**albatross around one's neck** A burden of guilt that becomes an obstacle to success, as in *The failed real estate scheme became an albatross around her neck, for now she could not interest other investors in a new project.*

**aleck** see SMART ALECK.

**alert** see ON THE ALERT.

**a little** **1.** A small amount, as in *Will you have some more meat? Yes, just a little.* **2.** Somewhat or rather, slightly, as in *I am a little annoyed with you.* For a synonym, see A BIT.

**a little bird** see LITTLE BIRD.

**alive** In addition to the idioms beginning with ALIVE, also see COME ALIVE; EAT SOMEONE ALIVE; LOOK ALIVE; MORE DEAD THAN ALIVE; SKIN ALIVE.

**alive and kicking** Also, **alive and well**. Alive and alert; living and healthy. For example, *She's completely recovered; she's alive and kicking*, or *You're quite mistaken; our lawyer is alive and well.* The first expression, sometimes shortened to **live and kicking**, originally was used by people selling fish to convince customers of their freshness. The variant originated as a denial of someone's reported death.

**alive with** Full of something, as in *During the sale, the store was alive with customers.*

**all** In addition to the idioms beginning with ALL, also see ABOVE ALL; AFTER ALL; AGAINST ALL ODDS; AS ALL GET-OUT; AT ALL; AT ALL COSTS; BE-ALL AND END-ALL; BEAT ALL; BY ALL ACCOUNTS; BY ALL MEANS; BY ALL ODDS; CAP IT ALL; DOWNHILL ALL THE WAY; FALL ALL OVER; FIRST OF ALL; FOR ALL; FOR ALL (ONE CARES); FOR ALL (ONE KNOWS); FOR ALL ONE IS WORTH; FOR ALL THAT; GET AWAY (FROM IT ALL); GET ONE'S ACT (IT ALL) TOGETHER; GO ALL THE WAY; HAVE ALL ONE'S MARBLES; HAVE IT (ALL OVER SOMEONE); HAVE IT BOTH WAYS (ALL); HOLD ALL THE ACES; IN (ALL OF) A DITHER; IN ALL; IN ALL ONE'S BORN DAYS; IN ALL PROBABILITY; IN (ALL GOOD) CONSCIENCE; (ALL) IN THE SAME BOAT; IT'S ALL OVER WITH; IT TAKES ALL SORTS; JUMP ALL OVER; KNOW ALL THE ANSWERS; KNOW-IT-ALL; LAUGH ALL THE WAY TO THE BANK; LEAST OF ALL; LET IT ALL HANG OUT; NOT ALL IT'S CRACKED UP TO BE; NOT FOR ALL THE TEA IN CHINA; NO TIME AT ALL; OF ALL THINGS; ONCE AND FOR ALL; ONE AND ALL; PULL OUT ALL THE STOPS; PUT ALL ONE'S EGGS IN ONE BASKET; SEEN ONE, SEEN THEM ALL; TILL ALL HOURS; TO ALL INTENTS AND PURPOSES; TOP IT ALL OFF; (ALL) TO THE GOOD; TURN OUT ALL RIGHT; WALK ALL OVER; WARTS AND ALL; WHEN ALL'S SAID AND DONE; WITH ALL DUE RESPECT; WITH ALL ONE'S HEART; YOU CAN'T WIN 'EM ALL.

**all along** From the start, throughout, as in *I've known he was innocent all along.* Also see ALL ALONG THE LINE.

**all along the line** Also, **(all the way) down the line**. At every point, stage, or moment. For example, *We've had problems with this company all along the line*, or *He's been very helpful all the way down the line.* The *line* originally referred to a row of troops. Also see SOMEWHERE ALONG THE LINE.

**all at once** **1.** All at the same time, as in *We can't get inside all at once, so please wait your turn.* **2.** Suddenly, unexpectedly, as in *All at once the sky darkened.* For a synonym, see ALL OF A SUDDEN.

**all at sea** see AT SEA, def. 2.

**all better** Completely healed or cured, as in *Once we've bandaged it up, you'll be all better.* This term is often used to comfort a child who has been hurt. It uses *all* in the sense of "entirely" and *better* in the sense of "cured."

**all but** Almost, nearly, as in *I've all but finished the book.*

**all-clear, give *one* the** Also, **get the all-clear**. Be told or tell somebody that a potentially dangerous situation is over. For example, *Did you get the all-clear on the project?* or *Give me the all-clear when she leaves.* The verbs in these phrases indicate whether one is making a signal or receiving it.

**all day, (not) take** Also, **(not) take all week** or **(not) take all year; (not) have all day** or **(not) got all day**. A phrase used to tell somebody to move or do something faster. For example, *Please don't take all day to give me an answer*, or *Let's get this over with; I don't have all day.*

**all dressed up with no place to go** Also, **all dressed up but** or **and** or **but with** or **and with no place to go**. Ready to go somewhere or do something but finding out that the event has been canceled or your help is no longer needed. For example, *There I was, all dressed up with no place to go after the concert was canceled.*

**all ears** Eager to hear something, listening attentively, as in *Tell me who else was invited? I'm all ears.* Also see ALL EYES.

**alley** see BLIND ALLEY; RIGHT UP ONE'S ALLEY.

**all eyes** Watching very closely, as in *The reporters at the fashion show were all eyes.* Also see ALL EARS.

**all for** Completely in favor of something or someone, as in *I'm all for eating before we leave*, or *The players are all for the new soccer coach.*

**all for the best** Also, **for the best**. The best despite problems. It is often a response to an unhappy outcome, as in *They had to sell their business, but since they weren't making money, it's probably all for the best*, or *The dress had* *been sold when she went back, but because it was a little too tight, it's for the best.*

**all gone** Completely finished or used up, as in *There's no milk left; it's all gone.*

**all hours** At unusual times, as in *You can't come home at all hours and expect your supper to be ready.* The expression can also mean "late at night," as in *College students like to stay up talking until all hours.* It is sometimes expanded into **all hours of the day and night**.

**all in, be** **1.** Be tired out or exhausted, as in *I can't walk another step; I'm all in.* **2.** In card games, especially poker, be out of money, as in *I'm finished for the night; I'm all in.*

**all in a day's work** Also, **all in the day's work**. Expected and normal, as in *I had 20 phone calls in an hour—it's all in the day's work.* This phrase is sometimes used as an ironic comment on an unpleasant but not abnormal situation.

**all in all** Considering everything, as in *All in all our trip to Europe was a success.*

**all in good time** see IN GOOD TIME.

**all in one piece** Also, **in one piece**. Entirely undamaged or unharmed, as in *Given all the airport delays and bad weather, we were glad to arrive all in one piece*, or *She was relieved when they returned from Nepal in one piece.*

**all in the family** Kept within or limited to one's nearest relatives or very close friends, as in *We're trying to keep news of her illness all in the family*, or *Of course I loaned her the money; it's all in the family.*

**all in the same boat** see IN THE SAME BOAT.

**all is not lost** There's still a way to achieve a goal or get what is desired, as in *The car has a flat tire, but all is not lost, we'll find a ride to the airport.*

**all joking aside** Also, **all kidding aside**. Seriously, as in *I know I said I'd quit, but all joking aside, this job is too much for one person*, or *All kidding aside, I hate to lose at chess.* This phrase often accompanies a joking or ironic statement.

**all kinds of** **1.** Also, **all manner of** or **all sorts of**. All or many varieties of something, as in *Before the banquet, they served all kinds of drinks*, or *The store sold fruit of all sorts*, or *The museum featured all manner of historical exhibits.* **2.** A large amount of something, as in *She has all kinds of money.*

**all of** **1.** The entire amount of something, as in *The baby ate all of her cereal.* **2.** No less than, at least, as in *Although he looked much younger, he was all of seventy.*

**all of a sudden** Entirely without warning, abruptly, as in *All of a sudden the lights went out.* Also see ALL AT ONCE, def. 2.

**all of it** Absolutely the best; superior. For example, *You can tell by the way he walks that he thinks he's all of it.* Also see ALL THAT.

**all of the above** Also, **none of the above**. Each one (not any) of the above-named alternatives. For example, *Have you decided to quit, or do you want to find another job first? None of the above.* These phrases originated as answers to a multiple-choice question on a test but are now often used as a form of avoiding a direct answer. They use *above* in the sense of "preceding."

**all of the best** see ALL THE BEST.

**all one** see ALL THE SAME, def. 1.

**all out** With all one's strength, ability, or resources. For example, *They are going all out to make the party a success.* This term once meant "completely" or "wholly." It now refers to making a great effort and is also used as an adjective, as in *They made an all-out effort to finish the project.* This usage earlier referred to races and other kinds of athletic events. Also see GO WHOLE HOG.

**all outdoors, big as** see BIG AS LIFE, def. 2.

**all over** **1.** Also, **all over the place**. Everywhere. This phrase may be used alone, as in *I've looked all over for that book*, or *The very thought of a wool sweater makes me itch all over.* In addition, versions can be used to mean "throughout," as in *The news spread all over the place.* Also see FAR AND WIDE. **2.** In all respects, as in *He is his grandfather all over.* **3.** Also, **all over again**. Again from the beginning. For example, *They're going to play the tape all over*, or *Are you starting all over again?* **4.** Also, **all over with**. Finished, completed, as in *By the time I arrived, the game was all over*, or *Now that she passed the test, her problems are all over with.* Also see ALL OVER BUT THE SHOUTING; HAVE IT (ALL OVER SOMEONE).

**all over but the shouting** The end result is a certainty, as in *When the batter hit the ball over the fence, it was all over but the shouting.* A common British version is **all over bar the shouting**.

**all over for one** see IT'S ALL OVER WITH.

**all over one** **1.** In close physical contact. For example, *Whenever I visit, that dog of Jane's is all over me.* **2.** Affecting one in a very annoying way, as in *His attitude gets all over me.* Also see FALL ALL OVER ONE; HAVE IT (ALL OVER SOMEONE).

**all over the place** Also, **all over town** or **all over the world** See ALL OVER, def. 1.

**all over with** see ALL OVER, def. 4; IT'S ALL OVER WITH.

**allowance** see MAKE ALLOWANCE FOR.

**allow for** Leave room for something, permit, as in *We have enough chairs to allow for forty extra guests*, or *Our church allows for a large variety of beliefs.* Also see MAKE ALLOWANCE FOR.

**all present and accounted for** All members or items of a group are here or where they are is known, as in *Is everyone ready to board the bus? All present and accounted for.* This expression almost certainly originated in the armed forces as a response to roll call. Now the expression is used to offer assurance that no person or thing is missing.

**all right** **1.** Completely correct, as in *You have a perfect score—your answers are all right.* (It could also be "all your answers are right.") **2.** In proper or working order, in a satisfactory way, as in *The engine is running all right now.* Also see TURN OUT ALL RIGHT. **3.** In good health, as in *I had the flu, but I'm all right now.* **4.** Not injured, safe, as in *It was just a minor accident, and everyone is all right.* **5.** Yes, as in *Do you want to leave now? All right,* or *All right, we'll stay home.* Also see ALL RIGHT WITH ONE. **6.** Certainly, without a doubt, as in *It's late all right, but we should still go.* **7.** Hurrah! Good for you, as in *All right! Our team has done it again!* **8.** Also, **all-right**. Good, satisfactory. For example, *This restaurant is all right,* or *Harry is an all-right guy.*

**all right for you** I'm angry with you. This expression usually accompanies a threat of revenge, as in *All right for you! I won't ever go out with you again.*

**all right with one** Also, **all right by one**. Agreeable to someone. For example, *If you want to practice now, that's all right with me,* or *It's all right by her if you stay at home.*

**all set** Ready, in position for some action, as in *I'm all set to leave for work.* This term uses *set* in the sense of "put in proper position or order." The same meaning appears in the traditional *Ready, get set, go* for starting a race; here *set* means "in position to start."

**all's fair in love and war** Any behavior is permissible in certain circumstances, as in *Of course he called her—all's fair in love and war.* This saying sometimes is altered by an addition or a substitution, as in *All's fair in love and the World Series,* or *All's fair in love and war and an election year.*

**all shook up** Greatly disturbed or upset, as in *Your letter left her all shook up.* This idiom uses *shook* instead of the grammatically correct *shaken* and adds *all* for emphasis.

**all sorts of** see ALL KINDS OF.

**all's well that ends well** The result is satisfactory, even though the outcome had been uncertain. For example, *My lawyer persuaded me to plead guilty, but the court merely put me on probation—all's well that ends well.*

**all systems go** Everything is ready for proceeding, as in *They've rented a hall and hired the band, so it's all systems go for the concert.* This expression originally referred to launching space missiles and vehicles and has since been transferred to general use.

**all talk (and no action)** Much discussion but no action or results, as in *Don't count on their help—they're all talk,* or *You have been saying for months that you'll get a summer job, but you're all talk and no action.*

**all that** **1.** Too, very, usually used in a negative context meaning not too, not very. For example, *The new house is not all that different from your old one.* Also see NONE TOO. **2.** That and everything else of the kind. For example, *She enjoys wearing nice clothes and perfume and all that.* Also see AND ALL. **3.** The best, superior. For example, *You may think you're all that, but you're really nothing much.* **4.** See FOR ALL THAT.

**all that glitters is not gold** Something attractive is not always what it seems, as in *This house is really beautiful, but a closer look will show a bad roof—all that glitters is not gold.*

**all the** **1.** Even, more so, as in *Painting the room white will make it all the lighter,* or *They liked her all the better for not pretending,* or *You don't care for dessert? Good, all the more for us.* For a synonym, see SO MUCH THE. **2.** The entire amount of, as in *These two cousins were all the family he had.* In this usage *all the* is short for *all of the*.

**all the best** **1.** Also, **all of the best**. The entire number or amount of the highest quality of something, as in *All the best fruit was on display,* or *All of the best students competed for the award.* **2.** Best wishes, as in *I've got to go now—all the best to you and the family.* This idiom is used as an oral farewell or to close an informal letter or note.

**all the rage** Also, **all the thing**. The current or latest fashion, suggesting that it will be short-lived, as in *In the 1930s the lindy was all the rage.* The use of *rage* reflects the transfer of an angry passion to an enthusiastic one; *thing* is vaguer, as in *Snowboarding is all the thing now.* These terms are heard less often today than the synonym THE THING.

**all there** Mentally competent, as in *He may seem absent-minded, but believe me, he's all there.* This phrase is often used negatively as **not all there**, meaning "without one's full faculties." For example, *I wonder about John; sometimes it seems as if he's not all there.*

**all the same** **1.** Also, **all one**. Equally acceptable, making no difference. For example, *If it's all the same to you, I'd prefer the blue car,* or *Hot or cold, it's all one to me.* **2.** Also, **just the same**. Nevertheless, still. For example, *She wants to stay another week, but I'm going home all the same,* or *Even if you vote against it, this measure will pass just the same.*

**all the thing** see ALL THE RAGE.

**all the time** **1.** Also, **all the while**. Throughout a specific period, as in *All the time the *music was playing, she tapped her foot*, or *The baby slept all the while the loud music played.* **2.** Continuously, without interruption, as in *That old refrigerator is running all the time.* **3.** Often, repeatedly, as in *We go to that store all the time.*

**all the way 1.** Also, **the whole way**. The entire distance, from start to finish, as in *We ran all the way home*, or *The baby cried the whole way home.* **2.** Completely, as in *I'm on your side all the way.* **3.** See GO ALL THE WAY.

**all things being equal** see OTHER THINGS BEING EQUAL.

**all things considered** Thinking about everything important to a particular situation or event. For example, *All things considered, I think we should leave tomorrow*, or *Would you still vote for that person, all things considered?*

**all things to all people, be** Satisfy everyone completely, as in *The trouble with the governor's campaign is that she is trying to be all things to all people.* This expression often appears in a political context, but phrased negatively, as in *He wants to be a good school committee member, but he can't be all things to all people.*

**all thumbs** Physically awkward, especially with respect to the hands, as in *When it comes to sewing, Mary is all thumbs.*

**all told** Added up, in all, as in *The boat will hold 80 passengers all told*, or *All told, his proposal makes some good points.* This idiom uses the verb *tell* in the sense of "count."

**all to the good** see TO THE GOOD.

**all very well** All right or quite true as far as it goes. For example, *It's all very well for Jane to drop out, but how will we find enough women to make up a team?* This idiom is generally used before a question beginning with "but," as in the example. Also see WELL AND GOOD.

**all well and good** see WELL AND GOOD.

**all wet** Completely wrong, mistaken, as in *If you think you can beat the system and win, you're all wet.* The original reference in this expression is unclear, that is, how moisture or dampness is related to wrongness.

**all work and no play (makes Jack a dull boy)** Hard work without time for recreation is not good for one's health, as in *If she keeps up that heavy schedule, she'll get sick—all work and no play isn't healthy.* This phrase is so familiar that it is often shortened, as in the example.

**all year round** Also, **year round**. Throughout the entire year, without regard to seasons. For example, *Thanks to the indoor courts, we can play tennis all year round.* The variant is also used as an adjective, as in *Basketball is a year-round game.*

**alma mater** Also, **Alma Mater**. The school or college one attended and, usually, graduated from, as in *During football season I always check to see how my alma mater is doing.* This expression sometimes refers to the institution's official song, as in *I never did learn the words to my college's alma mater.* The term is Latin for "kind mother."

**alone** see GO IT ALONE; LEAVE SOMEONE ALONE; LEAVE WELL ENOUGH ALONE; LET ALONE.

**along** In addition to the idioms beginning with ALONG, also see ALL ALONG; ALL ALONG THE LINE; BE ALONG; COME ALONG; FOLLOW ALONG; GET ALONG; GO ALONG; PLAY ALONG; RUN ALONG; STRING ALONG.

**along for the ride** Participating but not actively, as in *Don't ask me how long this job will take; I'm just along for the ride.* This term is often preceded by *just* to emphasize the passive role of the "passenger."

**along in years** Also, **on in years**. Elderly, old. For example, *Grandma's along in years now and doesn't hear too well.* It is often put as **get along** or **on in years**, as in *Our dog is not as playful now that it's getting on in years.* This idiom transfers the length of *along* (and the "onward" of *on*) to the passage of time.

**along the lines of** Also, **on the lines of**. Roughly similar. For example, *We told the architect we want a design along the lines of his own house but smaller*, or *They asked the caterer for a menu on the lines of the Morgans' big party.* This idiom uses *line* in the sense of "a direction or procedure."

**along with 1.** In association with, as in *For his second birthday, we sent him a fireman's hat, along with some books*, or *The audience was invited to sing along with the star.* **2.** Together with, as in *Along with what I told you before, that's the whole story of what happened.* For a synonym, see TOGETHER WITH. Also see GO ALONG, def. 2 and 3.

**a lot** Very many, a large number; also, very much. For example, *A lot of people like pizza*, or *Sad movies always made her cry a lot.* It is sometimes put as **a whole lot** for greater emphasis, as in *I learned a whole lot in this class.* It may also emphasize a comparative indication of amount, as in *We need a whole lot more pizza to feed everyone*, or *She had a lot less nerve than I expected.*

**also-ran** A loser or failure, an unsuccessful individual, as in *I feared that my candidate, a terrible speaker, would end up as an also-ran*, or *As for the promotions, he found himself among the also-rans.* This term comes from racing, where it describes a horse that finishes in fourth place or lower or does not finish a race at all. It has been transferred to losers in any kind of competition, and also more broadly to persons who simply don't do well.

**ambulance chaser** An attorney who seeks to profit from someone's injury or accident; also, an inferior lawyer. For example, *She refused to join any law firm that included ambulance chasers.* This term refers to lawyers who actively seek out people who are injured in accidents and require an ambulance and then sue for damages on behalf of the injured person or persons in exchange for a contingency fee—usually a large percentage of the amount of money won.

**amends** see MAKE AMENDS.

**amiss** see under TAKE SOMETHING THE WRONG WAY.

**amok** see RUN AMOK.

**amount to 1.** Add something up, develop into, as in *Even though she's careful with her money, her savings don't amount to much,* or *All parents hope that their children will amount to something.* **2.** Be equivalent to something, as in *Twenty people won't amount to a large crowd.* Also see AMOUNT TO THE SAME THING.

**amount to the same thing** Also, **come to the same thing**. Make no difference, be the same, as in *It's supposed to rain all day, so whether I go out now or later will amount to the same thing,* or *Paying in cash or with a credit card, it comes to the same thing.*

**a must 1.** A necessity; a requirement. For example, *This book is a must for serious students of English.* **2.** Also, **a must see**. A thing or a place everyone should see or visit, as in *The Louvre is a must see for visitors to Paris.*

**an apple a day** see APPLE A DAY.

**an arm and a leg** see ARM AND A LEG.

**ancient history** A past event, as in *She's talking about her vacation, but that's ancient history,* or *And then there was his divorce, but you don't want to hear ancient history.* This exaggerated idiom transfers the field of ancient history to a story told too often.

**and all** Also, **and all that**. Et cetera, and so on; whatever else goes with this statement. For example, *We can't afford eating out, since it's hard to find a baby sitter, they charge a lot, and all,* or *The builder will supply the paint and all that.* Also see AND SO FORTH; AND THE LIKE.

**and how!** Emphatically so. This idiom is used to stress agreement, as in *Did you enjoy the play? And how! It was wonderful.* This expression probably originated as a direct translation of the German *Und wie!*

**and/or** Both or either of two options. For example, *His use of copyrighted material shows that the writer is careless and/or dishonest.* This idiom comes from legal terminology.

**and so forth** Also, **and so on**. And more of the same, also, and others. For example, *At the mall, we shopped, had lunch, shopped some more, and so forth,* or *She planned to buy an entire outfit in blue—dress, shoes, hat, and so on.* Also see AND ALL; AND THE LIKE.

**and the like** And more of the same, as in *I just love hot dogs, hamburgers, french fries, and the like.* Also see AND ALL; AND SO FORTH.

**and then some** And much more, as in *I need all the help I can get and then some,* or *The speaker went on for an hour and then some.* This idiom may originally have come from **and some**, an old Scottish expression used in the same way.

**an eye for an eye** see EYE FOR AN EYE.

**another** In addition to the idiom beginning with ANOTHER, also see HAVE ANOTHER GUESS COMING; HORSE OF A DIFFERENT (ANOTHER) COLOR; ONE GOOD TURN DESERVES ANOTHER; ONE MAN'S MEAT IS ANOTHER MAN'S POISON; ONE WAY OR ANOTHER; SING A DIFFERENT (ANOTHER) TUNE; TOMORROW IS ANOTHER DAY; WEAR ANOTHER HAT.

**another county heard from** Also, **another country hear from**. An unexpected person has said something or arrived, as in *Our cousin from California decided to come at the same time—another county heard from.* This idiom originally referred to the counting of returns on election night.

**an ounce of prevention** see OUNCE OF PREVENTION.

**answer** In addition to the idioms beginning with ANSWER, also see KNOW ALL THE ANSWERS; TAKE NO FOR AN ANSWER.

**answer back** see TALK BACK.

**answer for 1.** Take responsibility for something, take charge of, as in *The new alarm system has to answer for the security of the grounds.* **2.** Take the blame for something, as in *The kids who were caught shoplifting have a lot to answer for.* **3.** To vouch for or sponsor someone, as in *I'll answer for him as a reliable employee.*

**answer to** Explain or justify something to someone, as in *If you don't help us finish this project, you'll have to answer to the boss.* This expression was at first used mainly for replying to legal charges.

**ante** In addition to the idiom beginning with ANTE, also see RAISE THE ANTE.

**ante up** Pay what is due, contribute; do one's share. For example, *The trustees were asked to ante up $10,000 each for the new scholarship,* or *Tired of watching Joe sit around while they cleaned up, the roommates told him to ante up or move out.* This expression comes from poker and other betting games, where *ante* means to make a bet or contribute to the pot before the cards are dealt. Also see RAISE THE ANTE.

**ants in one's pants, have** Be extremely restless, uneasy, impatient, or anxious, as in *This child just can't sit still; she must have ants in her pants*. This rhyming idiom gives a vivid image of what might cause a person to be jumpy.

**a number of** A collection of people or things; several. For example, *A number of tours are available*, or *We've visited a number of times*. This idiom often is modified by an adjective giving some idea of quantity, as in *Only a small number are going*. Also see ANY NUMBER OF.

**any** In addition to the idioms beginning with ANY, also see AT ANY RATE; BY ANY MEANS; BY ANY STRETCH OF THE IMAGINATION; GO TO ANY LENGTH; IN ANY CASE; NOT HAVE (ANY OF) IT; UNDER ANY (NO) CIRCUMSTANCES.

**any day 1.** No particular time, as in *It doesn't matter when; any day is fine with me*. **2.** Also, **any day now**. Quite soon, as in *I might get a call any day*, or *There could be a snowstorm any day now*. **3.** Also, **any day of the week**. Every day, as in *I could eat fresh corn any day of the week*. All three senses use *any* in the sense of "no matter which."

**any longer 1.** With added length, as in *If this skirt were any longer, it would touch the floor*. **2.** Still, any more, as in *They don't make that car any longer*. This negative form also appears as NO LONGER.

**any number of** Many; also, no particular amount of. The meaning here depends on the context. *I can give you any number of reasons for his absence* means "I can offer many reasons." *Any number of workers might stay home* means that an unknown number will not be present.

**any old** No particular, whichever or whatever, as in *Any old brand of detergent suits me*.

**anyone's guess** Also, **anybody's guess**. Something that no one knows for sure, as in *Will it rain next Sunday? That's anyone's guess*. Also see YOUR GUESS IS AS GOOD AS MINE.

**anything** In addition to the idioms beginning with ANYTHING, also see CAN'T DO ANYTHING WITH; IF ANYTHING; LIKE ANYTHING; NOT ANYTHING LIKE.

**anything but** By no means, not at all, as in *He is anything but worried about the test*.

**anything goes** Everything is permitted, as in *You're wearing sneakers to the office? Why not? Anything goes these days*. This idiom began life as **everything goes**.

**anything like** see NOT ANYTHING LIKE.

**any time 1.** Whenever it is best or most convenient, as in *We can leave any time*. **2.** At no particular time, as in *You could have told me at any time how you really felt*.

**A-one** Also, **A-1** or **A-number-one**. First-class, of the best quality, as in *This is an A-one pizza*. The term comes from Lloyd's, the British insurance company, which in an early shipping register designated the condition of a ship's hull by a letter grade (A, B, etc.) and of its cables, anchor, and other equipment by a number grade (1, 2, etc.). Later, A-1, the best possible grade, was transferred to anything of superior quality.

**apart** In addition to the idiom beginning with APART, also see COME APART AT THE SEAMS; FALL APART; PICK APART; POLES APART; SET APART; TAKE APART; TEAR APART; TELL APART; WORLDS APART.

**apart from** Also, **aside from**. Besides, except for. For example, *Apart from jogging occasionally in the park, she gets no exercise*, or *Aside from Sunday dinner with his parents, they have not gone out for months*.

**appearance** see KEEP UP (APPEARANCES); PUT IN AN APPEARANCE.

**appear as** Act the part of some role in public. For example, *She got wonderful reviews when she appeared as Portia*. This idiom uses *appear* in the sense of "come before the public."

**appetite** see WHET ONE'S APPETITE.

**apple** In addition to the idioms beginning with APPLE, also see ROTTEN APPLE; UPSET THE APPLECART.

**apple a day** A small preventive treatment helps prevent serious problems, as in *He exercises regularly—an apple a day is his motto*. This idiom shortens the proverb **An apple a day keeps the doctor away**.

**apple of one's eye** Special favorite, beloved person or thing, as in *The student was the apple of her teacher's eye*. This term rests on the ancient idea that the eye's pupil is apple-shaped and that eyes are particularly precious.

**apple-pie order** Extreme neatness, as in *David keeps his room in apple-pie order*. This term is generally believed to be an English corruption of the French *nappes pliées*, "neatly folded linen."

**apples and oranges** Unlike objects or people, as in *Comparing a neighborhood grocery to a giant supermarket is comparing apples and oranges*. This term for dissimilarity began as **apples and oysters**. It is nearly always accompanied by a warning that one cannot compare such different categories.

**appointment** see MAKE AN APPOINTMENT.

**approval** see ON APPROVAL; SEAL OF APPROVAL.

**apron strings** see TIED TO SOMEONE'S APRON STRINGS.

**apropos of** Concerning, in connection with, as in *Apropos of keeping in touch, I haven't heard from her in months*. This idiom was a borrowing of the French *à propos de* ("to the purpose of"). At first it was used without *of* and meant "fitting" or "opportune," as in *Their prompt arrival was very apropos.* Later, it began to be used with *of,* as in the current idiom, for "concerning" or "by way of."

**area** see GRAY AREA.

**argument** see FOR THE SAKE OF ARGUMENT; PICK A QUARREL (AN ARGUMENT).

**arm** In addition to the idioms beginning with ARM, also see AT ARM'S LENGTH; BABE IN ARMS; FOREWARNED IS FOREARMED; GIVE ONE'S EYETEETH (RIGHT ARM); LONG ARM OF THE LAW; ONE-ARMED BANDIT; PUT THE ARM ON; SHOT IN THE ARM; TAKE UP ARMS; TALK SOMEONE'S ARM OFF; TWIST SOMEONE'S ARM; UP IN ARMS; WITH ONE ARM TIED BEHIND ONE'S BACK; WITH OPEN ARMS.

**arm and a leg** A ridiculously high amount of money, as in *Some hotels charge an arm and a leg for a decent meal,* or *Fixing the car is going to cost an arm and a leg.* This exaggerated idiom is always used with verbs such as *cost, charge,* or *pay.*

**armchair quarterback** A football fan, especially a man, who thinks he knows the best play for a quarterback to call, even though he is watching the game on television, as in *That armchair quarterback couldn't throw a pass if he tried.* This expression is now also used to refer to anyone who offers advice, especially someone who is not involved in a situation, as in *We don't need any armchair quarterbacks on this project.* Also see BACKSEAT DRIVER; MONDAY-MORNING QUARTERBACK.

**armed to the teeth** Overly well equipped or prepared, as in *With her briefcase and new suit, she was armed to the teeth for her first day on the job.* The expression *to the teeth* meant "well equipped" in the days when knights often wore head-to-foot armor. The idiom later became popular as a reference to weapons or other military equipment. Today it is used even more figuratively.

**arm in arm** With one person's arm linked around another's; also, closely allied, as in *Both couples walked arm in arm around the grounds of the estate,* or *This candidate is arm in arm with the party's liberal wing.* Also see HAND IN HAND.

**armor** see CHINK IN ONE'S ARMOR; KNIGHT IN SHINING ARMOR.

**around** In addition to the idioms beginning with AROUND, also see BEAT AROUND THE BUSH; BEEN AROUND; BOSS ONE AROUND; BRING AROUND; CAST ABOUT (AROUND); COME AROUND; EVERY TIME ONE TURNS AROUND; FOOL AROUND; FUCK AROUND; GET AROUND; GET AROUND TO; GO AROUND (IN CIRCLES); HANG AROUND; HORSE AROUND; KICK AROUND; KID AROUND; KNOCK ABOUT (AROUND); KNOW ONE'S WAY AROUND; MESS AROUND; NOSE ABOUT (AROUND); PAL AROUND WITH; PLAY AROUND; POKE AROUND; PUSH AROUND; RALLY AROUND; ROLL AROUND; RUN AROUND IN CIRCLES; RUN AROUND LIKE A CHICKEN; RUN AROUND WITH; RUN RINGS AROUND; SCREW AROUND; SCROUNGE AROUND; SHOP AROUND; SLEEP AROUND; STICK AROUND; TALK AROUND; TEAR AROUND; THINK THE WORLD REVOLVES AROUND ONE; THROW ONE'S WEIGHT AROUND; TURN AROUND; TWIST AROUND ONE'S FINGER; UP AND ABOUT (AROUND). Also see under ROUND.

**around the bend** **1.** Around a curve or corner on a road or pathway, as in *Peter's house is just around the bend.* Also see AROUND THE CORNER, def. 1 and 2. **2.** Also, **round the bend**. Not having all one's senses or reason, as in *Throwing out that perfectly good steak? Have you gone round the bend?*

**around the corner** **1.** On the other side of a street corner, as in *The doctor's office is around the corner from our house.* **2.** Nearby, a short distance away, as in *The nearest grocery store is just around the corner.* **3.** Very soon, imminent, as in *You never know what lies just around the corner.*

**arrangements** see MAKE ARRANGEMENTS FOR.

**arrears** see IN ARREARS.

**arrest** see UNDER ARREST.

**arrive at** Reach an objective, as in *It took Harry only a few minutes to arrive at a solution.*

**art** see FINE ART; STATE OF THE ART.

**as . . . as** Also, **so . . . as**. Used with an adjective or an adverb to show similarity or equality of one thing with another. The *as . . . as* construction appears in numerous similes, including the idioms *as big as life, as good as done, as old as the hills.* (In this book, when such idioms occur without the first *as,* they can be found under the adjective or adverb: BIG AS . . . ; GOOD AS . . . ; OLD AS . . . , etc.; those that do not, like *as far as, as long as, as well as,* are found under *as* below.) The construction *so . . . as* is often preferred in negative statements, such as *I couldn't sleep, not so much as a wink.* Also see AS FAR AS.

**as all get-out** To the greatest degree possible, as in *She made him furious as all get-out.*

**as a matter of course** see MATTER OF COURSE.

**as a matter of fact** see MATTER OF FACT.

**as a rule** In general, usually, as in *As a rule Irene does not eat meat.*

**as a whole** All parts or aspects considered, altogether, as in *I like the movie as a whole, though the first half seemed somewhat slow.* Also see ON THE WHOLE.

**as best one can** To the best of one's ability, as in *We'll have to get along without it as best we can.* Also see DO ONE'S BEST.

**as big as life** see BIG AS LIFE.

**as far as** Also, **so far as**. To the extent, degree, or amount that. This phrase alone is always used to modify a verb, as in *As far as I can tell, it's a real diamond*, or *It's a good job as far as it goes, but it may need more work*, or *James said that, so far as he can remember, he's never met Mike*. Also see the following idioms beginning with AS FAR AS.

**as far as I can see** Also, **so far as I can see**. According to my judgment or understanding, as in *As far as I can see, you've got an excellent chance of getting that job.*

**as far as possible** Also, **so far as possible**. To the greatest extent, degree, or amount. For example, *I want to drive as far as possible today*, or *It was very complicated, but he promised to explain it so far as possible.*

**as far as that goes** Also, **so far as that goes**; **as far as that is concerned** or **so far as that is concerned**. Concerning that, actually. For example, *As far as that goes, I don't understand it*, or *My husband has never gotten along with his boss, and so far as that goes, his boss doesn't like him either*, or *As far as that is concerned, she can take care of herself.* Also see AS FOR.

**as follows** What comes next, usually in the form of a list. For example, *She planned her day as follows: answering her e-mail, a department meeting, lunch with her colleagues, library research.* This term is always put in the singular (*follows*), even though it applies to numerous items.

**as for** Also, **as to**. With regard to a particular thing, concerning. For example, *As for dessert, I'd better skip it today*, or *We are not sure as to how to pay the bill.* Also see AS TO.

**as good as** see GOOD AS.

**aside** see ALL JOKING ASIDE; LAY ASIDE; SET ASIDE; TAKE ASIDE.

**aside from** see APART FROM.

**as if** Also, **as though**. As it would be, as in *He decided to accept, as if it really mattered*, or *John scowled as though he were really angry*. Also see MAKE AS IF.

**as I live and breathe** **1.** For sure, definitely, as in *As I live and breathe, I've never seen a more beautiful view.* This expression is generally used to emphasize the truth of a statement. **2.** What a surprise! For example, *As I live and breathe, I thought you wouldn't be here!*

**as is** Just the way something is, with no changes. For example, *Used cars are sold as is*. This expression is used for goods to be sold that may be slightly worn, damaged, or less than perfect.

**as it stands** see AS THINGS STAND.

**as it were** Seemingly, in a way, as in *He was living in a dream world, as it were*. This phrase is one of the remaining examples of the subjunctive mood in English. Also see SO TO SPEAK.

**ask** In addition to the idioms beginning with ASK, also see DON'T ASK; FOR THE ASKING.

**askance** see LOOK ASKANCE.

**ask a stupid question and you'll get a stupid answer** Also, **ask a silly question**. Used for a question that does not deserve a proper answer, as in *Am I hungry? Ask a stupid question!*

**ask for** Also, **ask for it**. Persist in an action despite the probability that it will bring trouble on oneself, as in *Speeding as much as he does, he has been asking for a ticket*, or *She deserved that low grade; she asked for it by not studying*.

**ask for the moon** Make an unreasonable demand, request something impossible to get, as in *A thousand dollars for her birthday? Mary might as well be asking for the moon.*

**ask out** Invite someone to a social event, such as dinner, the theater, or a date. For example, *We've been asked out to dinner twice this week*, or *Mary felt shy about asking John out.*

**asleep** In addition to the idiom beginning with ASLEEP, also see FALL ASLEEP.

**asleep at the switch** Also, **asleep at the wheel** or **asleep on the job**. Not attentive, not doing one's job, as in *The guard was asleep at the switch and called the fire department when it was already too late*. This term came from U.S. railroading when it was the trainman's duty to switch cars from one track to another by means of levers operated by hand. If he failed to do so, trains could collide. It was later transferred to any lack of alertness. The *wheel* in the variant is a steering wheel; similarly terrible results are implied.

**as likely as not** see LIKE AS NOT.

**as long as** **1.** For the period of time that, as in *You may keep the book as long as you want*, that is, keep it for whatever time you wish to. **2.** Also, **so long as**. Because, since, as in *Please pick up some milk as long as you are going to the store*, or *So long as you're here, you might as well stay for dinner*. **3.** Also, **so long as**; **just so**. Provided that, as in *As long as you don't expect it by tomorrow, I'll write the report*, or *So long as sales continue, the company will make a profit*, or *You may have another cookie, just so you don't take the last one.*

**as luck would have it** How things turned out, as it happened, as in *As luck would have it, he missed his train*, or *The check arrived in time, as luck would have it*. The *luck* referred to can mean either good luck or bad.

**as many** **1.** The same number of. For example, *He changed jobs four times in as many years* means he changed jobs four times in four years. **2. as many as.** A phrase used to qualify the meaning of *many* as a very large number, depending on what follows it. For example, *You can take as many pens as you need.* Also see AS . . . AS ; AS MUCH AS.

**as much** The same or almost the same. For example, *He's resigning? I thought as much* means I thought he was doing just that. Also see AS MUCH AS.

**as much as** **1.** The same quantity as. As with AS MANY (def. 2), the meaning of *much* as a large amount here is qualified by what follows. For example, *Please help yourself to as much of the meat as you want* means you can have whatever amount you wish. **2.** Also, **however much** or **much as.** Even though, no matter how much, as in *As much as I hate to, I must stay home tonight*, or *However much it hurts, you ought to admit you were wrong*, or *Much as she would love to go, she already has plans.* **3.** Also, **so much as.** In effect, nearly the same as, as in *Mom as much as told Jane she couldn't go*, or *The clerk so much as accused the customer of shoplifting.*

**as of** From, at, or until a given time. For example, *As of five o'clock, the store will be closed for inventory*, or *As of last December, our meetings have been open to the public*, or *As of now, I'm not sure how I'll vote.* This idiom was first used in business but came into more general use.

**as one** Also, **as one man** or **as one woman.** All together, unanimously. For example, *The marchers shouted as one*, "*We shall overcome!*" or *They replied as one woman*, "*Of course we'll stay and help.*" For synonyms, see TO A MAN (WOMAN); WITH ONE VOICE.

**as regards** see IN REGARD TO.

**ass** In addition to the idiom beginning with ASS, also see BREAK ONE'S ASS; CHEW OUT (ONE'S ASS OFF); COVER ONE'S ASS; DRAG ONE'S ASS; KICK ASS; KICK IN THE PANTS (ASS); KISS ASS; MAKE A FOOL (AN ASS) OF; PAIN IN THE NECK (ASS); STICK IT (UP ONE'S ASS); YOU BET (YOUR ASS).

**ass in a sling, have one's** Also, **get one's ass in a sling.** Be (or get) in trouble or in a painfully awkward position, as in *When the news about the sale gets out, he'll have his ass in a sling.* Probably originating in the American South, this idiom may refer to so vigorous a kick in the buttocks (for which *ass* is a rude synonym) that the injured person requires a sling of the kind used to support a broken arm. [Vulgar slang]

**as soon** see AS SOON AS; JUST AS SOON.

**as soon as** **1.** When, just after, as in *Please call me as soon as dinner is ready*, or *As soon as the sun goes down, the temperature drops.* **2.** At the earliest possible moment, as in *Telephone me as soon as you can.* It often takes the form **as soon as possible**, as in *He'll finish the work as soon as possible.* This expression uses *possible* in the sense of "if it can or could be."

**as such** **1.** In itself, as in *The job as such was easy, but it required a lot of time.* **2.** In that capacity, as in *In the director's absence, the assistants, as such, were in charge.*

**as the crow flies** In a straight line, by the shortest route, as in *It's only a mile as the crow flies, but it's about three miles by this mountain road.* This idiom is based on the fact that crows, very intelligent birds, fly straight to the nearest food supply.

**as things stand** Also, **as it stands.** How a particular situation is at the present moment. For example, *As things stand, I don't think I'll be able to take a vacation*, or *As it stands, we're still not speaking to each other.*

**as though** see AS IF.

**as to** **1.** According to, as in *They were asked to sort the shirts as to color.* **2.** See AS FOR.

**astray** see BEST-LAID PLANS GO ASTRAY; GO ASTRAY; LEAD ONE ASTRAY.

**as usual** In the normal, habitual, or accustomed way, as in *As usual, he forgot to put away the milk.* Also see BUSINESS AS USUAL.

**as well** **1.** In addition, besides, also. For example, *Mary is going to Italy and to France as well*, or *A fine pianist, he plays the violin as well.* **2.** With an equal or similar result, as in *Since she can't get there in time, she might as well stay at home*, or *It's just as well that you came today, since another customer is here, too.*

**as well as** **1.** In as satisfactory or good a way as possible. For example, *After the operation, she walked around as well as she could without limping.* **2.** To the same extent as, as much as. For example, *He is an excellent teacher as well as being a fine musician.* **3.** In addition to, as in *The editors as well as the proofreaders are working overtime.*

**as yet** So far, up to now, as in *No one has found a solution as yet.*

**as you please** **1.** However you wish, whatever you choose, as in *We can have meat or fish tonight, as you please*, or *Go or don't go—do as you please.* **2.** Very, extremely, as in *After winning the contract, he was happy as you please*, or *She sat there in her new dress, as pretty as you please.*

**at a blow** see AT ONE STROKE.

**at about** At approximately, as in *We'll start at about nine.* This phrase, most often used with respect to time (as in *at about four o'clock*), is sometimes criticized for being redundant. Although one of the two words sometimes can

be omitted without changing the meaning—for example, *About four o'clock is when most guests will arrive*—in other instances both are needed, as in *This stock is now selling at about its original offering price.*

**at a crossroads** see AT THE CROSSROADS.

**at a discount** At a lower than usual price; also, held in low esteem. For example, *I'm not buying a computer until I can get one at a discount,* or *Liberals are at a discount in the present administration.* The first usage is mainly found in business.

**at all 1.** In any way or manner, as in *Is she able to sing at all?* **2.** To any extent, as in *Was he at all surprised?* **3.** For any reason, as in *Why bother at all?* **4.** In the slightest degree, under any circumstances, as in *She simply refused to talk at all.* This construction often occurs in the negative, as in *He was not at all frightened.*

**at all costs** Also, **at any cost** or **at any price**. Regardless of the expense or effort involved, by any means. For example, *Ann told the doctor to preserve her mother's sight at all costs,* or *It seems the company plans to develop the product at any cost,* or *I'm determined to get vacation time at any price.*

**at all times** Continuously, without interruption, as in *At the airport we were warned to keep our carryon bags in sight at all times.*

**at a loss 1.** Below cost, as in *The store was doing so badly that it was selling merchandise at a loss.* **2.** Puzzled, bewildered, uncertain, as in *When his letters were returned unopened, John was at a loss as to what to do next.* This usage was originally applied to hounds who had lost the scent or track of their prey. **3. at a loss for words**. Unable or uncertain as to what to say. For example, *Her tirade left us all at a loss for words.*

**at a low ebb** At a low point, in a state of decline or depression. For example, *The current recession has put our business at a low ebb.* This idiom transfers the low point of a tide to a decline in human affairs.

**at any cost** Also, **at any price**. See AT ALL COSTS.

**at any rate** In any event, whatever the case may be; also, at least. For example, *At any rate, I promise to be there even if I'm a little late,* or *It may not pay well, but at any rate it's a job.* Also see IN ANY CASE.

**at a premium** At a higher price than usual because of being rare; also, considered more valuable, held in high esteem. For example, *Since that article came out, the firm's stock has been selling at a premium,* or *Space is at a premium in most stores.* This idiom uses *premium* in the sense of "bounty" or "bonus." Also see PUT A PREMIUM ON.

**at a price** How much an action or involvement will cost in terms of one's energy or resources. For example, *We can meet our deadline, but only at a price,* or *Everything can be achieved, at a price.*

**at arm's length** At a distance, avoiding intimacy or familiarity, as in *Bill disliked seeing his colleagues outside the office, preferring to keep them at arm's length,* or *She was friendly only when he was safely at arm's length.* Now often used with the verb *keep,* this term for distancing oneself from a person, an organization, or an issue began as *at arm's end.*

**at a sitting** At one time, during one period. For example, *The cruise ship could feed 500 passengers at a sitting,* or *We read the entire poem at a sitting.* Since the word *sitting* suggests just that posture, the term means "during a period when one is seated and engaged in a single continuous activity."

**at a stretch** Also, **at one stretch**. At one time, during one period. For example, *Working quickly, she hoped to finish all the drawings at a stretch.* In contrast to the nearly synonymous AT A SITTING, this idiom does not imply being seated while engaging in a single continuous activity. Rather, it transfers the meaning of *stretch* as "a continuous length" to a continuous time period.

**at a stroke** see AT ONE STROKE.

**at a time** see AT ONE TIME, def. 1.

**at a word** In immediate response, in an instant. For example, *At a word from the captain they lined up in order.*

**at bat** Taking one's turn. For example, *At this conference, it's hard to tell which speaker is at bat,* or *I was nervous while waiting for the interview, but once at bat I felt better.* This idiom comes from baseball. Also see ON DECK.

**at bay** Cornered, desperate, as in *Angry bystanders chased the thief into an alley and held him at bay until the police arrived.* This idiom originally came from hunting, where it describes an animal that has been chased and now faces the pursuing hounds.

**at best** Under the most favorable circumstances, as in *At best, we'll be just one week behind schedule,* or *Cleaning out the attic is a boring job at best.* This idiom today is most often used in situations that are actually far from ideal, as in the examples above. For an antonym, see AT WORST.

**at bottom** Fundamentally, basically; also, in reality. For example, *He may speak somewhat openly, but at bottom he's always honest.*

**at close quarters** Crowded, in a very small space, as in *We could use a lot more room; this tiny office puts us at close quarters.* This idiom makes figurative use of *quarters* in the

sense of "military lodgings," but it originated in naval warfare. When the enemy boarded a ship, the crew would retreat behind wooden barriers erected for this purpose and would continue to fire through small holes. They thus were very near the enemy, fighting **in close quarters**.

**at close range** Very nearby, as in *At close range, the rock band was extremely loud. Range* here refers to the distance that a missile or projectile can travel. This expression soon came to mean anything that is close.

**at cross purposes** With aims or goals that work against or interfere with each other, as in *I'm afraid the two departments are working at cross purposes.*

**at death's door** On the point of dying, very ill, as in *Whenever he has a bad cold, he acts as though he were at death's door.* This expression associates death with a doorway. Today it is often used as an exaggeration of ill health.

**at each other's throats** Arguing or fighting. For example, *By the end of the long vacation, the children were constantly at each other's throats.* This idiom, with its vivid image of two persons trying to strangle each other, is often applied to less physical forms of disagreement.

**at ease 1.** Also, **at one's ease**. Comfortable, relaxed, not embarrassed, as in *I always feel at ease in my grandmother's house.* The related idiom **put at ease** means "make comfortable, reassure," as in *I was worried that the letter would not arrive in time, but the postmaster put me at ease.* For an antonym, see ILL AT EASE. **2.** In a relaxed position in military ranks. The phrase is often used as a command for troops standing at attention to relax, as in *At ease, squadron.*

**at every turn** Everywhere; also, continually, at every moment. For example, *He found garbage thrown about at every turn*, or *Life holds surprises at every turn.* The *turn* here does not mean change of direction but change of circumstances, and the phrase generally is an exaggeration.

**at face value, take something** Accept something from its appearance, as in *You can't always take a manufacturer's advertisements at face value; they usually exaggerate.* Literally this idiom refers to the monetary value printed on a bank note, stock certificate, bond, or other financial instrument.

**at fault** Responsible for a mistake, trouble, or failure; deserving blame. For example, *At least three cars were involved in the accident, so it was hard to determine which driver was at fault*, or *He kept missing his class and wondered if his watch was at fault.* Also see IN THE WRONG.

**at first** Initially, at the start, as in *At first the berries were green, but when they ripened, they turned bright red.*

**at first glance** Also, **at first sight**. When first seen. For example, *At first glance we thought it was an elegant restaurant, but it soon became obvious that it was not the place for a special dinner*, or *At first sight the contract looked just fine.* Also see LOVE AT FIRST SIGHT.

**at full tilt** see FULL TILT.

**at gunpoint** Also, **at knifepoint**. While being threatened with a weapon, as in *I'm going to hold him at gunpoint for that raise he promised me last year.* Both these phrases were at first used literally and later also figuratively.

**at half-mast** Also, **at half-staff**. Halfway up or down, as in *The church bells tolled off and on all day, and the flags were at half-mast.* This term refers to placing a flag halfway up a ship's mast or a flagpole. This practice is used as a mark of respect for a person who has died or, at sea, as a distress signal. Occasionally the term is transferred to other objects, as in *Tom's pants were at half-mast as he raced around the playground*, or *The puppy's tail was at half-mast.*

**at hand 1.** Also, **close at hand** or **near at hand**. Within easy reach, nearby, as in *I like to keep my tools close at hand.* **2.** Also, **on hand**. Nearby in time, soon, as in *The day of judgment is at hand*, or *A change of administration is on hand.* Also see ON HAND.

**at heart 1.** Fundamentally, basically, as in *He's a good fellow at heart.* **2.** In one's deepest feelings, as a great concern, as in *The governor has the party's best interests at heart.*

**at home 1.** In one's own residence, town, or country. For example, *Mary was not at home when I called*, or *Tourists in a foreign country often behave more rudely than they do at home.* **2.** Ready to receive a visitor, as in *We are always at home to our neighbor's children.* **3.** Also, **at home with**. Comfortable and familiar, as in *You always make us feel at home*, or *I've never been at home with his style of management.* Also see AT EASE, def. 1. **4.** Also, **at home with**. Proficient, skilled, as in *She is so much at home with numbers that she may well become a mathematician*, or *Some people are really at home in French.* **5.** In team sports, playing on one's own field or in one's own town. For example, *The Red Sox always do better at home than they do at away games.* For an antonym, see ON THE ROAD, def. 1.

**at issue 1.** In question, being discussed; also, to be decided. For example, *Who will pay for the food was the point at issue.* **2.** In conflict, in disagreement, as in *Physicians* *are still at issue over the appropriate use of hormone therapy.*

**at it** Engaging in an activity with great energy, especially a fight but also sex or some other activity. For example, *Whenever they play tennis, they really go at it* (fight), or *The new job keeps her at it day and night* (works hard), or *In the spring the dogs are always at it* (sex).

**at large** **1.** Free, unconfined, especially not in prison, as in *The bank robbers are still at large.* **2.** At length, fully; also, as a whole, in general. For example, *The chairman talked at large about the company's plans for the coming year.* **3.** Elected to represent an entire group of voters rather than those in a particular district. For example, a *councilman at large* represents all the areas of a city instead of just one.

**at last** Also, **at long last**. After a long time, finally, as in *At last the speeches ended and dinner was served*, or *Harry got his degree at long last.* Also see AT LENGTH, def. 2.

**at least** **1.** Also, **at the least**. According to the lowest possible estimate, no less than. For example, *At least a dozen more chairs are needed*, or *The job will take four hours at the least.* **2.** Anyway, anyhow, as in *At least you got there on time*, or *The children enjoyed the dessert at least.* For synonyms, see AT ANY RATE; IN ANY CASE.

**at leisure** Slowly, without hurrying, as in the famous proverb, *Marry in haste and repent at leisure.* Also see AT ONE'S LEISURE.

**at length** **1.** For a long time, extensively. For example, *The preacher went on at length about sin*, or *I have read at length about these cameras.* **2.** After a long time, finally, as in *At length the march ended.* Also see IN THE LONG RUN.

**at liberty** Free, not obligated. For example, *I am not at liberty to tell you the whole story.* This idiom is often used in the negative, as in the example.

**at loggerheads** In a quarrel or an argument, as in *The two brothers were always at loggerheads, making it difficult to celebrate holidays together.* Also see AT ODDS.

**at long last** see AT LAST.

**at loose ends** In an uncomfortable or uncertain situation. For example, *This whole visit has left me feeling restless, constantly at loose ends*, or *Jane couldn't find a job this year, so she is at loose ends for the summer.*

**at most** Also, **at the most** or **at the outside**. At the largest amount, the extreme limit; also, in the most extreme case. For example, *She'll be finished in two weeks at the most*, or *It'll take two weeks at the outside*, or *At most the chef uses a tiny bit of pepper.* Also see AT BEST.

**at odds** Disagreeing, opposed. For example, *It is only natural for the young and old to be at odds over money matters.* This idiom uses *odds* in the sense of "a condition of being unequal or different" and transfers it to a difference of opinion or quarrel.

**at once** **1.** At the same time, as in *We can't all fit into the kitchen at once.* Also see AT ONE TIME, def. 1. **2.** Immediately, as in *Mother told the children to come inside at once.*

**at one** In agreement, united, as in *John and Pat were at one on every subject except her cat, which made him sneeze*, or *Springtime always makes me feel at one with nature.*

**at one blow** see AT ONE STROKE.

**at one fell swoop** see ONE FELL SWOOP.

**at one's** In addition to idioms beginning with AT ONE'S, also see idioms beginning with AT SOMEONE'S.

**at one's best** In one's most excellent state or condition. For example, *The photographer tried hard to show the bride at her best.*

**at one's convenience** Also, **at one's earliest convenience**. Whenever one wishes; also, as soon as one can. For example, *Pick up the car any time, at your convenience*, or *We need that report very soon, so please finish it at your earliest convenience. Convenience* is used here in the sense of "ease" or "absence of trouble."

**at one's door** Also, **on one's doorstep**. Very close, as in *The bus stop was practically on our doorstep*, or *The Mexican currency crisis is literally at our door.* Also see LAY AT SOMEONE'S DOOR.

**at one's ease** see AT EASE, def. 1.

**at one's expense** see AT THE EXPENSE OF.

**at one's fingertips** Easily or immediately available. This idiom is used both literally, as in *This new design keeps all the important controls at the driver's fingertips*, and figuratively, as in *Tom was so familiar with the proposal that he had all the details at his fingertips.*

**at one's leisure** Whenever one wishes, at one's convenience, as in *At your leisure, please look over this manuscript and give me your comments.* Also see AT LEISURE.

**at one stretch** see AT A STRETCH.

**at one stroke** Also, **at one blow**; **at a stroke** or **at a blow**; **in one stroke** or **in one blow**. At the same time, with one forceful or quick action. For example, *I managed to please both buyer and seller at one stroke.*

**at one's wit's end** Also, **at wits' end**. Completely puzzled and confused, not knowing what to do. For example, *I've tried every possible source without success, and now I'm at my wit's end.* This idiom uses *wit* in the sense of "mental faculties."

**at one's word** see TAKE ONE AT ONE'S WORD.

**at one time** **1.** At the same time, as in *All the boys jumped into the pool at one time*. For synonyms, see AT ONCE, def. 1; AT THE SAME TIME, def. 1. **2.** Formerly, in the past, as in *At one time very few houses in town were for sale*.

**at one time or another** On various separate occasions. For example, *At one time or another I've considered replacing the stove, but so far I haven't done so*.

**at pains to, be** Also, **take pains to**. Make a special effort or take extra trouble to do something. For example, *Bob was at pains to make a good first impression and wore his best suit*, or *Mary took pains to make sure her speech would interest the audience*.

**at peace** In a state of agreement or friendliness, not at war; also, in a state of inner harmony or quiet. For example, *Whatever their disagreements, Mexico and Belize have remained at peace*, or *In his last illness he seemed finally to be at peace with himself*.

**at present** Also, **at the present time**. Now, as in *I don't have enough cash at the present time to lend you any*, or *At present the house is still occupied*. Also see AT THIS POINT.

**at random** Without order or fixed purpose, as in *Some artists drop paint on canvas seemingly at random*. Originally this phrase meant "very speedily" and "without concern."

**at rest** **1.** In a state of inactivity or quiet rest, either physical or mental. For example, *The doctor's clear explanation put her mind at rest*. Also see LAY AT REST. **2.** Dead, as in *His soul is now at rest with his ancestors*. This expression, using *rest* to refer to death, is less common today.

**at risk** **1.** In danger, as in *Their house's location on a major fault puts them at risk in the next earthquake*. **2.** Legally responsible to pay for loss or damage, as in *If he can't pay the insurance premiums, he is at risk for any liability claims on the property*.

**at sea** **1.** Aboard a ship, on the ocean, as in *Within a few hours, the ship would be out at sea*. **2.** Also, **all at sea**. Confused, bewildered, as in *She felt all at sea in these new surroundings*. This idiom transfers the condition of a ship that has lost its way to the human mind.

**at someone's** In addition to idioms beginning with AT SOMEONE'S, also see idioms beginning with AT ONE'S.

**at someone's beck and call** Required to follow or obey someone's requests or commands, as in *The boss expects the entire staff to be at his beck and call*. The noun *beck*, now used only in this idiom, means "a gesture or signal of command, such as a nod of the head or a hand movement," whereas *call* means "a vocal summons."

**at someone's elbow** Next to someone, close by, as in *The new dog was constantly at its master's elbow*. This idiom can mean either that someone is so close as to be a nuisance or to provide help easily.

**at someone's feet, be** Also, **sit at someone's feet**. Be enchanted or fascinated by someone, as in *Dozens of people are at her feet*, or *Bill sat at his mentor's feet for nearly three years, but he gradually became disillusioned and left the university*. For a quite different meaning, see UNDER ONE'S FEET.

**at someone's heels** Also, **on someone's heels**. Following directly behind, in close pursuit. This idiom is used both literally, as in *Jean's dog was always at her heels*, and figuratively, as in *Although his company dominated the field, he always felt that his competitors were on his heels*. The same idea is sometimes expressed more informally as **hard on someone's heels** or **hot on someone's heels**. Also see ON THE HEELS OF.

**at someone's mercy** see AT THE MERCY OF.

**at someone's request** When asked to do something, as in *At my request they'll move us to another room*, or *I'm speaking at his request*. Also see BY REQUEST.

**at someone's service** Ready to help someone, at someone's disposal, as in *The tour guide said he was at our service for the rest of the afternoon*.

**at stake** At risk to be won or lost, as in *We have a great deal at stake in this transaction*. This phrase uses *stake* in the sense of something that is wagered, a bet.

**attach** see NO STRINGS ATTACHED.

**attention** see PAY ATTENTION; UNDIVIDED ATTENTION.

**at that** **1.** In addition, besides, as in *The seats were good, and quite cheap at that*. **2.** In spite of, nevertheless, as in *Although I had to wait a long time for delivery, it was worth it at that*. **3.** As it stands, without further changes, as in *She wasn't happy with her grade in the course but decided to leave it at that*.

**at that point** Also, **at that point in time**. Then, as in *At that point we had finished the first chapter and had begun the second*. This phrase refers to a particular time when an event or a circumstance occurred, as opposed to "now" (see AT THIS POINT).

**at that rate** see AT THIS RATE.

**at that stage** see AT THIS STAGE.

**at the crossroads** Also, **at a crossroads**. At a point of decision or a critical place, as in *Because of the proposed merger, the company is standing at the crossroads*. This phrase is based on the importance given to the intersection of two roads.

**at the drop of a hat** Immediately, without delay, as in *We were ready to pack our bags*

A

*and go on vacation at the drop of a hat.* This phrase probably refers to signaling the start of a race or other contest by dropping a hat.

**at the end of one's rope** see END OF ONE'S ROPE.

**at the expense of** Also, **at one's expense.** **1.** Paid for by someone, as in *The hotel bill for the sales force is at the expense of the company.* **2.** With the risk of damage or injury to a person or thing, as in *We can't speed up production at the expense of quality,* or *The laughter was all at Tom's expense.*

**at the hand of** Also, **at the hands of.** Performed or done by someone, as in *The slaves suffered greatly at the hands of their new masters.* Also see AT HAND.

**at the helm** In charge, in command, as in *With Charles at the helm, the company will prosper.* This phrase transfers the idea of steering a ship to directing other activities. For a synonym, see AT THE WHEEL.

**at the last minute** At the latest possible moment or opportunity. For example, *Jim couldn't get a reservation because he had called at the last minute.* Also see AT THE LATEST; ELEVENTH HOUR.

**at the latest** No later than. For example, *We have to be in New York by Monday at the latest.*

**at the least** see under AT LEAST.

**at the mercy of 1.** Also, **at someone's mercy.** Under the power of someone, helpless against, as in *The captured rebels were at the mercy of the army commander.* **2.** Without any protection against, as in *On top of Mount Washington we were at the mercy of the elements.*

**at the most** see AT MOST.

**at the outset** Also, **from the outset.** At the start, from the start. For example, *He wanted to explain his position from the outset, but there wasn't time,* or *At the outset the problem seemed simple, but then it became quite complex.* The noun *outset* is rarely heard today except in these phrases.

**at the outside** see AT MOST.

**at the point of** see ON THE POINT OF.

**at the present time** see AT PRESENT.

**at the ready** Available for immediate use, as in *Umbrellas at the ready, we were prepared to brave the storm.* This idiom was originally a military term in which *the ready* referred to the position of a firearm prepared to be raised and aimed or fired.

**at the same time 1.** Simultaneously, as in *We were all scheduled to leave at the same time.* For synonyms, see AT ONCE, def. 1; AT ONE TIME, def. 1. **2.** Nevertheless, however, as in *Mary agreed with her mother's criticism, but at the same time she wanted to defend her sister's views.*

**at the time** At a particular time in the past, as in *She wasn't thinking clearly at the time.*

**at the top of one's lungs** Also, **at the top of one's voice.** With an extremely loud voice. For example, *The babies in the nursery all were crying at the top of their lungs.* The noun *top* here refers to the greatest volume (that is, loudest) rather than high pitch.

**at the wheel** In command, in control. For example, *Ann hated being told what to do; she wanted to be at the wheel by herself.* The comparison in this phrase is to the steering wheel of an automobile or a ship. For a synonym, see AT THE HELM.

**at the worst** see AT WORST.

**at this point** Also, **at this point in time** or **at this juncture** or **at this moment.** Now, as in *At this point in time we don't need a new car.* All four phrases imply that what is true now may not always have been so or may not remain so. For example, *At this point she is by far the best athlete on the team* suggests that she may not have been the best in the past or may not be the best in the future. Similarly, *Buying a new car seems wise at this juncture* indicates that this purchase may not have been wise in the past and may not be wise at some future time. Also see AT THAT POINT.

**at this rate** Also, **at that rate. 1.** Progressing at this (or that) speed, as in *At this rate we'll never finish in time.* **2.** Under these circumstances, in that case. For example, *At this rate they'll never agree on anything.*

**at this stage** Also, **at that stage** or **at this stage of the game** or **at that stage of the game.** At this (that) step, phase, or position in a process or activity, as in *I'm not sure if you can help at this stage, but perhaps you can later,* or *I don't need an assistant at this stage of the game.* The variant uses *game* in the sense of "a particular process or activity."

**at times** Occasionally, sometimes, as in *Away from home for the first time, I was homesick at times.* Also see AT ONE TIME OR ANOTHER.

**attitude** see HAVE AN ATTITUDE.

**at variance 1.** Differing, not in agreement. For example, *John's and Mary's answers are at variance.* **2.** In a state of conflict, as in *John was at variance with his in-laws.*

**at war 1.** In armed conflict. For example, *The Greeks and Turks have been at war for many years.* **2.** In a state of disagreement, as in *The two families were at war about the bill for the wedding reception.*

**at will** Freely, as one pleases, as in *The building is open to the public, and one can wander about at will,* or *With this system you can adjust the room temperature at will.*

**at wits' end** see AT ONE'S WIT'S END.

**at work** **1.** Engaged in a job or other activity, as in *The contractor is hard at work on the new building*, or *The little boy was fascinated to see the washing machine at work.* **2.** At one's office or other place of business, as in *Is it all right if I telephone you at work?*

**at worst** Also, **at the worst**. **1.** In the least favorable circumstance; under the most difficult conditions. For example, *At worst we will get home an hour late because of the traffic.* **2.** In the least favorable view, as in *No harm done; at the worst I'll copy the report again.* For an antonym, see AT BEST.

**avail** In addition to the idiom beginning with AVAIL, also see TO NO AVAIL.

**avail oneself of** **1.** Take advantage of something, gain by. For example, *To get a better mortgage, he availed himself of the employee credit union.* **2.** Use something, employ, as in *I'll avail myself of the first cab to come along.*

**avoid someone like the plague** Evade or stay away from someone at any cost. For example, *Since Bob was arrested, his friends have been avoiding him and his family like the plague.* The plague, a deadly infectious disease in the early Middle Ages, has largely been wiped out, but the term remains current.

**away** see BACK AWAY; BANG AWAY; BLOW AWAY; BREAK AWAY; BY FAR (FAR AND AWAY); CARRY AWAY; CART OFF (AWAY); CAST AWAY; CLEAR OUT (AWAY); DIE AWAY; DO AWAY WITH; DRAW AWAY; EAT AWAY AT; EXPLAIN AWAY; FADE OUT (AWAY); FALL AWAY; FIRE AWAY; FOOL AWAY; FRITTER AWAY; GET AWAY; GET AWAY WITH; GIVE AWAY; GO AWAY; HAMMER AWAY AT; LAY ASIDE (AWAY); MAKE AWAY WITH; OUT AND AWAY; PASS AWAY; PISS AWAY; PLUG AWAY AT; PULL AWAY; PUT AWAY; RIGHT AWAY; RUN AWAY; RUN AWAY WITH; SALT AWAY; SEND AWAY; SHY AWAY FROM; SLINK AWAY; SLIP OUT (AWAY); SOCK AWAY; SPIRIT AWAY; SQUARE AWAY; SQUIRREL AWAY; STOW AWAY; TAKE AWAY FROM; TAKE ONE'S BREATH AWAY; TEAR AWAY; THROW AWAY; TUCK AWAY; TURN AWAY; WALK AWAY FROM; WALK OFF (AWAY) WITH; WASTE AWAY; WEAR OFF (AWAY); WHALE AWAY AT; WHEN THE CAT'S AWAY; WHILE AWAY.

**a while back** Also, **a while ago**. Some time in the past, as in *I ran into Barbara a while back but didn't get her new address*, or *John wrote me a while ago about his new baby.* This term uses *a while* in the sense of "a short or moderate time."

**AWOL** see ABSENT WITHOUT LEAVE.

**ax** In addition to the idiom beginning with AX, also see GET THE AX.

**ax to grind** A selfish aim or motive for complaining, as in *The article criticized the new software, but the author had an ax to grind because the manufacturer had fired his son.* This frequently used idiom comes from a story about a boy who was talked into turning the grindstone for a man who was sharpening his ax. The boy worked hard until the school bell rang, when the man, instead of thanking the boy, began to scold him for being late and told him to hurry to school. "Having an ax to grind" then began to be used for having a personal motive for some action.

# Bb

**babe in arms** An infant, as in *She's been a family friend since I was a babe in arms.* This phrase describes a child who is too young to walk and therefore must be carried.

**babe in the woods** An innocent or very naive person who may easily be tricked, as in *She was a babe in the woods where the stock market was concerned.* The term originated in a popular ballad, "The Children in the Wood," about two young orphans who are abandoned in a forest and die.

**baby** see THROW OUT THE BABY WITH THE BATH WATER.

**back** In addition to the idioms beginning with BACK, also see A WHILE BACK; BEHIND SOMEONE'S BACK; BREAK ONE'S BACK; BREAK THE BACK OF; BROAD SHOULDERS (A BROAD BACK); CALL BACK; CHOKE BACK; COME BACK; CUT BACK; DOUBLE BACK; DRAW BACK; DROP BACK; EYES IN THE BACK OF ONE'S HEAD; FALL ALL OVER ONESELF (FALL OVER BACKWARD); FALL BACK; FALL BACK ON; FLAT ON ONE'S BACK; FROM WAY BACK; GET BACK; GET SOMEONE'S BACK UP; GIVE THE SHIRT OFF SOMEONE'S BACK; GO BACK ON ONE'S WORD; HANG BACK; HOLD BACK; IN ONE'S OWN BACK YARD; KICK BACK; KNOCK BACK; KNOW LIKE A BOOK (THE BACK OF ONE'S HAND); LEFT-HANDED (BACKHANDED) COMPLIMENT; LIKE WATER OFF A DUCK'S BACK; LOOK BACK; MONKEY ON ONE'S BACK; OFF SOMEONE'S BACK; PAT ON THE BACK; PAY BACK; PIN SOMEONE'S EARS BACK; PLAY BACK; PLOW BACK; PULL BACK; PUT ONE'S BACK UP; ROLL BACK; SCRATCH SOMEONE'S BACK; SEE THE BACK OF; SET BACK; SET BACK ON ONE'S HEELS; SET ONE BACK; SIT BACK; SLAP ON THE BACK; SNAP BACK; STAB IN THE BACK; TAKE ABACK; TAKE A BACK SEAT; TAKE BACK; TALK BACK; THINK BACK; THROW BACK; TURN BACK; TURN ONE'S BACK ON; WHEN ONE'S BACK IS TURNED; WITH ONE ARM TIED BEHIND ONE'S BACK.

**back against the wall** see BACK TO THE WALL.

**back alley** see BACK STREET.

**back and forth** Also, **backward(s) and forward(s).** To and fro, moving in one direction and then the opposite and making no progress in either direction. For example, *The trees moved back and forth in the wind.* The term is also used figuratively, as in *The lawyers argued the point backward and forward for an entire week.*

**back away** **1.** Walk backward, as in *He cautiously backed away from the dog.* **2.** Gradually retreat, withdraw, as in *Since he couldn't convince his boss, he's backing away from his original idea.* Both senses use the verb *back* in the sense of "retreat." Also see BACK DOWN; BACK OUT.

**back burner, on a** Delayed or postpone because unimportant. For example, *I haven't forgotten his letter; I've just put it on a back burner for now.* This term refers to a cook's putting items requiring less attention at the back of the stove. Also see FRONT BURNER.

**back door** **1.** An entry at the rear of a building, as in *Deliveries are supposed to be made at the back door only.* **2.** A secret, unauthorized, or illegal way of working. For example, *Salesmen are constantly trying to push their products by offering special gifts through the back door.* This term refers to the fact that the back door cannot be seen from the front.

**back down** **1.** Reverse one's upward movement, descend. For example, *When she saw the wasps' nest on the roof, she quickly backed down the ladder.* This literal usage usually refers to something one has climbed, such as a ladder or mountain. **2.** Also, **back off.** Retreat or yield. For example, *As the watchdog began to snarl, the letter carrier backed off,* or *You have a good point; now don't back down when you present it to your boss.* Also see BACK AWAY, def. 2.

**backhanded compliment** see LEFT-HANDED COMPLIMENT.

**back in circulation** see IN CIRCULATION.

**back of** Also, **at the back of** or **in back of.** Behind. For example, *The special brands were stored back of the counter.*

**back off** **1.** See BACK DOWN, def. 2. **2.** Abandon one's position. For example, *The chairman wanted to close several plants but later backed off.*

**back of one's hand** Showing rejection or contempt, as in *Unimpressed with the man, she gave the back of her hand to his suggestion.* This phrase is usually the object of a verb such as *give* or *show.* **Back of the hand** similarly means "an insult" in the term **backhanded compliment** (see under LEFT-HANDED COMPLIMENT) but has a quite different meaning in **know someone like the back of one's hand** (see under KNOW SOMEONE LIKE A BOOK).

**back of one's mind** The distant part of one's mind or memory, as in *With the idea of quitting in the back of his mind, he did not accept the next assignment.*

**back on one's feet** see ON ONE'S FEET.

**back order** An item not currently in stock but to be sold or delivered when it becomes available, as in *We don't have the shoes in white, but we can make them a a back order.* The verb **back-order** means "obtain such an item," as in *The furniture store is going to back-order the sofa for us.*

**back out** **1.** Move or retreat backward without turning; similar to BACK AWAY, def. 1. For example, *She backed out of the parking space.* **2.** Also, **back out of.** Withdraw from a situation, break an agreement or engagement. For example, *After the announcement appeared in the papers, Mary found it doubly difficult to back out of her engagement to Todd.* Also see GO BACK ON.

**backseat driver** A passenger who gives unwanted and/or unneeded directions to the driver; also, a person who interferes in situations. For example, *Aunt Mary drives us all crazy with her comments on our driving; she's an incurable backseat driver.* This term began in the United States, where it was first used for a passenger legitimately directing a chauffeur. It was quickly transferred to figurative use. For synonyms, see ARMCHAIR QUARTERBACK; MONDAY-MORNING QUARTERBACK. Also see TAKE A BACK SEAT.

**back street** Also, **back alley.** **1.** A less visible or an inferior location. For example, *The highway department is very slow to clear snow from the back streets.* **2.** A scene of secret or illegal dealings, as in *Before they were made legal, abortions were often performed in back alleys. Back street* literally means "one away from the main or business area of a town or city," but this term quickly became associated with illegal dealings. *Back alley* is always used in a negative sense.

**back to back** **1.** With backs close together or touching, as in *The chairs were back to back in two rows.* This term also can be applied to people who stand facing in opposite directions and with their backs touching. **2.** Consecutively, one after another, as in *I'm exhausted; I had three meetings back to back.*

**back to basics** Back to basic principles, as in *The plans are much too expensive; to stay within our budget, we have to get back to basics.* At first this term was used mainly for schooling that stresses excellence in reading, writing, and mathematics (also see THREE R'S), but it was quickly transferred to other areas.

**back to the drawing board** Also, **back to square one.** Back to the beginning because the current attempt did not succeed, as in *When the town refused to fund our music program, we had to go back to the drawing board,* or *I've put this together the wrong way, so it's back to square one.* The first term originated in the caption of a World War II cartoon in which a man who holds a set of blueprints is watching an airplane explode. The variant is thought to come from a game in which an unlucky throw of dice sends the player back to the beginning of the course.

**back to the salt mines** Resume work, usually with some reluctance, as in *Well, the holiday is over. Now, it's back to the salt mines.* This term refers to the Russian practice of punishing prisoners by sending them to work in the salt mines of Siberia. Today the term is only used ironically. Also see KEEP ONE'S NOSE TO THE GRINDSTONE.

**back to the wall, have one's** Also, **have one's back against the wall.** Be in a difficult situation; also, have no way of escape. For example, *In the closing minutes, our team had its back to the wall but continued to fight bravely,* or *The bank has him with his back against the wall; he'll have to pay up now.* This term was used originally for a military force making a last stand.

**back up** **1.** Move or drive a vehicle backward, as in *He told her to back up into the garage.* **2.** Bring or come to a standstill, as in *The water had backed up in the drains,* or *The accident backed up traffic for miles.* **3.** Support or strengthen something, as in *The photos were backed up with heavy cardboard so they wouldn't bend,* or *I'll back up your plan.* **4.** Duplicate a computer file or program so that the original is not lost. For example, *Every computer manual warns you to back up your work frequently in case of a loss of power or a computer failure.*

**backward** In addition to the idiom beginning with BACKWARD, also see BEND OVER BACKWARD; FALL ALL OVER ONESELF (FALL OVER BACKWARD); KNOW LIKE A BOOK (BACKWARD AND FORWARD).

**backward and forward** Also, **backwards and forwards.** **1.** See BACK AND FORTH. **2.** Thoroughly, completely, as in *He read the speech over and over, until he knew it backward and forward.*

**back yard** see IN ONE'S OWN BACK YARD.

**bacon** see BRING HOME THE BACON.

**bad** In addition to the idioms beginning with BAD, also see COME TO AN END (A BAD END); FEEL BAD; FROM BAD TO WORSE; GET OFF ON THE WRONG FOOT (TO A BAD START); GIVE A BAD NAME; GIVE BAD MARKS TO; GO BAD; HAVE IT BAD; IN A BAD MOOD; IN A BAD WAY; IN BAD FAITH; IN BAD WITH; IN SOMEONE'S BAD GRACES; LEAVE A BAD TASTE IN ONE'S MOUTH;

MAKE THE BEST OF (A BAD BARGAIN); NOT A BAD SORT; NOT BAD; POOR (BAD) TASTE; RUN OF (BAD) LUCK; TOO BAD; TURN UP (LIKE A BAD PENNY); WITH BAD GRACE.

**bad blood** Anger or hostility between people or groups, as in *There's been bad blood between the two families for years.* This term is based on the old association between blood and an emotion, particularly anger. Versions such as *ill blood* preceded it.

**bad egg** A person who turns out to be very bad, as in *You can't trust him—he's simply a bad egg.* Although *egg* has long been used for various kinds of person (young, good, bad), this transfer of an apparently good food that, when opened, turns out to be rotten is a relatively modern expression. The schoolyard saying **last one in is a rotten egg** does not have any special significance other than as a way of urging others to join an activity, jump into the water, or do something similar. Also see GOOD EGG.

**bad hair day** A day when one's appearance, especially one's hair, does not look attractive. For example, *What have I done to upset you? Nothing, I'm just having a bad hair day.* This term began as a humorous statement but was soon broadened to mean simply having a bad day, that is, a day when everything seems to go wrong. Also see NOT ONE'S DAY.

**bad luck** see under RUN OF LUCK.

**badly off** see BAD OFF.

**bad mouth** Criticize or talk meanly about someone, as in *Why do you constantly bad mouth your colleagues?* This term is believed to be of African origin, where the phrase *bad mouth* means a curse or an evil spell.

**bad name** see GIVE A BAD NAME TO.

**bad news** **1.** An unwelcome thing or person, trouble. For example, *That accident was bad news; the driver that hit us had no insurance,* or *No one wants her at the party—she's bad news.* This term transfers literal bad news—the report of an unhappy recent event—to an unwanted or undesirable person or circumstance. **2.** The amount charged for something, as in *Waiter, bring our check—I want to see the bad news.*

**bad off** Also, **badly off.** In unfortunate circumstances, poor. For example, *Her husband's death left her bad off,* or *She had her pension and wasn't too badly off.* Also see WELL OFF.

**bad press** Criticism or unfavorable reports, as in *That company has always gotten bad press.*

**bad sort, a** An unpleasant, mean person, as in *We cautioned Bill about his friend, who was clearly a bad sort.* The antonym is **a good sort,** a pleasant, kind person, as in *She's a good sort, always helping her neighbors.* The latter is stronger than **not a bad sort,** as in *He seems to get angry now and then, but he's not a bad sort.* All three terms use *a sort* in the sense of "kind of person."

**bad taste** see LEAVE A BAD TASTE; POOR TASTE.

**bad time** see under HAVE A GOOD TIME.

**bad trip** A frightening or an otherwise very unpleasant experience, as in *Given the poor results, her book tour was a bad trip.* The term comes from drug slang, where it meant experiencing hallucinations, pain, or other terrible effects from taking a drug, especially LSD. It was later extended to any extremely unpleasant experience.

**bag** In addition to the idioms beginning with BAG, also see BROWN BAGGER; GRAB BAG; IN THE BAG; LEAVE ONE HOLDING THE BAG; LET THE CAT OUT OF THE BAG; MIXED BAG; USE SOMEONE AS A PUNCHING BAG.

**bag it** **1.** Pack things in a bag, as in *"Please bag it," the customer said to the checkout clerk.* This usage mainly describes packing groceries or other purchases into a bag. **2.** Stop doing something or leave someone suddenly, quit. For example, *The class is not very good, so I've decided to bag it.* This idiom first became widespread among students. **3.** Be quiet, stop doing something, go away. For example, *I've heard enough about that, so just bag it!*

**bag lady** A woman, sometimes an elderly or mentally ill one, who wanders the streets going through garbage containers looking for things that can still be used. For example, *If you're not careful, you'll end up a bag lady.*

**bag of tricks** One's stock of mental resources and strategies, as in *Mom can fix anything—you never know what she will pull out of her bag of tricks.* This expression refers to a magician's bag of equipment for performing magic tricks.

**bail** In addition to the idiom beginning with BAIL, also see MAKE BAIL; OUT ON BAIL; SKIP BAIL.

**bail out** **1.** Empty water out of a boat, usually by filling a bucket or other container. For example, *We had to keep bailing out water from our leaky canoe.* **2.** Rescue someone in an emergency, especially a financial crisis of some kind, as in *They were counting on an inheritance to bail them out.* **3.** Jump out of an airplane, using a parachute. For example, *When the second engine failed, the pilot decided to bail out.* **4.** Give up on something, abandon a responsibility, as in *The company was not doing well, so John decided to bail out while he could still find another job.* **5.** See MAKE BAIL.

**bait** In addition to the idiom beginning with BAIT, also see FISH OR CUT BAIT; JUMP AT (THE BAIT); RISE TO THE BAIT; SWALLOW THE BAIT.

**bait and switch** A dishonest business practice. Customers are persuaded to visit a store for an advertised sale item, but when they arrive, they are told that it is out of stock or that it is far inferior to some more expensive item. For example, *I won't buy anything from that store; they're notorious for their bait and switch tactics.* The verb *bait* here means to place a small piece of food on a hook or in a trap so as to attract a fish or an animal; the verb *switch* means to change, alter, or transfer from one thing to another. It is called **switch-selling** in Britain.

**baker's dozen** Thirteen items instead of twelve, as in *The new bagel store always gives you a baker's dozen.* The origins of this term are unclear.

**balance** In addition to the idiom beginning with BALANCE, also see CHECKS AND BALANCES; HANG IN THE BALANCE; OFF BALANCE; ON BALANCE; STRIKE A BALANCE; TIP THE BALANCE.

**balance the books** **1.** Add up the debits and credits of an account and determine the difference; also, bring the two sides into equilibrium. For example, *It's my job to balance the books each quarter.* **2.** Settle an account by paying what is due, as in *We can't balance the books till your last check clears.*

**ball** In addition to the idioms beginning with BALL, also see BEHIND THE EIGHT BALL; BREAK ONE'S ASS (BALLS); CARRY THE BALL; CRYSTAL BALL; DROP THE BALL; EYEBALL TO EYEBALL; GET THE BALL ROLLING; HAVE A BALL; HAVE ONE'S EYE ON THE BALL; HAVE SOMEONE BY THE BALLS; KEEP THE BALL ROLLING; ON THE BALL; PLAY BALL; PUT SOMETHING IN MOTHBALLS; SNOWBALL'S CHANCE IN HELL; THAT'S HOW THE BALL BOUNCES; WHOLE BALL OF WAX.

**ball and chain** A heavy load and limitation, as in *She regarded her job as a ball and chain, but she needed the money.* This term originally referred to chaining a heavy iron ball to a prisoner's leg. Later it was transferred to other kinds of burdens. The slang phrase is also used figuratively by a man to mean "my wife," especially when he thinks his relationship with her is a burden, as in *It's late; got to get home to the old ball and chain.*

**ball game** see WHOLE NEW BALL GAME.

**ballistic** see GO BALLISTIC.

**ball of fire** A dynamic, energetic, and successful individual, as in *I hope your friend joins us; she's a real ball of fire.*

**balloon** see GO OVER (LIKE A LEAD BALLOON); TRIAL BALLOON.

**ballot** see STUFF THE BALLOT BOX.

**ballpark figure** An acceptable, roughly accurate estimate, as in *I know you can't tell me the exact cost; just give me a ballpark figure.* This term refers to a baseball field, which is always an enclosed space. The expression is basically an extension of the somewhat earlier idiom **in the ballpark,** meaning within a reasonable range, and **out of the ballpark,** meaning beyond a reasonable range.

**ball's in one's court, the** It's one's responsibility now; it's up to someone else. For example, *I've done all I can; now the ball's in your court.* This term comes from tennis, where it means it is the opponent's turn to serve or return the ball. It has since been transferred to other activities.

**ball *something* up** **1.** Roll something into a ball, as in *Her dirty clothes were all balled up in the corner.* **2.** Confuse or mess something up, as in *Jane got all balled up at the beginning of her speech,* or *Henry really balled up that exam.* This term may come from the fact that when a horse is driven over snow, the snow becomes packed into icy balls in its hoofs. Another theory is that it refers to the vulgar term *balls* for testicles.

**banana** see DRIVE SOMEONE CRAZY (BANANAS); GO BANANAS; TOP BANANA.

**band** see ON THE BANDWAGON; TO BEAT THE BAND.

**bang** In addition to the idioms beginning with BANG, also see BEAT (BANG) ONE'S HEAD AGAINST THE WALL; GET A BANG OUT OF; GO OVER (WITH A BANG); MORE BANG FOR THE BUCK.

**bang away** **1.** Strike repeatedly, as in *Mary is always banging away on the piano,* or *The doorbell must be broken; see who is banging away at the door.* Also see BANG SOMETHING OUT. **2.** Go ahead; begin or continue. This slang command usually calls only for energetic action, as in *You can start without me—bang away.* Also see GO TO (IT), def. 3. **3.** Have intercourse, as in *The couple next door banged away all night long.* [Vulgar slang]

**bang for the buck** see MORE BANG FOR THE BUCK.

**bang *something* in** Also, **bang *something* into.** Strike something heavily so as to drive in; also, persuade. For example, *I've been banging nails into the house all day trying to attach this nameplate,* or *I can't seem to bang it into his head that time is precious.*

**bang into** Crash noisily into something, collide with, as in *A clumsy fellow, Bill was always banging into furniture.* Also see BANG SOMETHING IN; BUMP INTO.

**bang one's head against** see BEAT ONE'S HEAD AGAINST THE WALL.

**bang *something* out** Produce something loudly or rapidly by striking something, such as a musical instrument or a typing keyboard. For example, *The pianist banged out the melody on the piano,* or *John planned to bang out his paper in a couple of hours.*

**bang *something* up** Damage something, injure, as in *Banging up the car a second time* *will make Dad very unhappy,* or *Mother fell down the stairs and was all banged up.* This expression led to the adjective **bang-up,** meaning excellent or very successful, as in *David did a bang-up job baking the birthday cake.*

**bank** In addition to the idiom beginning with BANK, also see BREAK THE BANK; LAUGH ALL THE WAY TO THE BANK.

**bank on** Rely on, count on. For example, *You can bank on my friend to do a good job.* This expression refers to a *bank* as a reliable storage place for money.

**baptism of fire** A severe ordeal or test, especially an initial one, as in *This interview would be Robert's baptism of fire.* This term transfers the original religious practice of baptism to various kinds of ordeals. At first it meant the death of martyrs burned at the stake. Later it was used for a soldier's first time in combat. Today it is used more loosely for any difficult first encounter. Also see TRIAL BY FIRE.

**bar** In addition to the idiom beginning with BAR, also see BEHIND BARS; NO HOLDS BARRED.

**bare bones** The essentials or plain, undecorated framework of something, as in *This outline gives just the bare bones of the story; details will come later.* This phrase transfers the naked skeleton of a body to figurative use.

**barefaced lie** A shameless falsehood. For example, *Bill could tell a barefaced lie with a straight face.* The adjective *barefaced* means "beardless," and one theory is that in early days being without a beard was considered improper in all but the youngest males. Later, *barefaced* also meant "brazen" or "bold," the meaning referred to in this phrase.

**bare hands, with one's** With one's hands but without weapons or tools. For example, *Jean assembled the new stove with her bare hands.* This phrase extends the literal meaning, "with uncovered (that is, without gloves) and therefore unprotected hands," to "unaided by tools."

**bare necessities** Just enough resources, with nothing to spare. For example, *The room was furnished with just the bare necessities—bed, table, chair.* This idiom uses *bare* in the sense of "basic, and nothing else."

**bare one's soul** Reveal one's most private thoughts and feelings. For example, *Teenagers rarely bare their souls to their parents; they prefer their peers.* This figurative use of the verb *bare* literally means "make bare" or "uncover."

**bargain** In addition to the idiom beginning with BARGAIN, also see DRIVE A HARD BARGAIN; INTO THE BARGAIN; MAKE THE BEST OF IT (A BAD BARGAIN); MORE THAN ONE BARGAINED FOR; STRIKE A BARGAIN.

**bargain for 1.** Also, **bargain over.** Negotiate about something, usually a price. For example, *In open-air markets it is common practice to bargain for the best price.* **2.** Also, **bargain on.** Expect something, be prepared for, as in *In planning the picnic, we hadn't bargained for bad weather,* or *I hadn't bargained on John's coming along.* For a synonym, see COUNT ON.

**barge in** Enter rudely or abruptly, intrude. For example, *Her mother never knocks but just barges in.* The term is also put as **barge into** or **barge in on** to mean interrupt something, as in *Who asked you to barge into our conversation?* These phrases use *barge* in the sense of "bump into" or "knock against," which may refer to the tendency of barges to collide with other craft.

**bark is worse than one's bite, one's** A person seems more hostile or aggressive than is actually the case, as in *Dad sounds very grouchy in the morning, but his bark's worse than his bite.*

**bark up the wrong tree** Waste one's efforts by pursuing the wrong thing or path, as in *If you think I will lend you more money, you're barking up the wrong tree.* This term comes from the nighttime hunting of animals using dogs. Occasionally the animal fools the dogs, which crowd around a tree, barking loudly, not realizing their prey has gone a different way.

**barn** see CAN'T HIT THE BROAD SIDE OF A BARN; LOCK THE BARN DOOR AFTER THE HORSE IS STOLEN.

**bar none** Also, **barring none.** Without exception, as in *This is the best book I've read all year, bar none.*

**barrel** In addition to the idiom beginning with BARREL, also see BOTH BARRELS; BOTTOM OF THE BARREL; CASH ON THE BARRELHEAD; LIKE SHOOTING FISH IN A BARREL; LOCK, STOCK, AND BARREL; MORE FUN THAN A BARREL OF MONKEYS; OVER A BARREL; PORK BARREL; ROTTEN APPLE (SPOILS THE BARREL).

**barrel of laughs** A lot of fun, as in *Your friend is a real barrel of laughs.* This idiom is also used negatively to say that somebody is not having a good time. For example, *My last year in graduate school was no barrel of laughs,* or *His life has been no barrel of laughs.*

**base** see GET TO FIRST BASE; OFF BASE; TOUCH BASE WITH.

**basis** see ON A FIRST-NAME BASIS.

**basket** In addition to the idiom beginning with BASKET, also see PUT ALL ONE'S EGGS IN ONE BASKET.

**basket case** A person or thing not functioning well. For example, *The stress of moving twice in one month left her a basket case,* or *The republics of the former Soviet Union are economic basket cases.* This term originated in World War I for a soldier who had lost all four limbs in combat and had to be carried in a litter ("basket"). The term was then transferred to an emotionally or mentally unstable person and later to anything that failed to function.

**bat** In addition to the idioms beginning with BAT, also see AT BAT; BLIND AS A BAT; GO TO BAT FOR; LIKE A BAT OUT OF HELL; RIGHT OFF THE BAT.

**bat an eye** see WITHOUT BATTING AN EYE.

**bat *something* around 1.** Hit something around, often with a baseball bat or another object, as in *We batted the tennis ball around this morning.* This term originated in baseball but came to be applied to more violent action as well, as in *Jerry left after being batted around by his father.* **2.** Discuss or debate something, as in *We batted the various plans around for at least an hour before we came to a decision.* This usage transfers batting a ball to a back-and-forth exchange of ideas. **3.** Drift aimlessly, roam, as in *After graduating, they batted around Europe for a year.*

**bath** see TAKE A BATH; THROW OUT THE BABY WITH THE BATH WATER.

**bat one thousand** Also, **bat a thousand.** Have a perfect record, as in *In meeting deadlines, she's batting one thousand,* or *So far, we're batting a thousand.* The term comes from baseball statistics, where it signifies getting a hit for every turn at bat. It was later transferred to other activities.

**bats in one's belfry, have** Be crazy or at least very strange, as in *Sally thought her aunt's belief in ghosts indicated she had bats in her belfry.* This term compares the bat's apparently unpredictable flight in the dark to ideas flying around in a person's head.

**batten down the hatches** Prepare for trouble, as in *Here comes the boss—batten down the hatches.* This term originated in the navy, where it meant preparing for a storm by fastening down canvas over doorways and hatches (openings) with strips of wood called *battens.*

**battle** see HALF THE BATTLE; LOSING BATTLE; PITCHED BATTLE; RUNNING BATTLE.

**bawl *something* or *someone* out 1.** Call out something loudly, announce, as in *Some of the players were quite hard of hearing, so the rector bawled out the bingo numbers.* **2.** Scold or reprimand someone loudly, as in *The boss was always bawling out the workers for not paying attention.*

**bay** see AT BAY.

**be** In addition to the idioms beginning with BE, also see LET BE.

**bead** see DRAW A BEAD ON.

**be-all and end-all, the** The most important item or goal, as in *Buying a house became the be-all and end-all for the newlyweds.*

**be along** Will come, will arrive, as in *John said he'd be along in a few minutes,* or *The doctor's report will be along by the end of the week.* This phrase always indicates a future event.

**beam** see BROAD IN THE BEAM; OFF THE BEAM.

**bean** see FULL OF BEANS; NOT KNOW BEANS; NOT WORTH A DAMN (HILL OF BEANS); SPILL THE BEANS.

**bear** In addition to the idioms beginning with BEAR, also see BRING SOMETHING TO BEAR; CAN'T STAND (BEAR); CROSS TO BEAR; GRIN AND BEAR IT.

**bear a grudge** Also, **have a grudge** or **hold a grudge.** Feel resentment or anger against someone for a past offense. For example, *They held up my claim for months, but I won't bear a grudge against them,* or *His grandfather was always one to hold a grudge.*

**bear down 1.** Press or weigh down on someone or something. For example, *This pen doesn't write unless you bear down hard on it.* **2.** Try hard, intensify one's efforts, as in *If you'll just bear down, you'll pass the test.* **3.** Move forward in a pressing or threatening way, as in *The ferry bore down on our little canoe.* This usage was originally nautical.

**bear fruit** Produce results, have a favorable outcome, as in *This new idea of his is bound to bear fruit.* This term transfers the production of fruit by a tree or plant to other kinds of useful production.

**bearings** see GET ONE'S BEARINGS.

**bear *something* in mind** Also, **keep *something* in mind.** Remember something, as in *Bear in mind that I can't walk as fast as you,* or *Keep the voters in mind when you speak.*

**bear one's cross** see CROSS TO BEAR.

**bear *something* out** Back up or confirm something, as in *The results bear out what she predicted,* or *His story bears me out exactly.*

**bear the brunt** Experience the worst of some bad circumstance, as in *It was the secretary who had to bear the brunt of the doctor's anger.* This idiom uses *brunt* in the sense of "the main force of an enemy's attack," which was experienced by the front lines of the defenders.

**bear up** Go through, face a hardship, as in *Jane found it hard to bear up under the strain of her father's illness.* This term is also used as a command, as in *Bear up—the trip's almost over.*

**bear with** Put up with someone, allow for, as in *He'll just have to bear with them until they decide.* This phrasal verb can also be used as a command, as in *Bear with me—I'm getting to the point.*

**beat** In addition to the idioms beginning with BEAT, also see DEAD BEAT; HEART MISSES A

B

BEAT; IF YOU CAN'T BEAT THEM, JOIN THEM; MARCH TO A DIFFERENT BEAT; MISS A BEAT; OFF THE BEATEN TRACK; POUND THE PAVEMENT (A BEAT); TO BEAT THE BAND.

**beat a dead horse** Also, **flog a dead horse.** Try to revive interest in a hopeless issue. For example, *Politicians who favor the old single-tax idea are beating a dead horse.* The term *dead horse* has long been used figuratively to mean "something of no current value," specifically an advance in pay or other debt that had to be worked ("flogged") off.

**beat all** Surprising, especially in a strange or amazing way, as in *Adam finally got a job—doesn't that beat all!* This expression is often used in a negative way, as in the example. Also see TO BEAT THE BAND.

**beat a path to someone's door** Come to someone in great numbers, as in *Ever since she won a million dollars, relatives have been beating a path to her door.* The term *beat a path* refers to the trampling action of many feet.

**beat a retreat** Also, **beat a hasty retreat.** Reverse direction or withdraw, usually quickly. For example, *I really don't want to run into Jim—let's beat a retreat.* This term originally referred to the military practice of sounding drums to call back troops. Today it is used only figuratively, as in the example.

**beat around the bush** Also, **beat about the bush.** Approach indirectly, in a roundabout way, or too cautiously. For example, *Stop beating around the bush—get to the point.* This term originally may have referred to beating the bushes for game.

**beat *something* back** Force something to retreat or withdraw, as in *His findings beat back all their arguments to the contrary.* This phrase was often used in a military context (and still is), as in *Their armies were beaten back.*

**beat down 1.** Force or drive someone down; defeat or subdue. For example, *That wrestler can beat down all challengers.* **2.** Strike violently, as in the *The sun kept beating down on us all day long.* **3. beat someone down.** Make someone lower a price, as in *He's always trying to beat us down.*

**beaten track** see OFF THE BEATEN TRACK.

**beat *something* into one's head** Also, **knock *something* into one's head** or **drum *something* into one's head.** Force one to learn something. For example, *Hard as I try, I can't seem to beat the correct amount into my head,* or *He promised to drum the numbers into my head by morning,* or *Whether we liked it or not, the English department was determined to knock Shakespeare into our heads.* Although *beat* implies violence, the first term usually refers more to a repeated striking, that is, repetition or drilling. Likewise, *drum* refers to drumbeats.

**beat it** Go away, as in *We should beat it before the food's all gone.* This term is considered rude when used as a a command, as in *Stop pestering me—beat it!*

**beat off 1.** Repulse something, drive away by blows, as in *We tried to beat off the mosquitoes.* This term originated in a military context. **2.** Masturbate, as in *He's too young to be beating off.* [Vulgar slang]

**beat one's brains out** Make a great mental effort to understand, solve, or remember something, as in *Joe's beating his brains out to finish this puzzle.* Also see RACK ONE'S BRAINS.

**beat one's head against the wall** Also, **bang one's head against the wall** or **run one's head against a brick wall** or **bang one's head into a brick wall.** Waste one's time in a hopeless activity, as in *I have tried many times to convince him to stop smoking, but I'm beating my head against a brick wall.* The phrase refers to a physical expression of frustration.

**beat *someone* out 1.** Knock something into shape by beating, as in *She managed to beat out all the dents in the fender.* **2.** Be better than or defeat someone; be chosen over someone. For example, *He got to the head of the line, beating out all the others.* Also see BEAT THE PANTS OFF. **3. beat *something* out of.** Cheat someone of something, as in *He was always trying to beat the conductor out of the full train fare.*

**beats me** This surprises or puzzles me, as in *I don't know how he does it—beats me!* This term originally may have referred to a winning poker hand. It may also be related to the even earlier usage of *beat* for "surprised" or "at a loss."

**beat someone at his or her own game** Do better than someone in his or her own specialty or undertaking. For example, *Jean knew that if she matched the new store's discount, she would keep her customers and beat the new competitors at their own game.* *Game* is used here for any kind of activity.

**beat the bushes for** Look everywhere for something or someone, as in *I've been beating the bushes for a car but haven't had any luck.* This term originally referred to hunting, when beaters were hired to frighten birds out of the brush. Also see BEAT AROUND THE BUSH.

**beat the clock** Finish something or succeed just before time is up, as in *The paper was due at five o'clock, and she hurried to beat the clock.* The term comes from various sports or races in which contestants compete within a certain time limit.

**beat the drum for** Praise, promote, publicize, as in *He's always beating the drum for his division, which actually has done very well.* This term transfers the literal striking of a drum for ceremonial or other purposes to proclaiming the virtues of a person, group, or product.

**beat the living daylights out of** Also, **beat the shit out of** or **beat the stuffing out of** or **beat the tar out of** or **knock the living daylights out of** or **knock the shit out of** or **lick the hell out of.** Give a merciless beating to someone; also, defeat soundly. For example, *The coach said he'd like to beat the living daylights out of the people who damaged the gym floor,* or *Bob knocked the stuffing out of that bully,* or *He swore he'd beat the tar out of anyone who tried to stop him.* These phrases nearly always indicate a physical attack. In the first, *daylights* originally meant "the eyes" and later was extended to any vital (*living*) body organ. *Hell* is simply a swear word used for emphasis. The more vulgar *shit* and the politer *stuffing* refer simply to knocking out someone's insides. *Tar* is more puzzling but has been so used for at least a century.

**beat the meat** Masturbate, as in *He was always beating the meat.* This term is used for males, since it uses *meat* in the sense of "penis." [Vulgar slang]

**beat the pants off** Win decisively over someone, outdo. For example, *When it comes to the annual parade, Lexington beats the pants off the neighboring towns.* This phrase uses *beat* in the sense of "surpass." *Pants off* is used here as an intensifier.

**beat the rap** Escape punishment; be acquitted. For example, *The youngsters were caught shoplifting, but somehow they were able to beat the rap. Rap* in this idiom means "the legal charge against one."

**beat the system** Find a way to do or get something one wants in spite of the established rules of a group or an organization. For example, *He tried to beat the system in Las Vegas but lost everything,* or *You won't succeed by trying to beat the system.* Also see BUCK THE SYSTEM.

**beat time** Mark musical time by beating a drum, clapping, tapping the foot, or a similar action. For example, *Even as a baby, she always beat time when she heard music.* Also see KEEP TIME.

**beat *someone* to it** **1.** Get ahead of someone to obtain something, as in *There was only enough for one, so Jane ran as fast as she could in order to beat everybody to it.* **2.** Also, **beat *someone* to the draw** or **beat *someone* to the punch.** React more quickly than someone else. For example, *The new salesman tried to take one of my customers, but I beat him to the draw* or *Bill was determined to get there first and beat everyone else to the punch.* The variants imply aggression to get ahead, *draw* referring to the drawing of a pistol and *punch* to hitting with the fists.

**beat *someone* up** **1.** Strike someone repeatedly, as in *She told the police her husband had beaten her up.* **2.** Also, **beat up on.** Attack someone verbally, as in *That newspaper article really beat up on the town council.*

**beauty** In addition to the idiom beginning with BEAUTY, also see THAT'S THE BEAUTY OF.

**beauty is only skin deep** Physical attractiveness has no relation to one's goodness or essential quality. For example, *I judge people on the basis of their inner qualities; I've learned that beauty is only skin deep.*

**beaver** see BUSY AS A BEAVER; EAGER BEAVER; WORK LIKE A BEAVER.

**be busted** **1.** Also, **go bust.** Lose all one's money, become financially ruined. For example, *Who knew that the firm would be busted?* Also see under GO BROKE. **2.** Also, **get busted.** Be demoted, as in *If you're caught gambling, you'll get busted to private.* This usage originated in the military and still most often refers to a reduction in rank. **3.** Also, **get busted.** Be arrested or turned over to the police, as in *The gang members were sure they'd get busted.*

**beck** see AT SOMEONE'S BECK AND CALL.

**become** In addition to the idiom beginning with BECOME, also see idioms beginning with GET.

**become of** Happen to someone, be the fate of, as in *I haven't seen Joe in a year; what has become of his book?*

**bed** In addition to the idioms beginning with BED, also see EARLY TO BED; GET UP ON THE WRONG SIDE OF BED; GO TO BED WITH; IN BED WITH; MAKE ONE'S BED AND LIE IN IT; MAKE THE BED; PUT TO BED; SHOULD HAVE STOOD IN BED; STRANGE BEDFELLOWS.

**bed and board** Lodging and meals, as in *Housekeepers usually earn a standard salary in addition to bed and board.*

**bed-and-breakfast** Also, **bed and breakfast** or **B and B.** A hotel or other similar business that offers a room for the night and a morning meal at an inclusive price. For example, *We stayed at a lovely bed-and-breakfast in New England.* This term and the practice originated in Britain and have become widespread.

**bed of roses** A very comfortable position, as in *Taking care of these older patients is no bed of roses.* This expression is often used in a negative context, as in the example. Also see BOWL OF CHERRIES.

**be down** Be depressed, in low spirits, as in *During the winter months, Sue's always down, but spring cheers her up.*

**bee** In addition to the idiom beginning with BEE, also see BIRDS AND THE BEES; BUSY AS A BEAVER (BEE); MAKE A BEELINE FOR; NONE OF ONE'S BUSINESS (BEESWAX).

**beef** In addition to the idiom beginning with BEEF, also see HAVE A BEEF

**beef up** Strengthen something, make larger, as in *Mary wants us to beef up her part in the play.* This phrase relies on an older slang sense of *beef* as "muscles" or "power."

**bee in one's bonnet, have a** A strange idea or notion; also, an idea that is constantly brought up, an obsession. For example, *Bill's got a bee in his bonnet about burglars; he's always imagining strange noises.* This term, which replaced the earlier *have bees in one's head,* transfers the buzzing of a bee inside one's hat to a strange idea in one's head.

**beeline** see MAKE A BEELINE FOR.

**been around** Been present or active; especially, gained experience or sophistication. For example, *This book isn't new; it's been around for many years,* or *This strategy won't fool Bill; he's been around.* Also see GET AROUND.

**been around the block (a few times)** Very experienced, often sexually, or completely used up or worn out. For example, *I'd say he's been around the block a few times,* or *That car looks like it's been around the block.*

**been there, done that (got the T-shirt)** see under SEEN ONE, SEEN THEM ALL.

**been to the wars** Show signs of rough treatment or injury, as in *That car of yours looks as though it's been to the wars.*

**before** In addition to the idioms beginning with BEFORE, also see CART BEFORE THE HORSE; CAST PEARLS BEFORE SWINE; LOOK BEFORE YOU LEAP.

**before long** Soon, in the near future, as in *The baby will be walking before long.*

**before one's time** **1.** In the past, before someone was born, as in *Do you like this song, or was it before your time?* **2.** Early, at a young age, as in *He was always sure he'd die before his time.*

**before you can say Jack Robinson** Also, **quicker than you can say Jack Robinson.** Almost immediately, very soon, as in *I'll finish this book before you can say Jack Robinson.* The identity of the original Jack Robinson has been lost. A newer version of the expression is **before you know it,** meaning so soon that you don't have time to become aware of it (as in *He'll be gone before you know it*).

**beg** In addition to the idioms beginning with BEG, also see GO BEGGING.

**beg, borrow, or steal** Get something by any possible means, as in *You couldn't beg, borrow, or steal tickets to the baseball game.* This term is often used in the negative, to describe something that cannot be obtained, as in the example.

**beggar description** Also, **beg description.** Be more than any possible description, as in *The room was so elaborate, it beggared description,* or *The party begged description.* This term refers to the idea that words are not adequate to describe something.

**beggars can't be choosers** Those in great need must be satisfied with what they get. For example, *The cheapest model will have to do—beggars can't be choosers.*

**begin** In addition to the idiom beginning with BEGIN, also see CHARITY BEGINS AT HOME; (BEGIN TO) SEE THE LIGHT; TO START (BEGIN) WITH.

**beginner's luck** Good fortune in a first attempt or effort, as in *I often use a brand-new recipe for a dinner party; I trust beginner's luck.*

**beginning of the end, the** The start of a bad outcome (ruin, disaster, catastrophe, death), as in *Joe's failing two of his courses was the beginning of the end; he dropped out soon afterward.* At first this phrase was used only to describe someone's approaching death, but it has come to be used more generally to refer to an approaching end or defeat.

**begin to see daylight** Realize that a task is finally nearing completion, that success or the right solution is near at hand. For example, *I've been working on this experiment for two years, and I'm finally beginning to see daylight.* The noun *daylight* here refers to knowledge and solution. Also see LIGHT AT THE END OF THE TUNNEL; SEE THE LIGHT.

**begin to see the light** see SEE THE LIGHT.

**begin with** see TO START WITH.

**beg off** Ask to be released from a duty; turn down an invitation. For example, *He's asked me out to dinner three times already, but I have to beg off again,* or *Mother couldn't take on another committee, and so she begged off.*

**beg the question** Take for granted or assume the truth of the very thing being questioned. For example, *Shopping now for a dress to wear to the ceremony is really begging the question—she hasn't been invited yet.* Today people sometimes use this phrase as a synonym for "ask the question" (as in *The article begs the question: "What are we afraid of?"*).

**beg to differ** Disagree with someone, as in *John told me Max was sure to win, but I beg to differ—I don't think he has a chance.* This courteous formula for expressing disagreement echoes similar uses of *beg* in the sense of "ask," such as **I beg your pardon.** Also see EXCUSE ME.

**be had** **1.** Be fooled; also, be cheated, deceived. For example, *This lawyer is a real con artist; you've been had,* or *I've become very cautious about these schemes; it's too costly to be had more than once.* This expression uses the verb *have* in the sense of getting someone in one's power or at a disadvantage. **2.** Be bribed or influenced by dishonest means. For example, *Our senator cannot be had.*

**behalf** see IN BEHALF OF.

**behavior** see ON ONE'S BEST BEHAVIOR.

**behind** In addition to the idioms beginning with BEHIND, also see COME FROM BEHIND; DROP BEHIND; FALL BEHIND; GET BEHIND; POWER BEHIND THE THRONE; PUT BEHIND ONE; WET BEHIND THE EARS; WITH ONE ARM TIED BEHIND ONE'S BACK.

**behind bars** In prison, as in *Murderers should be put behind bars for life.* The bars here refer to the iron rods used to confine prisoners.

**behind closed doors** In secret, privately. For example, *The executive committee always meets behind closed doors, so that its deliberations won't become known prematurely.* Also see BEHIND THE SCENES.

**behind in 1.** Also, **behind on.** Late doing something; not progressing quickly enough with a task. For example, *The builders are behind on this project,* or *I can't take time out, or I'll be too far behind in my work.* The same idea is also expressed as **behind time,** where *time* means a schedule or an appointed time, as in *The bus should be here soon; it's behind time.* Also see FALL BEHIND. **2.** Owing back payments or more than one should. For example, *We're behind in our payments, so the interest will mount up.*

**behind someone's back** Out of one's presence or without someone's knowledge, as in *Joan has a nasty way of making fun of her friends behind their backs.*

**behind the eight ball** In trouble or in an awkward position, out of luck, as in *His girlfriend saw him at the party, leaving him behind the eight ball.* The term comes from billiards or pool. In certain games, if the number eight ball is between the "cue ball" and "object ball," the player cannot make a straight shot.

**behind the scenes** In secret or private, away from public view, as in *His struggle for the top position took place behind the scenes.* This term refers to the various activities that go on behind the curtain in theaters, out of the audience's view. Also see BEHIND CLOSED DOORS.

**behind the times** Not keeping up with current fashion, methods, or ideas, as in *Your accounting methods are behind the times.*

**behind time** see under BEHIND IN.

**being** see FOR THE MOMENT (TIME BEING); OTHER THINGS BEING EQUAL.

**be in on** see IN ON.

**be into 1.** Also, **get into.** Be interested in or involved with something. For example, *She's really into yoga,* or *Once you retire, it's important to get into some hobby you've always wanted to try.* **2.** Be completely attracted to someone, as in *He's really into his new girlfriend.*

**belabor the point** Repeat an argument or other issue over and over, obsess about something in an exaggerated way, as in *We've discussed her decision—let's not belabor the point.* This term derives from *belabor* in the sense of "attack with words."

**belfry** see BATS IN ONE'S BELFRY.

**believe** In addition to the idioms beginning with BELIEVE, also see LEAD ONE TO BELIEVE; MAKE BELIEVE; YOU'D BETTER BELIEVE IT. Also see SEEING IS BELIEVING.

**believe it or not** It's true, whether or not you agree, as in *Believe it or not, I finally finished painting the house.* This phrase gained popularity as the title of a cartoon series begun by Robert Ripley and continuing to run in American newspapers long after his death. Each drawing presented a strange but supposedly true phenomenon, such as a two-headed chicken.

**believe one's ears** Also, **believe one's eyes.** Trust one's own hearing or sight, as in *We couldn't believe our ears when we heard that he was accepted at Stanford,* or *I couldn't believe my own eyes when the movie stars walked in.* This expression of disbelief is nearly always stated negatively, as in the examples.

**believing** see SEEING IS BELIEVING.

**bell** In addition to the idiom beginning with BELL, also see CLEAR AS A BELL; RING A BELL; SAVED BY THE BELL; SOUND AS A BELL; WITH BELLS ON.

**bells and whistles** Extra things added to a product, such as a car or computer, that don't contribute to its performance in any way. For example, *The updated software is all bells and whistles; there's no real difference between it and the old version.* Such things are added so that people will think it's a worthwhile purchase.

**belly** see GO BELLY UP.

**belong** see TO THE VICTOR BELONG THE SPOILS.

**below par** Also, **under par.** Not up to the average, normal, or desired standard. For example, *I am feeling below par today, but I'm sure I'll recover by tomorrow.* This term uses *par* in the sense of "an average amount or quality."

**below the belt, hit** Not behave according to the rules of fairness, as in *Bringing up my mother's faults—that's really hitting below the belt.* The term comes from boxing, where according to the Marquis of Queensberry Rules, a fighter may punch his opponent only in the upper body or head. For a synonym, see LOW BLOW. Also see UNDER ONE'S BELT.

**belt** In addition to the idioms beginning with BELT, also see BELOW THE BELT; BIBLE BELT; SUN BELT; TIGHTEN ONE'S BELT; UNDER ONE'S BELT.

B

**belt down** Swallow something very quickly, as in *After the race, he belted down a whole quart of water.* This phrase is frequently used for guzzling whiskey or some other liquor.

**belt out** Sing or play music very loudly, as in *She belted out the national anthem before every game.*

**be my guest** Do as you wish. For example, *May I drive your car? Sure, be my guest,* or *Do you mind if I go to the play without you? No, be my guest.* This expression not only literally invites someone to behave as one's guest (using one's house, belongings, etc.) but also figuratively tells someone to feel free to act as he or she pleases. Also see FEEL FREE.

**bench** see ON THE BENCH; WARM THE BENCH.

**bend** In addition to the idioms beginning with BEND, also see AROUND THE BEND; CROOK (BEND) ONE'S ELBOW; ON BENDED KNEE. Also see under BENT.

**bend one's elbow** see CROOK ONE'S ELBOW.

**bend over backward** Also, **lean over backward.** Exert oneself to the fullest extent, as in *Dad bent over backward so as not to embarrass my new boyfriend.* This phrase transfers the gymnastic feat of a back bend to taking a great deal of trouble for someone or something. Also see under FALL ALL OVER ONESELF.

**bend someone's ear** Talk about a matter at great length; completely dominate someone's attention. For example, *She is always bending his ear about her financial problems.* This term may have come from the much older *bend one's ear to someone,* meaning "listen to someone," although the current phrase implies a less than willing audience.

**bend the rules** Allow one to break a rule just a little, as in *He begged me to bend the rules and let him stay up longer.*

**benefit** see GIVE THE BENEFIT OF THE DOUBT.

**bent on** Also, **bent upon.** Determined, resolved, as in *He is bent on winning the math prize.* This phrase always uses the past participle of the verb *bend* in the sense of "tend toward."

**bent out of shape** **1.** Angry, annoyed, as in *Don't let Paul get you bent out of shape—calm down.* **2.** Shocked, astonished, as in *That conservative audience was bent out of shape by his speech.* Also see IN CONDITION (SHAPE).

**be off** **1.** Leave, depart, as in *I'm off to the school; I'll be home around 5:00.* This phrase was once commonly used as a command, meaning "go away"—as in *Be off or I'll call the police*—but today it is rare in this context. **2.** Be in poor condition; be stale or spoiled; not work properly. For example, *This milk must be off; it tastes sour,* or *The clock is off by at least five minutes.* **3.** Be free from work, school, or some other regular job, as in *Our secretary is off today, but perhaps I can find it.* **4.** Decline, as in *The industrial stocks are off 50 points today.* This usage is nearly always applied to securities or other prices.

**be on** **1.** Be taking medication or an illegal drug, as in *Are you on some antibiotic?* or *He was definitely on drugs when it happened.* **2.** Be in favor of something or be willing to participate, as in *We're going dancing after the play—are you on?* **3.** Be engaged in some action, especially on the stage, as in *Hurry up, you're on in five minutes.* **4.** Perform extremely well, as in *I can't return Dan's serve—he's really on today.* **5.** Be scheduled, as in *Is the party still on for tonight?* **6. be on one.** Be at one's expense, either as a treat or as the object of a joke. For example, *This round of drinks is on me,* or *He enjoys a good laugh, even when the joke's on him.* **7. be on the ball.** See ON THE BALL.

**be oneself** **1.** Act in one's usual way; be in one's normal physical or mental state. For example, *Peter's finally recovered from the accident and is himself again,* or *I was completely distracted; I just wasn't myself.* **2.** Act without pretense; be unaffected, sincere. For example, *I really enjoy their company because I can be myself with them.*

**be on to** **1.** Be aware of or have information about someone, as in *They can't pull that trick again; we're on to them now.* **2.** Discover something important or profitable, as in *The researchers claim they are really on to something big.*

**berth** see GIVE ONE A WIDE BERTH.

**beside oneself** In a state of extreme nervousness or excitement, as in *She was beside herself when she found she'd lost her ring,* or *He was beside himself with joy—he'd won the poetry award.*

**beside the point** Also, **beside the mark** or **beside the question.** Irrelevant, off the subject. For example, *Whether you had insurance is beside the point; the accident is your fault.* Also see NEITHER HERE NOR THERE.

**best** In addition to the idioms beginning with BEST, also see ALL FOR THE BEST; ALL THE BEST; AS BEST ONE CAN; AT BEST; AT ONE'S BEST; COME OFF (SECOND-BEST); DO ONE'S BEST; GET THE BETTER (BEST) OF; GIVE IT ONE'S BEST SHOT; HAD BETTER (BEST); IN ONE'S (BEST) INTEREST; MAKE THE BEST OF IT; ON ONE'S BEST BEHAVIOR; PUT ONE'S BEST FOOT FORWARD; SECOND BEST; SUNDAY BEST; TO THE BEST OF ONE'S ABILITY; WITH THE BEST OF THEM; WITH THE BEST WILL IN THE WORLD. Also see under BETTER.

**best bet** A preferred choice among several alternatives that will be the most advantageous. For example, *If you ask me, leaving early tomorrow is your best bet.*

**best-laid plans go astray, the** Also, **the best-laid plans of mice and men** or **the best-laid schemes go astray.** Even very careful designs or projects do not always succeed. For example, *He spent all afternoon preparing this elaborate dish but forgot the most important ingredient—oh well, the best-laid plans go astray.* This phrase comes from Robert Burns's poem "To a Mouse": "The best-laid schemes o' mice an' men gang aft a-gley [that is, go often astray]." It is so well known that it is often abbreviated to **the best-laid plans.**

**best of both worlds, the** Benefits from two seemingly opposite alternatives, as in *She taught in the morning only and worked on her book afternoons, so she had the best of both worlds.* Also see MAKE THE BEST OF IT.

**best part of, the** Also, **the better part of.** Nearly all of some period of time, as in *The dentist was late; I waited for the best part of an hour.* The adjective *best* here does not concern quality but quantity.

**best shot** see GIVE IT ONE'S BEST SHOT.

**bet** see HEDGE ONE'S BETS; YOU BET.

**be that as it may** Nevertheless, it may be true but, as in *Be that as it may, I can't take your place on Monday.* This phrase has its roots in *be as be may* and is one of the remaining examples of the subjunctive mood in English.

**be the death of** Cause the death of something or someone, as in *This comedian is so funny, he'll be the death of me.* This phrase can be used literally, meaning "to kill someone or something," but it can also be used to exaggerate, as in *All that running around, going here and going there, will be the death of her.*

**be the end of** Be the cause of one's downfall, as in *His heavy drinking may well be the end of him,* or *That math assignment will be the end of me.* This phrase originally referred to something that would cause someone's death. Today, while it may be used seriously (as in the first example), it more often is used more lightly (as in the second example).

**be the making of** Be the means or cause of one's progress or success, as in *Marriage will be the making of him.* This idiom uses *making* in the sense of "advancement."

**bet one's ass** Also, **bet one's bottom dollar** or **bet one's (sweet) life.** See YOU BET.

**better** In addition to the idioms beginning with BETTER, also see AGAINST ONE'S BETTER JUDGMENT; ALL BETTER; BEST (BETTER) PART OF; DISCRETION IS THE BETTER PART OF VALOR; FOR BETTER OR FOR WORSE; GET BETTER; GET THE BETTER (BEST) OF; GO ONE BETTER; HAD BETTER (BEST); KNOW BETTER; SEEN BETTER DAYS; SO MUCH THE BETTER; SOONER THE BETTER; TAKE A TURN FOR THE BETTER; THINK BETTER OF; YOU'D BETTER BELIEVE IT. Also see under BEST.

**better half, the** **1.** Also, **the better part.** The larger amount or majority of something, as in *I won't be long; the better half of this job is complete,* or *I have spent the better part of my life in this city.* The variant appears in a well-known proverb, DISCRETION IS THE BETTER PART OF VALOR. **2.** Also, **one's better half.** One's spouse, as in *I'm not sure if we can go; I'll have to check with my better half.* Originally this expression meant "a close friend or lover." It later referred to either a wife or a lover. Today it tends to be used lightly for either husband or wife.

**better late than never** Being tardy is better than not arriving or not doing something at all, as in *We've been waiting for you for an hour—but better late than never.* It is often used to show annoyance over a delay, as in the example.

**better off** **1.** In a more favorable position. For example, *They were better off flying than driving there.* **2.** In better financial circumstances, as in *They were better off than most of their neighbors.* This phrase is the comparative form of WELL OFF.

**better part of** see BEST PART OF; BETTER HALF, def. 1.

**better safe than sorry** Being careful may avoid disaster, as in *I'm not taking any shortcuts—better safe than sorry.*

**better someone than one** Glad that another person will have to do something difficult or unpleasant. For example, *I hear they're going to move next week—better them than me,* or *Someone has to tell him he's fired—better you than me.*

**better than** **1.** Superior to someone, as in *He's no better than Tom at writing a memo.* **2.** More than another thing, larger in amount or greater in rate, as in *My new car can do better than 100 miles an hour,* or *The new plan will cut costs better than 15 percent.*

**between** In addition to the idioms beginning with BETWEEN, also see BETWIXT AND BETWEEN; COME BETWEEN; DRAW A LINE BETWEEN; FALL BETWEEN THE CRACKS; FEW AND FAR BETWEEN; HIT BETWEEN THE EYES; IN BETWEEN; IN BETWEEN TIMES; READ BETWEEN THE LINES; TAIL BETWEEN ONE'S LEGS.

**between a rock and a hard place** Also, **between the devil and the deep blue sea.** Between two equally difficult or unacceptable choices. For example, *Trying to please both my boss and his supervisor puts me between a rock and a hard place.* The *rock and hard place* version refers to being caught or crushed between two rocks. The second phrase may simply refer to a choice between hellfire with the devil and drowning in deep waters.

B

**between the lines** see READ BETWEEN THE LINES.

**between you and me** Also, **between ourselves; just between you and me and the bedpost** or **four walls** or **gatepost** or **lamppost.** In strict confidence. For example, *Just between you and me, it was James who proposed the tax increase.* This phrase is generally followed by some informative statement that the listener is being asked to keep secret. The variant with *bedpost* is often shortened to *post,* and *four walls* is often shortened to *the wall* or *the walls.*

**betwixt and between** Undecided, midway between two options. For example, *I'm betwixt and between canceling my trip entirely or just postponing it,* or *Jane is betwixt and between about accepting the offer.* The adverb *betwixt,* originally meaning "by two," is seldom heard except in this expression.

**beyond** In addition to the idioms beginning with BEYOND, also see ABOVE AND BEYOND; CAN'T SEE BEYOND THE END OF ONE'S NOSE.

**beyond a doubt** Also, **beyond the shadow of a doubt.** Certainly, undoubtedly, as in *Beyond a doubt this is the best view of the valley.* This phrase, along with the earlier **without doubt,** asserts the truth of some statement. Another variant is **beyond a reasonable doubt.** This phrase is often used in court when the judge instructs the jury that they must be convinced of the accused person's guilt or innocence beyond a reasonable doubt; *reasonable* here means "logical and rational." Also see BEYOND QUESTION; NO DOUBT.

**beyond comparison** Also, **without comparison** or **beyond compare.** Too superior to be compared, unrivaled, as in *This view of the mountains is beyond comparison,* or *That bakery is without comparison.*

**beyond measure** To an extreme degree; exceedingly. For example, *Her attitude annoys me beyond measure.*

**beyond one's depth** see OUT OF ONE'S DEPTH.

**beyond one's means** Too costly for one, more than one can afford. For example, *That house is well beyond our means.* The noun *means* here refers to financial resources.

**beyond price** So valuable that its cost cannot be estimated, as in *That chair is beyond price; it was mine when I was a child.*

**beyond question** Also, **beyond all question** or **without question.** Definitely, certainly, as in *Beyond question he is the best man for the job.* This idiom indicates that something is so sure it cannot be questioned. Also see BEYOND A DOUBT.

**beyond reach** see under IN REACH.

**beyond reproach** Blameless, faultless, as in *Jean's conduct at work is beyond reproach.* The phrase uses the verb *reproach* in the sense of "find blame or fault."

**beyond the call of duty** see under ABOVE AND BEYOND.

**beyond the pale** Outside the bounds of morality, good behavior, or judgment; unacceptable. For example, *She thought taking the boys into a bar was beyond the pale.*

**beyond the shadow of a doubt** see BEYOND A DOUBT.

**Bible belt** An area of the United States noted for religious fundamentalism, specifically parts of the American South and Midwest. For example, *They wouldn't dare try to run that ad in the Bible belt.* This term refers to the frequency of evangelical revivals, strict morals, belief in the literal truth of the Bible, and similar traits.

**bide one's time** Wait for the best time to do something, as in *The cat sat in front of the mousehole, biding its time.* This phrase uses the verb *bide* in the sense of "wait for," a usage surviving mainly in this phrase.

**bid up** Raise a price by raising one's offer, as in *We were hoping to get an Oriental rug cheaply, but the dealer kept bidding us up.* This phrase is used in business and commerce, particularly at auctions.

**big** In addition to the idioms beginning with BIG, also see (BIG) BLABBERMOUTH; GO OVER (BIG); GREAT (BIG) GUNS; HIT IT BIG; IN A BIG WAY; LAST OF THE BIG SPENDERS; LITTLE FROG IN A BIG POND; MAKE A FEDERAL CASE (BIG DEAL); TALK BIG; THINK BIG; TOO BIG FOR ONE'S BREECHES; WHAT'S THE (BIG) IDEA. Also see under BIGGER.

**big as life 1.** Also, **large as life.** In person, as in *And there was Mary, big as life, standing right in front of me.* This phrase transfers the same size as in real life (life-size) to an actual appearance. **2.** Also, **larger than life; big as all outdoors.** On a grand scale, as in *That friend of his is as big as all outdoors.* The first variant is also used as an adjective, as in *The soap opera could well be called a larger-than-life drama.* These phrases can be used either literally, for larger than life-size (first example) or figuratively. The phrase *all outdoors* compares a person or an object to something that is immense.

**Big Brother (is watching you)** An authoritarian government or organization that controls its citizens or members by limiting their freedom and constantly spying on them, as in *Don't leave too early—Big Brother is watching.* This expression is often shortened to **Big Brother,** as in *Who does he think he is, forbidding us to leave when we please? Big Brother?*

**big bucks** A large amount of money, as in *A swimming pool—that means you're spending big bucks. Buck* is a slang term for "dollar."

**big cheese** Also, **big shot** or **big gun** or **big wheel** or **big enchilada.** An important, powerful person; the boss. For example, *She loved being the big cheese of her company,* or *The big guns in Congress are certain to change the President's bill,* or *You'd better not act like such a big shot around your old friends,* or *Harry was the big wheel in his class,* or *You'll have to ask permission from the big enchilada.*

**big daddy 1.** A powerful man, a big shot, as in *You'll have to get permission from big daddy.* Also see BIG CHEESE. **2.** A male sweetheart or friend, often a man older than his female companion; a SUGAR DADDY. **3.** Grandfather. This usage originated in the South among African Americans. **4.** The largest or most important person or thing of its kind. For example, *The United States has long been the big daddy of the Western Hemisphere,* or *The blue whale is the big daddy of the ocean.*

**big deal 1.** A matter of great interest or importance, as in *Winning the prize is a big deal for everyone in our school.* Also see under MAKE A FEDERAL CASE OUT OF. **2.** So what? Who cares? This phrase is often used as an ironic comment. For example, *So you got the job after all—well, big deal!*

**big enchilada** see BIG CHEESE.

**big fish in a small pond, a** Also, **a big frog in a little pond.** A person who is important in a limited area; someone overqualified for a position or in relation to colleagues. For example, *Steve has both a Ph.D. and an M.D., yet he's content with his practice at a rural hospital; he prefers to be a big fish in a little pond.* The expression *big fish* is a slang term for an important or influential person; *in a small pond* refers to an unimportant organization. Another variant is the proverb *Better a big fish in a little puddle than a little fish in a big puddle.*

**bigger** In addition to the idiom beginning with BIGGER, also see EYES ARE BIGGER THAN ONE'S STOMACH.

**bigger they come, the harder they fall, the** People in important positions lose more when they fail, as in *Impeaching a President is very painful—the bigger they come, the harder they fall.* This expression is believed to come from boxing and was probably derived from similar adages, such as "The bigger the tree, the harder it falls."

**big gun** see BIG CHEESE.

**big head, have a** Be conceited; have an exaggerated sense of one's own importance or ability. For example, *The constant flattery of his subordinates is certain to give him a big head.* Also see SWELLED HEAD.

**big league** Also, **in the big leagues.** An area of tough competition and high rewards; the largest or most important of its kind. For example, *Winning an Oscar put this unknown actress in the big league.* The term refers to the major (big) leagues of American baseball. Also see BIG TIME, def. 2.

**big mouth, have a** Also, **have a loud mouth** or **be a loud mouth.** Talk too much, and often too loudly or boastfully; reveal secrets. For example, *Don't tell Peggy anything confidential; she's known for having a big mouth,* or *After a few drinks, Dick turns into a loud mouth about his accomplishments.*

**big of one** Generous of one, as in *It was big of you to give your brother your entire paycheck.* This expression may be used either literally (as above) or sarcastically, as in *How big of you to save the worst seat for me.*

**big on** In favor of something, enthusiastic about, as in *Dad is big on Christmas with the whole family.*

**big shot** see BIG CHEESE.

**big stink, make a** Also, **put up a big stink** or **cause a big stink** or **create a big stink.** Cause a major scandal or disturbance. For example, *If they don't improve the women's facilities, I will make a big stink about it.*

**big time 1.** An enjoyable or exciting time, as in *The children came home exhausted but happy; they really had a big time at the circus.* **2.** The highest or most important level in any organization, as in *I knew that when I made it through the last audition, I was finally in the big time.* Also see BIG LEAGUE.

**big top 1.** The main tent of a circus, as in *The high-wire act is almost always in the big top.* **2.** Underworld slang for a maximum-security prison, as in *He was sentenced to ten years in the big top.*

**big wheel** see BIG CHEESE.

**bill** see CLEAN BILL OF HEALTH; FILL THE BILL; FOOT THE BILL; SELL ONE A BILL OF GOODS.

**bind** In addition to the idiom beginning with BIND, also see IN A BIND. Also see under BOUND.

**bind *one* hand and foot** see BOUND HAND AND FOOT.

**bind over** Oblige someone to do or not do something; hold on bail or keep under bond. For example, *The sheriff will bind over the murder suspect to the homicide division.* This phrase is nearly always used in a legal context.

**binge** Overindulgence, especially in food or drink, as in *They went on a popcorn binge last weekend.* It is often put as **go on a binge,** meaning "eat or drink too much," as in the example. The term is also used as a verb, as in *We really binged on those snacks.*

B

**bird** In addition to the idioms beginning with BIRD, also see CATBIRD SEAT; EARLY BIRD CATCHES THE WORM; EAT LIKE A BIRD; FOR THE BIRDS; FREE AS A BIRD; KILL TWO BIRDS WITH ONE STONE; LITTLE BIRD TOLD ME; NAKED AS A JAYBIRD; RARE BIRD.

**bird in the hand, a** A benefit available now is more valuable than some possibly larger future benefit. For example, *Bob thinks he might do better in a bigger firm, but his wife insists he should stay, saying a bird in the hand.* This expression, which in full is **A bird in the hand is worth two in the bush,** was an ancient Greek proverb. It has been repeated so frequently that it is often shortened.

**birds and the bees, the** A euphemism for sex education, especially when taught informally. For example, *It's time Dad told the children about the birds and the bees.* This idiom refers to sexual behavior in animals to avoid explicit explanation of human behavior.

**bird's eye view, a** **1.** A view seen from above, as in *This balcony gives us a bird's eye view of the town.* **2.** An overview, as in *This course gives you a bird's eye view of history—from Eolithic people to the Gulf War in one semester.*

**birds of a feather (flock together)** Individuals of like character, taste, or background (tend to stay together), as in *The members of the club had no trouble selecting their yearly outing—they're all birds of a feather.* This idiom is so well known that it is often shortened, as in the example.

**birth** see GIVE BIRTH TO.

**birthday suit, one's** Naked, as in *The doorbell rang, and here I was in my birthday suit.* In Britain this term originally referred to the clothes one wore on the king's birthday. Later it was humorously transferred to bare skin, referring to the condition of a newborn baby.

**bit** In addition to the idioms beginning with BIT, also see A BIT; CHAMP AT THE BIT; DO ONE'S PART (BIT); EVERY BIT; GO (A BIT) TOO FAR; NOT A BIT; QUITE A BIT; TAKE THE BIT IN ONE'S MOUTH; TWO BITS.

**bit by bit** Also, **little by little.** Gradually, by small degrees, slowly. For example, *The dog dug up the lawn bit by bit, till we had almost no grass,* or *Little by little he began to understand what I was getting at.*

**bite** In addition to the idioms beginning with BITE, also see BARK IS WORSE THAN ONE'S BITE; PUT THE ARM (BITE) ON; SOUND BITE. Also see BITTEN.

**bite me!** I don't care whether you approve or not, as in *So what if I'm two hours late—bite me!*

**bite off more than one can chew** Take on more work or a bigger task than one can handle, as in *With two additional jobs, Bill is clearly biting off more than he can chew.* This expression refers to taking in more food than one can chew.

**bite one's nails** Show signs of anxiety, impatience, or nervousness, as in *We'll be biting our nails till she comes back.* Biting one's fingernails is a time-honored sign of emotional tension.

**bite one's tongue** Stop oneself from speaking out, as in *A new grandmother must learn to bite her tongue so as not to give unwanted advice,* or *I'm sure it'll rain during graduation. Bite your tongue!* This term refers to holding the tongue between the teeth in an effort not to say something one might regret. It is sometimes used as a humorous command, as in the second example, with the suggestion that speaking might bring bad luck. Also see HOLD ONE'S TONGUE.

**bite someone's head off** Also, **snap someone's head off.** Scold or speak very angrily to someone, as in *Ask her to give me another week off? She'd bite my head off!* The first expression replaced the much earlier **bite someone's nose off.**

**bite the big one** Die, as in *In spite off all the warnings about drinking and driving, he finally bit the big one.*

**bite the bullet** Behave bravely when facing pain or a difficult situation, as in *If they want to cut the budget deficit, they are going to have to bite the bullet and find new sources of revenue.* This phrase is of military origin, but the precise reference is uncertain. Some say it referred to treating a wounded soldier without anesthesia, so that he would be asked to bite on a lead bullet during the procedure.

**bite the dust** Suffer defeat or death, as in *The election this November saw both our governor and our mayor bite the dust.* This expression was popularized by U.S. Western films in which either cowboys or Indians were thrown from their horses to the dusty ground.

**bite the hand that feeds you** Behave in a mean or ungrateful way toward someone who has helped you. For example, *The college gave me a scholarship, so I shouldn't bite the hand that feeds me and criticize its hiring policies.* This expression refers to a dog biting its master.

**bit much, a** Slightly too exaggerated, strange, showy, or beyond some limit. For example, *Don't you think his outfit is a bit much?*

**bitten** see ONCE BITTEN, TWICE SHY. Also see BITE.

**bitter** In addition to the idioms beginning with BITTER, also see TAKE THE BITTER WITH THE SWEET.

**bitter end, the** The last extremity; also, death or ruin. For example, *I'm supporting* *the union's demands to the bitter end,* or *Even though they fight a lot, I'm sure Mom and Dad will stay together to the bitter end.*

**bitter pill to swallow, a** An unpleasant fact, disappointment, or humiliation that is difficult to endure. For example, *Failing the bar exam was a bitter pill to swallow, but she plans to try again next year.*

**blabbermouth, a (big)** A person who talks constantly and cannot keep secrets, as in *He's such a big blabbermouth—he probably told everyone about the deal.*

**black** In addition to the idioms beginning with BLACK, also see DIRTY (BLACK) LOOK; IN THE RED (BLACK); LOOK BLACK; PAINT BLACK; POT CALLING THE KETTLE BLACK.

**black and blue** Badly bruised, as in *That fall down the stairs left me black and blue all over.*

**black and white** **1.** A monochromatic picture, drawing, television image, computer monitor, or film, as opposed to one using many colors, as in *Photos in black and white fade less than those taken with color film.* **2.** Also, **black or white.** Involving a very clear distinction. For example, *He tended to view everything as a black and white issue—it was either right or wrong—whereas his partner always found gray areas.* This usage is based on the association of black with evil and white with virtue. Also see GRAY AREA. **3. in black and white.** Written down or in print, and therefore official. For example, *The terms of our agreement were spelled out in black and white, so there should be no question about it.* This term refers to black ink or print on white paper.

**black as night** Also, **black as coal** or **black as pitch.** Totally black; also, very dark. For example, *The well was black as night,* or *She had eyes that were black as coal.* These expressions have survived while others—black as ink, a raven, thunder, hell, the devil, my hat, the minister's coat, the ace of spades—are seldom if ever heard today.

**black book** **1.** A list of persons or things out of favor, as in *Tom's in my black book these days.* Also see BLACK LIST. **2.** Also, **little black book.** A personal telephone directory listing girlfriends or, less often, boyfriends. For example, *Now that he's engaged to Ellen, Jim won't be needing his little black book.*

**black eye, a** A mark of shame, a humiliating setback, as in *Yet another defeated bill in Congress is a black eye for the administration.* This expression refers to having discolored flesh around the eye resulting from a blow. The term is also used literally, as in *The mugger not only took Bill's wallet but gave him a black eye.*

**black hole** **1.** A terrible prison cell or other place of confinement. For example, *The punishment is solitary confinement, known as the black hole.* This term refers to an event known as the Black Hole of Calcutta. On the night of June 20, 1756, the ruler of Bengal confined 146 Europeans in a prison space of only 14 by 18 feet. By morning all but 23 of them had suffocated to death. Although historians have since questioned the truth of the story, it survives in this usage. **2.** A great void or a waste. For example, *Running a single small newspaper ad to launch a major campaign is useless; it amounts to throwing money into a black hole.* This usage refers to a region, so named by astronomers, whose gravitational field is so intense that no electromagnetic radiation can escape from it.

**black list** **1.** A list of persons or things considered undesirable or deserving punishment, as in *She is on her landlord's black list after her last party.* The practice of making such lists is quite old. Famous examples include 19th-century black lists of union members whom employers would not hire and the black lists of people suspected of being Communists as a result of the hearings held by Senator Joseph R. McCarthy in the early 1950s. Today the term is used more loosely, as in the example. Also see BLACK BOOK, def. 1. **2. blacklist.** Place a person's name on such a list. For example, *He was one of several movie directors who were blacklisted during the 1950s.* This verb is usually passive, as in the example.

**black look** see under DIRTY LOOK.

**black mark** An indication of failure, as in *If you refuse to work late, won't that be a black mark against you?* This phrase refers to a literal black mark, such as a cross, that was formerly put next to a person's name, indicating that he or she had been charged a penalty of some kind.

**black or white** see BLACK AND WHITE, def. 2.

**black out** **1.** Completely cover something with black, as in crossing out words on a page or print on a screen. For example, *They have blacked out all the obscene words in the subtitles to make this movie suitable for youngsters.* This usage may be derived from an earlier meaning, "stain or defame," which probably refers to "blackening" a person's reputation. **2.** Put out all lights. For example, *The whole town was asleep, as blacked out as London during World War II.* At one time this expression referred to the lights in a theater, but in Europe during World War II it meant darkening all the lights in an entire city to hide it from enemy bombers. **3.** Lose consciousness, faint; also, experience a temporary loss of memory. For example, *I couldn't remember a single note of the music; I blacked out completely,* or

B

*The man claims he blacked out from drinking.* This usage is thought to have originated with pilots, who sometimes fainted briefly when pulling out of a power dive. It soon was transferred to other losses of consciousness or memory.

**black sheep** The worst member of a group; a disgrace. For example, *My uncle was the black sheep of the family; we always thought he emigrated to Argentina to avoid going to jail.* This expression is based on the idea that black sheep were less valuable than white ones because it was more difficult to dye their wool different colors. Also, their black color was considered the devil's mark.

**blame** see LAY (THE BLAME) ON; TO BLAME.

**blank** In addition to the idiom beginning with BLANK, also see DRAW A BLANK; FILL IN (THE BLANKS); POINT-BLANK.

**blank check** Unlimited authority, a free hand, as in *I'll support most of the chairman's plan, but I'm not ready to give him a blank check.* Literally this term signifies a bank check that is signed by the issuer but does not indicate the amount of money, which is filled in by the person to whom it is given.

**blanket** see SECURITY BLANKET; WET BLANKET.

**blast** In addition to the idioms beginning with BLAST, also see FULL BLAST.

**blast away (at)** Shoot repeatedly. For example, *The boy blasted away at the targets on the computer screen.* Also see BLAST OFF.

**blast off** **1.** Also, **blast away.** Take off or be launched, especially into space, as in *They're scheduled to blast off on Tuesday.* This usage originated with the development of powerful rockets and spacecraft and the training of astronauts, to all of which it was applied. **2.** Depart, clear out, as in *This party's over; let's blast off now.* **3.** Become excited or high, especially from using drugs, as in *They give parties where people blast off.*

**blaze** In addition to the idiom beginning with BLAZE, also see HOT AS BLAZES; LIKE GREASED LIGHTNING (BLAZES).

**blaze a trail** Find a new path or method; begin a new undertaking. For example, *His research blazed a trail for new kinds of gene therapy.* This expression was first used literally for the practice of marking a forest trail by making blazes, that is, marking trees with notches or chips in the bark.

**bleed** In addition to the idiom beginning with BLEED, also see MY HEART BLEEDS FOR YOU.

**bleed someone white** Also, **bleed one dry.** Take someone's money until he or she is completely broke. For example, *That contractor would have bled the department white, but fortunately he was stopped in time,* or *That guy bled his family dry trying to keep him out of jail.* Presumably this term refers to losing so much blood that one turns pale (and perhaps also to the idea that money is the life blood of commerce).

**blessed event** The birth of a baby, as in *When is the blessed event expected?* This expression combines two senses of *blessed,* that is, "happy" and "sacred." Today, however, unless used ironically, it is considered too sentimental.

**blessing** In addition to the idiom beginning with BLESSING, also see GIVE THANKS FOR SMALL BLESSINGS; MIXED BLESSING.

**blessing in disguise, a** A misfortune that unexpectedly turns into good fortune, as in *Missing the train was a blessing in disguise, for if I hadn't, I wouldn't have met Ann.*

**blind** In addition to the idioms beginning with BLIND, also see FLY BLIND; LOVE IS BLIND; ROB SOMEONE BLIND; TURN A BLIND EYE.

**blind alley** A dead end; a position without hope of progress or success. For example, *That line of questioning led the attorney up yet another blind alley.* This term refers to a street or alley that has no outlet at one end.

**blind as a bat** Quite blind; also, unaware. For example, *Without my glasses I'm blind as a bat,* or *I had no idea they wanted me to take over his job; I was blind as a bat.* This expression, based on the mistaken idea that a bat's erratic flight means it cannot see properly, has survived even though it is now known that bats have a sophisticated built-in sonar system.

**blind date, a** A social engagement, usually arranged by a friend or relative, with someone who is a stranger. For example, *I've never met anyone I liked on a blind date.*

**blind drunk** So drunk that one is unable to see, as in *When I last saw him, he was blind drunk and stumbling around.*

**blindfolded** see DO BLINDFOLDED.

**blind leading the blind, the** Those lacking the skills or knowledge for something are being guided by equally unskilled individuals. For example, *He's teaching his son carpentry; that's a case of the blind leading the blind.*

**blind one with science** Purposely confused one by using unfamiliar words or the specialized vocabulary of a science or other discipline, as in *When I asked a simple question, I was blinded by science.*

**blind side** see under BLIND SPOT.

**blind spot** A subject about which one is ignorant or biased. For example, *The boss has a blind spot about Henry; he wouldn't fire him for anything,* or *Dad has a blind spot about opera; he can't see anything good about it.* This term uses *blind* in the sense of "covered or hidden from sight." It has two literal meanings: an insensitive part of the retina and an area outside one's field of vision. The phrase has largely replaced **blind side,** which survives mainly in the verb **blind-side,** meaning "hit someone on an unguarded side" and "deal an unexpected blow."

**blink** see IN THE BLINK OF AN EYE; ON THE BLINK; WITHOUT BATTING (BLINKING) AN EYE.

**block** see BEEN AROUND THE BLOCK; CHIP OFF THE OLD BLOCK; KNOCK SOMEONE'S BLOCK OFF; ON THE BLOCK; STUMBLING BLOCK.

**blood** In addition to the idiom beginning with BLOOD, also see BAD BLOOD; DRAW BLOOD; FLESH AND BLOOD; HAVE SOMEONE'S BLOOD ON ONE'S HANDS; IN COLD BLOOD; IN ONE'S BLOOD; MAKE ONE'S BLOOD BOIL; MAKE ONE'S BLOOD RUN COLD; NEW BLOOD; OUT FOR (BLOOD); SCREAM BLOODY MURDER; SHED BLOOD; SPORTING BLOOD; SWEAT BLOOD. Also see under BLEED.

**blood is thicker than water** Family ties are closer than other relationships. For example, *She will drop everything to help her sister; blood is thicker than water.* This proverb refers to the fact that water evaporates without leaving a mark whereas blood leaves a stain.

**blossom into** Also, **blossom out.** Develop, flourish, as in *She's blossomed into a fine young woman,* or *His business has blossomed out, and he's doing well.*

**blot out** Kill someone, wipe out of existence or memory, as in *Several Native American nations were blotted out as the pioneers moved west,* or *The trauma of the accident blotted out all her memory of recent events.* This idiom uses the verb *blot* in the sense of making something unreadable by spotting or staining it with ink.

**blow** In addition to the idioms beginning with BLOW, also see AT ONE STROKE (BLOW); BODY BLOW; COME TO BLOWS; KEEP (BLOW) ONE'S COOL; LOW BLOW; WAY THE WIND BLOWS.

**blow a fuse** Also, **blow a gasket.** Lose one's temper, express furious anger. For example, *When his paycheck bounced, John blew a fuse,* or *Tell Mom what really happened before she blows a gasket.* An electric fuse is said to "blow" (melt) when the circuit is overloaded, whereas a gasket, used to seal a piston, "blows" (breaks) when the pressure is too high. Also see BLOW ONE'S TOP; KEEP ONE'S COOL.

**blow away** **1.** Kill, especially by gunshot or explosion. For example, *The press reported that the suspect was blown away.* This usage became particularly widespread during the Vietnam War. **2.** Overcome someone or something easily; defeat decisively. For example, *Ann said the test would be easy; she would just blow it away,* or *Jim was sure his team could blow away their opponents.* Also see BLOW OFF, def. 3. **3.** Impress one greatly, overwhelm with surprise, delight, or shock, as in *That music really blew me away.* Also see BLOW ONE'S MIND.

**blow by blow** Described in great detail, as in *Tell me about last night's party, blow by blow.* This term originated in early radio broadcasts in which a sportscaster would give a detailed account of each punch struck in a boxing match. It soon was transferred to a detailed account of anything at all.

**blow hot and cold** Change one's mind, be indecisive, as in *Jean's been blowing hot and cold about taking a winter vacation.* This expression comes from one of Aesop's fables. On a winter day a man blew on his hands to warm them and then blew on his soup to cool it. The man was said to be an unreliable friend because he blew hot and cold out of the same mouth. The expression was repeated by many writers, most often referring to a person who could not be trusted.

**blow in** Arrive, especially unexpectedly. For example, *Just when we thought he wouldn't come, he blew in.*

**blow it** **1.** Spoil, ruin, or miss something, as in *That was a great opportunity, but now I've blown it.* **2. blow one's lines.** Make a mistake in speaking one's part in a theatrical production, as in *I blew my lines, but she came to the rescue.*

**blow off** **1.** Vent one's strong feelings; see BLOW OFF STEAM. **2.** Ignore something; avoid something important. For example, *If you blow off your homework, you're certain to run into trouble on the exam.* **3.** Overcome, defeat someone easily, as in *With you pitching, we'll have no trouble blowing off the opposing team.* Also see BLOW AWAY, def. 2. **4.** Ignore someone or something, abandon, refuse to attend or take part. For example, *The college is blowing off our request for a new student center.*

**blow off steam** Also, **let off steam.** Talk about or relieve one's true feelings with loud talk or vigorous activity. For example, *Joan's shouting did not mean she was angry at you; she was just blowing off steam,* or *After spending the day on very exacting work, Tom blew off steam by going for a long run.* This term refers to easing the pressure in a steam engine.

**blow one's brains out** **1.** Shoot oneself in the head, as in *Blowing one's brains out is more a man's type of suicide; women seem to prefer poison.* **2.** Become so frustrated with people or with a situation and just want them out of sight or ended, as in *Those children make me want to blow my brains out,* or *This job is so frustrating, sometimes I just want to blow my brains out.*

**blow one's cool** see under KEEP ONE'S COOL.

**blow one's cover** Give away one's secret identity by accident, as in *Mary came to the store to check out the competition's prices and hoped no one would blow her cover.* This expression uses *blow* in the sense of "expose or betray."

**blow one's mind** **1.** Surprise, shock, or amaze one, as in *This jazz group blows my mind,* or *Joe served a jail sentence? That blows my mind.* This expression is used rather loosely, as seen in the examples; the first refers to amazement and pleasure, the second refers to shock and dismay. **2.** Alter one's perceptions, especially through drug use, as in *Taking LSD really blows one's mind.* **3.** Make one insane, drive crazy, as in *Was it his wife's death that blew his mind?* or *Losing her savings blew her mind.*

**blow one's own horn** Also, **blow one's trumpet** or **toot one's own horn.** Brag about oneself, as in *Within two minutes of meeting someone new, Bill starts blowing his own horn.*

**blow one's top** **1.** Also, **blow one's stack.** Fly into a rage; lose one's control. For example, *If she calls about this one more time, I'm going to blow my top,* or *He is generally very easygoing, but today he blew his stack.* The *top* here has been compared to the top of an erupting volcano; the *stack* refers to a smokestack. **2.** Go crazy, become insane, as in *When she regains consciousness, she just may blow her top.* Also see FLIP ONE'S LID.

**blow out** **1.** Extinguish something, especially a flame. For example, *The wind blew out the candles very quickly.* **2.** Lose force or stop entirely, as in *The storm will soon blow itself out and move out to sea.* Also see BLOW OVER. **3.** Burst or explode suddenly, as in *This tire is about to blow out.* This usage refers to the escape of air under pressure. **4.** Also, **blow *one* out of the water.** Defeat one decisively, as in *With a great new product and excellent publicity, we could blow the competition out of the water.* This term originally was used in naval warfare, where it meant to blast or shoot another vessel to pieces. It later was transferred to athletic and other kinds of defeat.

**blow over** Pass away, lessen. For example, *The storm will blow over by afternoon,* or *After a couple of years, the scandal will blow over.* This term refers to storm clouds that pass over an area without descending.

**blow *something* sky-high** **1.** Destroy something by explosion, explode, as in *The old building was blown sky-high to make room for the new hotel.* Also see BLOW UP. **2.** Refute something completely, as in *The lab report has blown your theory sky-high.*

**blow the lid off** Also, **blow *something* wide open.** Expose something, especially a scandal or an illegal activity. For example, *The newspaper's investigation blew the lid off the governor's practice of awarding state contracts to his friends.*

**blow the whistle on** **1.** Expose corruption or other wrongdoing, as in *The President's speech blew the whistle on the members of the opposition who were leaking information.* **2.** Put a stop to something, as in *The registry decided to blow the whistle on new vanity plates.* This term originally referred to ending an activity (such as factory work) with the blast of a whistle.

**blow *something* to smithereens** Completely destroy something, especially with a bomb or similar weapon, as in *We can blow this hill to smithereens with dynamite.*

**blow up** **1.** Explode or cause something to explode. For example, *The squadron was told to blow up the bridge,* or *I was afraid his experiment would blow up the lab.* **2. blow up at.** Lose one's temper, as in *I'm sorry I blew up at you.* **3.** Inflate something, fill with air, as in *If you don't blow up those tires, you're sure to have a flat.* **4.** Enlarge something, especially a photograph, as in *If we blow up this picture, you'll be able to make out the expressions on their faces.* **5.** Exaggerate the importance of something or someone, as in *Tom has a tendency to blow up his own role in making company policy.* This term applies the "inflate" of def. 3 to importance. **6.** Collapse, fail, as in *Graduate-student marriages often blow up soon after the couple earn their degrees.* **7. blow up in one's face.** Have something go the opposite of what was planned. For example, *She tried to make her boyfriend jealous, but it blew up in her face.*

**blue** In addition to the idioms beginning with BLUE, also see BETWEEN A ROCK AND A HARD PLACE (THE DEVIL AND THE DEEP BLUE SEA); BLACK AND BLUE; BOLT FROM THE BLUE; FAIR-HAIRED (BLUE-EYED) BOY; HAVE THE BLUES; INTO THIN AIR (THE BLUE); LIKE GREASED LIGHTNING (A BLUE STREAK); ONCE IN A BLUE MOON; OUT OF A CLEAR BLUE SKY; TALK SOMEONE'S ARM OFF (A BLUE STREAK); TALK SOMEONE'S ARM OFF (UNTIL ONE IS BLUE IN THE FACE).

**blue-eyed boy** see FAIR-HAIRED BOY.

**blue funk, in a** **1.** In a state of panic or terror. For example, *Just because the bride's mother is late, you needn't get in a blue funk.* This term originated as **in a funk.** The adjective *blue,* meaning "affected with fear or anxiety," was added later. **2.** In a state of dejection, sad. For example, *Anne has been in a blue funk since her dog died.* This sense uses *blue* to mean "sad." Also see HAVE THE BLUES.

**blue in the face, until one is** Exhausted from anger, strain, or other great effort. For example, *You can talk until you're blue in the face, but I won't go.* This expression refers to the bluish skin color resulting from a lack of oxygen, which might result from talking until one was breathless. See also under TALK SOMEONE'S ARM OFF.

**blues** see HAVE THE BLUES.

**blue streak** see TALK SOMEONE'S ARM OFF.

**bluff** In addition to the idiom beginning with BLUFF, also see CALL SOMEONE'S BLUFF.

**bluff it** Also, **bluff one out** or **bluff one's way out.** Do something without knowing or understanding it in order to avoid admitting ignorance. For example, *I didn't study for the test, so I'll have to bluff it,* or *That fool can bluff his way out of any situation.*

**blurt out** Say something abruptly or accidentally, utter without thinking. For example, *Unfortunately, he blurted out how much he hated dinner parties just as his hostess walked in.*

**board** see ACROSS THE BOARD; BACK TO THE DRAWING BOARD; BED AND BOARD; BULLETIN BOARD; BY THE BOARD; GO OVERBOARD; ON BOARD; OPEN AND ABOVEBOARD; ROOM AND BOARD; STIFF AS A BOARD.

**boat** see IN THE SAME BOAT; MISS THE BOAT; ROCK THE BOAT; WHATEVER TURNS ONE ON (FLOATS ONE'S BOAT).

**bob up** Appear suddenly or unexpectedly. For example, *I didn't know anyone in the group until you bobbed up.* This term uses the verb *bob* in the sense of "bounce."

**bode well for** Also, **bode ill for.** Have good (or bad) expectations for someone or something. For example, *John's recovery from surgery bodes well for the team,* or *The Republican victory in the Congressional elections bodes ill for affirmative action.* The verb *bode* comes from an old word meaning "announce or foretell," and is rarely heard today except in this idiom.

**body** In addition to the idioms beginning with BODY, also see KEEP BODY AND SOUL TOGETHER; OVER MY DEAD BODY; WARM BODY.

**body blow** An action that causes severe damage, as in *This last recession dealt a body blow to our whole industry.* This term comes from boxing, where it refers to a punch that lands between the opponent's chest and navel.

**body English** Movements of the body that express a person's feelings, as in *His body English tells us just how tired he is.* This expression originated in such sports as bowling and ice hockey, where a player tries to influence the path of a ball or puck by moving his or her body in a particular direction. It was based on the earlier use of *English* to mean "spin imparted to a ball."

**bog down** Become stuck, be unable to progress, as in *Their research bogged down because they lacked the laboratory expertise.* This expression transfers sinking into the mud of a swamp to being hindered or halted.

**boggle the mind** Bewilder or astonish with complexity, novelty, or something similar, as in *The very magnitude of the universe boggles the mind.* The source of this usage is unclear, as the verb *boggle* has several other seemingly unrelated meanings—shy away, hesitate, bungle.

**boil** In addition to the idioms beginning with BOIL, also see MAKE ONE'S BLOOD BOIL; WATCHED POT NEVER BOILS.

**boil down** **1.** Simplify something, summarize or shorten, as in *John finally managed to boil his thesis down to 200 pages.* **2. boil down to.** Able to be reduced to basic elements, be the same as. For example, *What this issue boils down to is that the council doesn't want to spend more money.* These usages refer to reducing and concentrating a substance by boiling off liquid.

**boiling point** **1.** A climax or crisis; a high degree of fury, excitement, or outrage. For example, *The union's disgust with management has reached the boiling point.* This term refers to the temperature at which water boils. **2. have a low boiling point.** Become angry quite easily, as in *Don't tease her anymore—she has a low boiling point.* This phrase means that it takes less heat than usual for a boiling point to be reached. Also see BOIL OVER; MAKE ONE'S BLOOD BOIL.

**boil over** Erupt in anger, excitement, or other strong emotion. For example, *The mere mention of a tax increase will make her boil over.* This phrase refers to liquid overflowing while boiling.

**bold as brass** Without shame, spirited, impudent. For example, *No one had invited her to the wedding, but she showed up at the church, bold as brass.* This alliterative simile uses *brass* in the sense of "shamelessness."

**bolt** In addition to the idioms beginning with BOLT, also see NUTS AND BOLTS.

**bolt from the blue, a** Also, **a bolt out of the blue.** A sudden, unexpected event. For example, *Bill's asking for a divorce was a bolt from the blue for his wife.* This term refers to unforeseen lightning or thunder from a cloudless (blue) sky.

**bolt upright** Precisely vertical, completely erect, as in *She sat bolt upright in her chair.*

**bomb** In addition to the idiom beginning with BOMB, also see TIME BOMB.

**bomb, the** **1.** In U.S. football, a pass thrown by the quarterback that travels most of the length of the playing field and is intended to be caught for a touchdown. For example,

*I don't think he'll throw the bomb this early in the game.* **2.** Extremely beautiful or handsome, as in *She's the bomb.*

B

**bombshell** see DROP A BOMBSHELL.

**bone** In addition to the idioms beginning with BONE, also see BARE BONES; CHILLED TO THE BONE; CUT TO THE BONE; FEEL IN ONE'S BONES; FUNNY BONE; MAKE NO BONES ABOUT; SKIN AND BONES; WORK ONE'S FINGERS TO THE BONE.

**bone of contention** The main issue of an argument; something to quarrel about. For example, *Grandfather's will was a bone of contention for the whole family.* This expression refers to two dogs fighting (contending) over a single bone.

**bone to pick with someone** An unpleasant issue or complaint that needs discussion with someone. For example, *Concerning the room assignments, I have a bone to pick with you.* This term refers to a dog chewing on a bone.

**bone up** Also, **bone up on.** Study intensely, as in *I'll have to bone up on my Spanish if I'm going to pass the language requirement.*

**bonnet** see BEE IN ONE'S BONNET.

**boob tube** Television, as in *He spends hours a day in front of the boob tube.* This expression shows a disapproval of television and the kind of entertainment it provides.

**book** see BALANCE THE BOOKS; BLACK BOOK; BY THE BOOK; CLOSED BOOK; CLOSE THE BOOKS; COOK THE BOOKS; CRACK A BOOK; HIT THE BOOKS; IN SOMEONE'S BAD GRACES (BOOKS); IN ONE'S BOOK; JUDGE A BOOK BY ITS COVER; KNOW LIKE A BOOK; MAKE BOOK; NOSE IN A BOOK; ONE FOR THE BOOKS; OPEN BOOK; TAKE A LEAF OUT OF SOMEONE'S BOOK; THROW THE BOOK AT; WROTE THE BOOK ON.

**boom** see LOWER THE BOOM.

**boot** In addition to the idiom beginning with BOOT, also see DIE WITH ONE'S BOOTS ON; GET THE AX (BOOT); KICK (BOOT) OUT; LICK SOMEONE'S BOOTS; PULL ONESELF UP (BY THE BOOTSTRAPS); QUAKE IN ONE'S BOOTS; TO BOOT; TOO BIG FOR ONE'S BREECHES (BOOTS); YOU BET (YOUR BOOTS). Also see under SHOE.

**boot *one* out** see KICK ONE OUT.

**boot up** Start a computer, as in *When you've booted up, it's best not to turn off the computer until you're done for the day.* The term is a shortening of **bootstrap,** another computer idiom referring to using one set of instructions to load another set of instructions. Also see LOG IN.

**bore *one* to death** Also, **bore *one* to tears** or **bore *one* stiff** or **bore the pants off.** Tire someone through extremely dull talk or uninteresting action. For example, *Sam was bored stiff by the play but didn't dare admit it,* or *Carol bores the pants off me with her constant talk about herself,* or *His books bore me to death.* All four expression convey the idea of such frustration that one dies, weeps, stiffens with annoyance, or has one's pants removed. Also see under PANTS OFF; TALK SOMEONE'S ARM OFF.

**born** In addition to the idioms beginning with BORN, also see IN ALL ONE'S BORN DAYS; NOT BORN YESTERDAY; THERE'S A SUCKER BORN EVERY MINUTE; TO THE MANNER BORN.

**born and bred** Born and educated in a single place or social class. For example, *She was a Bostonian, born and bred.*

**born under a lucky star** Very fortunate, as in *Peter comes out ahead no matter what he tries; he was born under a lucky star.* That stars influence human lives is an ancient idea, and *lucky star* has been used by writers from Shakespeare to the present. Also see THANK ONE'S LUCKY STARS.

**born with a silver spoon** Also, **born with a silver spoon in one's mouth.** Born wealthy, or fortunate, or both, as in *Paul can afford to go to medical school; he was born with a silver spoon.* Although some authorities believe this phrase refers to the custom of godparents giving a godchild a silver spoon, it is more likely that the spoon has come to symbolize wealth.

**born yesterday** see NOT BORN YESTERDAY.

**borrow** In addition to the idiom beginning with BORROW, also see BEG, BORROW, OR STEAL; ON BORROWED TIME.

**borrow trouble** Doing something even when one is aware that it may be harmful, as in *Just sign the paper—telling her about it ahead of time is borrowing trouble.* Also see ASK FOR.

**boss *one* around** Tell someone what to do, give orders. For example, *David complained that his older sister was always bossing him around.* The verb *boss* is used here in the sense of "dominate."

**both** In addition to the idioms beginning with BOTH, also see BEST OF BOTH WORLDS; BURN THE CANDLE AT BOTH ENDS; CUT BOTH WAYS; FOOT IN BOTH CAMPS; HAVE IT BOTH WAYS; PLAY BOTH ENDS AGAINST THE MIDDLE; SWING BOTH WAYS; WORK BOTH SIDES OF THE STREET.

**both barrels, with** With full force, as in *When I scolded her for stealing, I let her have it with both barrels,* or *I gave it to her with both barrels when she came in late again.* This term is often put as **let someone have it with both barrels** or **give it to someone with both barrels,** as in the examples above. The idiom refers to firing both barrels of a double-barreled shotgun.

**bother** see GO TO THE TROUBLE (BOTHER); HOT AND BOTHERED.

**both feet on the ground** Also, **with both feet on the ground** or **with one's feet on**

**the ground.** Sensible, realistic, or practical. For example, *You can count on Tom not to get cheated on that deal; he has both feet on the ground,* or *Jean is a dreamer, but her husband is a man with his feet on the ground.*

**bottle** In addition to the idiom beginning with BOTTLE, also see CRACK A BOTTLE; HIT THE BOTTLE.

**bottle up** **1.** Keep an emotion inside, contain, hold back. For example, *The psychiatrist said she had been bottling up her anger for years.* **2.** Confine or trap, as in *The accident bottled up traffic for miles.* This idiom compares other kinds of restraint to liquid being contained in a bottle.

**bottom** In addition to the idioms beginning with BOTTOM, also see AT BOTTOM; FROM HEAD TO TOE (TOP TO BOTTOM); FROM THE BOTTOM OF ONE'S HEART; GET TO THE BOTTOM; HIT (TOUCH) BOTTOM; KNOCK THE BOTTOM OUT OF; ROCK BOTTOM; TOUCH BOTTOM; YOU BET (YOUR BOTTOM DOLLAR).

**bottom dollar** see YOU BET (YOUR BOTTOM DOLLAR).

**bottom drops out, the** Also, **the bottom falls out.** A collapse occurs, as in *The bottom dropped out of the steel market,* or *When they lost the game, the bottom fell out of their hopes to make the playoffs.* This term refers to collapsing deeper than the very lowest point, or bottom.

**bottom feeder** The lowest or worst kind of person, someone who is satisfied with the very worst, as in *Those bottom feeders are always quick to point out someone else's mistake.* This expression refers to catfish and other fish that live and feed along the bottom of bodies of water.

**bottom line, the** The ultimate result; also, the main point or crucial factor. For example, *The bottom line is that the chairperson wants to dictate all of the board's decisions,* or *Whether or not he broke the law is the bottom line.* This originally was an accounting term that referred to the earnings figures that appear on the bottom (last) line of a financial statement. It was later transferred to other contexts.

**bottom of the barrel, the** The least desirable, the worst, as in *The nominating committee had trouble finding candidates; they were settling for the bottom of the barrel.* The phrase often is put as **scrape the bottom of the barrel,** meaning "use the least desirable elements" (because one has no other choice), as in *Bringing up that minor point proves that you're scraping the bottom of the barrel.*

**bottom of the ladder** Also, **bottom of the heap.** Lowest or most junior position in a hierarchy or a group. For example, *If we hire you, you'll have to begin at the bottom of the ladder,* or *He began as a good lawyer, but now he's at the bottom of the heap.* The rungs of a ladder have long been compared to a progress by steps. Also see LOW MAN ON THE TOTEM POLE. For an antonym, see TOP OF THE LADDER.

**bottom out** Reach the lowest level, as in *The recession appears to have bottomed out.* This expression tends to be used mostly in the context of trade and finance.

**bottoms up!** Finish your drinks now, especially in a single gulp, as in *Bottoms up everybody, we're already late!*

**bounce** In addition to the idioms beginning with BOUNCE, also see GET THE AX (BOUNCE); MORE BANG FOR THE BUCK (BOUNCE FOR THE OUNCE); THAT'S HOW THE BALL BOUNCES.

**bounce around** **1.** Move around from one person or place to another. For example, *The staff spent the morning bouncing around ideas to improve sales,* or *She had been bouncing around from one job to another.* This term refers to a ball bouncing among players. **2.** Treat someone roughly or unfairly, as in *Quit bouncing me around; I won't stand for it.* This usage is based on a somewhat earlier meaning of *bounce,* "beat up" or "coerce."

**bounce back** Recover quickly, as in *She has pneumonia, but we think she'll bounce back.* This expression refers to the rebound of a ball or some elastic material.

**bounce ideas off** To present an idea to someone in order to get his or her advice before making a decision or to clarify one's own thinking. For example, *Do you mind if I bounce a couple of ideas off you?*

**bound** In addition to the idioms beginning with BOUND, also see BY LEAPS AND BOUNDS; DUTY BOUND; HONOR BOUND; KNOW NO BOUNDS; OUT OF BOUNDS; WITHIN BOUNDS. Also see under BIND.

**bound and determined to** Firmly committed to, as in *He was bound and determined to finish the assignment on time.* This phrase is a redundancy used for emphasis, since *bound* and *determined* both mean "resolved to." Also see BOUND TO.

**bound for** On the way to, heading for. For example, *This bus is bound for New York.* This phrase stems from a very early meaning of *bound* as "ready" or "prepared."

**bound hand and foot** Completely obligated, unable to free oneself. For example, *These rules have us bound hand and foot; we can't even discuss the matter.* This term transfers the literal meaning, having one's hands and feet tied and therefore unable to move, to legal, moral, or social obligations.

**bound to, be** Be certain or destined to; also, be determined or resolved to. For example, *We are bound to hear from them soon,* or *No* *matter what they say, she is bound to run for mayor.* This usage is derived from the older sense of *bound* as "obliged."

B

**bound up in** Also, **bound up with.** Deeply involved in something. For example, *She is bound up in her church activities,* or *Obviously the candidate was bound up with the negotiations on the party platform.*

**bow** In addition to the idioms beginning with BOW, also see TAKE A BOW.

**bow and scrape** Behave submissively or flatter too much, as in *In this fashionable store, the salespeople really bow and scrape before customers.* This term refers to the old-fashioned custom of bowing so deeply that one's foot draws back and scrapes the ground. This idiom may be dying out.

**bowl of cherries, life is just a** These are happy circumstances; life is wonderful. This phrase is often used ironically, as in *My husband is about to lose his job—life is just a bowl of cherries, right?* Originating as the title of a song written during the Depression, this term expressed the idea that everything was going very well. Its ironical use was established later. Also see BED OF ROSES.

**bowl *one* over** Astonish one, surprise greatly, overwhelm, as in *I was bowled over by their wonderful performance.* This term originated in cricket.

**bow out** Depart, withdraw, resign, as in *After five years as head of the committee, I felt it was time I bowed out,* or *We'll have to defeat them; they'll never bow out.*

**box** In addition to the idiom beginning with BOX, also see IN A BIND (BOX); ON ONE'S SOAPBOX; PANDORA'S BOX; STUFF THE BALLOT BOX.

**box office** **1.** An office where tickets for a play, concert, or other form of entertainment may be purchased, as in *Tickets are available at the box office.* It is called this because originally it was the place for hiring a box, a special compartment of theater seats reserved for women. **2.** The financial receipts from a performance; also, a show's relative success in attracting a paying audience. For example, *You may not consider it great art, but this play is good box office.*

**boy** In addition to the idiom beginning with BOY, also see FAIR-HAIRED BOY; MAMA'S BOY; SEPARATE THE MEN FROM THE BOYS; WHIPPING BOY.

**boys will be boys** **1.** One can expect boys to act childishly or misbehave, said with resignation, as in *We told the kids not to eat in the living room, but when we got home there was a big mess there—oh well, boys will be boys.* **2.** Adult men never grow up but are more dangerous than boys because their toys are more dangerous, said sarcastically, as in *Another invasion of Nicaragua? Boys will be boys.*

**brace up** Also, **brace oneself.** Summon up one's courage or resolve, as in *Brace up, we don't have much farther to go,* or *Squaring his shoulders, he braced himself for the next wave.* This idiom uses *brace* in the sense of "strengthen."

**bragging rights** The ability to boast about an accomplishment or a triumph, as in *You beat me again, so I guess that gives you bragging rights for a while.*

**brain** In addition to the idioms beginning with BRAIN, also see BEAT ONE'S BRAINS OUT; BLOW ONE'S BRAINS OUT; ON ONE'S MIND (THE BRAIN); PICK SOMEONE'S BRAINS; RACK ONE'S BRAINS.

**brain drain** The departure of educated or talented people for better pay or jobs in another country, as in *Many Third World countries have experienced a brain drain to the United States.*

**brains behind *something*, be the** The person or group of people who are responsible for thinking of and carrying out an idea, a plan, or a project. For example, *I'd like to meet the brains behind this new policy,* or, ironically, *Who's the brains behind this idiocy?*

**brain someone** Hit someone hard on the head. For example, *The roof collapsed, and a bunk of plaster brained him,* or *I'll brain you if you don't get to those dishes!* This term is used both literally (first example) and as an exaggeration (second example).

**brain trust** A group of experts who serve as unofficial but vital advisers. For example, *Each town manager seemed to have his or her own brain trust, which of course changed with every election.* This term was closely associated with President Franklin D. Roosevelt's advisers on domestic and foreign policy, especially during the early 1930s.

**branch** In addition to the idioms beginning with BRANCH, also see OLIVE BRANCH.

**branch off** Split, subdivide, as in *It's the house on the left, just after the road branches off,* or *English and Dutch branched off from an older parent language, West Germanic.* This term refers to a tree, in which branches grow in separate directions from the main trunk. Also see BRANCH OUT.

**branch out** Spread into new areas; start in a new direction. For example, *Our software business is branching out into more interactive products,* or *Bill doesn't want to concentrate on just one field; he wants to branch out more.* This term refers to the growth habits of a tree's limbs. Also see BRANCH OFF.

**brass** In addition to the idioms beginning with BRASS, also see BOLD AS BRASS; GET DOWN TO BRASS TACKS; HAVE A NERVE (THE BRASS).

**brass hat** A high-ranking official, as in *All the brass bats were invited to the sales con-*

*ference.* The terms **big brass, top brass,** and **the brass** all refer to high officials considered as a group. For example, *John's one of the top brass in town—he's superintendent of schools.* Authorities believe these idioms first referred to senior officers of the British army, who had gold leaves on their cap brims. After World War II these terms began to be used for top executives in business and other organizations.

**brass ring** A chance to achieve wealth or success; a prize or reward. For example, *When you see the brass ring, grab it! You may never have another chance at success.* The term comes from the practice of giving a free ride to the person who succeeded in picking a ring out of a box while riding a merry-go-round.

**brave face, put on a** Also, **put up a brave front. 1.** Face hardship or difficulties cheerfully. For example, *Even though she had been passed over for promotion, she put on a brave face.* **2.** Try to appear brave even though very frightened. For example, *Harry was terrified of animals, but his boss was a dog lover, so he put up a brave front.*

**brave it out 1.** Face danger or a difficult situation with courage. For example, *They had far fewer votes than the opposition, but they decided to brave it out.* **2.** Also, **brazen it out.** Swagger, act with arrogant self-confidence. For example, *They hadn't been invited but decided to stay and brazen it out.*

**brave new world** A better era brought about by social changes that improve the quality of life. For example, *The candidate promised us a brave new world and lower taxes.* This phrase is also used ironically, as in *Your brave new world looks a lot like the old one.*

**brave the elements** Go out in stormy weather, as in *We've just about run out of food; I'll brave the elements and walk to the store.* The use of *elements* for weather is rare today except in this expression, which is often used in an exaggerated way.

**bread** In addition to the idiom beginning with BREAD, also see BREAK BREAD; GREATEST THING SINCE SLICED BREAD; KNOW WHICH SIDE OF ONE'S BREAD IS BUTTERED; TAKE THE BREAD OUT OF SOMEONE'S MOUTH.

**bread and butter 1.** The essential, sustaining element, as in *The quality of the schools is the bread and butter of town property values.* This idiom refers to a basic food, bread that is spread with butter. **2.** Means of livelihood, as in *Her job is the family's bread and butter.* **3.** Ordinary, routine, as in *Don't worry about it; this is just a bread and butter assignment.*

**break** In addition to the idioms beginning with BREAK, also see GET A BREAK; GIVE SOMEONE A BREAK; MAKE A BREAK FOR IT; MAKE OR BREAK; TAKE A BREAK; TOUGH BREAK. Also see under BROKE.

**break a leg** Good luck! as in *Play well, folks—break a leg!* The origin of this command to a performer about to go onstage is unclear; it may have been a translation of the German *Hals und Beinbruch* (that is, "Break your neck and leg"), also of unknown origin. Equally mysterious is the Italian equivalent, *In bocca di lupe,* "Into the mouth of the wolf."

**break away 1.** Leave hurriedly, escape, get loose. For example, *The boy tried to break away, but his mother held onto his coat,* or *On the last lap the horse broke away from the pack.* **2.** Sever connections with a group. For example, *It was hard for me to break away from that organization, but I knew it was necessary.* **3.** Stop doing something, as in *She broke away from work long enough to go out for lunch.*

**break bread** Have a meal, eat. For example, *It's hard to remain enemies when you've broken bread together.* This term occurs in numerous places in the New Testament, where it sometimes means to share bread and other times to distribute food to others.

**break camp** Take down a tent and pack up other gear; also, leave a place, move out. For example, *The landlord has to return my rent deposit before I'll break camp.* Originally *camp* meant a military encampment, but later it was transferred to temporary outdoor sites used by hunters and other people.

**break cover** Suddenly come out from a hiding place, as in *The soldiers broke cover and made a run for it.* This term originally referred to animals being hunted. Now it is also used for human beings.

**break down 1.** Demolish something, destroy, either physically or figuratively, as in *The carpenters broke down the wall between the bedrooms,* or *The interrogators finally broke down the spy and learned exactly what he knew about the plot.* **2.** Separate something into parts, analyze. For example, *I insisted that they break down the bill into separate charges for parts and labor,* or *The chemist was trying to break down the compound's molecules.* **3.** Stop functioning, cease to be effective or operable, as in *The old dishwasher finally broke down.* **4.** Become distressed or upset, as in *The funeral was too much for her, and she broke down in tears.* **5.** Have a physical or mental collapse, as in *After seeing all his work come to nothing, he broke down and had to be treated by a psychiatrist.*

**break even** Neither gain nor lose in some business, get back the amount invested. For example, *If the dealer sells five cars a week, he'll break even.* This expression probably came from a card game. It soon was transferred to balancing business gains and losses. The usage led to the noun **break-even point,** for the amount of sales or production needed for a firm to get back its investment.



**breakfast** see HAVE FOR BREAKFAST.

**break ground** Also, **break new ground. 1.** Begin digging into the earth for new construction of some kind. For example, *When will they break ground for the town hall?* This usage refers to breaking up soil with a plow. **2.** Take the first steps for a new venture; advance beyond previous achievements. For example, *She is breaking new ground in intellectual property law.*

**break in 1.** Enter by force, as in *The thieves broke in through the back door of the building.* Also see BREAK INTO. **2.** Also, **break in on.** Interrupt or disturb something unexpectedly, as in *His assistant broke in with the bad news just as we were ready to sign the agreement,* or *She broke in on our private talks.* **3.** Train or instruct someone in a new job or enterprise, as in *Every semester she has to break in a new teaching assistant.* **4.** Loosen or soften something with use, as in *It takes a while to break in a pair of new shoes.*

**break into 1.** Make a forcible entry into, as in *The alarm went off as soon as they tried to break into the house.* Also see BREAK IN, def. 1. **2.** Interrupt something, as in *I couldn't help but break into your conversation.* **3.** Suddenly begin some activity, as in *Without warning she broke into tears.* Also see BURST INTO. **4.** Enter or be admitted to an occupation or a profession, as in *Without connections it is virtually impossible to break into acting.*

**break it up** see under BREAK UP.

**break loose** Escape from restraint, as in *The dog broke loose,* or *He finally broke loose from his mother's influence.* This expression also appears in **all hell breaks loose,** which indicates a state of fury or extreme confusion, as in *When Dad finds out you wrecked the car, all hell will break loose,* or *When the children saw the dead bird in the hall, all hell broke loose.*

**break of day** Dawn, early morning, as in *We'll leave at break of day, as soon as it's light,* or *I feel as though I've been working since the break of day.* This term uses *break* in the sense "burst out of darkness." A similar term is **daybreak.**

**break off 1.** Stop abruptly, as in *The trade talks broke off yesterday.* **2.** Separate something, sever a connection, as in *The baby broke off the tops of all the flowers,* or *The new sect has broken off from the older church.* **3.** End a relationship or friendship, as in *Mary broke off her engagement to Bob.*

**break one** In addition to the idioms beginning with BREAK ONE, also see under BREAK SOMEONE.

**break one's ass** Also, **bust one's ass; break** or **bust one's balls** or **one's butt** or **one's chops. 1.** Exert oneself to the maximum, try very hard, as in *I've been breaking my ass to finish early.* Both *ass,* for backside or buttocks, and *balls,* for male genitals, are rude; *butt,* for buttocks, and *chops,* for either the mouth or the legs, are informal and emphatic but not quite as offensive. For a politer synonym, see BREAK ONE'S BACK. [Vulgar slang] **2. break someone's ass.** Also, **bust someone's chops.** Beat or bother someone, as in *Jim threatened to break Tom's ass,* or *The boss broke his workers' chops to improve service.* [Vulgar slang]

**break one's back** Also, **break one's neck.** Make a great effort, work very hard. For example, *I've been breaking my back over this problem for the past week,* or *Don't break your neck to get there; we'll wait for you.* Both versions of this expression, polite equivalents of BREAK ONE'S ASS, transfer the literal fracture of one's back or neck to figurative effort. However, **break one's neck** has the secondary sense of proceeding with reckless speed, a sense also conveyed by the term **breakneck pace.** Originally this idiom referred literally to breaking one's neck by rushing carelessly along, but it has long been used figuratively as well. Also see BREAK THE BACK OF.

**break one's fall** Interrupt a fall or descent, as in *It's a long way down over this cliff, with nothing to break your fall.*

**break one's word** Fail to keep a promise or contract one has made. For example, *You can trust him completely; I've never known him to break his word.*

**break out 1.** Develop suddenly and forcefully. For example, *A fire broke out last night,* or *He broke out in a sweat.* **2.** Be affected with a skin eruption, such as a rash, as in *A teenager's face often breaks out in pimples.* **3.** Prepare something for consumption, action, or use, as in *Let's break out the champagne,* or *It's such a fine day—let's break out the fishing rods.* **4. break out of.** Force out by breaking; also, escape from confinement. For example, *The hurricane broke the glass out of all the windows,* or *He broke out of prison but was soon caught.* **5.** Isolate a portion of a body of data, as in *Please break out the sales figures from the quarterly report.*

**break ranks 1.** Fall out of line or fall into disorder. For example, *The recruits were warned that they must not break ranks.* **2.** Fail to conform, as in *Harry was told to follow the party platform and not break ranks.* This idiom uses *rank* in the sense of "soldiers standing in line," and the term originally referred to their falling into disorder.

**break someone** In addition to the idioms beginning with BREAK SOMEONE, also see under BREAK ONE.

**break someone of doing something** Cause someone to discontinue a habit or practice, as in *Mom tried for years to break Betty of biting her nails.*

**break someone's heart** Cause great emotional pain or grief. For example, *If Anna moves away, it will break her mother's heart.* In noun form this expression appears as both **a broken heart** and **heartbreak.**

**break someone's serve** In tennis and related sports, win a game served by one's opponent, as in *The only way he'll win the match is to break Bill's serve.* The use of *serve,* from the earlier *service,* means "starting play" in these sports.

**break someone up** see BREAK UP, def. 5.

**break the back of** Overpower, overcome; also, get through the hardest part of something. For example, *This new offense has broken the back of the opposing team,* or *We're well over halfway there; we've broken the back of this journey.*

**break the bank** Ruin one financially, exhaust one's resources, as in *I guess the price of a movie won't break the bank.* This term began in gambling, where it means that a player has won more than the banker (the house) can pay. It also may be used ironically, as in the example.

**break the ice 1.** Make a start, pave the way, as in *Newton's theories broke the ice for modern physics.* This idiom refers to breaking ice in a channel so that a ship can pass. Also see BREAK GROUND. **2.** Relax a tense or very formal situation, as in *Someone at the conference table will have to break the ice.*

**break the news** Make something known, as in *We suspected that she was pregnant but waited for her to break the news to her in-laws.* A variant is the journalistic phrase **break a story,** meaning "reveal a news item or make it available for publication."

**break the record 1.** Do better than an earlier achievement, as in *He broke the record for the high jump.* This usage is applied primarily to sports. **2.** Move very fast, as in *The lecture was so dull that we broke the record getting to the door.*

**break through** Penetrate a barrier or an obstruction, as in *They broke through the wall to get into the vault,* or *It won't be long before we break through the code and map all human genes.*

**break up 1.** Divide something into many pieces. For example, *Now break up the head of garlic into separate cloves.* **2.** Interrupt the continuity of something, as in *A short walk will break up the long morning.* **3.** Also, **break it up.** Scatter, as in *The crowd broke up as soon as they reached the streets.* This phrase is also used as a command, meaning "stop doing something," as in *"Break it up!" shouted the police officer.* **4.** Bring or come to an end, as in *His gambling is sure to break up their marriage.* **5.** Also, **break someone up.** Burst into or cause one to burst into laughter or tears. For example, *His jokes always break me up,* or *That touching eulogy at the funeral broke us all up,* or *I looked at her and just broke up.* The precise meaning depends on the context. This sense grew out of an earlier usage that meant "upset" or "disturb."

**break wind** Expel intestinal gas, as in *Beans always make him break wind.*

**break with 1.** Separate from something, end relations with someone. For example, *On this issue the prime minister was forced to break with his cabinet.* Also see BREAK OFF, def. 2 and 3. **2.** Depart from social conventions, reject, as in *The couple broke with tradition and decided to write their own marriage vows.*

**breast** see KEEP ABREAST OF; MAKE A CLEAN BREAST OF.

**breath** In addition to the idiom beginning with BREATH, also see CATCH ONE'S BREATH; HOLD ONE'S BREATH; IN THE SAME BREATH; OUT OF BREATH; SAVE ONE'S BREATH; TAKE ONE'S BREATH AWAY; UNDER ONE'S BREATH; WASTE ONE'S BREATH; WITH BATED BREATH.

**breathe** In addition to the idioms beginning with BREATHE, also see AS I LIVE AND BREATHE; NOT BREATHE A WORD.

**breathe down someone's neck 1.** Pursue someone closely; pose a threat to one, as in *The immigration authorities were breathing down his neck.* **2.** Watch or supervise someone very closely, as in *The boss is always breathing down our necks.*

**breathe easy** Also, **breathe easily** or **breathe freely.** Relax, feel relieved from anxiety, stress, or tension. For example, *Now that exams are over, I can breathe easy,* or *Whenever I'm back in the mountains, I can breathe freely again.* This idiom originally was *breathe again,* implying that one had stopped breathing (or held one's breath) while feeling anxious or nervous.

**breathe life into** Also, **breathe new life into.** Revive someone or something. For example, *Cardiopulmonary resuscitation (CPR) shows one how to breathe life into a drowning victim,* or *Her appointment breathed new life into the firm.* This term is used both literally, for reviving a person who has stopped breathing temporarily, and figuratively, for energizing or renewing some project. Also see BREATH OF FRESH AIR.

**breathe one's last** Die, as in *My aunt breathed her last on Tuesday.* This term is considered poetic.

B

**breathing space** **1.** Room in which to breathe, as in *In that crowded hall, there was hardly any breathing space.* Earlier this term was put as **breathing room. 2.** Also, **breathing time.** A rest or pause. For example, *I can't work at this all day; I need some breathing space.*

**breath of fresh air, a** New and refreshing, as in *His arrival was a breath of fresh air.* This term transfers the idea of fresh air to a new approach or welcome arrival.

**bred** see BORN AND BRED. Also see under BREED.

**breed** see FAMILIARITY BREEDS CONTEMPT.

**breeze** In addition to the idioms beginning with BREEZE, also see HANDS DOWN (IN A BREEZE); SHOOT THE BREEZE.

**breeze, be a** Also, **be a snap.** Be very easy to do, as in *That test will be a breeze,* or *Finding our way here was a snap.*

**breeze in** **1.** Arrive in a casual way, as in *She breezed in, two hours late.* This phrase transfers the blowing of a light wind to human entrances. **2.** Win easily, as in *A fine golfer, he breezed in first.* This usage at first referred to horseracing but soon was transferred to more general use.

**breeze out** Leave a place quickly, especially showing an attitude of indifference. For example, *He thinks he can just breeze out of here whenever he pleases.*

**breeze through** **1.** Pass through a place quickly, as in *They breezed through town without even stopping for gas,* or, more figuratively, go through something without paying attention to it. For example, *The committee breezed through my report.* **2.** Do something very easily, as in *She breezed through final exams.*

**brick** In addition to the idiom beginning with BRICK, also see DROP A BRICK; LIKE A CAT ON A HOT TIN ROOF; LIKE A TON OF BRICKS; RUN INTO A STONE (BRICK) WALL; SHIT A BRICK.

**bricks shy of a load, a few** Mentally impaired, either unintelligent or merely strange. For example, *He may be handsome, but he's not too bright—a few bricks shy of a load.* This term transfers a light load to lightweight mental capacity and can also be preceded by a specific number such as **two.**

**bride** see GIVE AWAY (THE BRIDE).

**bridge** In addition to the idiom beginning with BRIDGE, also see BURN ONE'S BRIDGES; CROSS A BRIDGE WHEN ONE COMES TO IT; WATER OVER THE DAM (UNDER THE BRIDGE).

**bridge the gap** Find a way to make a connection between two people or things, especially in order to make a situation easier. For example, *I doubt those two will ever be able to bridge the gap that divides them,* or *We're having trouble bridging the gap between one payday and the next.*

**brief** see IN BRIEF.

**bright and early** Early in the morning, at dawn, as in *It's a long trip, so we'll have to leave bright and early.* The *bright* here may refer to the brilliance of the dawning sun.

**bright-eyed and bushy-tailed** Eager and alert, as in *Here is my new kindergarten class, all bright-eyed and bushy-tailed.* The reference here is to the appearance of a squirrel, which with its bright eyes and bushy tail looks ready for anything.

**bright idea** A clever thought or plan. For example, *John had a bright idea for saving space—we would each have a terminal but share the printer.* This term uses *bright* in the sense of "intelligent" or "quick-witted" and may be used either literally, as in the example above, or ironically, as in *Jumping in the pool with your clothes on—that was some bright idea.*

**bright lights, the** A big city when it is thought of as a place to find entertainment at night, especially enjoyment of activities that are not quite respectable. For example, *He's settling down now and has had enough of the bright lights.*

**bright side, the** Considering something favorably or hopefully, as in *Bob tends to look on the bright side of everything.* This idiom uses *bright* in the sense of "lit up with gladness or hope." Also see GLASS IS HALF FULL.

**bring about** Also, **bring *something* to pass.** Make something happen, accomplish or result in something. For example, *The revised tax code brought about considerable changes in accounting.* Also see BRING ON, def. 1.

**bring around** Also, **bring round. 1.** Conduct someone or transfer something to others. For example, *Anne brought around the new intern to meet the nursing staff,* or *The clerk will bring round the papers for you to sign.* **2.** Also, **bring *someone* around** or **bring *someone* to.** Restore someone to health or consciousness. For example, *Some fresh air will help bring him to.* **3.** Convert or persuade someone, as in *The senator was sure he could bring around the other committee members.*

**bring down** **1.** Cause something to fall, collapse, or die. For example, *The pilot won a medal for bringing down enemy aircraft,* or *The bill's defeat was sure to bring down the party.* **2.** Cause a punishment or judgment, as in *The bomb threats brought down the public's wrath on the terrorists.* **3.** Also, **bring oneself down.** Reduce something, lower, as in *I won't buy it till they bring down the price,* or *He refused to bring himself down to their level.* This usage may be literal, as in the first example, or figurative, as in the second.

**bring down the curtain** see RING DOWN THE CURTAIN.

**bring down the house** Evoke a lot of applause and cheers, as in *Her solo brought the house down.* This exaggerated expression suggests noise loud enough to pose a threat to the building—an unlikely event.

**bring forth** **1.** Give rise to something, introduce. For example, *I may be new, but I can still bring forth any proposals I consider necessary.* **2.** Give birth; see BRING INTO THE WORLD.

**bring home** Get to the heart of a matter, make perfectly clear. For example, *The crash brought home the danger of drinking and driving.* This term uses *home* in the figurative sense of "touching someone or something closely."

**bring home the bacon** **1.** Earn a living, provide the necessities of life, as in *Now that she had a job, Patricia could bring home the bacon.* **2.** Be successful, accomplish something of value, as in *George went to Washington and brought home the bacon—he got the funding we needed.* This idiom is widely believed to come from the old game of catching a greased pig, a popular competition at country fairs, in which the winner was awarded the pig.

**bring into line** see under FALL IN LINE.

**bring into the world** Also, **bring forth.** Give birth, as in *It's certainly easier to bring a child into the world when you have a definite means of support,* or *Our dog brought forth a fine litter of six puppies.* Both versions of this term are somewhat archaic.

**bring off** Accomplish something, achieve successfully, as in *We managed to bring off a wonderful performance.*

**bring on** **1.** Cause something to happen, produce, as in *His cold brought on an asthma attack.* Also see BRING ABOUT. **2.** Cause to appear or bring into action, as in *Bring on the jugglers.*

**bring out** **1.** Expose or reveal something; make conspicuous. For example, *His book brought out some new facts about the war,* or *Her photographs bring out the play of light on her subjects.* **2.** Nurture or develop a quality, as in *A gifted teacher brings out the best in students.* **3.** Present something to the public. For example, *The publisher decided to bring out this dictionary in a single volume,* or *Young upper-class women traditionally are brought out at a ball.* **4.** Play an important role in another person's acknowledgment of his or her homosexuality, as in *Ann brought Mary out a couple of years ago.* The gay sense of this expression is derived from def. 3 as illustrated by its second example, but presentation to the public is not an element of the sense. If someone announces that another person is a lesbian or a gay man, it is called *outing,* because many homosexuals choose to live in secrecy rather than risk exposure. Also see COME OUT, def. 6.

**bring round** see BRING AROUND.

**bring *someone* to** **1.** Restore someone to consciousness, as in *I'll see if these smelling salts will bring her to.* Also see BRING AROUND, def. 2. **2.** Cause a ship or boat to stop by heading into the wind or some other means. For example, *As they neared the dock, they brought the boat to.*

**bring *something* to a head** Cause something to reach a turning point or crisis. For example, *Management's newest policy has brought matters to a head.* The related phrase **come to a head** means "reach a crisis," as in *With the last break-in, the question of security came to a head.* These phrases refer to the medical sense of *head,* the tip of an infected lump that is about to burst.

**bring *something* to bear** Exert some force or pressure, apply, as in *All his efforts are brought to bear on the new problem,* or *The union is bringing pressure to bear on management.*

**bring *someone* to heel** Force someone to obey, conquer. For example, *The prisoners were quickly brought to heel.* This term transfers commanding a dog to come close behind its master to similar control over human beings or their activities.

**bring *someone* to life** Animate or energize a person or thing. For example, *The promise of a big part in the play brought Jane to life,* or *The author's changes really brought this screenplay to life.* Also see COME TO LIFE.

**bring *something* to light** Reveal or disclose something hidden or secret, as in *After careful investigation all the facts of the case were brought to light.* This term uses *light* in the sense of "public knowledge."

**bring to mind** Cause something or someone to be remembered, as in *The film brought to mind the first time I ever climbed a mountain.* Also see COME TO MIND.

**bring *one* to one's knees** Make one submit; reduce to an inferior position. For example, *Solitary confinement usually brings prisoners to their knees.*

**bring *something* to pass** see BRING ABOUT.

**bring *one* to terms** Force someone to agree or to continue negotiations, as in *The creditors were determined to bring the company to terms.* The *terms* here mean "the conditions for agreement." Also see COME TO TERMS.

**bring to the table** Supply experience or a skill to a task or negotiation, as in *We know she wants the job, but what does she bring to the table?*

**bring up** **1.** Raise someone from childhood, rear. For example, *Bringing up children is both* *difficult and rewarding.* **2.** Introduce a subject into discussion, mention, as in *Let's not bring up the cost right now.* **3.** Vomit, as in *She still felt sick but couldn't bring up anything.*

**bring *one* up short** Cause one to stop very suddenly in surprise, as in *Your warning certainly brought him up short.*

**bring up the rear** Be last in a line or series, as in *As a slow walker, I'm used to bringing up the rear,* or *In test results Tom always brought up the rear.* This term almost certainly came from the military.

**bring *one* up to date** Provide information up to the present; also, make one aware of or conform to new ideas, improvements, or styles. For example, *Bring me up to date on the test results,* or *We've been bringing Grandma up to date with a new personal computer.* This term comes from bookkeeping, where it means enter account figures to the present time. A shortened form, **up-to-date,** is also used as an adjective, as in *I need up-to-date sales figures for my report.*

**broad** In addition to the idioms beginning with BROAD, also see CAN'T HIT THE BROAD SIDE OF A BARN.

**broad daylight** A great deal of obvious natural light, as in *You don't need your flashlight—it's broad daylight,* or *She was attacked on her own street in broad daylight.*

**broad in the beam** Having broad hips or large buttocks. For example, *I've grown too broad in the beam for these slacks.* This expression originally described the width of a ship.

**broad shoulders, have** Also, **have a broad back.** Be able to accept a lot of responsibility, as in *With his broad shoulders, he can easily handle both departments,* or *Parents must have broad backs in order to raise children.*

**broke** see FLAT BROKE; GO BROKE; GO FOR (BROKE); IF IT AIN'T BROKE DON'T FIX IT. Also see under BREAK.

**broom** see NEW BROOM SWEEPS CLEAN.

**broth** see TOO MANY COOKS SPOIL THE BROTH.

**brow** see BY THE SWEAT OF ONE'S BROW; CAUSE RAISED EYEBROWS.

**brown bagger** A person who brings his or her own lunch, as in *The architects of the new office designed a space for brown baggers to eat lunch.* This term originated in Britain for serious students who carried their books about with them in brown briefcases or bags. However, in the United States, it has primarily been used for people who take their lunch to work or bring their own wine or liquor in a brown paper bag to a public place or a restaurant that is not licensed to sell alcoholic beverages.

**brownie points** Credit or recognition for a good deed, as in *John earned a lot of brownie points for doing his boss's report for him.* The term came from the points earned for various achievements by the youngest group of the Girl Scouts, called Brownies. Later it was transferred to general use.

**brown nose** Seek favor in an obviously insincere way, flatter someone in an excessive way. For example, *Harry was always brown nosing, but it didn't help his grades.* This term originated in the military; it refers to ass-kissing when the backside being kissed is less than clean. Despite its vulgar origin, today this slang term is not considered particularly offensive.

**brunt** see BEAR THE BRUNT.

**brush** In addition to the idioms beginning with BRUSH, also see GIVE SOMEONE THE BRUSHOFF; HAVE A BRUSH WITH; TARRED WITH THE SAME BRUSH.

**brush aside** Dismiss one, ignore something, as in *The teacher brushed aside our questions.*

**brush off** Dismiss someone or reject something, as in *She brushed off the poor reviews with a shrug,* or *You can't brush off a boyfriend and expect him to do you a favor.* This expression transfers sweeping off crumbs to a curt dismissal. Also see GIVE SOMEONE THE BRUSHOFF.

**brush under the rug** Also, **brush under the carpet.** See SWEEP UNDER THE RUG.

**brush up** **1.** Clean something, make neat and presentable, as in *We plan to get the house brushed up in time for the party.* **2.** Also, **brush up on.** Review something, refresh one's memory, as in *We brushed up on our Spanish before going to Honduras,* or *I'm brushing up my knowledge of town history before I speak at the club.*

**brute force** Also, **brute strength.** Extreme violence, unreasoning strength, as in *We hope that reason will triumph over brute force.* Although this expression is also used literally to mean exceptional physical power, the figurative sense reflects the origin for *brute,* which comes from a Latin word meaning "heavy, stupid, unreasoning."

**buck** In addition to the idioms beginning with BUCK, also see BIG BUCKS; FAST BUCK; MORE BANG FOR THE BUCK; PASS THE BUCK.

**bucket** see DROP IN THE BUCKET; KICK THE BUCKET; RAIN CATS AND DOGS (BUCKETS); WEEP BUCKETS.

**bucking for, be** Be working for a promotion or an award, aiming for, as in *She's bucking for Editor of the Year.* Strongly associated with seeking a promotion in the military, this expression is now applied more widely.

**buckle down** Set to work, apply oneself with determination, as in *We need to buckle down now and study for exams.*

**buckle under** Give way, collapse physically or mentally as a result of weight or stress, as in *One more heavy snowfall, and the roof may buckle under,* or *The stress of two jobs made her buckle under.*

**buckle up** Fasten a seat belt, as in *All the children must learn to buckle up as soon as they get in a car.* This term came into wide use after seat belts became required automobile equipment. Earlier they had been used mainly in airplanes.

**buck stops here, the** I'll take full responsibility, as in *You needn't call my boss; the buck stops here.* This saying gained fame as a sign on the desk of President Harry S. Truman. It refers to another expression that means the opposite, PASS THE BUCK.

**buck the system** Resist or fight against something, especially a government or social conventions, as in *She'll buck the system until she's dead.*

**Buck up!** A saying meaning "Cheer up," as in *Buck up! We'll soon be done.* A variant, **buck one up,** means "encourage or become encouraged," as in *Even the thought of a vacation did not buck her up.*

**bud** see NIP IN THE BUD.

**buddy up** Be very friendly, as in *He is always wanting to buddy up with me, but I don't really like him.*

**buff** see IN THE BUFF.

**bug** In addition to the idioms beginning with BUG, also see CUTE AS A BUTTON (BUG'S EAR); PUT A BUG IN SOMEONE'S EAR; SNUG AS A BUG IN A RUG; WHAT'S EATING (BUGGING) ONE.

**bug off** Also, **bugger off.** Go away, as in *Bug off before I call the police.* Both terms are often used as commands, as in the example, and the variant, which is considered vulgar, is used more in Britain than in the United States. For a synonym, see BUZZ OFF.

**bug out** **1.** Bulge, as in *The news will make her eyes bug out with astonishment.* This expression was originally used literally for bulging eyes and later used more loosely as a sign of astonishment. **2.** Leave, run out, as in *This conference is a bore; I think I'll bug out.* This usage originated as military slang for deserting and today is used more loosely.

**build** In addition to the idioms beginning with BUILD, also see LIGHT (BUILD) A FIRE UNDER. Also see under BUILT.

**build down** Reduce, become less, as in *Because of increased vigilance, traffic in narcotics is finally building down.* This term, the antonym of BUILD UP, first referred to reducing a stockpile of nuclear weapons and soon was applied more widely.

**build in** Also, **build into.** Construct or include something as an important part; also, make something automatic or intrinsic. For example, *Frank Lloyd Wright liked to build in as much furniture as possible, not just bookcases but desks and tables as well,* or *We've got to build some extra time into the schedule for this project.* Both terms are frequently used in the past participle, that is, **built in** or **built into.** The adjective and noun form is hyphenated, as in *I wanted built-in bookcases, but they would have cost too much,* or *The apartment features lots of built-ins, such as shelves in the closets for shirts and sweaters.*

**build on** Also, **build upon.** Add as an extension; use as a basis or foundation. For example, *They decided to build on an addition,* or *She was building all her hopes on passing the exam.*

**build *something* on sand** Use an insecure foundation, as in *If you buy nothing but high-risk stocks, your portfolio will be built on sand.*

**build up** **1.** Fill an area with houses or other buildings. For example, *We want to protect the wetlands against those who want to build up the area.* **2.** Gradually develop something, increase in stages. For example, *I want to build up my endurance for the race.* **3.** Accumulate or collect something, as in *A lot of rust has built up on the farm machinery.* **4.** Increase, strengthen, develop toward, as in *The sound built up until it was nearly deafening,* or *His argument was building up to a grand climax.* **5.** Establish or enhance a reputation; praise or flatter. For example, *Months before the official campaign could begin, they had been building up the senator's image.*

**built** see MADE (BUILT) TO ORDER; NOT BUILT THAT WAY; ROME WASN'T BUILT IN A DAY. Also see under BUILD.

**bulk** In addition to the idiom beginning with BULK, also see IN BULK.

**bulk up** Become more physically strong, either by exercising, taking a food supplement, or increasing one's carbohydrate intake. For example, *She has started lifting weights so she can bulk up for the Olympics,* or *I try to bulk up on carbohydrates before I exercise.*

**bull** In addition to the idioms beginning with BULL, also see COCK AND BULL STORY; HIT THE BULL'S-EYE; SHOOT THE BREEZE (BULL); TAKE THE BULL BY THE HORNS.

**bullet** see BITE THE BULLET; SWEAT BULLETS.

**bulletin board** Also, **electronic bulletin board.** A computer service that provides facilities for people to leave messages on the Internet. For example, *Many groups concerned with environmental issues have bulletin boards through which members can communicate via their computers.* The term refers to the older board for posting notices by hand.

**bull in a china shop** A very clumsy person, as in *Her living room, with its delicate furni-*

*ture and knickknacks, made him feel like a bull in a china shop.* The precise origin for this term has been lost.

B

**bull session** An informal discussion, as in *College students love late-night bull sessions about anything and everything, from professors to poetry to politics.* This expression originally referred to an exchange of opinions and anecdotes, including stories of sexual activities, by men, and then came to be used more broadly.

**bullshit artist, a** Also, **a bull artist.** A person who habitually exaggerates, flatters, or talks nonsense. For example, *Don't believe a word of it—he's a bullshit artist.* [Vulgar slang]

**bum** In addition to the idioms beginning with BUM, also see ON THE BLINK (BUM).

**bum around 1.** Loaf, wander without a destination, as in *After graduating, he decided to bum around Europe for a year.* **2.** Visit bars or nightclubs, as in *Her father accused her of bumming around half the night and threatened to cut off her allowance.*

**bum out 1.** Depress someone, sadden, as in *He's been really bummed out since his girlfriend moved to California.* **2.** Annoy someone, irritate, bother, as in *That haircut will really bum out his parents.* **3.** Fail badly, as in *I got through the midterm, but I bummed out totally on the final exam.* This usage is student slang.

**bump** In addition to the idioms beginning with BUMP, also see GOOSE PIMPLES (BUMPS); LIKE A BUMP ON A LOG.

**bump into 1.** Also, **bump against.** Collide with someone or something, come in contact with. For example, *It's easy to bump into furniture in the dark.* Also see BANG INTO. **2.** Encounter someone, meet by chance, as in *While I was downtown, I bumped into your cousin.* Also see RUN INTO.

**bump off** Kill someone, murder, as in *The convict bragged about bumping off his partner,* or *The first fighter plane bumped off three enemy aircraft.* This term was at first principally criminal slang and somewhat later, military jargon.

**bump up 1.** Suddenly increase something, as in *Oil-producing nations decided to bump up the price of oil.* This term is used mainly for prices or other figures. **2.** Give someone a promotion, move someone up. For example, *He hoped to be bumped up to first class on the flight,* or *After five years, she expected they would bump her up to vice president.*

**bum rap, a** A false accusation or conviction; also, unfair criticism or action. For example, *He claimed he was in prison on a bum rap,* or *The theater critics gave her last play a bum rap.* This expression originated as underworld slang and was soon used figuratively for any injustice.

**bum's rush** Forcible ejection, abrupt dismissal or removal. For example, *When he started shouting, the bouncer at the club gave him the bum's rush,* or *Within hours of being fired, Alice was given the bum's rush.* This idiom uses *bum* in the sense of "a vagrant or tramp."

**bum steer** False or misleading information; poor advice. For example, *She felt her doctor had given her a bum steer, as she hadn't gained any weight on the diet.*

**bundle** In addition to the idiom beginning with BUNDLE, also see MAKE A BUNDLE.

**bundle of nerves** A very nervous, tense, or fearful person, as in *For months after the accident, I was a bundle of nerves.*

**burden of proof** The obligation of proving a charge false. For example, *Are you sure you mailed the tax return on time? The burden of proof's on you.* Originally a legal term, this expression has also been used more loosely in recent times.

**burn** In addition to the idioms beginning with BURN, also see CRASH AND BURN; EARS ARE BURNING; FIDDLE WHILE ROME BURNS; (BURN) IN EFFIGY; MONEY BURNS A HOLE IN ONE'S POCKET; MONEY TO BURN; SLOW BURN.

**burn at the stake** Execute someone by tying to a stake and burning; also, punish severely. This expression refers to a method used in the Middle Ages for putting nonbelievers to death, but now it is used as an exaggerated term for harsh punishment, as in *She was sure she'd be burned at the stake for losing the contract.* In fact, *the stake* can be used loosely for any extreme punishment.

**burn down 1.** Completely consume something by fire, burn to the ground, as in *Their house burned down, and they had nowhere to go.* **2.** Become weaker for lack of fuel, as in *The fire will soon burn down.*

**burn in effigy** see IN EFFIGY.

**burning question** An urgent or crucial issue under vigorous discussion. For example, *Real estate taxes are always a burning question for the town leaders.* This term has exact equivalents in French (*question brûlante*) and German (*brennende Frage*).

**burn into** Make an unforgettable impression on, as in *An event like the Holocaust burns into the minds of all who see the movie,* or *The scene was burned into her memory.* This expression refers to such processes as etching or engraving, where an acid is used to make a design in a solid plate.

**burn off 1.** Clear something by heat, as in *The sun will soon burn off the morning fog.* **2.** Clear land by burning vegetation, as in *They've decided to burn off part of the field to prepare it for another planting.*

**burn one's bridges** Commit oneself to a plan or course of action that cannot be changed. For example, *Criticizing one's boss in a written resignation means one has burned one's bridges.* This idiom refers to ancient military tactics, when troops would cross a body of water and then burn the bridge they had used both to prevent retreat and to stop a pursuing enemy. Also see CROSS THE RUBICON.

**burn oneself out** see BURN OUT, def. 3.

**burn one's fingers** Harm oneself, as in *I'm staying away from risky stocks; I've burned my fingers often enough.*

**burn out** **1.** Stop functioning because something, such as fuel, has been used up. For example, *There's nothing wrong with the lamp; the light bulb just burned out.* **2. be burned out.** Lose one's home, place of work, or school as the result of a fire. For example, *Hundreds of businesses are burned out every year because of arsonists.* **3.** Also, **burn oneself out.** Make or become exhausted or indifferent, especially with one's work or schooling. For example, *Many young lawyers burn themselves out after a few years of 70-hour weeks.* This term refers to a fire going out for lack of new fuel.

**burn rubber** Drive very fast, as in *We'll have to burn rubber to get there in time.* In this automotive slang, the *rubber* refers to tires that heat up when they rotate suddenly at great speed.

**burn someone up** see BURN UP, def. 1.

**burn the candle at both ends** Exhaust one's energies or resources by leading a stressful life. For example, *Joseph's been burning the candle at both ends for weeks, working two jobs.*

**burn the midnight oil** Stay up late working or studying, as in *The semester is almost over, and we're all burning the midnight oil before exams.* This expression refers to the oil in oil lamps.

**burn *something* to a crisp** Also, **burn *something* to a cinder.** Destroy something by fire; overcook. For example, *If I stay in the sun too long, I'll be burnt to a crisp,* or *He's an awful cook—dinner was burnt to a crisp.* Although both expressions can be used literally, they are also used as exaggerations, as in the examples.

**burn up** **1. burn someone up.** Make someone angry or very irritated, as in *He was really burned up at his son for denting the new car,* or *Those careless drivers just burn me up.* **2.** Travel very fast, as in *This car will burn up the road.* **3.** Easily surpass or outdo someone, as in *They'll burn up the other teams.*

**burst a gut** see BUST A GUST.

**burst at the seams** Be filled to or beyond normal capacity. For example, *On her wedding day the church was bursting at the seams,* or *That was a wonderful meal, but I'm bursting at the seams.* This expression refers to tearing the seams of a garment that is too tight for the wearer and is generally used to exaggerate a situation. Also see COME APART AT THE SEAMS.

**burst into** **1.** Also, **burst out in** or **burst out into.** Break out into sudden activity. For example, **burst into flames** means "break out in a fire," as in *This dry woodpile may well burst into flames.* **2.** Also, **burst out.** Suddenly express an emotion. For example, **burst into tears** or **laughter** or **song** or **speech** or **burst out crying** or **laughing** or **singing,** etc., mean "begin suddenly to weep, laugh, sing," and so on, as in *When she saw him, she burst into tears,* or *I burst out laughing when I saw their outfits,* or *When they brought in the cake, we all burst into song.*

**burst with** Be overfull with something, be unable to contain oneself with an emotion. For example, *Jane's award made her parents burst with pride,* or *Harry is bursting with the news about his promotion.*

**bury one's head in the sand** see HIDE ONE'S HEAD IN THE SAND.

**bury the hatchet** Make peace; settle one's differences. For example, *Toward the end of the year, the roommates finally decided to bury the hatchet.* Although some believe this term comes from a Native American custom for declaring peace between warring tribes, others say it comes from **hang up one's hatchet,** a term used long before Columbus landed in the New World.

**bush** see BEAT AROUND THE BUSH; BEAT THE BUSHES FOR; BRIGHT-EYED AND BUSHY-TAILED.

**bushel** see HIDE ONE'S LIGHT UNDER A BUSHEL.

**business** In addition to the idiom beginning with BUSINESS, also see FUNNY BUSINESS; GO ABOUT (ONE'S BUSINESS); HAVE NO BUSINESS DOING; IN BUSINESS; LIKE CRAZY (NOBODY'S BUSINESS); MAKE IT ONE'S BUSINESS; MEAN BUSINESS; MIND ONE'S OWN BUSINESS; MONKEY BUSINESS; NONE OF ONE'S BUSINESS; OUT OF BUSINESS; SEND SOMEONE ABOUT HIS OR HER BUSINESS; THE BUSINESS.

**business as usual** The normal course of some activity, as in *The fire destroyed only a small section of the store, so it's business as usual.* This term originated as an announcement that a commercial establishment was continuing to operate in spite of fire, construction, or some similar interruption. Today it may be used in this positive sense and also negatively, as in *Never mind that many people are homeless—the authorities seem to regard their job as business as usual.*

**busman's holiday** Free time spent in much the same activity as one's work. For example, *Weather permitting, the lifeguard spent all her days off at the beach—a real busman's holiday.* The term refers to a bus driver spending his or her day off taking a long bus ride.

**bust** In addition to the idiom beginning with BUST, also see BREAK (BUST) ONE'S ASS; GO BROKE (BUST).

**bust a gut** Also, **burst a gut. 1.** Exert oneself to the greatest extent. For example, *He was busting a gut trying to please us.* This term refers to hurting one's midsection through physical straining. For synonyms, see BREAK ONE'S ASS; BREAK ONE'S BACK. **2.** Explode with strong feeling, especially laughter or anger. For example, *I almost bust a gut laughing,* or *The boss will burst a gut when he's told that the machine isn't repaired.*

**bust one's ass** see BREAK ONE'S ASS.

**busy** In addition to the idioms beginning with BUSY, also see GET BUSY.

**busy as a beaver** Also, **busy as a bee.** Hardworking, very industrious, as in *With all her activities, she is always busy as a bee,* or *He is busy as a beaver trying to finish painting before it rains.* Also see EAGER BEAVER; WORK LIKE A BEAVER.

**busy work** Activity meant to take up time but not actually be productive. For example, *We have to put in an eight-hour day, even if we do nothing but busy work.*

**but** In addition to the idioms beginning with BUT, also see ALL BUT; ALL OVER BUT THE SHOUTING; ANYTHING BUT; CAN'T HELP (BUT); CLOSE BUT NO CIGAR; EVERYTHING BUT THE KITCHEN SINK; LAST BUT NOT LEAST; LONG ON SOMETHING, BUT SHORT ON; NO IFS OR BUTS; NOTHING BUT; SADDER BUT WISER; SEPARATE BUT EQUAL; SLOW BUT SURE; SPIRIT IS WILLING BUT THE FLESH IS WEAK; THERE BUT FOR THE GRACE OF GOD.

**but for** Except for something, were it not for someone. For example, *But for the afternoon shower, it was a perfect day,* or *But for the children, they would have gotten a divorce long ago.*

**but good** Surely, thoroughly, as in *We decided to clean up the whole yard but good.* The word *but* in this expression functions as an intensive. Also see AND HOW.

**butter** In addition to the idioms beginning with BUTTER, also see BREAD AND BUTTER; KNOW WHICH SIDE OF ONE'S BREAD IS BUTTERED.

**butterflies in one's stomach** Fluttering sensations caused by a feeling of nervous anticipation. For example, *I always get butterflies in my stomach before making a speech.* This term compares a nervous feeling to the imaginary one resulting from swallowing live butterflies that fly about inside one.

**butter up** Excessively praise or flatter someone, usually to gain a favor. For example, *If you butter up Dad, he'll let you borrow the car.* This term transfers the oily quality of butter to lavish praise.

**butter wouldn't melt in one's mouth** Be too flattering; be insincere. For example, *She looked innocent, as though butter wouldn't melt in her mouth, but we knew better.* This expression suggests that one is literally so cool that butter inside the mouth would not melt.

**butt in** Also, **butt in on.** Interfere, interrupt someone, intrude. For example, *Mom is always butting in on our conversations,* or *It's against the law for employers to butt in on personal matters.* This term refers to the way an animal uses its horns.

**button** In addition to the idiom beginning with BUTTON, also see CUTE AS A BUTTON; ON THE BUTTON; PUSH (PRESS) SOMEONE'S BUTTONS; PUSH THE PANIC BUTTON.

**buttonhole someone** Approach and speak to a person in an insistent manner, detain in conversation. For example, *The reporter tried to buttonhole the senator, but she got away.* This term refers to grasping someone by a buttonhole on his or her clothing.

**button one's lip** see BUTTON UP, def. 2.

**button up 1.** Close something securely, fasten, as in *The house was all buttoned up,* or *Button up your coat—it's very cold.* **2.** Also, **button one's lip.** Not speak, be quiet. For example, *Please button your lip about the surprise.* A variant of this usage is **button one's mouth. 3.** Finish something successfully, as in *I've got this report all buttoned up.*

**buy into 1.** Purchase a membership, a share, or an interest in something. For example, *I'd love to buy into this partnership, but I can't afford it.* **2.** Accept a rumor, a lie, or an opinion as fact, as in *I can't believe you bought into that story,* or *Don't buy into his stories; they're all lies.* Also see BUY SOMETHING.

**buy it 1.** Suffer a severe reversal, as in *If they can't raise the money in time, they'll buy it.* **2.** Be killed; die. For example, *By the time we could get to the hospital, he had bought it.* First used during World War I as military slang, this term later was extended to peacetime forms of death. A later slang equivalent is **buy the farm.** For example, *He'll soon buy the farm riding that motorcycle.* **3.** Believe it; see BUY INTO, def. 2; BUY SOMETHING.

**buy off** Pay to get rid of a claim or opposition, or to avoid prosecution, as in *He was caught trying to buy off the judge.*

**buy out** Purchase the entire stock, rights, or interests of a business. For example, *A rival store owner offered to buy out my grandfather, but he refused,*

**buy something** Believe something; accept as true or satisfactory. For example, *You think he's a millionaire? I just won't buy that.*

**buy the farm** see under BUY IT.

**buy time** Increase the time available for a specific purpose. For example, *Renting an apartment buys them time to look around for a new house.*

**buy up** Purchase all that is available, as in *They want to buy up all the land in this area.*

**buzz off** Go away, leave. For example, *The store owner told the teenagers to buzz off and find another place to hang out.* This curt command originated during World War I. Also see BUG OFF.

**by a hair** Also, **by a hairbreadth** or **by a whisker.** Very narrowly. For example, *His serve was out of bounds by a hair,* or *We made our flight by a hairbreadth,* or *Dad missed hitting the pole by a whisker. Whisker* here means "a small amount." Also see BY THE SKIN OF ONE'S TEETH; HANG BY A HAIR.

**by all accounts** Also, **according to all accounts.** From all reports available, from what everyone is saying. For example, *By all accounts the party was a great success,* or *They spent a fortune on their cruise, according to all accounts.* These phrases use *account* in the sense of "a particular report or description of some event."

**by all means 1.** Also, **by all manner of means.** In every possible way, as in *I plan to make use of him by all means.* **2.** Also, **by all manner of means.** At any cost, as in *Losing the contract is to be avoided by all means.* **3.** Certainly, yes, as in *Are you coming tonight? By all means, I'll be there.* Also see BY ANY MEANS; BY NO MEANS.

**by all odds** By far, as in *She is by all odds the best player on the team.* This idiom uses *odds* in the sense of "the amount by which one thing excels or exceeds."

**by a long shot** see under LONG SHOT.

**by a mile** see MISS BY A MILE.

**by and by** After a while, soon, as in *She'll be along by and by.* The expression probably relies on the meaning of *by* as a succession of quantities (as in "two by two"). This adverbial phrase came to be used as a noun, meaning either procrastination or the future.

**by and large** For the most part, generally speaking, as in *By and large the novel was a success.* For a synonym, see FOR THE MOST PART.

**by any means** In any possible way, no matter how, as in *By any means I've got to get there.* Also see BY HOOK OR CROOK; BY MEANS OF; BY NO MEANS.

**by any stretch** Also, **by any stretch of the imagination.** Beyond ordinary limits. For example, *She could not, by any stretch of the imagination, be considered a great actress.* The phrase sometimes is put in the negative, **by no stretch,** as in *By no stretch can that house be called a mansion.*

**by a thread** see HANG BY A THREAD.

**by a whisker** see BY A HAIR.

**by chance** Casually, accidentally, as in *I ran into Bill purely by chance.* Also see BY COINCIDENCE.

**by choice** Deliberately, as a matter of preference. For example, *No one told me to come; I'm here by choice.*

**by coincidence** Through an accidental event at which two things happen at the same time, as in *By coincidence both researchers discovered the same solution.* Also see BY CHANCE.

**by cracky** see BY JOVE.

**by definition** According to an understood agreement, as a given. For example, *This antibiotic is by definition the most effective now on the market.*

**by degrees** Gradually, by steps or stages. For example, *By degrees he began to delegate more and more of his duties to his staff.* Also see BY INCHES.

**by design** On purpose, deliberately, as in *Whether by luck or by design, his application was accepted.* This term uses *design* in the sense of "plan."

**by dint of** By means of, as in *By dint of hard work he got his degree in three years.* The word *dint,* which survives only in this expression, originally meant "a stroke or blow," which signified the force behind such a blow. The current term preserves the sense of vigorous or persistent means.

**by far** Also, **far and away.** To the greatest degree, by a large margin. For example, *She is by far the most experienced member of the cast,* or *He is far and away the best teacher I've ever had.* Also see BY HALF.

**by fits and starts** see FITS AND STARTS.

**bygones** see LET BYGONES BE BYGONES.

**by half** Considerably better, a great deal more, as in *He was too good a cook by half for this small restaurant.* Also see BY HALVES.

**by halves** Imperfectly, reluctantly, or halfheartedly, as in *You really can't paint a house by halves.*

**by hand** With a hand or the hands, manually (as opposed to by a machine or some other means). For example, *This letter was delivered by hand,* or *You can make these drawings by hand, but computer graphics are more efficient.*

**by heart** Also, **by rote.** From memory; also, mechanically. For example, *Betty had trouble learning the song by heart, but her teacher insisted on it,* or *Some schools put heavy emphasis on learning by rote.* These terms are often put as **know *something* by heart** or **learn *something* by rote.** The variant often implies mere memorization without deeper understanding.

**by hook or crook** Also, **by hook or by crook.** By any means possible, in one way or another. For example, *My car broke down, but I'll get to the party by hook or crook.* Also see BY ANY MEANS.

**by inches** Also, **inch by inch.** Gradually, bit by bit, as in *We found ourselves in rush hour traffic, moving by inches.* This expression is often an exaggeration of the actual circumstance. A variant phrase, **to inch along,** means "to move bit by bit," as in *There was a long line at the theater, just inching along.*

**by Jove** Also, **by cracky.** Used to express surprise or emphasis. For example, *By Jove, I was glad to see her,* or *It was a great day, by cracky.* These mild oaths are euphemisms, the first for "by Jesus" or "by God" (Jove is another name for Jupiter, the principal Roman god), and the folksy variant **by cracky,** for "by Christ."

**by leaps and bounds** Rapidly or with fast progress, as in *The corn is growing by leaps and bounds,* or *School enrollment is increasing by leaps and bounds.* This term is redundant, since *leap* and *bound* both mean "spring" or "jump."

**by means of** Through the use of something, because of, as in *We plan to pay for medical school by means of a second mortgage,* or *He'll succeed by means of sheer persistence.* Also see BY DINT OF.

**by mistake** Erroneously, as in *He took my coat by mistake.*

**by no means** Also, **not by any means.** In no way, certainly not. For example, *She is by no means a weak opponent,* or *Not by any means will I go along with that decision.*

**by no stretch** see under BY ANY STRETCH.

**by one's bootstraps** see under PULL ONESELF UP.

**by oneself** Alone, without a companion; also, unassisted. For example, *She enjoyed being by herself much of the time,* or *You can pick up your toys by yourself.*

**by one's wits** see LIVE BY ONE'S WITS.

**by reason of** Because of something, as a result of, as in *By reason of a crop failure, the price of coffee is certain to rise.* This expression is considered quite formal today.

**by request** Also, **on request** or **upon request.** In response to being asked to do something. For example, *The band is playing our favorite song by request.*

**by rights** Justly, in fairness, as in *By rights he should have been chosen first.* This term was originally used as *by right.*

**by rote** see BY HEART.

**by storm** see TAKE BY STORM.

**by surprise** see TAKE BY SURPRISE.

**by the balls** see HAVE SOMEONE BY THE BALLS.

**by the board** No longer useful, discarded. This expression is usually put as **go by the board,** as in *With all the crime today, the practice of leaving the house unlocked has gone by the board.*

**by the book** Strictly according to the rules, as in *Our trip leader is going by the book, allowing us to wander off only for short periods.* Also see BY THE NUMBERS.

**by the bye** Also, **by the by.** Incidentally, in passing, as in *By the bye, my wife is coming too,* or *Exactly where do you live, by the by?* The *bye* or second *by* in this term originally meant "a side path," which the current sense of "off the track" or "of secondary importance" comes from. Also see BY THE WAY.

**by the day** Also, **by the hour** or **by the week** or **by the month** or **by the year.** According to a specific time period, as in *I'm renting this car by the day,* or *He's being paid by the hour.* This usage generally describes some amount paid per unit of time.

**by the dozen** Also, **by the hundred** or **by the thousand.** According to a definite quantity, as in *She buys tapes by the dozen.*

**by the numbers** In a strict sequence, step by step; also, mechanically. For example, *The only way to assemble this computer is to do it by the numbers,* or *Writing a novel is not something one can do by the numbers.* This expression has nothing to do with actual numerical figures (like BY THE DOZEN) but uses *numbers* in the sense of "a strict order or sequence."

**by the same token** **1.** In the same way, for the same reason. For example, *He has a good ear for music, and by the same token he finds it easy to pronounce foreign words.* This phrase today is used in a general way to connect statements that have some logical association with one another. **2.** As supporting or additional evidence, as in *Boston's population has grown very fast, and by the same token its urban problems have also increased.*

**by the seat of the pants** see SEAT OF THE PANTS.

**by the short hairs** Under one's complete control. This expression is often used with *get* or *have,* as in *The voters have the senator by the short hairs.* It is in effect a euphemism for HAVE SOMEONE BY THE BALLS, the hairs in question being pubic hair.

**by the skin of one's teeth** Just barely, very narrowly, as in *I passed the exam by the skin of my teeth.* Also see SQUEAK BY.

**by the sweat of one's brow** By hard work, as in *The only way he'll succeed is by the sweat of his brow.*

**by the way** **1.** In passing, incidentally, as in *She's my wife's cousin, and by the way, a good friend.* **2.** Parenthetically, in addition, as in *By the way, did Tom call you?*

**by turns** Alternately, one after another, as in *She is by turns cheerful, serious, and sad.*

**by virtue of** Also, **in virtue of.** On the grounds of something, by reason of, as in *By virtue of a large inheritance she could easily afford not to work.*

**by way of 1.** Through a particular place, via, as in *I'm flying to Australia by way of Hawaii.* **2.** As a means of accomplishing something, as in *He paid for our meal by way of apology.*

**by weight** According to weight rather than height, volume, or some other measure. For example, *In Europe bread often is sold by weight rather than by the loaf.*

**by word of mouth** see WORD OF MOUTH.

# Cc

C

**cabin fever** Distress or nervousness caused by a long confinement in a small or remote place, as in *We've been snowed in for a week and everyone has cabin fever.* Originating in the West, this term at first referred to being shut up in a remote cabin during a long winter but has since been applied more broadly.

**caboodle** see WHOLE KIT AND CABOODLE.

**cage** see RATTLE SOMEONE'S CAGE.

**cahoots** see under IN LEAGUE WITH.

**Cain** see RAISE CAIN.

**cake** see EAT ONE'S CAKE AND HAVE IT, TOO; FLAT AS A PANCAKE; ICING ON THE CAKE; NUTTY AS A FRUITCAKE; PIECE OF CAKE; SELL LIKE HOTCAKES; SLICE OF THE PIE (CAKE); TAKE THE CAKE.

**calculated risk** A chance taken after careful estimation of the probable outcome, as in *Taking their landlord to court was definitely a calculated risk.* This term uses *calculated* in the sense of "planned." Its pairing with *risk* comes from World War II, when the chances for losing planes were taken into account before a bombing mission was sent out. After the war the term was transferred to other situations where taking a chance to succeed had to be weighed against the costs of failure.

**calf** see PUPPY (CALF) LOVE.

**call** In addition to the idioms beginning with CALL, also see ABOVE AND BEYOND (THE CALL OF DUTY); AT SOMEONE'S BECK AND CALL; CLOSE CALL; NO CALL FOR; ON CALL; PAY A CALL; POT CALLING THE KETTLE BLACK; TOO CLOSE TO CALL; UNCALLED FOR; WAKE-UP CALL.

**call a halt** Also, **call a halt to.** Order something stopped, as in *It was getting too dark to see the ball, so the referee called a halt to the match,* or *They'd played the song four times, so the conductor called a halt.*

**call a spade a spade** Speak frankly and bluntly, be explicit, as in *You can always trust Mary to call a spade a spade.* This term comes from a Greek saying, *call a bowl a bowl,* that was mistranslated into Latin and later came into English. Also see TELL IT LIKE IT IS.

**call back 1.** Ask someone to return, as in *He passed the first audition and was waiting to be called back.* **2. call someone back.** Telephone someone in return, as in *May I call you back next week?* **3.** Ask for the return of a product because of a defect, as in *The company has called back all of its luxury cars.*

**call down 1.** Invoke something, as from heaven. For example, *He called down the wrath of God.* **2. call someone down.** Scold or reprimand someone, as in *The conductor called her down for playing out of tune.* For a synonym, see DRESS DOWN, def. 1.

**call for 1.** Go to get someone or something, as in *John said he'd call for Mary at eight,* or *Someone's at the door, calling for the package.* **2.** Ask for someone or something. For example, *The audience called for the playwright,* or *The judge called for the verdict.* **3.** Require something or someone, demand, as in *This job calls for a lot of patience.* Also see NO CALL FOR; UNCALLED FOR.

**call in 1.** Summon someone for help or advice, as in *We've decided to call in a specialist to look at Father.* **2.** Withdraw something from circulation, as in *We're calling in all the old models.* **3.** Communicate by telephone, as in *In this office salespeople must call in once a day.*

**call in sick** Telephone one's employer or school that one is ill and cannot come to work or attend school. For example, *He called in sick and told his boss he would miss the meeting.*

**call *something* into question** Also, **call *something* in question.** Argue about the truth or validity of something, challenge; also, cast doubt on. For example, *How can you call her honesty into question?*

**call it a day** Stop a particular activity for the rest of the day, as in *It's past five o'clock, so let's call it a day.* Similarly, **call it a night** means "stop something for the rest of the night," as in *One more hand of cards, and then we should call it a night.* Also see CALL IT QUITS.

**call it quits** Stop working, stop doing something, give up, as in *We're calling it quits for now,* or *This ground is far too stony for a garden, so I'm calling it quits.* Also see CALL IT A DAY.

**call of duty** see under ABOVE AND BEYOND.

**call off 1.** Summon a person or an animal away, restrain, as in *Please call off your dog.* **2.** Cancel some plan or undertaking, as in *She decided to call off their engagement,* or *In case of rain, the picnic will be called off.*

**call of nature** The need to urinate or defecate, as in *He left to answer the call of nature.* Also see NATURE CALLS.

**call on** Also, **call upon. 1.** Make a request, ask for, choose, as in *We are calling upon you* *to run for chairman,* or *The teacher called on Joe to answer.* **2.** Pay someone a brief visit, as in *The salesman said he'd call on me in the morning.* **3.** Draw on or gather all of one's strength, courage, or other ability, as in *If you hope to climb Mount Everest, you'll have to call on everything you have inside you.*

**call one names** Direct unpleasant names at another person, as in *The teacher told the children to stop calling each other names.*

**call one's own** Claim or regard something as one's possession or under one's control, as in *Victorian women had almost nothing to call their own.* This expression today is often used in a negative context, as in the example. It also appears in **can't call one's time one's own,** which means that one spends much of one's time in someone else's service, as in *The hours in this job are terrible; I can't call my time my own.*

**call *one* on the carpet** Summon one for a scolding or rebuke, as in *Suspecting a leak to the press, the governor called his press secretary on the carpet.* This term began as **on the carpet,** which referred to a cloth (carpet) covering a conference table and therefore came to mean "under consideration or discussion." In the United States, however, *carpet* meant "a floor covering," and the expression referred to being called before or reprimanded by a person rich or powerful enough to have a carpet.

**call out** Summon people or a group into action or service, as in *The governor called out the militia.*

**call someone back** see CALL BACK, def. 2.

**call someone down** see CALL DOWN, def. 2.

**call someone's bluff** Expose someone's lying or pretense, invite a showdown, as in *I don't believe they have enough money; I'm going to call their bluff.* This term comes from poker, where bluffing (pretending) that one has better cards than one's opponents is an essential part of the game, and calling someone's bluff means forcing that person to show his or her cards. It has since been applied to other activities. Also see SHOW ONE'S HAND.

**call the shots** Control what other people do, be in charge, as in *It's up to the boss to call the shots.* Also see CALL THE TUNE.

**call the tune** Make important decisions, control what other people do, as in *I think that it's her turn to call the tune.* The full term is **who pays the piper calls the tune,** meaning whoever bears the cost of an activity should have authority over it. Also see CALL THE SHOTS.

**call *something* to mind** Remember something, recall, as in *I've tried, but I can't call his name to mind.*

**call *someone* to order** Formally open a meeting; also, bid people to obey the rules. For example, *The chairman used his gavel to call everyone to order,* or *The judge called the spectators to order and threatened to make them leave.*

**call up 1.** Make someone report for military service, as in *He was called up for active duty.* **2.** Cause to remember something, bring to mind, as in *These stories call up old times.* Also see CALL SOMETHING TO MIND. **3.** Telephone someone, as in *I'll call up the theater and find out about tickets.* **4.** Retrieve data from a computer memory, as in *I asked him to call up the last quarter's sales figures.*

**call upon** see CALL ON.

**camel** see under LAST STRAW.

**camp** In addition to the idioms beginning with CAMP, also see BREAK CAMP; FOOT IN BOTH CAMPS; HAPPY CAMPER.

**camp follower 1.** A civilian who follows or settles near a military camp, especially a prostitute who does so. For example, *The recruits were told not to associate with camp followers.* **2.** A person who sympathizes with a cause or group but does not join it. For example, *She's only a camp follower, so we can't count on her for a contribution.*

**camp it up** Make an extravagant, affected, or vulgar display, as in *Amateur actors often camp it up, trying to be more dramatic.* Originating as slang for flamboyant behavior stereotypically associated with gay men, this term later began to be used more loosely. Also see HAM (IT) UP.

**camp out** Sleep outdoors; also, stay somewhere for an unusually long time. For example, *Let's camp out this weekend.* This term was originally used literally, but it was later extended to figurative uses, as in *She camped out at the stage door, hoping for an autograph.*

**can** In addition to the idioms beginning with CAN, also see AS BEST ONE CAN; BEFORE YOU CAN SAY JACK ROBINSON; BITE OFF MORE THAN ONE CAN CHEW; CATCH AS CATCH CAN; GAME THAT TWO CAN PLAY; GET THE AX (CAN); IN THE CAN; MORE THAN ONE CAN SHAKE A STICK AT; NO CAN DO; YOU BET (CAN BET YOUR BOTTOM DOLLAR); YOU CAN LEAD A HORSE TO WATER; YOU CAN SAY THAT AGAIN; YOU NEVER CAN TELL. Also see under CAN'T.

**canary** see LOOK LIKE THE CAT THAT ATE THE CANARY.

**cancel out** Neutralize the effect of something, offset, render void. For example, *Anne's kindness to her neighbor could not cancel out her irritability.*

**candle** see BURN THE CANDLE AT BOTH ENDS; HOLD A CANDLE TO.

**can do with** Might profit from something, needs, as in *This room can do with a good* *cleaning,* or *You can do with a new suit.* Also see COULD DO WITH; DO WITH.

**canned laughter** Prerecorded sound effects that can be played repeatedly, as in *That canned laughter doesn't make his jokes any funnier.* Canned laughter today is often used in broadcasting to replace the reaction of a nonexistent live audience.

C

**cannot** see under CAN'T.

**canoe** see PADDLE ONE'S OWN CANOE.

**can of worms** A complex unexpected problem or an unsolvable dilemma, as in *Tackling the budget cuts is sure to open a can of worms.* This expression refers to a container of bait used for fishing, which when opened reveals a tangle of worms.

**can't** In addition to the idioms beginning with CAN'T, also see BEGGARS CAN'T BE CHOOSERS; IF YOU CAN'T BEAT 'EM, JOIN 'EM; YOU CAN'T TAKE IT WITH YOU; YOU CAN'T WIN 'EM ALL. Also see under CAN.

**can't abide** Also, **can't bear.** See CAN'T STAND.

**can't but** Also, **cannot but.** See CAN'T HELP.

**can't complain** Used as a response meaning "fairly good" or "well" to questions such as "How are you?" or "How is business?" For example, *How've you been? Can't complain.* This term means that nothing serious is wrong.

**can't do anything with** Be unable to cope with or manage someone or something. For example, *I can't do anything with my hair,* or *My teenage daughter is very difficult—I can't do anything with her.*

**can't fight City Hall** Be unable to win against the rules of an institution or organization, as in *I couldn't get a permit without going through lots of paperwork—you can't fight City Hall!*

**can't help** Also, **can't help but** or **cannot but.** Be unable to avoid doing something. For example, *Maybe it's crazy, but I can't help thinking that he'll come back to her,* or *He couldn't help but believe he would pass the entrance exam,* or *I cannot but applaud his efforts.* The first phrase, *can't help,* is always followed by a present participle.

**can't hit the broad side of a barn** Have very poor aim. For example, *That new pitcher is terrible. He can't hit the broad side of a barn.* This term at first meant poor aim with a gun. Later it also began to be used in baseball.

**can't make a silk purse out of a sow's ear** Be unable to turn something ugly or inferior into something attractive or of value, as in *No matter how expensive his clothes, he still looks sloppy—you can't make a silk purse out of a sow's ear.*

**can't make head or tail of** Also, **can't make heads or tails of.** Fail to understand or be quite confused about something, as in *I can't make head or tail of these directions.* The source of this expression is unclear; *head* and *tail* may mean top and bottom, beginning and end, or the two sides of a coin.

**can't punch one's way out of a paper bag** Be awkward and unskilled, as in *Ask him to program the VCR? He can't punch his way out of a paper bag.* This exaggerated term for someone with no skill comes from boxing, where people used it to show disrespect or contempt for a weak or fearful boxer.

**can't see beyond the end of one's nose.** Also, **can't see farther than the end of one's nose.** Lack foresight, thinking only of immediate events or problems, as in *He still hasn't hired an orchestra for the party; he just can't see beyond the end of his nose.* This expression originated as a French proverb.

**can't seem to** Appear to be unable to do something, as in *No matter how hard I try, I can't seem to concentrate on this book.* This phrase gives added emphasis to a statement, as in the example.

**can't see the forest for the trees** Focus only on small details and fail to understand larger plans or principles, as in *He can't lead the company effectively because he worries too much about little things—he can't see the forest for the trees.*

**can't stand** Also, **can't abide** or **can't bear** or **can't stomach.** Thoroughly dislike, be unable to tolerate something or someone. For example, *I can't stand the sight of her; she's a terrible liar,* or *I can't bear to leave the country,* or *I can't stomach a dirty kitchen.*

**can't wait** Be very eager, anxious, or impatient, as in *We can't wait for the baseball season to begin,* or *I can't wait to see her—it's been a year.*

**cap** In addition to the idiom beginning with CAP, also see FEATHER IN ONE'S CAP; PUT ON ONE'S THINKING CAP. Also see under HAT.

**cap in hand** see under HAT IN HAND.

**cap it all** **1.** Also, **cap it all off.** Finish or complete something, as in *To cap it all off they served three kinds of dessert.* **2.** Also, **cap them all.** Go beyond or outdo something, as in *This last story of Henry's caps them all.* Both senses use *cap* to mean "topping" something.

**captive audience** Listeners or observers who listen or watch because they have to. For example, *It's a required course, and knowing he has a captive audience, the professor talks endlessly.* This expression uses *captive* in the sense of "unable to escape."

**carbo load** Eat a large amount of carbohydrate food, as in *Karen began carbo loading three days before the road race.* This term, a shortening of "carbohydrate loading," originated among marathon runners.

C

**carbon copy** A person or thing that closely resembles another, as in *Our grandson is a carbon copy of his dad.*

**card** In addition to the idioms beginning with CARD, also see HOLD ALL THE ACES (THE TRUMP CARD); HOUSE OF CARDS; IN THE CARDS; LAY ONE'S CARDS ON THE TABLE; PLAY ONE'S CARDS CLOSE TO ONE'S CHEST; PLAY ONE'S CARDS RIGHT; TRUMP CARD; WILD CARD.

**cards are stacked against, the** Many difficulties face someone or something, as in *The cards are stacked against getting approval for the new highway project.* This term came from gambling, where **stack the cards** or **stack the deck** means to arrange cards secretly and dishonestly in one's own favor or against another player.

**card up one's sleeve, have another** Also, **have an ace up one's sleeve.** Have a hidden or secret advantage or resource, as in *The union is gaining support, but let's see if management has another card up its sleeve,* or *You can count on John to have an ace up his sleeve when things get hopeless.* The practice of storing something in one's sleeve comes from the time when clothes rarely had pockets. The current term comes from gambling because a dishonest player might hide an ace or other winning card in his sleeve.

**care** In addition to the idiom beginning with CARE, also see COULDN'T CARE LESS; FOR ALL (ONE CARES); IN CARE OF; IN CHARGE (IN THE CARE OF); TAKE CARE; TAKE CARE OF; TENDER LOVING CARE; THAT'S (THAT TAKES CARE OF) THAT.

**career** see CHECKERED CAREER.

**care package** A gift package of food or other items not easily available to the person receiving it, as in *While I was in college, Mom sent me a care package of homemade cookies just about every month.* This term originated after World War II with CARE, an organization that sent needed food, clothing, and other items to war-torn nations. Later the expression was also used for packages of treats sent to children at camp, students away at school, etc.

**carpe diem** Enjoy the present and don't worry about the future, as in *It's a beautiful day, so forget tomorrow's test—carpe diem!* This term is Latin for "seize the day."

**carpet** see CALL ONE ON THE CARPET; RED CARPET.

**carried away** see CARRY AWAY.

**carrot and stick** Also, **the carrot or the stick.** Reward and punishment used to persuade someone to do something, as in *Management dangled the carrot of a possible raise before the striking workers, but at the same time waved the stick of taking away the workers' benefits.* This term refers to getting a horse or donkey to move by dangling a carrot in front of it and also beating it with a stick.

**carry** In addition to the idioms beginning with CARRY, also see FETCH AND CARRY.

**carry a torch for** Also, **carry the torch for.** Continue to feel the pain of love that is not returned, as in *Jane has been carrying the torch for Bill for at least a year.* The *torch* in this term refers to the heat of love or passion.

**carry a tune** Sing a melody accurately, as in *He loves to listen to music, but he can't carry a tune.*

**carry away** Move or excite someone greatly. This expression is usually used in the passive, **be carried away** or **get carried away,** as in *He was carried away talking about what he'd buy if he won the lottery,* or *Take it easy; don't get carried away and do too much.*

**carry coals to Newcastle** Do or bring something unnecessary, as in *Watering the garden while it's raining is like carrying coals to Newcastle.* This term refers to Newcastle-upon-Tyne in England, which was once a major coal-mining center. The phrase is heard less often today but is not yet obsolete.

**carry forward** **1.** Also, **carry over.** Transfer a bookkeeping entry to the next column or page or to another account or the next accounting period, as in *Let's carry forward this loss to next year for a saving in taxes,* or *She made an error in carrying over this column.* **2.** Make progress in, advance, as in *His successor hoped to carry forward his work.* Also see CARRY ON.

**carrying charge** **1.** Interest charged on the balance owed when paying on an installment plan, as in *What is the carrying charge for this credit card?* **2.** The cost to an owner when an asset is unproductive, as when airplanes are grounded during a strike or real estate cannot be developed because of zoning laws. For example, *The carrying charge for owning this vacant building is more than we can afford.*

**carry off** **1.** Handle something successfully, win, as in *It was a difficult situation, but he managed to carry it off gracefully,* or *They carried off first prize.* **2.** Cause the death of someone, as in *The new African virus carried off an entire village.* This usage is less common today.

**carry on** **1.** Maintain or conduct something, as in *The villagers carried on a busy trade,* or *They carried on a secret love affair.* **2.** Continue or progress, persevere, as in *I'm sure you can carry on without me.* **3.** Behave in an excited, improper, or silly manner, as in *They laughed and sang and carried on noisily.* **4.** Flirt or engage in a love affair, as in *She accused her friend of carrying on with her husband.*

**carry out** Put something into practice or effect, as in *They carried out the mission successfully,* or *Please carry out my instructions.*

C

**carry over 1.** See CARRY FORWARD, def. 1. **2.** Keep something, usually merchandise, for a later period. For example, *We'll carry over this summer's bathing suits for next winter's resort season.* **3.** Continue from one time or situation to another, as in *His leadership in sports carried over to the classroom.*

**carry the ball** Take charge, handle an assignment or problem, as in *In our lab, any of the assistants can carry the ball.* This usage comes from sports with a ball-carrying player. It later was transferred to other team efforts.

**carry the day** Win, succeed, as in *The best-organized candidates usually carry the day.*

**carry the torch for** see CARRY A TORCH FOR.

**carry through 1.** Continue with something or persevere to the end, as in *She carried the project through despite being ill.* **2.** Survive or persist in something, as in *His excellent technique carries through all his work.* **3.** Also, **carry someone through.** Enable someone to endure; sustain. For example, *His faith helped carry him through the operation and recovery.*

**carry *something* too far** Also, **carry *something* to excess.** Extend something too much in a single direction, as in *I know that athletes need to get into good shape, but that coach carries things too far,* or *Let's not carry our plans for reforms to excess.*

**carry weight** Also, **carry authority** or **carry conviction.** Have and use influence, authority, or persuasion, as in *No matter what the President says, his words always carry weight.*

**cart** In addition to the idioms beginning with CART, also see UPSET THE APPLECART.

**cart before the horse, put the** Reverse the proper order of things or events, as in *Don't put the cart before the horse and buy all the textbooks before you register for the classes.*

**carte blanche** Unlimited power to act as one thinks best. For example, *They gave the architect carte blanche in designing their house.*

**cart off** Also, **cart away.** Transport or remove someone or something with no show of respect or formality, as in *The police carted them all off to jail,* or *Who can we get to cart away this trash?* This term owes its meaning to *cart,* a poor kind of vehicle compared to a carriage.

**case** In addition to the idiom beginning with CASE, also see BASKET CASE; GET OFF (ONE'S CASE); IN ANY CASE; IN CASE; IN NO CASE; IN THE CASE OF; JUST IN CASE; MAKE A FEDERAL CASE OF; OFF SOMEONE'S BACK (CASE); OPEN AND SHUT (CASE).

**case in point** A relevant example or illustration of something, as in *He said there should be speed limits for bicycles, and a case in point was last week's collision of a cyclist with a pedestrian crossing the bike path.*

**cash** In addition to the idioms beginning with CASH, also see COLD CASH.

**cash cow** A dependable source of profit, as in *The small-appliance division is this company's cash cow.*

**cash in 1.** Settle an account, close a matter, quit, as in *I'm simply going to cash in and leave,* or *The partners have cashed in and sold the business.* **2.** Make a lot of money, as in *When the stock price went up, we really cashed in.* This phrase often is extended to **cash in on,** meaning to take advantage of something.

**cash in one's chips** Die, as in *If this new treatment fails, the poor guy may be cashing in his chips before long.* This usage transfers dying to quitting a poker game.

**cash on the barrelhead** Also, **cash on the barrel.** Immediate payment, as in *They won't extend credit; it's cash on the barrelhead or no sale.*

**cast** In addition to the idioms beginning with CAST, also see DIE IS CAST.

**cast about** Also, **cast around.** Look, make a search, as in *We cast about for the necessary tools but couldn't find them in the garage.*

**cast adrift** see CAST LOOSE.

**cast away 1.** Also, **cast aside.** Discard, reject, as in *He picked up a book, then cast it aside,* or *She cast away all thoughts of returning home.* **2.** Spend or use foolishly, waste, as in *She cast away a fortune on jewelry.*

**cast doubt on** Cause something or someone to be questioned. For example, *The prosecutor cast doubt on the wife's story.* This idiom uses *cast* in the sense of "throw."

**cast down 1.** Throw down, hurl to the ground, as in *She cast down her coat on the grass.* **2.** Lower or direct something down, as in *He cast down his eyes.*

**cast in stone** Also, **etched in stone.** Definite, fixed, as in *We may choose to stay longer—our plans aren't cast in stone,* or *When he announces a plan, you can safely assume it's etched in stone.* Both expressions refer to sculpture, with the first using the verb *cast* in the sense of pouring and hardening some material into a final form. The second uses *etched* to mean cut or corroded into a permanent design.

**cast in the same mold** Having a close resemblance, as in *All his detective stories are cast in the same mold.* This term uses the verb *cast* in the sense of forming an object by running hot, liquid metal into a mold.

**castles in the air** Dreams about future success, as in *Thinking about the bestseller list, the writer tended to build castles in the air.*

**cast loose** Also, **cast adrift.** Let go, freed, as in *After he was suspended from college, he was cast loose with nowhere to go,* or *Selling her home meant she was cast adrift with no* *financial ties or responsibilities.* This expression originally referred to releasing a boat from its moorage or anchorage.

**cast off 1.** Discard, reject, as in *He cast off his old friends and tried to create a new identity for himself.* **2.** Let something go, set loose, as in *He cast off the line, and the boat drifted from the dock.*

**cast one's lot with** Also, **throw in one's lot with.** Join or side with someone, no matter what the result, as in *Bill took a risk when he cast his lot with the new company.*

**cast out** Forcibly drive out or expel someone or something, as in *We have to cast out these old-fashioned ideas and methods.*

**cast pearls before swine** Give something of value to someone who won't appreciate it, as in *Why give them a fine painting when they would be just as happy with a poster? You would be casting pearls before swine.*

**cast the first stone** Also, **throw the first stone.** Be quick to blame, criticize, or punish, as in *She's always criticizing her colleagues, casting the first stone no matter what the circumstances.* Also see PEOPLE WHO LIVE IN GLASS HOUSES; POT CALLING THE KETTLE BLACK.

**cat** In addition to the idioms beginning with CAT, also see CURIOSITY KILLED THE CAT; FAT CAT; GRIN LIKE A CHESHIRE CAT; LET THE CAT OUT OF THE BAG; LIKE A CAT ON A HOT TIN ROOF; LOOK LIKE SOMETHING THE CAT DRAGGED IN; LOOK LIKE THE CAT THAT ATE THE CANARY; MORE THAN ONE WAY TO SKIN A CAT; NOT ENOUGH ROOM TO SWING A CAT; PLAY CAT AND MOUSE; RAIN CATS AND DOGS; WHEN THE CAT'S AWAY, THE MICE WILL PLAY.

**catbird seat, the** A situation of advantage or superiority, as in *His promotion put Charles in the catbird seat.* This term may refer to the noisy catbird's usual high place to sit.

**catch** In addition to the idioms beginning with CATCH, also see EARLY BIRD CATCHES THE WORM; GET (CATCH) THE DRIFT; IT TAKES ONE TO KNOW ONE (A THIEF TO CATCH A THIEF). Also see under CAUGHT.

**catch as catch can** By whatever means or in any way possible, as in *There was no formal language program; we simply learned Spanish catch as catch can.*

**catch at** Grab, grasp, as in *The cold wind made us keep catching at our coats.* Also see GRASP AT STRAWS.

**catch cold** Also, **catch a cold** or **catch one's death (of cold).** Become infected with a cold virus, as in *Jane manages to catch cold on every important business trip,* or *I caught a bad cold,* or *Put on your hat, or you'll catch your death.*

**catch fire 1.** Start burning, ignite, as in *This wood is dry enough to catch fire.* Also see SET ON FIRE. **2.** Become the subject of great interest and enthusiasm, as in *His ideas caught fire all over the country.*

**catch *someone* flat-footed** Catch someone unprepared, take someone by surprise, as in *The reporter's questions caught the President flat-footed.* This expression comes from sports, in which a player should be on his or her toes, ready to act.

**catch *someone* in the act** see under CATCH SOMEONE RED-HANDED.

**catch it** Also, **get it.** Receive a punishment or scolding, as in *If I forget anything on the shopping list, I'll catch it,* or *I'm really going to get it when I turn in my paper late.*

**catch *someone* napping** Surprise someone who is not paying attention. This term is often used in the passive, as in *Our company was caught napping when the competition introduced a revolutionary new technology.* Also see under OFF GUARD.

**catch *someone* off guard** see under OFF GUARD.

**catch on 1.** Also, **catch on to.** Understand, as in *Aunt Mary doesn't catch on to any jokes.* Also see GET IT, def. 2. **2.** Become popular, as in *This new dance is really beginning to catch on.*

**catch one's breath 1.** Resume normal breathing after effort of some kind, as in *These stairs are steep; wait a minute till I catch my breath.* This phrase used to mean the same as HOLD ONE'S BREATH, that is, stop breathing for a while. **2.** Relax, slow down, stop to think or take a rest, as in *Events have been moving so fast I'd like to stop and catch my breath.*

**catch one's death (of cold)** see CATCH COLD.

**catch *someone* red-handed** Also, **catch *someone* in the act.** Catch someone in the act of wrongdoing, as in *The boys were trying to steal a car, and the police caught them red-handed,* or *He tried to cheat on the exam, but his teacher walked in and caught him in the act.* The first term referred to blood on a murderer's hands and first meant only that crime. The second term is a translation of the Latin *in flagrante delicto.*

**catch sight of** See someone or something suddenly or unexpectedly, as in *When I first caught sight of the Alps, I was overwhelmed.*

**catch *someone's* eye** Attract someone's attention, as in *That window display really catches my eye.*

**catch some rays** Sunbathe, as in *I want a good tan, so I think I'll go catch some rays.*

**catch some z's** Take a nap, go to sleep, as in *I stayed up all night studying, so I'd better catch some z's.* This term refers to the buzzing sound of snoring.

C

**catch the drift** see GET THE DRIFT.

**Catch-22** Also, **a Catch-22 (situation).** A no-win situation, dilemma, or paradox, similar to DAMNED IF ONE DOES, DAMNED IF ONE DOESN'T. For example, *You can't get a job without experience, but you can't get experience unless you have a job—it's Catch-22.*

**catch up 1.** Also, **catch up with.** Come from behind, overtake. This usage can be either literal, as in *You run so fast it's hard for me to catch up,* or figurative, as in *The government finally caught up with those tax-evaders.* **2.** Become involved, fall under an influence, as in *We all were caught up in the magical mood of that evening.* **3.** Also, **catch up on.** Become or bring some up to date on something missed, as in *Let's get together soon and catch up on all the news.*

**cat got someone's tongue** A comment made when someone is surprisingly quiet, as in *We haven't heard from you all morning—has the cat got your tongue?* Often put as a question, this term is used to ask someone to speak.

**cat's paw** A person who is tricked or used by someone, as in *You always try to make a cat's paw of me, but I refuse to do any more of your work.* This term refers to an old story about a monkey that persuades a cat to pull chestnuts out of the fire so as to avoid burning its own paws.

**caught** In addition to the idioms beginning with CAUGHT, also see under CATCH.

**caught dead, wouldn't be** Also, **wouldn't be seen dead.** Would never have any connection with, detest, as in *I wouldn't be caught dead in that outfit,* or *He wouldn't be seen dead drinking a cheap wine.* This expression is always used negatively.

**caught in the middle** Also, **caught in the crossfire.** Between two opposing sides, as in *I feel caught in the middle when my boss and our customers want different things,* or *When parents don't get along, the children are often caught in the crossfire.* These terms originally were used literally in military situations and later began to be used figuratively.

**caught short** Found to be lacking something one needs, especially money, as in *Can you pay the check? I seem to be caught short.* This idiom uses *short* in the sense of "lacking money."

**caught with one's pants down** Surprised in an embarrassing or guilty position, as in *We spent a lot of time preparing for the inspection; we didn't want to get caught with our pants down.* This phrase probably refers to someone's pants being down in the bathroom but is not considered offensive. It is similar to OFF GUARD and, if wrongdoing is discovered, CATCH SOMEONE RED-HANDED.

**cause** In addition to the idioms beginning with CAUSE, also see LOST CAUSE.

**cause a commotion** Also, **cause a stir.** Create a disturbance, raise a fuss. For example, *The opening debate was so bitter it caused a commotion in the legislature,* or *She was so beautiful that her entrance always caused a stir.*

**cause raised eyebrows** Also, **raise an eyebrow** or **raise eyebrows.** Cause surprise or disapproval, as in *At school his purple hair rarely causes raised eyebrows anymore,* or *Nobody raised an eyebrow when she came in late.* These terms are often used in a negative sense. The expression transfers a physical act (raising one's eyebrows) to the feelings it may express.

**caution** see THROW CAUTION TO THE WINDS.

**cave in 1.** Fall in, collapse, as in *The earthquake made the walls cave in.* **2.** Give in, admit defeat, as in *The lawyer's questions soon made the witness cave in.* **3.** Collapse or faint from exhaustion, as in *After a twenty-mile hike, I caved in.*

**cease** In addition to the idiom beginning with CEASE, also see WONDERS WILL NEVER CEASE.

**cease and desist** Stop doing something, as in *The judge has ordered the developer to cease and desist.* This term often appears in legal documents.

**ceiling** see GLASS CEILING; HIT THE CEILING.

**cent** see FOR TWO CENTS; NOT WORTH A DAMN (RED CENT).

**center** In addition to the idiom beginning with CENTER, also see FRONT AND CENTER.

**center of attention, the** A person that everyone looks at and is interested in, as in *They're very different—he's extremely shy, but she loves being the center of attention.*

**center of attraction, the** Something or someone that attracts the most interest or curiosity. For example, *His new car is always the center of attraction wherever he goes,* or *Their new baby will be the center of attraction at the party.* This expression comes from physics.

**century** see TURN OF THE CENTURY.

**ceremony** see STAND ON (CEREMONY).

**certain** see FOR CERTAIN.

**chain** In addition to the idioms beginning with CHAIN, also see BALL AND CHAIN; PULL SOMEONE'S CHAIN.

**chain reaction** A series of events in which each event influences or causes the next event, as in *If one person collects a lot of money by suing a company, you can expect a chain reaction of such lawsuits.* The term came from the physical sciences, first chemistry and later physics; in the latter it refers to a process of nuclear fission.

**chain smoker** A person who smokes continually, often by lighting a new cigarette from the one being finished, as in *Before they set* *no-smoking rules, bridge tournaments often attracted players who are chain smokers.*

**chair** see MUSICAL CHAIRS.

**chalk up 1.** Score or earn, as in *She chalked up enough points to be considered the best basketball player in the school's history.* This term refers to recording accounts (and later, scores) in chalk on a slate. **2.** Credit something to a source or cause, as in *They chalked their success up to careful preparation.* **3. chalk something up to experience.** Regard a failure or disappointment as a useful lesson, as in *I didn't get the job, but I understand why, and I'll chalk that one up to experience.*

**champ** In addition to the idiom beginning with CHAMP, also see LIKE A CHAMP.

**champ at the bit** Show impatience at being held back or delayed, as in *The dismissal bell hadn't rung, but the students were champing at the bit to leave.* This term compares someone to a horse that impatiently bites the bit in its mouth.

**chance** In addition to the idioms beginning with CHANCE, also see BY CHANCE; FAT CHANCE; FIGHTING CHANCE; GHOST OF A CHANCE; JUMP AT (THE CHANCE); NOT HAVE AN EARTHLY CHANCE; ON THE CHANCE THAT; SNOWBALL'S CHANCE IN HELL; SPORTING CHANCE; STAND A CHANCE; TAKE A CHANCE; TAKE ONE'S CHANCES.

**chance it** Take the risk of something, as in *I don't know if there's a later bus, but let's chance it.* Also see TAKE A CHANCE.

**chance on** Also, **chance upon.** Find or meet someone or something accidentally, as in *In Paris we chanced on a wonderful little restaurant,* or *Andrew chanced upon his karate teacher in the health-food store.*

**change** In addition to the idioms beginning with CHANGE, also see CHUNK OF CHANGE; FOR A CHANGE; LEOPARD CANNOT CHANGE ITS SPOTS; PIECE OF CHANGE.

**change hands** Pass from one owner to another. For example, *That house has new owners; it seems to change hands often,* or *The contract is valid only when money changes hands.*

**change horses in midstream, not** Also, **not swap horses in midstream.** It's unwise to change methods or choose new leaders during a crisis, as in *I don't agree with the idea of getting a new manager right now— let's not swap horses in midstream.* This expression is used in the negative.

**change off** Alternate, or take turns. This phrase is used either for two people alternately performing a task, as in *Lifting cement blocks is such heavy work that they decided to change off periodically,* or for one person alternately performing two tasks, as in *I can concentrate on this book only for short periods, so I frequently change off and work in the garden.* Also see CHANGE OF PACE.

**change of heart** A change in feelings or attitude, as in *Paul didn't like his new job, but a raise gave him a change of heart and he became quite enthusiastic.*

**change of life, the** Also, **the change.** Menopause. For example, *After nine pregnancies, she was actually looking forward to the change of life,* or *She became quite moody during the change.*

**change of pace, a** A shift in normal routine, a variation in usual activities or pattern, as in *After six hours at my desk I need a change of pace, so I'm going for a swim.*

**change one's mind** Change one's opinion or intentions, as in *I might change my mind about going on the trip.*

**change one's stripes** see under LEOPARD CANNOT CHANGE ITS SPOTS.

**change one's tune** Also, **sing another tune** or **sing a different tune.** Reverse one's views or behavior, switch sides, as in *When she realized she was talking to the boss's wife, she quickly changed her tune,* or *I bet Dan will sing a different tune when he finds out how small the salary is.* Also see DANCE TO ANOTHER TUNE.

**change the subject** Change to another topic, as in *If someone asks you an embarrassing question, just change the subject.* This term uses *subject* in the sense of "a topic of conversation."

**channel** In addition to the idiom beginning with CHANNEL, also see GO THROUGH CHANNELS.

**channel surfing** Switching from one television station (channel) to another frequently, either to look for an interesting program or to follow several programs at the same time. For example, *What did you see on TV last night? Nothing much; I was just channel surfing.* This practice became widespread with the use of remote-control devices for changing channels. A more recent version is **Internet surfing,** a similar process for searching cyberspace.

**chapter and verse** The precise authority supporting a statement or view; established rules for or detailed information about something. For example, *You can't take back a card after you've played it; I'll cite you the rules, chapter and verse.* The term refers to the chapter and verse of a quotation from the Bible.

**character** see IN CHARACTER; OUT OF CHARACTER.

**charge** In addition to the idioms beginning with CHARGE, also see CARRYING CHARGE; GET A BANG (CHARGE) OUT OF; IN CHARGE; TAKE CHARGE.

C

**charge off** **1.** Leave in a hurry, run away, as in *After a few minutes, she charged off to the next meeting.* This term refers to the military meaning of *charge,* that is, "rush forward in attack." **2.** Also, **charge against.** Consider or count something as an accounting loss or expense, as in *I'm charging off this purchase to overhead,* or *Let's charge the new computer against office supplies.* Also see WRITE OFF. **3.** Give the blame for something to a cause, as in *We can charge off these errors to inexperience.*

**charge up** Excite or stimulate someone, as in *The new preacher at our church can really charge up the congregation,* or *Planning Beth's wedding got her mom all charged up.* This term originally was used for stimulation from drugs but now is used more broadly.

**charge with** **1.** Give a duty or task to someone, as in *He was charged with getting this message to each committee member.* **2.** Accuse someone of a crime, as in *He was charged with murder.*

**charity begins at home** Be generous to one's own family before helping others. For example, *She spends hours and hours on volunteer work and neglects the children, forgetting that charity begins at home.*

**charley horse** A cramp or stiffness in a muscle, most often in the leg, as in *After working in the garden I frequently get a bad charley horse.*

**charm** In addition to the idioms beginning with CHARM, also see (CHARM THE) PANTS OFF; WORK LIKE A CHARM.

**charmed life** A life that seems protected by extreme good luck, as in *Robert came out of that accident without a scratch; he must lead a charmed life.* The adjective *charmed* once meant "magical." Later it was extended to anyone who narrowly escaped from danger or was similarly lucky.

**charm the pants off** see under PANTS OFF.

**chase** see AMBULANCE CHASER; CUT TO THE CHASE; GIVE CHASE; GO FLY A KITE (CHASE YOURSELF); RUN (CHASE) AFTER; WILD GOOSE CHASE.

**chat up** **1.** Talk flirtatiously to someone, as in *Leave it to Charlie to chat up the girls.* This usage is mostly but not entirely British. **2.** Engage in light, friendly talk with someone, as in *He was soon chatting up all the board members.*

**cheap** In addition to the idioms beginning with CHEAP, also see DIRT CHEAP; ON THE CHEAP.

**cheap at twice the price** Very inexpensive, a good value for the money. For example, *Pete got a $3,000 rebate on his new car—it would have been cheap at twice the price.* For a synonym, see DIRT CHEAP.

**cheap shot** An unfair criticism or verbal attack, as in *When a candidate jokes about an opponent's family, that's really taking a cheap shot.* This term originated in sports, especially American football, where it refers to an attack on an unprepared opponent.

**cheapskate** A stingy person, a person who does not like to spend money, as in *He's a real cheapskate when it comes to tipping.*

**cheat on** Be sexually unfaithful to someone, as in *They divorced soon after she found he was cheating on her.*

**check** In addition to the idioms beginning with CHECK, also see BLANK CHECK; CLAIM CHECK; IN CHECK; PICK UP (THE CHECK); RAIN CHECK; REALITY CHECK; RUBBER CHECK.

**checkered career** A background that includes many changes, especially of employment. For example, *He has had a checkered career, moving from one city to another and one job to another.* This expression uses *checkered* in the sense of "constantly alternating," much like the squares on a checkerboard.

**check in** Record one's arrival at a place such as a hotel or at a conference or some other function, as in *I asked the manager if we could check in early.* Also see CHECK INTO, def. 2; CHECK OUT, def. 1.

**check into** **1.** Investigate something, as in *I don't know when they open, but I'll check into it.* Also see CHECK OUT, def. 5. **2.** Register one's arrival at a place such as a hotel, as in *She was about to check into the hospital.* Also see CHECK IN.

**check off** Mark something as entered, examined, or passed, as in *He checked off the students' names as they arrived.*

**check on** Also, **check up on** or **check over** or **check in on.** Investigate something, inspect, as in *I'll check on the brakes and make sure they're all right,* or *We need to check up on his work from time to time,* or *Let's check over the books together,* or *I want to check in on the baby.* Also see CHECK OUT, def. 5.

**check out** **1.** Record one's departure from a place such as a hotel or from a conference or some other function, as in *As soon as my bags are packed, I'll check out of the motel.* **2.** Leave in a hurry, make a quick exit, as in *As soon as I get paid, I'm checking out.* **3.** Take out an item after recording the withdrawal, as in *I'll check out the tapes on your library card.* **4.** Record, total the prices, and receive payment for a purchase, as in *The cashier checked out and bagged my groceries in record time.* **5. check something or someone out.** Investigate or observe something or someone carefully. For example, *I don't know if you'll like the film; check it out yourself,* or *That man who's staring is probably just checking us out.* **6.** Pass close inspection, as in *That rattle made me suspicious, but the repairman said the machine checked out completely.*

**check over** see CHECK ON.

**checks and balances** Methods by which each branch of an organization can limit the powers of the other branches, as in *The union has used a system of checks and balances to prevent any large local within it from dominating its policies.* A system of checks and balances was set up by the Constitution of the United States to prevent any of the three branches of the federal government from dominating the other two branches.

**check up on** see CHECK ON.

**cheek** In addition to the idiom beginning with CHEEK, also see TONGUE IN CHEEK; TURN THE OTHER CHEEK.

**cheek by jowl** Also, **cheek to cheek.** Side by side, close together, as in *In that crowded subway car we stood cheek by jowl, virtually holding one another up.*

**cheer** In addition to the idioms beginning with CHEER, also see THREE CHEERS FOR.

**cheer on** Encourage someone, as in *The crowd was cheering on all the marathon runners.*

**cheer up** Become or make someone happy, raise the spirits of, as in *She'll cheer up after she gets a good night's sleep,* or *This fine weather should cheer you up.*

**cheese** see BIG CHEESE.

**chest** see OFF ONE'S CHEST; PLAY ONE'S CARDS CLOSE TO ONE'S CHEST.

**chew** In addition to the idioms beginning with CHEW, also see BITE OFF MORE THAN ONE CAN CHEW.

**chew out** Scold someone harshly, as in *Dad will chew you out for taking the car without permission.* This slang term began to be used by the military during World War I and soon spread to civilian life. Several vulgar versions, such as **chew someone's ass out,** should be avoided in polite speech.

**chew the cud** Also, **chew over.** Think over a question, meditate, as in *John tends to chew the cud before he answers,* or *Let me chew that over and let you know.* The first term compares a person deep in thought to a cow chewing its cud.

**chew the fat** Talk in a friendly, relaxed way, as in *Let's get together for coffee and chew the fat,* or *John and Dave spend hours just chewing the fat.*

**chicken** In addition to the idioms beginning with CHICKEN, also see COUNT ONE'S CHICKENS (BEFORE THEY HATCH); GO TO BED WITH (THE CHICKENS); LIKE A CHICKEN WITH ITS HEAD CUT OFF; NO SPRING CHICKEN.

**chicken feed** A small and unimportant amount of money, as in *I'm not going to mow lawns for $5 an hour—that's chicken feed.* This expression refers to the fact that chickens can be fed corn and wheat grains too small for other uses.

**chicken out** Refuse or fail to do something as planned because of one's fear, lose one's nerve, as in *In the end I chickened out and took the easier route down the mountain. Chicken* is a popular synonym for "cowardly."

**chickens come home to roost** The consequences of doing wrong always hurt the wrongdoer in the end, as in *Now that you're finally admitting your true age, no one believes you—chickens come home to roost.*

**chicken shit** **1.** Something without any value or importance. For example, *He has spent his life making up chicken shit rules that nobody follows anyway.* [Vulgar slang] **2.** Cowardly, as in *You're not too chicken shit to come along, are you?* [Vulgar slang]

**chicken with its head cut off** see LIKE A CHICKEN WITH ITS HEAD CUT OFF.

**chief cook and bottlewasher** A person in charge of numerous duties, both important and not, as in *We have no secretaries or clerks; the department head is chief cook and bottlewasher and does it all.*

**child** In addition to the idiom beginning with CHILD, also see SECOND CHILDHOOD.

**child's play** Something easily done, an unimportant matter. For example, *Finding the answer was child's play for Robert,* or *The fight we had was child's play compared to the one I had with my mother!*

**chilled to the bone** Also, **chilled to the marrow.** Feeling extremely or bitterly cold, as in *After skiing in the wind for five hours straight, I was chilled to the bone.*

**chill out** Calm down or relax, as in *Don't let it bother you—just chill out,* or *Rob decided to come home and chill out for a while.* Also see COOL IT.

**chime in** **1.** Join in, either literally (with music) or figuratively (joining a conversation to express agreement). For example, *At this point in the song, I want the altos to chime in with the tenors,* or *When Mary agreed to go, her sister chimed in that she'd join her.* **2. chime in with.** Be in agreement with someone or something, as in *His views chime in with the paper's editorial position.*

**chin** see KEEP ONE'S CHIN UP; LEAD WITH ONE'S CHIN; TAKE IT ON THE CHIN.

**china, China** see BULL IN A CHINA SHOP; NOT FOR ALL THE TEA IN CHINA.

**chink in one's armor** A vulnerable area, as in *Putting things off to the last minute is the chink in Pat's armor and will get her in trouble one day.* This term uses *chink* in the sense of "a crack or gap."

**chip** In addition to the idioms beginning with CHIP, also see CASH IN ONE'S CHIPS; IN THE MONEY (CHIPS); LET THE CHIPS FALL WHERE THEY MAY; WHEN THE CHIPS ARE DOWN.

**chip in** Also, **chip in on.** Contribute money, help, or advice, as in *If we all chip in, we'll have enough to buy a refrigerator,* or *Everyone chipped in with ideas for the baby shower,* or *We all chipped in on the gifts.*



**chip off the old block, a** A person who is very much like a parent, as in *Like her mother, Karen has very little patience—she's a chip off the old block.* This term refers to a chip of stone or wood that closely resembles the larger block.

**chip on one's shoulder** An attitude that shows a readiness to fight and a sense of being treated unfairly, as in *Mary is easily offended; she always has a chip on her shoulder.*

**choice** see BY CHOICE; OF CHOICE; PAY YOUR MONEY AND TAKE YOUR CHOICE. Also see under CHOOSE.

**choke back** Control and hold in the expression of a feeling, as in *He choked back his tears.*

**choke off** **1.** Put a stop to something, as in *Higher interest rates are choking off the real estate boom.* **2.** Prevent something from growing, as in *Weeds choked off the garden.* **3.** Stop someone from speaking or complaining, as in *Throughout the debate, the congressman had to be choked off to give the other candidate a chance to speak.*

**choke up** **1.** Block a channel or other passage, as in *A traffic accident choked up the bridge.* **2.** Be too emotional or upset to speak, as in *She became so emotional about winning that she choked up and was unable to give an interview.* **3.** Become too nervous or tense to perform under pressure, as in *He's fine during practice, but in a game he tends to choke up.* This usage, also shortened to **choke,** is especially common in sports.

**choose** In addition to the idiom beginning with CHOOSE, also see BEGGARS CAN'T BE CHOOSERS; PICK AND CHOOSE. Also see under CHOICE.

**choose up** Select players and form teams for a game, as in *Jean was always afraid she'd be last when it was time to choose up.*

**chops** see BREAK ONE'S ASS (CHOPS); LICK ONE'S CHOPS.

**chord** see STRIKE A CHORD.

**chorus** see IN CHORUS.

**chow down** Eat, as in *He's always ready to chow down at dinner time.* Originally military slang, this term is now more widely used. The noun *chow* in the sense of "food" also appears in such terms as **chow line,** a line of people waiting for food, and **chow time,** mealtime.

**chump change** A small and unimportant matter or amount of money. For example, *Dave was sick of working for chump change; he wanted a decent salary,* or *Don't put that on the agenda; it's chump change.* This expression uses *chump* in the sense of "a fool or sucker who should be ignored." Also see CHICKEN FEED.

**chunk of change** A lot of money, *I bet that car cost a chunk of change.*

**church** see POOR AS A CHURCHMOUSE.

**churn out** Produce something in large amounts in an automatic manner, as in *He churned out a novel every six months.* This idiom transfers the turning of milk into butter to other kinds of production.

**cinder** see BURN TO A CRISP (CINDER).

**circle** see FULL CIRCLE; GO AROUND (IN CIRCLES); RUN RINGS (CIRCLES) AROUND; VICIOUS CIRCLE.

**circulation** see IN CIRCULATION; OUT OF CIRCULATION.

**circumstance** see EXTENUATING CIRCUMSTANCES; UNDER THE CIRCUMSTANCES.

**circus** see THREE-RING CIRCUS.

**civil tongue** see KEEP A CIVIL TONGUE IN ONE'S HEAD.

**claim** In addition to the idiom beginning with CLAIM, also see LAY CLAIM TO; STAKE A CLAIM.

**claim check** A receipt for property that has been left or deposited, as in *Give me your claim check, and I'll pick up your laundry for you.* This term most often refers to a receipt for such items as laundry (left for washing), clothes (for dry cleaning), or baggage (for short-term storage).

**clam** In addition to the idiom beginning with CLAM, also see HAPPY AS THE DAY IS LONG (AS A CLAM).

**clamp down on** Also, **put the clamps on.** Become stricter or put tighter controls on something; put a stop to. For example, *The company was clamping down on expenses like business lunches,* or *It's time we put the clamps on polluters.*

**clam up** Refuse to talk or respond, as in *Whenever she asks her teenager about his activities, he clams up.* This term refers to the tightly closed valves of a live clam.

**class** In addition to the idiom beginning with CLASS, also see CUT CLASS.

**class act** Someone or something of superior quality, as in *The last rider was definitely the class act of the competition.*

**clean** In addition to the idioms beginning with CLEAN, also see COME CLEAN; HAVE A CLEAR (CLEAN) CONSCIENCE; KEEP ONE'S NOSE CLEAN; MAKE A CLEAN BREAST OF; MAKE A CLEAN SWEEP; NEW BROOM SWEEPS CLEAN; TAKE SOMEONE TO THE CLEANERS; WIPE THE SLATE CLEAN.

**clean as a whistle** Completely, entirely, thoroughly, as in *He chopped off the branch, clean as a whistle.*

**clean bill of health** A report confirming the absence of illness, fault, or guilt in a person or thing, as in *The doctor gave her a clean bill of health,* or *Jeff checked every component and gave the computer a clean bill of health,* or *He had proof that he was somewhere else at the time of the robbery, so the police had to give him a clean bill of health.* This term comes from the old practice of requiring ships to produce a medical document (*bill*) stating that there was no infectious disease on board before landing.

**clean breast** see MAKE A CLEAN BREAST OF.

**clean hands, have** Be innocent or guiltless, as in *John's got clean hands; he had nothing to do with it.* It is sometimes put as **one's hands are clean,** meaning "one has done nothing wrong," as in *Don't look at me—my hands are clean.*

**clean house** Wipe out corruption or inefficiency, usually in an organization, as in *It's time the Republican Party cleaned house.*

**cleanliness is next to godliness** Being clean is a sign of spiritual purity or goodness, as in *Don't forget to wash your ears—cleanliness is next to godliness.* This expression is used to urge someone to wash or clean up.

**clean out 1.** Clear something out to make it neater, *I really need to clean out the drawers of my desk.* **2.** Empty something of its contents. For example, *The crows cleaned out the whole field of corn.* **3.** Deprive someone of money or other material resources, *He'd better not play cards with them again—they cleaned him out!* **4.** Drive someone out by force, as in *The new company president tried to clean out all employees over the age of 60.*

**clean slate, a** A fresh start; another chance after wiping out old offenses or debts. This idiom often appears as **wipe the slate clean.** For example, *Henry's boss assured him that the matter was finished and he could start with a clean slate,* or *He wished he could wipe the slate clean, but it was too late to save his marriage.* This expression refers to the slate boards on which school work was done in the past.

**clean someone's clock** Beat or defeat someone decisively, as in *He's much bigger than you and could easily clean your clock.* This term originated in the military.

**clean sweep** see MAKE A CLEAN SWEEP.

**clean up 1.** Make clean or orderly, as in *She cleaned up the cellar after the flood.* **2.** Also, **wash up.** Wash or tidy oneself, as in *Do I have time to clean up before dinner?* **3.** Settle or dispose of something, as in *He cleaned up all the bills that had arrived during his vacation.* **4.** Bring something to a certain standard of order or morality, as in *This script is not acceptable; we'll have to clean up the language.* This expression can also refer to personal behavior when it is put as **clean up one's act,** as in *He'll have to clean up his act and obey the rules.* **5.** Succeed, especially financially, as in *We had fantastic luck at the races and really cleaned up.* **6.** Defeat or kill someone, as in *We're cleaning up all the other teams.*

**clear** In addition to the idioms beginning with CLEAR, also see COAST IS CLEAR; FREE AND CLEAR; HAVE A CLEAR CONSCIENCE; IN THE CLEAR; LOUD AND CLEAR; OUT OF A CLEAR BLUE SKY; SEE ONE'S WAY (CLEAR); STEER CLEAR OF.

**clear as a bell** Very easy to understand, as in *Did you understand the message I left you? Yes, it was clear as a bell.*

**clear as crystal** see CRYSTAL CLEAR.

**clear as mud** Hard to understand, totally unclear, as in *These directions are clear as mud.* This phrase always means that something is far from clear.

**clear away** Remove something, as in *He cleared away the dishes after dinner.*

**clear off 1.** Remove objects from the surface of something, as in *I'll help you clear off the table.* **2.** Become clear after cloudiness, fog, or other bad weather conditions, as in *I hope this fog clears off before morning.* Also see CLEAR UP.

**clear one's name** Also, **clear someone** or **clear oneself.** Prove someone or oneself innocent. For example, *She not only wanted to be acquitted, she wanted to clear her name entirely.* The verb *clear* has the sense of "purify" or "wash away a stain."

**clear out 1.** Remove the contents of something, as in *I'll clear out this closet so you can use it.* **2.** Leave suddenly or run away, as in *We cleared out before our landlord could stop us.* **3.** Drive or force everyone out of a place, as in *The police cleared out the restaurant in no time.*

**clear the air** Clear up confusion, or ease controversy or emotional tension, as in *His letter has cleared the air; we now know where he stands.* This idiom compares the improvement of a tense situation to air that is fresher after a storm.

**clear the decks** Prepare for action, as in *I've finished all these memos and cleared the decks for your project,* or *Clear the decks—here comes the coach.* This expression originated in naval warfare, where it described preparing for battle by removing or fastening down all loose objects on the ship's decks.

**clear the table** Remove everything from the top of a table, as in *You clear the table, and I'll wash the dishes.*

**clear up 1.** Clarify, explain, or solve something confusing, as in *Let's try to clear up this misunderstanding.* **2.** Become clear, as in *After the storm, it cleared up very quickly.*

**3.** Return something to a normal condition, cure, as in *This new medicine will clear up your rash.*

**clear *something* with** Obtain approval or permission. For example, *Before you proceed, you'll have to clear it with the main office.*

C

**climb the walls** Show extreme frustration, impatience, or anxiety, as in *That long, boring dinner made me want to climb the walls,* or *If he says that one more time, I'll be ready to climb the walls.* Also see under DRIVE SOMEONE CRAZY.

**clinging vine, a** An overly dependent person, as in *She has been A clinging vine since her marriage, and she's never made a decision on her own.* Nearly always applied to a woman, this term for a climbing plant criticizes dependency.

**clip someone's wings** Limit or reduce someone's freedom, as in *If you take his car keys, you're really clipping his wings.* This expression refers to clipping a bird's wings to prevent it flying away.

**clock** In addition to the idioms beginning with CLOCK, also see AGAINST THE CLOCK; BEAT THE CLOCK; CLEAN SOMEONE'S CLOCK; LIKE CLOCKWORK; SET BACK (THE CLOCK); STOP THE CLOCK.

**clock in** Begin work or punch a timecard at the start of the workday, as in *She clocked in late again.* The opposite expression is **clock out,** end work or punch a timecard at the end of the workday, as in *Please wait for me; I forgot to clock out.* The reference here is to punching a time clock, a device that records the time on a card to show when an employee arrives and departs.

**clock is ticking, the** The time (for something to be done) is passing quickly; hurry up. For example, *The clock is ticking on that project.* This reference to a stopwatch is often used to tell someone to speed something up. It also is used in more specific form—**one's biological clock is ticking**—meaning that a woman may soon be too old to bear a child, as in *Her biological clock is ticking—she just turned forty.*

**close** In addition to the idioms beginning with CLOSE, also see AT CLOSE QUARTERS; AT CLOSE RANGE; BEHIND CLOSED DOORS; COME CLOSE TO; KEEP (A CLOSE) WATCH; NEAR (CLOSE) TO ONE'S HEART; PLAY ONE'S CARDS CLOSE TO ONE'S CHEST; TOO CLOSE FOR COMFORT; TOO CLOSE TO CALL.

**close at hand** see AT HAND.

**close but no cigar** Nearly correct or a winner, as in *He almost guessed the winning number—close but no cigar.* This expression refers to awarding a cigar to the winner of some competition, such as hitting a target.

**close call** Also, **close shave.** A narrow escape from some bad event, a near miss. For example, *That skier just missed the tree—what a close call,* or *That was a close shave, nearly leaving your passport behind.* The first phrase comes from sports, referring to an official's decision (*call*) that could have gone either way. The second phrase refers to the narrow space between closely shaved skin and a razor cut. Also see TOO CLOSE FOR COMFORT.

**closed book, a** A secret, mystery, or puzzle, as in *I can't figure her out; she's a closed book to me.* This term refers to information one can't get or comprehend (because the book is closed).

**closed door 1.** Something that blocks or limits one's choices or movement, as in *There are no closed doors in the new field of gene therapy.* **2. close one's doors.** See CLOSE DOWN. Also see BEHIND CLOSED DOORS; CLOSE THE DOOR ON.

**close down 1.** Also, **close one's doors** or **shut down.** Go out of business, end business operations. For example, *If the rent goes up, we'll have to close down,* or *After fifty years in business the store finally closed its doors,* or *The warehouse had a clearance sale the month before it shut down.* Also see CLOSE UP. **2.** Force someone to go out of business, as in *The police arrested the gun dealer and closed his shop down.*

**close in 1.** Surround and enclose someone, as in *The fog closed in, and we couldn't see two yards in front of us,* or *She felt the room was closing in.* **2.** Also, **close in on** or **close in upon.** Come closer or move toward someone or something, as in *The police closed in on the suspect.*

**close one's eyes to** Also, **shut one eyes to.** Refuse to notice someone or something, especially something that deserves attention. For example, *Jill closed her eyes to the danger and pushed off downhill,* or *The professor shut her eyes to the students who were reading during her lecture.* For a synonym, see TURN A BLIND EYE.

**close out 1.** Dispose of a stock of goods; end a business. For example, *The store is closing out all their china,* or *They've decided to close out their downtown branch.* This expression is most often used in business and commerce but occasionally refers to other matters. **2.** Prevent someone's entry or inclusion, as in *No one will tell us anything—they've closed us out.*

**close ranks** Unite, work together, as in *The members decided to close ranks and confront the president.* This expression comes from the military. It means bringing troops closely together so there are no gaps in the fighting line.

**close shave** see CLOSE CALL.

**closet** see COME OUT (OF THE CLOSET); SKELETON IN ONE'S CLOSET.

**close the books** Stop buying and selling; end a matter. For example, *Our client has formally accepted the project as complete, so we can close the books on it,* or *The detective was glad to close the books on this case.*

**close the door on** Also, **shut the door on.** End something or block it from consideration, discussion, or action. For example, *His lack of qualifications closed the door on further promotions,* or *Last quarter's poor sales figures have shut the door on any plans to expand the business.*

**close the sale** Also, **close the deal** or **close on a sale** or **close on a deal.** Complete a business transaction, as in *Jack was delighted to close the sale.* This term applies to such transactions as the sale of a house, also put as **closing on a house,** as well as negotiations leading up to a sale.

**close to home** Also, **where one lives.** Affecting someone very personally, as in *That description of orphans really upset her—it was too close to home,* or *The teacher's criticisms of her work got her where she lives.* The noun *home* here means "the heart of something." The verb *hit* often comes before these expressions, that is, something can **hit close to home** or **hit one where one lives,** as in *That remark about their marriage hit close to home.* Also see TOO CLOSE FOR COMFORT (TO HOME).

**close up** Also, **close up shop.** Stop doing business, temporarily or permanently; also, stop one's work. For example, *The bank is closing up all its overseas branches,* or *That's enough work for one day—I'm closing up shop and going home.*

**cloth** see OUT OF WHOLE CLOTH.

**clothing** see WOLF IN SHEEP'S CLOTHING.

**cloud** In addition to the idiom beginning with CLOUD, also see HEAD IN THE CLOUDS; ON CLOUD NINE; (EVERY CLOUD HAS A) SILVER LINING; UNDER A CLOUD.

**cloud over** Also, **cloud up. 1.** Become overcast with clouds, as in *It's clouding over now, so it may rain soon,* or *It was hot and sunny, but after a while the sky clouded up.* **2.** Become opaque or covered with moisture, making it hard to see through, as in *I'm sweating so much that my eyeglasses are clouded over.*

**clover** see LIKE PIGS IN CLOVER.

**club** see JOIN THE CLUB.

**clue *someone* in** Also, **clue *someone* in on.** Give someone guiding information, as in *It's time someone clued us in on what's happening.* This expression uses the verb *clue* in the sense of "inform." It is sometimes put simply as **clue,** as in *I'll clue you—this isn't going to work.* Also see NOT HAVE A CLUE.

**clutch** see GRASP (CLUTCH) AT STRAWS.

**coal** see CARRY COALS TO NEWCASTLE; RAKE SOMEONE OVER THE COALS.

**coast is clear, the** No one is watching, so one can proceed safely. For example, *Let's make sure the coast is clear before we set up this surprise party.*

**coattails** see ON SOMEONE'S COATTAILS.

**cock and bull story** An unbelievable tale that is intended to fool someone; a tall tale. For example, *Jack told us some cock and bull story about getting lost, but that wasn't really why he was late.*

**cocked** see GO OFF HALF-COCKED.

**cockles of one's heart** see WARM THE COCKLES OF ONE'S HEART.

**cog** In addition to the idiom beginning with COG, also see SLIP A COG.

**cog in the wheel** Also, **cog in the machine.** A person who holds a minor but necessary job in a large organization, as in *Frank knew he was just a cog in the wheel of this giant corporation.* This term refers to the role of the mechanical *cog,* one of the teeth on a wheel or gear. It engages or fits together with other teeth and transmits or receives motion. This expression sometimes is put as **small cog in a large wheel,** emphasizing a person's lack of importance.

**coin** see OTHER SIDE OF THE COIN; PAY BACK (IN SOMEONE'S OWN COIN).

**cold** In addition to the idioms beginning with COLD, also see BLOW HOT AND COLD; CATCH COLD; COME IN FROM THE COLD; IN A COLD SWEAT; IN COLD BLOOD; IN COLD STORAGE; IN THE COLD LIGHT OF DAY; KNOCK OUT (COLD); LEAVE SOMEONE COLD; MAKE SOMEONE'S BLOOD RUN COLD; OUT COLD; OUT IN THE COLD; POUR COLD WATER ON; STONE COLD; STOP COLD.

**cold cash** Also, **hard cash.** Bills and coins; money immediately available, paid at the time of a purchase. For example, *Will you lower the price if I pay in cold cash instead of using a credit card?* or *We have only a limited amount of hard cash—most of our money is tied up in investments.*

**cold comfort** News that makes someone feel little or no better about a bad situation. For example, *He can't lend us his canoe but will tell us where to rent one—that's cold comfort.*

**cold feet, get** Also, **have cold feet.** Lose the nerve or courage to do something as planned. For example, *I got cold feet when I learned the trip involves mountain climbing.*

**cold fish** A hardhearted, unfeeling person who shows no emotion, as in *Not even the sight of hungry children moved him; he's a real cold fish.*

**cold hands, warm heart** Not showing one's feelings does not mean that one doesn't have feeling. For example, *Dan rarely sends flowers or anything, but he's a case of cold hands, warm heart.* Why a literally cold hand should indicate sympathy or affection is not really clear.

C

**cold shoulder** Deliberate coldness or disregard. For example, *When I said hello to her in the library, she gave me the cold shoulder and walked away.* This term may refer to the custom of welcoming a desired guest with a meal of roasted meat but serving only a cold shoulder of beef or lamb to unwelcome guests.

**cold shower** A cool reception, reaction, or response that surprises someone with its lack of enthusiasm or approval, as in *The small voter turnout was a cold shower to the campaign workers.*

**cold snap** Also, **cold spell.** A short period of unusually cold weather, as in *The recent cold snap has threatened the crop.*

**cold storage** see IN COLD STORAGE.

**cold sweat** see IN A COLD SWEAT.

**cold turkey** **1.** Immediate, complete withdrawal from something, especially an addictive drug. For example, *My bad shoulder forced me to quit playing tennis cold turkey.* **2.** Without planning or preparation, as in *I'd never done any rock climbing but decided to try it cold turkey.* This term may have come from the earlier expression TALK TURKEY (for blunt speaking). At first it was used strictly for withdrawal from drugs or alcohol, but it soon was transferred to quitting any habit or activity.

**collar** see HOT UNDER THE COLLAR.

**collected** see COOL, CALM, AND COLLECTED.

**collector's item** An object of great interest, value, or rarity, as in *This necklace is a collector's item.*

**color** In addition to the idiom beginning with COLOR, also see FALSE COLORS; HORSE OF A DIFFERENT COLOR; LEND COLOR TO; SEE THROUGH ROSE-COLORED GLASSES; WITH FLYING COLORS.

**color of *someone's* money, see the** Get proof that someone can pay, as in *Before we talk any more about this car, let's see the color of your money.* This term probably comes from gambling.

**comb** see FINE-TOOTH COMB.

**come** In addition to the idioms beginning with COME, also see BIGGER THEY COME; CROSS A BRIDGE WHEN ONE COMES TO IT; DREAM COME TRUE; EASY COME, EASY GO; FIRST COME, FIRST SERVED; FULL CIRCLE, COME; GET ONE'S COMEUPPANCE; HOW COME; IF WORST COMES TO WORST; JOHNNY-COME-LATELY; MAKE A COMEBACK; (COME) OF AGE; (COME) ON THE SCENE; (COME) OUT OF NOWHERE; PUSH COMES TO SHOVE; TILL THE COWS COME HOME; (COME) TO THE POINT; WHEN IT COMES DOWN TO; WHEN ONE'S SHIP COMES IN. Also see under COMING.

**come about** Also, **come to pass.** Happen, take place, as in *How did this quarrel come about?* or *When did this new development come to pass?*

**come across** **1.** Also, **come upon** or **run across.** Meet or find by chance, as in *I came across your old letters today,* or *He came upon her looking in the store window,* or *If I run across it, I'll call you.* **2.** Also, **come across with.** Pay or give what is expected or demanded, as in *He finally came across with the money he owed me,* or *The landlord wants the rent, so come across.* **3.** Make a particular impression, as in *He comes across as a very sincere person,* or *Her meaning doesn't really come across; she'll have to revise the speech.* Also see GET ACROSS; PUT ACROSS.

**come again?** What did you say? as in *Come again? I didn't hear you.* This expression is used to ask someone to repeat a statement, either because it wasn't heard clearly or because it is hard to believe.

**come alive** Also, **come to life.** **1.** Become very active or lively. For example, *It took some fast rhythms to make the dancers come alive,* or *As soon as he mentioned ice cream, the children came to life.* **2.** Appear real or believable, as in *The characters in this story don't really come to life.* Also see LOOK ALIVE.

**come along** **1.** Accompany or go with someone. For example, *Are you coming along with us to the mall?* **2.** Advance toward a goal, make progress, as in *How are you coming along with your piano lessons?* **3.** Appear or happen, as in *I'm hoping another job offer will come along soon.*

**come a long way** Make considerable progress or improvement, as in *That student has brought his grade point average up from a D to a B—he has certainly come a long way.*

**come and get it** Said when a meal is ready, as in *She called to the children, "Come and get it!"*

**come and go** **1.** Arrive and depart, either briefly or repeatedly, as in *It's a busy shop—people come and go all day.* **2.** Alternately appear and disappear, as in *This rash is odd; it comes and goes.* Also see COMING AND GOING; COMING OR GOING; EASY COME, EASY GO.

**come apart at the seams** Also, **come unglued.** Become extremely upset and be unable to function. For example, *After he lost his job, Brad seemed to come apart at the seams* or *The director is losing control of the show and coming unglued.*

**come around** Also, **come round.** **1.** Arrive casually or visit. For example, *You should come round to see us more often.* Also see COME BY, def. 2. **2.** Change one's opinion and be in agreement with others, as in *I was sure you would come around and see it my way.*

**3.** Recover consciousness, return to a normal condition, as in *She fainted from loss of blood but came around after a minute.*

**come at 1.** Get hold of something, as in *You can come at a classical education with serious study.* **2.** Rush at or attack someone, as in *They came at him in full fore.*

**come back 1.** Return to or regain past success or popularity, as in *It's hard to come back from two goals down and win the game,* or *Long skirts are coming back this fall.* **2.** Return to one's mind, as in *Her name came back to me after I saw her picture.* **3.** Reply in a quick and forceful way. For example, *No matter how many insults he throws at me, I can always come back with another.*

**come between** Divide people and cause them to be in disagreement, as in *I wouldn't want to come between husband and wife.*

**come by 1.** Acquire or get something, as in *A good assistant is hard to come by.* A related expression is **come by *something* honestly,** meaning "to get something in some honorable or logical way." For example, *I'm sure she didn't come by that information honestly,* or *He does have an unusual voice, but he came by it honestly; his father's is the same.* **2.** Stop in, visit, as in *Please come by whenever you're in the neighborhood.*

**come clean** Confess everything, as in *If you come clean about what happened, I will promise not to tell anyone.*

**come close to** Almost do something, as in *I came close to telling that idiot what I really think of him.*

**come down 1.** Become reduced in size or amount, be lowered, as in *Interest rates will have to come down before the economy recovers.* **2.** Be passed down by inheritance, tradition, or a higher authority. For example, *This painting has come down to us from our great-grandparents,* or *These stories have come down through the generations,* or *The court's decision finally came down.* **3.** Also, **go down.** Happen, occur, as in *What's coming down tonight?*

**come down in the world** Lose money or social position. For example, *Since her divorce, she has really come down in the world.*

**come down on 1.** Also, **come down hard on.** Punish or reprimand someone severely. For example, *My professor is going to come down on me for not completing the paper,* or *The judge promised to come down hard on drug dealers.* Also see LIKE A TON OF BRICKS. **2.** Speak in opposition to something, as in *The President came down on the new budget cuts, promising to veto them.* **3. come down on the side of.** Make a choice or decision in favor of something, as in *I'll come down on the side of those who are needy.*

**come down the pike** Appear and become well known, as in *He was the best writer to come down the pike in a long time.* The noun *pike* here is short for "turnpike" or "road."

**come down to** Also, **come right down to. 1.** Amount to or be reduced to something basic, as in *It all comes down to a matter of who was first in line.* Also see BOIL DOWN (TO), def. 2. **2.** Face or deal with something honestly, as in *When you come right down to it, you have to admit he was mistaken.*

**come down with** Become ill with something, as in *The whole family came down with the flu.*

**comedy of errors** A complex and funny series of events, as in *Mary and John went to the Smiths', while the Smiths went to the Parkers', and the Parkers wondered why no one answered the door at John and Mary's—a true comedy of errors.*

**come forward** Present oneself, offer one's services, as in *The boss asked for more help, but no one wanted to come forward.*

**come from 1.** See COME OUT OF. **2.** Arrive from someone or somewhere, as in *This package just came from Alice,* or *Where did these chairs come from?* Also see WHERE ONE IS COMING FROM.

**come from behind** Also, **come up from behind.** Advance from the rear or from a losing position, as in *You can expect the team to come from behind before the season is over,* or *The polls say our candidate is coming up from behind.* This idiom comes from horseracing. It was first transferred to scores in various sports and later to more general use.

**come full circle** see FULL CIRCLE.

**come hell or high water** see HELL OR HIGH WATER.

**come home to roost** see CHICKENS COME HOME TO ROOST.

**come in 1.** Arrive, become available for use or begin to produce, as in *Has the new book order come in yet?* or *The latest reports are coming in now,* or *This oil well has just begun to come in.* **2.** Also, **come in on.** Join an effort or a business, as in *Do you want to come in on our venture?* **3.** Be one of those who finish a contest or race, as in *My horse came in last.* **4.** Perform, function, or play a role, as in *Where does my department come in?* Also see COME IN HANDY. **5.** Enter into an account, an issue, or a list, as in *Where does this question come in?* or *Please explain where in this long process I come in.* Also see COME INTO.

**come in for** Receive or be the object of something, especially blame, as in *His last book came in for some heavy criticism.*

**come in from the cold** Also, **come in out of the cold.** Return to shelter and safety, be welcomed into a group. For example, *Bill was tired of traveling on his own for the company and hoped they'd let him come in from the cold,* or *After years of waiting for an invitation from the group, Steve was finally asked to come in out of the cold.* Also see COME IN OUT OF THE RAIN.

**come in handy** Be useful or convenient, as in *This check will really come in handy.*

**come in out of the rain, know enough to** Show common sense. This expression means someone has enough sense to seek shelter from the weather. It is often used in the negative, as in *Peter doesn't know enough to come in out of the rain.*

**come into 1.** Inherit or acquire money or property, as in *She expected to come into a fortune when she turned 21.* **2.** Gain power or public office, as in *He came into office in 1820 and served three terms.* **3. come into one's own.** Get the recognition that one deserves or something else that belongs to one. For example, *The younger members of the orchestra have finally come into their own.*

**come of** see COME OUT OF.

**come of age** see OF AGE.

**come off 1.** Happen, occur, as in *The trip came off on schedule.* **2.** Perform or result in a certain way. This usage always includes a modifier, as in *Whenever he tries to be funny, he comes off badly,* or *This model will surely come off second-best.* **3.** Succeed, as in *Our dinner party really came off.*

**come off it** Stop acting or speaking foolishly, as in *Oh, come off it! You're no smarter than they are.* This term is often used as a command, as in the example.

**come on 1.** Move forward, progress, develop. For example, *We stopped as soon as darkness began to come on.* **2.** Hurry up, as in *Come on now, it's getting late.* **3.** Also, **come upon.** Meet or find someone or something unexpectedly, as in *We came on him while walking down the street,* or *I came upon an old friend in the bookstore today.* **4.** Make a stage entrance, as in *At the beginning of the play, she comes on from the right.* **5.** Please be more agreeable or cooperative, as in *Come on, that's no excuse for leaving,* or *Come on, you'll really like this restaurant.* **6.** Give people a specific personal image or impression, as in *He comes on as unfriendly, but he's really rather timid.* **7.** Also, **come on strong.** Behave or speak in an aggressive way, as in *Take it easy; you're coming on awfully strong.* **8.** Also, **come on to.** Make sexual advances to someone, as in *She reported her boss for coming on to her.*

**come on in** Please enter, as in *Come on in, the door's open.* This phrase is a friendly invitation to enter one's house or some other place. The related expression **come on in, the water's fine** began as an encouragement (or, sometimes, a command) to a reluctant or fearful swimmer, but now it can refer to other activities, as in *Come on in, the water's fine—this is a great office to work in!*

**come on strong** see COME ON, def. 7.

**come on to** see COME ON, def. 8.

**come out 1.** Become known, be discovered, as in *The whole story came out at the trial.* **2.** Be issued or brought to public attention, as in *My new book is coming out this month.* **3.** Make a formal debut in society or on the stage, as in *In New York City debutantes come out in winter.* **4.** End up, result, as in *Everything came out wrong.* Also see COME OUT AHEAD. **5. come out for** or **come out against.** Make a public statement in favor of or opposed to someone or something, as in *The governor came out for a tax cut,* or *Many senators came out against the bill.* **6.** Also, **come out of the closet.** Tell people that one is homosexual, as in *He came out to his friends before he told his parents,* or *The military has specific policies regarding soldiers who come out of the closet.* Also see the following idioms beginning with COME OUT.

**come out ahead** Succeed, make a profit. For example, *By the end of the year we expect to come out ahead.* Also see AHEAD OF THE GAME.

**come out for** see COME OUT, def. 5.

**come out in the wash, it will** A problem will be solved or difficulties will disappear. For example, *Don't worry about the fight you got into—it'll all come out in the wash.*

**come out of** Also, **come from** or **come of.** Follow or result from, as in *What good can come out of all this arguing?* or *What do you think will come of this change?* Also see WHERE ONE IS COMING FROM.

**come out of nowhere** see OUT OF NOWHERE.

**come out of the closet** see COME OUT, def. 6.

**come out with** Also, **come right out with. 1.** Put something into words; speak frankly. For example, *He always comes right out with the truth,* or *She can always come out with a joke.* **2.** Make something public, publish, as in *I don't know why they're coming out with yet another biography of President Truman.*

**come over 1.** Change sides or positions, as in *He's decided to come over to our side.* **2.** Happen to or affect someone, as in *Why are you leaving? What's come over you?* or *A sudden fit of impatience came over her.* **3.** Pay a casual visit, as in *I want to show you my garden, so please come over soon.* This term uses *come over* in the sense of "crossing a space" (from somewhere to one's home).

**come rain or shine** see RAIN OR SHINE.

**come right down to** see COME DOWN TO.

**come round** see COME AROUND.

**come someone's way** Present itself to someone, happen, as in *I sure hope a good opportunity will come her way.*

**come through 1.** Also, **come through with.** Do what is required, expected, or hoped for. For example, *My parents really came through for me when I needed help,* or *He took the test and came through with flying colors.* **2.** Become visible or be communicated, as in *He tried to keep a straight face, but his true feelings came through nevertheless.* **3.** Be approved, as in *If the bank loan comes through, we can afford to expand.*

**come to 1.** Recover consciousness, as in *She fainted but quickly came to.* Also see COME AROUND, def. 3. **2.** Change over time, learn, as in *I came to see that Tom was right.* **3.** See AMOUNT TO, def. 2. **4.** See WHEN IT COMES TO. Also see the following entries beginning with COME TO.

**come to a halt** Also, **come to a standstill.** Stop, either permanently or temporarily. For example, *The class came to a halt when the fire alarm rang,* or *With the strike, construction came to a standstill.*

**come to a head** see BRING TO A HEAD.

**come to an end 1.** Arrive at a conclusion or closing, as in *The school year will come to an end in June.* **2. come to a bad end** or **come to no good.** Have a bad result or die in an unpleasant way. For example, *I always suspected this plan would come to no good,* or *His parents feared he would come to a bad end.* **3. come to an untimely end** or **meet an untimely end.** Die at a young age, end much sooner than desired or expected. For example, *The blow was fatal, causing the young boxer to meet an untimely end,* or *Our partnership came to an untimely end when I became too ill to work.*

**come to blows** Begin to fight. For example, *It hardly seems worth coming to blows over a dollar!*

**come to grief** Meet with disaster or failure. For example, *The icy runway caused at least one light plane to come to grief.*

**come to grips with** Face something directly, deal decisively with something, as in *Her stories help the children come to grips with upsetting events.*

**come to life** see COME ALIVE.

**come to light** Be clearly revealed or shown to people, as in *New facts about his life have come to light during the trial.*

**come to mind** Enter one's thoughts, as in *A new idea just came to mind.* Also see BRING TO MIND; CALL SOMETHING TO MIND; ENTER ONE'S MIND.

**come to no good** see COME TO AN END, def. 2.

**come to nothing** Also, **come to naught.** Fail, as in *All his efforts have come to nothing,* or *The last round of peace talks came to naught.*

**come to one's senses 1.** Return to thinking or behaving sensibly and reasonably. For example, *I wish he'd come to his senses and stop playing around.* **2.** Recover consciousness, as in *When the boxer came to his senses, he was lying on the floor.* Also see TAKE LEAVE (OF ONE'S SENSES).

**come to pass** see COME ABOUT.

**come to terms 1.** Reach an agreement, as in *The landlord and his tenants soon came to terms regarding repairs.* **2. come to terms with.** Learn to understand and accept something, as in *He'd been trying to come to terms with his early life.*

**come to that** see WHEN IT COMES TO.

**come to the point** see TO THE POINT.

**come to the same thing** see AMOUNT TO THE SAME THING.

**come to think of it** Suddenly remembering or thinking about it. For example, *Come to think of it, I've got to send in my order now,* or *I was going to lend him a saw, but come to think of it, he already has one.*

**come true** Happen as predicted or as hoped, as in *Her dream of a movie career came true.*

**come under 1.** Fit into a category or classification, as in *This document comes under the heading "classified."* **2.** Be the responsibility of someone, as in *My department comes under your jurisdiction.*

**come unglued** see COME APART AT THE SEAMS.

**come up 1.** Come to someone's attention, present itself, as in *This question never came up.* **2.** Also, **come up to.** Approach or come near someone, as in *He came up and said hello,* or *The dog came right up to Nora.* **3.** Also, **come up to.** Rise in status or value, often so as to be equal to something else, as in *This officer came up through the ranks,* or *His paintings will never come up to his teacher's.* A variant is **come up in the world** or **rise in the world,** used for someone who has risen in rank, wealth, or status. For example, *He has really come up in the world—he now owns a software company,* or *I could see at once that she was a woman who would rise in the world.* Also see the following idioms beginning with COME UP.

**come up against** Meet something, especially an obstacle or problem. For example, *I've never come up against anything I can't handle,* or *Dealing with Malcolm is like coming up against a brick wall.*

**come up in the world** see COME UP, def. 3.

C

**come upon** see COME ACROSS, def. 1; COME ON, def. 3.

**come up smelling like a rose** see COMING UP ROSES.

**come up to** see COME UP, def. 2 and 3.

**come up with** **1.** Produce or supply something. For example, *Henry always comes up with the wrong answer,* or *How will they come up with the money?* **2.** Discover or think of something, as in *We're hoping they come up with a cure in time to help Aunt Alice.*

**come what may** No matter what happens, as in *Come what may, I'll be home in time for dinner.*

**come with the territory** Be a natural or usual part of a job or other situation, as in *You may not like the new coach, but he comes with the territory,* or *As the editor, you may not like listening to complaints, but it comes with the territory.* This term uses *territory* in the sense of "sales district." The phrase originally meant that traveling salesmen had to accept whatever problems or benefits they found in their assigned region.

**comfort** see COLD COMFORT; TOO CLOSE FOR COMFORT.

**comfortable as an old shoe** Familiar and very much at ease, as in *Kathy's really enjoying her third summer at the same camp—for her it's comfortable as an old shoe.*

**coming** In addition to the idioms beginning with COMING, also see GET WHAT'S COMING TO ONE; HAVE ANOTHER GUESS COMING; HAVE IT COMING; WHERE ONE IS COMING FROM. Also see under COME.

**coming and going, have someone** Give someone no choice to control in a situation. For example, *If Jane accepted the transfer she would have to move, but if she turned it down she would have to travel more—they had her coming and going.* Also see COMING OR GOING.

**coming or going, not know if one is** Be in a state of confusion, as in *He has so much to do that he doesn't know if he's coming or going.*

**coming out of one's ears** Amounting to too much, more than can be managed, as in *We miscalculated—new orders are coming out of our ears.* Also see EMBARRASSMENT OF RICHES.

**comings and goings** Movements, activities, as in *He's in and out of the office; I don't try to follow all his comings and goings,* or *In her job on the school board Mrs. Smith keeps track of all the comings and goings in town.*

**coming up roses** Also, **come up smelling like roses.** Succeed in coming out of a difficult situation with no stain on one's character or reputation, as in *He was suspended for a month but still came up smelling like a rose.*

**command** In addition to the idiom beginning with COMMAND, also see HAVE A GOOD COMMAND.

**command performance** An occasion a person must attend, as in *Dinner at my boss's house is always a command performance.* This term first meant a theatrical or musical performance presented for a king, queen, or head of state.

**commission** see ON COMMISSION; OUT OF (IN) COMMISSION.

**commit something to memory** Memorize something, as in *The director insisted that the altos commit their part to memory by Tuesday.*

**common** In addition to the idioms beginning with COMMON, also see IN COMMON.

**common ground** Shared beliefs or interests, a basis for understanding. For example, *The different interest groups within our church are struggling to find common ground.*

**common touch** The ability to appeal to the ordinary person's feelings and interests. For example, *The governor is an effective state leader who also happens to have the common touch.* This phrase uses *common* in the sense of "everyday" or "ordinary."

**commotion** see CAUSE A COMMOTION.

**company** In addition to the idioms beginning with COMPANY, also see KEEP COMPANY; MISERY LOVES COMPANY; PART COMPANY; TWO'S COMPANY.

**company man** A male worker who is more loyal to management than to his fellow workers; also, one who informs on fellow employees. For example, *He'll never join in a strike; he's a company man.* This term uses *company* in the sense of "a business concern." It has often been used as a criticism by supporters of labor unions, especially in times of trouble between workers and management.

**company manners** One's best behavior, as in *George never interrupts when we have guests; he has fine company manners.* This term uses *company* in the sense of "guests." The term implies that someone is more polite with invited guests than with family.

**compare** In addition to the idiom beginning with COMPARE, also see BEYOND COMPARISON.

**compare notes** Exchange information, observations, or opinions about something, as in *Michael and Jane always compare notes after a department meeting.* This term originally referred to written notes.

**complain** see CAN'T COMPLAIN.

**compliment** see LEFT-HANDED COMPLIMENT; PAY A COMPLIMENT; RETURN THE COMPLIMENT.

**concern** see AS FAR AS THAT GOES (IS CONCERNED); TO WHOM IT MAY CONCERN.

**conclusion** see FOREGONE CONCLUSION; JUMP TO A CONCLUSION.

C

**condition** see IN (OUT OF) CONDITION; MINT CONDITION; ON CONDITION THAT.

**confidence** see IN CONFIDENCE; TAKE INTO ONE'S CONFIDENCE.

**con game** Also, **confidence trick** or **confidence game.** A situation in which a person cheats someone out of money or property after winning his or her trust. For example, *The police warned of a confidence game in which people were asked to leave their valuables for a so-called appraisal,* or *The typical confidence trick is easy to catch if you know what to look for,* or *I almost became a victim of her con game—she seemed so sincere.* These terms use *confidence* in the sense of "trust." They were the source of **confidence man** (or **con man**) or **con artist** for the cheater.

**conk out** **1.** Stop functioning, fail, as in *The engine finally conked out.* **2.** Fall asleep, as in *Every evening he conked out in front of the television set.* **3.** Faint or collapse, as in *I don't know if it was the heat, but she suddenly conked out.*

**conniption** see HAVE A FIT (CONNIPTION).

**conquer** see DIVIDE AND CONQUER.

**conscience** see HAVE A CLEAR CONSCIENCE; IN CONSCIENCE.

**consequence** see IN CONSEQUENCE; OF CONSEQUENCE.

**consideration** see IN CONSIDERATION OF; TAKE INTO ACCOUNT (CONSIDERATION); UNDER CONSIDERATION.

**conspicuous by its absence** Also, **conspicuous by one's absence.** Extremely obvious because of being missing when expected. For example, *The bride's father was conspicuous by his absence.*

**conspiracy of silence** An agreement to keep something secret. For example, *In this state's medical society there is a conspiracy of silence regarding irresponsible doctors.* This expression often refers to remaining silent about something that is either unfavorable or criminal.

**contempt** see FAMILIARITY BREEDS CONTEMPT.

**content** see TO ONE'S HEART'S CONTENT.

**contention** see BONE OF CONTENTION.

**contradiction in terms** A statement with parts that seem to say opposite things, with one part of it denying another. For example, *I've always believed that "a poor millionaire" was a contradiction in terms.*

**contrary** see ON THE CONTRARY; TO THE CONTRARY.

**control** see OUT OF CONTROL; SPIN CONTROL.

**convenience** see AT ONE'S CONVENIENCE.

**conventional wisdom** A belief that most people hold. For example, *According to conventional wisdom, the person already in office nearly always wins more votes than a new candidate.* Today this term is used in any context where public opinion has great influence on events.

**conversation** In addition to the idiom beginning with CONVERSATION, also see MAKE CONVERSATION.

**conversation piece** An unusual object that causes comment or interest, as in *That painting in the living room is ugly, but it's an excellent conversation piece.*

**conviction** see COURAGE OF ONE'S CONVICTIONS.

**cook** In addition to the idioms beginning with COOK, also see CHIEF COOK AND BOTTLEWASHER; SHORT ORDER (COOK); TOO MANY COOKS SPOIL THE BROTH; WHAT'S COOKING.

**cookie** see HAND IN THE TILL (COOKIE JAR); THAT'S HOW THE BALL BOUNCES (COOKIE CRUMBLES); TOSS ONE'S COOKIES.

**cooking with gas** Also, **cooking.** Doing very well, making rapid progress. For example, *The first half is finished already? Now you're cooking with gas,* or *Two promotions in two years—she's really cooking!*

**cook someone's goose** Ruin someone, upset someone's plans. For example, *He thinks he can steal my idea, but I'm going to cook his goose.*

**cook the books** Enter false information in a company's financial records, as in *An independent audit showed that they have been cooking the books for years.*

**cook up** Invent or create something, especially to fool someone, as in *She's always cooking up some excuse.*

**cool** In addition to the idioms beginning with COOL, also see KEEP COOL; KEEP ONE'S COOL; PLAY IT COOL.

**cool as a cucumber** Calm and composed, self-possessed, as in *Throughout the emergency she was cool as a cucumber.* This idiom may be based on the fact that in hot weather the inside of cucumbers remains cooler than the air.

**cool, calm, and collected** Calm and composed, self-possessed. For example, *No matter what the board decides, you have to appear cool, calm, and collected in front of the stockholders.*

**cool down** Also, **cool off.** **1.** Cause a lower temperature, especially of the body following exercise. For example, *After a race the coach makes the entire team do stretches to cool down,* or *First let the eggs cool off.* **2.** See COOL OFF, def. 2.

**cool it** **1.** Calm down, relax, as in *John was beginning to get angry, but I told him to cool it.* **2.** Stop what one is doing, especially stop talking or behaving in a way that attracts attention, as in *We'd be wise to cool it until things quiet down.* It is also used as a command, as in *Cool it! We'll be in trouble if anyone hears you.*

**cool off 1.** see COOL DOWN. **2.** Also, **cool down** or **cool out.** Calm down, become less angry or emotional, as in *We can't discuss it until you've cooled off.* Also see CHILL OUT.

**cool one's heels** Wait or be kept waiting, as in *I've been cooling my heels in the doctor's waiting room for at least an hour.* This term first meant to cool one's feet when they become hot from walking. Then it began to be used ironically for being forced to rest (or wait).

C

**cool out** see COOL OFF, def. 2.

**coon's age, a** Also, **a dog's age.** A very long time, as in *I haven't seen Sam in a coon's age,* or *It's been a dog's age since I went to the ballpark.* The first phrase refers to the mistaken idea that raccoons ("coons") live a long time. Also see DONKEY'S YEARS.

**coop** see FLY THE COOP.

**cop a feel** Secretly touch someone in a sexual manner. For example, *The female clerks complained that Mr. Hardy was always trying to cop a feel.*

**cop a plea 1.** Plead guilty or confess to a crime in exchange for a lighter sentence; also, plead guilty to a lesser charge in exchange for not being tried for a more serious charge. For example, *On the advice of his lawyer, he decided it was safer to cop a plea.* **2.** Plead for mercy; make excuses. For example, *He copped a plea about not knowing his way around.*

**cop out** Back out of a responsibility or commitment; also, take the easy way out. For example, *Don't count on him; he's likely to fake illness and cop out,* or *She'll cop out and let her assistant do all the work.*

**core** see ROTTEN TO THE CORE.

**corner** In addition to the idiom beginning with CORNER, also see AROUND THE CORNER; CUT CORNERS; FOUR CORNERS OF THE EARTH; IN A TIGHT CORNER; OUT OF THE CORNER OF ONE'S EYE; PAINT ONESELF INTO A CORNER; TURN THE CORNER.

**corner the market** Buy all or most of a stock, or anything that is sold or traded, so that its price goes up. For example, *They cornered the market in silver and got rich.*

**correct** see STAND CORRECTED.

**corridors of power, the** The offices of powerful leaders. For example, *As clerk to a Supreme Court justice, Jim thought he'd get inside the corridors of power.*

**cost** see (COST AN) ARM AND A LEG; AT ALL COSTS; (COST A) PRETTY PENNY.

**cotton to 1.** Like or get along with someone, as in *This dog doesn't cotton to strangers.* **2.** Also, **cotton on to.** Begin to understand or grasp, as in *She didn't really cotton on to what I was saying.*

**couch potato** A person who spends a lot of time sitting or lying down, usually watching TV. For example, *Doctors warn couch potatoes to get some exercise.*

**cough up 1.** Hand over or give up something, especially money. For example, *It's time for him to cough up what he owes.* **2.** Confess or tell something that was secret, as in *Pretty soon she'll cough up the whole story about last night.*

**could** In addition to the idiom beginning with COULD, also see (COULD) SEE WITH HALF AN EYE. Also see under CAN; COULDN'T.

**could do with** Need or might benefit from something, as in *This room could do with a good cleaning,* or *He could do with a haircut.*

**couldn't** In addition to the idiom beginning with COULDN'T, also see under CAN'T.

**couldn't care less** Also, **could care less.** Be completely uninterested. For example, *Pick whatever dessert you want; I couldn't care less,* or *I could care less about the editor's opinion.*

**counsel** see KEEP ONE'S OWN COUNSEL.

**count** In addition to the idioms beginning with COUNT, also see DOWN FOR THE COUNT; EVERY MINUTE COUNTS; OUT COLD (FOR THE COUNT); STAND UP AND BE COUNTED.

**count against** Have a negative effect on someone or something, as in *His past troubles in school will count against him when he applies to colleges.*

**count down 1.** Count backward from any number to zero to mark time, as in *They counted down the final seconds before takeoff: 10, 9, 8, etc.* The *down* in this term refers to the decreasing size of the numbers. This usage began with the firing of missiles and spacecraft. **2.** Make final preparations for an event, as in *She was counting down to the day of the wedding.* This usage comes from def. 1.

**counter** see RUN COUNTER TO; UNDER THE COUNTER.

**count for 1.** Have importance or worth, as in *Doesn't his long service count for anything?* This term uses *count* in the sense of "enter into a calculation." **2. count for nothing.** Have no influence or effect, as in *All his work counts for nothing since they've dropped the project.*

**count in** Include someone or something, as in *Can all the members be counted in?* or *I'd love to come; count me in.*

**count noses** Also, **count heads.** Count up the number of people present. For example, *The theater seemed only half-full, so the producer decided to count noses,* or *Our tour leader was always careful to count heads before the bus started off.*

**count off 1.** Count aloud from one end of a line of persons to the other, each person saying a number in turn. For example, *The soldiers counted off one by one.* This usage and the practice it describes come from the military. **2.** Place things in separate groups by counting, as in *The office counted off the telephone books for each delivery route.*

**count on** Also, **count upon.** Rely on or depend on, as in *You can always count on him to be punctual,* or *Carol was counting upon getting a raise in spring.*

**count one's chickens (before they hatch)** Make plans based on events that may or may not happen. For example, *You might not win the prize, and you've already spent the money? Don't count your chickens before they hatch!* or *I know you have big plans for your consulting business, but don't count your chickens.* This expression comes from Aesop's fable about a milkmaid carrying a full pail of milk on her head. She daydreams about buying chickens with the money from selling the milk and becoming rich from selling eggs. But then she spills the milk. The term often appears shortened and usually in the negative as a warning (**don't count your chickens**).

**count out 1.** Declare a boxer (or other contestant) to have lost, as in *He was counted out in the first round of the match.* This term refers to the ten seconds allowed for a boxer to get up after being knocked down. If he does not rise in time, he is "out." Also see DOWN FOR THE COUNT. **2.** Also, **count someone out.** Leave someone out of consideration, as in *As for skiing this winter, you'll have to count me out.* Also see COUNT IN. **3.** Count and separate things, especially into shares. For example, *They counted out four pieces of music for each band member.*

**count sheep** Count imaginary sheep in an attempt to put oneself to sleep. For example, *I had too much coffee and was counting sheep at 1 o'clock in the morning.*

**count the cost 1.** Think about possible results before doing something. For example, *Count the cost in terms of your family life before you decide about that job.* **2.** Have problems as a result of something, especially an earlier action or decision. For example, *He didn't take the doctor's advice, and now he's counting the cost.*

**count to ten** Calm down, get hold of oneself. For example, *Before you tell him what you think of him, count to ten.* This phrase is often used as a command, meaning "take the time to count from one to ten so as to cool your temper."

**courage** In addition to the idiom beginning with COURAGE, also see PLUCK UP ONE'S COURAGE.

**courage of one's convictions, have the** Behave according to one's beliefs. For example, *Carl wouldn't give his best friend any of the test answers; he had the courage of his convictions.*

**course** see CRASH COURSE; IN DUE COURSE; MATTER OF COURSE; OF COURSE; PAR FOR THE COURSE; RUN ITS COURSE; STAY THE COURSE.

**court** see BALL'S IN ONE'S COURT; DAY IN COURT; FRIEND IN COURT; HOLD COURT; KANGAROO COURT; LAUGH OUT OF COURT; PAY COURT TO.

**cousin** see FIRST COUSIN; KISSING COUSINS; SECOND COUSIN.

**cover** In addition to the idioms beginning with COVER, also see BLOW ONE'S COVER; BREAK COVER; JUDGE A BOOK BY ITS COVER; (COVER A) MULTITUDE OF SINS; TAKE COVER; UNDER COVER.

**cover all the bases** Also, **cover the bases.** Deal with all aspects of a situation, especially to prevent problems or protect oneself from criticism. For example, *Be sure you've covered all the bases before you make a public statement.*

**cover for 1.** Also, **cover up for.** Hide the truth so as to protect someone, as in *I covered up for my friend when her mother called to find out where she was.* Also see COVER UP, def. 2. **2.** Substitute for someone, handle someone's responsibilities, as in *Mary was asked to cover for the manager while he was on jury duty.* **3. cover something for.** Provide protection against some hazard, as in *This policy covers the house for fire but not for theft.* This idiom uses the verb *cover* in the sense of "protect" or "shield."

**cover girl** An attractive woman whose photograph is on a magazine cover; also, a woman attractive enough to be on a magazine cover. For example, *All models hope to be cover girls some day,* or *She's gorgeous—a real cover girl.*

**cover ground** Also, **cover the ground** or **cover a lot of ground. 1.** Go a certain extent or a great distance, especially at a satisfactory speed. For example, *She really knows how to cover ground when she researches something,* or *That salesman covers a lot of ground.* **2.** Deal with or accomplish something in a certain way, as in *This history text covers the ground quite well.* Also see COVER THE FIELD.

**cover one's ass** Also, **cover one's hide** or **cover oneself.** Make excuses or take action to avoid being blamed, punished, or harmed. For example, *The first thing you learn in the army is to cover your ass,* or *Jane is very good at finding ways to cover her hide.* The variants are more polite. [Vulgar slang]

**cover one's tracks** Hide one's whereabouts, activities, intentions, or the evidence of one's involvement. For example, *No one knows* *much about his role in the decision—he's very good at covering his tracks.* This term transfers hiding one's footprints to more general activities. Also see COVER UP, def. 2.

C

**cover story 1.** A featured story in a magazine that concerns the illustration on the cover, as in *The earthquake is this week's cover story for all the news magazines.* **2.** A false story intended to mislead or deceive; also, an alibi. For example, *Their cover story while investigating local repair services was that they had just bought the house and were having problems,* or *The suspect gave the police some cover story about being out for a drive.*

**cover the bases** see COVER ALL THE BASES.

**cover the field** Also, **cover the territory** or **cover the waterfront.** Be comprehensive or all-inclusive. For example, *The review course will cover the field very well,* or *Bob's new assignment really covers the territory,* or *The superintendent's speech covered the waterfront on the drug problem.* These expressions all use the verb *cover* in the sense of "extend over" or "include," with the nouns (*field, territory, waterfront*) each meaning "whole area."

**cover the ground** see COVER GROUND.

**cover up 1.** Wrap up or enfold in order to protect. For example, *Be sure to cover up the outdoor furniture in case of rain,* or *It's cold, so be sure to cover up the baby.* **2.** Hide something, especially a crime, as in *The opposition accused the President of covering up his assistant's suicide.*

**cover up for** see COVER FOR, def. 1.

**cow** In addition to the idiom beginning with COW, also see CASH COW; HOLY COW; SACRED COW; TILL THE COWS COME HOME.

**cow college** An agricultural college; any small, relatively unknown rural college. For example, *He's never published a paper, but he might do all right teaching in some cow college.* This term uses *cow* in the pejorative sense of "provincial."

**cozy up** Also, **cozy up to.** Try to get on friendly or close terms with someone. For example, *That new woman is cozying up to club members so she'll be asked to join.*

**crack** In addition to the idioms beginning with CRACK, also see BY JOVE (CRACKY); FALL BETWEEN THE CRACKS; GET A MOVE ON (GET CRACKING); HARD NUT TO CRACK; HAVE A CRACK AT; MAKE A CRACK; NOT ALL IT'S CRACKED UP TO BE; PAPER OVER (THE CRACKS).

**crack a book** Open a book to study or read, as in *He passed the exam without cracking a book.*

**crack a bottle** Open a bottle so as to drink its contents, as in *Let's celebrate by cracking a bottle of champagne!*

**crack a joke** Make a joke, say something funny, as in *You can count on Grandpa to crack a joke on every occasion.*

**crack a smile** Smile, as in *Betty was a very serious person; she rarely cracked a smile.* This expression transfers *crack* in the sense of "break" to changing a serious facial expression into a smile.

**crack down** Also, **crack down on.** Act more forcefully to regulate, repress, or control someone or something. For example, *The police cracked down on speeding.*

**cracked up 1.** See CRACK UP. **2. be cracked up to be.** Supposed to be. This expression is always used in a negative way, as in *I don't think this book is all it's cracked up to be.* **3.** Under the influence of crack (a form of cocaine). For example, *The police were sure the suspect was cracked up.*

**crack of dawn** Very early morning, daybreak. For example, *I got up at the crack of dawn.* Originally the term was put as **crack of day.**

**crack the whip** Behave in a domineering and demanding way toward people one has control over. For example, *He's been cracking the whip ever since he got his promotion.* This expression refers to drivers of horse-drawn wagons who snapped their whips hard, producing a loud cracking noise.

**crack up 1.** Suffer an emotional breakdown, become crazy, as in *He might crack up under the strain.* **2.** Damage or wreck a vehicle or boat. For example, *I'm always afraid that he'll crack up the car.* **3.** Experience a crash, as in *We cracked up on the freeway in the middle of the ice storm.* **4.** Also, **crack someone up.** Burst or cause someone else to burst out laughing, as in *The audience cracked up,* or *That joke really cracked me up.* Also see BREAK UP, def. 5. All of these expressions come from *crack* in the sense of "break into pieces" or "collapse." Also see CRACKED UP.

**cradle** see FROM THE CRADLE TO THE GRAVE; ROB THE CRADLE.

**cramp one's style** Restrict or prevent one from free action or expression, as in *It really cramps my style when Mom looks over my shoulder while I'm making dinner.*

**crank call** Also, **crank letter.** A telephone call or letter from someone who is hostile or strange. For example, *Harriet was upset enough by the crank calls to notify the police,* or *The mayor's office was flooded with mail, including a lot of crank letters.* This expression uses *crank* in the sense of "irrational person."

**crank out** Produce something, especially mechanically or rapidly, as in *I don't know how he can crank out a novel a year.*

**crank up 1.** Get started, as in *The baseball season is cranking up with four exhibition* *games.* This expression transfers the sense of *crank* meaning "operate a motor by turning a crank" to starting any activity. **2.** Cause something to start or grow. For example, *We've got to crank up enthusiasm for this new product.* **3.** Make or become more intense, as in *Crank up the volume on that radio!* or *Close to the election, the campaign really cranked up.*

**cranny** see NOOK AND CRANNY.

**crap** In addition to the idioms beginning with CRAP, also see CUT THE COMEDY (CRAP); FULL OF CRAP.

**crap out 1.** Back down, quit, *When it got to the point of investing his money, Jack crapped out.* **2.** Go to sleep. This usage was military slang for sleeping during work hours or during a game of craps.

**crap up 1.** Burden or clutter something up, as in *They crapped up the look of that building with too many additions in too many different styles.* **2.** Ruin or foul something up, as in *I've really crapped up this speech; can I just start over again?* This idiom uses *crap* in the sense of "defecate." [Vulgar slang]

**crash and burn 1.** Fail completely, as in *Dale crashed and burned three times before passing the bar exam.* This idiom refers to a car or airplane that has crashed and caught fire. **2.** In skateboarding and other sports, be taken out of competition by a collision, accident, or fall, as in *Although she was favored to win the downhill race, she crashed and burned on her first run.*

**crash course** A short, intensive training course, as in *I planned to take a crash course in auto repair before I bought a car.*

**crash the gate** Manage to get in, as to a party or concert, without being invited or without paying. For example, *The concert was outdoors, but heavy security prevented anyone from crashing the gate.* This term first applied to people getting through the gate at sports events without buying tickets. It was extended to entering other gatherings uninvited and led to the noun **gatecrasher** for one who did so.

**craw** see STICK IN ONE'S CRAW.

**crazy** In addition to the idioms beginning with CRAZY, also see DRIVE SOMEONE CRAZY; LIKE CRAZY.

**crazy about, be** Also, **be mad about.** Be extremely fond of or infatuated with somebody or something, as in *I'm crazy about lobster,* or *George is mad about his new girlfriend.*

**crazy like a fox** Seemingly foolish but actually very smart and cunning. For example, *You think Bob was crazy to turn it down? He's crazy like a fox because they've now doubled their salary offer.*

**cream of the crop, the** The best of anything, as in *The apples from this orchard are definitely the cream of the crop.*

**create a scene** see MAKE A SCENE.

**creature comfort** Things that contribute to physical comfort, such as food, clothing, or housing. For example, *Dean always stayed in the best hotels; he valued his creature comforts.*

**credibility gap** Distrust of a public statement or position, as in *The current credibility gap at City Hall is the result of a lack of communication between the mayor's office and the press.* This term originated at a time when the American public no longer believed government statements about the Vietnam War. It soon was extended to individuals and corporations as well as government agencies to express a lack of confidence in the truth of their statements, or a discrepancy between words and actions.

**credit** see DO SOMEONE PROUD (DO CREDIT TO SOMEONE); EXTEND CREDIT TO; GET CREDIT FOR; GIVE SOMEONE CREDIT (GIVE CREDIT WHERE CREDIT IS DUE).

**creek** see UP A CREEK.

**creep** In addition to the idioms beginning with CREEP, also see MAKE ONE'S FLESH CREEP; THE CREEPS.

**creep in** Enter slowly or gradually, as in *She crept in the house because it was late and she didn't want to wake her parents,* or *If I try to do the accounts when I'm too tired, mistakes creep in.*

**creep up** Also, **creep up on.** Approach someone or something slowly or secretly, as in *Her skirt kept creeping up,* or *The cat crept up on the bird,* or *Autumn is creeping up on us.*

**cricket** see NOT CRICKET.

**crime does not pay** Lawbreakers do not benefit from their actions. For example, *He cheated on his taxes, but they caught him, and he's learned the hard way that crime does not pay.* This saying began as a slogan of the FBI.

**crisp** see BURN SOMETHING TO A CRISP.

**crocodile tears** A false show of grief, as in *When the star of the play broke her leg, the understudy who replaced her wept crocodile tears.* This term comes from the mistaken idea that crocodiles cry while eating their prey.

**crook** In addition to the idiom beginning with CROOK, also see BY HOOK OR CROOK.

**crook one's elbow** Also, **bend one's elbow.** Drink liquor, especially a great deal. For example, *Bill will crook his elbow now and then,* or *Uncle Joe overdoes it with bending his elbow.* Both slang expressions refer to the motion of lifting a drink to one's lips, which involves bending the elbow.

**crop** see CROP UP; CREAM OF THE CROP.

**crop up** Appear unexpectedly or occasionally, as in *One theory that crops up periodically is the influence of sunspots on stock prices,* or *We hope new talent will crop up in the next freshman class.*

C

**cross** In addition to the idioms beginning with CROSS, also see AT CROSS PURPOSES; AT THE CROSSROADS; CAUGHT IN THE MIDDLE (CROSSFIRE); DOT THE I'S AND CROSS THE T'S; DOUBLE CROSS; GET ONE'S WIRES CROSSED.

**cross a bridge when one comes to it** Also, **cross that bridge when one comes to it.** Deal with a situation when, and not before, it happens. For example, *If we can't sell the house—well, we'll cross that bridge when we come to it.*

**cross my heart and hope to die** I swear to the truth of what I say. For example, *I did lock the door—cross my heart and hope to die!* This phrase most likely began as a religious oath based on the sign of the cross.

**cross one's fingers** Also, **keep one's fingers crossed. 1.** Wish for luck by crossing the first two fingers of one hand. For example, *I'm crossing my fingers that I get the job,* or *Keep your fingers crossed that the hurricane goes out to sea.* This superstitious statement probably refers to the much older practice of making the sign of the cross to keep evil away. **2.** Tell a small and harmless lie with one's fingers crossed. For example, *I told Mom I didn't eat any cookies, but I had my fingers crossed.* The statement and practice come from the childish belief that if one keeps one's fingers crossed, one may lie without suffering any later punishment for it.

**cross one's mind** Also, **pass through one's mind.** Suddenly enter one's thoughts, as in *It never crossed my mind that they would refuse our proposal,* or *It passed through her mind that he might have gotten lost.*

**cross over 1.** Change from one field or affiliation to another, as in *He crossed over from the Anglican to the Roman Catholic Church,* or *She's a country and western singer who has crossed over into rock and pop music.* **2.** Also, **cross over to the other side.** Die, as in *It's a year since my grandmother crossed over to the other side.*

**cross someone's path** Meet someone, especially unexpectedly. For example, *John didn't know her name, so he was hoping she would cross his path again soon,* or *She would scream if a snake crossed her path.*

**cross swords** Fight, either with words or physically. For example, *At every policy meeting the two vice presidents crossed swords.*

**cross that bridge when one comes to it** see CROSS A BRIDGE WHEN ONE COMES TO IT.

**cross the Rubicon** Commit to a course of action, make a fateful and final decision. For example, *Once he submitted his resignation, he had crossed the Rubicon.* This phrase refers to Julius Caesar crossing the Rubicon River (between Italy and Gaul) in 49 B.C., thereby starting a war against Pompey and the Roman Senate.

**cross to bear** A burden or trial one must accept, as in *Their grandfather's illness is a cross to bear for the whole family,* or used jokingly, *Mowing that huge lawn once a week is Brad's cross to bear.* This phrase refers to the cross carried by Jesus to his Crucifixion. Today it may be used either seriously or lightly.

**crow** In addition to the idiom beginning with CROW, also see AS THE CROW FLIES; EAT CROW.

**crowd** see FOLLOW THE CROWD; THREE'S A CROWD.

**crown jewels 1.** A prized possession or asset, as in *The software products are the company's crown jewels.* This usage transfers the value of royal jewels to some other object. **2.** Also, **family jewels.** The male genitals, especially the testicles. For example, *She gave the man a hard kick in the family jewels and ran for her life.*

**crow over** Talk loudly about something one is proud of, especially someone's defeat. For example, *In most sports it's considered bad manners to crow over your opponent's loss.*

**crumble** see THAT'S HOW THE BALL BOUNCES (COOKIE CRUMBLES).

**crunch numbers** Perform many calculations or process a large amount of numerical data. For example, *Preparing John's presentation to the Federal Reserve Board required many hours of crunching numbers.* This term began with the computer age. It still applies mostly to the operations of computers.

**crunch time** A period when pressure to succeed is great, often toward the end of a big project. For example, *It's crunch time—we only have two more days to finish.* This term uses *crunch* in the sense of "a critical situation or test."

**crush** see HAVE A CRUSH ON.

**crust** see UPPER CRUST.

**crux of the matter, the** Also, **the heart of the matter.** The basic, central, or critical point of an issue. For example, *In this trial, the bloodstains represent the crux of the matter,* or *We think the second question gets to the heart of the matter.*

**cry** In addition to the idioms beginning with CRY, also see BURST INTO (OUT CRYING); FAR CRY FROM; FOR CRYING OUT LOUD; HUE AND CRY; IN FULL SWING (CRY).

**crying shame, a** An unfortunate situation, as in *It's a crying shame that Bob can't find a job.*

**crying towel** An imaginary towel for wiping the tears of someone who shouldn't feel so sorry for himself or herself. For example, *So you didn't make the first team? Get out the crying towel.* This expression is always used sarcastically.

**cry off** Break or withdraw from a promise or an agreement, as in *We thought we'd bought the car, but the owner cried off at the last minute.*

**cry one's eyes out** Also, **cry one's heart out.** Cry long and hard. For example, *Wendy was so homesick that she was crying her eyes out,* or *At funerals Ruth always cries her heart out.*

**cry on someone's shoulder** Tell one's problems to someone so as to gain sympathy or consolation, as in *When James had a problem at the office, he generally cried on his sister's shoulder.* It is also put as **a shoulder to cry on,** as in *When Mom came home, Jane had a shoulder to cry on.*

**cry out for** Also, **have a crying need for.** Be in great need of, as in *This car is crying out for a good washing,* or *There is a crying need for order in this house.*

**cry over spilt milk, don't** Also, **don't cry over spilled milk** or **no use crying over spilt milk** or **no use crying over spilled milk.** Don't regret what cannot be undone or changed, as in *The papers you wanted went out in last week's trash, so don't cry over spilt milk,* or *There's no use crying over spilled milk—you left the gate open and the dog has run away.*

**crystal ball** A means of predicting the future, as in *So what does your crystal ball say about the coming election?* The term refers to the crystal or glass ball used by fortunetellers.

**crystal clear, be** Also, **be clear as crystal.** Be easy to understand, have a very obvious meaning. For example, *The directions for installing the door are crystal clear,* or *Her intentions are clear as crystal.*

**cry uncle** Also, **say uncle.** Concede defeat, as in *He knows he has lost, but he won't cry uncle,* or *If you say uncle right now, I'll let you go first in the next game.*

**cry wolf** Raise a false alarm, as in *Helen's always crying wolf about attempted break-ins, but the police can never find any evidence.* This term comes from the story of a young shepherd watching sheep. He felt lonely and fearful, so he called for help by shouting "Wolf!" After people came several times and saw no wolf, they ignored his cries when a wolf really did attack his sheep.

**cucumber** see COOL AS A CUCUMBER.

**cudgel one's brains** see RACK ONE'S BRAINS.

**cue** In addition to the idiom beginning with CUE, also see ON CUE; TAKE ONE'S CUE FROM.

**cue *someone* in** Give someone information or instructions, for example, *She said she'd cue us in on their summer plans.* This is a verbal use of the noun *cue* in the sense of "guiding suggestion."

**cuff** see OFF THE CUFF.

**culture shock** A state of confusion and anxiety experienced by someone entering a strange environment. For example, *It's not just feeling tired from the trip—it's the culture shock of being in a new country.* This term was first used by social scientists to describe, for example, the feelings of a person moving from the country to a big city.

**cup** In addition to the idiom beginning with CUP, also see IN ONE'S CUPS.

**cupboard is bare, the** The resources someone is asking for are not available, as in *The schools are asking for a budget increase, but the cupboard is bare.*

**cup of tea, one's** Something that agrees with one's liking or taste. For example, *Quiz shows are just my cup of tea,* or *Baseball is not her cup of tea.*

**cure** see KILL OR CURE; OUNCE OF PREVENTION (IS WORTH A POUND OF CURE); SURE CURE.

**curiosity killed the cat** It's best to mind one's own business. For example, *Don't ask about his business dealings—curiosity killed the cat.*

**curl one's hair** see MAKE ONE'S HAIR STAND ON END (CURL).

**curl up 1.** Sit or lie with the legs drawn up; settle down for sleep in this posture. For example, *I love to curl up with a good book.* **2. curl up and die.** Retreat, fall suddenly, die, as in *At first the horse was ahead but near the end she curled up and died,* or *I'll just curl up and die if he comes here.*

**curry favor** Try to get something from someone by flattery, as in *Edith was famous for currying favor with her teachers.*

**curtain** In addition to the idioms beginning with CURTAIN, also see DRAW THE CURTAIN; RAISE THE CURTAIN; RING DOWN THE CURTAIN.

**curtain raiser** An event that comes just before another bigger, more important event, as in *This limited attack on the chairman is just a curtain raiser for a major campaign to remove him.* This term comes from a short play presented before the main theatrical production.

**curtains for, be** Also, **it's curtains.** Be the end for someone, especially death. For example, *If he hadn't worn a bulletproof vest, it would have been curtains for him,* or *It's curtains if she doesn't finish on time.* This expression refers to the falling curtain in a theater at the end of a performance.

**curve** see THROW A CURVE.

**customer** see UGLY CUSTOMER.

**cut** In addition to the idioms beginning with CUT, also see FISH OR CUT BAIT; HAVE ONE'S

WORK CUT OUT; LIKE A CHICKEN WITH ITS HEAD CUT OFF; MAKE (CUT) A LONG STORY SHORT; UNKINDEST CUT; YOU COULD CUT IT WITH A KNIFE.

**cut above, a** Someone or something that is better than others of the same kind, as in *This book is a cut above his previous one.*

**cut across** Go or pass beyond the usual limits of something, as in *The problem of drug use cuts across class lines.*

**cut a deal** Offer or arrange an agreement or compromise, as in *The President is hoping to cut a trade deal with Japan.* This expression uses *deal* in the sense of "business transaction."

**cut *someone* adrift** Separate someone, dismiss or free. For example, *Anyone who didn't seem completely loyal was cut adrift after the election.* This expression refers to cutting the rope of a floating boat so that it drifts without direction or purpose.

**cut a long story short** see MAKE A LONG STORY SHORT.

**cut and dried** Also, **cut-and-dried. 1.** Already decided and not changeable. For example, *The procedure is not quite cut and dried—there's definitely room for your own ideas.* **2.** Ordinary, routine, as in *He disappointed his listeners by telling the story of the crash in a very cut-and-dried manner.* This expression originally referred to dried herbs, as opposed to fresh, growing herbs.

**cut and paste 1.** Requiring or involving little thought or effort. For example, *The revision was easy, just cut and paste.* This term refers to simple artwork done by small children—cutting out pictures and gluing them to paper. **2.** A computer term used to describe the process of copying text, removing it, and placing it elsewhere. For example, *We can just cut and paste the changes.*

**cut and run** Leave quickly or escape, as in *He wished he could just cut and run.* Also see CUT OUT, def. 7.

**cut a wide swath** Draw a lot of attention, make a big impact, as in *Although he was new to the company, he cut a wide swath.*

**cut back 1.** Shorten something by cutting, as in *It's time we cut back these bushes.* **2.** Reduce or decrease something, as in *We have to cut back production.* Also see CUT TO THE BONE.

**cut both ways** Have a mixed effect, have advantages and disadvantages. For example, *Their solution will cut both ways; it'll take longer but is permanent.* This expression refers to a double-edged sword.

**cut class** Stay away from a class or another required event, as in *If he cuts one more class, he'll fail the course.*

**cut corners 1.** Do something in the easiest or least expensive way. For example, *Cutting corners in production led to a definite loss in product quality.* **2.** Act illegally by not following all the rules. For example, *If the accountant cuts corners, the tax man is sure to find out.* This term refers to rounding a corner as closely as possible in order to shorten the distance traveled and/or save time.

**cut down 1.** Kill, as in *The soldiers were cut down one by one as they crossed the field.* **2.** Also, **cut down on.** Reduce or decrease something, as in *I want to cut down my caffeine intake,* or *We have to cut down on our expenses.* **3. cut *someone* down to size** or **knock *someone* down to size.** Reduce the self-importance of a person who is too proud, as in *He's so arrogant—I wish someone would cut him down to size,* or *She really got knocked down to size when she lost the race after all her boasting.*

**cute as a button** Also, **cute as a bug's ear.** Pretty or attractive in a dainty way, as in *That baby is cute as a button.*

**cut in 1.** Move oneself between others, take a place ahead of one's proper turn. For example, *She was very aggressive, always cutting in when people were waiting in the cafeteria line.* **2.** Also, **cut in on** or **cut into.** Interrupt a conversation. For example, *Before we were done talking, Marion cut into our conversation,* or *I was starting to answer her question when he cut in.* **3.** Also, **cut in on.** Interrupt two people dancing together and take one person's place. For example, *He tapped the man on the shoulder and asked, "May I cut in?"* **4.** Also, **cut someone in on.** Include someone in a profitable business deal or share of the profit, as in *Do you want to be cut in on this deal?* or *We plan to cut you in on this moneymaker.*

**cut into** see CUT IN, def. 2.

**cut it 1.** Also, **cut that.** Stop doing something, as in *I won't stand for that—cut it!* or *If you don't cut that, I'll tell Mom.* Also see CUT IT OUT. **2.** Manage or tolerate something, as in *His job is so stressful, I don't know how he can cut it.* **3.** Be effective, prove satisfactory, as in *That player is getting old and can no longer cut it.* For a synonym, see CUT THE MUSTARD. Also see the following idioms beginning with CUT IT.

**cut it fine** Do something closely with a very slight margin, as in *Tom always cuts it fine, arriving at the airport at the last minute.* This term uses *fine* in the sense of "narrow."

**cut it out** Stop doing something, as in *Cut it out, stop teasing your sister.* Also see CUT IT, def. 1.

**cut loose 1.** Speak or act without control or restraint, as in *He cut loose with a string of curses.* **2.** Leave quickly, as in *Let's cut loose right now.*

**cut no ice** Have no effect, make no impression, as in *That excuse cuts no ice with me.*

**cut off** **1.** Separate someone from others, isolate, as in *With no phone or electricity, we felt cut off from the world.* **2.** Stop something suddenly, as in *He quickly cut off the engine,* or *The TV show was cut off by a news flash about storm warnings.* **3.** Shut something off, discontinue, as in *Their phone service was cut off when they didn't pay the bill,* or *Tom's father threatened to cut off his allowance.* **4.** Also, **cut off without a penny** or **cut off without a cent** or **cut off without a shilling.** Disinherit someone so that person gets nothing after one's death, as in *Grandfather cut him off without a penny.*

**cut off one's nose to spite one's face** Do something against another (out of anger) that really hurts oneself more. For example, *If you stay home because Meg was invited first, you're just cutting off your nose to spite your face.*

**cut off without a penny** see CUT OFF, def. 4.

**cut of someone's jib** A person's general appearance or personality, as in *I don't like the cut of Ben's jib.* In former times the shape of the jib sail often identified a ship's nationality, and so whether it was hostile or friendly. The term is usually used to express like or dislike for someone.

**cut one's losses** Get out of a losing situation to prevent losing any more, as in *They decided to close down the unprofitable branch and cut their losses.* This expression uses *cut* in the sense of "reduce." Also see CUT DOWN, def. 2.

**cut one's teeth on** Also, **cut one's eyeteeth on.** Get one's first experience by doing, or learn early in life, as in *I cut my teeth on sailing in conditions like these,* or *He cut his eyeteeth on magazine editing.* This term refers to the expression **cut teeth,** meaning "have teeth first come through a baby's gums."

**cut out** **1.** Remove something as if by cutting; also, form or shape something as if by cutting or carving. For example, *We're trying to cut fat and sugar out of our diet,* or *The first step is cutting out the dress pattern.* **2.** Replace or take the place of someone, as in *He cut out all her other boyfriends.* **3.** Also, **cut out for.** Suited or fitted by nature for something, as in *Dean's not cut out for a job in sales.* **4.** Also, **cut out for.** Assigned beforehand, already prepared for someone, as in *We have our work cut out for us.* **5.** Block someone from sharing in something, as in *He cut her out of his will.* **6.** Stop something, as in *He cut out the motor,* or *Cut out that noise!* Also see CUT IT OUT. **7.** Leave, especially in a hurry; also, run away. For example, *I'm cutting out right now,* or *At the first hint of a police raid they cut out.* Also see CUT AND RUN.

**cut out of whole cloth** see OUT OF WHOLE CLOTH.

C

**cut short** Interrupt or stop abruptly, as in *The thunderstorm cut short our picnic,* or *She cut me short, saying she'd already heard the story.*

**cut *someone's* throat** **1.** Cause someone's ruin, as in *Joe would cut her throat if she got in his way.* One can also **cut one's own throat,** that is, spoil one's own chances, as in *Alice cut her own throat by her repeated absences.* **2. cut one another's throats.** Engage in destructive competition. For example, *With their price war the two stores were cutting each other's throats.* This usage led to the idiom **cutthroat competition,** meaning vicious competitive practices.

**cut teeth** see CUT ONE'S TEETH ON.

**cut that** see CUT IT, def. 1.

**cut the comedy** Also, **cut the crap.** Stop talking or behaving foolishly, as in *Cut the comedy! We have work to do,* or *It's time you cut the crap and got to work.* The variant of this slang expression is considered rude.

**cut the cord** Stop depending on someone, especially one's parents. For example, *It's time he cut the cord and moved into a place of his own.*

**cut the ground from under** Also, **cut the ground out from under.** Unexpectedly take away one's support from someone. For example, *The city councilors cut the ground from under the mayor when they passed a vote of no confidence.* This phrase refers to removing the solid earth from under someone.

**cut the mustard** Perform satisfactorily, as in *We need a better computer; this one just doesn't cut the mustard.* This expression is often used in a negative way, as in the example.

**cutting edge, at the** Also, **on the cutting edge.** In the forefront, in a position of greatest advantage, importance, or technical knowledge. For example, *In my youth I was at the cutting edge of medical research,* or *Our company is on the cutting edge of software development.* This expression refers to the sharp edge of a knife or some other cutting tool.

**cut to the bone** Severely reduced, as in *During hard economic times, the city budget is cut to the bone.* The phrase *to the bone* means "through the flesh to the inmost part or core." This expression means that everything extra has been cut away so that only bone remains.

**cut to the chase** Get to the point without wasting time, as in *We don't have time to go into that, so let's cut to the chase.* This usage refers to editing (cutting) film so as to get to the exciting chase scene in a movie.

**cut to the quick** Deeply hurt or upset someone, as in *His criticism cut her to the quick.* This phrase uses *the quick* in the sense of a vital or very sensitive part of the body, such as under the fingernails.

**cut up 1.** Divide something into smaller parts, break the continuity of, as in *These meetings have cut up my whole day.* **2.** Severely criticize something, as in *The reviewer cut up the book mercilessly.* **3. be cut up.** Be upset or saddened, as in *I was terribly cut up when she left.* **4.** Behave in a playful or comic way, as in *On the last night of camp the children usually cut up.* **5. cut up rough.** Act in an angry or violent way, as in *After a beer or two the boys began to cut up rough.*

# Dd



**daddy** see BIG DADDY; GRANDDADDY OF THEM ALL; SUGAR DADDY.

**dagger** see LOOK DAGGERS.

**daily bread, one's** The money one needs to live, as in *It won't be easy to earn his daily bread as an artist.*

**daisy** In addition to the idiom beginning with DAISY, also see FRESH AS A DAISY; PUSH UP DAISIES.

**daisy chain** **1.** A series of connected events, activities, or experiences. For example, *The daisy chain of lectures on art history covered the last 200 years.* This term compares something to a string of the flowers linked together. **2.** A series of securities transactions intended to give the impression of active trading so as to drive up the price. For example, *Government investigators found dishonest brokers engaging in daisy chains.*

**dam** see WATER OVER THE DAM.

**damage** In addition to the idioms beginning with DAMAGE, also see DO SOMEONE WRONG (DAMAGE); THE DAMAGE.

**damage control** Measures to minimize or stop loss or harm. For example, *As soon as the story about the senator appeared in the news, his staff worked night and day on damage control.* This term was first used for limiting the effect of an accident on a ship.

**damn** In addition to the idioms beginning with DAMN, also see DO ONE'S BEST (DAMNEDEST); NOT GIVE A DAMN; NOT WORTH A DAMN.

**damned if one does, damned if one doesn't** A situation in which one can't win. For example, *If I invite Aunt Jane, Mother will be angry, and if I don't, I lose Jane's friendship—I'm damned if I do and damned if I don't.* Also see CATCH-22.

**damn well** Also, **damned well.** Certainly, without doubt. For example, *You damn well better improve your grades,* or *I know damned well that he's leaving me out.* The *damn* in this phrase is used mainly an intensifier.

**damn with faint praise** Compliment someone or something so weakly that it amounts to no compliment at all, or even implies disapproval. For example, *The reviewer damned the singer with faint praise, admiring her dress but not mentioning her voice.*

**damper** see PUT A DAMPER ON.

**damsel in distress** A girl or woman in need of help or rescue, as in *Who was the actress that played the damsel in distress?* This expression is now usually used as a joke.

**dance** In addition to the idiom beginning with DANCE, also see SONG AND DANCE.

**dance to another tune** Change one's manner, behavior, or attitude. For example, *He'll be dancing to another tune when he finds out that the board means business.* Also see CHANGE ONE'S TUNE.

**dander** see GET ONE'S BACK (DANDER) UP.

**dandy** see FINE AND DANDY.

**dangerous** see LITTLE KNOWLEDGE IS A DANGEROUS THING; LIVE DANGEROUSLY.

**dare say** see I DARE SAY.

**dark** In addition to the idioms beginning with DARK, also see IN THE DARK; LEAP IN THE DARK; SHOT IN THE DARK; WHISTLE IN THE DARK.

**darken one's door** Come unwanted to one's home, as in *I told him to get out and never darken my door again.* The verb *darken* here refers to casting one's shadow.

**dark horse** A little known, unexpectedly successful entrant in a race, as in *You never can tell—some dark horse may come along and win a Senate seat.* This expression originally referred to an unknown horse winning a race. It soon began to be transferred to political candidates.

**dash off** **1.** Write or sketch in a hurry, as in *I'm just going to dash off a letter.* **2.** Hurry away, leave hastily, as in *He dashed off as though he was being chased.*

**dash one's hopes** Destroy one's plans, disappoint or disillusion someone. For example, *That fall dashed her hopes of a gold medal.* This term uses *dash* in the sense of "destroy," a usage surviving only in this idiom.

**date** In addition to the idiom beginning with DATE, also see BRING UP TO DATE; DOUBLE DATE; MAKE A DATE; OUT OF DATE; TO DATE.

**date rape** Sexual intercourse forced on a person by the victim's date. For example, *Date rape is much more common on college campuses than people used to think.*

**dawn** In addition to the idiom beginning with DAWN, also see CRACK OF DAWN; LIGHT DAWNED.

**dawn on** Also, **dawn upon.** Become clear to someone or understood, as in *It finally dawned on him that they expected him to call them,* or *Around noon it dawned upon me that I had never eaten breakfast.* This expression transfers the beginning of daylight to the beginning of a thought process.

**day** In addition to the idioms beginning with DAY, also see ALL IN A DAY'S WORK; ANY DAY; APPLE A DAY; BAD HAIR DAY; BREAK OF DAY; BY THE DAY; CALL IT A DAY; CARRY THE DAY; DIFFERENT AS NIGHT AND DAY; DOG DAYS; EVERY DOG HAS ITS DAY; FIELD DAY; FOREVER AND A DAY; FROM DAY ONE; GLORY DAYS; GOOD DAY; HAD ITS DAY; HAPPY AS THE DAY IS LONG; HEAVENLY DAYS; IN ALL ONE'S BORN DAYS; IN THE COLD LIGHT OF DAY; IN THIS DAY AND AGE; LATE IN THE DAY; MAKE A DAY OF IT; MAKE ONE'S DAY; NAME THE DAY; NIGHT AND DAY; NOT GIVE SOMEONE THE TIME OF DAY; NOT ONE'S DAY; ONE OF THESE DAYS; ONE OF THOSE DAYS; ORDER OF THE DAY; OTHER DAY; PASS THE TIME (OF DAY); PLAIN AS DAY; RAINY DAY; RED-LETTER DAY; ROME WASN'T BUILT IN A DAY; SAVE THE DAY; SEEN BETTER DAYS; SEE THE LIGHT OF DAY; THAT'LL BE THE DAY; TIME OF DAY; TOMORROW IS ANOTHER DAY.

**day after day** Also, **day in, day out.** For many days, continuously; also, every day. For example, *Day after day the rain spoiled our vacation,* or *Day in, day out, all I ever do is work.*

**day and night** see under NIGHT AND DAY.

**day by day** On each successive day, daily, as in *Day by day he's getting better.*

**day in court, have one's** Have an opportunity to be heard, as in *By asking John for an explanation, the professor showed she was willing to let him have his day in court.* This expression transfers the idea of a hearing in a court of law to more general use.

**day in, day out** see DAY AFTER DAY.

**daylight** see BEAT THE LIVING DAYLIGHTS OUT OF; BEGIN TO SEE DAYLIGHT; BROAD DAYLIGHT; SCARE OUT OF ONE'S WITS (THE LIVING DAYLIGHTS OUT OF).

**daylight robbery** see HIGHWAY ROBBERY.

**day off** A day away from work, school, or a similar obligation; a free day. For example, *Sophie always uses her day off to do her grocery shopping.*

**days are numbered, one's** The usefulness or life of someone or something is nearly ended. For example, *When they announced the layoffs, she knew her days at the company were numbered,* or *My car's days are numbered—the transmission won't last much longer.*

**day to day** Also, **from day to day. 1.** Continuously, without interruption, on a daily basis. For example, *Running this office day to day is not an easy task.* **2. live from day to day.** Be interested only in immediate concerns, without thought for the future. For example, *Jean lives from day to day, planning nothing in advance.* Also see LIVE FOR THE MOMENT.

**dead** In addition to the idioms beginning with DEAD, also see BEAT A DEAD HORSE; CAUGHT DEAD; DROP DEAD; KNOCK DEAD; MORE DEAD THAN ALIVE; OVER MY DEAD BODY; STOP COLD (DEAD); TO WAKE THE DEAD. Also see under DEATH.

**dead ahead** Directly or straight in front of someone, as in *There's the house, dead ahead.*

**dead and buried** Also, **dead and gone.** Long forgotten, no longer in use, as in *That argument is dead and buried,* or *There's no point in bringing up issues that are long dead and gone.* This use of "having died" is usually applied to some issue.

**dead as a doornail** Also, **dead as a dodo.** Totally or definitely dead; also, finished. For example, *The cop announced that the body in the dumpster was dead as a doornail,* or *The plan to build a casino is now dead as a dodo.* **Dead as a dodo** refers to the extinct bird.

**dead beat 1.** Defeated; also, exhausted. For example, *That horse was dead beat before the race even began.* **2.** Also, **deadbeat.** A lazy person; also, one who does not pay debts. For example, *Her housemates discovered that she was a deadbeat and also didn't do her share of the chores,* or *He's a deadbeat; don't count on getting that money back.*

**dead drunk** Completely intoxicated (under the effect of alcohol), as in *I can't remember a thing about last night; I was dead drunk.*

**dead duck, a 1.** A person doomed to failure or death, a hopeless case. For example, *If they can't find a heart to transplant soon, he's a dead duck.* **2.** A useless, worthless, or no longer desirable person or thing. For example, *They didn't interview the outgoing senator; to the press he's a dead duck.*

**dead end 1.** A passage that has no exit, as in *This street's a dead end, so turn back.* **2.** A situation that offers no solution or benefit, allowing no progress to be made. For example, *This job is a dead end; I'll never be able to advance.*

**dead from the neck up** Extremely stupid, as in *That news commentator sounds dead from the neck up.*

**dead heat, a** A contest in which the competitors are equally matched and neither can win, a tie. For example, *The two companies are in a dead heat to get a new personal computer on the market,* or *The race was a dead heat.*

**dead horse** see BEAT A DEAD HORSE.

**dead in one's tracks** see under STOP COLD.

**dead in the water, be** Unable to function or move. For example, *Without an effective leader, our plans for expansion are dead in the water.* This term originally referred to a badly damaged ship.

**dead letter** An unclaimed or undelivered letter that is eventually destroyed or returned to the sender. For example, *She moved without leaving a forwarding address, so her mail ended up in the dead letter office.*

**dead loss 1.** A total loss, as in *The building was not insured, so when it burned, it was a dead loss.* **2.** A worthless person or thing; also, a complete waste of time. For example, *With an injured knee, he's a dead loss to the team,* or *It rained every day, so our week at the beach was a dead loss.*

**dead of, the** The period of greatest intensity of something, such as darkness or cold. For example, *I love looking at catalogs in the dead of winter, when it's below zero outside.*

**dead on one's feet** Also, **dead tired.** Extremely tired, as in *Mom was in the kitchen all day and was dead on her feet,* or *I'd love to go, but I'm dead tired.*

**dead ringer** A person or thing that closely resembles another. For example, *Brian's a dead ringer for his Dad,* or *That red bike is a dead ringer for Mary's.*

**dead set against** Completely opposed to, as in *His parents were dead set against John's taking a year off from college.*

**dead tired** see DEAD ON ONE'S FEET.

**dead to rights** In the act of committing an error or crime, red-handed. For example, *They caught the burglars dead to rights with the jewelry.*

**dead to the world** Sound asleep or unconscious, as in *The alarm clock went off, but Joseph was dead to the world.*

**dead weight** A heavy burden, as in *That police record will be a dead weight on his career.*

**dead wood** People in an organization who are useless or no longer needed. For example, *When management cut jobs, they got rid of some dead wood.*

**deaf** see FALL ON DEAF EARS; STONE DEAF; TURN A DEAF EAR.

**deal** In addition to the idioms beginning with DEAL, also see BIG DEAL; CLOSE THE SALE (DEAL); CUT A DEAL; DONE DEAL; GOOD DEAL; MAKE A FEDERAL CASE (BIG DEAL); RAW DEAL; SQUARE DEAL; SWEETEN THE KITTY (DEAL); WHEEL AND DEAL.

**deal in 1.** Also, **deal with.** Be occupied or concerned with something, as in *He refuses to deal in rumors or guesses,* or *This book deals with idioms.* **2.** Do business or trade in something, as in *They deal in diamonds.* Also see DEAL WITH. **3. deal someone in.** Also, **deal someone a hand.** Include someone, give someone a share, as in *I hope they'll deal me in on this new enterprise.* This usage comes from card games, where *deal* means "distribute cards."

**deal out 1.** Distribute something, as in *He dealt out more and more work.* Also see DEAL IN, def. 3. **2. deal someone out.** Exclude someone, as in *I don't have time for this project, so deal me out.* This usage is the opposite of DEAL IN, def. 3.

**deal with 1.** See DEAL IN, def. 1. **2.** Do business with someone, as in *I like dealing with this company.* Also see DEAL IN, def. 2. **3.** Take action in, handle, or administer something, as in *The committee will deal with this matter.* **4.** Act in a specified way toward someone, as in *He dealt extremely fairly with his competitors.*

D

**dear** In addition to the idiom beginning with DEAR, also see FOR DEAR LIFE; NEAREST AND DEAREST.

**dear me** Also, **oh dear.** A polite exclamation expressing surprise, distress, sympathy, or another emotion. For example, *Dear me, I forgot to mail the letter,* or *Oh dear, what a bad time you've been having.* These usages may originally have called on God, as in **dear God** or **oh God,** which also continue to be so used.

**death** In addition to the idioms beginning with DEATH, also see AT DEATH'S DOOR; BE THE DEATH OF; BORE TO DEATH; CATCH COLD (ONE'S DEATH); FATE WORSE THAN DEATH; IN AT THE DEATH; KISS OF DEATH; LOOK LIKE DEATH; MATTER OF LIFE AND DEATH; PUT TO DEATH; SCARE OUT OF ONE'S WITS (TO DEATH); SIGN ONE'S OWN DEATH WARRANT; SUDDEN DEATH; THRILL TO PIECES (TO DEATH); TICKLED PINK (TO DEATH); TO DEATH. Also see under DEAD.

**death and taxes, certain as** Also, **sure as death and taxes.** Sure to happen, inevitable, as in *His business is going to fail, certain as death and taxes.* This phrase was coined by Benjamin Franklin.

**death knell** Something that shows the end or failure of something will soon come. For example, *His low scores sounded the death knell for his ambitions.* The noun *knell,* referring to the ringing of a bell, is rarely heard today.

**death of** see BE THE DEATH OF.

**deck** In addition to the idiom beginning with DECK, also see CLEAR THE DECKS; HIT THE DECK; ON DECK.

**deck out** Decorate something or dress someone up, as in *They were all decked out in their best clothes.*

**declare war on** Also, **declare war against.** Announce one's intent or plan to put an end to something or someone. For example, *The police have declared war on drug dealing in the neighborhood,* or *Several gangs have declared war against each other.*

**deep** In addition to the idioms beginning with DEEP, also see BEAUTY IS ONLY SKIN DEEP;

BETWEEN A ROCK AND A HARD PLACE (THE DEVIL AND THE DEEP BLUE SEA); GO OFF THE DEEP END; IN DEEP; STILL WATERS RUN DEEP.

**deep down** At bottom, basically. For example, *Although he would never admit it, deep down he was very fond of her.*

**deep end** see GO OFF THE DEEP END.

D

**deep pockets** A source of wealth or financial support, as in *The college relies on the deep pockets of one particular alumna.* This term refers to money-filled pockets.

**deep six 1.** Burial at sea (by putting a body overboard). For example, *When our boat hit the rocks, I was sure we'd get the deep six.* This expression refers to the customary six-foot depth of most graves. **2.** The act of rejecting or getting rid of something, as in *They gave the new plan the deep six.* This usage comes from the slang for tossing something overboard (see def. 1). It was later transferred to more general kinds of disposal and led to the verb **deep-six,** for "throw away."

**deep water** see IN DEEP, def. 2.

**defensive** see ON THE DEFENSIVE.

**defiance** see IN DEFIANCE OF.

**degree** see BY DEGREES; THIRD DEGREE; TO SOME DEGREE; TO THE NTH DEGREE.

**deliver** In addition to the idiom beginning with DELIVER, also see SIGNED, SEALED, AND DELIVERED.

**deliver the goods** Do what is required, meet expectations. For example, *Kate delivered the goods and got us the five votes we needed.* This phrase refers to delivering an order of groceries or other items.

**delusions of grandeur** Mistaken beliefs in one's own importance or power. For example, *He has developed delusions of grandeur since he was elected.*

**demand** see IN DEMAND; MAKE DEMANDS ON; ON DEMAND.

**dent** see MAKE A DENT IN.

**depth** see IN DEPTH; OUT OF ONE'S DEPTH.

**description** see BEGGAR DESCRIPTION.

**desert** In addition to the idiom beginning with DESERT, also see JUST DESERTS.

**desert a sinking ship** Abandon something that is failing before it is too late. For example, *After seeing the company's financial statement, he knew it was time to desert a sinking ship.* This negative expression refers to rats, which leave a vessel when it sinks so as to escape drowning.

**deserve** see ONE GOOD TURN DESERVES ANOTHER.

**design** see BY DESIGN; HAVE DESIGNS ON.

**desire** see LEAVE A LOT TO BE DESIRED.

**desist** see CEASE AND DESIST.

**detail** see IN DETAIL.

**determine** see BOUND AND DETERMINED.

**device** see LEAVE TO ONE'S OWN DEVICES.

**devil** In addition to the idioms beginning with DEVIL, also see BETWEEN A ROCK AND A HARD PLACE (THE DEVIL AND THE DEEP BLUE SEA); FULL OF IT (THE DEVIL); GIVE SOMEONE HELL (THE DEVIL); GIVE THE DEVIL HIS DUE; GO TO HELL (THE DEVIL); LUCK OF THE DEVIL; RAISE CAIN (THE DEVIL); SPEAK OF THE DEVIL.

**devil and the deep blue sea** see BETWEEN A ROCK AND A HARD PLACE.

**devil-may-care 1.** Not caring about danger, reckless, as in *The driver's devil-may-care attitude worried his passengers.* **2.** Cheerful and dashing in style, as in *I envied his devil-may-care approach to life.*

**devil of a** Also, **one devil of a** or **the devil of a; one hell of a.** Extremely annoying or difficult, as in *This is a devil of a job,* or *She had one devil of a time getting through the traffic,* or *I had one hell of a morning sitting in that doctor's office.* Also see HELL OF A, def. 2.

**devil's advocate** One who argues against a cause or position either for the sake of argument or to help determine the truth of it. For example, *The teacher played devil's advocate with the class to get them to think hard about their political beliefs.*

**devil take the hindmost, the** Let everyone put his or her own interest first, not caring about what happens to others. For example, *I don't care if she makes it or not—the devil take the hindmost.* This expression probably referred to a children's game in which the last child (coming "hindmost") is the loser.

**devil to pay, the** Serious trouble resulting from some action, as in *There'll be the devil to pay if you let that dog out.* This expression originally referred to trouble resulting from making a bargain with the devil.

**diamond in the rough, a** Also, **a rough diamond.** A person of great character or potential but without good social skills or a smooth manner. For example, *Jack is intelligent and trustworthy but lacks manners—he's a diamond in the rough.*

**dibs** see HAVE DIBS ON.

**dice** see LOAD THE DICE; NO DICE.

**dice are loaded, the** see under LOAD THE DICE.

**Dick** see EVERY TOM, DICK, AND HARRY.

**die** In addition to the idioms beginning with DIE, also see CURL UP (AND DIE); DO OR DIE; IT'S TO DIE; NEVER SAY DIE.

**die away** Also, **die down.** Gradually become less or fade, slowly come to an end. For example, *As we watched them move higher up the mountain, their voices died away,* or *The rain seems to be dying down.* The first term today is most often applied to a diminishing sound. It was originally used to describe the wind slowing down or ceasing to blow.

**die down** see DIE AWAY.

**die for** Also, **be dying for.** Long for, have an extreme desire for, as in *I'm dying for some ice cream.* Also see DYING TO.

**die hard** Take a long time to end or be forgotten. For example, *Old prejudices die hard,* or *The board of directors voted down the proposal, but it will die hard among the members.* This idiom refers to struggling against physical death. The related noun **die-hard** or **diehard** means a person who stubbornly resists change or refuses to quit a hopeless cause. For example, *Everyone in the office uses e-mail now, except for a few die-hards.*

**die in harness** see DIE WITH ONE'S BOOTS ON.

**die is cast, the** The decision or course of action has been determined and cannot be changed. For example, *Now that I've announced my resignation, the die is cast.*

**die laughing** Feel very great amusement, as in *When his pants fell down, I thought I'd die laughing.* Also see SPLIT ONE'S SIDES.

**die off** Die one by one, as in *My grandmother's friends seem to be dying off.*

**die out** Gradually become extinct, as in *As modern culture spreads, many traditions are dying out.*

**die with one's boots on** Also, **die in harness.** Die while working, keep working to the end, as in *He'll never retire—he'll die with his boots on,* or *She knows she'll never get promoted, but she wants to die in harness.*

**differ** see AGREE TO DIFFER; BEG TO DIFFER. Also see under DIFFERENCE; DIFFERENT.

**difference** see MAKE A DIFFERENCE; SAME DIFFERENCE; SPLIT THE DIFFERENCE. Also see under DIFFERENT.

**different** In addition to the idioms beginning with DIFFERENT, also see CHANGE ONE'S (SING A DIFFERENT) TUNE; HORSE OF A DIFFERENT COLOR; (A DIFFERENT) KETTLE OF FISH; MARCH TO A DIFFERENT BEAT; WEAR ANOTHER (A DIFFERENT) HAT.

**different as night and day** Also, **different as day and night.** Totally unlike. For example, *Although they are sisters, they are as different as night and day.* Also see NIGHT AND DAY.

**different strokes for different folks** see under NO ACCOUNTING FOR TASTES.

**dig down 1.** Pay with money from one's own pocket, especially with difficulty. For example, *We've got to dig down deep to make the next payment.* **2.** Also, **dig deep.** Be generous, as in *Please dig deep when you make your donation.*

**dig in 1.** Prepare to defend oneself in battle and hold one's position, as in *The battalion dug in and held on.* This usage gained currency in the trench warfare of World War I. **2.** Also, **dig in one's heels.** Adopt a firm position without any willingness to change. For example, *Arthur refused to argue the point and simply dug in,* or *The dog dug in its heels and refused to move.* **3.** Begin to work intensively, as in *If we all dig in it'll be done before dark.* **4.** Also, **dig into.** Begin to eat heartily, as in *Even before all the food was on the table, they began to dig in,* or *When the bell rang, the kids all dug into their lunches.*

**dig one's own grave** Seriously harm oneself, cause one's own ruin or downfall. For example, *If he continues the way he's behaving at work, he'll be digging his own grave.*

**dig out 1.** Remove something from its surroundings, as in *He dug his car out of the snow.* **2.** Find something by searching for it, as in *He dug out his first contract from the file.*

**dig up 1.** Search out, find, or manage to get something, as in *I'm sure I can dig up a few more supporters.* **2. dig up some dirt** or **dig up the dirt.** Find embarrassing or negative information about someone or something. For example, *The editor assigned him to dig up all the dirt on the candidates.* The noun *dirt* here is slang for "embarrassing or scandalous information."

**dilemma** see HORNS OF A DILEMMA.

**dim** see TAKE A DIM VIEW.

**dime** In addition to the idiom beginning with DIME, also see DROP A DIME; NOT WORTH A DAMN (DIME); ON A DIME.

**dime a dozen, a** So plentiful or common as to be valueless. For example, *Don't bother to buy one of these—they're a dime a dozen.* The dime referred to is the American ten-cent coin.

**dine** see EAT (DINE) OUT; WINE AND DINE.

**dint** see BY DINT OF.

**dip into 1.** Explore or read about a subject briefly, as in *He began to dip into poetry,* or *She's just dipping into psychology.* This expression refers to plunging something briefly into a liquid. **2.** Take or use a small amount of something, usually money, as in *I'll have to dip into my savings.* This term uses *dip into* in the sense of plunging one's hand into a pot of water, for example, for the purpose of taking something out.

**dip one's toes into** Also, **get one's toes into** or **get one's toes wet.** Begin to do something unusual or unfamiliar, as in *I have been dipping my toes into Asian cooking,* or *She's eager to go to Europe and has been getting her toes wet by sending for travel information.* Also see GET ONE'S FEET WET.

**direction** see STEP IN THE RIGHT DIRECTION.

**dirt** In addition to the idiom beginning with DIRT, also see DIG UP (DIRT); DISH THE DIRT; HIT

THE DECK (DIRT); PAY DIRT; TREAT LIKE DIRT. Also see under DIRTY.

**dirt cheap** Very inexpensive, as in *Their house was a real bargain, dirt cheap.*

**dirty** In addition to the idioms beginning with DIRTY, also see DOWN AND DIRTY; WASH ONE'S DIRTY LINEN IN PUBLIC.

D

**dirty joke** A story about sex that is intended to be funny and is usually offensive, as in *Those boys love to tell dirty jokes. Dirty* is used here in the sense of "morally offensive" or "indecent." The same sense also appears in such expressions as **dirty book,** for a pornographic book; **dirty old man,** for a middle-aged or older man with a constant interest in sex; and **dirty word** or **talk dirty,** for an offensive expression or talk about sex.

**dirty look, give *someone* a** Look at someone in an angry or disapproving way. For example, *When I asked about the money he owed, he gave me a really dirty look.* This expression has largely replaced the earlier and more formal **black look.**

**dirty one's hands** Also, **get one's hands dirty** or **soil one's hands. 1.** Do something shameful or illegal. For example, *He refused to dirty his hands and give jobs to the people who'd given money to his campaign,* or *She would not soil her hands by cheating.* **2.** Perform manual labor, as in *She's always afraid to dirty her hands.* This phrase is used in a negative way.

**dirty tricks** Secret operations and dishonest acts in politics and espionage. For example, *This campaign has been dominated by the dirty tricks of both political parties.* The adjective *dirty* here is used in the sense of "unfair." The term originally referred to secret operations by the CIA (Central Intelligence Agency). It later was extended to illegal activity against opponents in politics or business.

**dirty work** An unpleasant or thankless task or job. For example, *Jane complained that she had to do all the dirty work while her colleagues took long vacations.*

**discount** see AT A DISCOUNT.

**discretion** In addition to the idiom beginning with DISCRETION, also see THROW CAUTION (DISCRETION) TO THE WINDS.

**discretion is the better part of valor** It is better to be careful than do something brave but risky, as in *I'm signing up for the easy course first; discretion is the better part of valor.*

**disguise** see BLESSING IN DISGUISE.

**dish** In addition to the idioms beginning with DISH, also see DO THE DISHES.

**dish out 1.** Deal or give something out, as in *He dishes out advice to one and all.* This expression refers to serving food from a dish. **2. dish it out.** Freely give out criticism or punishment, as in *He can dish it out with the best of them, but he can't take it.*

**dish the dirt** Spread gossip or scandal, as in *Be careful what you tell her—she loves to dish the dirt.*

**dishwater** see DULL AS DISHWATER.

**dispense with 1.** Manage without something that may be usual or desirable, as in *We can dispense with the extra help.* **2.** Get rid of something unwanted, as in *Let's dispense with these foolish arguments and get the job done!*

**disposal** see PUT AT SOMEONE'S DISPOSAL.

**dispose of 1.** Attend to, settle, or deal with something, as in *He quickly disposed of the problem.* **2.** Transfer responsibility for or ownership of something, as by giving away or selling. For example, *They wanted to dispose of the land as soon as possible.* **3.** Get rid of or throw out something, as in *Can we dispose of the trash in this barrel?* **4.** Kill or destroy. For example, *The king was determined to dispose of his enemies.*

**dispute** see IN DISPUTE.

**distance** see GO THE DISTANCE; KEEP ONE'S DISTANCE; SPITTING DISTANCE.

**ditch** see LAST-DITCH EFFORT.

**divide and conquer** Win by getting one's opponents to fight among themselves. For example, *Management hoped to divide and conquer, but the striking union members stuck together.*

**do** In addition to the idioms beginning with DO, also see CAN'T DO ANYTHING WITH; COULD DO WITH; HAVE NOTHING TO DO WITH; HAVE TO DO WITH; HOW DO YOU DO?; LEFT HAND DOESN'T KNOW WHAT THE RIGHT HAND IS DOING; MAKE DO; NO CAN DO; NOTHING DOING; TAKE DOING; THAT WILL DO; UP AND ABOUT (DOING). Also see under DOES; DONE; DON'T.

**do a disappearing act** Vanish, as in *As soon as the teacher came outside, Mary did a disappearing act.* This expression describes a sudden disappearance, as if by a magician's performance.

**do a double take** see DOUBLE TAKE.

**do a job on** Also, **do a number on.** Damage or harm someone or something, as in *The cat really did a job on the upholstery,* or *The teacher did a number on the class with that assignment.*

**do an about-face** Also, **do a flip-flop** or **do a one-eighty.** Reverse one's opinion or course of action. For example, *The board did an about-face after learning all the facts of the matter,* or *We expected Dad to do a flip-flop concerning our vacation plans,* or *They had relied on Jim for the plan, but he did a one-eighty and voted against it.* The first term refers to the army command to turn around. The last term refers to a 180-degree change of direction.

**do any good** Improve a situation or cause a favorable result, as in *Tell me if this new medicine does any good.* A negative version is **do no good;** for example, *All his explanations will do no good.*

**do as I say** Obey my instructions, as in *Never mind about the other mothers—you do as I say.* A related saying is **do as I say, not as I do.** This means "don't imitate my behavior—I don't always do the right thing—but obey my instructions."

**do away with** **1.** Make an end of something. For example, *The class wanted to do away with homework.* **2.** Destroy or kill someone or something, as in *The animal officer did away with the injured deer lying by the side of the road.*

**do *something* blindfolded** Also, **do *something* standing on one's head.** Perform something very easily, as in *Dave said he could do the income tax return blindfolded,* or *He could fix just about anything standing on his head.* Also see WITH ONE ARM TIED BEHIND ONE'S BACK.

**do credit to** see DO SOMEONE PROUD, def. 1.

**doctor** see APPLE A DAY (KEEPS THE DOCTOR AWAY); JUST WHAT THE DOCTOR ORDERED; SPIN DOCTOR.

**dodo** see DEAD AS A DOORNAIL.

**does, doesn't** see EASY DOES IT; HANDSOME IS AS HANDSOME DOES; LEFT HAND DOESN'T KNOW WHAT THE RIGHT HAND IS DOING; THAT DOES IT.

**dog** In addition to the idioms beginning with DOG, also see COON'S (DOG'S) AGE; EVERY DOG HAS ITS DAY; GO TO POT (THE DOGS); HAIR OF THE DOG; HANGDOG LOOK; HOT DOG; IN THE DOGHOUSE; LET SLEEPING DOGS LIE; PUT ON THE DOG; RAIN CATS AND DOGS; SEE A MAN ABOUT A DOG; SHAGGY-DOG STORY; SICK AS A DOG; TAIL WAGGING THE DOG; TEACH AN OLD DOG NEW TRICKS; THROW SOMEONE TO THE WOLVES (DOGS); TOP BANANA (DOG).

**dog-and-pony show** A special presentation to impress people and gain approval for a product or policy. For example, *I wish the administration would skip the dog-and-pony show and just give us the facts.* This term refers to a traveling variety show.

**dog days** Hot, humid summer weather; also, a period of no activity. For example, *It's hard to get much work done during the dog days,* or *Every winter there's a week or two of dog days when sales drop dramatically.* The term refers to the period between early July and early September, when Sirius, the Dog Star, rises and sets with the sun.

**dog eat dog** Hard competition with no concern for anything but success, as in *With shrinking markets, it's dog eat dog for every company in this field.*

**doghouse** see IN THE DOGHOUSE.

**dog in the manger** A selfish person who prevents others from enjoying something despite having no use for it. For example, *Why be a dog in the manger? If you aren't going to use those tickets, let someone else have them.* This expression refers to Aesop's fable about a snarling dog that prevents horses from eating hay that the dog itself doesn't want.

**dog it** **1.** Do less than is required, make little effort. For example, *I'm afraid our donors are dogging it this year.* **2.** Move slowly, as in *We just dogged it along from California to Oregon.* **3.** Run away, as in *Let's dog it out of here right now.*

**do good** Act in an upright, moral way; help people in need. For example, *Social workers are trained to help people to help themselves, not simply go around doing good.* Also see DO ANY GOOD; DO ONE GOOD.

**dog's age** see COON'S AGE.

**dog's life** A miserably unhappy existence, as in *He's been leading a dog's life since his wife left him.*

**do *someone* in** **1.** Tire someone out, as in *Running errands all day did me in.* Also see DONE IN. **2.** Kill someone, possibly oneself, as in *She was always threatening to do herself in.* **3.** Ruin someone completely; also, cheat someone out of something. For example, *The five-alarm fire did in the whole block,* or *His so-called friend really did him in.*

**do justice to** **1.** Treat someone or something fairly or adequately, with full appreciation, as in *That review doesn't do the play justice.* **2. do oneself justice.** Perform so as to show all one's abilities, as in *She finally got a position in which she could do herself justice.*

**doldrums** see IN THE DOLDRUMS.

**dollar** In addition to the idiom beginning with DOLLAR, also see LOOK LIKE A MILLION DOLLARS; YOU BET (YOUR BOTTOM DOLLAR).

**dollars to doughnuts, it's** It's a sure bet, as in *It's dollars to doughnuts that the team will make the playoffs.*

**dolled up** Also, **all dolled up.** Dressed in one's best clothes, usually for a special occasion. For example, *There's no need to get all dolled up—it's just a picnic.* This expression refers to a person being as attractive as a pretty doll. Also see GUSSIED UP.

**done** In addition to the idioms beginning with DONE, also see EASIER SAID THAN DONE; GOOD AS DONE; HAVE DONE (WITH); NO SOONER SAID THAN DONE; NOT DONE; OVER AND DONE WITH; SEEN ONE, SEEN THEM ALL (BEEN THERE, DONE THAT); WHAT'S DONE IS DONE; WHEN ALL'S SAID AND DONE. Also see under DO.

**done deal** An agreement that cannot be changed or undone, as in *Once you've signed the lease, it's a done deal.*

**done for 1.** Exhausted, worn out, as in *This old computer is just about done for.* Also see DONE IN. **2.** Sure to meet death or destruction, as in *Before he went to the hospital, it seemed as if he was done for.*

D

**done in** Exhausted, very tired, as in *After that hike I felt absolutely done in.* Also see DONE FOR, def. 1.

**done to a T** see TO A T.

**donkey's years** A long time, as in *I haven't seen her in donkey's years.* This expression is a pun that refers to the length of the animal's ears.

**do no good** see under DO ANY GOOD.

**don't ask** A phrase used to avoid answering questions about an awkward, unpleasant, or unsatisfactory situation. For example, *How did we do in the game? Don't ask!*

**don't change horses at midstream** see CHANGE HORSES IN MIDSTREAM.

**don't cross that bridge till you come to it** see CROSS A BRIDGE WHEN ONE COMES TO IT.

**don't hold your breath** see HOLD ONE'S BREATH.

**don't mention it** see under YOU'RE WELCOME.

**do one** In addition to the idioms beginning with DO ONE, also see under DO SOMEONE.

**do one good 1.** Benefit or make someone feel better, as in *I'm sure some fresh air will do her good.* **2.** Also, **do one's heart good.** Please or give satisfaction to someone. For example, *It does my heart good to see the young couple so happy.*

**do one's best** Also, **do one's level best** or **do one's damnedest.** Perform as well as one can, try as hard as possible, as in *I'm doing my best to balance this bank statement,* or *She did her level best to pass the course,* or *He did his damnedest to finish in time.*

**do one's duty 1.** Do one's tasks or what is expected of one. For example, *He was only doing his duty when he made the children finish their work.* **2.** Defecate or urinate, pass wastes out of the body. For example, *Please keep the dog outdoors until it does its duty.*

**do one's heart good** see DO ONE GOOD.

**do one's homework** Prepare well for something, as in *Steve had done his homework before the meeting and could answer all of the client's questions.* This usage transfers a school assignment to a broader context.

**do one's part** Also, **do one's bit.** Make an individual contribution to an overall effort. For example, *Each player on the team must do her part,* or *I'm anxious to do my bit as a board member.*

**do one's thing** Also, **do one's own thing.** Follow one's interests or desires; do what one does best or enjoys the most. For example, *That artist just does his thing and doesn't care what the critics say,* or *Phyllis isn't interested in a traditional career—she is busy doing her own thing.*

**door** see AT DEATH'S DOOR; AT ONE'S DOOR; BACK DOOR; BEAT A PATH TO SOMEONE'S DOOR; BEHIND CLOSED DOORS; CLOSE THE DOOR ON; DARKEN ONE'S DOOR; FOOT IN THE DOOR; KEEP THE WOLF FROM THE DOOR; LAY SOMETHING AT SOMEONE'S DOOR; LEAVE THE DOOR OPEN; LOCK THE BARN DOOR; NEXT DOOR TO; OPEN DOORS; OPEN THE DOOR TO; SEE OUT (SOMEONE TO THE DOOR); SHOW SOMEONE THE DOOR.

**do or die** Make a supreme effort because the danger of failure is near, as in *Jonathan was going to set up the computer, do or die.*

**doornail** see DEAD AS A DOORNAIL.

**doorstep** see under AT ONE'S DOOR (ON ONE'S DOORSTEP).

**door to door 1.** Calling at each house, apartment, store, etc., in an area, in order to deliver, sell, or ask for something. For example, *We went door to door to collect enough voters' signatures.* **2.** Sent from a place of origin or pickup to a place of delivery. For example, *They quoted me a price for door to door, as well as a lower one if I would pick up the furniture myself.* This usage is nearly always applied to a shipment of merchandise.

**do *someone* out of** Cheat or deprive someone of something. For example, *Jane tried to do me out of my share.*

**do over** Also, **do something over. 1.** Also, **do over again.** Repeat something, as in *I did the problem wrong; I'll have to do it over.* **2.** Redecorate a place, as in *We've decided to do over the living room.*

**dope out** Work out or figure out something, as in *I've been trying to dope out this new computer program.*

**dope up** Treat a person or animal with strong drugs. For example, *He was doped up for the operation.*

**do's and don'ts** Rules or customs concerning some activity, as in *It's important to know the do's and don'ts of diplomatic receptions.* This expression refers to what one should and should not do or say.

**dose of one's own medicine, a** Also, **a taste of one's own medicine.** Giving someone the same bad treatment he or she has given others. For example, *It's time we give them a dose of their own medicine and simply not call them back,* or *Joe was upset at their criticism, but they were just giving him a taste of his own medicine.*

**do someone** In addition to the idioms beginning with DO SOMEONE, also see under DO ONE.

**do someone proud** **1.** Also, **do credit to someone.** Be a source of honor, distinction, or pride for someone. For example, *She did us proud, handling the problem with such calm,* or *Your new title does you credit.* **2.** Treat someone or oneself generously, as in *You really did us proud with that banquet.*

**do someone wrong** Also, **do someone damage** or **do someone harm.** Hurt someone by being unfaithful or disloyal; act unjustly or unfairly toward someone. For example, *John's done her wrong, and I intend to tell him so,* or *She did him real damage when she started that rumor.* Also in use are the verbal phrases **wrong someone, harm someone,** and **damage someone.**

**do something over** see DO OVER.

**dot** In addition to the idiom beginning with DOT, also see ON THE DOT; SIGN ON THE DOTTED LINE.

**do tell** A phrase used to express surprise about something, as in *Jane's getting married again? Do tell.* This expression does not necessarily ask the speaker to provide more details but merely expresses one's surprise. For a synonym, see YOU DON'T SAY.

**do the dishes** Wash the plates, glasses, and silverware used at a meal. For example, *If you walk the dog, I'll do the dishes.*

**do the honors** Act as a host or hostess, performing introductions, pouring drinks, and otherwise attending to guests. For example, *At home Mary leaves it to Bill to do the honors when they have guests.*

**do the legwork** Do the work to prepare for a project, such as collecting information, usually with walking or traveling required. For example, *I count on my assistant to get out and do the legwork.*

**do the trick** Also, **turn the trick.** Bring about a desired result. For example, *One more nail should do the trick,* or *Bill wanted to finish all the errands in one day, but he couldn't quite turn the trick.* The second expression should not be confused with TURN A TRICK.

**do time** Serve a prison sentence, as in *Many of the gang members did time while they were still teenagers.*

**dot the i's and cross the t's** Be very careful and precise with details, as in *We have a general agreement about the contract, but we haven't yet dotted all the i's and crossed the t's.*

**double** In addition to the idioms beginning with DOUBLE, also see LEAD A DOUBLE LIFE; ON THE DOUBLE; SEE DOUBLE.

**double back** Also, **double back on someone.** Change direction and go back the way one has come, especially to escape someone. For example, *The officer lost the suspect, who had doubled back on him.*

**double bill** see DOUBLE FEATURE.

**double cross** A deliberate breaking of a promise, especially so as to cheat someone. For example, *Two of the robbers planned a double cross, intending to keep all of the money for themselves.* This term began with sports gambling. It referred to the action of a contestant who promises to lose but then wins. A variant is the verb **double-cross,** as in *We learned she was planning to double-cross us and take all the credit for herself.*

**double date** A date in which two couples go together, as in *They went on a double date to the movies with her brother and his girlfriend.*

**double Dutch** A game of jump rope in which players jump over two ropes swung in a crisscross fashion.

**double duty, do** Perform or fulfill two different functions, as in *Our pickup truck does double duty; it is used for the business and for family outings.*

**double feature** Also, **double bill.** A program of two full-length films shown for the price of a single ticket. For example, *It was a double feature and lasted five hours.* This expression is occasionally used for other paired events, as in *The women's conference had a double bill, first speakers from China and then visiting guests from the rest of the world.*

**double life** see LEAD A DOUBLE LIFE.

**doublespeak** see DOUBLE TALK, def. 2.

**double standard** **1.** A set of principles that unfairly treats one group more severely than another. For example, *He says that athletes at the school can break rules but not get into trouble for it, while other students do—there's a double standard.* **2.** Rules allowing men more sexual freedom than women. For example, *She complained that her father had a double standard—her brothers were allowed to date, but she was not, even though she was older.*

**double take, do a** Show a reaction to an unusual remark or circumstance after a short delay due to surprise. For example, *He did a double take when his ex-wife appeared at his wedding.*

**double talk** **1.** Meaningless speech mixing real and invented words. For example, *Some popular songs are actually based on double talk.* **2.** Also, **doublespeak.** Deliberately unclear and evasive language. For example, *I got tired of her double talk and demanded to know the true story,* or *His lawyer was very good at doublespeak.*

D

**double up** **1.** Bend over suddenly, as in pain or laughter. For example, *She doubled up with a cramp.* **2.** Share space meant for one person, as in *The hotel ran out of rooms, so we had to double up.*

**doubt** see BEYOND A DOUBT; CAST DOUBT ON; GIVE THE BENEFIT OF THE DOUBT; NO DOUBT.

**doubting Thomas** A person who is always doubtful. For example, *He was a doubting Thomas about the coming merger, not believing it would ever happen.* The term refers to the disciple Thomas, who doubted Jesus's resurrection until he had firsthand evidence of it.

**do unto others as you would have them do unto you** Behave toward other people as you would like them to behave toward you, as in *Of course I'll help him out; it's a case of do unto others, and I may be in the same situation one day.* This so-called **golden rule** is in just about every ancient writing about rules for behavior. It is so well known that it is often shortened.

**do up** **1.** Fasten or tie up something. For example, *Let's do up all the gifts in matching paper,* or *Please help me do up the collar button.* **2.** Make something or someone look nice or neat, as in *Jane did up her hair for the dance,* or *The children were all done up in their best outfits.*

**do well** **1.** Succeed or make steady progress, as in *He's done well in the stock market.* **2. do well to do something.** Have a better result or act wisely by doing something, as in *She would do well to ask permission before she leaves.*

**do well by** Behave toward or treat well, as in *John was determined to do well by his children.*

**do with** Survive or manage with, as in *They seem to do with very little sleep.* Also see COULD DO WITH; HAVE TO DO WITH; MAKE DO (WITH).

**do without** Manage in spite of being without something. For example, *They will just have to do without a vacation this year,* or *There was no telephone in the cabin, but we soon learned to do without.*

**down** In addition to the idioms beginning with DOWN, also see BACK DOWN; BATTEN DOWN THE HATCHES; BEAR DOWN; BEAT DOWN; BE DOWN; BELT DOWN; BOG DOWN; BOIL DOWN; BREAK DOWN; BREATHE DOWN SOMEONE'S NECK; BRING DOWN; BRING DOWN THE HOUSE; BUCKLE DOWN; BURN DOWN; CALL DOWN; CAST DOWN; CAUGHT WITH ONE'S PANTS DOWN; CHOW DOWN; CLAMP DOWN ON; CLOSE DOWN; COME DOWN; COME DOWN ON; COME DOWN THE PIKE; COME DOWN TO; COME DOWN WITH; COOL DOWN; COUNT DOWN; CRACK DOWN; CUT DOWN; DEEP DOWN; DIE AWAY (DOWN); DIG DOWN; DRAW DOWN; DRESS DOWN; FACE DOWN; FALL DOWN; FLAG DOWN; GET DOWN TO BRASS TACKS; GO DOWN; GO DOWNHILL; GO DOWN THE DRAIN; HAND DOWN; HANDS DOWN; HOLD DOWN; JUMP DOWN SOMEONE'S THROAT; KEEP DOWN; KNOCK DOWN; KNOCK FOR A LOOP (DOWN WITH A FEATHER); KNUCKLE DOWN; LAY DOWN; LAY DOWN THE LAW; LEAD DOWN THE GARDEN PATH; LET ONE'S HAIR DOWN; LET SOMEONE DOWN; LIE DOWN (ON THE JOB); LIVE DOWN; LOOK DOWN ON; MARK DOWN; MOW DOWN; NAIL DOWN; PIN DOWN; PIPE DOWN; PLAY DOWN; PLUNK DOWN; PULL DOWN; PUT DOWN; PUT DOWN ROOTS; PUT ONE'S FOOT DOWN; RAM DOWN SOMEONE'S THROAT; RING DOWN THE CURTAIN; RUB DOWN; RUN DOWN; SCALE DOWN; SELL DOWN THE RIVER; SET DOWN; SETTLE DOWN; SHAKE DOWN; SHOOT DOWN; SHOUT DOWN; SHUT DOWN; SIMMER DOWN; SIT DOWN; SLAP DOWN; SLOW DOWN; SPLASH DOWN; STAND DOWN; STARE DOWN; STEP DOWN; STRIKE DOWN; TAKE DOWN; TAKE DOWN A NOTCH; TAKE SOMETHING LYING DOWN; TALK DOWN TO; TEAR DOWN; THE LOWDOWN ON; THROW DOWN THE GAUNTLET; THUMBS UP (DOWN); TIE DOWN; TONE DOWN; TOUCH DOWN; TRACK DOWN; TRADE DOWN; TURN DOWN; TURN UPSIDE DOWN; UPS AND DOWNS; VOTE DOWN; WASH DOWN; WATER DOWN; WEAR DOWN; WEIGH DOWN; WHEN IT COMES (DOWN) TO; WHEN THE CHIPS ARE DOWN; WIND DOWN; WRITE DOWN.

**down and dirty** Also, **get down and dirty.** **1.** Not controlled by rules of fairness or decency, as in *The candidates are getting down and dirty early in the campaign.* **2.** Openly sexual in a crude way. For example, *Those two really get down and dirty on the dance floor.*

**down and out** With no money or hope of any. For example, *After losing his job, car, and home, he was completely down and out.* This term probably originated in boxing. Also see DOWN FOR THE COUNT.

**down cold, have *something*** Also, **have *something* down pat.** Learn or be able to do something perfectly. For example, *I have this song down cold.*

**down for the count** Defeated, finished, as in *I doubt if he'll ever leave the hospital; his illness really has him down for the count.* This expression refers to a losing boxer, unable to get to his feet before an official has counted to ten.

**downhill all the way** Also, **all downhill from here.** **1.** Easy from this point, without any difficulties the rest of the way. For example, *Once we had the basic design, it was downhill all the way.* **2.** Becoming worse or declining from this point on, as in *When the cancer couldn't be removed, it was downhill all the way for him.* The context should make clear which of these opposite meanings is intended. Also see GO DOWNHILL.

**down in the dumps** Also, **down in the mouth.** Discouraged, depressed, or sad, as in *She's been down in the dumps ever since she lost her job,* or *What's wrong with him? He's so down in the mouth about everything.* The noun *dumps* here means "a state of depression." **Down in the mouth** refers to the downturned corners of the mouth as a sign of unhappiness.

**down on, be** Unfriendly, angry, or negative toward something or someone. For example, *All the reviewers were down on this play,* or *Ever since he was injured, he's been down on skiing.* Also see DOWN ON ONE'S LUCK.

**down one's alley** see RIGHT UP ONE'S ALLEY.

**down one's neck** see BREATHE DOWN SOMEONE'S NECK.

**down one's nose** see LOOK DOWN ONE'S NOSE.

**down on one's luck** Experiencing bad luck or misfortune, as in *They've been down on their luck ever since they moved out West.*

**down someone's throat** see JUMP DOWN SOMEONE'S THROAT; RAM SOMETHING DOWN SOMEONE'S THROAT.

**down the drain** On the way to being lost or wasted; disappearing. For example, *Buying new furniture when they can't take it with them is just pouring money down the drain.* The phrase often occurs as **go down the drain.** For example, *When my computer crashed, a lot of hard work went down the drain.* This term compares something of value to water going down a drain. For a synonym, see DOWN THE TUBES.

**down the hatch** Drink up, as in *"Down the hatch," said Bill, as they raised their glasses.* This phrase, often used as a toast, uses *hatch* in the sense of "a trap door found on ships."

**down the line 1.** Also, **all along the line.** All the way, throughout. For example, *We've found repeated errors right down the line.* **2.** Also, **down the road.** At a future point or end. For example, *Somewhere down the road I think he'll be elected to high office.*

**down the pike** see COME DOWN THE PIKE.

**down the road** see DOWN THE LINE, def. 2.

**down the tubes** Also, **down the tube.** Into a state of failure or ruin, as in *If he failed the test, his chances went down the tubes.* Also see DOWN THE DRAIN.

**down to** In addition to the idioms beginning with DOWN TO, also see COME DOWN TO; GET DOWN TO.

**down to earth 1.** Back to reality. For example, *It's time the employees came down to earth concerning the budget.* **2.** Also, **down-to-earth.** Realistic or interested in everyday concerns, as in *She is a very down-to-earth person, not at all involved with the glamour of Hollywood.*

**down to size** see CUT DOWN, def. 3.

**down to the ground** Thoroughly, completely, as in *This new job suits him down to the ground.*

**down to the wire** To the last minute; to the very end. For example, *We're just about down to the wire with this project.* This term comes from horseracing. In the past it was the practice to stretch a wire across and above the track at the finish line.

**down with 1.** Inactive because of a certain sickness, as in *He's down with the flu.* Also see COME DOWN WITH. **2.** A phrase used to express one's feeling against someone or something and call for change. For example, *Down with the king!* **3. be down with** or **get down with.** Be close friends with, as in *I'm down with that crowd.*

**do you read me?** Do you understand me? For example, *I'm sick of all these meetings—do you read me?* This phrase originally applied to messages received by radio or telephone.

**dozen** see BAKER'S DOZEN; BY THE DOZEN; DIME A DOZEN; SIX OF ONE, HALF DOZEN OF THE OTHER.

**doze off** Fall into a light sleep, as in *Watching the ballet always made her doze off.*

**drab** see DRIBS AND DRABS.

**drag** In addition to the idioms beginning with DRAG, also see A DRAG; IN DRAG; LOOK LIKE SOMETHING THE CAT DRAGGED IN; WILD HORSES COULDN'T DRAG ME.

**drag in** Introduce something unnecessarily or forcefully. For example, *Whenever we argue, he drags in all sorts of unrelated issues, just to confuse matters.* Also see LOOK LIKE SOMETHING THE CAT DRAGGED IN.

**drag on** Also, **drag out.** Become or make longer, in a tiresome way. For example, *The speech dragged on for another hour,* or *He dragged out the story until his listeners were sick and tired of it.*

**drag one's ass 1.** Also, **drag ass** or **drag it.** Leave, depart, as in *I'm dragging my ass out of this place,* or *It's really late, let's drag ass!* [Vulgar slang] **2.** Also, **drag one's tail.** Move or act with deliberate slowness, as in *Hurry up, stop dragging your tail.* [Vulgar slang] For a politer synonym, see DRAG ONE'S FEET.

**drag one's feet** Also, **drag one's heels.** Act or work with intentional slowness, deliberately hold back or delay. For example, *Stop dragging your feet and get that job done!*

**dragon lady** A domineering or angry and unfriendly woman, as in *They called her the neighborhood dragon lady—she was always yelling at the children.*

**drag queen** A man, especially a performer, who dresses and acts like a woman. For example, *He was surprised to find out that Roxanne was actually a drag queen.* This term, sometimes considered offensive, uses the slang noun *drag* in the sense of "female clothes worn by a man." Also see IN DRAG.

**drain** see BRAIN DRAIN; DOWN THE DRAIN.

**draw** In addition to the idioms beginning with DRAW, also see BACK TO THE DRAWING BOARD; BEAT TO IT (THE DRAW); LUCK OF THE DRAW; QUICK ON THE DRAW.

D

**draw a bead on** Take careful aim at someone, as in *The debater drew a bead on his opponent.*

**draw a blank** Fail to find or remember something, as in *He looks familiar, but I've drawn a blank on his name.* This expression refers to drawing a lottery ticket with nothing on it (so one cannot win a prize).

**draw a line between** Also, **draw the line between.** Define a limit between two groups, courses of action, or similar things. For example, *Legally it's important to draw a line between private and public enterprises,* or *We'll have to draw the line between our different areas of responsibility.* Also see DRAW THE LINE AT.

**draw and quarter** Punish someone severely, as in *Mom'll draw and quarter me if even one scratch appears on her new car.* This expression refers to two brutal forms of execution practiced in the past.

**draw an inference** Guess or conclude, as in *From his wording, we can draw the inference that he disapproves.*

**draw a veil over** Conceal or avoid discussing something; keep something from public knowledge. For example, *The company president drew a veil over the accounting errors.*

**draw away** Also, **draw away from. 1.** Pull back, as in *He drew his chair away from the fire.* **2.** Move ahead of competitors, as in *On the last lap Jim drew away from the other runners.*

**draw back 1.** Retreat, as in *The army drew back to a stronger position.* **2.** Be afraid or unwilling to do something, refuse to go ahead with something. For example, *She promised to come—she can't draw back now.*

**draw blood** Injure someone physically or emotionally. For example, *The bullet skimmed his shoulder and barely drew any blood,* or *That reviewer really knows how to draw blood.*

**draw down** Lower or use up the supply of something by consuming or spending, as in *The government worries about drawing down our oil reserves.*

**drawer** see TOP DRAWER.

**draw fire** Meet with or be subject to criticism, as in *His recent article was bound to draw fire.* This expression uses the verb *draw* in the sense of "attract" or "provoke" and *fire* in the sense of "gunfire."

**draw in** Persuade someone to enter or participate. For example, *They tried to draw in as many new members as possible,* or *I refused to be drawn in to his scheme.*

**drawing board** see BACK TO THE DRAWING BOARD.

**drawing card** A feature or an event that attracts a large audience. For example, *This comedian is always a good drawing card.*

**draw in one's horns** see PULL IN ONE'S HORNS.

**draw in the reins** Bring something to a stop. For example, *During a recession, many businesses are forced to draw in the reins on expansion.* This expression transfers the means of stopping a horse to other kinds of restraint.

**draw on 1.** Approach, as in *Winter is drawing on, and the days are getting shorter.* **2.** Put on a piece of clothing, as in *She drew on her gloves.* **3.** Also, **draw upon.** Make use of something or someone. For example, *This dictionary draws on many different sources,* or *The coach was good at drawing upon the various members of the team.*

**draw out 1.** Pull out or remove something, as in *She drew out her pen,* or *Let's draw some money out of the bank.* **2.** Make something last, as in *This meal was drawn out over four hours.* The related expression **long-drawn-out** means "greatly extended or continued," as in *The dinner was a long-drawn-out affair.* **3.** Get someone to speak freely, as in *The teacher was good at drawing out the children.*

**draw straws** Also, **draw lots.** Decide something by a lottery using straws of different lengths. For example, *Let's draw straws to see who will have to write the first draft.* A related expression is **draw the short straw,** meaning to be the unlucky one who has to do a particular task.

**draw the curtain 1.** Pull a curtain back or to one side to let in more light or to discover what is behind it. For example, *The sun was so pleasant I drew the curtains.* **2.** Block or conceal something. For example, *Let's draw the curtain over this matter; no one needs to know more.* Also see DRAW A VEIL OVER.

**draw the line at** Refuse to go any further than a certain point, often due to disapproval, as in *I draw the line at giving them more money.* This expression refers to a line drawn at a stopping point of some kind.

**draw to a close** Approach or come to an end, as in *People started to leave as the game drew to a close.*

**draw up 1.** Compose or write something out in a set form, as in *The lawyer drew up the contract.* **2.** Arrange people or things in order or formation, as in *The bandleader drew up his players,* or *The officer drew up the troops.* **3.** Bring or come to a stop, as in *The car drew up to the door.* **4. draw oneself up.** Stand up straight to express dignity or indignation. For example, *She drew herself up and protested.*

**dream** In addition to the idioms beginning with DREAM, also see LIKE A DREAM; PIPE DREAM; SWEET DREAMS; WOULDN'T DREAM OF.

**dream come true, a** A wild fancy or hope that is realized. For example, *Winning a trip to Paris was a dream come true for her.*

**dream up** Invent or create something using one's imagination, as in *Count on her to dream up some explanation for her absence.*

**dress down** **1.** Scold or criticize someone strongly, as in *The sergeant will dress down the entire unit.* A variant is the noun **dressing down** for punishment with words. For example, *The teacher gave the girls a severe dressing down.* **2.** Wear informal clothes, as in *It's best to dress down for a beach party.* For an antonym, see DRESS UP.

**dressed to kill** Also, **dressed to the nines.** Wearing fancy clothes chosen with great care, as in *For the opening of the restaurant she was dressed to kill,* or *At the opera everyone was dressed to the nines.* Also see GUSSIED UP.

**dress up** **1.** Wear formal or one's best clothes, as in *I love to dress up for a party.* For an antonym, see DRESS DOWN, def. 2. **2.** Put on a costume of some kind, as in *The children love dressing up for Halloween.* **3.** Change or disguise something in order to make it more interesting or appealing. For example, *She has a way of dressing up her stories with fanciful details.*

**dribs and drabs** Bits and pieces, very small amounts, as in *There's not much left, just some dribs and drabs of samples.*

**drift** see GET THE DRIFT.

**drink** In addition to the idioms beginning with DRINK, also see DRIVE SOMEONE CRAZY (TO DRINK); INTO THE DRINK; MEAT AND DRINK TO; NURSE A DRINK.

**drink like a fish** Drink large amounts of alcoholic beverages, as in *He always drinks like a fish at holiday dinners.* The expression refers to the way fish take in oxygen, so that they seem to be constantly drinking.

**drink someone under the table** Drink more alcohol than someone else without getting as drunk. For example, *She claims she can drink me under the table.*

**drink to** Salute a person or an occasion with a toast, as in *Let's drink to our continued success.*

**drive a hard bargain** Insist on getting a lot, or refuse to give much, when making an agreement. For example, *It's more than I planned to pay, but you drive a hard bargain.* This expression uses the verb *drive* in the sense of "forcefully carry through."

**drive at** Mean to do or say, as in *I don't understand what he's driving at.* Today this idiom is used mainly with the participle *driving,* as in the example.

**drive home** Make something clearly understood, as in *The network news programs drive home the fact that violence is part of urban life.* This expression uses the verb *drive* in the sense of "force by a blow or thrust" (as in driving a nail).

**driven** see PURE AS THE DRIVEN SNOW.

**driver** see BACKSEAT DRIVER; IN THE DRIVER'S SEAT.

**drive someone crazy** Also, **drive someone mad** or **bananas** or **bonkers** or **nuts** or **up the wall; drive someone to drink.** Greatly annoy or irritate someone. For example, *His habitual lateness drives me crazy,* or *Apologizing over and over drives me bananas,* or *These messy workmen drive me up the wall,* or *Your complaints are driving me to drink.* All of these expressions describe a person's extreme frustration, supposedly to the point of insanity (*crazy, mad, nuts, bonkers,* and *bananas* all mean "insane"). *Up the wall* refers to climbing the walls to escape, and *to drink* refers to using alcohol as a kind of escape.

**driving force** The power or energy behind something in motion, as in *He was clearly the driving force in the new administration.* This term compares the force that sets in motion an engine or vehicle to the force behind other activities.

**drop** In addition to the idioms beginning with DROP, also see AT THE DROP OF A HAT; BOTTOM DROPS OUT; GET THE DROP ON; HEAR A PIN DROP; LET DROP; WAIT FOR THE OTHER SHOE TO DROP.

**drop a bombshell** Make an unexpected or shocking announcement. For example, *Bill dropped a bombshell when he said he was quitting.* This expression refers to the destruction caused by a falling bomb.

**drop a brick** Say something carelessly offensive, commit a social error. For example, *John dropped a brick when he called her by his ex-wife's name.*

**drop a dime** Inform on or betray someone, as in *No one can cheat in this class—someone's sure to drop a dime and tell the teacher.* This expression refers to the ten-cent coin long used for making a telephone call. It originated as slang for phoning the police to inform on a criminal.

**drop a line** Also, **drop someone a line.** Write a short letter or note. For example, *I hope you'll drop me a line soon.* This idiom uses *line* in the sense of "a few words in writing."

**drop back** Step back, retreat. For example, *When it was time for a group picture, Mary dropped back,* or *The player dropped back to kick the ball.*

**drop behind** Fail to continue at the normal pace or rate of progress. For example, *The teacher said Greg was dropping behind the class and needed extra help.*

**drop by** Also, **drop in** or **drop over.** Pay a short, informal, and usually unannounced visit. For example, *I asked her to drop by whenever she was in the neighborhood,* or *Joan loves to have friends drop in,* or *We'd love to drop over, but we don't have time on this trip.*

D

**drop dead** A phrase used to express one's anger toward someone. For example, *I should do all that work for you? Drop dead!* By contrast, the adjective (and adverb) **drop-dead** is not at all insulting. Rather, it means "dazzling" or "very impressive," as in *She wore a drop-dead outfit that all the other women admired.*

**drop in one's tracks** **1.** Suddenly lose all strength from tiredness or illness. For example, *I packed all day until I could have dropped in my tracks.* **2.** Die suddenly, as in *Grandfather's died; he just dropped in his tracks.* The phrase *in one's tracks* means "where one is at the moment" or "instantly."

**drop *something* in someone's lap** Give something to someone suddenly or without warning. It may be something desirable, as in *I'm just going to drop the promotion in her lap this afternoon,* or it may be something unwanted, as in *They simply dropped the employment problem in our laps.*

**drop in the bucket, a** A very small quantity, especially one that is too small. For example, *These contributions are just a drop in the bucket; the new church wing will cost thousands more.*

**drop *something* like a hot potato** see HOT POTATO.

**drop like flies** Rapidly fall, die, or fail to continue, usually referring to a group rather than one person. For example, *The race was so difficult that runners were dropping like flies.*

**drop names** Refer to important people that one knows in order to impress the listener. For example, *Her habit of dropping names made everyone very skeptical about her honesty.*

**drop off** **1.** Fall asleep, as in *When I looked at Grandma, she had dropped off.* **2.** Decrease; also, become less frequent. For example, *Sales have dropped off markedly,* or *As time passed, her visits dropped off.* **3.** Deliver or unload something or someone, as in *Bill dropped off the package at the office,* or *Could you drop me off downtown?*

**drop out** Also, **drop out of.** Fail to continue, end one's participation in a group such as a school, club, or game. For example, *He couldn't afford the club's membership dues and had to drop out,* or *She planned to drop out of college for a year.*

**drop the ball** Make an error; miss an opportunity. For example, *She really dropped the ball when she forgot to call back,* or *I think he dropped the ball when he refused their offer.* This expression comes from sports where a player who fails to catch a ball is charged with an error.

**drown** In addition to the idioms beginning with DROWN, also see LIKE A DROWNED RAT.

**drown one's sorrows** Drink alcohol to escape one's unhappiness. For example, *After the divorce, she took to drowning her sorrows at the local bar.*

**drown out** Overwhelm a sound with a louder sound, as in *Their cries were drowned out by the passing train,* or *The loud music drowned out their voices.*

**drug on the market** A commodity whose supply is much greater than the demand for it. For example, *The farmer complained that butter was a drug on the market, with everybody on low-fat diets now.*

**drum *something* into someone's head** see BEAT SOMETHING INTO SOMEONE'S HEAD.

**drummer** see MARCH TO A DIFFERENT DRUMMER.

**drum out** Expel or dismiss publicly and in disgrace, as in *They drummed him out of the club.* This usage refers to dismissal from a military service to the beat of a drum.

**drum up** **1.** Cause something to happen or appear by persistent effort, as in *I'm trying to drum up more customers,* or *We have to drum up support for this amendment.* **2.** Create, invent, or get something, as in *He hoped to drum up an alibi.*

**drunk as a skunk** Also, **falling-down drunk** or **roaring drunk.** Extremely drunk, as in *He came home drunk as a skunk.* The expression with *skunk* was undoubtedly chosen for the rhyme. The second expression refers to someone too drunk to keep his or her balance, as in *He couldn't make it up the stairs; he was falling-down drunk.* **Roaring drunk** refers to being extremely noisy as well as drunk. Also see DEAD DRUNK.

**druthers** see HAVE ONE'S DRUTHERS.

**dry** In addition to the idioms beginning with DRY, also see CUT AND DRIED; HANG OUT TO DRY; HIGH AND DRY; KEEP ONE'S POWDER DRY; WELL'S RUN DRY.

**dry as dust** Dull, boring, as in *The material in this book is dry as dust; it's putting me to sleep.*

**dry behind the ears** see under WET BEHIND THE EARS.

**dry out** Undergo a treatment for alcoholism, as in *After years of constant drinking, he realized that he needed to dry out.*

**dry run** A trial exercise or rehearsal, as in *Let's have a dry run this afternoon for tonight's ceremony.*

**dry up** **1.** Gradually become unproductive, as in *After two collections of short stories, his* *ability to write fiction dried up.* Also see WELL'S RUN DRY. **2.** Stop talking; also, cause to stop talking. For example, *Dry up! You've said enough.*

**duck** In addition to the idioms beginning with DUCK, also see DEAD DUCK; GET ONE'S DUCKS IN A ROW; LAME DUCK; LIKE WATER OFF A DUCK'S BACK; SITTING DUCK; TAKE TO (LIKE A DUCK TO WATER); UGLY DUCKLING.

**duck out** Also, **duck out on.** Leave hurriedly or secretly, especially to escape responsibility. For example, *If I can, I'll duck out of the office early,* or *He simply ducked out on his entire family.*

**duck soup** An easily accomplished task or assignment, as in *Fixing this car is going to be duck soup.*

**due** In addition to the idiom beginning with DUE, also see GIVE CREDIT (WHERE CREDIT IS DUE); GIVE THE DEVIL HIS DUE; IN DUE COURSE; PAY ONE'S DUES; WITH ALL DUE RESPECT.

**due to** **1.** Likely to, expected to, as in *Betty bought more of the stock, believing it was due to rise,* or *The play is due to open next week.* **2.** Because of, as in *Due to scanty rainfall, we may face a crop failure.* Also see ON ACCOUNT OF. **3.** Owing or payable to, as in *We must give our staff whatever vacation is due to them.*

**dull** In addition to the idiom beginning with DULL, also see NEVER A DULL MOMENT.

**dull as dishwater** Boring, tedious, as in *That lecture was dull as dishwater.*

**dumb bunny** A stupid person, as in *She was a bit of a dumb bunny but very nice.* This expression implies some toleration of or affection for the person.

**dumps** see DOWN IN THE DUMPS.

**dust** In addition to the idiom beginning with DUST, also see BITE THE DUST; DRY AS DUST; IN THE DUST; MAKE THE DUST FLY; SHAKE THE DUST FROM ONE'S FEET; THROW DUST IN SOMEONE'S EYES; WATCH MY DUST; WHEN THE DUST HAS SETTLED.

**dust off** Restore something to use. For example, *I've dusted off last year's menu for the party,* or *I'll have to dust off my skills in French if we're going to Paris.*

**Dutch** In addition to the idioms beginning with DUTCH, also see IN DUTCH.

**Dutch treat** An outing or a date in which each person pays his or her own expenses. For example, *Her parents agreed that she could date if it was a Dutch treat.* The related expression **go Dutch** means "to go on a date with each person paying his or her own way," as in *Students often agree to go Dutch.*

**Dutch uncle** A stern, candid critic or adviser, as in *When I got in trouble with the teacher again, the principal talked to me like a Dutch uncle.* This expression often occurs as **talk to someone like a Dutch uncle.**

**duty** In addition to the idiom beginning with DUTY, also see ABOVE AND BEYOND (THE CALL OF DUTY); ACTIVE DUTY; DO ONE'S DUTY; DOUBLE DUTY; OFF DUTY; ON DUTY.

**duty bound** Obliged, having a responsibility, as in *You're duty bound to help your little brother.*

**dwell on** Also, **dwell upon.** Think, speak, or write at length about something. For example, *Let's not dwell on this topic too long; we have a lot to cover today.*

**dying** In addition to the idiom beginning with DYING, also see under DIE.

**dying to do something** Very eager to do something, as in *I'm dying to go to Alaska.* Also see DIE FOR.

# Ee

**each** In addition to the idioms beginning with EACH, also see AT EACH OTHER'S THROATS; MADE FOR EACH OTHER.

**each and every one** Also, **every last one** or **every single one.** Every individual in a group, as in *Each and every student must register by tomorrow,* or *I've graded every last one of the exams,* or *Every single one of his answers was wrong.* All of these phrases are generally used for emphasis. Also see EVERY TOM, DICK, AND HARRY. **Every mother's son** and **every man Jack** are earlier versions that refer only to males.

**each other** Also, **one another.** Each one the other, as in *The two boys like each other,* or *The birds were fighting one another for the food.* Both of these phrases indicate a reciprocal relationship or action between the subjects (*the boys, the birds*). Also see AT EACH OTHER'S THROATS.

**eager beaver** A person who habitually takes on more tasks or works harder than others, especially so as to make a good impression. For example, *Bill is a real eager beaver, always volunteering to stay late.* This expression became popular during World War II. It was often applied to new soldiers anxious to impress their commanding officers.

**eagle eye, an** Unusually sharp sight; also, sharp intellectual vision. For example, *Antiques dealers have an eagle eye for valuable objects,* or *A good manager has an eagle eye for employee errors.*

**ear** In addition to the idioms beginning with EAR, also see ALL EARS; BELIEVE ONE'S EARS; BEND SOMEONE'S EAR; CAN'T MAKE A SILK PURSE OUT OF SOW'S EAR; COMING OUT OF ONE'S EARS; CUTE AS A BUTTON (BUG'S EAR); FALL ON DEAF EARS; HAVE SOMEONE'S EAR; IN ONE EAR AND OUT THE OTHER; LEND ONE'S EAR; MUSIC TO ONE'S EARS; OUT ON ONE'S EAR; PIN SOMEONE'S EARS BACK; PLAY BY EAR; PRICK UP ONE'S EARS; PUT A BUG IN SOMEONE'S EAR; TURN A DEAF EAR; UP TO ONE'S EARS; WALLS HAVE EARS; WET BEHIND THE EARS.

**early** In addition to the idioms beginning with EARLY, also see BRIGHT AND EARLY.

**early bird 1.** See EARLY BIRD CATCHES THE WORM. **2.** Someone who gets up early, as in *You can call me at seven—I'm an early bird.* **3.** Someone who eats dinner early, as in *The restaurant has early-bird specials at lower prices.*

**early bird catches the worm, the** Also, **the early bird gets the worm.** The one who arrives first has the best chance for success, as in *She's always the first one in line and does well at these auctions—the early bird catches the worm!* This proverbial saying is so familiar that it is often shortened to **early bird.**

**early on** At an early stage in a process or course of events, as in *He started using computers very early on.*

**early to bed, early to rise (makes a man healthy, wealthy, and wise)** Go to bed early and get up early, for good health and also for success in life. This proverb is often shortened, as in *With final exams coming, you should remember, early to bed and early to rise.*

**earn** In addition to the idioms beginning with EARN, also see PENNY SAVED IS A PENNY EARNED.

**earnest** see IN EARNEST.

**earn one's keep** Make enough money to cover one's own living expenses, as in *Get a job—it's time for you to earn your keep.*

**earn one's stripes** Gain a position through hard work and experience over time. For example, *She'd earned her stripes by serving for years as the governor's secretary and personal aide.* This expression refers to a military promotion or award, shown by strips of material added to the person's uniform.

**ears are burning, one's** Know or sense that people are talking about one. For example, *Were your ears burning? Jim was telling us about your success.* The related expression **make someone's ears burn** means "to embarrass someone by talking about the person," as in *Mom's stories about us as babies make my ears burn.* These expressions refer to a person's ears turning red from blushing.

**earth** see DOWN TO EARTH; ENDS OF THE EARTH; FOUR CORNERS OF THE EARTH; MOVE HEAVEN AND EARTH; NOT HAVE AN EARTHLY CHANCE; ON EARTH; SALT OF THE EARTH.

**ear to the ground, have one's** Also, **keep one's ear to the ground.** Be or remain well informed; be on the watch for new trends and information. For example, *She knew she'd succeed as a reporter if she kept her ear to the ground.* This expression probably refers to listening for distant horses by putting one's ear close to the ground.

**ease** In addition to the idioms beginning with EASE, also see AT EASE; ILL AT EASE. Also see under EASILY; EASY.

**ease off** **1.** Also, **ease up.** Become less severe, relax. For example, *I wish you'd ease off on Harold; he's doing the best he can,* or *The wind's eased up, so I think the storm is just about over.* Also see LET UP. **2.** Slow down, gradually decrease, as in *The market's easing off, so we may get some stocks more cheaply.*

**ease out** Extract or remove someone or something gradually or gently. For example, *He carefully eased the car out of the garage,* or *We were trying to ease him out of office without a public scandal.*

**easier said than done** Also, **more easily said than done.** An expression used to say that a suggested plan would be difficult to accomplish, as in *Keeping the cats off the sofa is easier said than done.*

**easily** see BREATHE EASY (EASILY); EASIER (MORE EASILY) SAID THAN DONE.

**easy** In addition to the idioms beginning with EASY, also see BREATHE EASY; FREE AND EASY; GET OFF (EASY); GO EASY; LET SOMEONE DOWN (EASY); TAKE IT EASY.

**easy as pie** Also, **easy as falling off a log** or **easy as rolling off a log.** Not at all difficult to do, as in *This crossword puzzle is easy as pie.* The first term probably refers to eating pie (since making pie requires both effort and skill). The variants most likely refer to standing on a log in the water, a feat in which falling off is a lot easier than staying on. For a synonym, see PIECE OF CAKE.

**easy come, easy go** Easily won and easily lost, as in *Easy come, easy go—that's how it is for Mark when he plays the stock market.*

**easy does it** Go carefully, don't hurry, as in *That chest is heavy, so easy does it.* Also see GO EASY.

**easy money** Money that someone gets easily, with little effort and, often, illegally. For example, *Winning the lottery—that's easy money!* or *I was suspicious when they described this as easy money.* Also see FAST BUCK.

**easy on the eyes** Also, **easy to look at.** Attractive, beautiful, as in *That model is definitely easy on the eyes.*

**easy sledding** Effortless progress, as in *It's easy sledding from here on.* This expression refers to coasting smoothly down a snow-covered hill and was first put as **smooth sledding.** Also see SMOOTH SAILING and the antonym TOUGH SLEDDING.

**easy street, be on** Have financial security and comfort, as in *If he actually gets that job, he will be on easy street.* Also see FAT CITY.

**eat** In addition to the idioms beginning with EAT, also see DOG EAT DOG; WHAT'S EATING ONE.

**eat and run** Leave immediately after eating a meal; also, leave in a hurry. For example, *Sorry, but I'll have to eat and run or I'll miss the last train,* or *Jim runs a meeting so efficiently that in effect it's eat and run.*

**eat away at** **1.** Destroy something gradually, erode. For example, *The sea has been eating away at the outer banks for years.* **2.** Worry someone constantly, as in *The fact that he failed the test is eating away at him.*

**eat crow** Also, **eat dirt** or **eat humble pie.** Be forced to admit a very embarrassing mistake, as in *When the reporter got the facts all wrong, his editor made him eat crow. Crow* meat tastes terrible, and *dirt* obviously tastes bad. *Humble pie* refers to a pie made from *umbles,* the undesirable parts of a deer (heart, liver, entrails). Also see EAT ONE'S WORDS.

**eat high off the hog** see HIGH OFF THE HOG.

**eat in** Have a meal at home, as in *Are we eating in tonight?* Also see EAT OUT.

**eat like a bird** Eat very little, as in *Jan is very thin—she eats like a bird.* This simile refers to the mistaken idea that birds don't eat much (they actually do, relative to their size). An antonym is **eat like a horse.** For example, *I never have enough food for Ellen—she eats like a horse!*

**eat one's cake and have it, too** Also, **have one's cake and eat it, too.** Have the benefits or advantages of two things that can't both exist. For example, *Doug was engaged to Ann and still dating Jane; he was trying to eat his cake and have it, too.* This expression is often put negatively.

**eat one's hat** Declare one's certainty that something will not happen or is untrue. This expression almost always follows an *if* clause, as in *If he's on time, I'll eat my hat,* that is, "I'll consume my headgear if I'm wrong."

**eat one's heart out** Feel bitter emotional pain, grief, worry, or jealousy. For example, *She is still eating her heart out over being fired,* or *Eat your heart out—my new car is being delivered today.*

**eat one's words** Be forced to take back something one has said, as in *To my surprise, he won easily, so I had to eat my words.*

**eat out** Have a meal outside one's home, usually dinner at a restaurant. For example, *We're almost out of groceries, so let's eat out tonight.* For the antonym, see EAT IN.

**eat out of someone's hand** Be controlled or dominated by another, do whatever someone wants, as in *He had the press eating out of his hand.* This expression refers to a tame animal eating out of one's hand.

**eat shit** Also, **eat crap.** Tolerate or submit to treatment that humiliates, degrades, or dishonors one, as in *He refused to eat shit from the coach.* [Vulgar slang]

**eat someone alive** Overwhelm or defeat someone thoroughly. For example, *Because he lacked experience in manufacturing, he was eaten alive by his competitors.* A newer version of this expression is **eat someone's lunch;** for example, *It was a decisive victory; he ate his opponent's lunch.*

E

**eat someone out of house and home** Eat so much as to use up someone's resources, as in *The kids are eating her out of house and home.*

**eat someone's lunch** see under EAT SOMEONE ALIVE.

**eat up 1.** Eat or use completely, as in *No television until you eat up your dinner,* or *Increased expenses have eaten up all my spare cash.* **2.** Enjoy something eagerly, as in *She simply eats up the publicity.* **3.** Believe something unquestioningly, as in *He'll eat up whatever the broker tells him.* **4.** Defeat someone completely, as in *This new fighter just eats up every opponent.*

**ebb** In addition to the idiom beginning with EBB, also see AT A LOW EBB.

**ebb and flow** Declines and increases, constant rising and falling in amount. For example, *He was fascinated by the ebb and flow of the Church's influence over the centuries.* This expression refers to the outward and inward movement of ocean tides.

**edge** In addition to the idioms beginning with EDGE, also see CUTTING EDGE; GET A WORD IN EDGEWISE; HAVE AN EDGE; ON EDGE; ON THE EDGE; OVER THE EDGE; SET ONE'S TEETH ON EDGE; TAKE THE EDGE OFF.

**edge in** Work or fit something or oneself into a limited space or time. For example, *The train was crowded, but I managed to edge in,* or *Everyone was talking at once, and he barely managed to edge in a word.* Also see GET A WORD IN EDGEWISE.

**edge out** Beat or defeat someone by a small margin, as in *She edged out her opponent on the home stretch.*

**edgewise** see GET A WORD IN EDGEWISE.

**educated guess, an** A guess or estimate based on past experience or knowledge, as in *I'm not sure how much meat we need to feed twelve, but I'll make an educated guess and say six pounds.*

**eel** see SLIPPERY AS AN EEL.

**effect** see IN EFFECT; TO THAT EFFECT.

**effigy** see IN EFFIGY.

**effort** see ALL OUT (EFFORT); LAST-DITCH EFFORT.

**egg** In addition to the idioms beginning with EGG, also see BAD EGG; GOOD EGG; GOOSE EGG; KILL THE GOOSE THAT LAYS THE GOLDEN EGGS; LAY AN EGG; PUT ALL ONE'S EGGS IN ONE BASKET; WALK ON EGGS.

**egg *someone* on** Urge or encourage someone to do something, often something they shouldn't, as in *Jack is always egging me on to drive faster,* or *I think she eggs her brother on to quarrel.*

**egg on one's face, have** Look foolish or be embarrassed, as in *If you ask any more personal questions, you'll end up with egg on your face.* This expression may refer to dissatisfied audiences throwing raw eggs at performers.

**ego trip** Something that one does because it gives one a sense of great importance. For example, *She's really on an ego trip, trying out for the lead in the play.*

**eight** see BEHIND THE EIGHT BALL.

**eke out 1.** Make something last, as in *The survivors eked out their food and water until they were rescued.* **2.** Get something with great difficulty or effort, as in *The soil was terrible, but the farmers managed to eke out a living.*

**elbow** In addition to the idioms beginning with ELBOW, also see AT SOMEONE'S ELBOW; CROOK ONE'S ELBOW; OUT AT THE ELBOWS; RUB ELBOWS WITH.

**elbow grease** Great physical effort, as in *You'll have to use some elbow grease to get the house painted in time.* This term refers to vigorous use of one's arm in cleaning, polishing, or the like.

**elbow room** Enough space to move about, as in *Two hundred actors on the stage? There won't be any elbow room.* This term refers to having enough room to extend one's elbows.

**element** see BRAVE THE ELEMENTS; IN ONE'S ELEMENT.

**elephant** see WHITE ELEPHANT.

**eleventh hour, the** The latest possible time, as in *We turned in our report at the eleventh hour.*

**else** see IN SOMEONE'S (SOMEONE ELSE'S) SHOES; OR ELSE; SOMETHING ELSE; SOMETHING ELSE AGAIN.

**embarrassment of riches, an** More than enough of something, too much of a good thing, as in *All four of them have their own cars, but there's no room in the driveway—an embarrassment of riches.*

**empty** In addition to the idioms beginning with EMPTY, also see GLASS IS HALF FULL (HALF EMPTY); RUNNING ON EMPTY.

**empty calories** Food that has little or no nutritional value. For example, *Snacking on beer and potato chips gets you nothing but a lot of empty calories.*

**empty nest** The home of parents whose children have grown up and moved out. For example, *Now that they had an empty nest, Jim and Jane opened a bed-and-breakfast.* This expression refers to a nest from which baby birds have flown. It is the source of such related expressions as **empty-nester,** for a parent whose children have moved out, and **empty-nest syndrome,** for the state of mind of parents whose children have left.

**empty suit** An unimportant person; also, a phony. For example, *Don't pay any attention to him—he's just an empty suit,* or *She acts as though she knows what she's doing, but she's really an empty suit.* This expression suggests an empty suit of clothes.

**enchilada** see BIG CHEESE (ENCHILADA); WHOLE BALL OF WAX (ENCHILADA).

**end** In addition to the idioms beginning with END, also see ALL'S WELL THAT ENDS WELL; AT LOOSE ENDS; AT ONE'S WIT'S END; BE-ALL AND END-ALL; BEGINNING OF THE END; BITTER END; BURN THE CANDLE AT BOTH ENDS; CAN'T SEE BEYOND THE END OF ONE'S NOSE; COME TO AN END; DEAD END; GO OFF THE DEEP END; HOLD ONE'S END UP; IN THE END; LIGHT AT THE END OF THE TUNNEL; MAKE ENDS MEET; MAKE SOMEONE'S HAIR STAND ON END; NEVER HEAR THE END OF; ODDS AND ENDS; ON THE RECEIVING END; PLAY BOTH ENDS AGAINST THE MIDDLE; PUT AN END TO; REAR END; SHORT END OF THE STICK; TAIL END; WRONG END OF THE STICK.

**endangered species** A group threatened with extinction or destruction. For example, *People willing to put in work overtime without extra pay are an endangered species,* or *With the new budget cuts, public television has become an endangered species.* This expression originally referred to species of plants or animals in danger of dying out. It later began to be used for anything or anyone becoming rare.

**end game** The final stage of some process, as in *The book discussed the diplomatic end game resulting in the treaty.* This term comes from chess, where it refers to the stage of a game when most of the pieces have been removed from the board.

**end in itself** A purpose or goal desired for its own sake (rather than as a way to get something else). For example, *For me, writing books is an end in itself; they don't really make that much money.* This expression uses the noun *end* in the sense of "final cause or purpose."

**end justifies the means, the** A good result excuses any wrongs someone commits to reach it. For example, *He's campaigning with illegal funds with the idea that if he wins the election the end will justify the means,* or *The officer tricked her into admitting her guilt—the end sometimes justifies the means.*

**end of one's rope, at the** At the limits of one's patience, resources, or endurance. For example, *The workmen are driving me crazy; I'm at the end of my rope.* This expression refers to a tied-up animal that can graze only as far as the rope permits.

**end of the line** Also, **end of the road.** The conclusion or the point where something must stop. For example, *The editorial pointed out that it was the end of the line for the President; he'd never be reelected,* or *When the star quit, it was obviously the end of the road for this television series.*

**end run** Action taken to avoid something, as in *The new department head was making an end run around the limits on hiring when she brought in temporary help.* This term comes from U.S. football. It refers to a play in which the ball carrier runs around one end of the opposing team's line.

**ends of the earth, the** The farthest possible limit, as in *She would go to the ends of the earth for him.*

**end to end 1.** In a row with the ends touching. For example, *The pipes were laid end to end.* **2. from end to end.** Throughout the length of something, as in *We hiked the Appalachian Trail from end to end.*

**end up** Arrive at a final point, result in, finish. For example, *He thought he'd end up living in the city,* or *We don't know how this situation will end up.* Also see WIND UP.

**English** see BODY ENGLISH; IN PLAIN ENGLISH.

**en masse** In one group or body; all together. For example, *The activists marched en masse to the capitol.*

**enough** In addition to the idioms beginning with ENOUGH, also see FAIR ENOUGH; LEAVE WELL ENOUGH ALONE; NOT ENOUGH ROOM TO SWING A CAT; SURE ENOUGH; (ENOUGH) TO WAKE THE DEAD.

**enough is enough** One should be satisfied; stop, there should be no more. For example, *No more speeches—enough is enough.*

**enough rope, give someone** Allow someone to continue on a course of action and then suffer its consequences. For example, *We suspected the accountant was cheating us but decided to give him enough rope.* This expression is a shortening of **enough rope to hang oneself.**

**enough said** Say no more, I understand; also, I agree completely. For example, *She didn't even bother to call you? Enough said.*

**enough to sink a ship** Also, **enough to sink a battleship.** An amount that is more than enough, as in *They brought enough food to sink a ship.*

**en route** On or along the way, as in *We'll pick up Dan en route to the restaurant,* or *We can finish our discussion en route.*

**enter into 1.** Participate in, take an active role or interest in, as in *We had to think carefully before we entered into these negotiations.* **2.** Commit oneself to a contract, bind oneself, as in *The nations entered into a new agreement.* **3.** Become or form a part of, as in

*Finances soon entered into the discussion.* **4.** Also, **go into.** Consider, investigate, as in *The report entered into the effect of high interest rates,* or *Let's not go into that problem now.*

**enter on** Also, **enter upon.** Begin to do or become involved in something, as in *We are entering on a new era,* or *They entered upon the most difficult part of the research.*

**enter one's mind** Also, **enter one's head.** Come into one's thoughts. This expression is most often used negatively, as in *It didn't enter my mind that he'd want to join us,* or *Run for office? It never entered my head.*

**enterprise** see FREE ENTERPRISE.

**enter the fray** Become involved in a fight or competition, as in *Whenever people disagreed, she was eager to enter the fray.*

**envy** see GREEN WITH ENVY.

**equal** In addition to the idiom beginning with EQUAL, also see OTHER THINGS BEING EQUAL; SEPARATE BUT EQUAL.

**equal to** Capable enough to succeed at something, as in *I'm not sure I'm equal to the task.* Also see FEEL UP TO; UP TO.

**errand** see FOOL'S ERRAND; RUN AN ERRAND.

**error** see COMEDY OF ERRORS; TRIAL AND ERROR.

**escape** In addition to the idiom beginning with ESCAPE, also see NARROW ESCAPE.

**escape *someone's* notice** Miss being seen or heard by someone, as in *It must have escaped the editor's notice, so I'll write again.*

**etched in stone** see CAST IN STONE.

**eve** see ON THE EVE OF.

**even** In addition to the idioms beginning with EVEN, also see BREAK EVEN; ON AN EVEN KEEL.

**evening** see GOOD DAY (EVENING).

**even money** Equal odds that something will or will not happen, as in *It's even money that he'll get the contract.* The term comes from gambling.

**even so** Nevertheless, still, in spite of that. For example, *His story may be true, but even so, we will investigate further,* or *She claimed it contained no garlic, but even so, I could taste it.*

**even-steven** Exactly equal; also, with nothing due or owed on either side. For example, *I've paid it all back, so now we're even-steven.* This rhyming phrase is used as an intensifier for *even.*

**event** see BLESSED EVENT; IN ANY CASE (EVENT); IN CASE (IN THE EVENT); IN THE UNLIKELY EVENT.

**ever** see HARDLY EVER; LIVE HAPPILY EVER AFTER.

**every** In addition to the idioms beginning with EVERY, also see AT EVERY TURN; EACH AND EVERY ONE; FINGER IN THE (EVERY) PIE; NOOK AND CRANNY, EVERY.

**every bit** **1.** All of something, as in *Eat every bit of that broccoli!* **2.** In all ways, equally. For example, *He is every bit as smart as his sister.* Also see EVERY LITTLE BIT HELPS.

**every cloud has a silver lining** see SILVER LINING.

**every dog has its day** Even the least important or respected will sometimes get a share of attention or luck. For example, *They may not listen to me now, but just wait, every dog has its day.* Also see HAD ITS DAY.

**every inch** Completely, throughout, as in *He was every inch a leader,* or *I had to argue this case every inch of the way.*

**every last one** see EACH AND EVERY ONE.

**every little bit helps** Even a small contribution can be useful, as in *He can only give us one day, but every little bit helps.*

**every man for himself** Each person puts his or her own interests first, without concern for others. For example, *In this company no one helps anyone—it's every man for himself.* Despite the wording, the term applies to either sex.

**every man has his price** Any person can be bribed in some way, as in *They had trouble persuading her to join, but when they offered her a car—well, every man has his price.* This cynical observation applies to either sex.

**every minute counts** Also, **every moment counts.** It is extremely important to act fast. For example, *Hurry up with those tools—every minute counts,* or *In performing surgery, every moment counts.*

**every nook and cranny** see NOOK AND CRANNY.

**every now and then** Also, **every now and again** or **every once in a while** or **every so often.** Occasionally, from time to time; also, periodically. For example, *Every now and then I feel an urge for a piece of chocolate,* or *We take long walks every now and again,* or *Every once in a while he'll call,* or *Every so often she washes the car.* Also see FROM TIME TO TIME; ONCE IN A WHILE.

**everyone** see entries under **every man.**

**every other** Every second one in a series, as in *I'm supposed to take this pill every other day.*

**every single one** see EACH AND EVERY ONE.

**every so often** see EVERY NOW AND THEN.

**everything** In addition to the idiom beginning with EVERYTHING, also see HOLD EVERYTHING.

**everything but the kitchen sink** Also, **everything under the sun.** Including just about everything, whether it's appropriate or not. For example, *Our new car has every feature—everything but the kitchen sink.* The variant expression uses *under the sun* in the sense of "on earth."

**every time one turns around** Very often; too often. For example, *Every time I turn around, he's asking for more money,* or *Some-*

*thing in this house breaks down every time I turn around.*

**every Tom, Dick, and Harry** Everyone, especially all ordinary men, as in *This model should appeal to every Tom, Dick, and Harry.*

**everywhere** see ALL OVER (EVERYWHERE); HERE, THERE, AND EVERYWHERE.

**every which way** In all directions, as in *Papers were blowing every which way.*

**evidence** see IN EVIDENCE.

**evil eye 1.** The power to cause injury or bad luck by looking at someone or something, as in *The tomatoes died shortly after I planted them—I must have an evil eye.* **2. give someone the evil eye.** Look at someone as if wishing harm to them, as in *We'd better be quiet, the librarian's giving us the evil eye.* The source of this expression is the ancient superstitious belief that some people could hurt others simply by looking at them.

**example** see FOR EXAMPLE; MAKE AN EXAMPLE OF; SET AN EXAMPLE.

**except for** Also, **with the exception of.** Other than, including all but. For example, *Except for Jack, everyone came to the party,* or *With the exception of the weather, everything went extremely well.*

**exception** In addition to the idiom beginning with EXCEPTION, also see EXCEPT FOR (WITH THE EXCEPTION OF); MAKE AN EXCEPTION; TAKE EXCEPTION TO.

**exception proves the rule, the** An instance that does not obey a rule shows that the rule exists. For example, *John's much shorter than average, but he's good at basketball—the exception proves the rule.*

**excess** see CARRY TOO FAR (TO EXCESS); IN EXCESS OF.

**exchange** see IN EXCHANGE.

**excuse me** Also, **I beg your pardon** or **pardon me.** Forgive me, as in *Excuse me, did I step on your toe?* or *Pardon me, do you know the time?* or *I beg your pardon, but I disagree.* These phrases are used to get someone's attention or as an apology for something (interrupting a conversation, bumping into someone, asking a speaker to repeat something, politely disagreeing, and so on).

**excuse oneself** Apologize and leave, as in *I'm afraid I must excuse myself, but please continue without me,* or *She excused herself from the table.*

**exert oneself** Try or work very hard, as in *We exerted ourselves to raise funds.*

**exhibition** see MAKE AN EXHIBITION OF ONESELF.

**expect** see WHEN LEAST EXPECTED.

**expedition** see FISHING EXPEDITION.

**expense** see AT THE EXPENSE OF; GO TO THE TROUBLE (EXPENSE); MONEY (EXPENSE) IS NO OBJECT.

**explain away** Dismiss or minimize the importance of something, especially one's mistake or failure. For example, *There's no way they can explain away the missing money.*

**explain oneself 1.** Explain what one has said or done, as in *If you have a few minutes, I'll try to explain myself.* **2.** Give an explanation or excuse for something wrong one has done. For example, *You're three hours late—can you explain yourself?*

**express oneself** Show one's feelings or views through speech, writing, some form of art, or behavior. For example, *I find it hard to express myself in Italian,* or *People often express themselves through their clothes, haircuts, and the like.*

**extend credit to** Also, **extend someone credit.** Allow someone to buy something on credit; also, permit someone to owe money. For example, *The store is closing his charge account; they won't extend credit to him any more,* or *The normal procedure is to extend you credit for three months, and after that we charge interest.* This idiom uses the verb *extend* in the sense of "offer" or "provide."

**extent** see TO SOME DEGREE (EXTENT).

**extenuating circumstances** A situation or condition that provides an excuse for an action, as in *Although she missed a lot of work, there were extenuating circumstances, so she didn't lose her job.* This expression was originally a legal term. It meant circumstances that partly excuse a crime and suggest less punishment.

**eye** In addition to the idioms beginning with EYE, also see ALL EYES; APPLE OF ONE'S EYE; BELIEVE ONE'S EARS (EYES); BIRD'S-EYE VIEW; BLACK EYE; BRIGHT-EYED AND BUSHY-TAILED; CATCH SOMEONE'S EYE; CLOSE ONE'S EYES; CRY ONE'S EYES OUT; EAGLE EYE; EASY ON THE EYES; EVIL EYE; FEAST ONE'S EYES ON; GIVE SOMEONE THE ONCE-OVER (EYE); GREEN-EYED MONSTER; HAVE AN EYE FOR; HAVE ONE'S EYE ON; HIT BETWEEN THE EYES; HIT THE BULL'S-EYE; IN A PIG'S EYE; IN ONE'S MIND'S EYE; IN THE EYE OF; IN THE PUBLIC EYE; IN THE TWINKLING OF AN EYE; KEEP AN EYE OUT; KEEP ONE'S EYE ON THE BALL; KEEP ONE'S EYES OPEN; LAY EYES ON; LOOK SOMEONE IN THE FACE (EYE); MAKE EYES AT; MORE THAN MEETS THE EYE; MY EYE; NAKED EYE; ONE EYE ON; OPEN ONE'S EYES; OUT OF THE CORNER OF ONE'S EYE; PRIVATE EYE; PULL THE WOOL OVER SOMEONE'S EYES; RUN ONE'S EYES OVER; SEE EYE TO EYE; SEE WITH HALF AN EYE; SIGHT FOR SORE EYES; STARS IN ONE'S EYES; THROW DUST IN SOMEONE'S EYES; TURN A BLIND EYE; UP TO ONE'S EARS (EYES); WITH AN EYE TO; WITH ONE'S EYES OPEN; WITHOUT BATTING AN EYE.

**eyeball to eyeball** Face to face; especially, about to begin a conflict. For example, *We are eyeball to eyeball with the enemy,* or *In*

E

*the first debate our candidate's going eyeball to eyeball with his opponent.* This term was originally used only in a military context. Later it entered civilian language, particularly in political or sports confrontations.

**eyebrow** see CAUSE RAISED EYEBROWS.

**eye for an eye, an** Punishment in which someone who did wrong suffers the same hurt the victim has suffered, as in *Joe believed in an eye for an eye.* Also see TURN THE OTHER CHEEK.

**eye opener, an 1.** Startling or shocking news, as in *The first sentence of his speech was a real eye opener.* This expression refers to widening one's eyes with surprise. **2.** A strong alcoholic drink taken early in the morning, as in *After a late night and little sleep, he needed an eye opener to wake him up a bit.*

**eyes are bigger than one's stomach, one's** Someone wants more than he or she can handle, as in *He's thinking of having another sandwich, but we think his eyes are bigger than his stomach.* This expression refers to someone taking more food than he or she can manage to eat.

**eyes in the back of one's head, have** Be more aware of what is happening than people realize. For example, *Even when he's away, he always knows what the staff are doing—he has eyes in the back of his head,* or *With so many enemies in her department, she needs to have eyes in the back of her head.*

**eyes open, with** see KEEP ONE'S EYES OPEN; OPEN ONE'S EYES.

**eyeteeth** see GIVE ONE'S EYETEETH.

**eye to, with an** With a plan for or the hope of doing or getting something. For example, *With an eye to expansion, we'll have to be careful with expenses,* or *She always operates with an eye to the future.* This phrase also occurs in **have an eye to the main chance** or **with an eye to the main chance,** meaning "watching for opportunities or advantages for oneself." For example, *He'll probably go far in politics; he always has an eye for the main chance.*

**eye to eye** see SEE EYE TO EYE.

**face** In addition to the idioms beginning with FACE, also see AT FACE VALUE; BLUE IN THE FACE; BRAVE FACE; DO AN ABOUT-FACE; EGG ON ONE'S FACE; FLY IN THE FACE OF; HIDE ONE'S FACE; IN SOMEONE'S FACE; IN THE FACE OF; IN YOUR FACE; KEEP A STRAIGHT FACE; LAUGH OUT OF THE OTHER SIDE OF ONE'S MOUTH (FACE); LONG FACE; LOOK SOMEONE IN THE FACE; LOSE FACE; MAKE A FACE; ON THE FACE OF IT; PLAIN AS DAY (THE NOSE ON YOUR FACE); POKER FACE; PUT ONE'S FACE ON; RED IN THE FACE; SAVE FACE; SHOW ONE'S FACE; SLAP IN THE FACE; STARE IN THE FACE; STUFF ONE'S FACE; TALK SOMEONE'S ARM OFF (UNTIL BLUE IN THE FACE); THROW IN SOMEONE'S FACE; TO ONE'S FACE.

**face down 1.** With the upper surface put down, as in *Please put these papers face down.* This usage appears to come from card-playing. The antonym is **face up. 2.** Gain control in a situation by dealing with someone in a strong, confident way. For example, *She faced down her critics and won many people's respect.*

**face it** see FACE UP TO.

**face the music** Meet with unpleasantness, especially the results of one's errors. For example, *When his check bounced, he had to face the music.* Also see FACE UP TO.

**face to face 1.** In each other's presence, opposite one another; in direct communication. For example, *The two chairmen sat face to face,* or *It's time his parents met the teacher face to face.* **2.** Confronting each other, as in *When the earthquake hit, we were face to face with death.*

**face up** see under FACE DOWN.

**face up to** Also, **face it.** Have to deal with or accept an unpleasant or difficult situation. For example, *Jane had to face up to the possibility of being fired,* or *Face it—you were wrong.* Also see FACE THE MUSIC.

**face value** see AT FACE VALUE.

**face with** Make someone confront or deal with something, as in *When he was faced with the evidence, he admitted it.*

**fact** In addition to the idiom beginning with FACT, also see AFTER THE FACT; IN FACT; IS THAT A FACT; MATTER OF FACT.

**factor in** Figure in, include as a basic element. For example, *In preparing the schedule, we factored in vacation and sick days.* This term comes from mathematics.

**facts of life, the** Knowledge of sexual reproduction, as in *Some people feel that the facts of life should not be taught in school.* Also see BIRDS AND THE BEES.

F

**fade away** see FADE OUT, def. 2.

**fade out 1.** Gradually disappear or become impossible to hear. For example, *The pianist let the final chord fade out completely before he played the next movement.* The antonym is **fade in,** "appear gradually or become heard," as in *The images on the screen faded in until they could be seen clearly.* These terms originated in the radio and movie industries, where they apply to images and sounds. **2.** Also, **fade away.** Leave quietly, as in *The guests began to fade away at midnight.*

**fail** see WITHOUT FAIL; WORDS FAIL ME.

**faint** see DAMN WITH FAINT PRAISE.

**fair** In addition to the idioms beginning with FAIR, also see ALL'S FAIR IN LOVE AND WAR; PLAY FAIR; TURNABOUT IS FAIR PLAY.

**fair and square** Justly and honestly, as in *He won the race fair and square.* This redundant expression—*fair* and *square* mean essentially the same thing—probably owes its long life to its rhyme.

**fair enough** That's reasonable; I agree. For example, *I'll wait just one more day. Fair enough, you've been very patient.*

**fair game** Someone or something that it is OK to attack or ridicule. For example, *On his talk show, authors are considered fair game.* This expression refers to animals one may hunt.

**fair-haired boy** A favorite person, usually a man, who is given special treatment. For example, *Today the attorney general is the governor's fair-haired boy.*

**fair play** Behavior that follows established rules; good conduct and conditions. For example, *The coach insists on fair play.* Also see TURNABOUT IS FAIR PLAY.

**fair sex** Girls or women, as in *Many women would object to being called the fair sex nowadays.* This term uses *fair* in the sense of "physically beautiful" and is probably dying out.

**fair shake, a** A fair or just bargain or opportunity, as in *You can always count on the boss to give his workers a fair shake.* This expression probably refers to the shaking of dice.

**fair to middling** Mediocre, pretty good but not great, as in *I asked them how they liked* *their new home, and John answered, "Fair to middling."* This phrase is often a reply to a question about one's health, business, or the like. Also see CAN'T COMPLAIN.

**fair-weather friend** A person who is dependable in good times but is not in times of trouble. For example, *You can't rely on Sarah—she's strictly a fair-weather friend.*

**fairy** In addition to the idiom beginning with FAIRY, also see TOOTH FAIRY.

**fairy godmother** A person who gives generous help, often unexpectedly, as in *An anonymous fairy godmother donated the money for the new organ.* This expression refers to a woman with magical powers in fairy tales such as *Cinderella.*

**faith** see ACT OF FAITH; IN BAD (GOOD) FAITH; ON FAITH; PIN ONE'S HOPES (FAITH) ON.

**fall** In addition to the idioms beginning with FALL, also see BOTTOM DROPS (FALLS) OUT; BREAK ONE'S FALL; EASY AS PIE (FALLING OFF A LOG); LET DROP (FALL); LET THE CHIPS FALL WHERE THEY MAY; TAKE THE FALL.

**fall all over oneself** Also, **fall over backward(s).** Make too much of an effort to do something, try very hard or eagerly. For example, *They fell all over themselves to be helpful, but only got in the way,* or *She fell over backwards trying to please her boss, but it didn't help.*

**fall apart** Suddenly lose strength and come apart or break down, either physically or mentally and emotionally. For example, *This chair is about to fall apart,* or *After his wife died, he fell apart.* For synonyms for the latter usage, see COME APART AT THE SEAMS; GO TO PIECES.

**fall asleep** Go to sleep. For example, *As soon as the lights were turned off, he fell asleep.* Also see ASLEEP AT THE SWITCH.

**fall away 1.** Also, **fall off.** Withdraw one's friendship or support. For example, *After the divorce, her friends slowly fell away.* **2.** Also, **fall off.** Gradually become smaller, weaker, or milder, as in *The breeze slowly fell away.* **3.** Slowly move away from an established faith, cause, or principles. For example, *I fell away from the Catholic Church when I was a teenager.*

**fall back** Retreat, as in *The soldiers fell back as the enemy advanced,* or *He stuck to his argument, refusing to fall back.*

**fall back on** Also, **fall back upon.** Rely on, go to for support, as in *I fall back on old friends in time of need,* or *When he lost his job, he had to fall back upon his savings.*

**fall behind** Also, **get behind. 1.** Fail to keep up or progress as expected. For example, *You really must keep up with the others; if you fall behind, you could get lost.* **2.** Be late with something expected, especially financially, as in *He fell behind in his payments.*

**fall between the cracks** Also, **fall through the cracks.** Be neglected or go unnoticed; also, not fit either of two alternatives. For example, *Please make sure that either our department or yours deals with this account, so it doesn't fall between the cracks.*

**fall by the wayside 1.** Fail to continue, as in *At first she did well on the women's professional golf tour, but with all the pressure she soon fell by the wayside.* **2.** Stop being important and be forgotten, as in *Our original plan has fallen by the wayside..*

**fall down** Fail to meet expectations; perform badly. For example, *It was disappointing to see him fall down on the job.*

**fall flat** Fail, prove to be ineffective, as in *His jokes nearly always fell flat—no one ever laughed at them.*

**fall for 1.** Become attracted to, as in *I was sure he'd fall for her.* **2.** Be tricked or cheated by, as in *He fell for the con artist's scheme and lost a great deal of money.*

**fall from grace** Lose a favored position or the liking of someone in authority. For example, *The whole department has fallen from grace, and we may all lose our jobs.* This expression originally referred to losing the favor of God.

**fall guy 1.** A scapegoat, one who is blamed for the actions of others. For example, *He refused to be the fall guy for his colleagues.* This expression uses *fall* in the sense of "consequences" or "blame," which originated in prison slang. Also see TAKE THE FALL. **2.** An easy victim, one who is easily tricked. For example, *His friends had marked him as the fall guy—they knew he would believe anything they said.*

**fall in 1.** Take one's place in formation or in the ranks, as in *The sergeant ordered the soldiers to fall in.* A related expression is **fall into,** as in *They all fell into their places.* Also see FALL INTO. **2.** Sink inward, cave in, as in *The snow was so heavy that we feared the roof would fall in.* Also see the following idioms beginning with FALL IN; FALL INTO.

**falling down drunk** see under DRUNK AS A SKUNK.

**fall in line** Also, **fall into line.** Follow or stick to established rules or courses of action. For example, *This idea falls in line with company policy,* or *It wasn't easy to get all the teachers to fall into line concerning the new methods.* A related term is **bring into line,** meaning "to make someone fit established rules." For example, *It was her job to bring her department's way of doing things into line with the others.* These terms use *line* in the sense of "alignment."

**fall in love** Develop a romantic love, as in *John and Mary fell in love on their first date.*

**fall in place** Also, **fall into place.** Become clear; also, become organized. For example, *With that last piece of information, the entire sequence of events fell in place,* or *When the architect's plans were complete, the construction schedule fell into place.* This idiom uses *place* in the sense of "proper position."

**fall into** **1.** Enter or engage in, be drawn into, as in *I told Dad not to fall into conversation with them.* **2.** See FALL IN, def. 1. **3.** Be naturally divisible into, as in *These students fall into three categories.* **4. fall into a trap.** Be tricked, become involved in something without intending to. For example, *By admitting I had free time, I fell into the trap of having to help him with his work.* Also see under FALL IN; FALL IN LINE; FALL IN PLACE.

**fall in with** **1.** Agree with, accept and go along with, as in *We happily fell in with his plans.* **2.** Come together with, become acquainted with (especially by chance), as in *On the cruise we fell in with a couple from Boston.*

**fall off** see FALL AWAY.

**fall off the wagon** see ON (OFF) THE WAGON.

**fall on** Also, **fall upon. 1.** Attack someone suddenly and violently, as in *They fell on the guards and overpowered them.* **2.** Meet with or encounter something, as in *They fell on hard times.* **3.** Find something by chance, discover, as in *We fell upon the idea last Saturday night.* **4.** Be the responsibility or duty of someone, as in *It fell on Clara to support the entire family.* Also see the following idioms beginning with FALL ON.

**fall on deaf ears** Be ignored or disregarded by someone who does not want to listen, as in *Any advice we give them seems to fall on deaf ears.* Also see TURN A DEAF EAR.

**fall on one's face** Also, **fall flat on one's face.** Make a bad mistake or error of judgment, as in *That weatherman keeps falling on his face with his predictions.*

**fall out** **1.** Leave one's place in military ranks, as in *After inspection, the soldiers were ordered to fall out.* **2.** Also, **have a falling-out.** Disagree, quarrel, as in *The brothers fell out over their inheritance,* or *They no longer speak—they had a falling-out some years ago.*

**fall over backward(s)** see under FALL ALL OVER ONESELF.

**fall short** Fail to meet expectations, be less than needed or wanted. For example, *His skills fell short of the required standard.*

**fall through** Fail, end without reaching completion, as in *The proposed law fell through,* or *I hope our plans won't fall through.*

**fall through the cracks** see FALL BETWEEN THE CRACKS.

**fall to** Energetically begin an activity, as in *As soon as they had the right tools, they fell to work on the house.* This expression is also often used to mean "begin to eat," as in *As soon as the food was on the table, the men fell to.*

**fall under** **1.** Be classified as, as in *The costs of food, hotels, and transportation all fall under Travel Expenses.* **2.** Be subject to, as in *This matter falls under federal law.*

**false** In addition to the idioms beginning with FALSE, also see LULL INTO (A FALSE SENSE OF SECURITY); PLAY FALSE; RING FALSE.

**false alarm** A warning signal when there is no real cause for action, made either by mistake or to trick people. For example, *The rumor that we were all going to get fired was just a false alarm,* or *Setting off a false alarm is a criminal offense.* This expression is often used for a report of a fire that doesn't really exist.

**false colors** The pretense of being something that one really is not. For example, *She's sailing under false colors—she claims to be a Republican, but she supports Democratic legislation.* This term refers to the practice of pirate ships **sailing under false colors**—that is, showing a particular flag to bring another ship close enough to be captured.

**false start** A failed attempt to begin something, as in *After several false starts, she finally managed to write the first chapter.* The term originated in racing. It refers to beginning a race before the starting signal has been given.

**false step** A mistake in a course of action, as in *Signing the contract without reading it was clearly a false step.*

**familiar** see HAVE A FAMILIAR RING.

**familiarity breeds contempt** Long experience of someone or something can make one so aware of faults as to lose all one's respect. For example, *She knows them too well to be impressed by them—familiarity breeds contempt.*

**family** see RUN IN THE FAMILY.

**famine** see FEAST OR FAMINE.

**famous last words** A phrase used to express disbelief, especially in a promise or prediction. For example, *They said we'd get an extra bonus at Christmas—famous last words!* or *This book is bound to make the bestseller list—famous last words!* This expression refers to statements about human affairs that prove to be untrue, such as "This is the war to end all wars."

**fan** In addition to the idiom beginning with FAN, also see SHIT WILL HIT THE FAN.

**fancy** see FLIGHT OF FANCY; FOOTLOOSE AND FANCY-FREE; TAKE A FANCY TO; TICKLE ONE'S FANCY;.

**fan the flames** Stir up feelings or make them stronger; make an explosive situation worse. For example, *She already found him attractive, but his letters really fanned the*

F

*flames,* or *His speech fanned the flames of racial tensions.*

**far** In addition to the idioms beginning with FAR, also see AS FAR AS; AS FAR AS I CAN SEE; AS FAR AS POSSIBLE; AS FAR AS THAT GOES; BY FAR; CARRY SOMETHING TOO FAR; FEW AND FAR BETWEEN; GO FAR; GO SO FAR AS TO; GO TOO FAR; SO FAR; SO FAR SO GOOD.

**far afield** Far from the usual course, goal, or environment. For example, *His research led him far afield from his original question.*

**far and away** see BY FAR.

**far and near** Everywhere, at a distance and nearby. For example, *People came from far and near to see the Pope.*

F

**far and wide** For a great distance, over a large area. For example, *They searched far and wide for the lost child,* or *The message went out far and wide.*

**far be it from one to** One will not do or say something, as in *Far be it from me to criticize his decision.* This denial of an intention may be true or false, depending on the speaker or the context. For example, *Far be it from him to disagree* may be an honest prediction that he will not disagree, or it may be used ironically (meaning that he actually disagrees quite strongly). For a phrase used similarly, see GOD FORBID.

**far cry from, a 1.** Also, **far from.** Very different from, as in *Thinking someone is stupid is a far cry from saying so,* or *Far from being a help, she made our job more difficult.* **2. far from it.** An interjection expressing strong denial, as in *I thought you were bored. Far from it, I enjoyed the evening.*

**far from** see under FAR CRY FROM.

**far gone** Extremely advanced, referring to some progressive action or condition. For example, *These trees are diseased, and they're too far gone to be saved,* or *He's had a lot to drink and is too far gone to drive himself home.*

**farm** In addition to the idiom beginning with FARM, also see BUY IT (THE FARM).

**farm out** Assign something to an outsider; subcontract something. For example, *The contractor was so busy he had to farm out two of his jobs,* or *When their mother was hospitalized, the children had to be farmed out to relatives.* This term originally referred to letting or leasing land. Today it usually refers to subcontracting work or the care of a dependent to another.

**far out 1.** Unusual or eccentric; very advanced. for example, *Painting blindfolded? That's far out,* or *Her child-raising theories are far out.* **2.** An interjection meaning "great" or "cool," as in *All he could say when he won the lottery was "Far out!"*

**fart around** Waste time, as in *Tell those guys to stop farting around!* [Vulgar slang]

**farther** see CAN'T SEE BEYOND (FARTHER THAN) THE END OF ONE'S NOSE.

**fashion** see AFTER A FASHION; GO OUT (IN FASHION).

**fast** In addition to the idioms beginning with FAST, also see GET NOWHERE (FAST); HARD AND FAST; PULL A FAST ONE; STAND ONE'S GROUND (FAST); THICK AND FAST.

**fast and furious** Swiftly, intensely and energetically, as in *The storm moved in fast and furious,* or *The sale was going fast and furious, attracting large crowds.*

**fast and loose** see PLAY FAST AND LOOSE.

**fast buck** Money made quickly and easily and, often, dishonestly. For example, *He's all right, but his partner is just out for a fast buck.* This expression gave rise to **fast-buck artist,** a person, especially a swindler, who is intent on making money quickly. Also see EASY MONEY.

**fast lane** Also, **life in the fast lane.** A lifestyle that involves free spending and a focus on pleasure, and sometimes also danger. For example, *They're finding that living in the fast lane can be very stressful.* This term refers to the highway express lane used by faster vehicles to pass slower ones. Also see ON THE FAST TRACK.

**fat** In addition to the idioms beginning with FAT, also see CHEW THE FAT.

**fat cat** A rich and important person, as in *This neighborhood, with its million-dollar homes, is full of fat cats.* This term originally meant "a rich contributor to a political campaign." It is still used in this way, but it now is often applied more broadly, as in the example.

**fat chance** Very little or no possibility, as in *A fat chance he has of coming in first,* or *You think they'll get married? Fat chance!* A related expression is **a fat lot,** meaning "very little or none at all," as in *A fat lot of good it will do her.*

**fat city** Also, **Fat City.** A condition or situation marked by lots of money or other advantages. For example, *With that new job, she'll be in fat city.* Also see EASY STREET.

**fate** In addition to the idiom beginning with FATE, also see SEAL ONE'S FATE; TEMPT FATE.

**fate worse than death, a** A very unwanted event or result, as in *Dean thinks driving daily during rush hour is a fate worse than death.* In the past, this phrase was used to refer to a woman's loss of virginity outside of marriage.

**fat farm** A humorous or insulting term for a clinic or resort where people go to lose weight, as in *She spends all her vacations at a fat farm, but it hasn't helped so far.*

**father** see LIKE FATHER, LIKE SON.

**fat is in the fire, the** A course of action has begun that will surely lead to bad results;

there's trouble ahead. For example, *Now the fat's in the fire—the boss arrived early and will see we haven't even started work.* This expression refers to fat dropping into a fire and causing a burst of flames.

**fat lot** see under FAT CHANCE.

**fat of the land, the** The best or richest of anything, as in *The tiny upper class lived off the fat of the land while many people were starving.*

**fault** see AT FAULT; FIND FAULT; TO A FAULT.

**favor** see CURRY FAVOR; IN FAVOR OF; IN ONE'S FAVOR; OUT OF FAVOR; RETURN THE COMPLIMENT (FAVOR).

**favorite son** A person valued by his or her hometown or local organization for his or her achievements, usually political. For example, *Mary hoped they would treat her as a favorite son and nominate her for state senator.* Today this term may apply to a woman.

**fear** see FOOLS RUSH IN WHERE ANGELS FEAR TO TREAD; FOR FEAR OF; NEVER FEAR; PUT THE FEAR OF GOD INTO.

**feast one's eyes on** Be delighted or very happy at the sight of something, as in *I'm feasting my eyes on this new sculpture—it's wonderful.*

**feast or famine** Also, **either feast or famine.** Either too much or too little, too many or too few. For example, *Yesterday two hundred people showed up at the fair; today, only two dozen—it's either feast or famine.*

**feather** In addition to the idioms beginning with FEATHER, also see BIRDS OF A FEATHER; IN FINE FEATHER; KNOCK FOR A LOOP (OVER WITH A FEATHER); LIGHT AS A FEATHER; MAKE THE DUST (FEATHERS) FLY; RUFFLE SOMEONE'S FEATHERS; TAR AND FEATHER.

**feather in one's cap, a** An act or accomplishment; a distinctive achievement. For example, *Getting all three countries to accept the peace agreement would be a feather in his cap.*

**feather one's nest** Become rich, especially by taking advantage of one's position or using the property of others. For example, *While he was supposed to be managing the company's money, he was feathering his nest.* This expression refers to birds making a soft nest for their eggs.

**fed up** Also, **fed to the gills** or **fed to the teeth.** Disgusted, unable or unwilling to tolerate any more of something. For example, *I'm fed up with these delays,* or *He was fed to the teeth with her excuses.* Of these expressions, **fed up** refers to being too full from having overeaten. Also see UP TO ONE'S EARS.

**feed** In addition to the idioms beginning with FEED, also see BITE THE HAND THAT FEEDS YOU; CHICKEN FEED; OFF ONE'S FEED; PUT ON THE FEED BAG.

**feed one's face** Also, **stuff one's face.** Eat greedily, overeat, as in *When Dave comes home, he's apt to feed his face,* or *She won't lose any weight if she keeps stuffing her face like that.*

**feed someone a line** **1.** Also, **feed someone lines.** Cue an actor with his or her next line (or lines), or tell someone what to say, as in *Some contestants become tongue-tied, so someone has to feed them a line,* or *Eric still has trouble learning a part; he needs someone to feed him his lines.* **2.** Also, **hand someone a line.** Talk someone into believing something that's not really true. For example, *He really fed them a line about his important new position,* or *Don't hand me a line—I know exactly how much you paid for it.*

**feed the kitty** Contribute money to a common fund or reserve, as in *I can't make a big donation this year, but I'm willing to feed the kitty something.*

**feel** In addition to the idioms beginning with FEEL, also see (FEEL) AT HOME; COP A FEEL; GET THE FEEL OF; (FEEL) PUT UPON. Also see FEELINGS.

**feel bad** Also, **feel bad about.** Experience regret, sadness, embarrassment, or a similar unpleasant emotion. For example, *I feel bad about not attending the funeral,* or *The teacher's scolding made Bobby feel bad.*

**feel blue** Also, **have the blues.** Be depressed or sad, as in *I was really feeling blue after she told me she was leaving.* Also see BLUE FUNK, def. 2.

**feeler** see PUT OUT FEELERS.

**feel for** **1.** Reach for and try to something with one's hands, as in *It was pitch dark, and I felt for the doorknob.* **2. feel for someone.** Sympathize with or feel sorry for someone, as in *Tom was so upset that I felt for him.*

**feel free** Be welcome to do or say something. For example, *Feel free to borrow the car whenever you need it,* or *You want to suggest a better plan? Feel free.* For a synonym, see BE MY GUEST.

**feelings** see HARD FEELINGS; MIXED FEELINGS; NO HARD FEELINGS; SINKING FEELING.

**feel *it* in one's bones** Have an intuition or hunch about something in the future, as in *I'm sure he'll succeed—I can feel it in my bones.* This expression refers to the idea that persons with a healed broken bone or with arthritis experience bone pain that lets them predict a weather change.

**feel like** Have a desire for something or an interest in doing something, as in *I feel like going out tonight,* or *Do you feel like steak for dinner?*

**feel like death** see LOOK LIKE DEATH.

**feel like new** Also, **feel as good as new** or **feel like a new person.** **1.** Have a renewed sense of well-being, especially after something has happened, such as recovery from illness or receiving good news. For example, *The surgery went very well, and he now feels like new,* or *I am so relieved at the news, I feel like a new person.* **2. feel like a million.** Be in the best of health or good spirits. For example, *After winning that prize, I feel like a million.* The *million* refers to a million dollars. Also see LOOK LIKE A MILLION DOLLARS; ON TOP OF THE WORLD.

F

**feel like oneself** Feel well, be in a normal state of health or spirits. For example, *I'm finally over the flu and feel like myself again.* Also see FEEL UP TO.

**feel like two cents** Feel of little or no value or importance, feel worthless. For example, *Her criticism made me feel like two cents.* Also see FOR TWO CENTS.

**feel no pain** Be very drunk, as in *After six beers he was feeling no pain.*

**feel one's oats 1.** Feel very energized or full of high spirits, as in *School was out, and they were feeling their oats.* This phrase refers to the behavior of a horse after having been fed oats. **2.** Show self-importance, as in *He was feeling his oats, bossing everyone in the office around.*

**feel one's way** Proceed cautiously, as in *Until we know who we're dealing with, we'll have to feel our way.* This expression refers to finding the way by touch in the dark. Also see FEEL FOR, def. 1.

**feel out** Try cautiously or indirectly to find out someone's viewpoint. For example, *We'd better feel out the author before we commit him to a publicity tour.* Also see TAKE THE PULSE OF.

**feel put upon** see PUT UPON.

**feel someone up** Touch someone sexually, as in *She complained that her boss tried to feel her up.*

**feel the pinch** Be affected by hardship, especially a lack of money. For example, *This job pays much less, so we're bound to feel the pinch.*

**feel up to** Consider oneself capable or able to do something, as in *Do you feel up to a three-mile run?* or *I don't feel up to another evening out.* Also see EQUAL TO; UP TO.

**feet** see AT SOMEONE'S FEET; BOTH FEET ON THE GROUND; DEAD ON ONE'S FEET; DRAG ONE'S FEET; GET ONE'S FEET WET; GET TO ONE'S FEET; HOLD SOMEONE'S FEET TO THE FIRE; LET THE GRASS GROW UNDER ONE'S FEET; OFF ONE'S FEET; ON ONE'S FEET; PUT ONE'S FEET UP; SHAKE THE DUST FROM ONE'S FEET; SIX FEET UNDER; STAND ON ONE'S OWN FEET; TAKE THE LOAD OFF (ONE'S FEET); THINK ON ONE'S FEET; TWO LEFT FEET; UNDER ONE'S FEET; VOTE WITH ONE'S FEET. Also see under FOOT.

**feet on the ground** see BOTH FEET ON THE GROUND.

**fell** see ONE FELL SWOOP.

**fellow** see REGULAR GUY (FELLOW); STRANGE BEDFELLOWS.

**fence** In addition to the idioms beginning with FENCE, also see MEND FENCES; ON THE FENCE.

**fence *someone* in** Also, **hem *someone* in**. Restrict or confine someone, as in *The actor wanted to work in films, but his contract for his TV series fenced him in,* or *Their father was old-fashioned and the children were hemmed in by his rules.* The first phrase became widely used because of a popular song about a cowboy, "Don't Fence Me In."

**fence with** Avoid answering directly, as in *The mayor was very good at fencing with the press about his future plans.* This expression compares conversation to fencing with swords.

**fend for oneself** Also, **shift for oneself.** Provide for one's own needs, as in *Don't worry about me, I can fend for myself,* or *Both parents work, so the children have to shift for themselves after school.*

**ferret out** Uncover something by searching and make it known, as in *Sandy was a superb reporter, tireless in ferreting out whatever facts were needed for her story.* This expression refers to hunting with ferrets, weasel-like animals used in the past to drive rabbits out of hiding.

**fetch and carry** Do errands and other low-level tasks, as in *She was hired as administrative assistant, but all she does is fetch and carry for the department's supervisor.* This expression originally referred to dogs that were taught to carry things.

**fever** see CABIN FEVER; RUN A FEVER.

**few** In addition to the idiom beginning with FEW, also see A FEW; (A FEW) BRICKS SHY OF A LOAD; OF FEW WORDS; PRECIOUS FEW; QUITE A BIT (FEW).

**few and far between** At wide intervals, scarce, as in *Supporters of the amendment are few and far between.* This expression originally was used for objects such as houses separated by wide spaces.

**few bricks shy of a load** see BRICKS SHY OF A LOAD.

**few words** see OF FEW WORDS.

**fiddle** In addition to the idiom beginning with FIDDLE, also see FIT AS A FIDDLE; HANG UP (ONE'S FIDDLE); PLAY SECOND FIDDLE.

**fiddle while Rome burns** Keey busy with unimportant matters and neglect important ones during a crisis. For example, *His employees were threatening to strike, but he was more worried about missing his golf game—talk about fiddling while Rome burns!* This expression refers to the story that the Emperor Nero played his fiddle while watching Rome in flames.

**field** In addition to the idiom beginning with FIELD, also see COVER THE FIELD; FAR AFIELD; OUT IN LEFT FIELD; PLAY THE FIELD; TAKE THE FIELD.

**field day** A time of great pleasure, activity, or opportunity, as in *The press had a field day with this sensational murder trial.* This expression originally referred to a day for military exercises and later was extended to a school day for sports and games.

**fifth** In addition to the idiom beginning with FIFTH, also see TAKE THE FIFTH.

**fifth wheel, a** An extra and unnecessary person or thing, as in *He was the only one without a date, so he felt like a fifth wheel.* This expression refers to an unneeded wheel on a four-wheel vehicle.

**fifty-fifty** In addition to the idiom beginning FIFTY-FIFTY, also see GO HALVES (FIFTY-FIFTY).

**fifty-fifty chance, a** An equal probability that something will or will not happen. For example, *There's only a fifty-fifty chance he'll survive.*

**fig** see under NOT GIVE A DAMN.

**fight** In addition to the idioms beginning with FIGHT, also see CAN'T FIGHT CITY HALL.

**fight fire with fire** Fight back against at attack or a harmful situation using the same means. For example, *When the opposition began a smear campaign against our candidate, we decided to fight fire with fire.*

**fighting chance, a** A possibility of winning, but only with a struggle. For example, *It's going to be hard to beat that record, but I think he has a fighting chance.*

**fighting words** A statement that is sure to start a quarrel or fight. It is often expressed as **them's fighting words,** as in *You say your father's smarter than mine? Them's fighting words.* The ungrammatical use of *them's* for "those are" emphasizes the very informal tone of this expression.

**fight it out** Settle a disagreement by fighting, either physically or verbally. For example, *The two sides couldn't agree on a budget but were determined to fight it out to the end.*

**fight off** Defend oneself against something or someone, as in *I've been fighting off a cold all week.*

**fight tooth and nail** Fight very hard or make a very strong effort, using all one's resources. For example, *I'm going to fight tooth and nail for that promotion.* This expression refers to biting and scratching.

**figment of one's imagination, a** Also, **figments of one's imagination.** Something made up or invented, as in *The insults he's complaining about are just figments of his imagination.*

**figure** In addition to the idioms beginning with FIGURE, also see BALLPARK FIGURE; IN ROUND NUMBERS (FIGURES); IT FIGURES.

**figure in** **1.** Include, add something in. For example, *Did you figure in the travel expense?* **2.** Play a part in, as in *His speaking ability definitely figured in his being chosen for the lead role in the play,* or *Their need for money figures in all their recent decisions.*

**figure on** **1.** Depend on or count on something, as in *We figured on your support.* **2.** Take something into consideration, expect, as in *We figured on his being late.* **3.** Plan on something, as in *We'll figure on leaving at noon.*

F

**figure out** **1.** Discover or determine something, as in *Let's figure out a way to help.* **2.** Solve or find an answer to something, as in *Can you figure out this puzzle?*

**figure up** Calculate, total, as in *Please figure up just how many feet of lumber we need.*

**file** see ON FILE; RANK AND FILE; SINGLE FILE.

**fill** In addition to the idioms beginning with FILL, also see GET ONE'S FILL. Also see under FULL.

**filled to the brim** As full as possible; also, completely satisfied. For example, *We're filled to the brim with excitement,* or *The cup was filled to the brim.* This expression transfers the idea of a container filled to the very top.

**fill in** **1.** Complete something, especially by supplying more information or detail. For example, *Be sure to fill in your salary history on the application.* It is also put as **fill in the blanks,** as in *If you have any more questions, you can rely on Mary to fill in the blanks.* Yet another related usage is **fill someone in,** as in *I couldn't attend the meeting, so will you fill me in?* Also see FILL OUT. **2.** Also, **fill in for.** Take someone's place, substitute for. For example, *The teacher is absent, so who will fill in?* or *I can't come, but my wife will fill in for me.* Also see FILL SOMEONE'S SHOES.

**fill out** **1.** Complete something by supplying required information, especially in writing. For example, *Please fill out the application form.* **2.** Become or make something larger and rounded in outline. For example, *The wind filled out the sails,* or *He's put on weight and really filled out.*

**fill someone's shoes** Take the position of someone who has left and perform that person's duties, especially in a satisfactory way. For example, *It'll be hard to find someone to fill her shoes when she retires,* or *John expects his son to fill his shoes in the family business.* Also see IN SOMEONE'S SHOES.

**fill the bill** Serve a particular purpose well, as in *I didn't know how I should cook the chicken for dinner, but this recipe will fill the* *bill,* or *We're looking for experienced salesmen, and he just fills the bill.*

**filthy rich** Extremely rich, as in *With a huge house and cars like theirs, they must be filthy rich.*

**final** see IN THE FINAL ANALYSIS.

**find** In addition to the idioms beginning with FIND, also see HARD WAY (FIND OUT THE).

**finders, keepers** A phrase meaning that the person who finds something has the right to keep it. For example, *Someone left a dollar bill in this rented car—finders, keepers.* This expression is often stated as **finders keepers, losers weepers.**

F

**find fault** Also, **find fault with.** Criticize, express dissatisfaction with, as in *Grandma is always finding fault,* or *She was a difficult traveling companion, constantly finding fault with the hotel, meal service, and tour guides.*

**find it in one's heart** Persuade oneself to do something, as in *I hope you can find it in your heart to forgive me,* or *They were an hour late, but I couldn't find it in my heart to scold them.* This expression, today often used in the negative, relates to forgiveness.

**find one's bearings** see GET ONE'S BEARINGS.

**find oneself 1.** Become aware of what one wishes and can best do in life. For example, *At last he's found himself—he really loves teaching.* The same idea is sometimes put as **find one's feet,** transferring a baby's new ability to stand or walk to a person becoming conscious of his or her abilities. **2.** Discover where one is or how one is feeling. For example, *He suddenly found himself on the right street,* or *To my surprise I find myself agreeing with you.*

**find one's way** Reach a destination, especially with some difficulty. For example, *She finally found her way to the cabin in the woods,* or *Some slang phrases have found their way into standard English.*

**find out 1.** Discover something by asking questions or doing research, as in *You can find out his phone number by looking in the book.* **2.** Discover someone's true nature or character, especially in an offense. For example, *Cheaters risk being found out.*

**fine** In addition to the idioms beginning with FINE, also see COME ON IN (THE WATER'S FINE); CUT IT FINE; IN FINE FEATHER.

**fine and dandy** All right, excellent, as in *What you're proposing is fine and dandy with the rest of us.* This redundant phrase (*fine* and *dandy* both mean "excellent") today is more often used sarcastically in the sense of "not all right" or "bad," as in *You don't want to play tennis? That's just fine and dandy.*

**fine art** Something requiring highly developed techniques and skills, as in *He's turned lying into a fine art,* or *The contractor excels in the fine art of estimating costs.* This term refers to the *fine arts,* such as music, painting, and sculpture, which require both skill and talent. It is now often used to describe anything that takes skill to do.

**fine-tooth comb, a** Also, **a fine-toothed comb.** A method of searching or investigating in very great detail, as in *He examined the figures with a fine-tooth comb but found no errors.* The phrase refers to the practice of using a comb with close-set teeth to comb out head lice.

**finger** In addition to the idiom beginning with FINGER, also see AT ONE'S FINGERTIPS; BURN ONE'S FINGERS; CROSS ONE'S FINGERS; LAY A FINGER ON; LET SLIP (THROUGH ONE'S FINGERS); NOT LIFT A FINGER; POINT THE FINGER AT; PUT ONE'S FINGER ON; PUT THE FINGER ON; SNAP ONE'S FINGERS AT; STICKY FINGERS; TWIST AROUND ONE'S FINGER; WORK ONE'S FINGERS TO THE BONE.

**finger in the pie, have a** Also, **have one's finger in the pie.** Have an interest or involvement in something. For example, *When they nominated me for the board, I'm sure Bill had a finger in the pie.* Another form of this idiom is **have a finger in every pie,** meaning "have an interest in or be involved in everything," as in *She does a great deal for the town; she has a finger in every pie.*

**fingertips** see AT ONE'S FINGERTIPS.

**finish** see FROM SOUP TO NUTS (START TO FINISH); IN AT THE DEATH (FINISH).

**finishing touch** Also, **finishing touches.** A small change or addition that serves to complete something. For example, *The room still needed a few finishing touches, such as a flower arrangement.*

**fire** In addition to the idioms beginning with FIRE, also see ADD FUEL TO THE FIRE; BALL OF FIRE; CATCH FIRE; CAUGHT IN THE MIDDLE (CROSSFIRE); DRAW FIRE; FAT IS IN THE FIRE; FIGHT FIRE WITH FIRE; GET ALONG (ON LIKE A HOUSE AFIRE); HANG FIRE; HOLD ONE'S FIRE; HOLD SOMEONE'S FEET TO THE FIRE; IRONS IN THE FIRE; LIGHT A FIRE UNDER; LINE OF FIRE; NO SMOKE WITHOUT FIRE; ON FIRE; OPEN FIRE; OUT OF THE FRYING PAN INTO THE FIRE; PLAY WITH FIRE; SET ON FIRE; SET THE WORLD ON FIRE; SPREAD LIKE WILDFIRE; TRIAL BY FIRE; UNDER FIRE; WHERE'S THE FIRE. Also see under FIRING.

**fire away** Start to talk or ask questions. For example, *You've got more questions? Well, fire away.* This expression began as a military command to fire guns. Also see FIRE OFF.

**fire off** Say or write something and send it away rapidly, as in *He fired off three more questions,* or *She fired off a letter of complaint to the president.* This expression was, and still is, used in the sense of "fire a weapon or ammunition," as in *The police planned to fire off canisters of tear gas.*

**fire up 1.** Fill someone with enthusiasm, anger, or another strong emotion, as in *Her speech fired up the crowd in favor of her proposals.* This expression first referred to starting a fire in a furnace or boiler. **2.** Start the ignition of an engine, as in *Whenever he tried to fire up the motor, it stalled.*

**firing line, on the** In a position that forces one to deal with questions, criticism, or accusations. For example, *At the sales conference they asked so many questions that Anne felt she was on the firing line.* This expression originally meant the line of positions *from* which gunfire is directed at a target, and it is still used in a military context.

**first** In addition to the idioms beginning with FIRST, also see AT FIRST; AT FIRST GLANCE; CAST THE FIRST STONE; GET TO FIRST BASE; IF AT FIRST YOU DON'T SUCCEED; IN THE FIRST PLACE; IN THE (FIRST) FLUSH OF; LOVE AT FIRST SIGHT; NOT KNOW BEANS (THE FIRST THING); ON A FIRST-NAME BASIS.

**first and foremost** Also, **first of all.** Most important, primarily; also, to begin with. For example, *First and foremost, I want to thank our sponsors,* or *What we need, first and foremost, is a new secretary,* or *We have to deal, first of all, with the early history.* The first term is redundant, since *first* and *foremost* mean virtually the same thing. Both the first term and the second are used to give emphasis to the initial item in a list of several. Also see FIRST OFF; FIRST THING.

**first and last** Under all circumstances, always, as in *She was an artist first and last.* (For a synonym, see ABOVE ALL.) This expression should not be confused with **from first to last,** which means "from start to finish" or "throughout," as in *We cheered the runners on from first to last.*

**first come, first served** Those who arrive or act first will have their needs attended to earliest, as in *So many people showed up that we may not have enough free samples, so let it be "first come, first served."* Also see EARLY BIRD CATCHES THE WORM.

**first cousin** Something with a close relation or resemblance to something else, as in *This new machine is a first cousin to the previous model.*

**firsthand** Coming from the original source, not being reported by a third person. For example, *I prefer to hear his opinion firsthand, rather than having it passed on by my boss.* This phrase uses *hand* in the sense of "person" (coming directly from one person). Also see SECONDHAND.

**first of all** see FIRST AND FOREMOST.

**first off** From the start, immediately. For example, *He said to wash the car first off,* or *Why didn't someone tell her first off?* Also see under FIRST AND FOREMOST; FIRST THING.

**first refusal** The right to accept to refuse something before it is offered to others. For example, *I'm not ready to sell the car yet, but I'll give you first refusal.*

**first thing** Before anything else; without delay. For example, *Tom was supposed to call him first thing in the morning.* Also see under FIRST AND FOREMOST; FIRST OFF.

F

**first things first** The most important task gets attention first, as in *I very much wanted to see that movie, but first things first—the paper's due tomorrow.*

**fish** In addition to the idioms beginning with FISH, also see BIG FISH IN A SMALL POND; COLD FISH; DRINK LIKE A FISH; GOLDFISH BOWL; KETTLE OF FISH; LIKE SHOOTING FISH IN A BARREL; NEITHER FISH NOR FOWL; NOT THE ONLY FISH IN THE SEA; OTHER FISH TO FRY; SMELL FISHY.

**fish for 1.** Try to get something by indirect means or by tricks. For example, *He was always fishing for compliments.* **2.** Search for something, as in *I've fished for my watch in all the drawers.*

**fishing expedition** An attempt to find useful information by asking questions at random. For example, *The sales force was told to go on a fishing expedition to find out what they could about the company's competitors.*

**fish in troubled waters** Try to take advantage of a confused situation. For example, *He often buys up stock in companies in crisis; he manages to profit by fishing in troubled waters.* This term expresses the idea that fish bite more readily when seas are rough.

**fish or cut bait** Either go ahead with an activity or quit completely. For example, *You've been putting off calling him for hours; either fish or cut bait.* This expression is often used to tell someone to stop delaying or wasting time. It refers to a fisherman who should either be actively trying to catch fish or cutting up bait for others to use. A vulgar synonym is **shit or get off the pot.**

**fish out 1.** Discover and retrieve something from a pile or store. For example, *She finally fished out the right letter from the files.* This usage compares pulling fish from the sea to finding something. **2.** Use up the fish in a body of water by fishing, as in *This stream is completely fished out.*

**fish out of water, a** Also, **like a fish out of water.** A person away from his or her usual environment or activities. For example, *Using a computer for the first time, Carl felt like a fish out of water,* or *On the camping trip, Nell was a fish out of water.*

**fish story** A boastful story that's probably not true, as in *He came up with some fish story about winning a car.* This expression refers to the tendency of fishermen to exaggerate the size of their catch.

**fist** see HAND OVER FIST.

**fit** In addition to the idioms beginning with FIT, also see HAVE A FIT; IF THE SHOE FITS; SEE FIT; SURVIVAL OF THE FITTEST.

**fit as a fiddle** In excellent form or health. For example, *He's not just recovered, he's fit as a fiddle.*

F

**fit in 1.** Also, **fit into.** Provide a place or time for something. For example, *We can't fit in another appointment—there's no time.* **2.** Also, **fit in with.** Be suited to, belong. For example, *I just don't fit in here,* or *Her mood fitted in with the sad occasion.*

**fit like a glove** Be the right size and well suited; also, be in conformity with. For example, *That position fits him like a glove.* Also see TO A T.

**fit out** Also, **fit up.** Equip or supply someone or something with what is needed, as in *They promised to fit out the expedition free of charge.* This expression originally meant to furnish a ship with supplies, repairs, and equipment.

**fits and starts, by** Also, **in fits and starts.** With irregular intervals of action and in action, as in *The campaign is not progressing smoothly; it's proceeding by fits and starts.*

**fit to be tied** Furious, enraged, as in *I've been waiting for two hours and am fit to be tied.* This expression implies anger so extreme that one needs to be held down.

**fit to kill** Dressed in an extreme manner, as in *She was dressed up fit to kill.* Also see DRESSED TO KILL.

**five** see TAKE FIVE.

**fix** In addition to the idioms beginning with FIX, also see GET A FIX; GET A FIX ON; IF IT AIN'T BROKE, DON'T FIX IT; IN A FIX.

**fix someone's wagon** Get revenge on someone, spoil someone's chance of success. For example, *He may think he can win the election, but these ads will fix his wagon,* or *After what he did to her, her family intends to fix his wagon.* This term uses *fix* in the sense of "punish someone" or "put someone in an awkward position."

**fix up 1.** Repair or renew something or oneself. For example, *They're busy fixing up their house,* or *We fixed ourselves up before we headed out for the evening.* **2.** Provide or furnish someone with something, as in *He can fix you up with a new car,* or *Can you fix up my friend with a date for the dance?* **3.** Smooth over or settle a problem, as in *You'd think they could fix up these small differences.*

**fizzle out** Fail, end weakly, especially after a hopeful beginning. For example, *The plans for the party have fizzled out.* The word *fizzle* meant "to break wind without making noise." Later it was applied to hissing noises, such as those made by wet fireworks, and then to any action that ends in disappointment.

**flag down** Signal someone to stop, as in *The police were flagging down all cars.* This expression uses the verb *flag* in the sense of "catch the attention of, as by waving a flag."

**flake out 1.** Lose one's nerve, as in *Please don't flake out now.* **2.** Go crazy; also, cause someone to go crazy. For example, *She just flaked out, and we had to call an ambulance,* or *This project is flaking us out.* These usages probably are derived from the adjective *flaky,* meaning "eccentric."

**flame** see ADD FUEL TO THE FIRE (FLAMES); BURST INTO (FLAMES); FAN THE FLAMES; GO UP IN FLAMES; SHOOT DOWN (IN FLAMES).

**flare up 1.** Suddenly become angry, as in *She flared up at the slightest criticism.* This expression transfers a sudden burst of flame to sudden anger. **2.** Appear again. Used with health conditions that are not always present. For example, *Grandfather's arthritis flared up again.*

**flash** In addition to the idiom beginning with FLASH, also see IN A FLASH; QUICK AS A WINK (FLASH).

**flash in the pan, be a** An effort or a person that has a brief great success but fails to repeat or sustain it. For example, *We had high hopes for the new director, but she was only a flash in the pan.*

**flat** In addition to the idioms beginning with FLAT, also see CATCH SOMEONE FLAT-FOOTED; FALL FLAT; IN NO TIME (NOTHING FLAT); LEAVE ONE FLAT.

**flat as a pancake** Extremely level, especially too much so. For example, *There are no hills; the land around here is flat as a pancake.*

**flat broke** Also, **stone broke** or **stony broke.** With no money at all. For example, *I can't help you—I'm flat broke,* or *He's stone broke again.*

**flat-footed** see CATCH SOMEONE FLAT-FOOTED.

**flat on one's back 1.** Sick in bed. For example, *The flu has put her flat on her back.* **2.** Helpless, defeated, as in *I wish I could help, but the recession has left me flat on my back.*

**flat out 1.** In a direct manner, bluntly. For example, *He told the true story flat out.* **2.** At top speed, as in *She was running flat out to catch the train.*

**flatter oneself** Be too pleased with one's own achievement; exaggerate one's good points. For example, *He flattered himself that his presentation at the sales conference was a success,* or *She flattered herself that she was* *by far the best skater at the rink.* This usage is often put negatively, as in *Don't flatter yourself—we haven't won the contract yet.*

**flea** In addition to the idiom beginning with FLEA, also see NOT HURT A FLY (FLEA).

**flea market** A market, usually held outdoors, where used goods and antiques are sold. For example, *We picked up half of our furniture at flea markets.* The term is a direct translation of the French *marché aux puces* and implies that some of the used clothes and furniture might have fleas.

**flesh** In addition to the idioms beginning with FLESH, also see IN PERSON (THE FLESH); MAKE ONE'S FLESH CREEP; POUND OF FLESH; PRESS THE FLESH; SPIRIT IS WILLING BUT THE FLESH IS WEAK.

**flesh and blood 1.** Human beings, especially with respect to their failings or weaknesses. For example, *I can't do everything—I'm only flesh and blood.* **2. one's own flesh and blood.** One's blood relatives, as in *She can't refuse to help her own flesh and blood.*

**flesh out** Also, **put flesh on the bones of.** Give substance to something, provide with details. For example, *The editor told her to flesh out the story,* or *You need to put flesh on the bones of these characters.*

**flex one's muscles** Show off one's strength or power, as in *The boys love flexing their muscles,* or *The new department head has decided to flex her muscles by insisting on these changes.*

**flies** see AS THE CROW FLIES; DROP LIKE FLIES; NO FLIES ON SOMEONE; TIME FLIES. Also see under FLY.

**flight** In addition to the idiom beginning with FLIGHT, also see PUT TO FLIGHT; TAKE FLIGHT.

**flight of fancy** An unrealistic or fantastic idea. For example, *She engaged in flights of fancy, such as owning a million-dollar house.*

**fling** In addition to the idiom beginning with FLING, also see LAST FLING.

**fling oneself at someone** Try openly to make someone love one. For example, *She was constantly phoning him and inviting him over, really flinging herself at him.*

**flip one's lid** Also, **flip one's wig** or **flip out.** React very strongly or wildly, as with anger, surprise, or excitement; also, go crazy. For example, *I'm going to flip my lid if he doesn't do as he promised,* or *She really flipped out when she won first prize,* or *I think Rob has flipped his wig, he's acting so strangely.*

**flip through** Look quickly through the pages of something, as in *She flipped through the magazine while she waited.* This expression uses *flip* in the sense of "turn over pages."

**flog** see BEAT A DEAD HORSE.

**floor** In addition to the idiom beginning with FLOOR, also see GROUND FLOOR; MOP UP THE FLOOR WITH; SINK THROUGH THE FLOOR; TAKE THE FLOOR; WALK THE FLOOR.

**floor it** Make a car go fast by pressing the gas pedal to the floor, as in *The driver moved into the passing lane and floored it.*

**flotsam and jetsam 1.** A collection of various unwanted things, as in *Most of our things have been moved to the new house, but there's still some flotsam and jetsam to sort.* **2.** Homeless people, as in *The mayor was concerned about the flotsam and jetsam of the inner city. Flotsam* means things left floating after a ship sinks, and *jetsam* means things thrown into the sea from a ship in trouble. **Flotsam and jetsam** is used to describe any collection of objects found floating or washed onto a shore.

F

**flow** see EBB AND FLOW; GO WITH THE FLOW.

**flunk out 1.** Be forced out of a school because one's work does not meet the required standard. For example, *He flunked out of Harvard after just one year.* **2.** Fail at anything, as in *The camera ran out of film, so we flunked out as photographers.*

**fly** In addition to the idioms beginning with FLY, also see GET OFF THE GROUND (TO A FLYING START); GO FLY A KITE; LET FLY; MAKE THE DUST FLY; NOT HURT A FLY; ON THE FLY; SEND FLYING; WHEN PIGS FLY; WITH FLYING COLORS. Also see under FLIES; FLIGHT.

**fly at** Attack someone or something fiercely. For example, *The dogs flew at each other's throats.*

**fly blind** Try to do something without necessary information, proceed by guesswork, as in *There are no directions for assembling this furniture, so I'm flying blind.* This expression dates from World War II, when it was used by pilots who could not see the horizon and therefore had to rely on instruments. A similar expression is **fly by the seat of one's pants.**

**fly high** Be extremely happy and exited, as in *They were flying high after the baby's birth.*

**flying start** see under GET OFF THE GROUND.

**fly in the face of** Also, **fly in the teeth of.** Act in direct opposition to or defiance of someone or something. For example, *This foolish decision flies in the face of all our careful recommendations,* or *They went out without permission, flying in the teeth of house rules.*

**fly in the ointment, a** Something that spoils or prevents the success of something. For example, *The new library is wonderful, but there's a fly in the ointment: their catalog isn't complete yet.*

**fly off the handle** Lose one's temper, as in *Tom flies off the handle at even the smallest delay.* This expression refers to the loosened head of a hammer flying off after a blow.

F

**fly on the wall, a** An unseen observer or listener, as in *I wish I could be a fly on the wall when she tells him she's pregnant.*

**fly the coop** Escape, run away, as in *After years of fighting with my mother, my father finally flew the coop.* A *coop* is a type of cage for chickens or other birds.

**foam at the mouth** Be extremely angry, as in *She was foaming at the mouth over the judge's ruling.*

**fob off 1.** Sell or dispose of goods by fraud or trickery, as in *They tried to fob off the zircon as a diamond.* **2.** To calm or turn aside someone with demands or complaints by some dishonest means, as in *We needed her help, but she fobbed us off with promises.*

**fog** see IN A FOG.

**fold** In addition to the idioms beginning with FOLD, also see RETURN TO THE FOLD.

**fold one's tent** Quietly leave, as in *It's late, so let's fold our tents.*

**fold up 1.** Fail, especially go out of business. For example, *Three stores on Main Street have folded up.* **2.** Suddenly lose strength, break down. For example, *When she told him about the dog's death, she folded up.*

**folk** see JUST FOLKS.

**follow** In addition to the idioms beginning with FOLLOW, also see AS FOLLOWS; CAMP FOLLOWER; HARD ACT TO FOLLOW.

**follow along** Move or proceed in agreement or in time with someone. For example, *The children followed along with the song,* or *They followed along with the crowd.*

**follow in someone's footsteps** Also, **follow in someone's tracks.** Follow someone's example or guidance. For example, *He hoped his son would follow in his footsteps and also become an economist.*

**follow one's nose** Go straight ahead, as in *To get to the restaurant, just follow your nose down Baker Avenue.*

**follow suit** Imitate or do as someone else has done, as in *Bill decided to leave, and Mary followed suit.* This term comes from card games in which one must play a card from the same suit as the one led.

**follow the crowd** Go along with the majority, do what most others are doing. For example, *Make your own decision—don't just follow the crowd.*

**follow through** Also, **follow through on. 1.** In sports such as tennis or golf, carry a stroke to completion after striking the ball. For example, *You don't follow through on your backhand, so the ball goes into the net.* **2.** Also, **follow through on.** Carry an object, project, or intention to completion. For example, *She followed through on her promise to reorganize the department.* Also see FOLLOW UP, def. 1.

**follow up** Also, **follow up with. 1.** Carry something to completion. For example, *I'm following up their suggestions with concrete proposals.* Also see FOLLOW THROUGH. **2.** Increase the effectiveness or the success of something by further action. For example, *She followed up her interview with a phone call.*

**food for thought** An idea or issue to think about, as in *That interesting suggestion of yours has given us food for thought.*

**fool** In addition to the idioms beginning with FOOL, also see MAKE A FOOL OF; NOBODY'S FOOL; NO FOOL LIKE AN OLD FOOL; NOT SUFFER FOOLS GLADLY; PLAY THE FOOL. Also see under FOOLISH.

**fool and his money are soon parted, a** A silly or stupid person readily wastes money. For example, *Albert spends a lot on lottery tickets—a fool and his money are soon parted.*

**fool around 1.** Also, **mess around** or **monkey around.** Engage in meaningless or casual activity. For example, *Jim loved to fool around with his computer,* or *She was monkeying around with some figures in hopes of balancing the budget.* **2.** Engage in useless activity, waste time. For example, *Instead of studying, he spends all his time fooling around.* Also see FOOL AWAY. **3.** Engage in flirting or casual sexual acts; also, engage in adultery. For example, *He caught his wife fooling around with his best friend.*

**fool away** Waste something, especially money or time, as in *He was fooling away the entire afternoon.* Also see FOOL AROUND, def. 2.

**foolish** see PENNY WISE AND POUND FOOLISH.

**fool's errand** A mission or project with no chance of success, as in *Asking the bank for yet another loan was clearly a fool's errand.*

**fool's paradise** A state of contentment based on illusions or false hope. For example, *Joan lived in a fool's paradise, looking forward to a promotion she would never get.*

**fools rush in where angels fear to tread** Ignorant or inexperienced individuals get involved in situations that wiser persons would avoid, as in *I've never fixed a computer before—oh well, fools rush in where angels fear to tread,* or *He tried to resolve their unending argument—fools rush in.*

**foot** In addition to the idioms beginning with FOOT, also see BOUND HAND AND FOOT; CATCH SOMEONE FLAT-FOOTED; NOT TOUCH WITH A TEN-FOOT POLE; ONE FOOT IN THE GRAVE; ON FOOT; ON THE RIGHT FOOT; PLAY FOOTSIE; PUT ONE'S BEST FOOT FORWARD; PUT ONE'S FOOT DOWN; PUT ONE'S FOOT IN IT; SET FOOT; SHOE IS ON THE OTHER FOOT; SHOOT ONESELF IN THE FOOT; WAIT ON SOMEONE HAND AND FOOT. Also see under FEET.

**foot in both camps, have a** Support or have good relations with two opposing sides. For example, *He had a foot in both camps, making donations to candidates in both parties.* In this expression *camp* refers to camps of enemy soldiers in a battle.

**foot in one's mouth, put one's** Say something foolish, embarrassing, or tactless. For example, *Jane put her foot in her mouth when she called him by her first husband's name.* This notion is sometimes put as having **foot-in-mouth disease,** as in *He has a bad case of foot-in-mouth disease, always making some tactless remark.* The variant is a play on the *foot-and-mouth* (sometimes called *hoof-and-mouth*) *disease* that can affect cattle.

**foot in the door, get one's** Manage to get a start at something or an opportunity to do more; succeed with a first step. For example, *I think I could do well in an interview once I get my foot in the door with an appointment.* This term refers to the door-to-door salesperson who blocks the door with one foot so it cannot be closed.

**footloose and fancy-free** Having no attachments, especially romantic ones, and free to do as one pleases. For example, *When I was in my twenties, footloose and fancy-free, I would travel at a moment's notice.*

**footstep** see FOLLOW IN SOMEONE'S FOOTSTEPS.

**foot the bill** Pay the bill, as in *The bride's parents offered to foot the bill for the wedding.*

**for** In addition to the idioms beginning with FOR, also see ALL FOR; AS FOR; BUT FOR; EXCEPT FOR; GO FOR; GO IN FOR; GOOD FOR; IN FOR; OUT FOR; UNCALLED FOR; WHAT FOR.

**for a change 1.** For the sake of variety or a new experience, as in *Let's take a taxi for a change.* **2.** In contrast to the norm or past practice, as in *So you're on time for a change.*

**for all 1.** Also, **for all that.** In spite of, despite something. For example, *For all her protests she still loved the attention,* or *That actor was too old for the part, but he did a good job for all that.* **2. for all one cares** or **for all one knows.** So far as one knows; also, one doesn't really care or know. These phrases are used like a negative. For example, *He can buy ten houses for all I care,* meaning "I don't care at all," or *For all I know, she's gone to China,* meaning "I don't really know where she is."

**for all intents and purposes** see TO ALL INTENTS AND PURPOSES.

**for all one is worth 1.** To the limits of one's power or ability, as in *Nearing the end of the race, she ran for all she was worth.* **2. for all it's worth** or **for what it's worth** or **for whatever it's worth.** Even though it may not be important or valuable. For example, *Here's my opinion, for what it's worth,* or *For whatever it's worth, I've decided to take the first train in the morning.*

**for all that** see under FOR ALL.

**for all the world 1.** In all respects, precisely, as in *She looked for all the world like a movie star.* **2.** Also, **not for the world.** Not for anything, not at any price. For example, *I wouldn't give up chocolate for all the world,* or *Not for the world would I reveal your secret.* This expression is generally part of a negative statement. For a synonym, see NOT FOR LOVE OR MONEY.

**for a loop** see KNOCK FOR A LOOP.

**for a song** Very cheaply, for little money, especially for less than something is worth. For example, *She's such a smart shopper she decorated that room for a song.*

**for better or for worse** Also, **for better or worse.** Under good or bad circumstances, with good or bad effect. For example, *For better or for worse he trusts everyone.* This term often forms part of the traditional promises made during a wedding.

**forbid** see GOD FORBID.

**forbidden fruit** Unlawful pleasure or enjoyment. For example, *Smoking behind the school, that's a case of forbidden fruit.* This expression refers to Adam and Eve's breaking of God's commandment not to touch fruit from the tree in the Garden of Eden. In the form **forbidden fruit is sweet,** it appeared in numerous early English proverb collections.

**force** In addition to the idioms beginning with FORCE, also see BRUTE FORCE; DRIVING FORCE; IN FORCE; JOIN FORCES.

**for certain** Also, **for sure.** Without doubt. For example, *I can't tell for certain if this is the right color,* or *I know for sure that she has a new car.* The variant is also used to express agreement or to stress the truth of a statement, as in *Mary is really bossy—That's for sure,* or *Are you coming to the birthday party? For sure I am.*

**force someone's hand** Make someone act or speak sooner than desired or against his or her will. For example, *He didn't want to decide just then, but the board forced his hand.*

**force to be reckoned with** A person or group with influence or power. For example, *The success of their first computer game made them a force to be reckoned with in the industry.*

**for chicken feed** see CHICKEN FEED.

**for crying out loud** An exclamation of anger or exasperation, as in *For crying out loud, can't you do anything right?*

**for days on end** see ON END.

**for dear life** Also, **for one's life.** Desperately, urgently, so as to save one's life. For example, *When the boat turned over, I hung on for dear life,* or *With the dogs chasing* *them, they ran for their lives,* or *She wanted that vase, but I saw it first and held onto it for dear life.* These expressions do not always mean that someone's life is really in danger. Also see FOR THE LIFE OF ONE.

**fore** see TO THE FORE.

**foregone conclusion, a 1.** An outcome or result that people think will surely happen, as in *The victory was a foregone conclusion.* **2.** A conclusion formed too soon in a process of decision-making, as in *The jury was warned to consider all of the evidence and not base their decision on a foregone conclusion.*

F

**foremost** see FIRST AND FOREMOST.

**forest** see CAN'T SEE THE FOREST FOR THE TREES.

**forever and a day** Also, **for forever and a day. 1.** For a very long time, as in *He's been working on that book forever and a day.* **2.** Without a break, endlessly, as in *Will this noise never end? It's been going on forever and a day.*

**forewarned is forearmed** Knowledge in advance lets someone be prepared, as in *Let me know when he's in town so I can stay home—forewarned is forearmed.* This expression first referred to military preparations. *Forearm* means "supply with weapons ahead of time."

**for example** Also, **for instance.** As an illustration of something, as in *Dress casually, in blue jeans, for example,* or *This computer program has problems—for instance, it's hard to retrieve lost data.* The first expression is used throughout this book to illustrate how an idiom is used.

**for fear of** Also, **for fear that.** Because of a fear of something bad that might happen. For example, *They closed all the windows for fear of rain,* or *She opened the door carefully for fear of waking the children.* The variant is always used before a clause, as in *She wouldn't let her children climb trees for fear that they would fall.*

**for free** Without charge, as in *You can't expect the doctor to treat you for free.*

**for fun, (just) 1.** Also, **(just) in fun.** As a joke, not seriously. For example, *For fun he told her he'd won the lottery,* or *Their teasing was just in fun.* **2. (just) for the fun of it** or **(just) for kicks.** For pleasure or excitement. For example, *He played basketball for the fun of it,* or *They drove around for hours, just for kicks.* Also see FOR THE HELL OF IT.

**forget** In addition to the idioms beginning with FORGET, also see FORGIVE AND FORGET.

**forget it 1.** Don't bother to think about it, it's not important. For example, *Don't worry about the mess, forget it!* In *Thanks so much for helping. Forget it, it was nothing,* it is a substitute for YOU'RE WELCOME. **2.** You are wrong, as in *You think I'm going to trust him again? Forget it!* **3.** Don't think about or hope for it anymore, as in *Forget it—you'll never understand this math.*

**forget oneself** Lose one's reserve, temper, or self-restraint; do or say something that is not acceptable in one's position. For example, *A teacher should never forget herself and shout at the class.*

**forgive and forget** Both pardon and hold no resentment concerning a past event. For example, *After Meg and Mary decided to forgive and forget their differences, they became good friends.* For a synonym, see LET BYGONES BE BYGONES.

**for God's sake** Also, **for goodness sake.** See FOR THE SAKE OF, def. 3.

**for good** Also, **for good and all** or **once and for all.** Permanently, forever. For example, *I'm moving to Europe for good.* Also see FOR KEEPS.

**for good measure** In addition to the required amount. For example, *Whenever she bakes, she adds a little more cinnamon for good measure,* or *He didn't argue with my price, so I gave him some extra supplies for good measure.*

**for heaven's sake** see FOR THE SAKE OF, def. 3.

**for keeps 1.** For the winner to keep permanently, as in *You can't take the marbles back; we were playing for keeps.* **2.** For an indefinitely long time, forever, as in *She is leaving town for keeps.* **3.** In earnest, seriously, as in *We're separating for keeps.*

**fork over** Also, **fork out** or **fork up.** Pay or give up an amount of money because one has to. For example, *It's time you forked over what you owe,* or *He forked out a hundred dollars for that meal,* or *Fork up or we'll sue.*

**for love or money** see NOT FOR LOVE OR MONEY.

**form** see RUN TO FORM.

**for one** Also, **for one thing.** As the first of several possible instances. For example, *Everything seemed to go wrong; for one, we had a flat tire, and then we lost the keys,* or *I find many problems with your proposal; for one thing, you don't specify where you'll get the money.* **For one** can also be applied to a person, as in *He doesn't like their behavior, and I for one agree with him.*

**for one's money** According to one's opinion, choice, or preference. For example, *For my money, a trip to New York is not worth the trouble or expense.*

**for one's pains** As a poor return for the trouble one has taken, as in *And all he got for his pains was a failing grade.* This expression is nearly always used ironically to indicate that the return was not appropriate to the effort made.

**for one's part** Also, **on one's part** or **on the part of one.** So far as one is concerned, as regards one's share in the matter. For example, *You may want to go out, but for my part I want to stay home,* or *If they want to postpone the meeting, there'll be no objection on our part.*

**for one's sake** see FOR THE SAKE OF.

**for one thing** see under FOR ONE.

**for openers** Also, **for starters.** To begin with. For example, *Out of 50 possible candidates for the job, they eliminated 30, for openers,* or *She believed him, which shows, for starters, that she was a fool.* The word *starters* is also used for the appetizer or first course of a meal, as in *For starters we had shrimp cocktail.*

**for Pete's sake** Also, **for pity's sake.** See FOR THE SAKE OF, def. 3.

**for real** Serious and true, genuine, as in *Are your plans to move away for real?*

**for shame** Also, **shame on you.** An expression that criticizes someone for being dishonorable or disgraceful. For example, "*For shame,*" *said Carol to the puppy,* "*You shouldn't have done that,*" or "*Shame on you for cheating,*" *the teacher said.*

**for short** Also, **short for.** As an abbreviation. For example, *Richard prefers to be called Dick for short,* or *The word* lab *is short for* laboratory.

**for show** For the sake of appearances or display. For example, *They held a Grand Opening ceremony, mainly for show,* or *The police pretended to jail the informer, for show.*

**for starters** see FOR OPENERS.

**for sure** see FOR CERTAIN.

**fort** see HOLD THE FORT.

**forth** see AND SO FORTH; BACK AND FORTH; BRING FORTH; HOLD FORTH; PUT FORTH; SET FORTH.

**for that matter** As for that, so far as that is concerned, as in *Yes, I'm hungry—for that matter, I'm starving!*

**for the asking** On request, without charge, as in *My brother is a lawyer, so for us his advice is free for the asking,* or *If you want to borrow my car, it's yours for the asking.*

**for the best** see ALL FOR THE BEST.

**for the birds** Worthless, not to be taken seriously, no good. For example, *This conference is for the birds—let's leave now.*

**for the hell of it** Also, **(just) for the heck of it** or **just for the hell of it.** For no particular reason; on a sudden desire. For example, *We drove by our old house just for the hell of it.* In the first variant, *heck* is a euphemism for *hell.* Also see FOR FUN, def. 2.

**for the life of me** Also, **for the life of him** or **her.** Although trying hard, as in *I can't for the life of me remember his name.* This expression is used for emphasis, not to mean that one's life is in any danger.

**for the love of** **1.** For the sake of, in consideration of. For example, *She signed up for all these volunteer jobs for the love of praise.* **2. for the love of Pete** or **for the love of Mike** or **for the love of God.** An exclamation of surprise, exasperation, or some similar feeling, as in *For the love of Pete, give me the money! Pete* and *Mike* are euphemisms for God. Also see FOR THE SAKE OF, def. 3.

F

**for the moment** Also, **for the present** or **for the time being.** Temporarily, for now. For example, *For the moment I am too busy, but I'll get to it next week,* or *This room arrangement will be fine for the present,* or *Jim will act as secretary for the time being.*

**for the most part** In general, usually. For example, *For the most part she is very good-humored,* or *The committee members agree for the most part.* Also see the synonyms BY AND LARGE; ON THE WHOLE.

**for the present** see FOR THE MOMENT.

**for the record** see GO ON RECORD; JUST FOR THE RECORD.

**for the sake of** **1.** Also, **for one's sake.** Out of consideration or regard for a person or thing; for someone's or something's advantage or good. For example, *For Jill's sake we did not serve meat,* or *We have to stop fighting for the sake of family unity.* **2.** For the purpose or motive of, as in *You like to quarrel only for the sake of an argument.* **3. for God's sake.** Also, **for goodness** or **heaven's** or **Pete's** or **pity's sake.** An exclamation showing surprise, impatience, anger, or some other emotion, depending on the context. For example, *For God's sake, I didn't expect to see you here,* or *Hurry up, for goodness sake,* or *For heaven's sake, how can you say such a mean thing?* or *For pity's sake, finish your dinner.* The variants are euphemisms for God. For a synonym, see FOR THE LOVE OF, def. 2.

**for the time being** see FOR THE MOMENT.

**fortune** see MAKE A FORTUNE.

**for two cents** For nothing; for a very small sum of money. For example, *For two cents I'd quit this job today.* The related expressions **one's two cents** and **two cents' worth** mean "one's opinion for whatever it is worth." They are often used when one offers an opinion without being asked, as in *Well, I think he should go—there's my two cents' worth.*

**forty winks** A brief nap, as in *There's just time for forty winks before we have to leave.*

**forward** see BACKWARD AND FORWARD; CARRY FORWARD; COME FORWARD; KNOW LIKE A BOOK

(BACKWARDS AND FORWARDS); LOOK FORWARD TO; PUT FORWARD; PUT ONE'S BEST FOOT FORWARD; SET FORWARD.

**for what it's worth** see under FOR ALL ONE IS WORTH.

**foul** In addition to the idioms beginning with FOUL, also see RUN AFOUL OF.

**foul one's nest** Also, **foul one's own nest.** Hurt one's own interests, as in *With his constant complaints about his wife, he's only fouling his own nest.*

**foul play** Unfair action, especially involving violence. For example, *The police suspected that the missing man had met with foul play.* This term originally was and still is applied to unfair conduct in a sport or game.

F

**foul up** **1.** Make a mistake; spoil something because of mistakes. For example, *He's fouled up this report, but I think we can fix it.* **2.** Cause serious problems in something; ruin. For example, *Our plans were fouled up by the bad weather.*

**four** In addition to the idioms beginning with FOUR, also see BETWEEN YOU AND ME (AND THE FOUR WALLS); ON ALL FOURS.

**four corners of the earth, the** The far ends of the world; all parts of the world. For example, *Athletes come from the four corners of the earth to compete in the Olympics.*

**four-letter word** Any of several short English words that are generally regarded as vulgar or obscene. For example, *No four-letter words are permitted in this classroom.*

**fowl** see NEITHER FISH NOR FOWL.

**fox** see CRAZY LIKE A FOX.

**frame of mind** Mental or emotional attitude or mood, as in *You have to be in the right frame of mind to enjoy hiking in the rain.*

**fray** see ENTER THE FRAY.

**freak out** **1.** Experience or cause someone to experience hallucinations, paranoia, or other frightening feelings as a result of taking a mind-altering drug. For example, *They were freaking out on LSD or some other drug.* **2.** Behave or cause someone to behave in a wild manner due to enthusiasm, excitement, or fear. For example, *The band's wild playing made the audience freak out,* or *It was such a close accident, it really freaked me out.* Also see FLIP ONE'S LID.

**free** In addition to the idioms beginning with FREE, also see BREATHE EASY (FREELY); FEEL FREE; FOOTLOOSE AND FANCY-FREE; FOR FREE; GET OFF (SCOT-FREE); HOME FREE; OF ONE'S OWN ACCORD (FREE WILL).

**free agent** **1.** A person not forced to do anything, not responsible to any authority for his or her actions. For example, *After he quit his job, he decided to pursue the same line of work as a free agent.* **2.** A professional athlete who is free to sign a contract with any team. For example, *After he was released from the Yankees, he was a free agent and could shop around for the team that offered the most money.*

**free and clear** Without any legal conditions attached, such as a lien or mortgage. For example, *After the mortgage was paid off, they owned the house free and clear.*

**free and easy** **1.** Casual, relaxed, as in *His style of writing is free and easy.* **2.** Careless, sloppy, or morally loose, as in *This administration was free and easy with the taxpayers' money,* or *Those girls hate to be considered free and easy.*

**free as a bird** At liberty, without obligations, as in *Can you join us tonight? Yes, I'm free as a bird,* or *He's free as a bird—he can travel wherever he chooses.* Also see FOOTLOOSE AND FANCY-FREE.

**free enterprise** Also, **private enterprise.** A business venture for one's own benefit, especially an unfair or illegal one. For example, *The city treasurer didn't bother with competitive bids; the spirit of free enterprise just led him to his brother-in-law,* or *The sergeant indulged in a little private enterprise, selling cigarettes on the black market.* This is a sarcastic use of a term that literally means the freedom of private businesses to operate with little government control.

**free fall** A rapid, uncontrolled drop or decline, as in *The markets threatened to go into free fall, and investors came close to panic.* This term was first used for a free fall through the air without anything to slow it, such as a parachute.

**free hand, a** Also, **free rein.** Freedom to do or decide as one thinks is right. For example, *The teacher gave her assistant a free hand with the class,* or *They gave me free rein to reorganize the department.*

**free lunch** Something gained without any effort or cost. For example, *In politics there is no free lunch; every favor calls for repayment.* This expression is often used in a negative way, as in the example.

**free rein** see FREE HAND.

**free will** see OF ONE'S OWN ACCORD.

**freeze one's blood** see MAKE ONE'S BLOOD RUN COLD.

**freeze out** **1.** Shut out or exclude someone by unfriendly treatment, as in *They tried to freeze me out of the conversation.* **2.** Force someone to retire or withdraw from membership, a job, or the like. For example, *After Bill was frozen out of the case, they hired a new lawyer.*

**fresh** In addition to the idioms beginning with FRESH, also see BREATH OF FRESH AIR.

**fresh as a daisy** Well rested, energetic, as in *I got a good night's sleep and feel fresh as a daisy.*

**fresh out of** Also, **clean out of.** Recently or completely reach the end of one's supply of something. For example, *Sorry, I'm fresh out of sugar and can't lend you any,* or *We're clean out of small change.*

**Friday** see GIRL FRIDAY.

**friend** In addition to the idiom beginning with FRIEND, also see FAIR-WEATHER FRIEND; MAKE FRIENDS.

**friend in court** Also, **friends in high places.** A person or persons who can help because of their important position. For example, *With a friend in court, he has a good chance of getting the contract,* or *Jim thinks he can escape paying the fine; he has friends in high places.* This expression refers to the power of a person at the royal court.

**frighten** see SCARE OUT OF ONE'S WITS.

**fritter away** Foolishly spend or waste something little by little; wear down gradually. For example, *She frittered away her salary on odds and ends and saved nothing.*

**fritz** see ON THE BLINK.

**fro** see TO AND FRO.

**frog in one's throat** A thick feeling in the throat, as in *Can you understand me? I have a frog in my throat.*

**frog in a small pond** see under BIG FISH IN A SMALL POND.

**from bad to worse, go** Become unacceptable, be on a steady downward course. For example, *Mary's grades have gone from bad to worse.* Also see IF WORST COMES TO WORST.

**from day one** Since the day something began, as in *She's complained about the job from day one.*

**from first to last** see under FIRST AND LAST.

**from hand to hand** see HAND TO HAND.

**from hand to mouth** see HAND TO MOUTH.

**from head to toe** Also, **from head to heels** or **from head to foot; from tip to toe** or **from top to toe.** Over someone's entire body. For example, *He was dressed in black from head to toe,* or *She ached all over, from tip to toe.*

**from Missouri, I'm** I'm extremely skeptical, so you'll have to prove it. For example, *You won the lottery? Come on, I'm from Missouri.* The full expression is **I'm from Missouri and you'll have to show me.**

**from now on** Also, **from this day forward** or **from this day on.** Beginning now and continuing forever, as in *From now on I'll be more careful,* or *They promised to follow instructions from this day forward.*

**from pillar to post** From one thing or place to another. For example, *After Kevin joined the Air Force, the family kept moving from pillar to post.*

**from rags to riches** From being poor to being rich, especially through one's own efforts. For example, *The invention carried the scientist from rags to riches.*

**from scratch** From the very beginning, from nothing. For example, *We made the cake from scratch.* Similarly, **to start from scratch** means "to start from the very beginning," as in *After the business failed, they decided to reorganize and start from scratch.* Also see FROM THE GROUND UP.

**from soup to nuts** Also, **from A to Z** or **from start to finish** or **from stem to stern.** From beginning to end, throughout, as in *We discussed all their concerns, from soup to nuts,* or *She had to learn a whole new system from A to Z,* or *It rained from start to finish,* or *We cleaned the whole house from stem to stern.* The first expression refers to the first and last courses of a meal. The second expression refers to the first and last letters of the Roman alphabet. The third refers to the entire course of a race. The last variant refers to the front (the *stem*) and back (the *stern*) of a vessel.

**from the bottom of one's heart** Most sincerely, unreservedly. For example, *I want to thank all of my supporters from the bottom of my heart,* or *She wished, from the bottom of her heart, that her daughter would get well.*

**from the cradle to the grave** From birth to death, throughout life, as in *This health plan will cover you from cradle to grave.*

**from the ground up** From the very beginning; also, completely, thoroughly. For example, *We've had to learn a new system from the ground up,* or *The company changed all of the forms from the ground up.* This expression refers to the construction of a house.

**from the horse's mouth** From a reliable source of information. For example, *I have it from the horse's mouth that he plans to retire next month.* It is also put as **straight from the horse's mouth,** meaning "directly from the best source of accurate information."

**from the outset** see AT THE OUTSET.

**from the sublime to the ridiculous** From the beautiful to the silly, from something great to something that can't compare in quality. For example, *They played first Bach and then some stupid popular song—from the sublime to the ridiculous.* The reverse, **from the ridiculous to the sublime,** is used with the opposite meaning.

**from the word go** From the start, as in *I've had trouble with this computer from the word go.* This expression probably refers to the start of a race, signaled by the word *go.*

**from time to time** Occasionally, once in a while. For example, *From time to time we have dinner with the Carters.* Also see AT TIMES; EVERY NOW AND THEN; ONCE IN A WHILE.

**from way back** Since long ago; for a long time. For example, *Our family has owned this painting from way back,* or *We know the Smiths from way back.*

**front** In addition to the idioms beginning with FRONT, also see BRAVE FACE (FRONT); IN FRONT OF; OUT FRONT; UP FRONT.

**front and center** In the most prominent or visible position, as in *You couldn't miss John—he was front and center in that presentation.* This expression refers to the best and usually most expensive seats in a theater.

F

**front burner, on a** Also, **on the front burner.** A position of relatively great importance or high priority. For example, *The boss said this project is now on a front burner.* This expression refers to a cook's putting the items requiring the most attention at the front of the stove. Also see BACK BURNER.

**front office** The top executives or decision-makers in an organization, as in *I'll have to check with the front office before I can give you a discount.*

**frosting on the cake** see ICING ON THE CAKE.

**frown on** Regard something with disapproval or distaste, as in *Pat frowns on bad language.* This idiom transfers the disapproving facial expression to the thought it expresses.

**fruit** see BEAR FRUIT; FORBIDDEN FRUIT.

**fruitcake** see NUTTY AS A FRUITCAKE.

**fry** see OTHER FISH TO FRY; OUT OF THE FRYING PAN; SMALL FRY.

**fuck around 1.** Fool around, engage in unimportant activity, as in *Stop fucking around and get the job done,* or *I'm tired of fucking around—let's go home.* [Vulgar slang] **2. fuck someone around.** Cheat, treat badly or make trouble for someone, as in *Stop fucking me around; I know what you're up to.* [Vulgar slang] **3.** Be sexually active, as in *Doesn't he have a reputation for fucking around?* [Vulgar slang]

**fuck off 1.** Go away, get out of here, as in *Fuck off or I'll call the police.* This idiom is used only as a command. [Vulgar slang] **2.** Spend time idly, loaf or avoid one's duty. For example, *After twelve years of school some kids feel they're entitled to fuck off,* or *You're always fucking off instead of working.* [Vulgar slang] **3. be fucked off.** To be furious, as in *They didn't show up, and I am really fucked off.* [Vulgar slang] Also see PISS OFF.

**fuck over** Treat unfairly, take advantage of, as in *This so-called reform is really fucking over the taxpayer.* [Vulgar slang]

**fuck up 1.** Ruin, spoil. For example, *Don't tell me you're going to fuck up again.* It is also put as **be fucked up,** meaning "be ruined or spoiled," as in *This entire project is fucked up.* [Vulgar slang] **2.** Act, carelessly or foolishly, mess up, as in *I'm sorry, I really fucked up when I invited them.* [Vulgar slang] **3.** Break down, fail, as in *If the flashbulb fucks up again, I won't get a picture.* [Vulgar slang] **4. be fucked up.** Be very confused or mentally ill; also, be intoxicated. For example, *He was so fucked up they had to drive him home,* or *What a party—I sure got fucked up.* [Vulgar slang]

**fuck you** Also **get fucked; go fuck yourself.** A curse meaning "go to hell." For example, *Fuck you—go make your own dinner!* or *Get out of here, get fucked!* [Vulgar slang] Also see GIVE THE FINGER.

**fuel** see ADD FUEL TO THE FIRE.

**full** In addition to the idioms beginning with FULL, also see GLASS IS HALF FULL; HAVE ONE'S HANDS FULL; IN FULL SWING; TO THE FULL. Also see under FILL.

**full blast** Also, **at full blast.** At full power, with great energy; also, as loud as possible. For example, *The committee is working full blast on the plans,* or *He played the car radio at full blast.* This expression transfers the strong currents of air used in furnaces to anything being done at full power.

**full circle, come** Also, **go full circle.** Complete an entire cycle; return to the original position or condition. For example, *After a whole year of debate we have come full circle on this issue and will follow our original plan.*

**full-court press** An all-out effort to apply pressure. For example, *She'd learned over the years how to deliver a full-court press of guilt.* The term refers to a basketball tactic in which the defenders play hard against the team with the ball all over the entire court.

**full of beans 1.** Lively, energetic, in high spirits, as in *The children were full of beans today, looking forward to their field trip.* **2.** Also, **full of prunes.** Acting foolish, talking nonsense, as in *One cup of coffee won't hurt you—you're full of prunes.* Also see FULL OF CRAP.

**full of crap** Also, **full of bull** or **full of shit.** Talking nonsense or saying things that aren't exactly true, as in *She doesn't know what she's talking about; she's full of crap.* [Vulgar slang] Also see FULL OF IT, def. 2; HOT AIR.

**full of hot air** see HOT AIR.

**full of it 1.** Also, **full of the devil.** Mischievous, naughty. For example, *The children were full of it today, giving the teacher a hard time,* or *Bill is full of the devil, hiding his brother's things and teasing him constantly.* **2.** Talking nonsense, as in *He claims he caught a lot of fish, but I think he's full of it.* This usage is a euphemism for ruder idioms like FULL OF CRAP.

**full of oneself** Conceited, self-centered, as in *Ever since she won the prize Mary's been so full of herself that no one wants to talk to her.*

**full speed ahead** Also, **full steam ahead.** As fast and as strongly as possible. For example, *There's only one way we'll get there on time, so go full speed ahead,* or *Production will go full steam ahead as soon as the orders are received.* It is also put as **with a full head of steam,** as in *She was traveling with a full head of steam—she was due there at noon.* These expressions all refer to the steam engine, where *full steam* signifies that a boiler has developed maximum pressure.

**full swing** see IN FULL SWING.

**full tilt** Also, **at full tilt.** As fast or forcefully as possible, as in *Running full tilt on that very uneven ground, she was certain to trip and fall,* or *Trying to keep up with new orders, the factory was running at full tilt.*

**full well** Very well, as in *You know full well how much this costs.*

**fun** In addition to the idiom beginning with FUN, also see FOR FUN; LIKE FUN; MAKE FUN OF; MORE FUN THAN A BARREL OF MONKEYS. Also see under FUNNY.

**fun and games** Activity for pure pleasure or enjoyment. For example, *This job isn't all fun and games, you know,* or *We're just out for fun and games tonight.*

**funeral** see IT'S ONE'S FUNERAL.

**funny** In addition to the idioms beginning with FUNNY, also see under FUN.

**funny bone** **1.** A point on the elbow where the ulnar nerve runs close to the surface and produces a sharp tingling sensation when knocked against the bone. For example, *Ouch! I just banged my funny bone.* **2.** A sense of humor, as in *That comedian really tickles my funny bone.* This expression is derived from def. 1.

**funny business** Activities or behavior that is dishonest, illegal or, unethical. For example, *We suspect their company has been up to some funny business.*

**funny money** Counterfeit money; also, money from a secret or questionable source. For example, *The police warned storekeepers that some funny money was being passed around town.*

**fur** see MAKE THE DUST (FUR) FLY.

**furious** see FAST AND FURIOUS.

**further** see WITHOUT FURTHER ADO.

**fury** see HELL HAS NO FURY LIKE A WOMAN SCORNED.

**fuse** see BLOW A FUSE.

**fuss** see KICK UP A FUSS; MAKE A FUSS.

**future** see IN THE NEAR FUTURE.

**futz around** Also, **futz with.** Waste time or effort on unimportant things, play around. For example, *He spent all morning futzing around with the report,* or *No more futzing with the car—we have to go now.*

# Gg

**gab** see GIFT OF GAB.

**gain** In addition to the idiom beginning with GAIN, also see ILL-GOTTEN GAINS; NO PAIN, NO GAIN; NOTHING VENTURED, NOTHING GAINED.

**gain ground** **1.** Advance, make progress; also, win acceptance. For example, *The new conservation policy is gaining ground among the voters.* This expression refers to a military advance in which an army takes territory from the enemy. For an antonym, see LOSE GROUND. **2. gain ground on** or **gain ground upon.** Advance at the expense of someone, make progress in competition with someone. For example, *Door-to-door contact with voters helped them gain ground on the opposition.* Also see LOSE GROUND.

**gallery** see PLAY TO THE GALLERY.

**game** In addition to the idioms beginning with GAME, also see AHEAD OF THE GAME; AT THIS STAGE (OF THE GAME); BEAT SOMEONE AT HIS OR HER OWN GAME; CON GAME; END GAME; FAIR GAME; FUN AND GAMES; LOSING BATTLE (GAME); NAME OF THE GAME; ONLY GAME IN TOWN; PLAY A WAITING GAME; PLAY GAMES; PLAY THE GAME; WHOLE NEW BALL GAME.

**game is up, the** Also, **the jig is up.** The trick or deception has been discovered. For example, *When they took inventory they realized what was missing, and the game was up for the department head.*

**game plan** A strategy or plan for reaching a goal or result, as in *Any new business has to have a clear game plan.*

**game that two can play, that's a** Also, **two can play at that game.** Another person can behave in the same way or do the same thing, usually something unfriendly or damaging. For example, *He refused to share any information with us, but that's a game two can play.* This expression is generally used as a threat.

**gander** see TAKE A GANDER AT.

**gang** In addition to the idiom beginning with GANG, also see LIKE GANGBUSTERS.

**gang up** **1.** Also, **gang up with.** Act together as a group. For example, *The residents ganged up to make the neighborhood safer.* **2. gang up on** or **gang up against.** Join in opposition or attack against, as in *The big kids were always ganging up on the little ones,* or *The students all ganged up against the substitute teacher.*

**garden** In addition to the idiom beginning with GARDEN, also see LEAD DOWN THE GARDEN PATH.

**garden variety** Ordinary, common, as in *I don't want anything special in a VCR—the garden variety will do.* This term refers to a common plant as opposed to a specially developed one.

**gas** In addition to the idiom beginning with GAS, also see COOKING WITH GAS; RUN OUT OF (GAS).

**gasket** see under BLOW A FUSE.

**gasp** see LAST GASP.

**gas up** Supply a vehicle with gasoline, as in *I want to be sure to gas up before we go.* Also see TANK UP.

**gate** see CRASH THE GATE.

**gather** In addition to the idiom beginning with GATHER, also see ROLLING STONE GATHERS NO MOSS.

**gather dust** Be forgotten or left unused, as in *They submitted their report, but it's just gathering dust on the president's shelf.*

**gauntlet** see RUN THE GAUNTLET; THROW DOWN THE GAUNTLET.

**gear** see HIGH GEAR.

**gee whiz** An expression of surprise, dismay, or enthusiasm. For example, *Gee whiz, Dad, I thought you'd let me borrow the car,* or *Gee whiz, they finally won a game!*

**gender gap** A broad difference between men and women, as in *There is still an enormous gender gap in the wages people earn.* This expression at first referred to the difference between men and women in voting preferences.

**general** see IN GENERAL; ON (GENERAL) PRINCIPLE.

**generation gap** A broad difference in values and attitudes between one generation and another, especially between parents and their children. For example, *There's a real generation gap in their choice of music, restaurants, clothing—you name it.*

**generous to a fault** see TO A FAULT.

**get** In addition to the idioms beginning with GET, also see BE (GET) BUSTED; COME AND GET IT; DIP (GET) ONE'S TOES INTO; EARLY BIRD CATCHES (GETS) THE WORM; GIVE AS GOOD AS ONE GETS; GROUND FLOOR, GET IN ON THE; IT TAKES GETTING USED TO; LAY (GET ONE'S) HANDS ON; MARCHING ORDERS, GET ONE'S; PLAY HARD TO GET; SQUEAKY WHEEL GETS THE GREASE; TELL (SOMEONE WHERE TO GET) OFF;

WHEN THE GOING GETS TOUGH; YOU GET WHAT YOU PAY FOR. Also see under BECOME; GIVE; HAVE.

**get a bang out of** Also, **get a charge out of** or **get a kick out of.** Get a feeling of excitement from, get a thrill from. For example, *I get a bang out of taking the kids to the amusement park,* or *I get a charge out of her imitations.*

**get about** Also, **get around. 1.** Move around, be active, especially after an illness. For example, *At 85 Jean still gets around very well,* or *Arthritis makes it hard for him to get about.* **2.** Become known by many people, as in *The news of her engagement got about very quickly.* **3.** Be socially active, as in *After her husband died, she didn't get about much for a year.*

**get a break** Receive special consideration or treatment; get a lucky chance at something. For example, *The new price is higher, but you are getting a break on service,* or *Farmers got a break when it finally rained.* Also see GIVE SOMEONE A BREAK.

**get a charge out of** see GET A BANG OUT OF.

**get across 1.** Also, **get *something* across.** Make something understandable or clear, as in *I tried to get my point across,* or *He'll have to get it across to the others.* **2.** Be convincing, communicate effectively, as in *How can I get across to the students?* Also see COME ACROSS; PUT ACROSS.

**get a dirty look** see DIRTY LOOK.

**get a fix** Get a needed dose of something, especially but not necessarily a narcotic drug. For example, *Heroin addicts will do anything to get their fix,* or *She says she has to have her daily chocolate fix.* Also see GET A FIX ON.

**get a fix on** Also, **have a fix on; get** or **have a handle on; get** or **have a grasp of.** Get (or have) a clear understanding of something. For example, *I was finally able to get a fix on the specifics of this problem,* or *No one in the press room had a handle on Balkan history,* or *Do you have a grasp of the situation?*

**get after** Urge or scold someone about doing something. For example, *Dad should get after Billy to mow the lawn,* or *Mom got after Jane for forgetting her house key.* Also see KEEP AFTER.

**get a grip on** Also, **have a grip on.** Get mastery or control over something or oneself (meaning one's emotions). For example, *Get a grip on yourself or the reporters will give you a hard time,* or *Does the old man still have a grip on the family business?* This expression transfers a firm physical hold to emotional or intellectual control.

**get a hand** see GIVE A HAND.

**get a handle on** see under GET A FIX ON.

**get ahead 1.** Succeed or make progress, especially in one's career or in society. For example, *She put in many hours of overtime in order to get ahead.* **2.** Save a little money, as in *After we settle the hospital bill, we hope to get ahead enough to buy a new car.* **3. get ahead of.** Move in front of, as in *I got ahead of her in line.* **4. get ahead of.** Make better progress than someone else in a competition, as in *We were determined to get ahead of the competition.* Also see AHEAD OF THE GAME.

**get a head start** see HEAD START.

**get a kick out of** see GET A BANG OUT OF.

**get a life** Develop some interests or relationships of one's own. For example, *Stop sitting around and complaining—get a life.*

**get a line on** Also, **have a line on.** Get information about something or someone. For example, *Sue got a line on some possible tennis partners,* or *The Realtor has a line on a number of vacant apartments.* Similarly, **give someone a line on** means "provide information about," as in *The librarian gave me a line on the books I would need.* Also see GET A FIX ON.

G

**get a load of** Look at or listen to, as in *Get a load of Mike feeding the baby.*

**get along 1.** Also, **get on.** Be or continue to be on friendly terms. For example, *She finds it hard to get along with her in-laws,* or *He gets on well with all of his neighbors except one.* A colloquial synonym for *get along well* is **get on like a house afire,** comparing increasingly good relations to the rapid progress of a fire. **2.** Also, **get on.** Manage, fare; also, prosper or progress. For example, *I can just get along in this town on those wages,* or *How are you getting on in school?* **3. get along without.** Manage without something, as in *With that new car loan, he can't get along without a raise.* **4.** Also, **get on.** Progress; advance, especially in years. For example, *How are you getting along with the work?* or *Dad doesn't hear too well; he's getting on, you know.* Also see ALONG IN YEARS; GET ON, def. 5. **5. get along with you.** Go away; also, be quiet, stop talking about the subject, as in *Get along with you, I'm trying to read.* Also see GET ON.

**get a move on** Also, **get cracking** or **get going** or **get rolling.** Hurry up; also, start working. For example, *Get a move on, it's late,* or *Let's get cracking, kids,* or *It's time we got going,* or *The alarm went off ten minutes ago, so get rolling.* **Get rolling** refers to setting wheels in motion. Also see GET BUSY; GET GOING; GET ON THE STICK.

**get an in with** Also, **have an in with.** Acquire (or have) influence with someone in authority. For example, *The only way they'll allow us to film the play is if we get an in with the director,* or *We should have no problem, since Dad has an in with the inspector.* This idiom uses the noun *in* in the sense of "an introduction to someone of power, fame, or authority."

**get a rise out of** Cause an angry or irritated reaction in someone, as in *His teasing always got a rise out of her.* This expression refers to a fisherman dropping a fly on the water in the hope that a fish will rise to this bait.

**get around 1.** Also, **get round.** Find a way to avoid or evade someone in authority or a requirement. For example, *He managed to get around the rules for visiting hours.* **2.** Also, **get round.** Convince or win over someone by flattery or persuasion, as in *Karen knew just how to get around her father,* or *I'll try to get round him, but I'm not sure it'll work.* **3.** Travel from place to place; also, be active socially. For example, *It's hard to get around without a car,* or *Mary is never without a date—she really gets around.* Also see GET ABOUT. **4.** Become known by many people, as in *Reports of her resignation got around quickly.* Also see GET ABOUT. **5. get around to** or **get round to.** Find the time or occasion for something, as in *Dean never gets around to cleaning up the garage.*

**get at 1.** Touch or reach something successfully, as in *Mom hid the peanut butter so we couldn't get at it.* **2.** Try to make something understandable; hint at or suggest something. For example, *I think I see what you're getting at.* **3.** Discover or learn something, as in *We must get at the facts of the case.* **4.** Bribe or influence someone by improper or illegal means, as in *He got at the judge, and the charges were dismissed.* **5.** Start on, begin work on, or attend to something, as in *There's a lot to do, so let's get at it.*

**get away 1.** Become free, escape, as in *The suspect ran down the street and got away,* or *I wanted to come but couldn't get away from the office.* A variant is **get away from it all,** meaning "go away and leave one's surroundings or problems or work behind." For example, *Joe is taking a few days off—he needs to get away from it all.* **2.** Start out or leave quickly, as in *The horses got away from the starting gate.* **3.** Go, move off. For example, *Get away from my desk!* or *Get away—I don't want you near that hot stove.* Also see GET AWAY WITH.

**get away with 1.** Escape without punishment or blame for something one did wrong, as in *Bill often cheats on exams but usually gets away with it.* **2. get away with murder.** Escape punishmen for killing someone; also, do anything one wishes. For example, *If the jury doesn't convict him, he'll have gotten away with murder,* or *He talks all day on the phone—the supervisor is letting him get away with murder.*

**get a word in edgewise** Also, **get a word in edgeways.** Be heard in a conversation or express one's opinion despite competition from other speakers. For example, *So many people had questions for the lecturer that it was hard to get a word in edgewise,* or *Nancy loves to talk, and I couldn't get a word in edgeways.*

**get back 1.** Also, **get back to.** Return to a place, topic, or condition. For example, *What time will you get back?* or *I hope he'll get back to the subject of this report.* **2. get back to someone.** Contact someone with the answer to a question or more information. For example, *The builder promised to get back to the client with an estimate for the work.* **3.** Recover something, as in *When will I get this book back?*

**get back at** Take revenge on someone, as in *Watch out for Peter; he's sure to get back at you.* Similarly, **get one's own back** means simply "get revenge," as in *She finally saw a chance to get her own back.*

**get back to** see GET BACK.

**get behind 1.** See FALL BEHIND. **2.** Support someone or something; also, help promote someone or something. For example, *We must find as many workers as we can to get behind the union.*

**get better** Improve or recover one's health. For example, *The doctor said I could expect to get better within a couple of days.* Also see GET WELL.

**get busy** Start working, become active, as in *Stop wasting time; get busy,* or *We'd better get busy on this paper.* Also see GET A MOVE ON; GET GOING; GET ON THE STICK.

**get by 1.** Move past, as in *There isn't room for this car to get by.* **2.** Manage to succeed or get along; also, barely succeed. For example, *He's getting by even though he only works half-time,* or *If he tried, Paul could be getting A's, but instead he's just getting by.* **3.** Be unnoticed, as in *She keeps a close watch on those kids; nothing gets by her.* **4.** Get approval or pass inspection. For example, *He hoped the paint job would get by.*

**get cracking** see under GET A MOVE ON.

**get credit for** Receive acknowledgment or praise for some accomplishment, as in *Bill got all the credit for attracting a big audience.* Similarly, **give credit for** means "acknowledge" or "praise," as in *We should give the pianist credit for her work in the program.*

**get down 1.** Go down or descend; bring something down. For example, *He's getting down from the ladder,* or *Can you get the cat down from the tree?* **2. get down to.** Give one's attention to something, as in *Let's get down to work,* or *It's time we got down to* *business.* For the most important variants, see under GET DOWN TO BRASS TACKS. **3. get down on.** See DOWN ON. **4. get one down.** Discourage or depress someone. For example, *Don't let Mary's troubles get you down,* or *Day after day of rain really gets me down.* **5.** Describe or record something in writing, as in *Can you get down all he's saying?* **6.** Lose one's self-restraint, enjoy oneself fully. For example, *At our reunion we got down with all our old friends.* **7.** Swallow something, as in *I can't seem to get the pill down.*

**get down to brass tacks** Also, **get down to bedrock** or **get down to the nitty-gritty.** Deal with the essentials; address the main issues. For example, *Stop delaying and get down to brass tacks,* or *We really need to get down to bedrock,* or *He has a way of getting down to the nitty-gritty.* The origin of the first phrase is unclear. The noun *bedrock* refers to the hard rock underlying mineral deposits. The noun *nitty-gritty* refers to the detailed ("nitty") and possibly unpleasant ("gritty") issue in question. Also see TO THE POINT.

**get even** Also, **get even with.** Get revenge, as in *He cheated them, and now they want to get even,* or *She swore she'd get even with him for the pain he caused.*

**get going 1.** See GET A MOVE ON. **2. get something going.** Start something, get something into full action. For example, *Once we get production going, we'll have no more problems.* Also see SWING INTO ACTION. **3.** Make someone talkative or active, as in *Once he got her going on her grandchildren, there was no stopping her.*

**get goose pimples** see GOOSE PIMPLES.

**get gray hair from** Be very worried or upset by something. For example, *I know I'm going to get gray hair from his driving.* Similarly, **give gray hair to** means "worry someone," as in *The boy's love of rock climbing gave his parents gray hair.* This idiom refers to the idea that extreme anxiety or grief can cause one's hair to turn gray.

**get hold of 1.** Grasp, get a grip on, or acquire something. For example, *If you can just get hold of one end, I'll get the other,* or *Jane had no luck getting hold of the book she needed.* **2.** Contact or get in touch with someone, as in *I've phoned a dozen times, but I can't seem to get hold of him.* Also see LAY HOLD OF.

**get in 1.** Enter a place, as in *We managed to get in just before the doors closed.* **2.** Arrive, as in *We got in late last night.* **3.** Be elected to office or become accepted, as in a club. For example, *Marge asked the club if she could get in.* The variant **get into** takes an object, as in *Things changed after he got into office.* **4.** Succeed in including, delivering, or finishing something, as in *Can you get in that last paragraph?* or *I hope you'll get it in on time.* Also see GET IN WITH.

**get in a snit** see IN A SNIT.

**get in a stew** see IN A STEW.

**get in bad with** Also, **get in good with.** See IN BAD WITH; IN GOOD WITH.

**get in bed with** Also, **get into bed with.** Form a close association with a person or group, usually for political or financial gain. For example, *There's always the danger that inspectors will get in bed with the industries they're supposed to be inspecting.* Also see GO TO BED WITH.

**get in on** see IN ON. Also see GET INTO THE ACT; (GET IN ON THE) GROUND FLOOR.

**get in one's hair** see IN SOMEONE'S HAIR.

**get in someone's face** see IN SOMEONE'S FACE.

**get in the way** see IN THE WAY.

**get into 1.** Become involved in, as in *He got into trouble by stealing cars,* or *I don't want to get into the long history of this problem.* Also see GO INTO, def. 4. **2.** Put on clothes, as in *Wait till I get into my suit.* **3.** Take control of someone and cause that person to act differently or inappropriately, as in *You're voting for that nut? What has got into you?* or *I don't know what gets into you children.* **4.** See BE INTO. Also see the following idioms beginning with GET INTO.

**get into hot water** see HOT WATER.

**get *something* into one's head** Also, **get it into one's head** or **take it into one's head.** Form an impression, idea, or plan about something. For example, *What strange idea has she got into her head?* or *He took it into his head that you want to quit.* Also see GET IT THROUGH ONE'S HEAD.

**get into the act** Also, **get in (on) the act.** Become involved in some activity or venture, as in *Everybody wants to get into the act on this offer,* or *I'm sure his agent plans to get in the act and start negotiations.*

**get into the swing of things** Become active, make progress. For example, *She only started work last week, but she quickly got into the swing of things.*

**get into trouble** see IN TROUBLE WITH.

**get in touch** see IN TOUCH.

**get involved** Become associated, especially in an emotional or sexual way. For example, *He joined the club last year but never really got involved in its activities,* or *It's been two years since Tom got involved with Jean.*

**get in with** Become involved or associated with, as in *She got in with the right crowd,* or *These loans got me in deeper and deeper with the bank.*

**get it 1.** See CATCH IT. **2.** Understand something, as in *He claims his plan is reasonable, but I'm not sure I get it.* The expression **You**

**just don't get it, do you?** is often used to express exasperation at someone's failure to understand something. The phrase is also put in the past tense, **got it,** meaning "understood." For example, *We're leaving tomorrow. OK, got it.* Also see GET THE MESSAGE.

**get it on 1.** Become filled with energy or excitement; enthusiastically begin. For example, *If you're ready to start rehearsing, let's get it on.* **2.** Have sex, as in *They were about to get it on when the doorbell rang.*

**get lost** Go away, as in *Get lost, we don't want you around.* This is a rude imperative.

**get mileage out of** Make use of, get a benefit or service from, as in *The actor got a lot of mileage out of that publicity,* or *You won't get much mileage out of that old TV set.* This expression refers to the number of miles of travel gained from a given amount of fuel, a tire, or other auto equipment.

G

**get nowhere** Also, **not get anywhere.** Make no progress, as in *I've tried to fix the problem, but I'm getting nowhere with it,* or *We couldn't get anywhere with him.* This expression is sometimes intensified as **get nowhere fast,** as in *I tried phoning but got nowhere fast.* Also see GET SOMEWHERE; GET THERE.

**get off 1.** Also, **get off of.** Leave a vehicle, as in *Let's get off the train at the next stop,* or *He got off and walked his bike across the street.* **2.** Start, as on a trip; leave. For example, *We got off at the crack of dawn.* **3.** Fire a round of ammunition; also, send something away. For example, *He got off two shots, but the deer fled,* or *I got off that letter just in time.* **4.** Escape from punishment; also, get a less severe penalty or a release for someone. For example, *He apologized so fully that he was sure to get off,* or *The attorney got her client off with a fine and no jail time.* This sense is sometimes expressed as **get off easy** or **get off lightly.** Where there is no punishment at all, the expression is sometimes put as **get off scot-free. 5.** Also, **get off of.** Remove or take off something, as in *I can't seem to get this paint off the car.* **6.** Succeed in saying something, especially a joke. For example, *Carl always manages to get off a good one before he gets serious.* **7. where does someone get off.** An expression spoken as a challenge to someone's right to do or say something. For example, *Where does he get off telling me what to do?* **8.** Experience orgasm, as in *She never did get off.* **9.** Also, **get off of one** or **get off one's case.** Stop bothering or criticizing one, as in *If you don't get off of me I'm walking out,* or *Get off my case right now!* Also see GET OFF ON; OFF SOMEONE'S BACK.

**get off on 1.** Feel the effects of or take a mind-altering drug. For example, *He was getting off on crack.* **2.** Enjoy, feel intense pleasure from, as in *I really get off on good jazz.*

**get off one's chest** see OFF ONE'S CHEST.

**get off one's tail** Also, **get off one's butt.** Stop being lazy and start doing something. For example, *Get off your tail and help your mother,* or *I should get off my butt, but I'm exhausted.*

**get off on the wrong foot** see under ON THE RIGHT FOOT.

**get off scot-free** see GET OFF, def. 4.

**get off someone's back** see OFF SOMEONE'S BACK.

**get off the ground** Make a start; get something started, as in *Because of legal difficulties, the construction project never got off the ground.* This expression refers to getting a plane into the air. The similar-sounding **get off to a flying start,** meaning "make a successful start," refers not to flight but to a quick start in a race. For example, *He's off to a flying start with his dissertation.*

**get off the hook** see OFF THE HOOK.

**get on 1.** Climb on or board a vehicle. For example, *I was the first passenger to get on the plane,* or *The bicycle was too big for him, so he had trouble getting on.* **2.** See GET ALONG, def. 1. **3.** See GET ALONG, def. 2. **4.** See GET ALONG, def. 4. Also see ALONG IN YEARS. **5. get on in.** Prosper or succeed (in life as general or in a specific situation), as in *How's your brother getting on in the world these days?* or *Dad asked if Bill was getting on in the company.* **6. get on with it.** Move ahead, do work. For example, *We've spent enough time talking about it; now let's get on with it.* **7. get on for** or **getting on toward.** Advance toward an age, amount, time, and so on. For example, *It's getting on for noon, so we'd better eat lunch.* This usage is often put in the participial form **getting on.** Also see the following idioms beginning with GET ON.

**get one down** see GET DOWN, def. 4.

**get one's** In addition to the idioms beginning with GET ONE'S, also see **get someone's.**

**get one's 1.** Get one's due punishment or reward, as in *If they keep ignoring their schoolwork, sooner or later they'll get theirs,* or *The union members were prepared to go on strike; they were determined to get theirs.* **2.** Be killed, as in *That soldier got his on the first day of fighting.* This usage originated in the military.

**get one's act together** Also, **get one's shit together** or **get it all together.** Start to behave more appropriately or effectively; get organized. For example, *Once Joe gets his act together, he'll get a raise,* or *You'd better get it all together before the boss comes back.* The variant using *shit* is considered vulgar. Also see GET ONE'S DUCKS IN A ROW.

**get one's bearings** Also, **find one's bearings.** Figure out one's position or situation relative to one's surroundings. For example, *She's still new to the company and needs time to get her bearings.* Naturally, one can also **lose one's bearings,** as in *After we missed the turnpike exit, we completely lost our bearings.*

**get one's comeuppance** Receive the treatment one deserves, especially punishment. For example, *She behaved badly, but I'm sure she'll get her comeuppance soon.*

**get one's ducks in a row** Also, **have one's ducks in a row.** Complete one's preparations, become efficient and well organized, as in *I'm trying to get my ducks in a row before I go to Europe.* This synonym for GET ONE'S ACT TOGETHER probably refers to lining up target ducks in a shooting gallery.

**get one's feet on the ground** Also, **have** or **keep one's feet on the ground.** See BOTH FEET ON THE GROUND.

**get one's feet wet** Start a new venture, start into new territory. For example, *I've only had a few guitar lessons—I've barely gotten my feet wet.* This expression refers to a timid swimmer slowly getting into the water.

**get one's fill** Also, **have one's fill.** Be satisfied; have enough (or more than enough) of something. For example, *I love shopping—I can never get my fill of it,* or *He's had his fill of dirty jobs.* This expression refers to having enough (or too much) to eat. Also see FED UP.

**get one's hands dirty** see DIRTY ONE'S HANDS.

**get one's hands on** see LAY HANDS ON.

**get one's head examined** Also, **have one's head examined.** An expression used to say someone is crazy or absolutely wrong. For example, *You like this food? Go get your head examined,* or *If you believe that story, you should have your head examined.*

**get one's money's worth** Receive good value, as in *They performed four extra songs, so we really got our money's worth,* or *We got our money's worth at the beach—there wasn't a cloud in the sky.* This expression often but not always refers to money spent.

**get one's own back** see GET BACK AT.

**get one's teeth into** see SINK ONE'S TEETH INTO.

**get one's walking papers** see WALKING PAPERS.

**get one's way** Also, **get one's own way** or **have one's own way** or **have it one's way.** Be allowed to or make others do as one wishes. For example, *Two-year-olds often scream until they get their own way,* or *All right, I give in—have it your way.*

**get one's wires crossed** Also, **have one's wires crossed.** Become or be confused or mistaken about something, as in *If you think there's a meeting today, you really have your wires crossed; it's not till next month.* This expression transfers a wrongly wired telephone or telegraph connection to human misunderstanding.

**get on one's feet 1.** Also, **get back on one's feet.** Reach or return to a secure or healthy state after an illness or difficulties with money. For example, *Business started out slowly, but they're getting on their feet now,* or *She got back on her feet quickly after the operation.* **2.** See GET TO ONE'S FEET.

**get on someone's good side** Win someone's approval or support, as in *Kate offered to walk the dog in order to get on her aunt's good side.* Also see IN GOOD WITH.

G

**get on someone's nerves** Irritate someone, as in *His fooling around gets on the teacher's nerves,* or *Please stop whistling—it's getting on my nerves.*

**get on the bandwagon** see ON THE BANDWAGON.

**get on the stick** Start working, as in *I have to get on the stick and start preparing dinner.* This synonym for GET GOING or GET BUSY refers to putting a car in motion by using the gearshift, or *stick.*

**get on with it** see GET ON, def. 6.

**get out 1.** Leave, escape, as in *There's a fence around the yard so the dog can't get out,* or *In case of a fire, we just want to get out alive.* Also see GET OUT OF, def. 1. **2.** Become known, as in *Somehow the secret got out.* Also see OUT IN THE OPEN. **3. get something out.** Publish something, as in *Once we get the newsletter out, we can concentrate on other projects.* **4.** Produce a sound, as in *The singer had a sore throat and could hardly get out a note.* Also see the following idioms beginning with GET OUT.

**get out from under** see OUT FROM UNDER.

**get out of 1.** Leave or escape from, as in *I hate to get out of bed on cold mornings,* or *He'll be lucky to get out of this mess.* Also see GET OUT, def. 1. **2.** Go beyond, as in *The cat climbed into the tree and got well out of my reach.* Also see OUT OF CONTROL; OUT OF SIGHT. **3.** Escape or avoid doing something, as in *He tried to get out of answering their questions.* Also see OUT OF THE WAY.

**get *something* out of 1.** Elicit or draw out something from someone. For example, *I can't get a straight answer out of him,* or *Getting a contribution out of her is hard work.* **2.** Remove or get rid of something, as in *Get these cats out of the house,* or *I can't get this melody out of my head.* Also see OUT OF ONE'S SYSTEM. **3.** Take something desired out of, obtain some benefit from. For example, *You can get a lot of juice out of these* *oranges,* or *She got little or nothing out of this investment.* It is also put as **get the most out of,** meaning "use to the greatest advantage," as in *He gets the most out of his staff.* Also see GET A BANG OUT OF; GET A RISE OUT OF; GET MILEAGE OUT OF.

**get *something* out of one's system** see OUT OF ONE'S SYSTEM.

**get out of someone's face** see under IN SOMEONE'S FACE, def. 2.

**get out of someone's sight** see OUT OF SIGHT, def. 1.

**get out of the way** see OUT OF THE WAY.

**get out while the getting is good** Leave while one can or has the chance to, as in *He just had a good offer from a rival firm and decided to get out while the getting is good.*

**get over 1.** Fight successfully against, as in *We have finally gotten over our difficulties.* **2.** Recover from, as in *I just got over the flu,* or *I hope the children get over their parents' divorce quickly.* **3.** Also, **get *something* over with.** Complete something unpleasant so as to be done with it. For example, *I'm glad to get all that dental work over with.* It also is put as **get it over with,** as in *I might as well sign the check and get it over with.*

**get physical** Make physical contact, either forcefully or sexually. For example, *Stop pushing—there's no need to get physical,* or *Thirteen is too young to get physical in that way.*

**get ready** Also, **make ready.** Become prepared or make preparations for something. For example, *It'll take me another hour to get ready for the painter,* or *Jane promised to make the room ready for our guests.* Also see GET SET.

**get real** Be realistic, stop dreaming or hoping, as in *You think you'll win the lottery if you buy one ticket a week? Get real!*

**get religion 1.** Accept and follow religious beliefs, as in *After the children were born, John got religion and joined the church.* **2.** Decide to behave in an upright, ethical way. For example, *After years of total selfishness, she suddenly got religion and is doing all kinds of volunteer work.*

**get rid of** Also, **be rid of.** Eliminate or free oneself from something unwanted. For example, *It's time we got rid of these old newspapers,* or *He kept calling for months, but now we're finally rid of him.* Also see GET SOMETHING OUT OF, def. 2.

**get *something* right** Understand something accurately or do something correctly, as in *If I get it right, you're not leaving until tomorrow,* or *The faucet works perfectly; the plumber finally got it right.*

**get rolling** see GET A MOVE ON.

**get round** see GET AROUND, def. 1, 2, and 5.

**get set** Prepare to go, as in *Get set; the taxi's coming.* This phrase is also a synonym for GET READY. Also see under ALL SET.

**get sick 1.** Also, **take sick** or **get ill** or **take ill.** Become sick, as in *It's just my luck to get sick on vacation,* or *When was she taken ill?* **2.** Become disgusted, as in *We got sick as we learned how much money was wasted,* or *I get sick when I hear about his debts.* Also see MAKE ONE SICK. **3.** Also, **get sick to one's stomach; be sick.** Become nauseous, vomit, as in *If you eat any more candy, you'll get sick,* or *Sick to her stomach every morning? She must be pregnant.*

**get someone's back up** Also, **get someone's dander up; put** or **set someone's back up.** Make someone angry, as in *Bill's arrogance really got my back up,* or *The foolish delays at the bank only put her back up.* **Get one's back up** and **get one's dander up** mean "become angry," as in *Martha is quick to get her dander up.* The *back* in these phrases refers to a cat arching its back when annoyed. Also see GET SOMEONE'S GOAT; RAISE ONE'S HACKLES.

**get someone's goat** Annoy or anger someone, as in *By teasing me about that article I wrote, he's trying to get my goat, but I won't let him.*

**get someone's number** Also, **have someone's number.** Determine or know one's real character or motives, as in *You can't fool Jane; she's got your number.*

**get someone wrong** Misunderstand someone, as in *I think you got him wrong.* This expression is often put as **Don't get me wrong,** used to make sure that one's feelings or opinions are clear, as in *Don't get me wrong—I'm happy about the outcome.* Also see MAKE NO MISTAKE.

**get something into one's head** see GET INTO ONE'S HEAD.

**get something on someone** Also, **have something on someone.** Get or have damaging knowledge about someone. For example, *They hoped to get something on the candidate,* or *Once Tom had something on his boss, he knew he would not be pressured again.* Also see BE ON TO.

**get somewhere** Make progress. For example, *The foundation for the building has been completed, so we're finally getting somewhere.* Also see GET NOWHERE; GET THERE.

**get *something* straight** Also, **have *something* straight.** Understand something correctly or make something clear, as in *Now let's get it straight—you'll come at four,* or *Do I have it straight about when you're leaving?* This expression uses *straight* in the sense of "in proper order" or "not confused."

**get stuffed** An imperative used to express anger at someone. For example, *When the taxi cut in front of him, he yelled at the driver, "Get stuffed!"* [Vulgar slang]

**get the advantage over** Also, **get the advantage of** or **have the advantage of.** Be in a superior position to, as in *He had the advantage over me, since I couldn't even remember his name, let alone his position.* Also see GET THE BETTER OF; GET THE DROP ON.

**get the ax** Also, **get the boot** or **can** or **heave-ho** or **hook** or **sack.** Be discharged or fired from a job, expelled from school, or rejected from another situation. For example, *The new TV show got the ax at the end of the first week,* or *The manager was stunned when he got the boot himself,* or *Bill finally gave his brother-in-law the sack.* All these expressions have variations using **give** that mean "fire or expel someone," as in *Are they giving Ruth the ax?* **Get the ax** refers to the *ax* used to cut off someone's head, and **get the boot** to *booting* or kicking someone out. **Get the can** comes from the verb *can,* meaning "dismiss," perhaps referring to being sealed in a container. **Get the heave-ho** refers to *heave* in the sense of lifting someone bodily, and **get the hook,** to a fishing hook. **Get the sack** refers is to a workman's sack for his tools, which was given back to him when he was fired. Also see GIVE SOMEONE THE GATE.

**get the ball rolling** Also, **keep the ball rolling.** Start something happening, such as a project; also, keep something in progress from slowing down. For example, *Let's get the ball rolling by putting up some posters,* or *The hostess kept the ball rolling, talking to each of the guests in turn.* This expression originated in one or another sport in which it was important to keep a ball moving. Also see GET THE SHOW ON THE ROAD.

**get the better of** Also, **get the best of; have the better of** or **have the best of.** Become superior to or master someone or something. For example, *John's common sense got the better of his pride, and he apologized,* or *Her older sister was always trying to get the best of her,* or *He was determined to have the better of his competitors.* Also see GET THE DROP ON.

**get the business** see THE BUSINESS.

**get the can** see GET THE AX.

**get the drift** Also, **catch the drift; get someone's drift** or **catch someone's drift.** Understand the general meaning or intention. For example, *I didn't get the drift—do they want to go or not?* or *Over all the noise he barely managed to catch the drift of their conversation.*

**get the drop on** Also, **get the jump on** or **have the jump on.** Achieve a distinct advantage over someone, especially through early or quick action; get a head start. For example, *Their book on electronic communication has the drop on all the others,* or *We really got the jump on the competition.*

**get the feel of** Also, **have the feel of.** Become or be accustomed to; get or have skill in. For example, *It took me a while to get the feel of the new car,* or *After a few months Jack had the feel of his new position.*

**get the goods on** Also, **have the goods on.** Get or have confidential information about someone, especially of a damaging or incriminating kind. For example, *The police have the goods on that guy, and they're about to arrest him.* Also see GET SOMETHING ON SOMEONE.

**get the hang of** Learn the proper way of doing, using, or handling something. For example, *I finally got the hang of this computer program.*

**get theirs** see GET ONE'S.

**get the jump on** see GET THE DROP ON.

**get the lead out** Also, **get the lead out of one's pants.** Hurry up, move faster. For example, *Get the lead out of your pants, kids, or we'll be late,* or *Arthur is the slowest talker—he can't seem to get the lead out and make his point.* This expression implies that lead, the heaviest of the base metals, is preventing someone from moving.

**get the message** Also, **get the picture.** Understand the real meaning or substance of something. For example, *He gestured to the waiter, who got the message and brought the bill,* or *Kate got the picture and decided to keep her mouth shut about the error.* Also see GET IT.

**get the most out of** see GET SOMETHING OUT OF, def. 3.

**get the nod** Receive approval or permission, as in, *The contestant got the nod from the judges.* Similarly, **give the nod** means "show approval or permission." These expressions refer to the quick movement of the head to show approval.

**get the picture** see GET THE MESSAGE.

**get there** Achieve success, as in *He always wanted to be a millionaire, and he finally got there.* In this expression, *there* indicates one's goal. The participial form of this phrase, **getting there,** means "making progress toward a goal," as in *I haven't finished the book, but I'm getting there.* Also see GET SOMEWHERE.

**get the runaround** Be treated misleadingly or get answers that are not honest or direct, especially in response to a request. For example, *Every time I ask about next year's plans, I get the runaround.* The related expression

G

**give the runaround** means "treat evasively or misleadingly," as in *He gives her the runaround whenever she asks for time off.*

**get the sack** see GET THE AX.

**get the show on the road** Start a project; begin work. For example, *After months of training, the astronauts were eager to get the show on the road.* This synonym of GET GOING refers to a theatrical production going on tour. Also see GET THE BALL ROLLING.

**get the upper hand** see UPPER HAND.

**get the worst of it** Also, **have the worst of it.** Be defeated, experience a disadvantage, or suffer the most harm. For example, *In any argument Joe usually gets the worst of it,* or *The car got the worst of it, and no one was hurt.* Also see GET THE BETTER (BEST) OF.

**get through** **1.** Reach the end, finish, as in *Now that our computer system is working again, I should get through by mid-afternoon.* It is also put as **get through with,** as in *As soon as we get through with painting the kitchen, I'll call you.* **2.** Succeed in passing or surviving something, as in *This epidemic is awful, but I'm sure we'll get through it somehow.* **3.** Also, **get through to.** Make contact with or reach someone, as in *After trying to reach them all night, we got finally through,* or *He tried to get through to the family.* **4.** Also **get through to.** Make oneself understood, as in *Am I getting through to you?*

**get *it* through one's head** Understand, believe, or be convinced of something. For example, *Bill cannot get it through his head that John is moving out.*

**get through to** see GET THROUGH, def. 3 and 4.

**getting there** see under GET THERE.

**get to** **1.** Arrive at, reach, as in *When we get to the store, we'll talk to the manager.* **2.** Begin doing something or start to deal with something. For example, *We got to talking about college days,* or *Let's get to this business right now.* **3.** Have to receive the chance to do something, as in *They went to the concert and got to meet the band afterward.* **4.** Influence or affect, especially adversely, as in *This loud music really gets to me,* or *Mother's crying always gets to him.* Also see GET UNDER SOMEONE'S SKIN. **5.** Bribe someone, as in *We're sure the dealer got to one of the narcotics agents.*

**get to first base** Also, **reach first base.** **1.** Succeed in the first phase of something; meet with preliminary approval. For example, *They were delighted that they'd gotten to first base in the negotiations.* This term refers to the *first base* of baseball, which is the first step toward scoring a run. **2.** Reach the first stage of sexual intimacy, such as kissing. For example, *Mary is so shy that I can't even get to first base with her.*

**get together** **1.** Gather things together, as in *Go get all the firewood together.* **2.** Come together, meet, as in *Let's get together next week.* The variant **get together with** means "meet with someone," as in *I can't get together with them today, but I'll have time next week.* **3.** Arrive at an agreement, as in *The jury was unable to get together on a verdict.* **4. get something together** or **get oneself together.** See under GET ONE'S ACT TOGETHER.

**get to one's feet** Also, **get on one's feet.** Stand up, as in *They all got to their feet when the President came in.* Also see GET ON ONE'S FEET.

**get to the bottom of** Find the basic quality or cause of something. For example, *He was determined to get to the bottom of the problem.* Also see AT BOTTOM.

**get to the heart of** Find or determine the most important or essential facts or meaning of something. For example, *It's important to get to the heart of the matter before we make any decisions.*

**get to the point** see TO THE POINT.

**get tough with** Become harsh or severe with someone. For example, *We have to get tough with these people, or they won't finish the work on time.*

**get under someone's skin** **1.** Irritate someone, as in *She really knows how to get under my skin with her nagging.* This expression refers to insects that cause itching or similar skin irritations. **2.** Fill someone's mind constantly or affect someone's deep feelings, as in *Jean's really gotten under his skin; he misses her terribly.*

**get up** **1.** Leave one's bed; also, sit or stand up. For example, *Once I get up and have coffee, I'm ready to work,* or *He got up and offered her his chair.* **2.** Climb, as in *I hate to get up on a ladder.* **3.** Create or organize something, as in *She got up the petition against expanding the airport.* **4.** Dress or decorate something or oneself, as in *She plans to get herself up as Cleopatra for the party.* This usage is most often put in the form of the past participle, **got up,** as in *The tables in the restaurant were got up with new tablecloths and bunches of flowers.* **5.** Create or find something in oneself, as in *I finally got up the nerve to quit,* or *Joe got up his courage and told the boss he was leaving.* Also see GET SOMEONE'S BACK UP; also see the following idioms beginning with GET UP.

**get up one's nerve** see GET UP, def. 5.

**get up on the wrong side of bed** Be in a grouchy, irritable state, as in *What's got into Max today? Did he get up on the wrong side of bed?* This expression refers to the ancient superstition that it was bad luck to put one's left foot down first.

**get up steam** Prepare to work hard, summon up energy. For example, *If we can just get up steam, we can finish in an hour.* This expression refers to producing enough steam to work an engine. Also see under FULL SPEED AHEAD.

**get used to** Be accustomed to. For example, *It took a while to get used to the new apartment.* Also see IT TAKES GETTING USED TO; USED TO.

**get well** Recover from illness, as in *I hope you get well soon.* This idiom uses *well* in the sense of "in good health."

**get what's coming to one** Receive what one deserves or is due, especially something unpleasant, such as a punishment. For example, *When they suspended Steve for cheating, he was only getting what was coming to him.*

**get wind of** Learn of new information; hear a rumor about something. For example, *The President's advisers knew there would be trouble if the news media got wind of the story.* This expression refers to an animal smelling a scent carried by the wind.

**get wise to** Also, **be wise to.** Become aware of something, especially something false or a dishonest person. For example, *It took a while, but she finally got wise to Fred's lies,* or *I'm wise to the fact that her clothes were borrowed.*

**get with it** see WITH IT.

**ghost** In addition to the idioms beginning with GHOST, also see GIVE UP THE GHOST.

**ghost of a chance, a** A very small chance, as in *They don't have a ghost of a chance of winning this game.* This expression is most often used in the negative.

**ghost town** A town that has been completely abandoned, as in *Many of the old mining communities are ghost towns now,* or *The resort is a ghost town in the winter.* This idiom implies that there are no living people left in town.

**gift** In addition to the idiom beginning with GIFT, also see GOD'S GIFT; LOOK A GIFT HORSE IN THE MOUTH.

**gift of gab** Talent for talking easily, especially the ability to talk persuasively. For example, *His gift of gab made him a wonderful salesman.*

**gilded cage** The problems or limitations that often accompany being rich, as in *She had furs, jewelry, whatever money could buy, but was trapped in a gilded cage.*

**gild the lily** Add unnecessary decorations or supposed improvement. For example, *Offering three different desserts after that elaborate meal would be gilding the lily.*

**gills** see FED UP (TO THE GILLS); GREEN ABOUT THE GILLS.

**girl Friday** Also, **gal Friday.** An efficient and faithful female assistant, as in *I'll have my girl Friday get the papers together.* The expression plays on **man Friday,** a name for a devoted male servant or assistant. Today these expressions are usually considered condescending and, when applied to a woman, sexist.

**give** In addition to the idioms beginning with GIVE, also see HARD TIME (GIVE SOMEONE A); NOT GIVE A DAMN; NOT GIVE SOMEONE THE TIME OF DAY; WHAT'S COOKING (GIVES). Also see under idioms beginning with GET and HAVE.

**give a bad name to** Also, **give someone a bad name** or **give something a bad name.** Spoil the reputation of, as in *Late deliveries are giving the company a bad name.*

**give a break** see GIVE SOMEONE A BREAK.

**give a damn** see NOT GIVE A DAMN.

**give a good account of oneself** Behave or perform well, as in *Harry gave a good account of himself over the last few months,* or *The company will probably give a good account of itself in the next quarter.* This expression transfers a financial reckoning to other affairs.

**give a hand** Also, **give someone a hand. 1.** Also, **lend a hand** or **lend someone a hand.** Help a person, as in *Let me give you a hand with those chairs,* or *Jane is always willing to lend a hand with refreshments.* **2.** Also, **give a big hand.** Give a round of applause, clap, as in *Please give her a hand.* One can also receive applause or **get a big hand,** as in *This speaker always gets a big hand.*

**give *someone* a hard time** see HARD TIME.

**give a hoot** see NOT GIVE A DAMN.

**give *one* a leg up** see LEG UP.

**give and take 1.** The practice of compromise, as in *Every marriage involves some give and take.* **2.** Lively exchange of ideas or conversation, as in *The legislature is famous for noisy give and take.*

**give an inch and they'll take a mile** Give or permit something small, and they'll take advantage of you. For example, *I told her she could borrow the car for one day, and she's been gone a week—give an inch!* This expression is often shortened, as in the example.

**give *someone* a piece of one's mind** see PIECE OF ONE'S MIND.

**give as good as one gets** Return the same kind of treatment that one receives, as in *In an argument Laura can give as good she gets,* or *Don't worry about the bullies in Bobby's class—he can give as good as he gets.*

**give a shit** see NOT GIVE A DAMN.

**give away 1.** Make a gift of, as in *I decided to give away all my plants.* **2.** Present a bride to the groom in a marriage ceremony, as in *Her father gave Karen away.* **3.** Reveal or make something known, often accidentally; also, betray or expose someone. For example, *She gave away her true feelings,* or *He confessed to the police and gave away his accomplices.* This idiom is sometimes put as **give oneself away,** as in *If you don't want the family to know about your gambling, don't give yourself away by spending your winnings.*

**give a wide berth** Avoid, as in *After Jane informed on them to the boss, they gave her a wide berth.* This expression refers to giving a ship enough room to swing at anchor so as to avoid a collision.

**give bad marks to** Judge something as unsatisfactory, as in *They gave bad marks to the President's program.* This expression transfers the grades given to schoolwork to other efforts.

G

**give birth to** **1.** Bear a child, as in *She gave birth to her first child exactly at midnight.* **2.** Also, **give rise to.** Be the cause or origin of. For example, *His hobby gave birth to a very successful business,* or *The economic situation gave rise to widespread dissatisfaction.*

**give chase** Follow and try to catch, as in *The police gave chase to the robber.*

**give color to** see LEND COLOR TO.

**give *someone* credit** **1.** Also, **extend *someone* credit.** Trust someone to pay at some future time what he or she owes. For example, *I haven't had an auto loan before this, so I hope they'll give me credit.* **2.** Acknowledge an accomplishment, as in *They really should give her credit for the work she's done.* The phrase is sometimes used in **give credit where credit is due,** meaning the acknowledgment should be to the person who deserves it. It is sometimes put as **give someone their due,** as in *We should really give Nancy her due for trying to sort out this mess.*

**give ground** Yield to a stronger force, retreat, as in *He began to give ground on that point, although he didn't stop arguing entirely.* This expression first referred to a military force retreating and so giving up territory to the enemy.

**give in** **1.** Hand in or submit something, as in *She gave in her report today.* **2.** Stop fighting against someone or something, relent, as in *I'll give in on this point,* or *You can have the car—I give in to your arguments.*

**give it one's best shot** Make one's hardest or most enthusiastic attempt, as in *I don't know if I can do it, but I'll give it my best shot.*

**give it to** Punish or reprimand someone, as in *Dad really gave it to Tom for coming in so late.* This expression implies a physical or verbal attack. Also see GIVE SOMEONE HELL.

**give it to someone straight** Tell someone something honestly and directly. For example, *I asked the doctor to give it to use straight about Mother's condition.*

**give me a break** see GIVE SOMEONE A BREAK, def. 2.

**give notice** **1.** Inform or warn someone of something, as in *He's prompt about giving us notice of any mistakes in the accounts.* **2.** Tell one's employer that one is quitting, as in *Our housekeeper gave notice last week.*

**given to** Tending toward, inclined to, as in *She was given to offering advice without being asked.*

**give off** Send out, emit, as in *Certain chemical changes give off energy,* or *This mixture gives off a very strange odor.*

**give of oneself** Give time and energy to an unselfish activity. For example, *The minister's sermons always emphasize giving of oneself in ways that help people in need.*

**give one** See below and also under GIVE SOMEONE.

**give oneself airs** see PUT ON AIRS.

**give oneself away** see GIVE AWAY, def. 3.

**give oneself up** **1.** Surrender, as in *They gave themselves up to the police.* **2.** Devote or apply oneself completely, as in *She gave herself up to her research.* Also see GIVE UP.

**give one's eyeteeth** Also, **give one's right arm.** Do whatever is necessary to get something desired, as in *She'd give her eyeteeth for a raise,* or *He'd give his right arm for a new car.* These expressions both refer to something precious, the eyeteeth (or canines) and the right arm.

**give or take** Plus or minus a small amount, approximately, more or less. For example, *We have ten acres of land, give or take a bit,* or *It should take a couple of hours, give or take.*

**give out** **1.** Allow something to be known, declare something publicly, as in *They gave out that she was ill.* **2.** Send something forth, emit, as in *The machine gave out a steady buzzing sound.* **3.** Distribute things to people, as in *The teacher gave out the tests to the class.* **4.** Stop functioning, fail; also, become exhausted or used up. For example, *The motor gave out suddenly,* or *My strength simply gave out.*

**give over** **1.** Hand something over, especially a responsibility or something valuable, as in *They gave over all the papers to the library.* **2.** Also, **give oneself over.** Devote or surrender something or oneself to a particular purpose or use, as in *The whole day was given over to partying,* or *He gave himself over to fear.*

**give pause** Cause someone to hesitate, as in *The high monthly payments gave me pause, and I decided not to buy it.*

**give rise to** see GIVE BIRTH TO, def. 2.

**give short shrift** see SHORT SHRIFT.

**give someone** See below, or under GIVE ONE, or look up the expression by its other words, as GIVE A HAND.

**give someone a break** **1.** Give someone a chance or special consideration. For example, *She begged the professor for an extension on her term paper, saying "Please give me a break."* Also see GET A BREAK. **2. give me a break.** Stop trying to fool or upset or bother me. For example, *Don't tell me the party's been postponed again—give me a break!* This interjection is usually uttered in a semihumorous way.

**give someone a ring** Also, **give someone a buzz.** Call someone on the telephone, as in *Give me a ring next week,* or *Bill said he'd give her a buzz.* Both these expressions refer to the sound of a telephone's ring.

**give someone enough rope** see ENOUGH ROPE.

**give someone fits** see HAVE A FIT.

**give someone heart failure** Frighten or startle someone very much, as in *You nearly gave me heart failure when you told me you were quitting.* It is also put as **have heart failure,** meaning "be frightened or startled," as in *I just about had heart failure when I heard about her accident.* Also see HEART MISSES A BEAT.

**give someone hell** Also, **give someone the devil.** Speak to someone harshly and critically. For example, *The boss gave them hell for not finishing in time,* or *Mom will give her the devil if she doesn't get home soon.* Also see GIVE IT TO.

**give someone his or her due** see under GIVE SOMEONE CREDIT, def. 2.

**give someone his or her head** Also, **let someone have his or her head.** Allow someone to proceed as he or she wishes, give someone freedom. For example, *He usually gave his assistant her head when it came to scheduling appointments,* or *Sometimes it's wise for parents to let a teenager have his head.* This expression refers to loosening a horse's reins and letting it go where it wants to.

**give someone the brushoff** Show in a rude way that one doesn't want to talk to or associate with someone. For example, *His old friends gave him the brush off.*

**give someone the gate** Also, **give someone the old heave-ho.** End a relationship with someone, as in *Mary cried and cried when he gave her the gate,* or *The company gave him the old heave-ho after only a month.* Also see GET THE AX.

**give someone the evil eye** see under EVIL EYE.

**give someone the once-over** Also, **give someone the eye.** Look or stare at someone with interest. For example, *The new coach gave the team the once-over before introducing himself,* or *He gave her the eye and she blushed.* The first expression generally implies a quick survey or assessment. The variant often signifies an inviting glance. Also see MAKE EYES AT.

**give something a whirl** Make a brief or experimental try, as in *I've never made a pie, but I'll give it a whirl.*

**give thanks for small blessings** Express gratitude for a small advantage or a bit of good luck, as in *My bag didn't get on the plane, but it did arrive in time—give thanks for small blessings.* This expression is usually used when one has an unexpected bit of good luck.

**give the back of one's hand** see BACK OF ONE'S HAND.

**give *someone* the benefit of the doubt** Regard someone as innocent until proven otherwise; lean toward a favorable view of someone. For example, *Let's give her the benefit of the doubt and assume that she's right.*

**give *someone* the business** see THE BUSINESS.

**give *someone* the creeps** see THE CREEPS.

**give the devil his due** Give credit for what is good in a disagreeable or disliked person. For example, *I don't like what the new management has done, but give the devil his due, sales have improved.*

**give the eye** Also, **give the once-over.** See GIVE SOMEONE THE ONCE-OVER.

**give *someone* the finger** Make an angry and obscene gesture by closing one's fist and extending one's middle finger upward. For example, *Herb has a dangerous habit of giving the finger to motorists who cut in front of him.*

**give the go-ahead** see GO AHEAD, def. 1.

**give the shirt off one's back** Give anything and everything one owns. For example, *Tom is truly generous—he'll give you the shirt off his back.*

**give *someone* the slip** Escape or evade someone. For example, *He saw the police approaching but managed to give them the slip.*

**give the time of day** see NOT GIVE SOMEONE THE TIME OF DAY.

**give the word** Also, **say the word.** Give an order, tell or show when something is to be done, as in *If you want us to move out, just give the word,* or *When you want the car, just say the word.* The first expression originally referred to saying a password in response to a challenge from a military guard.

**give *someone* the works** see THE WORKS.

**give *someone* to understand** Lead someone to think, as in *They gave me to understand that the President was coming here.*

**give up** **1.** Also, **give oneself up.** Surrender, as in *The suspect gave himself up to the* *police.* **2.** Stop doing or performing something, as in *They gave up the search,* or *She gave up smoking almost thirty years ago.* **3.** Let something go, often with regret, as in *They gave up their New York apartment,* or *We gave up all hope of finding the lost tickets.* **4.** Lose hope for, as in *We had given you up as lost.* **5.** Admit defeat, as in *I give up—what's the right answer?* **6. give up on.** Lose one's faith in something or someone, as in *I gave up on writing a novel,* or *She gave up on him; he'll never change.* Also see GIVE ONESELF UP TO.

**give up the ghost** Die, as in *At ten o'clock he gave up the ghost.* This expression uses *ghost* in the sense of "the soul or spirit."

G

**give vent to** Express a negative emotion, as in *He didn't dare give vent to his annoyance in front of his girlfriend's parents.*

**give voice to** Say or express something, especially an opinion or feeling. For example, *The faculty gave voice to their anger over the salary increase.*

**give way 1.** Retreat or withdraw, as in *The army gave way before the enemy.* **2.** Yield the right of way; also, take a lesser role or position, as in *The cars must give way to the ambulance,* or *The children were called inside as day gave way slowly to night.* **3.** Suddenly fail or break down, as in *The ladder gave way,* or *His health gave way under the strain.* **4.** Also, **give way to.** Yield to urging or demand, as in *At the last minute he gave way and avoided a fight,* or *The owners gave way to their demands for a pay increase.* **5.** Also, **give way to.** Lose self-control and allow a feeling to come forward, as in *She gave way to fear,* or *Don't give way to despair.*

**give way to** see GIVE WAY, def. 4 and 5.

**give *someone* what for** see WHAT FOR, def. 2.

**glad** In addition to the idiom beginning with GLAD, also see NOT SUFFER FOOLS GLADLY.

**glad hand** A warm and hearty but often insincere welcome or greeting, as in *Politicians are apt to give the glad hand to anyone and everyone.*

**glance** see AT FIRST GLANCE.

**glass** In addition to the idioms beginning with GLASS, also see PEOPLE WHO LIVE IN GLASS HOUSES.

**glass ceiling** A limit to professional advancement by women and minorities, caused by the attitudes and traditional practices of those in power. For example, *Harriet knew she'd never be promoted—she would never get through the glass ceiling.*

**glasses** see SEE THROUGH ROSE-COLORED GLASSES.

**glass is half full, the** A person views the situation optimistically or hopefully. For example, *Betty was not upset by the last-minute change, since it gave her extra time—she always sees the glass as half full.* The opposite—that is, the pessimistic view—is **the glass is half empty.** Also see BRIGHT SIDE.

**glitter** see ALL THAT GLITTERS IS NOT GOLD.

**glory** In addition to the idiom beginning with GLORY, also see IN ONE'S GLORY.

**glory days** A time in the past when one was admired, as in *He often remembers his glory days as a high school basketball star.*

**gloss over** Treat a problem or flaw lightly or somewhat dishonestly in order to make something attractive or acceptable. For example, *His résumé* glossed over his lack of experience, or *She tried to gloss over the mistake by insisting it would make no difference.*

**glove** see FIT LIKE A GLOVE; HAND IN GLOVE; HANDLE WITH GLOVES; HANG UP (ONE'S GLOVES); WITH THE GLOVES OFF.

**glutton for punishment** Someone who habitually takes on unpleasant tasks or unreasonable amounts of work. For example, *Rose agreed to organize the church fair for the third year in a row—she's a glutton for punishment.*

**gnash one's teeth** Express a strong emotion, usually anger, as in *When Jonah found out he was not going to be promoted, he gnashed his teeth.* This expression is actually redundant, since *gnash* means "strike the teeth together."

**go** In addition to the idioms beginning with GO, also see (GO) ALL OUT; ALL SYSTEMS GO; ANYTHING GOES; AS FAR AS THAT GOES; BEST-LAID PLANS GO ASTRAY; COME AND GO; COMING AND GOING; COMING OR GOING; COMINGS AND GOINGS; DUTCH TREAT (GO DUTCH); EASY COME, EASY GO; FROM THE WORD GO; GET A MOVE ON (GOING); GET GOING; HAVE A CRACK (GO) AT; HAVE A GOOD THING GOING; HAVE SOMETHING GOING FOR; HEART GOES OUT TO; HEAVY GOING; IN EFFECT (GO INTO EFFECT); HERE GOES; LET GO; MAKE A GO OF; NO DICE (NO GO); ON THE GO; OUT OF THE (GO OUT THE) WINDOW; PAY AS YOU GO; RARING TO GO; SHOW MUST GO ON; TOUCH AND GO; WHERE DO WE GO FROM HERE. Also see under GONE.

**go about 1.** Also, **go around.** Move here and there; also, circulate. For example, *She's been going about telling everyone the news,* or *A report went around that the dollar was dropping.* **2.** Begin or approach something, as in *I'm not sure how to go about making a pie.* **3. go about one's business.** Proceed with one's own job or concern. For example, *Don't bother with that—just go about your business.*

**go after** Pursue, try to get, as in *The officer went after the thief,* or *Ed was going after a new job.*

**go against** Oppose, be in conflict with, as in *Serving in the army would go against his religious beliefs.* Also see AGAINST THE GRAIN.

**go ahead 1.** Move forward or act without restraint. For example, *If you want to borrow the car, go ahead.* The term is the source of the phrase **give the go-ahead,** meaning "give permission to move or act in some way." **2.** Continue with something, as in *Despite the bad weather, construction is going ahead.* This expression is often put as **go ahead with,** as in *Are you going ahead with the party?* **3. go ahead of.** Make one's way before or to the front of, as in *They went ahead of me to talk to the boss.*

**go all out** see ALL OUT.

**go all the way 1.** Continue on a course to the end, as in *The town agreed to put in a sewer but would not go all the way with widening the street.* Also see GO THE DISTANCE. **2.** Have sex, as in *Her mother told her some boys will always try to make her go all the way.*

**go along 1.** Move on, proceed, as in *She was going along, singing a little song.* This expression is also used as an imperative meaning "get away from here," as in *The police ordered them to go along.* **2.** Also, **go along with.** Cooperate, agree. For example, *Don't worry about our votes—we'll go along,* or *I'll go along with you on that issue.* **3.** Also, **go along with.** Accompany someone, as in *I'll go along with you until we reach the gate.* This usage is the source of the phrase **go along for the ride,** meaning "accompany someone but without playing an active part," as in *I won't be allowed to vote at this meeting, so I'm just going along for the ride.*

**go a long way** see GO FAR.

**go a long way toward** Have a great effect or influence on. For example, *This research goes a long way toward proving the scientists are wrong.*

**go and** This phrase is an intensifier that expresses strong feeling about the verb that follows it. For example, *Don't go and eat all the leftover chicken* is stronger than "Don't eat all the leftover chicken." Sometimes the *and* is omitted, as in *Go tell Dad dinner is ready,* or *Go fly a kite,* colloquial imperatives telling someone to do something.

**go ape** Become wildly excited or enthusiastic. For example, *The audience went ape over the band.* This idiom is a modern version of the older GO BERSERK. It humorously equates frenzy with an ape's behavior. Also see GO BANANAS.

**go around 1.** Also, **go round.** Satisfy a demand or need, as in *Is there enough food to go around?* **2.** Same as GO ABOUT, def. 1. **3. go around with.** Same as GO WITH, def. 1. **4. go around in circles** or **run around in circles.** Engage in excited but useless activity. For example, *Bill ran around in circles trying organize us.*

**go astray** Wander off the right path or subject; also, wander into evil or error. For example, *It was hard to follow the lecturer's gist, since he kept going astray,* or *The gang members led him astray, and he ended up in court.* This expression refers to sheep or other animals that stray from the rest of the group.

**goat** see GET SOMEONE'S GOAT.

**go at** Attack, especially with energy; also, proceed vigorously. For example, *The dog went at the postman's legs,* or *Tom went at the chicken, eating away.* This idiom is sometimes put as **go at it,** as in *The bell sounded, and the boxers went at it.*

**go away** Leave a place, travel somewhere. For example, *They went away this morning,* or *Are you going away this winter?* This expression also can be used as an imperative ordering someone to leave: *Go away!* It can also be used to mean "disappear," as in *This fever just doesn't go away.*

**go back 1.** Return to a place or former condition. For example, *I'm going back to my hometown,* or *We want to go back to the old way of doing things.* **2.** Extend backward in space or time, as in *Our land goes back to the stone wall,* or *The family name goes back to Norman times.* Also see GO BACK ON.

**go back on** Fail to honor or keep a promise, as in *You can't go back on your word,* or *One should never go back on a promise.*

**go bad** Spoil, decay; also, turn to crime. For example, *You can tell from the smell that this milk has gone bad,* or *If he keeps running around with that street gang, he's sure to go bad.*

**go ballistic** Become extremely upset or angry, as in *Dad will go ballistic when he sees you dented the new car.* This expression, a variation on GO BERSERK, originally referred to a guided missile going out of control.

**go bananas** Act crazy, as in *When it comes to animal rights, some people go bananas.*

**go begging** Be in little or no demand, as in *At this time of year, apples go begging.*

**go belly-up** Fail, go bankrupt, as in *This company's about to go belly-up.* This expression refers to a dead fish in the water. Also see GO BROKE.

**go berserk** Show sudden furious emotion, usually rage, become crazily violent. For example, *When they announced the gymnast's score, her coach went berserk.* Also see GO APE.

**go broke** Also, **go bust.** Lose most or all of one's money. For example, *The company's about to go broke,* or *The producer of that movie went bust.*

**go by 1.** Pass, as in *Our time together went by quickly.* **2.** Pass without being taken advantage of, as in *You shouldn't let this opportunity go by.* For the related **go by the board,** see BY THE BOARD. **3.** Rely on, believe in, as in *I'm going by the numbers on this list,* or *We'll have to go by what she tells us.* **4. go by the name of.** Be known by or use a specific name. For example, *She continued to go by her maiden name, Mary Smith.*

**God** In addition to the idioms beginning with GOD, also see ACT OF GOD; FOR THE SAKE OF (GOD'S SAKE); GOD'S GIFT; HONEST TO GOD; MY GOD; PUT THE FEAR OF GOD INTO; SO HELP ME (GOD); THANK GOD; THERE BUT FOR THE GRACE OF GOD.

G

**God forbid** Also, **heaven forbid.** I hope that God will prevent something from happening or being the case. For example, *God forbid that they actually meet a bear,* or *Heaven forbid that the tornado pull off the roof.* These terms do not necessarily imply a belief in God's direct action; they merely express a strong wish. For a synonym, see PERISH THE THOUGHT.

**God knows** Also, **goodness knows; heaven knows. 1.** Truly, certainly, definitely, as in *God knows I need a winter coat.* This expression does not necessarily imply that God is all-knowing but merely emphasizes the truth of a statement. The variants using *goodness* and *heaven* are euphemisms that avoid misuse of God's name. **2.** Also, **God only knows.** Only God knows, that is, neither I nor anyone else knows, as in *God knows where I've stored those photos,* or *God only knows how many people will join the march.*

**go down 1.** Drop below the horizon, fall to the ground, or sink. For example, *The sun went down behind the hill,* or *I was afraid the plane would go down,* or *The ship went down, and everyone drowned.* **2.** Experience defeat or ruin, as in *They went down fighting,* or *The boxer went down in the first round.* **3.** Decrease, become less, as in *After Christmas, prices will go down,* or *As soon as the swelling goes down, it won't hurt as much.* **4.** Be swallowed, as in *This huge pill just won't go down,* or *That wine goes down very smoothly.* **5.** Also, **go down with.** Be accepted or believed, as in *How did your speech at the convention go down?* or *It's hardly the truth, but it still goes down with many voters.* **6.** Also, **go down in history.** Be recorded or remembered, as in *This event may go down in her book as one of the highlights of the year,* or *This debate will go down in history.* **7.** Occur, take place, as in *Really crazy behavior was going down in the sixties.* Also see COME DOWN, def. 3. **8.** Be sent to prison, as in *He went down for a five-year term.* Also see the subsequent idioms beginning with GO DOWN.

**go downhill** Deteriorate, become worse, as in *Ever since the recession began, the business has been going downhill,* or *Her health has gone downhill since she broke her hip.* Also see DOWNHILL ALL THE WAY.

**go down in history** see GO DOWN, def. 6.

**go down the drain** see DOWN THE DRAIN.

**God's gift** Someone extremely special or attractive, specially to a particular group, as in *He thinks he's God's gift to women.* This term is usually used in describing someone's idea of his or her own importance, as in the example.

**go Dutch** see under DUTCH TREAT.

**go easy 1.** Act or proceed with caution, as in *Go easy moving that bookcase,* or *Go easy on the subject of layoffs.* Also see EASY DOES IT; TAKE IT EASY. **2. go easy with** or **go easy on; go light on.** Use something in small amounts only, as in *Go easy with the makeup; a little lipstick is enough,* or *Go light on the salt.*

**goes to show** see GO TO SHOW.

**goes without saying, it** Be so clear or well understood that no one needs to say it. For example, *It goes without saying that success is the product of hard work.* This expression is a translation of the French *cela va sans dire.*

**go far** Also, **go a long way. 1.** Be enough for nearly all that is required; also, last for a long time. For example, *This turkey will go far to feed the people at the shelter,* or *She can really make that small amount of cash go a long way.* **2.** Be successful in life, as in *He's a smart boy; he'll go far.* Also see GO A LONG WAY TOWARD; GO SO FAR AS TO.

**go fifty-fifty** see GO HALVES.

**go fly a kite** Also, **go chase yourself** or **go climb a tree** or **go jump in the lake** or **go sit on a tack** or **go soak your head.** Go away and stop bothering me, as in *Quit it, go fly a kite,* or *Go jump in the lake.* All of these impolite imperatives use *go* as described under GO AND.

**go for 1.** Go in order to get, as in *I'll go for the paper,* or *He went for the doctor.* This usage is the source of the noun **gofer,** a person who is often sent on routine errands. **2.** Be valued as or sell for. For example, *All our efforts are going for very little,* or *That silver went for a lot of money.* **3.** Aim or try for, especially making a strong effort. For example, *They're going for the league championship.* This idiom is also put as **go for it,** as in *When Steve said he'd like to change careers, his wife told him to go for it.* The related phrase **go for broke** means "commit all one's resources toward achieving a goal," as in *Our competitors are going for broke to get some of our accounts.* Also see ALL OUT;

GO OUT FOR. **4.** Attack, as in *She went for him with a knife.* A variant, **go for the jugular**, is used for a fierce attack on the most vital part, as in *In political arguments he always goes for the jugular.* The jugular is an important blood vessel in the neck. **5.** Have a special liking for; respond favorably to, as in *I really go for progressive jazz,* or *He won't go for that idea.* **6.** Be valid for or applicable to, as in *Kevin hates broccoli, and that goes for Dean, too.* Also see HAVE SOMETHING GOING FOR ONE.

**go for nothing** Be useless, serve no purpose. For example, *He lost the case, so all our efforts on his behalf went for nothing.* Also see GO FOR, def. 2.

**go great guns** see GREAT GUNS, def. 1.

**go halfway** Also, **meet someone halfway.** Compromise, give up something for the sake of an agreement. For example, *The Smiths are willing to go halfway and pay their share for repairs,* or *I'll make peace with Nancy if she'll just meet me halfway.*

**go halves** Also, **go fifty-fifty.** Share equally. For example, *Ann suggested that they go halves on the rent,* or *The brothers are going fifty-fifty in their new business.*

**go hand in hand** see HAND IN HAND.

**go hard with** Be to one's harm or disadvantage. For example, *If this case gets to a jury, it will go hard with the defendant.*

**go haywire** Become wildly confused, out of control, or crazy. For example, *The plans for the party have gone haywire,* or *His enemies accused the mayor of going haywire.*

**go hog wild** Become crazy with excitement, as in *The shoppers went hog wild at the sale.*

**go in** **1.** Enter, especially into a building. For example, *It's cold out here, so can we go in?* **2.** Become hidden by clouds, as in *After the sun went in, it got quite chilly.* **3. go in with.** Join others in some venture or group project. For example, *He went in with the others to buy her a present.* Also see the subsequent idioms beginning with GO IN.

**go in for** **1.** Have a particular interest in or liking for, as in *He really goes in for classical music.* **2.** Be active or participate in, especially as a specialty. For example, *She's going in for tennis this year.*

**going for one** see HAVE SOMETHING GOING FOR ONE.

**going, going, gone** No longer available, as in *If you want this last doughnut speak up—going, going, gone!* This expression is used by auctioneers to warn of the acceptance of a final bid for an item.

**going my way** see GO ONE'S WAY, def. 2.

**going on** Also, **going on for.** Approaching, especially an age or time. For example, *She's twelve, going on thirteen,* or *It's going on for midnight.* Also see GO ON.

**going to, be** Be about to, will, as in *I'm going to start planting now,* or *Do you think it's going to rain?* This phrase is used with a verb (*start* or *rain* in the examples) to show the future tense. Occasionally the verb is omitted because it is understood. For example, *That paint hasn't dried yet, but it's going to soon,* or *Will you set the table? Yes, I'm going to.* Also see GO TO.

**go in on** Join together on a project or investment. For example, *Everyone in the office went in on a wedding gift for her.* Also see GO IN, def. 3.

**go in one ear and out the other** see under IN ONE EAR AND OUT THE OTHER.

**go into** **1.** Fit inside something; divide. For example, *The truck is too big to go into the garage,* or *Five goes into twenty four times.* **2.** Enter a particular state or condition, as in *She's about to go into tears,* or *I'm afraid he went into a coma.* **3.** Enter a profession or line of work, as in *She decided to go into politics.* For synonyms, see GO IN FOR, def. 2; TAKE UP. **4.** Investigate or discuss, especially in detail. For example, *We don't have time to go into the entire history of the project.* Also see ENTER INTO, def. 4. Also see the subsequent entries beginning with GO INTO.

**go into a huddle** Gather together privately to talk about or plan something, as in *The attorneys went into a huddle with their client before asking the next question.* This usage comes from football, where the team goes into a huddle to decide on the next play.

**go into a tailspin** Lose emotional control, panic. For example, *If she fails the bar exam again, she's sure to go into a tailspin.* This expression refers to the downward movement of an airplane out of control.

**go into effect** see IN EFFECT, def. 2.

**go it alone** Undertake a project, trip, or responsibility without others. For example, *If you decide not to help, I'll just go it alone.*

**gold, golden** In addition to the idioms beginning with GOLD or GOLDEN, also see ALL THAT GLITTERS IS NOT GOLD; GOOD AS GOLD; HEART OF GOLD; SILENCE IS GOLDEN; WORTH ONE'S WEIGHT IN GOLD.

**golden age** A period of prosperity or excellent achievement, as in *Some consider the baroque period the golden age of choral music.*

**golden handcuffs** Financial benefits that an employee will lose if he or she resigns, as in *The company has presented all the middle managers with golden handcuffs, so they can't afford to leave.*

**golden handshake** Generous severance pay to an employee, often as an incentive for early retirement. For example, *With a de-*

*creasing school population, the town decided to offer golden handshakes to some of the teachers.* A close relative is **golden parachute,** a generous severance agreement in an executive's contract.

**golden rule** see under DO UNTO OTHERS.

**goldfish bowl** A situation that allows no privacy, as in *Being in a goldfish bowl comes with the senator's job—there's no avoiding it.* This expression refers to a glass bowl allowing one to view goldfish from every direction.

**gold mine** An excellent source of money or some other desirable thing, as in *That business proved to be a gold mine,* or *She's a gold mine of information about the industry.*

G

**go light on** see GO EASY, def. 2.

**go native** Adopt another culture's way of life, especially that of a culture in a less developed country. For example, *Ben's decided to go native, sleeping in a hammock and eating all kinds of new foods.* This expression may be offensive. It is closely associated with the view of British colonists who had no respect for native cultures.

**gone** In addition to the idioms beginning with GONE, also see A GONER; ALL GONE; DEAD AND BURIED (GONE); FAR GONE; GOING, GOING, GONE; HERE TODAY, GONE TOMORROW; TO HELL AND GONE. Also see under GO.

**gone goose, a** A person in a hopeless situation; a DEAD DUCK. For example, *When he passed me, I knew I was a gone goose.*

**gone with the wind** Disappeared, gone forever, as in *With these unforeseen expenses, our profits are gone with the wind.* This phrase became famous as the title of Margaret Mitchell's 1936 novel, which refers to the Civil War causing the disappearance of a Southern way of life. It mainly serves as an intensifier of *gone.*

**good** In addition to the idioms beginning with GOOD, also see BAD (GOOD) SORT; BUT GOOD; DO ANY GOOD; DO GOOD; DO ONE GOOD; FOR GOOD; FOR GOOD MEASURE; GET ON SOMEONE'S GOOD SIDE; GET OUT WHILE THE GETTING IS GOOD; GIVE A GOOD ACCOUNT OF ONESELF; GIVE AS GOOD AS ONE GETS; HAVE A GOOD COMMAND OF; HAVE A GOOD MIND TO; HAVE A GOOD THING GOING; HAVE A GOOD TIME; HOLD GOOD; ILL WIND (THAT BLOWS NO ONE ANY GOOD); IN BAD (GOOD) FAITH; IN (GOOD) CONDITION; IN (ALL GOOD) CONSCIENCE; IN DUE COURSE (ALL IN GOOD TIME); IN GOOD HANDS; IN GOOD PART; IN GOOD SPIRITS; IN GOOD TIME; IN GOOD WITH; IN SOMEONE'S GOOD GRACES; KEEP (GOOD) TIME; MAKE GOOD; MAKE GOOD TIME; MAKE SOMEONE LOOK GOOD; MISS IS AS GOOD AS A MILE; NEVER HAD IT SO GOOD; NO GOOD; NO NEWS IS GOOD NEWS; NOT THE ONLY FISH (LOTS OF GOOD FISH) IN THE SEA; ONE GOOD TURN DESERVES ANOTHER; ON GOOD TERMS; ON ONE'S BEST (GOOD) BEHAVIOR; PUT IN A GOOD WORD; PUT TO GOOD USE; SHOW SOMEONE A GOOD TIME; SHOW TO (GOOD) ADVANTAGE; SO FAR SO GOOD; STAND IN GOOD STEAD; THROW GOOD MONEY AFTER BAD; TO GOOD PURPOSE; TOO GOOD TO BE TRUE; TOO MUCH OF A GOOD THING; TO THE GOOD; TURN SOMETHING TO GOOD ACCOUNT; UP TO (NO GOOD); WELL AND GOOD; WHAT'S THE GOOD OF; WITH GOOD GRACE; WORLD OF GOOD; YOUR GUESS IS AS GOOD AS MINE. Also see under GOODNESS; GOODS.

**good and** Very, as in *I'll go when I'm good and ready,* or *Mike was good and mad at Tom.* This phrase is used to intensify the words that follow.

**good as, as** Practically, in effect, almost the same as, as in *He as good as promised to buy a new car,* or *The house is as good as sold.* This idiom is very widely used to modify just about any verb, adverb, or adjective. However, it has been used so often with certain words that together they themselves now make up idioms (see the following idioms beginning with GOOD AS ).

**good as done, as** Almost completely finished or accomplished, as in *Your printing job is as good as done.*

**good as gold, as** Very well behaved. For example, *The children were as good as gold.* With this idiom the opening *as* is sometimes dropped.

**good as one's word, as** Completely trustworthy, dependable, as in *The boss said we could leave early on Friday, and she was as good as her word.*

**good day** Also, **good afternoon** or **good evening** or **good morning.** Formal ways of saying "Hello" or "Good-bye." For example, *He began by addressing the audience with "Good day,"* or *"Good afternoon, ladies," said the sales clerk as we walked out.* Also see GOOD NIGHT.

**good deal, a** Also, **a great deal. 1.** A large but indefinite quantity; to a large extent or degree, as in *They have a good deal of money,* or *He travels a lot.* Also see GOOD MANY. **2.** A very successful transaction or business agreement; a bargain. For example, *The new agent got him a great deal,* or *Only $50,000 for all that land? That's a good deal.*

**good egg, a** Also, **a good scout.** An amiable, basically nice person. For example, *You can always count on her to help; she's a good egg,* or *His friends all think Dad's really a good scout.*

**good evening** see GOOD DAY.

**good faith** see under IN BAD FAITH.

**good for 1.** Helpful or beneficial to, as in *Milk is good for children.* **2.** Financially reliable, able to pay or repay, as in *They know he's good for the loan.* **3.** Able to serve or continue to function, as in *This furniture's* *good for at least ten more years,* or *I hope you're not tired—I'm good for another three miles or so.* **4.** Equivalent in value; also, valid for. For example, *These coupons are good for a 20 percent discount,* or *This contract is good for the entire life of the book* **5. good for someone.** An expression of approval, as in *Good for Bill—he's sold the car,* or *Good for you! You passed the exam.* This usage differs from the others in that orally a slight emphasis is placed on *you* or whoever is being mentioned.

**good-for-nothing** A person, animal, or thing of little use or value. For example, *His brother is a good-for-nothing.* This phrase is also used to describe something, as in *Get your good-for-nothing cat off my table!*

**good graces** see IN SOMEONE'S GOOD GRACES.

**good grief** An exclamation expressing surprise, alarm, dismay, or some other, usually negative emotion. For example, *Good grief! You're not going to start all over again,* or *Good grief! He dropped the cake.* The term is a euphemism for "good God."

**good head on one's shoulders, have a** Be intelligent or shrewd; have good sense or good judgment. For example, *We can depend on George to figure it out—he has a good head on his shoulders.*

**good life, the** A very comfortably, rich style of living. For example, *Aunt Agatha left them a fortune, so now they're enjoying the good life.*

**good luck 1.** Good fortune or a happy outcome, especially by chance. For example, *It was good luck that brought this offer my way.* **2.** Also, **good luck to you.** I wish you success. This term is sometimes used sarcastically, implying that what someone is trying probably won't succeed. For example, *If you think you'll find that long-lost letter, good luck to you.*

**good many, a** Also, **a great many.** A large number of, as in *A good many checks have come in already,* or *We saw only a few hikers on the trail, although we expected a great many.* Also see A LOT; QUITE A BIT (FEW).

**good mind** see HAVE A GOOD MIND.

**good morning** see GOOD DAY.

**good nature** A cheerful, helpful disposition, as in *Ted is known for his good nature—he's always willing to help.*

**goodness** In addition to the idiom beginning with GOODNESS, also see FOR THE SAKE OF (GOODNESS SAKE); GOD (GOODNESS) KNOWS; HONEST TO GOD (GOODNESS); MY GOD (GOODNESS).

**goodness gracious** Also, **good gracious; gracious sakes.** Exclamation of surprise, dismay, or alarm, as in *Goodness gracious! You've forgotten your ticket.*

**goodness knows** see GOD KNOWS.

**good night 1.** Expression used when saying good-bye at night or when going to sleep, as in *He stood at the door, saying good night to each of the guests as they left,* or *Mother came to tuck the children in and kiss them good night.* **2.** Exclamation of surprise or irritation, as in *Good night, Joe! You can't mean what you said,* or *Good night, Anne—it's time you learned how to throw a ball.*

**good riddance** Also, **good riddance to bad rubbish.** A phrase used to express one's relief or pleasure that someone or something troublesome is gone. For example, *The principal has finally retired, and most of the teachers are saying, "Good riddance!"* or *When Jean decided to give up her violin, her relieved family quietly said, "Good riddance to bad rubbish."*

G

**goods** see DELIVER THE GOODS; GET THE GOODS ON; SELL A BILL OF GOODS; STRAIGHT GOODS.

**good Samaritan** A person who unselfishly helps others, as in *In this neighborhood you can't count on a good Samaritan if you get in trouble.*

**good scout** see GOOD EGG.

**good sort** see under BAD SORT.

**good thing** see HAVE A GOOD THING GOING.

**good time** see HAVE A GOOD TIME.

**good-time Charlie, a** A friendly man who enjoys company, as in *Joe was a typical good-time Charlie, always ready for a party.*

**good turn** A favor, an act of goodwill, as in *Pat did her a good turn by sending her an important client.*

**good word** see PUT IN A GOOD WORD.

**good works** Acts of kindness or goodwill, as in *She spent much of her life in doing good works, especially for the homeless.*

**goody two-shoes** A girl or woman who is too concerned with following rules and too proud of being morally right. For example, *Phyllis was a real goody two-shoes, tattling on her friends to the teacher.*

**goof around** Play around, as in *The boys were goofing around in the schoolyard.*

**go off 1.** Explode, fire; also, make noise or sound, especially abruptly. For example, *I heard the gun go off,* or *The sirens went off at noon.* This expression led to the related **go off half-cocked,** now meaning "act prematurely." It originally referred to the slipping of a gun's hammer so that the gun fires (goes off) unexpectedly. **2.** Leave, especially suddenly, as in *Don't go off mad,* or *They went off without saying good-bye.* **3.** Keep to the expected plan or course of events, succeed, as in *The project went off smoothly.* **4. go off on a tangent.** See under ON A TANGENT. **5. go off one's head.** See OFF ONE'S

HEAD. Also see the following idioms beginning with GO OFF.

**go off half-cocked** see under GO OFF, def. 1.

**go off the deep end 1.** Become too excited or angry. For example, *When he heard about John's smashing into his car, he went off the deep end.* **2.** Be unreasonable, act irresponsibly. For example, *Just because you like her looks doesn't mean you should go off the deep end and propose.* In both of these usages *deep end* refers to the deep end of a swimming pool.

**goof off** Ignore one's work or responsibility; fool around. For example, *We were supposed to be studying, but we were really goofing off,* or *If you ever feel like goofing off, please call me.*

G

**goof up** Make a mistake, spoil something. For example, *I really goofed up and got all the dates wrong,* or *The waiter goofed up our order.* Quite often *up* is omitted, as in *Sorry, I goofed.*

**go on 1.** Happen, take place, as in *What's going on here?* **2.** Continue, as in *The show must go on.* **3.** Advance, as in *She may go on to become a partner.* **4.** Act or behave, especially badly. For example, *Don't go on like that; stop throwing things.* **5.** Also, **go on and on; run on.** Talk without stopping, chatter, especially tiresomely. For example, *She certainly does go on and on about her grandchildren,* or *His date was running on about her job.* **6.** A phrase used to express disbelief, surprise, or the like, as in *Go on, you must be joking!* **7.** Approach; see GOING ON. **8.** Use as a starting point or as evidence, as in *The investigator doesn't have much to go on in this case.*

**go on and on 1.** See GO ON, def. 5. **2.** Continue without stopping, last for a long time, as in *This trail goes on and on,* or *The movie went on and on.*

**go one better** Perform better or do more than someone, as in *He went one better than his teacher and came up with five more famous scientists.*

**go one's way** Also, **go one's own way. 1.** Do what one pleases, especially differing from what others are doing, as in *You go your way and I'll go mine,* or *He always insisted on going his own way.* **2.** Proceed according to one's plans or wishes, as in *Let's hope things will go my way this time.* Applied to both events and people's actions, this thought is often expressed as **everything's going one's way** or **everything's going my way.** For example, *With her husband in charge, everything's going her way,* or *I trust you'll be going my way when we vote on this issue.*

**go on line** Also, **go online** or **go on-line.** Use a computer to connect with a network of computers. For example, *She went online and checked her e-mail.*

**go on record** Take a position publicly. For example, *I want to go on record in favor of the mayor's reelection.* It is also put as **for the record,** as in *For the record, we support sending troops there.* The *record* in both signifies either publication or public knowledge. Also see JUST FOR THE RECORD; OFF THE RECORD.

**goose** In addition to the idioms beginning with GOOSE, also see COOK SOMEONE'S GOOSE; GONE GOOSE; KILL THE GOOSE THAT LAYS THE GOLDEN EGGS; SAUCE FOR THE GOOSE; WILD GOOSE CHASE.

**goose egg** Zero, nothing, especially a score of zero. For example, *Our team did badly, earning a goose egg,* or *My income from writing this year was goose egg.*

**goose pimples** Also, **goose bumps** or **goose flesh.** Temporary rough skin caused by small raised bumps. For example, *Horror movies always give me goose pimples,* or *This cool breeze is giving me goose bumps.* This expression compares the skin of a plucked goose to the condition of human skin when a person is cold or afraid.

**go out 1.** Stop glowing, giving light, or burning, as in *All the lights went out.* **2.** Die; also, faint. For example, *I want to go out before I become senile,* or *At the sight of blood, he went out like a light.* For the variant, see under OUT COLD. **3.** Participate in social life outside the home, as in *We go out a lot during the holiday season.* This usage led to **go out with someone,** meaning "date someone," as in *She's going out with someone she met at school,* or *They've been going out for a year.* **4.** Stop working, as in *To show their support of the auto workers, the steel workers went out too.* This expression is short for **go out on strike. 5.** Become unfashionable, as in *Bell-bottom pants went out in the 1970s but made a comeback in the 1990s.* This usage is short for **go out of fashion** or **go out of style,** as in *This kind of film has gone out of fashion,* or *These boots are going out of style.* Also see the following idioms beginning with GO OUT.

**go out for** Try to become a participant in, as in *I'm going out for soccer.* Also see GO FOR, def. 3.

**go out of fashion** Also, **go out of style.** See under GO OUT, def. 5.

**go out of one's mind** Lose one's mental stability, become insane, as in *After he heard that the his bank had failed, the man went out of his mind.* This phrase is often used as a humorous exaggeration, as in *I'm going out of my mind waiting for the results of the test.* Also see LOSE ONE'S MIND.

**go out of one's way** Take extra trouble to do something beyond what is required. For example, *He went out of his way to introduce me to everyone there,* or *She went out of her way to be kind.* This usage refers to leaving one's intended path or normal procedures.

**go out the window** see OUT OF THE WINDOW.

**go out with** see GO OUT, def. 3; GO WITH.

**go over 1.** Examine or review something. For example, *They went over the contract with great care,* or *I think we should go over the whole business again.* **2.** Gain acceptance or approval, succeed, as in *I hope the play goes over.* This term is sometimes expanded to **go over big** or **go over with a bang** for a big success, and **go over like a lead balloon** for a complete failure. **3.** Rehearse, as in *Let's go over these lines one more time.*

**go overboard** Show too much enthusiasm, act in an excessive way. For example, *It's easy for investors to go overboard with a new stock offering,* or *She really went overboard buying presents for everyone.*

**go over someone's head** see OVER ONE'S HEAD.

**go places** Make progress, succeed, as in *I suspect that the company will be going places with the new product.*

**go postal** Become extremely angry and behave in a violent or crazy way, as in *When he heard the news, he went postal, so I got out of there fast.*

**go public 1.** Announce news or information, often of a private nature. For example, *She plans to go public about her relationship with the senator.* **2.** Become a publicly held company, that is, issue ownership shares in the form of stock. For example, *As soon as the company grows a little bigger and begins to show a profit, we intend to go public.*

**go right** Succeed, happen correctly, as in *If everything goes right, we should be in Canada by Tuesday,* or *Nothing has gone right for me today.* This idiom uses *right* in the sense of "in a satisfactory state."

**go right through someone** see under GO THROUGH SOMEONE.

**go so far as to** Also, **go as far as to.** Proceed to the point of doing something. For example, *I wouldn't go so far as to call him useless, but he does need a lot of help,* or *Would she go as far as to sell the house before she's found another?*

**go south** Get into bad or worse condition, decline, as in *The stock market is headed south again.* Also see GO WEST.

**gospel truth, the** Something that is unquestionably true. For example, *Every word he said was the gospel truth.* The word *gospel* refers to the Christian Bible. Also see TAKE SOMETHING AS GOSPEL.

**go stag** Go to a social event without being paired with a person of the opposite sex, as in *John decided to go stag to the party,* or *Some of the girls are going stag to the dance.* Although this term originally applied only to men attending an event without dates, it is now applied to women as well.

**go steady** Date one person exclusively, as in *Parents often don't approve of their children's decision to go steady.* Also see GO TOGETHER, def. 2; GO WITH, def. 1.

**go straight** Stop criminal activities and live an honest life. For example, *Once he got out of jail, he swore he would go straight.* The use of *straight* in the sense of "honest" probably refers to the opposite of *crooked* in the sense of "dishonest."

**got** see under GET; HAVE; HAVE TO.

**go the distance** Carry through a course of action to completion. For example, *He said he's willing to go the distance with this project.* For a synonym, see ALL THE WAY, def. 1.

**go the limit** see GO WHOLE HOG.

**go through 1.** Examine something carefully, as in *I went through all the students' papers.* **2.** Experience or suffer something, as in *We went through hell trying to find an answer.* **3.** Perform or rehearse something for performance. For example, *The team went through the play in practice,* or *Let's go through the third act again.* **4.** Use up or complete something, as in *The children went through all the milk we bought in one day.* **5.** Succeed, be approved, as in *I'm sure this new deal will go through.* **6. go through with.** Complete something planned, as in *They got engaged last year, but I'm not sure they'll go through with the wedding.*

**go through channels** Also, **go through proper channels.** Use the correct procedure, especially in a hierarchy or bureaucracy. For example, *You'll have to go through channels to get approval.*

**go through someone 1.** Use someone to help achieve a goal, as in *If you want to communicate with him, go through his agent.* Also see GO THROUGH CHANNELS. **2.** Also, **go right through someone (like a dose of salts).** Pass quickly through the body without being digested. For example, *I don't know why, but some food goes right through me.*

**go through the mill** see THROUGH THE MILL.

**go through the motions** Do something without thinking or caring, or merely pretend to do it. For example, *The team is so far behind that they're just going through the motions,* or *She didn't really grieve at his death; she just went through the motions.*

**go through the roof 1.** Also, **hit the ceiling** or **hit the roof.** Lose one's temper, become very angry, as in *Marge went through*

G

*the roof when she heard she'd been fired.* **2.** Reach new or unexpected heights, as in *After the war, food prices went through the roof.*

**go through with** see GO THROUGH, def. 6.

**got it** see under GET IT.

**go to 1.** See GOING TO. **2.** Also, **go toward.** Contribute to a result, as in *Can you name the bones that go to make the arms and legs?* or *The money will go toward her college expenses.* **3.** Begin, start, as in *By the time she went to call, she'd forgotten what she wanted to say.* The related idiom **go to it** means "get started, get going."

**go to any length** Also, **go to great lengths.** Take a great deal of trouble for something. For example, *He'll go to great lengths to make a perfect chocolate cake,* or *They would go to any length to win.*

**go to bat for** Take the side of, support or defend someone. For example, *Dad will always go to bat for his kids.* This term originated in baseball and refers to helping one's team.

**go to bed with 1.** Have sex with someone. Also see GO ALL THE WAY, def. 2. **2. go to bed with the chickens.** Go to sleep very early, as in *She made the children go to bed with the chickens.* **3. go to bed.** Start being printed. This phrase is used of a newspaper or other publication. It relates to the fact that the morning newspaper is usually printed sometime during the night before. For example, *It's too late for your story; the paper went to bed half an hour ago.* Also see GET IN BED WITH.

**go together 1.** Be suitable, appropriate, or harmonious together, as in *Pink and purple can go together well,* or *I don't think champagne and hot dogs go together.* **2.** Date on a regular basis. For example, *Are Bill and Ann still going together?* Also see GO STEADY; GO WITH.

**go to hell** Also, **go to the devil** or **go to the dickens.** A rude and angry expression used to tell someone to go away or to stop saying something. For example, *Nancy was very direct and simply told him to go the devil,* or *Go to hell, Tom, I won't give you another cent. Dickens* is a euphemism for "devil." *Hell* refers to the home of the devil, from which a person would never return.

**go to it** see GO TO, def. 3.

**go too far** Behave in a way that goes beyond some limit, as in *I wouldn't go too far with those remarks or they'll get you into trouble,* or *If the children go too far, she'll send them to their rooms.*

**go to one's head 1.** Make one dizzy or drunk, as in *Wine always goes to her head.* **2.** Make one proud or vain, as in *All this attention is going to his head.*

**go to pieces** Experience an emotional or a mental breakdown, as in *When she heard of his death, she went to pieces.* For a synonym, see FALL APART.

**go to pot** Also, **go to the dogs.** Get into bad or worse condition, decline; come to a bad end. For example, *My lawn has gone to pot during the drought,* or *The city schools are going to the dogs.* The first of these expressions refers to inferior pieces of meat being cut up for the stewpot. The second refers to the traditional view of dogs as inferior creatures. Also see RACK AND RUIN; RUN TO SEED.

**go to show** Help to prove or serve as evidence. For example, *His research goes to show that the medication is ineffective.*

**go to the devil** see GO TO HELL.

**go to the dogs** see GO TO POT.

**go to the expense** see GO TO THE TROUBLE.

**go to the mat** Fight until one side or another wins, as in *The governor said he'd go to the mat for this bill.* This term comes from wrestling. It suggests holding an opponent when both contestants are down on the mat, the padded floor covering used in matches.

**go to the trouble** Also, **take the trouble; go to the bother** or **go to the expense.** Make the effort or spend the money for something. For example, *He went to the trouble of calling every single parent,* or *She took the trouble to iron all the clothes,* or *Don't go to the bother of writing them,* or *They went to the expense of taking a taxi.* Also see PUT ONESELF OUT.

**go to the wall 1.** Lose a conflict, be defeated; also, yield. For example, *In spite of their efforts, they went to the wall,* or *When it's a matter of family versus friends, friends must go to the wall.* **2.** Fail in business, go bankrupt. For example, *First one branch and then another did poorly, and the store finally went to the wall.* **3.** Take an extreme position, try hard to the end. For example, *The President went to the wall to defend his choice to head the FBI.* Also see GO TO THE MAT.

**go to town** Also, **go to town on. 1.** Do something efficiently and energetically. For example, *She really went to town, not only developing and printing the film but making both mat and frame.* **2.** Act without restraint, do something to an extreme, as in *He went to town on the desserts, finishing nearly all of them.* **3.** Be successful, as in *After months of hard work, their business is really going to town.*

**go to waste** Fail to be used or taken advantage of. For example, *I hate to see such talent go to waste,* or *We bought so much food that some will be going to waste.*

**got to** see HAVE TO.

**go under 1.** Suffer defeat or destruction; fail. For example, *We feared the business would* *go under after the president died.* **2.** Lose consciousness. For example, *Ether was the first anesthetic to make patients go under quickly and completely.* **3.** Sink, as in *This leaky boat is about to go under.*

**go up 1.** Be constructed or put up, as in *New buildings are going up all over town.* **2.** Rise; increase. For example, *His temperature is going up at an alarming rate,* or *The costs of construction are going up all the time.* Also see the following idioms beginning with GO UP.

**go up in flames** Also, **go up in smoke.** Be completely destroyed, as in *This project will go up in flames if the designer quits,* or *All our work is going up in smoke.* This idiom transfers a fire to other kinds of destruction.

**go west** Die, as in *He declared he wasn't ready to go west just yet.*

**go whole hog** Also, **go the limit.** Do something completely or thoroughly; proceed as far as possible. For example, *Instead of just painting one room, why not go whole hog and paint the whole apartment?* or *Let's go the limit and spend and whole check.* Also see ALL OUT.

**go with 1.** Also, **go out with.** Accompany; also, date regularly. For example, *Is she going out with anybody these days?* or *Jerry has been going out with Frieda for two years.* **2.** Be associated with, as in *His accent goes with his background.* **3.** Take the side of someone, as in *I'll go with you in defending his right to speak freely.* Also see GO ALONG, def. 2. **4.** Also, **go well with.** Look good with, match. For example, *This chair goes well with the rest of the furniture,* or *That color doesn't go with the curtains.*

**go with the flow** Also, **go with the tide.** Move along in the same direction as other people, accept and do what others are doing, as in *Rather than leading others, he tends to go with the flow,* or *Pat isn't particularly original; she just goes with the tide.* The *flow* in the first and more informal term refers to the ebb and flow of tides.

**go wrong 1.** Make a wrong move or a mistake. For example, *We made a left turn and somehow went wrong from then on,* or *You won't go wrong if you follow the recipe.* **2.** Start behaving in immoral or illegal ways, become a criminal, as in *As soon as he turned thirteen, Billy made a bad set of friends and began to go wrong.* **3.** Fail, result, as in *Everything about this party has gone wrong.* **4.** Fail to work properly, as in *The car starts fine, but as soon as you put it in gear, something goes wrong.*

**grab** In addition to the idiom beginning with GRAB, also see HOW DOES THAT GRAB YOU; UP FOR GRABS.

**grab bag** A collection of varied things, as in *The meeting was only a grab bag of petty complaints.* This term refers to a container offered at a party or fair, where one reaches in for a party favor or prize without knowing what one will get.

**grace** see FALL FROM GRACE; IN SOMEONE'S BAD GRACES; IN SOMEONE'S GOOD GRACES; SAVING GRACE; SAY GRACE; THERE BUT FOR THE GRACE OF GOD; WITH GOOD GRACE.

**gracious** see GOODNESS GRACIOUS.

**grade** see MAKE THE GRADE.

**grain** see AGAINST THE GRAIN; WITH A GRAIN OF SALT.

**granddaddy of them all, the** The first, oldest, or most respected of its kind, as in *That mountain is the granddaddy of them all for climbers.*

**grand slam** A great success or total victory, as in *This presentation gave us a grand slam—every buyer placed an order.* This term is also used in various card games and sports, where it has different meanings: in baseball, a home run hit with runners on all three bases, resulting in four runs for the team; in tennis, winning all four national championships in a single calendar year; in golf, winning all four major championships.

**grandstand play, make a** Behave in a proud, showy way in front of others. For example, *His colleagues were annoyed with Tom for constantly making a grandstand play at sales conferences.* This expression was first used for a baseball play made to impress the crowd in the grandstand (the section of high-priced seats at ballparks). Also see PLAY TO THE GALLERY.

**grand tour** A comprehensive tour, survey, or inspection. For example, *They took me on the grand tour of their new house,* or *The new chairman will want to make a grand tour of all the branches.* This term was once used for a tour of the major European cities. Such a tour was a traditional part of a rich young man's education.

**granted** see TAKE FOR GRANTED.

**grape** see SOUR GRAPES.

**grasp** In addition to the idiom beginning with GRASP, also see GET A FIX ON (GRASP OF).

**grasp at straws** Also, **clutch at straws.** Make a desperate attempt to save oneself. For example, *He had lost the argument, but he kept grasping at straws..* This expression refers to a drowning person grabbing at reeds to try to save himself or herself.

**grass** In addition to the idiom beginning with GRASS, also see LET THE GRASS GROW UNDER ONE'S FEET; SNAKE IN THE GRASS.

**grasshopper** see KNEE-HIGH TO A GRASSHOPPER.

**grass is greener, the** A different situation always seems better than one's own. For example, *Bob always thinks the grass is greener elsewhere, which accounts for his constant* *job changes.* The complete proverb is **the grass is always greener on the other side.**

**grave** see DIG ONE'S OWN GRAVE; FROM THE CRADLE TO THE GRAVE; ONE FOOT IN THE GRAVE; TURN IN ONE'S GRAVE.

**gray** In addition to the idioms beginning with GRAY, also see GET GRAY HAIR FROM.

**gray area** An area where it's difficult to form opinions or make decisions because there are no clear rules or limits. For example, *There's a large gray area between what is legal and what is not.* This term uses *gray* in the sense of "neither black nor white" (or halfway between the two).

G

**gray matter** Brains, intelligence, as in *If you'd only use your gray matter, you'd see the answer in a minute.* This expression refers to actual brain tissue that is gray in color.

**grease** In addition to the idioms beginning with GREASE, also see ELBOW GREASE; LIKE GREASED LIGHTNING; SQUEAKY WHEEL GETS THE GREASE.

**grease someone's palm** Also, **oil someone's palm** or **oil someone's hand.** Give someone money in exchange for a favor; also, bribe someone. For example, *If you want your luggage to make the plane, be sure to grease the porter's palm.*

**grease the wheels** Also, **oil the wheels.** Make things run smoothly, as in *You can count on Ben to grease the wheels, so we'll get fast service.*

**greasy spoon** A cheap restaurant, especially one serving short-order fried foods. For example, *College students without much money tend to eat a lot in that greasy spoon.* This expression also implies that the restaurant is not very clean.

**great** In addition to the idioms beginning with GREAT, also see GOOD (GREAT) DEAL; GOOD (GREAT) MANY; GO TO ANY LENGTH (GREAT LENGTHS); MAKE GREAT STRIDES; NO GREAT SHAKES; SET (GREAT) STORE BY.

**great deal** see GOOD DEAL.

**greatest thing since sliced bread, the** Also, **the best thing since sliced bread.** An excellent new invention, as in *Harry swears that this new program is the greatest thing since sliced bread.* This phrase refers to the convenience of buying bread that is already sliced.

**great guns** **1.** Very energetically or successfully. This expression usually occurs in the phrase **go great guns,** as in *They're going great guns with plans for the celebration.* **2. Great guns!** An expression spoken to show surprise or astonishment, as in *Great guns! You're not leaving now?* **3. great gun.** See BIG GUN.

**great many** see under GOOD MANY.

**great minds run in the same channel, (all)** Also, **great minds think alike.** Intelligent persons think alike or arrive at similar ideas. For example, *I see you brought your tennis racket—thank goodness for great minds.* This term is often spoken (sometimes jokingly) when two persons seem to find the same answer at the same moment. It is often shortened.

**great shakes** see NO GREAT SHAKES.

**great white hope, the** Something or someone that is expected or depended on to succeed. For example, *Mark is the great white hope of the company's international division.* This expression refers to the early 20th-century heavyweight boxing champion Jack Johnson. He was black and seemed impossible to beat. The term was used for any white opponent who might defeat him.

**Greek to me, it's** Also, **it's all Greek to me.** I can't understand it at all, as in *This new computer program is all Greek to me.* This expression was first used by Shakespeare.

**green** In addition to the idioms beginning with GREEN, also see GRASS IS GREENER.

**green about the gills** Also, **green around the gills.** Looking sick or nauseous, sometimes from shock or fear, as in *After that bumpy ride she looked quite green about the gills,* or *The news of the stock market crash left him looking green around the gills. Gills* (meaning the breathing organs of a fish) refers to the flesh around human jaws and ears.

**green-eyed monster** Jealousy, as in *Bella knew that her husband was sometimes a victim of the green-eyed monster.* This expression was first used by Shakespeare. It is thought to refer to cats, often green-eyed, who tease their prey. Also see GREEN WITH ENVY.

**green light, the** Permission to go ahead, as in *The chief gave us the green light for starting this project.* This term refers to the signal used by railroads to indicate that a train could proceed.

**green thumb, a** A knack for making plants grow well, as in *Just look at Louise's plants—she really has a green thumb.* This term probably refers to the green-stained fingers of an enthusiastic gardener.

**green with envy** Full of desire for someone's possessions or advantages. For example, *Her new car makes me green with envy.* Also see GREEN-EYED MONSTER.

**grey** see GRAY.

**grief** see COME TO GRIEF; GOOD GRIEF.

**grievance** see AIR ONE'S GRIEVANCES.

**grin and bear it** Tolerate or react to a bad situation with good humor, as in *It's no fun being sick for the holidays, but I'll just have to grin and bear it.*

**grind** In addition to the idiom beginning with GRIND, also see AX TO GRIND.

**grindstone** see NOSE TO THE GRINDSTONE.

**grind to a halt** Also, **come to a grinding halt.** Gradually come to an end of activity. For example, *Once the funding stopped, the project ground to a halt,* or *She's come to a grinding halt with that book she's writing.* This expression refers to a clogged engine that gradually stops or a ship that runs aground.

**grin like a Cheshire cat** Smile broadly, especially in a self-satisfied way. For example, *John won the game and couldn't help grinning like a Cheshire cat.*

**grip** see COME TO GRIPS WITH; GET A GRIP ON; LOSE ONE'S GRIP.

**grist for the mill** Something that can be used to advantage, as in *For a writer of fiction, all of life's experiences are grist for the mill.* This expression refers to *grist,* which means the amount of grain that can be ground at one time.

**grit one's teeth** Summon up one's strength to face unpleasantness or a difficulty. For example, *Gritting his teeth, he dove into the icy water.* This expression uses *grit* in the sense of both clamping one's teeth together and grinding them with effort.

**groove** see IN THE GROOVE.

**gross someone out** Disgust or offend someone, as in *Chewing gum in church grosses me out,* or *His explicit language grossed her out.*

**ground** In addition to the idioms beginning with GROUND, also see BOTH FEET ON THE GROUND; BREAK GROUND; COMMON GROUND; COVER GROUND; CUT THE GROUND FROM UNDER; DOWN TO THE GROUND; EAR TO THE GROUND; FROM THE GROUND UP; GAIN GROUND; GET OFF THE GROUND; GIVE GROUND; HIT THE GROUND RUNNING; LOSE GROUND; ON ONE'S HOME GROUND; RUN INTO THE GROUND; STAMPING GROUND; STAND ONE'S GROUND; WORSHIP THE GROUND SOMEONE WALKS ON.

**ground floor, get in on the** Participate in the beginning of a project, especially a business venture, and gain some advantage. For example, *Investors were eager to get in on the ground floor of the new development.*

**ground rules** Basic procedures of conduct, as in *The press secretary sets the ground rules for all of the President's press conferences.* The term comes from baseball, where it refers to specific rules based on the conditions in a particular ballpark.

**grow** In addition to the idioms beginning with GROW, also see ABSENCE MAKES THE HEART GROW FONDER; LET THE GRASS GROW UNDER ONE'S FEET.

**growing pains** Problems that happen while beginning or enlarging an enterprise, as in *The company is undergoing growing pains but should be running smoothly by next year.* This expression originally referred to the joint and limb aches experienced by youngsters who are growing rapidly.

**grow into** **1.** Develop so as to become, as in *The army makes a boy grow into a man.* **2.** Develop or change so as to fit, as in *He'll soon grow into the next shoe size,* or *She has grown into her job.*

**grow on** Also, **grow upon. 1.** Gradually become clear or known to someone. For example, *A feeling of distrust grew upon him as he learned more about the way the account was handled.* **2.** Gradually become more pleasurable or acceptable to someone, as in *This music is beginning to grow on me.*

**grow out of** **1.** Develop or come into existence from a source. For example, *This article grew out of a short conversation,* or *Their mutual trust grew out of long acquaintance.* **2.** Also, **outgrow.** Become too large or mature for something, as in *The baby's grown out of all her dresses,* or *He outgrew his interest in cartoons.*

**grow up** **1.** Become an adult, as in *Sam wants to be a policeman when he grows up.* **2.** Come into existence, begin, as in *Similar social problems grew up in all the big cities.* **3.** Become mature or sensible, as in *It's time you grew up and faced the facts.* This usage may also be in the form of an imperative (as in *Don't bite your nails—grow up!*)

**grudge** see BEAR A GRUDGE; NURSE A GRUDGE.

**guard** see OFF GUARD; STAND GUARD.

**guess** In addition to the idiom beginning with GUESS, also see ANYONE'S GUESS; EDUCATED GUESS; HAVE ANOTHER GUESS COMING. I SUPPOSE (GUESS) SO; YOUR GUESS IS AS GOOD AS MINE.

**guess again** see HAVE ANOTHER GUESS COMING.

**guess what** An expression spoken to introduce some surprising or exciting news. For example, *Guess what—I got the job!*

**guest** see BE MY GUEST.

**gum up** Ruin or spoil something, as in *The front office has gummed up the sales campaign thoroughly.* This idiom is also put as **gum up the works,** as in *John's changes in procedures have gummed up the works in the shipping department.*

**gun** In addition to the idiom beginning with GUN, also see AT GUNPOINT; BIG GUN; HIRED GUN; HOLD A GUN TO SOMEONE'S HEAD; JUMP THE GUN; SMOKING GUN; SON OF A BITCH (GUN); STICK TO ONE'S GUNS; UNDER THE GUN.

**gun for** **1.** Chase or try to attack someone so as to destroy the person. For example, *He was sure they were gunning for him and asked for police protection,* or *The senator felt that the reporters were gunning for him with that arti-*

*cle about his brother.* **2.** Try hard to get something. For example, *He's been gunning for a raise all year.*

**gung ho** Also, **gung-ho.** Extremely enthusiastic or dedicated, as in *She was gung ho about her new job.* This expression was introduced during World War II as a training slogan for a U.S. Marine battalion. An American officer thought these were Mandarin Chinese words for "work together." The phrase was actually an abbreviation for the name of Chinese industrial cooperatives.

**gussied up** Also, **all gussied up.** Dressed up, as in *Dana loves to get all gussied up and go to a fine restaurant.*

**gut** see BUST A GUT; HATE SOMEONE'S GUTS; HAVE THE GUTS; SPILL ONE'S GUTS.

**gutter** see IN THE GUTTER.

**guy** see FALL GUY; NICE GUYS FINISH LAST; NO MORE MR. NICE GUY.

# Hh

**habit** see KICK A HABIT.
**hackles** see RAISE ONE'S HACKLES.
**had** In addition to the idioms beginning with HAD, also see under HAVE.
**had, to be** see BE HAD.
**had better** Also, **had best.** Ought to, should. For example, *You had better finish this one before starting another,* or *We had best be going.* Also see YOU'D BETTER BELIEVE IT.
**had enough** see HAVE HAD ENOUGH.
**had it** see HAVE HAD IT.
**had its day, has** Is no longer useful or popular or successful, as in *Some people think the railroad has had its day.*
**had one's fill** Also, **have one's fill.** See GET ONE'S FILL.
**had rather** Also, **had sooner.** Would prefer. For example, *I had rather you let me do the driving,* or *He'd sooner let them have their way than fight.* This idiom today is often replaced by WOULD RATHER. Also see JUST AS SOON.
**hail from** Come from, as in *He hails from Oklahoma.* This term originally referred to the port from which a ship had sailed.
**hair** In addition to the idioms beginning with HAIR, also see BAD HAIR DAY; BY A HAIR; BY THE SHORT HAIRS; FAIR-HAIRED BOY; GET GRAY HAIR FROM; HANG BY A THREAD (HAIR); HIDE NOR HAIR; IN SOMEONE'S HAIR; LET ONE'S HAIR DOWN; MAKE ONE'S HAIR STAND ON END; PUT LEAD IN ONE'S PENCIL (HAIR ON ONE'S CHEST); SPLIT HAIRS; TEAR ONE'S HAIR.
**hair of the dog that bit you** An alcoholic drink taken to treat a headache resulting from too much alcohol the night before. For example, *A little hair of the dog will cure that hangover in no time.* This expression is based on the past treatment for dog bite of putting a burnt hair of the dog on the wound. It is often shortened, as in the example.
**hair shirt** A difficult or uncomfortable situation someone suffers or chooses as punishment. For example, *I apologized a dozen times—do you want me to wear a hair shirt forever?* This term refers to wearing a coarse, scratchy hair shirt for religious reasons.
**hale and hearty** In robust good health, as in *After her long bout with pneumonia, I was glad to see her hale and hearty.* This redundant expression, since both *hale* and *hearty* here mean "healthy," probably survives because of its pleasing alliteration.
**half** In addition to the idioms beginning with HALF, also see AT HALF-MAST; BETTER HALF; BY HALF; GLASS IS HALF FULL; GO HALFWAY; GO OFF (HALF-COCKED); HOW THE OTHER HALF LIVES; IN HALF; LISTEN WITH HALF AN EAR; NOT BAD (HALF BAD); SEE WITH HALF AN EYE; SIX OF ONE, HALF DOZEN OF THE OTHER; TIME AND A HALF. Also see under HALFWAY; HALVES.
**half a heart, with** With only moderate enthusiasm, as in *After his transfer he worked with half a heart, looking forward to early retirement.* For an antonym, see WITH ALL ONE'S HEART.
**half a loaf is better than none** Something is better than nothing, even if it is less than one wanted. For example, *He had asked for new skis but got used ones—oh well, half a loaf is better than none.* This expression, often shortened, was originally a proverb, "For better is half a loaf than no bread."
**half a mind** A thought about doing something that is not definite or firm. For example, *I have half a mind to drop the course,* or *He went out with half a mind to walk all the way there.* Also see HAVE A GOOD MIND TO.
**half a minute 1.** Also, **half a second.** A brief period of time. For example, *Just give me half a minute and I'll join you,* or *This will take only half a second.* **2.** Stop, used as a command. For example, *Half a minute, there. I never said I'd buy your dinner.*
**half of it, the** Only part of something, as in *You saw them together, but that's just the half of it; she moved in with him.* This phrase, meaning the most important portion (more than half), is often put negatively as **not the half of it,** as in *You thought they played badly? That's not the half of it—they've also been kicked out of the league.*
**half the battle** A successful beginning, as in *You've got the shopping list done—that's half the battle.* This expression is an abbreviation of a proverb, "The first blow is half the battle."
**half the fun** A large part of what makes something enjoyable, as in *Half the fun of traveling is meeting new people.*
**half the time 1.** A large part of the time, most of the time. For example, *Half the time she doesn't even answer her phone.* **2.** Very

quickly, as in *The will get us there in half the time.*

**half the trouble 1.** A large part of what makes something difficult or unpleasant. For example, *Half the trouble of preparing a meal is figuring out what to eat.* **2.** A great deal of effort and time, as in *If you'd gone to half the trouble I have to make this cake from scratch, you'd also be upset because no one ate any.*

**halfway** In addition to the idiom beginning with HALFWAY, also see GO HALFWAY.

**halfway house** A place where people go to live after being released from an institution, such as a prison or drug rehabilitation center, so that they have time to adjust to living in the world again. For example, *He's now in a halfway house and looking for his own place to live.*

H

**halt** see CALL A HALT; COME TO A HALT; GRIND TO A HALT.

**halves** see BY HALVES; GO HALVES. Also see under HALF.

**hammer** In addition to the idioms beginning with HAMMER, also see UNDER THE HAMMER.

**hammer and tongs** Forcefully, with great energy. For example, *She went at the weeds hammer and tongs, determined to clean up the flower bed.* Often put as **go at it hammer and tongs,** this phrase refers to a blacksmith's tools.

**hammer away at** Keep at someone or something continuously, as in *The reporters hammered away at the candidate.* This phrase uses *hammer* in the sense of "beat repeatedly."

**hammer home** Also, **hammer *something* into someone's brain** or **skull.** Repeat something many times and with much emphasis because someone has previously not paid attention. For example, *Maybe being broke for a while will hammer home the importance of learning a skill,* or *No matter what I say, I can't seem to hammer this into his brain.*

**hammer out** Work something out with great effort, as in *It took weeks of negotiations to hammer out an acceptable compromise.* This usage compares intellectual effort to shaping metal with the blows of a hammer.

**ham up** Exaggerate or overdo something, especially with too much emotion, as in *Hamming up the song was disgraceful, especially since he didn't even know the words.* It is also put as **ham it up,** meaning "overact," as in *She loves to ham it up in front of the class.* This idiom probably refers to the *hamfat* (lard) used to remove stage makeup.

**hand** In addition to the idioms beginning with HAND, also see AT HAND; AT THE HAND OF; BACK OF ONE'S HAND; BARE HANDS; BIRD IN THE HAND; BITE THE HAND THAT FEEDS YOU; BOUND HAND AND FOOT; BY HAND; CATCH RED-HANDED; CHANGE HANDS; CLEAN HANDS; COLD HANDS, WARM HEART; DEAL IN (ONE A HAND); DIRTY ONE'S HANDS; EAT OUT OF SOMEONE'S HAND; FEED (HAND) SOMEONE A LINE; FORCE SOMEONE'S HAND; FREE HAND; FROM HAND TO HAND; GIVE A HAND; GLAD HAND; GREASE SOMEONE'S PALM (OIL SOMEONE'S HAND); HAT IN HAND; HAVE A HAND IN; HAVE ONE'S HANDS FULL; HEAVY HAND; IN GOOD HANDS; IN HAND; IN ONE'S HANDS; IN THE HANDS OF; IRON HAND; KEEP ONE'S HAND IN; KNOW LIKE A BOOK (THE BACK OF ONE'S HAND); LAY HANDS ON; LEFT HAND DOESN'T KNOW WHAT THE RIGHT HAND IS DOING; LEFT-HANDED COMPLIMENT; LEND A HAND; OFF SOMEONE'S HANDS; ON HAND; ON ONE'S HANDS; ON THE ONE (THE OTHER) HAND; OUT OF CONTROL (HAND); OUT OF HAND; PLAY INTO THE HANDS OF; PUTTY IN SOMEONE'S HANDS; RAISE A HAND AGAINST; RIGHT-HAND MAN; SHAKE HANDS; SHOW OF HANDS; SHOW ONE'S HAND; SIT ON ONE'S HANDS; SLEIGHT OF HAND; TAKE IN HAND; TAKE INTO ONE'S HANDS; TAKE SOMEONE'S LIFE (IN ONE'S HANDS); TAKE THE LAW INTO ONE'S HANDS; THROW IN ONE'S HAND; THROW UP ONE'S HANDS; TIE ONE'S HANDS; TIME HANGS HEAVY ON ONE'S HANDS; TIME ON ONE'S HANDS; TIP ONE'S HAND; TO HAND; TRY ONE'S HAND; TURN ONE'S HAND TO; UPPER HAND; WAIT ON HAND AND FOOT; WASH ONE'S HANDS OF; WITH ONE ARM (HAND).

**hand and foot** see BOUND HAND AND FOOT; WAIT ON HAND AND FOOT.

**hand down 1.** Leave something to one's heirs, as in *The silver and jewels have been handed down from generation to generation in that family.* **2.** Make and pronounce an official decision, especially the verdict of a court. For example, *The judge wasted no time in handing down a long sentence.* Also see HAND ON; HAND OVER.

**hand in glove** On very friendly terms, in close association, as in *The lawyer is hand in glove with the police, so you'd better be careful.*

**hand in hand** Working together, jointly, as in *Industrial growth and urbanization often go hand in hand.* This phrase is often put as **go hand in hand with.**

**hand in the till, with one's** Also, **with one's fingers in the till; have one's hand in the cookie jar.** Stealing from one's employer. For example, *He was caught with his hand in the till and was fired immediately,* or *They suspected she had her hand in the cookie jar but were waiting for more evidence.*

**hand it to** Give credit to someone, congratulate, as in *You've got to hand it to her; she knows what she's doing.*

**handle** In addition to the idioms beginning with HANDLE, also see FLY OFF THE HANDLE; GET A FIX (HANDLE) ON; TOO HOT TO HANDLE.

**handle *someone* with gloves** Also, **handle *someone* with kid gloves.** Treat someone with great care or very gently, as in *She has a terrible temper, so try to handle her with kid gloves.* Gloves made of kidskin, the hide of a young goat, are soft and comfortable, thus the transfer to delicate treatment.

**hand *something* on** Give something to another person, as in *When you've read the memo, please hand it on to Sam.* This term can also be used in the sense of "leave to one's heirs" (see HAND DOWN, def. 1).

**hand out** Distribute something, as in *The teacher handed out the test papers.* For a synonym, see PASS OUT, def. 1.

**hand over** Release or give something to another person's possession or control. For example, *You may as well hand over the money,* or *He decided to hand the store over to his children.* For a synonym, see TURN OVER, def. 5.

**hand over fist** Rapidly, at a fast rate, as in *He's making money hand over fist.* This expression is derived from the nautical **hand over hand,** describing how a sailor climbed a rope.

**hand over hand** see HAND OVER FIST.

**hands are tied** see TIE ONE'S HANDS.

**hands down 1.** Also, **in a breeze; in a walk.** Easily, without effort, as in *She won the election hands down,* or *They won in a breeze, 10-0,* or *The top players get through the first rounds of the tournament in a walk.* All of these expressions originated in sports. **Hands down** comes from horseracing, where jockeys drop their hands downward and relax their hold when they are sure to win. **In a breeze,** from baseball, refers to the rapid and easy passage of moving air; **in a walk,** also from baseball, refers to taking a base on balls, that is, reaching first base without having hit a pitched ball because of the pitcher's mistakes. **2.** Without question, without a doubt, as in *Hands down, it was the best thing I've ever done.*

**handshake** see GOLDEN HANDSHAKE.

**hands off** An order to stop touching or interfering with something, as in *Hands off the cake, children!* This idiom is also put as **keep one's hands off,** as in *She knew she had to keep her hands off so he could learn to tie his shoes by himself.*

**handsome is as handsome does** How one acts is more important than how one looks. For example, *He may be homely, but he's the kindest man I've ever met—handsome is as handsome does.*

**hands up** A direction or order to hold one's hands high, as in *Hands up or I'll shoot!* This command is used by police officers and criminals so that they can see if someone is holding a weapon.

**hand to hand 1.** In close combat; also, at close quarters. For example, *If the enemy came any closer, they would soon be fighting hand to hand.* This expression is usually restricted to military contexts but occasionally sees more general use. **2. from hand to hand.** From one person to another; through a succession of people. For example, *The instructions were passed from hand to hand until everyone had seen them,* or *Over the generations the family albums went from hand to hand.*

**hand to mouth, from** With only the bare essentials, barely existing. For example, *After she lost her job, she was living from hand to mouth.* This expression refers to eating immediately whatever is at hand.

**hand *something* to *one* on a silver platter** Also, **serve *something* up on a plate.** Provide one with something valuable for nothing, or give an unearned reward to; also, make it easy for one. For example, *She did no work at all, expecting to have everything handed to her on a silver platter,* or *Just ask them—they'll serve up the data on a plate.* Both terms refer to being elaborately served at the table. Also see BORN WITH A SILVER SPOON.

H

**handwriting on the wall, the** Also, **the writing on the wall.** A warning or hint of danger, as in *The company was losing money, and seeing the handwriting on the wall, she started to look for another job.*

**handy** see COME IN HANDY.

**hang** In addition to the idioms beginning with HANG, also see DRAW AND QUARTER (HANGED, DRAWN AND QUARTERED); GET THE HANG OF; I'LL BE HANGED; LEAVE HANGING; LET IT ALL HANG OUT; NOT GIVE A DAMN (HANG); THEREBY HANGS A TALE; TIME HANGS HEAVY.

**hang a left** Also, **hang a right.** Make a left (or right) turn, as when driving an automobile. For example, *Hang a left at the traffic light and then hang a right at the next intersection.*

**hang around 1.** Spend time idly, loiter, as in *Every afternoon they could be found hanging around the mall.* Also see HANG OUT, def. 4. **2.** Keep company with someone, as in *The younger campers loved to hang around the older ones.* Also see HANG OUT, def. 5.

**hang back** Be reluctant to move ahead, hold back. For example, *They hung back at the entrance, fearful that they wouldn't be admitted,* or *We hung back to let our parents go in first.*

**hang by a thread** Also, **hang by a hair.** Be in a risky or unstable situation, as in *His promotion was hanging by a thread,* or *With the lead actor sick, the success of our play hung by a hair.* This expression refers to the proverb of Damocles, who found himself seated under a sword suspended by a single hair, symbolizing his insecure position at court.

**hangdog look** A facial expression of shame or guilt. For example, *I suspected he had done something wrong when I saw his hangdog look.*

**hanged, drawn, and quartered** see DRAW AND QUARTER.

**hang fire** Delay, as in *The advertising campaign is hanging fire until they decide how much to spend on it.*

**hang in** Also, **hang in there.** Keep at something, be persistent. For example, *We decided to hang in until we had figured out why the experiment failed,* or *Hang in there! You'll soon catch on to the language.*

**hang in the balance** Be in an unsafe condition or in a state of suspense. For example, *The doctor said her life was hanging in the balance.* This expression refers to the suspended balance scale where an object is placed in one pan and weights are added one by one to the other pan until the two are balanced.

**hang it** Also, **hang it all.** An expression of irritation. For example, *Hang it! I locked my keys inside the car,* or *Hang it all, you don't need to push me.*

**hang it up** Give up on doing something, as in *It's too dark to continue playing; we might as well hang it up,* or *Why don't you just hang it up?*

**hang loose** Relax, take it easy, as in *Just hang loose and it will all work out.*

**hang on 1. hang on to.** Cling tightly to something, keep, as in *Hang on to those papers before they blow away.* Also see HANG ON TO YOUR HAT. **2.** Continue with determination, persist, as in *This cough is hanging on much longer than I expected,* or *He was hanging on, hoping business would improve when interest rates went down.* **3.** Keep a telephone connection open, as in *Please hang on, I'll see if he's in.* **4.** Wait for a short time, be patient, as in *Hang on, I'm getting it as fast as I can.* **5.** Depend on something, as in *Our plans hang on their decision about the new park.* **6.** Blame something on someone, as in *They'll try to hang that robbery on the same gang, but I don't think they'll succeed.* **7. hang one on.** Get very drunk, as in *Come on, let's go and hang one on.* Also see the following idioms beginning with HANG ON.

**hang one on** see HANG ON, def. 7.

**hang one's head** Show shame or regret. For example, *No need to hang your head—you've done the best you can.*

**hang on someone's words** Listen very attentively to someone. For example, *You don't need to hang on his words—just remember the gist of it.* It is also put as **hang on to every word,** as in *Whenever Mother read their favorite book to them, the children hung on to every word.*

**hang on to your hat** Also, **hold your hat.** An expression warning someone of a big surprise. For example, *Hang on to your hat, we're about to go public,* or *Hold your hat—we just won the lottery.* This expression may refer to a wild ride.

**hang out 1.** Stick out downward, as in *The dog's tongue was hanging out,* or *The tree branches hung out over the driveway.* **2.** Display a flag or sign of some kind, as in *They hang out the flag on every holiday.* **3.** Reside, live, as in *I've found a new apartment, and I'll be hanging out there beginning next week.* **4.** Spend one's free time in; also, pass time idly. For example, *They hung out downtown,* or *They spent the evening just hanging out.* **5. hang out with.** Keep company with someone, appear in public with, as in *She's hanging out with her ex-boyfriend again.* Also see LET IT ALL HANG OUT. Also see the following idiom beginning with HANG OUT.

**hang out one's shingle** Open an office, especially a professional practice, as in *She's renting that office and hanging out her shingle next month.* This idiom refers to the time when at first lawyers, and later also doctors and business concerns, used shingles for signboards.

**hang *someone* out to dry** Abandon someone to danger, as in *The soldiers withdrew and just hung us out to dry.* This expression refers to hanging wet laundry on a clothesline.

**hang over 1.** Remain suspended or unsettled, as in *They plan to let the vote hang over until the next session.* This usage refers to something suspended or floating in the air. **2.** Also, **hang over one's head.** Threaten or be about to happen, as in *I've got that test hanging over me,* or *A stiff fine is hanging over his head.* Also see HANG BY A THREAD.

**hang together 1.** Stand united, stay together, as in *We must all hang together and tell the same story.* **2.** Make sense, amount to a consistent whole. For example, *The plot lines in that movie don't hang together.*

**hang tough** Remain firmly resolved, as in *We're going to hang tough on this point and not give in.* This slangy idiom uses *tough* in the sense of "aggressively unyielding."

**hang up 1.** Suspend on a hook or hanger, as in *Let me hang up your coat for you.* **2.** Also, **hang up on.** End a phone conversation. For example, *She hung up the phone,* or *He hung up on her.* **3.** Delay or hinder something; also, become halted or stopped, as in *Budget problems hung up the project for months,* or *Traffic was hung up for miles.* **4. hang one up.** Have or cause one to have emotional difficulties, as in *Being robbed at gunpoint can hang one up* *for years to come.* **5. hung up on** Obsessed with something or someone, as in *For years the FBI was hung up on Communist spies.* **6. hang up one's hat.** Settle somewhere, reside, as in *Home is wherever I hang up my hat.*

**happen** see ACCIDENT WAITING TO HAPPEN, SHIT HAPPENS.

**happily** see LIVE HAPPILY EVER AFTER.

**happy** In addition to the idioms beginning with HAPPY, also see MANY HAPPY RETURNS; TRIGGER HAPPY.

**happy as the day is long** Also, **happy as a lark** or **happy as a clam (at high tide).** Extremely glad, delighted, very cheerful, as in *He was happy as the day is long,* or *When she heard the news, she was happy as a lark,* or *Once I got the test results, I was happy as a clam at high tide.* The second of these expressions refers to the lark's beautiful, seemingly very happy song. The third refers to the fact that clams can only be dug at low tide and therefore are safe at high tide; it is often shortened to **happy as a clam.**

**happy camper** A satisfied participant, a contented person, as in *She loved the challenge of her new job; she was one happy camper.* This expression is also often put in the negative, as in *She hated the heat and humidity of the southern summer; she was not a happy camper.*

**happy hour** A period in the late afternoon or early evening when a bar sells drinks at reduced prices. For example, *The hotel bar has a happy hour from five to seven every day.*

**happy medium** The midway point between two extremes. For example, *We need to find a happy medium between spending too much on gifts and not giving anything.* This expression was once known as **the golden mean** and is based on ancient mathematical principles.

**hard** In addition to the idioms beginning with HARD, also see BETWEEN A ROCK AND A HARD PLACE; COLD (HARD) CASH; COME DOWN (HARD) ON; DIE HARD; DRIVE A HARD BARGAIN; GO HARD WITH; HIT HARD; LEARN THE HARD WAY; NO HARD FEELINGS; PLAY HARDBALL; PLAY HARD TO GET; SCHOOL OF HARD KNOCKS; TOUGH (HARD) ROW TO HOE.

**hard act to follow, a** Also, **a tough act to follow.** An outstanding performance or individual. For example, *Lucy was a terrific group leader—hers is a hard act to follow,* or *Bob's record is excellent—it will be a tough act to follow.* This expression was originally used for a particularly good vaudeville act that made the next act look poor by comparison. It soon was extended to other activities.

**hard and fast** Defined, fixed, unchanging, as in *We have hard and fast rules for this procedure.* This term originally was applied to a ship that is out of the water and is therefore unable to move.

**hard as nails** Unyielding, unsympathetic, as in *Don't ask her for a contribution—she's hard as nails.*

**hard at it** Working on a task for a long period of time without stopping. For example, *You've been hard at it all day. Why not take a break?*

**hard bargain** see DRIVE A HARD BARGAIN.

**hard cash** see COLD CASH.

**harden one's heart** Feel no sympathy for, as in *We can't afford to give them more; we'll just have to harden our hearts when they ask.*

**hard feelings** see NO HARD FEELINGS.

**hard hat** A working-class person. For example, *They were counting on a large number of votes from the hard hats.* This term refers to the rigid protective headgear worn by construction workers.

H

**hard hit, be** Be negatively affected or be severely hurt, as in *The clinics were hard hit by the new insurance laws.* This idiom must be distinguished from the similar-sounding adjective **hard-hitting,** which refers to great exertion, as in *They were a hard-hitting team.*

**hard line** A firm, uncompromising policy or position. For example, *The President took a hard line on the budget.*

**hard liquor** Distilled alcoholic beverages, such as gin or whiskey. For example, *We're serving wine and beer but no hard liquor.* The *hard* here refers to their high alcoholic content.

**hard luck** Misfortune, bad luck, as in *He's had a lot of hard luck in his day.* This expression is also used in the phrase **hard-luck story,** a tale of one's misfortune that is told in order to get sympathy (or money). For example, *We can't ignore her hard-luck story, even if you doubt that it's true.* Also see TOUGH BREAK.

**hardly ever** Also, **rarely ever** or **scarcely ever.** Very seldom, almost never, as in *This kind of thief is hardly ever caught,* or *He rarely ever brings up his wartime experiences.* The *ever* in these expressions is an intensifier.

**hard nut to crack, a** Also, **a tough nut to crack.** A difficult problem; also, an individual who is difficult to deal with. For example, *This assignment is a hard nut to crack,* or *It won't be easy getting her approval; she's a tough nut to crack.* This metaphoric expression refers to hard-shelled nuts like walnuts.

**hard of hearing** Somewhat deaf, having a partial loss of hearing. For example, *You'll have to speak distinctly; Dad's a little hard of hearing.* The use of *hard* in the sense of "difficulty in doing something" survives only in this expression.

**hard on, be 1.** Be close by or near, as in *The police were hard on the heels of the thieves.*

**2.** Deal severely with someone or something, cause damage to. For example, *He asked the teacher not to be too hard on those who forgot the assignment,* or *That cat has really been hard on the upholstery.* Also see HARD TIME, def. 2.

**hard on someone's heels** see AT SOMEONE'S HEELS.

**hard-pressed** Overburdened, put upon, as in *With all these bills to pay we find ourselves hard-pressed.*

**hard put, be** Find something very difficult, as in *The show was so bad that I was hard put to hide my feelings,* or *Manufacturers will be hard put to meet the new standards.*

**hard row to hoe** see TOUGH ROW TO HOE.

H

**hard sell, a 1.** An aggressive, high-pressure sales practice or advertisement, as in *Used-car salesmen tend to give you a hard sell.* This expression gave rise to the antonym **a soft sell,** a low-key sales approach that relies on gentle persuasion. **2.** A difficult sales prospect, one who resists sales pressure. For example, *Those companies that call us at dinnertime find me a hard sell—I usually just hang up on them.*

**hard time, a 1.** Also, **hard times.** A period of difficulty or hardship, especially financial hardship. For example, *Since Mom died, Christmas has been a hard time for Dad,* or *It's been hard times for both of them since they split up.* It is also put as **have a hard time,** as in *I'm having a hard time finishing this book.* A more recent version is **have a time of it,** which despite its ambiguity (not specifying either "good" or "bad") nearly always means "experiencing difficulty"; for example, *We had quite a time of it in that hurricane.* **2. give someone a hard time.** Annoy or harass someone. For example, *Don't let him give you a hard time; he's often late himself.*

**hard to come by** Very difficult to find, rare. For example, *Our team found hits hard to come by in that game,* or *Some orchids are hard to come by.*

**hard to stomach** Also, **difficult to stomach.** Very unpleasant. For example, *His presence is hard to me to stomach,* or *It's difficult to swallow one's anger, but it's often necessary.* Also see BITTER PILL TO SWALLOW.

**hard to swallow** Also, **difficult to swallow** or **not easy to swallow.** Difficult to accept or believe something, as in *I find that excuse hard to swallow,* or *Such an insult is difficult to swallow,* or *Sometimes it's not easy to swallow disappointment.*

**hard up** In need, poor, as in *Unemployment is rising, and many families are hard up,* or *With widespread emigration, Russia is finding itself hard up for scientists and other professional people.*

**hard way, the** By bad or unpleasant experiences; also, by one's own efforts. For example, *Bill found out the hard way that interest on his credit-card debt can mount up fast,* or *No one can teach you how—you'll just have to learn it the hard way.*

**hare** see MAD AS A HATTER (MARCH HARE).

**hark back to** Return to an earlier time or point, as in *Let us hark back to my first statement.*

**harm** see DO SOMEONE WRONG (HARM); OUT OF HARM'S WAY.

**harness** see DIE WITH ONE'S BOOTS ON (IN HARNESS).

**harp on** Dwell on something; talk or write about something to a boring and excessive extent. For example, *She kept harping on the fact that she had no household help at all.* This expression is a shortening of **harp on the same string,** meaning "to play the same note over and over."

**has** see under HAVE.

**hash** In addition to the idiom beginning with HASH, also see SLING HASH.

**hash over** Also, **hash out.** Discuss something carefully, review, as in *Let's hash over these plans again,* or *The department was hashing out the new syllabus.* This idiom uses the verb *hash* in the sense of "cut into small pieces."

**haste** In addition to the idiom beginning with HASTE, also see MAKE HASTE.

**haste makes waste** Proceeding too quickly can spoil an activity, as in *Stop trying to rush through three things at once—haste makes waste, you know.*

**hat** In addition to the idioms beginning with HAT, also see AT THE DROP OF A HAT; BRASS HAT; EAT ONE'S HAT; HANG ON TO YOUR HAT; HANG UP (ONE'S HAT); HARD HAT; KEEP SOMETHING UNDER ONE'S HAT; OLD HAT; PASS THE HAT; PULL SOMETHING OUT OF A HAT; TAKE ONE'S HAT OFF TO; TALK THROUGH ONE'S HAT; THROW ONE'S HAT IN THE RING; WEAR ANOTHER HAT. Also see under CAP.

**hatch** see BATTEN DOWN THE HATCHES; COUNT ONE'S CHICKENS BEFORE THEY HATCH; DOWN THE HATCH.

**hatchet** In addition to the idiom beginning with HATCHET, also see BURY THE HATCHET.

**hatchet job** see HATCHET MAN, def. 2.

**hatchet man 1.** A person assigned or hired to carry out a disagreeable task or an unethical order. For example, *When it came to firing an employee, the vice president was his boss's hatchet man.* This expression originally referred to a hired assassin but was later transferred to less evil activities. **2.** A person who attacks the reputation of others, especially a journalist hired to do so, as in *You can count on Mary's column to destroy the mayor—she's the perfect hatchet man.* This usage gave rise to **hatchet job,** meaning "harsh destructive criticism."

**hate** In addition to the idiom beginning with HATE, also see SOMEBODY UP THERE LOVES (HATES) ME.

**hate someone's guts** Thoroughly despise someone, as in *I hate Peter's guts.* The *guts* here refers to a person's inner essence.

**hat in hand** Also, **cap in hand.** In a humble manner. For example, *They went to her, hat in hand, asking for a change of assignment.* This expression refers to removing one's headgear as a sign of respect.

**hat in the ring** see THROW ONE'S HAT IN THE RING.

**hats off to** Congratulations to someone, as in *Hats off to you! You've set a new record for the mile.* This expression refers to taking off one's hat as a sign of respect.

**hatter** see MAD AS A HATTER.

**hat trick** An extremely clever performance, as in *It looked as though the party was going to achieve a hat trick in this election.*

**haul** In addition to the idioms beginning with HAUL, also see LONG HAUL; RAKE (HAUL) OVER THE COALS.

**haul off 1.** Draw back slightly, in preparation for some action. For example, *He hauled off and smacked his brother in the face.* **2.** Also, **haul out.** Shift operations to a new place, move away. For example, *The group gradually hauled off to the West Coast,* or *The train hauled out just as I arrived.*

**haul over the coals** see RAKE OVER THE COALS.

**haul up 1.** Come to a halt, stop, as in *We hauled up in front of the hotel.* **2.** Bring someone before a superior or other authority, call someone to account. For example, *This was the third time he'd been hauled up before the judge.*

**have** In addition to the idioms beginning with HAVE, also see I MUST HAVE DOZED OFF; NOT HAVE IT. Also see under GET, HAD, and KEEP.

**have a ball** Enjoy oneself enormously, as in *It was a great trip—I had a ball.* This idiom uses the noun *ball* in the sense of "a gala dance."

**have a beef** Be unhappy or dissatisfied about something, as in *We have a beef about the cost of our hotel room.* This idiom also is used as a negative meaning "everything is fine," as in *I have no beef with you.* Also see BONE TO PICK.

**have a big mouth** see BIG MOUTH.

**have a bone to pick** see BONE TO PICK.

**have a broad back** see BROAD SHOULDERS.

**have a brush with** Have an encounter or come in conflict with, as in *This was not the first time that Bob had a brush with the law.* This expression refers to the noun *brush* in the sense of "a hostile collision."

**have a case on** see HAVE A CRUSH ON.

**have a clear conscience** Also, **have a clean conscience.** Feel free of guilt or responsibility. For example, *I have a clear conscience—I did all I could to help.* This idiom is also put as **one's conscience is clear** or **one's conscience is clean,** as in *His conscience is clean about telling the whole story.* The adjectives *clear* and *clean* are used here in the sense of "innocent."

**have a clue** see NOT HAVE A CLUE.

**have a crack at** Also, **get** or **have a go at** or **shot at** or **whack at; take a crack at.** Make an attempt or have a turn at doing something. For example, *Let me have a crack at fixing it,* or *I had a shot at it but failed,* or *Dad thinks he can—let him have a go at it,* or *Dave had a whack at changing the tire,* or *Jane wants to take a crack at it.* **Have a shot at** refers to firing a gun.

**have a crush on** Also, **have a case on.** Be infatuated with someone, as in *He's had a crush on her for years,* or *Teenage girls often have a case on a friend's older brother.*

**have a familiar ring** Sound or seem as though one has already heard of something. For example, *That story has a familiar ring; I'm sure I've read it before.*

**have a feel for** Show a natural ability for something. For example, *She has a wonderful feel for music,* or *I'm not trained enough to understand the subject, but I have a feel for it.* Also see GET THE FEEL OF.

**have a fit** Also, **have fits** or **have a conniption fit** or **throw a fit** or **have kittens.** Become extremely upset. For example, *She'll have a fit when she sees you wearing the same dress,* or *Mom had a conniption fit when she heard about the broken mirror,* or *Don't throw a fit—the car's not really damaged,* or *He was having kittens over the spoiled cake.* One can also **give someone a fit** or **fits,** as in *His fussing about punctuation is enough to give me fits. Fit* and *fits,* along with *conniption fit,* have long been used in exaggerated expressions to denote extreme anger; **have kittens** refers to being so upset as to bear kittens.

**have against** see HAVE SOMETHING AGAINST.

**have a go at** see HAVE A CRACK AT.

**have a good command of** Have the ability to use or control something; have mastery of. For example, *She has a remarkably good command of Japanese,* or *He had a good command of his emotions.*

**have a good day** see HAVE A NICE DAY.

**have a good head on one's shoulders** see GOOD HEAD ON ONE'S SHOULDERS.

**have a good mind to** Be strongly inclined to, as in *She had a good mind to tell him everything.* A slightly weaker form of this

H

idiom is **have a mind to,** as in *I have a mind to spend my next vacation in the desert.* Also see HALF A MIND.

**have a good thing going** Have matters arranged to one's benefit or profit. For example, *Joe's got a good thing going with this new franchise.* It also may be put as **make a good thing of,** meaning "make something work to one's benefit," as in *If we work hard we can make a good thing of this job.* Also see HAVE GOING FOR.

**have a good time** Enjoy oneself, as in *I hope you have a good time at the beach.* This idiom is also used as a command. Also see HARD TIME; SHOW SOMEONE A GOOD TIME.

**have a grasp of** see GET A FIX ON.

**have a hand in 1.** Also, **take a hand in.** Participate in something, be involved, as in *I'd like to have a hand in planning the publicity.* **2. have one's hand in** or **keep one's hand in.** Be actively engaged or remain in practice doing something. For example, *He has a hand in every aspect of running the office,* or *Write a few pages every day, just to keep your hand in.*

**have a hard time** see HARD TIME.

**have a head for** Also, **have a good head for** or **have a strong head for. 1.** Be able to tolerate, as in *He has no head for liquor,* or *Luckily I have a good head for heights.* **2.** Have a mental ability for, as in *She has a good head for figures and straightened out the statistics in no time.*

**have a heart** Be merciful, show pity; also, be reasonable. For example, *Have a heart—I can't pay you back until next month,* or *Have a heart and stop your arguing now.* This expression is often put as a command, as in the examples. Also see HARDEN ONE'S HEART.

**have a high old time** see HIGH TIME, def. 2.

**have a hold over** Also, **have a hold on.** Have a controlling influence over one. For example, *Blackmailers have a hold over their victims,* or *Rhythm has a hold on me.*

**have all one's marbles** Be completely sane and rational. For example, *I'm not sure he has all his marbles.* For an antonym, see LOSE ONE'S MARBLES.

**have a lot on one's plate** Also, **have too much on one's plate.** Have a great deal (or too much) to cope with, as in *With the new baby and the new house, they have a lot on their plate,* or *I can't take that on now; I've got too much on my plate already.* This expression transfers a filled dinner plate to other activities.

**have a mind to** see HAVE A GOOD MIND TO.

**have an active fantasy life** Be unrealistic, expect something is going to happen that will never happen. For example, *If he thinks she'll go out with him, he has an active fantasy life.*

**have an attitude** Also, **cop an attitude.** Act in a way that shows hostility, contempt, or dislike in a situation, as in *He's had an attitude all day,* or *Don't cop an attitude in this office.* This idiom and its variant assume a bad attitude rather than a good one. A related expression, **have attitude,** is used to indicate approval of a person's self-confidence or a thing's good qualities, as in *Your sister really has attitude,* or *I like music that has attitude.*

**have an edge** Also, **have the edge.** Have an advantage over, as in *Our team has an edge on them,* or *In this competition our town has the edge.* The use of *edge* here refers to the power to cut, transferred to a margin of superiority.

**have a nerve** Also, **have some nerve.** Act in a disrespectful or impudent way. For example, *You have a nerve telling me what to do,* or *She had some nerve, criticizing the people who donated their time.* The related **have the nerve** and **have the brass** can be used with an infinitive, as in *He had the nerve to scold his boss in public,* or *You'll have to have a lot of brass to challenge him.* These expressions are also used with *a lot* as an intensifier, as in **have a lot of nerve** and **have a lot of brass.** They are also used as exclamations about someone's behavior, as in *The nerve of her! Taking credit for what we accomplished.* These idioms use *nerve* in the sense of "courage" or "audacity."

**have an eye for 1.** Be discriminating or perceptive about something, as in *She has an eye for decorating.* **2. have eyes for.** Also, **have eyes only for.** Be attracted to or desire someone or something (exclusively). For example, *It's obvious she has eyes for him,* or *He has eyes only for the top award.*

**have a nice day** Also, **have a good day** or **have a good one.** A friendly good-bye to you. For example, *Thanks for the order, have a nice day,* or *See you next week—have a good day,* or *The car's ready for you—have a good one.* These expressions have become synonymous with a polite farewell.

**have another guess coming** Also, **have another think coming** or **have another thing coming.** Be mistaken and therefore have to reconsider or rethink one's answer. For example, *If you think you can fool me, you have another guess coming,* or *John thinks he convinced me; well, he has another think coming.* A related idiom is **guess again,** often used as a command, as in *You think that car cost $20,000? Guess again!*

**have an out** Have a means of escape or an excuse, as in *I'm supposed to go to the meeting, but I have an out—Sam invited me first to come to his wedding.* One can also **give someone an out,** as in *She was hoping someone would give her an out; other-*

*wise she'd be stuck visiting relatives all afternoon.*

**have a penchant for** Have a liking or taste for something. For example, *He has a penchant for saying the wrong thing,* or *She has a strong penchant for baroque music.*

**have a point** Have said something about an event, issue, or situation that is important to consider, as in *He has a point—we should think about canceling the event.*

**have a right to** Have a just or legal claim on something or on some action, as in *The accused has a right to legal counsel.* The related **have the right to** is often used with an infinitive, as in *You have the right to remain silent.* The antonym is **have no right to,** as in *He has no right to push you aside.* Also see IN THE RIGHT.

**have a say in 1.** Also, **have a voice in.** Have the right or power to influence or make a decision about something. For example, *I want to have a say in this matter,* or *Citizens want to have a voice in their local government.* **2. have one's say.** Express one's views, as in *As soon as I've had my say, I'll sit down.* **3. have the say.** Be in command, as in *The general has the say over which troops will be sent.*

**have a screw loose** Be mentally unstable or behave strangely, as in *Anyone who approves that purchase must have a screw loose.* This term compares a mental weakness to a machine in which a part is not securely fastened. An antonym is **have one's head screwed on right;** for example, *She's very capable; she has her head screwed on right.*

**have a shot at** see HAVE A CRACK AT.

**have a stake in** Have a share, interest, or involvement in something or someone. For example, *Every member had a stake in the business,* or *She knew that she had a stake in her children's future.* This term uses *stake* in the sense of "something to gain or lose," as in gambling.

**have at** Attack someone; also, make an attempt at something. For example, *Urging the dog on, he said, "Go on, Rover, have at him,"* or *It's time to have at straightening out these files.*

**have a strong stomach** Able to see or listen to something that might make one nauseous, as in *She told me about the accident—good thing I have a strong stomach.* This idiom is also often used negatively, meaning "unable to see or listen to something sickening." For example, *He refuses to go see the new horror movie because he doesn't have a strong stomach.*

**have a thing about** Be obsessed or preoccupied with something. For example, *He has a thing about spiders in the garage,* or *She has a thing about watching movie previews.*

**have a thing going** see HAVE A GOOD THING GOING; HAVE GOING FOR.

**have a tight rein on** see TIGHT REIN ON.

**have a time of it** see under HARD TIME, def. 1.

**have attitude** see HAVE AN ATTITUDE.

**have a way with** Be successful in dealing with something or someone, as in *She has a way with mechanical things,* or *He has a way with young children.*

**have a weakness for** Be prone to, indulge in something; also, like or enjoy. For example, *She has a weakness for chocolate,* or *Bill has a weakness for gambling.*

**have a whack at** see HAVE A CRACK AT.

**have a word with** Speak with someone, discuss something with, as in *Jerry asked to have a word with you,* or *I must have a word with the company about the repairs.* This expression was at one time used interchangeably with HAVE WORDS WITH, but it no longer is.

**have a yen for** Crave or desire something or someone, as in *I have a yen for a thick juicy steak.* The *yen* in this expression comes from the Chinese *yan,* meaning "a craving" (probably for opium).

**have been had** Tricked, fooled, or badly treated. For example, *You've been had; there's no money buried in the garden,* or *Tell me I haven't been had. I invested all my savings in that stock,* or *She's tired of being had by her so-called friends.*

**have designs on** Make a secret plot or scheme, especially with selfish motives. For example, *I think he has designs on my job,* or *Mary has designs on her sister's boyfriend.* This term uses *design* in the sense of "a crafty plan."

**have dibs on** Have a first claim on something, as in *If you don't want it, I have dibs on the next available apartment.* This term was originally schoolyard slang.

**have done** Stop or cease, as in *Have done—enough of this nonsense.* This idiom is also put as **have done with it,** as in *This arrangement won't work; let's find a new one and have done with it.* The past participle *done* is used here in the sense of "finished." Also see HAVE TO DO WITH.

**have eyes for** Also, **have eyes only for.** See HAVE AN EYE FOR, def. 2.

**have fits** see HAVE A FIT.

**have for breakfast** Also, **eat for breakfast.** Dispose of or deal with someone very easily, as in *He won't let you get away with that. He has folks like you for breakfast,* or *You're in trouble now; I eat jerks like you for breakfast.*

**have going for** Have in one's favor or of benefit to one. For example, *They have enough going for them that their new store* *should be a success,* or *Mary is very talented; she has a lot going for her.* Also see HAVE A GOOD THING GOING.

**have got to** see HAVE TO.

**have had enough** Want no more of something, as in *I've had enough of their quarreling.* This phrase uses *enough* in the sense of "an adequate amount." For synonyms, see FED UP; HAVE HAD IT, def. 1.

**have had it 1.** Also, **have had it up to here.** Have endured all one can, as in *I've had it with their delays,* or *She has had it up to here with her hour-long commute.* **2.** Be in a state beyond remedy or repair, as in *That old coat has had it.* **3.** Be dead, as in *His heart just stopped; he'd had it.* All three usages appear to be shortenings of HAVE HAD ENOUGH.

H

**have in common** see IN COMMON.

**have in one's hands** see IN ONE'S HANDS.

**have it 1.** Receive or learn something, as in *I have it on the best authority that he's running for office again.* **2.** Possess a solution, understand, as in *Is this the new phone number? Do I have it straight?* or *I think I have it now.* **3.** Take it, as in *There's some ice cream left; go ahead and have it.* This usage is always put as a command. **4.** Have the victory, win, as in *We've counted the votes, and the nays have it.* The related expressions **have it over someone** or **have it all over someone** mean "be superior to someone." For example, *Jane has it all over Mary when it comes to reading aloud.* **5. let someone have it.** Give someone a beating, scolding, or punishment. For example, *When she gets home, Dad will let her have it.* **6. have it off.** Have sex with, as in *The two dogs were having it off in the back yard.* Also see NOT HAVE IT. Also see the following idioms beginning with HAVE IT.

**have it bad 1.** Be completely in love with someone or something, as in *He really has it bad for his new neighbor.* Also see HAVE A CRUSH ON. **2.** Be in a difficult or stress situation. For example, *You think you have it bad, wait until I tell you what happened to her.*

**have it both ways** Achieve two mutually exclusive objectives, as in *Bill wants to have it both ways—to enjoy Christmas at home and to travel with his friends.* The related **have it all** means "get everything one wants," as in *It's too bad we can't have it all—the wisdom of experience and the fresh enthusiasm of youth.*

**have it coming** Deserve what one receives, as in *You may not like being punished, but you have to admit you had it coming,* or *When he won the Nobel Prize, everyone said he'd had it coming for a long time.*

**have it in for** Intend to harm someone, especially because of a grudge. For example, *Ever since he called the police about their dog, the neighbors have had it in for Tom.*

**have it in one 1.** Have the ability to accomplish something, as in *I don't think you have it in you to stand up to the boss.* **2.** Be without a specific inner quality, as in *He doesn't have it in him to be mean.*

**have it made** Be sure of success; also, have achieved success. For example, *Since he knows all the important people, that lawyer has it made,* or *She was accepted every place she applied—she has it made.*

**have it out** Settle decisively, especially in an argument or discussion. For example, *I'm tired of doing all the work. I'm going to have it out with him once for all.*

**have kittens** see HAVE A FIT.

**have no business** see NONE OF ONE'S BUSINESS.

**have no heart for** Also, **not have the heart for.** Lack enthusiasm for, as in *After the dog died, he had no heart for taking long walks,* or *I should go through the family albums, but I don't have the heart for it.* Also see HEART IN IT.

**have no idea 1.** Be lacking any knowledge about something and so be unable to provide information, as in *I have no idea when she'll return.* **2.** Be unaware of something, as in *I had no idea you were coming.*

**have none of** see under NOT HAVE IT.

**have no stomach for** see NO STOMACH FOR.

**have nothing on** Also, **not have anything on. 1.** Have no advantage over something or someone, as in *This car has nothing on my old one.* **2.** Have no damaging information or proof of wrongdoing about someone, as in *The police had nothing on him and so were forced to let him go.* This usage is the antonym of **have something on someone,** as in *Blackmail requires that you have something on someone wealthy.* **3.** Have nothing scheduled for a certain time, as in *We have nothing on tonight, so why don't you come over?* This expression, and its antonym, **have something on,** are abbreviations of *have nothing* (or *something*) *going on.* **4.** Be naked, as in *Please bring in the mail; I just took a bath and don't have anything on.*

**have nothing to do with** Also, **not have anything to do with. 1.** Be irrelevant, be unrelated, as in *Their visit has nothing to do with the holiday.* **2.** Avoid someone, as in *Dad insisted that we have nothing to do with the neighbors,* or *I won't have anything to do with people who act like that.* Also see HAVE TO DO WITH.

**have no time for** see NO TIME FOR.

**have no truck with** Have no dealings with, as in *The doctor said he wanted no truck with midwives. Truck* is used here in the sense of "dealings."

**have no use for** **1.** Not require something, as in *I don't smoke, so I have no use for a lighter.* **2.** Dislike something or someone, as in *I have no use for people who won't answer letters.*

**haven't** see under **not have.**

**have on** **1. have something on.** See HAVE NOTHING ON, def. 3. **2. have someone on; put someone on.** Deceive or fool someone, as in *There was no answer when I called; someone must be having me on,* or *You can't mean you're taking up ballet—you're putting me on!*

**have one's ass in a sling** see ASS IN A SLING.

**have one's cake and eat it, too** see EAT ONE'S CAKE.

**have one's druthers** Have one's choice, as in *If I had my druthers, I'd go to London first.* The noun *druthers* is a contraction of "would rather."

**have oneself** Enjoy something, as in *Be sure to have yourself a good nap,* or *They were having themselves a great time at the fair.* The *oneself* in this expression adds emphasis to the verb *have.*

**have one's eye on** **1.** Also, **keep an eye on.** Look at someone or something, especially attentively or continuously; watch. For example, *The teacher has his eye on the boys in the back row,* or *Please keep an eye on the stew.* Also see KEEP AN EYE OUT FOR. **2.** Also, **have an eye to.** Have as one's objective, as in *We had our eyes on that birthday cake,* or *The Republicans have an eye to a big majority in the House.* **3.** Also, **with an eye to.** With a view to, regarding as a goal, as in *With an eye to her inheritance, she was very attentive to her aunt.* Also see HAVE AN EYE FOR.

**have one's hands full** Be very busy, as in *With the new baby she really has her hands full.*

**have one's head in the sand** see HIDE ONE'S HEAD IN THE SAND.

**have one's head screwed on right** see under HAVE A SCREW LOOSE.

**have one's heart in it** see HEART IN IT.

**have one's moments** Also, **have its moments.** Experience or undergo brief periods of superior performance. For example, *She's not a great basketball player, but she has her moments,* or *It wasn't an outstanding performance, but it had its moments.*

**have one's own way** see GET ONE'S WAY.

**have one's say** see HAVE A SAY IN, def. 2.

**have one's undivided attention** see UNDIVIDED ATTENTION.

**have one's way with** Have sex with someone, as in *He wanted to have his way with her.* This usage is nearly always used of a man trying to get a woman to have sex. It may be dying out.

**have one's wits about one** Also, **keep one's wits about one.** Remain alert or calm, especially in a crisis. For example, *After the collision, I had my wits about me and got his name and license number,* or *Being followed was terrifying, but we kept our wits about us and got home safely.*

**have one's work cut out for one** Face a difficult task, as in *This is a very large house to manage, so I have my work cut out for me.* This expression refers to cloth cut out to make a garment.

**have on the ball** see ON THE BALL.

**have out** see HAVE IT OUT.

**have pity on** see TAKE PITY ON.

**have pull with** Have a means of gaining advantage with someone, have influence on, as in *She had pull with several of the board members.*

**have rocks in one's head** see ROCKS IN ONE'S HEAD.

**have second thoughts** Change one's mind as a result of rethinking an earlier decision, as in *He's having second thoughts about running for office.* Another version of this idiom, **on second thought,** in which *thought* is singular, is used to mean that one has changed his or her mind, as in *On second thought, let's stay home tonight.*

**have someone by the balls** Have someone at one's mercy, as in *You have to pay up—they've got you by the balls.* The *balls* here refer to the male genitals. [Vulgar slang]

**have someone right where you want them** Also, **have someone just where you want them.** Succeed in putting someone in a position or situation of maximum advantage to oneself, often by using deceit or trickery. For example, *When I have her right where I want her, then I'll make my move,* or *Wait until he has you just where he wants you; then you'll find out his true character.*

**have someone's blood on one's hands** Be responsible for something terrible happening to another person. For example, *Tell him that if he cancels the concert now, he'll have your blood on his hands.*

**have someone's ear** Get someone's attention, especially favorable attention. For example, *Harry has the boss's ear and could put in a good word about you.*

**have someone's hide** see TAN SOMEONE'S HIDE.

**have someone's number** see GET SOMEONE'S NUMBER.

**have something against** Be opposed to, especially for a particular reason. For example, *Do you have something against this plan?* or *Ann must have something against Mary, because she's always so mean when they're together.*

**have something coming** see HAVE IT COMING.

**have something going** see HAVE A GOOD THING GOING; HAVE GOING FOR.

**have something on** see under HAVE NOTHING ON.

**have something out the wazoo** Also, **coming out the wazoo; have** or **coming out the ying-yang.** Have something, especially money, in a great quantity, as in *His family is very wealthy. They have money coming out the wazoo,* or *She's got nerve out the wazoo.* In these idioms, both *wazoo* and *ying-yang* refer to the anus. [Vulgar slang]

**have something to show for** see HAVE TO SHOW FOR.

**have something written all over it** Be very obvious, as in *That prank has Joe's name written all over it.* In this idiom, *it* can be replaced by *one's face.* For example, *Mary had guilt written all over her face,* or *Do I have* sucker *written all over my face?*

**have the better of** see GET THE BETTER OF.

**have the blues** Also, **feel blue.** Feel depressed or sad, as in *After seeing the old house in such bad shape, I had the blues for weeks,* or *Some people tend to feel blue around the holidays.* The noun *blues* means "low spirits." Also see BLUE FUNK.

**have the brass** see HAVE A NERVE.

**have the courage of one's convictions** see COURAGE OF ONE'S CONVICTIONS.

**have the edge** see HAVE AN EDGE.

**have the feel** see GET THE FEEL OF.

**have the goods on** see GET THE GOODS ON.

**have the guts** Have the courage, as in *Does he have the guts to dive off the high board?*

**have the heart to** see NOT HAVE THE HEART TO. Also see HAVE A HEART; HEART IN IT.

**have the hots for** Be physically attracted to someone and eager to engage in sexual intercourse with him or her. For example, *He has the hots for her so bad he'll do anything she wants.*

**have the last laugh** see LAST LAUGH.

**have the makings of** Have the abilities or qualities needed to become something, as in *She has the makings of a fine teacher.*

**have the say** see HAVE A SAY IN, def. 3.

**have the world at one's feet** Have everything one could wish for, as in *Once she graduates from college, she'll have the world at her feet.*

**have to** Also, **have got to.** Be obliged to, must. For example, *We have to go now,* or *He has got to finish the paper today.*

**have to do with** Be concerned or associated with; deal with. For example, *This book has to do with the divisions within the church.* For the antonym, see HAVE NOTHING TO DO WITH.

**have to show for** Be able to point to something as a result of one's work or expense. For example, *I've been working all day, and I have absolutely nothing to show for it,* or *He has some very fine paintings to show for the vast amount of money he's spent.*

**have tunnel vision** see TUNNEL VISION.

**have two left feet** see TWO LEFT FEET.

**have words with** Quarrel with someone, scold, as in *If he keeps on pushing my son, I'm going to have words with him. Words* is used here to mean "a disagreement." Also see HAVE A WORD WITH.

**havoc** see PLAY HAVOC.

**haw** see HEM AND HAW.

**hawk** see WATCH ONE LIKE A HAWK.

**hay** see HIT THE HAY; MAKE HAY WHILE THE SUN SHINES; ROLL IN THE HAY; THAT AIN'T HAY.

**haystack** see NEEDLE IN A HAYSTACK.

**haywire** see GO HAYWIRE.

**haze** see IN A FOG (HAZE).

**head** In addition to the idioms beginning with HEAD, also see BEAT INTO ONE'S HEAD; BEAT ONE'S HEAD AGAINST THE WALL; BIG HEAD; BITE SOMEONE'S HEAD OFF; BRING TO A HEAD; CAN'T MAKE HEAD OR TAIL OF; COUNT NOSES (HEADS); DO BLINDFOLDED (STANDING ON ONE'S HEAD); ENTER ONE'S MIND (HEAD); EYES IN THE BACK OF ONE'S HEAD; FROM HEAD TO TOE; GET INTO ONE'S HEAD; GET ONE'S HEAD EXAMINED; GET THROUGH ONE'S HEAD; GIVE SOMEONE HIS OR HER HEAD; GOOD HEAD ON ONE'S SHOULDERS; GO TO ONE'S HEAD; HANG ONE'S HEAD; HANG OVER (ONE'S HEAD); HAVE A HEAD FOR; HAVE A SCREW LOOSE (ONE'S HEAD SCREWED ON RIGHT); HIDE ONE'S FACE (HEAD); HIDE ONE'S HEAD IN THE SAND; HIT THE NAIL ON THE HEAD; HOLD A GUN TO SOMEONE'S HEAD; HOLD ONE'S HEAD HIGH; IN DEEP (OVER ONE'S HEAD); KEEP ONE'S HEAD; LAUGH ONE'S HEAD OFF; LIKE A CHICKEN WITH ITS HEAD CUT OFF; LOSE ONE'S HEAD; MAKE ONE'S HEAD SPIN; NEED LIKE A HOLE IN THE HEAD; NOT RIGHT IN THE HEAD; OFF ONE'S HEAD; OFF THE TOP OF ONE'S HEAD; ON ONE'S HEAD; (PUT ONE'S HEAD) ON THE BLOCK; OVER ONE'S HEAD; PUT IDEAS INTO SOMEONE'S HEAD; PUT OUR HEADS TOGETHER; REAR ITS UGLY HEAD; ROCKS IN ONE'S HEAD; ROOF OVER ONE'S HEAD; SCRATCH ONE'S HEAD; SHAKE ONE'S HEAD; SOFT IN THE HEAD; STAND ON ONE'S HEAD; STAND SOMETHING ON ITS HEAD; SWELLED HEAD; TALK SOMEONE'S ARM (HEAD) OFF; THROW ONESELF AT (SOMEONE'S HEAD); TOUCHED IN THE HEAD; TROUBLE ONE'S HEAD; TURN ONE'S HEAD; UPSIDE THE HEAD; USE ONE'S HEAD.

**head above water, keep one's** Stay out of trouble, especially financial difficulties; also, keep up with work or other demands. For example, *With new bills coming in every day, they're barely keeping their heads above water,* or *The work's piling up, but I manage to keep my head above water.* This expression refers to keeping oneself from drowning. Also see IN DEEP.

**head and shoulders above** Greatly superior to something, as in *This book is head and shoulders above her first one,* or *His ability to cook is head and shoulders above his brother's.* This expression transfers physical stature to other kinds of status.

**head for** Proceed or go in a certain direction, as in *I'm heading for town,* or *I believe those two are heading for a big quarrel.* This expression, which uses *head* in the sense of "advance toward," occasionally includes a figurative destination, especially in the western United States. For example, **head for the hills** means "run away to high and safer ground" or "flee from danger." It is often used humorously, as in *Here comes that old bore—head for the hills!*

**head in the clouds, have one's** Be absent-minded or impractical, as in *She must have had her head in the clouds when she made the reservations, because they never heard of us,* or *He'll never be able to run the business—he's always got his head in the clouds.*

**head in the sand** see HIDE ONE'S HEAD IN THE SAND.

**head off** Block the progress or completion of something; also, intercept someone. For example, *They worked round the clock to head off the flu epidemic,* or *Try to head him off before he gets home.* This expression gave rise to **head someone off at the pass,** which in Western films meant "block someone at a mountain pass." It then became a general expression for intercepting someone, as in *Jim is going to the boss's office—let's head him off at the pass.*

**head on 1.** With the face or front first, as in *The two bicycles collided head on.* **2.** In direct conflict, in open opposition, as in *They decided to meet the opposition head on.*

**head or tail** see CAN'T MAKE HEAD OR TAIL.

**head out 1.** Depart, begin a journey, as in *The ship was heading out to sea,* or *When do you head out again?* **2. head out after.** Follow or pursue someone, as in *Since they knew the way, we headed out after them,* or *A police car headed out after the thieves.*

**head over heels** Completely, thoroughly, as in *They fell head over heels in love.* This expression originated as *heels over head* and meant literally being upside down.

**heads or tails** An expression used when tossing a coin to decide between two alternatives, as in *Let's just flip a coin to decide who pays—do you want heads or tails?* Each person involved chooses a different side of the coin, either "heads" or "tails," and whichever side lands facing up is considered the winner. This usage is sometimes turned into **heads I win, tails you lose,** meaning "I win no matter what," which probably originated in an attempt to trick someone.

**head start, a** An early start that gives an advantage, as in *This year we'll get a head start on the competition by running more ads.* The expression comes from racing, where it was used for a horse being given an advantage of several lengths over the others.

**heads up** A warning to watch out for potential danger, as in *Heads up, that tree is coming down now!* The expression is generally in the form of a command.

**heads will roll** Someone will be severely punished, as in *If no one meets the chairman's plane, heads will roll.* This exaggerated expression refers to the punishment of being beheaded.

**head trip, be on a** Feel very superior and proud of an accomplishment, as in *She's been on a head trip ever since she was promoted.* This idiom refers to the high that results from hallucinogenic drugs.

**head up** Be in charge of something, lead, as in *She headed up the commission on conservation.*

**headway** see MAKE HEADWAY.

**health** see CLEAN BILL OF HEALTH.

**heap** see BOTTOM OF THE LADDER (HEAP); TOP OF THE LADDER (HEAP).

**hear** In addition to the idioms beginning with HEAR, also see ANOTHER COUNTY HEARD FROM; HARD OF HEARING; NEVER HEAR THE END OF; NOT HAVE IT (WON'T HEAR OF); UNHEARD OF.

**hear a peep out of** Hear the slightest noise from, as in *I don't want to hear another peep out of those children.* This expression is often used negatively, as in *I didn't hear another peep out of them.*

**hear a pin drop, can** Be able to hear even the smallest noise because of the quiet, as in *When he entered the room, you could have heard a pin drop.*

**hear from 1.** Receive a letter, call, or other communication from someone, as in *I haven't heard from my daughter in two weeks.* **2.** Be scolded by someone, as in *If you don't get home on time, you'll be hearing from your father.*

**hear, hear** An expression used to express approval, as in *Whenever the senator spoke, he was greeted with cries of "Hear! hear!"* This expression was originally *Hear him! hear him!* and was used to call attention to a speaker's words. It gradually came to be used simply as a cheer.

**hear of** Be informed about someone or something, as in *I'd never heard of that jazz singer before, but she was very good.* Also see NOT HAVE IT (WON'T HEAR OF).

**hear oneself think, can't** Be unable to concentrate because there is too much noise.

For example, *There was so much noise from the traffic we couldn't hear ourselves think.*

**hear *someone* out** Listen to what someone says until the end, allow someone to speak fully, as in *Please hear me out before you jump to any conclusions.*

**heart** In addition to the idioms beginning with HEART, also see ABSENCE MAKES THE HEART GROW FONDER; AFTER ONE'S OWN HEART; AT HEART; BREAK SOMEONE'S HEART; BY HEART; CHANGE OF HEART; COLD HANDS, WARM HEART; CROSS MY HEART; CRY ONE'S EYES (HEART) OUT; DO ONE (ONE'S HEART) GOOD; EAT ONE'S HEART OUT; FIND IT IN ONE'S HEART; FROM THE BOTTOM OF ONE'S HEART; GET TO THE HEART OF; GIVE SOMEONE HEART FAILURE; HALF A HEART; HARDEN ONE'S HEART; HAVE A HEART; HAVE NO HEART FOR; HEAVY HEART; IN ONE'S HEART OF HEARTS; LOSE HEART; LOSE ONE'S HEART TO; MY HEART BLEEDS FOR YOU; NEAR TO ONE'S HEART; NOT HAVE THE HEART TO; OPEN ONE'S HEART; POUR OUT ONE'S HEART; SET ONE'S HEART ON; SICK AT HEART; STEAL SOMEONE'S HEART; STEEL ONE'S HEART AGAINST; TAKE HEART; TAKE TO HEART; TO ONE'S HEART'S CONTENT; WARM HEART; WARM THE COCKLES OF ONE'S HEART; WEAR ONE'S HEART ON ONE'S SLEEVE; WITH ALL ONE'S HEART; YOUNG AT HEART.

**heart and soul** All one's energies or affections. For example, *He put heart and soul into his music.*

**heart goes out to, one's** One's sympathy is extended to someone, as in *She's had a terrible time of it; my heart goes out to her.*

**hear the wheels turning, can** Know that another person is thinking about something, as in *I know she's thinking about our proposal—I can hear the wheels turning.*

**heart in it, have one's** Also, **put one's heart in it.** Be emotionally involved in something, undertake something enthusiastically, as in *Nancy puts her heart in her teaching.* This expression may also be put negatively as **one's heart is not in it,** as in *She decided to quit; her heart just wasn't in this kind of work.* Also see HAVE NO HEART FOR.

**heart in one's mouth, have one's** Be extremely frightened or anxious, as in *When the plane was about to take off, my heart was in my mouth.* This usage refers to the heart beating so violently that it appears to leap upward.

**heart in the right place, have one's** Have good intentions, as in *Her plan raise money for the poor succeed, but she had her heart in the right place.*

**heart is set on** see SET ONE'S HEART ON.

**heart misses a beat, one's** Also, **one's heart skips a beat** or **one's heart stands still.** Be startled, frightened, or very excited. For example, *Her heart missed a beat when she heard her name called out as the winner,* or *When the bear appeared in front of us, my heart skipped a beat,* or *My heart stands still at the thought of flying through a thunderstorm.* All these exaggerated expressions can also be used with **make,** meaning "cause one to be startled," as in *That blast from the ship's whistle made my heart skip a beat.*

**heart not in it** see under HEART IN IT.

**heart of gold** A very kind and good nature, as in *Bill is very generous; he has a heart of gold.* This expression refers to gold in the sense of "something valued for its goodness."

**heart of stone** A very cold and unfeeling nature, as in *You'll get no sympathy from her; she has a heart of stone.* This idea dates from ancient times.

**heart of the matter** see ROOT OF THE MATTER.

**heart on one's sleeve** see WEAR ONE'S HEART ON ONE'S SLEEVE.

**heart's content** see TO ONE'S HEART'S CONTENT.

**heart sinks, one's** One's courage or hope fails; one is very disappointed or sad. For example, *An hour before the picnic I heard thunder and my heart sank.*

**heart stands still** see HEART MISSES A BEAT.

**heart to heart** Honestly, sincerely, as in *We need to talk heart to heart about your coming marriage.* This expression is nearly always applied to a conversation of some kind.

**hearty** see HALE AND HEARTY.

**heat** In addition to the idioms beginning with HEAT, also see DEAD HEAT; IF YOU CAN'T STAND THE HEAT, GET OUT OF THE KITCHEN; IN HEAT; IN THE HEAT OF THE MOMENT; TURN UP THE HEAT ON.

**heat is on, the** Be under extreme pressure to do or accomplish something, as in *We need to finish quickly; the heat is on.* This idiom can also be used negatively as **the heat is off,** meaning that there's no longer any pressure. For example, *We can relax now; the heat is off.*

**heat up** Become acute or intense, as in *If inflation heats up, the interest rate will surely rise,* or *The debate over the budget was heating up.*

**heave-ho, give *someone* the** see under GET THE AX; GIVE SOMEONE THE AIR.

**heaven** In addition to the idiom beginning with HEAVEN, also see FOR THE SAKE OF (HEAVEN'S SAKE); GOD (HEAVEN) FORBID; GOD (HEAVEN) KNOWS; IN SEVENTH HEAVEN; IN THE NAME OF (HEAVEN); MANNA FROM HEAVEN; MOVE HEAVEN AND EARTH; PENNIES FROM HEAVEN; SEVENTH HEAVEN; STINK TO HIGH HEAVEN; THANK GOD (HEAVEN).

**heaven knows** see GOD KNOWS.

**heavenly days** An exclamation similar to **for heaven's sake.** See under FOR THE SAKE OF, def. 3.

**heaven on earth** A perfect place or situation, as in *She's in love and thinks she's found heaven on earth.* This expression can also be used negatively, as in *Let me tell you, this town is no heaven on earth*

**heavy** In addition to the idioms beginning with HEAVY, also see HOT AND HEAVY; PLAY THE HEAVY; TIME HANGS HEAVY.

**heavy going** Also, **heavy weather.** Difficult, as in *Tom found calculus heavy going,* or *It's going to be heavy weather for us from here on.* The first expression originally referred to a road or path that was hard to negotiate; the variant refers to bad weather at sea.

**heavy hand, with a 1.** In a clumsy manner, as in *You can't use that delicate equipment with a heavy hand.* **2.** Too severely, as in *Children brought up with a heavy hand often rebel in later years.*

**heavy heart, with a** In a sad or miserable state, unhappily, as in *He left her with a heavy heart, wondering if she would ever recover.* The adjective *heavy* is used here in the sense of "weighed down with grief or sadness." Its antonym, *light,* survives only in **light heart,** meaning "freedom from the weight of sorrow"—that is, "a happy feeling." For example, *She left for Europe with a light heart, knowing that the kids would be fine.*

**heavy hitter** An important or powerful individual or organization. For example, *This publishing house is one of the heavy hitters in the textbook industry.* This expression originated in sports such as boxing, where it literally meant "hitting hard."

**hedge one's bets** Lessen one's chance of loss by counterbalancing it with other bets, investments, or the like. For example, *I'm hedging my bets by putting some of my money in bonds in case there's another drop in the stock market.* This term transfers *hedge,* in the sense of "a barrier," to a means of protection against loss.

**heel** see ACHILLES' HEEL; AT SOMEONE'S HEELS; BRING SOMEONE TO HEEL; COOL ONE'S HEELS; DIG IN (ONE'S HEELS); DRAG ONE'S FEET (HEELS); HEAD OVER HEELS; KICK UP ONE'S HEELS; ON THE HEELS OF; OUT AT THE ELBOWS (HEELS); SET BACK ON ONE'S HEELS; SHOW ONE'S HEELS; TAKE TO ONE'S HEELS; TO HEEL; TURN ON ONE'S HEEL.

**hell** In addition to the idioms beginning with HELL, also see (ALL HELL BREAKS) BREAK LOOSE; DEVIL (HELL) OF A; FOR THE HELL OF IT; GIVE SOMEONE HELL; GO TO HELL; HOT AS BLAZES (HELL); LIKE A BAT OUT OF HELL; LIKE HELL; MAD AS A HORNET (HELL); NOT A HOPE IN HELL; RAISE CAIN (HELL); ROAD TO HELL IS PAVED WITH GOOD INTENTIONS; SEE SOMEONE IN HELL FIRST; SHOT TO HELL; SNOWBALL'S CHANCE IN HELL; TILL HELL FREEZES OVER; TO HELL AND GONE; TO HELL WITH; WHAT THE HELL.

**hell-bent for leather** Moving recklessly fast, as in *Out the door she went, hell-bent for leather. Hell-bent* is used here in the sense of "recklessly determined." *Leather* refers to a horse's saddle and to riding on horseback.

**hell-bent on** Determined to do or accomplish something, as in *I've tried to talk her out of it, but she's hell-bent on leaving town.*

**hell has no fury like a woman scorned** No anger is worse than that of a jilted woman. For example, *Nancy has nothing good to say about Tom—hell has no fury, you know.*

**hell of a** Also, **one hell of a 1.** See DEVIL OF A. **2.** This phrase is used to emphasize certain qualities about the noun it modifies. By itself the idiom is ambiguous, because its exact meaning depends on the context. For example, *He is a hell of a driver* can mean either that he is very skillful or that he is a terrible driver. Similarly, *We had one hell of a time* can mean either that we enjoyed ourselves greatly or that we had an awful or difficult time.

**hell on wheels, be** Tough, aggressive, wild, or mean, as in *Watch out for the boss—he's hell on wheels this week.*

**hell or high water, come** Also, **in spite of hell or high water** or **despite hell or high water.** No matter what difficulty or obstacle, as in *I'm going to finish this week, come hell or high water.* This expression refers to the destructive forces of hellfire or flood.

**hell to pay** Great trouble, as in *If we're wrong, there'll be hell to pay.*

**helm** see AT THE HELM; TAKE THE HELM.

**help** In addition to the idioms beginning with HELP, also see CAN'T HELP (BUT); EVERY LITTLE BIT HELPS; NOT IF ONE CAN HELP IT; SO HELP ME.

**helping hand** see under LEND A HAND.

**help oneself 1.** Make an effort on one's own behalf. For example, *No one can help you now, you'll have to help yourself.* It also appears in the old proverb, *God* (or *heaven*) *helps those who help themselves.* Also see CAN'T HELP. **2.** Serve oneself, as in *The food's in the kitchen; just help yourself.* When it takes an object, this phrase is put as **help oneself to,** as in *I helped myself to more meat.* It also is used as a euphemism for stealing, as in *She simply helped herself to the hotel towels and left.*

**help out** Give additional assistance, as in *I offered to help out with the holiday rush at the store.*

**hem and haw** Be hesitant and indecisive; avoid committing oneself, as in *When asked about their wedding date, she hemmed and hawed,* or *The President hemmed and hawed* *about new Cabinet appointments.* This expression imitates the sounds of clearing one's throat.

**hem *someone* in** see FENCE SOMEONE IN.

**hen** see MAD AS A HORNET (WET HEN); SCARCE AS HEN'S TEETH.

**herd** see RIDE HERD ON.

**here** In addition to the idioms beginning with HERE, also see BUCK STOPS HERE; DOWNHILL ALL THE WAY (ALL DOWNHILL FROM HERE); HAVE HAD IT (UP TO HERE); LOOK HERE; NEITHER HERE NOR THERE; SAME HERE; WHERE DO WE GO FROM HERE.

**here and now 1.** At this moment, as in *We must reach a decision here and now.* **2. the here and now.** This life, the present, as in *We'd better think of the here and now before worrying about future generations.*

**here and there 1.** In various places, as *She's lived here and there..* **2.** In various directions, as in *She turned her eyes here and there, looking for him in the audience.* Also see HERE, THERE, AND EVERYWHERE.

**here goes 1.** An expression or exclamation declaring one's determination to do something, as in *This hill is steeper than any I've climbed before, but here goes!* This usage is sometimes expanded to **here goes nothing,** meaning one is starting something that one doubts will succeed, as in *I've never tried this before, so here goes nothing.* **2. here someone goes again.** Someone is repeating the same action or speech, especially an undesirable one. For example, *Here he goes again, criticizing all his colleagues,* or *The power's out—here we go again.*

**here's to** A salute to someone or something. For example, *Here's to you on your retirement,* or *Here's to the new project.* This phrase is nearly always used as a toast to someone or something.

**here, there, and everywhere** In every possible place. For example, *Flags hung here, there, and everywhere, making it a colorful occasion.*

**here today, gone tomorrow** Also, **here today and gone tomorrow.** Lacking permanence, lasting only a short time. For example, *His book attracted a great deal of attention but quickly went out of print—here today and gone tomorrow.* This idiom originally referred to the briefness of human life.

**here to stay** Permanent or continuing, as in *I'm afraid the uncertainty about energy costs is here to stay.*

**here we go again** An exclamation that shows displeasure or annoyance at someone or something, as in *Here we go again! Doesn't he ever shut up?*

**herring** see DEAD AS A DOORNAIL (HERRING); RED HERRING.

**he who hesitates is lost** One who cannot come to a decision will suffer for it, as in *I couldn't make up my mind, and now they has hired someone else—he who hesitates is lost.*

**hidden agenda** A secret plan or motive for accomplishing a goal. For example, *Don't let him fool you, he always has a hidden agenda.*

**hide** In addition to the idioms beginning with HIDE, also see COVER ONE'S ASS (HIDE); TAN SOMEONE'S HIDE.

**hide and seek** see PLAY HIDE AND SEEK.

**hide nor hair, neither** Also, **hide or hair.** No trace of something or someone lost or missing. For example, *I haven't seen hide nor hair of the children.* This expression refers to the entire outer coat of an animal.

**hide one's face** Also, **hide one's head.** Feel shame or embarrassment. For example, *You needn't hide your face—you're not to blame,* or *Whenever the teacher asked her a question, the shy little child hid her head.* This idiom refers to the gesture indicative of these feelings.

**hide one's head in the sand** Also, **bury one's head in the sand.** Refuse to face something by pretending not to see it. For example, *For years we have been hiding our heads in the sand, refusing to admit that the store is losing money,* or *When it comes to a family quarrel, he just buries his head in the sand.* This expression refers to the belief that ostriches burrow in sand thinking they will not be seen because they cannot see. In fact, however, when they do this, they are consuming sand and gravel to aid their digestive system.

**hide one's light under a bushel** Show extreme modesty, as in *Even after she won the scholarship, she went on hiding her light under a bushel.* This expression, which does not necessarily express approval of this behavior, has its origin in the New Testament.

**hide out** Go into or stay in hiding, especially from the authorities. For example, *The burglars hid out in the building,* or *He decided to hide out from the press.*

**high** In addition to the idioms beginning with HIGH, also see BLOW SKY-HIGH; FLY HIGH; FRIEND IN COURT (FRIENDS IN HIGH PLACES); HELL OR HIGH WATER; HIT THE HIGH SPOTS (POINTS); HOLD ONE'S HEAD HIGH; KNEE-HIGH TO A GRASSHOPPER; ON HIGH; ON ONE'S HIGH HORSE; RIDE HIGH; RUN HIGH; STINK TO HIGH HEAVEN; THINK A LOT (HIGHLY) OF; TURN ON (GET HIGH).

**high and dry** Left alone or without support, as in *They walked out on the party, leaving me high and dry.* This expression originally referred to a ship that was out of the water.

**high and low** Everywhere, as in *We searched high and low but couldn't find the ring,* or *He hunted high and low for a parking space.*

**high and mighty** Have too high an opinion of oneself, as in *She was too high and mighty* *to make her own bed.* This expression originally referred to high-born rulers.

**high as a kite** Intoxicated, as by alcohol or drugs, as in *After three beers she's high as a kite.*

**high five** An informal sign of enthusiastic agreement made by hitting one's open upstretched hand against another person's. For example, *Give me a high five!*

**high gear** A state of great and energetic activity or force. For example, *His mind was in high gear as he studied for the medical exam,* or *The political campaign is finally moving into high gear.* This expression refers to the high gear of an engine transmission, used at the fastest speeds.

**high hopes** see IN HOPES OF.

**high horse** see ON ONE'S HIGH HORSE.

**high jinks** Playful or noisy activity, often involving pranks. For example, *All sorts of high jinks go on at summer camp after "lights out."* This term originally referred to a gambling game accompanied by much drinking.

**high off the hog, eat** Also, **live high on the hog.** Do well, live luxuriously, as in *When their aunt dies and they inherit her estate, they'll be eating high off the hog,* or *Since their loan was approved, they've been living high on the hog.* These expressions refer to the choicest cuts of meat, which are found on a pig's upper flanks.

**high on 1.** Under the influence of alcohol or a drug. For example, *I think he got high on marijuana before he came to the party.* **2.** Very enthusiastic about, as in *They were high on video games.*

**high places, friends in** see under FRIEND IN COURT

**high seas** Open waters of an ocean, beyond the territorial rule of a country. For example, *Commercial fishermen are being forced to go out on the high seas in order to make a living.*

**high sign** A secret signal intended to warn or inform, as in *Dad gave us the high sign when it was time to leave.* This expression presumably refers to a gesture such as a hand wave.

**high spot** The very best part of an event, as in *Her solo was the high spot of the concert,* or *His college years were the high spot of his life.* For a synonym, also see HIGH-WATER MARK.

**hightail it** Go as fast as possible, especially in leaving; rush off. For example, *With the police now searching for them, they hightailed it out of town,* or *When I remembered it was his birthday, I hightailed it to the bakery for a cake.* This expression refers to the raised tail of a rabbit or other animal that is running away.

**high time 1.** The appropriate time for something; also, past the appropriate time. For example, *It's high time we did something about that dog,* or *It's high time you children were in bed.* The precise meaning of this term depends on the tone of voice and/or the context. For a synonym, see ABOUT TIME. **2. have a high old time.** Have a wonderful time, as in *We'll have a high old time at the picnic this year.*

**high-water mark** The peak of something, especially an achievement. For example, *This composition is the high-water mark of his entire work.* This expression refers to the highest mark left on shore by the tide.

**highway robbery** Also, **daylight robbery.** The charge of an unreasonably high price or fee. For example, *You paid ten dollars for that meat? That's highway robbery,* or *The amount they're charging for that stove is daylight robbery.* This term refers to literal robbery of travelers on or near a public road.

**high-wire act** A risky job or operation, as in *She had to balance work and family—that's a high-wire act.* This expression refers to a performer on a tightrope stretched high above the ground.

**hike** see TAKE A HIKE.

**hill** see DOWNHILL ALL THE WAY; GO DOWNHILL; HEAD FOR (THE HILLS); MAKE A MOUNTAIN OUT OF A MOLEHILL; NOT WORTH A DAMN (HILL OF BEANS); OLD AS THE HILLS; OVER THE HILL.

**hilt** see TO THE HILT.

**hindmost** see DEVIL TAKE THE HINDMOST.

**hinge on** Also, **hinge upon.** Depend on, as in *This plan hinges on her approval.*

**hint** see TAKE A HINT.

**hip** see JOINED AT THE HIP; SHOOT FROM THE HIP.

**hired gun 1.** A person, especially a professional killer, employed to kill someone, as in *They thought the murder had been done by a hired gun.* **2.** A person with special knowledge or expertise who is employed to resolve a complex problem. For example, *The legal team was looking for a hired gun to testify.*

**hired hand** Also, **hired man** or **hired girl.** A person hired to assist with farm or household chores, as in *We need extra hired hands during the harvest,* or *She was looking for a hired girl to do the laundry.* This use of *hired* once referred to someone employed for wages as opposed to a slave. The use of *girl* now may be offensive.

**hire out** Obtain work; also, rent the services or temporary use of something for a fee, as in *He hired out as a cook,* or *They hired out the cottage for the summer.*

**history** see ANCIENT HISTORY; GO DOWN (IN HISTORY); MAKE HISTORY; REPEAT ONESELF (HISTORY REPEATS ITSELF).

**hit** In addition to the idioms beginning with HIT, also see (HIT) BELOW THE BELT; CAN'T HIT

THE BROAD SIDE OF A BARN; HEAVY HITTER; MAKE A HIT; PINCH HITTER; SMASH HIT.

**hit a brick wall** Also, **hit a stone wall.** Encounter an obstacle that stops all activity or progress, as in *Everything seemed to be going fine, and then we hit a brick wall when the parts we needed weren't available,* or *I warned her that she'd hit a stone wall if she suggested any changes.* Also see RUN INTO A STONE WALL.

**hit and run** **1.** Cause a traffic accident and leave before the police arrive, as in *I heard on the radio that there's been a hit and run.* **2.** Do something very quickly and inadequately without thinking about what one is doing. For example, *What he calls cleaning his room, she calls a hit and run.* This expression is also used as an adjective, as in *She was in a hit-and-run accident last week,* or *They had what you might call a hit-and-run romance.* Also see HIT OR MISS.

H

**hit a nerve** Also, **hit a raw nerve.** Be absolutely correct about something said to or about another person, as in *I've never seen him so angry. Your remark about his appearance must have hit a nerve.*

**hit a snag** Encounter a problem or an obstacle. For example, *We've hit a snag with this building project.* The noun *snag* is used here in the sense of "a sharp or rough projection" that would make passage difficult.

**hit below the belt** see BELOW THE BELT.

**hit *someone* between the eyes** Also, **hit *someone* right between the eyes.** Make someone suddenly aware of something, have a sudden impact on. For example, *News of their divorce hit me right between the eyes.*

**hit bottom** Also, **hit rock bottom** or **touch bottom.** Reach the worst or lowest point. For example, *When he lost his job again, they knew they had hit bottom,* or *When wheat prices touch bottom, many farmers will lose their farms.*

**hitch a ride** Also, **thumb a ride.** Ask for a free ride, especially by hitchhiking. For example, *I have no car; can I hitch a ride home with you?* or *He was hoping to thumb a ride to the stadium.* Raising one's *thumb* is the traditional signal for stopping a car on the road.

**hitch one's wagon to a star** Aim high, as in *Bill's hitching his wagon to a star—he plans to own the company by age thirty.*

**hither and yon** Also, **hither and thither.** Here and there, as in *Ruth went hither and yon, searching for her sister,* or *I've been wandering about, hither and thither.* These old words for "here" and "there" are rarely heard outside these expressions, which themselves may be dying out.

**hit *one* hard** Affect one deeply in a saddening way, as in *She was really hit hard by her mother's death.*

**hit home** Also, **strike home.** Insult someone or make a remark that cannot be misunderstood and causes deep hurt or some realization. For example, *Your comment must have really hit home. He's leaving now,* or *Her observation struck home for many of us.*

**hit it big** Score a major success, especially a profit, as in *Some investors hit it big in the stock market.* The adverb *big* here means "with great success."

**hit it off** Get along well together, as in *I was so glad that our parents hit it off.*

**hit list** A list of people who are to be killed or harmed in some way. For example, *I hear you're on their hit list for taking their clients,* or *He's going to be fired; I hear he's at the top of the management's hit list.*

**hit on** **1.** Also, **hit upon.** Discover something, happen to find, as in *I've hit upon a solution to this problem.* **2.** Make sexual advances to someone, especially unwanted ones, as in *You can't go into that bar without being hit on.*

**hit one's stride** **1.** Reach a steady, effective pace, as in *After the first few laps around the track, he hit his stride.* This expression comes from horseracing, *stride* referring to the regular pace of the horse. **2.** Reach the highest level of competence, as in *Jack didn't really hit his stride until he started college.*

**hit one where one lives** see under CLOSE TO HOME.

**hit or miss** In a careless way, at random. For example, *She took dozens of photos, hit or miss, hoping that some would be good.*

**hit out** Make a violent verbal or physical attack; also, strike aimlessly. For example, *The star hit out at the press for their lukewarm reviews,* or *The therapist said patients often hit out in frustration.*

**hit the books** Study with great effort, as in *At exam time we all hit the books.*

**hit the bottle** Also, **hit the booze** or **hit the sauce.** Drink alcoholic beverages, especially a great deal, as in *I don't know if it will be a problem, but he hits the bottle every weekend,* or *She hardly ever hits the booze, but when she does, watch out,* or *It doesn't show in her work, but she hits the sauce every night.*

**hit the bull's-eye** Also, **hit the mark** or **hit the nail on the head.** Be absolutely right, as in *Your remark about finances hit the bull's-eye,* or *Jane hit the mark with her idea for moving personnel,* or *The governor's speech on attracting new businesses hit the nail on the head.* The round black center of a target has long been called a *bull's-eye; mark* similarly refers to a target; and *nail on the head* refers to driving home a nail by hitting it on its head. Also see OFF THE MARK.

**hit the ceiling** Also, **hit the roof.** Explode in anger, as in *Jane hit the ceiling when she saw her grades,* or *Dad hit the roof when he didn't get his usual bonus.* The second expression is a version of an earlier expression meaning "enraged."

**hit the deck** Also, **hit the dirt.** Fall to the ground, usually for protection. For example, *As the planes approached, we hit the deck,* or *We heard shooting and hit the dirt.* The first expression once was nautical slang for "jump out of bed" or "wake up," and somewhat later, "get going."

**hit the fan** see SHIT WILL HIT THE FAN.

**hit the ground running** Take an opportunity; begin at full speed. For example, *As soon as the front office gave its approval for the new department, we hit the ground running.*

**hit the hay** Also, **hit the sack.** Go to bed, as in *I usually hit the hay after the eleven o'clock news,* or *I'm tired; let's hit the sack.*

**hit the high spots** Also, **hit the high points.** Pay attention only to the most important places or parts. For example, *We only had a week in New York, but we managed to hit the high spots,* or *His speech was brief, but he hit all the high points.* Also see HIGH SPOT.

**hit the jackpot** Be highly successful, especially unexpectedly; win, especially a lot of money. For example, *She hit the jackpot at the auction; that painting turned out to be a masterpiece.*

**hit the mark** see HIT THE BULL'S-EYE.

**hit the nail on the head** see HIT THE BULL'S-EYE.

**hit the road** Also, **hit the trail.** Start out, as on a trip. For example, *Come on, it's time to hit the road,* or *Jack hit the trail at dawn.*

**hit the roof** see HIT THE CEILING.

**hit the sack** see HIT THE HAY.

**hit the spot** Give total satisfaction, as in *This coffee really hits the spot.* This expression became popular with an advertising jingle, in which a popular soda was said to *hit the spot.*

**hit the wall** Suddenly encounter an obstacle and be unable to continue an activity; also, become very tired. For example, *We worked all night trying to finish the project, but at dawn we hit the wall.*

**hit *someone* up for** Ask someone for a loan or favor, as in *He hit me up for ten bucks,* or *I hit her up for a job.*

**hit upon** see HIT ON.

**hoe** see TOUGH ROW TO HOE.

**hog** In addition to the idiom beginning with HOG, also see GO HOG WILD; GO WHOLE HOG; HIGH OFF THE HOG; ROAD HOG.

**hog heaven** An extremely pleasing or excellent situation, as in *She's in hog heaven now that she has a new car.*

**hold** In addition to the idioms beginning with HOLD, also see BEAR (HOLD) A GRUDGE; GET HOLD OF; HANG ON TO; (HOLD) YOUR HAT; HAVE A HOLD OVER; LAY HOLD OF; LEAVE HOLDING THE BAG; NO HOLDS BARRED; ON HOLD; (HOLD THE) PURSE STRINGS; STAND (HOLD) ONE'S GROUND; TAKE HOLD.

**hold a candle to, not** Also, **not fit to hold a candle to** or **cannot hold a candle to.** Be inferior to someone or something, as in *This hotel can't hold a candle to the Palace,* or *This new friend of his is not fit to hold a candle to his former buddies.* This expression refers to holding a candle to provide light for someone, in the least considered a menial chore.

**hold against** Think badly of someone because of some fault or event. For example, *Even if you're late, I won't hold it against you,* or *She backed right into his new car, so he's certain to hold it against her.* Also see BEAR A GRUDGE.

**hold a grudge** see BEAR A GRUDGE.

**hold a gun to someone's head** Exert pressure on someone, as in *How could I refuse when she was holding a gun to my head?* Also see AT GUNPOINT; HOLD SOMEONE'S FEET TO THE FIRE.

**hold all the aces** Also, **hold all the cards** or **hold all the trumps.** Be in a winning position, as in *We can't argue with him; he holds all the aces,* or *If she refuses, he'll reveal that he holds all the trumps and force her to give in.* These expressions refer to card games in which the ace or a trump card outranks all the others. Also see PLAY ONE'S CARDS RIGHT; TRUMP CARD.

**hold back** Also, **keep back. 1.** Keep something in one's possession or control, as in *He held back vital information,* or *I managed to keep back my tears.* **2.** Restrain oneself, as in *She held back from joining the others,* or *I wanted to denounce him right there, but I kept back for fear of making a scene.* **3.** Block the progress of something, as in *The barriers held back traffic during the parade,* or *Her daughter was kept back and had to repeat first grade.*

**hold court** Be surrounded by and command the attention of admirers or inferiors. For example, *After a match, the tennis star generally held court in the locker room.* This expression refers to royalty convening courtiers as well as a judge convening a court of law.

**hold down 1.** Also, **keep down.** Limit something, restrain, as in *Please hold down the noise.* Also see KEEP DOWN. **2.** Work at one's duties satisfactorily, as in *He managed to hold down two jobs at the same time.*

**hold everything** Also, **hold it.** Stop, wait. These expressions are usually used as commands, as in *Hold everything, we can't unload the truck yet,* or *Hold it, you've gone far enough.*

**hold forth** Speak in public, especially at great length. For example, *She loved to hold forth on the latest discoveries in astronomy.*

**hold good** Also, **hold true.** Be valid, be relevant. For example, *Does that version of events still hold good?* or *The story he told ten years ago holds true today.*

**hold it** see HOLD EVERYTHING.

**hold off 1.** Keep someone or something at a distance, resist, delay, as in *This payment should hold off the creditors.* **2.** Stop or delay from action, as in *Let's hold off until we know more.*

**hold on 1.** Also, **hold on to.** Maintain one's grip, cling, as in *Hold on to your hat in this wind,* or *The early Christians held on to their beliefs despite strong opposition.* **2.** Continue to do something, persist, as in *Please hold on for a while longer.* **3.** Stop, wait, as in *Hold on! We can't go past this gate.* **4.** Remain on a telephone line, as in *If you can hold on a minute, I'll go and find her.*

**hold one's breath 1.** Be excited, anxious, or nervous. For example, *The election was so close that I held my breath until the final results were in,* or *I'm holding my breath until everyone's been heard from.* This expression refers to the interruption of normal breathing. **2. not hold one's breath.** An expression used to mean one is *not* awaiting something, as in *I'm hoping to hear if I got the job, but I'm not holding my breath.* It often is put as a command, **don't hold your breath,** meaning "don't expect it, it's not likely," as in *They may get married this summer, but don't hold your breath.* This expression in effect implies it is not wise to stop breathing until a particular event happens, since it may never come to pass.

**hold one's end up** Also, **keep one's end up.** Do one's share. For example, *John always holds his end up, but Jerry is less reliable,* or *Let's hope she can keep up her end.* In these expressions *end* refers to one of two sides of something that must be lifted by two people.

**hold one's fire** Refrain from comment or criticism, especially for the time being. For example, *Hold your fire, Jim, she's not finished yet,* or *Nancy decided to hold her fire until she had more information.* This expression refers to refraining from shooting a gun and originated in the military.

**hold one's head high** Also, **hold one's head up** or **hold up one's head.** Behave proudly; maintain one's dignity. For example, *After the bankruptcy they still held their heads high,* or *Grandma told him he could hold his head up because he'd tried extremely hard,* or *After that newspaper article, I'm not sure I'll ever hold up my head again.* All these expressions refer to a posture of pride.

**hold one's horses** Slow down, be patient, as in *Dad told us to hold our horses on Christmas shopping since it was only July,* or *Hold your horses, I'm coming.* This expression refers to a driver making horses wait by holding the reins tightly.

**hold one's own** Do reasonably well in spite of opposition, competition, or criticism. For example, *The team held its own against their opponents,* or *Rumors often hold their own against facts.*

**hold one's peace** see HOLD ONE'S TONGUE.

**hold one's temper** Also, **keep one's temper.** Refrain from expressing violent anger, maintain control or remain calm. For example, *Billy has to learn to hold his temper when he's frustrated,* or *If the chairman can keep his temper, the matter will get settled.* For an antonym, see LOSE ONE'S TEMPER.

**hold one's tongue** Also, **hold one's peace** or **keep one's peace.** Keep quiet, remain silent, as in *If you don't hold your tongue, you'll have to go outside,* or *Mother kept her peace about the wedding.* The idiom with *tongue* uses *hold* in the sense of "restrain," while the others use *hold* and *keep* in the sense of "preserve." The variant appears in the traditional wedding service, telling anyone who knows that a marriage should not take place to "speak now or forever hold your peace." Also see KEEP QUIET.

**hold on to** see HOLD ON, def. 1.

**hold on to your hat** see HANG ON TO YOUR HAT.

**hold out 1.** Extend something, stretch forth; also, present or offer something. For example, *He held out his hand and she took it,* or *The new policy held out promise of major changes in the welfare program.* **2.** Last, continue to be in supply or service, as in *The food is holding out nicely.* Also see HOLD UP, def. 4. **3.** Continue to resist, as in *The troops held out for another month.* **4.** Withhold cooperation, agreement, or information, as in *We've asked for a better deal, but they've been holding out for months.* It is also put as **hold out on,** as in *They were still holding out on some of the provisions,* or *He's not telling us what happened; he's holding out on us.* **5. hold out for.** Insist on obtaining something, as in *The union is still holding out for a better contract.*

**hold out on** see HOLD OUT, def. 4.

**hold *something* over 1.** Postpone or delay something, as in *Let's hold this matter over until the next meeting.* **2.** Keep something in a position or state beyond the normal period, as in *The film was to be held over for another* *week.* **3.** Continue in office past the normal period, as in *The committee chair held the group over until they could find a suitable replacement.* **4. hold something over someone.** Have an advantage or use a threat to control someone. For example, *They knew he'd been caught stealing and were sure to hold it over him.*

**hold someone's feet to the fire** Also, **keep someone's feet to the fire.** Pressure someone to agree to something or to do something, as in *The only way you'll get him to agree is to hold his feet to the fire.* This idiom refers to an ancient test of courage or form of torture in which a person's feet were placed to the fire. Also see HOLD A GUN TO SOMEONE'S HEAD.

**hold still for** Also, **stand still for.** Accept or tolerate something, as in *Do you think he'll hold still for your decision?* These terms are often put negatively, as in *The town won't hold still for another increase in property taxes,* or *The teacher won't stand still for this kind of behavior.*

**hold sway over** Dominate, have a controlling influence over, as in *He held sway over the entire department.* This idiom uses the noun *sway* in the sense of "power."

**hold the bag** see LEAVE ONE HOLDING THE BAG.

**hold the floor** Take one's turn at speaking in a public meeting and talk for so long that other people cannot speak. For example, *I can't believe he held the floor for an hour!*

**hold the fort** Assume responsibility, especially in another person's absence; also, maintain a secure position. For example, *He did a good job of holding the fort until his boss recovered,* or *Can you hold the fort in the kitchen?*

**hold the line** Maintain the existing position or state of affairs. For example, *We'll have to hold the line on spending until our profits rise.* This term refers to former military tactics, in which a line of troops was supposed to prevent an enemy breakthrough. Eventually, it was transferred to civilian activities.

**hold the phone** Stop what one is doing, as in *Hold the phone! There's no sense in continuing this argument.* This expression is often put as a command, as in the example. Also see HOLD EVERYTHING.

**hold the purse strings** see PURSE STRINGS.

**hold to** Remain loyal or faithful to something, abide by, as in *She held to her resolutions,* or *He held to his view that the interest rate should be lowered.* Also see STICK BY; STICK TO.

**hold true** see under HOLD GOOD.

**hold up 1.** Offer or present something as an example, as in *The teacher held Bernie's essay up as a model for the class to follow.* **2.** Obstruct or delay, as in *We were held up in traffic.* **3.** Rob, as in *He was held up in a dark alley, with no help nearby.* This usage, which gave rise to the noun **holdup** for a robbery, refers to the robbers' demand that the victims hold their hands high. **4.** Also, **hold out.** Continue to function without losing force or effectiveness, endure. For example, *We held up through that long hard winter,* or *The nurse was able to hold out until someone could relieve her.* **5.** See HOLD ONE'S HEAD HIGH.

**hold water** Stand up to critical examination, be sound and valid, as in *This argument just won't hold water,* or *Her reasons for quitting don't hold water.* This expression refers to a container that can hold water without leaking.

**hold with** Agree with something, support, as in *I don't hold with that view of the situation.*

**hold your** see under HOLD ONE'S.

**hole** In addition to the idioms beginning with HOLE, also see ACE IN THE HOLE; BLACK HOLE; IN A BIND (HOLE); IN THE HOLE; MONEY BURNS A HOLE IN ONE'S POCKET; NEED LIKE A HOLE IN THE HEAD; PICK HOLES IN; SQUARE PEG IN A ROUND HOLE.

**hole in one** A perfect achievement, as in *Tim scored a hole in one on that test.* The term refers to a perfect stroke in golf, where one drives the ball from the tee into the hole with a single stroke.

**hole in the wall** A small, modest, or obscure place, as in *My new apartment is just a hole in the wall,* or *Believe it or not, that little hole in the wall is a great restaurant.* This graphic term is often used as an insult.

**hole up** Take refuge or shelter, hide, as in *I spent most of the cruise holed up in my cabin.* This usage refers to animals hibernating in winter or hiding from attack in caves or holes.

**holiday** see BUSMAN'S HOLIDAY.

**hollow** see BEAT THE PANTS OFF (HOLLOW); RING HOLLOW.

**holy cow** Also, **holy mackerel** or **Moses** or **moly** or **smoke.** An exclamation of surprise, astonishment, delight, or dismay, as in *Holy cow, I forgot the wine,* or *Holy mackerel, you won!* or *Holy Moses, here comes the teacher!* or *Holy smoke, I didn't know you were here too.* None of these slangy expressions has any literal significance, and *moly* is a creation devised to rhyme with *holy* and possibly a euphemism for "Moses."

**holy of holies** A place that many people regard as special or that is available only to a few. For example, *Elvis Presley's home in Memphis is the holy of holies for his fans.*

**holy terror** A frustrating or bothersome individual, as in *He was only five, but he was a holy terror, running wild through the house* *and throwing whatever he could lay his hands on.* The adjective *holy* here is an intensifier.

**home** In addition to the idioms beginning with HOME, also see AT HOME; BRING HOME; BRING HOME THE BACON; CHARITY BEGINS AT HOME; CHICKENS COME HOME TO ROOST; CLOSE TO HOME; DRIVE HOME; EAT SOMEONE OUT OF HOUSE AND HOME; HAMMER HOME; HIT HOME; MAKE ONESELF AT HOME; NOBODY HOME; NOTHING TO WRITE HOME ABOUT; TILL THE COWS COME HOME.

**home away from home** A place where someone spends a lot of time that is not where he or she lives, as in *You can usually find her at the office; it's her home away from home.*

**home free** In a secure or comfortable position, especially because of being certain to succeed. For example, *Once I meet the schedule, I'll be home free,* or *I think we have enough support for this measure—we're home free.* This expression probably refers to safely reaching baseball's *home plate,* meaning one has scored a run. Also see HOME STRETCH.

**home in on** Move toward or focus on a goal, as in *He began with a couple of jokes before homing in on the main subject of his talk.* This expression originally referred to a ship, aircraft, or missile being guided to its target by a radio beam or some other means.

**home run** A highly successful achievement; also, doubling one's profits. For example, *We scored a home run with that drug stock, buying it at 15 and selling at 30.* This expression originated in baseball, where it refers to a pitched ball batted so far that the batter can round all three bases and reach home plate, scoring a run.

**home stretch** The final part or phase of something, such as a project, when the pressure is over. For example, *Now that we have the parts we need, we're in the home stretch.* This idiom comes from horseracing and refers to the final part of the race. Also see HOME FREE.

**homework** see DO ONE'S HOMEWORK.

**honest** In addition to the idiom beginning with HONEST, also see COME BY (HONESTLY); OPEN (HONEST) AND ABOVEBOARD.

**honest to God** Also, **honest to goodness** or **honest to Pete** or **honest Injun.** Truly, really, as in *Honest to God, I didn't know it was yours,* or *Honest to goodness, we had exactly the same experience,* or *I promise I'll finish in time, honest to Pete.* **Honest Injun** is today considered offensive.

**honeymoon is over, the** The initial harmonious period in a new relationship has ended, as in *After the first ninety days, the honeymoon between the new President and the press was over.* The figurative use of *honeymoon* refers to the first month of marriage.

**honor** In addition to the idiom beginning with HONOR, also see DO THE HONORS; IN HONOR OF; ON ONE'S HONOR; WORD OF HONOR.

**honor bound** Obliged by one's personal values, as in *She was honor bound to admit that it was her fault and not her sister's.* Also see ON ONE'S HONOR.

**hoof it** **1.** Go on foot, as in *The car's being repaired—we'll have to hoof it.* **2.** Dance, as in *He was always a good dancer, and he's still able to hoof it.*

**hook** In addition to the idioms beginning with HOOK, also see BY HOOK OR CROOK; OFF THE HOOK; ON ONE'S OWN ACCOUNT (HOOK).

**hook, line, and sinker** Without reservation, completely, as in *He swallowed our excuse hook, line, and sinker.* This expression refers to a fish swallowing not only the baited hook but the leaden sinker and the entire fishing line between them.

**hook or crook** see BY HOOK OR CROOK.

**hook up** **1.** Assemble a mechanism or device, as in *She helped us hook up the VCR.* **2.** Connect a mechanism with a main source, as in *The printer had not yet been hooked up to the computer.* **3. hook up with.** Form a tie or association with someone, as in *She had hooked up with the wrong crowd.*

**hooky** see PLAY HOOKY.

**hoop** see JUMP THROUGH HOOPS; SHOOT HOOPS.

**hoot** see NOT GIVE A DAMN (HOOT).

**hop** In addition to the idioms beginning with HOPE, also see MAD AS A HORNET (HOPS).

**hope** In addition to the idioms beginning with HOPE, also see GREAT WHITE HOPE; IN HOPES OF; LIVE IN HOPE; NOT A HOPE IN HELL; PIN ONE'S HOPES ON; WHILE THERE'S LIFE THERE'S HOPE.

**hope against hope** Hope or wish for something with little reason or justification, as in *I'm hoping against hope that someone will return my wallet.*

**hope springs eternal** People will keep on hoping, no matter what the odds. For example, *I keep buying lottery tickets—hope springs eternal.*

**hopped up** **1.** Relating to a motor, especially a car engine, whose power has been increased. For example, *Kids loved to ride around in hopped-up cars.* Also see SOUP UP. **2.** Stimulated with, or as if with, a narcotic. For example, *Their idea of a good time is to get all hopped up on marijuana or worse.*

**hopping mad** Enraged, furious, as in *I was hopping mad when they left my name off the list.* This expression creates an image of jumping up and down with rage.

**hop, skip, and a jump, a** A short distance, as in *It's just a hop, skip, and a jump from my house to yours.* This expression originally referred to a game involving these movements, but it later was also used figuratively for the short distance so covered.

**hop to it** Begin to do something quickly and energetically, as in *We've got to hop to it and get our shopping done.*

**hop up** see HOPPED UP.

**horizon** see ON THE HORIZON.

**horn** In addition to the idioms beginning with HORN, also see BLOW ONE'S OWN HORN; LOCK HORNS; PULL IN ONE'S HORNS; TAKE THE BULL BY THE HORNS.

**hornet** see MAD AS A HORNET; STIR UP A HORNET'S NEST.

**horn in on** Intrude, join in something without being invited. For example, *She has a rude way of horning in on our conversations.* This expression refers to a bull pushing in with its horns.

**horns of a dilemma, on the** Faced with two equally undesirable alternatives. For example, *I'm on the horns of a dilemma—if I sell the house, now I have no place to live, but if I wait, I may not get as good a price.* The idea of being caught on either one horn or the other (of an animal) was expressed in Roman times.

**horror** see under THROW UP ONE'S HANDS.

**horse** In addition to the idioms beginning with HORSE, also see BEAT A DEAD HORSE; CART BEFORE THE HORSE; CHANGE HORSES IN MIDSTREAM; CHARLEY HORSE; DARK HORSE; EAT LIKE A BIRD (HORSE); FROM THE HORSE'S MOUTH; HOLD ONE'S HORSES; IF WISHES WERE HORSES; LOOK A GIFT HORSE IN THE MOUTH; ONE-HORSE TOWN; ON ONE'S HIGH HORSE; WAR HORSE; WILD HORSES COULDN'T DRAG ME; WORK LIKE A BEAVER (HORSE); YOU CAN LEAD A HORSE TO WATER.

**horse around** Engage in meaningless activity or play. For example, *The boys were horsing around all afternoon.* This term presumably refers to *horseplay,* meaning "rough or boisterous play."

**horse of a different color, a** Also, **a horse of another color.** Another matter entirely, something else. For example, *I thought he was her boyfriend, but he turned out to be her brother—that's a horse of a different color.*

**horse sense** Sound practical sense, as in *She's got too much horse sense to believe his story.*

**horse trading** Negotiation marked by hard bargaining and clever exchange. For example, *The restaurant owner is famous for his horse trading; he just exchanged a month of free dinners for a month of free television commercials.* This expression refers to the well-known cleverness of **horse traders,** who literally bought and sold horses.

**hot** In addition to the idioms beginning with HOT, also see BLOW HOT AND COLD; HAVE THE HOTS FOR; LIKE A CAT ON A HOT TIN ROOF; MAKE IT HOT FOR; PIPING HOT; SELL LIKE HOTCAKES; STRIKE WHILE THE IRON'S HOT; TOO HOT TO HANDLE.

**hot air** Empty, exaggerated talk, as in *That last speech of hers was pure hot air.* It is also put as **full of hot air,** as in *Pay no attention to him—he's full of hot air.* This term transfers heated air to meaningless talk.

**hot and bothered** In a state of nervous excitement, worried, as in *She was all hot and bothered before her big opening.*

**hot and heavy** **1.** Very enthusiastic and excited, as in *That was a hot and heavy debate.* This slangy expression uses *hot* in the sense of "characterized by intense feeling," and *heavy* in the sense of "serious." **2.** Passionate, lustful, as in *They were awfully young to be so hot and heavy about their romance.* This slangy term uses *hot* in the sense of "sexually aroused."



**hot as blazes** Also, **hot as hell.** Extremely warm, as in *It was hot as blazes in that room,* or *I'm hot as hell and would love a cold shower.*

**hot at** see HOT ON, def. 2.

**hot dog** **1.** A person who performs showy, often dangerous stunts, especially but not exclusively in sports; also, a showoff. For example, *He was a shameless hot dog on the tennis court, smashing every ball,* or *She was a hot dog behind the wheel, screeching her tires at every turn.* The relation of this term to the edible hot dog is unknown. The activity of showing off is called **hot-dogging.** **2.** Also, **hot diggety dog.** An expression of delight or enthusiasm, as in *Hot dog! What a great gift.*

**hotfoot it** Go in haste, walk fast or run. For example, *I'll have to hotfoot it to the airport if I'm to meet them.*

**hot for** see HOT ON, def. 1.

**hot line** A telephone line that gives quick and direct access to a source of information or help. For example, *Our state has an AIDS hot line in every county.* This term was originally (and is still) used for a direct link between heads of government for use during a crisis, but it was quickly extended to wider applications.

**hot number, a** Also, **hot stuff.** Someone or something that is currently popular or fashionable; also, someone or something unconventional or daring. For example, *That new song is going to be a hot number,* or *He really thinks he's hot stuff.* These slangy expressions use *hot* in the sense of "recent" or "fresh."

**hot off the press** Newly printed; sensational and exciting. For example, *I've got it hot off the press—he's resigning,* or *This design is hot off the press.*

**hot on** **1.** Also, **hot for.** Enthusiastic about, as in *She's really hot on golf,* or *He's hot for* *another skiing vacation.* Also see MAKE IT HOT FOR. **2.** Also, **hot at.** Very good, impressive, as in *He's hot at anything involving numbers.* This expression is frequently used in the negative, as in *I'm not so hot at new computer programs.*

**hot on someone's heels** see AT SOMEONE'S HEELS.

**hot potato** A problem so controversial and sensitive that it is risky to deal with. For example, *Gun control is a political hot potato.* This term refers to a slightly older expression, **drop like a hot potato,** meaning "abandon something or someone quickly" (lest one be burned). The idiom refers to the fact that cooked potatoes retain considerable heat because they contain a lot of water.

H

**hot rod** An automobile modified to increase its speed and acceleration, as in *Kids love to work with cars and try to convert them into hot rods.* Also see HOPPED UP.

**hot seat, in the** Also, **on the hot seat.** In a position of extreme stress or discomfort, as when subjected to harsh criticism. For example, *When the negotiations broke down, he was in the hot seat with the government.* This expression extends *hot seat* in the sense of "the electric chair" (for executing someone) to wider use.

**hot spot 1.** A region of a country or the world where there is violent conflict or where violent conflict is likely to happen, as in *The Middle East is only one of many hot spots.* **2.** A place where entertainment or good food can be found that is very popular. For example, *We hit all the hot spots on our trip to New York.*

**hot stuff** see HOT NUMBER.

**hot to trot 1.** Ready and willing, eager. For example, *We should let them start putting up posters; they're hot to trot.* **2.** Sexually avid, lustful, as in *He's hot to trot and asked her out almost as soon as he met her.* Both slangy usages refer to a horse eager to get going.

**hot under the collar** Angry, as in *She is quick to get hot under the collar, but once the problem is ironed out, she forgets it entirely.* This expression refers to the heat of anger.

**hot water, in** In trouble or difficulty, as in *She's deep in political hot water,* or *We got in hot water over the car deal.* The opposite is **out of hot water,** as in *He's finally paid his tuition and is out of hot water with the school.* Both terms refer to water hot enough to burn one. Also see IN TROUBLE WITH.

**hound** see RUN WITH (THE HARE, HUNT WITH THE HOUNDS).

**hour** see AFTER HOURS; ALL HOURS; BY THE DAY (HOUR); ELEVENTH HOUR; HAPPY HOUR; KEEP LATE HOURS; ON THE HOUR; SMALL HOURS.

**house** In addition to the idiom beginning with HOUSE, also see BRING DOWN THE HOUSE; CLEAN HOUSE; EAT SOMEONE OUT OF HOUSE AND HOME; GET ALONG (LIKE A HOUSE AFIRE); HALFWAY HOUSE; KEEP HOUSE; ON THE HOUSE; OPEN HOUSE; PEOPLE WHO LIVE IN GLASS HOUSES; PUT ONE'S HOUSE IN ORDER.

**house of cards** A weak and fragile structure, plan, or organization, as in *Her scheme to reorganize the school sounds like another house of cards,* or *Jerry built his entire business on what turned out to be a house of cards.* This expression refers to the structure made by balancing playing cards against one another.

**how** In addition to the idioms beginning with HOW, also see AND HOW.

**how about?** What is your thought, feeling, or desire concerning? For example, *How about a cup of tea?* or *How about joining us for lunch?* It is also put as **how about it?** as in *How about it? Do you want to come along?* Also see WHAT ABOUT?

**how about that?** Isn't that surprising, remarkable, or pleasing. For example, *They're engaged—how about that?*

**how are you?** see HOW DO YOU DO?

**how come?** How is it that? as in *How come you're not attending the conference?* Sometimes **how come?** follows a statement and asks the question "why" or "in what way," as in *You're not going? How come?* The related phrase **how so?** functions the same way, as in *You say she's changed her mind—how so?* **How come?** is short for *how did it come about that;* **how so?** is short for *how is it so* or *how is it that.*

**how dare someone?** An expression of extreme surprise that someone would do something. For example, *How dare he come here after firing me?* or *How dare you call again?*

**how does that grab you?** What do you think of that? For example, *They want to put his name at the top of the list—how does that grab you?* This expression uses the verb *grab* in the sense of "excite one's interest or attention."

**how do you do?** A common greeting used mostly after being introduced to someone, as in *And this is our youngest—say "How do you do" to your uncle.* Although it is a question, it requires no reply. Originally, this question was asked about a person's health. Today we usually express this as **how are you?** or **how are you doing?** or **how goes it?** or **how's it going?** Even more general are the slangy expressions **how are things?** or **how's tricks?**

**however much** see AS MUCH AS, def. 2.

**how goes it?** see HOW DO YOU DO?

**howling success** A great triumph, as in *Their first play was a howling success.* This expression uses *howling* in the sense of "very pronounced" or "extreme."

**how so?** see under HOW COME?

**how's that?** Also, **how's that again?** What did you say? Please repeat it. For example, *How's that? I didn't quite hear you.*
**how's tricks?** see HOW DO YOU DO?
**how the land lies** see LAY OF THE LAND.
**how the other half lives** The way a group of people, usually those who have more or less money than oneself, lives. For example, *You should get a job and find out how the other half lives,* or *I could find out how the other half lives if I win the lottery.*
**how the wind blows** see WAY THE WIND BLOWS.
**huddle** see GO INTO A HUDDLE.
**hue and cry** A loud public protest or demand. For example, *The reformers raised a hue and cry about political corruption.* This redundant expression (*hue* and *cry* both mean "an outcry") originally meant "an outcry calling for the pursuit of a criminal."
**huff** In addition to the idiom beginning with HUFF, also see IN A HUFF.
**huff and puff** Make noisy, empty threats; bluster. For example, *You can huff and puff about leaving, but we'll believe it when we see it.* This expression uses two very old words, *huff,* meaning "emit puffs of breath in anger," and *puff,* meaning "blow in short gusts." Rhyme has helped this idiom survive.
**human** see MILK OF HUMAN KINDNESS.
**humble** see EAT CROW (HUMBLE PIE).
**humor** In addition to the idiom beginning with HUMOR, also see OUT OF SORTS (HUMOR).
**humor me** Used as a command to tell someone to allow you to say or do something, especially when that person thinks you're wrong. For example, *Humor me! Let's look for your watch one more time.*
**hump** In addition to the idiom beginning with HUMP, also see OVER THE HUMP.
**hump day** Wednesday, because it is the middle day of the workweek, as in *Thank goodness it's hump day. I can't wait for Friday!*
**hundred** see BY THE DOZEN (HUNDRED).
**hung up** see under HANG UP.
**hunt** see RUN WITH (THE HARE, HUNT WITH THE HOUNDS).
**hurry up and wait** Move quickly and then have to wait for something or someone. For example, *We did our share in good time, but the others were several days behind, so we couldn't finish—it was another case of hurry up and wait.* This expression probably originated in the armed services.
**hurt** see NOT HURT A FLY.
**hush money** A bribe paid to keep something secret, as in *No amount of hush money will keep that scandal from coming out.*
**hush up** Keep from public knowledge, suppress mention of. For example, *They tried to hush up the damaging details.*
**Hyde** see JEKYLL AND HYDE.

**i** see DOT THE I'S AND CROSS THE T'S.

**I beg your pardon** see under EXCUSE ME.

**ice** see BREAK THE ICE; CUT NO ICE; ON ICE; ON THIN ICE; PUT ON ICE; TIP OF THE ICEBERG.

**icing on the cake** Also, **frosting on the cake. 1.** An additional benefit to something already good. For example, *All these letters of congratulation are icing on the cake,* or *After that beautiful sunrise, the rainbow is just frosting on the cake.* This expression refers to the sweet creamy coating used to enhance a cake. **2.** A final event that makes something that is already bad worse, as in *Purposely avoiding me was just the icing on the cake,* or *Running out of gas was the frosting on the cake.*

I

**I dare say 1.** I can assert or affirm something with certainty, as in *I dare say my point of view will be heard.* **2.** Also, **I daresay.** I presume or assume to be likely, as in *I daresay you'll be invited.* This usage is more common in Britain than in America.

**idea** see BOUNCE IDEAS OFF; BRIGHT IDEA; HAVE NO IDEA; PUT IDEAS IN SOMEONE'S HEAD; WHAT'S THE IDEA.

**idiot box** A television set, as in *There they sit in front of the idiot box, hour after hour.*

**if** In addition to the idioms beginning with IF, also see AS IF; DAMNED IF ONE DOES, DAMNED IF ONE DOESN'T; MAKE AS IF; NO IFS OR BUTS; NOTHING IF NOT; (IF) PUSH COMES TO SHOVE; WHAT IF.

**if anything** If at all, if in any degree. For example, *If anything, we have too much food rather than too little.*

**if at first you don't succeed, try, try again** Don't let a first-time failure stop further attempts. For example, *I know it's hard at first to shift gears without stalling, but if at first you don't succeed.* This saying has become so well known that it is often shortened, as in the example.

**if it ain't broke, don't fix it** Don't try to repair something that is working well. For example, *Since they like our proposal, let's not change it; if it ain't broke, don't fix it.* For a synonym, see LEAVE WELL ENOUGH ALONE.

**if only** I wish that. For example, *If only I had known you were coming, I would have met your plane,* or *If only it would snow on Christmas Eve.* For a synonym, see WOULD THAT.

**if the shoe fits, wear it** Also, **if the cap fits, wear it.** If something applies to you, accept it, as in *These problems are hard to solve, and most people would need help, so if the shoe fits, wear it!* This expression originated as *if the cap fits,* which referred to a fool's cap. Although this version has not died out entirely, *shoe* today is more common and probably became more popular through the Cinderella fairy tale, in which the prince searches for her by means of the slipper she lost at the ball.

**if wishes were horses** If one could readily have what one wanted, life would be easy. For example, *She would love a brand-new car for her sixteenth birthday but—if wishes were horses.* This expression is a shortening of **if wishes were horses, beggars would ride.**

**if worst comes to worst** Also, **if worse comes to worst.** In the least favorable situation, if the worst possible result happens. For example, *If worst comes to worst and the budget is not approved, the government will shut down,* or *Go ahead and go to school with a cold; if worse comes to worst, the teacher will send you home.* This expression is nearly always followed by a solution.

**if you can't beat 'em, join 'em** Also, **if you can't lick 'em, join 'em.** If you can't defeat your opponents, you might be better off switching to their side. For example, *No one else was willing to stick with the old software program, so she learned the new one, noting if you can't beat 'em, join 'em,* or *I opposed a new school library, but the town voted for it, so I'll support it—if you can't lick 'em, join 'em.* This expression originally referred to political opponents.

**if you can't stand the heat, get out of the kitchen** If the pressure or stress is too great, leave or give up. For example, *It'll take a lot of weekend overtime to finish, so if you can't stand the heat, get out of the kitchen.* This folksy saying has been attributed to President Harry S. Truman, who certainly said it and may have originated it.

**ignorance is bliss** What you don't know won't hurt you. For example, *She decided not to read the critics' reviews—ignorance is bliss.* This idea has been expressed since ancient times.

**ill** In addition to the idioms beginning with ILL, also see under GET SICK.

**ill at ease** Uncomfortable, as in *Large parties made him feel ill at ease.* For an antonym, see AT EASE.

**I'll be hanged** **1.** I am very surprised, as in, *Well, I'll be hanged; there's my taxi.* **2. I'll be hanged if I.** Under no circumstances will I, as in *I'll be hanged if I let you do that.* Both of these usages refer to being executed by hanging.

**I'll believe it when I see it** see SEEING IS BELIEVING.

**I'll be seeing you** Also, **see you.** Good-bye, as in *I have to go now; I'll be seeing you,* or *All right, see you.* These expressions do not necessarily imply a future meeting.

**ill-gotten gains** Benefits obtained in an evil manner or by dishonest means, as in *They tricked their uncle into leaving them a fortune and are now enjoying their ill-gotten gains.*

**I'll say** Absolutely, I strongly agree. For example, *Did you enjoy the film? I'll say.* This phrase is generally used alone and for emphasis. For a synonym, see YOU CAN SAY THAT AGAIN.

**ill wind that blows no one any good, it's an** A loss or misfortune usually benefits someone. For example, *They lost everything when their house burned down, but they got rid of a lot of junk as well—it's an ill wind.* This expression is so well known that it is often shortened, as in the example.

**image** see SPITTING IMAGE.

**imagination** see BY ANY STRETCH (OF THE IMAGINATION); FIGMENT OF ONE'S IMAGINATION.

**I'm from Missouri** see FROM MISSOURI.

**immemorial** see TIME IMMEMORIAL.

**impose *something* on *one*** **1.** Force something on someone; also, levy a tax or duty. For example, *Don't try to impose your ideas on me,* or *The British government imposed a new tax on tea.* **2.** Force oneself on others; take unfair advantage of. For example, *Am I imposing on you if I stay overnight?* or *He's always imposing on us, dropping in unexpectedly with numerous friends.*

**impression** see MAKE AN IMPRESSION; UNDER THE IMPRESSION.

**improve on** Make beneficial additions or changes to, as in *The company is trying to improve on the previous model.*

**I must have dozed off** Also, **I must have missed a paragraph.** Perhaps I have missed a step in the logic because I cannot follow the discussion. For example, *How did he get on this subject? I must have dozed off,* or *That movie was frustrating. I felt like I must have missed a paragraph between one scene and the next.*

**in** In addition to the idioms beginning with IN, also see under OUT OF.

**in a bad light** see IN A GOOD LIGHT.

**in a bad mood** In an irritable or depressed state of mind. For example, *Dad's in a bad mood, so don't ask for anything right now.* The antonym **in a good mood** refers to a cheerful, contented state of mind, as in *When the boss is in a good mood, our whole day goes well.* Also see IN THE MOOD.

**in a bad way** In trouble; also, in the process of declining. For example, *If he can't get that bank loan, he'll be in a bad way,* or *The business is in a bad way, with profits declining every month.*

**in a big way** To a great extent, quite obviously. For example, *I could go for a hamburger in a big way,* or *This hotel chain is expanding in a big way.*

**in a bind** Also, **in a box** or **in a hole** or **in a jam** or **in a tight corner** or **in a tight spot.** In a difficult, threatening, or embarrassing position; also, unable to solve a difficult problem. For example, *He's put us in a bind: we can't refuse, but at the same time we can't fill the order,* or *She's in a box; she can't afford to pay what she owes us,* or *He quit without giving notice, and now we're really in a hole,* or *We always end up in a jam during the holiday season,* or *He's in a tight corner with those new customers,* or *We'll be in a tight spot unless we can find another thousand dollars.* All these terms refer to places from which it is hard to get out. Also see IN A FIX.

**in a breeze** see under HANDS DOWN.

**in absentia** While not present, as in *He was tried and convicted in absentia,* or *He was awarded his degree in absentia.* This expression is Latin for "in absence."

**in a cold sweat** Feeling nervous or terrified, as in *When I looked over the cliff, I broke out in a cold sweat.* This expression refers to perspiring accompanied by a feeling of cold, which can be caused by fear as well as by fever.

**in addition** **1.** Also, as well as. For example, *They study their instruments and, in addition, theory and music history.* **2. in addition to.** Over and above, besides, as in *In addition to a new muffler, the truck needs new brakes.*

**in a dither** Also, **all of a dither** or **in a flutter** or **in a tizzy.** In a state of nervousness, as in *Planning the wedding put her in a dither,* or *He tried to pull himself together, but he was all of a dither,* or *She showed up in such a flutter that our meeting was useless.* Also see IN A LATHER.

**in advance** **1.** Beforehand, ahead of time. For example, *He insisted on being paid half his fee in advance.* **2. in advance of.** In front of, as in *The forward man moved in advance of the line.*

**in a fix** Also, **in a pickle** or **in a spot.** In a difficult or embarrassing situation. For example, *I was really in a fix when I missed the plane,* or

*Lost and out of gas—how did we get in such a pickle?* or *John had lost all his money in the poker game—now he was in a spot.* **In a pickle** is sometimes put as **in a pretty pickle. In a spot** is also put as **in a bad spot** or **in a tough spot.** Also see IN A BIND; IN DEEP, def. 2; IN THE SOUP; IN TROUBLE; ON THE SPOT.

**in a flash** Also, **in a jiffy** or **in a second** or **in a trice.** Quickly, immediately. For example, *I'll be with you in a flash,* or *He said he'd be done in a jiffy,* or *I'll be off the phone in a second,* or *I felt a drop or two, and in a trice there was a downpour.* The first idiom refers to a flash of lightning. The word *jiffy* here means "a short time," and *a second,* literally one sixtieth of a minute, is used vaguely to mean "a very short time." *Trice* originally meant "a single pull at something."

**in a flutter** see IN A DITHER.

I

**in a fog** Also, **in a haze.** Thinking of something else, not paying attention; also, at a loss, confused. For example, *After the accident he went about in a fog, even though he had not been injured,* or *She always seems to be in a haze; she never knows what's going on.* These expressions refer to fog or haze that makes it hard to see.

**in a good light** Under favorable circumstances, as in *They thought he'd make a wonderful mayor, but they'd only seen him in a good light,* or *The book portrayed their actions in a good light.* Both this expression and its antonym, **in a bad light,** transfer physical light in which something can (or cannot) be seen clearly to figurative use.

**in a hole** see IN A BIND.

**in a huff** In an offended manner, angrily, as in *When he left out her name, she left in a huff.* This idiom transfers *huff* in the sense of a gust of wind to a burst of anger. Also see IN A SNIT.

**in a jam** see IN A BIND.

**in a lather** Also, **in a state.** Agitated and anxious, as in *Don't get yourself in a lather over this,* or *She was in a state over the flight cancellation.* The first term refers to the frothy sweat of a horse, the second to an upset state of mind. Also see IN A DITHER; IN A STEW.

**in all** All together, considering everything, as in *There are four cars in all,* or *They won ten games and lost two, doing very well in all.* Also see ALL IN ALL.

**in all one's born days** Ever, as in *I've never seen so much snow, not in all my born days.* This folksy usage literally means "since I was born."

**in all probability** Also, **in all likelihood.** Most likely, almost certainly. For example, *In all probability we'll be home for Christmas.*

**in a manner of speaking** In a way; so to speak. For example, *He was, in a manner of speaking, asked to leave the group.*

**in and of itself** Inherently, considered alone. For example, *In and of itself the plan might work, but I doubt that it will be approved.* This expression is also put simply as **in itself,** as in *This account may be true in itself.*

**in a nutshell** Briefly, in a few words, as in *Here's our proposal—in a nutshell, we want to sell the business to you.* This exaggerated expression refers to the Roman writer Pliny's description of Homer's *Iliad* being copied in so tiny a hand that it could fit in a nutshell. For a time it referred to anything shortened, but later on it referred mainly to written or spoken words.

**in any case** Also, **at all events** or **in any event.** No matter what happens, certainly; also, whatever the fact is, anyway. For example, *In any case, I plan to go,* or *Call me tomorrow, at all events,* or *He may not be getting a raise, but in any event his boss thinks highly of him.* For an antonym, see IN NO CASE.

**in a pig's eye** Under no condition, not at all, as in *In a pig's eye he'll pay me back,* or *You think he's competent? In a pig's eye!* This expression, a euphemism for *in a pig's ass,* is generally used as a strong negative.

**in a pinch** In an emergency, as in *This music isn't what I would have chosen, but it will do in a pinch.*

**in a quandary 1.** Unable to make a choice or decision. For example, *We're in a quandary about whether to rent or buy an apartment.* **2.** Confused, as in *His angry response left me in a quandary.*

**in arms** see BABE IN ARMS; UP IN ARMS.

**in arrears** Late or behind in payment of money. For example, *He's been in arrears on his rent so often that he may be evicted.*

**in a rut** In a settled or established habit or course of action, especially a boring one. For example, *We go to the seashore every summer—we're in a rut,* or *After ten years at the same job, she says she's in a rut.* This expression refers to having a wheel stuck in a groove in the road.

**in a sense** Also, **in some sense.** Sort of, in some ways but not others. For example, *In a sense our schools are the best in the state, but the test scores don't always show that,* or *In some sense I agree with you, but not entirely.* Also see IN A WAY.

**inasmuch as** Also, **insomuch as. 1.** Since, because of the fact that, as in *Inasmuch as I have to go anyhow, I'll pick up the book for you,* or *Insomuch as they are friends, we can seat them together.* **2.** Also, **insofar as.** To the extent or degree that, as in *You will become a good pianist only inasmuch as you keep practicing,* or *He's lost interest insomuch as he has stopped attending church* *altogether,* or *Insofar as this is a temporary measure, we can't complain.*

**in a snit** In a state of anxiety or irritation, as in *He is in a snit over the guest list.* It is also put as **get in a snit** or **get into a snit,** as in *She tends to get in a snit every time things don't go her way.* The origin of this expression is uncertain.

**in a state** see IN A LATHER.

**in a stew** Excited, alarmed, or anxious. For example, *Mary was in a stew about how her request for a promotion would turn out.* This expression is also put as **get in a stew** or **get into a stew,** as in *Every Saturday the minister got in a stew about Sunday's sermon.* This expression transfers the mixture of meat and vegetables in a stew to overheated, mixed emotions.

**in at the death** Also, **in at the finish** or **in at the kill.** Involved in or present at the end, especially a terrible end but sometimes merely the climax of an important event. For example, *He had a hand in their breakup, but he didn't want to be in at the death,* or *They've done really well this year, and we want to be in at the kill.* These expressions originally referred to hunters and hounds being present at the death of a fox they had hunted.

**in a tight corner** Also, **in a tight spot.** See IN A BIND.

**in a tizzy** see IN A DITHER.

**in a vacuum** Without having any information about or experience with something. For example, *He has so little social grace, it's as though he's lived in a vacuum all his life.*

**in a walk** see under HANDS DOWN.

**in a way** To a certain extent, with reservations; also, in some respects. For example, *In a way I like the new styles,* or *You're right, in a way, but we have to consider the price.* Also see IN A SENSE.

**in awe of, be** Also, **stand in awe of.** Respect and revere someone or something, experience a feeling of solemn wonder, as in *All of us are in awe of his many achievements.* This expression originally meant "fear something or someone." Later *awe* came to mean "dread mingled with respect," and eventually it meant reverence alone.

**in a while** Also, **after a while.** After a period of time, usually a fairly short time. For example, *Go ahead, I'll be along in a while,* or *After a while we turned off the television and went for a walk.*

**in a whirl, be 1.** Very confused, very excited. For example, *All those people talking at once had my head in a whirl,* or *She's in a whirl making plans for her annual party.* **2. in the social whirl.** Completely involved in many social activities, as in *He's gotten caught up in the social whirl and rarely calls us.*

**in a word** see IN BRIEF.

**in a world of one's own** see IN ONE'S OWN WORLD.

**in back of** see BACK OF.

**in bad** see IN BAD WITH.

**in bad faith** With the intention of tricking someone or doing harm, as in *I'm sure they were acting in bad faith and never planned to pay us.* The antonym **in good faith** means "sincerely and honestly," as in *I signed that contract in good faith.*

**in bad with, be** Be disliked; be out of favor. For example, *She was afraid she would be in bad with her new supervisor.* Also see IN GOOD WITH.

**in bed with, be** Doing business with someone, closely connected with someone. For example, *I hear that company is in bed with a big communications monopoly,* or *Watch what you say to him. He's in bed with upper-level management.*

**in behalf of** Also, **on behalf of. 1.** For someone else, as someone's agent or representative. For example, *In behalf of the board, I want to thank you for your help,* or *She was speaking on behalf of the entire staff.* **2.** For someone's benefit or interest, as in *He was collecting the dues in my behalf.* Some authorities insist that **in behalf of** should be used only to mean "for someone's benefit" and **on behalf of** only to mean "as someone's agent." In practice, however, the terms are so often used interchangeably that this distinction no longer applies.

**in between** In an intermediate situation, as in *My roommates disagreed, and I was caught in between.*

**in between times** During an intervening period, as in *He has written several books, and in between times he teaches.*

**in black and white** see BLACK AND WHITE, def. 3.

**in brief** Also, **in short** or **in a word.** Concisely, in few words, to sum up. All three phrases usually precede or follow a summary statement, as in *In brief, we didn't get much out of his speech,* or *There was no agenda; in short, they could discuss whatever they wanted to,* or *The sun was shining, the sky was clear—in a word, it was a beautiful day.*

**in bulk 1.** Unpackaged, loose, as in *It's cheaper to buy rice in bulk.* **2.** In large amounts or volume, as in *The ship was carrying wheat in bulk.*

**in business** Able to engage in an activity or achieve some goal. For example, *If she remembers the hamburger, we'll be in business,* or *Once you pay off your debt, you'll be in business.*

**in cahoots** see IN LEAGUE WITH.

**in care of** Through someone, by way of someone, as in *I sent the gift in care of your parents.*

This phrase indicates that something is to be delivered to someone at someone else's address.

**in case** **1.** Also, **just in case.** If it should happen that. For example, *In case he doesn't show up, we have a backup speaker.* The variant also is used without a following clause to mean simply "as a precaution," as in *I took an umbrella just in case.* **2. in the case of** or **in the event of.** If there should happen to be. For example, *Here is a number to call in case of an emergency,* or *In the event of rain, we'll have to change our plans.* Similarly, **in that case** means "if that should happen," as in *You're going to the store? In that case, could you get me some eggs?* Also see IN ANY CASE; IN NO CASE; IN THE CASE OF.

**in cement** Firmly settled or determined; unchangeable. For example, *Their policy on admissions was set in cement.* For a synonym, see CAST IN STONE.

I

**inch** In addition to the idiom beginning with INCH, also see BY INCHES; EVERY INCH; GIVE AN INCH; WITHIN AN INCH OF.

**inch along** Move or progress at a very slow pace. For example, *The traffic was terrible; it just inched along,* or *Work on the building is inching along.* Also see BY INCHES.

**in character** Consistent with someone's general personality or behavior. For example, *Her failure to answer the invitation was completely in character.* The antonym is **out of character,** as in *It was out of character for him to refuse the assignment.*

**in charge** **1.** In a position of leadership or supervision, as in *Who's in charge here?* or *He's the agent in charge at the ticket counter.* **2. in charge of.** Having control over or responsibility for, as in *You're in charge of making the salad.* **3. in the charge of** or **in the care of.** Under someone's care or supervision, as in *We left the children in the charge of their grandparents.*

**inch by inch** see BY INCHES.

**in check** Unable to move or act freely: under control. For example, *The troops held the enemy in check,* or *We kept our emotions in check.*

**in chorus** All together, in unison, as in *The children answered the teacher in chorus.* This expression transfers group singing to simultaneous utterance of any kind.

**in circles** see GO AROUND (IN CIRCLES).

**in circulation** Also, **into circulation.** A return to business or social life, especially after a period of absence. For example, *After a month in the hospital Bill was eager to get back in circulation.* The antonym is **out of circulation,** as in *Since we had twins, we've been out of circulation, but we're hoping to get out more often soon.*

**inclined to** Tending or disposed toward, as in *I'm inclined to believe his story.*

**in clover** Prosperous, living well. For example, *After we make our first million, we'll be in clover.* This expression refers to cattle happily feeding on clover. Slightly different versions are **like pigs in clover** and **rolling in clover.**

**in cold blood** In a purposely ruthless and unfeeling manner, as in *The whole family was murdered in cold blood.* This expression refers to the notion that blood is the seat of emotion and is hot in passion and cold in calm. The term therefore means *not* "in the heat of passion" but "in a calculated, deliberate manner."

**in cold storage** In a state of delay or postponement. For example, *We can't consider these design changes now; let's put them in cold storage for a year or so.* This expression refers to the literal storage of food, furs, or other objects in a refrigerated place.

**in commission** see under OUT OF COMMISSION.

**in common** Shared characteristics, as in *One of the few things those two have in common is a love of music.* **2.** Held equally, in joint possession or use, as in *This land is held in common by all the neighbors.*

**in concert** **1.** Together, jointly, as in *They worked in concert on the script,* or *When mind is in concert with body, one can accomplish a great deal.* **2.** Performing music for an audience, as in *They will be in concert on March 17th and 18th.*

**in condition** Also, **in good condition** or **in good shape** or **in shape.** Physically fit; also, in a state of readiness. For example, *I've got to get in condition before the next race,* or *This project's in good shape now,* or *Is this report in shape to show to the president?* The antonyms of these expressions include **out of condition** and **out of shape.** For example, *Don't buy a racehorse that's out of condition,* or *I'm so out of shape that I can barely run a mile.*

**in confidence** Also, **in strict confidence** or **in strictest confidence.** Privately, on condition that what is said will not be repeated to anyone else. For example, *The doctor told her in confidence that her mother was terminally ill,* or *He told us in strict confidence that she was pregnant.* Also see TAKE INTO ONE'S CONFIDENCE.

**in conscience** Also, **in all good conscience** or **in good conscience.** In all truth or fairness, as in *I can't in conscience say that the meeting went well,* or *In all good conscience we can't support their stand on cutting taxes.*

**in consequence** As a result, therefore, as in *She was away for years and in consequence has few friends here.* The prepositional phrase

**in consequence of** means "as a result of," as in *In consequence of this finding, there is sure to be further investigation.*

**in consideration of 1.** In view of, on account of, as in *We turned back in consideration of the worsening weather.* **2.** In return for, as in *She received a small amount of money in consideration of her key contributions.*

**in creation** see under ON EARTH.

**incumbent on** Also, **incumbent upon.** Imposed on someone as an obligation or duty on, obligatory for. For example, *He felt it was incumbent on us all to help the homeless.*

**in deep 1.** Also, **in too deep.** Seriously involved; far advanced. For example, *He was in deep with the other partners and couldn't sell his shares of the business,* or *She used her credit cards for everything, and before long she was in deep.* **2. in deep water.** Also, **in over one's head** or **in deep shit.** In trouble, with more problems than one can manage, as in *The business was in deep water after the president resigned,* or *I'm afraid Bill got in over his head,* or *You'll be in deep shit if you're late again.* These expressions transfer the difficulties of being submerged in water to other problems. Also see OVER ONE'S HEAD.

**in defiance of** In spite of, with obvious disdain for, as in *She left early in defiance of her boss.*

**in demand** Popular, as in *The general was in demand as an after-dinner speaker.*

**in depth** Completely, thoroughly, as in *It will take years to cover the entire subject in depth.*

**in detail** With close attention to particulars; thoroughly. For example, *She explained her theory in detail.* It is also put as **go into detail,** meaning "to explain thoroughly," as in *You know what I mean, so I needn't go into detail.*

**Indian giver** One who takes or demands back one's gift to another, as in *She wanted to take back my birthday present, but Mom said that would make her an Indian giver.* This term, now considered offensive, originally referred to the Native American practice of expecting a gift in return for one that is given.

**Indian summer** A period of mild, sunny weather occurring in late autumn, usually following a seasonable cold spell. For example, *We had two whole days of Indian summer this year, and then it turned cold again.*

**in dispute** In disagreement about. For example, *This land is in dispute; it is claimed by several people,* or *The origin of this phrase is in dispute.*

**in drag 1.** Wearing clothes normally worn by the opposite sex, as in *All of the actors in the play were in drag.* This expression originally referred to male actors wearing women's apparel on stage, especially for comic purposes, but it also refers to cross-dressing by homosexuals. **2.** Wearing clothes that are so uncomfortable that one wears them only when the occasion requires it. For example, *I'm wearing jeans, but she'll be in drag. She had a job interview today.*

**in due course** Also, **in due course of time** or **in due time; in time** or **all in good time.** After an appropriate interval, in a reasonable length of time. For example, *In due course we'll discuss the details of this arrangement,* or *In due time the defense will present new evidence,* or *You'll learn the program in time,* or *We'll come up with a solution, all in good time.* Also see IN GOOD TIME.

**in Dutch, be** Be in trouble or disfavor, as in *If I don't finish on time I'll really be in Dutch.*

**in earnest 1.** With sincere intent, as in *We settled down to study in earnest.* **2.** Also, **in dead earnest.** Serious, as in *We thought he was joking, but he was in earnest,* or *I'm in dead earnest about selling the business.* In the variant, *dead* means "completely" or "thoroughly" and is used for emphasis.

**in effect 1.** For all practical purposes, as in *This testimony in effect contradicted her earlier statement.* **2.** In or into operation, as in *This law will be in effect in January.* Related phrases include **go into effect** and **take effect,** which mean "become operative," as in *This law goes into effect January 1,* or *It takes effect January 1.* Similarly, **put into effect** means "make operative," as in *When will the judge's ruling be put into effect?* Also see IN FORCE, def. 2.

**in effigy** Symbolically. For example, *That umpire was completely unfair—let's burn him in effigy.* Now used only figuratively, this term formerly signified a way of carrying out the sentence of a criminal who had escaped, such as **burn in effigy** or **hang in effigy.** A dummy was made of the criminal or a detested political figure and subjected to the prescribed punishment.

**in escrow** In trust with a third party for delivery after certain conditions are fulfilled. For example, *Our down payment on the house is in escrow until the current owner makes the promised repairs.*

**in essence** Basically, by nature, as in *He is in essence a very private person,* or *In essence, they were asking the wrong question.* This term uses *essence* in the sense of "intrinsic nature."

**in evidence 1.** Also, **much in evidence.** Plainly visible, obvious, as in *The car's new dents were very much in evidence.* **2.** As testimony in a court of law, as in *The attorney submitted the photograph in evidence.*

**in excess of** Greater than, more than, as in *The book sold in excess of a million copies.*

**in exchange** Also, **in exchange for.** In return (for something or someone), as in *She lent me her motorcycle, and I offered my car in exchange,* or *At the party the guests were given cookies in exchange for the gifts they brought.*

**in fact** Also, **in point of fact.** In reality, in truth; actually. For example, *She was, in fact, eager to join the club,* or *In point of fact, his parents never had much influence on him.*

**in fashion** Also, **in style.** See under GO OUT, def. 5.

**in favor of 1.** In support of, approving, as in *We are in favor of her promotion,* or *All the reviews were in his favor.* **2. in one's favor.** To the advantage of, as in *The court decided in favor of the defendant.* **3.** Written or made out to the benefit of, as in *The check was made out in favor of the charity.* **4. in one's favor.** Out of a preference for, as in *The mayor turned down the new road in favor of better sewers.*

I

**inference** see DRAW AN INFERENCE.

**in fine feather** In excellent form, health, or humor. For example, *He was in fine feather, joking with all his visitors.* These expressions all refer to a bird's healthy plumage, a usage no longer very common.

**influence** see UNDER THE INFLUENCE.

**in for 1.** Guaranteed to get or have, as in *We're in for a difficult time.* **2. in for it.** Certain to have trouble or be punished, as in *When Harry finds out we left early, we'll be in for it.* **3.** Involved or entered for some purpose, as in *We're in for the profits.* Also see HAVE IT IN FOR; IN FOR A DIME.

**in for a dime, in for a dollar** Once involved, one must not stop at half-measures. For example, *All right, I'll drive you all the way there—in for a dime, in for a dollar.* This idiom began as **in for a penny, in for a pound,** and meant that if one owes a penny, one might as well owe a pound. It came from Britain into American usage without changing the British monetary unit. Later, however, U.S. and Canadian currency terms replaced the British ones.

**in force 1.** In full strength, in large numbers, as in *Demonstrators were out in force.* This usage originally referred to a large military force. **2.** Being observed, binding, as in *This rule is no longer in force.* This usage originally referred to the binding power of a law.

**information** see under GOLD MINE.

**in front of 1.** Facing someone or a group, as in *He was shy about speaking in front of a large audience.* **2.** In someone's presence, as in *Let's not fight in front of the children.*

**in full** Completely, as in *His talk covered the subject in full,* or *The debt was repaid in full.*

**in full swing** In full operation, at the highest level of activity. For example, *After the strike it will be some time before production is in full swing.* This expression refers to the energetic movement of a swinging body.

**in general 1.** Referring to a group of people or a subject as a whole, as opposed to particular ones. For example, *I am speaking about contracts in general,* or *Girls in general mature at a younger age than boys.* For an antonym, see IN PARTICULAR. **2.** For the most part; commonly, usually. For example, *In general the children behaved very well,* or *Our winters are quite mild in general.*

**in glowing terms** Spoken of with great praise. For example, *She described her trip to Hawaii in glowing terms,* or *Used-car commercials always talk about the vehicles for sale in glowing terms*

**in good condition** Also, **in good shape.** See IN CONDITION

**in good faith** see under IN BAD FAITH.

**in good hands** In reliable or safe care. For example, *I know the children are in good hands when they visit my mother.* The term *good hand* is here used in the sense of "skill" or "ability."

**in good part 1. take in good part.** Accept good-naturedly or with good grace; without taking offense. For example, *She took her brother's teasing in good part.* **2.** Mostly, to a great extent, as in *Their failure is in good part the result of poor management.* Also see FOR THE MOST PART.

**in good spirits** Also, **in high spirits.** Happy, cheerful, as in *Grandmother was in good spirits today. High spirits* also can indicate liveliness and excitement, as in *The children were in high spirits at the prospect of a trip to the beach.*

**in good stead** see STAND IN GOOD STEAD.

**in good time 1.** See IN DUE COURSE. **2.** In a short time, quickly; also, earlier than expected. For example, *We want to get home in good time for the show,* or *They sent us the bids in good time.*

**in good with, be** Also, **be in with; get on someone's good side.** Be in someone's favor, be well liked by someone. For example, *He's in good with the boss, so we can expect approval of our application,* or *I'd love to be in with that popular crowd, but I don't quite know how,* or *I don't know how he got on her good side after that fight they had.* Also see IN BAD WITH; IN SOMEONE'S GOOD GRACES.

**in half** In two equal or roughly equal parts. For example, *Let's cut this sandwich in half.*

**in hand 1.** Available at the present time, as in *The company has very little cash in hand.* **2.** Under one's control or authority, as in *The police had the situation well in hand.* **3.** In process, being settled, as in *He was willing to give full attention to the matter in hand.* Also see IN ONE'S HANDS.

**in heat** In a state of sexual excitement immediately preceding ovulation. For example, *Our cat's in heat, so we have to keep her inside.* This expression applies to most female mammals and indicates the period when the animal is fertile and most receptive to mating.

**in honor of** In celebration of, as a mark of respect for, as in *We are holding a banquet in honor of the president.*

**in hopes of** Also, **in hopes that; in the hope of** or **in the hope that; in high hopes of** or **in high hopes that.** Expecting and wishing for, as in *We went in hopes of finding a vacancy,* or *They met in the hope of bringing about a peaceful settlement.* The phrases with *that* are used with clauses, as in *In hopes that something good might come of it, he began to work,* or *We are in high hopes that a cure for leukemia will be found soon.*

**initiative** see ON ONE'S OWN ACCOUNT (INITIATIVE); TAKE THE INITIATIVE.

**in itself** see under IN AND OF ITSELF.

**injury** see ADD INSULT TO INJURY.

**in keeping with** In agreement with, in harmony with, as in *The new wing is in keeping with the house's original architecture,* or *His actions are not in keeping with his words.* This expression uses *keeping* in the sense of "harmony," as does its antonym, **out of keeping with,** as in *The funeral arrangements were out of keeping with the family's wishes.* Also see IN KEY; IN LINE.

**in key** In harmony with other factors, in a matching style, as in *This furniture is perfectly in key with the overall design.* This term uses *key* in the musical sense, that is, "notes related to one another." The antonym **out of key** means "not in harmony with other factors" or "unsuitable," as in *He is out of key with his time.*

**in kind 1.** With services or products rather than money. For example, *I edited Bob's book for payment in kind; he gave me guitar lessons in exchange.* **2.** In the same manner or with something equal, as in *He returned the insult in kind.*

**in large measure** see under IN SOME MEASURE.

**in large part** see IN PART.

**in league with** Also, **in cahoots with.** In close cooperation or in partnership with, often secretly or in a plot. For example, *He finally realized that his brother is in league with his enemies,* or *We suspect that the mayor is in cahoots with the construction industry.* The variant may come from the French *cahute,* "a small hut or cabin," and may refer to the limited space in such a dwelling.

**in left field** see OUT IN LEFT FIELD.

**in less than no time** see LESS THAN.

**in lieu of** see INSTEAD OF.

**in light of** Also, **in the light of** or **in view of.** With regard to, in relationship to. For example, *In light of recent developments, we're postponing our meeting,* or *In the light of the weather forecast, we've canceled the picnic,* or *He got a special bonus in view of all the extra work he had done.*

**in limbo 1.** In a condition of uncertainty or neglect, as in *They kept her application in limbo for months.* **2.** An intermediate or temporary state, as in *After his editor left the firm, the author's book was in limbo.* Both usages refer to the religious meaning of *limbo,* that is, a place outside hell and heaven to which unbaptized infants and the righteous who died before Christ's coming were sent.

**in line 1.** Also, **in line with.** In agreement with; within ordinary or proper limits. For example, *The new policy was intended to keep prices in line with their competitors,* or *It's up to the teacher to keep the students in line.* Also see FALL IN LINE. **2.** Waiting behind others in a row. For example, *The children stood in line for their lunches.* **3. in line for.** Next in order for, as in *He is next in line for the presidency.* All of these terms use *line* in the sense of "an orderly row or series of people or objects."

**in love** see FALL IN LOVE.

**in luck** Fortunate, enjoying success, as in *You're in luck—we found your car keys.*

**in memory of** As a reminder of something or as a memorial to someone who has died. For example, *In memory of Grandma, we put flowers on her grave on her birthday,* or *In memory of our happy times here, we've planted a little garden.*

**in mind** see BEAR IN MIND; PUT ONE IN MIND OF.

**in name only** Also, **only in name.** Not actually, without any authority. For example, *He's the chief executive in name only; his vice president makes all the decisions,* or *Theirs was a marriage only in name; they lived in different cities.*

**in no case** Never, under no circumstances, as in *She should in no case be told that her father has a terminal illness.* For an antonym, see IN ANY CASE.

**in nothing flat** see IN NO TIME.

**in no time** Also, **in no time at all** or **in less than no time** or **in nothing flat.** Almost instantly, immediately, as in *The train will be here in no time at all,* or *He'll be finished in less than no time,* or *I'll be there in nothing flat.* All these exaggerated terms equate a very short time with "at once."

**in no uncertain terms** Explicitly, definitely so. For example, *My sister told them in* *no uncertain terms that she wanted no part of their practical joke.* The double negative in this idiom serves for emphasis. Also see IN SO MANY WORDS.

**in on, be** Also, **get in on.** Be or become a participant; be or become one of a group who have information. For example, *Is she in on our secret?* or *I'd like to get in on this deal.* Also see BARGE IN; GROUND FLOOR, GET IN ON THE; IN GOOD WITH.

**in one blow** see AT ONE STROKE.

**in one breath** see IN THE SAME BREATH.

**in one ear and out the other** Quickly forgotten, as in *Their advice to her just went in one ear and out the other.* This expression calls up a graphic image of sound traveling through one's head.

**in one fell swoop** see ONE FELL SWOOP.

**in one piece** see ALL IN ONE PIECE.

I

**in one's** In addition to the idioms beginning with IN ONE'S, also see under IN SOMEONE'S; OUT OF ONE'S.

**in one's behalf** see IN BEHALF OF.

**in one's blood** Also, **in the blood.** Part of one's basic nature. For example, *The whole family loves music; it's in their blood,* or *Sailing somehow gets in your blood.* Also see RUN IN THE FAMILY (BLOOD).

**in one's book** According to one's opinion or one's way of thinking. For example, *In my book, he's a wonderful father.* Also see BLACK BOOK.

**in one's cups** Drunk, as in *You can't believe anything he says when he's in his cups.*

**in one's element** Also, **in one's own element.** In an environment naturally suited to or associated with one; doing what one enjoys. For example, *He's in his element when he's working in the garden.* This term refers to one's natural place, as does the antonym **out of one's element.** Also see IN ONE'S GLORY.

**in one's eyes** see IN ONE'S MIND'S EYE.

**in one's favor** see IN FAVOR OF, def. 2 and 4.

**in one's glory** At one's best, happiest, or most contented. For example, *She was in her glory playing her first big solo,* or *In the classroom, this teacher's in his glory.* Also see IN ONE'S ELEMENT.

**in one's hands** Also, **in the hands of.** In one's responsibility, charge, or care. For example, *The selling of the property is in his hands,* or *Let's put this part of that project in the hands of Christine.* For the antonym, see OFF ONE'S HANDS. Also see IN THE HANDS OF; ON ONE'S HANDS; TAKE INTO ONE'S HANDS; TAKE ONE'S LIFE (IN ONE'S HANDS); TAKE THE LAW INTO ONE'S OWN HANDS.

**in one's heart of hearts** According to one's truest, innermost feelings, especially when secret. For example, *It's a wonderful job offer, but in my heart of hearts I don't want to leave this area.*

**in one's interest** Also, **in the interest of** or **in one's own interest** or **in one's best interest.** For one's benefit or advantage, as in *It's obviously in their interest to increase profits,* or *Is this policy in the interest of the people?* or *I think it's in your own best interest to quit now.*

**in one's mind's eye** In one's imagination or memory. For example, *I can just see the old farm in my mind's eye.* This term pairs *mind* and *eye* in the sense of "a mental view."

**in one's midst** see IN THE MIDST.

**in one's name** see IN THE NAME OF.

**in one's own back yard** In one's own territory, in a position very close to one. For example, *You didn't expect to find a first-class artist in your own back yard.* A variant of this expression, **not in my back yard** (and its acronym NIMBY), is used to describe the attitude of some people to the disposal of nuclear waste or the location of halfway houses, rehabilitation centers, or similar facilities—that is, they don't care where it is disposed of or located as long as it isn't near where they live, as in *I understand the need for assisted-care housing, but not in my back yard.* Also see CLOSE TO HOME.

**in one's own right** Through one's own skills or qualifications, as in *He's a fine violinist in his own right,* or *She has a fortune in her own right.* This term originally referred to a legal title or claim, as in *She was queen in her own right,* but it has long been used more loosely.

**in one's own world** Also, **in one's own little world** or **in a world of one's own.** In deep thought or concentration. For example, *Our manager was really in her own world at the meeting this morning,* or *Like many mathematicians, Bill lives in his own little world,* or *Bob's in a world of his own when he's listening to music.*

**in one's pocket** **1.** In one's power or possession, under one's influence. For example, *The defense lawyer had the jury in his pocket.* **2. in each other's pockets.** Very close to or showing dependence, as in *They work in the same office, live in the same house, belong to the same clubs—they're constantly in each other's pockets.*

**in one's prime** see PRIME OF LIFE.

**in one's right mind** In a healthy mental state; sane and rational. For example, *No one in his right mind would drive so fast.* This expression is often used in a negative construction, as in the example. The antonym is **out of one's mind,** as in *You must be out of your mind to swim in that icy lake.* Also see GO OUT OF ONE'S MIND.

**in one's shell** Also, **into one's shell.** In a quiet or withdrawn state. For example, *Dad is extremely shy; if you try to get him to talk, he immediately goes into his shell.* This usage refers to the shell as a protective covering, as does the antonym **out of one's shell,** as in *Once she is out of her shell, she's very talkative.*

**in one stroke** see AT ONE STROKE.

**in one's tracks** see DROP IN ONE'S TRACKS; FOLLOW IN ONE'S TRACKS; STOP COLD (DEAD IN ONE'S TRACKS).

**in one's way 1.** Also, **in one's own way.** According to one's personal manner. For example, *She's serious but kind in her own way,* or *Both of them are generous in their way.* This phrase is often used to limit an expression of praise, as in the examples. **2.** Also, **put something in one's way** or **put something in the way of.** Before one, within reach or experience, as in *That deal put an unexpected sum of money in my way,* or *He promised to put her in the way of new business.* **3. in someone's way.** Also, **in the way.** In a position to block or interfere with someone or something. For example, *That truck is in our way,* or *You're standing in the way; please move to one side.*

**in orbit** Thrilled, delighted, as in *He's in orbit over his son's success.* This expression refers to the successful launching into orbit of a satellite or other spacecraft. Also see IN THE ORBIT OF.

**in order 1.** In proper order or arrangement, as in *The children lined up in order of size,* or *Are the letters all in order?* **2.** Suitable, correct, appropriate, as in *A few words on this subject are in order now.* **3.** See IN SHORT ORDER. **4. in order that.** So that, to the end or purpose that, as in *In order that Bob can meet my husband, we've come early.* **5. in order to.** For the purpose of, as a means to, as in *We'll have to hire more help in order to finish on time.* This usage always precedes a verb, as in the example.

**in other words** Saying something differently, usually more simply or clearly. For example, *The weather was terrible, the plane took off several hours after the scheduled time, and then fog prevented their landing—in other words, they never got to the wedding at all.*

**in over one's head** see under IN DEEP, def. 2.

**in part** Also, **in large part** or **in small part.** To some degree, not completely, somewhat. For example, *We didn't get to Chicago, in part because we didn't have time,* or *He was the one to blame, in large part because he was the one who hired the contractor,* or *The attorney herself was in small part responsible for this witness.*

**in particular** Especially; also, separately, individually, in detail. For example, *The principal talked about the curriculum, the core courses in particular,* or *The orchestra was outstanding, the strings in particular.*

**in passing** Incidentally, by the way, as in *In passing, she told me a bit of news.*

**in perpetuity** For all time, forever, as in *This land was given to the state in perpetuity.*

**in person** Also, **in the flesh.** In one's physical presence, as in *He applied for the job in person,* or *I couldn't believe it, but there she was, in the flesh.*

**in phase** see IN SYNC.

**in place 1.** In the proper or usual position or order. For example, *With everything in place, she started the slide show.* Also see PUT SOMEONE IN HIS OR HER PLACE. **2.** In the same spot, without advancing or retreating, as in *While marching in place, the band played six more songs.*

**in place of** see IN SOMEONE'S SHOES; INSTEAD OF.

**in plain English** In clear, understandable language, as in *The doctor's diagnosis was too technical; please tell us what he meant in plain English.* Also see IN SO MANY WORDS.

**in play 1.** In action or operation. For example, *A number of conflicting forces were in play, so the outcome was uncertain.* It is also put as **bring into play,** meaning "put into action," as in *The surprise witness brought new evidence into play.* **2.** In sports, in a position to be legally or easily played, as in *The ball is now in play.* **3.** In business, in a position for a possible corporate takeover, as in *After a news item said the company was in play, the price of its stock began to rise.*

**in point 1.** Relating to a subject being discussed in a direct way, as in *That is a case in point.* **2. in point of.** With reference to, in the matter of, as in *In point of the law, he is obviously wrong.* **3. in point of fact.** See IN FACT.

**in practice 1.** Actually, in fact, especially as opposed to in theory. For example, *In practice this device seems to work, although no one knows how or why.* Also see IN PRINCIPLE; PUT SOMETHING INTO PRACTICE. **2.** In the exercise of a particular profession, as in *She's a doctor and has been in practice for at least ten years.* **3.** In a state of being exercised so as to maintain one's skill, as in *This trumpeter is always in practice.* For an antonym, see OUT OF PRACTICE.

**in principle** Fundamentally, in general, but not necessarily in all details. For example, *The ambassadors accepted the idea in principle but would rely on experts to work out all the particulars.*

**in print 1.** In printed or published form, as in *You can find this information in print.* **2.** Offered for sale by a publisher, as in *The* *library has a list of all the books in print.* The antonym is **out of print,** describing material no longer offered for sale by a publisher, as in *Most of his books are out of print.*

**in private** Not in public; secretly, confidentially. For example, *The hearings will be conducted in private,* or *May I speak to you in private?* For an antonym, see IN PUBLIC.

**in progress** Going on, under way, happening, as in *She has another book in progress,* or *The game was already in progress when I arrived.*

**in proportion** see OUT OF PROPORTION.

**in public** Openly, open to public view. For example, *They've never appeared together in public.* For an antonym, see IN PRIVATE.

**in question** Under consideration, referring to the subject being discussed, as in *I don't know where he was during the period in question.* Also see CALL SOMETHING INTO QUESTION.

I

**in quest of** see IN SEARCH OF.

**inquire after** Ask about the health or condition of someone or something. For example, *She was inquiring after you in class.*

**in reach** Also, **within reach.** Within one's means or abilities or understanding. For example, *The heirs were extremely greedy, taking whatever of their aunt's came within reach,* or *Don't price this item too high; it should be in reach of the average customer.* The antonyms **out of reach** and **beyond reach** mean "unattainable"; for example, *The tickets are out of reach for most people,* or *His explanation is beyond my reach.*

**in reality** Actually, in fact, as in *He may seem slow to you, but in reality he's very intelligent.*

**in reason** Also, **within reason.** Inside the limits of good sense, justification, or practicality. For example, *We need to keep our prices in reason,* or *He promised to do what he can to help us, within reason.*

**in reference to** see IN REGARD TO.

**in regard to** Also, **as regards; in reference to** or **with reference to; with regard to; in respect to** or **with respect to.** Concerning, about. For example, *In regard to your letter, I cannot agree with your decision,* or *As regards your order, I'm not sure why it was canceled,* or *In reference to your inquiry, I'll have to ask my boss,* or *We have a few questions with regard to your recent offer,* or *With respect to your latest request, we'll be happy to oblige.* Also see RELATIVE TO.

**in relation to** see RELATIVE TO.

**in reserve** Kept back, set aside, or saved. For example, *We have a fair amount of cash in reserve,* or *The coach decided to keep the best player in reserve until the last quarter.*

**in residence** Committed to live and work in a certain place, often for a specific length of time. For example, *He loved being the college's poet in residence.* This expression originally referred to clerics whose presence was required in a specific church. It was later extended to other positions.

**in respect to** Also, **with respect to.** See IN REGARD TO.

**in retrospect** Looking backward, reflecting on the past. For example, *In retrospect, he regarded his move as the best thing he'd ever done.* This idiom uses *retrospect* in the sense of "a view of the past."

**in return** Also, **in return for.** In repayment or in order to offer something that is mutually advantageous, as in *I did her many favors and got nothing in return,* or *In return for your patience, I promise to do a really good job.*

**inroads** see MAKE INROADS INTO.

**in round numbers** Also, **in round figures.** As an estimate. For example, *How much will the new highway cost, in round numbers?* or *In round figures, a diamond of this quality is worth five thousand dollars, but it depends on the market at the time of selling.* Also see BALLPARK FIGURE.

**ins and outs** The complicated details of a situation or process. For example, *It takes a new student some time to learn the ins and outs of the school,* or *He really knows the ins and outs of how this engine works.* This usage refers to the windings and turnings of a road or path.

**in search of** Also, **in quest of.** Looking for, seeking, as in *They went to California in search of gold,* or *I went to the library in quest of a quiet place to read.*

**in season** **1.** At the right time, at the appropriate time, as in *We tried to return from our trip in good season.* **2.** Available and ready for eating, or other use; also, legal for hunting or fishing. For example, *Strawberries are now in season,* or *Let me know when trout are in season, and I'll go fishing with you.* The antonym **out of season** is used for "inopportunely," "unavailable," and also for "not in fashion." For example, *Sorry, oysters are out of season this month,* or *This style used to be very popular, but it's been out of season for several years.*

**in secret** Unknown to others, privately. For example, *They met in secret,* or *All the negotiations were done in secret.*

**in seventh heaven** In a state of bliss or extreme happiness, as in *John was in seventh heaven when the director praised his speech.* This term refers to the dwelling place of God.

**in shape** see IN CONDITION.

**in shit up to one's eyeballs** Also, **in it up to one's eyeballs.** In very serious trouble. For example, *He's in shit up to his eyeballs for writing bad checks,* or *Now we're in it up to our eyeballs.* The variant of this expression can also be used to mean that one is deeply and eagerly involved in a situation or an activity, as in *I heard he was part of the group planning the escape and in it up to his eyeballs.* [Vulgar slang]

**in short** see IN BRIEF.

**in short order** Quickly, without delay, as in *The children got ready in short order to go to the mall.*

**in short supply** Less than is needed, lacking. For example, *Skilled operators were in short supply,* or *The hotels are all full, and beds are in short supply.*

**inside** In addition to the idioms beginning with INSIDE, also see ON THE INSIDE.

**inside of** Within, in less than the whole of a period of time. For example, *They promised to return the book inside of a month.* Although some authorities believe *inside* alone expresses the same meaning, the full term is widely used.

**inside out 1.** With the inner surface turned out or revealed, as in *He wore his shirt inside out.* This expression is also used figuratively, as in *He turned the verses inside out and revealed their hidden sense.* **2.** Also, **inside and out.** Extremely well, thoroughly, especially referring to knowing something. For example, *He knows this system inside out,* or *She understands how the company works inside and out.*

**inside track, on the** A position of special advantage, as in *His relationship with me put him on the inside track with the company.* This expression refers to the inner, shorter track of a racecourse.

**in sight 1.** Within one's range of vision, as in *The sailboat was still in sight on the horizon.* **2.** Also, **in one's sight** or **in one's sights.** Before one's eyes; also, within one's awareness. For example, *In the world's sight he was at fault,* or *She had that promotion firmly in her sights.*

**in single file** see SINGLE FILE.

**in small part** see IN PART.

**insofar as** see INASMUCH AS, def. 2.

**in so many words** In those precise words; also, plainly, directly. For example, *He didn't tell me in so many words, but I understood that he planned to apply,* or *The owner has threatened, but not in so many words, to close the store.*

**in some measure** To a certain extent, as in *In some measure we owe them our thanks.* Similarly, **in large measure** means "to a considerable degree," as in *In large measure, the two sides agree.*

**in someone's** In addition to the idioms beginning with IN SOMEONE'S, also see under IN ONE'S.

**in someone's bad graces** Also, **in someone's bad books.** Out of favor with someone. For example, *The student's tardiness put him in the teacher's bad graces,* or *Making fun of the director is certain to get you in his bad books.* Also see IN SOMEONE'S GOOD GRACES.

**in someone's face 1.** In front of or against someone directly, as in *He slammed the door in her face.* **2. get in someone's face.** Annoy or pester someone. For example, *He's always getting in my face when I'm trying to meet a deadline.* Closely related is the command **get out of someone's face,** which means "stop annoying someone," as in *Get out of my face before I punch you!* Also see IN YOUR FACE; THROW IN SOMEONE'S FACE.

**in someone's good graces** Also, **in someone's good books** or **in the good graces of.** In someone's favor or good opinion, as in *The child is back in her mother's good graces,* or *He is anxious to get in the boss's good books,* or *She was always in the good graces of whoever happened to be in charge.* An antonym is **out of someone's good graces,** as in *Walking out on his speech got him out of the professor's good graces.* Another is IN SOMEONE'S BAD GRACES.

I

**in someone's hair** Annoying or bothering someone. For example, *She was constantly in my hair, overseeing everything I did,* or *Dad was working on taxes, and the children were getting in his hair.* This expression refers to entangling one's hair. The antonym **out of someone's hair** is often used as a command, as in *Get out of my hair!*

**in someone's shoes** Also, **in someone else's shoes; in someone's place** or **in someone's stead.** Acting for another person or experiencing something as another person might; in another's position or situation. For example, *If you were in my shoes, would you ask the new secretary for a date?* or *In your shoes I wouldn't accept the offer,* or *Can you go to the theater in my place?* or *He was speaking in her stead.* The idioms referring to *shoes,* with their image of stepping into someone's shoes, are generally used in a conditional clause beginning with *if.* Also see FILL SOMEONE'S SHOES; PUT SOMEONE IN HIS OR HER PLACE.

**in someone's stead** see IN SOMEONE'S SHOES; INSTEAD OF.

**insomuch as** see INASMUCH AS.

**in spades** Considerably, in the extreme; also, without restraint. For example, *They were always having money problems, in spades,* or *I told him what I really thought of him, in spades.* This expression refers to spades as the highest-ranking suit in various card games and transfers "highest" to other extremes.

**in spite of** Regardless of, in defiance of, as in *They kept on in spite of their fears,* or *In spite of my warning, the children continued to play in the street.*

**instance** see under FOR EXAMPLE.

**in state** With great ceremony, as in *The foreign leaders were dining in state at the White House.* This expression also appears in **lie in state,** said of a dead body ceremoniously presented for public view before being buried. The latter usage is generally limited to important public figures, as in *The king lay in state in the palace.*

**instead of** Also, **in lieu of** or **in place of** or **in someone's stead.** In substitution for, rather than. For example, *She wore a dress instead of slacks,* or *They had a soprano in lieu of a tenor,* or *In place of soft drinks they served fruit juice,* or *The chairman spoke in her stead.* Also see IN SOMEONE'S SHOES.

**in step 1.** Moving to a rhythm or following the movements of others, as in *The kids marched in step to the music.* **2. in step with.** Conforming to or in harmony with, as in *He was in step with the times.* The antonym to both usages is **out of step,** as in *They're out of step with the music,* or *His views are out of step with those of the committee.* Also see IN PHASE; OUT OF PHASE.

**in stitches** Laughing uncontrollably, as in *Joke after joke had me in stitches. Stitches* here refers to the sharp local pain (known as **a stitch in the side**) that can make one double over, much as a fit of laughter can.

**in stock** Available for sale or use, on hand, as in *We have several dozen tires in stock.* The antonym **out of stock** means "not available for sale," usually only temporarily. For example, *This item is out of stock now, but we expect a new order next week.*

**in store 1.** In readiness, in preparation for future use, as in *I'm keeping several videos in store for your visit.* **2. in store for.** About to experience, awaiting, as in *There's trouble in store for you.*

**in stride** see TAKE IN STRIDE.

**in style** see under GO OUT, def. 5.

**in substance 1.** In reality, essentially, as in *The mayor was in substance a civil authority.* **2.** In essence, basically, as in *I don't remember all the details, but in substance this was the plan.*

**insult** see ADD INSULT TO INJURY.

**in sync** Also, **in phase.** In a matching or synchronized way; in accord, in harmony. For example, *John and Pat often say the same thing at the same time; their minds are perfectly in sync,* or *If everyone were in phase, we could speed up the schedule.* Also see IN STEP; PHASE IN. For the antonym, see OUT OF PHASE.

**intent** see TO ALL INTENTS AND PURPOSES.

**interest** see IN ONE'S INTEREST; TAKE AN INTEREST; VESTED INTEREST; WITH INTEREST.

**interim** see IN THE INTERIM.

**in terms of 1.** As measured or indicated by, on the basis of. For example, *How far is it in terms of miles?* This usage originated in mathematics, where it refers to numerical units. **2.** In relation to, with reference to, as in *This film offers nothing in terms of entertainment.*

**in that** For the reason that, because, as in *In that you will be busy for the next few days, let's go over your paper now.*

**in that case** see IN CASE, def. 2.

**in the act 1.** Also, **in the act of.** In the process of doing something. For example, *The police caught the robber in the act,* or *I was in the act of closing the window.* **2.** Performing sexual intercourse, as in *Her father caught them in the act.*

**in the aggregate** Considered as a whole, as in *Our profits in the aggregate have been slightly higher this year.*

**in the air** In addition to the following idiom, also see CASTLES IN THE AIR; LEAVE HANGING (IN THE AIR); NOSE IN THE AIR; UP IN THE AIR.

**in the air 1.** Often thought of, in people's thoughts. For example, *There's a rumor in the air that the store is closing,* or *Christmas is in the air.* Also see IN THE WIND. **2.** See UP IN THE AIR.

**in the altogether** Also, **in the buff** or **stripped to the buff; in the raw.** Naked, nude, as in *The art class wanted a model to pose in the altogether,* or *She was stripped to the buff when the doorbell rang,* or *He always sleeps in the raw.*

**in the back** see EYES IN THE BACK OF ONE'S HEAD; STAB ONE IN THE BACK.

**in the bag** Certain of success, nearly won. For example, *The coach thought the game was in the bag,* or *Our new contract is in the bag.* Also see under WRAP UP.

**in the balance** see HANG IN THE BALANCE.

**in the ballpark** Also, **out of the ballpark.** See under BALLPARK FIGURE.

**in the bargain** see INTO THE BARGAIN.

**in the black** see under IN THE RED.

**in the blink of an eye** see WITHOUT BATTING AN EYE.

**in the blood** see IN ONE'S BLOOD.

**in the bud** see NIP IN THE BUD.

**in the buff** see IN THE ALTOGETHER.

**in the can 1.** In the bathroom, as in *He can't come to the phone; he's in the can.* The related **on the can** means "sitting on the toilet." The noun *can* is used for both the room and the toilet in this expression. **2.** Completed, as in *About a hundred pages of her next book are in the can.* This usage began in filmmaking to describe a completed motion picture, when film was literally put into a can or canister.

**in the cards** Likely or certain to happen, as in *I don't think Jim will win—it's just not in* *the cards.* This term, often used in the negative, refers to the cards used in fortunetelling.

**in the care of** see IN CHARGE, def. 3.

**in the case of** Regarding, in the matter of, in that instance. For example, *In the case of James, they decided to promote him to the next grade.* Also see IN CASE, def. 2.

**in the chips** see IN THE MONEY, def. 1.

**in the circumstances** see UNDER THE CIRCUMSTANCES.

**in the clear 1.** Free from danger or suspicion of wrongdoing, as in *The evidence showed that the suspect was actually in the clear.* **2.** Having enough money to make a profit, as in *When they added up the ticket sales, they found they were several thousand dollars in the clear.*

**in the clouds** see HEAD IN THE CLOUDS.

**in the cold light of day** Without bias or passion, without emotion, especially at a later time. For example, *They had a terrible fight about the mix-up, but in the cold light of day they realized they were both at fault.*

**in the course of** Also, **during the course of.** In the process or progress of, as in *In the course of cleaning out my closet, I found the coat you loaned me,* or *We saw some beautiful scenery during the course of our trip.* These phrases have been criticized as needlessly wordy (*in* or *during* alone are adequate), but they have a stressed rhythm that keeps them alive.

**in the dark 1.** In secret, as in *This agreement was concluded in the dark.* **2.** In a state of ignorance, uninformed, as in *I was in the dark about their plans.* This expression often appears as **keep in the dark,** meaning "intentionally keep someone uninformed," as in *They kept me in the dark about their plans.* For an antonym, see IN THE KNOW.

**in the doghouse** In disfavor, in trouble, as in *Jane knew that forgetting the check would put her in the doghouse.* This expression refers to punishing a dog that misbehaves by sending it to its outdoor kennel.

**in the doldrums** Depressed. For example, *He's been in the doldrums for most of the winter.* This expression refers to the doldrums in the ocean, a belt of calms and light winds north of the equator in which sailing ships were often left stranded when there was no wind. Also see DOWN IN THE DUMPS.

**in the driver's seat** Also, **in the saddle.** In control, in a position of authority. For example, *With the boss on vacation, he was in the driver's seat and enjoying it,* or *She waited until after the election, knowing that she'd be in the saddle then.* Also see AT THE HELM.

**in the dumps** see DOWN IN THE DUMPS.

**in the dust, leave someone** Leave someone far behind, as in a race or competition. For example, *This marketing strategy will leave the others in the dust.* This expression refers to the dust raised by a fast-moving horse or vehicle.

**in the end** Eventually, finally, as in *All will turn out well in the end.*

**in the event of** See IN CASE, def. 2.

**in the eye** In addition to the idiom beginning with IN THE EYE, also see IN ONE'S MIND'S EYE; IN THE PUBLIC EYE; LOOK SOMEONE IN THE FACE (EYE).

**in the eye of 1.** In the central point of something, as in *They were right in the eye of this controversy.* This term uses *eye* in the sense of "a central spot." **2. in the eyes of.** In the view or opinion of, from the standpoint of. For example, *In the eyes of his fans, Elvis could do no wrong,* or *In the eyes of the law, he was a fugitive.* The *eyes* here refer to their function, seeing.

**in the face** In addition to the idiom beginning with IN THE FACE, also see BLUE IN THE FACE; FLY IN THE FACE; LOOK SOMEONE IN THE FACE; RED IN THE FACE; SLAP IN THE FACE; STARE IN THE FACE; TALK SOMEONE'S ARM OFF (UNTIL ONE IS BLUE IN THE FACE).

**in the face of 1.** Despite the evidence, as in *In the face of published statistics, they insist they don't need to wear seat belts.* Also see FLY IN THE FACE OF. **2.** When confronted with something, as in *It is hard for brokers to be cheerful in the face of a falling stock market.*

**in the family way** Pregnant, as in *My niece is in the family way again.*

**in the final analysis** Also, **in the last analysis.** When all things are considered. For example, *In the final analysis, we must find ways to improve our sales,* or *I can, in the last analysis, talk only about my own work.*

**in the first place 1.** From the beginning, from the start, before anything else. For example, *Why didn't you tell me in the first place that you've decided to leave?* or *He should have bought a new car in the first place.* **2.** As the first of several items in order of importance. This phrase is usually accompanied by **in the second place, in the third place,** and so on, as in *I'm not joining the health club because, in the first place, I don't like their hours, and in the second place, I can't afford the dues.* Also see FOR ONE.

**in the flesh** see IN PERSON.

**in the flush of** Also, **in the first flush of** or **in the full flush of.** During a sudden rush of a strong positive feeling about something, as in *In the first flush of victory, he decided to take all his friends to dinner.* This expression uses *flush* in the sense of "a feeling of emotion or passion."

**in the fullness of time** Within the proper or destined time, as in *We'll know if it's a boy* *or a girl in the fullness of time.* This expression uses *fullness* in the sense of "a complete or ample measure or degree."

**in the good graces of** see IN SOMEONE'S GOOD GRACES.

**in the groove** Performing very well, excellent; also, in fashion, up-to-date. For example, *The band was slowly getting in the groove,* or *To be in the groove this year you'll have to get a fake fur coat.* This idiom originally referred to running accurately in a channel or groove. It was taken up by jazz musicians and later began to be used more loosely. A variant, **back in the groove,** means "returning to one's old self," as in *He was very ill, but now he's back in the groove.*

**in the gutter** Proper to or from a dirty, repulsive condition. For example, *The language in that book belongs in the gutter.* An antonym, **out of the gutter,** means "away from vulgarity or filth," as in *That joke was quite innocent; get your mind out of the gutter.* This idiom uses *gutter* in the sense of "a way to move filthy waste."

**in the hands of** In the possession of someone; under the authority of. For example, *In the hands of the decorator, the hall was completely transformed.* Also see IN HAND; IN ONE'S HANDS.

**in the heat of** In the most intense or active stage of some activity or condition. For example, *One never knows how soldiers will behave in the heat of battle,* or *In the heat of the moment she accepted his proposal.*

**in the hole 1.** In debt; in trouble, especially financial trouble. For example, *Her sister spends too much money; she's always in the hole,* or *Buying all these Christmas presents will put us in the hole for the next few months.* Also see IN A BIND. **2.** In trouble in a competitive sport. For example, *At three balls and no strikes, the pitcher's in the hole.* **3.** In a card game, scoring lower than zero. For example, *Only one hand's been dealt, and I'm already three points in the hole.* This expression refers to the practice of circling a minus score in some card games. The antonym for all three usages is **out of the hole,** as in *It took careful financial management to get us out of the hole,* or *An experienced pitcher often can manage to get out of the hole.* Also see ACE IN THE HOLE.

**in the hope of** see IN HOPES OF.

**in the hot seat** see HOT SEAT.

**in the interest of** see IN ONE'S INTEREST.

**in the interim** In the meantime, as in *Her brother is in Israel, so in the interim she will handle their business.*

**in the know** Having access to special or secret information, as in *Not too many people are in the know about this project.*

**in the lap of luxury** see LAP OF LUXURY.

**in the least** Also, **in the slightest.** At all, in the smallest degree. These terms are nearly always used in a negative context. For example, *I don't care in the least what you do with the money,* or *It doesn't matter in the slightest whether or not you come.* They may also be put as **not in the least** or **not in the slightest,** as in *I am not in the least worried about the outcome,* or *The heat doesn't bother me in the slightest.* **In the slightest** is used here in the sense of "very unimportant."

**in the limelight** Also, **in the spotlight.** At the center of public attention. For example, *John loves being in the limelight,* or *The reporters made sure the new actress would be in the spotlight.* Both terms come from the theater and refer to focusing light on an important person. Also see IN THE PUBLIC EYE; STEAL THE SHOW.

**in the long run** Also, **over the long run.** Over a long period of time, in the end. For example, *He realized that in the long run, their move wouldn't seem so awful,* or *Over the long run, we should make back our money.* This expression originated as *at the long run* and may refer to a runner who continues on his course to the end. The antonym **in the short run** means "over a short period of time."

**in the loop** Provided with information and included in a decision-making process. For example, *She's new to the board, but be sure to keep her in the loop.* This expression uses *loop* in the sense of "a circle of individuals among whom information or responsibility circulates." The antonym **out of the loop** means "left out of such a circle." For example, *The chairman was consistently left him out of the loop.*

**in the lurch** see LEAVE SOMEONE IN THE LURCH.

**in the main** For the most part, chiefly, as in *It was an excellent conference in the main.*

**in the making** In the process of developing or growing, being made, as in *The reporters agreed it was history in the making.* This term is frequently used to describe the course of events, as in the example.

**in the market for** Wanting to possess, eager to have, seeking. For example, *The crowd was in the market for more entertainment,* or *I'm sure he's in the market for another fast car.*

**in the middle of 1.** Also, **in the midst of.** During, while engaged in, as in *He stopped me in the middle of my speech,* or *I'm in the midst of calculating my income tax.* Also see IN THE MIDST. **2. in the middle of nowhere.** In a very remote location, as in *We found a great little hotel out in the middle of nowhere.*

**in the midst 1.** Also, **in one's midst.** Surrounded by, among, as in *I saw a familiar* *face in the midst of the crowd,* or *To think there was a Nobel Prize winner in our midst!* **2.** See IN THE MIDDLE OF, def. 1.

**in the money** **1.** Also, **in the chips.** Rich, wealthy. For example, *When he's in the money, he's extremely generous to his friends,* or *After that box-office success, she's in the chips.* The *chips* in the variant may refer to poker chips. **2.** Placing first, second, or third in a contest on which a bet has been made, especially a horse race. For example, *My luck held today, and I ended up in the money.*

**in the mood** Disposed or inclined toward something, as in *I'm in the mood for a good long walk.* This phrase is also put in the negative, *I'm not in the mood to argue.*

**in the mouth** see DOWN IN THE DUMPS (MOUTH); LOOK A GIFT HORSE IN THE MOUTH.

**in the name of** **1.** By the authority of, as in *Open up, in the name of the law!* **2.** Also, **in someone's name.** On behalf of, as in *She made a donation in her daughter's name.* **3. in God's name** or **in heaven's name; in the name of God** or **in the name of heaven.** Requesting, as in *In the name of God, stop that noise!* or *What in heaven's name are you doing?* **4.** Under the pretext of, as in *People were killed in the name of freedom.* **5.** Under the possession or ownership of, as in *The car was in my name.* **6. in one's own name.** On one's own behalf, as in *Mary signed the check for John in her own name.*

**in the near future** Very soon, within a short time. For example, *We'll be needing a new car in the near future.* This term uses *near* in the sense of "close at hand." Also see AT HAND, def. 2.

**in the neck** see PAIN IN THE NECK.

**in the neighborhood of** Also, **in the region of.** Close to, about, as in *They paid in the neighborhood of a million dollars,* or *I don't know exactly what the exchange rate is—somewhere in the region of 95 yen to the dollar.*

**in the nick of time** Also, **just in the nick of time** or **just in time.** At the last moment, as in *The police arrived in the nick of time,* or *He got there just in time for dinner.* Also see IN TIME, def. 1.

**in the offing** In the near or immediate future; soon to come. For example, *We were delighted that exams were finished and graduation was in the offing.* This expression originally meant "in the part of the ocean visible between shore and horizon." Also see IN THE WIND.

**in the orbit of** Also, **within the orbit of.** Within a particular area or very close to someone who has a great deal of influence, as in *I hear he's currently in the orbit of the next president,* or *She's an engineer, so higher mathematics is well within her orbit.*

**in the picture, be** Understand, be informed about or be involved in a particular situation or activity. For example, *The new ambassador wanted to be in the picture for every event, small or large.* This term is also used in such expressions as **put someone in the picture,** meaning "inform or include someone," as in *Put me in the picture about the new staff,* or **out of the picture,** meaning "left ignorant of or excluded from some activity," as in *The local authorities were out of the picture when it came to drug dealers.* Also see GET THE MESSAGE (PICTURE).

**in the pink** In good health, as in *We're glad to hear you're in the pink again.* This idiom uses *pink* in the earlier sense of "the bodily form of perfection."

**in the pipeline** **1.** In process, under way, as in *The new software is in the pipeline, but it will take months to get it finished.* Also see IN THE WORKS. **2.** Budgeted for something but not yet spent, as in *There's $5 million more in the pipeline for the city schools.*

**in the public eye** Under the attention and scrutiny of the public, as in *Rock stars live in the public eye.* This usage, which is similar to IN THE LIMELIGHT, should not be confused with the similar-sounding **in the eyes of the public,** which means "in the opinion or views of the general public" (as in *In the eyes of the public, the mayor was guilty of perjury*). Also see IN THE EYE OF, def. 2.

**in the raw** see IN THE ALTOGETHER.

**in the red** In debt, as in *The owner can't keep track of funds, so half the time his company is in the red.* This expression refers to the bookkeeping practice of marking debits in red ink and credits in black. It survives even in the age of computerized accounts. So does the antonym **in the black,** for being financially solvent or out of debt, as in *Bill was happy to say they were in the black.*

**in the region of** see IN THE NEIGHBORHOOD OF.

**in there pitching** Putting forth one's best effort, trying actively. For example, *After the flood, everyone was in there pitching to clean up the streets.* This term refers to the pitcher's important role in baseball.

**in the right, be** Have the support of fact, justice, or reason. For example, *Her parents were in the right when they grounded her.* For an antonym, see IN THE WRONG.

**in the right place at the right time** Able to take advantage of an opportunity, as in *He got the job because he was in the right place at the right time.*

**in the rough** see DIAMOND IN THE ROUGH.

**in the round** Visible from all sides, as in *Jerry's done an excellent job in this interview, really portraying the senator in the round.*

**in the running 1.** Entered as a competitor in a contest. For example, *Is Mary in the running for this election?* The antonym **out of the running** means "not entered as a competitor," as in *My uncle is out of the running for the job now that he's living in another state.* **2.** Having a chance to win, as in *Jean is still in the running for the promotion.* Again, **out of the running** means the opposite, as in *He's too old—he's out of the running.* Both usages refer to the entry and chances of a horse in a race.

**in the saddle** see IN THE DRIVER'S SEAT.

**in the same boat** Also, **all in the same boat.** In a similar situation, in the same position. For example, *Everyone's got too much work—we're all in the same boat.* This expression refers to the risks shared by passengers in a small boat at sea.

I

**in the same breath 1.** Also, **in one breath.** At or almost at the same time. For example, *Ed complains about having too much homework, and in the same breath he talks about going out every night,* or *The twins said, in one breath, "more cake, please."* **2. not in the same breath.** Not to be compared. For example, *Karen's a good runner, but you can't speak of her in the same breath as an Olympic athlete.* Also see IN THE SAME LEAGUE.

**in the same league** On the same level of skill, in the same class, as in *As a woodworker, Bill wishes he were in the same league as Carl, who is a master carpenter.* This expression refers to the leagues of baseball clubs, categorized as major or minor. It is often put negatively as **not in the same league,** as in *This restaurant is not in the same league as the French café across the street.*

**in the same mold** see CAST IN THE SAME MOLD.

**in the second place** see under IN THE FIRST PLACE.

**in the short run** see under IN THE LONG RUN.

**in the slightest** see IN THE LEAST.

**in the social whirl** see IN A WHIRL.

**in the soup** In trouble, as in *She mailed all the checks with the wrong postage, and now she's really in the soup.*

**in the spotlight** see IN THE LIMELIGHT.

**in the street** see under ON THE STREET.

**in the swim** Actively participating, as in *He was new in town, but he soon got in the swim at school.* This expression refers to the fishing term for a large number of fish in one area, a *swim.*

**in the teeth of 1.** Also, **into the teeth of.** Straight into, confronting, as in *The ship was headed in the teeth of the gale.* **2.** In opposition to or against the wishes of, as in *She stuck to her position in the teeth of criticism by the board members.* Also see FLY IN THE FACE OF. **3.** Facing danger or threats, as in *The tribe was in the teeth of starvation.*

**in the thick of 1.** Also, **in the thick of it.** In the center of a confused situation. For example, *Before she knew it, she found herself in the thick of the controversy,* or *If you open your mouth, you'll be in the thick of it before you know what has happened.* **2.** In the most crowded or densest part of something, as in *I was in the thick of doing my homework when she called.*

**in the throes of** In the midst of, especially of a difficult struggle. For example, *The country was in the throes of economic collapse,* or *We were in the throes of giving a formal dinner when my in-laws arrived.* The noun *throe,* meaning "a severe pain," was at first used mainly for such physical events as childbirth or dying. Today it is used both seriously (first example) and more lightly (second example).

**in the twinkling of an eye** In an instant, as in *The breakup of Yugoslavia created many warring nations in the twinkling of an eye.* This exaggerated expression refers to the very brief time it takes for an eye to blink.

**in the unlikely event that** In case something unexpected happens. For example, *In the unlikely event that I'm late, please cover for me,* or *In the unlikely event that we should have snow in May, we're still well equipped to handle it.* Also see IN CASE, def. 2.

**in the wake of 1.** Following directly, as in *In the wake of the parade came a number of small children.* This usage refers to the waves made behind a ship **2.** In the aftermath of, as a result of, as in *Famine often comes in the wake of war.*

**in the way 1.** See IN ONE'S WAY, def. 3. **2. in the way of.** In the nature of, as in *He was getting nothing in the way of pay,* or *They had nothing in the way of an excuse.*

**in the wind 1.** About to happen, as in *He knew what was in the wind and was pretty unhappy about it.* **2.** See IN THE AIR, def. 1. Both expressions refer to something being brought or blown by the wind. Also see GET WIND OF.

**in the wings** Also, **waiting in the wings.** Nearby in the background, available on short notice. For example, *Some police were in the wings in case of trouble at the rally,* or *There are at least a dozen young managers waiting in the wings for him to retire.* This expression refers to the theater, where a player waits in the wings or backstage area, unseen by the audience, for his or her turn to come on stage.

**in the works** In preparation, under development. For example, *The agent said there was a movie deal in the works,* or *He assured her that a promotion was in the works.* Also see IN THE PIPELINE, def. 1.

**in the world** see COME UP (IN THE WORLD); ON EARTH (IN THE WORLD); WITH THE BEST WILL IN THE WORLD.

**in the worst way** Desperately, very much, as in *He wanted a new computer in the worst way.*

**in the wrong** Mistaken, to blame. For example, *The banker was clearly in the wrong but refused to admit it,* or *Since he had driven straight through a red light, the other driver was the one in the wrong.* Also see AT FAULT.

**in thing, the** see under THE THING.

**in this day and age** Now, in the present, as in *In this day and age, divorce is a very common occurrence.* This phrase is redundant, since *this day* and *this age* both mean "now."

**in time** In addition to the idiom beginning with IN TIME, also see AT THIS POINT (IN TIME); IN DUE COURSE (TIME); IN GOOD TIME; IN THE NICK OF (JUST IN) TIME; ON TIME; STITCH IN TIME.

**in time** **1.** Before a time limit expires, early enough, as in *His speech begins at eight, so we've arrived in time.* It is often put as **in time for,** as in *Please come in time for dinner.* Also see IN GOOD TIME. **2.** Eventually, within an indefinite period, as in *In time you'll see that Dad was right.* Also see IN DUE COURSE. **3.** In the proper musical tempo or rhythm, as in *It's important to dance in time to the music.*

**into** In addition to the idioms beginning with INTO, also see BE INTO.

**into account** see TAKE INTO ACCOUNT.

**into circulation** see IN CIRCULATION.

**into effect** see IN EFFECT, def. 2.

**in token of** As a sign or symbol of, as in *He gave her a ring in token of his love,* or *In token of our esteem, we dedicate this hospital wing to Dr. Salk.*

**into line** see FALL IN LINE.

**in too deep** see IN DEEP, def. 1.

**into one's head** see BEAT INTO ONE'S HEAD; GET INTO ONE'S HEAD.

**into one's shell** see IN ONE'S SHELL.

**into question** see CALL SOMETHING INTO QUESTION.

**into the bargain** Also, **in the bargain.** In addition, over and above what is expected. For example, *The new researcher was an excellent chemist and a good programmer in the bargain,* or *It was very cold, and then rain and sleet were added into the bargain.*

**into the blue** see INTO THIN AIR.

**into the drink** Into the water, especially the ocean. For example, *One more wave and I thought I'd fall off the boat into the drink.*

**into the teeth of** see IN THE TEETH OF, def. 1.

**into thin air** Also, **into the blue.** Completely disappeared, as in *The report was here on my desk and now it's gone, vanished into thin air,* or *I don't know where they've gone—into the blue, for all I know.* Both of these exaggerated expressions, often preceded by *vanish,* as in the first example, use the thin atmosphere far above the earth as a reference to an unknown location. An antonym for both is **out of thin air,** meaning "from an unknown place or source." For example, *She made up this excuse out of thin air,* or *The car appeared out of thin air.* However, **out of the blue** is not precisely an antonym (see under OUT OF A CLEAR BLUE SKY).

**into trouble with** see under IN TROUBLE WITH.

**in touch, be** Also, **be in touch with.** Be in communication or contact with, as in *Be sure to be in touch once you've arrived,* or *Our representative is really in touch with the voters.* Related idioms are **get in touch,** meaning "initiate contact," as in *We tried to get in touch with you, but you were out of town;* **keep in touch** or **stay in touch,** meaning "remain in communication or contact," as in *With Jim stationed in Korea, it was hard to keep in touch,* or *Do stay in touch with us;* and **put one in touch,** which means to provide someone with the information needed to contact another person or organization. For example, *She can put you in touch with her insurance agent,* or *Could you put me in touch with a good lawyer?* All these idioms transfer physical touch to communication.

**in tow** In one's charge or close guidance; along with one. For example, *The older girl took the new student in tow,* or *Peter always had his family in tow.* This expression refers to the literal meaning of being pulled along.

**in trouble with** In difficulties with someone, especially an authority. For example, *If they don't paint their house, they'll be in trouble with their neighbors.* This idiom is also put as **get in trouble with** or **get into trouble with,** as in *Watch what you say, or you'll get into trouble with the teacher.* Also see HOT WATER; IN A FIX.

**in trust** In the legal possession or care of a trustee, as in *The money was held in trust for the children's education.*

**in tune** Also, **in tune with.** **1.** In agreement in musical pitch or intonation, as in *It's hard to keep a violin in tune during damp weather,* or *Dave is always in tune with the other instrumentalists.* **2.** In harmony or agreement, as in *He was in tune with the times.* The antonyms for this idiom are **not in tune** and **out of tune,** as in *My ideas are not in tune with those of the rest of the committee,* or *The lawyer was out of tune with his partners.*

**in turn** Also, **in turns.** In the proper order or one after the other; also, one at a time. For example, *Each generation in turn must deal with the same budget problems,* or *Someone must be awake at all times, so let's sleep in turns.* Also see OUT OF TURN; TAKE TURNS.

**in two shakes** Also, **in two shakes of a lamb's tail.** Very quickly, very soon, as in *I'll be with you in two shakes,* or *She'll be finished in two shakes of a lamb's tail.* The longer idiom refers to the friskiness of lambs; the shorter one may be an abbreviation of the longer one, or it may refer to the shaking of dice or any two quick movements.

**in vain** Without success, useless, as in *The project was canceled, so all our work was in vain.* Also see TAKE SOMEONE'S NAME IN VAIN.

**invent the wheel** see REINVENT THE WHEEL.

**in view 1.** Also, **within view.** Visible, in sight, as in *The end of the project is in view,* or *The mountains are just within view.* **2.** Under consideration, as in *Let's keep this suggestion in view while we talk about the project.* **3.** As an end or a goal one aims at. For example, *With the coming election in view, we should present a united front on the issues.* Also see IN VIEW OF.

**in view of 1.** See IN LIGHT OF. **2.** Also, **with a view to.** Considering, in prospect or anticipation of, as in *In view of the economic situation, he should look for a better job,* or *I started saving money with a view to going to law school.*

**involve** see GET INVOLVED WITH.

**in wait** see LIE IN WAIT.

**in waiting** In attendance, especially on a royal person. For example, *The priests who were in waiting asked him to take the last rites.* This usage still survives but has become less common with the disappearance of royalty and royal courts.

**in with, be 1.** Be in league or association with, as in *She was in with the wrong crowd.* It is also put as **get in with** or **keep in with,** meaning "become or remain in league or association with," as in *He really kept in with his high school friends even while he was in college.* **2.** See IN GOOD WITH.

**in working order** Able to function properly, as in *That company keeps our office machine in working order.*

**in your face** Defiant, confrontational; also, an exclamation of contempt. For example, *This show is not suitable for youngsters; its attitude about sex is in your face,* or *In your face, mister!* This slangy expression originated in basketball as a phrase of contempt used against the opposing team and was soon extended to other areas. Also see IN SOMEONE'S FACE, def. 2.

**iota** see NOT ONE IOTA.

**Irish** see LUCK OF THE DEVIL (IRISH).

**iron** In addition to the idioms beginning with IRON, also see PUMP IRON; STRIKE WHILE THE IRON IS HOT.

**iron hand** Absolute control, as in *He ruled the country with an iron hand.* This usage is sometimes put as **iron hand in a velvet glove,** meaning "firm but seemingly gentle control," as in *She runs the town with an iron hand in a velvet glove.*

**iron out** Work out, resolve, settle. For example, *They managed to iron out all the problems with the new production process,* or *Her daughters finally ironed out their differences.* This expression uses ironing wrinkled fabric as a reference to smoothing differences.

**irons in the fire, too many** Too many activities at once. For example, *We have too many irons in the fire to cope with moving this year.* This expression originally referred to a blacksmith heating too many irons at once and therefore spoiling some in the forging.

**I see** Also, **I see what you mean.** I understand, as in *I see, you'd rather go running in the morning while it's cool,* or *It's too early to run an ad? I see what you mean.* This idiom uses *see* in the sense of "perceive" or "comprehend." Also see AS FAR AS I CAN SEE.

**Is my face red!** see under RED IN THE FACE.

**issue** see AT ISSUE; TAKE ISSUE WITH.

**is that a fact?** Also, **is that so?** Phrases indicating that one is following what another person is saying. These expressions, which require no reply, can be used either straightforwardly, as in *You mean you've flown to Paris three times just this month? Is that a fact?* or sarcastically, expressing disbelief or contempt, as in *Just wait, I'll be promoted over you before the year is out. Oh yeah, is that so?*

**I suppose so** Also, **I guess so.** I reluctantly agree, as in *Do you want tickets to the concert? I suppose so,* or *Do you think it's going to rain? I guess so.*

**it** In addition to the idioms beginning with IT, also see HARD AT IT; THAT DOES IT; WHEN IT RAINS, IT POURS.

**itch for, have an 1.** Also, **itch to.** Have a continual restless desire for, as in *She has an itch for excitement.* **2.** Eager to do something, as in *I'm just itching to read her new novel,* or *Why are you itching to leave so early?*

**itchy fingers** Always looking for a chance to obtain or steal something. For example, *Hide your valuables when he's around; he has itchy fingers,* or *Don't get itchy fingers around my baseball cards.*

**itchy palm** Also, **itching palm.** A desire for money, greed; also, wanting a bribe. For example, *The waiter has an itchy palm; he wants a big tip,* or *The mayor was known for* *his itchy palm.* This expression refers to placing money in the palm of the hand.

**it figures** Also, **that figures.** It's (or that's) reasonable; it makes sense. For example, *Hanging it upside down sounds like a weird idea, but it figures,* or *It figures that they won't be coming this year,* or *So she's complaining again; that figures.* This idiom refers to reckoning up numbers.

**it never rains but it pours** see WHEN IT RAINS, IT POURS.

**I told you so** I warned you in advance, especially about something bad. For example, *It's too bad you missed the bus again, but remember, I told you so,* or *I admit I was wrong, but please don't say I told you so.*

**it's about time** Also, **it's high time.** See ABOUT TIME; HIGH TIME.

**it's all downhill** Also, **it's all downhill from here.** See under DOWNHILL ALL THE WAY. Also see UPHILL BATTLE.

**it's all over with** Also, **all over for.** Something or someone is completely finished, defeated, or dead. The precise meaning of this phrase depends on the context. In *This loss means that it's all over with the company,* it refers to defeat, whereas in *The vet can do no more; it's all over for the dog,* it refers to the dog's death, either approaching or actual.

**it's an ill wind** see ILL WIND.

**it's a small world** One encounters the same people, events, or situations in unexpected places. For example, *I never thought I'd run into you at a ball game—it's a small world.*

**it's a zoo** Also, **what a zoo.** This is a place or situation of confusion and/or disorder. For example, *Mary's got all these houseguests with children and pets—it's a zoo,* or *We're in the midst of moving our office, and files are all over the place—what a zoo!*

**it's no laughing matter** see NO JOKE.

**it's no use** see NO USE.

**it's one's funeral** Also, **it's not one's funeral.** One must take the consequences of one's destructive or foolish actions. This expression is used to show one's lack of sympathy for another's actions. For example, *Suppose they do get caught speeding—it's their funeral,* or *I don't care whether you quit your job—it's not my funeral.* This exaggerated term implies that an action is so bad it will result in death.

**it stands to reason** It's reasonable or to be expected. For example, *It stands to reason that if we leave late, we'll arrive late.*

**it's the thought that counts** What is important is a person having had a kind or generous idea, whether or not he or she was able to do it. For example, *The boss wanted to give all of us a raise but couldn't afford it. Oh, well, it's the thought that counts.*

**it's to die** Also, **it's to die for.** It's beyond the ordinary; it's deeply appreciated and/ or greatly desired. For example, *Her performance, it's to die!* or *That diamond ring—it's to die for!* This exaggeration is usually put as an exclamation.

**it takes all sorts** Also, **it takes all kinds.** Many different kinds of people make up the world. For example, *I would never go swimming in April, but it takes all sorts,* or *He insists on wearing sunglasses indoors and out—I guess it takes all kinds.* This expression originated as *It takes all sorts to make a world* and is often used to comment on one's own difference from others or someone else's oddity. Also see NO ACCOUNTING FOR TASTES.

**it takes getting used to** One needs to become accustomed to something. For example, *We've always had a small car, so driving a big van like this—well, it takes getting used to.* This idiom employs *used to* in the sense of "accustomed to."

**it takes one to know one** The person who expressed criticism has similar faults to the person being criticized. This is a classic response to an insult. For example, *You say she's a terrible cook? It takes one to know one!* For a synonym, see POT CALLING THE KETTLE BLACK. A near equivalent is **it takes a thief to catch a thief,** a proverb meaning "no one is better at finding a wrongdoer than another wrongdoer."

**it takes two to tango** The active cooperation of both people or groups is needed for some activity, as in *We'll never pass this bill unless both sides work out a compromise—it takes two to tango.* This expression dates from the time when the Latin American tango became a very popular dance.

**ivory tower, an** A place or attitude of retreat, isolation from everyday affairs, as in *What does the professor know about student life, living as he does in an ivory tower?* This term is a translation of the French *tour d'ivoire* and is used most often in reference to intellectuals and artists who are not interested in daily affairs.

# Jj

**jack** In addition to the idiom beginning with JACK, also see BEFORE YOU CAN SAY JACK ROBINSON.

**jack off** see JERK OFF.

**jackpot** see HIT THE JACKPOT.

**Jack Robinson** see BEFORE YOU CAN SAY JACK ROBINSON.

**jack up** Raise or increase the price of something, as in *The cartel is jacking up oil prices again.* This term refers to the literal meaning of *jack up,* that is, "hoist with a jack."

**jam** see under GET IN A BIND.

J

**Jane Doe** see JOHN DOE, def. 2.

**jaybird** see NAKED AS A JAYBIRD.

**jazz up 1.** Enliven something, make more interesting, as in *They jazzed up the living room with a new rug,* or *They decided to include a comedy act to jazz up the program.* **2.** Modify a vehicle so as to increase its performance, as in *He wanted to jazz up his motorbike with a stronger engine.* Also see JUICE UP.

**Jekyll and Hyde** A personality alternating between good and evil behavior, as in *You never know whether my father will be a Jekyll or a Hyde.* This expression comes from a novel by Robert Louis Stevenson, *The Strange Case of Dr. Jekyll and Mr. Hyde.* Also see LEAD A DOUBLE LIFE.

**jerk *someone* around** Take unfair advantage of someone, manipulate or deceive, as in *Leave me alone; quit jerking me around!* or *He was jerking you around when he said he was home all evening.*

**jerk off** Also, **jack off.** Masturbate, as in *His roommate was always jerking off.* [Vulgar slang]

**jetsam** see FLOTSAM AND JETSAM.

**jib** see CUT OF SOMEONE'S JIB

**jiffy** see under IN A FLASH.

**jig is up** see GAME IS UP.

**jinks** see HIGH JINKS.

**job** see DO A JOB ON; HATCHET MAN (JOB); LIE DOWN (ON THE JOB); ON THE JOB; PUT-UP JOB; SOFT JOB.

**jockey for position** Maneuver or manipulate for one's own benefit, as in *The singers are always jockeying for position on stage.* This expression originally meant maneuvering a racehorse into a better position for winning. It was later transferred to other kinds of manipulation.

**Joe Six-pack** A lower-middle-class male. For example, *I don't think opera will appeal to Joe Six-pack; he'd prefer a wrestling match.* This insulting term creates the image of a man in an undershirt and a construction helmet who spends his evenings watching television and drinking an entire six-pack (six cans or bottles of beer sold in a package).

**jog someone's memory** Remind someone of something that one knows but is no longer remembering, as in *Give me a hint, something that will jog my memory.*

**John Doe 1.** Also, **John Q. Public** or **Joe Blow.** An average undistinguished man; also, the average citizen. For example, *This television show is just right for a John Doe,* or *It's up to John Q. Public to go to the polls and vote.* Originally used on legal documents as an alias to protect a witness, *John Doe* later acquired the sense of "ordinary person." Also see JOE SIX-PACK. **2.** Also, **Jane Doe.** An unknown individual, as in *The police found a John Doe lying on the street last night,* or *The judge issued a warrant for the arrest of Jane Doe No. 1 and Jane Doe No. 2.*

**John Hancock** Also, **John Henry.** One's signature, as in *Just put your John Hancock on the dotted line.* This expression refers to John Hancock's prominent signature on the Declaration of Independence. The variant simply substitutes a common name.

**Johnny-come-lately** A newcomer, as in *She may be a Johnny-come-lately on the committee, but she's doing a fine job with publicity.*

**Johnny-on-the-spot** A person who is available when needed, as in *He always is there at the right time, a real Johnny-on-the-spot.* Also see ON THE SPOT, def. 2.

**John Q. Public** see JOHN DOE.

**joined at the hip** Hard to separate or unwilling to be separated. For example, *You and your new friend seem to be joined at the hip,* or *She doesn't want to be joined at the hip to anyone.*

**join forces** Act together, combine efforts. For example, *The public relations people joined forces to get better coverage for their candidates.* This expression originally referred to combining military forces.

**joint** see NOSE OUT OF JOINT; OUT OF JOINT.

**join the club** A phrase used to express sympathy for a common experience. For example, *You waited three hours for the doctor? Join the club!*

**joke** see CRACK A JOKE; DIRTY JOKE; NO JOKE; SICK JOKE; STANDING JOKE; TAKE A JOKE.

**joking** see ALL JOKING ASIDE.

**Jones** see KEEP UP (WITH THE JONESES).

**jowl** see CHEEK BY JOWL.

**joy** see BURST WITH (JOY); PRIDE AND JOY.

**judge** In addition to the idiom beginning with JUDGE, also see SOBER AS A JUDGE. Also see JUDGMENT.

**judge a book by its cover, one can't** One can't rely on outward appearances to know what something or someone is really like. For example, *He seems very quiet, but you can't judge a book by its cover.*

**judgment** see AGAINST ONE'S BETTER JUDGMENT; SIT IN JUDGMENT; SNAP JUDGMENT.

**jugular** see GO FOR, def. 4.

**juice** In addition to the idiom beginning with JUICE, also see STEW IN ONE'S OWN JUICE.

**juice up** **1.** Give something energy, spirit, or interest. For example, *They tried to juice up the party by playing loud music.* **2.** Change something to improve its performance, as in *That old jeep's motor got juiced up in the shop,* or *Lowering interest rates is one way to juice up the economy.*

**jump** In addition to the idioms beginning with JUMP, also see GET THE DROP (JUMP) ON; GO FLY A KITE (JUMP IN THE LAKE); HOP, SKIP, AND A JUMP; NOT KNOW WHERE TO TURN (WHICH WAY TO JUMP); ONE JUMP AHEAD; SKIP (JUMP) BAIL.

**jump all over** Also, **jump on** or **land on.** Scold or criticize someone. For example, *He jumped all over his son for being late,* or *The editor jumped on me for getting the names wrong,* or *She was always landing on me for something or other.* Also see JUMP DOWN SOMEONE'S THROAT.

**jump at** Also, **jump at the chance** or **jump at the bait.** Take prompt advantage of, respond quickly to an opportunity. For example, *When Dad said he'd help pay for my vacation, I jumped at the offer,* or *When the lead singer became ill, I jumped at the chance to replace her,* or *They offered a large reward, hoping that someone would jump at the bait.*

**jump bail** see SKIP BAIL.

**jump down someone's throat** Strongly criticize or disagree with someone. For example, *Just because I was ten minutes late, you needn't jump down my throat.* Also see JUMP ALL OVER.

**jump in** Also, **jump in with both feet** or **jump into the ring.** Enter into something enthusiastically; also, act too quickly. For example, *When Don found out what his job was to be, he was ready to jump in immediately,* or *As soon as they asked me to join, I jumped in with both feet,* or *When buying securities, Anne's apt to jump into the ring, no matter what the risks.* The first two usages refer to jumping into water; the third refers to entering a boxing ring.

**jumping-off place** Also, **jumping-off point** **1.** A starting point for a journey or venture, as in *This tiny village is the jumping-off place for our trip into the desert.* **2.** A very remote spot; also, the last place to be reached. For example, *This was the jumping-off point for the first gold miners in Alaska.*

**jump on** see JUMP ALL OVER.

**jump out of one's skin** Be extremely surprised or frightened. For example, *When he came in so quietly, I nearly jumped out of my skin.*

**jump the gun** Start doing something too soon, act too hastily. For example, *The local weather station jumped the gun on predicting a storm; it didn't happen for another two days.* This expression refers to starting a race before the starter's gun has gone off.

**jump the track** Suddenly switch from one thought or activity to another. For example, *Joe was describing his trip to Australia and, jumping the track, began complaining about the airline,* or *They couldn't decide on the next step, and now the whole reorganization plan has jumped the track.* This expression refers to a train going off the rails.

**jump through hoops** Do just about anything to please someone. For example, *The boss expects the entire staff to jump through hoops for him,* or *This violinist will jump through hoops for the conductor.* This expression refers to circus animals that have been trained to jump through hoops.

**jump to a conclusion** Form an opinion or a judgment too quickly, as in *Wait till you have the facts; don't jump to a conclusion.* The expression **jump to the wrong conclusion** describes an opinion that is or may be in error, as in *Let's not jump to the wrong conclusion; maybe he's just working late.*

**juncture** see AT THIS POINT (JUNCTURE).

**jungle** see LAW OF THE JUNGLE.

**junk food** Prepackaged snack food that is high in calories but low in nutritional value; also, anything attractive but having little value. For example, *She loves potato chips and other junk food,* or *When I'm sick in bed, I often resort to TV soap operas and similar junk food.*

**junk mail** Third-class mail, such as unsolicited advertisements and flyers, that is sent to everyone. For example, *While we were on vacation, the front hall filled up with junk mail.*

**jury is still out, the** No decision has been made; the public's opinion is not known. For example, *As for a possible merger, the jury is still out,* or *The jury is still out on the new* *spring fashions.* This expression refers to the jury that decides a legal case.

**just** In addition to the idioms beginning with JUST, also see ALL (JUST) THE SAME; (YOU JUST DON'T) GET IT; TAKE IT (JUST SO MUCH). Also see under JUSTICE.

**just about 1.** Almost, very nearly, as in *This job is just about done,* or *At just about midnight we'll open the champagne.* This phrase is sometimes used alone, as in *Are you finished yet? Just about.* **2. just about to.** Almost ready to do something, as in *I don't have time to talk. I was just about to leave.* These expressions use *about* in the sense of "nearly."

**just a minute** Also, **just a moment. 1.** Wait a little bit. This expression is used before explaining oneself, as in *Just a minute, I didn't mean that he was wrong,* or to stop someone from something, as in *Just a moment, I was here first.* Also see HOLD EVERYTHING. **2.** Only a very short time, as in *I'll be with you in just a minute.*

J

**just as 1.** In precisely the same way as. For example, *He made the cake just as he's always done it.* **2.** Also, **just so.** To the same degree as. For example, *She's running just as fast as her friend,* or *He intended to give them just so much work as they could do in a day.* Also see JUST SO.

**just as soon** Also, **as soon.** Rather, more readily; also, equally. For example, *I'd just as soon you took care of it,* or *I'd as soon have the lamb as the beef,* or *I would just as soon shoot myself as go to that party.* As in the last example, this expression is often used to emphasize something one does not want to do.

**just as well** Good thing that an event appearing to be an unexpected obstacle happened, as in *It's just as well you're late; dinner isn't ready yet.*

**just deserts** A deserved punishment or reward, as in *He got his just deserts when Mary divorced him.* This idiom uses *desert* in the sense of "what one deserves." The usage now occurs only in this expression. Also see JUST REWARD.

**just folks** Friendly, casual, without pretension. For example, *Politicians meeting the public like to pretend they are just folks, but that's not always true.*

**just for the record** Let's me tell you; also, let me make myself clear. For example, *Just for the record, we never agreed to the plan,* or *Just for the record, I didn't vote for him.* This expression uses *record* in the sense of "public knowledge." Also see GO ON RECORD; SET (THE RECORD) STRAIGHT.

**justice** see DO JUSTICE TO; MISCARRIAGE OF JUSTICE; POETIC JUSTICE.

**just in case** see IN CASE, def. 1.

**just in time** see IN THE NICK OF TIME.

**just like that 1.** Suddenly and, sometimes, unexpectedly. For example, *The alarm went off, just like that,* or *And then they walked out, just like that.* **2.** Also, **like that.** Very friendly or intimate with one another. For example, *Bill and his boss often see each other socially; they are just like that,* or *Those two are always together; they're like that.* This expression is usually strengthened by the speaker's holding up two fingers and either keeping them together or crossing them to show the closeness or intimacy of the parties being discussed.

**just now 1.** Exactly at this time, as in *She isn't here just now; can she call you back?* **2.** Only a moment ago, as in *As she was saying just now, they are nearly finished.*

**just one of those things** A random occurrence that can't be explained. For example, *It wasn't your fault that she failed; it was just one of those things.* Also see ONE OF THOSE DAYS.

**just reward** Also, **just rewards.** Exactly what someone has earned, either good or bad. For example, *He thinks he's getting away with cheating, but he'll get his just reward,* or *She's worked hard but will probably never get her just rewards.* Also see JUST DESERTS.

**just say the word** see SAY THE WORD.

**just so 1.** Exactly in that way, very carefully and properly, as in *The children had to be dressed just so for their aunt's wedding.* **2.** I agree, that is correct, as in *The house was a mess. Just so; I told her to clean the place up.* **3.** See JUST AS, def. 2. **4.** See AS LONG AS, def. 3.

**just the same** see ALL THE SAME, def. 2.

**just the thing** Exactly what is needed, as in *Going swimming is just the thing on a day like this,* or *Her suggestion proved to be just the thing.* Also see JUST THE TICKET.

**just the ticket** Also, **that's the ticket.** Exactly what is needed; exactly right. For example, *This van is just the ticket for carrying all our luggage,* or *That's the ticket—you're using the software very well.* Also see JUST THE THING. For a synonym, see WAY TO GO.

**just think** Consider the possibilities, as in *Just think! Tomorrow we'll be in London.* Also see TO THINK THAT.

**just what the doctor ordered** Exactly what was needed. For example, *This meat is just what the doctor ordered,* or *You've been a great help in our office—just what the doctor ordered.* This expression refers to a physician's prescription for a cure. Also see JUST THE THING.

# Kk

**kangaroo court** A self-appointed legal group that violates established legal procedure; also, a dishonest or incompetent court of law. For example, *The rebels set up a kangaroo court and condemned the prisoners to execution,* or *That judge runs a kangaroo court—he tells rape victims they should have been more careful.* This expression compares the jumping ability of kangaroos to a court that jumps to conclusions on an invalid basis.

**keel** In addition to the idiom beginning with KEEL, also see ON AN EVEN KEEL.

**keel over** Collapse, as if in a faint; also, faint. For example, *When she heard the awful news, she keeled over.* This term refers to a ship rolling on its keel and capsizing.

**keen about, be** Be enthusiastic about. For example, *He's been keen about going to law school for a long time.* It is also put as **be keen on,** which has the additional meaning "be in love with," as in *Jim's been keen on Jane for years.*

**keep** In addition to the idioms beginning with KEEP, also see EARN ONE'S KEEP; FINDERS KEEPERS (LOSERS WEEPERS); FOR KEEPS; GET (KEEP) THE BALL ROLLING; IN KEEPING WITH; (KEEP SOMEONE) IN THE DARK.

**keep abreast of** Also, **stay abreast of.** Stay or cause to stay up to date with, as in *Please keep me abreast of any change in his condition,* or *He's staying abreast of the latest weather reports.*

**keep a civil tongue in one's head** Speak politely, as in *The teacher won't allow swearing; she says we must keep a civil tongue in our heads.* This expression uses *tongue* in the sense of "a manner of speaking."

**keep after** Make a determined effort regarding something; also, continuously urge someone to do something. For example, *We'll have to keep after the dust,* or *He won't get anything done unless you keep after him.* Also see KEEP AT.

**keep a level head** Stay calm, not panic and do something that might be regretted later, as in *I was surprised that she was able to keep a level head during the crisis.* As an adjective, this idiom appears as **level-headed,** as in *He's the most level-headed person in the office.*

**keep a low profile** Stay out of public notice, avoid attracting attention to oneself. For example, *Until her appointment becomes official, she is keeping a low profile.*

**keep an eye on** see HAVE ONE'S EYE ON, def. 1.

**keep an eye out for** Also, **keep a sharp lookout for.** Be watchful for something or someone, as in *Keep an eye out for the holes in the road,* or *They told him to keep a sharp lookout for the police.* The first expression is sometimes expanded to **keep a sharp eye out for.** Also see HAVE ONE'S EYE ON; KEEP ONE'S EYES OPEN; LOOK OUT.

**keep a sharp lookout** see KEEP AN EYE OUT FOR.

**keep a stiff upper lip** Show courage in the face of pain or hard times. For example, *I know you're upset about losing the game, but keep a stiff upper lip.* This expression may refer to the trembling lips that precede bursting into tears.

**keep a straight face** Not showing one's feelings, especially not laughing. For example, *The school orchestra played so many wrong notes that I had trouble keeping a straight face.*

**keep at 1.** Persevere or persist at doing something. For example, *If you keep at your math, you'll soon master it.* It is also put as **keep at it,** as in *He kept at it all day and finally finished the report.* **2.** Nag, harass, or annoy someone, as in *You have to keep at him if you want him to do the work,* or *He keeps at me all the time.* Also see KEEP AFTER.

**keep at arm's length** see AT ARM'S LENGTH.

**keep back** see HOLD BACK.

**keep body and soul together** Stay alive, support life, as in *He earns barely enough to keep body and soul together.* This expression refers to the belief that the soul gives life to the body, which therefore cannot survive without it. Today it most often is applied to earning a living.

**keep company 1.** Also, **keep company with.** Associate with someone; also, carry on a courtship. For example, *He keeps company with a wild bunch,* or *They kept company for two years before they married.* **2. keep someone company.** Accompany or remain with someone, as in *She kept Mother company at the doctor's office,* or *Do you want me to stay and keep you company?*

**keep cool** Also, **keep a cool head; stay cool** or **be cool; take it cool.** Remain calm and under control, as in *Keep cool, they'll* *soon show up,* or *Be cool, the surprise is not spoiled,* or *You have to keep a cool head in these tense situations,* or *Sit tight, take it cool, they won't bother you again.* All these terms use *cool* in the sense of "not heated by strong emotion." Also see KEEP ONE'S COOL; PLAY IT COOL.

**keep down 1.** Hold something under control, repress; also, retain food. For example, *Keep your voice down,* or *The governor vowed to keep down the rebellion,* or *With morning sickness, she had a hard time keeping down her breakfast.* **2.** Prevent from increasing or succeeding, as in *The government was determined to keep prices down,* or *She felt that her lack of an advanced degree kept her down in terms of promotions.*

**keep from 1.** Withhold; also, prevent. For example, *What information are you keeping from me?* or *Please keep your dog from running through our garden.* **2.** Restrain oneself, hold oneself back, as in *I can hardly keep from laughing.*

**keep house** Manage a household, especially do the housework. For example, *It's difficult to find time to keep house when you work full-time.*

K

**keeping up with the Joneses** see KEEP UP, def. 1.

**keep in mind** see BEAR IN MIND.

**keep in the dark** see IN THE DARK, def. 2.

**keep in touch** see IN TOUCH.

**keep in with** see IN WITH.

**keep it up** Continue to do something, as in *They were playing loud music, and they kept it up all night long.* Also see KEEP UP, def. 4.

**keep late hours** Stay awake until late at night. For example, *Never call me before noon; I keep late hours and sleep all morning.*

**keep off 1.** Ward off something, avert, as in *She used a bug spray to keep off the mosquitoes.* **2.** Stay away from, not trespass on; also, prevent from trespassing. For example, *They put up a sign asking the public to keep off their property.* **3. keep something** or **someone off.** Not touch; also, prevent from touching, as in *Please keep your feet off the sofa.* Also see HANDS OFF.

**keep on 1.** Continue, persist, as in *They kept on singing all night.* **2.** Maintain an existing job or situation, as in *After he died, the housekeeper wondered if she would be kept on.* **3.** Cause to stay on or remain attached, as in *Keep your coat on; it's cold in here.*

**keep *someone* on a tight leash** Limit someone's freedom to act, restrain something. For example, *He keeps his children on a tight leash,* or *Say nothing, and keep your temper on a tight leash.* Also see TIGHT REIN ON.

**keep one's chin up** Be brave and firm in a difficult situation, as in *Don't let the officer intimidate you; keep your chin up,* or *Despite all the difficulty, he kept his chin up.* This expression refers to a posture of firm resolution.

**keep one's cool** Retain one's calm and poise, as in *Billy keeps his cool, no matter what the situation.* Antonyms for this slang expression include **blow one's cool** and **lose one's cool,** as in *Try not to blow your cool in front of the team,* or *Dad lost his cool when he saw Jim playing with matches.* Also see KEEP COOL.

**keep one's distance** Stay away; also, remain emotionally distant. For example, *It's wise to keep one's distance from any wild animal,* or *Since the family argued with him, Harry's been keeping his distance.*

**keep one's end up** see HOLD ONE'S END UP.

**keep one's eye on the ball** Remain alert and attentive, as in *The professor told her students to keep their eye on the ball when it came to accurate footnotes.* This expression refers to numerous sports in which players must watch a ball's path.

**keep one's eyes open** Also, **keep one's eyes peeled** or **keep one's eyes skinned.** Be watchful and observant. For example, *We should keep our eyes open for a change in the wind direction,* or *Keep your eyes peeled for the teacher.*

**keep one's fingers crossed** see CROSS ONE'S FINGERS.

**keep one's hand in** see under HAVE A HAND IN.

**keep one's hands off** see HANDS OFF.

**keep one's head 1.** Stay calm, maintain self-control, as in *When the elevator stopped between floors, Samantha said that we should keep our head.* The antonym **lose one's head** means "become confused and upset," as in *Whenever the stock market goes down sharply, people seem to lose their heads and sell.* **2. keep one's head above water.** See HEAD ABOVE WATER.

**keep one's mouth shut 1.** Be quiet. For example, *The teachers told us to keep our mouths shut during the entire presentation.* **2.** Not reveal secret or confidential information, as in *You can't tell Carol anything; she's incapable of keeping her mouth shut.* Also see HOLD ONE'S TONGUE; KEEP QUIET.

**keep one's nose clean** Stay out of trouble. For example, *Dad told me to keep my nose clean from now on or he'd cut off my allowance.*

**keep one's nose to the grindstone** see NOSE TO THE GRINDSTONE.

**keep one's own counsel** Say little or nothing about one's opinions or intentions. For example, *That teacher is notorious for keeping her own counsel; you never know what she really thinks.* This expression uses *counsel* in the sense of "a secret."

**keep one's powder dry** Stay alert, be careful, as in *Go ahead and take on the opposition, but keep your powder dry.* This expression, which originally referred to keeping gunpowder dry so that it would ignite, has long been used figuratively. Today it is less common than TAKE CARE.

**keep one's shirt on** Stay calm, be patient; not give way to temper or excitement. For example, *Keep your shirt on, Bob, they'll be here in time for the wedding.*

**keep one's temper** see HOLD ONE'S TEMPER.

**keep one's wits about one** see HAVE ONE'S WITS ABOUT ONE.

**keep one's word** Honor one's promises, as in *You can count on Richard; he'll keep his word.* This expression uses *word* in the sense of "a promise." For an antonym, see GO BACK ON.

**keep pace** Also, **keep up.** Go at the same rate or speed as others, not fall or lag behind. For example, *The runners kept pace,* or *The teacher told Jimmy's mother that he was not keeping up with the class.*

**keep *one* posted** Supply one with up-to-date information, as in *Keep me posted about your new job.* This usage refers to the accounting practice of posting the latest figures in a ledger.

**keep quiet** Also, **keep still. 1.** Also, **be quiet** or **be still.** Remain silent. For example, *Please keep quiet about the party.* Also see HOLD ONE'S TONGUE; KEEP ONE'S MOUTH SHUT. **2.** Refrain from moving, stay in the same position. For example, *The doctor gave the young boy a toy to keep him quiet while on the examining table,* or *It's hard for the baby to keep still unless she's sleeping.*

**keep tabs on** Observe carefully, keep a record of. For example, *I hate having my boss keep tabs on my every move,* or *We've got to keep tabs on outgoing mail so we can keep track of postage.* This expression uses *tab* in the sense of "an account." Also see KEEP TRACK.

**keep the ball rolling** see GET THE BALL ROLLING.

**keep the lid on** see PUT THE LID ON.

**keep the peace** Maintain public order; prevent violence. For example, *The President ordered troops to the area to keep the peace.* This expression was originally used more in the sense of police keeping public order. It gained extra usage when military forces were sent to places such as Lebanon, Haiti, and Bosnia to stop warring factions.

**keep the wolf from the door** Prevent starvation or financial ruin. For example, *In many countries, people are working simply to keep the wolf from the door, and owning a car or washing machine is just a dream,* or *Gail would take any job now, just to keep the wolf from the door.* This term refers to the wolf's fabled hunger.

**keep time 1.** Maintain the correct tempo and rhythm of music; also, mark the rhythm by foot-tapping, hand movements, or something similar. For example, *The children love to keep time by clapping their hands.* **2.** Also, **keep good time.** Indicate the correct time, as in *This watch does not keep good time.*

**keep to 1.** Stay with something, conform to, as in *Let's keep to the original purpose of this will.* **2.** Confine oneself to, as in *Whenever she didn't feel well, she kept to her bed.* Also see KEEP TO ONESELF.

**keep to oneself 1.** Avoid the company of others, value one's privacy, as in *She kept to herself all morning.* **2.** Not tell, hold secret, as in *He promised to keep the news to himself.* For a synonym, see KEEP SOMETHING UNDER ONE'S HAT.

**keep track** Remain informed, follow the course of, as in *Are you keeping track of the time?* This usage refers to following a literal track, as of footsteps. The antonym **lose track** refers to straying or wandering from a track, as in *I've lost track—what day are you leaving?*

**keep *something* under one's hat** Maintain the secrecy of something, as in *I'll tell you about it if you promise to keep it under your hat.* This usage refers to hiding a secret in one's head, covered by a hat.

**keep under wraps** see UNDER WRAPS.

**keep up 1.** Also, **keep up with.** Proceed at the same pace, continue alongside another, as in *We try to keep up with the times.* This usage, also put as KEEP PACE, appears in the phrase **keeping up with the Joneses,** which was coined by cartoonist Arthur R. Momand for the title of a series in the *New York Globe.* It means "trying to match the lifestyle of wealthier neighbors or acquaintances." For example, *Their buying a new van is just another attempt to keep up with the Joneses.* **2.** Support something, maintain, as in *They're trying to keep up their spirits while they wait for news of the crash.* Also see KEEP ONE'S CHIN UP. **3.** Maintain something in good condition, as in *Joan really kept up the property.* This usage also appears in the idiom **keep up appearances,** meaning "maintain a good front, make things look good even if they're not," as in *She was hit hard by the bad news but is trying hard to keep up appearances for the children.* **4.** Persevere, carry on, prolong, as in *Keep up the good work,* or *How long will this noise keep up?* Also see KEEP IT

UP. **5.** Also, **keep up with** or **keep up on.** Stay in touch, remain informed. For example, *Ann and I haven't seen each other since college, but we keep up through our annual Christmas letters,* or *We subscribe to three papers so as to keep up on current events.* **6. keep someone up.** Cause someone to remain out of bed, as in *He's keeping the children up beyond their bedtime.*

**keep watch** Also, **keep a watch on** or **keep a close watch on; watch over.** Observe with continuous attention, especially to act as a guard or for protection. For example, *Afraid that the men would return, she kept watch while the others slept,* or *They kept a close watch on the harbor, looking for signs of enemy ships.* Also see KEEP AN EYE OUT FOR.

**keg** see SITTING ON A POWDER KEG.

**kettle** In addition to the idiom beginning with KETTLE, also see POT CALLING THE KETTLE BLACK.

**kettle of fish 1.** Also, **a fine kettle of fish** or **a pretty kettle of fish.** An unpleasant or a messy situation, as in *They haven't spoken in years, and they'll both be at the wedding—that's a fine kettle of fish.* **2. a different kettle of fish** or **another kettle of fish.** A very different matter or issue, not necessarily a bad one. For example, *They're paying for the meal? That's a different kettle of fish.*

**key** In addition to the idiom beginning with KEY, also see IN KEY; UNDER LOCK AND KEY.

**key up** Make intense, excited, or nervous. For example, *The excitement of the gallery opening has me all keyed up.* This expression uses *key* in the sense of "wind up a spring-driven mechanism such as a clock."

**kibosh** see PUT THE KIBOSH ON.

**kick** In addition to the idioms beginning with KICK, also see ALIVE AND KICKING; FOR FUN (KICKS); GET A BANG (KICK) OUT OF.

**kick a habit** Also, **kick it** or **kick the habit.** Overcome or give up habitual use, especially of narcotics. For example, *Smoking is addictive; it's not easy to kick the habit.* This idiom uses *kick* in the sense of "get rid of."

**kick around 1.** Treat someone badly, abuse, as in *I'm sick and tired of being kicked around by my supervisor.* **2.** Also, **kick about.** Move from place to place, as in *They spent three years kicking around the country on their bikes,* or *We've no address; we're just kicking about until we find somewhere to settle.* **3.** Also, **kick about.** Consider, think about or discuss something; examine or try out. For example, *Let's kick this plan around for a while and see what we come up with,* or *We've been kicking about various schemes to make money.* **4.** Be available or unused, as in *This old computer has been kicking around for months—no one seems to want it.*

**kick ass** Also, **kick butt. 1.** Punish or discipline someone harshly; also, defeat soundly. For example, *That foreman's furious; he's going to kick ass before the day is over,* or *Our team is out to kick butt today.* [Vulgar slang] **2.** Be really great, as in *Her new truck really kicks butt.* [Vulgar slang]

**kick back 1.** Recoil unexpectedly and violently, as in *This rifle kicks back a lot when you fire it.* **2.** Pay back a part of one's earnings, as in *The workers were forced to kick back half their pay to the agent.* **3.** Relax, become calm, as in *When she gets home from work, she just kicks back and forgets her problems*

**kick in 1.** Contribute one's share, as in *We'll kick in half if you take care of the rest.* **2.** Also, **kick off.** Die, as in *No one knows when he'll kick in,* or *He finally kicked off yesterday.* Also see KICK THE BUCKET. **3.** Begin to operate, as in *Finally the motor kicked in and we could get started.*

**kick in the pants, a 1.** Also, **a kick in the teeth.** A humiliating setback or rejection. For example, *That rejection was a real kick in the pants,* or *That review was a kick in the teeth.* A vulgar version of these colloquial terms is **a kick in the ass,** with its variants **a kick in the butt** and **a kick in the behind. 2.** A cause of enjoyment, as in *That show was a real kick in the pants.* This meaning is virtually the opposite of def. 1 and can be distinguished from it only by the context.

**kick it** see KICK A HABIT.

**kick off 1.** Start something, begin, as in *They kicked off the celebration with a parade.* This term refers to starting play by kicking the ball in soccer, football, and similar sports. **2.** See KICK IN, def. 2.

**kick oneself** Blame oneself, scold oneself, as in *I've been kicking myself all day for forgetting the keys.*

**kick out 1.** Also, **boot out.** Throw out, dismiss, especially in a humiliating way. For example, *George said they'd been kicked out of the country club,* or *The owner booted them out of the restaurant for being loud and disorderly.* This idiom refers to expelling someone with a KICK IN THE PANTS. **2.** Supply something, especially in a sorted fashion, as in *The bureau kicked out the precise data for this month's production.*

**kick the bucket** Die, as in *All of my goldfish kicked the bucket while we were on vacation.* This moderately impolite usage has an unclear origin.

**kick the habit** see KICK A HABIT.

**kick up** Malfunction, cause trouble or pain, as in *My grandmother's arthritis is kicking up again.* Also see ACT UP. Also see the following idioms beginning with KICK UP.

**kick up a fuss** Also, **kick up a row** or **kick up a storm.** Create a disturbance; start a fight. For example, *The soup was cold, and Aunt Mary began to kick up a fuss, calling for the manager,* or *There's no need to kick up a row; the boys will leave quietly,* or *If they fire him, Carl is ready to kick up a storm.*

**kick up one's heels** Enjoy oneself, as in *When she retires, she plans to kick up her heels and travel.* Originally this expression meant "be killed." The modern sense refers to a prancing horse or energetic dancer.

**kick *someone* upstairs** Promote someone to a higher but less desirable position, especially one with less authority. For example, *Paul never forgave the company for kicking him upstairs at age 55.* This expression refers to its antonym, **kick *someone* downstairs,** simply meaning "eject."

**kid** In addition to the idioms beginning with KID, also see HANDLE WITH (KID) GLOVES; LIKE A KID IN A CANDY STORE. Also see KIDDING.

**kid around** Engage in good-humored fooling, joking, or teasing. For example, *He's always kidding around with the other boys.*

**kidding** see ALL JOKING (KIDDING) ASIDE; NO KIDDING.

**kid gloves** see HANDLE WITH GLOVES.

**kid stuff** Something very easy or simple, as in *That new computer program is kid stuff.* This usage refers to something suitable for young children, or "kids."

**kid the pants off** see PANTS OFF.

**kill** In addition to the idioms beginning with KILL, also see CURIOSITY KILLED THE CAT; DRESSED TO KILL; FIT TO KILL; IN AT THE DEATH (KILL); MAKE A KILLING.

**kill off 1.** Cause to be extinct, eliminate completely, as in *The plague killed off entire villages and towns.* **2.** Represent as dead, as in *This mystery writer kills off a new victim in almost every chapter.*

**kill or cure** Either cure what ails someone or kill the person, as in *A good long vacation will either kill you or cure you.*

**kill the goose that lays the golden eggs** Destroy a source of riches through stupidity or greed, as in *If he never gives his loyal customers a break on some items in his store, he'll kill the goose that lays the golden eggs.* This expression refers to Aesop's fable about a farmer whose goose lays one golden egg a day and who kills the goose in the mistaken belief that he'll get all the eggs at once.

**kill time** Pass time aimlessly. For example, *There was nothing to do, so I sat around killing time until dinner was ready.*

**kill two birds with one stone** Achieve two results with a single effort, as in *As long as I was in town on business, I thought I'd kill two birds and visit my uncle.* This expression is so well known that it is often shortened, as in the example.

**kill *someone* with kindness** Overwhelm or harm someone with mistaken or extreme kindness. For example, *She constantly sends me chocolates, even though she's been told I'm allergic to them—nothing like killing with kindness.*

**kilter** see OUT OF KILTER.

**kin** see KITH AND KIN.

**kind** In addition to the idiom beginning with KIND, also see ALL KINDS OF; IN KIND; NOTHING OF THE KIND; OF A KIND; TWO OF A KIND.

**kindly** see TAKE KINDLY TO.

**kindness** see KILL SOMEONE WITH KINDNESS; MILK OF HUMAN KINDNESS.

**kind of** Also, **sort of.** Rather, somewhat, as in *I'm kind of hungry,* or *The bird looked sort of like a sparrow.* This usage should not be confused with **a kind of** or **a sort of,** which refer to a member of a given category (as in *a kind of a shelter* or *a sort of a bluish color*). Also see OF A KIND.

**kindred spirit** Also, **kindred soul.** An individual with the same beliefs, attitudes, or feelings as oneself. For example, *She and I are kindred spirits when it comes to spending money.*

**king** In addition to the idiom beginning with KING, also see LIVE LIKE A KING.

**king's ransom** A huge sum of money, as in *That ring must have cost a king's ransom.* This expression originally referred to the sum required to release a king from captivity.

**kiss and make up** Settle one's differences, resolve an argument, as in *The two friends decided to kiss and make up.*

**kiss and tell** Tell a secret, as in *A real lady doesn't kiss and tell.* This idiom originally referred to betraying a romantic or sexual intimacy. It is still so used, as well as more loosely, as in *Don't ask how I voted; I don't kiss and tell.*

**kiss ass** Also, **kiss someone's ass** or **kiss up to.** Seek or gain favor by fawning or flattery, as in *I am not going to kiss as to get the raise I deserve,* or *If I could find a good way to kiss up to my boss, I would be promoted.* The first two are vulgar slang usages. The third term is a politer blend of **kiss ass** and SUCK UP TO. [Vulgar slang]

**kiss *something* good-bye** Also, **say good-bye to.** Be forced to regard as lost, ruined, or hopeless, as in *Now that both kids are sick, we'll have to kiss our vacation in Florida good-bye,* or *After causing that accident, you can say good-bye to car insurance.* This usage ironically refers to a genuine good-bye kiss and the probability that the two people will never see each other again. Also see KISS OFF, def. 2.

**kissing cousins** Two or more things that are closely related or very similar. For example, *They may be made by different manufacturers, but these two cars are kissing cousins.* This term refers to a distant relative who is well known enough to be greeted with a kiss.

**kiss of death** An action, event, or relationship that will ultimately be destructive. For example, *Some regard a royal divorce as a kiss of death to the monarchy.* This term refers to the betrayal of Jesus by Judas Iscariot, who kissed him as a way of identifying him to the soldiers who came to arrest him. It was previously called a **Judas kiss.**

**kiss off** **1.** Dismiss or reject something, as in *He kissed off their offer.* This usage refers to kissing something good-bye. **2.** Be forced to give up or regard as lost, as in *You can kiss off that promotion.* **3.** Get out, go away, as in *She told the reporters to kiss off.*

**kit and caboodle** see WHOLE KIT AND CABOODLE.

**kitchen** see EVERYTHING BUT THE KITCHEN SINK; IF YOU CAN'T STAND THE HEAT, GET OUT OF THE KITCHEN.

K

**kite** see GO FLY A KITE; HIGH AS A KITE.

**kith and kin** Friends and family, as in *Everyone was invited, kith and kin as well as distant acquaintances.* This expression originally meant "countrymen" (*kith* meaning "one's native land") and "family members." It gradually took on the present looser sense.

**kitten** see HAVE A FIT (KITTENS); WEAK AS A KITTEN.

**knee** In addition to the idioms beginning with KNEE, also see BRING TO ONE'S KNEES; KNEE-JERK REACTION; ON BENDED KNEE.

**knee-high to a grasshopper, be** Be quite young, as in *I haven't seen him since I was knee-high to a grasshopper.* This exaggerated expression refers to someone's youth.

**knee-jerk reaction, a** An automatic, unthinking response to a situation, event, or what someone has said. For example, *She hasn't really thought about what you said. Her anger was just a knee-jerk reaction.* This idiom refers to a knee's involuntary jerk when a doctor strikes it in order to test someone's reflexes.

**knell** see DEATH KNELL.

**knife** see AT GUNPOINT (KNIFEPOINT); STICK THE KNIFE IN; TURN THE KNIFE; UNDER THE KNIFE; YOU COULD CUT IT WITH A KNIFE.

**knight in shining armor** A rescuer or defender, as in *What this political party needs is a knight in shining armor to change its tarnished image.* This expression refers to a medieval knight and the rules of courtly love.

**knock** In addition to the idioms beginning with KNOCK, also see BEAT (KNOCK) INTO SOMEONE'S HEAD; BEAT (KNOCK) THE LIVING DAYLIGHTS OUT OF; CUT (KNOCK) DOWN (TO SIZE); (KNOCK ONE) OFF ONE'S FEET; SCHOOL OF HARD KNOCKS.

**knock about** Also, **knock around. 1. knock someone about** or **knock someone around** Be rough or brutal with someone, mistreat, as in *He was known to knock his wife about on a regular basis.* **2.** Wander from place to place, as in *They were knocking around Europe all summer.* **3.** Discuss or consider something, as in *They met to knock about some new ideas.* Also see KICK AROUND.

**knock back** Also, **knock it back.** Gulp down an alcoholic beverage, as in *He knocked back glass after glass of wine,* or *I hear you've been knocking it back a bit.*

**knock cold** see KNOCK OUT, def. 1.

**knock *one* dead** Greatly amuse, astonish, or thrill someone, as in *This new song will knock them dead.* Also see KNOCK THE SOCKS OFF.

**knock down** **1.** Take something apart for storage or shipping, as in *We need to knock down this chest to ship it safely overseas.* **2.** Declare something sold at an auction, as by striking a blow with a gavel. For example, *That was the last bid, and the first edition was knocked down for only three hundred dollars.* **3.** Reduce the price of something, as in *They knocked it down by another hundred dollars,* or *An overabundant harvest will knock down corn prices.* **4.** Earn something as wages, as in *She knocks down a hundred grand a year.* **5.** Steal or embezzle something, as in *He was caught knocking down the box-office receipts.* This usage may be archaic. Also see KNOCK OVER, def. 2.

**knock-down, drag-out, a** Also, **a knock down, drag out.** An extremely vicious argument or fight, as in *I just had a knock-down, drag-out with my neighbor about his kids.*

**knock *one* down with a feather** see under KNOCK ONE FOR A LOOP.

**knock 'em dead** Perform something so well, especially a public presentation, that observers are impressed, as in *You've rehearsed your role for weeks. Now go out there and knock 'em dead.*

**knock *one* for a loop** Also, **throw *one* for a loop; knock *one* down with a feather** or **knock *one* over with a feather; knock *one* sideways.** Overcome someone with surprise or astonishment, as in *The news of his death knocked me for a loop,* or *Being fired without any warning threw me for a loop,* or *Jane was knocked sideways when she found out she had won.*

**knock it off** Quit or stop doing something, as in *Knock it off, boys! That's enough noise.* This term is often used as a command. Also see KNOCK OFF.

**knock off** **1.** Take a break or rest from, stop doing something, especially quit working.

For example, *He knocked off work at noon,* or *Let's knock off at five o'clock.* Also see KNOCK IT OFF. **2.** Also, **knock out.** Dispose of or produce something easily or hastily, finish, as in *A writer of detective novels, he knocks off a book a year,* or *We can knock out a rough drawing in a few minutes.* **3.** Get rid of something, reduce, as in *She knocked off twelve pounds in a month,* or *They knocked off one third of the original price.* **4.** Kill someone, murder, as in *They decided to knock off the boss.* **5.** Copy or imitate something, especially without permission, as in *They are knocking off designer Swiss watches and selling them for a few dollars.* **6.** Hold up something, rob, as in *The gang knocked off two liquor stores in half an hour.*

**knock oneself out 1.** Make a great effort, as in *I was knocking myself out to finish on time.* This expression also is put negatively, **don't knock yourself out,** meaning "don't exert yourself; it's not worth that much effort." For a synonym, see BREAK ONE'S ASS. **2.** Enjoy yourself, have a good time, as in *You're off to Europe? Knock yourself out.* This sense is also used ironically, as in *You want to wash the dishes? Knock yourself out.* Both usages refer to knocking oneself unconscious (see KNOCK OUT).

**knock on wood** Also, **touch wood.** Express a wish that something will or will not happen, as in *This last round of treatment should cure her, knock on wood.* This expression refers to an ancient superstition that literally knocking on or touching wood will ward off evil spirits.

**knock out 1. knock someone out** or **knock someone out cold.** Make someone unconscious by a blow or some other means. For example, *It was just a swinging door, but it knocked her out,* or *Just one of those sleeping pills can knock you out cold.* **2. knock someone out.** Make someone tired, exhaust, as in *That sightseeing tour knocked me out.* **3.** Make something useless or inoperative, as in *The storm knocked out the power.* **4.** Produce something very quickly, as in *I can knock out my term paper in a week.* **5.** Be very impressed by someone or something, as in *Her new novel really knocked me out.* **6.** See KNOCK OFF, def. 2. **7.** See KNOCK ONESELF OUT.

**knock *one* over 1.** Astonish one, overcome, as in *Their resemblance completely knocked me over.* Also see KNOCK ONE FOR A LOOP. **2.** Steal something or burgle a place, as in *They knocked over one bank and headed for another.*

**knock *one* over with a feather** see KNOCK ONE FOR A LOOP.

**knock *one* sideways** see KNOCK ONE FOR A LOOP.

**knock someone's block off** Beat up someone, as in *If he doesn't leave at once, I'll knock his block off.* This exaggerated term uses *block* in the sense of "head." Also see BEAT THE LIVING DAYLIGHTS OUT OF; KNOCK THE STUFFING OUT OF.

**knock someone's socks off** see KNOCK THE SOCKS OFF.

**knock the bottom out of** Also, **knock the props out from under.** Cause to become invalid, undermine. For example, *The discovery of another planet that might support life knocks the bottom out of many theories,* or *The candidate's skilled debating knocked the props out from under her opponent.*

**knock the living daylights out of** Also, **knock the shit out of** or **knock the stuffing out of** or **knock the tar out of.** See BEAT THE LIVING DAYLIGHTS OUT OF.

**knock the socks off** Also, **knock someone's socks off.** Overwhelm, bedazzle, or amaze someone, as in *The young pianist knocked the socks off of the judges,* or *That display will knock their socks off.*

**knock the stuffing out of 1.** Give one a serious beating, as in *Try to avoid him. He's threatened to knock the stuffing out of you.* **2.** Surprise or thrill someone completely. For example, *Winning the tournament knocks the stuffing out of our coach.*

**knock together** Make or assemble something quickly or carelessly, as in *We knocked together the bookcases in about half an hour.*

**knock up 1.** Make a woman pregnant, as in *The young girl said she was afraid of getting knocked up.* **2.** Injure or damage something, as in *This coffee table got all knocked up in the moving van.*

**knot** see TIE ONE INTO KNOTS; TIE THE KNOT.

**know** In addition to the idioms beginning with KNOW, also see BEFORE YOU CAN SAY JACK ROBINSON (KNOW IT); (KNOW) BY HEART; COME IN OUT OF THE RAIN, KNOW ENOUGH TO; COMING OR GOING, NOT KNOW IF ONE IS; FOR ALL (ONE KNOWS); GOD KNOWS; IN THE KNOW; IT TAKES ONE TO KNOW ONE; LEFT HAND DOESN'T KNOW WHAT THE RIGHT HAND IS DOING; NOT KNOW BEANS; NOT KNOW SOMEONE FROM ADAM; NOT KNOW WHERE TO TURN (WHICH WAY TO JUMP); WHAT DO YOU KNOW; WHAT HAVE YOU (WHO KNOWS WHAT); WHICH IS WHICH, KNOW; YOU KNOW; YOU KNOW WHO.

**know all the answers** Also, **know a thing or two** or **know it all** or **know one's way around.** Be very knowledgeable or experienced. These idioms may be used somewhat differently, expressing overconfidence, as in *Helen always knew all the answers, or thought she did,* or competence, as in *Bob knows a thing or two about battery technology,* or surprise, as in *I thought I knew it all about plants, and then I got poison ivy,* or real expertise, as in *John knows his way around tax forms.* Also see KNOW ONE'S STUFF; KNOW THE ROPES; TRICKS OF THE TRADE.

**know a thing or two** see KNOW ALL THE ANSWERS.

**know beans** see NOT KNOW BEANS.

**know best** Be very experienced and understand the best thing to do in a situation. For example, *I'd do things differently, but you know best,* or *Let's ask the teacher what to do; she knows best.*

**know better** Be able to recognize something as wrong or not possible, as in *Mary knows better than to leave her child alone in the house,* or *Try to get in without a ticket? You should know better.*

**know by heart** see BY HEART.

**know *someone* by sight** Recognize someone or something by appearance but not know the name or other details. For example, *I know a lot of people by sight from the tennis courts.*

K

**know different** Also, **know otherwise.** Believe that one has access to information different from what other people have. For example, *He spends money like he's rich, but I know different,* or *If she knows otherwise, she'll tell you.*

**know enough to come in out of the rain** see COME IN OUT OF THE RAIN.

**know from Adam** see NOT KNOW SOMEONE FROM ADAM.

**know if one is coming or going** see COMING OR GOING.

**know it all** see KNOW ALL THE ANSWERS.

**knowledge** see LITTLE KNOWLEDGE IS A DANGEROUS THING.

**know *someone* like a book** Also, **know *something* like the back of one's hand; know *something* backwards and forwards** or **backward and forward.** Be very familiar with or knowledgeable about something; understand perfectly. For example, *I know him like a book—I'm sure he'll come,* or *I know this town like the back of my hand,* or *John knew his part backwards and forwards.* The first of these exaggerations has a close cousin in **read *someone* like a book,** which means "discern someone's intent," as in *I can read you like a book;* also see under OPEN BOOK. Also see BACKWARD AND FORWARD, def. 2; INSIDE OUT, def. 2; KNOW ALL THE ANSWERS.

**know no bounds** Have no limits, especially of an emotion, as in *My joy knew no bounds when I received your letter*

**know one's own mind** Be certain about what one wants; be decisive. For example, *Don't ask him; he's so tired that he doesn't know his own mind,* or *She certainly knows her own mind when it comes to building a house.*

**know one's place** Behave properly for one's position, rank, or status. This idiom often has the sense of "behave humbly, not criticize one's superiors," as in *Sorry, I know my place, and I can't tell you more about my supervisor's plans.* Also see PUT ONE IN ONE'S PLACE.

**know one's stuff** Be experienced or knowledgeable in one's field or in the matter at hand. For example, *She knows her stuff when it comes to Mexican history.*

**know one's way around** see KNOW ALL THE ANSWERS.

**know only too well** see under ONLY TOO.

**know perfectly well** see WELL AWARE.

**know the meaning of the word** Be aware of a particular sense of a term, as in *Does he know the meaning of the word* work? This expression is used sarcastically when the speaker is drawing attention to someone's indifference to an activity. Its negative version, **not know the meaning of the word,** is used to assert the speaker's judgment of someone's inadequacy. For example, *That child doesn't know the meaning of the word* no.

**know the ropes** Be informed about the details of a situation or task. For example, *Don't worry about her taking over that reporter's job—she already knows the ropes.* This expression refers to sailors learning the rigging so as to handle a sailing vessel's ropes. The same reference is present in **show someone the ropes,** meaning "familiarize someone with the details," as in *Your assistant is very experienced—he'll show you the ropes.*

**know the score** Also, **know what's what.** Understand what is happening; be familiar with the real story or the full situation. For example, *It will take the new boss some time to know the score,* or *When it comes to teaching youngsters to read, she knows what's what.* The first expression refers to *score* as a tally of points in a game.

**know what one is talking about** Also, **know whereof one speaks.** Be so experienced in a particular subject or area that one can usually provide useful information, as in *Listen to her advice. She knows what she's talking about,* or *Don't hang around with such people; I know whereof I speak.*

**know what's what** Be aware of what is really happening, as in *He may not talk about it much, but he knows what's what.*

**know where one is going** Have a very clear idea of one's goals and how to achieve them, as in *Since childhood he's known where he's going and has done whatever it takes to get there.*

**know where one stands** **1.** Be aware of one's position relative to others, or how one is regarded by others, as in *I'd love to know where I stand with the new boss.* **2.** Be aware of one's own opinion or feelings about something, as in *He knows where he stands on the issue of public housing.*

**know where someone is at** Aware of how someone feels about a particular subject. For example, *I have no idea of where she's at about our money situation.*

**know which side of one's bread is buttered** Be aware of where one's best interests lie, as in *He always helps out his boss; he knows which side of his bread is buttered.* This expression refers to the more favorable, or buttered, side of bread.

**know which way is up** Also, **know which end is up.** Aware of one's position; not confused or disoriented, as in *I wish I knew which way is up,* or *It will take a while for you to learn which way is up.* This idiom is also often used in the negative. For example, *She's so tired she doesn't know which way is up,* or *We've been so busy we haven't known which end is up for weeks.*

**knuckle** In addition to the idioms beginning with KNUCKLE, also see RAP SOMEONE'S KNUCKLES.

**knuckle down** **1.** Apply oneself seriously to some task or goal, as in *The professor insisted that we knuckle down and get our papers in by Friday.* This term also has a rhyming synonym, **buckle down.** **2.** See KNUCKLE UNDER.

**knuckle under** Also, **knuckle down.** Give in, acknowledge defeat, as in *The dean refused to knuckle under to the graduate students' demands,* or *He was forced to knuckle down as a result of their threats of violence.* This idiom appears to refer to a kneeling position with hands on the ground, knuckles down.

# Ll

**labor of love** Work done for one's satisfaction rather than monetary reward. For example, *The research took three years, but it was a labor of love.*

**ladder** see BOTTOM OF THE LADDER.

**ladies' man** Also, **lady's man.** A man who enjoys and attracts the company of women. For example, *Because women seemed to seek him out at parties, Dick got the reputation for being quite a ladies' man.*

**laid back** Very casual and relaxed, and sometimes, indifferent, as in *Don't worry about being late. She's pretty laid back.*

**laid up** **1.** Also, **sick in bed.** Ill and confined to bed, as in *I was laid up for a week with the flu,* or *Sally can't come outside; she's sick in bed.* **2.** Put in a safe place, as in *The ship was laid up in dock with engine trouble,* or *The hikers were laid up in a cave during the storm.* Also see under LAY IN; LAY SOMEONE LOW.

**la-la land** **1.** Los Angeles, California (often abbreviated L.A.). This expression pokes fun at the rumored oddness of the city's inhabitants. For example, *What do you expect? He has lived in la-la land for ten years, and it has rubbed off on him.* **2.** A state of being out of touch with reality, as in *I don't know what's going on with my sister—she seems to be in la-la land.* Also see NEVER-NEVER LAND.

**lam** see ON THE LAM.

**lamb** see IN TWO SHAKES (OF A LAMB'S TAIL); LIKE A LAMB TO THE SLAUGHTER.

**lame duck** An elected officeholder whose term of office has not yet expired but who has failed to be reelected and therefore cannot find much political support for programs. For example, *This lame duck President won't get much accomplished; he's only got a month left in office.*

**land** In addition to the idioms beginning with LAND also see FAT OF THE LAND; LA-LA LAND; LAY OF THE LAND; NEVER-NEVER LAND.

**land in** Also, **end up.** Arrive at, end in something. For example, *This situation could land you in a terrible mess,* or *I never thought I'd end up with a reward for excellence.* This expression uses *land* in the sense of "end."

**land of milk and honey** A goal achieved, a position with all the good things in life. For example, *He was so certain the new job would his land of milk and honey.*

**land of the living, in the** Once again up and able to participate in daily life after an illness or injury, as in *You must be feeling better. It's good to see you in the land of the living again.*

**land on** see under JUMP ALL OVER.

**lane** see FAST LANE; LOVERS' LANE.

**lap** In addition to the idioms beginning with LAP, also see DROP IN SOMEONE'S LAP.

**lap of luxury, in the** In wealthy circumstances, equipped with anything money can buy. For example, *Jane grew up in the lap of luxury.*

**lap *something* up** Take in or receive something very eagerly, as in *She loves to travel—she just laps it up,* or *The agency is lapping up whatever information their spies send in.* This expression refers to an animal drinking greedily.

**large** see AT LARGE; BIG (LARGE) AS LIFE; BY AND LARGE; COG IN THE (A LARGE) WHEEL; IN (LARGE) PART; IN SOME (LARGE) MEASURE; LOOM LARGE.

**large as life** Also, **larger than life.** See BIG AS LIFE.

**lark** see HAPPY AS THE DAY IS LONG (AS A LARK).

**lash out** Make a sudden blow or fierce verbal attack. For example, *The mule lashed out with its hind legs,* or *After listening to Dad's criticism of his driving, my brother lashed out at him.*

**last** In addition to the idioms beginning with LAST, also see AT LAST; AT THE LAST MINUTE; BREATHE ONE'S LAST; EACH AND EVERY (EVERY LAST ONE); FAMOUS LAST WORDS; FIRST AND LAST; HEAD FOR (THE LAST ROUNDUP); IN THE FINAL (LAST) ANALYSIS; ON ONE'S LAST LEGS; SEE THE LAST OF; TO THE LAST.

**last analysis** see FINAL ANALYSIS.

**last but not least** Last in order but not least in importance, as in *Last but not least, I want to thank you for sending me copies of my article in the paper.*

**last-ditch effort** A desperate final attempt, as in *We're making a last-ditch effort to finish on time.* This expression refers to the military sense of *last ditch,* "the last line of defense."

**last fling** A final enjoyment of freedom. For example, *He's planning to have one last fling before joining the army.*

**last gasp** The moment before something ends, as in *He was determined to stay at the* *party until the last gasp.* This idiom transfers taking one's last breath to any kind of ending.

**last laugh, have the** Succeed in the end, after some earlier difficulties. For example, *We'll have the last laugh when they learn we got the contract.* This expression, referring to laughing at the loser, gave us to the modern proverbial phrase, **he who laughs last laughs best** (or **he laughs best who laughs last**).

**last of the big spenders, the** A person who enjoys spending a lot of money. For example, *He doesn't earn that much money, but he acts like he's the last of the big spenders.* This idiom is often used sarcastically or to show mild disapproval.

**last resort** A final method to achieve some end or settle a difficulty. For example, *If you don't feel better, we'll try this new medication as a last resort.* This term originally referred to a court of law from which there was no appeal.

**last straw, the** The final irritation or problem, which even though minor makes one lose patience. For example, *I could put up with his delays and missed deadlines, but when he claimed the work was unimportant—that was the last straw!* This term is a shortening of **the straw that broke the camel's back,** which creates the vivid image of an overloaded animal being given one slight additional weight. The expression replaced the earlier *the last feather that breaks the horse's back.*

**last word, the 1.** The final statement in a verbal argument, as in *She is never satisfied unless she has the last word.* **2.** A conclusive or expert statement or treatment. For example, *This report is considered to be the last word on genetic counseling.* **3.** The power or authority of final decision, as in *In financial matters, the treasurer has the last word.* **4.** The latest thing; the newest, most fashionable of its kind. For example, *Our food processor is the last word in kitchen equipment.*

**latch onto** Also, **latch on to. 1.** Get hold of something, grasp; also, understand, grasp mentally. For example, *They latched onto a fortune in the diamond trade,* or *I quickly latched on to how the sewing machine works.* **2.** Attach oneself to someone, join in with, as in *He didn't know the way, so he latched on to one of the older children.*

**late** In addition to the idioms beginning with LATE, also see AT THE LATEST; BETTER LATE THAN NEVER; JOHNNY-COME-LATELY; KEEP LATE HOURS; OF LATE; THE LATEST; TOO LITTLE, TOO LATE. Also see under LATER.

**late in life** In old age. For example, *Isn't it rather late in life for your grandmother to go skydiving?*

**late in the day** Far advanced; also, too far advanced. For example, *It's late in the day to change the kitchen layout since we've already ordered the cabinets,* or *It's a bit late in the day for apologizing.*

**later** In addition to the idiom beginning with LATER, also see SOONER OR LATER. Also see under LATE.

**later on** After something else has happened, afterward, as in *They served the main course and, later on, the dessert,* or *When can I use the computer? Later on, when I'm done.*

**lather** see IN A LATHER.

**laugh** In addition to the idioms beginning with LAUGH, also see DIE LAUGHING; LAST LAUGH; NO JOKE (LAUGHING MATTER); SHAKE WITH LAUGHTER.

**laugh all the way to the bank** Also, **cry all the way to the bank.** Be very happy about a financial gain from something that had either been ridiculed or thought worthless. For example, *You may not think much of this comedian, but he's laughing all the way to the bank.* Despite the seeming difference between *laugh* and *cry,* the two terms are almost synonymous, the one with *cry* being used ironically and the one with *laugh,* literally.

**laugh and the world laughs with you** Keep your sense of humor, and people will sympathize with you, as in *She's always cheerful and has dozens of friends; laugh and the world laughs with you.* This expression actually is part of an ancient Latin saying that concludes, *weep and the world weeps with you.*

**laugh at** Treat something or someone lightly, make fun of. For example, *He said the other children all laughed at his jacket,* or *They stopped laughing at his theory when it proved to be correct.*

**laughing matter** see under NO JOKE.

**laugh off** Also, **laugh away.** Dismiss something as absurd or irrelevant, as in *He laughed off the suggestion that his career was over.*

**laugh one's head off** see SPLIT ONE'S SIDES.

**laugh *someone* out of court** Dismiss someone with ridicule or scorn, as in *When he told them the old car could be repaired, they laughed him out of court.* This expression originally referred to a case so laughable or unimportant that a court of law would dismiss it.

**laugh out of the other side of one's mouth** Also, **laugh on the wrong side of one's mouth** or **face.** Change from happiness to sadness, disappointment, or irritation. For example, *He'll be laughing out of the other side of his mouth when he learns that he'll have to pay for the trip.*

**laugh up one's sleeve** Celebrate secretly, hide one's amusement, as in *When she tripped over her long dress, her sister couldn't help*

L

*laughing up her sleeve.* This expression refers to hiding one's laughter in big loose sleeves.

**laundry** In addition to the idiom beginning with LAUNDRY, also see WASH ONE'S DIRTY LINEN (LAUNDRY).

**laundry list** A long list of related items, some of them unimportant. For example, *I have a whole laundry list of complaints to discuss with my boss,* or *We asked if we could pick anything up for them, and they gave us a laundry list of errands!*

**laurel** see LOOK TO ONE'S LAURELS; REST ON ONE'S LAURELS.

**law** In addition to the idioms beginning with LAW, also see ABOVE SUSPICION (THE LAW); LAY DOWN THE LAW; LETTER OF THE LAW; LONG ARM OF THE LAW; MURPHY'S LAW; POSSESSION IS NINE POINTS OF THE LAW; TAKE THE LAW INTO ONE'S HANDS; UNWRITTEN LAW.

**law and order** Strict enforcement of laws, especially for controlling crime. For example, *That candidate is always talking about law and order.*

**law of averages, the** The idea that probability will influence all events in the long term, that one will neither win nor lose all of the time. For example, *If it rains every day this week, by the law of averages we're certain to get a sunny day soon.* This term is a popular interpretation of a statistical principle, Bernoulli's theorem.

**law of the jungle, the** Survival of the strongest, as in *The recent price war among the major airlines was governed by the law of the jungle.* This term refers to the jungle as a place without ethics where brutality and self-interest are common.

**law unto oneself** A person who is totally independent, especially one who ignores established rules. For example, *You can't tell Marge how to punctuate; she's a law unto herself.*

**lay** In addition to the idioms beginning with LAY, also see LET IT LAY. Also see under LIE; PUT.

**lay about one** **1.** Strike blows on all sides, as in *When the dogs cornered the old man, he laid about him with his cane.* **2.** Act energetically, make extreme efforts, as in *When there was an opportunity for profit, he laid about him.*

**lay a finger on** Also, **put a finger on.** Barely touch something or someone, as in *You'd better not lay a finger on those documents!* or *If you lay a finger on me, I'll sue.* This expression is nearly always used as a warning. Also see PUT ONE'S FINGER ON.

**lay an egg** Fail, especially in a public performance; make a humiliating error. For example, *Carol really laid an egg last night when she forgot her lines,* or, as *Variety* put it after the stock market crash of October 1929: "Wall Street Lays An Egg." The term began in live theater and was later extended to nontheatrical failures.

**lay aside** **1.** Give up something, abandon, as in *He laid aside all hopes of winning first prize.* **2.** Also, **lay away** or **lay by.** Set apart for a reason, save for the future, as in *They lay aside enough to pay the rent,* or *Because coffee prices were rising, she laid by enough for a month,* or *The store laid away the winter coat I wanted.* The first variant gave rise to the term **layaway plan,** in which merchandise is *laid away* for a buyer who pays a deposit and receives it when payment is made in full. Also see LAY DOWN, def. 4; SET ASIDE.

**lay *something* at rest** Also, **lay *something* to rest** or **set *something* at rest.** Satisfy something, settle, as in *I'll take care of it; you can set your mind at rest,* or *The professor is sure to lay these questions to rest.* Also see AT REST; LAY TO REST.

**lay *something* at someone's door** Attribute or place the blame on someone; make someone responsible for something (usually bad). For example, *That this law failed to pass can be laid at your door, Senator.*

**lay a wager** see under LAY ODDS.

**lay away** see LAY ASIDE, def. 2.

**lay by** see LAY ASIDE, def. 2.

**lay claim to** Assert one's right to or ownership of, as in *You can't just lay claim to my office because you want it,* or *He lays claim to several fine novels.* Also see STAKE A CLAIM.

**lay down** **1.** Give something up, surrender, as in *They laid down their arms.* **2.** State something, specify, as in *The club laid down new membership rules.* **3.** Also, **lay down one's life.** Sacrifice one's life, as in *He would willingly lay down his life for his children.* **4.** Store for the future, as in *It was a great vintage year for burgundy, and Mark laid down several cases.* Also see LAY ASIDE, def. 2.

**lay down the law** Assert something positively and often arrogantly, state something rigidly. For example, *Dad laid down the law about locking up the house.* This expression uses LAY DOWN in the sense of "state something specifically."

**lay eyes on** Also, **set eyes on.** Look at, see, as in *As soon as I laid eyes on him, I knew he would be perfect for the lead in our play,* or *I'd never set eyes on such a beautiful gown.*

**lay for** Be waiting to attack someone; also, lie in wait for, as in *The gang members were laying for him in that dark alley,* or *The reporters were laying for the Vice President when he came out of the meeting.*

**lay hands on 1.** Also, **get one's hands on.** Get someone or something in one's grasp, especially to do harm. For example, *Tom's gone off with the keys again; just wait till I lay my hands on him.* **2.** Also, **get one's hands on** or **lay one's hands on** or **put one's hands on.** Find something, obtain, as in *As soon as I lay my hands on the book, I'll call you,* or *He couldn't seem to put his hands on last year's sales figures.* Also see GET HOLD OF.

**lay hold of** Grab something, seize on, as in *He clutched at branches, shrubs, anything he could lay hold of to break his fall.* Also see GET HOLD OF.

**lay in** Also, **lay up.** Stock or store something for future use, as in *We laid in supplies for the winter,* or *Are you sure you've laid up enough material?* Also see LAY ASIDE, def. 2; LAY DOWN, def. 4.

**lay into 1.** Attack someone physically, *The boys ganged up and laid into the young child.* **2.** Scold someone vigorously, as in *The teacher laid into her aide when she learned he had left the children alone in the schoolyard.* Also see PITCH INTO.

**lay it on the line** see LAY SOMETHING ON THE LINE.

**lay it on thick** Also, **lay it on with a trowel.** Exaggerate something, overstate; also, flatter someone in an extreme or insincere way. For example, *That critic laid it on thick when she said this was the greatest book she'd ever read,* or *The principal thought he'd get the senator to waive the speaker's fee if he just laid it on with a trowel.* This idiom refers to applying a thick coat of paint or plaster.

**lay low** see LAY SOMEONE LOW; LIE LOW.

**lay odds** Make a bet on terms favorable to the other party, as in *I'll lay odds that it will rain before the week is out.* The closely related **lay a wager** means "make a bet," as in *He laid a wager that Don would be late.*

**lay off 1.** Terminate a person from employment. For example, *When they lost the contract, they had to lay off a hundred workers.* This expression formerly referred to temporary dismissals, as during a recession, with the idea that workers would be hired back when conditions improved, but with the recent tendency of businesses to downsize, it has come to mean "terminate permanently." **2.** Stop doing something, quit, as in *Lay off that noise for a minute, so the baby can get to sleep,* or *She resolved to lay off smoking.* **3.** Stop bothering or annoying someone, as in *Lay off or I'll tell the teacher.*

**lay of the land, the** The nature, arrangement, or order of something, the general state of affairs, as in *Once we know the lay of the land, we can plan our advertising campaign.* A related expression is **how the land lies,** as in *Let's be cautious till we know how the land lies.* This usage originated in Britain as *the lie of the land* and is still so used there.

**lay on 1.** Cover with something, apply; also, use. For example, *He decided to lay on a second coat of primer,* or *She laid on a thick Southern accent.* Also see LAY IT ON THICK. **2.** Impose or cast something on someone, as in *The government laid a tax on landholders,* or *Dad had a way of laying the guilt for his shortcomings on his partners.* This usage is also found in **lay the blame on** or **put the blame on,** as in *Nancy could always find someone to lay the blame on,* or *Jerry put the blame on Bill.*

**lay one's cards on the table** Also, **put one's cards on the table.** Be open and honest, reveal one's position or intentions, as in *John laid his cards on the table and told her how much they could afford.* This expression refers to showing the poker hand one holds. Also see SHOW ONE'S HAND.

**lay oneself out** see PUT ONESELF OUT.

**lay *something* on the line 1.** Make something ready for payment, as in *They laid hundreds of thousands of dollars on the line to develop the new software.* **2. lay it on the line.** Speak frankly and firmly, make something clear. For example, *The professor laid it on the line: either hand in a term paper or fail the course.* **3.** Put something at risk, as in *The troops sent overseas were laying their lives on the line.*

**lay open** Also, **lay oneself open.** Expose something; also, make vulnerable to. For example, *The accountant laid open some suspicious dealings,* or *She had not laid herself open to any charge of wrongdoing.* Also see LEAVE SOMETHING OPEN, def. 2.

**lay out 1.** Make a detailed plan, design, or explanation, as in *They laid out the exact dimensions in order to construct the new display,* or *Robert laid out next year's plans for his staff.* **2.** Prepare a dead body for burial, as in *He died that morning and was laid out for the wake by afternoon.* **3.** Scold someone harshly, as in *She laid me out for breaking the vase.* **4. lay someone out.** Knock someone unconscious or to the ground, make helpless, as in *He laid him out with one good punch.* **5.** Spend something, as in *She laid out a fortune on jewelry.* **6.** Display or arrange something, especially in a particular order, as in *He asked her to lay out the merchandise in an attractive way.*

**lay over 1.** Delay dealing with something, as in *This issue will have to be laid over until our next meeting.* **2.** Make a stop in the course of a journey, as in *They had to lay over* *for two days in New Delhi until the next flight to Katmandu.* This sense gave rise to the noun **layover** for such a stopover.

**lay someone low** Overcome someone, as in *He laid him low with one good punch,* or *The flu laid us low for two weeks.* Also see LIE LOW.

**lay *something* to rest** **1.** See LAY SOMETHING AT REST. **2.** Bury someone, as in *She wanted to be laid to rest beside her husband.* This usage replaced the earlier **go to rest.**

**lay up** see LAID UP; LAY IN.

**lay waste** Ravage something, ruin, as in *The hurricane laid waste the entire seashore.* Originally referring to the destruction caused by attackers, this term has come to be used more generally.

**lead** In addition to the idioms beginning with LEAD, also see BLIND LEADING THE BLIND; GET THE LEAD OUT; GO (LEAD) ASTRAY; GO OVER (LIKE A LEAD BALLOON); YOU CAN LEAD A HORSE TO WATER.

**lead a dog's life** see DOG'S LIFE.

**lead a double life** Live as if one were two people, usually one good and one bad. For example, *They learned that his frequent travels were actually lies, and he was leading a double life, with a second home on the other side of town.* This phrase is often used for a married person who establishes a second household with a lover. Also see JEKYLL AND HYDE.

**lead *one* astray** Talk one into doing something that is wrong or illegal, as in *She told me that gang would lead me astray.*

**lead by the nose** Dominate or control someone, as in *I don't understand why she lets him lead her around by the nose.* This expression refers to an animal being led by a ring passed through its nostrils.

**lead *someone* down the garden path** Also, **lead *someone* up the garden path.** Deceive someone. For example, *Bill had quite different ideas from Tom about their new investment strategy; he was leading him down the garden path.* This expression may refer to the garden path as an intentional detour. Also see LEAD ON.

**leading question, a** A question worded so as to get particular information or a particular answer, as in *When are you selling the business?* This example assumes that the person is going to sell the business, an action that may not have been established or revealed.

**lead off** Begin, start, go first. For example, *We have a panel of three speakers, so will you lead off?*

**lead on** Trick or tempt someone into proceeding, mislead; also, deceive someone, especially pretending romantic interest. For example, *He's leading her on to reveal more of her family history,* or *She's just leading him on; she has a serious boyfriend at home.*

**lead one to** Cause one to do something. For example, *This report leads me to believe that we're in an economic recession,* or *Her unexpected pregnancy led her to take a leave of absence.*

**lead-pipe cinch** A certainty, an assured success. For example, *Finding work isn't always a lead-pipe cinch.*

**lead the way** **1.** Act as a guide, go in advance of others. For example, *We asked him to lead the way since he'd hiked this mountain before.* **2.** Be first or most important in some field or action, as in *Our teacher led the way in finding new methods of teaching algebra.*

**lead *someone* up the garden path** see LEAD SOMEONE DOWN THE GARDEN PATH.

**lead up to** Prepare gradually for something, result in gradually, as in *These events clearly led up to the attack,* or *His remarks led up to the main point of the speech, that he was going to resign next year.*

**lead with one's chin** Take a risk, behave without caution. For example, *He always says exactly what he thinks; he never minds leading with his chin.* This term refers to a boxer leaving his or her chin, a vulnerable point, unprotected.

**leaf** In addition to the idiom beginning with LEAF, also see QUAKE IN ONE'S BOOTS (LIKE A LEAF); TAKE A LEAF OUT OF SOMEONE'S BOOK; TURN OVER A NEW LEAF.

**leaf through** Turn pages, as in browsing or searching for something. For example, *There she sat, leafing through the various catalogs.* This expression uses *leaf* in the sense of "turn over the leaves of a book."

**league** see BIG LEAGUE; IN LEAGUE WITH; IN THE SAME LEAGUE.

**lean on** **1.** Rely on someone, depend on, as in *He's leaning on me for help.* **2.** Exert pressure on one, especially to obtain something or make one do something against one's will. For example, *The gangsters were leaning on local storekeepers to pay them protection money.*

**lean over backward** see BEND OVER BACKWARD.

**leap** In addition to the idioms beginning with LEAP, also see BY LEAPS AND BOUNDS; LOOK BEFORE YOU LEAP; QUANTUM LEAP. Also see under JUMP.

**leap in the dark, a** An act whose results cannot be predicted. For example, *Given today's high divorce rate, he considered marriage a leap in the dark.*

**leap of faith, a** A belief or trust in something invisible or incapable of being proved. For example, *It required a leap of faith to* *take the unusual step of transplanting an animal's heart into a human patient.*

**learn** In addition to the idioms beginning with LEARN, also see (LEARN) BY HEART; LITTLE KNOWLEDGE (LEARNING) IS A DANGEROUS THING; LIVE AND LEARN.

**learn *something* by heart** Also, **learn *something* by rote.** See under BY HEART.

**learn one's lesson** Profit from experience, especially an unhappy one. For example, *From now on she will read the instructions first; she has learned her lesson.* Also see HARD WAY.

**learn the hard way** see HARD WAY.

**learn to live with** Get used to or accustom oneself to something that is painful, annoying, or unpleasant. For example, *The doctor said nothing more could be done about improving her sight; she'd just have to learn to live with it,* or *Pat decided she didn't like the new sofa but would have to learn to live with it.*

**lease** see NEW LEASE ON LIFE.

**leash** see KEEP ON A TIGHT LEASH; STRAINING AT THE LEASH.

**least** In addition to the idioms beginning with LEAST, also see AT LEAST; IN THE LEAST; LAST BUT NOT LEAST; TO SAY THE LEAST.

**least of all** Especially not. For example, *No one cared, least of all the manager,* or *None of them will attend, least of all Jim.*

**least one can do, the** The smallest thing one can do to make something right, help someone. For example, *You've wrecked by car; the least you can do is say you're sorry,* or *The least you can do is help me with the laundry.*

**least resistance, the line of** Also, **the path of least resistance.** The easiest method, way, or course of action. For example, *He tends to do what most people seem to want, taking the line of least resistance.* This term uses *resistance* in the sense of "the physical opposition of one thing or force to another."

**leather** see HELL-BENT FOR LEATHER.

**leave** In addition to the idioms beginning with LEAVE, also see ABSENT WITHOUT LEAVE; LIKE IT OR LUMP (LEAVE) IT; TAKE IT OR LEAVE IT; TAKE LEAVE OF; TAKE ONE'S LEAVE. Also see under LET.

**leave a bad taste in one's mouth** Make a bad impression on one, as in *The argument left a bad taste in my mouth, so after that I avoided talking politics.* This expression transfers the bad taste left by eating unpleasant food to a distasteful experience.

**leave alone** see LEAVE SOMEONE ALONE.

**leave a lot to be desired** Also, **leave a great deal to be desired** or **leave much to be desired.** Be imperfect or unsatisfactory. For example, *His account of the accident leaves a lot to be desired.* This usage can also be put in a more positive way, that is, **leave nothing to be desired,** meaning "to be perfectly satisfactory," as in *His account leaves nothing to be desired.*

**leave *one* flat** Forsake or abandon someone completely, especially without warning. For example, *He didn't tell her he wasn't picking her up; he just left her flat.* Also see HIGH AND DRY; LEAVE ONE IN THE LURCH.

**leave *someone or something* hanging** Also, **leave *someone* hanging in the air** or **leave *someone* in midair.** Keep someone or something undecided, uncertain, or in suspense. For example, *Since we hadn't found a big enough hall, we left the final date for the wedding hanging,* or *She couldn't figure out a good ending for the book, so her audience was left hanging in midair.*

**leave her lay** see LET IT LAY.

**leave high and dry** see HIGH AND DRY.

**leave *someone* holding the bag** Also, **leave *someone* holding the baby.** Abandon someone, force someone to bear the responsibility or blame. For example, *Her friends said they were too busy to help with cleaning up and left her holding the bag.* This expression is often put as **be left holding the bag,** as in *When they quit the clean-up committee, Lucy was left holding the bag.* Also see LEAVE IN THE LURCH.

**leave *one* in the lurch** Abandon or desert someone in a difficult time. For example, *Jane was angry enough to quit without giving notice, leaving her boss in the lurch.* Also see (LEAVE) HIGH AND DRY; LEAVE ONE TWISTING IN THE WIND.

**leave no stone unturned** Make every possible effort, use every possible source or resource. For example, *To raise ten thousand dollars to keep the shelter open, we must leave no stone unturned.* This expression refers to an ancient Greek legend about a general who buried a large treasure in his tent when he was defeated in battle. Those seeking the treasure consulted the Oracle of Delphi, who advised them to move every stone.

**leave off 1.** Stop doing something, cease; also, stop doing or using. For example, *Mother told the children to leave off running around the house,* or *Please use a bookmark to show where you left off reading.* **2.** Omit something, as in *We found she had left off our names.*

**leave one cold 1.** Fail to impress or interest someone, as in *The orchestra's performance left us cold.* **2.** Suddenly withdraw support or help from something. For example, *He just left us cold, without even offering us a ride.*

This expression uses *cold* in the sense of "unenthusiastic" or "indifferent."

**leave *something* open 1.** Keep something undecided or unscheduled, as in *We don't know how much fabric will be needed; let's leave that open,* or *The doctor leaves Fridays open for consultation.* This expression uses *open* in the sense of "undetermined." **2. leave oneself open.** Be vulnerable to something; also, remain willing to consider. For example, *Her actions left her open to widespread criticism,* or *I left myself open to further suggestions about how to proceed.* Also see under LAY OPEN.

**leave out** Omit something, fail to include, as in *This sentence doesn't make sense; a key word has been left out.*

**leave *one* out in the cold** see OUT IN THE COLD.

**leave *something* out of account** see TAKE SOMETHING INTO ACCOUNT.

**leave someone alone** Also, **let someone alone.** Restrain from disturbing or interfering with someone. For example, *She'll manage very well if you just leave her alone,* or *Stop teasing the dog; let him alone.* Also see LEAVE SOMEONE IN PEACE; LET ALONE; LET SOMEONE OR SOMETHING BE.

**leave someone in peace** Avoid disturbing or bothering someone, as in *It's best to leave Dean in peace when he's paying the bills.* This expression uses *peace* in the sense of "undisturbed." Also see LEAVE ONE ALONE; LET SOMEONE OR SOMETHING BE.

**leave someone to his or her resources** Let one rely on oneself to do what one likes or to get out of trouble. For example, *Left to his own resources, he might well turn the hose on the dog,* or *Refusing to pay for my traffic ticket, Dad insisted on leaving me to my resources.*

**leave the door open 1.** Allow for further action or discussion. For example, *This will's terms leave the door open for fighting among the heirs.* **2.** Remain open to other possibilities or opportunities, as in *Don't take the first job you're offered. Leave the door open for better positions.* This expression transfers the invitation implied by an open door to future events. Also see OPEN THE DOOR TO.

**leave to one's own devices** Allow one to do as one wishes. For example, *Left to his own devices, he would hire someone to do the yard work.* This expression uses *device* in the sense of "a plan or scheme."

**leave *one* to someone's tender mercies** Submit to another's power or discretion, especially to an unsympathetic individual. Today this expression is always used ironically, as in *We left him to the tender mercies of that stiff-necked, arrogant nurse.*

**leave *one* twisting in the wind** Abandon someone in a time of great need, especially if he or she has relied on another person, as in *You can't just go off and leave him twisting in the wind.* Also see HIGH AND DRY; LEAVE ONE IN THE LURCH.

**leave well enough alone** Also, **let well enough alone.** Not try to change something because you might make it worse. For example, *This recipe has turned out fine in the past, so leave well enough alone.* Also see LET SLEEPING DOGS LIE.

**leave *one* without a leg to stand on** see WITHOUT A LEG TO STAND ON.

**leave word** Leave a message, as in *Please leave word at the desk when you check out,* or *I left word about my plans with the secretary; didn't she tell you?* This expression uses *word* in the sense of "information."

**left** In addition to the idioms beginning with LEFT, also see HANG A LEFT; OUT IN LEFT FIELD; RIGHT AND LEFT; TWO LEFT FEET.

**left field** see OUT IN LEFT FIELD.

**left hand doesn't know what the right hand is doing, the** The actions of two groups are uncoordinated, especially when they contradict each other, as in *Our office has placed the order, but accounting says we can't pay for more supplies this month; the left hand doesn't know what the right hand is doing.* This expression is nearly always used as a criticism.

**left-handed compliment, a** Also, **a back-handed compliment.** An insult that looks at first like an expression of praise. For example, *She said she liked my hair, but it turned out to be a left-handed compliment when she asked how long I'd been dyeing it.* This expression uses *left-handed* in the sense of "questionable or doubtful."

**left wing** The liberal or radical faction of a political group, as in *Many consider him a leader of the Democratic Party's left wing.* This expression originated in the seating practice of European legislatures, whereby those holding liberal views were assigned to the left side of the house.

**leg** In addition to the idiom beginning with LEG, also see ARM AND A LEG; BREAK A LEG; ON ONE'S LAST LEGS; PULL SOMEONE'S LEG; SHAKE A LEG; STRETCH ONE'S LEGS; TAIL BETWEEN ONE'S LEGS; WITHOUT A LEG TO STAND ON.

**leg up 1.** Assist someone, give someone a boost. For example, *Studying with her will give you a leg up for the final exam because she knows French history well.* This usage refers to helping a person get on a horse by getting a foot in the stirrup. **2.** Also, **have a leg up.** Be in a position of advantage, as in *Because of the advertising campaign, we had a leg up on the competition.*

**leisure** see AT LEISURE; AT ONE'S LEISURE.

**lend a hand** Also, **lend someone a hand** or **lend a helping hand.** Be of assistance, as in *Can you lend them a hand with putting up the flag?* or *Peter is always willing to lend a helping hand around the house,* or *Let's see if we can lend a hand.*

**lend an ear** see LEND ONE'S EAR.

**lend color to** Add to something, especially to give the appearance of truth. For example, *I'm sure he lied about reaching the summit; that part about losing his pack just lent color to the story.*

**lend itself to** Adapt to, be suitable for. For example, *The Bible lends itself to numerous interpretations,* or *This plot of land lends itself to a variety of uses.*

**lend one's ear** Also, **lend an ear.** Pay attention, listen, as in *If you'll lend me your ear, I'll tell you a secret.*

**length** see AT ARM'S LENGTH; AT LENGTH; GO TO ANY LENGTH.

**leopard cannot change its spots, a** Also, **the tiger cannot change its stripes.** One can't change one's essential nature. For example, *He's a conservative, no matter what he says; a leopard cannot change its spots.*

**less** In addition to the idioms beginning with LESS, also see COULDN'T CARE LESS; IN (LESS THAN) NO TIME; MORE OR LESS; MUCH LESS.

**lesser of two evils, the** The slightly less unpleasant of two poor choices. For example, *I'd rather stay home and miss the picnic altogether than run into my ex-boyfriend—it's the lesser of two evils.*

**lesson** see LEARN ONE'S LESSON; TEACH ONE A LESSON.

**less said the better, the** In a tense situation, saying nothing or very little is often the best thing to do. For example, *Don't respond to that remark; the less said the better.*

**less than** Not at all or hardly at all. For example, *He had a less than favorable view of the matter,* or *She had a less than adequate grasp of the subject.* This expression uses *less* in the sense of "a smaller quantity, number, or degree than is implied." The same sense appears in **less than no time,** an exaggerated term for a very short time, as in *Don't worry, he'll be here in less than no time.*

**let** In addition to the idioms beginning with LET, also see BLOW (LET) OFF STEAM; GIVE SOMEONE (LET SOMEONE HAVE) HIS OR HER HEAD; (LET SOMEONE) HAVE IT; LIVE AND LET LIVE. Also see under LEAVE.

**let alone 1.** See LEAVE SOMEONE ALONE. **2.** Not to mention, as in *We have no room for another houseguest, let alone an entire family.*

**let *someone or something* be** Leave someone or something undisturbed, not interfere with. For example, *Stop fussing with the tablecloth; let it be,* or *Stop bothering your sister. Just let her be!* Also see LEAVE SOMEONE ALONE; LEAVE SOMEONE IN PEACE.

**let bygones be bygones** What's done is done; not worry about the past, especially past errors or regrets. For example, *Bill and Tom shook hands and agreed to let bygones be bygones.*

**let down 1.** Cause something to descend, lower, as in *They let down the sails.* **2.** Also, **let up.** Slow down, lessen, as in *Sales are letting down in this quarter,* or *They didn't let up in their efforts until the end.* **3.** See LET SOMEONE DOWN. Also see LET ONE'S HAIR DOWN.

**let down easy** see under LET SOMEONE DOWN.

**let down one's hair** see LET ONE'S HAIR DOWN.

**let drop** Also, **let fall.** Say something or give a hint, either casually or by accident. For example, *He let drop the fact that he'd decided to run for office,* or *She let fall some bits of gossip about the other teachers.*

**let fly 1.** Throw an object or fire a weapon. For example, *He let fly a rotten egg at the speaker.* **2.** Attack verbally, as in *They let fly some insults laced with four-letter words.*

**let go 1.** Allow someone to escape, set free, as in *The police decided to let him go.* **2.** Also, **let go of.** Release one's hold on, as in *Please let go of my sleeve,* or *Once he starts on this subject, he never lets go.* **3. let it go.** Allow something to stand or be accepted. For example, *Let it go; we needn't discuss it further.* This usage is sometimes expanded to **let it go at that,** meaning "allow matters to stand as they are." **4.** Cease to employ someone, dismiss, as in *The company had to let twenty workers go.*

**let grass grow** see LET THE GRASS GROW UNDER ONE'S FEET.

**let her rip** see LET IT RIP.

**let *one* in on** Allow one to know about or participate in something, as in *I'm going to let you in on a little secret.*

**let it all hang out** Be totally honest in expressing feelings and opinions; hold nothing back. For example, *His friends urged him not to spare any details, to let it all hang out.*

**let it go at that** see under LET GO, def. 3.

**let it lay** Also, **leave her lay.** Allow something to rest; leave it alone. For example, *Don't discuss their gift anymore; let it lay.* The use of *her* in the variant is a slangy version of "it."

**let it rip** Also, **let her rip.** Go ahead, proceed unchecked. For example, *Once you get the tractor started, let it rip.* The use of *her* in the variant comes from the habit, primarily among men, of referring to vehicles as though they were women.

**let loose 1.** Also, **turn loose.** Release an animal or a person from confinement or restraint, as in *The next thing we knew, they'd let loose all the dogs,* or *You shouldn't turn loose a tame animal.* **2.** Say many angry words, as in *He was mad when he got home, and he let loose a stream of obscenities.*

**let me see** Also, **let's see.** I'm thinking about it or trying to remember, as in *Let me see, I'll be in Boston tomorrow and the next day,* or *Let's see, where were we when we were interrupted?*

**let off 1.** Release something by exploding; see BLOW OFF STEAM. **2.** Allow someone to go free or escape; excuse from punishment. For example, *They let her off from work early,* or *The teacher let him off with a reprimand.* Also see OFF THE HOOK.

**let off steam** see BLOW OFF STEAM.

**let on 1.** Reveal one's true feelings or a fact, allow something to be known, as in *Don't let on that you met her before.* **2.** Pretend, as in *He let on that he was very angry, but in fact he didn't care a bit.* Also see LET IN ON.

**let oneself go 1.** Behave without restraint, abandon one's inhibitions. For example, *When the music began, Jean let herself go and started a wild dance.* **2.** Neglect one's personal appearance or hygiene, as in *After her husband's death she let herself go, forgetting to bathe and staying in her nightgown all day.*

**let one's hair down** Also, **let down one's hair.** Drop one's reserve or inhibitions, behave casually or informally, as in *Whenever the two sisters get together, they let their hair down and discuss all their problems.* This expression refers to the old practice of women taking down their pinned-up long hair only in the privacy of the bedroom.

**let out 1.** Allow something to escape or run free, as in *Did you let the dog out of the yard?* Also see GET OUT; GET OUT OF. **2.** Make something known, reveal, as in *I thought it was a secret—who let it out?* Also see LET THE CAT OUT OF THE BAG. **3.** Finish, end, as in *What time does school let out?* **4.** Increase the size of a garment, as in *This coat needs to be let out across the shoulders.* This usage refers to opening some of the seams.

**let *something* ride** Also, **let *something* slide.** Allow something to be ignored or to continue in its natural course. For example, *Bill disagreed with Mary's description, but he let it ride,* or *He had a way of letting things slide.* The first term refers to things moving along as though they were riding a horse or vehicle; the variant uses *slide* in the sense of "pass by." Also see under LET SLIP.

**let sleeping dogs lie** Allow inactive problems to remain inactive, as in *She knew she should report the accident but decided to let sleeping dogs lie.* This suggestion to avoid stirring up trouble refers to waking up a fierce watchdog.

**let *something* slide** see LET SOMETHING RIDE; LET SOMETHING SLIP.

**let *something* slip 1.** Also, **let *something* slip by** or **let *something* slide by; let *something* slide.** Miss an opportunity; waste time. For example, *We forgot to buy a ticket and let our big chance slip by,* or *He let the whole day slide by.* **2.** Also, **let *something* slip out** or **let slip that.** Reveal something, usually without intending to, as in *He let it slip out that he had applied for the vacant position.* **3. let *something* slip through one's fingers.** Fail to seize an opportunity, as in *We could have won the trophy, but we let it slip through our fingers.*

**let someone** In addition to the idiom beginning with LET SOMEONE, also see under LET ONE'.

**let someone down 1.** Fail to support someone; also, disappoint someone. For example, *I was counting on John, but he let me down,* or *The team didn't want to let down the coach.* **2. let someone down easy.** Give someone bad or disappointing news in a kind way. For example, *The teacher knew that Paul would have to repeat the course and that there was no way to let him down easy.* Also see LET DOWN.

**let someone have it** see HAVE IT, def. 5.

**let's see** see LET ME SEE.

**letter** In addition to the idiom beginning with LETTER, also see CRANK CALL (LETTER); DEAD LETTER; FOUR-LETTER WORD; POISON-PEN LETTER; RED-LETTER DAY; TO THE LETTER.

**letter of the law, the** The exact wording rather than the spirit or intent. For example, *Since it was the first time he'd broken the rules, the school decided to ignore the letter of the law and just give him a warning.*

**let the cat out of the bag** Give away a secret, as in *Mom let the cat out of the bag and told us Karen was engaged.* This expression refers to the old, dishonest practice of a merchant substituting a worthless cat for a valuable pig, which is discovered only when the buyer gets home and opens the bag. Also see PIG IN A POKE.

**let the chips fall where they may** No matter what the consequences, as in *I'm going to tell the truth about what happened, and let the chips fall where they may.* This term refers to chopping wood and is usually joined to a statement that one should do what is right; that is, the woodcutter should pay attention to the main task of cutting logs and not worry about small chips.

**let the grass grow under one's feet** Delay and lose valuable time. For example,

*Write your applications today; don't let the grass grow under your feet.* This expression refers to waiting so long before doing something that grass can grow under one's feet. It is most often used in the negative, as in the example.

**let up 1.** See LET DOWN, def. 2. **2.** Cease, stop entirely, as in *The rain has let up, so we can go out.* **3. let up on.** Be or become less harsh with someone, take the pressure off, as in *Why don't you let up on the child?*

**let well enough alone** see LEAVE WELL ENOUGH ALONE.

**level** In addition to the idioms beginning with LEVEL, also see DO ONE'S (LEVEL) BEST; KEEP A LEVEL HEAD; ON THE LEVEL.

**level best** see under DO ONE'S BEST.

**level-headed** see KEEP A LEVEL HEAD.

**level off** Move toward stability or consistency, as in *Prices have leveled off.* This idiom transfers a physical flattening to a figurative one.

**level with someone** Speak honestly and openly to someone, as in *His companions advised him to level with the customs inspector.* Also see ON THE LEVEL.

**liberty** see AT LIBERTY; TAKE THE LIBERTY OF.

**lick and a promise, a** A superficial effort made without care or enthusiasm. For example, *I haven't time to do a good job of vacuuming, just enough for a lick and a promise.* This expression is believed to allude to the quick lick a cat or other animal might give itself and a promise to do more or better at some future time.

**lick *something* into shape** Also, **whip *something* into shape.** Bring something or someone into satisfactory condition or appearance, as in *The garden looks neglected, but Dad will soon lick it into shape,* or *We need at least three more practices before the team is whipped into shape.*

**lick one's chops** Also, **lick one's lips.** Show great eagerness; anticipate with great pleasure. For example, *The kids were licking their chops as Mother described the family vacation plans,* or *I couldn't help but lick my lips when she talked about the menu.* Both expressions refer to anticipating tasty food.

**lick one's wounds** Recover from injuries or hurt feelings. For example, *They were badly beaten in the debate and went home sadly to lick their wounds.* This expression refers to an animal's behavior when wounded.

**lick someone's boots** Flatter someone insincerely in order to gain an advantage, as in *This man wanted every employee to lick his boots, so he had a hard time keeping his staff.*

**lick the stuffing out of** Also, **lick the tar out of.** See under BEAT THE LIVING DAYLIGHTS OUT OF.

**lid** see BLOW THE LID OFF; FLIP ONE'S LID; PUT THE LID ON.

**lie** In addition to the idioms beginning with LIE, also see BAREFACED LIE; (LIE) IN STATE; LAY OF THE LAND (HOW THE LAND LIES); LET SLEEPING DOGS LIE; MAKE ONE'S BED AND LIE IN IT; TAKE LYING DOWN; WHITE LIE.

**lie down** Also, **lie down on the job.** Fail to perform well, be lazy. For example, *They fired him because he was always lying down on the job.* This expression refers to lying down in the sense of "resting."

**lie in** Also, **lie in one's hands** or **lie in one's power.** Rest or depend on something or someone, as in *The solution lies in research,* or *The decision lies in the President's hands,* or *It does not lie in my power to turn this situation around.* Also see LIE IN WAIT; LIE THROUGH ONE'S TEETH.

**lie in state** see under IN STATE.

**lie in wait** Remain hidden while preparing to attack, as in *The opposition was quietly lying in wait for the mayor to make his first big mistake.* This expression originally referred to physical attacks and is now often used figuratively. Also see LAY FOR.

**lie low** Also, **lay low.** Keep oneself or one's plans hidden; wait until the appropriate time. For example, *The children lay low, hoping the broken window would not be noticed,* or *The senator decided to lay low until his opponent had committed herself to raising taxes.* This expression calls up the image of a hunter in the brush, waiting for game.

**lie one's way out of** Tell a lie in order to get out of a situation, as in *She couldn't lie her way out of trouble this time.* The opposite idiom, **lie one's way into,** means to tell a lie in order to reach a goal. For example, *He lied his way into his current position because he wasn't qualified for it.*

**lie through one's teeth** Also, **lie in one's teeth.** Speak outrageous lies, as in *He was lying through his teeth when he said he'd never seen her before; they've known each other for years.*

**lieu** see under INSTEAD OF.

**lie with** Be decided by someone, dependent on. For example, *The choice of restaurant lies with you.*

**life** In addition to the idioms beginning with LIFE, also see BIG AS LIFE; BREATHE NEW LIFE INTO; BRING TO LIFE; CHANGE OF LIFE; CHARMED LIFE; COME ALIVE (TO LIFE); DOG'S LIFE; FACTS OF LIFE; FOR DEAR LIFE; FOR THE LIFE OF ONE; GET A LIFE; GOOD LIFE; HAVE AN ACTIVE FANTASY LIFE; LATE IN LIFE; LAY DOWN (ONE'S LIFE); LEAD A DOUBLE LIFE; MATTER OF LIFE AND DEATH; NEW LEASE ON LIFE; NOT ON YOUR LIFE; OF ONE'S LIFE; ONCE IN A LIFETIME; PRIME OF LIFE; PUT YEARS ON ONE'S LIFE; RISK

LIFE AND LIMB; RUN FOR IT (ONE'S LIFE); SLICE OF LIFE; SPRING TO LIFE; STAFF OF LIFE; STORY OF MY LIFE; TAKE ONE'S LIFE INTO ONE'S HANDS; TAKE SOMEONE'S LIFE; TAKE YEARS OFF ONE'S LIFE; TO SAVE ONE'S LIFE; TRUE TO (LIFE); VARIETY IS THE SPICE OF LIFE; WALK OF LIFE; WHILE THERE'S LIFE THERE'S HOPE; YOU BET (YOUR LIFE).

**life and death** see MATTER OF LIFE AND DEATH.

**life in the fast lane** see FAST LANE.

**life is too short** Not waste time on unimportant matters or unworthy emotions, such as anger or anxiety. For example, *I could get him fired, but life's too short,* or *Don't spend all day waiting for his call—life is too short.* This phrase is often used to dismiss an unimportant or unworthy concern.

**life of Riley, the** Also, **the life of Reilly.** An easy life, as in *She had enough money to take off the rest of the year and live the life of Riley.* This phrase originated in a popular song, which described what its hero would do if he suddenly came into a fortune.

**life of the party, the** A lively, amusing person who is the center of attention at a social gathering. For example, *Your cousin was the life of the party, telling one good story after another.*

L

**lift a finger** see NOT LIFE A FINGER.

**lift a hand against** see RAISE A HAND AGAINST.

**lift off** Begin flight, as in *The spacecraft was due to lift off at ten o'clock.* The *off* in this idiom means "off the ground."

**lift the curtain** see RAISE THE CURTAIN.

**lift the roof** see RAISE THE ROOF.

**light** In addition to the idioms beginning with LIGHT, also see BEGIN TO SEE DAYLIGHT; BRING TO LIGHT; COME TO LIGHT; GO LIGHT ON; GREEN LIGHT; HEAVY (LIGHT) HEART; HIDE ONE'S LIGHT UNDER A BUSHEL; IN A GOOD (BAD) LIGHT; IN LIGHT OF; IN THE COLD LIGHT OF DAY; MAKE LIGHT OF; ONCE OVER LIGHTLY; OUT COLD (LIKE A LIGHT); SEE THE LIGHT; SHED LIGHT ON; SWEETNESS AND LIGHT; TRAVEL LIGHT.

**light a fire under** Also, **build a fire under.** Urge or goad someone to action, as in *If we don't light a fire under that committee, they'll never do any work.* This idiom uses *light* in the sense of "ignite."

**light as a feather** Also, **light as air.** Extremely light in weight. This simile can be used to refer either to physical weight, as in *This load is light as a feather,* or to texture, as in *This cake is light as air.*

**light at the end of the tunnel, the** The end of a difficult situation or task, the solution to a difficult problem. For example, *It's taken three years to complete the building, but we're finally seeing the light at the end of the tunnel.*

**light dawned, the** Understanding finally came, as in *They couldn't figure out where they went wrong, but then the light dawned—they'd turned right instead of left.* This expression transfers the beginning of the day to human understanding.

**lighten up** Become or cause to become less serious or gloomy and more cheerful. For example, *Lighten up, friend—it'll turn out all right.* This slang expression transfers reducing a physical weight to a change of mood or attitude.

**light heart** see under HEAVY HEART.

**light into** Attack someone, assail, as in *She lit into him for forgetting the tickets.*

**lightly** see GET OFF (LIGHTLY); ONCE OVER LIGHTLY.

**lightning** In addition to the idiom beginning with LIGHTNING, also see LIKE GREASED LIGHTNING.

**lightning never strikes twice (in the same place)** The same misfortune will never occur again, as in *Go ahead and try your luck investing again; lightning never strikes twice.* This saying is based on a longstanding notion about lightning, which has been proved to be untrue. Nevertheless, it is so well known it is often shortened, as in the example.

**light on** Also, **light upon.** Happen upon something, come across, discover. For example, *John was delighted to light on a new solution to the problem,* or *We were following the path when suddenly we lit upon a cave.*

**light out** Leave hastily, run away, as in *Here comes the teacher—let's light out.*

**lights are on but nobody's home, the** Not really capable of performing adequately, in spite of having the appearance of being mentally competent, as in *We can't count on him to do his share; the lights are on but nobody's home.* This idiom is also often used humorously to mean "distracted or not paying attention," as in *Don't bother me right now; the lights are on but nobody's home.*

**light up** **1.** Become or cause to become more cheerful, as in *Her laughter lit up the whole room,* or *His face lit up when he saw her.* This expression transfers physical light to human moods. Also see LIGHTEN UP. **2.** Start smoking a cigar, cigarette, or pipe, as in *The minute he got outside the church, he lit up.*

**like** In addition to the idioms beginning with LIKE, also see AND THE LIKE; AVOID LIKE THE PLAGUE; COME UP (SMELLING LIKE) ROSES; CRAZY LIKE A FOX; DRINK LIKE A FISH; DROP LIKE FLIES; (TALK TO LIKE A) DUTCH UNCLE; EAT LIKE A BIRD; FEEL LIKE; FIT LIKE A GLOVE; GET ALONG (LIKE A HOUSE AFIRE); GO OVER (LIKE A LEAD BALLOON);

GRIN LIKE A CHESHIRE CAT; (DROP LIKE A) HOT POTATO; JUST LIKE THAT; KNOW LIKE A BOOK; LIVE LIKE A KING; LOOK LIKE A MILLION DOLLARS; LOOK LIKE DEATH; LOOK LIKE SOMETHING THE CAT DRAGGED IN; LOOK LIKE THE CAT THAT ATE THE CANARY; MAKE OUT LIKE A BANDIT; MIND LIKE A STEEL TRAP; NEED LIKE A HOLE IN THE HEAD; NO FOOL LIKE AN OLD FOOL; NOT ANYTHING LIKE; NO TIME LIKE THE PRESENT; OUT COLD (LIKE A LIGHT); PACKED IN LIKE SARDINES; SELL LIKE HOTCAKES; SLEEP LIKE A LOG; SOMETHING LIKE; SPREAD LIKE WILDFIRE; STICK OUT (LIKE A SORE THUMB); SWEAR LIKE A TROOPER; TAKE TO (LIKE A DUCK TO WATER); TELL IT LIKE IT IS; TREAT LIKE DIRT; TURN UP (LIKE A BAD PENNY); WAIL LIKE A BANSHEE; WATCH LIKE A HAWK; WORK LIKE A BEAVER; WORK LIKE A CHARM.

**like a bat out of hell** Moving extremely fast, as in *She ran down the street like a bat out of hell.* For a synonym, see LIKE GREASED LIGHTNING.

**like a bump on a log** Unmoving, inactive, stupidly silent. For example, *He just sat there like a bump on a log while everyone else joined in the fun.*

**like a cat on a hot tin roof** Restless or nervous, unable to remain still, as in *Nervous about the lecture he had to give, he was like a cat on a hot tin roof.*

**like a champ** Very well, very successfully, as in *He got through that job interview like a champ.* This expression, in which *champ* is short for *champion,* refers to the winner of a sports competition.

**like a chicken with its head cut off** In a frenzied manner, crazily. For example, *She ran around the station looking for her lost bag like a chicken with its head cut off.* This graphic simile refers to the fact that the body of a chicken whose head has been cut off sometimes moves about crazily before dying.

**like a dream** Very well, as in *This car handles like a dream.*

**like a drowned rat** Also, **wet as a drowned rat.** Soaking wet and a complete mess, as in *When she came in out of the rain, she looked like a drowned rat.*

**like a fish out of water** see FISH OUT OF WATER.

**like a house afire** see under GET ALONG, def. 1.

**like a kid in a candy store** Very excited, as in *When she opened her presents, she was like a kid in a candy store.* This comparison is used to describe adults who are overjoyed by something

**like a lamb to the slaughter** Also, **as lambs to the slaughter.** Innocently and helplessly, without realizing the danger. For example, *She agreed to testify, little knowing she would go like a lamb to the slaughter.*

**like anything** Extremely, intensely, as in *She cried like anything when the dog died.* This idiom substitutes *anything* for a swearword.

**like a shot** Very rapidly, as in *When they asked for volunteers, he raised his hand like a shot.* This expression refers to the rapidity of gunfire.

**like as not** Also, **as like as not** or **as likely as not.** In all probability, with an even chance, as in *Like as not, it'll rain by afternoon,* or *Likely as not, the governor will run for a second term.* In the first two terms, *like* is short for *likely* in the sense of "probably," that is, "It is as likely as it is not likely."

**like as two peas in a pod** Very similar, having a close resemblance. For example, *They're not even sisters, but they're like as two peas in a pod.* This expression refers to the peas contained in a pea pod, which do indeed look very much alike.

**like a ton of bricks** Very heavily, sparing nothing. For example, *If he doesn't like your work, he'll come down on you like a ton of bricks.* This expression often appears with COME DOWN ON (def. 1). The reference here is to the considerable weight of such a load.

L

**like clockwork** Also, **regular as clockwork.** With extreme regularity, as in *The nurse arrives every Wednesday morning just like clockwork,* or *You can count on his schedule, which is regular as clockwork,* or *Their assembly line runs like clockwork.* This idiom refers to the mechanical and therefore very regular action of a clock.

**like crazy** Also, **like mad** or **like nobody's business.** With a great deal of enthusiasm or speed, without restraint. For example, *We shopped like crazy and bought all our furniture in one day,* or *Once he's on the highway, he drives like mad,* or *The choir sang the chorus like nobody's business.*

**like death warmed over** see LOOK LIKE DEATH.

**like father, like son** In the same manner from generation to generation, as in *He's decided to run for mayor—like father, like son.* This ancient proverb sometimes appears with the counterpart **like mother, like daughter.** Also see CHIP OFF THE OLD BLOCK; FOLLOW IN SOMEONE'S FOOTSTEPS.

**like fun** Not really, certainly not. For example, *She said she'd been skiing for years—like fun she had!* or *Do I want to eat raw oysters—like fun I do.* This expression originated with the quite different meaning "energetically," a sense that is now obsolete. Also see FOR FUN.

**like gangbusters** Energetically, forcefully, loudly. For example, *They should have been quiet in the hospital, but they came in like* *gangbusters.* This expression refers to a popular radio series called *Gangbusters,* which featured explosive sound effects, such as gunfire and sirens, at the beginning of each episode.

**like greased lightning** Also, **like a blue streak** or **like the wind** or **like blazes.** Very fast, as in *He climbed down that ladder like greased lightning,* or *She kept on talking like a blue streak,* or *The children ran like the wind when they heard there'd be free ice cream.*

**like hell** **1.** Recklessly, extremely, as in *We ran like hell to catch the train.* **2.** Not at all, on the contrary, as in *You think I called her stupid? Like hell I did!* or *Like hell I can't say that to my boss.*

**like hotcakes, go** Also, **sell like hotcakes.** Be a great commercial success, as in *I'm sure this new line of coats will go like hotcakes,* or *She was thrilled that her new book was selling like hotcakes.* This term refers to *hotcakes,* another name for pancakes, which are usually eaten as quickly as they are cooked.

**like it or lump it** Also, **if you don't like it you can lump it** or **like it or leave it.** Whether or not you want to, as in *Like it or lump it, we're staying home this summer,* or *You can like it or leave it, I'm not going to their wedding.*

L

**likely as not** see LIKE AS NOT. Also see under UNLIKELY.

**like mad** see LIKE CRAZY.

**like nobody's business** see LIKE CRAZY.

**like nothing on earth** see ON EARTH, def. 2.

**like pigs in clover** Very happily, as in *They had a handsome pension and lived like pigs in clover.* This expression refers to pigs being allowed to eat as much clover, a favorite plant, as they wish.

**like pulling teeth** Very difficult, especially to get information from someone. For example, *It's like pulling teeth to get a straight answer from him.*

**like rolling off a log** see EASY AS ROLLING OFF A LOG.

**like shooting fish in a barrel** Very easy, as in *Setting up a computer nowadays is like shooting fish in a barrel.* This exaggerated comparison refers to the fact that fish make an easy target inside a barrel (as opposed to swimming freely in the sea).

**likes of, the** Also, **the like of one.** An identical or very similar person or thing; an equal or match. For example, *I've never seen the likes of this before,* or *We'll never see his like again.* This expression today is almost always put in a negative context.

**like something the cat dragged in** see LOOK LIKE SOMETHING THE CAT DRAGGED IN.

**like that** **1.** In that way or manner, having those characteristics, as in *I told him not to talk to her like that,* or *I wish I had told him what I really think, but I'm not like that.* **2.** See JUST LIKE THAT.

**like the devil** An intensifier meaning very or very bad, as in *He ran like the devil to get away from the dog,* or *You look like the devil today.*

**like there's no tomorrow** As if there will not be a next day, very quickly, as in *She's been working on that project like there's no tomorrow.*

**like to** Also, **liked to.** Come close to, be on the point of. For example, *We like to froze to death,* or *He liked to have never got away.* This expression is now used mainly in the southern United States.

**like water off a duck's back** Easily and without apparent effect. For example, *The criticism rolled off him like water off a duck's back.* This expression refers to the fact that duck feathers shed water.

**lily** see GILD THE LILY.

**limb** see OUT ON A LIMB; RISK LIFE AND LIMB; TEAR SOMEONE LIMB FROM LIMB.

**limbo** see IN LIMBO.

**limit** see GO WHOLE HOG (THE LIMIT); SKY'S THE LIMIT; THE LIMIT.

**line** In addition to the idioms beginning with LINE, also see ALL ALONG THE LINE; ALONG THE LINES OF; BLOW IT (ONE'S LINES); BOTTOM LINE; CHOW DOWN (LINE); DOWN THE LINE; DRAW A LINE BETWEEN; DRAW THE LINE AT; DROP A LINE; END OF THE LINE; FALL IN LINE; FEED SOMEONE A LINE; FIRING LINE; GET A LINE ON; GO ON (LINE); HARD LINE; HOLD THE LINE; HOOK, LINE, AND SINKER; HOT LINE; IN LINE; LAY ON THE LINE; LEAST RESISTANCE, LINE OF; ON LINE; OUT OF LINE; PARTY LINE; READ BETWEEN THE LINES; SIGN ON THE DOTTED LINE; SOMEWHERE ALONG THE LINE; STEP OUT OF LINE; TOE THE LINE.

**linen** see WASH ONE'S DIRTY LINEN IN PUBLIC.

**line of fire, in the** In the path of an an attack, as in *Whenever Ann and Jeff quarreled, I was in the line of fire.* The opposite idiom is **out of the line of fire,** as in *Don't blame me. I'm just trying to stay out of the line of fire.* This expression originally referred to the path of a bullet or other projectile, a meaning that is still in use. Also see FIRING LINE.

**line one's pockets** Accept a bribe or other illegal payment, as in *The mayor found dozens of ways to line his pockets.*

**line up** **1.** Arrange something in or form a line, as in *Betty lined up the books on the shelf,* or *The children lined up for lunch.* **2.** Organize something, make ready, make the arrangements for, as in *They lined up considerable support for the bill,* or *Nancy was supposed to line up a hall for the concert.*

**lining** see SILVER LINING.

**lion** In addition to the idiom beginning with LION, also see THROW SOMEONE TO THE WOLVES (LIONS).

**lion's share, the** The greater part or most of something, as in *Whenever they won a tennis match, Ethel claimed the lion's share of the credit,* or *As usual, Uncle Bob took the lion's share of the cake.* This expression refers to Aesop's fable about a lion that got all of a kill because its fellow hunters, an ass, a fox, and a wolf, were afraid to claim their share.

**lip** In addition to the idioms beginning with LIP, also see BUTTON UP (ONE'S LIP); KEEP A STIFF UPPER LIP; LICK ONE'S CHOPS (LIPS); PASS ONE'S LIPS.

**lips are sealed, one's** One will reveal nothing, especially about a secret. For example, *You can trust me with the details of the contract—my lips are sealed.*

**lip service** Verbal but insincere expression of agreement or support. It is often put as **pay lip service** or **give lip service,** as in *They paid lip service to holding an election next year, but they had no intention of doing so.*

**list** see BLACK LIST; SUCKER LIST.

**listen in 1.** Hear or overhear the conversation of others; eavesdrop. It is also put as **listen in on,** as in *She listened in on her parents and learned they were planning a surprise party.* **2.** Tune in and listen to a broadcast, as in *Were you listening in the other night when they played that new CD?*

**listen to reason** Pay attention to reasonable advice or argument, as in *We can't let him rush into that job—it's time he listened to reason.*

**listen with half an ear** Not give someone or something one's full attention. For example, *I was so occupied with what I was doing that I only listened to her with half an ear.*

**little** In addition to the idioms beginning with LITTLE, also see A LITTLE; EVERY LITTLE BIT HELPS; IN ONE'S OWN (LITTLE) WORLD; MAKE LITTLE OF; PRECIOUS FEW (LITTLE); THINK LITTLE OF; TO LITTLE PURPOSE; TOO LITTLE, TOO LATE.

**little bird told one, a** A source one cannot or will not identify gave this information, as in *How did you learn they were getting a divorce? Oh, a little bird told me.* Versions of this idiom date from ancient times.

**little by little** see BIT BY BIT.

**little frog in a big pond, a** Also, **a small frog in a large pond.** An unimportant or unqualified individual in a large organization or other setting. For example, *Coming from a small school, she felt lost at the state university—a little frog in a big pond.* This phrase is the counterpart of BIG FISH IN A SMALL POND.

**little knowledge is a dangerous thing, a** Also, **a little learning is a dangerous thing.** Knowing a little about something may cause one to overestimate one's abilities. For example, *I know you've assembled furniture, but that doesn't mean you can build an entire wall system; remember, a little knowledge.* This saying is sometimes shortened, as in the example.

**little pitchers have big ears** Young children often overhear something they should not. For example, *Don't use any swearwords around him—little pitchers have big ears.* This expression compares the curved handle of a pitcher to the human ear.

**live** In addition to the idioms beginning with LIVE, also see ALIVE (LIVE) AND KICKING; AS I LIVE AND BREATHE; CLOSE TO HOME (WHERE ONE LIVES); (LIVE FROM) DAY TO DAY; HIGH OFF THE HOG (LIVE HIGH ON THE HOG); HOW THE OTHER HALF LIVES; LEARN TO LIVE WITH; PEOPLE WHO LIVE IN GLASS HOUSES SHOULDN'T THROW STONES. Also see LIVING.

**live and learn** Acquire experience, as in *I ignored the garden book, planted my beans in March, and they all died—live and learn.*

**live and let live** Show tolerance for those different from oneself. For example, *I'm not going to tell my sister what to do—live and let live, I say.*

**live beyond one's means** see BEYOND ONE'S MEANS.

**live by one's wits** Manage by clever methods rather than hard work or wealth. For example, *He's never held a steady job but manages to live by his wits.*

**live dangerously** Take numerous risks, be daring, as in *Bill never knows if he'll have enough money to pay the next month's rent—he likes to live dangerously.*

**live down** Overcome or reduce the shame of a mistake. It is often put in the negative, as in *I'm afraid I'll never live down that remark I made.*

**live for the moment** Focus on the present, with little or no concern for the future. For example, *Instead of putting aside money for the children's education, Jane and Jim live for the moment, spending whatever they earn.* Also see DAY TO DAY, def. 2; FOR THE MOMENT.

**live from day to day** see DAY TO DAY, def. 2.

**live from hand to mouth** see HAND TO MOUTH.

**live happily ever after** Spend the rest of one's life in happiness, as in *In her romantic novels the hero and heroine marry and live happily ever after.* This exaggerated phrase ends many fairy tales.

**live high on the hog** see HIGH OFF THE HOG.

**live in** Live where one works or attends school, as in *They wanted a baby sitter who could live in,* or *Joe was planning to live in at the college.* This expression is used primarily for household workers or students.

L

**live in fear** Continue to be afraid that something harmful or destructive will happen, as in *She lives in fear of being poor again,* or *We're all tired of living in fear.*

**live in hope** Continue to hope that something pleasant or beneficial will happen, as in *He lived in hope of becoming a teacher,* or *She insists that it's better to live in hope.*

**live in sin** Live together but not marry, as in *Bill and Anne lived in sin for years before they got married.* This term is mostly used in a joking fashion today, when customs and views are more liberal in this regard. Also see LIVE TOGETHER.

**live in the past** Also, **live in the present** or **live in the future.** Think mostly about people or events from one's past, as in *Some people live in the past because they cannot bear the present.* The variants of this expression mean the same thing with respect to a different time. For example, *She's concerned only with living in the present,* or *Visionaries live in the future.*

**live it up** Enjoy oneself, often to excess. For example, *They came into some money and decided to live it up with a trip around the world.*

**live like a king** Also, **live like a prince.** Enjoy a wealthy style of living, as in *He spared no expense, preferring to live like a king as long as he could,* or *Since they got their inheritance, our neighbors are living like princes.* This expression continues to be used despite the much smaller role royalty plays in the present day.

**live on 1.** Be financially supported by something, as in *His pension is too small to live on.* **2.** Continue to survive, especially unexpectedly, as in *They thought the cancer would kill her, but she lived on for another twenty years.* **3.** Remain in human memory, as in *This book will live on long after the author's death.*

**live on borrowed time** see ON BORROWED TIME.

**live on the edge** see ON THE EDGE.

**live out of** Lead a lifestyle characterized by a particular item. This phrase appears in such idioms as **live out of a suitcase,** meaning "travel so much that one has no time to unpack one's belongings," or **live out of cans,** meaning "eat only prepared food for lack of other foods or time to prepare them." For example, *Traveling for months on end, he got very tired of living out of a suitcase,* or *We had neither gas nor electricity for a week and had to live out of cans.*

**live out one's days** Also, **live out one's life.** Complete or survive to the end of a period of time, as in *I want to live out my days in a warmer climate.*

**live through** Endure something, survive. This idiom is used both seriously, as in *Those who have lived through a depression never forget what it was like,* or as an exaggeration, as in *That speech was endless—I thought I'd never live through it.*

**live together** Share a house or an apartment, especially when not married. For example, *How long have the two of you been living together?* Also see LIVE IN SIN.

**live to tell the tale** Survive a dangerous or difficult situation in order to be able to tell the story, as in *You can tell this story to your friends, if you live to tell the tale.*

**live up to 1.** Live or act in a way that fits an ideal. For example, *Children rarely live up to their parents' ideals,* or *This new technology has not lived up to our expectations.* **2.** Carry something out, fulfill, as in *She certainly lived up to her end of the bargain.*

**live wire, a** A highly alert or energetic person. For example, *Sally's a real live wire; she brightens up any gathering.* This term compares a wire carrying electric current to a lively individual.

**live with 1.** Share a house or an apartment with someone, live as if married to, as in *I don't approve of my daughter living with her boyfriend.* Also see LIVE TOGETHER. **2.** Put up with something, tolerate, as in *I think I can live with this new agreement.* Also see LEARN TO LIVE WITH. **3. live with oneself.** Keep one's self-respect, as in *I don't know how he can live with himself after violating their trust.*

**live within one's means** Not spend more money than one earns, as in *Sooner or late he'll have to learn to live within his means.*

**living** In addition to the idioms beginning with LIVING, also see BEAT THE LIVING DAYLIGHTS OUT OF; THINK THE WORLD OWES ONE A LIVING.

**living end, the** The most extreme act in any situation, something quite extraordinary, as in *When he threw the stereo out the window—well, that was the living end!* or *That performance was the living end.*

**living proof** Actual evidence of something, as in *It's an excellent school, and my daughter is living proof.*

**living soul** A person. For example, *Every living soul in this town has a stake in the decision to ban smoking,* or *The place was empty—not a living soul could be found.*

**load** In addition to the idioms beginning with LOAD, also see CARBO LOAD; FEW BRICKS SHY OF A LOAD; GET A LOAD OF; TAKE THE LOAD OFF.

**loaded question, a** A question heavy with meaning or emotional impact, as in *When he inquired after Helen's ex-husband, that was a loaded question.*

**load off one's feet** see TAKE THE LOAD OFF.

**load off one's mind, a** Relief from a mental burden or anxiety, as in *Good news about the baby took a load off my mind.*

**load the dice** Fix the odds so there is little chance for another person to win, cheat. For example, *There's no way we can win this contest; they've loaded the dice.* This expression is also put as **the dice are loaded,** as in *There's no point in trying; the dice are loaded.* The term refers to adding weight to one side or another of dice so that they will always come up with certain numbers facing upward.

**loaf** see HALF A LOAF IS BETTER THAN NONE.

**local yokel** A native or resident of a particular locale, as in *She's only gone out with local yokels, so she's not used to more sophisticated men.* This insulting rhyming term was first used by military troops stationed away from home.

**lock** In addition to the idioms beginning with LOCK, also see UNDER LOCK AND KEY.

**lock horns** Become engaged in conflict, as in *At the town meeting the mayor and one of the council members locked horns over increasing the property tax.* This expression refers to how male deer and bulls use their horns to fight one another.

**lock in 1.** Enclose something, surround, as in *The ship was completely locked in ice.* **2.** Also, **lock *something* into.** Fix something firmly in position, commit to something, as in *We locked in the interest rate on our home loan with the bank.* This phrase often occurs as **be locked in** or **be locked into,** as in *She felt she was locked in a binding agreement,* or *Many of the teachers are locked into their present positions.*

**lock out 1.** Keep out someone, prevent from entering. For example, *Karen was so angry at her brother that she locked him out of the house.* **2.** Withhold work from employees during a labor dispute, as in *The company threatened to lock out the strikers permanently.*

**lock, stock, and barrel** All of something; completely. For example, *Jean moved out of the house, lock, stock, and barrel.*

**lock the barn door after the horse has bolted** Also, **lock the stable door after the horse is stolen.** Take preventive action after damage has occurred. For example, *After the burglary they installed an alarm system, but it's locking the barn door,* or *Deciding to negotiate now after they've been fired—that's a matter of locking the stable door after the horse is stolen.*

**lock up 1.** Close a house or place of work, fastening all the doors and windows, as in *The boss locks up at eleven o'clock every night,* or *Did you remind her to lock up?* **2.** Invest in something not easily converted into cash, as in *Most of their assets were locked up in real estate.* **3.** Confine or imprison someone, as in *The princes were locked up in the Tower of London.*

**log** In addition to the idiom beginning with LOG, also see EASY AS PIE (FALLING OFF A LOG); LIKE A BUMP ON A LOG; SLEEP LIKE A LOG.

**loggerheads** see AT LOGGERHEADS.

**log in** Also, **log on.** Enter into a computer the information needed to begin a session, as in *I logged in at two o'clock,* or *There's no record of your logging on today.* These expressions refer especially to large systems shared by numerous individuals, who need to enter a user name or password before starting a program. The antonyms are **log off** and **log out,** meaning "end a computer session." All these expressions come from the use of *log* in the sense of entering information about a ship in a journal called a *logbook.*

**lone wolf** A person who prefers to be without the company or assistance of others. For example, *Her nursery school teacher described my daughter as a lone wolf, an assessment I found astonishing.* This expression refers to the tendency of some species of wolf to hunt alone rather than in packs.

**long** In addition to the idioms beginning with LONG, also see AS LONG AS; AT (LONG) LAST; BEFORE LONG; COME A LONG WAY; DRAW OUT (LONG-DRAWN-OUT); GO A LONG WAY TOWARD; HAPPY AS THE DAY IS LONG; IN THE LONG RUN; MAKE A LONG STORY SHORT; SO LONG. Also see under LONGER.

**long ago** A time well before the present, the distant past. For example, *I read that book long ago,* or *The battles of long ago were just as fierce.*

**long and short of it, the** The substance or main point of something, as in *The first page of this report will give you the long and short of it.*

**long arm of the law, the** The far-reaching power of the authorities. For example, *You'll never get away with leaving work early; the long arm of the law is certain to catch you.*

**longer** see ANY LONGER; NO LONGER.

**long face** A facial expression showing sadness or disappointment, as in *His long face was a clear indication of his feelings.*

**long haul 1.** A great distance over which something must travel or be carried. For example, *It's a long haul from my house to yours.* The antonym is **short haul,** as in *The movers charge just as much for a short haul as for a long one.* **2.** A great length of time, an extended period, as in *This investment is one for the long haul.* It is often put as **over the long haul,** as in *Over the long haul we needn't worry about production.* Also see IN THE LONG RUN.

**long in the tooth** Getting on in years, old, as in *My aunt's a little long in the tooth to be helping us move.* This expression refers to a horse's teeth that appear longer as it ages.

**long on something but short on** Also, **short on something but long on.** Having a great deal of one quality and very little of another, or the reverse. For example, *He's long on talk but short on action,* or *As a friend, she's short on patience but long on loyalty.*

**long shot, a** A very small possibility of success, as in *It's a long shot that Joan will actually finish the marathon,* or *He may be a good programmer, but he's a long shot for that job.* This expression refers to the inaccuracy of early guns, which when shot over a distance rarely hit the target. The idiom is commonly used in horseracing for a bet made at great odds. A related phrase is **not by a long shot,** meaning "not even remotely," as in *I'll never make it to California in three days, not by a long shot.*

**long suit** One's strong point or advantage, as in *Organizing has never been Nancy's long suit.* This expression refers to card games in which holding numerous cards in a single suit may be a strong advantage.

L

**long time no see** It's been a long time since last we met, as in *Hi there! Long time no see.* This joking imitation of broken English originated in the English used in Chinese and Western commerce.

**look** In addition to the idioms beginning with LOOK, also see DIRTY LOOK; MAKE SOMEONE LOOK GOOD; TAKE A LOOK AT; THINGS ARE LOOKING UP.

**look after** Also, **look out for; see after.** Take care of someone or something, attend to the safety or well-being of, as in *Please look after your little brother,* or *We left my cousin to look out for the children,* or *Please see after the luggage.*

**look a gift horse in the mouth, not** Be critical or suspicious of something received for free. For example, *Dad's old car is full of dents, but we shouldn't look a gift horse in the mouth.* This term is generally expressed as a warning, as in *Don't look a gift horse in the mouth.* It refers to determining the age of a horse by looking at its teeth.

**look alive** Also, **look lively.** Act lively, hurry up, as in *Look alive! This job has to be finished today,* or *Look lively! Here comes the boss.* This phrase is often used as a command.

**look as if butter wouldn't melt** see BUTTER WOULDN'T MELT.

**look a sight** Appear to be feeling sick or unable to present oneself or something well. For example, *You look a sight! Have you been ill?* or *Ignore the house. It's looked a sight since the children came to visit.*

**look askance** View with mistrust, as in *They looked askance at him when he said he'd just made a million in the stock market.* The original literal meaning of this idiom was "look at an angle, with a side glance." Also see LOOK SIDEWAYS AT.

**look back 1.** Remember or think about the past, as in *When Mom looked back on the early days of their marriage, she wondered how they'd managed with so little money.* **2. not look back** or **never look back.** Never show signs of interrupted progress, never return to past events. For example, *Once he'd won the Pulitzer Prize, he never looked back.*

**look before you leap** Think of the consequences before you act, as in *You'd better check out all the costs before you buy a cellular phone—look before you leap.* This expression refers to Aesop's fable about the fox who is unable to climb out of a well and persuades a goat to jump in. The fox then climbs on the goat's horns to get out, while the goat remains trapped.

**look black** Appear threatening or unfavorable, as in *The future looked black for him after he dropped out of school.* Also see under DIRTY LOOK.

**look blank** Be expressionless, appear dazed or overwhelmed. For example, *When I asked her how to get to the hospital, she looked blank.*

**look daggers** Glare at someone, stare fiercely, as in *When she started to discuss their finances, he looked daggers at her.* This term compares an angry expression to a dagger's thrust.

**look down on** Also, **look down one's nose at.** Regard someone with contempt, consider oneself superior to. For example, *When it comes to baking, my sister is a purist—she looks down on anyone who buys cookies,* or *Seniors have a way of looking down their noses at juniors.*

**look for 1.** Search for something; also, seek out. For example, *A search party was sent to look for the lost fliers,* or *Those kids are just looking for trouble.* **2.** Expect something, anticipate, as in *Look for a change of weather in March.*

**look forward to** Eagerly expect something, as in *I'm looking forward to their visit,* or *My father looked forward to the day when he could retire.*

**look here** Pay attention because the speaker is angry or frustrated, as in *Look here! I'm tired of your being late to work,* or *Look here! You have to listen to what other people say.*

**look in on** Pay someone a brief visit, as in *I'm just going to look in on my friend and her new baby; I won't stay long.* Also see LOOK SOMEONE IN THE FACE.

**look into** Also, **see into.** Investigate, as in *He promised to look into the new law,* or *We must see into the matter of the missing checks.*

**look like 1.** Have the appearance of something, as in *This letter looks like an acceptance.* **2. it looks like.** It seems likely that, as in *It looks like it will rain.* Also see the following idioms beginning with LOOK LIKE.

**look like a million dollars** Appear attractive. For example, *The painter did a good job—the house looks like a million dollars.* The related **feel like a million dollars** means "feel healthy," as in *Helen came back from her winter vacation feeling like a million dollars.*

**look like death** Also, **look like death warmed over** or **feel like death warmed over.** Look or feel very ill or tired. For example, *After two nights without sleep, Bill looked like death warmed over,* or *This cold makes me feel like death warmed over.*

**look like something the cat dragged in** Appear very messy or neglected, as in *After walking around in the rain for hours, I looked like something the cat dragged in.* This expression refers to a cat's bringing home birds or mice it has killed.

**look like the cat that ate the canary** Also, **look like the cat that swallowed the canary.** Appear happy with oneself or self-satisfied. For example, *After she hit her third winning shot, the player looked like the cat that ate the canary.*

**look on 1.** Also, **look upon.** Regard in a certain way, as in *I looked on him as a second father,* or *We looked upon her as a good manager.* **2.** Be a spectator, watch, as in *She rode the horse around the ring as her parents looked on.* **3.** Also, **look on with.** Read from someone's book, paper, or music at the same time, as in *I forgot my copy; can I look on with you?*

**look oneself** Appear to be the way other people are accustomed to seeing somebody, as in *It's good to see you looking yourself again after your long illness.* This expression is also used negatively, **not look oneself,** as in *He hasn't looked himself since the divorce.*

**look on the bright side** see BRIGHT SIDE.

**lookout** see KEEP AN EYE OUT (A SHARP LOOKOUT) FOR; ON THE LOOKOUT. Also see the following idioms beginning with LOOK OUT.

**look out** Also, **watch out.** Be careful, be watchful, as in *Look out that you don't slip and fall on the ice,* or *Watch out! There's a car coming.* Also see LOOK OUT FOR.

**look out for 1.** See to the well-being of someone, as in *An older student was assigned to look out for the youngsters on the playground.* Similar to LOOK AFTER, this phrase appears in such terms as **look out for number one,** meaning "see to one's own best interests," as in *Looking out for number one is his first priority.* There are many versions of this expression, such as **take care of number one. 2.** Be careful of or watchful for something or someone, as in *Look out for the broken glass on the floor,* or *Look out for the boss—she'll be coming any minute.* Also see LOOK OUT.

**look over** Also, **look *someone* up and down.** Examine or inspect something or someone. For example, *Jerry was looking over the books when he found an error,* or *They looked the new boy up and down.* The variant often refers to examining someone who is sexually attractive, as in *It made her uncomfortable when the man looked her up and down.*

**look sharp** Get moving, be alert, as in *The coach told the team they would have to look sharp if they wanted to win.*

**look sideways at** Glance at someone suspiciously or lovingly, as in *I thought the detective was looking sideways at me, and it made me very nervous,* or *They were looking sideways at each other, and I don't think it was innocent.* Also see LOOK ASKANCE.

**look small** Also, **feel small.** Be humiliated or made to feel inferior by someone else. For example, *There was no reason to make me look small in front of my friends,* or *He seems to enjoy making other people feel small.* **Look small** describes another person's perception, while **feel small** describes one's own feelings.

**look someone in the face** Also, **look someone in the eye.** Face someone directly. These expressions imply honesty—or at least the appearance of honesty—in what is said, as in *Can you look me in the face and tell me you don't want that prize?* or *John looked me in the eye and told me he didn't break the window.* Also see STARE IN THE FACE.

**look the other way** Deliberately overlook something, especially something of an illegal nature. For example, *They're not really entitled to a discount, but the sales manager decided to look the other way.* This expression uses *the other way* in the sense of "away from what is normal or expected."

**look the part** Also, **look every inch the part.** Have an appearance that suggests one has a particular role or position, as in *I don't know if she's a lawyer, but she certainly looks the part,* or *If you want that job, you'll have to look every inch the part.*

**look through rose-colored glasses** see SEE THROUGH ROSE-COLORED GLASSES.

**look to 1.** Pay attention to something, take care of, as in *You'd best look to your own affairs.* **2.** Anticipate or expect, as in *We look to hear from her soon.* **3. look to be.** Seem to be, promise to be, as in *This looks to be a very difficult assignment.*

**look to one's laurels** Protect one's well-earned reputation or position, especially against a threat of losing it. For example, *Your opponent's done very well in the practice, so you'd better look to your laurels in the actual game.* This idiom refers to *laurels* as the traditional leaf used to make a victor's crown.

**look up** **1.** Search for something in a book or other source, as in *I told her to look up the word in the dictionary.* **2.** Call on or visit someone, as in *I'm going to look up my friend in Chicago.* **3.** Become better, improve, as in *Business is finally looking up.* **4. look up to.** Admire someone, respect, as in *The students really looked up to their teacher.*

**look *someone* up and down** see LOOK OVER.

**look up to** see LOOK UP, def. 4.

**look who's talking** You're in no position to criticize, as in *I wish Kate would be on time for once. You do? Look who's talking!*

**loom large** Appear about to happen in a threatening, magnified form. For example, *The possibility of civil war loomed large on the horizon,* or *Martha wanted to take it easy for a week, but the exam loomed large.* This term uses *loom* in the sense of "come into view."

**loop** see IN THE LOOP; KNOCK ONE FOR A LOOP.

**loose** In addition to the idioms beginning with LOOSE, also see AT LOOSE ENDS; BREAK LOOSE; CAST LOOSE; CUT LOOSE; FOOTLOOSE AND FANCY-FREE; HANG LOOSE; HAVE A SCREW LOOSE; LET LOOSE; ON THE LOOSE; PLAY FAST AND LOOSE.

**loose cannon, a** One who is uncontrolled and therefore a serious and unpredictable danger. For example, *We can't trust her to talk to the press—she's a loose cannon.* This expression refers to cannon mounted on the deck of a sailing ship, which if dislodged during combat or a storm could cause serious damage to both vessel and crew by sliding about.

**loose ends** Also, **loose ends to tie up.** Unfinished details, incomplete business. For example, *We've not quite finished the project; there are still some loose ends.* This expression refers to the ends of a rope or cable that should be fastened. Also see AT LOOSE ENDS.

**loosen one's tongue** Make one become careless and talk too much about things that one wants to be silent about. For example, *A couple of beers will loosen his tongue.*

**lord it over** Dominate someone, act as though one is superior to others, as in *After Mary was elected president, she tried to lord it over the other girls.*

**lose** In addition to the idioms beginning with LOSE, also see GET (LOSE) ONE'S BEARINGS; KEEP (LOSE) ONE'S COOL; KEEP (LOSE) TRACK; WIN SOME, LOSE SOME. Also see under LOST.

**lose face** Be embarrassed or humiliated, especially publicly. For example, *That executive lost face when his assistant was promoted and became his boss.* Both this expression and the underlying concept come from Asia; the term itself is a translation of the Chinese *tiu lien.* Also see SAVE FACE.

**lose ground** Fail to hold one's position; fall behind, get worse. For example, *The Democrats were losing ground in this district,* or *We thought Grandma was getting better, but now she's quickly losing ground.* This expression originally referred to territory lost by a retreating army.

**lose heart** Become discouraged, as in *The rescuers worked hard for the first few hours, but then they lost heart.* This term uses *heart* in the sense of "courage" or "spirit." Also see LOSE ONE'S HEART TO.

**lose it** see LOSE ONE'S GRIP; LOSE ONE'S TEMPER.

**lose no time** see under LOSE TIME, def. 2.

**lose one's bearings** see under GET ONE'S BEARINGS.

**lose one's cool** see under KEEP ONE'S COOL.

**lose oneself in** Become deeply absorbed or involved in, as in *Doctors are notorious for losing themselves in their work.* This expression refers to becoming so absorbed as to forget oneself.

**lose one's grip** Also, **lose it. 1.** Fail to maintain control or one's ability to function, as in *He wasn't running things the way he used to, and his boss thought he might be losing his grip,* or *I thought I was losing it when I couldn't remember the words to that old song.* **2.** Fail to remain in control of oneself, as in *When Billy broke the window, Dad just lost his grip and let him have it,* or *I just can't deal with this many visitors—I must be losing it.* Also see LOSE ONE'S TEMPER.

**lose one's head** see under KEEP ONE'S HEAD, def. 1.

**lose one's heart to** Fall in love with someone or something, as in *I totally lost my heart to the new puppy.*

**lose one's lunch** Vomit, as in *When Anne saw the injury, she thought she would lose her lunch.* This expression does not usually refer to a specific meal and probably survives because of the repeated consonant in *lose* and *lunch.*

**lose one's marbles** Also, **lose all one's marbles.** Become unable to function in a rational way, as in *She'll lose her marbles when she finds out how much we spent.* Also see HAVE ALL ONE'S MARBLES.

**lose one's mind** Also, **lose one's reason.** Go crazy, lose one's sanity, as in *I thought* *she'd lost her mind when she said she was going ice fishing,* or *That assignment is enough to make me lose my reason.* Also see GO OUT OF ONE'S MIND; LOSE ONE'S MARBLES.

**lose one's nerve** Become frightened or timid, lose courage. For example, *I wanted to ski down the expert slope, but then I lost my nerve.* This expression uses *nerve* in the sense of "courage or boldness."

**lose one's shirt** Face financial ruin, go bankrupt, as in *He lost his shirt in the last recession.* This expression implies that one has lost everything including one's shirt.

**lose one's temper** Also, **lose it.** Become angry, lose self-control. For example, *When she found out what Ann had done, she lost her temper,* or *He arrived without that important check, and then I just lost it completely.*

**lose one's touch** No longer be able to do or handle something skillfully. For example, *I used to make beautiful cakes, but I seem to have lost my touch.* This expression refers to an older sense of *touch* as a musician's skill or an artist's skill.

**lose out 1.** Fail to succeed, be defeated, as in *The election's over, and you've lost out.* **2.** Also, **lose out on** or **lose out in.** Miss an opportunity to participate, as in *We came so late that we lost out on our chance to see her dance,* or *The Republicans lost out in last fall's elections.* Also see MISS OUT ON.

**loser** see under FINDERS, KEEPERS.

**lose sight of** Overlook something, fail to take into account, as in *We must not lose sight of our main objective,* or *That star never lost sight of her humble beginnings.* This expression refers to physical sight and transfers it to mental awareness. For an antonym, see BEAR IN MIND.

**lose sleep over** Worry about something, as in *It's too bad the experiment failed, but I'm not going to lose sleep over it.* This expression, often put negatively, refers to an inability to sleep caused by worry.

**lose the thread** Stop following the sense of what is said. For example, *It was such a long story that I soon lost the thread.*

**lose time 1.** Operate too slowly. For example, *My watch loses time,* or *This clock loses five minutes a day.* This usage is always applied to a timepiece. **2.** Waste time, delay, as in *We wanted to paint the entire porch today, but we lost time trying to find a color that matched the house.* This expression is sometimes put negatively as **lose no time,** meaning "act immediately" or "not delay," as in *We must lose no time in getting him to the hospital.* Also see MAKE UP FOR (LOST TIME).

**lose touch** Fail to keep in contact or communication, as in *The two sisters lost touch years ago,* or *Please don't lose touch with me after you move away.* For an antonym, see IN TOUCH.

**lose track** see under KEEP TRACK.

**losing battle, a** Also, **a losing game.** A failing effort or activity. For example, *He's fighting a losing battle against putting on weight,* or *We think his candidacy is a losing game.* These expressions refer to both literal and figurative unsuccessful battles or games. Also see LOST CAUSE.

**loss** see AT A LOSS; CUT ONE'S LOSSES; DEAD LOSS.

**lost** In addition to the idioms beginning with LOST, also see ALL IS NOT LOST; GET LOST; HE WHO HESITATES IS LOST; MAKE UP FOR (LOST TIME); NO LOVE LOST; YOU'VE LOST ME. Also see LOSE.

**lost cause, a** A hopeless activity, as in *Trying to get him to quit smoking is a lost cause.* Also see LOSING BATTLE.

**lost in the shuffle** Failing to be seen among others, as in *In that huge economics class Jane's afraid she'll get lost in the shuffle.* This term refers to mixing playing cards before dealing them.

**lost in thought** Concentrating on or pondering something. For example, *I didn't hear a word you said; I was lost in thought.*

**lost on one** Have no effect or influence on one, as in *His attempts at humor were lost on me,* or *David's kindness was not lost on his aunt.* This expression uses *lost* in the sense of "wasted." Also see YOU'VE LOST ME.

**lost without, be** Unable to function properly without someone or something. For example, *Since she moved, I'm lost without her company,* or *He'd be lost without his television.*

**lot** see A LOT; CAST ONE'S LOT WITH; FAT CHANCE (LOT); HAVE A LOT ON ONE'S PLATE; LEAVE A LOT TO BE DESIRED; QUITE A BIT (LOT); THINK A LOT OF.

**loud** In addition to the idioms beginning with LOUD, also see ACTIONS SPEAK LOUDER THAN WORDS; BIG (LOUD) MOUTH; FOR CRYING OUT LOUD; OUT LOUD; THINK ALOUD; (LOUD ENOUGH) TO WAKE THE DEAD.

**loud and clear** Easily heard and understandable. For example, *They told us, loud and clear, what to do in an emergency,* or *You needn't repeat it—I hear you loud and clear.* This expression became popular in the military during World War II to acknowledge radio messages (**I read you loud and clear**).

**loud mouth** see BIG MOUTH.

**louse up** Spoil or ruin something. For example, *The bad weather loused up our plans,* or *Your change of mind really loused me up.*

**lousy with** Abundantly supplied, as in *He's lousy with money.*

**love** In addition to the idioms beginning with LOVE, also see ALL'S FAIR IN LOVE AND WAR;

FALL IN LOVE; FOR THE LOVE OF; LABOR OF LOVE; MAKE LOVE; MISERY LOVES COMPANY; NO LOVE LOST; NOT FOR LOVE OR MONEY; PUPPY LOVE; SOMEBODY UP THERE LOVES ME.

**love affair** **1.** An intimate sexual relationship, as in *They had a love affair many years ago.* This expression originally referred merely to the experience of being in love. **2.** A strong enthusiasm, as in *We can't ignore America's love affair with the automobile.*

**love at first sight** An instant attraction to someone or something. For example, *With that couple, it was a case of love at first sight,* or *When Dave saw that car, it was love at first sight.*

**lovers' lane** An isolated road or area used by lovers seeking privacy. For example, *The police liked to embarrass teenagers parked in lovers' lane.*

**loving** see TENDER LOVING CARE.

**love is blind** The intensity of love makes someone unable to see the obvious flaws in someone he or she loves, as in *Why did she marry him? Oh well, love is blind.*

**low** In addition to the idioms beginning with LOW, also see AT A LOW EBB; (LOW) BOILING POINT; HIGH AND LOW; KEEP A LOW PROFILE; LAY SOMEONE LOW; LIE LOW; RUN LOW ON.

**low blow, a** An unfair attack; an insult. For example, *When my roommate moved out without a word of warning, leaving me to pay the entire rent, that was a low blow,* or *She wanted to win the argument, but bringing up his failed marriage was a low blow.* This term refers to the illegal practice of hitting an opponent in boxing BELOW THE BELT.

**low boiling point** see BOILING POINT, def. 2.

**lower one's sights** Reduce one's goals or hopes, as in *Once he got the job I'd applied for, I had to lower my sights.* This expression refers to taking aim through the sights of a firearm. Also see RAISE ONE'S SIGHTS; SET ONE'S SIGHTS ON.

**lower the boom on** Scold someone harshly or punish severely; also, put a stop to something. For example, *If you're caught smoking in school, the principal will lower the boom on you,* or *The new radar equipment enabled the police to lower the boom on speeding.* This slang expression refers to the boom of a sailboat. In a changing wind, the boom can swing wildly, leaving one at risk of being struck.

**low man on the totem pole** Low in rank, least important person, as in *I just joined the company, so I'm low man on the totem pole.*

**low profile** see KEEP A LOW PROFILE.

**luck** In addition to the idioms beginning with LUCK, also see AS LUCK WOULD HAVE IT; BEGINNER'S LUCK; DOWN ON ONE'S LUCK; GOOD LUCK; HARD LUCK; IN LUCK; OUT OF LUCK; PUSH ONE'S LUCK; RUN OF LUCK; TAKE POT LUCK; TOUGH BREAK (LUCK); TRY ONE'S HAND (LUCK).

**luck into** see LUCK OUT.

**luck of the devil, the** Also, **the luck of the Irish.** Extremely good fortune, as in *You've the luck of the devil—that ball landed just on the line,* or *Winning the lottery—that's the luck of the Irish.*

**luck of the draw, the** Pure chance, as in *It isn't anyone's fault—it's just the luck of the draw.* This expression refers to the random drawing of a playing card.

**luck out** Also, **luck into.** Gain success or something desirable through good fortune. For example, *We lucked out and found the same rug for half the price,* or *She's lucked into a terrific apartment.*

**lucky** see BORN UNDER A LUCKY STAR; STRIKE IT RICH (LUCKY); THANK ONE'S LUCKY STARS.

**lull *someone* into** Deceive someone into trusting something, as in *The steadily rising market lulled investors into a false sense of security.* This idiom often appears with the phrase **a false sense of security,** as in the example.

**lump** In addition to the idiom beginning with LUMP, also see LIKE IT OR LUMP IT; TAKE ONE'S LUMPS.

**lump in one's throat** A feeling of tightness in the throat caused by emotion, as in *The bride's mother had a lump in her throat.* This expression compares the sense of a physical swelling to the tight sensation caused by strong feelings.

**lunch** see EAT SOMEONE ALIVE (SOMEONE'S LUNCH); FREE LUNCH; LOSE ONE'S LUNCH; OUT TO LUNCH.

**lung** see AT THE TOP OF ONE'S LUNGS.

**lurch** see LEAVE ONE IN THE LURCH.

**luxury** see LAP OF LUXURY.

**lying down** see TAKE SOMETHING LYING DOWN. Also see LIE DOWN.

# Mm

**mad** In addition to the idioms beginning with MAD, also see CRAZY (MAD) ABOUT; DRIVE SOMEONE CRAZY (MAD); HOPPING MAD; LIKE CRAZY (MAD); STARK RAVING MAD.

**mad about** Also, **mad for.** See CRAZY ABOUT.

**mad as a hatter** Also, **mad as a March hare.** Not able to think clearly or act rationally, as in *She is throwing out all his clothes; she's mad as a hatter.* This expression refers to exposure to the chemicals formerly used in making felt hats, which caused serious symptoms. The variant refers to the strange behavior of hares during mating season, mistakenly thought to be only in March.

**mad as a hornet** Also, **mad as hell** or **mad as hops** or **mad as a wet hen.** Very angry, enraged as in *My mother was mad as a hornet when her purse was stolen,* or *Upset? He was mad as hell,* or *The teacher was mad as a wet hen.*

**made** In addition to the idioms beginning with MADE, also see HAVE IT MADE. Also see under MAKE.

**made for each other** Also, **made for one another.** Perfectly suited, as in *Pat and Peter were just made for each other.*

**made of money** Very rich, as in *I can't afford a limousine! Do you think I'm made of money?*

**made to measure** Also, **tailor-made.** Fashioned to fit a particular need or purpose, very suitable. For example, *Jane thinks her new position is made to measure for her,* or *This film is tailor-made for a teenage audience.* These terms originally referred to clothes made to fit a particular person very precisely. Also see MADE TO ORDER.

**made to order** Also, **built to order.** Very suitable, as in *Her new assignment was made to order for her.* In its literal use, this idiom refers to an item created or built according to particular instructions.

**madness** see METHOD IN ONE'S MADNESS.

**mad rush** Also, **mad dash.** A wild hurry, as in *I was in a mad rush to get to the bank on time to cash my check,* or *Why the mad rush? We have lots of time before the concert starts.* The use of *mad,* for "with great confusion or excitement," serves merely as an intensifier.

**maiden voyage** The first experience, as in *This tennis tournament is my maiden voyage in statewide competition.* This term originally referred to the first voyage of a ship.

**main** In addition to the idioms beginning with MAIN, also see IN THE MAIN.

**main drag, the** The principal street of a city or town, as in *Several stores on the main drag have closed.*

**main squeeze** One's sweetheart, as in *Nancy is his main squeeze.* This slang usage refers to the "squeeze" of a hug.

**make** In addition to the idioms beginning with MAKE, also see ABSENCE MAKES THE HEART GROW FONDER; ALL WORK AND NO PLAY MAKES JACK A DULL BOY; CAN'T MAKE A SILK PURSE OUT OF A SOW'S EAR; CAN'T MAKE HEAD OR TAIL OF; KISS AND MAKE UP; MIGHT MAKES RIGHT; ON THE MAKE; PRACTICE MAKES PERFECT; PUT IN (MAKE) AN APPEARANCE; PUT THE MAKE ON; THAT MAKES TWO OF US; TWO WRONGS DO NOT MAKE A RIGHT; WHAT MAKES ONE TICK. Also see under MADE.

**make a beeline for** Go straight to, as in *He made a beeline for the food.* In this expression, *beeline* means "the shortest distance between two points." It refers to the route of worker bees bringing nectar and pollen from pollen back to the hive.

**make a break for** Also, **make a run for.** Run toward or escape from something. For example, *As soon as the class ended, they made a break for the door,* or *I'll have to make a run for the plane.* Both terms may be put as **make a break for it** or **make a run for it,** meaning "escape or get away quickly." For example, *With the guards asleep, he decided to make a break for it,* or *The rain's stopped; let's make a run for it.*

**make a bundle** Also, **make a pile.** Make a great deal of money, as in *When the market went up, they made a bundle,* or *He made a pile from that department store.* The first term comes from an earlier use of *bundle* for a roll of bank notes.

**make a clean breast of** Confess fully, as in *After they were caught shoplifting, the girls decided to make a clean breast of it to their parents.* This expression uses *clean breast* in the sense of baring of one's heart or secret feelings.

**make a clean sweep** **1.** Remove or eliminate unwanted persons or things, as in *The new owners made a clean sweep of the place, intending to replace all the equipment.* **2.** Win a series of competitions, as in *Our candidate made a clean sweep of all the districts.* This usage most often refers to success in a sports competition or an election.

**make a comeback** Also, **stage a comeback.** Achieve a success after retirement or failure, as in *After years in small roles on TV, she made a comeback in a major film,* or *The fashions from that period are about to stage a comeback.* Also see COME BACK, def. 1.

**make a crack** Make a disrespectful joke; comment with a sarcastic or ironic remark, as in *She's constantly making cracks about the store's management.* The noun *crack* here refers to a hunter's shot at an animal.

**make a date** Arrange a meeting with someone, as in *Let's get the department heads together and make a date for lunch next week,* or *I've made a date with Jean; can you join us?* At first this term referred only to social engagements, especially with a member of the opposite sex. It is now used more broadly.

**make a day of it** Also, **make a night of it.** Devote a day (or night) to some pleasurable activity, as in *If we're going all that way to the beach, let's make a day of it,* or *Since they missed the seven o'clock train, they decided to make a night of it.*

**make a dent in** Begin to accomplish, use, or do something, as in *I've barely made a dent in this pile of correspondence,* or *Help us put a dent in this pie.*

M

**make a difference 1.** Also, **make the difference.** Cause a change in effect, change the nature of something, as in *His score on this test will make the difference between passing and failing the course,* or *These curtains sure make a difference in the lighting.* **2.** Be important, matter, as in *Her volunteer work made a difference in many lives.* The antonym of this usage is **make no difference,** as in *It makes no difference to me if we go immediately or in an hour.*

**make advances 1.** Try to start a friendly relationship or alliance, as in *The ambassador knew that the ministers would soon make advances to him.* **2.** Try to start a sexual relationship, as in *His wife accused him of making advances to the baby sitter.* Also see MAKE A PASS AT, def. 1.

**make a face** Change one's facial features to be funny or express a feeling, as in *The teacher told Joan to stop making faces at Mary.*

**make a federal case of** Also, **make a big deal of.** Give too much importance to an issue, as in *I'll pay you back next week—you needn't make a federal case of it,* or *Jack is making a big deal of filling out his passport application.* The first expression is almost always used in a negative context. It refers to taking a legal action before a high (federal) court. The second may refer to an important business transaction (see BIG DEAL, def. 1).

**make a fool of** Also, **make an ass of** or **make a monkey out of.** Cause someone or oneself to look foolish or stupid. For example, *John doesn't mind making a fool of himself at parties,* or *They made an ass of me by giving me the wrong instructions,* or *Just watch him make a monkey out of this amateur chess player.* The first variant is sometimes put more rudely as **make a horse's ass of.**

**make a fortune** Also, **make a small fortune.** Earn a great deal of money, as in *He made a fortune on the stock market.* Similar expressions include **be worth a fortune** or **be worth a small fortune,** as in *Now that their parents have died, they're worth a small fortune.*

**make a fuss 1.** Cause an unnecessary disturbance or display, as in *I'm sure he'll be here soon; please don't make a fuss.* It is also often put as **make a fuss about** or **make a fuss over,** as in *He's making a fuss about nothing,* or *If you make a fuss over the small budget items, what will it be like when we discuss the big ones?* **2. make a fuss over.** Treat someone with a great or too great amount of attention, concern, or affection, as in *Grandma makes a fuss over the children whenever they visit.*

**make a go of** Achieve success in, as in *He has made a go of his new business.*

**make a hit 1.** Also, **be a hit.** Achieve or be a success, especially a popular one, as in *She made a big hit in this performance,* or *After just one week the play was already a hit.* This term transfers the meaning of *hit* as "a stroke or blow" to theatrical performances, books, songs, and the like. **2.** In underworld slang, commit a murder, as in *Known for his deadly accuracy, he was about to make his third hit.* This usage also has been extended to such terms as **hit list,** a list of persons to be killed, and **hit man,** a killer who is usually hired by someone else.

**make a killing** Enjoy a large and quick profit, as in *They made a killing in real estate.* This expression refers to a hunter's success.

**make a laughingstock of** Make someone the subject of ridicule, as in *They made a laughingstock of the chairman by inviting him to the wrong meeting place,* or *She felt she was making a laughingstock of herself by always wearing the wrong clothes for the occasion.*

**make a living** Earn enough to support oneself, as in *Can he make a living as a musician?*

**make allowance for** Also, **make allowances for.** Take into account circumstances or conditions that excuse a failure or bad behavior, as in *We have to make allowance for Jeff; he's very new to the business,* or *Grandma is always making allowances for the children's bad manners.*

**make a long story short** Also, **cut a long story short.** Leave out details and get to the point, as in *To make a long story short, they got married and moved to Omaha,* or *To cut a long story short, he was arrested and went to jail.*

**make amends** Compensate someone for a grievance or injury, as in *They must make amends for the harm they've caused you.*

**make a mess of** Ruin or spoil something, as in *They've made a mess of their financial affairs.*

**make a monkey out of** see MAKE A FOOL OF.

**make a mountain out of a molehill** Make small difficulties seem bigger than they are, as in *If you forgot your tennis racket, you can borrow one—don't make a mountain out of a molehill.* This expression is often used in the negative, as in the example.

**make a name for oneself** Become prominent or well known, usually because of one's successes, as in *Martha is making a name for herself as an excellent chef.* Also see MAKE ONE'S MARK.

**make an appearance** see PUT IN AN APPEARANCE.

**make an appointment 1.** Assign someone to a particular office or position, as in *When the head of White House security resigned, it was up to the President to make a new appointment.* **2.** Schedule a meeting with someone, as in *Do I need to make another appointment with the doctor?*

**make an ass of** see MAKE A FOOL OF.

**make an end of** see PUT AN END TO.

**make an example of** Punish someone as a warning to others, as in *The teacher made an example of the boy she caught cheating,* or *The judge gave the car thieves a tough sentence to make an example of them.*

**make an exception** Free someone or something from a general rule or practice, as in *Because it's your birthday, I'll make an exception and let you stay up as late as you want.*

**make an exhibition of oneself** Act so as to draw too much attention or embarrass oneself in public, as in *When Mike has too much to drink, he's apt to make an exhibition of himself.*

**make a night of it** see MAKE A DAY OF IT.

**make an impression** Produce a strong effect on someone. The particular type of impression is often described with an adjective such as *good, bad, strong,* or the like. For example, *He tried to make a good impression on his girlfriend's parents,* or *Be careful or you'll make a bad impression on the jury,* or *You made quite a strong impression with that speech.*

**make a note of** Write down so as to remember; also, remember. For example, *I'll make a note of the fact that the tires are low.*

**make a nuisance of oneself** Bother or annoy others, as in *That child is making a nuisance of himself.*

**make a pass at 1.** Flirt or make advances to someone, especially of a sexual nature, as in *He makes passes at all the pretty girls he meets.* **2.** Also, **take a pass at.** Make an attempt, as in *I've made a pass at opening it but had no luck,* or *Jake, will you take a pass at fixing my bike?* Also see MAKE A STAB AT.

**make a pig of oneself** Eat too much, as in *I really made a pig of myself at the buffet.* Also see PIG OUT.

**make a pile** see MAKE A BUNDLE.

**make a pitch for** Say or do something in support of someone or something, as in *That announcer really made a pitch for Sunday's concert,* or *Her agent's been making a pitch for her books all over town.* This expression originally referred to a sales talk that was "pitched" (in the sense of "thrown") at the listener.

**make a play for** Try to attract someone's interest, especially romantic interest. For example, *Bill has been making a play for Anne, but so far it hasn't gotten him anywhere.*

**make a point of** Treat something as important or essential, as in *She made a point of thanking everyone in the department for their efforts.* This expression uses *point* in the sense of "an objective or purpose." Also see MAKE ONE'S POINT.

**make a practice of** Do something regularly, as a habit, as in *Bill makes a practice of checking the oil and gas before every long trip.*

**make arrangements for** Plan or prepare for someone or something, as in *Who is making all the arrangements for our sales meeting?*

**make a run for** see MAKE A BREAK FOR.

**make a scene** Also, **create a scene** or **make an uproar.** Make a public disturbance or an excited emotional display. For example, *Joan made a scene when the restaurant lost her dinner reservation,* or *Ted made an uproar when the airline lost his luggage.*

**make as if** Also, **make as though** or **make like.** Behave as if, pretend that. For example, *Jean made as if she really liked the soup,* or *Dad made as though he had not heard them,* or *She makes like she's a really important person.*

**make a silk purse** see CAN'T MAKE A SILK PURSE OUT OF A SOW'S EAR.

**make a stab at** Try to do something, as in *I don't know the answer, but I'll make a stab at it.* This expression derives from *stab* in the sense of "a vigorous thrust." Also see MAKE A PASS AT, def. 2.

**make a stand** Hold firm against something or someone, as in *The government was determined to make a stand against all forms of terrorism.* This idiom first referred to holding ground against an enemy. Also see TAKE A STAND.

**make a statement** Create a certain impression; communicate an idea or mood without using words. For example, *The furnishings of their offices make a statement about the company.*

**make a stink** Also, **raise a stink.** Create a great fuss; complain, criticize, or otherwise make trouble about something. For example, *They promised to fix the printer today; you don't need to make a stink about it,* or *The parents were raising a stink about the principal's new rules.* This idiom transfers an offensive smell to a public fuss. Also see MAKE A SCENE.

**make a virtue of necessity** Find a benefit or gain an advantage out of a situation one can't avoid. For example, *Since he can't break the contract, Bill's making a virtue of necessity.* Also see MAKE THE BEST OF.

**make away with** Escape with something, steal, as in *The burglars made away with all their jewelry.*

**make bail** Pay an amount of money to ensure that someone released from prison will appear for trial, as in *He didn't think he could make bail for his brother.*

**make believe** Pretend, as in *Let's make believe we're the last people on Earth.* This expression refers to making oneself believe in an illusion.

**make book** Accept bets on a race, game, or contest, as in *No one's making book on the local team.* This expression uses *book* in the sense of "a record of the bets made by different individuals."

**make conversation** Engage someone in talking purely for its own sake, as in *She had a real talent for making conversation with strangers.*

**make demands on** Urgently require something of someone, as in *Her mother's illness has made considerable demands on her time.*

**make do** Also, **make do with.** Manage with whatever is available, especially when it's less than enough. For example, *We'll just have to make do with one potato each.*

**make ends meet** Manage so that one's money is enough for one's needs, as in *On that salary Enid had trouble making ends meet.*

**make eyes at** Look at in a way that shows romantic interest, flirt with, as in *To her sister's disgust, she was always making eyes at the boys.* Also see GIVE SOMEONE THE ONCE-OVER.

**make fast work of** see MAKE SHORT WORK OF.

**make for** **1.** Have or cause to have a particular effect; also, help promote or further. For example, *That letter of yours will make for hard feelings in the family,* or *This system makes for better communication.* **2.** Go toward, as in *They turned around and made for home.*

**make friends** Form one or more friendships, develop an easy relationship, as in *I hope Brian will soon make friends at school,* or *She's done a good job of making friends with influential reporters.*

**make fun of** Also, **poke fun at** or **make sport of.** Talk about and laugh at, as in *The girls made fun of Mary's shoes,* or *They poked fun at Willie's haircut,* or *I wish you wouldn't make sport of the new boy.*

**make good** **1.** Complete something successfully, make sure of something, as in *He made good his escape.* **2.** Fulfill or act on something as agreed, as in *She made good her promise.* **3.** Do or pay something as compensation for, as in *They made good the loss.* **4.** Succeed, as in *He made good as a writer.*

**make good time** Travel far in a short time, as in *We made good time, getting to Vermont in only four hours.*

**make great strides** Advance successfully, make good progress, as in *He made great strides in his study of Latin.* This expression has taken a number of forms, including **take strides** and **make rapid strides.** All of them compare a long walking step to other kinds of progress.

**make haste** Also, **make it snappy.** Hurry up, move or act quickly, as in *If you don't make haste, we'll be late,* or *Make it snappy, kids.*

**make hay while the sun shines** Take advantage of good but temporary conditions, as in *Car sales have finally improved, so we're making hay while the sun shines.* This expression refers to the best weather for cutting grass.

**make head or tail of** see CAN'T MAKE HEAD OR TAIL OF.

**make headway** Advance, make progress, as in *We haven't made any headway with this project.* This expression uses *headway* in the sense of "a ship's forward movement."

**make history** Do something memorable or important enough to influence the course of history, as in *That first space flight made history.*

**make inroads into** Advance into an area and cause another to lose power or popularity. For example, *The Japanese rapidly made inroads into the computer-chip market.* The noun *inroad* originally meant "an invasion."

M

**make it** **1.** Also, **make it to.** Reach a certain point or goal, as in *Do you think she'll make it to graduation?* or *We drove to Chicago and made it in seven hours.* **2.** Succeed; also, win acceptance. For example, *When he won the prize, he realized he'd finally made it,* or *Jane longed to make it with the crowd from Society Hill.* **3.** Also, **make it with.** Have sexual intercourse, as in *The basketball star bragged that he'd made it with hundreds of women.*

**make it hot for** Cause trouble or discomfort for someone, as in *They made it so hot for Larry that he had to resign,* or *The police were making it hot for shoplifters.*

**make it one's business** Choose to be responsible for a task, as in *I'll make it my business to find out their plans.*

**make it snappy** see MAKE HASTE.

**make it up** see under MAKE UP.

**make it up to** Do something nice for someone because of feeling sorry about some loss or disappointment he or she felt. For example, *I know I promised to be there, and I'll make it up to you somehow.*

**make it with** see MAKE IT, def. 3.

**make light of** Also, **make little of.** Treat something as unimportant, as in *He made light of his allergies,* or *She made little of the fact that she'd won.* The first term uses *light* in the sense of "trivial." For an antonym, see MAKE MUCH OF.

**make like** see MAKE AS IF.

**make little of** see MAKE LIGHT OF.

**make love** Have sexual intercourse, as in *They'd been making love for months before they married.*

**make mincemeat of** **1.** Hit and hurt someone badly, as in *That bully will make mincemeat of my son.* **2.** Defeat someone completely, as in *The other team will make mincemeat out of us.* This idiom refers to finely chopping up meat.

**make mischief** Cause trouble, as in *Don't listen to her gossip—she's just trying to make mischief.* The related noun is **mischief-maker,** used for a person who causes trouble especially by passing information on.

**make much of** Treat or consider something as very important; also, pay someone a lot of favorable attention. For example, *Bill made much of the fact that he'd been to Europe three times,* or *Whenever Alice came home for a visit, her relatives made much of her.*

**make my day** see MAKE ONE'S DAY.

**make no bones about** Act or speak openly about something, without hesitation or evasion. For example, *Tom made no bones about wanting to be promoted,* or *Make no bones about it—she's very talented.*

**make no difference** see under MAKE A DIFFERENCE, def. 2.

**make no mistake** Have no doubt, certainly, as in *Make no mistake—I'll vote Republican no matter who runs.* This expression is usually used as a command, as in the example. Also see GET SOMEONE WRONG.

**make nothing of** **1.** Regard something as unimportant, make light of, as in *He made nothing of walking three miles to buy a newspaper.* **2. can make nothing of.** Fail to accomplish, understand, or solve something, as in *I could make nothing of that long speech.*

**make off** **1.** Leave in a hurry, run away, as in *The cat took one look at Richard and made off.* **2. make off with.** Take something away; also, steal something, as in *I can't write it down; Tom made off with my pen,* or *The burglars made off with the stereo and computer as well as jewelry.*

**make one's bed and lie in it** Suffer the consequences of one's actions. For example, *It's a shame that she's in such a bad situation, but Sara made her bed and now she must lie in it.* This idiom refers to times when a permanent bed was a luxury, and most people had to stuff a sack with straw every night for use as a bed.

**make one's blood boil** Make one very angry, as in *Whenever Jim criticizes his father, it makes my blood boil.*

**make one's blood run cold** Also, **freeze one's blood.** Cause someone to shiver from fright or horror, as in *Strange noises at night made George's blood run cold,* or *Movies about vampires always freeze my blood.* Also see MAKE ONE'S FLESH CREEP.

**make one's day** Give one great pleasure, as in *Hearing you won first prize just made my day.* This phrase uses *make* in the sense of "secure success in."

**make one's ears burn** see EARS ARE BURNING.

**make oneself at home** Relax and act as though one were in one's own home. For example, *I have to make a phone call, but please make yourself at home,* or *Tim has a way of making himself at home just about anywhere.* Also see AT HOME, def. 3.

**make oneself scarce** Leave quickly, go away, as in *The children saw Mrs. Frost coming and made themselves scarce.* This idiom uses *scarce* in the sense of "seldom seen."

**make one's flesh creep** Also, **make one's skin crawl.** Cause one to shudder with disgust or fear, as in *That picture makes my flesh creep,* or *Cockroaches make my skin crawl.* This idiom refers to the feeling of having something crawl over one's body or skin.

**make one's hair stand on end** Also, **make one's hair curl.** Terrify one, as in *The very thought of an earthquake makes my hair* *stand on end,* or *Diving off a high board is enough to make my hair curl.* The first term refers to goose pimples caused by fear, which make the hairs around them stand up.

**make one's head spin** Cause one to be dizzy, dazed, or confused, as in *The figures in this tax return make my head spin.* This phrase uses *spin* in the sense of "rapidly turning."

**make one sick** Disgust one, as in *Your constant complaining makes me sick.* This expression transfers physical illness to strong negative reactions.

**make one's mark** Become know and respected for one's abilities or achievements, as in *Terry soon made his mark as an organist.* Also see MAKE A NAME FOR ONESELF.

**make one's mouth water** Cause one to eagerly want or look forward to something, as in *The sight of that chocolate cake made her mouth water,* or *Those travel folders about Nepal make my mouth water.* This term refers to an increase of saliva in the mouth when one anticipates food and is also used figuratively, as in the second example.

**make one's peace with** Restore or create friendly relations with, as in *He's repented and made his peace with God.* Also see MAKE PEACE.

**make one's point** Effectively express one's idea, as in *I see what you mean about skateboards being dangerous—you've made your point.* This expression uses *point* in the sense of "an important or essential argument or suggestion." Also see MAKE A POINT OF; TAKE SOMEONE'S POINT.

**make one's way** **1.** Go in a particular direction or to a particular destination, as in *I'm making my way to the china department,* or *How are we going to make our way through this crowd?* **2.** Also, **make one's own way.** Advance in life by one's own efforts, *His family hasn't much money, so he'll just have to make his own way in the world.*

**make one's wishes known** Also, **make one's feelings known.** Let others know what one wants or feels, as in *He hadn't made his wishes known, so we didn't know he wanted to leave.* This idiom is often used in the negative or as a suggestion, as in *You need to make your feelings known.*

**make or break** Cause either total success or total ruin, as in *This assignment will make or break her as a reporter.*

**make out** **1.** Manage to see, especially with difficulty, as in *I can hardly make out the number on the door.* **2.** Manage, get along, as in *How did you make out with the accountant?* **3.** Engage in long kisses or in sexual foreplay, as in *Bill and Jane were making out on the sofa.* **4.** Understand, as in *I can't make out what she is trying to say.* Also see CAN'T MAKE HEAD OR TAIL OF. **5.** Try to establish or prove, as in *He made out that he was innocent.* **6.** Imply or suggest, as in *He made out that it was all my fault.* This usage often occurs with an object plus a base verb, as in *Are you making me out to be a liar?* **7.** Write something out; fill in a written form. For example, *He made out the check for ten dollars,* or *Jane started making out job applications.*

**make out like a bandit** Succeed extremely well, as in *He invested in real estate and made out like a bandit.* This expression compares other forms of success to that of a successful robber. It may come from the use of *bandit* (or *one-armed bandit*) for a slot machine, which is far more profitable for the casino than for gamblers.

**make over** **1.** Redo, renovate, as in *We're making over the playroom into an additional bedroom.* **2.** Change or transfer ownership, usually through a legal document, as in *She made over the house to her daughter.*

**make peace** Achieve friendly relations or an end to hostilities. For example, *The United Nations sent a task force to make peace,* or *Mom was good at making peace among the children.* Also see MAKE ONE'S PEACE WITH.

**make ready** see GET READY.

**make rounds** see MAKE THE ROUNDS, def. 2.

**make sail** see SET SAIL.

**make sense** **1.** Be understandable. This usage is often used in a negative context, as in *This explanation doesn't make sense.* It may also be put as **make any sense,** as in *This proposal doesn't make any sense.* **2.** Be reasonable, wise, or practical, as in *It makes sense to find out first how many will attend the conference.* This term uses *sense* in the meaning of "what is reasonable."

**make short work of** Complete or use up something quickly, as in *The children made short work of the ice cream,* or *They made short work of cleaning up so they could get to the movies.* This term in effect means "turn something into a brief task."

**make someone look good** Cause someone to appear in a favorable light, as in *Harry's staff does most of the important work and makes him look good.*

**make something of** **1.** Also, **make something of oneself.** Make important or useful; improve. For example, *Dad hoped Tim would make something of himself.* **2.** Give too much importance to something, especially a problem or disagreement, as in *Ann decided to make something of it when Bob said women's studies is not a real discipline.* This usage sometimes is put as **make something out of nothing,** as in *You shouldn't worry just because he had coffee with your girlfriend—*

*don't make something out of nothing.* For an antonym, see MAKE NOTHING OF, def. 1.

**make sport of** see MAKE FUN OF.

**make *something* stick** Make effective or permanent, as in *They tried to appeal, but our lawyers made the verdict stick.*

**make sure 1.** Make certain, establish something without doubt, as in *Make sure all the doors are locked.* It is also put as **make sure of,** as in *Before you make that speech, make sure of your facts.* **2. make sure of.** Act so as to be certain of something, as in *He wanted to make sure of support in his own district before looking for support elsewhere.*

**make the bed** Put the coverings of a bed in order after sleeping it it. For example, *Mom taught us all to make the bed every morning.* Also see MAKE ONE'S BED AND LIE IN IT.

**make the best of it** Also, **make the best of a bad bargain.** Manage as well as possible in a bad situation, as in *Jeff ended up in a class without his friends but decided to make the best of it,* or *She got the worst possible position, but Dad told her to make the best of a bad bargain.*

**make the dust fly** Also, **make the feathers fly** or **make the fur fly.** Cause a disturbance or a lot of sudden noisy activity or arguing. For example, *When she saw the dog sleeping on her new bedspread, she really made the dust fly,* or *As soon as he learns who dented his car, he'll make the feathers fly,* or *She'd better not interfere, or he'll make the fur fly.* The first usage refers to the results of a vigorous housecleaning effort. The two variants refer to what happens when a hunting dog finds a bird or rabbit.

**make the grade** Satisfy the requirements, qualify; also, succeed. For example, *Angela hoped that the photos she entered in the contest would make the grade,* or *Barbara certainly has made the grade as a trial lawyer.* This expression uses *grade* in the sense of "accepted standard."

**make the most of** Use something to the greatest advantage, as in *She planned to make the most of her trip to Europe,* or *The class quickly made the most of the teacher's absence.*

**make the rounds 1.** Follow a given series of places on a route, as in *The watchman makes the rounds every hour,* or *The gossip soon made the rounds of the school.* There are many versions of this expression, such as **go the rounds, follow the rounds,** and **march the rounds. 2. make rounds.** Visit each hospitalized patient who is under the care of a specific doctor, as in *The surgery residents make rounds with their chief every morning.*

**make the scene** Appear at or participate in an event, as in *I'll miss most of the party, but I hope to make the scene before midnight.* This expression uses *scene* in the sense of "a place where an action occurs."

**make the sparks fly** Also, **make sparks fly.** Start a fight or argument, as in *If Mary finds out he went to the races without her, that will make the sparks fly.* In this idiom, the small particles of a fire called *sparks* are transferred to a tense situation.

**make time 1.** Act quickly, as in *We have to make time if we don't want to miss the first part of the movie.* This usage refers to compensating for lost time. Also see MAKE GOOD TIME. **2. make time for.** Arrange one's schedule to include doing something or seeing someone, as in *Harold always manages to make time for tennis,* or *I'm pretty busy, but I can make time for you tomorrow morning.* **3. make time with.** Flirt with or attract the romantic interest of someone, as in *Jerry is trying to make time with Beth.*

**make tracks** Move or leave in a hurry, as in *If we're going to catch the first show, we'd better make tracks.* This term refers to the footprints left by running.

**make up 1.** Put together, construct or compose something, as in *The druggist made up the prescription,* or *The tailor said he could make up a suit from this fabric.* **2.** Combine to form something, as in *One hundred years make up a century.* **3.** Change the appearance of or apply cosmetics to someone. For example, *He made himself up as an old man.* **4.** Create or invent a story, an excuse, a song, or something similar. For example, *Mary is always making up stories for her children,* or *Is that account true, or did you make it up?* **5.** Do or give something to fill the place of what's missing. For example, *I only have twenty dollars, so can you make up the difference in the bill?* or *What that basketball player lacks in height he makes up in skill.* Also see MAKE UP FOR. **6.** Repeat a course, take a test, or do an assignment at a later time because of an earlier absence or failure. For example, *Steve will have to make up calculus this summer,* or *The professor is letting me make up the exam tomorrow.* **7.** Also, **make it up.** Resolve a quarrel, as in *The Sweeneys argue a lot, but they always make up before going to sleep,* or *Will you two ever make it up?* **8.** Put something in order, as in *We asked them to make up the room for us,* or *Can you make up another bed in this room?* Also see the following idioms beginning with MAKE UP.

**make up for 1.** Do something good to take away the bad effects of an action or event, as in *How can she make up for all the trouble she caused?* **2. make up for lost time** Also, **make up ground.** Hurry to compensate for wasted time, as in *They started late but hoped* *to make up for lost time,* or *We're behind in the schedule, and we'll just have to make up ground as best we can.*

**make up one's mind** Decide between choices, come to a decision, as in *I had trouble making up my mind about which coat I liked best.*

**make up to** Try to please or gain favor with, flirt with, as in *She was always making up to the boss's assistant.*

**make use of** Utilize, use, as in *I hope readers will make use of this dictionary.*

**make waves** Cause a disturbance or an argument, as in *We've finally reached an agreement, so please don't make waves.* This expression refers to causing turbulence in the water. Also see ROCK THE BOAT.

**make way 1.** Allow room for passage, move aside, as in *Please make way for the wheelchair.* **2.** Also, **make way for.** Allow someone to take one's position, as in *It's time he retired and made way for some younger professor.* **3.** Progress, advance, as in *Is this enterprise making way?* For a synonym, see MAKE HEADWAY.

**make whoopee** Have sexual relations, as in *They were caught making whoopee.* This slang expression is now used only in a humorous way.

**make with** Use, concern oneself with, as in *Why are you making with that strange group?* or *Let's go—make with the feet!* This expression is a translation of the Yiddish *mach mit.*

**mama's boy** A boy or man seen as too attached to and protected by his mother. For example, *The children called Tom a mama's boy because he ran home with every little problem.*

**man** In addition to the idioms beginning with MAN, also see AS ONE (MAN); COMPANY MAN; DIRTY JOKE (OLD MAN); EVERY MAN FOR HIMSELF; EVERY MAN HAS HIS PRICE; GIRL (MAN) FRIDAY; HATCHET MAN; HIRED HAND (MAN); LADIES' MAN; LOW MAN ON THE TOTEM POLE; MARKED MAN; NO MAN IS AN ISLAND; ODD MAN OUT; OF FEW WORDS, A MAN; ONE-MAN SHOW; ONE MAN'S MEAT IS ANOTHER MAN'S POISON; OWN PERSON (MAN); RIGHT-HAND MAN; SEE A MAN ABOUT A DOG; TO A MAN. Also see under MEN.

**man about town** A man who frequently attends fashionable social functions, as in *Fred is quite the man about town these days.* This expression uses *town* in the sense of "a sophisticated place," as opposed to the country.

**man in the street, the** Also, **the woman in the street.** An ordinary, average person, as in *It will be interesting to see how the man in the street will answer that question.* This expression came into use when the votes of ordinary citizens began to influence public affairs. Today it is used especially in the news media, where reporters try to learn the political opinions of the average person.

**manna from heaven** An unexpected help or advantage, as in *After all the criticism in the media, that favorable evaluation was like manna from heaven.* This expression refers to food (*manna*) that miraculously appeared in the desert in the biblical account of the Israelites' journey from Egypt to the Promised Land.

**manner** see ALL KINDS (MANNER) OF; BY ALL (MANNER OF) MEANS; COMPANY MANNERS; IN A MANNER OF SPEAKING; TO THE MANNER BORN.

**man of few words** see OF FEW WORDS.

**man of his word, a** A man who keeps promises, who can be trusted, as in *You can count on Rudy—he's a man of his word.* This expression uses *word* in the sense of "a promise."

**man of the moment** see OF THE MOMENT.

**man of the world, a** Also, **a woman of the world.** A sophisticated person with wide experience of the world. For example, *You can discuss anything with him—he's a man of the world,* or *She's a woman of the world and understands these delicate issues.*

**many** In addition to the idioms beginning with MANY, also see AS MANY; GOOD (GREAT) MANY; IN SO MANY WORDS; IRONS IN THE FIRE, TOO MANY; SO MANY; TOO MANY COOKS SPOIL THE BROTH.

**many a** A large number, as in *Many a little boy has wanted to become a firefighter,* or *I've seen that happen many a time.* This adjective is always used with a singular noun, as in the examples. Also see MANY IS THE.

**many happy returns** Also, **many happy returns of the day.** Happy birthday and many more of them, as in *I came by to wish you many happy returns.*

**many is the** There are a great number of, as in *Many is the time I've told her to be careful,* or *Many is the child who's been warned against strangers.* This phrase is always used at the beginning of a sentence and with a singular noun. Also see MANY A.

**map** see PUT ON THE MAP; WIPE OFF THE MAP.

**marble** see HAVE ALL ONE'S MARBLES.

**marching orders, get one's 1.** Be ordered to move on or proceed. For example, *The sales force got their marching orders yesterday, so now they'll be on the road with the new product.* **2.** Be fired or dismissed from a job, as in *It's too bad about Jack—the boss gave him his marching orders Friday.* This expression originally referred to a military command.

**march to a different drummer** Also, **march to a different beat.** Act independently; behave differently or hold different ideas from most others, as in *Joe wanted to be married on a mountain top—he always* *marches to a different beat,* or *Sarah has her own ideas for the campaign; she marches to a different drummer.* This idiom refers to being out of step in a parade.

**mark** In addition to the idioms beginning with MARK, also see BLACK MARK; GIVE BAD MARKS TO; HIGH-WATER MARK; HIT THE BULL'S-EYE (MARK); MAKE ONE'S MARK; OFF THE MARK; QUICK OFF THE MARK; TOE THE LINE (MARK); UP TO PAR (THE MARK); X MARKS THE SPOT.

**mark down** Reduce the price of something, as in *If they mark down these shoes, I'll buy two pairs.* The *mark* here refers to the writing on the price tag.

**marked man, a** Also, **a marked woman.** A person that others suspect or plan to attack. For example, *As a witness to the robbery, he felt he was a marked man,* or *After her lawsuit, she was a marked woman—no one would hire her.*

**market** see CORNER THE MARKET; FLEA MARKET; IN THE MARKET FOR; ON THE MARKET; PLAY THE MARKET.

**mark my words** Pay attention to what I say, as in *Mark my words, that man is not to be trusted.*

**mark time** Pass time waiting for something to occur, as in *We were just marking time until we received our instructions.* This idiom refers to marching in place to the *time,* or beat, of music.

**mark up 1.** Spoil the appearance of something by drawing, cutting, or another means of covering something with marks. For example, *John was punished for marking up his desk,* or *These shoes really mark up the floor.* **2.** Raise the price of something, as in *This small shop marks up its merchandise much more than department stores do.*

**mast** see AT HALF-MAST.

**master** see PAST MASTER.

**mat** see GO TO THE MAT; WELCOME MAT.

**match** see MEET ONE'S MATCH; MIX AND MATCH; WHOLE BALL OF WAX (SHOOTING MATCH).

**matter** In addition to the idioms beginning with MATTER, also see CRUX OF THE MATTER; FOR THAT MATTER; GRAY MATTER; MINCE MATTERS; MIND OVER MATTER; NO JOKE (LAUGHING MATTER); NO MATTER; WHAT'S THE MATTER.

**matter of course, a** Something that is expected, as in *It was a matter of course that police officers received special training.* It is also put as **as a matter of course,** meaning "as part of a standard procedure," as in *The employer checked John's references as a matter of course.* This idiom uses *course* in the sense of "the natural or logical order of events."

**matter of fact, a** Something that is really true, as in *The records showed it to be a matter of fact that they were married in 1960.* This idiom often occurs in the phrase **as a matter of fact,** as in *As a matter of fact, you are absolutely right.*

**matter of life and death, a** A very urgent issue, situation, or circumstance. This expression is sometimes used literally, as in *She told the doctor to hurry, since it was a matter of life and death,* but not always, as in *She desperately wants to win—it's a matter of life and death to her.*

**matter of opinion, a** A question on which people hold different views, as in *I rather like that design, but really, it's a matter of opinion,* or *The quality of that new restaurant is a matter of opinion.*

**max out 1.** Reach one's limit by producing or performing to the maximum, as in *The weight lifter maxed out at 180 kilograms.* **2.** Reach a point at which no more growth, improvement, or benefit is possible, as in *The salary for this job maxes out at $90,000.*

**may** see BE THAT AS IT MAY; COME WHAT MAY; LET THE CHIPS FALL WHERE THEY MAY; TO WHOM IT MAY CONCERN.

**me** see DEAR ME; SO HELP ME.

**meal** In addition to the idiom beginning with MEAL; also see SQUARE MEAL.

**meal ticket** A person or thing depended on as a source of income, as in *That player is a real meal ticket for his team,* or *Her ability to get along with other people will be her meal ticket when she goes into sales.* This expression refers to the practice of handing out tickets for meals, as in a school cafeteria.

**mean** In addition to the idioms beginning with MEAN, also see under MEANS.

**mean business** Be serious or in earnest. For example, *He really means business with this deadline.* This idiom uses *business* in the sense of "a serious effort."

**means** see BEYOND ONE'S MEANS; BY ALL MEANS; BY ANY MEANS; BY MEANS OF; BY NO MEANS; END JUSTIFIES THE MEANS.

**mean to** Intend to, as in *I meant to go running this morning but got up too late,* or *I'm sorry I broke it—I didn't mean to.*

**measure** In addition to the idiom beginning with MEASURE, also see BEYOND MEASURE; FOR GOOD MEASURE; IN SOME MEASURE; MADE TO MEASURE; TAKE SOMEONE'S MEASURE.

**measure up** Also, **measure up to. 1.** Be the equal of, as in *Is he a good enough actor to measure up to the other members of the cast?* **2.** Be good enough or well-prepared enough for, as in *His latest book hasn't measured up to the reviewers' expectations.*

**meat** In addition to the idioms beginning with MEAT, also see BEAT THE MEAT; ONE'S MAN'S MEAT IS ANOTHER MAN'S POISON.

**meat and drink to one** A source of great satisfaction or delight, as in *Good music is meat and drink to her.*

**meat and potatoes** The fundamental part or parts of something, as in *That paragraph is the meat and potatoes of the contract.* This term transfers basic foods to the basics of an issue.

**medicine** see DOSE OF ONE'S OWN MEDICINE; TAKE ONE'S MEDICINE.

**medium** see HAPPY MEDIUM.

**meet** In addition to the idioms beginning with MEET, also see GO (MEET) HALFWAY; MAKE ENDS MEET; MORE THAN MEETS THE EYE.

**meeting of the minds, a** Agreement, a shared understanding, as in *The teachers and the principal had a meeting of the minds regarding smoking in school.*

**meet one's match** Find someone equal in ability to oneself, as in *The chess champion was about to meet his match in a computer.*

**meet one's Waterloo** Suffer a major defeat, as in *Our team's done well this season but is about to meet its Waterloo.* This term refers to Napoleon's military defeat at Waterloo, Belgium, which marked the end of his domination of Europe. It was soon transferred to other kinds of defeat.

**meet the requirements** Satisfy the conditions, as in *His work does not meet graduation requirements,* or *Lynn did not meet the requirements for this position.* This expression uses *meet* in the sense of "satisfy." Also see MEASURE UP, def. 2.

M

**meet up with** Come into contact with, especially by accident, as in *We hadn't gone far along the trail when we met up with another mule train.*

**meet with** Experience or face, as in *The housing bill met with their approval,* or *Drunk and homeless, he's bound to meet with a bad end.*

**mellow out** Calm down, relax, as in *The teacher mellowed out when they explained what had happened.* This expression uses *mellow* in the sense of "ripening," with the idea of softness and sweetness.

**melt** In addition to the idiom beginning with MELT, also see BUTTER WOULDN'T MELT.

**melt in one's mouth** Taste very good, as in *This cake is wonderful—it just melts in your mouth.* This expression at first referred to the tenderness of food that did not require chewing. Also see BUTTER WOULDN'T MELT.

**memory** see IN MEMORY OF.

**men** see SEPARATE THE MEN FROM THE BOYS. Also see under MAN.

**mend** In addition to the idioms beginning with MEND, also see ON THE MEND.

**mend fences** Improve poor relations; do things to soften the anger of personal, political, or business contacts. For example, *The senator always goes home weekends and spends time mending fences.*

**mend one's ways** Improve one's behavior, as in *After he was threatened with suspension, Jerry promised to mend his ways.* This expression transfers a repair of clothes to fixing problems in one's character.

**mention** see NOT TO MENTION; YOU'RE WELCOME (DON'T MENTION IT).

**mercy** see AT THE MERCY OF.

**merit** see ON ITS MERITS.

**merry** see MORE THE MERRIER.

**mess** In addition to the idioms beginning with MESS, also see MAKE A MESS OF.

**message** see GET THE MESSAGE.

**mess around** see FOOL AROUND.

**mess up** **1.** Create disorder in; ruin. For example, *On rainy days the children really mess up the house,* or *The wind messed up my hair.* **2.** Make a mistake, especially from nervousness or confusion, as in *He messed up and took the wrong folder to the meeting,* or *Jill swore she would never mess up again.* **3.** Beat up, manhandle, as in *Joe got messed up in a barroom brawl.*

**mess with** **1.** Become involved or associate with. For example, *Our music society won't mess with those street musicians.* **2.** Annoy, bother, as in *I told him not to mess with me or there would be trouble.*

**meter is running, the** Costs or other consequences are growing, as in *We'd better come to a decision soon, for the meter is running.* This expression refers to the charge adding up on a taxi's meter.

**method in one's madness** Also, **method to one's madness.** A plan or purpose in crazy behavior, as in *Harry's trips around the country seem random, but there's method to his madness—he's checking on real estate values.* Also see CRAZY LIKE A FOX.

**mice** see BEST-LAID PLANS OF MICE AND MEN; WHEN THE CAT'S AWAY, THE MICE WILL PLAY. Also see under MOUSE.

**midair** see under LEAVE HANGING.

**middle** In addition to the idiom beginning with MIDDLE, also see CAUGHT IN THE MIDDLE; IN THE MIDDLE OF; PLAY BOTH ENDS AGAINST THE MIDDLE.

**middle of nowhere, in the** A very remote location, as in *They live in the middle of nowhere in the mountains of Oregon.*

**middling** see FAIR TO MIDDLING.

**midnight oil** see BURN THE MIDNIGHT OIL.

**midstream** see CHANGE HORSES IN MIDSTREAM.

**might makes right** Superior strength can make the rules or force agreement, as in *The generals dismissed the parliament and imprisoned the premier—might makes right in that country.*

**mighty** see HIGH AND MIGHTY.

**mildly** see PUT IT MILDLY.

**mile** In addition to the idioms beginning with MILE, also see MISS BY A MILE; MISS IS AS GOOD AS A MILE; STICK OUT (A MILE).

**mile a minute, a** Very rapidly, as in *She was talking a mile a minute about the accident.* This expression refers to the actual speed of 60 miles per hour.

**miles and miles** A long distance; also, a large interval, by far. For example, *We drove for miles and miles before we saw a gas station,* or *She was miles and miles a better pianist than her brother.*

**milk** In addition to the idiom beginning with MILK, also see CRY OVER SPILT MILK.

**milk of human kindness, the** Kindness, sympathy, as in *There's no milk of human kindness in that girl—she's totally selfish.*

**mill** see GRIST FOR THE MILL; THROUGH THE MILL; TILT AT WINDMILLS.

**million** see FEEL LIKE ONESELF (A MILLION); LOOK LIKE A MILLION DOLLARS; ONE IN A MILLION.

**millstone around one's neck** A heavy burden, as in *Her demanding relatives are a millstone around her neck.* The hanging of a millstone around the neck is mentioned as a punishment in the Bible.

**mince matters** Also, **mince words.** Moderate or restrain one's language to be polite or avoid giving offense. Today these phrases are nearly always put negatively, as in *Not to mince matters, I feel he should resign,* or *Don't mince words—say what you mean.*

**mincemeat** see MAKE MINCEMEAT OF.

**mind** In addition to the idioms beginning with MIND, also see BACK OF ONE'S MIND; BEAR IN MIND; BLOW ONE'S MIND; BOGGLE THE MIND; BRING TO MIND; CALL SOMETHING TO MIND; CHANGE ONE'S MIND; COME TO MIND; CROSS ONE'S MIND; FRAME OF MIND; GO OUT OF ONE'S MIND; GREAT MINDS RUN IN THE SAME CHANNEL; HALF A MIND; HAVE A GOOD MIND TO; IN ONE'S MIND'S EYE; IN ONE'S RIGHT MIND; KNOW ONE'S OWN MIND; LOAD OFF ONE'S MIND; LOSE ONE'S MIND; MAKE UP ONE'S MIND; MEETING OF THE MINDS; NEVER MIND; OF TWO MINDS; ONE-TRACK MIND; ON ONE'S MIND; OPEN MIND; OUT OF SIGHT (OUT OF MIND); PIECE OF ONE'S MIND; PRESENCE OF MIND; PUT SOMEONE IN MIND OF; READ SOMEONE'S MIND; SET ONE'S MIND AT REST; SLIP SOMEONE'S MIND; SPEAK ONE'S MIND; TO MY MIND.

**mind like a steel trap, have a** Be very quick to understand something, as in *Aunt Ida may be old, but she still has a mind like a steel trap.* This expression compares the closing of an animal trap to a quick mental grasp.

**mind of one's own, have a** Think independently, reach one's own opinions or conclusions. For example, *You can't tell Karen what she should wear—she has a mind of her own.* Also see KNOW ONE'S OWN MIND.

**mind one's own business** Keep from interfering in other people's lives, pay attention to one's own affairs, as in *If she would only mind her own business, there would be a lot fewer family quarrels.*

**mind one's p's and q's** Practice good manners, be precise and careful in one's behavior and speech, as in *Their grandmother often told the children to mind their p's and q's.* The origin of this expression is not certain. One theory is that bartenders kept track of customers' drinks in terms of *pints* (*p's*) and *quarts* (*q's*), and the phrase referred to an honest accounting. Another theory relates the expression to the fact that schoolchildren were taught to be careful in writing the letters *p* and *q*.

**mind over matter** The strength of one's will or desire to do something can win over physical limitations or difficulties. For example, *Margaret was determined to go to the wedding, even on crutches—mind over matter.*

**mind the store** Attend to local or family matters, as in *Ask Dad for permission; he's minding the store while Mom's away.* This expression transfers looking after an actual business to more general activities.

**mine** see BACK TO THE SALT MINES; GOLD MINE; YOUR GUESS IS AS GOOD AS MINE.

**mint condition, in** In excellent condition, perfect, as in *This car is in mint condition.* This expression refers to the condition of a new coin.

**minute** see AT THE LAST MINUTE; EVERY MINUTE COUNTS; JUST A MINUTE; MILE A MINUTE; WAIT A MINUTE.

**miscarriage of justice** An unfair decision, especially one in a court of law. For example, *Many felt that his being expelled from the school was a miscarriage of justice.* This expression uses *miscarriage* in the sense of "making a blunder."

**mischief** see MAKE MISCHIEF.

**misery** In addition to the idiom beginning with MISERY, also see PUT SOMEONE OUT OF HIS OR HER MISERY.

**misery loves company** Its easier to bear unhappiness when others are suffering too, as in *She secretly hoped her friend would fail, too—misery loves company.*

**miss** In addition to the idioms beginning with MISS, also see HEART MISSES A BEAT; HIT OR MISS; NEAR MISS; NOT MISS A TRICK.

**miss a beat** Hesitate for a moment because of embarrassment or confusion. This expression is most often used in a negative context, as in *He sidestepped the reporter's question about his personal life without missing a beat,* or *Not missing a beat, she outlined all the reasons for her decision.* This expression refers to the regular beat of musical time.

**miss by a mile** Fail by a lot, as in *Your guess as to the winner missed by a mile.* This expression uses *miss* in the sense of "fail to hit something aimed at." *By a mile* means by a great distance or interval.

**miss is as good as a mile, a** Coming close to success but failing is no better than failing by a lot, as in *He was beaten by just one vote, but a miss is as good as a mile.*

**miss much** see under NOT MISS A TRICK.

**Missouri** see FROM MISSOURI.

**miss out on** Lose a chance for or the opportunity to enjoy, as in *Ruth came late to the party and missed out on all the fun,* or *Trudy missed out on the promotion.* Also see LOSE OUT, def. 2.

**miss the boat** **1.** Fail to take advantage of an opportunity, as in *Jean missed the boat on that club membership.* This expression first referred to not being in time to catch a boat. It has since been applied more widely. **2.** Fail to understand something, as in *I'm afraid our legislator missed the boat on that amendment to the bill.* Also see MISS THE POINT.

**miss the point** Fail to understand the essential or important part of something, as in *He missed the point of Gwen's complaint, thinking she was upset about something else.*

**mistake** In addition to the idiom beginning with MISTAKE, also see BY MISTAKE; MAKE NO MISTAKE.

**mistake for** Confuse someone or something with someone or something else, as in *I'm sorry, I mistook you for your sister,* or *Don't mistake that friendly smile for good intentions; he's a tough competitor.*

**mix and match** Combine different items in a number of ways. For example, *The store displayed skirts, blouses, and pants in colors that one could mix and match.*

**mixed bag, a** A collection of various people, items, activities, or the like; an assortment. For example, *The school offers a mixed bag of after-school activities—team sports, band practice, a language class.* This idiom presents an image of a sack full of different items.

**mixed blessing, a** Something that has both good and bad features, as in *Being accepted by the college was a mixed blessing, since she couldn't afford the tuition.*

**mixed feelings** A partly positive and partly negative reaction to something, as in *I have mixed feelings about this trip; I'd love to go but don't want to ride in that tiny car.*

**mix it up** Get in a fight, as in *The driver got out and began to mix it up with the other driver.*

**mix up** **1.** Confuse someone, as in *His explanation just mixed me up even more.* **2.** Confuse one person or thing with another, as in *I always mix up the twins.* Also see MISTAKE FOR. **3.** Change the order or arrangement of things, as in *I've organized those papers, so don't mix them up.* **4. mixed up.** Involved, connected, or associated, as in *He got mixed up with the wrong crowd.*

**mold** see CAST IN THE SAME MOLD.

**molehill** see MAKE A MOUNTAIN OUT OF A MOLEHILL.

**moment** In addition to the idiom beginning with MOMENT, also see AT THIS POINT (MOMENT); EVERY MINUTE (MOMENT) COUNTS; FOR THE MOMENT; HAVE ONE'S MOMENTS; JUST A MINUTE (MOMENT); LIVE FOR THE MOMENT; NEVER A DULL MOMENT; NOT FOR A MOMENT; OF THE MOMENT; ON THE SPUR OF THE MOMENT; WEAK MOMENT.

**moment of truth, the** A very important or decisive time, when one faces the final test, as in *Now that all the bills are in, we've come to the moment of truth—can we afford to live here or not?*

**Monday-morning quarterback** A person who criticizes or passes judgment after something has already happened and it's easier to know what's best. For example, *Ethel was a Monday-morning quarterback about the failure of the program and claimed that she had known it wouldn't work.* This expression refers to fans who criticize the decisions by the coach and quarterback in Sunday's football game the next day. The *quarterback,* of course, is the team member who calls the plays.

**money** In addition to the idioms beginning with MONEY, also see COLOR OF SOMEONE'S MONEY; EASY MONEY; EVEN MONEY; FOOL AND HIS MONEY ARE SOON PARTED; FOR ONE'S MONEY; FUNNY MONEY; GET ONE'S MONEY'S WORTH; HUSH MONEY; IN THE MONEY; MADE OF MONEY; NOT FOR LOVE OR MONEY; ON THE MONEY; PAY YOUR MONEY AND TAKE YOUR CHOICE; PIN MONEY; POCKET MONEY; PUT MONEY ON; PUT ONE'S MONEY WHERE ONE'S MOUTH IS; RUN FOR ONE'S MONEY; THROW GOOD MONEY AFTER BAD; TIME IS MONEY.

**money burns a hole in one's pocket** A person can't keep from spending whatever money he or she has. For example, *As soon as she gets paid, she goes shopping; money burns a hole in her pocket.* This expression suggests that someone must take out the money before it actually burns a hole.

**money is no object** Also, **expense is no object.** It doesn't matter how much it costs, as in *Get the very best coat you can find—money is no object.* In this expression *no object* means "presenting no obstacle."

**money talks** People with money have great influence, as in *Big contributors to campaigns are generally rewarded with important posts—in politics, money talks.*

**money to burn** More than enough money for what is required or expected, as in *After they paid off the creditors, they still had money to burn.* The expression implies that one has so much that one can afford to burn it. This sense of the verb *burn* is occasionally used in other phrases, such as **time to burn** ("more than enough time").

**monkey** In addition to the idioms beginning with MONKEY, also see FOOL (MONKEY) AROUND; MAKE A FOOL OF (MONKEY OUT OF); MORE FUN THAN A BARREL OF MONKEYS; THROW A MONKEY WRENCH INTO.

**monkey business** Silly, mischievous, or dishonest actions, as in *The teacher told the children to stop the monkey business and get to work,* or *I don't trust that lawyer—there's some monkey business going on.* This expression compares the tricks of monkeys to human behavior.

**monkey on one's back** **1.** Drug addiction, as in *He'd had a monkey on his back for at least two years.* **2.** An annoying problem or burden, as in *This project has proved to be a monkey on my back—there seems to be no end to it.* Both usages refer to being unable to shake off the animal from one's back.

**monster** see GREEN-EYED MONSTER.

**month** In addition to the idiom beginning with MONTH, also see BY THE DAY (MONTH).

**month of Sundays, a** A long time, as in *I haven't seen Barbara in a month of Sundays.* This exaggerated expression may have first meant a long, boring time, since games and other kinds of amusement were often forbidden on Sunday.

**mood** see IN A BAD MOOD; IN THE MOOD.

**moon** see ASK FOR THE MOON; ONCE IN A BLUE MOON.

**moot point, a** A matter of no importance because it is irrelevant; also, a subject people disagree on. For example, *It's a moot point whether the chicken or the egg came first.*

**mop up** **1.** Clear an area of remaining enemy troops after a victory, as in *They left behind just one squadron to mop up.* **2.** Perform the minor tasks that complete a project or activity, as in *Go ahead, I'll mop up these last invoices.* Both usages transfer the task of housecleaning with a mop to other kinds of cleanup.

**mop up the floor with** Also, **wipe the floor with.** Defeat thoroughly, overwhelm, as in *The young boxer said he was sure to mop up the floor with his opponent,* or *I just know we'll wipe the floor with the competition.*

**moral support** Emotional or psychological support, as opposed to financial or physical help. For example, *There's not much I can do at the doctor's office, but I'll come with you to give you moral support.*

**more** In addition to the idioms beginning with MORE, also see BITE OFF MORE THAN ONE CAN CHEW; WEAR ANOTHER (MORE THAN ONE) HAT; WHAT IS MORE.

**more and more** Increasingly, to a steadily growing extent or degree. For example, *As night came on, we were getting more and more worried,* or *More and more I lean toward thinking he is right.*

**more bang for the buck** Also, **more bounce to the ounce.** More value for one's money, a greater return on an investment. For example, *Buying a condominium is better than renting for years and years—more bang for the buck,* or *We always get the largest packages of dog food—more bounce to the ounce.*

**more dead than alive** Exhausted, in poor condition, as in *By the time I got off that mountain I was more dead than alive.*

**more fun than a barrel of monkeys** Very amusing or lots of fun, as in *That video game was more fun than a barrel of monkeys.* This expression refers to the playful behavior of these animals.

**more often than not** Also, **often as not.** Fairly frequently, more than half the time, as in *More often than not we'll have dinner in the den,* or *Dean and Chris agree on travel plans, often as not.*

**more or less** **1.** Approximately, as in *The truck will hold two tons of dirt, more or less.* **2.** Basically, essentially, as in *We more or less agree on what needs to be done.*

M

**more power to** Best wishes to someone, as in *He's decided to climb Mount Everest—well, more power to him.* For a synonym, see RIGHT ON.

**more than meets the eye** A hidden meaning or part of something that is greater than one can understand at first. For example, *This sudden agreement involves more than meets the eye.*

**more than one bargained for** An unexpected result, especially an unfavorable one, as in *Serving on the board this year has involved more work than I bargained for.* This expression refers to a higher than anticipated cost for a transaction.

**more than one can shake a stick at** A large quantity, more than one can count, as in *Our town has more banks than you can shake a stick at.*

**more than one way to skin a cat** More than one method to reach the same end, as in *We can solve that problem by renting instead of buying a computer—there's more than one way to skin a cat.*

**more the merrier, the** As the number of people involved grows, the better the occasion becomes. For example, *John's invited all his family to come along, and why not? The more the merrier.*

**morning** In addition to the idioms beginning with MORNING, also see GOOD DAY (MORNING); MONDAY-MORNING QUARTERBACK.

**morning after, the** The unpleasant results of an evening's activity, especially drinking too much alcohol. For example, *A headache is just one of the symptoms of the morning after.* This expression originated as a synonym for a hangover (and was often put as *the morning after the night before*). It is now also used more loosely for the aftereffects of staying up late.

**morning, noon, and night** Constantly or repeatedly, as in *I'm sick of hearing the TV morning, noon, and night.* This phrase is usually used to complain about something that happens too often.

**moss** see ROLLING STONE GATHERS NO MOSS.

**most** see AT MOST; FOR THE MOST PART; MAKE THE MOST OF.

**mothballs** see PUT IN MOTHBALLS.

**mother** In addition to the idioms beginning with MOTHER, also see NECESSITY IS THE MOTHER OF INVENTION.

**mother of** The best or greatest of a type, as in *That was the mother of all tennis matches.* This expression originated during the Gulf War as a translation of Iraqi leader Saddam Hussein's term *umm al-ma'arik,* for "major battle"; the Arabic "mother of" is a figure of speech for "major" or "best." It was quickly adopted and applied to just about any person, event, or activity.

**mother tongue** A person's first language, learned as a child. For example, *She's from Switzerland and speaks three languages well, but her mother tongue is French.*

**motion** see GO THROUGH THE MOTIONS; SET IN MOTION.

**mountain** see MAKE A MOUNTAIN OUT OF A MOLEHILL.

**mouse** see PLAY CAT AND MOUSE; POOR AS A CHURCHMOUSE; QUIET AS A MOUSE. Also see under MICE.

**mouth** In addition to the idiom beginning with MOUTH, also see BAD MOUTH; BIG MOUTH; BUTTER WOULDN'T MELT IN ONE'S MOUTH; DOWN IN THE DUMPS (MOUTH); FOAM AT THE MOUTH; FOOT IN ONE'S MOUTH; FROM THE HORSE'S MOUTH; HAND TO MOUTH; HEART IN ONE'S MOUTH, HAVE ONE'S; KEEP ONE'S MOUTH SHUT; LAUGH OUT OF THE OTHER SIDE OF ONE'S MOUTH; LEAVE A BAD TASTE IN ONE'S MOUTH; LOOK A GIFT HORSE IN THE MOUTH; MAKE ONE'S MOUTH WATER; MELT IN ONE'S MOUTH; NOT OPEN ONE'S MOUTH; OUT OF THE MOUTHS OF BABES; PUT ONE'S MONEY WHERE ONE'S MOUTH IS; PUT WORDS IN SOMEONE'S MOUTH; RUN OFF AT THE MOUTH; SHOOT OFF ONE'S MOUTH; TAKE THE BIT IN ONE'S MOUTH; TAKE THE BREAD OUT OF SOMEONE'S MOUTH; TAKE THE WORDS OUT OF SOMEONE'S MOUTH; WORD OF MOUTH.

**mouthful** see SAY A MOUTHFUL.

**mouth off 1.** Complain or express one's opinions loudly and without care for who might hear, as in *She was always mouthing off about the other members of the class.* **2.** Speak disrespectfully, talk back, as in *He got in trouble by mouthing off to his teacher.*

**move** In addition to the idioms beginning with MOVE, also see GET A MOVE ON; ON THE MOVE.

**move a muscle** Move oneself even slightly. This idiom is usually put negatively, sometimes with implied criticism, as in *She won't move a muscle to help get dinner,* and sometimes not, as in *When I saw the deer, I stayed quite still, not daring to move a muscle.*

**move heaven and earth** Make the greatest possible effort, as in *I'd move heaven and earth to get an apartment here.*

**move in 1.** Begin to live in or use a place, as in *We are scheduled to move in next month,* or *Helen is moving in with her sister.* **2. move in on.** Disturb by moving into the area of; also, try to take control of. For example, *Their sales force is moving in on our territory,* or *The police moved in on the gang.*

**move on** Continue moving or progressing; also go away. For example, *It's time we moved on to the next item on the agenda,* or *The police ordered the spectators to move on.*

**move one's bowels** Go to the bathroom; defecate. For example, *Has the baby moved her bowels yet?*

**mover** In addition to the idiom beginning with MOVER, also see PRIME MOVER.

**mover and shaker** A person who holds power and influence in a particular activity or field, as in *He's one of the movers and shakers in the art world.*

**move up** Also, **move up in the world.** Advance, rise to a higher level, succeed, as in *Gene hoped he would move up in the new division,* or *That new house and car show they are moving up in the world.* Also see COME UP, def. 3.

**mow down 1.** Destroy in great numbers, especially in battle, as in *The machine gun mowed them down as they advanced.* **2.** Overpower and defeat, as in *He mowed down the opposition with his arguments.* This usage, like the first, refers to *mowing,* the cutting of grass.

**much** In addition to the idioms beginning with MUCH, also see AS MUCH; AS MUCH AS; MAKE MUCH OF; NOT MISS A TRICK (MUCH); NOT THINK MUCH OF; PRETTY MUCH; SO MUCH; SO MUCH FOR; SO MUCH THE BETTER; (MUCH) SOUGHT AFTER; TAKE IT (JUST SO MUCH); TOO MUCH OF A GOOD THING; WITHOUT SO MUCH AS.

**much ado about nothing** A big fuss over something very unimportant, as in *Jerry had everyone running around looking for his gloves—much ado about nothing.*

**much as** see AS MUCH AS, def. 2.
**much less** And certainly not, as in *He rarely talks about his outside activities, much less his family.*
**much sought after** see SOUGHT AFTER.
**muck up** Damage, make a mess of, as in *Don't let him write the review; he's sure to muck it up.* This idiom refers to the verb *muck* in the sense of "spread manure on." For a synonym, see FOUL UP.
**mud** see CLEAR AS MUD; NAME IS MUD; SLING MUD AT.
**muddle through** Complete something but in a confused manner, manage to do though awkwardly, as in *The choir never knows how to line up, but we muddle through somehow.*
**muddy the waters** Confuse the issue, as in *Bringing up one irrelevant fact after another, he succeeded in muddying the waters.* This expression refers to making a pond or stream hard to see through by stirring up mud from the bottom.
**mule** see STUBBORN AS A MULE.
**mull over** Think about something, consider slowly, as in *She mulled over the offer for some time and then said no.*
**multitude of sins, cover a** Do something good to balance the bad effects of a number of other things. For example, *You may not be offering to help with the fair, but that big donation covers a multitude of sins.*
**mum's the word** Say nothing about this, it's a secret, as in *Mum's the word on tonight's surprise party.*
**munchies, have the** Be very hungry for a snack. For example, *I have the munchies. What do you have to eat?* This idiom was previously associated with the use of marijuana, but it is now more widely applied.
**murder** In addition to the idiom beginning with MURDER, also see GET AWAY WITH (MURDER); SCREAM BLOODY MURDER.
**murder will out** Certain news cannot be kept secret, as in *The company discovered he was cheating them—murder will out, you know.*
**Murphy's law** If anything can go wrong, it will, as in *We may think we've covered all the details for the conference, but remember Murphy's law.*
**muscle** In addition to the idiom beginning with MUSCLE, also see FLEX ONE'S MUSCLES; MOVE A MUSCLE.
**muscle in** Also, **muscle in on.** Use force or strong influence to become involved with, get control of, or interfere with something, as in *The children were determined not to allow the school bully to muscle in,* or *No more muscling in on our policy decisions!*
**museum piece** A very old or an old-fashioned item or person, as in *When are you going to sell that museum piece of a car?* or *Aunt Jane's ideas come from another era—she's a real museum piece.* This expression first referred to an article valuable enough for museum display but soon began to be used disparagingly.
**music** In addition to the idiom beginning with MUSIC, also see FACE THE MUSIC.
**musical chairs, play** Move around from position to position, such as the jobs in an organization. For example, *Bob now has Mary's job, and she has Tom's, and he has Bob's—the boss loves to play musical chairs with the staff.* This expression refers to the game in which children walk around a number of seats (one less than the number of participants) while music plays. When the music stops, the players must sit down, and the player who is left standing is out of the game. Then another chair is removed, and the game continues until only one player is left.
**music to one's ears** Very pleasing information, excellent news, as in *So they're getting married? That's music to my ears.*
**must** see A MUST; SHOW MUST GO ON.
**mustard** see CUT THE MUSTARD.
**muster** In addition to the idiom beginning with MUSTER, also see PASS MUSTER.
**muster in** Bring someone into military service. For example, *They were mustered in at Fort Dix.* The antonym is **muster out,** meaning "leave or be discharged from military service," as in *He was mustered out and given a dishonorable discharge.*
**mutual admiration society** A relationship in which two people have strong feelings of respect for each other and often exchange compliments. The term may refer to either real or pretended admiration, as in *Each of them praised the other's book—it was a real mutual admiration society.*
**my eye** I don't believe it, that's nonsense, as in *You were at the library all day? My eye, you were!*
**my God** Also, **my goodness.** Expressions of shock, surprise, or dismay, as in *My God, you mean that he's dying?* or *My goodness, what luck! Goodness* here is a euphemism for *God.*
**my heart bleeds for you** I don't feel at all sorry for you, I don't sympathize, as in *You only got a 5 percent raise? My heart bleeds for you.*
**my name is mud** see under NAME IS MUD.

# Nn

**nail** In addition to the idioms beginning with NAIL, also see BITE ONE'S NAILS; FIGHT TOOTH AND NAIL; HARD AS NAILS; HIT THE BULL'S-EYE (NAIL ON THE HEAD).

**nail down** Find out or settle something so there is no doubt, as in *We still need to nail down our vacation plans,* or *The reporter nailed down the story by checking all the facts.* This expression refers to fixing or fastening something down with nails.

**nail in one's coffin** Something that might hasten or contribute to one's death, as in *Every cigarette you smoke is another nail in your coffin.* This expression, referring to fastening down a coffin lid, is almost always used today for a harmful habit such as tobacco use.

**naked as a jaybird** Bare, unclothed, as in *I came straight out of the shower, naked as a jaybird.*

**naked eye, the** Human sight without the help of an instrument such as a microscope or telescope. For example, *These insects are too small to be seen with the naked eye.*

N

**naked truth, the** Plain facts, adding to them or hiding anything. For example, *What I've told you is the naked truth.* This expression may refer to a story in which Truth and Falsehood went swimming. Afterward, Falsehood dressed in Truth's clothes, and Truth, refusing to take another's clothes, went naked.

**name** In addition to the idioms beginning with NAME, also see CALL ONE NAMES; CLEAR ONE'S NAME; DROP NAMES; GIVE A BAD NAME TO; GO BY (THE NAME OF); IN NAME ONLY; IN THE NAME OF; MAKE A NAME FOR ONESELF; ON A FIRST-NAME BASIS; TAKE SOMEONE'S NAME IN VAIN; TO ONE'S NAME; WORTHY OF THE NAME; YOU NAME IT.

**name after** Also, **name for.** Give someone or something the name of another person or place. For example, *They named the baby after his grandfather,* or *The mountain was named for President McKinley.*

**name is mud, one's** One is in trouble, disgraced, or will lose his or her reputation, as in *If they find out I broke it, my name will be mud,* or *If his estimate is completely wrong, his name will be mud. Mud* was once a slang term for a stupid person or fool.

**name names** Specify persons by name, especially those who are accused of something. For example, *Others were involved in the robbery, so the police pressured him to name names.* It is also put negatively, **name no names,** as in *Some of our neighbors disobey the town's leash law, but I'm naming no names.*

**name of the game, the** The central part of the matter; also, the main goal. For example, *Getting them to admit they're wrong—that's the name of the game,* or *That coach insists that winning any way one can is the name of the game.* This rhyming idiom uses *name* in the sense of "identity."

**name the day** Decide on the date for a wedding, as in *Her parents pressed her to name the day.*

**napping** see CATCH NAPPING.

**narrow** In addition to the idiom beginning with NARROW, see STRAIGHT AND NARROW.

**narrow escape** A barely successful escape from or avoidance of danger or trouble, as in *He had a narrow escape, since the bullet came within inches of his head.* This expression uses *narrow* in the sense of "barely enough." For a synonym, see CLOSE CALL.

**nary a** Not one, as in *There's nary a mention of taxes in that speech,* or *Nary an officer could be seen.* This is an old contraction of "never a."

**natural** see under BIG AS LIFE.

**nature** In addition to the idiom beginning with NATURE, also see CALL OF NATURE; GOOD NATURE; SECOND NATURE.

**nature calls** Said when one feels the need to urinate or defecate, as in *I'll be back in a moment. Nature calls.*

**naught** see COME TO NOTHING (NAUGHT).

**near** In addition to the idioms beginning with NEAR, also see FAR AND NEAR; IN THE NEAR FUTURE; NOT ANYTHING LIKE (ANYWHERE NEAR).

**near at hand** see AT HAND.

**nearest and dearest** One's closest friends, companions, or relatives, as in *It's a small party—we're inviting only a dozen or so of our nearest and dearest.* This rhyming expression is used both ironically, as in *They've invited 200 of their nearest and dearest,* and straightforwardly, as in the first example.

**near miss** An incident or event that was almost an accident or a mistake; also, a failed attempt that almost succeeded. For example,

*It was a near miss for that car—luckily, the truck stopped in time,* or *Her horse kept having a near miss in every race, so she decided to sell it.* This expression originated during World War II, when it referred to a bomb exploding in the water close enough to a ship to damage it.

**near thing** Something that almost failed to happen or be achieved, as in *That election was a near thing—he won by a handful of votes.*

**near to one's heart** Also, **close to one's heart** or **dear to one's heart.** Loved by or important to one, as in *This last painting was very near to her heart,* or *His first grandson is close to his heart.*

**necessary evil, a** Something unpleasant or bad that must be accepted because it also does some good. For example, *Houses in this area all have those ugly bars in the windows—they're a necessary evil.*

**necessity** In addition to the idiom beginning with NECESSITY, also see MAKE A VIRTUE OF NECESSITY; OF NECESSITY.

**necessity is the mother of invention** A real need for something that will often lead to creative ideas and inventions. For example, *The first prisoner to tie together bedsheets to escape knew that necessity was the mother of invention.*

**neck** In addition to the idioms beginning with NECK, also see ALBATROSS AROUND ONE'S NECK; BREAK ONE'S BACK (NECK); BREATHE DOWN SOMEONE'S NECK; DEAD FROM THE NECK UP; MILLSTONE AROUND ONE'S NECK; PAIN IN THE NECK; RISK LIFE AND LIMB (ONE'S NECK); SAVE ONE'S NECK; STICK ONE'S NECK OUT; UP TO ONE'S EARS (NECK).

**neck and neck** So close that the advantage or lead shifts from one to the other or is impossible to see, as in *The two are neck and neck in developing a new operating system for the computer.* This term comes from horseracing, where the necks of two horses in competition appear to be side by side. For a synonym, see NIP AND TUCK.

**neck of the woods, one's** A neighborhood or region, as in *He's one of the wealthiest men in our neck of the woods.* This expression first referred to a forest settlement and is now used more loosely, for urban as well as rural areas.

**need** In addition to the idiom beginning with NEED, also see CRY OUT (HAVE A CRYING NEED) FOR.

**needle** In addition to the idiom beginning with NEEDLE, also see ON PINS AND NEEDLES.

**needle in a haystack, a** An item that is very hard or impossible to find, as in *Looking for that screw in his workshop amounts to looking for a needle in a haystack.*

**needless to say** Obviously, as anyone knows, as in *Needless to say, the availability of assault weapons is closely connected with crime.* This phrase is generally used for emphasis. Also see GOES WITHOUT SAYING.

**need like a hole in the head** Have neither a need nor a desire for something, as in *I needed that extra work like I need a hole in the head.*

**neither fish nor fowl** Not one or the other, not something fitting any category under discussion. For example, *They felt he was neither fish nor fowl—not qualified to lead the department, yet not appropriate to work as a staff member either.*

**neither here nor there** Unimportant, irrelevant, as in *You pay for the movie, and I'll get the dinner check, or vice versa—it's neither here nor there.* Also see BESIDE THE POINT.

**neither hide nor hair** see HIDE NOR HAIR.

**neither rhyme nor reason** see RHYME OR REASON.

**Nellie** see NERVOUS NELLIE.

**nerve** see BUNDLE OF NERVES; GET ON SOMEONE'S NERVES; HAVE A NERVE; LOSE ONE'S NERVE.

**nervous Nellie** Someone who is too timid or anxious, as in *He's a real nervous Nellie, calling the doctor about every little symptom.*

**nervous wreck** A person suffering from extreme nervousness or worry, as in *Pat was a nervous wreck until her mother arrived at the wedding.* Also see BASKET CASE.

**nest** In addition to the idiom beginning with NEST, also see EMPTY NEST; FEATHER ONE'S NEST; FOUL ONE'S NEST; STIR UP A HORNET'S NEST.

**nest egg** An amount of money saved for the future, as in *She'll have a nice nest egg by the time she retires.*

**never** In addition to the idioms beginning with NEVER, also see BETTER LATE THAN NEVER; IT NEVER RAINS BUT IT POURS; LIGHTNING NEVER STRIKES TWICE; NOW OR NEVER; WATCHED POT NEVER BOILS; WONDERS WILL NEVER CEASE; YOU NEVER CAN TELL.

**never a dull moment** Something is always changing or happening, as in *First she changes jobs, then she wrecks her car, then she falls in love—never a dull moment with my sister.*

**never fear** Don't worry that a thing will or won't occur, be confident, as in *I'll get there, never fear.*

**never had it so good** Be in a better situation now than one has ever been before, as in *She keeps complaining about her new job, but the truth is that she's never had it so good.*

**never hear the end of** Be constantly reminded of, as in *If you don't send a wedding present to them, you'll never hear the end of it from your mother.*

**never mind 1.** Don't worry about something, don't trouble yourself, it doesn't matter. For example, *Never mind what I said, it* *wasn't important,* or *Never mind, you can always take the driver's test again.* This expression uses *mind* in the sense of "care about something." **2.** Also, **never you mind.** Don't concern yourself with that, it's none of your business, as in *Never you mind where I plan to buy the new TV.*

**never miss a trick** see NOT MISS A TRICK.

**never-never land** A fantasy land, an imaginary place, as in *I don't know why she's so distracted and careless these days—she's way off in never-never land.*

**never put off until tomorrow** see under PUT OFF.

**never say die** Don't ever give up, do not lose hope, as in *This plan doesn't look too good, but never say die, we may be able to fix it.* This maxim today is often used ironically for something that has already failed.

**never say never** Nothing is impossible, anything can happen, as in *Mary said Tom would never call her again, but I told her, "Never say never."*

**new** In addition to the idioms beginning with NEW, also see BREAK (NEW) GROUND; BREATHE (NEW) LIFE INTO; FEEL LIKE NEW; NOTHING NEW UNDER THE SUN; TEACH AN OLD DOG NEW TRICKS; TURN OVER A NEW LEAF; WHAT'S COOKING (NEW); WHOLE NEW BALL GAME.

**new ball game** see WHOLE NEW BALL GAME.

**new blood** People who join a group or organization and bring in fresh ideas and energy. For example, *The board could really use some new blood next year.* This expression refers to a blood transfusion and uses *new* in the sense of "fresh."

**new broom sweeps clean, a** A fresh leader or administration gets rid of the old and brings in new ideas and people. For example, *Once he takes office, you can be sure the President will replace most of the people on the staff—a new broom sweeps clean.*

**new leaf** see TURN OVER A NEW LEAF.

**new lease on life** A fresh start; renewed energy and good health, as in *Since they bought his store, Dad has had a new lease on life.* This term uses *lease* to mean a rental agreement. The phrase originally referred only to recovery from illness. Later it was applied to any kind of fresh beginning.

**new one** see under THAT'S ONE ON ME.

**new person** see under FEEL LIKE NEW.

**news** see BAD NEWS; BREAK THE NEWS; NO NEWS IS GOOD NEWS.

**new wrinkle, a 1.** A new and clever way to do something, as in *The players added a new wrinkle to victory celebrations by tossing their shirts to the crowd after the game.* **2.** A new development or factor to be considered, as in *I thought our travel plans were set, but now there's a new wrinkle: she wants to bring her dog.*

**next** In addition to the idioms beginning with NEXT, also see CLEANLINESS IS NEXT TO GODLINESS.

**next best thing, the** The best alternative to or substitute for something that's not possible. For example, *If she can't get a summer job near the beach, then working at the camp would be the next best thing.*

**next door to** Very close to, as in *The old dog was next door to death.* This expression refers to a neighboring house.

**next to 1.** Beside, to or at the side of, as in *The car next to mine has a flat tire.* **2.** Following in order or degree, as in *Next to skiing, she likes hiking best.* **3.** Almost, nearly, as in *It's next to impossible to predict the outcome,* or *I earned next to nothing last year.*

**nice guys finish last** An expression that claims people have to think only of themselves to succeed in business or in life. For example, *You have to demand more from your employees—nice guys finish last.*

**nick** see IN THE NICK OF TIME.

**nickel** see NOT WORTH A DAMN.

**night** In addition to the idioms beginning with NIGHT, also see BLACK AS NIGHT; CALL IT A DAY (NIGHT); DIFFERENT AS NIGHT AND DAY; GOOD NIGHT; MAKE A DAY (NIGHT) OF IT; SHIPS THAT PASS IN THE NIGHT.

**night and day** Also, **day and night.** Continually, without stopping. This phrase is used either literally, as in *The alarm is on night and day,* or to exaggerate, as in *We were working day and night on these drawings.*

**night owl** A person who usually stays up late and is active at night, as in *You can call her after midnight; she's a night owl.*

**nine** see DRESSED TO KILL (TO THE NINES); ON CLOUD NINE; POSSESSION IS NINE POINTS OF THE LAW; WHOLE NINE YARDS.

**nine to five** Involving a traditional work schedule, as in *He's a musician, and he's never had a nine to five job.*

**nip and tuck** Very close, so that the advantage or lead of competitors keeps changing, as in *It was nip and tuck whether they would win the contract to design the building.* Also see NECK AND NECK.

**nip in the bud** Stop something at an early stage, or thoroughly check something. For example, *By arresting all the leaders, they nipped the rebellion in the bud.* This expression refers to a spring frost that kills flower buds.

**no** In addition to the idioms beginning with NO, also see ALL TALK (AND NO ACTION); ALL WORK AND NO PLAY; BY NO MEANS; CLOSE BUT NO CIGAR; COME TO AN END (NO GOOD); CUT NO ICE; DO ANY (NO) GOOD; FEEL NO PAIN; HELL HAS NO FURY; IN NO CASE; IN NO TIME; IN NO

UNCERTAIN TERMS; LEAVE NO STONE UNTURNED; LESS THAN (NO TIME); LONG TIME NO SEE; LOSE (NO) TIME; MAKE NO BONES ABOUT; MAKE NO DIFFERENCE; MAKE NO MISTAKE; MONEY IS NO OBJECT; NONE OF ONE'S (HAVE NO) BUSINESS; POINT OF NO RETURN; PULL NO PUNCHES; ROLLING STONE GATHERS NO MOSS; TAKE NO FOR AN ANSWER; THERE'S NO TELLING; TO LITTLE (NO) PURPOSE; TO NO AVAIL; UNDER THE (NO) CIRCUMSTANCES; UP TO NO GOOD; YES AND NO.

**no accounting for tastes, there's** Individual likes and dislikes cannot be explained, as in *They painted their house purple—there's really no accounting for tastes.* A synonym that originated in the American South is **different strokes for different folks.** For another synonym, see ONE MAN'S MEAT IS ANOTHER MAN'S POISON.

**nobody** In addition to the idioms beginning with NOBODY, also see LIKE CRAZY (NOBODY'S BUSINESS).

**nobody home** **1.** No one is paying attention, as in *She threw the ball right past him, yelling "Nobody home!"* **2.** The person being discussed is not normal mentally and so cannot understand, as in *When the woman did not answer his question, he concluded it was a case of nobody home.*

**nobody's fool** A person who cannot be fooled or taken advantage of, as in *You can't trick Ryan—he's nobody's fool.*

**no-brainer, a** **1.** Something that's very easy to do or to understand, as in *You won't have any trouble with the last math problem—it's a no-brainer.* **2.** Something that's so obvious it requires no thought, as in *I know I should quit smoking—I mean, that's a no-brainer.*

**no buts** see NO IFS OR BUTS.

**no call for** Also, **no call to.** No requirement or reason for doing something, as in *There was no call for your getting upset; she knew quite well what to do.* This idiom uses *call* in the sense of "duty" or "need." The variant is always used with a verb, as in *There was no call to get the police involved, because it was a simple dispute between neighbors.*

**no can do** It's impossible; I can't do this. For example, *When Bill asked me to write a speech, I told him bluntly no can do.*

**nod** In addition to the idiom beginning with NOD, also see GET THE NOD.

**nodding acquaintance** A slight or superficial knowledge of someone or something, as in *I have a nodding acquaintance with the company president,* or *She has a nodding acquaintance with that software program.* This expression refers to knowing someone just well enough to nod when meeting him or her.

**no dice** Also, **no go** or **no soap** or **no deal.** No, certainly not; also, impossible. For example, *Anthony wanted to borrow my new coat, but I said no dice,* or *We tried to rent the church for the wedding, but it's no go for the date you picked,* or *Jim asked Dad to help pay for the repairs, but Dad said no deal. No dice* refers to an unlucky throw in gambling; *no go,* to lack of progress. *No soap* may refer to the phrase **it won't wash,** meaning "it won't find acceptance." Also see NOTHING DOING; WON'T WASH.

**nod off** Fall asleep briefly, as in *Grandma spends a lot of time in her rocking chair, nodding off now and then.* This expression refers to the quick involuntary dropping of one's head from an upright position when drowsy or napping. Also see DROP OFF, def. 1.

**no doubt** **1.** Probably, most likely, as in *No doubt you've heard the news about Mother.* **2.** Also, **without doubt** or **without a doubt.** Certainly, without question, as in *He's guilty, no doubt, but he doesn't deserve such a long sentence,* or *That basketball player is without doubt the tallest man I've ever seen.* Also see BEYOND A DOUBT.

**no end** **1.** A large number, a great deal, as in *He made no end of campaign promises.* This expression sometimes is put as **no end to** or **no end of,** meaning "no limit to" or "an endless amount of," as in *There is no end to the junk mail we get,* or *There are no end of books in this house.* **2.** To a very great degree, as in *This situation puzzles us no end.*

N

**no flies on someone** Someone is very alert; there is nothing slow or dull about the person. For example, *She may be new to this field, but there are no flies on her.* This slang expression refers to flies settling on a slow-moving animal.

**no fool like an old fool, there's** An old fool is the worst kind of fool, as in *He's marrying a woman fifty years younger—there's no fool like an old fool.* This saying is now considered somewhat offensive for stereotyping older people.

**no go** see NO DICE.

**no good** **1.** Unsatisfactory, not right or acceptable. For example, *This work is no good; it'll have to be done again.* **2.** Worthless, serving no purpose, as in *It's no good complaining since there's nothing we can do,* or *I tried to reason with him, but it did no good.* Also see COME TO AN END (TO NO GOOD), def. 2; DO ANY (NO) GOOD.

**no great shakes** Nothing special, ordinary or mediocre, as in *I'm afraid the new singer is no great shakes,* or *What I did with this room was no great shakes.*

**no hard feelings** No resentment or anger, as in *I hope there are no hard feelings about not being invited.* This idiom uses *hard* in the sense of "severe" or "harsh."

**no holds barred** Without any restrictions, as in *Telephone companies are entering the market for Internet users with no holds barred.* This expression comes from wrestling, where certain holds are illegal, or *barred.*

**no ifs or buts** Also, **no ifs, ands, or buts.** No reservations, restrictions, or excuses, as in *You'd better be there tomorrow, and no ifs, ands, or buts about it.* This expression uses the conjunctions to stand for the conditions and objections that they introduce.

**no joke** Also, **no laughing matter.** A serious issue, as in *Missing the last flight out was no joke,* or *This outbreak of flu is no laughing matter.*

**no kidding** Truly, seriously, as in *No kidding, I really did lose my wallet.*

**no longer** Not any more, as in *They no longer make this model of computer.*

**no love lost** Dislike, bad feelings, hate, as in *There's no love lost between those competitors.*

**no man is an island** Human beings need and depend on one another, as in *You can't manage this all by yourself; no man is an island.*

**no matter** **1.** It's not important, as in *She wasn't home when I came by, but no matter.* **2.** Also, **no matter what.** Regardless, it makes no difference, as in *No matter what I say, she'll do what she likes,* or *The car must be repaired, no matter what.*

**no matter how you slice it** Regardless of how one views something, as in *No matter how you slice it, he's still guilty.*

**no more Mr. Nice Guy** An expression used to say one will no longer try to be kind and fair. For example, *I've tried to be patient with them, but from now on, no more Mr. Nice Guy.*

**none** In addition to the idioms beginning with NONE, also see ALL (NONE) OF THE ABOVE; BAR NONE; NOT HAVE IT (HAVE NONE OF); SECOND TO NONE.

**none of one's business** Not one's concern, as in *How much I earn is none of your business.* This expression uses *business* in the sense of "one's affairs." (Also see MIND ONE'S OWN BUSINESS.) A slang variant is **none of one's beeswax.** The related verb phrase **have no business** is used to say that one should not meddle or interfere, as in *He has no business discussing the contract with outsiders.*

**none of the above** see under ALL OF THE ABOVE.

**none other than** That very person or thing, the same as. For example, *In the elevator I ran into none other than the woman we'd been talking about,* or *It turned out to be none other than Jim in a clown costume.* This expression is used to show surprise at finding someone or something in a particular situation.

**none the wiser** Knowing no more than before, as in *He tried to explain the tax structure, but in the end I was none the wiser.*

**none the worse for** **1.** Also, **none the worse for wear.** Not harmed from, as in *He was none the worse for walking the entire ten miles,* or *This carpet may be old, but it's none the worse for wear.* **2.** Be improved by, as in *The dog would be none the worse for a good brushing.*

**none too** Also, **not too.** Not very, as in *The application arrived none too soon,* or *I'm afraid this secretary is none too smart,* or *He was here not too long ago.*

**no news is good news** Having no new information means that things are probably fine, as in *I haven't heard from them in a month, but no news is good news.*

**nonsense** see STUFF AND NONSENSE.

**no offense** Please don't feel insulted, I don't mean to offend you, as in *No offense, but I think you're mistaken.* This expression generally accompanies a statement that could be regarded as insulting but is not meant to be so, as in the example.

**nook and cranny, every** Everywhere, as in *I've searched for it in every nook and cranny, and I still can't find it.*

**no pain, no gain** Suffering is needed to make progress, as in *I've worked for hours on those irregular French verbs, but no pain, no gain.* This idiom is often associated with athletic coaches who urge athletes to train harder.

**no picnic** Difficult, no fun, as in *Recovering from abdominal surgery is no picnic.* This expression refers to a picnic as a pleasant occasion.

**no problem** **1.** Also, **no sweat; not to worry.** There's no difficulty about this, don't be concerned. For example, *Of course I can change your tire—no problem,* or *You want more small time? No sweat,* or *We'll be there in plenty of time, not to worry.* **2.** You're welcome, as in *Thanks for the ride, Dad. No problem.*

**nor** see HIDE NOR HAIR; NEITHER FISH NOR FOWL; NEITHER HERE NOR THERE; RHYME OR REASON (NEITHER RHYME NOR REASON).

**nose** In addition to the idioms beginning with NOSE, also see BROWN NOSE; CAN'T SEE BEYOND THE END OF ONE'S NOSE; COUNT NOSES; CUT OFF ONE'S NOSE; FOLLOW ONE'S NOSE; KEEP ONE'S NOSE CLEAN; LEAD BY THE NOSE; LOOK DOWN ON (ONE'S NOSE AT); NO SKIN OFF ONE'S NOSE; ON THE NOSE; PAY THROUGH THE NOSE; PLAIN AS DAY (THE NOSE ON YOUR FACE); POKE ONE'S NOSE INTO; RUB SOMEONE'S NOSE IN IT; THUMB ONE'S NOSE; TURN UP ONE'S NOSE; UNDER ONE'S NOSE; WIN BY A NOSE.

**nose about** Also, **nose around.** Look for something, especially something private or hidden. For example, *She was always nosing about in my kitchen, looking in all the cupboards,* or *The detective nosed around the apartment.*

**nose in** Also, **nose into. 1.** Advance cautiously, front end first, as in *We nosed the boat toward the dock,* or *The car nosed in very slowly.* **2.** Try to find information about other people's private concerns, as in *He was nosing into our finances again.* Also see NOSE ABOUT; POKE ONE'S NOSE INTO.

**nose in a book, have one's** Be constantly reading, as in *Walter always has his nose in a book.*

**nose in the air, have one's** Behave as if one is better than others, as in *Ever since we moved in, our next-door neighbor has had her nose in the air.* The related phrase **with one's nose in the air** means "in a too proud way," as in *She thinks she's so smart; she's always walking around with her nose in the air.* Also see TURN UP ONE'S NOSE.

**nose into** see NOSE IN.

**nose out 1.** Defeat someone by a small amount, as in *She barely nosed out the other candidate.* This expression refers to a horse winning a race with its nose in front of the other horses. **2.** Discover, especially something hidden or secret, as in *This reporter has a knack for nosing out the truth.* This usage refers to following the scent of something.

**nose out of joint, have one's** Be upset or irritated, especially when displaced by someone. For example, *Ever since Sheila got promoted, he's had his nose out of joint.* Similarly, **put someone's nose out of joint** means to cause such an upset, as in *The boss's praise of her assistant put Jean's nose out of joint.* These terms may refer to the facial expression of someone who is displeased.

**nose to the grindstone, keep one's** Stay hard at work, as in *We expect John to get good grades again, since he really keeps his nose to the grindstone.* This expression refers to a tool that must be sharpened by being held to a grindstone.

**no shit** Really, do you mean it, as in *You took her to a prizefight? No shit!* This interjection is used to express surprise or disbelief. It can also be used as a statement of one's lack of surprise, as in *No shit the exam's tomorrow—where have you been, asleep?* [Vulgar slang]

**no sir** Also, **no sirree.** Certainly not. This strong denial is used without regard to the gender of the person addressed. For example, *No sir, I'm not doing that for free,* or *Live here? No sirree.*

**no skin off one's nose** Not harmful or any trouble to one, as in *I don't care if you stay home—it's no skin off my nose.*

**no smoke without fire, there's** Also, **where there's smoke there's fire.** A suspicion or rumor usually has a basis in fact, as in *When the sales figures continued strong but the company still wasn't making money, he suspected something was wrong—there's no smoke without fire.*

**no soap** see under NO DICE.

**no sooner said than done** Accomplished immediately, as in *He said we should leave, and no sooner said than done.* This expression uses *no sooner than* in the sense of "at once."

**no spring chicken** No longer a young person, as in *She's no spring chicken, but she plays a fine game of tennis.* This expression is now usually considered insulting to women and to older people.

**no stomach for, have** Dislike, be unable to tolerate, as in *Pat has no stomach for violent movies.* This expression uses *stomach* in the sense of "appetite" or "desire."

**no strings attached** Without conditions or restrictions, as in *They give each of the children $10,000 a year with no strings attached.*

**no such thing 1.** Nothing like that, nothing of the kind, as in *We've been looking for a car without air conditioning, but no such thing is available.* **2.** Certainly not, the opposite is true, as in *You thought I was quitting? No such thing!*

**no sweat** see under NO PROBLEM.

**not** In addition to the idioms beginning with NOT, also see ALL THAT GLITTERS IS NOT GOLD; (NOT) ALL THERE; BELIEVE IT OR NOT; COMING OR GOING, NOT KNOW IF ONE IS; DO AS I SAY (NOT AS I DO); (NOT A) GHOST OF A CHANCE; (NOT THE) HALF OF IT; HEART (ONE'S HEART IS NOT) IN IT; (NOT) HOLD ONE'S BREATH; (NOT) IN THE LEAST; IT'S (NOT) ONE'S FUNERAL; LAST BUT NOT LEAST; LIKE AS NOT; MORE OFTEN THAN NOT; NO PROBLEM (NOT TO WORRY); (NOT) TAKE NO FOR AN ANSWER; TWO WRONGS DO NOT MAKE A RIGHT; WASTE NOT, WANT NOT; WHETHER OR NOT; WITHOUT A (NOT HAVE A) LEG TO STAND ON. Also see under CAN'T; COULDN'T; WOULDN'T.

**not a bad sort** see BAD SORT.

**not a bit** Not at all, as in *She was not a bit interested.*

**not able** see under CAN'T.

**not about to** see ABOUT TO, def. 2.

**not a ghost of a chance** see GHOST OF A CHANCE.

**not a hope in hell** Also, **not a chance in hell** or **not a prayer.** No chance at all, as in *There's not a hope in hell that we'll win,* or *If you don't hurry, you won't have a prayer of being on time.* Also see SNOWBALL'S CHANCE IN HELL.

**not a leg to stand on** see WITHOUT A LEG TO STAND ON.

**not all it's cracked up to be** It is disappointing, it does not live up to its reputation, as in *The restaurant wasn't all it's cracked up to be.* This term uses *crack up* in the sense of "praise," which survives only in this expression.

**not all there** see ALL THERE.

**not anything like** Also, **nothing like** or **not anywhere near** or **nowhere near.** Quite different from, far from; also, not nearly. For example, *The town library isn't anything like the university library,* or *His attitude was nothing like his brother's,* or *It isn't anything like as cold as it was last winter,* or *That movie isn't anywhere near as exciting as I thought it would be,* or *Her diamond is nowhere near as big as mine.*

**not bad** Also, **not half bad** or **not so bad** or **not too bad** or **not too shabby.** Fairly good, as in *Not bad, said the conductor, but we still need to practice,* or *The movie wasn't half bad, but Jerry wanted to go home,* or *Our garden's not too bad this year,* or *How are things going? Not too shabby.* All of the terms involving *bad* imply that something is less bad than it might be. The last variant uses *shabby* in the sense of "inferior."

**not bat an eye** see WITHOUT BATTING AN EYE.

**not born yesterday** More experienced and less naive than one appears to be, as in *Don't think you can fool me; I wasn't born yesterday.*

N

**not breathe a word** Not reveal a secret, keep something secret, as in *You must promise not to breathe a word of what I'm about to tell you* or, *Don't worry, I won't breathe a word.* This phrase uses the verb *breathe* in the sense of "say."

**not built that way** Not inclined, ready, or willing to do something, as in *I can't apologize for something I didn't do—I'm just not built that way.*

**not by a long shot** see LONG SHOT.

**not by any means** see BY NO MEANS.

**notch** see TAKE SOMEONE DOWN A NOTCH.

**not cricket** Unfair, failing to follow the rules of good sportsmanship, as in *It's not cricket to fire him without notice.* This term compares the sport of cricket with fair and upright behavior. It survives in the United States even though cricket is not well known there.

**not done** Also, **just not done** or **simply not done.** Socially unacceptable, improper, as in *Bringing two friends to their house without asking, that's not done.*

**note** see COMPARE NOTES; MAKE A NOTE OF; OF NOTE; STRIKE THE RIGHT NOTE; TAKE NOTE; TAKE NOTES.

**no telling** see THERE'S NO TELLING.

**not enough room to swing a cat** Very little space, as in *There's not enough room to swing a cat in this tent.* This expression probably refers to a cat-o'-nine-tails, or "cat," a whip with nine lashes widely used to punish offenders in the British military.

**not feel oneself** see NOT ONESELF.

**not for all the tea in China** Not at any price, never, as in *I wouldn't give up my car, not for all the tea in China.* This term originated in Australia and refers to the presumed huge quantity of tea in China. Also see FOR ALL THE WORLD; NOT FOR LOVE OR MONEY.

**not for a moment** Also, **not for one moment** or **not for a single moment.** Never, not to any degree, as in *Not for a moment did I believe he was telling the truth.* This expression uses *moment* in the sense of "the tiniest length of time."

**not for love or money** Never, under no circumstances, as in *I'd never visit them again, not for love or money.* This expression refers to two powerful persuasive forces.

**not give a damn** Also, **not give a fig** or **hoot** or **rap** or **shit.** Not care about, not have any interest in, as in *I don't give a damn about him,* or *She doesn't give a fig if he comes or not.* The nouns in all these terms signify something totally worthless. *Damn* is mildly offensive, and *shit* is vulgar.

**not give someone the time of day** Ignore someone, refuse to pay any attention to someone, as in *He's tried to be friendly, but she won't give him the time of day.* This expression refers to refusing even to answer the question, "What time is it?"

**not half bad** see NOT BAD.

**no thanks to** see THANKS TO.

**not have a clue** Have no idea or understanding about something, as in *Jane doesn't have a clue as to why John won't call her,* or *Do you know what's wrong with the heater? No, I haven't a clue.*

**not have a dime** Also, **not have a penny.** Have no money, as in *She doesn't have a dime since she quit her job,* or *He doesn't have a penny to his name.*

**not have a leg to stand on** see WITHOUT A LEG TO STAND ON.

**not have an earthly chance** Also, **stand no earthly chance.** Have no chance at all, as in *She doesn't have an earthly chance of getting into medical school,* or *Bill stands no earthly chance of winning the lottery. No earthly* is used here in the sense of "no conceivable." Also see GHOST OF A CHANCE; NOT A HOPE IN HELL.

**not have anything on** see HAVE NOTHING ON.

**not have it** Also, **have none of; not** or **won't** or **wouldn't hear of.** Not allow; refuse to tolerate, accept, or endure. For example, *Mary wanted to get married at home,* *but her mother would not have it,* or *I'll have none of your back talk,* or *The minister wouldn't hear of a change in the service.*

**not have one's heart in it** see under HEART IN IT.

**not have the heart to** Be unable to make oneself say or do something, as in *He didn't have the heart to tell her the cat had died.* Also see HAVE A HEART.

**nothing** In addition to the idioms beginning with NOTHING, also see COME TO NOTHING; COUNT FOR (NOTHING); GO FOR NOTHING; HAVE NOTHING ON; HAVE NOTHING TO DO WITH; HERE GOES (NOTHING); IN NO TIME (NOTHING FLAT); LEAVE A LOT (NOTHING) TO BE DESIRED; MAKE NOTHING OF; MAKE SOMETHING OF (OUT OF NOTHING); MUCH ADO ABOUT NOTHING; NOT KNOW BEANS (FROM NOTHING); NOT TO MENTION (TO SAY NOTHING OF); STOP AT NOTHING; SWEET NOTHINGS; THINK NOTHING OF; WANT FOR NOTHING.

**nothing but** Only, as in *She thinks of nothing but money.*

**nothing could be further from the truth** What was said is not at all the way things really are. For example, *I thought she'd be happy about it, but nothing could be further from the truth—she's miserable.*

**nothing doing** Certainly not, as in *Can I borrow your down coat? Nothing doing.* Also see NO DICE.

**nothing if not** Above all else, very, as in *He was nothing if not discreet.*

**nothing less than** The equivalent of; very, completely, as in *It was nothing less than a revolution in the industry,* or *His success was nothing less than amazing.*

**nothing like** see NOT ANYTHING LIKE.

**nothing new under the sun** Everything has been seen before, as in *Those clothing designs remind me of the 1950s—there really is nothing new under the sun.* This saying expresses a lack of interest in or excitement about the world.

**nothing of the kind** Also, **nothing of the sort. 1.** No, certainly not, as in *Did you push Charlie? Nothing of the kind!* or *Do you think the kids were trying to shoplift? Nothing of the sort.* **2.** Not at all like what is mentioned or expected, as in *They thought we would come visit them, but we'd planned nothing of the kind.*

**nothing short of** The equivalent of, the same as, as in *What she's calling "a few changes" is really nothing short of a complete redesign!* This term is slightly stronger than **little short of,** meaning "almost the same as," as in *Her claim is little short of stupid.* Also see SHORT OF.

**nothing to do with** see HAVE NOTHING TO DO WITH.

**nothing to it, there's** It's not at all difficult, it's easy, as in *Of course I can fix the faucet—there's nothing to it.*

**nothing to sneeze at** see NOT TO BE SNEEZED AT.

**nothing to speak of** Not much, nothing worth talking about, as in *What's been happening in the stock market? Nothing to speak of,* or *They've done nothing to speak of about publicity.*

**nothing to write home about** Ordinary or unremarkable, as in *The restaurant was all right but nothing to write home about.* This idiom may have originated among military troops stationed far from home. It became widespread during World War I.

**nothing ventured, nothing gained** One must take risks to achieve something, as in *They quit their jobs, packed up, and moved to Hollywood, saying "nothing ventured, nothing gained."* For another version, see NO PAIN, NO GAIN.

**not hurt a fly** Also, **not hurt a flea.** Not cause harm to anyone, be gentle and mild, as in *Paul's the kindest man—he wouldn't hurt a flea,* or *Bert has a temper, but it's all talk; he wouldn't hurt a fly.* Both *fly* and *flea* are used in the sense of "a small insignificant animal."

**notice** see ESCAPE NOTICE; GIVE NOTICE; SHORT NOTICE; SIT UP AND TAKE NOTICE; TAKE NOTE (NOTICE).

**not if one can help it** Only if one cannot prevent it. For example, *Is he taking a second job? Not if his wife can help it,* or *He's not riding on the back of that motorcycle, not if I can help it.* This idiom uses *help* in the sense of "prevent" or "cause to be otherwise."

**not if you paid me** Under no circumstances, as in *I wouldn't jump off the high diving board, not if you paid me.*

**no time at all** see IN NO TIME.

**no time for, have** Can't be bothered with, dislike, as in *Dad has no time for her whining and complaining.* This expression refers to impatience with someone or something.

**no time like the present, there's** Do or say it now, as in *Go ahead and call him—there's no time like the present.*

**not in the least** see IN THE LEAST.

**not know beans** Also, **not know the first thing** or **not know from nothing.** Be ignorant about something, as in *I have no idea why my car won't start—I don't know beans about auto mechanics.*

**not know enough to come in out of the rain** see COME IN OUT OF THE RAIN.

**not know if one is coming or going** see under COMING OR GOING.

**not know someone from Adam** Be unable to recognize someone, as in *Although I have worked here for two months, I've never* *seen the department head; I wouldn't know her from Adam.*

**not know where to turn** Also, **not know which way to jump** or **not know which way to turn.** Have no idea of how to get help or what course to take. For example, *With all these offers coming in, he didn't know where to turn,* or *When her car was stolen, Meg did not know which way to jump.*

**not let the grass grow under one's feet** see LET THE GRASS GROW.

**not lift a finger** Refuse to make the effort to help or perform an action. For example, *Dad won't lift a finger to help them financially,* or *Early in the war, the United States officially would not lift a finger.*

**not miss a trick** Also, **never miss a trick** or **not miss much.** Not fail to see or be aware of what is happening. For example, *When it comes to saving money, Mark never misses a trick,* or *Dad may seem absent-minded, but he doesn't miss much.* The variant phrase uses *miss* in the sense of "fail to perceive."

**not my cup of tea** see CUP OF TEA.

**not one iota** Also, **not one bit.** Not even the smallest amount, as in *He got not one iota of thanks for his efforts.*

**not one's day, this is** Also, **just one of those days.** Nothing is going right for one today. For example, *The car wouldn't start, it rained unexpectedly—this is not my day,* or *The phone has rung nonstop all morning; it's just one of those days.*

N

**not oneself** Not feeling physically or mentally well, as in *I think there's something wrong; he's not himself,* or *She seemed to be improving last week, but she's just not feeling herself today.* Also see FEEL LIKE ONESELF.

**not on your life** Certainly not, as in *Go sky-diving? Not on your life.*

**not open one's mouth** Also, **shut one's mouth; not say a word** or **not utter a word.** Be silent, not express one's feelings or opinions, keep a secret. For example, *Don't worry, I'm not going to open my mouth on this issue,* or *She promised not to say a word about it to anyone.* Also see HOLD ONE'S TONGUE; KEEP ONE'S MOUTH SHUT.

**not put something past someone** Consider someone capable of doing something, especially something bad. For example, *I wouldn't put it past him to tell a lie or two.* This expression uses *past* in the sense of "beyond."

**not right in the head** Also, **not quite right.** Mentally unwell or abnormal, as in *Physically, she's quite healthy for ninety, but we suspect she's not right in the head.* This usage was first recorded as *right in his wits.*

**not see beyond one's nose** see CAN'T SEE BEYOND THE END OF ONE'S NOSE.

**not suffer fools gladly** Refuse to tolerate stupidity, as in *Chris sometimes loses her patience at these meetings; she does not suffer fools gladly.*

**not take no for an answer** see TAKE NO FOR AN ANSWER.

**not the end of the world** Not as bad or as serious as someone may think, as in *You didn't get the job? Well, that's too bad, but it's not the end of the world.*

**not the half of it** see HALF OF IT.

**not the only fish in the sea** Also, **lots of fish in the sea** or **plenty of good fish in the sea; not the only pebble on the beach.** Plenty of other suitable people, especially for a romantic relationship. For example, *When Bob walked out on Sally, all we could tell her was that he was not the only fish in the sea,* or *Bill knew she wasn't the only pebble on the beach, but he was determined to win her over.* Both *fish* and *pebble* here refer to something available in large quantities.

**not think much of** Have little regard for, have a low opinion of, as in *Bill doesn't think much of the carpentry work in that house.*

**not to be sneezed at** Also, **nothing to sneeze at.** Not to be ignored or dismissed as unimportant, as in *It's a great honor, not to be sneezed at,* or *That salary of his is nothing to sneeze at.*

**not to mention** Also, **not to speak of; to say nothing of.** In addition to, plus. For example, *I don't think the voters will want that type of program, not to mention the cost,* or *Dave teaches trumpet and trombone, not to speak of other brass instruments,* or *Their house is worth at least a million, to say nothing of their other assets.*

**not touch *something* with a ten-foot pole** Stay far away from something, avoid completely, as in *I'm not going to get involved in their argument—I wouldn't touch it with a ten-foot pole,* or *Sam won't touch garlic with a ten-foot pole.*

**not to worry** see NO PROBLEM.

**not up to** see UP TO.

**not worth a damn** Also, **not worth a plugged nickel** or **red cent** or **dime** or **hill of beans** or **fig** or **straw** or **tinker's damn.** Worthless, as in *That car isn't worth a damn,* or *My new tennis racket is not worth a plugged nickel.* Each of the nouns used in these expressions refers to something of little or no value.

**no two ways about it** No room for a difference of opinion, no alternative, as in *We have to agree on the date and time—no two ways about it.*

**no use, it's** **1.** It's impossible; it can't succeed. For example, *It's no use; these pieces just don't fit.* **2.** Also, **it's no use to man or**

**beast.** It's worthless, it serves no purpose, as in *This car is so old it's no use to man or beast.* Also see HAVE NO USE FOR.

**no use crying over spilt milk** see CRY OVER SPILT MILK.

**now** In addition to the idioms beginning with NOW, also see ANY DAY (NOW); EVERY NOW AND THEN; HERE AND NOW; JUST NOW.

**now and again** Also, **now and then.** See EVERY NOW AND THEN.

**no way** Also, **there is no way.** Certainly not; never; no possibility. For example, *No way can I forget what he did,* or *Are you coming along? No way!* or *There's no way our candidate can lose.*

**nowhere** see GET NOWHERE; IN THE MIDDLE OF (NOWHERE); OUT OF NOWHERE.

**nowhere near** see NOT ANYTHING LIKE.

**no-win situation, a** A situation certain to end in failure or disappointment, as in *If the in-laws visit them or they visit the in-laws, either way they see it as a no-win situation.*

**no wonder** Also, **small wonder.** It's not at all (or hardly) surprising, as in *With the goalie out with a sprained ankle, it's no wonder you lost the game,* or *If he finished off all of the turkey, small wonder that he now has a stomachache.*

**now or never, it's** It must be done now or not at all, as in *If you plan to state your case to the boss, it's now or never.*

**now that** Seeing that, because, as in *Now that you're here, you might as well stay for dinner.* For a synonym, see AS LONG AS.

**now you're talking** Good for you, that's a good idea, as in *You've decided to enter the contest? Now you're talking!*

**nth** see TO THE NTH DEGREE.

**nuisance** see MAKE A NUISANCE OF ONESELF.

**null and void** Canceled, invalid, as in *The lease is now null and void.* This phrase is actually redundant, since *null* means "void" or "ineffective."

**number** In addition to the idiom beginning with NUMBER, also see A NUMBER OF; ANY NUMBER OF; BY THE NUMBERS; CRUNCH NUMBERS; DAYS ARE NUMBERED; DO A JOB (NUMBER) ON; GET (HAVE) SOMEONE'S NUMBER; HOT NUMBER; IN ROUND NUMBERS; LOOK OUT FOR (NUMBER ONE); OPPOSITE NUMBER; SAFETY IN NUMBERS.

**number is up, one's** One is in serious difficulty or near death. For example, *She knew her number was up when she saw the look on her supervisor's face,* or *He looks terrible; I think his number's up.* This phrase may refer to an unfavorable lottery number, or it could refer to any number by which one is identified, such as the number on a military dog tag.

**nurse a drink** Drink something slowly, especially in order to conserve it. For example, *He nursed one drink for the whole evening.*

**nurse a grudge** Remain angry or resentful for a long time, as in *I don't know why Karl looks so angry; I think he's nursing a grudge against the family.*

**nut** In addition to the idioms beginning with NUTS, also see DRIVE SOMEONE CRAZY (NUTS); FROM SOUP TO NUTS; HARD NUT TO CRACK.

**nuts about, be** Be extremely enthusiastic about; also, be extremely fond of. For example, *Ellen is nuts about opera,* or *Kevin has been nuts about Megan since he met her.*

**nuts and bolts, the** The essential or basic aspects of something, as in *They have ambitious goals, but they don't specify the nuts and bolts of how to achieve them.* This expression refers to basic parts of machinery.

**nutshell** see IN A NUTSHELL.

**nutty as a fruitcake** Crazy, idiotic, as in *Mary's nutty as a fruitcake if she thinks she can change him.* This idiom refers to the fact that a fruitcake contains nuts as well as fruit.

# Oo

**oats** see FEEL ONE'S OATS; SOW ONE'S WILD OATS.

**object** see MONEY IS NO OBJECT.

**objection** see RAISE AN OBJECTION.

**occasion** see ON OCCASION; RISE TO THE OCCASION.

**occur to one** Come to mind, as in *It never occurred to me that he might refuse,* or *It wouldn't occur to him to ask directions.*

**odd couple** see under STRANGE BEDFELLOWS.

**odd jobs** A variety of temporary, short-term jobs. For example, *He did odd jobs such as yard work and painting while he was in college.*

**odd man out** **1.** A person who is left out of a group for some reason, as in *The invitation was for couples only, so Jane was odd man out.* **2.** Something or someone who differs markedly from the others in a group, as in *Among all those ranch-style houses, their Victorian was odd man out.*

**odds** In addition to the idioms beginning with ODDS, also see AGAINST ALL ODDS; AT ODDS; BY ALL ODDS; LAY ODDS.

O

**odds and ends** Varied items, fragments and leftovers, as in *I've finished putting everything away, except for a few odds and ends.*

**odds are, the** The chances are, as in *The odds are that they'll serve turkey for Thanksgiving.* This phrase refers to betting.

**of age** **1.** Old enough, according to the law, to be eligible for something, as in *In this state he's not of age for buying liquor, but he may vote,* or *Next year Jane's coming of age and will get her driver's license.* The term **under age** means too young to be eligible, as in *It's against the law to serve alcohol to anyone under age.* **2. come of age.** Mature or develop fully, as in *The school's bilingual program has finally come of age.*

**of a kind** **1.** Of some sort, but not a typical or perfect example. For example, *They have a backyard of a kind, but it's tiny.* For a synonym, see OF SORTS. **2. one of a kind.** A unique instance, as in *There are and will be no others like it; this event is one of a kind,* or *She's extremely generous, one of a kind.* Also see TWO OF A KIND.

**of all things** From all the possibilities, as in *The boy says he want to be a ballet dancer of all things!* This term generally expresses surprise.

**of a piece** Also, **all of a piece.** Of the same kind, as in *This legislation is of a piece with the previous bill,* or *Her rude behavior was all of a piece.* The *piece* in this idiom refers to a single mass of material.

**of a sort** see OF SORTS.

**of choice** Preferred above others, as in *A strike is the union's weapon of choice.* Also see BY CHOICE.

**of consequence** Important, as in *For all matters of consequence we have to consult the board of directors,* or *Only scientists of consequence have been invited to speak.*

**of course** **1.** In the customary or expected order, naturally, as in *The new minister did not, of course, fire the church secretary.* This phrase uses *course* in the sense of "ordinary procedure." **2.** Yes, certainly, as in *Of course I'll answer the phone,* or *Are you going to the meeting? Of course.* The negative version is **of course not,** meaning "certainly not," as in *You won't forget, will you? Of course not!* Also see MATTER OF COURSE.

**off** In addition to the idioms beginning with OFF, also see BACK OFF; BAD OFF; BEAT OFF; BEAT THE PANTS OFF; BEG OFF; BE OFF; BETTER OFF; BITE OFF MORE THAN ONE CAN CHEW; BITE SOMEONE'S HEAD OFF; BLAST OFF; BLOW OFF; BLOW OFF STEAM; BLOW THE LID OFF; BORE TO DEATH (THE PANTS OFF); BRANCH OFF; BREAK OFF; BRING OFF; BRUSH OFF; BUG OFF; BUMP OFF; BURN OFF; BUY OFF; BUZZ OFF; CALL OFF; CAP IT ALL (OFF); CARRY OFF; CART OFF; CAST OFF; CHANGE OFF; CHARGE OFF; CHECK OFF; CHIP OFF THE OLD BLOCK; CHOKE OFF; CLEAR OUT (OFF); COME OFF; COME OFF IT; COOL DOWN (OFF); COOL OFF; COUNT OFF; CRY OFF; CUT OFF; CUT OFF ONE'S NOSE TO SPITE ONE'S FACE; DASH OFF; DAY OFF; DIE OFF; DOZE OFF; DROP OFF; DUST OFF; EASE OFF; EASY AS PIE (FALLING OFF A LOG); FALL AWAY (OFF); FIGHT OFF; FIRE OFF; FIRST OFF; FISH OR CUT BAIT (SHIT OR GET OFF THE POT); FLY OFF THE HANDLE; FOB OFF; GET OFF; GET OFF ON; GET OFF ONE'S TAIL; GET OFF THE GROUND; GIVE OFF; GIVE THE SHIRT OFF ONE'S BACK; GO OFF; GO OFF THE DEEP END; GOOF OFF; HANDS OFF; HATS OFF TO; HAUL OFF; HAVE IT (OFF); HEAD OFF; HIGH OFF THE HOG; HIT IT OFF; HOLD OFF; HOT OFF THE PRESS; JERK OFF; JUMPING-OFF PLACE; KEEP OFF; KICK OFF; KILL OFF; KISS OFF; KNOCK IT OFF; KNOCK OFF; KNOCK SOMEONE'S BLOCK

OFF; KNOCK THE SOCKS OFF; LAUGH OFF; LAY OFF; LEAD OFF; LEAVE OFF; LET OFF; LEVEL OFF; LIFT OFF; LIKE A CHICKEN WITH ITS HEAD CUT OFF; LIKE WATER OFF A DUCK'S BACK; LOAD OFF ONE'S MIND; LOG IN (OFF); MAKE OFF; MOUTH OFF; NOD OFF; NO SKIN OFF ONE'S NOSE; ON (OFF) CAMERA; ON (OFF) DUTY; ON THE (OFF) CHANCE THAT; PACK OFF; PAIR OFF; PALM OFF; PANTS OFF; PASS OFF; PAY OFF; PEEL OFF; PICK OFF; PISS OFF; PLAY OFF; POLISH OFF; PULL OFF; PUSH OFF; PUT OFF; PUT ONE OFF; QUICK OFF THE MARK; RAKE OFF; RATTLE OFF; RIGHT AWAY (OFF); RIP OFF; ROUND OFF; RUB OFF ON; RUN AWAY (OFF); RUN OFF; RUN OFF AT THE MOUTH; RUN OFF WITH; SEAL OFF; SEE SOMEONE OFF; SELL OFF; SEND OFF; SET OFF; SHAKE OFF; SHOOT OFF ONE'S MOUTH; SHOW OFF; SHRUG OFF; SIGN OFF; SLACK OFF; SLIP OUT (OFF); SOUND OFF; SPIN OFF; SPLIT ONE'S SIDES (LAUGH ONE'S HEAD OFF); SPONGE OFF; SQUARE OFF; SQUEEZE OFF; STAND OFF; STAVE OFF; STOP OFF; STRAIGHT OFF; SWEAR OFF; SWITCH OFF; TAIL OFF; TAKE OFF; TAKE THE EDGE OFF; TALK SOMEONE'S ARM OFF; TAPER OFF; TEAR OFF; TEE OFF; TELL OFF; THROW OFF; TRADE OFF; WIPE OFF THE MAP. Also see under ON.

**off, be** see BE OFF.

**off again, on again** see OFF AND ON, def. 2.

**off and on** Also, **on and off. 1.** From time to time rather than continuously. For example, *I read his column off and on,* or *We've been working on the garden all summer, on and off.* **2.** Also, **off again, on again** or **on again, off again.** Uncertain, changing back and forth, as in *Theirs is an off again, on again relationship,* or *The peace talks are on again, off again.* Some believe this term originally referred to minor railroad accidents, where a train went off the track and then on again.

**off and running** Making a good start, progressing well, as in *After the first episode the new soap opera was off and running.* This phrase comes from horseracing, where it is the traditional announcement at the beginning of a race ("*They're off and running*").

**off balance 1.** Out of balance and therefore unsteady, as in *When learning how to ride a bicycle, it's easy to get off balance and fall,* or *She stood up and threw the canoe off balance.* **2.** Surprised, confused and uncertain, as in *The teacher's questions threw the class off balance.*

**off base** Wrong, relying on a mistaken idea, as in *His description of the accounting system was totally off base,* or *You shouldn't have said that. You were totally off base.* This term originated in baseball, where a runner who steps off a base can be put out.

**off duty** see under ON DUTY.

**offense** see NO OFFENSE; TAKE OFFENSE.

**of few words, a man.** Also, **a woman of few words.** A person who does not speak much; also, a person of action rather than words. For example, *A woman of few words, Susan hardly seemed like she'd be a successful lawyer,* or *Harry's a man of few words, but he gets things done.*

**off guard** Also, **off one's guard.** Not watchful, easily surprised. It is often put as **catch *someone* off guard** or **be caught off guard,** meaning "take (or be taken) by surprise." For example, *The chairman was caught off guard by that financial report,* or *With any luck the boss will be off guard when I come in late.* The antonym **on guard** or **on one's guard** means "watchful or prepared, especially to defend oneself." For example, *In this crowd we must be on guard against pickpockets,* or *I'm always on my guard when someone asks how I voted.*

**office** see BOX OFFICE; FRONT OFFICE; TAKE OFFICE.

**offing** see IN THE OFFING.

**off kilter** Also, **out of kilter.** Out of good condition or proper form, off balance. For example, *My life seems off kilter since you've been away.*

**off of** Away from, from, as in *Don't take your eyes off of the road,* or *Can I borrow ten dollars off of you?* This idiom is used more in oral than written communications. Also see GET OFF.

**off one's chest, get *something*** Relieve one's mind by confessing or saying something that has been kept secret. For example, *I've got to get this off my chest—I can't stand his parents,* or *He admitted taking the dollar and said he was glad to get it off his chest.* This expression uses *chest* for the seat of the emotions.

**off one's feed** With no desire to eat, without one's normal appetite, as in *Even though Mom's been gone only for a week, her absence puts Dad off his feed.* This expression was originally used only for animals.

**off one's feet 1. sweep** or **carry** or **knock one off one's feet.** Overwhelm someone emotionally; make a very favorable impression on someone. For example, *Winning first prize knocked me off my feet,* or *With his handsome looks and great charm, he swept her off her feet,* or *That fine speech carried him off his feet.* **2. run** or **rush someone off his** or **her feet.** Work someone to the point of exhaustion, hurry or pressure someone, as in *With all the preparations, they've been running me off my feet,* or *The waiters were rushed off their feet.* These expressions refer to running or hurrying so much that one falls down.

**off one's guard** see OFF GUARD.

**off one's head** Also, **out of one's head; off one's nut** or **rocker** or **trolley.** Crazy, out of one's mind, as in *You're off your head if you think I'll pay your debts,* or *I think Jerry's gone off his nut over that car,* or *When she said we had to sleep in the barn we thought she was off her rocker,* or *The old man's been off his trolley for at least a year.*

**off one's high horse** see under ON ONE'S HIGH HORSE.

**off one's rocker** Also, **off one's nut** or **trolley.** See OFF ONE'S HEAD.

**off someone's back** Also, **off someone's case.** No longer bothering someone or insisting that someone do something. It is often put as **get off someone's back** or **get off someone's case,** as in *I told her to get off my back—I'll mow the lawn tomorrow,* or *I wish Dad would get off my case about grades.* The antonym for the first of these slang terms is **on someone's back,** as in *He's been on my back about that report all morning.* The antonym for the variant is **on someone's case,** as in *He's always on my case.*

**off someone's hands** Out of or removed from someone's charge, possession, or responsibility. It is often put as **take *something* or *someone* off someone's hands,** as in *We hoped that once they saw the kittens they would take them off our hands,* or *I'm glad that job is finally off our hands.*

**off the air** Not being broadcast on radio or TV, as in *Once they knew they were off the air, the panelists burst out laughing.* The antonym is **on the air,** meaning "being broadcast,"

**off the beam** Off course, on the wrong track, as in *He's way off the beam with that argument.* This term and its antonym **on the beam,** meaning "on the right track," refer to directing aircraft by means of radio beams.

**off the beaten track** On an unusual route or in an unknown area, as in *We found a great vacation spot, off the beaten track.* This term refers to a well-worn path made by many feet passing that way. The phrase *beaten track* was first used to refer to the usual, unoriginal way of doing something.

**off the cuff** Without preparation, in words chosen at the moment, as in *His speech was entirely off the cuff.* This term may refer to the practice of a speaker making last-minute notes on the cuff of a shirtsleeve.

**off the deep end** see GO OFF THE DEEP END.

**off the ground** see GET OFF THE GROUND.

**off the handle** see FLY OFF THE HANDLE.

**off the hook** Also, **get *someone* off the hook** or **let *someone* off the hook.** Released from blame, freed from an annoying responsibility or obligation, as in *He was supposed to serve on the jury, but they settled the case, so he was off the hook,* or *I don't know how the robber got off the hook,* or *Once they found the person who really started the rumor, they let Mary off the hook.* This idiom refers to the fish that manages to free itself from the fisherman's hook and escape.

**off the mark** Also, **wide of the mark.** Inaccurate, wrong, as in *The economic forecast was off the mark, since unemployment is down,* or *His answers on the test were just wide of the mark.* It is also put as **miss the mark,** meaning "be mistaken," as in *The teacher missed the mark when he assumed everyone would finish the test in 30 minutes.* All these terms refer to *mark* in the sense of "a target," as do the antonyms **on the mark** and **hit the mark,** meaning "exactly right," as in *He was right on the mark with that budget amendment,* or *Bill hit the mark when he accused Tom of lying.*

**off the rack** Ready-made and available in stores, as in *She has all her clothes custom-made; she never buys a dress off the rack.* The *rack* here is a frame from which clothes are hung. Also see OFF THE SHELF.

**off the record** Unofficially, private, not for publication, as in *What he was about to say, he told the reporters, was strictly off the record.* This phrase probably refers to striking evidence from a court record (because it is irrelevant or improper). It later came into wide use with reference to persons who did not wish to be quoted by journalists. Also see GO ON RECORD; JUST FOR THE RECORD.

**off the shelf** Ready-made, already available in a store, as opposed to by special order. For example, *Sometimes you can get a better discount by buying an appliance off the shelf.* Also see OFF THE RACK; ON THE SHELF.

**off the top of one's head** In an unplanned way, without much thought, as in *Off the top of my head I'd say we'll double our profits in a year.* This idiom suggests one has not used the inside of one's head before making some statement.

**off the track** Also, **off track.** Away from one's goal, train of thought, or a sequence of events. It is often put as **get** or **put** or **throw *someone* off (the) track,** as in *Your question has gotten me off the track,* or *The interruption threw Mom off the track, and she forgot what she'd already put into the stew.* This term comes from railroading.

**off the wagon** see ON THE WAGON.

**off the wall** Unusual and unexpected, unconventional, as in *That idea of opening a 100-seat theater is off the wall.* This expression probably originated in baseball or some other sport in which the ball can bounce off a wall in unexpected directions.

**of it** see COME TO THINK OF IT; FOR FUN (THE FUN OF IT); FOR THE HELL OF IT; FULL OF IT; HALF OF IT; LONG AND SHORT OF IT; MAKE A DAY OF IT; ON THE FACE OF IT; OUT OF IT; SNAP OUT OF (IT); THAT'S ABOUT THE SIZE OF IT; WHAT OF IT.

**of late** Recently, lately, as in *She's been very quiet of late; is something wrong?*

**of necessity** Also, **out of necessity.** As the only possible result, unavoidably, as in *The prosecution has not proved him guilty. So the jury must, of necessity, find him not guilty.*

**of note** Important, of distinction, famous, as in *I have nothing of note to report,* or *The speaker was a man of note.* This idiom uses *note* in the sense of "importance" or "fame."

**of old** Formerly, at an earlier time, as in *In days of old, the whole town would come out to watch the parade.*

**of one's life** Being the greatest, worst, or best occasion of a lifetime, as in *She was having the time of her life at the party,* or *The threatened takeover of the company put the president in the fight of his life.*

**of one's own accord** Also, **of one's own free will.** Voluntarily, without being forced, as in *The entire audience rose of their own accord,* or *No, I'm climbing this mountain of my own free will.*

**of service to someone, be** Help someone, as in *How can I be of service to you?* This idiom uses *service* in the sense of "supplying someone's needs."

**of sorts** Also, **of a sort.** Of a kind, especially a mediocre or somewhat different kind. For example, *He was wearing a jacket of sorts but no tie,* or *They established a constitutional government of a sort.*

**often** see EVERY NOW AND THEN (SO OFTEN); MORE OFTEN THAN NOT.

**often as not** see under MORE OFTEN THAN NOT.

**of the devil** see SPEAK OF THE DEVIL.

**of the essence** Of the greatest importance, crucial, as in *Time is of the essence.* This idiom uses *essence* in the sense of "the most important element of something."

**of the kind** see NOTHING OF THE KIND.

**of the moment** Of importance at this time, as in *The issue of the moment is dealing with our budget deficit.* This expression led to **the man of the moment,** meaning "the most important person at this time," as in *When Alan scored a goal for his team, he was the man of the moment.*

**of two minds, be** Be undecided, hesitate to choose between two alternatives, as in *She's of two minds about her new job—it's much closer to home but also less challenging.*

**oil** see BURN THE MIDNIGHT OIL; GREASE (OIL) SOMEONE'S PALM; GREASE (OIL) THE WHEELS; POUR OIL ON TROUBLED WATERS; STRIKE IT RICH (OIL).

**ointment** see FLY IN THE OINTMENT.

**okey-dokey** Okay, as in *Okey-dokey, I'll get that ordered for you.* This somewhat old-fashioned expression plays with the rhyming sounds of the two invented words.

**old** In addition to the idioms beginning with OLD, also see ANY OLD; CHIP OFF THE OLD BLOCK; COMFORTABLE AS AN OLD SHOE; DIRTY JOKE (OLD MAN); GIVE SOMEONE THE GATE (OLD HEAVE-HO); NO FOOL LIKE AN OLD FOOL; OF OLD; RIPE OLD AGE; SAME OLD STORY; SETTLE A SCORE (OLD SCORES); (OLD) STAMPING GROUND; TEACH AN OLD DOG NEW TRICKS; UP TO ONE'S OLD TRICKS.

**old as the hills** Also, **old as Adam.** Extremely old, ancient, as in *That joke is as old as the hills,* or *He must be as old as Adam by now.* The first expression refers to the time in the distant past when mountains were created. The variant refers to the first human created by God, according to the Bible.

**old college try, the** One's best effort, as in *Come on, if we give it the old college try, we just might be able to cut down this tree.* This expression was originally a cheer to urge a team on.

**old flame** A former love interest, as in *Jim ran into an old flame that he had not seen in years.*

**old fogy** Also, **old fart.** A person who is old-fashioned in habits and attitudes. For example, *Grandpa has really become an old fogy.* The first is mildly insulting; the variant is somewhat vulgar.

**old hat** Overly familiar or routine, as in *Winning had become old hat.*

**old saw** A proverb or saying, as in *Mom's always repeating the old saw, "Haste makes waste."* This term uses *saw* in the sense of "saying," and *old* in the sense of "wise" rather than old-fashioned.

**old shoe** see COMFORTABLE AS AN OLD SHOE.

**old stamping ground** see STAMPING GROUND.

**old story, an** **1.** A common or excuse. For example, *Karen's headaches are an old story.* **2.** Something that often happens, as in *They're both in love with the same girl—it's an old story.* Also see SAME OLD STORY.

**old wives' tale** A belief that has persisted for a long time but isn't really true, a superstition, as in *Toads cause warts? That's an old wives' tale.*

**olive branch** A symbol of peace, an offering of goodwill, as in *They fought for years, but finally one side came over bearing an olive branch.*

**on, be** see BE ON.

**on account** In part payment of a debt, as in *He paid half the amount on account.*

**on account of** Because of the fact that, due to, as in *We canceled the beach picnic on account of the bad weather forecast.*

O

**on a dime** In a very small space, suddenly, as in *That horse is so well trained it can turn on a dime.* This expression refers to the fact that the dime is the smallest-size U.S. coin.

**on a first-name basis** Quite familiar and friendly, as in *Practically all the guests were on a first-name basis.* This idiom refers to the fact that using a person's given name is usually of a sign of familiarity.

**on again, off again** see under OFF AND ON.

**on a limb** see OUT ON A LIMB.

**on all fours** On one's hands and knees, as in *Seven of us were on all fours, looking for the lost earring in the sand.* In this idiom *fours* refers to the arms and legs.

**on and off** see OFF AND ON.

**on and on** Continuously, persistently, without stopping, as in *On and on they rode for three whole days.* Also see GO ON AND ON.

**on an even keel** Stable, balanced, as in *She kept the staff on an even keel in any emergency.* This term refers to keeping a ship's keel in a level position, assuring smooth sailing.

**on a par with** As good as, equal to, as in *This violinist may be an amateur, but he's on a par with professional orchestral players.*

**on a pedestal, put *someone*** Also, **set *someone* on a pedestal.** Greatly admire someone and believe them to be better or more important that they really are. For example, *Youngsters tend to put rock stars on a pedestal, forgetting that they're only human.* This expression refers to the raised position of a statue on a pedestal.

O

**on approval** To be returned if not satisfactory, as in *We took home the green curtains on approval.* This expression nearly always refers to the purchase of goods.

**on a rampage** Behaving violently, as in *There was a near riot after the game, when some of the spectators went on a rampage.* This term comes from the Old Scots verb *ramp,* meaning "storm and rage."

**on a roll** On a streak of success or intense activity, as in *The team's scored three goals in the last ten minutes; they're really on a roll,* or *Once the experiment succeeded, Tim was on a roll.* This term refers to the momentum in the act of rolling.

**on a shoestring** With very little money, as in *The just-married young couple was living on a shoestring.*

**on a string** Under someone's control, as in *She'll drop everything whenever Sam asks for something—he's got her on a string.* This expression refers to pulling an animal on a leash.

**on a tangent** On a sudden change of topic or change of course, on a digression, as in *The professor's lectures are hard to follow; he always goes off on a tangent.* This phrase often occurs in the idioms **fly off on a tangent** or **go off on a tangent,** as in *The witness was convincing until he went off on a tangent.* This expression refers to the geometric tangent—a line or curve that touches but does not intersect with another line or curve.

**on balance** Taking everything into consideration, as in *On balance, I think we've had a very good year.* This expression in effect means "balancing all the factors involved."

**on behalf of** see IN BEHALF OF.

**on bended knee** In a way that shows one's desperate desire for something, pleading, as in *They're desperate for funds; they're asking for contributions on bended knee.* This expression refers to kneeling to beg a favor. *Bended,* the past tense of *bend,* survives only in this idiom; elsewhere it was replaced by *bent.*

**on board** Joining in or participating, as in *The department head addressed the new employees, saying "Welcome on board,"* or *The opera company has a new vocal coach on board to help the soloists.* This expression refers to being on or in a vessel, an airplane, or another vehicle.

**on borrowed time, live** Live longer than reasonable expectations, as in *Our twenty-year-old car is living on borrowed time,* or *The vet said our dog is living on borrowed time.* This expression refers to time borrowed from death.

**on call** Available if asked to come, as in *Medical residents are required to be on call at least three nights a week.* Also see AT SOMEONE'S BECK AND CALL.

**on camera** Being filmed, as in *When the talk-show host began, I wasn't sure if we were on camera.* The antonym **off camera** means "outside the view of a movie or TV camera," as in *Go ahead and scratch—we're off camera now.*

**once** In addition to the idioms beginning with ONCE, also see ALL AT ONCE; AT ONCE; EVERY NOW AND THEN (ONCE IN A WHILE); GIVE SOMEONE THE ONCE-OVER.

**once and for all** As a settled matter, finally, permanently, as in *Once and for all, we're not going to buy you a horse!* or *We've settled that question once and for all.* This expression is in effect an abbreviation of "one time and for all time."

**once bitten, twice shy** After a person has been hurt, he or she is very cautious in the future, as in *He was two days late last time, so she's not hiring him again—once bitten, twice shy.* This expression probably refers to an animal biting someone.

**once in a blue moon** Rarely, once in a very long time, as in *We only see our daughter* *once in a blue moon.* A blue moon—that is, a second full moon in the same calendar month—occurs every 32 months or so, but the expression does not refer to that particular length of time.

**once in a lifetime** Extremely rare, especially as an opportunity. For example, *An offer like that will come just once in a lifetime.* Also see OF ONE'S LIFE.

**once in a while** Occasionally, not very often, as in *Once in a while I enjoy going fishing.* Also see EVERY NOW AND THEN; FROM TIME TO TIME.

**once over lightly** Quickly and not thoroughly, as in *I did read the program once over lightly, but perhaps I should study it more carefully.*

**once upon a time** On some past occasion, as in *I may have met him once upon a time, but I don't really remember.* This phrase is frequently used as the opening line of fairy tales and stories told to children, as in *Once upon a time there was a king who had three beautiful daughters.*

**on cloud nine** Extremely happy, as in *Ever since he proposed to her, she has been on cloud nine.* Also see IN SEVENTH HEAVEN.

**on commission** Making money based on sales completed or services provided, as in *Real estate agents rarely get a salary; they work largely on commission.* This use of the noun *commission* generally refers to a percentage of the total price.

**on condition that** Only if, provided that, with the restriction that, as in *She said she'd help with the costumes on condition that she would get ten free tickets to the play.*

**on consignment** Giving goods go an agent to sell, with the agreement that payment is made only on completed sales and that unsold goods may be returned by the agent. For example, *This secondhand shop accepts items of clothing on consignment.*

**on cue** Also, **right on cue.** At just the right moment, as if at a signal. For example, *We were asking about her when she called, right on cue.*

**on deck 1.** Available, ready for action, as in *We had ten kids on deck to clean up after the dance.* **2.** In baseball, scheduled to bat next, waiting near home plate to bat, as in *Joe was on deck next.* Both usages refer to crew members being on the deck of a ship and ready to perform their duties.

**on demand** When needed or asked for, as in *She's always ready to sing on demand,* or *Nowadays parents usually feed newborn babies on demand.* In finance, this phrase means "payable on being requested or presented," as in *This note is payable on demand.*

**on draft** Taken from a large container, such as a keg (as opposed to bottles). For example, *We much prefer the taste of beer on draft.*

**on duty** At one's post, at work, as in *The new nurse was on duty that evening,* or *The watchman was fired because he was drunk on duty.* The antonym **off duty** means "not engaged in one's work," as in *Captain Smith was much more relaxed and friendly when he was off duty.*

**one** In addition to the idioms beginning with ONE, also see ALL IN ONE PIECE; ALL THE SAME (ONE); A-1 (A-ONE); AS ONE; AT ONE; AT ONE STROKE; AT ONE TIME; AT ONE TIME OR ANOTHER; BACK TO THE DRAWING BOARD (SQUARE ONE); EACH AND EVERY ONE; EACH OTHER (ONE ANOTHER); FOR ONE (THING); GO ONE BETTER; HANG (ONE) ON; HOLE IN ONE; IN ONE EAR AND OUT THE OTHER; IN THE SAME (ONE) BREATH; IT TAKES ONE TO KNOW ONE; JUST ONE OF THOSE THINGS; LOOK OUT FOR (NUMBER ONE); MORE THAN ONE WAY TO SKIN A CAT; NOT ONE IOTA; ON THE ONE HAND; (ONE) PICTURE IS WORTH A THOUSAND WORDS; PULL A FAST ONE; PUT ALL ONE'S EGGS IN ONE BASKET; QUICK ONE; SEEN ONE, SEEN THEM ALL; SIX OF ONE, HALF A DOZEN OF THE OTHER; THAT'S ONE ON ME; TIE ONE ON; WEAR ANOTHER (MORE THAN ONE) HAT; WITH ONE ARM TIED BEHIND ONE'S BACK; WITH ONE VOICE. (Note that this listing does not include those idioms where ONE is a personal pronoun meaning "someone" or "oneself.")

**one and all** Everyone, as in *She's told one and all about their quarrel.*

**one and only** One's only love; one's only sweetheart. For example, *He swore she was his one and only, but the detective following him knew better.*

**one and the same** Identical, as in *Gloria's grandfather had been, at one and the same time, the king's doctor and a general in the army.* This expression is an emphatic form of "the same."

**one another** see EACH OTHER.

**one-armed bandit** A slot machine, as in *It's amazing how many people think they can make money playing a one-armed bandit.* This term refers to both appearance and function: the operating lever looks like an arm, and the machine in effect robs players, since it almost always "wins" and keeps the player's money.

**on earth 1.** Also, **in creation** or **in the world.** Ever, of all possible things. These phrases are all used for emphasis in questions or, less often, in a negative context. For example, *What on earth is he doing with a spade?* or *Where in creation did that child go?* or *How in the world do you expect me to carry all those bags?* **2. like nothing on**

**earth.** So special that nothing else can compare. For example, *That perfume smells like nothing on earth,* or *Her new hair color is like nothing on earth.*

**on easy street** see EASY STREET.

**one by one** Also, **one at a time.** One following another, as in *The ducklings jumped into the pond one by one,* or *One at a time they went into the office.*

**on edge** Tense, nervous, irritable, as in *We were all on edge as we waited for the doctor's report.* This expression transfers the edge of a cutting instrument to one's feelings. Also see ON THE EDGE; SET ONE'S TEETH ON EDGE.

**one eye on** Paying some but not full attention to, as in *He ran the rehearsal with one eye on the clock.* Also see HAVE ONE'S EYE ON; OUT OF THE CORNER OF ONE'S EYE; SEE WITH HALF AN EYE.

**one fell swoop, in** Also, **at one fell swoop.** All at once, in a single action, as in *This law has lifted all the controls on cable TV in one fell swoop.*

**one foot in the grave, have** Be close to death or in terrible condition, as in *Jane looks as though she has one foot in the grave.*

**one for the books** Also, **one for the book.** An outstanding or unusual achievement or event, as in *All of the main awards went to one film—that's one for the books.* This expression originally referred to record books kept for sports.

**one for the road** A final drink before leaving, as in *Won't you have just one for the road?* This term always refers to an alcoholic drink. If the person is going to drive away, then the practice is not only unwise but in many places illegal.

**one good turn deserves another** A favor should be returned with a favor of the same kind, as in *I'll give you a ride next time—one good turn deserves another.*

**one-horse town** A small and unimportant town, as in *Ours was just a one-horse town until the nuclear plant was built.* This expression probably originally referred to a town so small that a single horse would be all it needed.

**one in a million** Also, **one in a thousand** or **one in a billion.** Extremely special, extraordinary, rare, as in *She's the kindest soul—she's one in a million,* or *This ring is one in a thousand.*

**one jump ahead** Expecting and prepared for what will happen, as in *We have to keep one jump ahead of the opposition,* or *He was clever thief and stayed one jump ahead of the police.* Also see GET THE DROP (JUMP) ON.

**one-man show** Also, **one-man band.** A person who does or manages just about everything, as in *This department is a one-man show—the chairman runs it all,* or *The editor of that little newspaper conducts the interviews, writes the articles, sells ads, deals with the printer—he's a one-man band.* This idiom refers to an actor or artist responsible for an entire performance or exhibit, or to a musician who plays every instrument in the group.

**one man's meat is another man's poison** What is good for or enjoyed by one person is not necessarily the same for someone else. This expression is so well known that it is often shortened, as in *Pat loves to travel, but that's not for Doris—one man's meat, you know.* Also see NO ACCOUNTING FOR TASTES.

**on end** **1.** Continuously, without interruption, as in *It's been raining for days on end.* **2.** Upright, having its end down, as in *Let's put this box on end.*

**one of a kind** see under OF A KIND.

**one of these days** Also, **one day** or **some day.** On some day in the future, as in *One of these days I'm going to clean out my desk,* or *One day you'll see what it's like to have your child insult you,* or *They hoped to buy a brand-new car some day.*

**one of those days** Also, **just one of those days.** A day when everything goes wrong, as in *The car wouldn't start, I lost my glasses—it was one of those days.*

**one on, that's** see THAT'S ONE ON ME.

**one on one** In a direct meeting between two persons, especially a conflict, as in *The two department heads went one on one in competition for office space.* This expression almost certainly comes from sports. It is commonly used to refer to a two-person basketball game, but it is also applied to the interaction of two players on opposing teams in other sports.

**one picture is worth a thousand words** see PICTURE IS WORTH A THOUSAND WORDS.

**oneself** see AVAIL (ONESELF) OF; BE ONESELF; BESIDE ONESELF; BURN (ONESELF) OUT; BY ONESELF; COVER ONE'S ASS (ONESELF); EXCUSE ME (ONESELF); EXERT ONESELF; EXPLAIN ONESELF; EXPRESS ONESELF; FALL ALL OVER ONESELF; FEEL LIKE ONESELF; FIND ONESELF; FLATTER ONESELF; FLING ONESELF AT; FORGET ONESELF; FULL OF ONESELF; GIVE A GOOD ACCOUNT OF ONESELF; GIVE (ONESELF) AWAY; GIVE OF ONESELF; GIVE ONESELF UP; HAVE ONESELF; HEAR ONESELF THINK; HELP ONESELF; KEEP TO ONESELF; KICK ONESELF; KNOCK ONESELF OUT; LAW UNTO ONESELF; LEAVE (ONESELF) OPEN; LET (ONESELF) GO; LIVE WITH (ONESELF); LOSE ONESELF IN; MAKE A LAUGHINGSTOCK OF ONESELF; MAKE A NAME FOR ONESELF; MAKE AN EXHIBITION OF ONESELF; MAKE A NUISANCE OF ONESELF; MAKE A PIG OF ONESELF; MAKE ONESELF AT HOME; MAKE ONESELF SCARCE; NOT ONESELF; PAINT ONESELF INTO A

CORNER; PRIDE ONESELF ON; PULL ONESELF TOGETHER; PULL ONESELF UP; PUT ONESELF OUT; RELIEVE ONESELF; REPEAT ONESELF; SHIFT FOR ONESELF; SHOOT ONESELF IN THE FOOT; SPREAD ONESELF TOO THIN; SUIT ONESELF; SURE OF ONESELF; TAKE IT UPON ONESELF; THROW ONESELF AT; TIE ONESELF IN KNOTS; TROUBLE ONE'S HEAD WITH (ONESELF ABOUT).

**one-track mind** A mind limited to only one line of thought or action, as in *All you think about is sex—you have a one-track mind.* This expression refers to a train that runs only on one track or in one direction.

**one up** Also, **one up on.** Having an advantage or lead over someone, as in *Sara is one up on her sister because she already has her driver's license.* This expression comes from sports, where it means to be one point ahead of one's opponent.

**one way or another** Also, **one way or the other.** Somehow, in some fashion, as in *One way or another I'm sure we'll meet again,* or *He wasn't sure how to build the wall, but he was sure he would manage in one way or the other.*

**on faith, take it** Trust something, accept without proof, as in *I have no firm evidence that Bob's responsible for the errors—you'll just have to take it on faith.* This idiom uses *faith* in the sense of "belief or confidence in something."

**on file** In or as if in a record for easy reference. For example, *There's no job open right now, but we'll keep your résumé on file.* This expression uses *file* in the sense of "a collection of papers stored for ready reference."

**on fire** see SET ON FIRE; SET THE WORLD ON FIRE.

**on foot** Walking or running, not using a vehicle. For example, *There's no road to the beach; we have to get there on foot.* Also see HOOF IT; ON ONE'S FEET; ON THE RIGHT FOOT.

**on guard** see under OFF GUARD.

**on good terms** On a friendly basis, as in *I'm on good terms with the manager, so I'll ask him to help you.* Also see ON SPEAKING TERMS.

**on hand 1.** In one's possession, ready and available, as in *The business needs to have enough cash on hand.* **2.** Present, as in *Jim was always on hand to help.* **3.** Soon to happen. See AT HAND, def. 2.

**on high 1.** Up in the sky; also, in heaven. For example, *They fixed their eyes on high, looking for the comet.* **2.** In a position of authority, as in *Those on high have decided that we must work every other weekend.* Also see POWERS THAT BE.

**on hold 1.** In a state of temporary interruption, but not disconnection, during a telephone call, as in *While I was on hold, I had to listen to some awful music,* or *They had to put me on hold while they looked up my account.* **2.** In a state of postponement or delay, as in *When she was transferred, they had to put their romance on hold.*

**on ice 1.** In reserve or readiness. This idiom often occurs with *put,* meaning "place in reserve," as in *Let's put that proposal on ice until we have the money for it.* This usage refers to putting food in cold storage to preserve it. **2.** In prison, as in *He's been on ice for ten years.* This usage may come from the slang term *cooler* for "jail."

**on in years** see ALONG IN YEARS.

**on its merits** Also, **on one's merits** or **according to one's merits.** With regard only to the quality of something or someone. For example, *Who supports it doesn't matter; we have to consider the idea solely on its merits,* or *The agency doesn't care about her political connections; it wants to hire candidates according to their merits.*

**on line** Actively linked to a computer or network of computers, as in *They haven't got the printer on line yet,* or *Mark's been on line all morning.* Also see GO ONLINE.

**only** In addition to the idioms beginning with ONLY, also see BEAUTY IS ONLY SKIN DEEP; HAVE AN EYE (EYES ONLY) FOR; IF ONLY; IN NAME ONLY; NOT THE ONLY FISH IN THE SEA; ONE AND ONLY

**only game in town, the** The only choice, so one must accept it. For example, *Out here, this bank is the only game in town when it comes to financial services.* This term originally was used as a response to a gambler looking for a game in a strange town.

**only too 1.** More than enough or desired, as in *I know only too well that I can't win the lottery.* **2.** Very, extremely, as in *I am only too glad to help.*

**on no account** Also, **not on any account.** Under no circumstances, not for any reason, as in *On no account should you put anything metal in the microwave oven,* or *Dad said we can't go, not on any account.*

**on occasion** From time to time, now and then, as in *Nell was a vegetarian but now eats meat on occasion.*

**on one hand** see ON THE ONE HAND.

**on one's** In addition to the idioms beginning with ON ONE'S, also see under ON SOMEONE'S.

**on one's account** see ON ACCOUNT OF; ON ONE'S OWN ACCOUNT.

**on one's behalf** see IN BEHALF OF.

**on one's best behavior** Also, **on one's good behavior.** Very polite, as in *Mother told the children to be on their best behavior during Grandma's visit,* or *All the staff members were on their good behavior while the client inspected the premises.*

**on one's doorstep** see AT ONE'S DOOR.
**on oneself** see TAKE IT UPON ONESELF.
**on one's feet** In addition to the idiom ON ONE'S FEET, also see DEAD ON ONE'S FEET; GET TO (ON) ONE'S FEET; SET ONE BACK ON ONE'S FEET; STAND ON ONE'S OWN FEET; THINK ON ONE'S FEET.
**on one's feet 1.** Standing, as in *I'm tired—I've been on my feet all day.* Also see GET TO ONE'S FEET. **2.** Also, **back on one's feet.** Healthy, returned to good health, as in *I hope you get back on your feet very soon.*
**on one's good behavior** see ON ONE'S BEST BEHAVIOR.
**on one's guard** see under OFF GUARD.
**on one's hands 1.** In one's possession or care, often as a responsibility, as in *As long as she had three children on her hands, she couldn't get very much accomplished,* or *They had two houses on their hands because they hadn't sold the first before having to move.* For an antonym, see OFF SOMEONE'S HANDS. **2. time on one's hands.** Time in which one has nothing necessary to do, free time, as in *She has a lot of time on her hands now that the kids have moved out.* Also see IN ONE'S HANDS.
**on one's head** Also, **on one's own head.** As one's responsibility or fault, as in *If the police catch you speeding, it's on your own head.* Also see OFF ONE'S HEAD.
**on one's heels** see AT ONE'S HEELS.
**on one's high horse** In an arrogant manner, acting as if one is better than other people. For example, *When they started talking about music, David got on his high horse and said that classical music was only for educated ears.* This expression refers to the use of tall horses by important people. Similarly, **off one's high horse** means "less arrogantly, more humbly," as in *I wish she'd get off her high horse and be more friendly.*
**on one's home ground** Where one has the advantage of familiarity. For example, *Teams generally find it easier to win on their home ground,* or *The candidate from Maine was comfortable speaking on his home ground.*
**on one's honor** Entrusted to behave honorably and honestly without supervision. For example, *The students were on their honor not to consult notes during the exam.*
**on one's last legs** Extremely tired, close to collapsing, as in *We've been cleaning house all day, and I'm on my last legs.* This expression is sometimes applied to things that will not be in a usable condition much longer, as in *That furnace is on its last legs.*
**on one's mind** Also, **on the brain.** In one's thoughts, filling someone's mind. For example, *The book prize has been on my mind, but I haven't been able to discuss it with you.* It is often put as **have something on one's mind (or the brain),** meaning "be preoccupied with something," as in *I didn't mean to be rude; I just have a lot on my mind right now,* or *John has nothing but girls on the brain.*
**on one's own 1.** By one's own efforts or resources, as in *He built the entire addition on his own.* **2.** Responsible for oneself, independent of outside help or control, as in *Dave moved out last fall; he's on his own now.*
**on one's own account** Also, **on one's own hook** or **on one's own initiative.** For oneself; also, by one's own efforts, as in *I've gone into business on my own account,* or *He called the police on his own hook,* or *She went job-hunting on her own initiative.* The first term transfers the financial sense of *account* to one's own interest or risk. The third term uses *initiative* in the sense of "enterprise."
**on one's own time** During nonworking hours, especially when one is not being paid. For example, *Marcia wrote poetry evenings and weekends, on her own time.* This expression implies that the time a person spends working for someone else is no longer his or her possession.
**on one's part** see FOR ONE'S PART.
**on one's say-so** According to one's authority, as in *I'm reorganizing the files on the boss's say-so,* or *You can skip the exam? On whose say-so?*
**on one's shoulders** As one's responsibility, as in *The king carries his entire country on his shoulders,* or *The success of the conference rests on Nancy's shoulders. Shoulders* is used here as the burden-bearing part of the body.
**on one's soapbox** Expressing one's views passionately or self-importantly, as in *Dexter can't resist getting on his soapbox about taxes.* This expression comes from the past use of a soapbox as a platform for a speaker, usually outdoors.
**on one's tail** see GET OFF ONE'S TAIL; ON SOMEONE'S COATTAILS; ON SOMEONE'S TAIL.
**on one's toes** Alert, ready to act, as in *Orchestra players must be on their toes all the time, so as not to miss an entrance.* This expression probably refers to boxers or runners who must be on their toes in order to move or start quickly.
**on one's way 1.** See ON THE WAY. **2.** Also, **be on one's way.** Leave, get going, as in *"On your way," said the officer, trying to move the crowd,* or *It's been a wonderful party, but we must be on our way now.*
**on order** Requested but not yet delivered, as in *Our new sofa is on order.* This term is always used for goods of some kind, the noun *order* here meaning "a commission for goods."

**on pain of** Also, **under pain of.** Risking the penalty of a specific punishment. For example, *The workers knew that going on strike was on pain of losing their jobs.* At one time this idiom often referred to death as the penalty. Today, the expression is usually an exaggeration, as in *We'd better be back on time, under pain of death.*

**on paper** In theory as opposed to reality, as in *They are a good team on paper but not in the field.* This expression contrasts something written down with what really exists

**on pins and needles** Nervously anxious, as in *He was on pins and needles, waiting for the test results.* This expression refers to the tingling sensation experienced in recovering from numbness.

**on principle** **1.** For moral or ethical reasons. For example, *She won't wear fur or eat meat on principle.* **2.** According to a fixed rule or practice. For example, *The police were locking up the demonstrators on principle.* **3. on general principle.** For no special reason, in general, as in *Dean won't touch broccoli on general principle.*

**on purpose** **1.** Deliberately, intentionally, as in *He left some facts out of the story on purpose.* **2. accidentally on purpose.** Seemingly accidentally but actually deliberately, as in *She stepped on his foot accidentally on purpose.* This phrase is often used as a joke.

**on record** see GO ON RECORD.

**on relief** see ON WELFARE.

**on request** When asked for, as in *The agreement states that they will repay the loan on request.* Also see BY REQUEST.

**on sale** At a reduced price, as in *These rugs have been on sale for a month.*

**on schedule** At the announced or expected time, as in *Her first baby arrived right on schedule.* This expression originally referred to published railroad timetables.

**on second thought** Resulting from a revised opinion or change of mind, as in *I thought I'd go to the movies, but on second thought I'd rather stay home.* Similarly, **have second thoughts** means "change one's mind," as in *I've had second thoughts about moving to Florida.* This idiom refers to ideas that come later.

**on sight** Also, **at sight.** Immediately after seeing, as in *The soldiers threatened were ordered to shoot the enemy on sight,* or *He's able to multiply those three-digit figures at sight.*

**on someone's** In addition to the idioms beginning with ON SOMEONE'S, also see under ON ONE'S.

**on someone's back** Also, **on someone's case.** See under OFF SOMEONE'S BACK.

**on someone's coattails** Also, **on the coattails of.** Owing to another person's popularity or merits. For example, *He won the cabinet post by hanging on the senator's coattails,* or *He was elected to office on the coattails of the governor.* This expression dates from a time when coats with tails were in fashion.

**on someone's heels** see AT SOMEONE'S HEELS.

**on someone's nerves** see GET ON SOMEONE'S NERVES.

**on someone's side** In support of someone's views or interests, as in *I'm glad you're on my side in this debate,* or *With the Canadians on our side, we should be able to persuade the Mexicans of a North American policy.*

**on someone's tail** Following and watching someone closely, as in *The police were on the suspect's tail day and night.*

**on speaking terms** **1.** Friendly enough for conversation, as in *We're on speaking terms with the new neighbors.* **2.** Ready and willing to communicate. For example, *We are on speaking terms again after the quarrel.* Both senses of this idiom commonly occur in the negative, as in *Brett and his brother haven't been on speaking terms for years.*

**on spec** Done in hopes of making money but with no assurance of profit. For example, *We didn't design our house; the builder built it on spec. Spec* is used here as an abbreviation for *speculation.*

**on standby** Ready and waiting, as in *We've got three more painters on standby.* This expression originated in the navy during World War II, where it referred to someone being ready to come on duty as soon as required. More recently, it has been widely used for a passenger waiting to take the first available seat on a full flight.

**on strike** Engaged in a work stoppage, as in *The auto workers were on strike for the entire summer.* This expression originally used *strike* in the sense of a labor stoppage organized to gain something from employers, and the term is still used this way. But it is also used more loosely, as in *Where washing dishes is concerned, Mom has announced that she's on strike.* Also see GO OUT, def. 4.

**on tap** Available for immediate use, ready, as in *We have two more bands on tap for the parade.* This expression refers to a drink such as beer that is ready to be drawn from a cask.

**on target** Completely accurate, wholly valid, as in *Our cost estimates were right on target,* or *His criticisms were on target.*

**on tenterhooks** In a state of painful suspense, as in *We were on tenterhooks all through the game, hoping our team would win.*

**on the air** see under OFF THE AIR.

**on the alert** Watchful, fully prepared, as in *The inspectors are always on the alert for a manufacturing error.*

**on the average** In general, usually, as in *On the average, about 15 percent of the freshman class will drop out before graduation.* This expression uses *average* in the sense of "a norm or standard."

**on the ball, be** Also, **have something on the ball.** Be especially quick-thinking or efficient, as in *You need to be on the ball when you baby-sit an active two-year-old,* or *These programmers really have a lot on the ball.* This term originated in baseball and referred to throwing a pitch with great speed, spin, or some other deceptive motion.

**on the bandwagon, get** Also, **climb on the bandwagon** or **hop on the bandwagon** or **jump on the bandwagon.** Join a popular cause or movement, as in *More and more people are getting on the bandwagon to denounce cigarette smoking.* This expression refers to the horse-drawn wagons, carrying a brass band, that often accompanied political candidates on campaign tours. It was later extended to supporting a campaign or another cause.

**on the barrel** see CASH ON THE BARRELHEAD.

**on the beam** see under OFF THE BEAM.

**on the bench** **1.** Presiding as judge in a law court, as in *Lawyers are very careful when Judge Brown is on the bench.* The *bench* is the seat occupied by a judge. **2.** Waiting for a chance to participate; also, removed from participation. For example, *Mary complained that all her colleagues were going to the sales conference while she was left on the bench.* This usage comes from baseball and other sports. Players who are not considered ready or competent to play sit on a bench watching the game. Also see WARM THE BENCH.

**on the blink** Also, **on the bum** or **on the fritz.** Out of order, broken, working poorly or not at all, as in *The TV is on the blink again,* or *You drive—our car's on the bum.* The first of these slang expressions may refer to an electric light that flickers on and off ("blinks"). The second may come from *bum* in the sense of "a contemptible person." The third, *fritz,* is of unknown origin.

**on the block** **1. put on the block** or **go on the block.** Offer something or be offered for sale, as in *These paintings will all be put on the block.* This usage refers to the auction block, the platform from which the auctioneer sells goods. **2. put one's head on the block.** Take a great risk, make oneself vulnerable, as in *I'm not going to put my head on the block just to save her reputation.* This usage refers to the executioner's block, where victims once had their heads cut off.

**on the brain** see ON ONE'S MIND.

**on the bum** see ON THE BLINK.

**on the button** Exactly right, precisely, as in *Her review of the book was right on the button,* or *We're supposed to be there at six o'clock on the button.* Also see ON THE DOT.

**on the carpet** see CALL SOMEONE ON THE CARPET.

**on the chance that** On the possibility that, in case, as in *I came early on the chance that we might have time to chat.* This phrase uses *chance* in the sense of "a possibility or probability for some event." It is sometimes put as **on the off chance,** meaning "on the slight but unlikely possibility," as in *I came late on the off chance that I could avoid Thomas.*

**on the cheap** Economically, at very little cost, as in *We're traveling around Europe on the cheap.*

**on the chin** see TAKE IT ON THE CHIN.

**on the contrary** It's the opposite, as in *Is his shoulder hurting? On the contrary, it's all better,* or *We thought you didn't like opera. On the contrary, I love it.*

**on the defensive** Feeling a need to defend oneself against criticism or attack, as in *The debate team's plan was to keep their opponents on the defensive,* or *This teacher put students on the defensive about their mistakes.*

**on the dole** see ON WELFARE.

**on the dot** Exactly on time, as in *We had to be there at eight on the dot.* The *dot* in this idiom is the mark on the face of a watch or clock that shows the time in question. Also see ON THE BUTTON.

**on the double** Very quickly, as in *You'd better get here on the double.* This expression, also put as *at the double,* came from the military, where it means "double time"—that is, marching twice as fast as normally.

**on the edge** **1.** In a risky position; also, in a state of excitement, as from danger or risk. For example, *When the stock market crashed, their whole future was on the edge,* or *Skydivers obviously must enjoy living on the edge.* **2. on the edge of.** Very close to doing something, as in *He was on the edge of winning the election when the sex scandal broke.* Both senses refer to the danger of falling over the edge of a high elevation.

**on the eve of** Just before, as in *On the eve of the conference the main speaker had to cancel.* The word *eve* literally means "the night before."

**on the face of it** Based on available evidence, according to the way something appears, as in *On the face of it this project should take no more than six months.* This idiom uses *face* in the sense of "a superficial view."

**on the fast track** **1.** On a direct route to a more important job, expected to gain professional success. For example, *He started with the firm just a year ago, but he's definitely on the fast track.* **2.** In position for immediate action, as in *Because of the recent violence, Congress has put the gun-control bill on the fast track.*

**on the fence, be** Also, **straddle the fence.** Be undecided, not be committed, as in *I don't know if I'll move there; I'm still on the fence,* or *He's straddling the fence about the merger.* This expression suggests that one can jump to either side. At first it was applied mainly to political commitments.

**on the fly** In a hurry, while rushing somewhere, as in *I picked up some groceries on the fly.* This expression literally means "in midair or in flight."

**on the fritz** see ON THE BLINK.

**on the go** In constant activity, very busy, as in *I'm exhausted—I've been on the go since eight this morning.*

**on the heels of** Also, **hard on the heels of.** Immediately after or following, as in *Mom's birthday comes on the heels of Mother's Day,* or *Hard on the heels of the flood there was a tornado.* The *hard* in the variant acts as an intensifier, giving it the sense of "close on the heels of." Also see AT SOMEONE'S HEELS.

**on the horizon** Within view, not too far away, as in *The analysts see a huge rise in the stock market on the horizon.*

**on the horns of a dilemma** see HORNS OF A DILEMMA.

**on the hour** At every hour exactly; at one o'clock, two o'clock, and so on. For example, *Buses to New York depart on the hour.* An extension of this idiom is **every hour on the hour,** as in *The bus passes by the house every hour on the hour.*

**on the house** At the expense of the business, without charge to the customer, as in *This hotel serves an afternoon tea that's on the house.* This idiom uses *house* in the sense of "an inn, tavern, or other building serving the public."

**on the in, be** Have information known only to a few, as in *She was too new to the firm to be on the in for policy changes.* Also see GET AN IN WITH; IN ON.

**on the increase** Growing, happening more often, as in *Violent crime is on the increase.*

**on the inside** In a position of confidence or influence, as in *The new reporter said he got his facts from at least one official on the inside.*

**on the job** **1.** At work, busy, as in *We've got three men on the job.* **2.** Paying close attention, alert, as in *Trust Jim to find out the details—he's always on the job.*

**on the lam** Running away, especially from the police, as in *He's always in some kind of trouble and constantly on the lam.*

**on the level** Honest, straightforward, sincere, as in *You can believe her—she's on the level.*

**on the line** see LAY SOMETHING ON THE LINE.

**on the lines of** see ALONG THE LINES OF.

**on the lookout** Also, **on the watch.** Watchful, alert, as in *Be on the lookout for the twins—they're somewhere on this playground,* or *He was on the watch for her arrival.*

**on the loose** **1.** Free to move, not under control, as in *That dog of theirs is on the loose all the time.* **2.** Acting without restraint, as in *After the game the players celebrated on the loose.*

**on the make** **1.** Trying to get money and power, as in *Tom's a young man on the make—he doesn't care whom he offends.* **2.** Looking for sex, as in *After several affairs, Peter got the reputation of being on the make.*

**on the map** see PUT SOMETHING ON THE MAP.

**on the mark** see under OFF THE MARK.

**on the market** For sale; also, available for buying. For example, *We've put the boat on the market,* or *This is the only tandem bicycle on the market right now.* Also see DRUG ON THE MARKET.

**on the mend** Recovering one's health, as in *I heard you had the flu, but I'm glad to see you're on the mend.* This idiom uses *mend* in the sense of "repair."

**on the money** Also, **right on the money.** Exact, precise, as in *Your estimate is right on the money.* This term refers to a winning bet in horseracing.

**on the move** **1.** Busily moving about, very active, as in *A nurse is on the move all day long.* Also see ON THE GO. **2.** Going from one place to another, traveling, as in *The army was on the move again.* **3.** Making progress, advancing, as in *Their technology is clearly on the move.*

**on the nose** Exactly, precisely; especially, at the appointed time or estimated amount. For example, *The busload of students arrived at the museum at ten o'clock, right on the nose,* or *He guessed the final score on the nose.* This term may come from boxing, where the opponent's nose is a highly desired target.

**on the off chance** see under ON THE CHANCE THAT.

**on the one hand** Also, **on one hand.** As one point of view, from one standpoint. This phrase is often paired with **on the other hand** to indicate two sides of an issue. For example, *On the one hand, this car is expensive; on the other hand, it's available and we need it right now.*

**on the order of 1.** Approximately, as in *We need on the order of three cases of wine for the reception.* **2.** Like, of a kind similar to, as in *Their house is small, more on the order of a cottage.*

**on the other foot** see SHOE IS ON THE OTHER FOOT.

**on the other hand** see under ON THE ONE HAND.

**on the outs** No longer on friendly terms, as in *They've been on the outs with their in-laws for years.*

**on the part of** see FOR SOMEONE'S PART.

**on the point of** Also, **at the point of.** Close to doing something, as in *I was on the point of leaving when the phone rang.*

**on the prowl** Actively looking for something, as in *Their underpaid computer programmers are always on the prowl for better jobs.* This idiom refers to an animal's search for prey.

**on the Q.T.** Secretly, as in *They told her on the Q.T. that she was being promoted.* In this slang term *Q.T.* is an abbreviation for "quiet."

**on the rebound** Reacting to or recovering from an unhappy experience, especially the end of a love affair. For example, *A month after breaking up with Larry, Jane got engaged to Bob, a classic case of being on the rebound.* This term refers to the bouncing back of a ball.

**on the receiving end** In a position to be affected by someone's action, especially something unpleasant, as in *It seems I'm always on the receiving end of his bad moods.*

**on the right foot, get off** Also, **start off on the right foot.** Make a good beginning, establish good relations, as in *It's important to get off on the right foot in this new job.* This usage refers to walking correctly. The antonym is **get off on the wrong foot,** as in *I'm afraid we got off on the wrong foot with our daughter's in-laws.*

**on the right tack** Also, **on the right track.** Continuing or progressing in the right way; also, following the correct line of reasoning. For example, *He thinks the housing market is improving, and he's on the right tack there,* or *That's not exactly so, but you're on the right track.* The first term refers to the direction of a sailboat, the second to the direction of a path. The same is true of the antonyms, **on the wrong tack** and **on the wrong track,** which refer to thinking or a course that is mistaken. For example, *He's on the wrong tack for finding a solution,* or *The researchers were on the wrong track altogether when they assumed the virus was transmitted by mosquitoes.*

**on the road 1.** Traveling, as in *Our salesmen are on the road five days a week.* **2. on the road to.** On the way to, following a course that will end in. For example, *We could see Mary was on the road to recovery,* or *The business obviously was on the road to ruin.*

**on the rocks 1.** Ruined, spoiled, as in *Six months after the wedding, their marriage was on the rocks.* This expression refers to a ship running aground on rocks and breaking apart. **2.** Served over ice only, as in *He always drinks whiskey on the rocks.* The *rocks* here are the ice cubes. **3.** Without any money, bankrupt, as in *Can I borrow next month's rent? I'm on the rocks.* This usage is heard more often in Britain than in the United States.

**on the ropes** Close to defeat or collapse, helpless, as in *They acknowledged that their campaign was on the ropes, and they could not possibly win the election.* This expression refers to a boxer forced back to the ropes of the ring and leaning against them for support.

**on the run 1.** In rapid retreat; also, attempting to escape from someone chasing behind. For example, *The burglars were on the run from the police.* **2.** Hurrying from place to place, as in *The company officers were always on the run from New York to Los Angeles and back.*

**on the safe side** Avoiding risk or danger, with a margin for error, as in *Just to be on the safe side, let's order another hundred chairs.*

**on the same page** Sharing a point of view, understanding someone's ideas. For example, *All three of us are finally on the same page.*

**on the same wavelength** In complete accord, sharing similar opinions and feelings, rapport, as in *I like our new neighbors; we seem to be on the same wavelength.* This term refers to radio waves that carry a broadcast.

**on the scene, be** Also, **arrive on the scene** or **come on the scene.** Be or arrive where an action or event occurs, as in *They won't have a wild party because their parents will be on the scene,* or *Once Bob arrives on the scene, you can expect trouble.* This idiom refers to a theatrical setting, where a drama is being played.

**on the shelf 1.** Inactive, not employed, as in *Many useful employees are put on the shelf because they aren't allowed to work past age 65.* **2.** In a state of disuse, as in *We'll have to put her proposal on the shelf until we have more funds.* Both these usages refer to an article left on the shelf of a store, bookcase, or the like.

**on the side** In addition to the main portion of something; also, in addition to one's regular job. For example, *He ordered some French fries on the side,* or *She had full-time work as a bookkeeper, but she often prepared*

O

*tax returns on the side.* Also see ON SOMEONE'S SIDE.

**on the sidelines** Watching rather than participating, out of the action, as in *Nearby nations remained on the sidelines, waiting to see which political faction would win.* This idiom comes from sports. The *sidelines* are the two lines defining the sides of a court or playing field and the area immediately beyond them. The nonplaying team members and spectators sit here.

**on the skids** In the process of decline or ruin, as in *If she quit now, her career would be on the skids.* This idiom always implies a bad change. The *skids* here are runners such as those on a sled, which cause one to go downhill quickly.

**on the sly** Furtively, secretly, as in *She's always eating cookies on the sly.* The adjective *sly,* which means "cunning" or "crafty," is here used as a noun.

**on the spot** **1.** At once, without delay, as in *When the boss learned Tom had been lying, he fired him on the spot.* This usage suggests that one does not have time to move away from a particular spot. **2.** At the scene of action, as in *Whenever there's a bad accident or fire, you can be sure the station will have a reporter on the spot.* This usage also uses *spot* in the sense of "a particular location." **3.** Under pressure or in trouble, as in *He's on the spot, because he can't pay back the loan.* It is also phrased as **put *someone* on the spot,** meaning "put under pressure." For example, *The reporter's question put her on the spot; she didn't want to lie or to admit her part in the scandal.*

**on the spur of the moment** Impulsively, without prior preparation, as in *He decided to join a tour to England on the spur of the moment.* This expression refers to the spurring to a horse.

**on the street** Also, **in the street.** **1.** Without a job, unemployed, as in *After they fired her, she was on the street for two years.* **2.** Without a regular place of residence, homeless, as in *It's terrible to be on the street in winter.* **3.** Released from prison, as in *One more year and he'll be back on the street.*

**on the strength of** Mainly because of, on the basis of, for, as in *She was hired on the strength of her computer skills,* or *The newspaper won't print the story on the strength of just gossip and rumors.*

**on the surface** According to how something looks or seems, to all appearances, as in *On the surface he appeared brave and patriotic, but the truth was quite different.*

**on the table** **1.** Waiting to be discussed, as in *There are two new proposals on the table.* **2.** Postponed or put aside for later consideration, as in *When they adjourned, three items were put on the table until the next meeting.* The *table* in both idioms means a conference table. Also see LAY ONE'S CARDS ON THE TABLE.

**on the take** Accepting bribes or other illegal money or gifts, as in *The commission found a number of police officers on the take.*

**on the tip of one's tongue** Something is in one's mind, but one is unable to remember and say it at the moment, as in *I met him last year and his name is on the tip of my tongue—it'll come to me in a minute.*

**on the town** Also, **out on the town.** Enjoying entertainment offered by a town or city, as in *We went out on the town last night.*

**on the up-and-up** Open and honest, as in *Their boss has always been on the up-and-up with them.*

**on the uptake** In understanding or comprehension. This term is most often put as **quick on the uptake,** meaning quick to understand things, and **slow on the uptake,** meaning slow to comprehend. For example, *Shirley will have no trouble learning that new computer program—she's very quick on the uptake.* The expression refers to absorbing ("taking up") information.

**on the verge of** Close to doing something, as in *I was on the verge of calling the doctor when he suddenly got better,* or *Sara was on the verge of tears when she heard the news.* This term uses *verge* in the sense of "the brink or border of something."

**on the wagon** Abstaining from drinking alcohol, as in *Don't offer her wine; she's on the wagon.* The antonym is **off the wagon,** used for a return to drinking.

**on the warpath** Very angry and on a hostile course of action, as in *When the meat wasn't delivered, the chef went on the warpath.* This expression is an English translation of a Native American term that literally means "a path used by a war party." **Go on the warpath** thus meant "go to battle."

**on the watch** see ON THE LOOKOUT.

**on the way** **1.** Also, **on one's way.** In the process of coming, going, or traveling. For example, *The package is on the way,* or *She was on her way out the door,* or *Winter is on the way.* **2.** On the route of a journey, as in *I met him on the way to town,* or *We ran into them on the way.* **3. on the way to** or **well on the way to.** Close to experiencing or achieving, as in *James is on the way to becoming a full professor,* or *Nancy is well on her way to a nervous breakdown.* Also see ON THE WAY OUT.

**on the way out** **1.** Also, **on one's way out.** Ready and starting to go out, as in *We were on our way out when the phone rang.* **2.** Going

O

out of fashion, becoming obsolete, as in *Full-size cars are on the way out.*

**on the whole** Considering everything, as in *On the whole we enjoyed our vacation, although the hotel was not perfect.* Also see BY AND LARGE; FOR THE MOST PART.

**on the wing** In flight, usually referring to a bird as opposed to a plane. For example, *Louise is very good at identifying birds on the wing.*

**on the wrong foot** see under ON THE RIGHT FOOT.

**on the wrong side of bed** see GET UP ON THE WRONG SIDE.

**on the wrong tack** Also, **on the wrong track.** See under ON THE RIGHT TACK.

**on thin ice** In a dangerous or risky position, as in *After failing the midterm, he was on thin ice with his math teacher.* This metaphor is often put as **skate on thin ice,** as in *He knew he was skating on thin ice when he took his rent money with him to the racetrack.* This idiom refers to the danger that walking or being on thin ice will cause it to break.

**on time 1.** Punctually, according to schedule, as in *I hope the plane will be on time.* **2.** By paying in installments, on credit, as in *They are buying their car on time.* The *time* here refers to the designated period in which payments must be made.

**on tiptoe 1.** Eagerly waiting for something, as in *The children were on tiptoe before the birthday party.* **2.** Moving in a secretive and quiet way, as in *They went down the hall on tiptoe.* Both usages transfer standing or walking on one's toes to a particular reason for doing so.

O

**on to** see BE ON TO.

**on top** In a dominant or successful position, as in *Which team is on top in that league?* It is also put as **come out on top,** as in *As we expected, Paul again came out on top in the chess tournament.* Also see ON TOP OF.

**on top of 1.** In control of, fully informed about, as in *The weeds were terrible, but the new gardener was soon on top of them,* or *Our senator always manages to be on top of the issues.* **2.** In addition to, following closely on, as in *Several other benefits are being offered on top of a better salary,* or *On top of the flu, Jane caught her sister's measles.* **3.** Also, **on top of one another.** Very close to, crowded, as in *I didn't see her until she was right on top of us,* or *In these tiny apartments people are living right on top of one another.*

**on top of the world** Feeling very happy, delighted, as in *She was on top of the world after her roses won first prize.* This idiom refers to the peak of success or happiness.

**on trial 1.** In the process of being tried, especially in a court of law. For example, *He will be put on trial for the murder of his wife.* **2.** On a temporary basis, as a test of something, as in *They said we could take the vacuum cleaner on trial and return it if it was too noisy.*

**on view** So as to be seen, as in *They will put the antiques on view an hour before the auction begins.*

**on welfare** Also, **on relief** or **on the dole.** Receiving financial support from the government, as in *With the factories closed, half the people in this town are on welfare,* or *Don hated the idea of going on relief.* The first two terms originated in the United States during the Depression, when government assistance of this kind was first introduced. **On the dole** is used mainly in Britain.

**on your life** see NOT ON YOUR LIFE.

**open** In addition to the idioms beginning with OPEN; also see KEEP ONE'S EYES OPEN; LAY OPEN; LEAVE OPEN; LEAVE THE DOOR OPEN; NOT OPEN ONE'S MOUTH; OUT IN THE OPEN; THROW OPEN; WIDE OPEN; WITH ONE'S EYES OPEN; WITH OPEN ARMS.

**open and aboveboard** Also, **honest and aboveboard.** Candid and fair, without dishonesty or trickery, as in *I'll join you, but only if everything remains open and aboveboard. Aboveboard* comes from gambling. It refers to the fact that card players who do not keep their hands on the table (board) may be suspected of changing their cards under the table.

**open-and-shut** Simple, straightforward, easily solved, as in *With three eyewitnesses, the prosecutor said this case was open-and-shut.* This term suggests that one has immediate access to the facts of a situation.

**open book, an** Something or someone that can be readily examined or easily understood, as in *His entire life is an open book.* This expression is often expanded to **read someone like an open book,** meaning "see and understand someone's thoughts or feelings." For an antonym, see CLOSED BOOK.

**open doors** see OPEN THE DOOR TO.

**open fire** Also, **open fire on. 1.** Begin shooting, as in *He ordered the men to open fire on the enemy.* **2.** Begin a verbal attack, as in *In her second letter to the editor she opened fire, saying the reporter had deliberately lied.*

**open house 1.** A particular occasion or period when a home or an institution is open to visitors or prospective buyers. For example, *They held an open house on Sunday for potential home buyers.* **2.** A period of time, often during a special occasion, when hospitality is provided for visitors, as in *We held an open house for our daughter's graduation.*

**open mind** A mind receptive to different opinions and ideas, as in *Her open mind* *could see merit in the new method.* This phrase is often put as **keep an open mind,** as in *The judge cautioned the jury to keep an open mind while hearing the evidence.*

**open one's eyes** Become or make someone aware of the truth of a situation, as in *It's time you opened your eyes to the politics of this office,* or *The trip to Zimbabwe opened her eyes to the difficulties faced by developing nations.*

**open one's heart to** Confide in, reveal one's thoughts and feelings to, as in *Last night Meg opened her heart to her sister concerning her marriage.* This expression uses *heart* in the sense of "the center of thought and emotion."

**open one's mouth** see NOT OPEN ONE'S MOUTH.

**open question, an** An unresolved issue, one that has not been decided. For example, *Whether the town should pave all the dirt roads remains an open question.*

**open season on** A period of unrestrained criticism or attack on something or someone, as in *During an election year, it's open season on all officeholders.* This expression refers to the period during which one may legally hunt or fish.

**open secret, an** Something that is supposedly secret but is in fact widely known, as in *It's an open secret that both their children are adopted.*

**open the door to** Also, **open doors.** Create an opportunity for, as in *Legalizing marijuana may open the door to all kinds of drug abuse,* or *Her statement opened the door to further discussion,* or *Dad's connections at the hospital have opened doors for Richard at medical school.*

**open up** **1.** Spread out, unfold, as in *A green valley opened up before us.* **2.** Begin operation, as in *The new store opens up next month.* **3.** Begin firing, begin attacking, as in *The artillery opened up at dawn,* or, *The speaker opened up fiercely on the opposition.* Also see OPEN FIRE. **4.** Speak freely and candidly, as in *At last she opened up and told us what happened.* **5.** Make an opening in something by cutting, as in *The surgeon opened up the patient's chest.* **6.** Become available or accessible, as in *With new markets opening up all the time we hope to see an increase in international sales.* **7.** Increase the speed of a vehicle, as in *Let's see how fast the car will go if you open it up.* **8.** Open the door, as in *Open up! This is the police.* Note that in all of these usages except def. 4 and 7, *up* serves as an intensifier; that is, it emphasizes the verb *open* but does not change its meaning.

**open with** Begin with, as in *The singer opened the concert with her best-selling song.*

**opinion** see MATTER OF OPINION.

**opposite number, one's** One's counterpart, as in *He's my opposite number in the California office.* This expression is generally used for a person's equivalent in another organization or system (with *number* referring to one's position in a hierarchy).

**opt out** Choose not to participate, as in *Our school opted out of the state competition.*

**oranges** see APPLES AND ORANGES.

**orbit** see IN ORBIT.

**order** In addition to the idioms beginning with ORDER, also see APPLE-PIE ORDER; BACK ORDER; CALL TO ORDER; IN ORDER; IN SHORT ORDER; JUST WHAT THE DOCTOR ORDERED; LAW AND ORDER; MADE TO ORDER; MARCHING ORDERS; ON ORDER; ON THE ORDER OF; OUT OF ORDER; PECKING ORDER; PUT ONE'S HOUSE IN ORDER; SHORT ORDER; STANDING ORDERS; TO ORDER.

**order of the day, the** What is usually done or expected in a particular situation, as in *T-shirts and blue jeans were the order of the day for the picnic,* or *Fierce competition seems to be the order of the day among those boys.* This expression originally referred to the subject of debate in a legislature on a particular day, as well as to specific commands given to troops.

**order someone about** Give commands to someone in a domineering and offensive manner, as in *That teacher had better learn not to order the other teachers about.*

**ordinary** see OUT OF THE ORDINARY.

**or else** **1.** Otherwise, in different circumstances, as in *Present your case now, or else you won't have a chance.* **2.** Regardless of any excuses, no matter what, as in *Be there on time or else!*

**or other** Or another person, thing, or place. This phrase is used after indefinite words beginning with *some,* such as *someone, somehow, sometime,* or *somewhere.* It suggests the speaker doesn't think it's important to be more specific. For example, *Someone or other will be taking tickets at the door,* or *I can't remember where I put the lawn rake, but it's somewhere or other in the garage,* or *Somehow or other be found one that matched.*

**or so** Approximately, especially referring to a number, as in *Four hundred or so guests are invited.*

**or what?** A phrase following a statement that adds emphasis or suggests an option. For example, in *Is this a good movie or what?* the phrase asks for confirmation or agreement. However, it also may ask for an alternative, as in *Is this book a biography or what?*

**or whatever** Or any other thing that might be mentioned, as in *They've stocked wine,* *beer, soda, or whatever,* or *You can stay or leave, or whatever.*

**other** In addition to the idioms beginning with OTHER, also see AT EACH OTHER'S THROATS; DO UNTO OTHERS; EACH OTHER; EVERY OTHER; IN ONE EAR AND OUT THE OTHER; IN ONE'S POCKET (EACH OTHER'S POCKETS); IN OTHER WORDS; LAUGH OUT OF THE OTHER SIDE OF ONE'S MOUTH; LOOK THE OTHER WAY; MADE FOR EACH OTHER; NONE OTHER THAN; ON THE ONE (THE OTHER) HAND; OR OTHER; SHOE IS ON THE OTHER FOOT; SIX OF ONE, HALF A DOZEN OF THE OTHER; THIS AND THAT (THIS, THAT, AND THE OTHER); TURN THE OTHER CHEEK; WAIT FOR THE OTHER SHOE TO DROP.

**other day, the** One day recently, a short time ago, as in *I saw her in the museum the other day.*

**other fish to fry** Also, **better fish to fry** or **bigger fish to fry.** More important matters to attend to, as in *They asked me to help with the decorations, but I have other fish to fry.*

**other good fish in the sea** see NOT THE ONLY FISH IN THE SEA.

**other side of the coin** The opposite aspect, as in *I know you'd like to go, but the other side of the coin is that someone has to stay with the baby* or *The college is expensive, but the other side of the coin is that it's an excellent school.*

**other than 1.** Different from, besides, as in *They were shocked to find she has a lover other than her husband.* **2.** In a different manner than; anything different than, as in *How could she be other than happy with the new house?* **3. other than that.** Except that, as in *Other than that the nearest store was five miles away, it was a perfect location.*

**other things being equal** Also, **all else being equal** or **all things being equal.** Given the same circumstances, as in *Other things being equal, I prefer the green sofa,* or *All things being equal, we'll vacation at the same place again this year.*

**other way round, the** In the reverse direction, as in *I don't think the sofa will go through the door this way; let's try it the other way round.*

**ounce** In addition to the idiom beginning with OUNCE, also see MORE BANG FOR THE BUCK (BOUNCE TO THE OUNCE).

**ounce of prevention is worth a pound of cure, an** It is easier to prevent a disaster than to deal with it after it happens. For example, *The new law makes all children under twelve wear bicycle helmets—an ounce of prevention.* This ancient proverb is often used in shortened form, as in the example.

**out** In addition to the idioms beginning with OUT, also see ACT OUT; ALL OUT; ASK OUT; BACK OUT; BAIL OUT; BANG OUT; BAWL OUT; BEAR OUT; BEAT ONE'S BRAINS OUT; BEAT OUT; BELT OUT; BENT OUT OF SHAPE; BLACK OUT; BLOT OUT; BLOW ONE'S BRAINS OUT; BLOW OUT; BLURT OUT; BOTTOM OUT; BOW OUT; BRANCH OUT; BRAVE IT OUT; BREAK OUT; BRING OUT; BUG OUT; BUM OUT; BURN OUT; BURST INTO (OUT IN); BUY OUT; CALL OUT; CAMP OUT; CANCEL OUT; CARRY OUT; CAST OUT; CHECK OUT; CHEW OUT; CHICKEN OUT; CHILL OUT; CHURN OUT; CLEAN OUT; CLEAR OUT; CLOCK IN (OUT); CLOSE OUT; COME OUT; COME OUT AHEAD; COME OUT IN THE WASH; COME OUT OF; COME OUT WITH; CONK OUT; COOL OFF (OUT); COP OUT; COUNT OUT; CRANK OUT; CRAP OUT; CRY OUT FOR; CUT IT OUT; CUT OUT; DAY AFTER DAY (DAY IN, DAY OUT); DEAL OUT; DECK OUT; DIE OUT; DIG OUT; DISH OUT; DO OUT OF; DOPE OUT; DOWN AND OUT; DRAG ON (OUT); DRAW OUT; DROP OUT; DROWN OUT; DRUM OUT; DRY OUT; DUCK OUT; EASE OUT; EAT SOMEONE OUT OF HOUSE AND HOME; EAT ONE'S HEART OUT; EAT OUT; EAT OUT OF SOMEONE'S HAND; EDGE OUT; EKE OUT; FADE OUT; FALL OUT; FARM OUT; FAR OUT; FEEL OUT; FERRET OUT; FIGHT IT OUT; FIGURE OUT; FILL OUT; FIND OUT; FISH OUT; FISH OUT OF WATER; FIT OUT; FIZZLE OUT; FLAKE OUT; FLAT OUT; FLESH OUT; FLIP ONE'S LID (OUT); FLUNK OUT; FOR CRYING OUT LOUD; FORK OVER (OUT); FREAK OUT; FREEZE OUT; FRESH OUT OF; GET OUT; GET OUT OF; GET SOMETHING OUT OF; GET THE LEAD OUT; GIVE OUT; GO OUT; GO OUT OF ONE'S WAY; GROSS ONE OUT; GROW OUT OF; HAMMER OUT; HAND OUT; HANG OUT; HANG OUT ONE'S SHINGLE; HANG OUT TO DRY; HASH OVER (OUT); HAVE AN OUT; HAVE IT OUT; HAVE ONE'S WORK CUT OUT FOR ONE; HEAD OUT; HEAR OUT; HEART GOES OUT TO; HELP OUT; HIDE OUT; HIRE OUT; HIT OUT; HOLD OUT; IN ONE EAR AND OUT THE OTHER; IN (OUT OF) ONE'S ELEMENT; IN (OUT OF) PRINT; IN (OUT OF) REACH; INS AND OUTS; INSIDE OUT; INTO (OUT OF) THIN AIR; IN (OUT OF) TUNE; IRON OUT; JURY IS STILL OUT; KEEP AN EYE OUT; KICK OUT; KNOCK OUT; KNOCK THE BOTTOM OUT OF; LASH OUT; LAY OUT; LEAVE OUT; LET OUT; LET THE CAT OUT OF THE BAG; LIGHT OUT; LIKE A BAT OUT OF HELL; LIVE OUT OF; LOCK OUT; LOG IN (OUT); LOOK OUT; LOOK OUT FOR; LOSE OUT; LUCK OUT; MAKE A MOUNTAIN OUT OF A MOLEHILL; MAKE OUT; MAX OUT; MELLOW OUT; MISS OUT ON; MURDER WILL OUT; MUSTER IN (OUT); NOSE OUT; NOSE OUT OF JOINT; ODD MAN OUT; ON THE OUTS; ON THE WAY OUT; OPT OUT; PAN OUT; PARCEL OUT; PASS OUT; PAY OUT; PETER OUT; PHASE IN (OUT); PICK OUT; PIG OUT; PLAYED OUT; PLAY OUT; POINT OUT; POOP OUT; POUND OUT; POUR OUT ONE'S HEART; PRINT OUT; PROVE OUT; PSYCH OUT; PULL OUT; PULL OUT ALL THE STOPS; PULL OUT OF A HAT; PULL THE RUG OUT FROM UNDER; PUNCH OUT; PUT ONE OUT; PUT ONESELF OUT;

PUT OUT; PUT OUT FEELERS; PUT SOMEONE OUT TO PASTURE; PUT SOMEONE OUT OF HIS OR HER MISERY; PUZZLE OUT; RACK OUT; RAIN OUT; RIDE OUT; RIGHT OUT; RIGHT-SIDE OUT; ROLL OUT; ROOT OUT; ROUGH OUT; ROUND OFF (OUT); ROUND OUT; RUB OUT; RULE OUT; RUN OUT OF; RUN OUT ON; SACK OUT; SCARE OUT OF ONE'S WITS; SCREW SOMEONE OUT OF; SEE OUT; SELL OUT; SET OUT; SETTLE A (WIPE OUT AN OLD) SCORE; SHELL OUT; SHIP OUT; SHUT OUT; SIGN OUT; SING OUT; SINGLE OUT; SIT OUT; SKIP OUT; SLEEP OUT; SLIP OUT; SMOKE OUT; SNAP OUT OF; SNIFF OUT; SNUFF OUT; SOUND OUT; SPACE OUT; SPELL OUT; SPIN OUT; STAKE OUT; STAMP OUT; STAND OUT; START OUT; STEP OUT; STICK ONE'S NECK OUT; STICK OUT; STRAIGHTEN OUT; STRESS OUT; STRIKE OUT; STRING (STRUNG) OUT; SWEAR OUT; SWEAT OUT; TAKE A LEAF OUT OF SOMEONE'S BOOK; TAKE IT OUT ON; TAKE OUT; TAKE THE WIND OUT OF SOMEONE'S SAILS; TALKED OUT; TALK OUT; TALK OUT OF; TEASE OUT; TELL TALES (OUT OF SCHOOL); THINK OUT; THRASH OUT; THROW OUT; TIME OUT; TIRED OUT; TOP OUT; TOUGH IT OUT; TROT OUT; TRUTH WILL OUT; TRY OUT; TUCKERED OUT; TUNE OUT; TURN OUT; WAIT OUT; WALK OUT; WANT IN (OUT); WASHED OUT; WASH OUT; WEAR OUT; WEASEL OUT; WEAVE IN AND OUT; WEED OUT; WELL OUT OF; WHACKED OUT; WIG OUT; WIN OUT; WIPE OUT; WORK OUT; WORM OUT OF; WRITE OUT; YEAR IN, YEAR OUT; ZAP OUT.

**out and about** Well enough to come and go, especially after an illness. For example, *I'm glad to see you're out and about again.* Also see UP AND ABOUT.

**out and away** Also, **far and away.** Much more than all others, as in *He's out and away the best pitcher in the league.* Also see BY FAR.

**out at the elbows** Also, **out at the heels** or **out at the knees.** Wearing clothes that are worn out or torn; poor. For example, *When we last saw Phil, he was out at the elbows.* These expressions can also refer to clothes worn through at these points, as in *You can't wear those pants—they're out at the knees.*

**out back** see under OUT FRONT.

**out cold** Also, **out for the count** or **out like a light.** Unconscious; also, asleep. For example, *He crashed into the wall and was out cold,* or *Willie punched him too hard, and he was out for the count,* or *Don't call Jane; she's out like a light by ten every night.*

**outdoors** see BIG AS LIFE (ALL OUTDOORS).

**out for, be 1.** Be intent on, want, as in *The management is mostly out for bigger growth in sales.* **2. out for blood.** Intent on revenge, ready to fight with someone, as in *When Tom heard they'd cheated him, he was out for blood.* This term uses *blood* in the sense of "bloodshed" or "violent confrontation." Also see GO OUT FOR.

**out for the count** see OUT COLD.

**out from under** Free from difficulties, especially from a burden of debts or work. For example, *They've been using credit cards for everything and don't know how they'll get out from under,* or *We have loads of mail to answer, but we'll soon get out from under.*

**out front** In front of a building or house, as in *We really need to put another light out front,* or *I'll meet you at the museum, out front.* The antonym, referring to the back of a building, is **out back,** as in *John's out back fixing his bike.*

**out in left field** Also, **out of left field.** Strange, odd; also, mistaken. For example, *Don't listen to his ideas—he's out in left field,* or *His answer was out of left field; he was totally wrong.* This idiom refers to baseball's left field. Also see FAR OUT.

**out in the cold** Excluded from a group or activity, ignored or neglected, as in *Her stand on abortion left her out in the cold with the party.* This idiom refers to being left outdoors without shelter. Also see COME IN FROM THE COLD.

**out in the open** Also, **out into the open.** In or into public view or knowledge, as in *I wish he wouldn't talk behind our backs but bring his complaints out in the open,* or *It's important to bring the merger plans out into the open.* This term uses *open* to mean "an unconcealed state."

**out like a light** see OUT COLD.

**out loud** Aloud, so that others can hear, as in *I sometimes find myself reading the paper out loud,* or *That movie was hilarious; the whole audience was laughing out loud.* This idiom is used with verbs like *laugh* and *cry* more often than its synonym *aloud.* Also see FOR CRYING OUT LOUD.

O

**out of, be 1.** Have no more of, be lacking, as in *We're out of milk, so I'll run to the store.* Also see RUN OUT OF. **2.** See OUT OF IT.

**out of a clear blue sky** Also, **out of the clear blue sky** or **out of the blue.** Without warning, suddenly, as in *Her offer to help us buy the house came out of a clear blue sky,* or *We got a check from Aunt Ruby out of the blue.* These terms suggest something dropping unexpectedly from the sky. Also see OUT OF NOWHERE.

**out of all proportion** see OUT OF PROPORTION.

**out of bounds** Beyond accepted limits, breaking the rules, unreasonable. For example, *You can criticize the candidate's ideas and voting record, but criticizing his family—that's out of bounds.* This expression refers to the boundaries of the playing area in numerous sports. Also see WITHIN BOUNDS.

**out of breath** Breathing with difficulty, gasping for air. For example, *After five flights* *of stairs, I'm out of breath.* Also see CATCH ONE'S BREATH.

**out of business 1.** No longer continuing as a business, as in *He's decided to go out of business when he turns 65,* or *The supermarkets are putting the small grocers out of business.* **2.** Not in working order, as in *It looks as though the elevator is out of business tonight.* Also see OUT OF COMMISSION.

**out of character** see IN CHARACTER.

**out of circulation** see under IN CIRCULATION.

**out of commission** Not in working order, unable to function. For example, *The bridge is out of commission, so we'll have to take the tunnel.* This idiom originally referred to a ship that was waiting for repairs or held in reserve. Similarly, the antonym **in commission** referred to a ship armed and ready for action. The latter term is also used in more general contexts today, as in *My car's back in commission now, so we can drive to the theater.*

**out of condition** Also, **out of shape.** See under IN CONDITION.

**out of control** Also, **out of hand.** No longer under management, direction, or regulation; difficult or impossible to manage or control. For example, *Housing costs are out of control,* or *The children were getting out of hand again.* The first term uses *control* in the sense of "restraint," the variant uses *hand* in the sense of "power" or "authority."

**out of date 1.** Too old to be used, past the point of expiration, as in *This milk is out of date.* **2.** Old-fashioned, no longer in style, as in *Dean has three suits, but they're all out of date.*

**out of fashion** Also, **out of style.** See GO OUT, def. 5.

**out of favor** No longer liked or approved of, as in *Recent public opinion polls show the senator has fallen out of favor.*

**out of gas** see under RUN OUT OF.

**out of hand 1.** See OUT OF CONTROL. **2.** At once, immediately, as in *The second surgeon rejected the doctor's treatment plan out of hand.*

**out of harm's way** In a safe condition or place, as in *We fenced the yard to keep the children out of harm's way.*

**out of humor** see under OUT OF SORTS.

**out of it 1.** Not participating in or knowledgeable about a particular style, activity, or group. For example, *Dad looked really out of it in a bathing suit and long black socks,* or *Mary sometimes felt out of it because she didn't know anyone in the most popular crowd.* **2.** Confused about what is happening or where one is. For example, *Two or three beers and she was out of it,* or *He had no idea where he was or had been; he was totally out of it.*

**out of joint 1.** Dislocated, as in *Trying to break his fall, he put his shoulder out of joint.* **2.** See NOSE OUT OF JOINT. **3.** Out of order, unsatisfactory, as in *Our entire department's routine is out of joint.*

**out of keeping with** see under IN KEEPING WITH.

**out of key** see IN KEY.

**out of kilter** Also, **out of whack.** Not properly adjusted, not working well, out of order. For example, *This whole schedule is out of kilter with the rest of our projects,* or *The wheels on the trailer are out of whack.* Also see OFF KILTER.

**out of left field** see IN LEFT FIELD.

**out of line 1.** Improper, inappropriate. For example, *His remarks were totally out of line, and he should apologize.* It is often put as **get out of line** or **step out of line,** meaning "behave improperly," as in *She really stepped out of line when she called him incompetent in front of his boss.* **2.** Not in agreement with general practice, as in *Their prices are way out of line with other hotels.* Both def. 1 and 2 transfer being out of alignment (as in the wheels of a car) to various kinds of behavior. **3. out of one's line** or **not in one's line.** Not in one's occupation or field of interest. For example, *He offered her a generous salary, but she felt the work was out of her line,* or *I'd love to help, but handling animals is not in my line.* This idiom uses *line* in the sense of "a business or occupation."

**out of luck** Having bad fortune, as in *You're out of luck if you want a copy; we just sold the last one.* This expression assumes that good luck is something that one can run out of. However, it generally applies to more temporary circumstances than being DOWN ON ONE'S LUCK.

**out of necessity** see OF NECESSITY.

**out of nowhere** Suddenly, unexpectedly, as in *That anonymous letter arrived out of nowhere.* It is often put as **come out of nowhere,** as in *Their team came out of nowhere and won the state championship.* This term uses *out of* in the sense of "from," and *nowhere* in the sense of "an unknown place." For a synonym, see OUT OF A CLEAR BLUE SKY.

**out of one's** In addition to the idioms beginning with OUT OF ONE'S, also see under IN ONE'S.

**out of one's depth** Also, **beyond one's depth.** Outside one's understanding or competence, as in *He was out of his depth in that advanced math class,* or *The drama club members knew they couldn't present a play by Shakespeare—it was beyond their depth.*

This expression refers to being in water so deep that one might sink. Also see OVER ONE'S HEAD.

**out of one's element** see under IN ONE'S ELEMENT.

**out of one's hair** see under IN SOMEONE'S HAIR.

**out of one's head** see OFF ONE'S HEAD.

**out of one's mind** see GO OUT OF ONE'S MIND. Also see IN ONE'S RIGHT MIND.

**out of one's shell** see under IN ONE'S SHELL.

**out of one's system** Out of one's thoughts. It is often put as **get something out of one's system,** as in *You need to get your ex-husband out of your system,* or *At the annual all-chocolate buffet I try everything, which gets it out of my system for at least a month,* or *Let him complain as much as he wants so he'll get it out of his system.* This idiom uses *system* in the sense of "all one's physical and mental functions."

**out of one's way** see GO OUT OF ONE'S WAY; OUT OF THE WAY.

**out of order 1.** Not functioning well, not operating properly or at all, as in *The elevator is out of order again.* **2.** Improper, inappropriate, as in *Her comments about the management were out of order.* Also see OUT OF LINE, def. 1. **3.** Not following the rules of parliamentary procedure, as in *The chair called him out of order, but he still kept talking.*

**out of phase** Also, **out of sync.** In an unsynchronized way, not in accord with the timing of something else. For example, *A long plane trip usually means my internal clock gets out of phase and I suffer jet lag,* or *The traffic lights are out of sync and keep flashing at random.* For the antonym, see IN PHASE.

**out of place** Not in the proper situation, not belonging; inappropriate for the circumstances or location. For example, *She felt out of place among all the women in long dresses and wished she hadn't worn jeans,* or *This big sofa is out of place in such a small room.* This idiom uses *place* in the sense of "a fitting position."

**out of pocket** Referring to actual money spent, as in *I had to pay the hotel bill out of pocket, but I know I'll be reimbursed by the company.* This expression sometimes occurs as a hyphenated adjective, mainly in the phrase **out-of-pocket expenses,** as in *My out-of-pocket expenses for business travel amounted to more than a thousand dollars.*

**out of practice** No longer used to doing something, no longer good at something for lack of doing it, as in *Mom hadn't baked a cake in years—she said she was out of practice.* Also see IN PRACTICE.

**out of print** see under IN PRINT.

**out of proportion** Also, **out of all proportion.** Not in proper relation to other things, especially by being the wrong size or amount. For example, *This big vase looks out of proportion on this small table,* or *Her emotional response was out of all proportion—it was really a very minor problem.* The noun *proportion* means "an agreeable or harmonious relationship of one thing to another." The antonym **in proportion** also refers either to physical size or appropriate degree, as in *The bird's wings are huge in proportion to its body,* or *Her willingness to give money to the organization stands in direct proportion to her faith in its leadership.*

**out of reach** see under IN REACH.

**out of season** see under IN SEASON.

**out of shape** see under IN CONDITION. Also see BENT OUT OF SHAPE.

**out of sight 1.** Also, **out of someone's sight.** Out of someone's range of vision, as in *Stay out of sight while they're visiting, or you'll get stuck listening to them for hours,* or *Don't let the baby out of your sight in the yard.* This idiom is also used in the phrase **get out of someone's sight,** meaning "go away"; for example, *Jean was furious with Bill and told him to get out of her sight at once.* **2.** Unreasonable, excessive, as in *Our bill for the wine was out of sight.* **3.** Excellent, superb, as in *The graduation party was out of sight.* This phrase is also used as an interjection meaning "Wonderful!" as in *Do I like it? Out of sight!* **4. out of sight, out of mind.** People soon forget a person or thing that is no longer present or cannot be seen, as in *I don't think of them unless they send a Christmas card—out of sight, out of mind, I guess.*

**out of sorts** Irritable, grouchy, in a bad mood, as in *Don't ask him today—he's out of sorts.* This expression also implies that one's poor spirits result from feeling slightly ill. The synonym **out of humor** simply means "ill-tempered" or "irritable."

**out of step** see under IN STEP.

**out of stock** see under IN STOCK.

**out of style** see GO OUT, def. 5.

**out of sync** see OUT OF PHASE.

**out of the blue** Also, **out of the clear blue sky.** See OUT OF A CLEAR BLUE SKY.

**out of the corner of one's eye** Glancing casually or secretively, as in *Out of the corner of my eye, I saw Justin walking out the door.* This expression refers to looking sideways at something rather than directly.

**out of the frying pan into the fire** Also, **out of the frying pan and into the fire.** From a bad situation to one that is much worse. For example, *After Karen quit the first law firm, she went to one with even longer hours—out of the frying pan into the fire.*

**out of the hole** see under IN THE HOLE.

**out of the loop** see under IN THE LOOP.

**out of the mouths of babes** Young and inexperienced people often can be remarkably wise, as in *She's only six, but she said, quite rightly, that Harry was afraid of being alone—out of the mouths of babes.*

**out of the ordinary** Unusual, uncommon, exceptional, as in *The food they served was certainly out of the ordinary.* This expression sometimes, but not always, indicates that something is better than the usual. However, the negative version, **nothing out of the ordinary,** usually indicates that something is *not* special or any better than average, as in *It was an interesting lecture, but nothing out of the ordinary.*

**out of the picture** see under IN THE PICTURE.

**out of the question** Impossible, not worth considering, as in *Spending that much money is certainly out of the question.*

**out of the rain** see COME IN OUT OF THE RAIN.

**out of the running** see under IN THE RUNNING.

**out of the way 1.** Not blocking or interfering, as in *This chair is out of the way now, so you won't trip.* This phrase also appears in **get out of the way** or **get out of one's way,** as in *Would you please get your coat out of the way?* or *Get your car out of my way.* **2.** Taken care of, as in *I'm glad we got these details out of the way.* **3.** In a remote location, as in *This restaurant is a little out of the way.* **4.** Unusual, remarkable, as in *It was out of the way for him to praise his staff.* **5.** Wrong, in error, improper, as in *The security guard checked all the locks and saw nothing out of the way.* Also see GO OUT OF ONE'S WAY.

**out of the window** Discarded, tossed out. This term is often used in the phrase **go out the window,** as in *When the boss changed his mind about the project, all the work I'd done went out the window.* It refers to unwanted items being thrown out of the window.

**out of the woods** Out of difficulties, danger, or trouble, as in *We're through the worst of the recession—we're out of the woods now,* or *That illness was serious, but Charles is finally out of the woods.* This expression refers to having been lost in a forest.

**out of the woodwork** Coming or appearing from a hidden or little-known place or a place of seclusion. It often is put as **come out of the woodwork** or **crawl out of the woodwork,** as in *The candidates for this job were coming out of the woodwork.* The expression refers to insects crawling out of the interior wood of a house, such as baseboards and moldings.

**out of thin air** see under INTO THIN AIR.

**out of this world** Extraordinary, superb, as in *Her carrot cake is out of this world.* This term refers to something too good for this world.

**out of touch** No longer in contact or communication, as in *John and Mark have been out of touch for years,* or *That speech showed he's out of touch with the voters.* This expression refers to physical contact. Also see IN TOUCH.

**out of town** Away from the town or city under consideration; away from home. For example, *In his new job Tom will be going out of town nearly every week,* or *He's out of town, but I'll have him call you when he gets back.*

**out of turn 1.** Not in the proper order or sequence, as in *The meeting will be very formal, and you must not speak out of turn.* **2.** In an inappropriate manner or at an inappropriate time, as in *I may be out of turn telling you, but shorts are not permitted in the restaurant.*

**out of wedlock** Of parents not legally married, as in *Over the centuries many royal children were born out of wedlock.* The noun *wedlock,* for the state of being married, is rarely heard today except in this phrase.

**out of whack** see OUT OF KILTER.

**out of whole cloth** From pure invention or fiction; not based on fact. This expression is often put as **cut out of whole cloth** or **made out of whole cloth,** as in *That story was cut out of whole cloth.*

**out of work** Unemployed; also, having no work to do. For example, *He lost his job a year ago and has been out of work ever since.*

**out on a limb** In a difficult, awkward, or vulnerable position, as in *I filed a complaint about low salaries, but the people who had supported me left me out on a limb.* This expression refers to an animal climbing out on the limb of a tree and then being afraid or unable to retreat.

**out on bail** Released from jail on the basis of bail being paid, as in *The lawyer promised to get him out on bail.* This expression refers to a payment made to the court to ensure that the accused person will appear for trial.

**out on one's ear** Dismissed, thrown out in disgrace, as in *In this company you get only one chance, and if you fail, you're out on your ear.* This term refers to being physically thrown out head first.

**out on the town** see ON THE TOWN.

**outs** see INS AND OUTS; ON THE OUTS.

**outset** see AT THE OUTSET.

**outside** In addition to the idiom beginning with OUTSIDE, also see AT MOST (THE OUTSIDE).

**outside of** Except for, aside from, as in *Outside of a little lipstick, she wore no makeup.*

**out to lunch** Not in touch with the real world, crazy; also, inattentive. For example, *If he* *believes that story, he's really out to lunch,* or *Anne hasn't heard a word you said—she's out to lunch.* This expression transfers a temporary physical absence for the purpose of eating to a temporary or permanent mental absence.

**out with it** Say it, as in *Tell us what you really think—out with it!* This idiom is used as a command, as in the example.

**over** In addition to the idioms beginning with OVER, also see ALL OVER (and entries beginning with ALL OVER); BEND OVER BACKWARD; BLOW OVER; BOIL OVER; BOWL OVER; CARRY OVER; CHECK ON (OVER); CHEW THE CUD (OVER); CLOUD OVER; COME OVER; CROSS OVER; CROW OVER; CRY OVER SPILT MILK; DO OVER; DRAW A VEIL OVER; DROP BY (OVER); FALL ALL OVER ONESELF; FORK OVER; GET OVER; GET THE ADVANTAGE OF (OVER); GIVE OVER; GLOSS OVER; GO OVER; HAND OVER; HAND OVER FIST; HANG OVER; HASH OVER; HAVE A HOLD OVER; HAVE IT (ALL OVER SOMEONE); HEAD OVER HEELS; HOLD OVER; HONEYMOON IS OVER; IN DEEP WATER (OVER ONE'S HEAD); IT'S ALL OVER WITH; JUMP ALL OVER; KEEL OVER; KEEP WATCH (OVER); KNOCK FOR A LOOP (OVER WITH A FEATHER); KNOCK OVER; LAY OVER; LOOK LIKE DEATH (WARMED OVER); LOOK OVER; LORD IT OVER; LOSE SLEEP OVER; MAKE OVER; MIND OVER MATTER; MULL OVER; ONCE OVER LIGHTLY; PAPER OVER; PARTY'S OVER; PASS AWAY (OVER); PASS BY (OVER); PICK OVER; PULL OVER; PULL THE WOOL OVER SOMEONE'S EYES; PUT OVER; RAKE OVER THE COALS; RIDE ROUGHSHOD OVER; ROLL OVER; ROOF OVER ONE'S HEAD; RUN ONE'S EYES OVER; RUN OVER; SCOOT OVER; SIGN OVER; SLEEP OVER; SMOOTH OVER; STAND OVER; START OVER; STOP OFF (OVER); TAKE OVER; TALK OVER; THINK OVER; THROW OVER; TIDE OVER; TILL HELL FREEZES OVER; TURN (OVER) IN ONE'S GRAVE; TURN OVER; TURN OVER A NEW LEAF; WALK ALL OVER; WATCH OVER; WATER OVER THE DAM; WIN OVER; WORK OVER.

**over a barrel** In a weak or difficult position, as in *Once the competitors found a flaw in our product, they had us over a barrel.*

**over again** Once more, as in *The conductor had them start the symphony over again.*

**over and above** In addition to, besides, as in *Over and above travel expenses, he was given a daily allowance.*

**over and done with** Completed, finished, as in *That argument's over and done with, so stop talking about it.* This usage is more emphatic that OVER WITH.

**over and over** Also, **over and over again.** Repeatedly, many times, as in *I've told you over and over that he can't eat spicy food.* Also see AGAIN AND AGAIN.

**overboard** see GO OVERBOARD.

**over my dead body** In no way, under no circumstances, as in *Over my dead body will you drop out of high school.* This expression is often used jokingly.

**over one's head** **1.** To a position higher than another's, as in *She was furious when her assistant was promoted over her head.* Similarly, **go over someone's head** means "appeal to a higher authority," as in *Since she couldn't help me, I decided to go over her head and talk to her supervisor.* **2.** Beyond one's understanding or competence, as in *The math required for that course is way over my head.* For a synonym, see OUT OF ONE'S DEPTH. Also see IN DEEP (OVER ONE'S HEAD).

**over the edge** Insane, as in *I think he's gone over the edge.* This expression refers to the edge of sanity or mental health.

**over the hill** Past the prime of one's life, getting old, as in *I'm a little over the hill to be playing contact sports.* This term refers to a climber who has reached a mountaintop and is now descending.

**over the hump** Past the most difficult part, as in *She's over the hump with her dissertation; she'll soon be done.* This expression refers to a barrier that blocks progress.

**over the top** **1.** Going beyond a goal or quota, as in *The new salesmen are excellent; they were over the top within the first six months.* **2.** Up and over the edge of a military trench, as in *The lieutenant sent fresh troops over the top.* This usage dates from World War I. **3.** Extreme, outrageous, as in *This comedian's style goes over the top.*

**over with** Done, finished, as in *I'll be glad when exams are over with.* Also see OVER AND DONE WITH.

**owl** see NIGHT OWL.

**own** In addition to the idioms beginning with OWN, also see AFRAID OF ONE'S OWN SHADOW; AFTER ONE'S OWN HEART; BEAT SOMEONE AT HIS OR HER OWN GAME; BLOW ONE'S OWN HORN; CALL ONE'S OWN; COME INTO (ONE'S OWN); DIG ONE'S OWN GRAVE; DO ONE'S (OWN) THING; DOSE OF ONE'S OWN MEDICINE; GET BACK (ONE'S OWN BACK); GET ONE'S (OWN) WAY; GO ONE'S (OWN) WAY; HOLD ONE'S OWN; IN ONE'S (OWN) INTEREST; IN ONE'S OWN BACKYARD; IN ONE'S OWN RIGHT; IN ONE'S OWN WORLD; KEEP ONE'S OWN COUNSEL; KNOW ONE'S OWN MIND; LEAVE TO ONE'S OWN DEVICES; MIND OF ONE'S OWN; MIND ONE'S OWN BUSINESS; OF ONE'S OWN ACCORD; ON ONE'S OWN; ON ONE'S OWN ACCOUNT; ON ONE'S OWN TIME; PADDLE ONE'S OWN CANOE; PAY BACK (IN SOMEONE'S OWN COIN); PAY ONE'S (OWN) WAY; PICK ON (SOMEONE YOUR OWN SIZE); PULL ONE'S (OWN) WEIGHT; SIGN ONE'S OWN

O

DEATH WARRANT; STEW IN ONE'S OWN JUICE; TAKE THE LAW INTO ONE'S (OWN) HANDS; UNDER ONE'S OWN STEAM; WRITE ONE'S OWN TICKET.

**own person, be one's** Also, **be one's own man** or **be one's own woman.** Be independent, be responsible for oneself. For example, *We can't tell Jerry what to do—he's his own person.*

**own medicine** see DOSE OF ONE'S OWN MEDICINE.

**own up** Also, **own up to what one did.** Confess, make a full admission, as in *Come on, Tim, you'd better own up that you lost the car keys,* or *You need to own up to what you did to him.* This idiom uses the verb *own* in the sense of "acknowledge."

**oyster** see WORLD IS ONE'S OYSTER.

O

# Pp

**p** see MIND ONE'S P'S AND Q'S.

**pace** see CHANGE OF PACE; KEEP PACE; PUT SOMEONE THROUGH HIS OR HER PACES; SET THE PACE; SNAIL'S PACE.

**pack** In addition to the idioms beginning with PACK, also see JOE SIX-PACK; SEND SOMEONE ABOUT HIS OR HER BUSINESS (PACKING).

**pack a punch** Also, **pack a wallop. 1.** Be capable of a forceful blow; also, deliver a forceful blow. For example, *Knowing Bob could pack a wicked punch, they were careful not to anger him,* or *She swung her handbag, really packing a wallop.* **2.** Have a powerful effect, as in *That double espresso packed a wallop.*

**packed in like sardines** Extremely crowded, as in *I could barely breathe—we were packed in like sardines.* This term refers to how tightly sardines are packed in cans.

**pack it in** Stop working or abandon an activity, as in *Let's pack it in for the day.* This usage refers to packing one's things before departing. It also is used as a command ordering someone to stop, as in *Pack it in! I've heard enough out of you.* The expression is also put as **pack it up.**

**pack off** Also, **pack someone** or **something off.** Send someone or something away without ceremony or special attention, as in *As soon as the children are packed off to bed, I'll call you back,* or *She told Anne she'd pack her things off as soon as she had a chance.*

**pack them in** Attract a large audience, as in *A big star will always pack them in.* This idiom refers to tightly filling a hall.

**paddle** In addition to the idiom beginning with PADDLE, also see UP A CREEK (WITHOUT A PADDLE).

**paddle one's own canoe** Be independent and self-reliant, as in *It's time Bill learned to paddle his own canoe.* This idiom refers to moving one's own boat.

**paid** see under PAY.

**pain** In addition to the idiom beginning with PAIN, also see AT PAINS; FEEL NO PAIN; FOR ONE'S PAINS; GROWING PAINS; NO PAIN, NO GAIN; ON PAIN OF.

**pain in the neck** Also, **pain in the ass** or **pain in the butt.** A source of annoyance, a nuisance, as in *Joan is a real pain in the neck, with her constant complaining,* or *Jack told his brother to stop being a pain in the ass.* The two variants are mildly offensive.

**paint black** Represent someone or something as evil or harmful, as in *He's not so black as he's been painted.*

**paint oneself into a corner** Get oneself into a difficulty from which one can't get out. For example, *By volunteering to do more work in the office and then taking another job, George has painted himself into a corner.* This idiom uses the graphic image of painting all of the floor except for the corner one stands in, so that one cannot leave without stepping on wet paint.

**paint the town red** Celebrate something by going to bars, clubs, or similar establishments, as in *Whenever they go to New York, they want to paint the town red.*

**pair** In addition to the idiom beginning with PAIR, also see SHOW ONE'S (A CLEAN PAIR OF) HEELS.

**pair off 1.** Put two persons together; also, become one of a couple, as in *Jean mentally paired off her guests whenever she planned a party,* or *All the tennis players had to pair off for a round of doubles matches.* **2.** Also, **pair up.** Make a pair of, match, as in *I always have trouble pairing up the boys' socks.*

**pal around** Associate as friends, as in *Bill and Jim have been palling around for years.* This expression makes a verb of the noun *pal.*

**pale** see BEYOND THE PALE.

**palm** In addition to the idiom beginning with PALM, also see GREASE SOMEONE'S PALM; ITCHY PALM.

**palm off** Pass something off dishonestly, substitute something with intent to deceive, as in *The salesman tried to palm off a zircon as a diamond,* or *The producer tried to palm her off as a star from the Metropolitan Opera.* This expression refers to hiding something in the palm of one's hand.

**pan** In addition to the idiom beginning with PAN, also see FLASH IN THE PAN; OUT OF THE FRYING PAN.

**pancake** see FLAT AS A PANCAKE.

**Pandora's box** A source of unexpected trouble, as in *Revising the tax code is opening a Pandora's box.* This equivalent for the modern CAN OF WORMS comes from a Greek legend in which Pandora is entrusted with a box containing the world's ills and told not to open it. She is overcome by curiosity and opens the box, thereby releasing them.

**panic** see PUSH THE PANIC BUTTON.

**pan out** Turn out well, succeed, as in *If I don't pan out as a musician, I can always go back to school.* This expression refers to finding gold by washing it from dirt or gravel in a pan.

**pants** In addition to the idiom beginning with PANTS, also see ANTS IN ONE'S PANTS; BEAT THE PANTS OFF; CAUGHT WITH ONE'S PANTS DOWN; GET THE LEAD OUT (OF ONE'S PANTS); KICK IN THE PANTS; SEAT OF THE PANTS; TALK SOMEONE'S ARM (PANTS) OFF; WEAR THE PANTS.

**pants off, the** This phrase is used to intensify the meaning of verbs such as **bore** or **charm** or **kid** or **scare** or **talk.** For example, *That speech bored the pants off us,* or *It was a real tornado and scared the pants off me.* Also see BEAT THE PANTS OFF; BORE TO DEATH.

**paper** In addition to the idiom beginning with PAPER, also see ON PAPER; PUSH PAPER; WALKING PAPERS.

**paper over** Also, **paper over the cracks.** Hide something, especially flaws, as if by making minor repairs. For example, *He used some accounting trick to paper over a deficit,* or *It was hardly a perfect settlement, but they decided to paper over the cracks.* The reference here is to covering cracked plaster with wallpaper, thereby improving its appearance but not the problem underneath.

**par** In addition to the idiom beginning with PAR, also see BELOW PAR; ON A PAR WITH; UP TO PAR.

**parade** See RAIN ON ONE'S PARADE.

**paradise** see FOOL'S PARADISE.

**parcel** In addition to the idiom beginning with PARCEL, also see PART AND PARCEL.

**parcel out** Divide into parts and distribute, as in *She parceled out the remaining candy among the children.* This idiom uses *parcel* in the sense of "divide into small portions."

**pardon** see BEG TO DIFFER; EXCUSE ME.

**par for the course** An average or normal amount; just what one might expect. For example, *I missed three questions, but that's par for the course.* This term comes from golf, where it refers to the number of strokes needed by an expert golfer to finish the entire course.

**part** In addition to the idioms beginning with PART, also see BEST PART OF; BETTER HALF (PART); DISCRETION IS THE BETTER PART OF VALOR; DO ONE'S PART; FOOL AND HIS MONEY ARE SOON PARTED; FOR ONE'S PART; FOR THE MOST PART; IN GOOD PART; IN PART; TAKE PART; TAKE SOMEONE'S PART.

**part and parcel** An essential or basic element, as in *Traveling is part and parcel of her job.* Although both nouns have the same basic meaning, the redundancy lends emphasis.

**part company** Go separate ways; also, disagree about something. For example, *After they reached the shopping mall, Jeff and Jane parted company,* or *They parted company on their views of foreign policy.*

**particular** see IN PARTICULAR.

**parting of the ways** A point of separation, especially an important one, as in *When Jim decided to travel with the band and Jill wanted a more normal home life, they came to a parting of the ways.* This term transfers a fork in a road to separate courses of action.

**parting shot** A final insult or last word in an argument, as in *As she stalked out, Jane hurled as a parting shot, "And I quit!"* This idiom refers to ancient warriors who turned back to shoot at their pursuers.

**part with** Give up, let go of, as in *Janice hated to part with her cat, but the landlord wouldn't allow pets.*

**party** In addition to the idioms beginning with PARTY, also see LIFE OF THE PARTY.

**party line** The official policy of an organization or a government, as in *The current party line opposes legalized abortion in all cases.*

**party's over, the** It's time to be serious; carefree times have ended. For example, *Now that he's been promoted, the party's over; he has to write a report every week.* This expression uses *party* in the sense of "a pleasant social gathering."

**pass** In addition to the idioms beginning with PASS, also see BRING ABOUT (TO PASS); COME ABOUT (TO PASS); CROSS (PASS THROUGH) ONE'S MIND; HEAD OFF (AT THE PASS); IN PASSING; MAKE (TAKE) A PASS AT; SHIPS THAT PASS IN THE NIGHT.

**pass away** Also, **pass on** or **pass over.** Die, as in *He passed away last week,* or *After Grandma passes on, we'll sell the land,* or *I hear he's about to pass over.* All these terms are euphemisms for dying.

**pass by** **1.** Proceed past something, as in *If you pass by a white house, you've gone too far.* **2.** Also, **pass over.** Disregard, pay no attention to, as in *Just pass by the first few pages, and you'll get to the basics,* or *Ralph was passed over for promotion.*

**pass for** Be accepted as or believed to be something, usually something that is not so. For example, *Jean is 23 but could pass for a teenager,* or *They thought that copy would pass for an original.*

**pass muster** Meet a required standard, as in *That yard cleanup won't pass muster with Mom.* This expression originally meant "undergo a military review and prove acceptable," *muster* referring to an assembling of troops for inspection or a similar purpose.

**pass off** Also, **pass off as.** Misrepresent something or someone, as in *They tried to pass off that piece of glass as a gemstone,* or *Bill passed her off as his sister.* Also see PALM OFF.

**pass on** **1.** See PASS AWAY. **2.** Transfer something, as in *Sign the card and then pass it on to the others,* or *Grandpa passed his tools on to his favorite grandson.* Also see PASS THE TORCH.

**pass one's lips** Be spoken, as in *Not a word of it will pass my lips, I promise.*

**pass out** **1.** Distribute something, as in *He passed out the papers.* **2.** Also, **pass out cold.** Faint, as in *When she heard the news, she passed out cold.* Also see OUT COLD.

**pass over** **1.** See PASS BY, def. 2. **2.** See PASS AWAY.

**pass the buck** Shift responsibility or blame to someone else, as in *She's always passing the buck to her staff; it's time she accepted the blame herself.*

**pass the hat** Ask people to donate money, as in *Let's pass the hat so we can get her a nice going-away gift.* This expression refers to the actual practice of passing a hat around a gathering.

**pass the time** **1.** Keep oneself busy for a period, as in *The plane was six hours late, but I passed the time reading a book.* **2. pass the time of day.** Exchange greetings, have conversation, as in *Whenever I met her, we would stop to pass the time of day.*

**pass the torch** Also, **hand on the torch.** Give one's responsibilities, tradition, practice, or knowledge to another person, often someone younger. For example, *When the company's founder became too ill to continue, he passed the torch to his nephew.* This expression refers to an ancient Greek race in which a lighted torch was passed from one runner to the next.

**pass through one's mind** see CROSS ONE'S MIND.

**pass up** Let something go by, reject, as in *I can't believe Betty passed up the chocolate cake,* or *This opportunity is too good to pass up.*

**pass with flying colors** see WITH FLYING COLORS.

**past** In addition to the idioms beginning with PAST, also see LIVE IN (THE PAST); NOT PUT SOMETHING PAST SOMEONE.

**past master** A person who is thoroughly experienced or exceptionally skilled in some activity or craft. For example, *We're lucky to get Ella, because she's a past master at fund-raising.*

**past one's prime** Beyond the highest point of one's powers or abilities, as in *Jean still plays tennis, but at 79 she's obviously past her prime.* Also see OVER THE HILL; PRIME OF LIFE.

**pasture** see PUT SOMEONE OUT TO PASTURE.

**pat** In addition to the idiom beginning with PAT, also see STAND PAT.

**patch up** Mend or repair something, make something whole again. For example, *He managed to patch up the lawn mower so it's running,* or *John cut his hand badly, but they patched him up in the emergency room,* or *Mike and Molly have patched up their differences.* This term refers to mending something by putting patches of material on it.

**path** see BEAT A PATH TO SOMEONE'S DOOR; CROSS SOMEONE'S PATH; LEAD DOWN THE GARDEN PATH; (PATH OF) LEAST RESISTANCE; ON THE WARPATH.

**patience** see TRY ONE'S PATIENCE.

**pat on the back** A word or gesture of support, approval, or praise, as in *The bonus she gave her assistant was a pat on the back for doing a good job.*

**Paul** see ROB PETER TO PAY PAUL.

**pause** see GIVE PAUSE.

**pavement** see POUND THE PAVEMENT.

**pave the way** Make progress or development easier, as in *Her findings paved the way for developing a new medicine.* This expression refers to paving a road so it is easier to travel on.

**pawn off** Dispose of something by deception, as in *They tried to pawn off a rebuilt computer as new.*

**pay** In addition to the idioms beginning with PAY, also see (PAY THE PIPER) CALL THE TUNE; CRIME DOES NOT PAY; DEVIL TO PAY; HELL TO PAY; (PAY) LIP SERVICE; ROB PETER TO PAY PAUL; YOU GET WHAT YOU PAY FOR.

**pay a call** Also, **pay a visit** or **pay one's respects.** Make a short visit, especially as a formal courtesy or for business reasons. For example, *Bill decided to pay a call on his mother-in-law,* or *Each salesman was told to pay a visit to every new doctor in town,* or *We went to the wake to pay our respects.* The second variant is used specifically to refer to a courtesy visit made when someone dies, as in the last example. Also see CALL ON, def. 2.

**pay *someone* a compliment** Express praise or admiration to someone, as in *Meredith wanted to pay Christopher a compliment, so she told him she liked his new haircut.* This expression uses *pay* in the sense of "give something that is due."

**pay as you go** Pay for purchases immediately instead of later. For example, *Ruth and Bob had no credit cards; they believed in paying as you go.*

**pay attention** Carefully listen to, watch, or think about, as in *Now pay attention to these instructions.*

**pay a visit** see PAY A CALL.

**pay back** **1.** Repay a debt or a loan to someone, as in *I'll pay you back next month.* **2.** Also, **pay *someone* back in his** or **her own coin.** Get revenge on someone, make someone suffer for causing trouble or pain, as in *He thought he could get away with copying my plans, but I'll pay him back in his own coin.* This expression refers to repaying a debt in exactly the same currency in which the money was lent.

**pay court to** Try to gain the favor or affection of someone, as in *If you want to win the daughter, you'll have to pay court to her mother.*

**pay dirt, hit** Also, **strike pay dirt.** Make a valuable discovery or large profit, as in *We've been researching the source of that quotation for a month, and we finally hit pay dirt in the Library of Congress.* This idiom refers to a miner's finding gold or other precious metals while sifting soil.

**pay for** **1.** Cover the expenses of, pay the cost of, as in *I'll pay for your movie ticket,* or *This truck will pay for itself within a year.* **2.** Suffer for, as in *He may have looked like a good manager, but his successor will end up paying for his mistakes.*

**pay lip service to** see LIP SERVICE.

**pay off** **1.** Pay the full amount owed for something or owed to someone as wages, as in *The car's finally paid off,* or *Les pays off the workers every Friday evening.* **2.** Produce a profit, as in *That gamble did not pay off.* **3.** Also, **pay off an old score.** Get revenge on someone for some past wrong, as in *Jerry was satisfied; he'd paid off his ex-partner when he bought back the company at half-price,* or *Amy went out with her roommate's boyfriend, but she was paying off an old score.* **4.** Bribe someone, as in *The drug dealer paid off the local police so he could operate freely.*

P

**pay one's dues** Earn something through hard work, long experience, or suffering. For example, *She'd paid her dues in small-town shows before she finally got a Broadway part.* This expression transfers the cost of being a paid-up member in an organization to that of gaining experience over time.

**pay one's respects** see PAY A CALL.

**pay one's way** **1.** Also, **pay one's own way.** Pay in full for one's expenses, as in *She paid her way through college by working in the library.* **2. pay someone's way.** Pay someone's expenses, as in *Dad offered to pay my way if I went to Spain with him.*

**pay out** **1.** Distribute money, as in *He paid out the full amount.* **2.** Let out a rope by loosening it, as in *She paid out the rope until it was long enough to tie the canoe onto the car.*

**pay the piper** see under CALL THE TUNE.

**pay through the nose** Pay a very large amount for something, as in *We paid through the nose for that vacation.*

**pay up** Pay in full, pay all that is owing, as in, *It's late—let's pay up and go home.* Also see PAY OFF, def. 1.

**pay your money and take your choice** Also, **you pays your money and takes your choice.** Since you're paying, it's your decision, as in *We can take the train or the bus—you pays your money and takes your choice.*

**PC** Also, **p.c.** See POLITICALLY CORRECT.

**pea** see LIKE AS TWO PEAS IN A POD.

**peace** In addition to the idiom beginning with PEACE, also see AT PEACE; HOLD ONE'S TONGUE (PEACE); KEEP THE PEACE; LEAVE SOMEONE IN PEACE; MAKE ONE'S PEACE WITH; MAKE PEACE.

**peace and quiet** Calm and freedom from disturbance. This phrase is used in wishes for this condition, as in *All I want is a little peace and quiet.*

**peacock** see PROUD AS A PEACOCK.

**pearl** In addition to the idiom beginning with PEARL, also see CAST PEARLS BEFORE SWINE.

**pearls of wisdom** Good advice, wise words. This phrase is often used jokingly, as in *I'm sure Dad will have some pearls of wisdom for me before I go.*

**pebble** see NOT THE ONLY FISH IN THE SEA (PEBBLE ON THE BEACH).

**pecking order** The order of authority or importance in a group of people, as in *On a space mission the astronauts have a definite pecking order.* This expression was invented by biologists who discovered that chickens maintain such a hierarchy, with one bird pecking another of lower status.

**pedal** see SOFT PEDAL.

**pedestal** see ON A PEDESTAL.

**peel** In addition to the idiom beginning with PEEL, also see KEEP ONE'S EYES OPEN (PEELED).

**peel off** **1.** Remove an outer layer of skin, bark, paint, or something similar; also, come off in thin strips or pieces. For example, *Peeling off birch bark can kill the tree,* or *Paint was peeling off the walls.* **2.** Remove or separate something, as in *Helen peeled off her gloves and got to work,* or *Al peeled off a ten-dollar bill and gave it to the driver.* **3.** Also, **peel away.** Depart from a group, as in *Ruth peeled away when we got to the mall and went looking for a phone.* This expression originated in the Air Force during World War II. It was used for an airplane that left flight formation, a sight that suggested the peeling of skin from a banana.

**peep** see HEAR A PEEP OUT OF.

**peeping Tom** A person who secretly watches others, especially for sexual pleasure. For example, *The police caught a peeping Tom right outside her house.* This expression refers to the legend of the tailor Tom. He was the only person to watch the naked Lady Godiva as she rode by, and, as a punishment, he was struck blind.

**peg** see SQUARE PEG IN A ROUND HOLE; TAKE DOWN A NOTCH (PEG).

**pen** see SLIP OF THE TONGUE (PEN).

**penchant** see HAVE A PENCHANT FOR.

**pencil** see PUT LEAD IN ONE'S PENCIL.

**pennies from heaven** Unexpected good fortune, as in *They sent back our check—pennies from heaven.*

**penny** In addition to the idioms beginning with PENNY, also see PINCH PENNIES; PRETTY PENNY; TURN UP (LIKE A BAD PENNY).

**penny for your thoughts, a** What are you thinking about? For example, *You've been awfully quiet—a penny for your thoughts.*

**penny saved is a penny earned, a** What a person does not spend, he or she will have. This saying advises care in spending. It is so familiar that it often appears in shortened form, as in *Although they can afford to buy a house right now, they're putting it off, on the principle of "a penny saved."*

**penny wise and pound foolish** Stingy about spending small amounts and extravagant with large ones, as in *Dean clips all the coupons for supermarket bargains but insists on going to the best restaurants—penny wise and pound foolish.* This phrase refers to British currency. The phrase is also occasionally used for being very careful about unimportant matters and careless about important ones.

**people who live in glass houses shouldn't throw stones** Anyone who is open to criticism should not criticize others, as in *She has no right to talk about my spending habits when she's in debt herself—people who live in glass houses!* This proverb is so well known that it is often shortened, as in the example. Also see POT CALLING THE KETTLE BLACK.

**pep someone up** Give someone more energy or cheer someone up, as in *This drink will pep you up,* or *The good news about his recovery pepped us up.* Both the verb *pep* and the noun *pep,* referring to vigor and energy, are abbreviations for *pepper,* a spice with a pungent, biting quality. They also have led to **pep rally,** a meeting to inspire enthusiasm, and **pep talk,** a speech intended to strengthen someone's confidence or spirits.

**perish** In addition to the idiom beginning with PERISH, also see PUBLISH OR PERISH.

**perish the thought** Don't even think of it. This expression is used as a wish that what was just mentioned will never happen. For example, *He's going to give another speech? Perish the thought!* Also see GOD FORBID.

**perk up** Restore to good spirits, liveliness, or good appearance, as in *You're exhausted, but a cup of tea will perk you up,* or *The flowers perked up the whole room.*

**person** In addition to the idiom beginning with PERSON, also see FEEL LIKE ONESELF (A NEW PERSON); IN PERSON; OWN PERSON, BE ONE'S.

**person of color** A nonwhite person, such as someone of African or Native American descent. For example, *They have made an effort to promote persons of color to executive positions.*

**pet** In addition to the idiom beginning with PET, also see TEACHER'S PET.

**Pete** Also, **Peter.** See FOR THE SAKE OF (PETE'S SAKE); HONEST TO GOD (PETE); ROB PETER TO PAY PAUL.

**peter out** Become fewer in number or less in amount and then come to an end, as in *Their enthusiasm soon petered out.*

**pet peeve** A particular or frequent source of irritation, as in *My pet peeve is that neighbor's cat running through my herb garden.*

**physical** see GET PHYSICAL.

**phase in** Introduce one stage at a time. For example, *New technology must be phased in, or the office will be overwhelmed.* The antonym is **phase out,** meaning "bring or come to an end, one stage at a time," as in *The department is phasing out all the older computers.*

**PI** Also, **p.i.** See POLITICALLY INCORRECT.

**pick** In addition to the idioms beginning with PICK, also see BONE TO PICK; SLIM PICKINGS.

**pick a bone with** see BONE TO PICK.

**pick and choose** Select with great care, as in *John and Kate loved to go to the pastry shop, especially if they had time to pick and choose.*

**pick apart** Also, **pick holes in** or **pick *something* to pieces.** Find flaws in something by close examination, criticize sharply, as in *The lawyer picked apart the testimony,* or *He found it easy to pick holes in their argument,* or *The new editor picked the manuscript to pieces.* These expressions use *pick* in the sense of "pierce" or "poke."

**pick a quarrel** Also, **pick an argument** or **pick a fight.** Look for a chance to quarrel or argue with someone. For example, *I don't want to pick a quarrel with you,* or *Jason was always in trouble for picking fights.* These terms use *pick* in the sense of "select."

**pick at** **1.** Pluck or pull at something, especially with the fingers, as in *She was always picking at her skirt with her nails.* **2.** Eat very little of something and show no appetite for it, as in *He was just picking at his dinner.* **3.** Keep criticizing or complaining to someone, as in *He's picking at me all day long.*

**picked over** see under PICK OVER.

**pick holes in** see PICK APART.

**pickle** see IN A FIX (PICKLE).

**pick off** Shoot someone or something after singling that person or thing out, as in *The hunter picked off the ducks one by one.*

**pick of the litter, the** The best of a group, as in *He was first in the ticket line, so he had the pick of the litter.* This term refers to the most desirable one from a litter of puppies or kittens.

**pick on** Tease, bully, or victimize someone, as in *She told Mom the boys were always picking on her.* This expression is used in the command **pick on someone your own size,** meaning "don't bully someone who is younger, smaller, or weaker than yourself."

**pick one's way** Find and move through a passage carefully, as in *She picked her way through the crowd outside the theater,* or, more figuratively, *He picked his way through the mass of 19th-century journals, looking for references to his subject.*

**pick out 1.** Choose or select something or someone, as in *She picked out the best piece of fabric.* **2.** Distinguish or identify a person or thing from the surroundings, as in *They managed to pick out their mother from the crowd.* **3.** Identify the notes of a tune and play it on an instrument, as in *When she was four, she could pick out folk songs on the piano.*

**pick over** Sort out a group of things by examining item by item, as in *Dad hates to pick over the beans one by one.* This term is sometimes put as **picked over,** describing something that has already been examined and selected from, as in *They have almost nothing left; the stock of bathing suits has been picked over.*

**pick someone's brain** Get ideas or information from another person, as in *I'm out of ideas for decorating—let me pick your brain.*

P

**pick *something* to pieces** see PICK APART.

**pick up 1.** Lift or take up something by hand, as in *Please pick up that book from the floor.* **2.** Collect or gather things, as in *First they had to pick up the pieces of broken glass.* **3.** Put a place in order, as in *Let's pick up the bedroom,* or *I'm always picking up after Pat.* **4.** Take on passengers or freight, as in *The bus picks up commuters at three stops.* **5.** Get something casually, without great effort or by accident. For example, *I picked up a nice coat at the sale,* or *She had no trouble picking up French.* This usage is also extended to contracting diseases, as in *I think I picked up the baby's cold.* **6.** Claim or collect a possession, as in *He picked up his laundry every Friday.* **7.** Shop and buy something, as in *Please pick up some wine at the store on your way home.* **8. pick up the bill** or **pick up the check** or **pick up the tab.** Take the responsibility for paying for something, especially a meal in a restaurant, as in *They always wait for us to pick up the tab.* **9.** Increase speed or rate, as in *The plane picked up speed,* or *He wants his staff to pick up the work rate.* **10.** Gain ground, as in *The second runner picked up several meters on the last lap but couldn't catch the leader.* **11.** Take someone into custody, as in *The police picked him up for burglary.* **12.** Make a casual acquaintance with someone, especially for sexual relations, as in *A stranger tried to pick her up at the bus station.* **13.** Come upon, find, or detect something, as in *The dog picked up the scent,* or *They picked up two submarines on sonar,* or *I can't pick up that station on the car radio.* **14.** Resume something, as in *Let's pick up the conversation after lunch.* **15.** Improve or cause something or someone to improve in condition or activity, as in *Sales picked up last fall,* or *He picked up quickly after he got home from the hospital,* or *A cup of coffee will pick you up.* **16.** Gather one's belongings, as in *She just picked up and left him.* **17. pick oneself up.** Recover from a fall or other mishap, as in *Jim picked himself up and stood there waiting.* Also see the following idioms beginning with PICK UP.

**pick up on** Become aware of, notice, as in *The teacher picked up on her nervousness right away.*

**pick up the pieces** Recover from a bad situation, restore matters to normal, as in *She's trying to forget him and pick up the pieces of her life,* or *Once fighting ended, the task force picked up the pieces and restored democracy.*

**picnic** see NO PICNIC.

**picture** In addition to the idiom beginning with PICTURE, also see GET THE MESSAGE (PICTURE); IN THE PICTURE; PRETTY AS A PICTURE; TAKE A PICTURE; THE PICTURE.

**picture is worth a thousand words, one** A graphic illustration carries a stronger message than words, as in *The book jacket is a big selling point—one picture is worth a thousand words.*

**pie** In addition to the idiom beginning with PIE, also see APPLE-PIE ORDER; EASY AS PIE; EAT CROW (HUMBLE PIE); FINGER IN THE PIE; SLICE OF THE PIE.

**piece** In addition to the idioms beginning with PIECE, also see ALL IN ONE PIECE; CONVERSATION PIECE; GO TO PIECES; MUSEUM PIECE; OF A PIECE; PICK APART (TO PIECES); PICK UP THE PIECES; PUFF PIECE; SAY ONE'S PIECE; THRILL TO PIECES; TO PIECES.

**piece by piece** In stages, gradually, as in *He took the clock apart piece by piece,* or *Let's go over your exam paper, piece by piece.* Also see BIT BY BIT.

**piece of ass** Also, **piece of tail.** Sexual intercourse, as in *He was out for a piece of ass.* [Vulgar slang]

**piece of cake** Something that is easy to do, as in *I had no trouble finding your house—a piece of cake.* This expression originated in the Royal Air Force for an easy mission. Also see EASY AS PIE.

**piece of change** Also, **chunk of change.** A sum of money, especially a large amount, as in *That car is worth a piece of change.*

**piece of one's mind, a** Frank and severe criticism, as in *Chuck was furious and gave them a piece of his mind.* This expression always refers to a negative opinion.

**piece of the action** A share in an activity or in the profits, as in *They wanted a piece of the action in this land deal.*

**piece together** Join or combine parts into a whole, as in *With information from several observers, she pieced together an account of what had actually taken place.*

**pie in the sky** An empty wish or promise, as in *His dream of being hired as a sports editor proved to be pie in the sky.*

**pig** In addition to the idioms beginning with PIG, also see IN A PIG'S EYE; LIKE PIGS IN CLOVER; MAKE A PIG OF ONESELF; WHEN PIGS FLY.

**pigeon** see STOOL PIGEON.

**pig in a poke** An object offered in a manner that hides its low value. For example, *Eric believes that buying a used car is buying a pig in a poke.* This expression refers to the practice of substituting a worthless object, such as a cat, for the costly suckling pig a customer has bought and wrapping it in a *poke,* or sack. Also see LET THE CAT OUT OF THE BAG.

**pig it** Live in a messy way, as in *Ten roommates shared that small house, and as you might guess they were pigging it.*

**pig out** Eat a huge amount, as in *The kids pigged out on the candy they had collected on Halloween.*

**pile** In addition to the idioms beginning with PILE, also see MAKE A BUNDLE (PILE).

**pile into** Move in a disorderly group into, crowd into, as in *The team piled into the bus.* The related expression **pile in** takes no object, as in *Jack opened the car door and yelled, "Pile in!"*

**pile up** **1.** Grow larger or collect an increasing amount over time, as in *The leaves piled up in the yard,* or *He piled up a huge fortune.* In this idiom *pile* means "form a heap or mass of something." **2.** Be involved in a crash, as in *When the police arrived, at least four cars had piled up.*

**pill** see BITTER PILL TO SWALLOW; SUGAR THE PILL.

**pillar to post** see FROM PILLAR TO POST.

**pimple** see GOOSE PIMPLES.

**pin** In addition to the idioms beginning with PIN, also see HEAR A PIN DROP; ON PINS AND NEEDLES.

**pin back one's ears** see PIN SOMEONE'S EARS BACK.

**pinch** In addition to the idioms beginning with PINCH, also see FEEL THE PINCH; IN A PINCH; WITH A GRAIN (PINCH) OF SALT.

**pinch hitter** A substitute for another person, especially in an emergency. For example, *Pat expected her mother to help with the baby, but just in case, she asked her mother-in-law to be her pinch hitter.* This expression comes from baseball, where it is used for a player substituting for another hitter at a critical point or in a tense situation.

**pinch pennies** Be thrifty and spend as little as possible, as in *There's no need to pinch pennies now that you're working full-time.*

**pin down** **1.** Fix or establish something clearly, as in *The firefighters finally were able to pin down the source of the odor.* **2.** Force someone to give precise information or opinions, as in *The reporter pinned down the governor on the issue of conservation measures.*

**pink** see IN THE PINK; TICKLED PINK.

**pin money** Small amounts of money for little expenses, as in *Grandma usually gives the children some pin money whenever she visits.* This expression originally meant money given by a husband to his wife for small personal expenditures such as pins, which were very costly items in centuries past.

**pin *something* on** Put the blame for something on someone, especially the blame for a crime. For example, *They pinned the murder on the wrong man.* This expression uses *pin* in the sense of "attach."

**pin one's heart on** see WEAR ONE'S HEART ON ONE'S SLEEVE.

**pin one's hopes on** Also, **pin one's faith on.** Put one's hope or trust in someone or something, as in *She'd pinned her hopes on an early acceptance to the university, but it didn't come through.*

**pin someone's ears back** Defeat someone, overcome, punish, as in *The Red Sox had their ears pinned back by the Yankees,* or *You'll get your ears pinned back if you're late.*

**pipe** In addition to the idioms beginning with PIPE, also see IN THE PIPELINE; LEAD-PIPE CINCH; PUT THAT IN YOUR PIPE AND SMOKE IT.

**pipe down** Stop talking, be quiet, as in *I wish you children would pipe down.* This idiom is also used as a command, as in *Pipe down! We want to listen to the music.*

**pipe dream** A fantastic notion or vain hope, as in *I'd love to have one home in the mountains and another at the seashore, but that's just a pipe dream.* This term originally referred to the fantasies brought about by smoking an opium pipe.

**piper** see CALL THE TUNE (PAY THE PIPER).

**pipe up** Speak up, as in *Finally she piped up, "I think I've got the winning ticket,"* or *Pipe up if you want more pancakes.*

P

**piping hot** Very hot, as in *These biscuits are piping hot.* This idiom refers to something so hot that it makes a piping or hissing sound.

**piss and moan** Also, **bitch and moan.** Complain at length and in an annoying way. For example, *Ignore him. He's been pissing and moaning about the money all day.* [Vulgar slang]

**piss away** Spend money unwisely, waste money, as in *They've pissed away a fortune on those horses.* [Vulgar slang]

**piss into the wind** Also, **spit into the wind.** Engage in a useless activity that is not only futile but may backfire as well. For example, *Trying to talk to him is like pissing in the wind,* or *You might as well spit in the wind as try to discredit her.* [Vulgar slang]

**piss off** **1.** Make someone very angry, as in *That letter pissed me off,* or *She was pissed off because no one had called her.* [Vulgar slang] **2.** Go away, as in *Piss off and stop bothering me.* [Vulgar slang]

**pit** In addition to the idiom beginning with PIT, also see THE PITS.

**pit *someone* against** Oppose or compete directly with someone, as in *The Civil War pitted brother against brother,* or *She enjoys pitting her wits against me.* This idiom refers to setting fighting cocks or dogs against one another in a pit.

**pitch** In addition to the idioms beginning with PITCH, also see BLACK AS NIGHT (PITCH); IN THERE PITCHING; MAKE A PITCH FOR; SALES PITCH; WILD PITCH.

**pitched battle, a** An intense conflict, as in *Their disagreement turned into a pitched battle between the nurses and the doctors' assistants.*

**pitcher** see LITTLE PITCHERS HAVE BIG EARS.

**pitch in** **1.** Set to work energetically, as in *We pitched right in and started mowing the field.* **2.** Join forces with others; help, cooperate. For example, *We were hoping you'd pitch in and sort the books.* Also see PITCH INTO.

**pitch into** Attack or assault someone, either physically or verbally. For example, *Mom pitched into Dad when he forgot to go to the bank.*

**pity** see FOR THE SAKE OF (PITY'S SAKE); TAKE PITY ON.

**place** In addition to the idiom beginning with PLACE, also see ALL OVER THE PLACE; BETWEEN A ROCK AND A HARD PLACE; FALL IN PLACE; FRIEND IN COURT (HIGH PLACES); GO PLACES; HAVE ONE'S HEART IN THE RIGHT PLACE; IN PLACE; IN SOMEONE'S SHOES (PLACE); INSTEAD (IN PLACE) OF; IN THE FIRST PLACE; IN THE RIGHT PLACE AT THE RIGHT TIME; JUMPING-OFF PLACE; KNOW ONE'S PLACE; OUT OF PLACE; PUT SOMEONE IN HIS OR HER PLACE; RUN IN PLACE; TAKE PLACE.

**place in the sun** An important or favorable position or situation, as in *The Nobel prizewinners really enjoyed their place in the sun.*

**plague** see AVOID SOMEONE LIKE THE PLAGUE.

**plain** In addition to the idioms beginning with PLAIN, also see IN PLAIN ENGLISH.

**plain as day** Also, **plain as the nose on your face.** Very obvious, quite clear, as in *It's plain as day that they must sell their house before they can buy another,* or *It's plain as the nose on your face that she's lying.* The first term is probably a shortening of *plain as the sun at midday.*

**plain sailing** Easy going; straightforward, continuous progress. For example, *The first few months were difficult, but I think it's plain sailing from here on.* This term refers to navigating waters free of rocks or other obstructions.

**plan** In addition to the idiom beginning with PLAN, also see BEST-LAID PLANS; GAME PLAN.

**plank** see WALK THE PLANK.

**plan on** **1.** Have as an aim or purpose, as in *We had planned on going to the movies after dinner.* **2.** Anticipate something, prepare for, as in *We planned on you to make a speech,* or *They hadn't planned on such a big crowd.*

**plate** see HAND SOMETHING TO ONE ON A SILVER PLATTER (SERVE UP ON A PLATE); HAVE A LOT ON ONE'S PLATE.

**platter** see under HAND SOMETHING TO ONE ON A SILVER PLATTER.

**play** In addition to the idioms beginning with PLAY, also see ALL WORK AND NO PLAY; CHILD'S PLAY; FAIR PLAY; FOUL PLAY; GAME THAT TWO CAN PLAY; GRANDSTAND PLAY; IN PLAY; MAKE A PLAY FOR; MUSICAL CHAIRS, PLAY; SQUEEZE PLAY; WHEN THE CAT'S AWAY, THE MICE WILL PLAY.

**play along** Cooperate or pretend to cooperate, as in *They decided to play along with the robbers, at least for a while.*

**play a losing game** see under LOSING BATTLE.

**play around** **1.** Act playfully or without purpose, as in *Stop playing around the house,* or *I didn't mean to offend you; I was just playing around.* **2.** Engage in one or more casual sexual relationships. For example, *She got tired of his playing around and filed for divorce.*

**play at** Do or take part in an activity halfheartedly, as in *She was just playing at keeping house, letting the others do all the work.*

**play a waiting game** Delay an action or decision so as to force an opponent to move or to gain additional information. For example, *The lawyer advised her to play a waiting game and see if her husband would come up with a better settlement offer.*

**play back** Replay something, especially a recorded performance; also, repeat. For example, *When we played back the tape of the concert, we noticed a lot of missed notes,* or *He uses the same material again and again, playing back his old speech.*

**play ball 1.** Cooperate with someone, as in *The opposing attorneys refused to play ball with us.* **2.** Get going, start, as in *It's time to get a move on; let's play ball.* This usage comes from the baseball umpire's call to start a game.

**play both ends against the middle** Also, **play one off against another.** Gain an advantage by setting opposing parties or interests against one another. For example, *Some children are adept at manipulating their parents, playing both ends against the middle,* or *Their older sister had a nasty habit of playing the twins off against each other.*

**play *something* by ear 1.** Play a musical instrument without the aid of written music, as in *By the time she was four, she could play a dozen songs by ear.* **2. play it by ear.** Continue gradually, depending on what happens; decide what to do without advance planning. For example, *I'm not sure how much we should say about our plans, so let's play it by ear.*

**play cat and mouse** Amuse oneself or toy with, as in *She loved to play cat and mouse with an admirer, acting by turns friendly, indifferent, and jealous.* This expression refers to the way a cat will often toy with a helpless mouse.

**play dirty** Behave in a deceitful or an unfair way in order to get what one wants, as in *He doesn't mind playing dirty if it will get what he wants.* Also see PLAY FAIR; PLAY HARDBALL.

**play down 1.** Make little of something, make less important, as in *A skillful salesman plays down the drawbacks of the product and emphasizes its good features.* **2. play down to.** Lower one's standards to meet the demands of someone, as in *Some stand-up comics deliberately play down to the vulgar taste of their audiences.*

**played out** Exhausted, worn out, as in *This was the third trip the horses had made, and they were utterly played out.* Also see PLAY OUT.

**play fair** Behave honestly and honorably, obey the rules, as in *Not every supplier we deal with plays fair,* or *We can't just leave them to find their own way back—that's not playing fair.* This idiom refers literally to playing by the rules in some game or sport. Also see PLAY DIRTY; PLAY THE GAME.

**play false** Deceive or betray someone, as in *If my memory does not play false, I met them years ago in Italy.*

**play fast and loose** Be recklessly irresponsible, unreliable, or deceitful, as in *This reporter is known for playing fast and loose with the facts.*

**play footsie 1.** Behave coyly, flirt with someone, especially secretly. For example, *Get to the point, there's no need to play footsie with us.* This expression refers to two people secretly rubbing each other's feet. **2.** Cooperate or seek favor with someone in a sly or secret way, as in *The mayor's been playing footsie with various neighborhood business interests.*

**play for 1.** Take part for a particular reason, as in *We're not playing for money, just for fun.* A special usage of this idiom is **play for laughs,** that is, with the aim of causing laughter. **2. play someone for.** Manage someone for one's own ends, make a fool of, trick or cheat. For example, *I resent your playing me for a fool,* or *He suddenly found out she'd been playing him for a sucker.*

**play for keeps** see FOR KEEPS.

**play for laughs** see PLAY FOR, def. 1.

**play for time** Delay doing something until one is ready to act, as in *The defense attorney decided to play for time while they searched for an eyewitness.*

**play games** Be deceitful or refuse to be direct, as in *Don't play games with me—I want an honest answer.* Also see PLAY THE GAME.

**play hardball** Act aggressively and without concern for fairness, as in *It's only a month before the election, and I'm sure they'll start to play hardball.* This term originated in baseball, where it refers to using the standard ball as opposed to the slightly larger and softer ball of softball.

**play hard to get** Pretend to be unavailable or uninterested, especially with the opposite sex. For example, *I know he has no appointments tomorrow; he's just playing hard to get,* or *My sister is very popular, perhaps because she plays hard to get.*

**play havoc** Also, **raise havoc** or **wreak havoc.** Disrupt, damage, or destroy something, as in *The wind played havoc with her hair,* or *The fire alarm raised havoc with the children,* or *The earthquake wrought havoc in the town.*

**play hide and seek** Evade or seem to evade someone. For example, *Bill is hard to pin down—he's always playing hide and seek.* This expression refers to the children's game in which one player tries to find others who are hiding.

**play hooky** Be absent from school or some other obligation without permission, as in *It was such a beautiful day that we played hooky from work.*

**play in Peoria** Be acceptable to the average unsophisticated person. For example, *We've tested this new soup in several markets, but* *will it play in Peoria?* This expression originated among touring theater companies trying to make sure their productions would win favor in the U.S. heartland, symbolized by the small city of Peoria, Illinois.

**play into the hands of** Act so as to give an advantage to an opponent, as in *The senator played right into the hands of her opponents when she backed that unpopular amendment to the tax bill.*

**play it close to one's chest** Be secretive or cautious, give nothing away, as in *We've no idea how many tickets they sold; they play it close to their chests.* This expression, which is also put as **play one's cards close to one's chest,** refers to holding one's cards up against one's chest, so that no one else can see them.

**play it cool** **1.** Act cautiously or pretend indifference, as in *When they asked how much she earned, she played it cool.* **2.** Become or remain calm, as in *When they start to tease you, just play it cool.*

**play it safe** Also, **play safe.** Avoid extreme risks, as in *I played it safe and bet only a dollar,* or *Let's play safe and get a backup in case the announced speaker gets sick.*

**play musical chairs** see MUSICAL CHAIRS.

**play off** **1.** See PLAY BOTH ENDS AGAINST THE MIDDLE. **2.** Break a tie by playing an additional game or period, as in *Each team had won three games, so they had to play off the tie to decide the championship.*

**play on** Also, **play upon.** Take advantage of something or make use of for a desired effect, as in *These health care ads are meant to play on our fears.*

P

**play one's cards close to one's chest** see PLAY IT CLOSE TO ONE'S CHEST.

**play one's cards right** Act carefully or wisely in order to succeed, as in *She played her cards right and got a promotion.*

**play one's part** Be a factor in or do what is necessary in order for something to happen, as in *Missing classes played a part in the student's failure,* or *We'll get through this difficulty if we all play our part.*

**play on words** A word or turn of phrase with a double meaning, a pun or other humorous use of language. For example, *Shakespeare was a master at plays on words—his dramas are full of puns.*

**play out** **1.** Finish something, run out, as in *This concern for having the right clothes will soon play out,* or *The tension between the two groups will surely play itself out by next year.* **2.** Unwind something, unreel, as in *They slowly played out the cable.* Also see PLAYED OUT.

**play politics** Act for personal or political gain rather than principle, as in *I don't think this judge is fair—he's playing politics.*

**play possum** Pretend to be dead or asleep, as in *That boy always plays possum when it's time to clean up his room.* This expression refers to the fact that the opossum gives the appearance of death when it is caught.

**play safe** see PLAY IT SAFE.

**play second fiddle** Be in an inferior role to someone, as in *Mary resented always playing second fiddle to her older sister.* This term refers to the part of second violin in an orchestra. Although many would argue it is as important as first violin, it is the idea of less importance that was transferred in the figurative term.

**play the field** Date more than one person; avoid a commitment to one person. For example, *All of my brother's friends are married now, but he continues to play the field.* This term originated in British horseracing, where it meant "bet on every horse in a race except the favorite."

**play the fool** Act in a silly or stupid way, as in *Helen deliberately played the fool so they wouldn't realize she understood their strategy.*

**play the game** **1.** Behave according to accepted customs, obey the rules. For example, *Not every foreign company can be counted on to play the game.* The *game* here refers to a sport with a set of rules. **2. play someone's game.** To go along with what someone appears to be doing in order to find out what he or she wants or has planned, or in order to win in a competition. For example, *I can play your game as well as you can, but I don't like the rules,* or *Let's play their game and find out what they're up to.* In this idiom, *game* refers to a plan or an agenda. Also see PLAY GAMES.

**play the heavy** Act the part of an evil person; take the blame for unkind behavior. For example, *She can't bear firing an employee, so she relies on Jim to play the heavy.* This term comes from the theater, where *heavy* has long been used for a stern, serious role or that of an evil person.

**play the market** Trade in stocks and securities in order to make money, as in *He is always playing the market, with only mixed results.* This term uses *play* in the sense of "gamble."

**play to the gallery** Appeal to an audience for approval, as in *He peppers his speeches with humor and comments about his opponent, clearly playing to the gallery.* In this term *gallery* refers to the cheapest seats in a British theater and therefore to the least sophisticated audience.

**play up** Stress or publicize something, as in *In the press interview, the coach played up the importance of having a strong defense.* Also see PLAY DOWN; PLAY UP TO.

**play upon** see PLAY ON.

**play up to** Seek favor with, flatter insincerely, as in *There's no use playing up to the boss; it doesn't influence him.*

**play with fire** Take part in a dangerous undertaking, as in *You're playing with fire if you go behind his back and take over his department.*

**plea** see COP A PLEA.

**please** see AS YOU PLEASE.

**pleased as Punch** Delighted, as in *We were pleased as Punch when they asked us to be godparents.* This term refers to the character Punch in Punch and Judy shows, who is always very happy when his evil deeds succeed.

**plenty** see under NOT THE ONLY FISH IN THE SEA.

**plot thickens, the** A situation is becoming very complex or mysterious. Today this term is often used ironically or half-humorously, as in *His companion wasn't his wife or his partner—the plot thickens.* Originally this expression described the plot of a play that was very complicated. Later it began to be used for increasingly complex mysteries in detective stories.

**plow back** Reinvest earnings or profits in one's business, as in *This company plows back half its profits every year.* This term transfers the farming practice of turning the soil from top to bottom to financial activities.

**plow into** Strike something with force, crash into; also, attack energetically. For example, *The truck plowed into the retaining wall,* or *The writer plowed into the pile of correspondence.* This expression transfers the force of a farmer's plow to other activities.

**plow *something* under** Cause something to disappear, overwhelm, as in *The independent bookstores are being plowed under by the large chains.* This term refers to a farmer burying vegetation by turning it into the soil with a plow.

**pluck up one's courage** Also, **screw up one's courage.** Force oneself to overcome fear or timidity, as in *He was really afraid of falling, but he plucked up his courage and stepped onto the ice,* or *I screwed up my courage and dove off the high board.*

**plug** In addition to the idiom beginning with PLUG, also see PULL THE PLUG ON.

**plug away at** Continue to work at a job or task even though it is difficult or unpleasant. For example, *If you keep plugging away at algebra, it'll begin to make sense to you.* This idiom refers to the effort and persistence required to seal something by inserting a plug.

**plugged in, be** Be involved in, as in *He couldn't make any important social connections because he just wasn't plugged in.* The related expression **be plugged into** takes an object, as in *These collectors are plugged into the local art scene.* These terms refer to inserting a plug into an electrical socket.

**plunge** see TAKE THE PLUNGE.

**plunk down** Also, **plunk oneself down.** Throw or place or drop something heavily, as in *He plunked down the money and walked out,* or *It was hot work, so after an hour we plunked ourselves down in the shade.*

**pocket** In addition to the idiom beginning with POCKET, also see DEEP POCKETS; IN ONE'S POCKET; LINE ONE'S POCKETS; MONEY BURNS A HOLE IN ONE'S POCKET; OUT OF POCKET.

**pocket money** Also, **spending money.** Cash for unexpected or minor expenses, as in *They don't believe in giving the children pocket money without asking them to do chores,* or *Can I borrow a dollar? I'm out of all my spending money.* The first term refers to keeping small sums in one's pocket; the second refers to money that may be spent (as opposed to saved).

**poetic justice** An outcome in which good behavior is rewarded and evil punished, often in an especially appropriate or ironic manner. For example, *It was poetic justice for the known thief to go to jail for the one crime he didn't commit.*

**poetic license** Also, **artistic license.** The liberty taken by a writer or an artist in not following the usual or expected in order to achieve an effect. For example, *I've never seen grass or a tree of that color; but that's artistic license.*

**point** In addition to the idioms beginning with POINT, also see AT THAT POINT; AT THIS POINT; BELABOR THE POINT; BESIDE THE POINT; BOILING POINT; BROWNIE POINTS; CASE IN POINT; GET TO THE POINT; HAVE A POINT; HIT THE HIGH SPOTS (POINTS); IN (POINT OF) FACT; IN POINT; JUMPING-OFF PLACE (POINT); MAKE A POINT OF; MAKE ONE'S POINT; MISS THE POINT; ON THE POINT OF; POSSESSION IS NINE POINTS OF THE LAW; SCORE POINTS OFF OF; SORE POINT; STRETCH A POINT; STRONG POINT; TAKE SOMEONE'S POINT; TO THE POINT; UP TO A POINT; WIN ON POINTS.

**point-blank** Without trying to say something, such as a question or statement, indirectly, as in *She asked him point-blank if he was going out with someone else,* or *I told her point-blank that I wouldn't work extra hours.*

**point in time** A particular moment, as in *At no point in time had they decided to leave the country,* or *The exact point in time when he died has not been determined.* Also see AT THIS POINT.

**point of no return, the** The place in a course of action beyond which it is not possible to go back. For example, *Once the contract is signed, we've reached the point of no* *return.* This expression comes from aviation, where it means the point at which an aircraft does not have enough fuel to return to its starting place.

**point of view** An attitude or belief, how one sees or thinks of something. For example, *From the manufacturer's point of view, the critical issue is cost.* This expression originally referred to the point from which one looks at a building or painting or other object.

**point out** Identify or bring someone or something to notice, as in *He pointed out the oldest buildings in the city,* or *She pointed out an error in our reasoning.*

**point the finger at** Blame someone, accuse, as in *When they asked her who broke the window, she pointed the finger at Tom.* Also see PUT THE FINGER ON.

**point up** Stress something, draw attention to, as in *The recent robbery points up the need for more security at the store.*

**poison** In addition to the idiom beginning with POISON, also see ONE MAN'S MEAT IS ANOTHER MAN'S POISON.

**poison-pen letter** A letter, usually anonymous, that makes threatening statements to the person who receives it or to someone else. For example, *She told the police about the poison-pen letters, but they said they couldn't pursue the matter.*

**poke** In addition to the idioms beginning with POKE, also see MAKE FUN OF (POKE FUN AT); PIG IN A POKE; TAKE A POKE AT.

**poke around** Also, **poke about.** Look through things; also, make an investigation. For example, *I was poking around the attic when I found these old photos,* or *The detective was poking about, tracking where she went on that fatal night.* Also see NOSE ABOUT; POKE ONE'S NOSE INTO.

**poke fun at** see under MAKE FUN OF.

**poke one's nose into** Involve oneself in another's affairs, as in *I told her to stop poking her nose into our business.*

**poker** In addition to the idiom beginning with POKER, also see STIFF AS A BOARD (POKER).

**poker face** A facial expression that doesn't reveal any emotion that can be interpreted, as in *Whenever Betty attended one of her children's performances, she managed to keep a poker face.* This term refers to the facial expression of a poker player who is expert at concealing his or her feelings.

**pole** see LOW MAN ON THE TOTEM POLE; NOT TOUCH WITH A TEN-FOOT POLE.

**poles apart** Completely disagreeing, as in *The two brothers were poles apart in nearly all their views.* This expression refers to the two extremities of the earth's axis, the North and South poles.

**polish** In addition to the idiom beginning with POLISH, also see SPIT AND POLISH.

**polish off** Finish or use up something, especially quickly and easily. For example, *We polished off the pie in no time,* or *If everyone helps, we can polish off this job today.* This usage came from boxing, where it originally meant "defeat an opponent quickly and easily."

**politically correct** Also, **PC** or **p.c.** Showing an effort to make broad social and political changes to address injustices caused by prejudice. It often involves changing or avoiding language that might offend others, especially with respect to gender, race, or ethnic background. For example, *Editors of major papers have established guidelines concerning politically correct language.* This expression is often used sarcastically by people who aren't concerned about the feelings of other people.

**politically incorrect** Also, **PI** or **p.i.** Talking or acting in ways that show no concern for the feelings of other people, especially those who are different from oneself in some way. For example, *He doesn't care if he's politically incorrect; to him, women will always be chicks, babes, and broads.* This expression is often used defiantly to show that one does not care about offending other people.

**politics** see PLAY POLITICS.

**pond** see BIG FISH IN A SMALL POND; LITTLE FROG IN A BIG POND.

**pond scum** see SCUM OF THE EARTH.

**pony** In addition to the idiom beginning with PONY, also see DOG-AND-PONY SHOW.

**pony up** Pay money that is owed or due, as in *Come on, it's time you ponied up this month's rent.*

**poop out** **1.** Tire out, exhaust, as in *I ran about ten miles, but then I was too pooped out to go on.* **2.** Quit, decide not to participate, especially at the last minute. For example, *We had about twenty signed up for the seminar, but then half of them pooped out.*

**poor as a churchmouse** Having little or no wealth and few possessions, as in *She's poor as a churchmouse, so you can't expect her to donate anything.*

**poor relation** An inferior member of a group, as in *Many regard Turkey as the poor relation in the European alliance.* This expression originally referred to a family member living in poverty.

**poor taste, in** Also, **in bad taste.** Not suitable, inappropriate, offensive, as in *His criticism of the Pope was in poor taste,* or *That television interview was in very bad taste.* These idioms use *taste* in the sense of "sensitivity to what is appropriate."

**pop off** **1.** Also, **pop out.** Leave abruptly or hurriedly, as in *I'm just going to pop off and mail some letters.* The antonym is **pop in,** as in *Let's just pop in to see them for a minute.* **2.** Die suddenly, as in *No one expected her to pop off like that.* **3.** Speak thoughtlessly in an angry outburst, as in *Don't pop off at me—complain to whoever's responsible.* All these usages transfer *pop* in the sense of "explode" to other kinds of sudden or violent behavior.

**pop the question** Propose marriage, as in *He picked Valentine's Day to pop the question.*

**pop up** Suddenly appear, as in *After a brief warm period, all the flowers popped up,* or *He's constantly popping up where he's least expected.*

**pork barrel** Government funding of something that benefits a particular district, whose legislator wins favor with local voters. For example, *Our senator knows the value of the pork barrel.* This expression refers to the fatness of pork, which is equated with wasting the taxpayers' money.

**positive** see PROOF POSITIVE.

**possessed by** Driven by something, obsessed with, as in *He was possessed by the idea of becoming a millionaire.* This idiom uses *possess* in the sense of "dominate one's thoughts or ideas."

**possession is nine points of the law** Actually holding something is better than only claiming it. For example, *When I told John he must return the tools he'd borrowed, he said possession is nine points of the law.*

**possible** see AS FAR AS POSSIBLE; AS SOON AS POSSIBLE.

**possum** see PLAY POSSUM.

**post** see FROM PILLAR TO POST; KEEP POSTED.

**pot** In addition to the idiom beginning with POT, also see FISH OR CUT BAIT (SHIT OR GET OFF THE POT); GO TO POT; HIT THE JACKPOT; SWEETEN THE KITTY (POT); TAKE POTLUCK; TEMPEST IN A TEAPOT; WATCHED POT NEVER BOILS.

**potato** see HOT POTATO; MEAT AND POTATOES; SMALL POTATOES.

**pot calling the kettle black, the** Accusing someone of faults that one has oneself, as in *Tom's criticizing me for bad line calls is a case of the pot calling the kettle black, since Tom's about the worst line judge I've ever seen.* This expression dates from the days of cooking over a fire, which blackens all the utensils used.

**potluck** see TAKE POTLUCK.

**pound** In addition to the idioms beginning with POUND, also see PENNY WISE AND POUND FOOLISH.

**pound of flesh** A debt whose payment is harshly insisted on, as in *The other members of the cartel all want their pound of flesh from Brazil.*

**pound out** Produce something, especially on a keyboard, as in *I can pound out another résumé,* or *She was pounding out song after song on the piano.*

**pound the pavement** Walk the streets, especially in search of employment. For example, *He was fired last year, and he's been pounding the pavement ever since.* A similar usage is **pound a beat,** meaning "walk a particular route over and over"; it is nearly always applied to a police officer.

**pour** In addition to the idioms beginning with POUR, also see WHEN IT RAINS, IT POURS.

**pour cold water on** Also, **throw cold water on.** Ruin one's hopes or plans, discourage, as in *Cutting my year-end bonus poured cold water on my loyalty to the company,* or *Hearing about the outbreak of cholera threw cold water on our plans to visit Bolivia.*

**pour oil on troubled waters** Soothe or calm down something or someone, as in *The twins are quarreling, so I should go pour oil on troubled waters.* This term refers to an ancient practice of pouring oil on ocean waves to calm them.

**pour out one's heart** Express one's deepest thoughts and feelings to someone else, as in *Upset over the breakup, she poured out her heart to her mother.* Also see OPEN ONE'S HEART.

**powder** see KEEP ONE'S POWDER DRY; SITTING ON A POWDER KEG; TAKE A POWDER.

**power** In addition to the idioms beginning with POWER, also see CORRIDORS OF POWER; MORE POWER TO; STAYING POWER.

**power behind the throne, the** A person with great influence who stays behind the scenes and has no apparent authority. For example, *Doesn't your husband get tired of being the power behind the throne?*

**powers that be, the** Those in control, the authorities, as in *Our plan was vetoed by the powers that be.*

**practical** see TO ALL INTENTS AND (FOR ALL PRACTICAL) PURPOSES.

**practice** In addition to the idioms beginning with PRACTICE, also see IN PRACTICE; MAKE A PRACTICE OF; OUT OF PRACTICE; PUT INTO PRACTICE.

**practice makes perfect** Frequently doing something makes one better at doing it, as in *I've made at least a hundred cakes, but in my case practice hasn't made perfect.*

**practice what you preach** Behave as you would have others behave, as in *You keep telling us to clean up, but I wish you'd practice what you preach.* Also see DO AS I SAY.

**praise** In addition to the idiom beginning with PRAISE, also see DAMN WITH FAINT PRAISE; SING ONE'S PRAISES.

**praise *someone* to the skies** Compliment someone in an excessive way, as in *The critics praised the new movie to the skies.* Also see SING ONE'S PRAISES.

**prayer, not a** see under NOT A HOPE IN HELL.

**preach** In addition to the idiom beginning with PREACH, also see PRACTICE WHAT YOU PREACH.

**preach to the converted** Try to convince someone who already agrees, as in *Why tell me smoking is bad when I gave it up years ago? You're preaching to the converted.*

**precedent** see SET A PRECEDENT.

**precious few** Also, **precious little.** Very few, very little, as in *There are precious few leaves left on the trees,* or *We have precious little money left.* In these idioms *precious* serves as an intensive.

**premium** see AT A PREMIUM; PUT A PREMIUM ON.

**presence of mind** The ability to act sensibly, promptly, and appropriately, especially in a difficult situation or an emergency. For example, *Frantic about losing her wallet and passport, she had the presence of mind to notify the authorities at once.* This idiom in effect says that one's mind is present and functioning.

**present** see ALL PRESENT AND ACCOUNTED FOR; AT PRESENT; FOR THE MOMENT (PRESENT); NO TIME LIKE THE PRESENT.

**press** In addition to the idioms beginning with PRESS, also see BAD PRESS; HARD-PRESSED; HOT OFF THE PRESS; PUSH (PRESS) ONE'S LUCK; PUSH (PRESS) SOMEONE'S BUTTONS. Also see under PUSH.

P

**pressed for time** In a hurry, as in *How long will this take? I'm really pressed for time.*

**press *someone* into service** Convince or force someone to do something, as in *Can I press you into service to help people find their coats?* or *The concert drew such a large crowd that more police were pressed into service.* This idiom transfers *press* in the sense of "seize and force someone to serve," as seamen once were, to other activities.

**press on** see PUSH ON.

**press one's luck** see PUSH ONE'S LUCK.

**press someone's buttons** see PUSH SOMEONE'S BUTTONS.

**press the flesh** Shake hands and mingle with people, especially when running for public office. For example, *The candidate went through the crowd, pressing the flesh.*

**press the panic button** see PUSH THE PANIC BUTTON.

**pretty** In addition to the idioms beginning with PRETTY, also see IN A FIX (PRETTY PICKLE); (PRETTY) KETTLE OF FISH; SITTING PRETTY.

**pretty as a picture** Very attractive, as in *She looked pretty as a picture in her new hat.*

**pretty much** Also, **pretty well** or **pretty nearly.** Almost, nearly, approximately, as in *Our homework was pretty much finished,* or *We get along pretty well with our neighbors,* or *The police pretty nearly recovered all the stolen money.* This adverbial usage differs from the use of *pretty* for "considerable" (as in PRETTY PENNY ).

**pretty penny, a** A large sum of money, as in *That fur coat must have cost a pretty penny.*

**pretty well** see PRETTY MUCH.

**prevail on** Successfully persuade or influence someone, as in *They prevailed on me to speak at their annual luncheon.* This term uses *prevail* in the sense of "exert superior force."

**prey on 1.** Take advantage of, steal from; also, make a profit at someone else's expense, victimize. For example, *Pirates preyed on the coastal towns of England,* or *The rich have been preying on the poor for centuries.* **2.** Hunt something, especially in order to eat, as in *Their cat preys on all the birds in the neighborhood.* **3.** Exert a harmful effect, as in *Guilt preyed on his mind.*

**price** In addition to the idioms beginning with PRICE, also see AT ALL COSTS (AT ANY PRICE); AT A PRICE; BEYOND PRICE; CHEAP AT TWICE THE PRICE; EVERY MAN HAS HIS PRICE; PUT A PRICE ON; WHAT PRICE.

**price is right, the** The cost is very reasonable, it is a good value. This term is often used jokingly to describe something that is free but otherwise not particularly good. For example, *These golf balls we found in the pond may not look new, but the price is right.*

**price oneself out of the market** Charge so much for a product or service that no one will buy it, as in *Asking $10 each for those old CDs is pricing yourself out of the market.*

**price on someone's head** A reward for capturing or killing someone, usually someone guilty of a crime. For example, *He was a serial killer, and they put a price on his head.*

**prick up one's ears** Listen carefully, pay close attention, as in *When she heard them mention her boyfriend, she pricked up her ears.* This term refers to horses raising their ears at a sudden noise.

**pride** In addition to the idioms beginning with PRIDE, also see SWALLOW ONE'S PRIDE.

**pride and joy, one's** The object of one's great pleasure, as in *Our new grandson is our pride and joy,* or *That car is his pride and joy.*

**pride oneself on** Also, **take pride in.** Be proud of, take satisfaction in, as in *We pride ourselves on always being on time,* or *She took pride in her flower garden.*

**prime** In addition to the idioms beginning with PRIME, also see PAST ONE'S PRIME.

**prime mover** The initial source of energy directed toward a goal, someone or something that sets others in motion. For example, *Jean was the prime mover in getting us more laboratory space,* or *Patriotism was the prime mover of the revolution.*

**prime of life** The best years of one's life, when one is at the peak of one's powers, as in *She was in the prime of life when she began to lose her sight.* The related phrase **in one's prime** can be applied to objects as well as people. For example, *The roses were in their prime when you last saw them.* Also see PAST ONE'S PRIME.

**prime the pump** Encourage the growth or action of something, as in *The speaker tried to prime the pump by offering some new issues for discussion.* This expression originally was used for pouring liquid into a pump to force out the air and make the pump work. During the Depression it was applied to government efforts to stimulate the economy and later was extended to other activities.

**principle** see IN PRINCIPLE; ON PRINCIPLE.

**print** In addition to the idiom beginning with PRINT, also see GO OUT (OF PRINT); IN PRINT; SMALL PRINT.

**print out 1.** Write by drawing letters as opposed to cursive writing, as in *Please print out your name above your signature.* **2.** Use a computer printer, as in *This manuscript is too long to print out, so let's continue using floppy disks.*

**prisoner** see TAKE NO PRISONERS.

**private** In addition to the idioms beginning with PRIVATE, also see FREE (PRIVATE) ENTERPRISE; IN PRIVATE.

**private eye** A privately employed detective, as opposed to one working for the police or another authority. For example, *The children loved stories about private eyes, and Janey wanted to become one.* This expression comes from the term *private investigator,* with the "i" of investigator changed to "eye," which plays on the idea of a person looking into things.

**private parts** One's external sex organs, as in *He talks about his private parts constantly.*

**probability** see IN ALL PROBABILITY.

**problem** see NO PROBLEM.

**profile** see KEEP A LOW PROFILE.

**progress** see IN PROGRESS.

**promise** see LICK AND A PROMISE.

**proof** In addition to the idioms beginning with PROOF, also see LIVING PROOF.

**proof is in the pudding, the** Results are what count, as in *Let's see if this ad actually helps sales—the proof is in the pudding, you know.* The full form of this proverb is **The proof of the pudding is in the eating,** but it has become so well known that it is often shortened.

**proof positive** Evidence for something that is beyond question, as in *That delicious meal is proof positive that you're a good cook.*

**prop** see KNOCK THE BOTTOM (PROPS) OUT FROM.

**proportion** see OUT OF PROPORTION.

**pros and cons** Arguments or considerations for and against something, as in *We need to weigh all the pros and cons before we decide to add a new wing to the library.* This idiom is taken from the Latin *pro,* meaning "for," and *con,* meaning "against."

**proud** In addition to the idiom beginning with PROUD, also see DO SOMEONE PROUD.

**proud as a peacock** Having a very high opinion of oneself, filled with or showing too much self-esteem. For example, *She strutted about in her new outfit, proud as a peacock.* This simile refers to the male peacock, with its colorful tail that can be expanded like a fan, which has long symbolized vanity and pride.

**prove** In addition to the idiom beginning with PROVE, also see EXCEPTION PROVES THE RULE.

**prove out** Succeed, turn out well, as in *Farm-raised trout has proved out so well that the fish industry plans to experiment with other species.*

**prune** see FULL OF BEANS, def. 2.

**psych out 1.** Analyze or understand something; also, anticipate the intentions of someone, as in *It's hard to psych out the opposition's thinking, but we have to try.* **2.** Cause someone to lose confidence, intimidate. For example, *The basketball team managed to psych out their opponents' guards.* This expression is often used in the passive and can mean "lose one's nerve," as in *After I learned that he had two doctorates in the field, I was completely psyched out.*

**psych up** Excite emotionally, as in *The chorus was really psyched up for performing in Symphony Hall.*

**public** see GO PUBLIC; IN PUBLIC; IN THE PUBLIC EYE; JOHN DOE (Q. PUBLIC); WASH ONE'S DIRTY LINEN IN PUBLIC.

**publish or perish** Produce published work or fail to be promoted. For example, *The younger members of the department have a heavier teaching load, but they also know it's publish or perish.* This expression is nearly always used for college or university teachers, for whom advancement often is based on publishing research in their field.

**pudding** see PROOF IS IN THE PUDDING.

**puff piece** An approving or flattering article, as in *That was really a puff piece about the conductor, written by her cousin.*

**pull** In addition to the idioms beginning with PULL, also see HAVE PULL WITH; LIKE PULLING TEETH.

**pull a boner** Make a blunder, as in *I pulled an awful boner when I mentioned his ex-wife.* This expression comes from the noun *bonehead,* for "blockhead" or "stupid person."

**pull a fast one** Also, **put over a fast one.** Engage in a deceitful practice or play an unfair trick. For example, *He pulled a fast one when he gave me that fake employment record,* or *She tried to put over a fast one, but we found out in time to stop her.*

**pull away** **1.** Move away or withdraw from something, as in *The car pulled away from the curb.* **2.** Move ahead or forward, as in *His horse pulled away and took the lead.*

**pull back** **1.** Retreat, as in *The troops gradually pulled back.* **2.** Move away, often suddenly, as in *She pulled back her hand when she felt the heat.*

**pull down** **1.** Demolish something, destroy, as in *They pulled down several old office buildings downtown.* **2.** Lower something, reduce; also, depress someone in health or spirits. For example, *The bumper wheat crop is certain to pull down prices,* or *The flu really pulled him down.* **3.** Receive as wages, as in *He pulled down a hefty salary.*

**pull in** **1.** Arrive at a destination, as in *The train pulled in right on time.* **2.** Rein in someone or something, restrain, as in *She pulled in her horse,* or *The executives did not want to pull in their most aggressive salesmen.* **3.** Arrest a suspect, as in *The police said they could pull him in on lesser charges.*

**pulling teeth** see LIKE PULLING TEETH.

**pull in one's horns** Also, **draw in one's horns.** **1.** Retreat, back down, restrain oneself, as in *The town manager wanted higher taxes, but public reaction made him draw in his horns.* **2.** Reduce expenses, as in *That drop in profits will force the company to pull in its horns.*

**pull no punches** Behave or speak in a blunt way, hold nothing back, as in *The doctor pulled no punches but told us the whole truth.* This expression comes from boxing, where **pull one's punches** means "hit less hard than one can." This idiom, too, has been applied more generally, as in *They decided to pull their punches during these delicate negotiations.*

**pull off** Accomplish something, bring off, especially in the face of difficulties or at the last minute. For example, *I never thought we would win the game, but somehow we pulled it off.*

**pull oneself together** **1.** Regain one's calmness or self-control, as in *After that frightening episode, it took her a while to pull herself together.* **2.** Get ready, as in *Give me a few minutes to pull myself together, and I'll be right with you.*

**pull oneself up by the bootstraps** Succeed by one's own efforts, as in *She was homeless for nearly two years, but she managed to pull herself up by the bootstraps.* This expression refers to pulling on high boots by means of the straps attached at the top.

**pull one's punches** see under PULL NO PUNCHES.

**pull one's weight** Also, **pull one's own weight.** Do one's share, as in *We have a small organization, so we all must pull our own weight.* This term comes from rowing, where each crew member must pull on an oar.

**pull out** **1.** Leave, as in *The bus pulled out at noon.* **2.** Withdraw from an activity, as in *After the crash, many investors pulled out of the market,* or *Several teams pulled out of the tournament.*

**pull out all the stops** Use all the resources or force available, as in *The police pulled out all the stops to find the thief.*

**pull *something* out of a hat** Produce something suddenly and surprisingly, as if by magic. For example, *We can't just pull the answers out of a hat.* This expression refers to the magician's trick of pulling some unexpected object out of a hat. That object is often a rabbit, and the expression **pull a rabbit out of a hat** is frequently used to mean "get magical results," as in *Much as I would like to be able to pull a rabbit out of a hat, I doubt if I can find any more money for this project.*

**pull over** Bring a vehicle to the side of the road; also, instruct a motorist to stop. For example, *We pulled over to ask a passerby for directions,* or *The state trooper pulled the speeding motorist over.*

**pull rank** Use one's higher status to force someone to obey or obtain privileges for oneself, as in *She hated pulling rank in the office, but sometimes it was necessary.* This term comes from the military.

**pull round** Restore or be restored to good health, as in *It was good nursing that pulled him round so quickly,* or *Once on antibiotics, he pulled round quickly.*

**pull someone's chain** **1.** Make someone speak out of turn, as in *Who pulled your chain? It's none of your business.* **2.** Also, **yank someone's chain.** Make someone angry, especially deliberately, as in *Teenagers really know how to pull their parents' chains,* or *Don't yank his chain—he's in a bad mood.* Both expressions refer to the literal sense of pulling on a chain or leash to cause something to happen. Also see RATTLE SOMEONE'S CAGE.

**pull someone's leg** Play a joke on someone, tease, as in *Are you serious about moving back in, or are you pulling my leg?*

**pull something** Play a trick, deceive someone, as in *We thought he was trying to pull something when he claimed he had never picked up our tickets.* It is often put as **pull something on someone,** as in *I knew he was pulling something on me when he told me the wrong date.* Also see PULL A FAST ONE.

**pull strings** Also, **pull wires.** Use one's influence with important people in order to gain an advantage or get something desirable, as in *By pulling strings, he got us house seats to the opening,* or *His father pulled some wires and got him out of jail.* Both terms refer to moving a puppet with strings.

**pull the plug on** **1.** End something, as in *The government pulled the plug on that program.* **2.** Remove all life-supporting equipment, as in *The family debated whether it was time to pull the plug on him.* Although this idiom undoubtedly refers to cutting off electricity to an electrical device, it originally referred to the removal of a stopper that flushed an old-style toilet.

**pull the rug out from under** Remove all support and help from someone, usually suddenly. For example, *Stopping his allowance pulled the rug out from under him, forcing him to look for a job.* This term refers to pulling on a rug a person is standing on so that he or she falls.

**pull the wool over someone's eyes** Deceive or trick someone, as in *Her partner had pulled the wool over her eyes for years by keeping the best accounts for himself.* This term refers to the former custom of wearing a wig, which can slip down and cover the eyes temporarily.

**pull through** Survive a difficult situation or illness, as in *We've had to declare bankruptcy, but I'm sure we'll pull through,* or *they don't know if he'll pull through the surgery.*

**pull together** **1.** Make an effort together, cooperate, as in *If we pull together, I'm sure we'll meet our quota.* **2.** Assemble or gather something together, as in *Once we pull together all the facts, we'll understand the situation.* Also see PULL ONESELF TOGETHER.

**pull up** **1.** Stop or cause to stop, as in *He pulled up his horse,* or *They pulled up in front of the door.* **2.** Catch up, advance in relation to others, as in a race. For example, *She was behind at the start, but she quickly pulled up.* Also see PULL ONESELF UP BY THE BOOTSTRAPS.

**pull up stakes** Move away, leave one's home, job, or country. For example, *We've lived here for years, but now it's time to pull up stakes.* This expression refers to the stakes that mark property boundaries.

**pull wires** see PULL STRINGS.

**pulse** see TAKE THE PULSE OF.

**pump** In addition to the idioms beginning with PUMP, also see PRIME THE PUMP.

**pump iron** Lift weights, as in *She's started pumping iron three times a week.* This idiom refers to lifting weights.

**pump up** **1.** Inflate something with gas or air, as in *This tire needs pumping up.* **2.** Fill one with enthusiasm, strength, and energy, as in *The lively debate pumped us all up.*

**punch** In addition to the idioms beginning with PUNCH, also see BEAT TO IT (THE PUNCH); CAN'T PUNCH ONE'S WAY OUT OF A PAPER BAG; PACK A PUNCH; PLEASED AS PUNCH; PULL NO PUNCHES; ROLL WITH THE PUNCHES; SUCKER PUNCH; THROW A PUNCH.

**punch in** **1.** Also, **punch a clock** or **punch the clock.** Check in at a job on arrival, as in *You have to punch in or you won't get paid,* or *In this office no one has to punch a clock.* This usage refers to a time clock, which records the time of arrival on a card. Also see PUNCH OUT, def. 1. **2.** Keyboard data into a computer, as in *He was careful about punching in all the payments.*

**punching bag** see USE SOMEONE AS A PUNCHING BAG.

**punch out** **1.** Record one's time of departure from work, as in *We never punch out at exactly five o'clock.* This usage refers to a time clock, which records the time of departure on a card. Also see PUNCH IN, def. 1. **2.** Eject from a military aircraft, as in *The pilot punched out just before the plane blew up.*

**punishment** see GLUTTON FOR PUNISHMENT.

**puppy love** Young love, especially one that is not expected to last, as in *Our daughter is crazy about him, but we think it's just puppy love.*

P

**pure and simple** No more and no less, plainly so, as in *This so-called educational video is really a game, pure and simple.* This expression is nearly redundant, since *pure* and *simple* here mean "plain" and "unadorned."

**pure as the driven snow** Morally pure. This expression is especially used to describe a woman who is a virgin, as in *She's just sixteen and pure as the driven snow.*

**purpose** see AT CROSS PURPOSES; FOR ALL INTENTS AND PURPOSES; ON PURPOSE; SERVE A PURPOSE; TO GOOD PURPOSE; TO LITTLE (NO) PURPOSE.

**purse** In addition to the idiom beginning with PURSE, also see CAN'T MAKE A SILK PURSE OUT OF A SOW'S EAR.

**purse strings** Financial resources or control of them, as in *His mother doesn't want to let go of the purse strings because he may make some foolish investments.* This expression is often extended to **hold** or **tighten** or **loosen the purse strings,** as in *As long as Dad holds the purse strings, we have to consider his* *wishes,* or *The company is tightening the purse strings and will not be hiring many new people this year.* The *purse strings* in this idiom are used to open and close a drawstring purse.

**push *someone* around** Treat or threaten to treat someone roughly, bully, as in *I won't let him push me around.*

**push comes to shove, if** Also, **when push comes to shove.** When important matters must be dealt with, when a crucial point is reached, as in *If push comes to shove, the Federal Reserve Board will lower the interest rate,* or *They supposedly support equality, but when push comes to shove, they always seem to promote a man instead of a woman.* This term comes from Rugby, where, after an infraction of rules, forwards from each team face off and push against one another until one player can kick the ball to a teammate and resume the game. For a synonym, see IF WORST COMES TO WORST.

**push it** Be overly aggressive or insistent, as in *I promise to think over your proposal, but don't push it.* This idiom uses *push* in the sense of "force some activity or issue."

**push off** Also, **shove off.** Leave, set out, depart, as in *The patrol pushed off before dawn,* or *It's time to shove off.* This usage refers to the literal meaning of a person in a boat pushing against the bank or dock to move away from the shore.

**push on 1.** Also, **press on.** Continue or proceed along one's way, as in *The path was barely visible, but we pushed on,* or *It's time to push on to the next item on the agenda.* **2. push something on someone.** Force someone to accept something after he or she has refused it, as in *She's always pushing second helpings on her guests.*

**push one's luck** Also, **press one's luck.** Risk one's good fortune, often by acting too confidently, as in *We've gotten all but one of the benefits we asked for; demanding that last one would be pushing our luck,* or *You've done very well so far, but don't press your luck.*

**push paper** Do administrative, often unimportant paperwork. For example, *She spent the whole day pushing paper for her boss.*

**push someone's buttons** Also, **press someone's buttons.** Draw a strong emotional reaction from someone, especially anger or sexual arousal. For example, *My sister really knows how to push my buttons,* or *He seems to press everyone's buttons where he works.* This expression transfers starting a mechanism by pushing buttons to the arousal of human emotions.

**push the envelope** Go beyond the limits of what is normally done, start something new, as in *They are pushing the envelope in gene therapy.* This idiom comes from aviation, the *envelope* referring to the technical limits of a plane's performance.

**push the panic button** Also, **press the panic button.** Have an extreme emotional reaction to a situation, especially when it is probably not necessary. For example, *Don't worry; someone is always pushing the panic button, but I'm sure we'll get through this.*

**push up daisies** Be dead and buried, as in *There is a cemetery full of heroes pushing up daisies.* This slang expression refers to flowers growing over a grave.

**put** In addition to the idioms beginning with PUT, also see (PUT) AT EASE; BRAVE FACE, PUT ON A; CART BEFORE THE HORSE, PUT THE; CLAMP DOWN (PUT THE CLAMPS) ON; FLESH OUT (PUT FLESH ON THE BONES OF); FOR (PUT IN ONE'S) TWO CENTS; HARD PUT; (PUT) IN EFFECT; (PUT SOMEONE) IN THE PICTURE; LAY (PUT ONE'S) HANDS ON; LAY (PUT THE BLAME) ON; LAY (PUT) ONE'S CARDS ON THE TABLE; (PUT ONE'S) NOSE OUT OF JOINT; NOT PUT SOMETHING PAST SOMEONE; (PUT) OFF THE TRACK; (PUT) ON A PEDESTAL; (PUT ONE'S HEAD) ON THE BLOCK; PULL (PUT OVER) A FAST ONE; SET (PUT) SOMETHING IN MOTION; THROW OFF (PUT OFF THE SCENT). Also see under SET.

**put a bug in someone's ear** Give someone a hint about something, as in *She put a bug in her husband's ear about getting the children a dog for Christmas.*

**put *something* across 1.** Express one's ideas clearly, as in *She put her views across very well.* **2.** Attain something or carry through by tricking someone, as in *You can't put anything across this teacher.* Also see PUT SOMETHING OVER, def. 3.

**put a damper on** Stop someone from doing something, especially when he or she is excited about it, as in *Grandpa's death put a damper on our Christmas holidays.* This idiom uses the noun *damper* in the sense of "something that damps or depresses the spirits."

**put all one's eggs in one basket** Risk all of one's resources in a single venture, as in *He had warned us about investing heavily in a single stock; it was putting all our eggs in one basket.*

**put an end to** Also, **put a stop to.** End a particular activity, as in *It's time they put an end to their feud,* or *The police chief vowed to put a stop to crime.* This expression is more emphatic than the verbs *end* or *stop* alone.

**put an idea in someone's head** see PUT IDEAS INTO SOMEONE'S HEAD.

**put a premium on** Value something more highly than usual, as in *Her employer put a premium on honesty and hard work.*

**put a price on** Estimate the value of something in terms of money, as in *You can't put a price on friendship.*

**put aside 1.** Also, **put by** or **put away.** Save something, store up for future use, as in *We put aside all the toys for our grandchildren,* or *My parents put by dozens of cans of tomatoes this year,* or *She put away some of her salary every month.* **2.** Also, **set aside.** Place out of the way, as in *The clerk put the bruised fruit aside to sell at a reduced price,* or *We set aside the outdoor furniture before we water the lawn.*

**put a spin on** Give a certain meaning or interpretation to information. *Spin* is usually modified by an adjective in this expression, as in *The accountant was adept at putting a positive spin on weak financial reports,* or *This chef has put a new spin on seafood dishes.* Also see SPIN DOCTOR.

**put at ease** see AT EASE.

**put *something* at *someone's* disposal** Allow one to use, as in *They put their car at our disposal for our entire stay.*

**put away 1.** Place something in a particular spot for storage; also, place out of reach. For example, *Please put away your clothes,* or *This young tennis player can really put away the ball.* Also see PUT ASIDE, def. 1; SET ASIDE, def. 1. **2.** Get rid of something, discard, as in *Put away all those negative thoughts.* **3.** Eat quickly, as in *He put away his dinner in just a few minutes.* **4.** Confine someone to a mental health facility, as in *The doctor said we had to put her away.* **5.** Kill an animal, especially one that is old or ill, as in *The vet put our old cat away.*

**put back the clock** see SET BACK, def. 3.

**put *something* behind one** Try to forget something, make an effort not to be bothered by, as in *He had to put his failed marriage behind him and make a fresh start.*

**put by** see PUT ASIDE, def. 1; SET ASIDE, def. 1.

**put down 1.** Write something down; also, enter in a list. For example, *Please put down my name for a free ticket,* or *Put me down as a subscriber.* **2.** Bring something to an end, stop, as in *They managed to put down the rebellion in a single day,* or *We've got to put down these rumors about a takeover.* **3.** Kill a sick animal, as in *The vet said the dog must be put down.* Also see PUT AWAY, def. 5. **4.** Make someone feel inferior, as in *Her husband was always putting her down.* Also see RUN DOWN, def. 6. **5.** Identify as a cause or reason, as in *We put her poor performance down to stage fright.* **6.** Describe someone or something in a particular way, classify, as in *We put her down as a liar.* **7.** Pay a deposit for something, as in *We put down $2,000 for the car.* **8.** Store something for future use, as in *They've put down ten cases of this year's wine.* **9.** Land in an aircraft; also, land an aircraft, as in *What time will we put down at Heathrow?* or *She put the plane down exactly on the runway.* **10.** Put a child to bed, as in *The sitter said she'd put the baby down at 8:30.*

**put down roots** Settle somewhere, become established, as in *We've put down roots here and don't want to move away.* This expression compares the rooting of a plant to human settlement.

**put forth 1.** Grow something, as in *This tree puts forth new leaves each spring.* **2.** Bring something to bear, exert, as in *We'll have to put forth a great deal more effort.* **3.** Also, **set forth.** Offer something for consideration, as in *She put forth at least three new ideas.* **4.** Bring something to notice, publish, as in *The appendix puts forth a fresh analysis of events.* **5.** See SET FORTH, def. 1.

**put forward** Propose something for consideration, as in *His attorney put forward a claim on the property,* or *They put me forward for the post of chair.*

**put hair on one's chest** Make someone stronger or tougher, as in *His coffee is so strong it'll put hair on your chest.*

**put heads together** see PUT OUR HEADS TOGETHER.

**put ideas into someone's head** Also, **put an idea in someone's head.** Suggest something to someone, as in *No, we're not moving—what put that idea in your head?*

**put in 1.** Make a formal offer of, as in a court of law. For example, *He put in a plea of not guilty.* **2.** Give an opinion; interject; see PUT IN A GOOD WORD. **3.** Spend time at a location or job, as in *He put in three years at hard labor,* or *She put in eight hours a day at her desk.* **4.** Plant something, as in *We put in thirty new trees.* **5.** Enter a port or harbor, as in *The yacht will put in here for the night.* **6. put in for.** Request or apply for something, as in *I put in for a raise,* or *John put in for department supervisor.*

**put in a good word** Make a helpful remark or favorable recommendation. For example, *Please put in a good word for me with the supervisor,* or *When you see her, put in a good word for the department.* The phrase *good word* is used here in the sense of "a compliment."

**put in an appearance** Also, **make an appearance.** Be present, especially for a short time, as in *We were hoping the rock star would put in an appearance, but she didn't show up,* or *She was tired and didn't want to go to the party, but decided she had to make an appearance.*

**put in mind of** see PUT ONE IN MIND OF.

**put *something* in mothballs** Delay something indefinitely or for a very long time, as in *We've put the plans for a new library in mothballs.* This expression refers to storing woolen clothing or other items with marble-size balls of naphthalene or camphor to prevent them from being eaten by moths.

**put in one's place** see PUT SOMEONE IN HIS OR HER PLACE.

**put in one's two cents** see under FOR TWO CENTS.

**put *something* in order** Arrange something in proper sequence; see IN ORDER, def. 1. Also see PUT ONE'S HOUSE IN ORDER.

**put *something* in the way of** Also, **put *something* in one's way. 1.** Block something or keep someone from achieving a goal, as in *The police put a traffic barrier in the way of northbound motorists,* or *I don't want to put anything in the way of your advancement.* **2.** See IN ONE'S WAY, def. 2.

**put into effect** see IN EFFECT, def. 2.

**put *something* into practice** Also, **put *something* in practice.** Carry out in action, as in *It's time we put these new ideas into practice,* or *I plan to put her advice in practice.*

**put *something* into words** Express in language, as in *I find it hard to put my feelings into words.*

**put it mildly** Describe someone or something in order to downplay the actual situation, understate, as in *It's a fairly long way to walk, to put it mildly—twenty miles or so.*

**put it to 1.** Present something for consideration, as in *Let's put it to a vote,* or *I put it to you, I did the best I could under the circumstances.* **2.** Present something in a forceful, honest manner to someone, as in *I can't put it to you any more clearly—stay away from the electrical equipment.* **3.** Overload someone with tasks or work, as in *They really put it to him, expecting him to do all the packing.* **4.** Take unfair advantage of someone, cheat, as in *That used-car dealer really put it to you.*

**put lead in one's pencil** Enhance or restore sexual vigor, as in *Try one of these hot peppers; that'll put lead in your pencil.*

**put money on** Also, **put one's money on.** Bet on someone; also, consider something likely or nearly certain, expect. For example, *She put her money on the horse that came in last in the race,* or *I'm sure the President will speak to the crowd; I'd put money on it.*

**put off** Delay or postpone something, as in *He always puts off paying his bills.* This idiom led to the proverb **Never put off until tomorrow what you can do today.** Also see PUT ONE OFF, def. 2.

**put *someone* off the scent** see THROW OFF, def. 3.

**put on 1.** Clothe oneself with, as in *I put on my socks.* **2.** Apply something, activate, as in *He put on the brakes.* **3.** Pretend to have, as in *He put on a British accent.* **4. put someone on.** Tease or mislead another, as in *I don't believe you! You're putting me on.* **5.** Add something to, gain, as in *Please put this on our bill,* or *I've put on some weight.* **6.** Cause something to be performed, produce, as in *I hear they're putting a play this summer.*

**put on a brave face** see BRAVE FACE.

**put on airs** Assume a superior manner, pretend to be better than one is, as in *I'm sick of her and the way she puts on airs. Airs* here means "a manner of superiority."

**put on an act** Pretend, especially in order to deceive someone; also, show off. For example, *We were afraid he had hurt himself, but he was just putting on an act,* or *We know you're a good swimmer—stop putting on an act.*

**put *someone* on a pedestal** see ON A PEDESTAL.

**put one in mind of** Remind one of someone else, as in *You put me in mind of your grandmother.* For a synonym, see CALL SOMETHING TO MIND.

**put one into the picture** see IN THE PICTURE.

**put one off 1.** Cause someone to feel displeasure or discomfort, as in *His bad manners put her off,* or *They were put off by the bad smell.* **2. put someone off.** Persuade someone to delay further action, as in *He put off the creditors, promising to pay next week,* or *They managed to put him off from suing.*

**put one off one's stride** Also, **put one off one's stroke.** Interfere with one's progress, distract or disturb one, as in *The interruption put her off her stride for a moment, and she took several seconds to remember where she was in her speech,* or *The noise of the airplanes overhead put her off her stroke, and she missed the next ball.* The first term refers to the regular pace of a walker or runner; the variant refers to the regular strokes of a rower. Also see OFF THE TRACK.

**put one out 1.** Inconvenience one, as in *Will it put you out if we arrive early?* Also see PUT ONESELF OUT. **2.** Offend or irritate one, as in *His watching television while I visited put me out.* Also see PUT OUT.

**put one's back into it** Make a forceful, determined effort, as in *If you put your back into that report, you'll soon be done.* This idiom refers to physical labor involving the strength of one's back.

**put one's back up** see GET ONE'S BACK UP.

**put one's best foot forward** Try to make the best possible impression, make a good start, as in *Come on, let's put our best foot forward for this interview.*

**put one's cards on the table** see LAY ONE'S CARDS ON THE TABLE.

**put oneself in someone's place** Imagine being someone else, as in *Just put yourself in my place—how would you deal with it?*

**put oneself out** Make a large effort, go to a lot of trouble, as in *I put myself out trying to make everyone feel at home.* Also see PUT ONE OUT.

**put one's face on** Apply makeup, as in *My sister won't stir out of the house before she puts her face on.*

**put one's feet up** Rest, as in *After a day of gardening, I'm ready to put my feet up.*

**put one's finger on** **1.** Identify someone, as in *I can't put my finger on the man in that photo.* **2.** See LAY A FINGER ON.

**put one's foot down** Take a firm stand, as in *She put her foot down and said we could not go to the concert.* This idiom refers to setting down one's foot firmly, representing a firm position.

**put one's foot in it** Make a mistake, as in *I didn't know it was a surprise party; I guess I put my foot in it.* This expression may refer to setting one's foot down in mud or excrement. Also see FOOT IN ONE'S MOUTH.

**put one's hand to** see TURN ONE'S HAND TO.

**put one's head on the block** see ON THE BLOCK, def. 2.

**put one's house in order** Arrange one's business and personal affairs, as in *Stop meddling in your daughter's business and put your own house in order.*

**put one's mind to** Also, **set one's mind on.** Concentrate on something or be determined to do something, as in *She's put her mind to improving her test results,* or *I've set my mind on finding a job I really like.*

**put one's money on** see PUT MONEY ON.

**put one's money where one's mouth is** Support one's opinion with action, as in *He goes on and on about helping the homeless; I wish he'd put his money where his mouth is.*

**put one's nose out of joint** see NOSE OUT OF JOINT.

**put one's shoulder to the wheel** Work hard, make a great effort, as in *We'll have to put our shoulder to the wheel to get this job done.* This term refers to pushing a heavy vehicle that has gotten stuck.

**put *something* on hold** see ON HOLD.

**put *something* on ice** see ON ICE, def. 1.

**put on one's thinking cap** Think seriously, as in *A new slogan? I'll have to put on my thinking cap for that.*

**put on the dog** Also, **put on the ritz.** Behave or dress in an elegant, wealthy way, as in *They like to put on the dog when their daughter's in-laws visit,* or *They really put on the ritz for the wedding reception.*

**put on the feed bag** Also, **tie on the feed bag.** Eat a meal, as in *Come on, it's time to put on the feed bag.* This slang term refers to a horse's feed bag that is literally tied on.

**put *something* on the map** Make something famous, as in *The incident got on the national news and put our community on the map.* This expression refers to a locality that formerly was too small to put on a map.

**put *one* on the spot** see ON THE SPOT.

**put on weight** see PUT ON, def. 5.

**put our heads together** Also, **put their heads together.** Discuss or plan something among ourselves (or themselves), as in *Let's put our heads together and figure out what we can give him for his birthday.* This idiom refers to combining mental forces.

**put out** **1.** Extinguish something burning, as in *We put out the campfire before we went to bed.* **2.** Also, **put to sea.** Leave a port or harbor, as in *They put out yesterday morning.* **3.** Publish something, as in *They put out a weekly newsletter.* **4.** Engage in sex. This usage is applied only to women, as in *She had a reputation for putting out.* [Vulgar slang] Also see PUT ONE OUT.

**put out feelers** Try to learn something in a way that is not obvious or clumsy, as in *They put out feelers to see if anyone was interested in buying the company.* This idiom refers to an animal's feelers, such as antennae or tentacles, used to find food.

**put *one* out of business** see OUT OF BUSINESS.

**put *something* out of one's mind** Make oneself forget or overlook something, as in *You've lost, but put that out of your mind and focus on the job.*

**put *someone* out to pasture** Cause someone to retire, as in *That company puts workers out to pasture at 65.* This idiom refers to farm animals sent to graze when they are no longer able to work.

**put *something* over** **1.** Make something successful, as in *Do you think we can put this play over?* **2.** Make something or someone be understood or accepted, as in *The public relations staff helped put our candidate over to the public.* **3. put *something* over on.** Fool someone, deceive, as in *We can't put anything over on Tom.*

**put *something* right** Fix something, make amends, correct, as in *The wheel came off, but we can put that right in no time,* or *Our landlord thought we were moving out, but we put him right.*

**put someone away** see PUT AWAY, def. 4.

**put someone down** see PUT DOWN, def. 4.

**put someone in his or her place** Remind someone of his or her position, as in *She is entirely too rude; it's time you put her in her* *place.* The noun *place* here refers to one's rank or position.

**put someone off** see PUT ONE OFF, def. 2.

**put someone on** see PUT ON, def. 4.

**put someone out of his or her misery** **1.** Kill a wounded or suffering animal or person, as in *When a horse breaks a leg, there is nothing to do but put it out of its misery.* Also see PUT AWAY, def. 5; PUT DOWN, def. 3; PUT TO SLEEP, def. 2. **2.** End someone's feeling of suspense, as in *Tell them who won the tournament; put them out of their misery.* Both senses use *put out of* in the sense of "free from."

**put someone through his or her paces** Test thoroughly to see what someone can do, as in *We put the new programmer though her paces, and she passed with flying colors.* The idiom can refer to things as well, as in *When we put the electrical system through its paces, we blew a fuse.* The expression refers to testing a horse's ability in the various paces (trot, canter, and gallop).

**put someone up** see PUT UP, def. 6.

**put someone up to** Encourage someone to do something, especially a mischievous act. For example, *My brother put me up to making those prank telephone calls,* or *They didn't think of it on their own; someone put them up to it.*

**put something in motion** see SET SOMETHING IN MOTION.

**put that in your pipe and smoke it** Take that information and give it some thought, as in *I'm quitting at the end of the week—put that in your pipe and smoke it.*

P

**put the arm on** Also, **put the bite on** or **put the touch on.** Ask for or demand money, as in *He's the youngest, and he's always putting the arm on Dad.*

**put the blame on** see under LAY ON, def. 2.

**put the cart before the horse** see CART BEFORE THE HORSE.

**put the fear of God into** Terrify someone, as in *The school counselor put the fear of God into the girls when she talked about AIDS.*

**put the finger on** Inform on someone, as in *The witness put the finger on the defendant.*

**put the heat on** see TURN UP THE HEAT ON.

**put their heads together** see PUT OUR HEADS TOGETHER.

**put the kibosh on** Limit something, as in *The rain put the kibosh on our beach party,* or *The boss put the kibosh on the whole project.* The origin of the word *kibosh* is unknown.

**put the lid on** Also, **keep the lid on.** Suppress something, as in *I don't know how, but we'll have to put the lid on that rumor about her,* or *Let's keep the lid on our suspicions.* The word *lid* is used here in the sense of "a cover for a container."

**put the make on** Make unwanted sexual advances to, as in *He's always putting the make on his wife's friends.*

**put the screws on** see under TURN UP THE HEAT ON.

**put the skids on** Bring to a stop, as in *The school committee put the skids on the idea of a dress code.*

**put the skids under** Bring about the failure or defeat of, as in *It was lack of funds that put the skids under the new senior center.* The *skids* here are runners or rollers on which a heavy object may be moved.

**put through** **1.** Bring something to a successful conclusion, as in *We put through a number of new laws.* **2.** Make a telephone connection, as in *Please put me through to the doctor.* **3.** Cause someone to undergo, especially something difficult or troublesome, as in *He put me through a lot during this last year.* The related expression, **put someone through the wringer,** means "give someone a hard time," as in *The lawyer put the witness through the wringer.* The *wringer* referred to is an old-fashioned clothes wringer, in which clothes are pressed between two rollers to remove moisture.

**put *someone* through the wringer** see under PUT THROUGH, def. 3.

**put *something* to bed** Complete something and either set it aside or send it on to the next step, as in *We put the magazine to bed at ten,* or *They said they'd put the whole project to bed at least a month ago.* This expression was first applied to a newspaper, where it meant "send to press," that is, start to print.

**put *someone* to death** Kill someone, execute, as in *Another convicted murderer was put to death last night.*

**put *someone* to flight** Cause a person or an animal to run away, as in *The bombs put the civilians to flight.*

**put together** **1.** Build something, assemble parts or pieces, create, as in *We put together the new bookcase,* or *This writer can't put together a coherent sentence.* **2.** Combine ideas mentally, as in *Once she put things together, she knew exactly what had happened.* Also see PUT OUR HEADS TOGETHER; PUT TWO AND TWO TOGETHER.

**put to good use** Use something to the best advantage, as in *I'm sure this dictionary will be put to good use.*

**put to it, be** Be faced with a serious difficulty, as in *I was put to it to finish this book on time.*

**put *something* to rights** see SET SOMETHING TO RIGHTS. Also see PUT SOMETHING RIGHT.

**put to sea** see PUT OUT, def. 2.

**put *someone or something* to shame** Make someone or something seem inferior by comparison, as in *Your immaculate kitchen puts mine to shame.* This idiom modifies the literal sense of *put to shame,* that is, "disgrace someone," to the much milder "cause to feel inferior."

**put *someone* to sleep** **1.** Bore one utterly, as in *That show put me to sleep.* This exaggerated term suggests that something is so dull one could fall asleep. **2.** Kill an animal, especially as a kindness, as in *We had to put the cat to sleep.* Also see PUT AWAY, def. 5; PUT DOWN, def. 3; PUT SOMEONE OUT OF HIS OR HER MISERY, def. 1. **3.** Make someone unconscious, as in *This injection will put you to sleep so you won't feel any pain.*

**put *something* to the test** Try or check out something or someone, as in *This tall grass will put our new lawn mower to the test,* or *Let's put him to the test and see if he knows the last twenty World Series winners.*

**put two and two together** Figure something out from existing evidence, as in *Putting two and two together, it's not hard to guess who will be chosen for the lead role in the play.*

**putty in someone's hands** A person who is easily influenced or manipulated, as in *He adored his little granddaughter; he was putty in her hands.* This term transfers the softness of putty to human behavior. Also see TWIST SOMEONE AROUND ONE'S FINGER.

**put up** **1.** Erect something, build, as in *They put up three new houses on our street.* **2.** Place or wear something in a higher position, as in *She looks more grown-up when she puts up her hair in a bun.* **3.** Preserve food, can, as in *She put up countless jars of jam.* **4.** Propose someone for a position, as in *She put you up for president.* **5.** Provide funds, especially in advance, as in *They put up nearly a million for the new museum.* **6. put someone up.** Provide a place to sleep for, as in *We can put you up for the night.* **7.** Offer something for sale, as in *They had to put up their last antiques.* **8.** Make a display or appearance of something, as in *They were actually broke but put up a good front.* **9.** Do well in a contest, as in *They put up a good fight.* **10.** Stake money for a bet, as in *Each player put up ten dollars.*

**put up a brave front** see under BRAVE FACE.

**put-up job** A criminal plot, especially a crime such as a burglary. For example, *The police suspected that the butler was in on it—it was a put-up job.*

**put upon, be** Be taken advantage of, be imposed on, as in *My brother was always put upon by his friends, who knew he couldn't say no.* It also is put as **feel put upon,** as in *We felt quite put upon because the entire family insisted on spending every holiday at our house.*

**put up or shut up** Act on what you are saying or stop talking about it, as in *You've been citing evidence for months but never presented it—now put up or shut up.* This somewhat impolite term is often put as a command. Also see PUT ONE'S MONEY WHERE ONE'S MOUTH IS.

**put up with** Endure someone or something without complaint, as in *She's been very patient, putting up with all kinds of inconvenience.*

**put words in someone's mouth** Say what someone should say or misinterpret what someone said, as in *Give her a chance to answer my question; don't put words in her mouth.* Also see TAKE THE WORDS OUT OF ONE'S MOUTH.

**put years on one's life** Make someone look or feel older than he or she is, as in *Taking care of all these children will put years on your life.* For an antonym, see TAKE YEARS OFF ONE'S LIFE.

**puzzle out** Clarify or solve something, as in *It took him a while to puzzle out the significance of the statement.*

# Qq

**q** see MIND ONE'S P'S AND Q'S.
**Q.T.** see ON THE Q.T.
**quake in one's boots** Also, **shake in one's boots; quake like a leaf** or **shake like a leaf.** Tremble with fear, as in *The very thought of a hurricane makes me quake in my boots.* Both *quake* and *shake* here mean "tremble." The idioms with *leaf* refer to trembling leaves, as in *He was shaking like a leaf when the exams were handed back.*
**quandary** see IN A QUANDARY.
**quantity** see UNKNOWN QUANTITY.
**quantum leap** A dramatic increase, especially in knowledge or method, as in *Establishing a central bank represents a quantum leap in this small country's development.* This term originated in physics and was later transferred to other advances.
**quarrel** see PICK A QUARREL.
**quarter** see AT CLOSE QUARTERS; DRAW AND QUARTER.
**quarterback** see ARMCHAIR QUARTERBACK; MONDAY-MORNING QUARTERBACK.
**quest** see under IN SEARCH OF.
**question** see ASK A STUPID QUESTION; BEG THE QUESTION; BESIDE THE POINT (QUESTION); BEYOND QUESTION; BURNING QUESTION; CALL SOMETHING INTO QUESTION; IN QUESTION; LEADING QUESTION; LOADED QUESTION; OPEN QUESTION; OUT OF THE QUESTION; POP THE QUESTION; RHETORICAL QUESTION; WITHOUT QUESTION.
**quick** In addition to the idioms beginning with QUICK, also see CUT TO THE QUICK; (QUICK) ON THE UPTAKE.
**quick as a wink** Also, **quick as a bunny** or **quick as a flash.** Very fast, as in *He was out of here quick as a wink,* or *She answered, quick as a bunny.*
**quicker than you can say Jack Robinson** see BEFORE YOU CAN SAY JACK ROBINSON.
**quick off the mark** Fast to start or try something, as in *This physician is quick off the mark in trying the newest medications.* This expression comes from various kinds of races, where *mark* indicates the starting point.
**quick one, a** An alcoholic drink to be consumed rapidly, as in *We have time for a quick one before we board the plane.*
**quick on the draw** Also, **quick on the trigger.** Rapid in acting or reacting, as in *You have to be quick on the draw if you want to find low-cost housing here,* or *She was quick on the trigger when it came to answering questions.* The first expression came from the West's gunslingers and was later broadened to mean "a quick reaction."
**quick on the uptake** see ON THE UPTAKE.
**quid pro quo** An equal exchange or substitution, as in *I think it should be quid pro quo—you mow the lawn and I'll take you to the movies.* This Latin expression literally means "something for something."
**quiet** In addition to the idiom beginning with QUIET, also see KEEP QUIET; PEACE AND QUIET.
**quiet as a mouse** Also, **still as a mouse.** Silent, without noise, as in *She sneaked into the house, quiet as a mouse,* or *When he heard the news, he was still as a mouse.*
**quit** In addition to the idiom beginning with QUIT, also see CALL IT QUITS.
**quite a bit** Also, **quite a few** or **quite a lot.** A considerable or moderate amount, as in *There's still quite a bit of snow on the ground,* or *Quite a few parking spaces are open.*
**quit while one's ahead** Don't try to improve on something that is already done, as in *Those drapes we hung are even enough—let's quit while we're ahead.* This idiom also suggests that further action might spoil something. Also see LEAVE WELL ENOUGH ALONE.

# Rr

**R** see THREE R'S.
**rabbit** see PULL (A RABBIT) OUT OF A HAT.
**race** see RAT RACE; SLOW BUT SURE (STEADY WINS THE RACE).
**rack and ruin, go to** Also, **go to wrack and ruin.** Become decayed, decline or fall apart, as in *After the founder's death, the business went to rack and ruin.* The repetition of *rack* and *wrack* in these expressions is used for emphasis, since both words (which are different spellings of the same word) mean "destruction" or "ruin."
**rack one's brain** Strain to remember something or find a solution, as in *I've been racking my brain trying to recall where we put the key.* This term, first recorded as *rack one's wit,* refers to the *rack,* an old instrument of torture on which the victim's body was stretched until the joints were broken. Also see BEAT ONE'S BRAINS OUT.
**rack out** Go to sleep, as in *I racked out about midnight.* This slang expression, as well as the related **rack time,** for sleeping or snooze time, use *rack* to refer to being laid out on a bed.
**rack up** Accumulate or score a great deal of something, as in *The winning team racked up nine runs in the last inning.*
**rag** In addition to the idiom beginning with RAG, also see CHEW THE FAT (RAG); FROM RAGS TO RICHES; RUN SOMEONE RAGGED.
**rag doll** A weak, indecisive person, as in *You won't get a decision from her; she's a rag doll when it comes to making up her mind.* This expression transfers the limpness of a soft doll made from scraps of cloth to human behavior.
**rage** see ALL THE RAGE; ROAD RAGE.
**ragged** see RUN SOMEONE RAGGED.
**rags** see FROM RAGS TO RICHES.
**rail** see THIN AS A RAIL; THIRD RAIL.
**rain** In addition to the idioms beginning with RAIN, also see COME IN OUT OF THE RAIN; RIGHT AS RAIN; WHEN IT RAINS, IT POURS.
**rain cats and dogs** Also, **rain buckets.** Rain very heavily, as in *It was raining cats and dogs, so I couldn't walk to the store,* or *It's been raining buckets all day.*
**rain check** A promise that an unaccepted offer will be made again in the future, as in *I can't come to dinner Tuesday, but I hope you'll give me a rain check.* This term is used for tickets to entertainment events that are canceled because of bad weather or other unforeseen circumstances. It is also used for a coupon that a customer can use at a future time to buy an item, especially one on sale, that is currently out of stock.
**rain on one's parade** Spoil one's plans, as in *The minority party in the legislature has tried hard to rain on the speaker's parade, but so far his agenda has prevailed.* This expression creates the image of a downpour ruining a celebration such as a parade.
**rain or shine** No matter what the situation, as in *We promised we would finish the project tomorrow, rain or shine.* This term still refers to weather, as well as other uncertainty, and always implies that an activity will be carried out, no matter what. For a synonym, see HELL OR HIGH WATER.
**rain out** Force the cancellation or postponement of some event because of bad weather. For example, *Our picnic was rained out, but we hope to have it next week.*
**rainy day, a** A time of need or trouble, as in *We knew a rainy day would come sooner or later.* This idiom is often used in the context of **save for a rainy day,** which means put something aside for a future time of need.
**raise** In addition to the idioms beginning with RAISE, also see CAUSE RAISED EYEBROWS; CURTAIN RAISER; MAKE (RAISE) A STINK; PLAY (RAISE) HAVOC.
**raise a hand against** Also, **lift one's hand against.** Threaten to hit or actually hit someone, as in *She's never raised a hand against the children.*
**raise an objection** Protest, as in *I'll raise no objections to your proposed bill if you promise to support me next time.*
**raise a stink** see MAKE A STINK.
**raise Cain** Also, **raise hell** or **raise the devil.** Behave in a noisy and disorderly way, as in *He said he'd raise Cain if they wouldn't give him a refund,* or *The gang was out to raise hell that night,* or *The wind raised the devil with our picnic.* The first term refers to the son of Adam and Eve who killed his brother, Abel.
**raise eyebrows** see CAUSE RAISED EYEBROWS.
**raise havoc** see PLAY HAVOC.
**raise hell** see RAISE CAIN.
**raise one's hackles** Make one very angry, as in *That really raised my hackles when he pitched straight at the batter's head. Hackles* are the hairs on the back of an animal's neck,

which stick up when the animal is afraid or angry.

**raise one's sights** Establish higher goals for oneself, as in *She seemed content as a paralegal, but we thought she should raise her sights and get a law degree.* This idiom uses *sights* in the sense of "a device on a gun or optical instrument that helps one take aim." For an antonym, see LOWER ONE'S SIGHTS.

**raise one's voice** Talk louder, either to be heard more clearly or in anger, as in *You'll have to raise your voice if you expect the audience to hear you,* or *Don't you raise your voice at me!*

**raise the ante** **1.** Increase the price or cost of something, as in *We'd hoped to invest in some land, but they've raised the ante and now we can't afford it.* **2.** Also, **up the ante.** Increase demands, expectations, or risk in order to get more out of a situation. For example, *Our manager upped to ante to make us work faster.* These terms refer to the *ante* or stakes of gambling.

**raise the curtain** Also, **lift the curtain.** **1.** Begin or start something, as in *It's time to raise the curtain, guys—start shoveling.* **2.** Make something public, reveal. In this sense, both terms often occur with *on,* as in *We won't know what the new design is until they lift the curtain on it.* Both usages refer to the curtain raised at the beginning of a theatrical performance, revealing the stage.

**raise the devil** see RAISE CAIN.

**raise the roof** **1.** Be very noisy and disorderly, as in *They'd had a lot to drink and were really raising the roof last night.* **2.** Complain loudly and angrily, as in *When the landlord increased the rent, the tenants raised the roof about his lack of repairs and maintenance.* Both usages suggest the image of the roof being lifted because it cannot contain either noise or anger. Also see HIT THE CEILING.

R

**rake in** Collect a lot of money, as in *They're really raking it in after that ad campaign.*

**rake off** Make an illegal profit, as in *They suspected her of raking off some of the campaign contributions for her personal use.* This expression refers to the raking of chips by an attendant at a gambling table.

**rake *someone* over the coals** Also, **haul *someone* over the coals.** Scold someone severely, as in *When Dad finds out about the damage to the car, he's sure to rake you over the coals,* or *The coach hauled me over the coals for missing practice.*

**rake up** Revive something, bring to light, especially something unpleasant, as in *She was raking up old gossip.*

**rally around** Join in a common effort, as in *When Mom broke her leg, the entire family rallied around to help.*

**ramble on** Speak or write at length without saying very much, as in *The speaker rambled on for at least two hours, and the audience became restless.*

**ram *something* down someone's throat** Also, **shove *something* down someone's throat.** Compel to accept or consider something, as in *That salesman tried to ram a life insurance policy down my throat,* or *She has a way of shoving her political views down your throat.* These terms transfer forcing one to swallow something to forcing acceptance of an object or idea.

**rampage** see ON A RAMPAGE.

**random** see AT RANDOM.

**range** see AT CLOSE RANGE.

**rank** In addition to the idiom beginning with RANK, also see BREAK RANKS; CLOSE RANKS; PULL RANK; RISE THROUGH THE RANKS.

**rank and file** Followers, the general membership, as in *This new senator really appeals to the rank and file in the labor unions.*

**ransom** see KING'S RANSOM.

**rant and rave** Talk loudly and continuously, especially in anger, as in *There you go again, ranting and raving about the neighbor's car in your driveway.* This idiom is redundant, since *rant* and *rave* mean just about the same thing, but it probably survives because of the appealing repetition of the letter *r* at the beginning of both words.

**rap** In addition to the idiom beginning with RAP, also see BEAT THE RAP; NOT GIVE A DAMN (RAP); TAKE THE RAP.

**rap someone's knuckles** Punish someone mildly, as in *If I'd seen John take that last piece of cake, I'd have rapped his knuckles.* This term transfers a physical punishment to a verbal one.

**rare bird, a** An exceptional individual, a unique person, as in *That wife of yours is a rare bird; you're lucky to have her.* This idiom, generally used as a compliment, is a translation of the Latin *rara avis.*

**rarely ever** see HARDLY EVER.

**raring to go** Very eager to begin, as in *The children were all dressed and raring to go.* This idiom uses *raring* for *rearing,* and refers to a horse's standing on its hind legs when it is anxious to start moving.

**rat** In addition to the idioms beginning with RAT, also see LIKE A DROWNED RAT; SMELL A RAT.

**rate** see AT ANY RATE; AT THIS RATE; X-RATED.

**rather** see HAD RATHER.

**rat on** Betray a friend by giving information, as in *He ratted on the gang members to the police.*

**rat race** Fierce competition to maintain or improve one's position, especially in the workplace. For example, *You may not realize* *what a rat race it is to get research grants.* This term may refer to the rat's desperate struggle for survival.

**rattle off** Also, **reel off.** Say or perform rapidly or effortlessly, often at length. For example, *The treasurer rattled off the list of all those who had not paid their dues,* or *She reeled off song after song.* The verb *reel off* refers to unwinding something from a reel.

**rattle on** Talk without stopping about unimportant or boring topics, as in *After he'd rattled on for ten minutes, I stopped listening.*

**rattle someone's cage** Disturb or anger someone, often for no good reason, as in *He just enjoys rattling your cage,* or *You're in a bad mood today. Who rattled your cage?* This expression refers to rattling the bars of a captive animal's cage in order to upset it. Also see PULL SOMEONE'S CHAIN, def. 2.

**rave** see RANT AND RAVE; STARK RAVING MAD.

**raw** In addition to the idiom beginning with RAW, also see IN THE ALTOGETHER (RAW).

**raw deal** An instance of unfair or harsh treatment, as in *After 25 years with the bank she got a raw deal—no pension, no retirement benefits of any kind, just a gold watch. Raw* here means "crude" or "unfair."

**razor** In addition to the idiom beginning with RAZOR, also see SHARP AS A TACK (RAZOR).

**razor's edge** A very dangerous situation where a mistake could bring misfortune or failure, as in *The world has been on the razor's edge several times, but we've managed to avoid nuclear war so far.* This expression refers to the dangerous sharpness of a razor's blade.

**reach** In addition to the idiom beginning with REACH, also see GET TO (REACH) FIRST BASE; IN REACH.

**reach for the sky** **1.** Set very high goals, try for the best, as in *I'm sure they'll make you a partner, so reach for the sky.* The *sky* here stands for high aspirations. Also see SKY'S THE LIMIT. **2.** Put your hands up high, as in *One robber held the teller at gunpoint, shouting "Reach for the sky!"* This usage is always put as a command.

**reaction** see KNEE-JERK REACTION.

**read** In addition to the idioms beginning with READ, also see DO YOU READ ME; (READ SOMEONE LIKE AN) OPEN BOOK.

**read between the lines** Detect a hidden meaning in something, as in *They say that everything's fine, but reading between the lines, I suspect they have some marital problems.*

**read into** Find an additional hidden or unintended meaning in something that is said or written, as in *What I read into that speech on foreign policy is that the Vice President plans to run for President.*

**read *someone* like an open book** see OPEN BOOK.

**read someone's mind** Know what someone is thinking or feeling, as in *He often finished her sentences for her, almost as though he could read her mind.*

**read the riot act** Warn or scold someone forcefully or severely, as in *When he was caught throwing stones at the windows, the principal read him the riot act.* This term refers to an actual British law, the Riot Act of 1714, which required reading a proclamation so as to disperse a crowd; those who did not obey within an hour were guilty of a felony.

**read up on** Study or learn something by reading, as in *I don't know much about childhood illnesses, but I can always read up on them.*

**ready** In addition to the idioms beginning with READY, also see AT THE READY; GET READY; ROUGH AND READY.

**ready to roll** Prepared to leave or to begin an activity. For example, *Hurry up and get dressed; we're ready to roll,* or *The printing presses are ready to roll.*

**ready, willing, and able** Well prepared and eager to do something, as in *Any time you want me to baby-sit, I'm ready, willing, and able.*

**real** In addition to the idiom beginning with REAL, also see FOR REAL; GET REAL.

**reality check** A check to find out if one's situation or hopes conform to reality, as in *Time for a reality check—wasn't this supposed to be a money-making enterprise?*

**real McCoy, the** Also, **the McCoy.** The genuine thing, as in *That painting's not a reproduction—it's the real McCoy.*

**reap what one sows** Get back or experience the same treatment that you give, as in *I warned her not to be so mean; you reap what you sow.*

**rear** In addition to the idioms beginning with REAR, also see BRING UP THE REAR.

**rear end** **1.** The back part of anything, especially a vehicle, as in *There's a large dent in the rear end of the car.* **2.** The buttocks, as in *I'm afraid these pants don't fit my rear end.*

**rear its ugly head** Appear. This phrase is used only of something undesirable or unpleasant, as in *The interview went very well until a question about his academic record reared its ugly head.*

**reason** see BY REASON OF; IN REASON; IT STANDS TO REASON; LISTEN TO REASON; LOSE ONE'S MIND (REASON); RHYME OR REASON; SEE REASON; STAND TO REASON; WITH REASON.

**reasonable** see BEYOND A (REASONABLE) DOUBT.

**rebound** see ON THE REBOUND.

**receiving** see ON THE RECEIVING END.

**recharge one's batteries** Rest for a time in order to begin a new task or return to one unfinished with renewed energy, as in *Give* *me a little time to recharge my batteries, and we'll be able to finish the project on time.*

**recipe for disaster** A combination of people or factors in a situation that will certainly cause failure, as in *Those two working together? Now that's a recipe for disaster.* Also see ACCIDENT WAITING TO HAPPEN; SPELL DISASTER.

**reckon** In addition to the idiom beginning with RECKON, also see FORCE TO BE RECKONED WITH.

**reckon with 1.** Take someone or something into account, be prepared for, as in *The third-party movement is a force to be reckoned with during the primaries.* **2.** Deal with, as in *Your lost wallet isn't the only problem we have to reckon with.* Also see TAKE SOMETHING INTO ACCOUNT.

**record** see BREAK THE RECORD; GO ON RECORD; JUST FOR THE RECORD; OFF THE RECORD; SET (THE RECORD) STRAIGHT; TRACK RECORD.

**red** In addition to the idioms beginning with RED, also see CATCH SOMEONE RED-HANDED; IN THE RED; NOT WORTH A DAMN (RED CENT); PAINT THE TOWN RED; SEE RED.

**red carpet** Treatment worthy of nobility, lavish hospitality, as in *We'll have to get out the red carpet for the President's visit.* This term comes from the literal practice of rolling out a carpet to welcome a member of royalty or other esteemed guest. Indeed, it is often put as **roll out the red carpet.** The expression is also used as an adjective, as in *The company gave the new chairman red-carpet treatment.*

**red cent** see NOT WORTH A DAMN.

**redeeming feature** Also, **redeeming value.** A good quality or aspect that makes up for other less desirable features, as in *The house isn't very attractive, but the garden is the redeeming feature.* This idiom uses *redeem* in the sense of "compensate."

R

**red herring, a** Something that draws attention away from the central issue, as in *Talking about the new factory is a red herring to keep us from learning about the company's downsizing plans.* The *herring* in this expression is a fish that is red and strong-smelling from being preserved by smoking. The idiom refers to dragging a smoked herring across a trail to cover up the scent and throw off tracking dogs.

**red in the face, be** Suffer embarrassment or shame; also, exert oneself. For example, *He was red in the face from all of the mistakes he made while announcing the winners' names,* or *You can try until you're red in the face, but you still won't get straight A's.* This expression is also put as an interjection, **Is my face red!** meaning "I am very embarrassed or ashamed."

**red-letter day, a** A special occasion, as in *When Jack comes home from college, that'll be a red-letter day.* This term refers to the practice of marking feast days and other holy days in red on church calendars.

**red tape** Official forms and procedures, especially those that are complex and time-consuming. For example, *There's a lot of red tape involved in getting a building permit.* This expression refers to the former British custom of tying up official documents with red ribbon.

**reel off** see RATTLE OFF.

**reference** see IN REGARD (REFERENCE) TO.

**reflect on 1.** Consider or think carefully about something, as in *She reflected on her country's role in history.* A closely related phrase is **on due reflection,** meaning "after careful consideration." For example, *On due reflection I decided to vote for the new candidate.* **2. reflect on one.** Give evidence of one's qualities, as in *The poor preparation of this report will reflect on you.*

**regard** see IN REGARD TO.

**region** see IN THE NEIGHBORHOOD (REGION) OF.

**regular as clockwork** see LIKE CLOCKWORK.

**regular guy** Also, **regular fellow.** A nice or agreeable person, as in *Luke's a regular guy,* or *Hilda's a regular fellow.*

**rein** see DRAW IN THE REINS; FREE HAND (REIN) TIGHT REIN ON.

**reinvent the wheel** Do something again, from the beginning, especially in a needless or wasteful effort, as in *School committees need not reinvent the wheel every time they try to improve the curriculum.*

**relation** see POOR RELATION; RELATIVE (IN RELATION) TO.

**relative to** In terms of amount or proportion; also, pertaining to, as in *Relative to its size, Boston has a great many universities,* or *It's important to get all the facts relative to the accident.* Another form of this idiom is **in relation to** or **with relation to,** meaning "in reference or with regard to," as in *Demand is high in relation to supply,* or *That argument changes nothing with relation to our plans for hiring workers.*

**relieve oneself** Urinate or defecate, as in *The puppy relieved itself in the middle of the floor.*

**relieve someone of 1.** Take something away from someone, rob someone of something, as in *The pickpocket relieved the tourist of his wallet.* **2.** Take away a burden or responsibility, as in *The doorman relieved her of her packages,* or *He was relieved of all his duties.*

**religion** see GET RELIGION.

**remain** see WHO SHALL REMAIN NAMELESS.

**repeat oneself** Express oneself in the same way or with the same words, as in *Grandma forgets she has told us this story before and repeats herself over and over,* or *This architect tends to repeat himself—all his houses look alike.* A well-known version of this idiom is **history repeats itself,** as in *Her mother also married when she was 18—history repeats itself.*

**request** see AT SOMEONE'S REQUEST; BY REQUEST; ON REQUEST.

**requirement** see MEET THE REQUIREMENTS.

**resistance** see LEAST RESISTANCE.

**resort** see LAST RESORT.

**resources** see LEAVE SOMEONE TO HIS OR HER RESOURCES.

**respect** see IN REGARD (WITH RESPECT) TO; PAY A CALL (ONE'S RESPECTS); WITH ALL DUE RESPECT.

**rest** In addition to the idioms beginning with REST, also see AT REST; LAY AT REST; LAY TO REST; SET ONE'S MIND AT REST.

**rest assured** You can be sure, as in *Rest assured that the police will recover your diamonds.* This expression uses *assured* in the sense of "certain" or "confident."

**rest on one's laurels** Rely on one's past achievements, especially as a way of avoiding the work needed to advance professionally. For example, *Now that James is in his eighties, he's decided to rest on his laurels and let some of the younger agents do the work.* This term refers to the crown of laurels awarded in ancient times for a great achievement.

**retreat** see BEAT A RETREAT.

**return** In addition to the idioms beginning with RETURN, also see IN RETURN; MANY HAPPY RETURNS; POINT OF NO RETURN.

**return the compliment** Also, **return the favor.** Repay someone in the same manner, as in *Her political opponent came out with a negative campaign, and she returned the compliment.* Neither the *compliment* nor the *favor* in this idiom need to be pleasant.

**return to the fold** Come back to a group after an absence, as in *Our neighbor taught for a number of years, but now he's returned to the fold as vice president of the firm.* This term uses *fold* in the sense of "an enclosure for sheep."

**revolve** see THINK THE WORLD REVOLVES AROUND ONE.

**rev up** Increase the speed or rate of a machine or an activity, make more lively, stimulate, as in *Bill revved up the motor,* or *They looked for ways to rev up the ad campaign.* The verb *rev* is a shortening of *revolution,* which refers here to the rate of rotation of an engine.

**rhetorical question, a** A question asked for the sake of emphasis or effect. The expected answer is usually "yes" or "no." For example, *Can we improve the quality of our work? That's a rhetorical question—we all know the answer.*

**rhyme or reason, no** With no common sense or logic, as in *This memo has no rhyme or reason.* Closely related variants are **without rhyme or reason,** as in *The conclusion of her paper was without rhyme or reason,* and **neither rhyme nor reason,** as in *Neither rhyme nor reason will explain that lawyer's objections.*

**rib** see STICK TO THE RIBS.

**rich** see EMBARRASSMENT OF RICHES; FROM RAGS TO RICHES; STRIKE IT RICH.

**rid** see GET RID OF.

**riddance** see GOOD RIDDANCE.

**ride** In addition to the idioms beginning with RIDE, also see ALONG FOR THE RIDE; GO ALONG (FOR THE RIDE); HITCH A RIDE; LET RIDE; TAKE SOMEONE FOR A RIDE.

**ride hell-bent for leather** see HELL-BENT FOR LEATHER.

**ride herd on** Keep close watch or tight control over someone, as in *My aunt is always riding herd on her children, making sure they follow the rules.* This idiom refers to a cowboy who rides around a herd of cattle to keep them together.

**ride high** Enjoy success, as in *He's been riding high ever since they made him vice president.*

**ride out** Live through something difficult, outlast, as in *They rode out the storm,* or *Times were hard during the depression, but we managed to ride it out.* Also see WEATHER THE STORM.

**ride roughshod over** Act without regard for the feelings or interests of others, as in *She rode roughshod over her colleagues at the office.*

**ride shotgun** **1.** Guard someone or something while moving from one place to another, as in *The reporter found himself in the odd position of riding shotgun for an accused mobster.* **2.** Sit in the front passenger seat of a car, as in *My oldest son always wants to ride shotgun.* This term refers to the armed defender of a stagecoach who sat beside the driver to protect against robbers. Later it was transferred to anyone riding in the front passenger seat of a motor vehicle, as well as to the more general function of protection.

**ride up** Gradually move upward from a normal position, as in *This skirt is too tight and it constantly rides up.*

**ridiculous** see FROM THE RIDICULOUS TO THE SUBLIME.

**riding for a fall, be** Seek or encourage one's ruin, as in *I think that anyone who backs the governor is riding for a fall.* This idiom refers to a careless rider who risks a bad fall from a horse.

**rid of** see GET RID OF.

**right** In addition to the idioms beginning with RIGHT, also see ALL RIGHT; ALL RIGHT FOR YOU; ALL RIGHT WITH ONE; BRAGGING RIGHTS; BY RIGHTS; COME (RIGHT) OUT WITH; DEAD TO RIGHTS; GET RIGHT; GIVE ONE'S EYETEETH (RIGHT ARM); GO RIGHT; HANG A LEFT (RIGHT); HAVE A RIGHT TO; HAVE A SCREW LOOSE (ONE'S HEAD SCREWED ON RIGHT); HEART IN THE RIGHT PLACE; IN ONE'S OWN RIGHT; IN ONE'S RIGHT MIND; IN THE RIGHT; IN THE RIGHT PLACE AT THE RIGHT TIME; LEFT HAND DOESN'T KNOW WHAT THE RIGHT HAND IS DOING; MIGHT MAKES RIGHT; NOT RIGHT IN THE HEAD; (RIGHT) ON THE BUTTON; (RIGHT) ON THE MONEY; ON THE RIGHT FOOT; ON THE RIGHT TACK; PLAY ONE'S CARDS RIGHT; PRICE IS RIGHT; PUT SOMETHING RIGHT; SAIL (RIGHT) THROUGH; SERVE ONE RIGHT; SET SOMETHING RIGHT; SET SOMETHING TO RIGHTS; STEP IN THE RIGHT DIRECTION; STRIKE THE RIGHT NOTE; THAT'S RIGHT; TURN OUT ALL RIGHT; TWO WRONGS DO NOT MAKE A RIGHT; WHEN IT COMES (RIGHT DOWN) TO.

**right and left** Also, **left and right.** In or from all directions, on every side, as in *Questions were coming right and left,* or *She was giving orders left and right.* This idiom uses the directions *right* and *left* to mean all sides.

**right as rain** In good order or good health, satisfactory, as in *He was very ill, but he's right as rain now,* or *If she'd only worked on it another week, everything would have been as right as rain.*

**right away** Also, **right off.** Without delay, immediately, as in *Can you bring our dinners right away? We're in a hurry,* or *We liked her right off.* Also see RIGHT OFF THE BAT.

R

**right down one's alley** see RIGHT UP ONE'S ALLEY.

**right-hand man** Also, **right-hand woman.** A trusted helper, as in *Give it to my assistant, she's my right-hand man.* This idiom is based on the idea that in most people the right hand is stronger than the left.

**right in the head** see NOT RIGHT IN THE HEAD.

**right off** see RIGHT AWAY.

**right off the bat** Instantly, immediately, as in *I can't tell you how many right off the bat, but I can find out.* This term refers to a baseball being hit by a bat.

**right of way 1.** The right of one person or vehicle to travel over another's property, as in *The new owner doesn't like it, but hikers have had the right of way through these woods for years.* **2.** The right to precede another person or vehicle, as in *Sailboats always have the right of way over motorboats, and swimmers do over any kind of boat.*

**right on!** An exclamation of enthusiasm or encouragement, as in *You've said it really well—right on!* Also see WAY TO GO.

**right out** Also, **straight out.** Plainly, without holding back, as in *He told her right out that he didn't want to go,* or *When my sister told us she wanted to become a doctor, Dad said straight out that he couldn't afford medical school.*

**right side, on someone's** Also, **on someone's good side.** Liked or favored by someone. It is often put as **get** or **keep** or **stay on someone's right side,** as in *We must get on Bill's right side if we're to get approval of our plans,* or *Jane had a hard time staying on the good side of her difficult supervisor.* The antonym **on someone's wrong side** means "dislike by someone or in someone's disfavor," as in *I got on her wrong side by opening my mouth once too often.*

**right side of the tracks, the** The desirable part of town, as in *They were relieved to learn that his fiancée came from the right side of the tracks.* This expression refers to the fact that when a railroad ran through a town, it often divided the rich neighborhoods from the poor ones. Today this term is considered snobbish. For an antonym, see WRONG SIDE OF THE TRACKS.

**right-side out** Turned correctly, with the outer side on the outside, as opposed to INSIDE OUT, def. 1. For example, *I turned the sweater right-side out before putting it on.*

**right-side up** With the top correctly facing upward, as in *Please keep the box holding the china right-side up,* or *He turned his cards right-side up.*

**right tack** Also, **right track.** See ON THE RIGHT TACK (TRACK).

**right up one's alley** Also, **right down one's alley.** In one's specialty, to one's taste, as in *Writing press releases is right up her alley,* or *He loved opera, so this program was right down his alley.* Also see CUP OF TEA.

**Riley** see LIFE OF RILEY.

**ring** In addition to the idioms beginning with RING, also see BRASS RING; GIVE SOMEONE A RING; HAVE A FAMILIAR RING; RUN RINGS AROUND; THREE-RING CIRCUS; THROW ONE'S HAT IN THE RING.

**ring a bell** Remind one of something, as in *That name rings a bell—I think I've met him.* The *bell* here calls up a memory.

**ring down the curtain on** Bring something to an end, as in *We should stay at that grand old hotel before they ring down the curtain on it.* This idiom refers to the old practice of signaling that a theater curtain be lowered at the ring of a bell. Similarly, **ring**

up the curtain on refers to a bell rung to begin a performance and came to mean starting anything, as in *Their contribution rang up the curtain on the fund drive.*

**ring false** Also, **have a false ring** or **have a hollow ring; strike a false note.** Seem wrong or untrue, as in *Her denial rings false—I'm sure she was there when it happened,* or *His good wishes always seem to have a hollow ring,* or *Her congratulatory phone call really struck a false note.* **Ring false** and its antonym, **ring true,** which means "real or true," refer to the old practice of judging a coin to be genuine or fake by the sound it gives out when tapped. Also see RING HOLLOW.

**ring hollow** Sound insincere, lack substance, as in *Such flattery rings hollow after what he did,* or *Her assertions of undying love rang hollow to his ears.* Also see RING FALSE.

**ring one's chimes** Get one's attention, excite one, as in *That kind of music really rings my chimes.*

**ringside seat** A place providing a close view of something, as in *We lived right next door, so we had ringside seats for our neighbors' quarrels.* This term may have come from boxing, where it refers to the seats just outside the boxing ring.

**ring true** see under RING FALSE.

**ring up** **1.** Record a sale, especially by means of a cash register, as in *They had already rung up the sale so I decided not to get the extra items.* Although older cash registers usually signaled a recorded sale with the ringing of a bell, the idiom survives in the age of computers. **2.** Accomplish something, achieve, as in *They rang up an impressive string of victories.*

**riot** see READ THE RIOT ACT; RUN AMOK (RIOT).

**rip** In addition to the idioms beginning with RIP, also see LET IT RIP; TEAR (RIP) SOMEONE LIMB FROM LIMB.

**ripe** In addition to the idiom beginning with RIPE, also see TIME IS RIPE.

**ripe old age** An age advanced in years, as in *I expect to live to a ripe old age,* or *She lived to the ripe old age of 100.* The adjective *ripe* means "fully developed physically," but the current use of the idiom usually just signifies a long life span.

**rip into** Also, **tear into.** Attack or criticize something or someone vehemently, as in *She ripped into her opponent's voting record.* These expressions allude to the literal senses of the verbs *rip* and *tear,* that is, "cut" or "slash."

**rip off** **1.** Steal something, as in *They fired him when they caught him ripping off the merchandise.* **2.** Cheat someone, as in *These advertising claims have ripped off a great many consumers.* **3.** Steal someone else's ideas or work, as in *He was sued for ripping off someone else's thesis.*

**rise** In addition to the idioms beginning with RISE, also see COME UP (RISE IN THE WORLD); GET A RISE OUT OF; GIVE BIRTH (RISE) TO.

**rise and shine** An expression used when waking someone up, as in *It's past seven, children—rise and shine!*

**rise from the ashes** Emerge as new from something that has been destroyed, as in *A few months after the earthquake, large sections of the city had risen from the ashes.* This expression refers to a legendary bird, the phoenix, which supposedly rose from the ashes of its funeral pyre with renewed youth.

**rise in the world** see COME UP, def. 3.

**rise through the ranks** Also, **rise from the ranks; come up through the ranks.** Work one's way to the top, as in *He's risen through the ranks, starting in the mailroom and ending up as president.* Originally this term was used for a military officer who had worked his way up from the rank of private. Also see COME UP, def. 3.

**rise to the bait** Be tempted by or react to an appealing offer, as in *We told him there'd be lots of single young women at the party, and he rose to the bait.* This idiom compares a fish enticed by bait to human behavior.

**rise to the occasion** Show unexpected skill in dealing with a problem, as in *The actor broke his leg in the first act, but his understudy rose to the occasion and was rewarded with excellent reviews.*

**risk** In addition to the idiom beginning with RISK, also see AT RISK; CALCULATED RISK; RUN A RISK.

**risk life and limb** Also, **risk one's neck.** Take dangerous chances, as in *He was on the roof, risking life and limb to rescue the kitten,* or *I don't want to risk my neck contradicting him.* Also see STICK ONE'S NECK OUT.

**river** see SELL DOWN THE RIVER; UP THE RIVER.

**road** In addition to the idioms beginning with ROAD, also see DOWN THE LINE (ROAD); END OF THE LINE (ROAD); GET THE SHOW ON THE ROAD; HIT THE ROAD; ONE FOR THE ROAD; ON THE ROAD.

**road hog** A motorist whose vehicle occupies portions of two traffic lanes, as in *Stay in your own lane, you road hog!* This expression uses *hog* in the sense of "a greedy or selfish person."

**road rage** Anger or hostility directed at the drivers of other vehicles or at their way of driving, as in *That six-car accident was caused by road rage.*

**road show** A tour made for a particular purpose, especially a political campaign. For example, *Every would-be candidate was planning a road show.* This term originated for touring theatrical productions and later was transferred to other activities.

**road to hell is paved with good intentions, the** Well-intended acts can have very bad results, as in *She tried to help by defending Dad's position, and they haven't spoken since—the road to hell is paved with good intentions.*

**robbery** see DAYLIGHT ROBBERY; HIGHWAY ROBBERY.

**Robinson** see BEFORE YOU CAN SAY JACK ROBINSON.

**rob Peter to pay Paul** Take from one to give to another, transfer resources. For example, *They took out a second mortgage on their house so they could buy a condo in Florida—they're robbing Peter to pay Paul.*

**rob someone blind** Cheat someone in a very dishonest or complete manner, as in *The nurse was robbing the old couple blind.* This idiom may refer to robbing a blind beggar, who cannot see that the cup for donations is being emptied.

**rob the cradle** Have a romantic or sexual relationship with someone much younger than oneself, as in *The old actor was notorious for robbing the cradle, always trying to date some young actress.*

**rob the till** see HAND IN THE TILL.

**rock** In addition to the idioms beginning with ROCK, also see BETWEEN A ROCK AND A HARD PLACE; ON THE ROCKS; STEADY AS A ROCK.

**rock bottom** The lowest possible level, absolute bottom, as in *Wheat prices have reached rock bottom.* This idiom is also often used as an adjective, as in *That store sells furniture at rock-bottom prices.*

**rocker** see OFF ONE'S HEAD (ROCKER).

**rocks in one's head, have** Show poor judgment, act stupidly, as in *If you think that's an accurate summary, you've got rocks in your head.*

R

**rock the boat** Disturb a stable situation, as in *An easygoing manager, he won't rock the boat unless it's absolutely necessary.*

**rod** see HOT ROD; SPARE THE ROD AND SPOIL THE CHILD.

**roll** In addition to the idioms beginning with ROLL, also see EASY AS PIE (ROLLING OFF A LOG); GET ROLLING; GET THE BALL ROLLING; HEADS WILL ROLL; ON A ROLL; READY TO ROLL; RED CARPET, ROLL OUT THE.

**roll around** Return or happen again, as in *When income tax time rolls around, she is too busy to play tennis.*

**roll back** Decrease, cut back, or reduce, especially prices, as in *Unless they roll back oil prices, this summer's tourist traffic will be half of last year's.*

**rolled into one** Also, **all rolled into one.** Two or more people, things, or qualities combined, as in *This tool is a hammer, screwdriver, and drill rolled into one,* or *Working as a team, those workers have intelligence, experience, and skill, all rolled into one.*

**roll in** **1.** Go to bed for the night, as in *It's time to roll in—we'll see you in the morning.* **2.** Add something, as in *She tried to roll in several new clauses, but the publisher would not agree.* **3.** Arrive, flow, or pour in, as in *The football fans have been rolling in since this morning.* **4.** Enjoy ample amounts of something, especially wealth, as in *Ask the neighbors for a donation—they're rolling in money.* This idiom refers to having so much of something that one can roll around in it (as a pig might roll in mud). It is sometimes put as **rolling in it,** the *it* meaning money. Also see ROLL IN THE AISLES; ROLL IN THE HAY.

**rolling stone, a** A person who moves about a great deal and never settles down, as in *My sister lived in ten cities in as many years—she's a real rolling stone.* This expression is a shortening of the proverb **a rolling stone gathers no moss.**

**roll in the aisles** Laugh a lot, as in *The writer's new book had them rolling in the aisles.* This exaggerated idiom refers something that causes an audience to laugh so hard that they might roll about in the theater's aisles.

**roll in the hay** Sexual intercourse, as in *The main character in the movie was always looking for a roll in the hay.* This phrase refers to secret lovemaking in a hayloft.

**roll out** **1.** Get out of bed, as in *I rolled out around six o'clock this morning.* **2.** Introduce something, reveal, as in *They rolled out the new model cars with great fanfare.*

**roll out the red carpet** see RED CARPET.

**roll over** Reinvest profits from one investment back into that investment or into another, as in *Our broker advised us to roll over the proceeds into a tax shelter.*

**roll up** **1.** Accumulate something, as in *He rolled up a fortune in commodity trading,* or *She rolled up a huge number of votes in this district.* **2.** Arrive in a vehicle, as in *They rolled up in a taxi at exactly eight o'clock.*

**roll up one's sleeves** Get ready to work, as in *When he saw how much snow had fallen, he simply rolled up his sleeves and went to find the shovel.* This expression, which refers to turning up one's sleeves to avoid getting them wet or dirty, is used both literally and more loosely, as in the example here.

**roll with the punches** Deal with hard times or a bad situation successfully, especially by being able to change one's behavior as necessary. For example, *She'd had three different lawyers for her case, each with a different style, but she'd learned to roll with the punches.* This term refers to the boxer's ability to avoid the full force of an opponent's blow by quickly moving his body.

**Roman** see WHEN IN ROME DO AS THE ROMANS DO.

**Rome** In addition to the idiom beginning with ROME, also see FIDDLE WHILE ROME BURNS; WHEN IN ROME DO AS THE ROMANS DO.

**Rome wasn't built in a day** Important work takes time. This expression functions as a request for someone to be patient. For example, *You can't expect her to finish this project in one week; Rome wasn't built in a day.*

**roof** In addition to the idiom beginning with ROOF, also see GO THROUGH THE ROOF; HIT THE CEILING (ROOF); LIKE A CAT ON A HOT TIN ROOF; RAISE THE ROOF.

**roof over one's head, a** A shelter, especially a home, as in *I can barely afford to put a roof over my head, my salary is so low.*

**rooftop** see SHOUT FROM THE ROOFTOPS.

**room** In addition to the idiom beginning with ROOM, also see NOT ENOUGH ROOM TO SWING A CAT.

**room and board** A place to stay and one's meals, as in *The university's price for room and board has increased by another 10 percent.*

**roost** see CHICKENS COME HOME TO ROOST; RULE THE ROOST.

**root** In addition to the idioms beginning with ROOT, also see PUT DOWN ROOTS; TAKE ROOT.

**rooted to the spot** Unable to move, especially because of some strong emotion such as fear. For example, *The dog was terrified and stood rooted to the spot as the truck bore down on it.* This idiom compares the roots of a plant to a strong feeling that keeps one from moving.

**root for** Cheer on someone, give moral support to, as in *The fans were out rooting for their team,* or *I've been rooting for you to get that promotion.*

**root of the matter** Also, **heart of the matter** or **crux of the matter.** The most important part or cause of something, as in *We still don't understand what happened; we must get to the root of the matter.*

**root out** Search for a source or an explanation, seek to discover, as in *He was trying to root out the reason for her long absence.* This idiom refers to the way pigs dig in the ground.

**rope** In addition to the idiom beginning with ROPE, also see END OF ONE'S ROPE; ENOUGH ROPE; KNOW (SHOW SOMEONE) THE ROPES; ON THE ROPES.

**rope *someone* in** Also, **rope *someone* into.** Convince someone by lying or continued insistence to do something he or she does not want to do, as in *We didn't want to spend the night there, but we got roped in by my aunt,* or *The salesman tried to rope us into buying some worthless real estate.* These expressions refer to catching an animal by throwing a rope around it.

**rose** see BED OF ROSES; COMING UP ROSES; SEE THROUGH ROSE-COLORED GLASSES.

**rote** see BY HEART (ROTE).

**rotten apple** A bad person among many good ones who ruins the whole group. For example, *The roommates are having problems with Jane—she's the one rotten apple of the bunch.* This expression is a shortening of the proverb **a rotten apple spoils the barrel.**

**rotten egg** see under BAD EGG.

**rotten to the core** Completely bad or evil, as in *Those drug dealers are rotten to the core.* The noun *core* here refers to the central part or heart of anything or anyone.

**rough** In addition to the idioms beginning with ROUGH, also see DIAMOND IN THE ROUGH; RIDE ROUGHSHOD OVER; TAKE THE ROUGH WITH THE SMOOTH.

**rough and ready** Unfinished or hastily made but available for use, as in *The agenda is somewhat rough and ready, but it covers the main issues.*

**rough and tumble** Disorderly scuffling or fighting, as in *She had some concerns about entering the rough and tumble of local politics.* This expression originated in boxing, where it referred to a fight without rules.

**rough it** Be without the usual comforts and conveniences, as in *We spent our vacation roughing it in a log cabin.*

**rough on, be 1.** Be harmful to someone or something or difficult for, as in *The harsh winter has been rough on the highways,* or *Their divorce was rough on the whole family.* **2.** Treat someone or something harshly, be severe with, as in *The police have been very rough on thieves,* or *Don't be too rough on him; he's only a child.*

**rough out** Also, **rough in.** Prepare or indicate something in unfinished form, as in *He roughed out several plans for a merger,* or *They roughed in with the architect where they wanted the doors for the new patio.*

**rough up** Beat someone up, cause physical harm to, as in *The gang was about to rough him up when the police arrived.*

**round** In addition to the idioms beginning with ROUND, also see ALL YEAR ROUND; BRING AROUND (ROUND); COME AROUND (ROUND); GET AROUND (ROUND); IN ROUND NUMBERS; IN THE ROUND; MAKE THE ROUNDS; OTHER WAY ROUND; PULL ROUND; RALLY AROUND. Also see under AROUND.

**round and round** Also, **around and around.** In circles, as in *You've gone round and round with him, and he still won't listen.* This idiom transfers moving in a circle to mental or verbal activities.

**round figures** see IN ROUND NUMBERS.

**round off 1.** Change a number to the closest whole number or the closest multiple of 10.

R

For example, *Rounding it off, I expect the new school addition will cost a million dollars.* **2.** Also, **round out.** Finish something, complete, especially in an appropriate or perfect way. For example, *They rounded off the dinner with a magnificent dessert,* or *That stamp rounded out his collection.*

**round out 1.** See ROUND OFF, def. 2. **2.** Grow or develop to a round form, as in *The horse was thin when we first got it, but it has since rounded out nicely.*

**round peg in a square hole** see SQUARE PEG IN A ROUND HOLE.

**round robin** In sports, a tournament in which each player or team plays against all of the others in turn. For example, *The club always holds a tennis round robin on the Fourth of July.*

**round the bend** see AROUND THE BEND, def. 2.

**round trip** A journey to a given place and back again, usually over the same route; also, a ticket for such a trip. For example, *The fare for a round trip is generally lower than for two one-way journeys.* This expression is also used as an adjective, as in *I bought a round-trip ticket to Hawaii.*

**roundup** see HEAD FOR (THE LAST ROUNDUP). Also see ROUND UP.

**round up 1.** Bring together or gather people or things in a body, as in *We'll have to round up some more volunteers for the food drive,* or *The police rounded up all the suspects,* or *Please round up all the files that pertain to this project.* This usage comes from the West, where it has long been used for collecting livestock by riding around the herd and driving the animals together. **2.** Express a number as a higher amount, as in *Just round up the bill to the nearest dollar.*

R

**row** see GET ONE'S DUCKS IN A ROW; KICK UP A FUSS (ROW); SKID ROW; TOUGH ROW TO HOE.

**rub** In addition to the idioms beginning with RUB, also see THE RUB.

**rubber check** A check drawn on an account without the funds to pay it, as in *He's been writing rubber checks everywhere, but the police have finally caught up with him. Rubber* here refers to the fact that, like rubber, the check "bounces," in this case back from the bank.

**rubber stamp** A person or an organization that automatically approves or endorses a policy without judging its merit; also, such an approval or endorsement. For example, *The nominating committee is merely a rubber stamp; they approve anyone the chairman names,* or *The dean gave his rubber stamp to the recommendations of the tenure committee.* This term refers to a rubber printing device used to imprint the same words over and over.

**rubbish** see GOOD RIDDANCE (TO BAD RUBBISH).

**rub down** Briskly rub the body, as in a massage. For example, *The trainer rubs down marathon runners,* or *That horse needs rubbing down.*

**rub elbows with** Also, **rub shoulders with.** Mix or socialize with, as in *He likes rubbing elbows with the rich and famous,* or *At the reception diplomats were rubbing shoulders with heads of state.* Both of these terms refer to being in close contact with someone.

**rub in** Also, **rub it in.** Mention something over and over, especially an unpleasant matter, as in *She always rubs in the fact that she graduated with honors and I didn't,* or *I know I forgot your birthday, but don't keep rubbing it in.* Also see RUB SOMEONE'S NOSE IN IT.

**rub off on** Pass something on to or be affected by someone, influence through close contact, as in *We hoped some of their good manners would rub off on our children.* This idiom refers to transferring something like paint to another substance by rubbing against it.

**rub one's hands** Show pleased anticipation or self-satisfaction, as in *The owner rubbed his hands as the customer picked out item after item.* This term refers to the actual rubbing together of one's hands to show happiness.

**rub out 1.** Erase something by, or as if by, rubbing. For example, *The editor was so busy rubbing out the old markings that he forgot to put in new ones.* **2.** Murder someone, kill, as in *They threatened to rub him out if he didn't pay up.*

**rub salt in the wound** Make someone who feels upset or sad about an event or a situation feel even worse, as in *It was bad enough I couldn't go on the trip, but to rub salt in the wound, everyone sent me post cards saying what a great time they were having.* This idiom refers to an action that makes a wound more painful.

**rub someone's nose in it** Bring something, especially an error or fault, repeatedly and forcefully to someone's attention. For example, *I know I was wrong, but don't rub my nose in it.* This expression refers to the unkind practice of teaching a dog not to defecate in the house by rubbing its nose in its feces.

**rub *one* the wrong way** Affect one in a negative way, as in *His remarks about welfare rubbed a great many people the wrong way.* This idiom refers to rubbing an animal's fur in the wrong direction. Also see RUFFLE SOMEONE'S FEATHERS.

**ruffle someone's feathers** Annoy or offend someone, as in *Calling him greedy really ruffled his feathers.* This term refers to the stiff, upright feathers of an angry bird.

**rug** see PULL THE RUG OUT FROM UNDER; SWEEP UNDER THE RUG. Also see under CARPET.

**ruin** see RACK AND RUIN.

**rule** In addition to the idioms beginning with RULE, also see AS A RULE; BEND THE RULES; EXCEPTION PROVES THE RULE; GROUND RULES.

**rule of thumb** A rough and useful principle or method, based on experience rather than accurate measurements. For example, *As a rule of thumb, you'll need about one pound of meat for four people.*

**rule out** **1.** Eliminate someone or something from consideration, exclude, as in *We've ruled out the option of starting over again.* **2.** Prevent something, make impossible, as in *The snowstorm ruled out our weekly meeting.*

**rule the roost** Be in charge, boss others, as in *In our division the chairman's son rules the roost.* Also see RUN THE SHOW.

**run** In addition to the idioms beginning with RUN, also see BEAT (RUN) ONE'S HEAD AGAINST THE WALL; CUT AND RUN; DRY RUN; EAT AND RUN; END RUN; GO (RUN) AROUND IN CIRCLES; HIT AND RUN; HOME RUN; IN THE LONG RUN; MAKE A BREAK (RUN) FOR; MAKE ONE'S BLOOD RUN COLD; (RUN) OFF ONE'S FEET; ON THE RUN; STILL WATERS RUN DEEP; TRIAL RUN; WELL'S RUN DRY. Also see under RUNNING.

**run across** see COME ACROSS, def. 1.

**run a fever** Also, **run a temperature.** Suffer from a body temperature higher than normal, as in *She was running a fever, so I kept her home from school.* These idioms use *run* in the sense of "cause to move," in this case upward.

**run afoul of** Also, **run foul of.** Come into conflict with, as in *If you keep parking illegally, you'll run afoul of the police.*

**run after** Also, **chase after.** **1.** Follow someone, pursue with haste, as in *Our dog loves to run after cars,* or *The children were chasing after the geese in the park.* **2.** Seek the company or attention of someone, especially aggressively. For example, *He's run after her for a year, but she just ignores him.*

**run against** **1.** Also, **run up against** or **run into.** Encounter something, especially a difficulty, unexpectedly. For example, *We didn't know we'd run up against so much opposition,* or *He ran into trouble with his taxes.* **2.** Work against someone, as in *Public sentiment ran against her.* **3.** Oppose someone for elective office, as in *Susan decided to run against the current mayor.*

**run along** Go away, leave, as in *I'll be running along now; I'm already late.* This expression is also used as a command to tell someone to go away, as in *Run along, children, I have work to do.*

**run amok** Also, **run riot** or **run wild.** Behave in an excited or out-of-control manner. For example, *I was afraid that if I allowed the baby to stay up, she would run amok and have a hard time calming down,* or *The weeds are running riot in the lawn,* or *The children were running wild in the playground.*

**run an errand** Go to perform a task, as in *I spent the morning running household errands—to the cleaners, the supermarket, the hardware store.*

**run a risk** Also, **run the risk.** Be in danger of something, as in *Hiding anything from customs means running a risk that you'll be caught,* or *Without the right postage and address, this package runs the risk of being lost.*

**runaround** see GET THE RUNAROUND.

**run around** **1.** Hurry about here and there, as in *I have been running around all day, so I want to stay home tonight and relax.* **2.** Also, **run around with.** Spend time with someone socially, as in *At college she began to run around with a very liberal group.* **3.** Be sexually unfaithful, as in *She caught him running around and finally sued for divorce.*

**run around in circles** see GO AROUND.

**run around like a chicken** see CHICKEN WITH ITS HEAD CUT OFF.

**run around with** see RUN AROUND, def. 2.

**run a temperature** see RUN A FEVER.

**run a tight ship** see under TIGHT SHIP.

**run away** **1.** Avoid, escape, as in *Our dog is no watchdog; he runs away from strangers,* or *Our six-year-old said he'd run away from home.* **2.** Also, **run off.** Leave secretly, especially to elope, as in *She ran away from home when she was only thirteen,* or *They ran off to Maryland and got married by a justice of the peace.* **3. it won't run away.** An object, activity, or task will not disappear, as in *You can leave, but when you come back, the mess in the kitchen will still be there—it won't run away, you know!* Also see RUN AWAY WITH.

**run away with** **1.** Also, **run off with.** Quickly go off with someone or something, as in *She ran away with the boy next door,* or *The children ran off with the ball.* **2.** Win easily, as in *The star ran away with all the important awards.* **3.** Get the better of, as in *Sometimes his enthusiasm runs away with him.*

**run *something* by someone** Try something out on someone, as in *Let me run this idea by you and see what you think of it.*

**run circles around** see RUN RINGS AROUND.

**run counter to** Be in conflict with, oppose, as in *Practice often runs counter to theory.* This idiom uses *counter* in the sense of "in an opposite direction."

**run deep** Go very far or be very strong in someone's feelings, be in existence for a long time. For example, *His sense of justice runs deep,* or *We found that loyalty to the company ran deep.*

R

**run down** **1.** Stop because of lack of power or force, as in *The alarm clock finally ran down.* **2.** Make or be tired, cause to lose health or vigor, as in *His long illness ran him down, leaving him with no energy,* or *After that huge assignment, his strength ran down.* **3.** Collide with and knock someone over, as in *The speeding car ran down a pedestrian.* **4.** Chase and capture someone, as in *Police ran down the suspects.* **5.** Trace the source of, as in *She ran down all the references at the library.* **6.** Talk about someone in a negative way, as in *Don't run him down, he's a talented actor.* Also see PUT DOWN, def. 4. **7.** Also, **run one's eyes over.** Look over something quickly, review, as in *Let's run down the membership list again and see if we can find her name,* or *She ran her eyes over the crowd, looking for her husband.*

**run dry** see WELL'S RUN DRY.

**run for it** Also, **run for one's life.** Leave a place as fast as possible, either to escape danger or to reach something quickly. For example, *You'd better run for it before the teacher catches you,* or *The bully is coming after you—run for your life!* The *for it* in the first term almost certainly means "for one's life"—that is, to save one's life, a usage that can be literal or exaggerated. Also see FOR DEAR LIFE; MAKE A BREAK FOR IT.

**run for one's money, a** A close contest or a strong competition, as in *We may not win the game, but let's give them a run for their money.*

**run foul of** see RUN AFOUL OF.

**run high** Be intense, as in *Feelings are running high on the issue of raising taxes.*

**run in** **1.** Insert or include something extra, as in *Can you run this chart in with the text?* **2.** Also, **run someone in.** Take someone in a suspected criminal, as in *The police were going to run him in, but he got away.* **3.** Visit someone briefly, as in *If I have time, I'll run in to see your friend.* Also see RUN INTO.

**run-in** An unpleasant encounter, an argument. For example, *He had another run-in with the police.*

**run in place** Work or spend energy without making any change or progress. For example, *I've worked on this project for months, but I feel I'm running in place.* This idiom uses *in place* in the sense of "on one spot."

**run interference** Handle problems or help clear the way for another person, as in *The press secretary runs interference for the governor.*

**run in the family** Also, **run in the blood.** Be typical of a family or passed on from one generation to the next, as in *Big ears run in the family,* or *That happy-go-lucky trait runs in the blood.*

**run into** **1.** Meet or find someone by chance, as in *I ran into an old friend at the concert.* **2.** See RUN AGAINST, def. 1. **3.** Hit something, as in *The car ran straight into the retaining wall.* **4.** Get something undesirable and unexpected, as in *We've run into extra expenses with the renovation,* or *She said they've run into debt.* **5.** Add up, increase to, as in *Her book may well run into a second volume.* **6.** Follow something without stopping, as in *What with one day running into the next, we never knew just what day it was!* or *He spoke so fast his words ran into one another.* Also see RUN INTO A STONE WALL; RUN SOMETHING INTO THE GROUND.

**run into a stone wall** Also, **run into a brick wall.** Come to a barrier that makes additional progress hard or impossible, as in *We tried to get faster approval from the town and ran into a stone wall,* or *For him, learning a foreign language was like running into a brick wall.* Also see HIT A BRICK WALL.

**run *something* into the ground** **1.** Talk about a topic until there is nothing interesting left to say about it, as in *They've run the abortion issue into the ground.* **2.** Ruin or destroy something, as in *During her brief time as chief executive, Marjorie just about ran the company into the ground.* Both usages refer to pushing something so far that it is, in effect, buried.

**run its course** Come to a logical or natural end, as in *The doctor said the cold would probably run its course within a week.* This idiom uses *course* in the sense of "an onward movement in a particular path."

**run like clockwork** see LIKE CLOCKWORK.

**run low on** Be at the end of one's resources, such as time, money, or energy. For example, *I'm running low on sugar and have to go to the store,* or *He's running low on money, so I loaned him enough to pay his rent.* Also see RUNNING ON EMPTY.

**running** In addition to the idioms beginning with RUNNING, also see HIT THE GROUND RUNNING; IN THE RUNNING; METER IS RUNNING; OFF AND RUNNING.

**running battle, a** An ongoing argument or conflict between two or more people, groups, or organizations, as in *Trying to get the children to go to bed is a running battle,* or *Ignore them. This subject is a running battle between them.*

**running jump** see RUNNING START.

**running on empty** At the end of one's resources, out of money or energy, as in *I don't know how much longer we can live this way—we're running on empty with no jobs in sight.* This idiom refers to a car running when the gas gauge indicates it is out of fuel. Also see RUN LOW ON.

R

**running start** Also, **running jump.** An advantage at the start of something, as in *His background in biochemistry gave him a running start in the field of genetics,* or *If we want to be on time, we'll need to get a running jump in the morning.* Both these expressions refer to track events such as the running broad jump, in which one begins moving before reaching the actual takeoff point. The variant is also used as a command to tell someone to go away, as in *I asked him to work for me tomorrow, and he told me to take a running jump.* Also see under GET OFF THE GROUND.

**run off** **1.** Leave secretly; see RUN AWAY, def. 2. **2.** Flow off, drain, as in *By noon all the water had run off the street.* **3.** Print, duplicate, or copy something, as in *We ran off 200 copies of the budget.* **4.** Decide a contest or competition, as in *The last two events will be run off on Tuesday.* **5.** Also, **run someone out.** Force or drive someone away, as in *The security guard ran off the trespassers,* or *They ran him out of town.* **6.** Produce or perform something quickly and easily, as in *After years of practice, he could run off a speech in a couple of hours.*

**run off at the mouth** Talk for a long time without stopping, as in *He is always running off at the mouth about his investments.* This idiom compares a flow of water to an unending flow of words.

**run off with** **1.** Get away with someone or something; see RUN AWAY WITH, def. 1. **2.** Capture or carry off something, as in *The debaters ran off with the state championship.*

**run of luck, a** Also, **a run of bad luck.** A continued spell of good (or bad) fortune, as in *The builder had a run of luck with ten days of good weather,* or *Nothing was going right; he was having a long run of bad luck.*

**run of the mill** Ordinary, average, as in *There's nothing special about these singers—they're just run of the mill.* This expression refers to fabrics coming directly from a mill without having been inspected for quality.

**run on** **1.** Keep going, continue; also, remain in effect. For example, *That murder trial has been running on for months,* or *How much longer can this debt be allowed to run on?* **2.** Talk at length; see GO ON, def. 5.

**run oneself ragged** see RUN SOMEONE RAGGED.

**run one's eyes over** see RUN DOWN, def. 7.

**run one's head against the wall** see BEAT ONE'S HEAD AGAINST THE WALL.

**run one's own show** see under RUN THE SHOW.

**run out** **1.** Become used up, as in *Our supplies have run out.* **2.** Force something to leave; see RUN OFF, def. 5. **3.** Be no longer valid or in effect, as in *Our home insurance ran out last month.* Also see RUN OUT OF; RUN OUT ON.

**run out of** Use up a supply or quantity of something completely, as in *We're about to run out of coffee and sugar.* This expression can be used both literally and figuratively. Thus, **run out of gas** may mean one no longer has any fuel, but it has also acquired the figurative sense of using up a supply of energy, enthusiasm, or support and therefore causing some activity to come to a halt. For example, *After running ten laps, I ran out of gas and had to rest to catch my breath,* or *The economic recovery seems to have run out of gas.* On the other hand, **run out of steam,** which originally referred to a steam engine, today is used only figuratively to indicate a loss of energy of any kind.

**run out on** Desert someone or something, abandon, as in *He ran out on his family,* or *I hear they ran out on all their debts.*

**run over** **1.** Knock someone or something down and, often, pass over, as in *The car ran over our dog.* **2.** Review something quickly, as in *I'll run over the speech one more time.* **3.** Overflow, as in *This pot's running over.* **4.** Go beyond a limit, as in *I've run over the time I was given, but there are still questions.*

**run rings around** Also, **run circles around.** Be superior to, as in *She runs rings around me in chess,* or *In spelling, he runs circles around his classmates.*

**run riot** see RUN AMOK.

**run scared** Become frightened or aware of danger. For example, *The polls don't look too good for our candidate, and he's running scared,* or *The shrinking market has many businesses running scared.*

**run short** Use something up so that a supply runs out or decreases, as in *We ran short of envelopes,* or *The organization is running short of money.*

**run someone in** see RUN IN, def. 2.

**run someone off his or her feet** see OFF ONE'S FEET.

**run someone out** see RUN OFF, def. 5.

**run someone ragged** Also, **run oneself ragged.** Tire one out completely, as in *I've run myself ragged with this project.* This idiom refers to working so hard that one's appearance suffers.

**run the gamut** Go from one end to the other of an entire range, as in *His music runs the gamut from rock to classical.*

**run the gauntlet** Be exposed to danger, criticism, or hardship, as in *After he was misquoted in the interview, he knew he would have to run the gauntlet of his colleagues' anger.*

**run the risk** see RUN A RISK.

R

**run the show** Take charge of something, assume control, as in *Ever since Bill retired from the business, his daughter has been running the show.* The word *show* here simply means "kind of activity." A similar usage is **run one's own show,** meaning "control one's own activities" or "act independently." For example, *The high school drama club didn't ask permission to perform that play—they want to run their own show.*

**run through** **1.** Pierce someone or something, as in *The soldier was run through by a bayonet.* **2.** Use something up quickly, as in *She ran through her allowance in no time.* **3.** Practice something, review or rehearse quickly, as in *At rehearsal we ran through the whole play for the first time,* or *The crew ran through the rescue procedures.*

**run to** **1.** Amount to, as in *The total will run to thousands of dollars.* **2.** Lean toward something, favor, as in *My taste runs to chocolate desserts.* Also see RUN TO FORM.

**run to form** Also, **run true to form.** Act as one expects, especially in the same as earlier behavior. For example, *She ran to form, arriving an hour late,* or *The evening was running true to form, with solicitors calling at dinnertime.* This term at first referred to racehorses running as expected from their earlier record.

**run to seed** Also, **go to seed.** Lose energy or wear out, become worse, as in *I went back to visit my old elementary school, and sadly, it has really run to seed,* or *The gold medalist quickly went to seed after he left competition.* This term refers to plants that, when allowed to set seed after flowering, either taste bitter, as in the case of lettuce, or do not produce new buds, as is true of certain flowers.

**run up** **1.** Make or become greater or larger, as in *That offer will run up the price of the stock.* **2.** Gather or pile up something, as in *She ran up huge bills at the florist.* **3.** Raise a flag, as in *Let's run up the flag for the holiday.* This usage originated in the navy and led to the slang phrase **Let's run it up the flagpole and see if anybody salutes,** meaning, "Let's try this out."

**run up against** Encounter a difficulty, as in *We ran up against a problem with the car repairs.* Also see RUN AGAINST, def. 1.

**run wild** see RUN AMOK.

**run with** **1.** Also, **run around with.** Spend a lot of time with a person or a group; see RUN AROUND, def. 2. **2.** Take something as one's own, adopt; also, carry out with great energy. For example, *He wanted to run with the idea and go public immediately.* **3. run with it.** Make an effort to develop someone, take an opportunity to succeed at a task or project. For example, *Now that she has approval for the project, I'm sure she'll run with it,* or *With so many people supporting us, we'd be foolish not to run with it.*

**rush** see BUM'S RUSH; FOOLS RUSH IN WHERE ANGELS FEAR TO TREAD; MAD RUSH; (RUSH) OFF ONE'S FEET.

**rustle up** Get together food or some other needed item with some effort, as in *I don't know what we have, but I'll rustle up a meal somehow,* or *You boys need to rustle up some wood for a campfire.* The verb *rustle* here means "to assemble in a hurry."

**rut** see IN A RUT.

# Ss

**saber rattling** An excessive show of military power that is often intended to scare someone. For example, *There had been a great deal of saber rattling between the two nations, but hostilities had never broken out.* This term, originally indicating that an officer was about to draw his saber, at first referred to threatening military force but later was extended to more general use, as in *Both candidates engaged in pre-debate saber rattling.*

**sack** In addition to the idiom beginning with SACK, also see GET THE AX (SACK); HIT THE HAY (SACK); SAD SACK.

**sack out** Go to sleep, go to bed, as in *We sacked out about midnight.* This idiom is a verbal use of the noun *sack,* slang for "bed" or "sleeping bag." It also appears in such phrases as **in the sack,** meaning "in bed," and **sack time,** meaning "bedtime."

**sacred cow** A person or thing that cannot be criticized or questioned, as in *The rules governing press conferences have become a sacred cow in this administration.* This term refers to the honored status of cows in Hinduism.

**sadder but wiser** Unhappy but having learned from one's mistakes, as in *Sadder but wiser, she's never going near poison ivy again.*

**saddle** In addition to the idiom beginning with SADDLE, also see IN THE DRIVER'S SEAT (SADDLE).

**saddle someone with** Leave someone too much to do or take care of, as in *Before he left on vacation, he saddled his assistant with everything he hadn't had time to do himself.*

**sad sack** A person who is very clumsy or who fails at everything, as in *That poor guy is a hopeless sad sack.* This term refers to a cartoon character, Sad Sack, invented by George Baker during World War II and representing a soldier in an ill-fitting uniform who failed at whatever he tried to do. It was soon used to describe civilians who were clumsy or unable to do anything right.

**safe** In addition to the idiom beginning with SAFE, also see BETTER SAFE THAN SORRY; ON THE SAFE SIDE; PLAY IT SAFE.

**safe and sound** Out of danger and unharmed, as in *It was a long trip, so I'm relieved they got home safe and sound.*

**safety in numbers, there's** A group has more protection against harm than an individual, as in *Her parents won't allow her to date but do let her go to parties, saying there's safety in numbers.*

**said** see EASIER SAID THAN DONE; ENOUGH SAID; NO SOONER SAID THAN DONE; WHEN ALL'S SAID AND DONE; YOU SAID IT. Also see under SAY.

**sail** In addition to the idioms beginning with SAIL, also see (SAILING UNDER) FALSE COLORS; PLAIN SAILING; SET SAIL; SMOOTH SAILING; TAKE THE WIND OUT OF ONE'S SAILS; TRIM ONE'S SAILS.

**sailing under false colors** see FALSE COLORS.

**sail into** Attack or criticize someone with great force, as in *It was part of his technique to sail into the staff at the start of their end-of-the-year meeting.* This term uses *sail* in the sense of "move vigorously."

**sail through** Also, **sail right through.** Do something quickly and easily, make easy progress through, as in *He sailed through the written test in no time,* or *We sailed right through customs.* This expression refers to a boat moving quickly and easily through the water.

**sake** see FOR THE SAKE OF.

**sale** see CLOSE THE SALE; ON SALE; WHITE SALE.

**sales pitch** A line of talk that tries to convince someone to buy or to do something, as in *Let's hear your latest sales pitch for energy conservation.* This term uses the noun *pitch* in the sense of "a talk," or more literally, a throwing of words at one.

**salt** In addition to the idioms beginning with SALT, also see BACK TO THE SALT MINES; RUB SALT IN THE WOUND; WITH A GRAIN OF SALT; WORTH ONE'S SALT.

**salt away** Save something, store, as in *He salted away most of his earnings in a bank account.* This idiom refers to using salt to preserve food, especially meat.

**salt of the earth, the** The very best of their kind, as in *Those friends are the salt of the earth.*

**Samaritan** see GOOD SAMARITAN.

**same** In addition to the idioms beginning with SAME, also see ALL THE SAME; AMOUNT TO THE SAME THING; AT THE SAME TIME; BY THE SAME TOKEN; CAST IN THE SAME MOLD; GREAT MINDS RUN IN THE SAME CHANNEL; IN THE

SAME BOAT; IN THE SAME BREATH; IN THE SAME LEAGUE; ONE AND THE SAME; ON THE SAME WAVELENGTH; TARRED WITH THE SAME BRUSH.

**same difference** No difference at all, the same thing, as in *She's my sister, or stepsister—same difference.*

**same here** Also, **the same with me.** Me too, I agree, as in *I think she was lying all along. Same here,* or *I couldn't sleep because of the noise. The same with me.* The first phrase is also used in an order for food or drink to say that one wants the same thing as another person placing an order. For example, *One more beer, please. Same here.*

**same old story, the** Also, **the same old rigmarole** or **same old, same old.** An event or a situation that happens often. For example, *It's the same old story—they won't hire you without experience, but how can you get experience if you're not hired?* or *With him, it's the same old, same old—he'll never get a job.* These expressions originally referred to a boring, rambling talk, but today they are used mainly for an annoying repetition.

**same to you** I wish you the same (as you have wished me), as in *Merry Christmas! Same to you.*

**sand** see BUILD SOMETHING ON SAND; HIDE ONE'S HEAD IN THE SAND.

**sardine** see PACKED IN LIKE SARDINES.

**sauce** In addition to the idiom beginning with SAUCE, also see HIT THE BOTTLE (SAUCE).

**sauce for the goose is sauce for the gander, what's** Also, **what's good for the goose is good for the gander.** What applies to one applies to both, especially to both male and female. For example, *After her husband went off with his fishing buddies for a week, she decided to take a vacation without him—what's sauce for the goose, you know,* or *He'll be sorry he cheated on her—what's good for the goose is good for the gander.* These proverbial expressions are often shortened, as in the first example.

**save** In addition to the idioms beginning with SAVE, also see PENNY SAVED IS A PENNY EARNED; (SAVE FOR A) RAINY DAY; SCRIMP AND SAVE; TO SAVE ONE'S LIFE.

**saved by the bell** Rescued from a difficulty at the last moment, as in *I couldn't put off explaining his absence any longer, but then Bill arrived and I was saved by the bell.* This expression refers to the bell rung at the end of a boxing round.

**save face** Avoid humiliation or embarrassment, preserve dignity, as in *Rather than fire him outright, they let him save face by resigning.* The phrase, which uses *face* in the sense of "outward appearances," is modeled on the antonym LOSE FACE.

**save for a rainy day** see RAINY DAY.

**save it** Used to tell someone to stop talking, either because what the person is saying is not interesting or because it will not make any difference in the outcome of a situation. For example, *Save it, Carl—he's not listening to you anyway.*

**save one's neck** Also, **save one's skin.** Rescue one from a difficult situation or harm, as in *I was having a hard time changing the flat tire, but along came Bud, who saved my neck,* or *The boat sank in icy waters, but the life preservers saved our skins.*

**save one's breath** Stop arguing about a lost cause, as in *You can save your breath; I'm not going to change my mind.* For an antonym, see WASTE ONE'S BREATH.

**save the day** Keep a misfortune from happening, as in *They had forgotten the knife to cut the cake, but Elizabeth found one and saved the day.*

**save up** Collect something for a particular purpose, as in *Jan had been saving up her money for a new house.*

**saving grace, a** A quality that makes up for flaws or negative features. For example, *She may not be too knowledgeable, but her saving grace is that she doesn't pretend to be.* Also see REDEEMING FEATURE.

**saw** see OLD SAW.

**say** In addition to the idioms beginning with SAY, also see BEFORE YOU CAN SAY JACK ROBINSON; CRY (SAY) UNCLE; DO AS I SAY; GIVE (SAY) THE WORD; GOES WITHOUT SAYING; HAVE A SAY IN; I DARE SAY; I'LL SAY; NEEDLESS TO SAY; NEVER SAY DIE; NEVER SAY NEVER; NOT TO MENTION (SAY NOTHING OF); ON ONE'S SAY-SO; STRANGE TO SAY; SUFFICE IT TO SAY; THAT IS (TO SAY); TO SAY THE LEAST; YOU CAN SAY THAT AGAIN; YOU DON'T SAY. Also see under SAID.

**say a mouthful** Say something important or meaningful, as in *You said a mouthful when you called him a fine musician.* This term is often used to express agreement, much as YOU CAN SAY THAT AGAIN is.

**say good-bye** see KISS GOOD-BYE.

**say grace** Pronounce a short prayer before a meal, as in *Before we started in on the turkey, we asked Liz to say grace.* The word *grace* here means asking for God's blessing or giving thanks for the food being served.

**say no more** Enough has been said and the situation is understood, as in *Say no more—I'll help in any way I can.*

**say one's piece** see SPEAK ONE'S PIECE.

**says who?** This expression means "I don't believe this story." For example, *That horse of your will never win a race. Says who?* This slang expression of disagreement or disbelief may also be put as an exclamation, **says**

S

**you!,** meaning "I disagree with what you just said." For example, *It was an accident, I didn't mean to break it. Says you! You've always hated that vase.*

**say the word** see GIVE THE WORD.

**say uncle** see CRY UNCLE.

**say what?** Repeat what you just said because I don't believe I understood correctly, as in *Say what? She'll be here in five minutes?* or *Say what? You think I'd spread rumors about you?*

**say when** Tell me when you have food on your plate or liquid in your glass, as in *I'll pour the wine for you—just say when.*

**scale** In addition to the idiom beginning with SCALE, also see TIP THE BALANCE (SCALES).

**scale down** Reduce the size or cost of something, as in *The owners decided to scale down wages.* A related expression, **scale up,** refers to an increase.

**scarce** In addition to the idiom beginning with SCARCE, also see MAKE ONESELF SCARCE.

**scarce as hen's teeth** Also, **scarcer than hen's teeth.** Very rare, as in *On a rainy night, taxis are as scarce as hen's teeth.* Because hens have no teeth, this term says that something is so scarce that it does not exist at all.

**scarcely ever** see HARDLY EVER.

**scare** In addition to the idioms beginning with SCARE, also see RUN SCARED.

**scare *one* out of one's wits** Also, **frighten *one* out of one's wits; scare *one* stiff** or **silly** or **to death; scare the living daylights out of** or **scare the pants off.** Terrify one, make one panic, as in *When the lights went out, she was scared out of her wits,* or *I was scared stiff that I would fail the driver's test.*

**scare up** Also, **scrape together** or **scrape up.** Gather or produce something with great effort, as in *We managed to scare up extra chairs for the large audience,* or *He managed to scrape together enough cash to buy two more tickets.* Also see SCROUNGE UP.

**scarlet woman** A prostitute, as in *Malicious gossip had it that she was a scarlet woman, which was quite untrue.*

**scene** see BEHIND THE SCENES; MAKE A SCENE; MAKE THE SCENE; ON THE SCENE; SET THE SCENE FOR.

**scent** see THROW OFF, def. 3.

**schedule** see ON SCHEDULE.

**scheme** In addition to the idiom beginning with SCHEME, also see BEST-LAID PLANS (SCHEMES).

**scheme of things, the** The way the world is, as in *In the scheme of things, getting a promotion isn't that important.*

**school** In addition to the idioms beginning with SCHOOL, also see TELL TALES (OUT OF SCHOOL).

**school of hard knocks** The practical experience of life, including hardship and disappointment. For example, *A self-made man, he never went to college but came up through the school of hard knocks.* This idiom uses *knock,* meaning "a blow," as a reference to a setback.

**school of thought** The theories or opinions held by a group of people on a particular matter, as in *They belong to different schools of thought on raising children.*

**science** see BLIND ONE WITH SCIENCE.

**scoot over** Move to the side, especially to make room. For example, *If you scoot over a little, I'll have room to sit down.*

**score** In addition to the idiom beginning with SCORE, also see KNOW THE SCORE; PAY OFF (AN OLD SCORE); SETTLE A SCORE.

**score points off** Make oneself look better than someone else by criticizing or humiliating that person, as in *He has no interest in what you have to say—he's just trying to score points off you.*

**scoring position, in** About to succeed, as in *The author is in scoring position with that new book about the trial.* This term comes from sports, where it means being in a spot where scoring is likely.

**scot** see GET OFF (SCOT-FREE).

**scout** see GOOD EGG (SCOUT).

**scrape** see (SCRAPE THE) BOTTOM OF THE BARREL; BOW AND SCRAPE; SCARE (SCRAPE) UP.

**scrape together** Also, **scrape up.** See SCARE UP.

**scratch** In addition to the idioms beginning with SCRATCH, also see FROM SCRATCH; UP TO PAR (SCRATCH).

**scratch one's head** Show confusion or lack of understand, think hard, as in *They scratched their heads over this puzzling question, but no one knew the answer.*

**scratch someone's back** Do someone a favor in hopes that a favor will be returned. For example, *I don't mind driving this time—she has scratched my back plenty of times.* It also is put as **you scratch my back and I'll scratch yours,** as in *If you do the laundry, I'll do the cooking—you scratch my back and I'll scratch yours.*

**scratch the surface** Examine or treat something superficially, as in *This food program only scratches the surface of the hunger problem,* or *Her survey course barely scratches the surface of economic history.* This term transfers shallow marks made in the surface of a material to a shallow treatment of a subject.

**scream bloody murder** Angrily protest as loudly as possible, as in *When Jimmy took her teddy bear, Janet screamed bloody murder,* or *Residents are screaming bloody murder about the increase in property taxes.* The *scream* here may be either literal (as in the first example) or figurative, which is also true of using *murder* as though one were in danger of being killed.

**screw** In addition to the idioms beginning with SCREW, also see HAVE A SCREW LOOSE; PLUCK (SCREW) UP ONE'S COURAGE; TIGHTEN THE SCREWS; TURN UP THE HEAT (PUT THE SCREWS) ON.

**screw around** **1.** Fool around without a purpose, accomplish nothing, as in *If you boys would stop screwing around, we would have the fence painted in an hour.* It is also put as **screw around with,** as in *Stop screwing around with the new camera.* **2.** Be sexually active, often with multiple partners, as in *He has been screwing around behind her back for years.* [Vulgar slang]

**screw loose** see HAVE A SCREW LOOSE.

**screw someone out of** Cheat, deceive, or defraud someone, as in *They screwed me out of my overtime pay again.* It is often put in the passive, **be screwed** or **get screwed,** meaning "be cheated or deceived." For example, *We're getting screwed by this new income tax regulation.*

**screw up** **1.** Gather or summon up something; see PLUCK UP ONE'S COURAGE. **2.** Ruin an activity; also, make a mistake, as in *I really screwed up this report,* or *She said she was sorry, admitting that she had screwed up.* **3.** Injure something, damage, as in *I screwed up my back lifting all those heavy books.* **4.** Make neurotic or anxious, as in *Her family really screwed her up, but her therapist has helped her a lot.*

**screw up one's courage** see PLUCK UP ONE'S COURAGE.

**screw you!** Go to hell, as in *You won't help after all? Well, screw you!*

**scrimp and save** Barely manage to survive, spend as little money as possible, as in *For years we had to scrimp and save, but now we can enjoy life more.*

S

**scrounge around** Look about in an effort to obtain something at no cost, as in *We scrounged around their kitchen looking for a snack.*

**scrounge up** Find or gather something, as in *I'll have to scrounge up another microphone for today's speaker.* Also see SCARE UP.

**scrub up** Thoroughly wash one's hands and forearms, as before performing surgery. For example, *The residents had to scrub up in case they were called on to assist with the operation.*

**scruff of one's neck, the** The back of the neck of a person or animal, as in *The safest way to pick up a kitten is by the scruff of its neck.* This expression can also be used figuratively, as in *That child needs to be taken by the scruff of his neck and spanked.*

**scum of the earth** Also, **pond scum.** A person or a group of people thought to be worthless or without good qualities, as in *He seems to prefer to associate with the scum of the earth,* or *How can you associate with pond scum like her?*

**sea** In addition to the idiom beginning with SEA, also see AT SEA; BETWEEN A ROCK AND A HARD PLACE (THE DEVIL AND THE DEEP BLUE SEA); HIGH SEAS; NOT THE ONLY FISH IN THE SEA; PUT OUT (TO SEA).

**seal** In addition to the idioms beginning with SEAL, also see LIPS ARE SEALED; SET ONE'S SEAL ON; SIGNED, SEALED, AND DELIVERED.

**sea legs** The ability to adjust to a new situation or difficult conditions, as in *She's only spoken in public a few times; she hasn't found her sea legs yet.* This expression originally referred to, as it still does, the ability to walk steadily on a ship, especially in rough seas. It was later used to describe other difficult situations.

**seal of approval** A mark or sign showing that someone approves of something or someone, as in *Our candidate doesn't have the governor's seal of approval,* or *The new management gave the old refund policy their seal of approval.*

**seal off** Also, **seal up.** Close something tightly or block something to prevent entry or exit. For example, *We're sealing off the unused wing of the building,* or *The jar is tightly sealed up.*

**seal one's fate** Decide what will become of one, as in *The letter of rejection sealed his fate; he'd have to apply to other medical schools.*

**seam** see BURST AT THE SEAMS; COME APART AT THE SEAMS.

**seamy side** The unpleasant or worst aspect of something, as in *This nightclub certainly shows you the seamy side of the community.* This term refers to the inside of a garment, revealing the stitched seams.

**search** In addition to the idiom beginning with SEARCH, also see (SEARCH) HIGH AND LOW; IN SEARCH OF.

**search me** I don't know the answer to that, as in *Where's John? Search me, I haven't seen him for weeks.* This expression means "you can question me thoroughly for the information you want, but you won't get it."

**season** see IN SEASON; OPEN SEASON.

**seat** In addition to the idiom beginning with SEAT, also see BACKSEAT DRIVER; CATBIRD SEAT; HOT SEAT; IN THE DRIVER'S SEAT; RINGSIDE SEAT; TAKE A BACK SEAT.

**seat of the pants, by the** Using intuition and creative thinking rather than method or experience, as in *He ran the business by the seat of his pants.* This expression was invented by World War II fliers, who used it to describe flying when instruments were not working or weather interfered with their ability to see.

**second** In addition to the idioms beginning with SECOND, also see COME OFF (SECOND BEST); HAVE SECOND THOUGHTS; IN A FLASH (SECOND); IN THE FIRST (SECOND) PLACE; PLAY SECOND FIDDLE; SPLIT SECOND; TOP (SECOND) BANANA.

**second banana** see under TOP BANANA.

**second best** Also, **second class.** Next after the first in rank or quality, not equal to the best, as in *We aren't satisfied with being second best in sales,* or *This hotel is obviously second class.* Also see SECOND CLASS.

**second childhood** The tendency of some old people to behave in a childlike way because of a disease such as Alzheimer's; also, childlike playfulness in an adult. For example, *Grandpa has Alzheimer's and is in his second childhood,* or *Since he retired and started learning to fly, he's been in his second childhood.* Depending on the context, this term may refer either to such problems of old age as losing one's mental or physical capacities or to delighting in new pleasures in a childlike fashion. It is also offensive if one assumes that being mentally feeble is a natural result of old age.

**second class** **1.** Inferior; see SECOND BEST. **2.** Travel accommodations ranking below the highest or first class, as in *Traveling second class on European trains is not only cheaper but gives you more contact with local people.* **3.** In the United States and Canada, a type of mail consisting of periodicals and newspapers. **4. second-class citizen.** A person regarded or treated as inferior to others in status or rights, an oppressed person. For example, *All over the world women still are considered second-class citizens.* This term uses *second class* in the sense of "inferior."

**second cousin** Something that is related or similar but not quite the same, as in *This beef stew is second cousin to boeuf bourguignon.* This expression transfers the literal sense of *second cousin*—that is, the child of the first cousin of one's mother or father—to an object that is similar to something else.

**second fiddle** see PLAY SECOND FIDDLE.

**secondhand** **1.** Received from some source other than the original. For example, *I learned secondhand of Mary's divorce.* **2.** Relating to previously owned merchandise, as in *We bought the computer secondhand.* Also see FIRSTHAND.

**second nature** A habit or way of behaving so long practiced that it seems natural, as in *Driving in heavy traffic is second nature to Pat.*

**second thoughts** see HAVE SECOND THOUGHTS.

**second to none** The best, as in *Mom's chocolate cake is second to none.*

**second wind** Renewed energy or strength that enables one to continue an activity or task. For example, *I wasn't sure how far they'd get in a week, but now they have gotten their second wind and are making progress painting the mural.* This expression was at first (and still is) used for returned ease in breathing after becoming out of breath during physical exertion such as running. It soon began to be applied to nonphysical efforts as well.

**secrecy** see SWEAR SOMEONE TO SECRECY.

**secret** see IN SECRET; OPEN SECRET.

**security** In addition to the idiom beginning with SECURITY, also see LULL SOMEONE INTO (A FALSE SENSE OF SECURITY).

**security blanket** Something that calms anxiety or nerves, as in *I always carry my appointment calendar; it's my security blanket.* This term was originally used for the blanket or toy or other object held by a young child to reduce anxiety.

**see** In addition to the idioms beginning with SEE, also see AS FAR AS I CAN SEE; BEGIN TO SEE DAYLIGHT; CAN'T SEE BEYOND THE END OF ONE'S NOSE; CAN'T SEE THE FOREST FOR THE TREES; I'LL BE SEEING YOU; I SEE; LET ME SEE; LONG TIME NO SEE; WAIT AND SEE.

**see about** **1.** Also, **see to.** Attend to someone or something, take care of, as in *I'll see about the refreshments if you'll handle the tickets,* or *Will you see to the outdoor chores?* The variant is also put as **see to it,** as in *Yes, I'll see to it that everything's done.* **2.** Check something, as in *I'm not sure, but I'll see about the cost of renting a van.* Also see LOOK INTO.

**see after** see LOOK AFTER.

**see a man about a dog** Excuse oneself without giving the real reason for leaving, especially to go to the toilet or have an alcoholic drink. For example, *Excuse me, I have to see a man about a dog.*

**see *something* a mile off** Also, **tell a mile off.** Identify someone or something very quickly. For example, *I saw this problem coming a mile off,* or *He could tell a mile off that you aren't feeling well.*

**see beyond one's nose** see CAN'T SEE BEYOND THE END OF ONE'S NOSE.

**see both sides** Understand the two positions in an argument or unpleasant situation. For example, *A good lawyer can see both sides of a case.*

**seed** see RUN TO SEED.

**see daylight** see BEGIN TO SEE DAYLIGHT.

**see double** See two images of one object, either as an illusion or because of some visual problem, especially one caused by drunkenness. For example, *Those twins look so much*

S

*alike they make me think I'm seeing double,* or *One more drink and I'll be seeing double.*

**see eye to eye** Agree completely, as in *I'm so glad we see eye to eye on whom we should pick for department head.*

**see fit** Also, **think fit.** Judge to be fitting, as in *He's entitled to divide up his property as he sees fit,* or *Do whatever you think fit.* This expression uses *see* in the sense of "view as."

**see for oneself** Check on information to be sure that it's true, as in *The dog is still in the yard—see for yourself.*

**see *someone* in hell first** Refuse to do something under any conditions, as in *I'm never going to give in to their demands—I'll see them in hell first.*

**seeing is believing** Also, **I'll believe it when I see it.** Only physical or concrete evidence is convincing, as in *She wrote us that she's lost twenty pounds, but seeing is believing,* or *He swears he won't be late tonight, but I'll believe it when I see it.*

**seeing that** Also, **seeing as** or **seeing as how.** In view of, because. For example, *Seeing that you're coming anyhow, I decided not to take notes for you,* or *Seeing as they liked her first book, they were sure to make a good offer for the second one.*

**seeing things** Experiencing hallucinations or delusions, as in *I thought I saw my father, but I must have been seeing things; he died twenty years ago.*

**seek** see PLAY HIDE AND SEEK.

**seen better days, have** Be worn out, have fallen into a state of ruin, as in *This chair has seen better days,* or *The family business has seen better days.* This term was first used to describe a decline of fortune but soon was broadened to describe aging or deterioration in both humans and objects.

**seen one, seen them all** One example is enough, as in *I'm afraid I don't care for home movies—seen one, seen them all.* A newer idiom expressing a very similar view is **been there, done that (got the T-shirt),** indicating that it is boring to repeat an experience once it has lost its novelty. For example, *No, I don't want to climb Mount Washington; been there, done that.*

**see one's way to** Also, **see one's way clear to.** Find it possible or feel free to do something, as in *Can you see your way to lending me the car for the week?* or *I finally saw my way clear to taking a vacation in Costa Rica.* This expression transfers seeing one's path to something that is clear of obstacles.

**see out 1.** Also, **see someone out** or **see someone to the door.** Go with someone to the door, as in *The butler saw him out,* or *She refused to see him to the door.* Also see SEE SOMEONE OFF. **2.** Remain with a task or situation to the end; see SEE THROUGH, def. 2.

**see reason** Adopt a sensible course of action, let oneself be persuaded, as in *At ninety Grandma finally saw reason and gave up driving her car.* This expression uses *reason* in the sense of "good sense."

**see red** Become very angry, as in *I saw red when I learned they had not invited Tom and his family.* The exact reference in this term is not known, but it probably refers to the longstanding association of the color red with passion and anger.

**see service 1.** Be a member of one of the armed forces, as in *He saw service in the Korean War.* **2.** Be in use, as in *This chair has seen a lot of service.*

**see someone off** Take leave of someone, as in *We saw our guests off at the door,* or *They came to the airport to see us off.* Also see SEE OUT, def. 1.

**see stars** Perceive flashing lights, especially after a blow to one's head. For example, *A swinging door hit me, and I really saw stars.*

**see the back of** Be finished with, as in *I hope we've seen the back of Betsy; she is terribly rude.* This idiom transfers literally seeing someone's back because they are leaving to a more figurative and lasting departure. Also see SEE THE LAST OF.

**see the color of someone's money** see COLOR OF SOMEONE'S MONEY.

**see the last of** End one's dealings with someone or something, as in *I hope I've seen the last of those boring ice shows,* or *We haven't seen the last of Jerry—he'll be back.* Also see SEE THE BACK OF.

**see the light** Also, **begin to see the light.** Understand or begin to understand something; also, see the value of another's explanation or decision. For example, *Harry had been trying to explain that tax deduction for fifteen minutes when I finally saw the light,* or *Pat was furious she and her friends were not allowed to go hiking on their own in the mountains, but she began to see the light when a group got lost up there.* This term originally referred to religious conversion, the *light* meaning "true religion." Later it began to be was used more broadly for any kind of understanding. Also see LIGHT AT THE END OF A TUNNEL; SEE THE LIGHT OF DAY.

**see the light of day** Be published, brought out, or born. For example, *I wonder if her book will ever see the light of day,* or *The family reunion was a disaster, and I wish the idea for it had never seen the light of day,* or *When we visited Pittsburgh, we saw where Mom had first seen the light of day.*

**see the sights** Visit important features or see noteworthy objects, especially while touring a place. For example, *It's impossible to see all the sights of Paris in just a week.*

**see the world** Travel widely and visit many different places, as in *She's waiting until she retires to see the world.*

**see things** see SEEING THINGS.

**see through** **1. see through someone** or **something.** Understand the true character or nature of someone or something, as in *We saw through his superficial charm: he was obviously a liar.* **2.** Also, **see out.** Remain with a task or situation to the end; also, provide reliable support to. For example, *I saw the reorganization through, and then I left the company,* or *We'll see out the year in Florida and then decide if the move is permanent,* or *We'll see you through medical school, but then you're on your own.*

**see through rose-colored glasses** Also, **look through rose-colored glasses.** Take a very positive view of something, as in *Kate enjoys just about every activity; she sees the world through rose-colored glasses,* or *If only Martin wouldn't be so critical, if he could look through rose-colored glasses once in a while, he'd be much happier.* The adjectives *rosy* and *rose-colored* are used here in the sense of "hopeful" or "optimistic."

**see to** Also, **see to it.** See under SEE ABOUT.

**see what someone is made of** Find out if a person has a strong character and is able to endure hardship, as in *During the interview, we'll see what she's made of.*

**see which way the wind blows** Try to find out what kind of mood a person is in or how favorable a situation is. For example, *Don't ask Dad for money until you see which way the wind blows.*

**see with half an eye** Notice the obvious, tell at a glance, as in *I could see with half an eye that he was sleeping through the entire concert.* This exaggerated expression may refer to an eye that is only half-open.

**seize on** Also, **seize upon.** **1.** Grab or take hold of something suddenly, as in *He seized on the bell rope and started to pull vigorously,* or *She seized upon every opportunity to present her side of the story.* **2.** Resort to some action, especially out of great necessity, as in *He seized upon any excuse to justify his actions.*

**seize the day** Take advantage of a situation, as in *Seize the day—you never know when you'll have this chance again.* Also see CARPE DIEM.

**seize up** Come to a halt, as in *The peace talks seized up and were not rescheduled.* Originally this term referred to a machine of some kind that jams or locks because of too much heat or friction.

**sell** In addition to the idioms beginning with SELL, also see HARD SELL.

**sell *one* a bill of goods** Deceive someone, swindle or take unfair advantage of, as in *He was just selling you a bill of goods when he said he worked as a secret agent,* or *Watch out if anyone says he wants to trade bikes with you; he's apt to be selling you a bill of goods.* The *bill of goods* here means "a dishonest offer."

**sell *one* down the river** Betray a person or cause, as in *They kept the merger a secret until the last minute, so the employees who were laid off felt they'd been sold down the river.* This expression refers to slaves being sold down the Mississippi River to work as laborers on cotton plantations.

**sell like hotcakes** see LIKE HOTCAKES.

**sell off** Get rid of something by selling, often at reduced prices. For example, *The jeweler was eager to sell off the last of the diamond rings.* Also see SELL OUT, def. 1.

**sell oneself** **1.** Convince another of one's good qualities, present oneself in a favorable light, as in *A job interview is an ideal opportunity to sell oneself to a prospective employer.* Originally this idiom referred to selling one's services for money. **2.** Compromise one's principles for money. An early version was **sell oneself (**or **one's soul) to the devil,** which referred to having the devil's help in exchange for one's soul after death.

**sell out** **1.** Get rid of something entirely by selling. For example, *The rancher finally sold out to the oil company,* or *The tickets to the concert were sold out a month ago.* **2.** Betray one's cause or colleagues, as in *He sold out to the other side.*

**sell short** **1.** Contract for the sale of securities or commodities one expects to own at a later date and at a lower price, as in *Selling short runs the risk of a rise in the market, forcing one to pay more than one expected.* **2. sell someone short.** Fail to appreciate the true value or worth of someone, as in *Don't sell her short; she's an able lawyer.*

**sell someone on** Convince or persuade someone of the worth or desirability of something, as in *They were hoping to sell enough legislators on their bill so that it would pass easily,* or *Dave was really sold on that new car.*

**send around** see SEND ROUND.

**send away** Also, **send off.** **1.** Cause someone or something to leave, as in *We send the children away to camp every summer,* or *I sent off that letter last week.* **2.** Order an item, as in *I sent away for those gloves last month but they haven't arrived yet.* Also see SEND FOR, def. 2.

**send *something* or *someone* flying** Cause something or someone to be knocked or

S

scattered about, as in *She bumped into the table and sent all the papers flying,* or *I accidentally ran into Tina and sent her flying to the floor.*

**send for 1.** Request that someone come, as in *She sent for all the children when their father was dying.* **2.** Order a delivery of something, as in *The king sent for a bottle of wine.* Also see SEND AWAY, def. 2; SEND OUT, def. 2.

**send in 1.** Cause something to be sent or delivered, as in *Let's send in a letter of protest to the hiring committee.* **2.** Cause someone to become involved in a particular situation, as in *This disagreement is serious; it's time to send in the lawyers,* or *In the final few minutes of the game the coach sent in Richard.*

**send off** see SEND AWAY.

**send on 1.** Forward something, as in *He's moved; I'll send on this letter to his new address.* **2. send someone on.** Cause someone to go on an errand or path, as in *I sent your brother on an errand, but he should be back soon,* or *They've sent us on a wild goose chase.*

**send out 1.** Issue or mail something, as in *We sent out the wedding invitations last month,* or *When did you send out that message?* **2. send out for.** Order a delivery of something, as in *Every Wednesday we send out for Chinese food.*

**send round** Also, **send around.** Circulate something widely, as in *A notice about the new health plan is being sent round to all employees,* or *We sent a memo around telling everyone about the party.*

**send someone about his or her business** Also, **send someone packing.** Dismiss someone abruptly, as in *When I catch children teasing the dog, I sent them about their business,* or *The owner caught Jack taking small items from the store and sent him packing.* The first term tells people to tend to their own affairs; the variant tells people to pack their bags and leave. Also see SEND AWAY, def. 1.

S

**send someone packing** see SEND SOMEONE ABOUT HIS OR HER BUSINESS.

**send up 1.** Put in prison, as in *He'll be sent up for at least ten years.* **2.** Cause something to rise, as in *The gaseous emissions sent up by that factory are clearly poisonous.* **3.** Make a parody of something or someone, make fun of, as in *This playwright has a genius for sending up modern life.* **4. send up a trial balloon.** See TRIAL BALLOON.

**sense** see COME TO ONE'S SENSES; HORSE SENSE; IN A SENSE; LULL SOMEONE INTO (A FALSE SENSE OF SECURITY); MAKE SENSE; SIXTH SENSE; TAKE LEAVE OF (ONE'S SENSES); TALK SENSE.

**separate but equal** Relating to or affected by a policy whereby two groups are kept apart if they are given equal facilities and opportunities. For example, *They divided up the physical education budget so that the girls' teams were separate but equal to the boys' teams.*

**separate the men from the boys** Distinguish between mature, experienced individuals and those new to something, as in *The picket line will separate the men from the boys in the union.*

**separate the sheep from the goats** Distinguish between good and bad individuals, or superior and inferior ones. For example, *In a civil war where both sides commit terrible acts, you can't separate the sheep from the goats.*

**separate the wheat from the chaff** Sort the valuable from the worthless, as in *I hope we'll get a preview of the auction so we can separate the wheat from the chaff.* This idiom refers to the ancient practice of winnowing grain.

**serve** In addition to the idioms beginning with SERVE, also see BREAK SOMEONE'S SERVE; FIRST COME, FIRST SERVED; HAND SOMETHING TO ONE ON A SILVER PLATTER (SERVE UP ON A PLATE).

**serve a purpose** Also, **serve one's purpose** or **serve the purpose.** Be useful, meet the needs or requirements of a task or situation, satisfy, as in *I don't know why they've added all this information, but it probably serves a purpose,* or *It often serves his purpose to be vague,* or *We don't have a screwdriver, but this knife should serve the purpose.*

**serve one right** Be deserved under the circumstances. For example, *That punishment serves him right after what he's done to you.* It is also put as **serves you right,** as in *It wasn't accepted? Serves you right for applying so late.* These idioms use *serve* in the sense of "treat in a specified manner."

**serve time** Be in prison; also, work at a particular task, especially an undesirable one. For example, *We couldn't hire him when we learned that he had served time for robbery,* or *I applied for a transfer after serving time in that disorganized department.*

**serve up 1.** Dish out food, as in *Next they served up some chicken.* **2.** Provide something, as in *He served up joke after joke, delighting his audience.* Also see HAND SOMETHING TO ONE ON A SILVER PLATTER.

**service** see AT SOMEONE'S SERVICE; BREAK SOMEONE'S SERVE (SERVICE); LIP SERVICE; OF SERVICE TO SOMEONE; PRESS SOMEONE INTO SERVICE; SEE SERVICE.

**session** see BULL SESSION.

**set** In addition to the idioms beginning with SET, also see ALL SET; DEAD SET AGAINST; GET SET; GET (SET) SOMEONE'S BACK UP; GET (SET)

THE BALL ROLLING; LAY (SET) EYES ON; (SET) ON A PEDESTAL; SMART SET. Also see under PUT.

**set about** Begin something, start, as in *How do we set about solving this puzzle?* or *She set about looking for the money.* This idiom is followed by a gerund, as in the examples.

**set against** Be or cause someone to be opposed to, as in *Civil wars often set friend against friend,* or *The police chief's critics were set against his officers.* Also see DEAD SET AGAINST.

**set ahead** see SET FORWARD.

**set an example** Also, **set a good example** or **set a bad example.** Behave in a way that should (or will) be imitated, as in *Dad was always telling Bill to set a good example for his younger brother,* or *They were afraid of setting a bad example for the other students.*

**set apart** **1.** Reserve something for a particular use, as in *One group of tissue samples was set apart for further analysis.* **2.** Make someone or something noticeable, as in *Certain traits set her apart from her twin sister.*

**set a precedent** Establish a usage, tradition, or standard to be followed in the future. For example, *He set a precedent by having the best student lead the procession of teachers.*

**set aside** **1.** Separate and reserve something for a special purpose, as in *We have to set aside some chairs for latecomers.* Also see SET BY. **2.** Not consider something, as in *Setting aside all health considerations, do you believe this law is fair to smokers?* **3.** Declare something invalid, annul or overrule, as in *The higher court set aside the conviction.* Also see LAY ASIDE.

**set at** Also, **set upon.** Attack an animal or person, as in *The dog set at the postman,* or *The wolves set upon the wounded deer.*

**set at rest** see LAY SOMETHING AT REST.

**set back** **1.** Slow down the progress of something, make difficult, as in *The project was set back by the absence of crucial staff members.* **2.** Cost one, as in *That car set me back twenty thousand dollars.* **3.** Change something to a lower level or an earlier time, as in *We set back the thermostat whenever we go on vacation,* or *At the end of October we have to set back the clocks.* **Set back the clock** is also used figuratively to mean "return to an earlier era," as in *He wished he could set back the clock to those carefree high school days.* Also see SET FORWARD.

**set *one* back on one's heels** Surprise, shock, or confuse someone, as in *The news of their divorce set us back on our heels.* This idiom calls up an image of someone being pushed back literally onto the heels of his or her feet.

**set back the clock** see SET BACK, def. 3.

**set by** Put something aside for future use, as in *She had dozens of cans of food set by for an emergency.* Also see SET ASIDE, def. 1; SET STORE BY.

**set down** **1.** Place a person or thing in a lower position, as in *Set the baby down here,* or *Set the bags down on the table.* **2.** Put something in writing, record, as in *Just set down all the facts as you remember them.* **3.** Regard someone, consider, as in *Just set him down as a fool.* **4.** Assign something probable to a cause, as in *Let's set down his error to inexperience.* **5.** Land an aircraft, as in *The pilot set the plane down hard on the runway.* Also see PUT DOWN.

**set eyes on** see LAY EYES ON.

**set fire to** see SET SOMEONE OR SOMETHING ON FIRE.

**set foot** **1. set foot in.** Enter, as in *I'll never set foot in this house again.* **2. set foot on.** Step on something, as in *We were so happy to set foot on dry land.*

**set forth** **1.** Also, **put forth.** Start a journey, as in *We plan to set forth at daybreak,* or *They put forth for France tomorrow.* **2.** Present something for consideration; also, express in words, as in *She set forth a very sensible plan,* or *We need to set forth our ideas clearly.* **3.** See PUT FORTH, def. 3.

**set forward** Also, **set ahead.** Turn a clock to a later time, as in *For daylight-saving time we set the clocks forward.*

**set great store by** see SET STORE BY.

**set in** **1.** Insert something, put in, as in *I still have to set in the sleeves, and then the sweater will be done.* **2.** Begin to happen or appear, as in *Darkness was setting in as I left.* **3.** Move toward the shore, said of wind or water, as in *The tide sets in very quickly here.*

**set *something* in motion** Start something moving, propel something, as in *A press conference set the new project in motion.* It is also put as **set the wheels in motion,** as in *Let's set the wheels in motion for the new library wing.* This idiom was preceded by **put *something* in motion.**

**set in one's ways, be** Be unwilling to change or fixed in one's habits, as in *She's too set in her ways to go out and buy a dog.* This idiom uses *set* in the sense of "in a rigid position."

**set in stone, be** Be permanently fixed and impossible to change, as in *We can leave on another day; our schedule isn't set in stone.* This expression is usually used in the negative, as in the example.

**set off** **1.** Give rise to something, cause to happen, as in *The acid set off a chemical reaction.* **2.** Cause something to explode, as in *They set off a bomb.* **3.** Distinguish someone or something, show to be different, contrast with, as in *That black coat sets him off from the others in the picture,* or *Italics set this sentence off from the rest of the text.* **4.** Make something more attractive, as in *That color sets off her blonde hair.* **5.** Begin a journey, leave, as in *When do you set off for Europe?*

**set on** Also, **set upon. 1.** Attack someone; see SET AT. **2. be set on** or **be set upon.** Be determined to do something, as in *He's set on studying law.* This sense is followed by a gerund, as in the example.

**set on a pedestal** see ON A PEDESTAL.

**set one back** see SET BACK, def. 1 and 2.

**set one back on one's feet** Help restore one's position, reestablish one, as in *The agency promised to help set the unemployed workers back on their feet.* This idiom uses an upright position to refer to being active and productive.

**set one's back up** see PUT ONE'S BACK UP.

**set one's heart on** Also, **have one's heart set on.** Strongly desire something, as in *I'd set my heart on a vacation in New Mexico, but I got sick and couldn't go,* or *Harry had his heart set on a new pickup truck.*

**set one's mind at rest** Also, **put one's mind at rest.** Stop worrying, lessen one's worry. For example, *Your car has been found undamaged, so set your mind at rest.* Also see LAY SOMETHING AT REST.

**set one's mind on** see under PUT ONE'S MIND TO.

**set one's seal on** Also, **put one's seal on.** Authorize something, give one's approval to, as in *We can go ahead as soon as the boss sets his seal on it.* This idiom refers to the old practice of attaching a seal to a document as a way of showing its validity.

**set one's sights on** Have something as a goal, as in *She has set her sights on law school.* This expression refers to the optical device used for taking aim with a firearm.

**set one's teeth on edge** Irritate one, annoy, as in *That loud laugh sets my teeth on edge.* This expression refers to the shuddering feeling caused by a grating noise or similar irritation.

**set *someone* or *something* on fire 1.** Also, **set fire to.** Cause something to ignite and burn, as in *The drought and high wind combined to set the woods on fire.* **2.** Cause someone to become excited, as in *The music set the audience on fire.* Also see CATCH FIRE; SET THE WORLD ON FIRE.

**set out 1.** Begin a serious attempt, as in *He set out to prove his point,* or *We accomplished what we set out to do.* **2.** Lay something out in an orderly way, as in *She set out all the reports in chronological order.* **3.** Display something for exhibition or sale, as in *The Japanese restaurant set out samples of all the different kinds of sushi.* **4.** Plant something, as in *It was time to set out the seedlings.* **5.** Begin a journey, as in *They set out at dawn.*

**set *something* right** Also, **put *something* right. 1.** Place something in proper position; also, repair something. For example, *Your tie is crooked; let me set it right,* or *The faucets were in backward, but the plumber will soon put them right.* **2.** Correct someone, as in *They thought he was married, but he quickly set them right.* **3.** Make something accurate or fair, as in *He offered to pay for the meal to put things right.* Also see SET SOMEONE STRAIGHT.

**set sail** Also, **make sail.** Begin a voyage on water, as in *Dad rented a yacht, and we're about to set sail for the Caribbean,* or *We'll make sail for the nearest port.*

**set store by** Also, **set great store by.** Regard something as valuable or worthwhile, as in *I don't set much store by her judgment,* or *He sets great store by his good name.* The word *store* is used here in the sense of "something precious," a usage that is unknown except in these expressions.

**set *someone* straight** Correct someone by providing accurate information; also, make an arrangement honest or fair. For example, *Let me set you straight about Lisa; she's never actually worked for us,* or *To set matters straight, I'll pay you back Monday.* It is sometimes put as **set the record straight,** meaning "correct an inaccurate account," as in *Just to set the record straight, we arrived at ten o'clock, not midnight.*

**set the pace** Establish a standard for others to follow, as in *Jim has set the pace for the department, exceeding the monthly quota every time.* This expression comes from racing, where it is said of a horse that passes the others and leads the field.

**set the record straight** see SET SOMEONE STRAIGHT.

**set the scene for** Also, **set the stage for.** Provide the underlying basis or background for an event, make likely or certain, as in *Their fights about money set the scene for a divorce,* or *The company's profits last year set the stage for a takeover.*

**set the table** Also, **lay the table.** Arrange a tablecloth, plates, glasses, silverware, and other objects for a meal, as in *Please set the table for dinner.*

**set the tone for** Create the atmosphere of an event or a situation, as in *The threat of war set a hostile tone for the peace talks.*

**set the wheels in motion** see under SET SOMETHING IN MOTION.

**set the world on fire** Do something important and become famous, as in *An ambitious* *man, he longed to set the world on fire with his inventions.* This exaggerated expression is often used to describe what one hopes to do. Also see SET SOMEONE OR SOMETHING ON FIRE, def. 2.

**settle a score** Also, **settle an old score** or **wipe out an old score.** Get even for a wrong or an injury. For example, *Gail settled an old score with Bill when she made him wait for half an hour in the rain.* These expressions all use *score* in the sense of "an account" or "a bill." Also see PAY OFF, def. 3.

**settle down** **1.** Begin living a stable, orderly life; also, marry. For example, *After traveling all over the world for two years, he decided to settle down in his hometown,* or *Her parents wished she would settle down and raise a family.* **2.** Become calm, less nervous, or less active, as in *Come on, children, it's time to settle down.* **3.** Apply oneself seriously, as in *If you don't settle down to your homework, you'll never get pass those courses.*

**settle for** Accept or be satisfied with something that is less than what one wanted, as in *He really wanted a bigger raise but decided to settle for what they offered.*

**settle on** Also, **settle upon.** **1.** Decide something, as in *They finally settled on Bermuda for their vacation.* **2.** Give property or a title to someone, as in *She settled half her estate on her husband.*

**settle up** Also, **settle with.** Pay a debt or one's share of the cost, as in *When can you settle up for the tickets I bought for us?* or *Jean said she'd settle with the bank next month.*

**set to** **1.** Apply oneself, begin, work energetically, as in *We set to revising our policy on child care,* or *She set to studying for the exam.* **2.** Begin fighting, as in *Both of them were furious, and they set to immediately.*

**set *something* to rights** Also, **put *something* to rights.** Place something in proper condition or order. For example, *The children promised to set the room to rights before bedtime,* or *Don't worry, the lawyer will put the will to rights.* Also see SET SOMETHING RIGHT.

**set up** **1.** Place something in an upright position, as in *I keep setting up this lamp, but it won't stay up.* **2.** Elevate something, raise; also, put in a position of authority or power, as in *They set him up as their leader.* **3.** Put oneself forward, claim to be, as in *He set himself up as an authority on the banking system.* **4.** Assemble something, erect, make ready for use, as in *They set up the sound system last night.* **5.** Establish something, found, as in *They set up a new charity for the homeless.* **6.** Establish someone in business by providing money or other support, as in *His father set her up in a new dental practice.* **7.** Treat someone to drinks, pay for drinks, as in *Please let us set you up tonight.* **8.** Stimulate or exhilarate someone, as in *That victory really set up our team.* **9.** Lay plans for something, as in *I think they set up the kidnapping months ago.* **10.** Prepare someone for a trick, lie, or joke, as in *They set up their victim for the usual real estate scam,* or *Her friends set her up so that she was the only person in costume.* **11.** Cause something, bring about, as in *The new taxes set up howls of protest.*

**set up housekeeping** Move in together, as in *Couples today often set up housekeeping long before they marry.*

**set upon** see SET AT; SET ON.

**set up shop** Open a business, start a profession, as in *Now that you've got your degree, where do you plan to set up shop?*

**sew up** **1.** Complete an activity or project successfully, as in *Our team sewed up the championship.* **2.** Gain complete control of something, monopolize, as in *The construction company hopes to sew up all of the city's building projects.*

**sex** see FAIR SEX.

**shack up** **1.** Sleep together or live in sexual intimacy without being married. For example, *They dated for two months and then decided to shack up.* **2.** Stay or reside with someone, as in *I'm shacking up with my cousin till I find a place of my own.*

**shades of** A reminder of a person or situation in the past. For example, *He really played a fine game for a fifty-year-old—shades of his high school days,* or *They found themselves alone on the beach—shades of their childhood summers together.*

**shadow** In addition to the idiom beginning with SHADOW, also see AFRAID OF ONE'S OWN SHADOW; BEYOND A (THE SHADOW OF A) DOUBT.

**shadow of one's self** Also, **shadow of one's former self** or **shadow of one's old self.** A person, group, or thing that has become weaker in physical or mental abilities or in power or authority. For example, *After that long battle with the flu, he was just a shadow of his old self,* or *This new administration is but a shadow of itself,* or *The company is a shadow of its former self.* The term *shadow* originally referred to a weakened person and later began to be used for other kinds of decline.

**shaggy-dog story** A long story with an absurd ending. For example, *At first he had us laughing wildly at his shaggy-dog stories, but after the third or fourth one we were tired of them.* The term refers to a well-known series of such stories, which involved a talking dog.

**shake** In addition to the idioms beginning with SHAKE, also see ALL SHOOK (SHAKEN) UP;

FAIR SHAKE; IN TWO SHAKES; MORE THAN ONE CAN SHAKE A STICK AT; MOVER AND SHAKER; NO GREAT SHAKES; QUAKE (SHAKE) IN ONE'S BOOTS.

**shake a leg 1.** Hurry up, as in *Shake a leg or we'll miss the plane.* **2.** Dance, as in *Whenever there was music, he was eager to shake a leg.*

**shake a stick at** see MORE THAN ONE CAN SHAKE A STICK AT.

**shake down 1.** Demand money from, as in *They had quite a racket, shaking down merchants for so-called protection.* **2.** Make a thorough search of someone or something, as in *They shook down all the passengers, looking for drugs.* **3.** Try out a new vehicle or machine, do a test of, as in *We'll shake down the new aircraft next week.*

**shake hands 1.** Also, **shake someone's hand.** Take hold of another's hand in greeting, farewell, or congratulation or as a sign of friendship or goodwill. For example, *Stop fighting, boys; shake hands and be done with it,* or *You won first prize? Let me shake your hand.* **2. shake hands on.** Confirm a promise or bargain, as in *We didn't sign a contract; we simply shook hands on our agreement.*

**shake in one's boots** see QUAKE IN ONE'S BOOTS.

**shake off** Free oneself or get rid of something or someone, as in *I've had a hard time shaking off this cold,* or *She forged ahead, shaking off all the other runners.* It is also put as **give someone the shake,** as in *We managed to give our pursuers the shake.*

**shake one's head** Express disapproval, disagreement, or doubt, as in *That announcement had us shaking our heads in dismay.* This expression can be used both literally (for moving one's head from side to side) and figuratively.

**shaker** see MOVER AND SHAKER.

S

**shake the dust from one's feet** Leave in a hurry, especially from an unpleasant situation; also, go away forever. For example, *I couldn't wait to shake the dust from my feet; I never wanted to see either of them again.*

**shake up 1.** Stir or move something rapidly in order to mix or loosen, as in *I shook up the cough medicine,* or *Please shake up these pillows.* **2.** Upset someone greatly, as in *Even though no one was hurt, he was greatly shaken up by the accident.* This usage refers to being disturbed like a liquid being shaken. Also see ALL SHOOK UP. **3.** Cause something to undergo thorough change or reorganization, as in *The new management planned on shaking up each division.*

**shake with laughter** Have an extreme reaction to the humor of something, as in *When asked if he was planning to give away the bride, he shook with laughter at the very thought.*

**shall** see WHO SHALL REMAIN NAMELESS.

**shame** see CRYING SHAME; FOR SHAME; PUT ONE TO SHAME.

**shame on you** see under FOR SHAME.

**shape** In addition to the idiom beginning with SHAPE, also see BENT OUT OF SHAPE; IN CONDITION (SHAPE); LICK SOMETHING INTO SHAPE; TAKE SHAPE.

**shape up 1.** Turn out, develop; see TAKE SHAPE. **2.** Improve so as to meet a standard, as in *The coach told the team that they'd better shape up or they'd be at the bottom of the league.* **3. shape up or ship out** Behave or be forced to leave, as in *The new supervisor told Tom he'd have to shape up or ship out.* This expression originated during World War II as a threat that if one didn't behave in an appropriate military manner, one would be sent overseas to a combat zone. After the war it was transferred to other situations calling for improved performance.

**share** In addition to the idiom beginning with SHARE, also see LION'S SHARE.

**share and share alike** Distribute or receive something equally, as in *Mom told the children to share and share alike with their Halloween candy.*

**shark** see SWIM WITH THE SHARKS.

**sharp** In addition to the idiom beginning with SHARP, also see KEEP AN EYE OUT (A SHARP LOOKOUT) FOR; LOOK SHARP.

**sharp as a tack** Also, **sharp as a razor.** Very intelligent. For example, *She's very witty—sharp as a tack.*

**shave** see CLOSE CALL (SHAVE).

**shed blood** Also, **spill blood.** Wound or kill someone, especially violently. For example, *It was a bitter fight, but fortunately no blood was shed,* or *A great deal of blood has been spilled in this family feud.* Both of these terms refer to causing blood to flow and fall on the ground.

**shed light on** Also, **throw light on.** Make an event or situation easier to understand, as in *I was hoping the professor would shed light on how he arrived at his theory,* or *Can anyone throw some light on where these plants came from?* Originally these expressions were used literally, in the sense of "illuminate," but they soon were used figuratively as well.

**sheep** see BLACK SHEEP; SEPARATE THE SHEEP FROM THE GOATS; WOLF IN SHEEP'S CLOTHING.

**sheet** see THREE SHEETS TO THE WIND; WHITE AS A SHEET.

**shelf** see OFF THE SHELF; ON THE SHELF.

**shell** In addition to the idiom beginning with SHELL, also see IN ONE'S SHELL.

**shellacking** see TAKE A SHELLACKING.

**shell out** Pay money, hand over, as in *We had to shell out $1,000 for auto repairs.* This expression transfers taking a seed such as a nut out of its shell to taking money out of one's pocket.

**shift for oneself** Also, **fend for oneself.** Provide for one's own needs, as in *Don't worry about Anne; she's very good at shifting for herself,* or *The children had to fend for themselves after school.* The first term uses *shift* in the old sense of "manage"; the variant uses *fend for* in the sense of "look after."

**shilling** see CUT ONE OFF (WITH A SHILLING).

**shine** In addition to the idiom beginning with SHINE, also see MAKE HAY WHILE THE SUN SHINES; RAIN OR SHINE; RISE AND SHINE; TAKE A FANCY (SHINE) TO; TAKE THE SHINE OFF.

**shine up to** Try to impress or please someone, be attentive to, as in *George was always shining up to the teacher,* or *Her father warned her about men shining up to her for her money.*

**shingle** see HANG OUT ONE'S SHINGLE.

**ship** In addition to the idioms beginning with SHIP, also see DESERT A SINKING SHIP; ENOUGH TO SINK A SHIP; RUN A TIGHT SHIP; SHAPE UP (OR SHIP OUT); WHEN ONE'S SHIP COMES IN.

**ship of state** The nation, as in *We wonder who will be steering our ship of state a hundred years from now.*

**ship out** **1.** Leave, especially for a distant place, as in *The transport planes carried troops shipping out to the Mediterranean.* Although this usage originally meant "depart by ship," the expression is no longer limited to that means of transportation. **2.** Send something, export, especially to a distant place, as in *The factory shipped out many more orders last month.* **3.** Quit a job or be fired; see SHAPE UP, def. 3.

**ships that pass in the night** Individuals who are rarely in the same place at the same time. For example, *Jan works the early shift and Paula the late shift—they're two ships that pass in the night.*

**shirt** see GIVE THE SHIRT OFF ONE'S BACK; HAIR SHIRT; KEEP ONE'S SHIRT ON; LOSE ONE'S SHIRT; STUFFED SHIRT.

**shit** In addition to the idioms beginning with SHIT, also see FULL OF CRAP (SHIT); GET ONE'S ACT (SHIT) TOGETHER; IN SHIT UP TO ONE'S EYEBALLS; NO SHIT; NOT GIVE A DAMN (SHIT); THINK ONE'S SHIT DOESN'T STINK; TOUGH BREAK (SHIT); UP A CREEK (SHIT CREEK).

**shit a brick** Be very surprised or scared, as in *He almost shit a brick when we walked in,* or *The boss will shit a brick when he sees what you did.* [Vulgar slang]

**shit happens** Also, **doo-doo occurs.** Unpleasant events happen without apparent cause or reason. For example, *So you wife left you, your son's in jail, and you lost your job—shit happens,* or *I lost my car keys, was late to work, and missed an appointment—doo-doo occurs.* These expressions are cynical ways of dismissing events for which one has no explanation. The variant is often used humorously. [Vulgar slang]

**shit on one** Treat someone with hatred or disrespect, as in *I'm tired of all these administrators shitting on me every time I want to try something new.* [Vulgar slang]

**shit or get off the pot** see under FISH OR CUT BAIT.

**shit will hit the fan, the** Also, **when the shit hits the fan** or **then the shit hits the fan.** There will be major trouble, often following the disclosure of a piece of information. For example, *When they find out they were firing on their own planes, the shit will hit the fan.* [Vulgar slang]

**shock** see CULTURE SHOCK.

**shoe** In addition to the idiom beginning with SHOE, also see COMFORTABLE AS AN OLD SHOE; FILL SOMEONE'S SHOES; GOODY-TWO-SHOES; IF THE SHOE FITS; IN SOMEONE'S SHOES; STEP INTO SOMEONE'S SHOES; WAIT FOR THE OTHER SHOE TO DROP.

**shoe is on the other foot, the** The situation has changed, the participants have changed places, as in *I was one of his research assistants, subject to his orders, but now that I'm his department head the shoe is on the other foot.* Literally wearing the right shoe on the left foot would be quite uncomfortable, and this is implied in this idiom, which suggests that changing places is not equally comfortable for all parties concerned.

**shoestring** see ON A SHOESTRING.

**shoo-in, be a** Be able or certain to obtain or achieve something without any effort, as in *He thinks he's a shoo-in for that promotion.*

**shook up** see ALL SHOOK UP.

**shoot** In addition to the idioms beginning with SHOOT, also see LIKE SHOOTING FISH IN A BARREL; SURE AS SHOOTING; WHOLE BALL OF WAX (SHOOTING MATCH). Also see under SHOT.

**shoot down** **1.** Ruin the hopes of, disappoint, as in *Bill was hoping Sharon would go out with him, but she shot him down.* **2.** Reject something, defeat; also, expose as false. For example, *It was the best idea I could come up with, but they unanimously shot it down,* or *It was inevitable that they would shoot down any claim made by the opposing candidate.* This expression, which refers to bringing down an aircraft by shooting, is sometimes put as **shoot *something* down in flames.**

**shoot for** Try to achieve something, as in *We're shooting for higher production by* *spring.* This term refers to aiming at something with a weapon.

**shoot from the hip** Speak or act too honestly or recklessly, as in *Steve isn't very tactful; indeed, he's known for shooting from the hip.* Also see SHOOT OFF ONE'S MOUTH.

**shoot hoops** Play basketball. For example, *Let's shoot some hoops tomorrow.*

**shoot off one's mouth** Speak carelessly; also, brag or boast. For example, *Now don't go shooting off your mouth about it; it's supposed to be a surprise,* or *Terry is always shooting off his mouth about much money he makes.*

**shoot oneself in the foot** Foolishly harm one's own cause, as in *He really shot himself in the foot, telling the interviewer all about the others who were applying for the job he wanted.* This term refers to an accidental shooting as opposed to one done in order to avoid military service.

**shoot one's wad** Do all within one's power; use up one's resources. For example, *They were asking for more ideas, but Bob had shot his wad and couldn't come up with any,* or *Don't shoot your wad on that suit or you won't have any money left for dinner.* This idiom comes from gambling and refers to spending all of a wad of rolled-up bank notes. Also see SHOOT THE WORKS.

**shoot straight** Also, **shoot square.** Deal fairly and honestly, as in *You can't trust most car salesmen, but Jim always shoots straight,* or *We always shoot square with our customers.* These terms use *straight* and *square* in the sense of "straightforward and honest," and *shoot* in the sense of "deal with."

**shoot the breeze** Also, **shoot the shit, shoot the bull** or **throw the bull.** Talk idly, chat, as in *They've been sitting on the porch for hours, just shooting the breeze,* or *Let's have lunch sometime and shoot the shit,* or *The guys sat around the locker room, throwing the bull.* The first of these slang terms refers to talking into the wind. In the vulgar slang variants *shit* and *bull* are shortenings of *bullshit* and mean "empty talk" or "lies."

S

**shoot the works** Spend all one's money, use up one's resources, as in *He's broke after shooting the works on that new office building.* Also see THE WORKS.

**shoot up 1.** Grow or get taller very rapidly, as in *She has really shot up in the past year, and now she's taller than her mother.* **2.** Riddle something with bullets; damage or terrorize with gunfire. For example, *I liked the scene in which the cowboy stomps into the saloon, gets drunk, and shoots the place up.* **3.** Inject a drug into a vein, especially an illegal drug. For example, *The police caught him shooting up and arrested him.*

**shop** In addition to the idiom beginning with SHOP, also see BULL IN A CHINA SHOP; CLOSE UP (SHOP); SET UP SHOP; SHUT UP (SHOP); TALK SHOP.

**shop around 1.** Look for the best bargain, opportunity, or something similar, as in *This job offers only minimum wage, so she decided to shop around for one with better pay.* This expression refers to looking in different stores in search of bargains or a particular item. **2.** Look for a buyer for, offer for sale to various parties, as in *The company is now being actively shopped around.*

**shopping list** A list of things that one wants to obtain or hopes that someone else will do. For example, *A new car is on his shopping list if he wins the lottery,* or *She has a whole shopping list of complaints about her job.*

**shore up** Support something, prop up, as in *The new law was designed to shore up banks in danger of failure.*

**short** In addition to the idioms beginning with SHORT, also see BRING ONE UP SHORT; BY THE SHORT HAIRS; CAUGHT SOMETHING SHORT; CUT SHORT; FALL SHORT; FOR SHORT; IN BRIEF (SHORT); IN SHORT ORDER; IN SHORT SUPPLY; IN THE LONG (SHORT) RUN; LIFE IS TOO SHORT; LONG AND SHORT OF IT; LONG ON SOMETHING, BUT SHORT ON; LONG (SHORT) HAUL; MAKE A LONG STORY SHORT; MAKE SHORT WORK OF; NOTHING SHORT OF; RUN SHORT; SELL SHORT; STOP SHORT.

**short and sweet** Satisfyingly brief and pertinent, as in *When we asked about the coming merger, the chairman's answer was short and sweet—it wasn't going to happen.*

**short end of the stick, the** The inferior part, the worse side of an unequal deal. For example, *Helen got the short end of the stick when she was assigned another week of night duty.* Also see WRONG END OF THE STICK.

**short for** see FOR SHORT.

**short fuse, have a** Be unable to control one's temper, anger quickly. For example, *Don't annoy him—he has a short fuse.*

**short haul** see under LONG HAUL.

**short notice, on** Also, **at short notice.** With little advance warning or time to prepare, as in *They told us to be ready to move out on short notice.*

**short of 1.** Not having enough of something, as in *We're short of cash right now.* Also see FALL SHORT. **2.** Less than, inferior to, as in *Nothing short of her best effort was needed to make the team.* **3.** Other than, as in *Short of yelling, I had no other way of getting his attention.* **4.** See STOP SHORT, def. 3.

**short order 1.** Quickly; see IN SHORT ORDER. **2.** An order of food to be prepared and served quickly, as in *It's just a diner, serving short orders exclusively.* This expression led to the adjective **short-order,** used not only in **short-order cook,** a cook specializing in short orders, but in other terms such as **short-order divorce,** a divorce obtained quickly as a result of liberal divorce laws.

**short run** see under IN THE LONG RUN.

**short shrift, give** Also, **get short shrift.** Give (or receive) brief attention or little time. For example, *The architect made elaborate plans for the entry but gave short shift to the back of the house.*

**shot** In addition to the idioms beginning with SHOT, also see BIG CHEESE (SHOT); CALL THE SHOTS; CHEAP SHOT; GIVE IT ONE'S BEST SHOT; HAVE A CRACK (SHOT) AT; LIKE A SHOT; LONG SHOT; PARTING SHOT. Also see under SHOOT.

**shotgun** In addition to the idiom beginning with SHOTGUN, also see RIDE SHOTGUN.

**shotgun wedding** An agreement or compromise made through necessity, as in *Since neither side won a majority, the coalition government was obviously a shotgun wedding.* This expression refers to a marriage brought about by a woman's pregnancy, causing her father to point a literal or figurative gun at the responsible man's head.

**shot in the arm, a** A stimulus, something animating or encouraging, as in *Getting a new pianist was a real shot in the arm for the orchestra.* This expression refers to a drug given by injection.

**shot in the dark, a** A wild guess that has no basis to support it; also, an attempt that has little chance for success. For example, *It was a shot in the dark, but the engineers had a hunch that replacing the valve would make the system work,* or *You can try looking for your key on the beach, but I think it's a shot in the dark.*

**shot to hell** Worn out, ruined, as in *This carpet is shot to hell,* or *My privacy has been shot to hell because of all these reporters.* This term refers to being shot by gunfire.

**shot up** **1.** Severely wounded by gunfire; see SHOOT UP, def. 2. **2.** Drugged; see SHOOT UP, def. 3.

**should** In addition to the idiom beginning with SHOULD, also see (SHOULD) GET ONE'S HEAD EXAMINED.

**shoulder** In addition to the idiom beginning with SHOULDER, also see BROAD SHOULDERS; CHIP ON ONE'S SHOULDER; COLD SHOULDER; CRY ON SOMEONE'S SHOULDER; GOOD HEAD ON ONE'S SHOULDERS; HEAD AND SHOULDERS ABOVE; ON ONE'S SHOULDERS; PUT ONE'S SHOULDER TO THE WHEEL; RUB ELBOWS (SHOULDERS) WITH; SHRUG ONE'S SHOULDERS; SQUARE ONE'S SHOULDERS; STRAIGHT FROM THE SHOULDER.

**shoulder to shoulder** Close to or cooperating, as in *The volunteers worked shoulder to shoulder in the effort to rescue the lost children.* This expression originated in the military, at first referring to troops in close formation.

**should have stayed in bed, one** Also, **one should have stood in bed.** It has been such a bad day that one should never have gotten up at all. For example, *And then I got rear-ended at the stop sign—I should have stayed in bed,* or *It sounds like it's been one of those days when you should've stood in bed.* The ungrammatical variant is used humorously to express frustration or resignation.

**shout** In addition to the idioms beginning with SHOUT, also see ALL OVER BUT THE SHOUTING.

**shout down** Drown out or silence someone by yelling or jeering, as in *The audience went wild and shouted down the speaker.*

**shout from the rooftops** Announce publicly, as in *Just because I won first prize, you needn't shout it from the rooftops.* This term refers to climbing on a roof so as to be heard by more people.

**shove** see PUSH COMES TO SHOVE; PUSH (SHOVE) OFF; RAM (SHOVE) DOWN SOMEONE'S THROAT; STICK (SHOVE) IT.

**show** In addition to the idioms beginning with SHOW, also see DOG-AND-PONY SHOW; FOR SHOW; GET THE SHOW ON THE ROAD; GO TO SHOW; KNOW (SHOW) THE ROPES; ONE-MAN SHOW; ROAD SHOW; RUN THE SHOW; STEAL THE SHOW.

**show and tell** A public presentation or display, as in *It was a terrible bore, what with their show and tell of every last detail about their trip around the world.* This expression was first used to describe a learning exercise for young children in which each child in a group brings some object to show the others and talks about it.

**shower** see COLD SHOWER.

**show must go on, the** The activities must continue, no matter what unfortunate event has happened, as in *The chairman died yesterday, but the show must go on.* This expression comes from the theater and was later transferred to other situations.

**show off** Display something in an obvious, annoying way; also, seek attention by displaying one's accomplishments, abilities, or possessions. For example, *I'm wearing shorts to show off my Florida tan,* or *Karen loved showing off her new baby to her friends,* or *There's no need to show off, Fred; we all know you're a good dancer.*

**show of hands, a** An informal vote made by participants holding up one hand each to indicate a choice, as in *Let's have a show of hands—how many want the next meeting on Sunday?*

**show one's colors** see SHOW ONE'S TRUE COLORS.

**show one's face** Appear, as in *She was so upset that we were sure she'd never show her face at our house again.*

**show one's hand** Reveal one's plans, intentions, or resources, especially when they were previously hidden. For example, *We have to be careful not to show our hand to our competitors.* The *hand* here refers to a hand of cards, and showing them means turning them face up.

**show one's heels** Also, **show a clean pair of heels.** Run away, flee, as in *He wanted to ask her out, but she showed her heels before he had a chance,* or *As soon as the burglar alarm went off, the thief showed a clean pair of heels.*

**show one's true colors** Reveal oneself as one really is, as in *We always thought he was completely honest, but he showed his true colors when he tried to use a stolen credit card.* This expression refers to the antonym, FALSE COLORS, that is, sailing under a flag other than one's own.

**show signs of** Indicate or hint at something, as in *She definitely shows signs of accepting the appointment,* or *Terry's health shows no signs of improvement.*

**show someone a good time** Entertain someone, as in *I know Aunt Dorothy will show us a good time when we visit San Francisco.*

**show someone out** Also, **show someone to the door.** Escort someone who is leaving to the exit door, as in *Thanks for coming; please excuse me for not showing you out,* or *Please show Mr. Smith to the door.* Also see SEE OUT, def. 1; SHOW SOMEONE THE DOOR.

**show someone the door** Order someone to leave, as in *I never should have listened to him; I should have shown him the door at once.* This expression is not the same as **show someone to the door** (see under SHOW SOMEONE OUT ).

S

**show someone the ropes** see under KNOW THE ROPES.

**show someone who's boss** Act in a dominating way in order to convince other people that one is in control, as in *Just wait until he gets back—I'll show him who's boss.*

**show the way** Guide, as in *This division has shown the way to bigger profits.* This expression refers to the physical sense of guiding one in a particular direction. Also see LEAD THE WAY.

**show *something* to advantage** Also, **show *something* to good advantage** or **show *something* to one's advantage.** Display something in a flattering way, benefit, as in *This lighting shows the paintings to advantage,* or *Your extensive use of quotations shows your knowledge to good advantage.*

**show up** **1.** Be clearly visible, as in *The print doesn't show up against this dark background.* **2.** Put in an appearance, arrive, as in *I wonder if he'll show up at all.* **3.** Expose or reveal the true character of, as in *This failure showed up their efforts as a waste of time.* **4.** Perform better than someone, outdo someone, as in *John's high score on that math test really showed up the rest of the class.*

**shrift** see SHORT SHRIFT.

**shrinking violet, a** A very shy person, as in *She was a shrinking violet until she went away to college.*

**shrug off** **1.** Ignore something unpleasant, as in *That nasty review didn't bother him at all; he just shrugged it off.* **2.** Get rid of something, as in *She managed to shrug off her drowsiness and keep driving.* **3.** Wriggle out of a garment, as in *He shrugged off his coat.*

**shrug one's shoulders** Show an inability to make a decision or a lack of interest, as in *When I asked her if she minded staying home, she just shrugged her shoulders.* This idiom is repetitive, since *shrug* means "raise and contract the shoulders."

**shuffle** In addition to the idiom beginning with SHUFFLE, also see LOST IN THE SHUFFLE.

**shuffle off** **1.** Get rid of something, act evasively, as in *They've tried to shuffle off public questions about the safety of their planes.* **2.** Move away reluctantly, dragging one's feet, as in *The prisoners shuffled off to their work detail.*

**shut** In addition to the idioms beginning with SHUT, also see CLOSE (SHUT) DOWN; CLOSE (SHUT) ONE'S EYES TO; CLOSE (SHUT) THE DOOR ON; KEEP ONE'S MOUTH SHUT; OPEN AND SHUT CASE; PUT UP OR SHUT UP.

**shut down** **1.** See CLOSE DOWN, def. 1. **2.** Stop or switch off machinery, as in *They shut down all the machines for one week a year.* **3.** Stop speaking or force someone to be silent. For example, *After she criticized him, he shut down,* or *Without any concern for her feelings, the chairperson shut her down.*

**shut off** **1.** Stop the flow or passage of, as in *They shut off the water while they made the repairs.* **2.** Close off oneself, isolate, as in *Loners shut themselves off from the community.*

**shut one's eyes to** see CLOSE ONE'S EYES TO.

**shut out** **1.** Exclude someone or something, deny entry to, block, as in *Anyone convicted of a crime is shut out from the legal profession,* or *These curtains shut out all the light.* **2.** Prevent an opponent from scoring, as in *They were shut out in the last two games,* or *The President shut out his opponent in the New Hampshire primary.* Originating in baseball, this expression was later transferred to other sports and then to other situations.

**shut the door on** see CLOSE THE DOOR ON.

**shut up 1.** Imprison someone or something, confine, enclose, as in *The dog was shut up in the cellar for the night,* or *She shut up her memories and never talked about the past.* **2.** Close something completely, as in *The windows were shut up tightly, so no rain could come in.* This sense is also used in **shut up shop,** meaning "close the premises of a business," as in *It's late, let's shut up shop now.* Also see CLOSE UP. **3.** Cause someone to stop speaking, silence someone, as in *It's time someone shut him up.* **4.** Stop speaking, as in *I've told you what I think, and now I'll shut up.* This sense is also used as a rather rude imperative, as in *Shut up! You've said enough.*

**shy** In addition to the idiom beginning with SHY, also see BRICKS SHY OF A LOAD; ONCE BITTEN, TWICE SHY.

**shy away from** Avoid someone or something, evade, as in *He shied away from all questions concerning his private life.*

**sick** In addition to the idioms beginning with SICK, also see CALL IN SICK; GET SICK; MAKE ONE SICK; WORRY SICK.

**sick and tired** Also, **sick to death** or **tired to death.** Completely weary or bored, as in *I'm sick and tired of these phone calls from salespeople,* or *She was sick to death of that endless recorded music.* These exaggerated expressions of irritation and frustration suggest that one is weary to the point of illness or death.

**sick as a dog** Very ill, especially from a stomach problem. For example, *I don't know what was in that stew, but I was sick as a dog all night.* Why a dog should be viewed as particularly sick is not clear.

**sick at heart** Grieving, very disappointed, depressed, as in *We were sick at heart when we learned of her death.* This idiom compares heart disease to unhappiness.

**sick in bed** see LAID UP, def. 1.

**sick joke** A joke or story intended to be humorous but actually in very bad taste, as in *His stories always turn out to be sick jokes about people who are handicapped in some way.*

**sick to one's stomach** Also, **sick at one's stomach.** Nauseated, vomiting, as in *I always get sick to my stomach in the back seat of a car.*

**side** In addition to the idioms beginning with SIDE, also see BLIND SPOT (SIDE); BRIGHT SIDE; CAN'T HIT THE BROAD SIDE OF A BARN; CHOOSE UP (SIDES); GET ON SOMEONE'S GOOD SIDE; GET UP ON THE WRONG SIDE OF BED; IN GOOD WITH (ON SOMEONE'S GOOD SIDE); KNOW WHICH SIDE OF ONE'S BREAD IS BUTTERED; LAUGH OUT OF THE OTHER SIDE OF ONE'S MOUTH; LET SOMEONE (THE SIDE) DOWN; ON SOMEONE'S SIDE; ON THE SAFE SIDE; ON THE SIDE; OTHER SIDE OF THE COIN; RIGHT SIDE OF THE TRACKS; RIGHT-SIDE OUT; RIGHT-SIDE UP; SEAMY SIDE; SEE BOTH SIDES; SPLIT ONE'S SIDES; SUNNY SIDE; TAKE ASIDE (TO ONE SIDE); TAKE SIDES; THIS SIDE OF; THORN IN ONE'S SIDE; TIME IS ON ONE'S SIDE; WORK BOTH SIDES OF THE STREET; WRONG SIDE OF THE TRACKS.

**side against** Refuse to support someone, oppose in an argument, as in *The older club members sided against the new program director and her plans for change.* For an antonym, see SIDE WITH.

**side by side** Next to each other, close together, as in *They were walking down the street side by side when the taxi hit them,* or *In the new Russia, communism and capitalism are trying to live side by side.*

**sidelines** see ON THE SIDELINES.

**side of the tracks** see RIGHT SIDE OF THE TRACKS; WRONG SIDE OF THE TRACKS.

**side street** A minor road that has little traffic, as in *Our favorite hotel is on a quiet little side street.* The *side* in this idiom means "away from the main street." Also see BACK STREET.

**sideways** see KNOCK ONE FOR A LOOP (SIDEWAYS); LOOK SIDEWAYS AT.

**side with** Support or favor someone, as in *The Armenians traditionally side with the Greeks against the Turks.* For an antonym, see SIDE AGAINST.

**sight** In addition to the idioms beginning with SIGHT, also see AT FIRST GLANCE (SIGHT); CAN'T STAND (THE SIGHT OF); CATCH SIGHT OF; IN SIGHT; KNOW SOMEONE BY SIGHT; LOOK A SIGHT; LOSE SIGHT OF; LOVE AT FIRST SIGHT; LOWER ONE'S SIGHTS; ON SIGHT; OUT OF SIGHT; RAISE ONE'S SIGHTS; SEE THE SIGHTS; SET ONE'S SIGHTS ON; TWENTY-TWENTY HINDSIGHT.

**sight for sore eyes, a** One whom it is a relief or joy to see, as in *Linda, who had not seen him in 15 years, told him he was a sight for sore eyes.* This idiom suggests an appearance so welcome that it heals ailing eyes.

**sight unseen** Without having viewed the object in question, as in *He bought the car sight unseen.*

**sign** In addition to the idioms beginning with SIGN, see HIGH SIGN; SHOW SIGNS OF.

**signed, sealed, and delivered** Completed satisfactorily, as in *The house is sold—signed, sealed, and delivered.*

**sign in** Record one's arrival by signing a list, as in *He signed in both himself and his wife.* For an antonym, see SIGN OUT.

**sign off 1.** Announce the end of a communication, especially a broadcast. For example, *The station has signed off for the night.* **2.** Stop talking, become silent, as in *Every time the subject of marriage came up, Harold*

S

*signed off.* **3.** Also, **sign off on.** Express approval formally or conclusively, as in *The President got the majority leader to sign off on the tax proposal.*

**sign of the times, a** Something that one thinks shows how the world is changing, especially something that one does not approve of, as in *Trying to keep children from bringing guns to school—I guess it's a sign of the times.*

**sign on 1.** Enlist oneself as an employee or a volunteer, as in *Arthur decided to sign on with the new software company.* **2.** Begin radio or television broadcasting, especially at the beginning of the day, as in *What time does the station sign on?*

**sign one's own death warrant** Bring about one's own downfall, do oneself great harm, as in *By taking his secretary to a nightclub, the minister was signing his own death warrant.* This expression is used in an exaggerated way for severe results or punishments. Also see SHOOT ONESELF IN THE FOOT.

**sign on the dotted line** Agree formally or fully, as in *The deal is just about complete; all they have to do is sign on the dotted line.* This idiom refers to the broken line traditionally appearing at the bottom of a legal document, indicating the place for one's signature.

**sign out** Record the departure of a person or the removal of an object, as in *He turned in his room key and signed out about an hour ago,* or *I asked the librarian how many books I could sign out.*

**sign over** Legally give something to a different owner, as in *She signed over nearly all of her property to the church.*

**sign up** Enlist in an organization; also, register or subscribe to something. For example, *He signed up for four years in the navy,* or *Are you planning to sign up for that pottery class?*

**silence is golden** Keeping one's mouth shut is a great virtue, as in *Don't tell anyone else about it—silence is golden.* This expression is part of a much older proverb, **speech is silver and silence is golden.**

**silent majority, the** A group that makes up a majority of voters but does not widely express its views through speeches, marches, or demonstrations. For example, *They thought they had a convincing case, but they hadn't counted on the silent majority.* This idiom became popular when President Richard Nixon claimed that his policies were supported by a majority of citizens who did not bother to make their views known.

**silk** see CAN'T MAKE A SILK PURSE OUT OF A SOW'S EAR; SMOOTH AS SILK.

**silver** In addition to the idiom beginning with SILVER, also see BORN WITH A SILVER SPOON; HAND SOMEONE TO ONE ON A SILVER PLATTER.

**silver lining** An element of hope or a good quality in an otherwise bad situation, as in *Few people came to the charity sale, but the silver lining was that those who came spent a great deal of money.* This term is a shortening of **every cloud has a silver lining.**

**simmer down** Become calm after anger or excitement, as in *Simmer down, Mary; I'm sure he'll call you,* or *I haven't time to look at your report now, but I will when things have simmered down a bit.* This idiom comes from *simmer* in the sense of "cook at low heat, below the boiling point."

**simple** see PURE AND SIMPLE.

**sin** see LIVE IN SIN; MULTITUDE OF SINS; UGLY AS SIN; WAGES OF SIN.

**since** see GREATEST THING SINCE SLICED BREAD.

**sing a different tune** Also, **sing another tune.** See CHANGE ONE'S TUNE.

**sing for one's supper** Work for one's pay or reward, as in *Entertaining visiting scientists is part of the job; you know I have to sing for my supper.* This term refers to wandering musicians who performed in taverns and were paid with a meal.

**single** In addition to the idioms beginning with SINGLE, also see EACH AND EVERY (EVERY SINGLE).

**single file, in** Lined up one behind the other, as in *We have to walk in single file here.* This usage refers to a military formation.

**single *someone* out** Choose or distinguish from someone or something else, as in *We singled him out from all the other applicants.*

**sing one's praises** Praise someone or something with great enthusiasm, as in *The last I heard, critics were singing the praises of her new book.* Also see PRAISE SOMEONE TO THE SKIES.

**sing out** Call out loudly, shout, as in *One of them fell in the stream and sang out for help.*

**sink** In addition to the idioms beginning with SINK, also see DESERT A SINKING SHIP; ENOUGH TO SINK A SHIP; EVERYTHING BUT THE KITCHEN SINK; HEART SINKS.

**sinker** see HOOK, LINE, AND SINKER.

**sink in** Enter the mind, be absorbed, as in *The news of the crash didn't sink in right away.*

**sinking feeling, have a** Have a sense of dread or anxiety, as in *I had a sinking feeling that I'd forgotten my ticket.*

**sink one's teeth into** Also, **get one's teeth into.** Become fully engaged in, as in *He couldn't wait to sink his teeth into that problem.* This expression refers to an animal biting eagerly into its prey.

**sink or swim** Fail or succeed, no matter what, as in *Now that we've bought the farm, we'll have to make a go of it, sink or swim.* This

S

expression refers to the former practice of throwing a suspected witch, often weighted down, into deep water, where she usually drowned. If the victim did manage to swim, she was considered to be working with the devil and was then executed by other brutal means. This expression is also used as an adjective, as in *When it comes to teaching, he uses the sink-or-swim method.*

**sink through the floor** Suffer extreme embarrassment, as in *When she called our name on the list of those who owed dues, I sank through the floor.*

**sink to someone's level** Also, **stoop to someone's level.** Behave just as bad as someone else, as in *Don't react to his insults—you'll only be sinking to his level,* or *If they pick a fight with you, don't stoop to their level and fight back.*

**sit** In addition to the idioms beginning with SIT, also see AT A SITTING.

**sit at one's feet** see AT ONE'S FEET.

**sit back** **1.** Relax, as in *Now that the work's finished, we can just sit back.* **2.** Refrain from interfering or taking part, as in *Mom and Dad just sat back and watched as Sue tried to decide whether or not she should tell on her friends.* Also see SIT BY.

**sit bolt upright** see BOLT UPRIGHT.

**sit by** Also, **sit idly by.** Not interfere in a situation, remain passive, as in *I can't just sit by and let her get in trouble.*

**sit down** **1.** Take a seat, as in *Please sit down. I won't be long.* **2. sit down to.** Prepare to eat a meal, as in *At six we all sat down to dinner.*

**sit in** **1.** Attend or take part as a visitor, as in *My son's jazz group asked me to sit in tonight.* It is often put as **sit in on,** as in *They asked me to sit in on their poker game.* **2.** Take part in an organized protest in which seated participants refuse to move. For example, *The students threatened to sit in unless the dean was reinstated.* The protest itself is called a **sit-in. 3. sit in on.** Visit or observe something, as in *I'm sitting in on his class because I enjoy his lectures.* **4. sit in for.** Substitute for a regular member of a group, as in *I'm just sitting in for Harold, who couldn't make it.*

**sit in judgment** Make an unfavorable judgment of someone, especially a person thought to be one's inferior, as in *You have no right to sit in judgment on him—you've done worse things yourself.*

**sit on** Also, **sit upon. 1.** Talk about or debate over, as in *Another attorney was called to sit on the case.* **2.** Suppress or repress something or someone, as in *I know they were sitting on some evidence.* **3.** Postpone action or resolution on something, as in *I don't know why the city council is sitting on their decision.* **4.** Scold someone sharply, punish verbally, as in *If he interrupts one more time, I'm going to sit on him.*

**sit on one's hands** Take no action; also, fail to applaud. For example, *Instead of making a new will, George is sitting on his hands,* or *The audience was bored, sitting on their hands for the whole performance.*

**sit out** **1.** Also, **sit through.** Stay until the end of, as in *We decided to sit out the lecture instead of leaving early,* or *He was only eight when he sat through an entire opera—and it lasted nearly five hours.* **2.** Refrain from taking part in something, as in *Jane's foot hurt, so she sat out the last three dances.* **3.** Stay longer than someone else, as in *He sat out all the other guests, hoping to get a word alone with the host.*

**sit tight** Be patient, take no action, as in *If you just sit tight, I'm sure your passport will be returned to you.*

**sitting duck** An easy target, as in *If you park in front of a fire hydrant, you're a sitting duck for a ticket.* This term refers to the ease with which a hunter can shoot a duck that remains in one spot, in contrast to one in flight.

**sitting on a powder keg** In immediate danger, in an explosive situation, as in *Our office is sitting on a powder keg while management decides whether or not to close us down.* This term refers to sitting on a keg of gunpowder that could go off at any moment.

**sitting pretty** In a very good position; also, wealthy. For example, *The terms of the will left Mary sitting pretty.*

**situation** see NO-WIN SITUATION.

**sit up** **1.** Rise to a sitting position from lying down, as in *The sick child sat up and asked for a drink of water.* **2.** Stay up later than usual, as in *The nurse sat up with her all night long,* or *She sat up waiting for her daughter to get home.* **3.** Sit with the spine erect, as in *She was always telling the students to sit up.* **4.** Become suddenly alert, as in *The students sat up when he brought up the test.* The same sense appears in the related **sit up and take notice,** as in *When he mentioned the arrival of a movie star, they all sat up and took notice.*

**sit upon** see SIT ON.

**sit well with** Fit or suit, be acceptable to, please, as in *I don't think that explanation sits well with the teacher,* or *His sense of humor does not sit well with this serious audience.*

**six** In addition to the idioms beginning with SIX, also see DEEP SIX; JOE SIX-PACK.

**six feet under** Dead and buried, as in *No, you can't read my diary—not until I'm six feet under.* This expression refers to what has long been the traditional depth of a grave, that is, approximately the same as the length of the coffin.

**six of one, half a dozen of the other** The two choices are the same, as in *You can pay now or next week—it's six of one, half a dozen of the other.* This term simply equates two different ways of saying "six."

**sixth sense** Accurate intuition, as in *She had a sixth sense that they would find it in the cellar.* This term refers to a sense in addition to the five physical senses of sight, hearing, smell, taste, and touch.

**size** In addition to the idiom beginning with SIZE, also see CUT DOWN (TO SIZE); PICK ON (SOMEONE YOUR OWN SIZE); TAKE SOMEONE DOWN A NOTCH (TO SIZE); THAT'S ABOUT THE SIZE OF IT; TRY SOMETHING ON (FOR SIZE).

**size up** Make an estimate, opinion, or judgment of someone or something, as in *She sized up her opponent and decided to withdraw from the election.* This usage compares measuring the size of something to forming an opinion.

**skate** see CHEAP SKATE; (SKATE) ON THIN ICE.

**skeleton in one's closet** A shameful secret, as in *Both her parents were alcoholics; that was the skeleton in her closet.*

**skid** In addition to the idiom beginning with SKID, also see ON THE SKIDS; PUT THE SKIDS ON; PUT THE SKIDS UNDER.

**skid row** A neglected or rundown area inhabited the poor and the homeless. For example, *That part of town is our skid row,* or *His drinking was getting so bad we thought he was headed for skid row.* This expression originated in the lumber industry, where it referred to a road made of logs laid crosswise over which other logs were slid. Later the name *Skid Road* was used for the part of a town that had many bars, and the expression was later changed to *skid row,* with its current meaning.

**skin** In addition to the idioms beginning with SKIN, also see BEAUTY IS ONLY SKIN DEEP; BY THE SKIN OF ONE'S TEETH; GET UNDER SOMEONE'S SKIN; JUMP OUT OF ONE'S SKIN; MAKE ONE'S FLESH CREEP (SKIN CRAWL); MORE THAN ONE WAY TO SKIN A CAT; NO SKIN OFF ONE'S NOSE; SAVE ONE'S NECK (SKIN); SOAKED TO THE SKIN; THICK SKIN.

**skin *someone* alive** Punish someone severely, as in *If I find the guy who stole my car, I'll skin him alive.*

**skin and bones** So thin that one's bones are clearly visible beneath the skin. This phrase often is expanded to **nothing but skin and bones,** as in *She came home from her trip nothing but skin and bones.*

**skin deep** see BEAUTY IS ONLY SKIN DEEP.

**skin off one's nose** see NO SKIN OFF ONE'S NOSE.

**skin of one's teeth** see BY THE SKIN OF ONE'S TEETH.

**skip** In addition to the idioms beginning with SKIP, also see HEART MISSES (SKIPS) A BEAT; HOP, SKIP, AND A JUMP.

**skip bail** Also, **jump bail.** Fail to appear in court for trial and thereby give up the bail bond (paid to guarantee one's appearance). For example, *He can't afford to skip bail—he would lose half a million dollars,* or *We were sure she would jump bail, but she finally showed up.* This idiom uses *skip* and *jump* in the sense of "evade." Also see MAKE BAIL.

**skip it** Drop the subject, ignore the matter, as in *I don't understand what you mean. Oh, skip it for now.* This interjection uses *skip* in the sense of "don't bother."

**skip out** Leave quickly, as in *They just skipped out of town yesterday.* It is also put as **skip out on,** meaning "desert, abandon," as in *He skipped out on his wife, leaving her with the four children.*

**skip over** Leave something out or ignore somebody. For example, *Why don't we just skip over that question for now?* or *I think you skipped over me when you took attendance.*

**sky** In addition to the idiom beginning with SKY, also see BLOW SKY-HIGH; OUT OF A CLEAR BLUE SKY; PIE IN THE SKY REACH FOR THE SKY.

**sky's the limit, the** There is no limit (to ambition, hopes, expense, or the like). For example, *Order anything you like on the menu—the sky's the limit tonight,* or *He's so brilliant he can do anything—the sky's the limit.*

**slack off** Become less active or intense, as in *If business ever slacks off, we can go on vacation,* or *When the project fell behind schedule again, she thought we were slacking off.*

**slam dunk** A forceful, dramatic move, as in *That indictment was a slam dunk if ever there was one.* This expression is also often put as a verb, meaning "make a forceful move against someone," as in *This is a great chance for us to slam-dunk the opposition.* The idiom comes from basketball, where it refers to a dramatic shot in which the ball is thrust into the basket from above the rim.

**slap down** Restrain or correct someone in an emphatic way, as in *They thought he was getting far too arrogant and needed to be slapped down.* This idiom literally means "inflict a physical blow."

**slap in the face, a** A sharp verbal criticism or a rejection, as in *Being criticized in front of my staff was a real slap in the face,* or *We thought it quite a slap in the face when they returned our letter unopened.* This term can refer either to a literal blow or to a figurative one.

**slap on the back, a** A gesture of congratulations, as in *The coach gave him a slap on the back for coming in first.* This gesture is usually an actual light slap on someone's back to show support or approval.

**slap on the wrist, a** A mild reprimand, as in *I was fined heavily, and all my friend got from the judge was a slap on the wrist.* This idiom is used in a figurative sense.

**slate** see CLEAN SLATE.

**slated for, be** Be planned or scheduled, as in *The history test is slated for next Thursday,* or *He's slated for a second round of blood tests.*

**slaughter** see LIKE A LAMB TO THE SLAUGHTER.

**sleaze factor** The element in a political party, administration, or other organization that is corrupt, controversial, or touched by scandal. For example, *I can't see myself making a campaign contribution to them—there's too much of a sleaze factor.* This slang expression comes from the adjective *sleazy,* which means "vulgar" or "low-class."

**sledding** see EASY SLEDDING; SMOOTH SAILING (SLEDDING); TOUGH SLEDDING.

**sleep** In addition to the idioms beginning with SLEEP, also see LET SLEEPING DOGS LIE; LOSE SLEEP OVER; PUT TO SLEEP. Also see under ASLEEP.

**sleep around** Engage in sex without caring who one's partner is, as in *Fortunately, no one mentioned that both of them had slept around in their younger days.*

**sleep a wink, not** Not sleep at all, as in *I couldn't sleep a wink last night.* In this expression *wink* refers to closing the eyes for sleep.

**sleep in** **1.** Sleep late, either accidentally or on purpose. For example, *I slept in and missed my usual train,* or *On weekends we like to sleep in.* **2.** Sleep at one's place of employment, as in *They have a butler and maid who both sleep in.*

**sleep like a log** Sleep very soundly, as in *I slept like a log last night.* This idiom transfers a log's inability to move to a person who is sound asleep.

**sleep on something** Consider something for a time, especially overnight, before deciding, as in *I don't know if I want to go on such a long hike; let me sleep on it,* or *We should sleep on that idea before we make a decision.* This idiom is used figuratively.

**sleep out** **1.** Sleep at home, as opposed to where one works, as in *We have a nurse for her, but she sleeps out.* **2.** Sleep away from one's own home, as in *She's not here; she's sleeping out.*

**sleep over** Spend the night as a guest in another's home, as in *Karen's friend Betty is going to sleep over tonight.* This idiom often applies to children staying overnight at a friend or relative's house.

**sleep through** **1.** Sleep without waking for a period of time, usually the night, as in *At three months many babies have learned to sleep through.* **2.** Fail to pay attention to something, as in *She slept through the lecture, so she had trouble answering the teacher's question.*

**sleep with** Be sexually intimate with, as in *The director had made several attempts to sleep with the actress.* The related phrase **sleep together** means "have sexual relations," as in *We wondered if they were sleeping together but didn't dare ask them.* The verb *sleep* has long been associated with sex.

**sleeve** see CARD UP ONE'S SLEEVE; LAUGH UP ONE'S SLEEVE; ROLL UP ONE'S SLEEVES; WEAR ONE'S HEART ON ONE'S SLEEVE.

**sleight of hand** Trickery, cunning, as in *By some sleight of hand they managed to overlook all bonuses.* This term refers to performing magic tricks with the hands.

**slice** In addition to the idioms beginning with SLICE, also see GREATEST THING SINCE SLICED BREAD; NO MATTER HOW YOU SLICE IT.

**slice of life** A dramatic presentation that portrays life realistically, as in *We're tired of paying to see films that give us a slice of life; we prefer to be entertained.* It is also used as an adjective, **slice-of-life,** as in *She's always reading one of those slice-of-life novels.*

**slice of the pie** Also, **slice of the cake.** A share of the proceeds or benefits, as in *It's reasonable for a heavy contributor to ask for a big slice of the pie.* For a synonym, see PIECE OF THE ACTION.

**slick as a whistle** Very smooth and neat; also, smoothly, quickly, easily. For example, *That salesman is as slick as a whistle,* or *The bookcase went in place slick as a whistle.*

**slide** see LET SOMETHING RIDE (SLIDE); LET SOMETHING SLIP (SLIDE).

**slight** see IN THE LEAST (SLIGHTEST).

**slim pickings** A small amount left after others have taken a share. For example, *After each of the children took what they wanted of Mother's things, it was slim pickings for the rest of the family.* This expression refers to the way animals leave a carcass.

**sling** In addition to the idioms beginning with SLING, also see ASS IN A SLING.

**sling hash** Serve food in a restaurant, especially a cheap establishment. For example, *The only job she could find was slinging hash in the neighborhood diner.* This term refers to the unappealing nature of the food.

**sling mud at** Insult or discredit someone, as in *The paper became famous for slinging mud at movie stars.*

**slink away** Also, **slink off.** Leave in an ashamed or secretive way, as in *The shoplifter slipped the scarf into his coat pocket* *and slunk away,* or *After that severe scolding, she slunk off.* This term uses *slink* in the sense of "move stealthily."

**slink over** **1.** Approach a person or a group of people in a way that suggests a suspicious motive or the intent to be sexually appealing, as in *Did you see how she slunk over to our table?* or *It's only a matter of time until he slinks over and asks to join us.* **2.** Behave in a defeated or inferior way. For example, *After I'd called several times, the dog slunk over to me.*

**slip** In addition to the idioms beginning with SLIP, also see GIVE SOMEONE THE SLIP; LET SOMETHING SLIP.

**slip a cog** Also, **slip a gear** or **slip one's gears.** Lose one's ability to reason soundly or make correct judgments, as in *She must have slipped a cog or she would never have gone out barefoot in December,* or *What's the matter with him? Has he slipped his gears?* These slang usages refer to a mechanical failure resulting when a cog of a gear or a gear fails to mesh.

**slip of the tongue** Also, **slip of the lip** or **slip of the pen.** An unintentional mistake in speaking (or writing), as in *She didn't mean it; it was a slip of the tongue,* or *He intended to write "the honorable," but a slip of the pen turned it into "reverend."*

**slip one's mind** Forget or overlook something, as in *I meant to pick up the milk, but it slipped my mind.*

**slip out** **1.** See LET SOMETHING SLIP. **2.** Also, **slip away** or **slip off.** Leave quietly and unobtrusively, as in *She slipped out without telling anyone,* or *Let's slip away before the speech,* or *Joe and Sheila slipped off to Bermuda.*

**slippery as an eel** Hard to catch, cunning, as in *When it comes to talking about his personal life, Jim's slippery as an eel.* This idiom refers to the eel's skin, which has tiny scales and is quite slippery when wet.

S

**slippery slope** A dangerous course, one that leads easily to disaster, as in *He's on a slippery slope, compromising his values to please both the bosses and the union.* This expression refers to climbing a slick hillside, in constant danger of falling.

**slip something over on** Deceive someone, trick, as in *Her lawyer tried to slip one over on him, but his lawyer wouldn't let him get away with it,* or *Don't trust Dan—he's always slipping something over on his customers.*

**slip through one's fingers** see LET SOMETHING SLIP, def. 3.

**slip up** Make a mistake, commit an error, as in *I slipped up and sent the e-mail to the wrong person.*

**slow** In addition to the idioms beginning with SLOW, also see (SLOW) ON THE UPTAKE.

**slow as molasses** Also, **slow as molasses in January.** Extremely slow, as in *The old dog walked slow as molasses.* This expression refers to the fact that in cold weather molasses—a thick, brown liquid sugar—is too thick to pour.

**slow burn** Slowly increasing anger. It is often put as **do a slow burn,** meaning "gradually grow angrier," as in *I did a slow burn when he kept me waiting for three hours.* The *burn* in this idiom comes from *burn up* in the sense of "make furious."

**slow but sure** Also, **slowly but surely.** Gradual or plodding but certain to finish, as in *Slow but sure this book's getting written,* or *Slowly but surely he got better.* A related phrase appears in the proverb **slow and steady wins the race,** which is the moral of Aesop's fable about the race between a tortoise and a hare, which stopped to nap during the race and therefore lost.

**slow down** **1.** Delay, retard, reduce speed, as in *She slowed down the sled by dragging her foot,* or *Slow down, Bill; you're driving much too fast.* Also see SLOW UP. **2.** Become less active or energetic, as in *Now that Grandpa is in his seventies he has slowed down quite a bit.*

**slow on the uptake** see ON THE UPTAKE.

**slow up** Decrease or cause something to decrease speed, as in *The train slowed up as it approached the curve,* or *Come on, you're slowing me up.* Also see SLOW DOWN, def. 1.

**sly** see ON THE SLY.

**small** In addition to the idioms beginning with SMALL, also see BIG FISH IN A SMALL POND; (SMALL) COG IN THE WHEEL; GIVE THANKS FOR SMALL BLESSINGS; IN (SMALL) PART; IT'S A SMALL WORLD; LITTLE (SMALL) FROG IN A BIG POND; LOOK SMALL; MAKE A (SMALL) FORTUNE; NO (SMALL) WONDER.

**small potatoes** Of little importance, as in *It's silly to worry about that bill; it's small potatoes.* Also see SMALL FRY, def. 2.

**small cog in a large wheel** see COG IN THE WHEEL.

**small frog in a big pond** see LITTLE FROG IN A BIG POND.

**small fry** **1.** Young children, as in *This show is not suitable for small fry.* **2.** People of little importance or influence, as in *She wasn't about to invite the Washington small fry to the reception.* Both usages refer to *fry* in the sense of "young or small fish."

**small hours, the** Also, **the wee hours.** The hours following midnight, as in *I stayed up working through the small hours,* or *My parents didn't come home until the wee hours.* The adjectives *small* and *wee* both refer to the low numbers of those hours (one o'clock, two o'clock, etc.).

**small print** Also, **fine print.** The details in a contract or other document, often indicating limitations or other disadvantages. For example, *Be sure you read the small print before you sign your name to it,* or *The warranty terms were in fine print, so buyers wouldn't notice that it was only good for a month.* This idiom refers to the fact that such material is often printed in smaller type than the rest of the document.

**small talk** Casual or unimportant conversation, as in *We stood around making small talk until the guest of honor arrived.* The *small* in this expression refers to unimportant subjects of conversation, as opposed to serious ones.

**small time** A modest or minor level of achievement, as in *Her success took her out of the small time to prime-time television.* This expression is also used as an adjective. For example, *Small-time criminals took over the illegal gambling operations in our town.* The term was originally used for second-rate theaters and productions. Also see BIG TIME, def. 2.

**small wonder** see NO WONDER.

**smart aleck** An aggressively obnoxious individual, a wise guy, as in *New teachers often have a hard time coping with the smart alecks in their classes.*

**smart as a whip** Very intelligent or clever, as in *Little Brenda is smart as a whip; she's only three and she's already learning to read.* This expression refers to the sharp crack of a whip. Also see MIND LIKE A STEEL TRAP.

**smart set, the** A fashionable social group, as in *This restaurant has been discovered by the smart set.* This idiom is rarely used today.

**smash hit** An outstanding success, as in *She was a smash hit in the role of the lawyer,* or *His first book was a smash hit, but this one isn't doing well.*

**smear campaign** An attempt to ruin a reputation by spreading scandalous rumors, as in *This press agent is well known for starting smear campaigns against her clients' major competitors.*

**smell** In addition to the idioms beginning with SMELL, also see COMING UP (COME UP SMELLING LIKE) ROSES; STINK (SMELL) TO HIGH HEAVEN.

**smell a rat** Suspect something is wrong, especially a betrayal of some kind. For example, *When I didn't hear any more from my boyfriend, I began to smell a rat.* This expression refers to a cat sniffing out a rat.

**smell fishy** Be suspicious, as in *His explanation definitely smells fishy; my guess is that he's lying.* This idiom refers to the fact that fresh fish have no odor, but stale or rotten ones do.

**smell to high heaven** see STINK TO HIGH HEAVEN.

**smell up** Also, **stink up.** Cause a bad odor, as in *These onions smell up the whole house,* or *Your old sneakers are stinking up the closet; throw them out.*

**smile** In addition to the idiom beginning with SMILE, also see CRACK A SMILE.

**smile on** Look with favor or approval on someone, as in *The current administration smiles on anyone who gives it helpful publicity.*

**smithereens** see BLOW SOMETHING TO SMITHEREENS.

**smoke** In addition to the idiom beginning with SMOKE, also see CHAIN SMOKER; GO UP IN FLAMES (SMOKE); HOLY COW (SMOKE); NO SMOKE WITHOUT FIRE; WATCH ONE'S DUST (SMOKE).

**smoke out** Expose something, reveal, bring to public view, as in *Reporters thrive on smoking out a scandal.* This expression refers to driving a person or an animal out of a hiding place by filling it with smoke.

**smoking gun** Something that serves as unquestionable evidence or proof, especially of a crime. For example, *They claimed that there was no smoking gun in the Oval Office and that the President had no role in tampering with the evidence.*

**smooth** In addition to the idioms beginning with SMOOTH, also see TAKE THE ROUGH WITH THE SMOOTH.

**smooth as silk** Without problems or obstacles, as in *The contract negotiations went smooth as silk.* This expression refers to the slippery quality of silk. Also see SMOOTH SAILING.

**smooth over** Also, **smooth the way.** Get rid of obstacles or difficulties, as in *We tried to smooth things over between the families before the wedding but didn't succeed.*

**smooth sailing** Also, **smooth sledding.** Easy progress, as in *We had a hard time setting up the new computer system, but it'll be smooth sailing from here on,* or *I thought it would be smooth sledding once we got out of the city traffic.* Also see EASY SLEDDING; PLAIN SAILING.

**snag** see HIT A SNAG.

**snail mail** Ordinary postal service, as opposed to electronic communications. For example, *He doesn't have a computer, so he's still using snail mail.* This slang idiom, which refers to the slowness of a snail, became popular at least partly for its rhyme.

**snail's pace** A very slow pace, as in *They're making progress testing the new medicine, but at a snail's pace.*

**snake in the grass** A sneaky, untrustworthy person, as in *Ben secretly applied for the same job as his best friend; no one knew he was such a snake in the grass.* This expression refers to a poisonous snake concealed in tall grass.

**snap, be a** see BREEZE, BE A.

**snap at** Speak irritably or abruptly to someone, as in *This teacher was always snapping at the children.* This use of *snap* transfers an animal's sudden bite at something to a verbal attack.

**snap back** Return to normal after a setback, recover rapidly, as in *I think we'll snap back quickly from this business downturn.* This idiom transfers the sudden release of tension on, for example, a tree branch to other kinds of recovery.

**snap judgment** A hurried or thoughtless decision or finding, as in *George was known for making snap judgments on personnel questions; he rarely bothered to investigate enough.* This expression uses *snap* in the sense of "quick."

**snap one's fingers at** Treat something with contempt, scorn, disregard, as in *Peter just snapped his fingers at the speed limit and drove as fast he liked,* or *Joan snapped her fingers at the rumor about their bankruptcy.* This expression refers to the gesture of striking one's finger against one's thumb, thus making a sharp noise.

**snap out of** Suddenly recover, as in *You can't expect the economy to snap out of a recession overnight.* This expression is also put as a command, **snap out of it!,** which tells someone to return to his or her normal state of mind from an undesirable condition such as grief, self-pity, or depression; for example, *Snap out of it, Sue; it's over and done with.*

**snappy** see under MAKE HASTE.

**snap someone's head off** see BITE SOMEONE'S HEAD OFF.

**snap to** Move swiftly to an action, as in *The troops snapped to attention.* This phrase is sometimes expanded to **snap to it,** as in *You'd better snap to it if we're going to finish today.*

**snap up** Grab something for one's own use, as in *As soon as they lower the price, we intend to snap up the house; it's exactly what we want.*

**sneaking suspicion** A guess or hunch about someone or something that cannot be proven or demonstrated at the time, as in *She has a sneaking suspicion that her friend betrayed her.*

**sneak preview** An advance showing of something, as in *It was supposed to be bad luck, but she gave the bridegroom a sneak preview of her wedding gown.* This expression originally referred to a single public showing of a motion picture before its general release and was later transferred to other events.

**sneeze at** see NOT TO BE SNEEZED AT.

**sniff out** Uncover something, find, as in *If there's anything to that rumor, Gail will sniff it out.* This expression refers to an animal sniffing for prey.

**snit** see IN A SNIT.

**snow** In addition to the idioms beginning with SNOW, also see PURE AS THE DRIVEN SNOW.

**snowball's chance in hell, a** No chance at all, as in *He hasn't a snowball's chance in hell of getting there in two hours.* This idiom, nearly always used negatively, refers to the traditional view of hell as extremely hot, causing snow to melt at once.

**snow job, a** An effort to deceive, persuade, or overwhelm someone with insincere talk. For example, *Peter tried to give the officer a snow job about an emergency at the hospital, but he got a speeding ticket anyway.*

**snow under** Overwhelm, overpower, as in *I can't go; I'm just snowed under with work,* or *We were snowed under by more votes than we could have anticipated.* This expression refers to being buried in snow.

**snuff** In addition to the idiom beginning with SNUFF, also see UP TO PAR (SNUFF).

**snuff out 1.** Extinguish something, put a sudden end to, as in *Three young lives were snuffed out in that automobile accident.* This usage uses *snuff* in the sense of "put out a candle by pinching the wick." **2.** Kill someone, murder, as in *If he told the police what he knew, the gang would snuff him out.* **3.** Also, **snuff it.** Die or be killed, as in *He looked very ill indeed, as though he might snuff out any day,* or *Grandpa just snuffed it.*

**snug as a bug in a rug** Very cozy and comfortable, as in *During the blizzard we had plenty of firewood and stayed in the cottage, snug as a bug in a rug.* This expression, thought to refer to a moth larva happily feeding inside a rolled-up carpet, probably owes its popularity to the rhyme.

**so** In addition to the idioms beginning with SO, also see AND SO FORTH (AND SO ON); AS (SO) FAR AS; AS (SO) FAR AS POSSIBLE; AS (SO) FAR AS THAT GOES; AS (SO) LONG AS; AS (SO) MUCH AS; EVEN SO; EVERY NOW AND THEN (SO OFTEN); GO SO FAR AS TO; HOW COME (SO); IN SO MANY WORDS; IS THAT A FACT (SO); I TOLD YOU SO; JUST SO; NEVER HAD IT SO GOOD; NOT (SO) BAD; ON ONE'S SAY-SO; OR SO; TAKE IT (JUST SO MUCH); WITHOUT SO MUCH AS.

**soaked to the skin** Also, **soaked through** or **soaked through and through.** Drenched, extremely wet, as in *What a downpour; I'm soaked to the skin,* or *She fell in the stream and was soaked through.* This idiom implies that water has penetrated one's clothing, so one is thoroughly wet.

**soak up 1.** Absorb something, take in, as in *I lay on the beach, soaking up the sun,* or *She often went to hear poets read their work, soaking up every word.* This usage refers to absorbing a liquid. **2.** Drink to excess, as in *She can really soak up her beer.*

**so-and-so** **1.** A person or thing that is not named, as in *He told me to call so-and-so, but I can't remember her name.* **2.** Someone so despised that his or name is not mentioned, *Don't invite that foul-mouthed so-and-so to our party.* Also see WHO SHALL REMAIN NAMELESS.

**soap** In addition to the idiom beginning with SOAP, also see NO DICE (SOAP); ON ONE'S SOAPBOX; SOFT SOAP.

**soap opera** **1.** A radio or television serial with stock characters in domestic dramas that are noted for being sentimental and melodramatic. For example, *He doesn't work, he just watches soap operas all day long.* This term refers to the fact that the sponsors of the original radio shows were often soap manufacturers. **2.** A real-life situation resembling one that might happen in a soap opera, as in *She just goes on and on about her various medical and family problems, one long soap opera.*

**so as to** In order to, as in *We took off our shoes so as to avoid scratching the newly polished floors.* This idiom is always followed by an infinitive. For a synonym, see IN ORDER, def. 5.

**so be it** Let it be so, I accept it as it is. For example, *If you can't change the reservation, so be it; I'll travel on Monday.* This phrase is often given as a translation of the Hebrew (and Greek and Latin) *amen.*

**sober as a judge** Not at all intoxicated, quite clear-headed, as in *Even after three drinks he was sober as a judge.*

**sob story** A tale of personal hardship, true or invented, that is intended to arouse pity in the listener. For example, *She always came up with some sob story to excuse her absences, but no one believed her.*

**society** see MUTUAL ADMIRATION SOCIETY.

**sock away** Put money in a safe place for future use, as in *I've got about $2,000 socked away for a new car.* This usage may refer to putting one's savings in a sock.

**sock in** Engulf someone or something, especially an airport, in thick fog or other weather conditions that make it difficult to see, as in *The airport was socked in all morning, and air traffic was at a standstill,* or *We finally got to the peak and were totally socked in—there was no view at all.*

**sock it to** Deliver a physical blow, forceful comment, or reprimand to someone, as in *The judge often socks it to the jury in a murder case.* This expression uses *sock* in the sense of "strike hard." It is also put as a command, as in *Sock it to them, kid!* or *Sock it to me!* The idiom is sometimes used to give encouragement but can also have sexual overtones.

**so far** Also, **thus far.** Up to this point, as in *So far we haven't seen him in the crowd,* or *They've made very little progress on their report thus far.*

**so far as** see under AS FAR AS.

**so far, so good** Matters are fine up to this point, as in *You've done the research but not written the paper? Well, so far, so good.*

**soft** In addition to the idioms beginning with SOFT, also see HARD (SOFT) SELL.

**soften up** Reduce someone's resistance, as in *His sales motto was: a fine lunch and a few drinks often will soften up a prospective customer.*

**soft in the head** With limited mental ability; also, silly, foolish. For example, *He's nice enough but a bit soft in the head.* The *soft* in this idiom refers to a weakness in mental capacity.

**soft job** An easy job or task, as in *He really has a soft job—his assistants do nearly all the work.* This expression uses *soft* in the sense of "involving little or no hardship or discomfort."

**soft on** **1.** Attracted to or emotionally involved with, as in *He's been soft on Margaret for years.* **2.** Not stern, easygoing, especially too much so. For example, *Some think the court has been soft on young offenders.*

**soft pedal** Something that lessens, restrains, or plays down, as in *The mayor put a soft pedal on this potentially explosive situation.* This expression refers to the soft pedal of a piano, which reduces the volume of the sound. It led to the verb **soft-pedal,** meaning "make less emphatic, downplay," as in *They soft-pedaled their demands in order to speed up the negotiations.*

**soft sell** see HARD SELL, def. 1.

**soft soap** Flattery, coaxing, as in *She's only six, but she's already learned how to get her way with soft soap.* This expression is also used as a verb, as in *She soft-soaped her grandfather into buying her a pony.* The idiom refers to a wet bar of soap, comparing its slippery quality to insincere flattery.

**soft spot** **1.** A weak or vulnerable point, as in *That's the soft spot in his argument.* **2. have a soft spot for.** Have a tender or sentimental feeling for, as in *Grandpa had a soft spot for his first grandson.* This expression uses *soft* in the sense of "tender."

**soft touch, a** Someone easily persuaded or taken advantage of, especially in giving away money. For example, *Ask Dan for the money; he's always a soft touch.*

**so help me** Also, **so help me God.** I swear that what I am saying is true, as in *So help me, I haven't enough cash to pay for the tickets,* or *I wasn't there, so help me God.* This idiom became a formula for swearing a formal oath and is still so used in courts of law for swearing in a witness (*I swear to tell the truth, the whole truth, and nothing but the truth, so help me God*).

**soil one's hands** see DIRTY ONE'S HANDS.

**so long** Good-bye, as in *So long, we'll see you next week.*

**so long as** see AS LONG AS, def. 2 and 3.

**so many** **1.** Such a large number, as in *There were so many guests that we didn't have enough chairs.* **2.** An unspecified number, as in *There are supposed to be so many shrimp per pound, but of course the exact number depends on their size and weight.* **3.** Forming a group, as in *The reporters turned on the speaker like so many tigers let loose.*

**some** see AND THEN SOME; CATCH SOME RAYS; CATCH SOME Z'S; DIG UP (SOME DIRT); IN A (SOME) SENSE; IN SOME MEASURE; ONE OF THESE DAYS (SOME DAY); TAKE SOME DOING; TO SOME DEGREE; WIN SOME, LOSE SOME.

**somebody up there loves one** One is having very good luck right now; also, someone with power is favoring one. For example, *I won $40 on that horse—somebody up there loves me,* or *I don't know how he got that great assignment; maybe somebody up there loves him.* This idiom, generally used half-jokingly, refers either to heavenly help or to the aid of a worldly higher authority. Also see FRIEND IN COURT.

**somehow** see under OR OTHER.

**someone's word is law** Whatever a particular person says cannot be ignored and must be acted on, as in *In this house, Mom's word is law.*

**something** In addition to the idioms beginning with SOMETHING, also see BUY SOMETHING; GET (HAVE) SOMETHING ON SOMEONE; HAVE SOMETHING AGAINST; LOOK LIKE SOMETHING THE CAT DRAGGED IN; MAKE SOMETHING OF; NOT PUT SOMETHING PAST ONE; PULL SOMETHING ON; START SOMETHING; TAKE SOMETHING; YOU KNOW SOMETHING.

**something else** A person, thing, or event that is quite remarkable, as in *That player is something else,* or *Her new film is something else.* The *else* in this idiom means "other than ordinary."

**something else again** A different case entirely, as in *If he'd called to cancel, we wouldn't mind, but not showing up, that's something else again.*

**something is up** Also, **something must be up.** An unknown event is being planned, either to surprise or trick someone. For example, *I knew something was up when the boss called me in,* or *Something must be up—that's the third time he's left the table to make a phone call.*

**something like** Similar to, resembling, as in *They want a flower garden something like the ones they saw in England.*

**something of a** To some extent, as in *Our professor is something of a joker.*

**something or other** see under OR OTHER.

**something tells me** I suspect, I have a feeling, as in *Something tells me that she's not really as ill as she says,* or *Something told him that it was going to snow.*

**sometime thing, a** Something casual or quickly passing, as in *For most freelance musicians, work is a sometime thing.*

**somewhere** In addition to the idiom beginning with SOMEWHERE, also see GET SOMEWHERE; (SOMEWHERE) OR OTHER.

**somewhere along the line** At some point in time, as in *Somewhere along the line I'm sure I saw that photo.*

**so much** An unspecified amount or cost, as in *They sell the fabric at so much per yard.* Also see AS MUCH AS; SO MUCH FOR; SO MUCH THE.

**so much as** see AS MUCH AS, def. 3.

**so much for** We have adequately treated or are finished with something, as in *So much for this year's sales figures; now let's estimate next year's.*

**so much the** To that extent or degree, as in *You decided to stay home? So much the better, because now we won't need a second car.* This usage is always followed by a comparative adjective, such as *better* in the example.

**son** In addition to the idiom beginning with SON, also see FAVORITE SON; LIKE FATHER, LIKE SON.

**so near, yet so far** A greatly desired object or achievement was close to being achieved, but one failed, as in *I almost had all that money in my hands—so near, yet so far.*

**song** In addition to the idiom beginning with SONG, also see FOR A SONG; SWAN SONG.

**song and dance** A complicated story or effort to explain and justify something, or to deceive and mislead someone. For example, *Do you really believe his song and dance about the alarm not going off, being stopped for speeding, and then the car breaking down?* or *At every annual meeting the chairman goes through the same song and dance about the company's great future plans.* This term originally referred to a vaudeville act featuring singing and dancing.

**son of a bitch** Also, **SOB; son of a gun.** A mean, disagreeable individual, as in *He was regarded as the worst son of a bitch in the industry,* or *He ran out on her? What an SOB,* or *He's a real son of a gun when it comes to paying back the money he owes.* The first of these terms, calling a man the son of a female dog, is considered vulgar enough to have given rise to the two variants, both euphemisms. **Son of a gun** and **son of a bitch** are also put as exclamations expressing surprise, amazement, disgust, or disappointment, as in *Son of a bitch! I lost my ticket,* or *I'll be a* *son of a gun! That must be the governor.* [Vulgar slang]

**soon** see AS SOON AS; FOOL AND HIS MONEY ARE SOON PARTED; HAD RATHER (SOONER); JUST AS SOON; NO SOONER SAID THAN DONE; SPEAK TOO SOON.

**sooner or later** Eventually, at some unspecified future time, as in *Sooner or later we'll have to answer that letter,* or *It's sure to stop raining sooner or later.* This term suggests that some future event is certain to happen.

**sooner the better, the** As quickly or early as possible, as in *As for paying that bill, the sooner the better.*

**sore** In addition to the idiom beginning with SORE, also see SIGHT FOR SORE EYES; STICK OUT (LIKE A SORE THUMB).

**sore point, a** A sensitive or annoying issue, as in *Don't mention diets to Elsie; it's a sore point with her.*

**sorrow** see DROWN ONE'S SORROWS.

**sorry** see BETTER SAFE THAN SORRY.

**sort** see AFTER A FASHION (SORT); ALL KINDS (SORTS) OF; BAD SORT; IT TAKES ALL SORTS; KIND (SORT) OF; NOTHING OF THE KIND (SORT); OF SORTS; OUT OF SORTS.

**so that** **1.** In order that, as in *I stopped so that you could catch up.* **2.** With the result that, as in *Mail the package now so that it will arrive on time.* **3. so . . . that.** In such a way or to such an extent that, as in *The line was so long that I could scarcely find the end of it.* The first two usages are sometimes put simply as **so,** as in *I stopped so you could catch up,* or *Mail it now so it will arrive on time.*

**so there!** I'm right, and you're wrong, said to end an argument or to make someone feel inferior. For example, *My brother can beat your brother up any day, so there!* or *I'm going to camp and you're not—so there!*

**so to speak** Phrased like this, in a manner of speaking, as in *He was, so to speak, the head of the family, although he was only related by marriage to most of the family members.* Also see AS IT WERE.

**sought after** Also, **much sought after.** Very popular, in demand, as in *He was much sought after as a throat specialist, particularly by singers.* This expression uses the past participle of *seek* in the passive voice to mean "desired" or "searched for."

**soul** In addition to the idiom beginning with SOUL, also see BARE ONE'S SOUL; HEART AND SOUL; KEEP BODY AND SOUL TOGETHER; KINDRED SPIRIT (SOUL); LIVING SOUL.

**soul of, the** The essence of some quality, as in *You can trust her; she's the soul of discretion,* or *He's the very soul of generosity, but he can be cranky at times.*

**sound** In addition to the idioms beginning with SOUND, also see SAFE AND SOUND.

**sound as a bell** In excellent condition, as in *Now that the brakes have been fixed, the car is sound as a bell,* or *The surgery went perfectly, and now he's sound as a bell.* This expression rests on the assumption that the bell in question is not cracked (which would make it useless). It has outlasted numerous other expressions (*sound as a top* or *roach* or *dollar*), probably because of its pun on *sound.*

**sound bite** A short, striking, quotable statement well suited to a television news program. For example, *He's extremely good at sound bites, but a really informative speech is beyond him.* This slang expression originated in political campaigns in which candidates try to get across a particular message or get publicity by having it picked up in newscasts.

**sound off** Express one's views intensely and loudly, as in *Dad's always sounding off about higher taxes.*

**sound out** Seek the views or intentions of someone, as in *We'd better sound out Mom about who's using the car,* or *Let's sound out the staff before we decide which week we should close for vacation.*

**soup** In addition to the idiom beginning with SOUP, also see DUCK SOUP; FROM SOUP TO NUTS; IN THE SOUP; THICK AS THIEVES (PEA SOUP); TOO MANY COOKS SPOIL THE BROTH (SOUP).

**soup up** Make something more powerful; especially, add power to an engine. For example, *He was riding around in that car he'd souped up,* or *They had to soup up the sound system for the outdoor concert.*

**sour grapes** Ridiculing or speaking badly about something one cannot have or get, as in *The losers' scorn for the award is pure sour grapes.* This expression refers to Aesop's fable about a fox that cannot reach some grapes on a high vine and announces that they are sour.

**sour on** Cease to like someone or something, take a dislike to, as in *At first they liked the new supervisor, but now they've soured on her.*

S

**south** see GO SOUTH.

**sow** In addition to the idiom beginning with SOW, also see CAN'T MAKE A SILK PURSE OUT OF A SOW'S EAR.

**so what** Who cares? What does it matter? For example, *You're not going to the beach today? Well, so what, you can go tomorrow,* or *So what if she left without saying good-bye—she'll call you, I'm sure.* Also see WHAT OF IT.

**sow one's wild oats** Behave foolishly, excessively, or without discrimination when young, as in *Bill has spent the last couple of years sowing his wild oats, but now he seems ready to settle down.* This expression and its connection with seed suggests excessive sexual activity.

**space** In addition to the idiom beginning with SPACE, also see BREATHING SPACE.

**space out** Cease to be aware of one's surroundings, become disoriented, from or as if from a drug. For example, *This medication spaces me out so I can't think clearly,* or *I wonder what those kids are on—they look totally spaced out.* Also see ZONE OUT.

**spade** see CALL A SPADE A SPADE; IN SPADES.

**Spain** see CASTLES IN THE AIR (SPAIN).

**span** see SPICK AND SPAN.

**spare** In addition to the idioms beginning with SPARE, also see TO SPARE.

**spare the rod and spoil the child** Discipline is necessary for good upbringing, as in *She lets Richard get away with anything—spare the rod, you know.* This saying originally referred to corporal punishment. It is still used, often in shortened form, and today does not necessarily mean physical discipline.

**spare tire** Fat around one's middle, as in *He's determined to lose ten pounds and that spare tire he has.* This expression transfers the term for an extra tire carried in cars in case of a flat tire to excess fat around the waist.

**spark** see MAKE THE SPARKS FLY.

**sparring partner** An individual with whom one enjoys arguing, as in *Jim's my best sparring partner.* This expression refers to boxing, where it means the person one practices or trains with. Also see SPAR WITH.

**spar with** Argue or debate with someone, as in *You'd never know they were happily married because they're constantly sparring with each other.*

**speak** In addition to the idioms beginning with SPEAK, also see ACTIONS SPEAK LOUDER THAN WORDS; IN A MANNER OF SPEAKING; NOTHING TO SPEAK OF; NOT TO MENTION (SPEAK OF); ON SPEAKING TERMS; SO TO SPEAK; TO SPEAK OF.

S

**speak down to** see TALK DOWN TO.

**speak for** **1.** Recommend someone, as in *He spoke for the young applicant, praising her honesty.* **2.** Express the views of someone, as in *I can't speak for my husband, but I'd love to accept,* or *I don't care what Harry thinks—speak for yourself, Joe.* **3. speak for itself.** Be important or obvious, as in *They haven't called us in months, and that speaks for itself.* **4. spoken for.** Ordered, engaged, or reserved, as in *This rug is already spoken for,* or *Is this dance spoken for?* This use of the passive comes from an older verb, *bespeak,* meaning "to order."

**speak of the devil** The person just mentioned has appeared, as in *Speak of the devil—there's Jean.* This expression is a shortening of the older *Speak of the devil and he's sure to appear,* based on the superstition that pronouncing the devil's name will cause his arrival on the scene.

**speak one's mind** Also, **speak out.** Say what one really thinks, talk freely and fearlessly, as in *Will you give me a chance to speak my mind, or am I supposed to agree with everything you say?* or *Jan welcomed the chance to speak out about abortion.* Also see SPEAK ONE'S PIECE.

**speak one's piece** Also, **say one's piece.** Say what one thinks, or what one usually says or is expected to say. For example, *All right, you've spoken your piece; now let someone else have a turn.* The *piece* in this expression refers to a memorized poem or speech of the kind recited in a classroom.

**speak out** see SPEAK ONE'S MIND; SPEAK UP, def. 1.

**speak out of turn** see OUT OF TURN, def. 2.

**speak the same language** Understand one another very well, agree with each other, as in *Negotiations went on for days, but finally both sides realized they weren't speaking the same language.*

**speak too soon** Assume something prematurely, as in *I guess I spoke too soon about moving to Boston; I didn't get the job after all.*

**speak up** **1.** Also, **speak out.** Talk loudly, so as to be heard, as in *Speak up, child, I can't hear you,* or *He should speak out so that those in back can hear him.* **2.** Also, **speak up for.** Express one's opinion or one's support for someone or something. For example, *When it comes to speaking up about the town's needs, you can rely on Mary,* or *I'm glad you spoke up for me in that meeting.*

**speak volumes** Be important, indicate a great deal, as in *That house of theirs speaks volumes about their income.* This idiom uses *volumes* in the sense of "the information contained in volumes of books."

**spec** see ON SPEC.

**species** see ENDANGERED SPECIES.

**speed** In addition to the idiom beginning with SPEED, also see FULL SPEED AHEAD; UP TO PAR (SPEED).

**speed up** Go faster, make easier, increase the rate of something, as in *The car speeded up as it went downhill,* or *It's difficult to speed up production without new equipment.*

**spell** In addition to the idioms beginning with SPELL, also see COLD SNAP (SPELL); UNDER SOMEONE'S SPELL.

**spell disaster** Indicate that an event or a situation cannot turn out well, as in *His appearance now spells disaster for our plans.* Also see ACCIDENT WAITING TO HAPPEN; RECIPE FOR DISASTER.

**spell out** **1.** Make something plain or clear, as in *We asked her to spell out her goals.* **2.**

Read something slowly and with great effort, as in *He was only six, but he managed to spell out the instructions.* **3.** Puzzle something out, manage to understand with some effort, as in *It took years before anyone could spell out the inscriptions on the Rosetta Stone.* All three senses use *spell* in the sense of "proceed letter by letter."

**spend** see LAST OF THE BIG SPENDERS; POCKET (SPENDING) MONEY.

**spice** see VARIETY IS THE SPICE OF LIFE.

**spick and span** Neat and clean, as in *When Ruth has finished cleaning, the whole house is spick and span.*

**spike someone's drink** Add alcohol or a drug to someone's drink without his or her knowledge, as in *He claims someone spiked his drink and he doesn't remember anything.*

**spill** In addition to the idioms beginning with SPILL, also see SHED (SPILL) BLOOD; TAKE A SPILL.

**spill one's guts** Confess or tell secret information suddenly, as in *He spilled his guts as soon as his boss called him in.*

**spill the beans** Tell a secret or reveal something too soon, as in *You can count on Carol to spill the beans about the surprise.* In this expression *spill* means "say."

**spin** In addition to the idioms beginning with SPIN, also see GO INTO A TAILSPIN; MAKE ONE'S HEAD SPIN; PUT A SPIN ON; TAKE A SPIN.

**spin a yarn** Tell a story, especially a long drawn-out or totally fictitious one, as in *This author really knows how to spin a yarn,* or *Whenever he's late, he spins some yarn about a crisis.*

**spin control** Manipulation of news, especially political news, as in *The White House press secretary is a master of spin control.* This idiom uses *spin* in the sense of "interpretation," that is, how something will be interpreted by the public. Also see PUT A SPIN ON; SPIN DOCTOR.

**spin doctor** An individual charged with getting others to interpret a statement or event from a particular viewpoint, as in *Charlie is the governor's spin doctor.* This term uses *doctor* in the sense of "one who repairs something." Also see SPIN CONTROL.

**spin off** Derive or produce from something else, especially a small part from a larger whole. For example, *The corporation decided to spin off the automobile parts division,* or *Her column was spun off from her book on this subject.*

**spin one's wheels** Expend effort with no result, as in *We're just spinning our wheels here while management tries to make up its mind.* This idiom calls up an image of a vehicle in snow or sand that spins its wheels but cannot move.

**spin out** **1.** Protract or prolong something, as in *They spun out the negotiations over a period of months.* This idiom refers to drawing out a thread by spinning. **2.** Rotate out of control, as in *The car spun out and crashed into the store window.*

**spirit** In addition to the idioms beginning with SPIRIT, also see KINDRED SPIRIT; WHEN THE SPIRIT MOVES ONE.

**spirit away** Carry someone or something off mysteriously or secretly, as in *The police found that the documents had been spirited away from the office.* This term comes from the noun *spirit,* in the sense of "a supernatural being such as a ghost."

**spirit is willing but the flesh is weak, the** One would like to do something but hasn't the energy or strength to do so. For example, *Another set of tennis? The spirit is willing but the flesh is weak.* This idiom is often used today as an admission of weariness or other physical weakness. An equivalent expression is **I would if I could but I can't.**

**spit** In addition to the idioms beginning with SPIT, also see PISS (SPIT) INTO THE WIND.

**spit and polish** Close attention to appearance and order, as in *With a little spit and polish this house will sell very quickly.* This expression originated in the military and probably referred to literally shining up something with the aid of a little saliva.

**spite** see IN SPITE OF.

**spit something out** Say whatever it is one has to say, as in *What time did you get home last night? Come on—spit it out!*

**spitting distance** A very short distance, as in *We were in spitting distance of winning the championship, but then we lost three games in a row.* This idiom refers to the relatively short distance over which one's spit will carry.

**spitting image** An exact resemblance, especially in closely related persons. For example, *Dick is the spitting image of his grandfather.* This idiom refers to the earlier use of the noun *spit* for "likeness."

**spit up** Vomit, as in *Infants often spit up part of their milk.*

**splash down** Land in water, as in *The spacecraft splashed down within a few hundred yards of the pickup point.* The *splash* in this idiom refers to the impact of a solid body on water.

**spleen** see VENT ONE'S SPLEEN.

**splinter group** A part of an organization that breaks away from the main body, usually because of disagreement. For example, *Her supporters at first were only a splinter group, but they soon formed a third political party.* This idiom refers to the noun *splinter,* a fragment of wood or some other material that is split or broken off.

**split hairs** Make unimportant distinctions, argue over small things, as in *Let's not split hairs about whose turn it is to clean up; I'll do it today and you do it tomorrow.* This idiom transfers dividing an object as fine as a single hair to other petty divisions.

**split one's sides** Also, **laugh one's head off.** Be extremely amused, laugh very hard. For example, *That comedian had us splitting our sides,* or *Jane laughed her head off when she saw my costume.*

**split second** An instant, a fraction of a second, as in *Our best swimmer came in a split second before theirs.*

**split the difference** Compromise between two close amounts, divide the remainder equally. For example, *You're asking $5,000 for the car and I'm offering $4,000; let's split the difference and make it $4,500.*

**split ticket** A ballot cast for candidates of more than one party, as in *I'm registered as an Independent, and I usually vote a split ticket.* This idiom uses *ticket* in the sense of "a list of nominees for office." Also see STRAIGHT TICKET.

**spoil** In addition to the idiom beginning with SPOIL, also see SPARE THE ROD AND SPOIL THE CHILD; TOO MANY COOKS SPOIL THE BROTH; TO THE VICTOR BELONG THE SPOILS.

**spoil for** Be eager for something, as in *He's just spoiling for a fight.* This idiom nearly always refers to some kind of fight.

**spoken for** see SPEAK FOR, def. 4.

**sponge** In addition to the idiom beginning with SPONGE, also see THROW IN THE TOWEL (SPONGE).

**sponge off** Impose on another's hospitality or generosity, as in *He's been sponging off relatives for the past year.* This expression uses *sponge* in the sense of "soak up something."

**spoon** see BORN WITH A SILVER SPOON; GREASY SPOON.

S

**sporting blood** Willingness to take risks, as in *His sporting blood won't let him stay away from the races.* This idiom uses *sporting* in the sense of "associated with gambling."

**sporting chance, a** A fair chance for success, as in *She thinks she has a sporting chance of being named bureau chief.*

**spot** see BLIND SPOT; HIT THE HIGH SPOTS; HIT THE SPOT; IN A BIND (TIGHT SPOT); IN A FIX (SPOT); JOHNNY-ON-THE-SPOT; KNOCK THE SOCKS (SPOTS) OFF; LEOPARD CANNOT CHANGE ITS SPOTS; ON THE SPOT; ROOTED TO THE SPOT; SOFT SPOT; X MARKS THE SPOT.

**spotlight** see IN THE LIMELIGHT (SPOTLIGHT); STEAL THE SHOW (SPOTLIGHT).

**spread like wildfire** Disperse or circulate very quickly, as in *The rumor about their divorce spread like wildfire.* The noun *wildfire* means "a raging, rapidly spreading fire."

**spread oneself too thin** Overextend oneself, take on too many different activities or projects. For example, *Tom's exhausted; with work, volunteer activities, and social life he has spread himself too thin.* This expression refers to smearing something (like butter on bread) in such a thin layer that it does not cover the surface.

**spread one's wings** Have or find the self-confidence to experiment with new activities or ideas. For example, *After years of living with his parents, he seems to be ready to spread his wings.* This expression compares a person's self-confidence to the way a bird spreads its wings before taking flight.

**spring** In addition to the idioms beginning with SPRING, also see HOPE SPRINGS ETERNAL; NO SPRING CHICKEN.

**spring chicken** see NO SPRING CHICKEN.

**spring for** Pay another's expenses, treat, as in *I'll spring for the dinner this time.*

**spring *something* on someone** Present or make known unexpectedly, as in *They sprung the news of their engagement on the family last night.* This idiom uses *spring* in the sense of "make a sudden move."

**spring to life** Suddenly become very alert or active, as in *When I mentioned ice cream, she sprang to life.*

**spring to mind** see COME TO MIND.

**spruce up** Make something neat and clean, as in *She spruced up the chairs with new cushions.*

**spur** In addition to the idiom beginning with SPUR, also see ON THE SPUR OF THE MOMENT.

**spur on** Urge someone to continue at a task or endeavor, as in *The thought of winning a Pulitzer Prize spurred the reporter on.* This expression transfers using spurs to make a horse go faster to encouragement of other kinds.

**spy on** Secretly observe someone or something, as in *The children loved spying on the grownups,* or *The company sent him to spy on the competitor's sales force.*

**square** In addition to the idioms beginning with SQUARE, also see BACK TO THE DRAWING BOARD (SQUARE ONE); FAIR AND SQUARE; SHOOT STRAIGHT (SQUARE).

**square an account** Also, **square accounts. 1.** Repay money borrowed from someone, as in *The next payment will square my account with the store.* **2.** Do something equally harmful to someone who has hurt one. For example, *She swore to square accounts with him after he fired her.* Also see SQUARE WITH, def. 2.

**square away** Put something in order; also, get ready for. For example, *Once we've got the files squared away, we can decide on next year's projects,* or *She had to square away the house before leaving town.*

**square deal** A fair arrangement or transaction, as in *I know I'll get a square deal if I work with that supplier.* This idiom uses *square* in the sense of "fair" or "honest."

**square meal, a** A full or complete meal, as in *These airlines never feed you; I haven't had a square meal yet.*

**square off** Take a fighting position, prepare to fight, as in *As they squared off, the teacher came out and stopped them,* or *The ambassador said the two countries were squaring off.*

**square one's shoulders** Prepare to face hardship or difficulty, as in *She knew it wouldn't be easy, but she squared her shoulders and faced her boss.* This expression transfers standing erect with one's shoulders back to situations that call for such a stance.

**square peg in a round hole, a** Also, **a round peg in a square hole.** Someone who does not fit in his or her environment, especially a person unsuited for a position or an activity. For example, *Ruth doesn't have the skill for this job; she's a square peg in a round hole.* This idiom calls up an image of something that cannot fit.

**square the circle** Try to do the impossible, as in *Getting that bill through the legislature is the same as trying to square the circle.* This idiom refers to the impossibility of turning a circle into a square.

**square up** Settle a bill or debt, as in *The others went to get the car while he squared up with the waiter.* This idiom uses *square* in the sense of "set straight."

**square with 1.** Correspond to something, agree with, as in *His story doesn't square with what the witness saw.* **2.** Settle a disagreement or an account with someone, put a matter straight, as in *We've squared it with the manager to paint the apartment ourselves.*

**squeak by** Also, **squeak through.** Manage barely to pass, win, survive, or something similar, as in *They are just squeaking by on their income,* or *He squeaked through the driver's test.* This idiom transfers *squeak* in the sense of "barely produce a sound" to "narrowly manage something." Also see SQUEEZE THROUGH.

**squeaky wheel gets the grease, the** Also, **the squeaky wheel gets greased.** The loudest complaints get the most attention, as in *No matter what table they give her, Helen generally insists on a better one and gets it—the squeaky wheel gets the grease.*

**squeeze** In addition to the idioms beginning with SQUEEZE, also see MAIN SQUEEZE; PUT THE ARM (SQUEEZE) ON; TIGHT SQUEEZE.

**squeeze in 1.** Make room for one in a crowded space, as in *I think you can squeeze me in the front seat.* **2.** Make time available to see someone, especially for a meeting or an appointment. For example, *The dentist said she could squeeze us in tomorrow morning.*

**squeeze off** Fire a gun, as in *The officer squeezed off several rounds at the target.* The idiom refers to squeezing the trigger.

**squeeze play** A situation in which pressure is used to get an agreement or achieve a goal, as in *Workers sometimes feel caught in a squeeze play between union and management.* This expression originated in baseball.

**squeeze through** Also, **squeeze by.** Manage to pass, win, or survive something by a small amount, as in *We squeezed through the second round of playoffs,* or *There was just enough food stored in the cabin for us to squeeze by until the storm ended.* Also see SQUEAK BY.

**squirrel away** Hide or store something, as in *She squirreled away her savings in at least four different banks.* This expression refers to the squirrel's habit of hiding nuts and acorns in the ground.

**stab** In addition to the idiom beginning with STAB, also see MAKE A STAB AT.

**stab in the back, a** A betrayal of trust, an act of treachery, as in *Voting against our bill at the last minute was a real stab in the back.* It is also put as **stab someone in the back,** meaning "betray someone." For example, *Don't trust George; he's been known to stab his friends in the back.* The noun and verb forms of this idiom both refer to a physical attack when one's back is turned.

**stable** see LOCK THE BARN (STABLE) DOOR AFTER THE HORSE HAS BOLTED.

**stack** In addition to the idiom beginning with STACK, also see BLOW ONE'S TOP (STACK); CARDS ARE STACKED; NEEDLE IN A HAYSTACK; SWEAR ON A STACK OF BIBLES.

**stack the cards** see CARDS ARE STACKED.

**stack up 1.** Measure up, equal, as in *Their gift doesn't stack up against mine.* This usage refers to piling up one's chips at poker and comparing them to those of the other players. **2.** Make sense, seem believable, as in *Her explanation just doesn't stack up.* Also see ADD UP, def. 2.

**staff of life, the** A necessary food, especially bread. For example, *Rice is the staff of life for a majority of the earth's people.* This expression uses *staff* in the sense of "a support."

**stag** In addition to the idiom beginning with STAG, also see GO STAG.

**stage** In addition to the idioms beginning with STAGE, also see AT THIS STAGE; SET THE SCENE (STAGE) FOR.

**stage fright** Extreme nervousness when performing or speaking before an audience, as in *When John first had to present his findings to the committee, stage fright made him stutter.*

S

**stage whisper** A whisper loud enough to be overheard, as in *Our three-year-old behaved beautifully at the ceremony, but then he asked in a stage whisper, "Why is that woman wearing white hair?"* This expression refers to an actor's whisper on stage, which is meant to be heard by the audience.

**stag party** A social gathering for men only, often involving lewd entertainment. For example, *They wanted to give him a stag party before the wedding, but John wasn't interested.* This idiom uses *stag* in the sense of "a man unaccompanied by a woman."

**stake** In addition to the idioms beginning with STAKE, also see AT STAKE; BURN AT THE STAKE; HAVE A STAKE IN; PULL UP STAKES.

**stake a claim** Also, **stake out a claim.** Indicate something as one's own, as in *I'm staking a claim to the last piece of cake,* or *She staked out a claim for herself in the insurance business.* This term originally meant "register a claim to land by marking it with stakes."

**stake out** **1.** Keep an area or person under police watch; also, assign someone to conduct such a watch. For example, *They staked out the house,* or *He was staked out in the alley, watching for drug dealers.* **2.** Make it clear that something has been claimed, as in *We've staked out the area by the river for our picnic.* Also see STAKE A CLAIM.

**stamp** In addition to the idiom beginning with STAMP, also see RUBBER STAMP.

**stamping ground** Also, **stomping ground** or **old stamping ground.** A habitual or favorite place, as in *Whenever we visit, we go back to our old stamping ground, the drugstore nearest the high school.* This term refers to a traditional gathering place for horses or cattle, which stamp down the ground with their hooves.

**stamp out** Put out or destroy something, as in *The government stamped out the rebellion in a brutal way,* or *The police were determined to stamp out drug dealers.* This expression refers to extinguishing a fire by trampling on it.

S

**stand** In addition to the idioms beginning with STAND, also see AS THINGS STAND; CAN'T STAND THE SIGHT OF; HEART MISSES A BEAT (STANDS STILL); IF YOU CAN'T STAND THE HEAT, GET OUT OF THE KITCHEN; (STAND) IN AWE OF; IT STANDS TO REASON; KNOW WHERE ONE STANDS; MAKE A STAND; MAKE ONE'S HAIR STAND ON END; NOT HAVE (STAND) AN EARTHLY CHANCE; TAKE A STAND; (STAND THE) TEST OF TIME; WITHOUT A LEG TO STAND ON.

**stand a chance** Have a possibility or a hope of success, as in *Do you think Mary stands a chance of finishing the marathon?* or *I think we stand a fair chance of seeing the Queen arrive at Buckingham Palace.* Also see NOT HAVE AN EARTHLY CHANCE.

**stand at ease** see AT EASE, def. 2.

**stand by** **1.** Be ready or available to act, as in *I'm almost ready for you to carve the turkey, so please stand by.* **2.** Wait for something to start again, as in *We are all standing by until the power is restored.* Also see ON STANDBY. **3.** Be present but remain uninvolved, not acting, as in *I can't stand by and watch those kids shoplifting.* **4.** Remain loyal to someone, as in *She's my friend, and I'll stand by her, no matter what.* Also see STICK BY. **5.** Stay with something, as in *I'm going to stand by what I said yesterday.*

**stand corrected** Agree that one was wrong, as in *I stand corrected—we did go to Finland in 1985.*

**stand down** **1.** Leave a witness stand, as in *The judge told her to stand down.* **2.** Withdraw, as from a political contest or a game or race, as in *Harry decided to stand down as a candidate for mayor.* **3.** Go off duty, as in *The American forces were ordered to stand down.*

**stand fast** Also, **stand firm.** See STAND ONE'S GROUND.

**stand for** **1.** Represent something, symbolize, as in *The Stars and Stripes stands for our country.* **2.** Support something, uphold, as in *The National Writers Union stands for freedom of the press.* Also see STAND UP FOR. **3.** Put up with something, tolerate. This sense is generally used in a negative context, as in *Mother will not stand for rude behavior.* Also see HOLD STILL FOR. **4.** Have some value or importance, as in *She realized that appearances do stand for something.* This usage was preceded by **stand for nothing,** meaning "be worthless." Also see STAND IN FOR.

**stand guard** Watch over, act as a lookout, as in *We'll climb the tree and get the apples if you'll will stand guard,* or *There's a parking space; stand guard while I turn the car around.* This term refers to the military defense of posting guards to watch for the enemy.

**stand in awe** see IN AWE OF.

**stand in for** Take someone's place, as in *He has kindly agreed to stand in for me at work tonight.*

**standing joke** Something that is always funny even though it is often repeated. For example, *The fact that he's never on time is a standing joke around here.* This idiom uses *standing* in the sense of "established" or "regular."

**standing on one's head** see under DO BLINDFOLDED.

**stand in good stead** Be extremely useful, as in *That umbrella stood me in good stead on our trip; it rained every day.*

**standing order** **1.** A rule that is in force until it is specifically changed or withdrawn, as in *The waiters have standing orders to fill all glasses as they are emptied.* **2.** A regular order for something, especially a product. For example, *I have a standing order at the bookstore for new titles on insect behavior.*

**stand off** **1.** Stay at a distance, remain apart, as in *Carol stood off from the others.* This usage led to the adjective **standoffish,** meaning "aloof" or "reserved in an overly proud way." **2.** Put someone off, keep away, as in *The police stood off the angry strikers.*

**stand on** **1.** Be based on something, depend on, as in *Our success will stand on their support.* **2. stand on ceremony.** Insist on observance of something, as in *Let's not stand on ceremony.* This usage today is nearly always put in a negative context.

**stand one's ground** Also, **hold one's ground; stand fast** or **stand firm.** Be unyielding, as in *You've got to respect him for standing his ground when all the others disagree,* or *I'm going to hold my ground on this issue,* or *No matter how he votes, I'm standing fast,* or *Parents should stand firm about their children's bedtime.* Also see STAND PAT.

**stand *something* on its head** Distort or misinterpret an idea so that it no longer makes sense, as in *Even when she agrees with him, he takes her words and stands them on their head so he can disagree with her.*

**stand on one's head** Do the impossible. For example, *She did everything she could to help us but stand on her head.*

**stand on one's own feet** Act or behave independently, as in *You've got to learn to stand on your own feet and not always listen to your friends.*

**stand out** **1.** Stick out from a surface, project, as in *Those nails stand out from the walls.* **2.** Be very obvious, easy to identify, or prominent, as in *He's so tall that he always stands out in a crowd.*

**stand over** **1.** Watch or supervise someone closely, as in *I hate to cook when you're standing over me.* **2.** Delay something, as in *We'll have to let this budget item stand over till next year.*

**stand pat** Refuse to change one's position or opinion, as in *We're going to stand pat on this change to the rules.* Also see STAND ONE'S GROUND.

**standstill** see COME TO A HALT (STANDSTILL).

**stand still for** see HOLD STILL FOR.

**stand the sight of** see CAN'T STAND THE SIGHT OF.

**stand the test of time** see TEST OF TIME.

**stand to reason** Be logical or rational, as in *It stands to reason that if you don't like hot weather, you shouldn't move to Florida.*

**stand up** **1.** Remain valid, sound, or lasting, as in *His claim will not stand up in court,* or *Our old car stood up well over time.* **2.** Fail to keep a date or an appointment with someone, as in *If Al stands her up one more time, that will be the end of their relationship.* Also see STAND UP FOR; STAND UP TO.

**stand up and be counted** Reveal one's beliefs or opinions, especially when it requires courage to do so. For example, *Stop complaining about the government; stand up and be counted if you want something changed.* The *counted* in this expression refers to having one's vote on a matter acknowledged.

**stand up for** Also, **stick up for.** Side with someone, defend something, as in *Paul always stands up for what he thinks is right,* or *Virginia has learned to stick up for her family.*

**stand up to** Confront someone fearlessly, oppose boldly, as in *You've got to stand up to the boss if you want him to respect you.*

**star** In addition to the idiom beginning with STAR, also see BORN UNDER A LUCKY STAR; SEE STARS; THANK ONE'S LUCKY STARS.

**starch** see TAKE THE STARCH OUT OF.

**stare down** Cause someone to hesitate or yield by or as if by being stared at. For example, *Insisting on a better room, he stared down the manager until he got it.* This expression refers to staring at someone without being the first to blink or lower one's gaze.

**stare *one* in the face** Also, **look *one* in the face.** Be very obvious, although at first overlooked, as in *The solution to the problem had been staring me in the face all along,* or *I wouldn't know a Tibetan terrier if it looked me in the face.*

**stark raving mad** Totally crazy, as in *The constant worry about his job is making him stark raving mad.* This term, meaning "completely wildly insane," is used literally and as an exaggeration.

**stars in one's eyes, have** Be dazzled or enchanted, especially with romance; also, be too idealistic or optimistic. For example, *Thinking about their coming marriage, they both had stars in their eyes,* or *Kit had stars in her eyes when she talked about the millions who would buy her recording.* This idiom transfers the shining of stars to eyes shining with love or enthusiasm.

**start** In addition to the idioms beginning with START, also see FALSE START; FITS AND STARTS; FOR OPENERS (STARTERS); (START) FROM SCRATCH; FROM SOUP TO NUTS (START TO FINISH); GET OFF THE GROUND (TO A FLYING START); HEAD START; RUNNING START; TO START WITH.

**starters** see under FOR OPENERS.

**start from scratch** see FROM SCRATCH.

**start in** Begin, as in *He started in playing, without any practice.* This idiom is followed by a gerund, as in the example. Also see START OUT.

**start in on 1.** Begin doing something, as in *We started right in on the repairs.* Also see START IN. **2.** Attack someone, especially verbally, as in *Nancy was starting in on Carl again, complaining about the errors in his work.*

**start off 1.** Begin a trip, as in *We plan to start off in the morning.* Also see START OUT. **2. start someone off.** Cause someone to set out or to begin something, as in *Mother packed their lunches and started them off,* or *Paul started them off on their multiplication tables.* For **start off on the right foot,** see GET OFF ON THE RIGHT FOOT.

**start out** Begin a trip, as in *The climbers started out from base camp shortly after midnight.*

**start over** Begin again, as in *This composition is no good; I'll have to start over.*

**start something** Cause trouble, especially a quarrel or fight, as in *Stop bringing that up—do you want to start something?*

**start up 1.** Begin to operate something, especially a machine or an engine, as in *Start up the motor so we can get going.* **2.** Move suddenly or begin an activity, as in *When the alarm rang, I started up.* **3.** Organize a new business, as in *Starting up a company requires a lot of money.*

**state** In addition to the idiom beginning with STATE, also see IN A LATHER (STATE); IN STATE; SHIP OF STATE.

**state of the art** The highest level of development, the latest in ideas or improvements, as in *This new television set reflects the state of the art in screen technology.* In spite of including the word *art,* this term originated in technology. Today it is often used as an adjective, as in *This is a state-of-the-art camera,* and sometimes very loosely, as in *That movie is state-of-the-art George Lucas.*

**status quo** The existing condition or state of affairs, as in *We don't want to admit more singers to the chorus; we like the status quo.* This term is Latin for "state in which."

S

**status symbol** A position or an activity that allows one's social prestige to be displayed, as in *She doesn't even drive; that car of hers is purely a status symbol.*

**stave off** Keep or hold something unpleasant away, as in *The Federal Reserve Board is determined to stave off inflation.*

**stay** In addition to the idioms beginning with STAY, also see HERE TO STAY; (STAY) IN TOUCH; (STAY ON SOMEONE'S) RIGHT SIDE; SHOULD HAVE STAYED IN BED.

**stay one step ahead of** Also, **stay one jump ahead of.** Remain just a little bit ahead of someone in a situation or activity, either because of greater knowledge or the ability to predict his or her behavior. For example, *She seems to be able to stay one step ahead of her competition,* or *The escaped convict stayed one jump ahead of the police.*

**staying power** The ability to endure or last, as in *I'm not sure that this young actor will have staying power,* or *Our candidate definitely has staying power.*

**stay over** Remain overnight, as in *We hadn't planned to stay over, but the bad weather changed our plans,* or *She asked her mother if she could have a friend stay over.*

**stay put** Remain in a fixed or established position, as in *I can't get the baby to stay put,* or *I'm coming, just stay put till I get there.*

**stay the course** Hold or continue to the end, as in *No, he's not resigning; he's going to stay the course.* This expression refers to a horse running an entire race.

**stay with 1.** Remain in one's mind or memory, as in *That song has stayed with me all these years.* **2.** Keep up with someone; also, concentrate on something, continue with. For example, *The runner from Kenya stayed with Mark almost to the finish line,* or *She has a talent for staying with a problem until she solves it.* Also see STICK WITH.

**stead** see IN SOMEONE'S SHOES (STEAD); STAND IN GOOD STEAD. Also see under INSTEAD.

**steady** In addition to the idiom beginning with STEADY, also see GO STEADY; SLOW BUT SURE (STEADY WINS THE RACE).

**steady as a rock** Firm, dependable, as in *Betty always knows her part; she's steady as a rock.*

**steal someone blind** Also, **rob someone blind.** Rob or cheat someone of all he or she has, as in *Ann always maintained that children would steal their parents blind.*

**steal someone's heart** Win someone's love, as in *That puppy stole Brian's heart.*

**steal someone's thunder** Take or use another's idea, especially to one's advantage, as in *It was Harold's idea, but they stole his thunder and turned it into a big advertising campaign without giving him credit.* This idiom comes from an actual incident in which playwright and critic John Dennis (1657-1734) devised a "thunder machine" (by rattling a sheet of tin backstage) for one of his plays. A few days later he discovered the same device being used in a performance of *Macbeth,* whereupon he declared, "They steal my thunder."

**steal the show** Also, **steal the spotlight.** Be the center of attention, as in *The speeches were interesting, but her singing stole the show.* This idiom refers to one actor unexpectedly outshining the rest of the cast in a theatrical production.

**steam** see BLOW OFF STEAM; FULL SPEED (STEAM) AHEAD; GET UP STEAM; LET OFF STEAM; RUN OUT OF STEAM; UNDER ONE'S OWN STEAM.

**steamed up** Stirred up, aroused with passion, excitement, anger, or another strong emotion, as in *She was all steamed up about the test results.* The exact meaning of this expression depends on the context.

**steel** In addition to the idiom beginning with STEEL, also see MIND LIKE A STEEL TRAP.

**steel one's heart against** Also, **harden one's heart.** Not allow one's feelings to show or come out, as in *He finally steeled his heart against them and refused the loan,* or *You'll just have to harden your heart and tell them the truth.* Also see HEART OF STONE.

**steer** In addition to the idiom beginning with STEER, also see BUM STEER.

**steer clear of** Stay away from someone or something, avoid, as in *Dad warned us to steer clear of Dr. Smith and his poor advice,* or *Steer clear of that section of town.* This idiom is often used as a warning.

**stem** In addition to the idiom beginning with STEM, also see FROM SOUP TO NUTS (STEM TO STERN).

**stem the tide** Stop the course of a trend or tendency, as in *It is not easy to stem the tide of public opinion.*

**stem to stern** see under FROM SOUP TO NUTS.

**step** In addition to the idioms beginning with STEP, also see FALSE STEP; IN STEP; (STEP) OUT OF LINE; STAY ONE STEP AHEAD OF; TAKE STEPS; WATCH ONE'S STEP.

**step aside 1.** Move out of the way, as in *Please step aside—I've got my arms full of groceries.* **2.** Withdraw, make room for a replacement, as in *The senior researcher decided to step aside for a younger colleague.*

**step by step** By degrees, as in *You'll have to go through this recipe step by step.* This idiom transfers putting one foot in front of the other to other kinds of progress.

**step down 1.** Resign from office, as in *He threatened to step down if they continued to argue with him.* **2.** Reduce something, especially in stages, as in *They were stepping down the voltage.* Also see STEP UP, def. 1.

**step in** Enter into an activity or a situation; also, change the way a situation is developing or how an activity is carried out. For example, *The business was doing poorly until Stan stepped in,* or *They are going to make a mess of the dinner unless someone steps in and shows them what to do.* Also see STEP INTO.

**step in the right direction, a** A move that advances a course of action, as in *Asking Bill to resign is a step in the right direction.*

**step into** Involve oneself or alter an action or a situation, as in *He knew he'd be able to step into a job in his father's firm,* or *Jane asked Mary to step into the matter and settle it.* Also see STEP IN.

**step into someone's shoes** Take someone's place, as in *He has prepared his daughter to step into his shoes and run the business when he resigns.* Also see FILL SOMEONE'S SHOES; IN SOMEONE'S SHOES.

**step on it** Hurry up, go faster, as in *Step on it or we are going to be late.* This idiom refers to pressing down on a vehicle's gas pedal.

**step on someone's toes** Also, **tread on someone's toes.** Hurt or offend someone. For example, *Be careful what you say about her losing weight; don't step on her toes,* or *Would I be stepping on someone's toes if I offered to help out with the party arrangements?* This idiom transfers physical suffering to emotional pain.

**step out 1.** Walk briskly, as in *He stepped out in time to the music.* **2.** Also, **step outside.** Go outside briefly, as in *He just stepped out for a cigarette,* or *Let's step outside to discuss this.* **3.** Go out for an evening of entertainment, as in *They're stepping out again tonight.* **4. step out with.** Accompany a person, as when going on a date. For example, *She's been stepping out with him for a month.*

**step out of line** see OUT OF LINE, def. 1.

**step up 1.** Increase something, especially in stages, as in *We've got to step up production.* Also see STEP DOWN, def. 2. **2.** Come forward, as in *Step up to the table, and I'll show you how this gadget works.*

**stern** see FROM SOUP TO NUTS (STEM TO STERN).

**steven** see EVEN-STEVEN.

**stew** In addition to the idiom beginning with STEW, also see IN A STEW.

**stew in one's own juice** Suffer the consequences of one's actions, as in *He's run into debt again, but this time we're leaving him to stew in his own juice.* This term refers to cooking something in its own liquid.

**stick** In addition to the idioms beginning with STICK, also see CARROT AND STICK; GET ON THE STICK; MAKE SOMETHING STICK; MORE THAN ONE CAN SHAKE A STICK AT; SHORT END OF THE STICK; STAND (STICK) UP FOR; WRONG END OF THE STICK. Also see under STUCK.

**stick around** Remain, stay, as in *I hope you'll stick around till the end of the party.*

**stick at** Hesitate to do something because of one's conscience or ethics, as in *She sticks at nothing to gain her ends.* This idiom is nearly always used in a negative context. Also see STOP AT NOTHING.

**stick by** Also, **stick to.** Remain loyal to someone, as in *The brothers said they'd stick by one another, no matter what,* or *Pat promised to stick to Bert.* This idiom comes from *stick* in the sense of "adhere." Also see STAND BY, def. 4.

**stick in one's craw** Also, **stick in one's throat. 1.** Be unable to say something, as in

S

*I meant to apologize, but the words stuck in my craw.* **2.** Be so offensive that one can't tolerate it, as in *That obscene art exhibit stuck in my throat.*

**stick in one's mind** Remain vivid in one's mind for a long time, as in *That stupid toothpaste commercial is stuck in my mind.*

**stick-in-the-mud** A person who is unable to have fun or to show enthusiasm, or who resists change. For example, *Come swimming with us—don't be such a stick-in-the-mud,* or *Those stick-in-the-muds will never accept your new ideas.*

**stick it** Also, **stick it up one's ass** or **shove it up one's ass; stick where the sun don't shine.** Do whatever you like with it, I don't want it, as in *Do that job all over again? Why don't you stick it?* or *Tell the chef he can take this fish and shove it up his ass,* or *She can take her opinions and stick them where the sun don't shine.* These idioms, which use *stick* in the sense of "thrust inward or upward," also function as variants of UP YOURS. The ungrammatical use of *don't,* rather than *doesn't,* in the last variant emphasizes the slang nature of the idiom and may also add emphasis to the intended insult. [Vulgar slang]

**stick it to** Treat someone badly or unfairly, as in *The head nurse really stuck it to Judy when she made her work all three shifts.* This slang usage may come from STICK IT.

**stick one's neck out** Make oneself vulnerable, take a risk, as in *I'm going to stick my neck out and ask for a raise.* This expression probably refers to a chicken extending its neck before being slaughtered.

**stick out 1.** Also, **stick out a mile** or **stick out like a sore thumb.** Be very visible or obvious, as in *Dad's funny hat made him stick out in the crowd,* or *That purple house sticks out a mile,* or *John's lie sticks out like a sore thumb.* **2.** Continue doing something, endure something, as in *I know you don't like it, but you have to stick out the job for another month.* A variant is **stick it out,** as in *His new play's boring, but since he's my cousin we'd better stick it out.*

**stick the knife in** Hurt, insult, make someone feel bad, as in *You might as well have stuck the knife in when you left.* Also see TWIST THE KNIFE.

**stick to 1.** Remain loyal to someone; see STICK BY. **2.** Continue to maintain an idea or apply oneself to a task, as in *I'm sticking to my opinion that he's basically honest,* or *The music teacher told John to stick to the clarinet, at least until the end of the year.* Also see STICK TO ONE'S GUNS.

**stick together** Remain united, as in *It's important that we stick together on this issue.*

**stick to one's guns** Hold fast to a statement, an opinion, or a course of action, as in *The witness stuck to her guns about the exact time she was there.*

**stick to the ribs** Also, **stick to one's ribs.** Be substantial or filling, as in *It may not be health food, but steak really sticks to the ribs,* or *This soup will stick to your ribs.*

**stick up 1.** Project from a surface, as in *That little piece of his hair sticks up no matter what he does.* **2.** Put up a poster or notice, as in *Will you stick up this announcement on the bulletin board?* **3.** Rob someone, especially at gunpoint, as in *The gang concentrated on sticking up liquor stores and gas stations.* This usage led to the phrase **stick 'em up,** a robber's order to a victim to raise his or her hands in the air.

**stick up for** see STAND UP FOR.

**stick with 1.** Continue to support or be faithful to someone, as in *They stuck with us through all our difficulties.* **2.** Continue to maintain an opinion or to perform a task, as in *She plans to stick with her piano lessons.* Also see STICK TO, def. 2.

**sticky fingers** A tendency to steal, as in *You'd better not leave any cash around; she's known for her sticky fingers.* This expression suggests that valuable items adhere naturally to a thief's fingers.

**stiff** In addition to the idioms beginning with STIFF, also see BORE TO DEATH (STIFF); KEEP A STIFF UPPER LIP; SCARE ONE OUT OF ONE'S WITS (STIFF).

**stiff as a board** Also, **stiff as a poker.** Unable to bend, rigidly formal, as in *This cloth is stiff as a board; what happened to it?* or *There he stood, stiff as a poker, unwilling to give an inch.* The *board* in the first expression is a slab of wood. The second expression refers to an iron tool used to arrange logs in an open fire.

**stiff drink, a** A very strong alcoholic drink, usually one without water or some other liquid, as in *After what I've been through today, I need a stiff drink.*

**stiff upper lip** see KEEP A STIFF UPPER LIP.

**still** In addition to the idioms beginning with STILL, also see HEART MISSES A BEAT (STANDS STILL); HOLD STILL FOR; JURY IS STILL OUT; KEEP QUIET (STILL); QUIET (STILL) AS A MOUSE.

**still and all** Nevertheless, all the same, as in *But still and all, visiting in Nepal is an expensive undertaking.*

**still going strong** Continue to be active, healthy, or successful, especially after a long period of time, as in *In the ninth inning the pitcher was still going strong,* or *At 90 I'm still going strong.*

**still waters run deep** A quiet person may be very profound, as in *Susie rarely says much, but still waters run deep.*

S

**sting** see TAKE THE STING OUT OF.

**stink** In addition to the idiom beginning with STINK, also see MAKE A STINK; SMELL (STINK) UP.

**stink to high heaven** Also, **smell to high heaven. 1.** Smell very bad, as in *This fish stinks to high heaven.* **2.** Be of very poor quality; also, be suspect or have a bad reputation. For example, *This plan of yours stinks to high heaven,* or *His financial schemes smell to high heaven; I'm sure they're dishonest.* This expression refers an odor so bad that it can be smelled from a great distance away.

**stir** In addition to the idioms beginning with STIR, also see CAUSE A COMMOTION (STIR).

**stir up 1.** Mix together the ingredients or parts, as in *He stirred up some pancake batter,* or *Will you stir up the fire?* **2.** Cause someone to be moved to action, as in *He's always stirring up trouble among the tenants,* or *If the strikers aren't careful, they'll stir up a riot.* Also see STIR UP A HORNETS' NEST.

**stir up a hornets' nest** Make trouble, cause confusion, as in *Asking for an audit of the treasurer's books stirred up a hornets' nest in the association.* This term compares hornets to angry human beings.

**stitch** In addition to the idiom beginning with STITCH, also see IN STITCHES; WITHOUT A STITCH ON.

**stitch in time, a** A prompt action will avoid more serious trouble. For example, *Changing the car's oil every 3,000 miles is a stitch in time.* The complete form of this saying is **a stitch in time saves nine.**

**stock** In addition to the idioms beginning with STOCK, also see IN STOCK; LOCK, STOCK, AND BARREL; MAKE A LAUGHING STOCK OF; TAKE STOCK; TAKE STOCK IN.

**stocking feet, in one's** Wearing one's socks or stockings, but not shoes, as in *I got locked out of the house in my stocking feet.*

**stock in trade** A resource or an ability that one has, as in *Making everyone laugh is her stock in trade.*

**stock still** Motionless, not moving at all, as in *If we stand stock still, the deer will come to us.*

**stomach** see BUTTERFLIES IN ONE'S STOMACH; CAN'T STAND (STOMACH) THE SIGHT OF; EYES ARE BIGGER THAN ONE'S STOMACH; HARD TO STOMACH; HAVE A STRONG STOMACH; NO STOMACH FOR; SICK TO ONE'S STOMACH; TURN ONE'S STOMACH.

**stomping ground** see STAMPING GROUND.

**stone** In addition to the idioms beginning with STONE, also see CAST IN STONE; CAST THE FIRST STONE; FLAT (STONE) BROKE; HEART OF STONE; KILL TWO BIRDS WITH ONE STONE; LEAVE NO STONE UNTURNED; ROLLING STONE GATHERS NO MOSS; RUN INTO A STONE WALL; SET IN STONE.

**stone cold** Unable to react emotionally, unfeeling, as in *That sad story left her stone cold.*

**stone cold dead** Without life, as in *We found him stone cold dead on the floor.*

**stone deaf** Totally unable to hear, as in *Poor Grandpa, in the last year he's become stone deaf.*

**stoned out of one's mind, be** Also, **get stoned out of one's mind.** Be or get high on an illegal drug, usually marijuana. For example, *We were stoned out of our minds last night,* or *Did you get stoned out of your mind at that party?* These idioms are often shortened to **be stoned** or **get stoned.**

**stone's throw, a** A very short distance, as in *They live just a stone's throw from us.* This term refers to how far one can toss a stone.

**stood in bed** see under SHOULD HAVE STAYED IN BED.

**stool pigeon** A spy or an informer, especially a police spy. For example, *Watch out for Dick; I'm sure he's a stool pigeon for the supervisor.*

**stoop labor** Back-bending manual work, especially farm work. For example, *They had us picking strawberries all day, and that's too much stoop labor.*

**stoop so low** Behave in a way that is, or should be, beneath one's usual principles, as in *I heard you'd reported him for being late—how could you stoop so low?*

**stoop to** Agree to something beneath one's dignity, as in *She wouldn't stoop to listening to that obnoxious gossip.*

**stoop to someone's level** see SINK TO SOMEONE'S LEVEL.

**stop** In addition to the idioms beginning with STOP, also see BUCK STOPS HERE; PULL OUT ALL THE STOPS; PUT AN END (A STOP) TO.

**stop at nothing** Do everything in one's power, be prevented by no obstacle, as in *She'll stop at nothing to get her revenge.*

**stop by** Also, **stop in.** Pay a brief visit, as in *I hope you'll stop by this afternoon,* or *He stopped in at Martha's whenever he traveled to New York on business.*

**stop cold** Also, **stop dead; stop in one's tracks** or **stop on a dime; come to a dead stop.** Halt suddenly, come to a complete stop, as in *When the computer crashes, it just stops cold,* or *He was so surprised to see them in the audience that he stopped dead in the middle of his speech,* or *The deer saw the hunter and stopped in its tracks,* or *An excellent skateboarder, she could stop on a dime,* or *As the car approached, I panicked and came to a dead stop in the middle of the crosswalk.*

**stop in** see STOP BY.

**stop off** Also, **stop over.** Interrupt a journey for a short stay somewhere, as in *When we* *drove through Massachusetts, we stopped off for a few days at Cape Cod,* or *When you're in the area, try to stop over and see our new house.*

**stop payment** Instruct a bank not to honor a check one has written, as in *If that check was lost, we'll have to stop payment on it before writing another.*

**stop short** **1.** Also, **stop one short.** Halt abruptly, as in *When we tried to cross the street, the barrier stopped us short.* **2.** Cause someone to stop speaking, as in *I was about to tell them the date when my father stopped me short.* **3. stop short of.** Not go so far as to do or say something. For example, *He usually stops short of actually lying.*

**stop the clock** Delay a deadline by not counting the passing hours. For example, *Management agreed to stop the clock so that a new contract could be negotiated before the present one expired.*

**stop up** Fill a hole or gap, block an opening or passage. For example, *We need to stop up the holes in the walls,* or *The sink is stopped up; it won't drain.*

**storage** see IN COLD STORAGE.

**store** see IN STORE; LIKE A KID IN A CANDY STORE; MIND THE STORE; SET STORE BY; VARIETY STORE.

**storm** see KICK UP A FUSS (STORM); RIDE OUT (THE STORM); TAKE BY STORM; WEATHER THE STORM.

**story** In addition to the idiom beginning with STORY, also see COCK-AND-BULL STORY; COVER STORY; FISH STORY; HARD-LUCK STORY; MAKE A LONG STORY SHORT; OLD STORY; SAME OLD STORY; SHAGGY-DOG STORY; SOB STORY.

**story of my life, the** What typically happens to me, as in *I rushed through the meeting to get to the airport, and then the plane was three hours late—that's the story of my life.* This exaggerated expression is generally used to describe some mishap or misfortune.

S

**stow away** **1.** Put aside or store something until needed, as in *We generally stow away the lawn furniture in the garage during the winter.* **2.** Hide oneself on a ship or in a vehicle in order to get free transportation, as in *The youngsters planned to stow away on a freighter, but they never even got to the waterfront.* This usage led to the noun **stowaway.** **3.** Greedily consume food or drink, as in *Bob sure can stow away a lot in a short time.*

**straddle the fence** see ON THE FENCE.

**straight** In addition to the idioms beginning with STRAIGHT, also see (STRAIGHT) FROM THE HORSE'S MOUTH; GET SOMETHING STRAIGHT; GIVE IT TO (SOMEONE STRAIGHT); GO STRAIGHT; KEEP A STRAIGHT FACE; RIGHT (STRAIGHT) OUT; SET SOMEONE STRAIGHT; SHOOT STRAIGHT; THINK STRAIGHT.

**straight and narrow, the** The honest and virtuous way of living, as in *He led a wild life when he was young, but he's been on the straight and narrow for some years.*

**straight as an arrow** Honest, real, as in *You can trust Pat with the money; he's straight as an arrow.* This expression refers to an arrow's direct flight through the air.

**straight away** see STRAIGHT OFF.

**straighten out** **1.** Clear up disorder, a confusion, or a misunderstanding, as in *This is an awful mess; I hope you'll straighten it out,* or *I don't understand; please straighten me out.* **2.** Adopt an honest, virtuous course, as in *He's only sixteen; I'm sure he'll straighten out before long.*

**straighten up** **1.** Make something neat and organized, as in *Let's get this room straightened up.* **2.** Also, **straighten up and fly right.** Stop behaving in annoying or illegal ways and live in a proper or ethical manner, as in *If that child doesn't straighten up and fly right, he'll have to deal with the principal.*

**straight face** see KEEP A STRAIGHT FACE.

**straight from the horse's mouth** see FROM THE HORSE'S MOUTH.

**straight from the shoulder** In a direct, honest manner, as in *I'll tell you, straight from the shoulder, that you'll have to do better or they'll fire you.* This expression comes from boxing, where it describes a blow delivered with full force.

**straight goods** The truth, as in *Is that straight goods about how much you still owe?* or *I'm giving you the straight goods about her.*

**straight off** Also, **straight away.** Immediately, as in *I knew straight off that he was lying,* or *I'll get to the dishes straight away.*

**straight out** see RIGHT OUT.

**straight talk** Plain, honest speaking, as in *We have to have some straight talk with Harry before he goes away to college.*

**straight ticket** All the candidates of a single political party, as in *Are you going to vote a straight ticket again?* Also see SPLIT TICKET.

**straight up** Served without ice, generally said of an alcoholic drink, as in *He ordered a martini straight up.*

**straining at the leash** Eager to do something, especially go on a trip. For example, *He was straining at the leash to go to the dance,* or *I've been straining at the leash to get out of town for a few days.* This idiom uses the way a dog pulls at a leash to describe eagerness.

**strange bedfellows** An odd alliance or combination, as in *George and Arthur really are strange bedfellows, sharing the same job but totally different in their views.* Although strictly speaking *bedfellows* are persons who share a bed, such as a husband and wife, the term has long been used figuratively. Today a common extension is **politics makes strange bedfellows,** meaning that politicians form odd associations in order to win more votes. A similar term is **odd couple,** meaning a pair who share either housing or a business but are very different in most ways.

**strange to say** Also, **strangely enough.** Surprisingly, curiously, oddly, as in *Strange to say, all the boys in his class are six feet tall or taller,* or *I've never been to the circus, strangely enough.*

**strapped for** In need of, as in *We're strapped for cash this week.* This expression originated as simply *strapped,* meaning "in need of money." Now it is also used for other needs, as in *I can't give you any more firewood; I'm strapped for it myself.*

**straw** In addition to the idioms beginning with STRAW, also see DRAW STRAWS; GRASP AT STRAWS; LAST STRAW; NOT WORTH A DAMN (STRAW).

**straw boss** A subordinate boss, a worker who supervises other workers as well as performing regular duties. For example, *Jim was pleased when he was promoted to straw boss.* This term refers to the person's position as a **straw man,** that is, a front or cover for the real boss and of little real importance.

**straw in the wind** A slight hint of the future, as in *The public unrest is a straw in the wind indicating future problems for that country.* This expression refers to a straw showing the direction of the wind, an observation also behind the idiom STRAW VOTE.

**straw that breaks the camel's back** see LAST STRAW.

**straw vote** Also, **straw poll.** An unofficial vote or poll indicating how people feel about a candidate or an issue. For example, *Let's take a straw poll on the bill and see how it does.* This idiom refers to a straw used to show the direction of the wind, in this case the wind of public opinion.

**streak** see LIKE GREASED LIGHTNING (A BLUE STREAK); TALK SOMEONE'S ARM OFF (A BLUE STREAK); WINNING STREAK; YELLOW STREAK.

**stream** In addition to the idiom beginning with STREAM, also see CHANGE HORSES IN MIDSTREAM; SWIM AGAINST THE CURRENT (STREAM).

**stream out** Move out of a place in a constant flow, as in *People streamed out into the streets,* or *Vulgar language seemed to stream out of his mouth.*

**street** see BACK STREET; EASY STREET; MAN IN THE STREET; ON THE STREET; SIDE STREET; WORK BOTH SIDES OF THE STREET.

**strength** see BRUTE FORCE (STRENGTH); ON THE STRENGTH OF; TOWER OF STRENGTH.

**stress out** Cause someone to feel extreme pressure or strain, as from working. For example, *I badly need a vacation; I'm just plain stressed out from this job and its aggravations.*

**stretch** In addition to the idioms beginning with STRETCH, also see AT A STRETCH; BY ANY STRETCH; HOME STRETCH.

**stretch a point** Extend or enlarge beyond the usual limits, exaggerate, as in *It would be stretching a point to say this novel is the work of a great writer.*

**stretch one's legs** Stand up or go for a walk, especially after a long period of sitting. For example, *Let's go stretch our legs at intermission.*

**stride** see HIT ONE'S STRIDE; MAKE GREAT STRIDES; PUT ONE OFF ONE'S STRIDE; TAKE SOMETHING IN STRIDE.

**strike** In addition to the idioms beginning with STRIKE, also see GO OUT (ON STRIKE); (STRIKE A) HAPPY MEDIUM; LIGHTNING NEVER STRIKES TWICE; ON STRIKE; TWO STRIKES AGAINST.

**strike a balance** Find a middle ground between two extremes, as in *We have to strike a balance between what we want and what we can afford.* This expression refers to accounting, where it means finding a profit or loss by weighing income against expenses.

**strike a bargain** Reach an agreement, as in *They finally struck a bargain after weeks of arguing over who would get what.*

**strike a blow** Do something in order to support a case or group of people. For example, *Your support will strike a blow for justice,* or *The new law will strike a blow against unfair taxes.*

**strike a chord** Trigger a feeling or memory, as in *That poem strikes a chord in all those touched by the Holocaust.* This term refers to striking the strings or keys of a musical instrument. Also see STRIKE THE RIGHT NOTE.

**strike a happy medium** see HAPPY MEDIUM.

**strike down 1.** Knock down someone or something with a blow or misfortune, as in *The tree was struck down by lightning,* or *He was struck down by tuberculosis while in his twenties.* **2.** Cause something to become invalid, cancel, especially in a legal context. For example, *The appeals court struck down the verdict.*

**strike gold** Find someone or something very special or extraordinary, as in *You really struck gold when you hired that new employee.*

**strike home** see HIT HOME.

**strike it rich** Also, **strike oil** or **strike it lucky.** Experience sudden financial success, as in *He never dreamed that he'd strike it rich this soon,* or *They really struck oil with that investment,* or *One of these days we'll strike it lucky.* The first of these idioms originated in mining, where it referred to finding a rich mineral deposit.

**strike out** **1.** Cancel or erase something, as in *Strike out that last sentence, please.* **2.** Begin a course of action, set out energetically, as in *Elaine was determined to strike out on her own.* **3.** Fail in an endeavor, as in *His latest business venture has struck out.* This usage originated in baseball, where it refers to a batter's failure to put the ball in play, as in *Johnson struck out three times in yesterday's game,* as well as to a pitcher's success in eliminating a batter, as in *Thompson struck him out again in the fourth inning.*

**strike the right note** Say or do what is especially appropriate, as in *She struck the right note when she complimented the new parents on their baby.* This expression refers to playing the correct note on a musical instrument.

**strike while the iron is hot** Take advantage of favorable conditions, as in *They just made a huge profit, so let's strike while the iron is hot and ask for some money.* This saying refers to a blacksmith's forge. Also see MAKE HAY WHILE THE SUN SHINES.

**string** In addition to the idioms beginning with STRING, also see HARP ON (ONE STRING); NO STRINGS ATTACHED; ON A SHOESTRING; ON A STRING; PULL STRINGS; PURSE STRINGS; TIED TO SOMEONE'S APRON STRINGS.

**string along** **1.** Go along with someone, accompany or follow, as in *I decided to string along with them, just to see what might happen.* **2.** Agree, as in *We knew that three committee members would string along with us for now.* **3. string someone along.** Keep someone waiting or in a state of uncertainty; also, fool or deceive someone. For example, *We were stringing them along, hoping that we'd get a better offer,* or *She was in tears when she found out that he'd just been stringing her along.*

**string out** **1.** Stretch, extend; also, prolong. For example, *The parade strung out for miles,* or *The meetings strung out over weeks instead of days.* **2. strung out.** Addicted to, numbed by, or weakened by drug use, as in *She was completely strung out when they found her.*

**strings attached** see NO STRINGS ATTACHED.

**string together** Compose something, assemble, put things together, as in *There's more to devising an effective slogan than stringing together some words.* This expression refers to threading beads on a string.

**string up** Hang something; also, kill someone by hanging. For example, *They strung up their Christmas lights in October,* or *The mob wanted to string him up on the nearest tree.*

**stroke** see AT ONE STROKE; NO ACCOUNTING FOR TASTES (DIFFERENT STROKES FOR DIFFERENT FOLKS); PUT ONE OFF ONE'S STRIDE (STROKE).

**strong** In addition to the idioms beginning with STRONG, also see COME ON STRONG; HAVE A STRONG STOMACH; STILL GOING STRONG.

**strong point** Also, **strong suit.** An area in which someone or something excels, as in *That beautiful lobby is the building's strong point,* or *Writing is her strong suit.* The variant refers to various card games, in which it means the suit with the highest or most cards.

**strong silent type, the** A man of action who is reserved and hides his feelings. For example, *Paula always preferred the strong silent type to more extroverted men.* This phrase is almost never used for a woman.

**strong suit** see STRONG POINT.

**strung out** see STRING OUT, def. 2.

**strut one's stuff** Behave or perform in an arrogant, obvious way, show off, as in *The skaters were on the ice, strutting their stuff.* This expression uses *strut* in the sense of "display in order to impress others."

**stubborn as a mule** Extremely resistant or defiant, as in *He's stubborn as a mule about wearing a suit and tie.* This expression refers to the proverbial stubbornness of mules.

**stuck for, be** Be unable to obtain or think of something, as in *We're stuck for a fourth for bridge,* or *In this class I'm always stuck for an answer.*

**stuck on, be** Be very fond of someone, as in *She's been stuck on him ever since first grade.*

**stuck up** Believing that one is superior to other people, as in *I had no idea she was so stuck up.* It is also used as an adjective, as in *We couldn't stand his stuck-up attitude.*

**stuck with** Forced to tolerate something; also, unable to get rid of. For example, *Once again Dean was stuck with the check for all of the dinner guests,* or *She's my sister-in-law, so I'm stuck with her.*

**stuff** In addition to the idioms beginning with STUFF, also see GET STUFFED; HOT NUMBER (STUFF); KID STUFF; KNOW ONE'S STUFF; STRUT ONE'S STUFF.

**stuff and nonsense** Total foolishness or absurdity, as in *Stuff and nonsense, of course I can pack a suitcase.* This idiom is often used as an interjection.

**stuffed shirt, a** An overly formal or pompous person, as in *She's such a stuffed shirt that I'm surprised she would come to a barbecue.* This expression refers to a shirt filled with paper (instead of a real person).

**stuffing** see KNOCK THE STUFFING OUT OF.

**stuff it** Take back something, as in *As for that memo of yours, you can just stuff it.* This idiom is used, often as an interjection, to express scorn or defiance. It is probably short for the vulgar expression *Stuff it up your ass.* [Vulgar slang] Also see STICK IT.

**stuff one's face** see FEED ONE'S FACE.

**stuff the ballot box** Put invalid votes in a ballot box or otherwise cheat in an election. For example, *The only way he'll win is if we stuff the ballot box.*

**stumble across** Also, **stumble on.** Find something by accident, discover or meet with unexpectedly. For example, *When we were hiking up the mountain, we stumbled across a few abandoned cabins,* or *At the flea market Alfred stumbled on a quite valuable old painting.* This idiom uses *stumble* in the sense of "accidentally trip."

**stumbling block** Something that causes a plan or project to stop temporarily, obstacle, as in *His lack of a degree is a real stumbling block to his advancement.*

**style** see CRAMP ONE'S STYLE; GO OUT (OF STYLE); IN FASHION (STYLE).

**subject** In addition to the idiom beginning with SUBJECT, also see CHANGE THE SUBJECT.

**subject to, be** **1.** Be under the control or authority of something, as in *All citizens in this nation are subject to the law.* **2.** Be inclined or disposed to something, as in *This child has always been subject to colds.* **3.** Be likely to acquire or receive, as in *This memo is subject to misinterpretation.* **4.** Depend on something, be likely to be affected by, as in *Our vacation plans are subject to the boss's whims.*

**subscribe to** **1.** Agree to receive and pay for a given number of issues of a periodical, tickets to a series of performances or events, or a utility service. For example, *We subscribe to the local paper,* or *Betty and I have been subscribing to this concert series for years,* or *We have no choice; we have to subscribe to the local power company.* **2.** Feel or express approval of something, as in *I subscribe to your opinion, but I don't think Donald does.* **3.** Promise to pay or contribute money to, as in *We subscribe to many charities.* All of these usages come from *subscribe* in the sense of "sign one's name to something, such as a pledge."

**substance** see IN SUBSTANCE; SUM AND SUBSTANCE.

**such and such** Not specified, not mentioned, unknown, as in *They agreed to meet at such and such a time and place.*

**such as** For example, as in *She enjoys eating seafood, such as lobster and shrimp.*

**such as it is** In the form that it has, which is not very good but is all that's available, as in *Of course you can stay for supper, such as it is.* This expression is generally used apologetically, indicating that the item in question isn't very good or worth much.

**sucker** In addition to the idioms beginning with SUCKER, also see THERE'S A SUCKER BORN EVERY MINUTE.

**sucker list** A list of names of likely prospects for making purchases or donations, as in *Some charities raise money by selling their sucker lists to other organizations.*

**sucker punch** An unexpected blow, as in *They felt that suddenly raising the interest rate was a sucker punch to the administration.* This expression comes from boxing, where it is used for a punch delivered unexpectedly.

**suck in** **1.** Also, **suck someone in** or **suck someone into.** Draw into a course of action, as in *They sucked me into helping them raise money.* **2.** Take advantage of someone, cheat, swindle, as in *That used-car salesman sure sucked in my uncle and aunt.* This term uses *suck* in the sense of "take in."

**suck up to** Behave submissively toward someone, flatter insincerely, as in *Now that he's the boss they're all sucking up to him, hoping to get big raises.* [Vulgar slang]

**sudden** In addition to the idiom beginning with SUDDEN, also see ALL OF A SUDDEN.

**sudden death** Additional play to decide the winner of a tied game or other sports event, as in *Looks like this golf tournament is headed into sudden death.* The winner is the first player or team to score. This expression is also used as an adjective, as in *We won only after a sudden-death playoff.*

**suffer** see NOT SUFFER FOOLS GLADLY.

**suffice it to say** It is enough to say this and no more, as in *Suffice it to say that she was furious when the invitation was withdrawn.*

**sugar daddy** A wealthy, usually older man who gives expensive gifts to someone much younger in return for companionship or sexual favors. For example, *The aspiring young actress and the sugar daddy are a classic combination in Hollywood.* The *sugar* in this term refers to the sweetening role of the gifts, and *daddy* to the age difference between the pair.

**sugar the pill** Also, **sugarcoat the pill.** Make something unpleasant easier to bear, as in *There would be no Christmas bonus this year, but management sugared the pill by giving workers extra vacation time over the holidays,* or *Just give me the bad news—you don't have to sugarcoat the pill.*

**suit** In addition to the idioms beginning with SUIT, also see BIRTHDAY SUIT; EMPTY SUIT; FOLLOW SUIT; LONG SUIT; STRONG POINT (SUIT).

**suitcase** see LIVE OUT OF (A SUITCASE).

**suit oneself** Do as one pleases, as in *We had expected you, but if you don't want to come, suit yourself.* This idiom, which uses *suit* in the sense of "be agreeable or convenient," is often used as a command.

**suits, the** Men who wear dark suits to work, especially those who have a lot of economic power. For example, *I hear the suits are having a secret meeting in the conference room.*

**suit up** Put on clothes for a particular activity, as in *Come on, fellows, it's time to suit up for the hockey game.*

**sum and substance** The essence of something, as in *The sum and substance of their platform is financial conservatism.*

**sum total** The complete result, everything, as in *I spent all day in the kitchen, and the sum total of my efforts is this cake.*

**sum up** Present the important points of something, summarize, as in *They always sum up the important news in a couple of minutes,* or *That comment sums up my feelings about the matter.*

**sun** In addition to the idiom beginning with SUN, also see EVERYTHING BUT THE KITCHEN SINK (UNDER THE SUN); MAKE HAY WHILE THE SUN SHINES; NOTHING NEW UNDER THE SUN; PLACE IN THE SUN.

**sun belt, the** The southern and southwestern United States, as in *Retirees have been moving to the sun belt for years.* The area is called this because of its warm climate.

**Sunday** In addition to the idioms beginning with SUNDAY, also see MONTH OF SUNDAYS.

**Sunday best** One's finest clothes, as in *They were all in their Sunday best for the photographer.* This expression refers to saving one's best clothes for going to church. An older idiom is **Sunday-go-to-meeting clothes,** which uses *meeting* in the sense of "prayer meeting."

**Sunday driver** Someone who drives a vehicle at a very low speed, forcing other drivers to follow at the same speed, as in *I swear, the Sunday drivers in this town make me crazy.* The expression refers to the fact that Sunday formerly was the day when many families would go for a ride, traveling slowly through an area to look at houses and sightsee.

**sunny side** **1.** The pleasant or cheerful aspect of something, as in *Beth always sees the sunny side of events like graduations.* This idiom refers to the area on which sunlight falls. **2. on the sunny side of.** At an age less than, younger than, as in *He's still on the sunny side of forty.* **3. sunny-side up.** Fried so that the yolk of an egg remains intact and uppermost, as in *I ordered my eggs sunny-side up, and you brought me scrambled eggs.* This expression transfers the appearance of the sun to that of an egg yolk.

S

**supper** see SING FOR ONE'S SUPPER.

**supply** see IN SHORT SUPPLY.

**suppose** see I SUPPOSE SO.

**supposed to** **1.** Intended to; also, believed to, expected to. For example, *This pill is supposed to relieve your pain,* or *You're supposed to be my partner.* **2.** Required to, as in *He is supposed to call home.* **3. not supposed to.** Not allowed to, as in *You're not supposed to smoke in here.*

**sure** In addition to the idioms beginning with SURE, also see FOR CERTAIN (SURE); MAKE SURE; SLOW BUT SURE; TO BE SURE.

**sure as shooting** Most certainly, as in *It's going to snow tonight, sure as shooting,* or *That bear is sure as shooting going to make dinner out of us if we don't get out of here.*

**sure cure** A remedy that won't fail, as in *Hard work is a sure cure for brooding.*

**sure enough** Actually, as one thought would happen, as in *Sure enough, the plane was three hours late.*

**sure of oneself** Self-confident, as in *Now that Mary has graduated, she's much more sure of herself.* This expression uses *sure* in the sense of "confident" or "secure."

**sure thing** **1. a sure thing.** A certainty, as in *Making the bestseller list has been a sure thing for that novelist.* This usage originally referred to a bet that one could not lose. **2.** Yes indeed, certainly, as in *Are you coming tonight? Sure thing!* In this sense, the idiom is used as an interjection.

**surface** see ON THE SURFACE; SCRATCH THE SURFACE.

**surprise** see TAKE ONE BY SURPRISE.

**survival of the fittest** Those best adapted to particular conditions will succeed in the end, as in *They've had to close a dozen of their stores, but the ones in the western part of the state are doing well—it's the survival of the fittest.* This phrase originally referred to Charles Darwin's theory of natural selection of living species. It was later transferred to other areas.

**suspicion** see ABOVE SUSPICION; SNEAKING SUSPICION.

**swallow** In addition to the idioms beginning with SWALLOW, also see BITTER PILL TO SWALLOW; HARD TO SWALLOW.

**swallow one's pride** Humble oneself, as in *She decided to swallow her pride and apologize.*

**swallow one's words** Take back what one said, as in *If they win, I'll have to swallow my words.* For a synonym, see EAT ONE'S WORDS.

**swallow something whole** Believe whatever someone tells you and neglect to question whether it is true. For example, *We both heard that sales pitch—I can't believe you swallowed it whole!*

**swallow the bait** Also, **take the bait.** Accept something, such as an offer, that has been made to look tempting and very attractive and that is intended to get you to do something, as in *If we make our trip sound like a lot of fun, maybe he'll swallow the bait and do the driving for us,* or *I knew you'd take the bait—the temptation was too great.*

**swan song** A final accomplishment or performance, one's last work. For example, *I'm* *resigning tomorrow; this project was my swan song.* This term refers to the old belief that swans normally are mute but burst into beautiful song just before they die.

**swap horses** see CHANGE HORSES IN MIDSTREAM.

**swath** see CUT A WIDE SWATH.

**sway** see HOLD SWAY.

**swear at** Curse, use abusive, violent, or vulgar language against someone, as in *He always swears at all the other drivers on the road.*

**swear by 1.** Have great reliance on or confidence in someone or something, as in *She swears by her personal physician,* or *I swear by that new coffee grinder.* **2.** Also, **swear to.** Have reliable knowledge of something, be sure of, as in *I think she was going to the library, but I can't swear to it.* **3.** Take an oath by something, as in *I swear by all the saints in heaven.*

**swear in** Administer a legal or an official oath to, as in *The new mayor will be sworn in tomorrow.*

**swear like a trooper** Freely say vulgar or obscene words, as in *The teacher was shocked when she heard one of the fathers begin to swear like a trooper.* The *troopers* in this term were the cavalry, who were long known for their swearing.

**swear off** Promise to give up something, as in *I've sworn off cigarettes.* This expression was first used for giving up alcoholic drinks but has since come to refer to just about anything.

**swear on a stack of Bibles** Promise solemnly that what one is about to say is true, as in *I swear on a stack of Bibles that I had nothing to do with the dent in the car.* This term refers to the practice of placing one's hand on a sacred object while taking an oath. It is still used in courts of law, where a witness being sworn to tell the truth places a hand on a Bible.

**swear out** Obtain a warrant for someone's arrest by making a charge under oath, as in *The school principal swore out a warrant for the arrest of the vandals.*

**swear to** see SWEAR BY, def. 2.

**swear *someone* to secrecy** Make someone promise not to reveal information that is secret, as in *I had to swear everyone to secrecy about the surprise birthday party.*

**sweat** In addition to the idioms beginning with SWEAT, also see BY THE SWEAT OF ONE'S BROW; IN A COLD SWEAT; NO PROBLEM (SWEAT).

**sweat blood 1.** Also, **sweat one's guts out.** Work very hard, as in *The men were sweating blood to finish the roof before the storm hit.* **2.** Suffer mental anguish, worry intensely, as in *Waiting for the test results, I was sweating blood.*

**sweat bullets** Perspire a great deal; also, suffer mental anguish. For example, *We were sweating bullets, sitting in the sun through all those graduation speeches,* or *It was their first baby, and David was sweating bullets while Karen was in labor.* The *bullets* in this expression refer to drops of perspiration the size of bullets.

**sweat of one's brow** see BY THE SWEAT OF ONE'S BROW.

**sweat out** Wait for something anxiously, as in *He sweated out that last final exam,* or *I don't know if I made the team—I'm still sweating it out.* This idiom is often expanded to **sweat it out,** as in the second example.

**sweep** In addition to the idiom beginning with SWEEP, also see MAKE A CLEAN SWEEP; NEW BROOM SWEEPS CLEAN; (SWEEP) OFF ONE'S FEET.

**sweep off someone's feet** see OFF ONE'S FEET.

**sweep *something* under the rug** Hide something, as in *Their attempts to sweep the scandal under the rug were not very successful.* This idiom refers to sweeping dust under the rug so that it won't be seen.

**sweet** In addition to the idioms beginning with SWEET, also see SHORT AND SWEET; TAKE ONE'S (SWEET) TIME; TAKE THE BITTER WITH THE SWEET.

**sweet dreams** Sleep well, as in *Good night, children, sweet dreams.*

**sweeten the kitty** Also, **sweeten the pot** or **sweeten the deal.** Make something financially more attractive, as in *I am unable to give you a promotion, but I could sweeten the kitty a little by giving you a raise.* This idiom comes from card games such as poker, where it means "add money to the pool," and uses *sweeten* in the sense of "make more agreeable."

**sweetness and light** A show of friendliness, as in *One day she has a temper tantrum, the next day she's all sweetness and light.* This idiom is generally used ironically, either indicating a lack of trust in a person's seeming friendliness or for an unpleasant situation.

**sweet nothings** Special words or phrases, often whispered, between lovers. For example, *They sat in a corner all evening, whispering sweet nothings.* Also see SWEET TALK.

**sweet on, be** Be in love with someone, as in *I think Barbara's sweet on Nick.*

**sweet talk** Flattery, coaxing, as in *She uses sweet talk to get her way.*

**sweet tooth** A love for sugary foods, as in *You can always please Mary with cake or ice cream; she has a big sweet tooth.* Originally this term referred not only to sweets but to other delicacies as well.

**swelled head, have a** Be too impressed with one's accomplishments, as in *Winning all that money has not given her a swelled head, at least not yet.* For a synonym, see BIG HEAD.

**swim** In addition to the idioms beginning with SWIM, also see IN THE SWIM; SINK OR SWIM.

**swim against the current** Also, **swim against the stream** or **swim against the tide.** Go against common opinion or thought, as in *I'm voting for him even if that is swimming against the current.* For the antonym, see SWIM WITH THE TIDE.

**swim with the sharks** Be able to survive in the business world, as in *Anyone who expects to succeed in this business must be able to swim with the sharks.*

**swim with the tide** Go along with common opinion or thought, as in *Irene doesn't have a mind of her own; she just swims with the tide.* For the antonym, see SWIM AGAINST THE CURRENT.

**swine** see CAST PEARLS BEFORE SWINE.

**swing** In addition to the idioms beginning with SWING, also see GET INTO THE SWING OF THINGS; IN FULL SWING; NOT ENOUGH ROOM TO SWING A CAT.

**swing both ways 1.** Be able to leave an intimate relationship, as in *If you're not happy in this relationship, remember—the door swings both ways.* **2.** Be bisexual. For example, *She told us that her boyfriend swings both ways.*

**swing into action** Start doing something with a lot of energy, as in *Come on, let's swing into action before the others arrive.* This idiom uses *swing* in the sense of "move vigorously."

**switch** In addition to the idioms beginning with SWITCH, also see ASLEEP AT THE SWITCH; BAIT AND SWITCH.

**switch off** Stop paying attention, lose interest, as in *Whenever he starts in on economics, I switch off automatically.* This expression transfers turning off a light switch or similar device to diverting one's attention. Also see SWITCH ON.

**switch on** Produce something as if operating by a control, as in *She switched on the charm as soon as he walked in.* Also see SWITCH OFF.

**swoop** In addition to the idiom beginning with SWOOP, also see ONE FELL SWOOP.

**swoop down 1.** Descend suddenly from a great height, as in *The eagle swooped down from its nest.* **2.** Attack something as if descending quickly from a great height. For example, *The shoppers swooped down on the shoes that were on sale.*

**sword** In addition to the idiom beginning with SWORD, also see CROSS SWORDS.

**sword of Damocles** Also, **Damocles' sword.** A possible disaster, as in *The likelihood of layoffs has been a sword of Damocles over the department for months.* This expression refers to the legend of Damocles, a courtier to King Dionysius I. The king, weary of Damocles' insincere flattery, invited him to a banquet and seated him under a sword hung by a single hair in order to point out to him the danger of his position. The same story led to the related expression HANG BY A THREAD.

**symbol** see STATUS SYMBOL.

**system** see ALL SYSTEMS GO; BEAT THE SYSTEM; BUCK THE SYSTEM; OUT OF ONE'S SYSTEM.

# Tt

**T** see DOT THE I'S AND CROSS THE T'S; TO A T.

**tab** see KEEP TABS ON; PICK UP (THE TAB); RUN UP (A TAB).

**table** see BRING TO THE TABLE; CLEAR OUT (THE TABLE); LAY ONE'S CARDS ON THE TABLE; ON THE TABLE; SET THE TABLE; TURN THE TABLES; UNDER THE TABLE; WAIT TABLE.

**tack** see GET DOWN TO BRASS TACKS; ON THE RIGHT TACK; SHARP AS A TACK.

**tail** In addition to the idioms beginning with TAIL, also see BRIGHT-EYED AND BUSHY-TAILED; CAN'T MAKE HEAD OR TAIL OF; GET OFF ONE'S TAIL; HEADS OR TAILS; IN TWO SHAKES (OF A LAMB'S TAIL); ON SOMEONE'S COATTAILS; TIGER BY THE TAIL; TURN TAIL; WORK ONE'S FINGERS TO THE BONE (TAIL OFF).

**tail between one's legs, with one's** Saddened, ashamed, especially after a defeat or being proven wrong. For example, *After bragging about her great musical ability, she lost the competition and went off with her tail between her legs.* This idiom refers to a dog retreating in this way.

**tail end, the** **1.** The rear or last part, as in *Douglas was at the tail end of the academic procession.* **2.** The very end, the conclusion, as in *Only at the tail end of his speech did he thank his sponsors.*

**tail off** Also, **tail away.** Decrease gradually, subside, as in *The fireworks tailed off into darkness.*

**tailor-made for** see MADE TO MEASURE.

**tailspin** see GO INTO A TAILSPIN.

**tail wagging the dog, the** A small or unimportant factor or element governing an important one; a reversal of the proper roles. For example, *She found herself explaining the new therapy to her doctor—a case of the tail wagging the dog.*

**take** In addition to the idioms beginning with TAKE, also see AT (TAKE) PAINS; DEVIL TAKE THE HINDMOST; DOUBLE TAKE; GIVE AND TAKE; GIVE OR TAKE; GO TO (TAKE) THE TROUBLE; HAVE (TAKE) A CRACK AT; IN (TAKE) EFFECT; (TAKE) IN GOOD PART; (TAKE) IN TOW; IT TAKES ALL SORTS; IT TAKES GETTING USED TO; IT TAKES ONE TO KNOW ONE; (TAKE) OFF ONE'S HANDS; (TAKE) ON FAITH; ON THE TAKE; PAY YOUR MONEY AND TAKE YOUR CHOICE; PRIDE ONESELF (TAKE PRIDE IN); (TAKE A) RAIN CHECK; SIT UP (AND TAKE NOTICE); THAT'S (TAKES CARE OF) THAT; WHAT DO YOU TAKE ME FOR; WHAT IT TAKES; (TAKE) WITH A GRAIN OF SALT; YOU CAN LEAD (TAKE) A HORSE TO WATER; YOU CAN'T TAKE IT WITH YOU; YOU CAN'T TAKE SOMEONE ANYWHERE.

**take *one* aback** Surprise one, shock, as in *He was taken aback by her sarcastic remark.* This idiom comes from the earlier term **be taken aback,** which referred to a ship stalling because of a wind shift that made the sails lay back against the masts.

**take a back seat** Occupy an inferior position; allow another to be in control. For example, *Linda was content to take a back seat and let Nancy run the meeting.* This idiom uses *back seat* in contrast to the driver's seat, that is, the one in control.

**take a bath** Experience serious financial loss, as in *The company took a bath investing in that new product.* This idiom, which originated in gambling, transfers washing oneself in a bathtub to being "cleaned out" financially.

**take a bow** Acknowledge praise or applause, as in *The conductor asked the composer to take a bow.* This idiom uses *bow* in the sense of "inclining the body or head as a token of greeting."

**take a break** Interrupt one's activity briefly, as in *We've been working for two hours; let's take a break.* Also see TAKE FIVE.

**take account of** see TAKE SOMETHING INTO ACCOUNT.

**take a chance** Risk something, gamble, as in *I'll take a chance that he'll be on the next plane.*

**take a crack at** see HAVE A CRACK AT.

**take a dim view of** Regard something with disapproval, as in *I take a dim view of meeting every single week.* This idiom uses *dim* in the sense of "unfavorable."

**take advantage of** **1.** Put to good use. For example, *Let's take advantage of the good weather and go hiking.* **2.** Profit selfishly by someone, exploit, as in *They really take advantage of her good nature, getting her to do all the unpleasant chores.*

**take a fall** **1.** Also, **take a spill.** Fall down, as in *You took quite a fall on the ski slopes, didn't you?* or *Bill took a spill on the ice.* **2.** Be arrested or convicted, as in *He's taken a fall or two and spent some years in jail.*

**take a fancy to** Also, **take a liking to** or **take a shine to.** Be attracted to someone or something, as in *They took a fancy to spicy foods after their Mexican vacation,* or *I'm hoping he'll take a liking to the water, now that we have a cottage on a lake,* or *We think Bill's taken a shine to Betsy.*

**take after** **1.** Follow the example of someone; also, resemble in appearance, temperament, or character. For example, *Bill took after his uncle and began working as a volunteer for the Red Cross.* **2.** Go after someone, chase quickly, as in *After he hit me, I took after him and knocked him down.*

**take a gander at** Look at something, glance at, as in *Will you take a gander at that woman's red hair!* This slang idiom may have come from the verb *gander,* meaning "stretch one's neck to see," possibly referring to the long neck of the male goose. Also see TAKE A LOOK AT.

**take a hand in** see HAVE A HAND IN.

**take a hike** Go hiking; also, go away. For example, *We asked Jim to take a hike with us, but he didn't want to,* or *I've had enough of you—take a hike!* The latter usage is a slang command. Also see TAKE A WALK.

**take a hint** Also, **take the hint.** Accept an indirect or subtle suggestion, as in *Evelyn took the hint and quietly left the room.*

**take aim** Direct a missile or criticism at something or someone, as in *Raising his rifle, Charles took aim at the squirrel but missed it entirely,* or *In his last speech the President took aim at the opposition leader.*

**take a joke** Accept teasing at one's own expense, as in *Sam really couldn't take a joke.* This idiom is often used negatively. Also see TAKE IT.

**take a leaf out of someone's book** Imitate or follow someone's example, as in *Ann took a leaf out of her mother's book and began to keep track of how much money she was spending on food.* This idiom refers to tearing a page from a book.

**take a leak** Also, **take a piss.** Urinate, as in *Excuse me, I've got to take a leak.* [Vulgar slang]

**take a liking to** see TAKE A FANCY TO.

**take a load off one's mind** see LOAD OFF ONE'S MIND. Also see TAKE THE LOAD OFF.

**take a look at** Turn one's attention to something or someone, examine, as in *Take a look at that new building,* or *The doctor took a look at Gene's throat and swollen glands.* For a synonym, see TAKE A GANDER AT.

**take *something* amiss** see TAKE SOMETHING THE WRONG WAY.

**take an interest** **1.** Be concerned or curious, as in *She really takes an interest in foreign affairs,* or *I wish he'd take an interest in classical music.* **2.** Share in a right to or ownership of property or a business, as in *He promised to take an interest in the company as soon as he could afford to.*

**take apart** **1.** Break down into small pieces, disassemble something, as in *They had to take apart the stereo before they could move it.* **2.** Examine something thoroughly, analyze, as in *The teacher embarrassed Tom by taking his report apart in front of the class.* **3.** Beat someone up, as in *You'd better be careful; those boys will take you apart.*

**take a picture** **1.** Photograph something, as in *I'd love to take a picture of your garden.* This idiom was first used for making a drawing or other portrait and was later transferred to photography. **2.** Take a good look at someone, often in a rude way. For example, *Haven't you seen anyone like me before? Take a picture!* This phrase is used as a command in order to make fun of someone who is staring, as in the example.

**take a piss** see TAKE A LEAK.

**take a poke at** Hit someone with one's fist, as in *If you don't quit teasing me, I'll take a poke at you.*

**take a powder** Leave quickly, run away, as in *I looked around and he was gone—he'd taken a powder.* This slang idiom may be derived from the British dialect sense of *powder* as "a sudden hurry." It may also refer to the explosive quality of gunpowder.

**take a rain check** see RAIN CHECK.

**take *something* as gospel** Also, **take *something* for gospel.** Believe what someone says absolutely, regard as true, as in *We took every word of his as gospel, but in fact he was often mistaken.* This idiom uses *gospel* in the sense of the absolute truth. Also see GOSPEL TRUTH.

**take a shellacking** Be soundly beaten or defeated, as in *Our team took quite a shellacking last night.*

**take a shine to** see TAKE A FANCY TO.

**take *someone* aside** Also, **take *someone* to one side.** Talk to another privately or away from others, as in *The doctor took Pat aside to explain what she had to do,* or *The boss took William to one side rather than criticize his work in front of his colleagues.*

**take a spill** see TAKE A FALL.

**take a spin** Also, **go for a spin.** Go for a ride in a vehicle, usually without having any particular destination. For example, *How about taking a spin in my new car?* or *It's a beautiful day—let's go for a spin.*

**take a stand** Adopt a firm position about an issue, as in *She was more than willing to take a stand on abortion rights.* This idiom refers to the military sense of *stand,* meaning "hold one's ground against an enemy." Also see MAKE A STAND.

**take at face value** see AT FACE VALUE.

**take a toll** see TAKE ITS TOLL.

**take a turn for the better** Improve, as in *We thought she was on her deathbed, but now she's taken a turn for the better.* The antonym is **take a turn for the worse,** meaning "get worse, decline," as in *Unemployment has been fairly low lately, but now the economy has taken a turn for the worse.* This idiom uses *turn* in the sense of "a reversal."

**take a walk** Leave abruptly, walk out; also, go away. For example, *If she's rude again, I'm just going to take a walk,* or *The director would not put up with tantrums and ordered the young actress to take a walk.* Also see TAKE A HIKE; WALK OUT, def. 2.

**take away from** Make something less appealing, as in *Her messy hair takes away from her otherwise attractive appearance.*

**take a whack at** see HAVE A CRACK AT.

**take back 1.** Retract a statement, as in *I said you weren't much of a cook, but after that dinner I take it all back.* **2. take one back.** Return in thought to a past time, as in *That music takes me back to the first dance I ever went to.*

**take *something* by storm** Make a vivid impression on something or someone, quickly become popular, as in *The new rock group took the town by storm.* This usage transfers the original military meaning of the phrase, "assault in a violent attack," to more peaceful endeavors.

**take *one* by surprise** Encounter something unexpectedly, as in *The rainstorm took us by surprise.*

**take care 1.** Be careful, use caution, as in *Take care or you will slip on the ice.* **2.** Good-bye, as in *I have to go now; take care.* This apparent abbreviation of **take care of yourself** is used both orally and in writing, where it sometimes replaces the conventional *Sincerely* or *Love* in signing off correspondence.

**take care of 1.** Attend to a task, assume responsibility for, as in *Go ahead to the movies, I'll take care of parking the car,* or *They've hired someone to take care of the children for a week.* **2.** Beat up or kill someone, as in *If he didn't pay up, they threatened to take care of him and his family.*

**take charge** Assume control, command, or responsibility, as in *I'll take charge of selling the tickets if you'll do the publicity,* or *They're not happy about the counselor who took charge of the children.*

**take cover** Seek protection, find a hiding place, as in *It started to pour, so we took cover under the trees,* or *He wanted to avoid the reporters, so we said he could take cover in our summer cottage.* This term uses *cover* in the sense of "shelter" or "concealment."

**take doing** Require great effort to accomplish, as in *It'll take doing to get the whole house painted in a week.* This expression is sometimes put as **take some doing,** as in *You want the President to come? That'll take some doing!*

**take down 1.** Bring something from a higher position to a lower one, as in *After the sale they took down all the signs.* **2.** Take something apart, dismantle, as in *They took down the scaffolding.* **3.** Humiliate or humble someone; see TAKE SOMEONE DOWN A NOTCH. **4.** Record something in writing, as in *Please take down all these prices.*

**take *someone* down a notch** Also, **take *someone* down a peg.** Make someone who is arrogant feel less confident, humble, as in *He's so self-important; I wish someone would take him down a notch,* or *That defeat took them down a peg.* Also see CUT DOWN, def. 3.

**take effect** see IN EFFECT, def. 2.

**take exception to** Disagree with, object to, as in *I take exception to that remark about unfair practices.* This idiom uses *exception* in the sense of "objection," a meaning that is found in only a few current phrases.

**take five** Relax, take some time off from what one is doing, as in *We've been at it long enough; let's take five.* This term is short for **take five minutes off.** For a synonym, see TAKE A BREAK.

**take flight** Also, **take wing.** Run away, flee, go away, as in *When the police arrived, the demonstrators took flight,* or *The tenant took wing before paying the rent.* The first idiom comes from the earlier *take one's flight.*

**take *someone* for 1.** Regard someone as, as in *Do you take me for a fool?* **2.** Think of something in the wrong way, as in *Don't take our silence for approval,* or *I think they took us for foreigners.* Also see TAKE SOMETHING FOR GRANTED; WHAT DO YOU TAKE ME FOR.

**take for a ride** see TAKE SOMEONE FOR A RIDE.

**take *something* for gospel** see TAKE SOMETHING AS GOSPEL.

**take *something* for granted 1.** Consider something as true or real, anticipate correctly, as in *I took it for granted that they'd offer to pay for their share, but I was wrong.* **2.** Underestimate the value of someone or something, become used to, as in *The children felt that their parents were taking them for granted.*

**take heart** Be confident, be brave, as in *Take heart, we may still win this game.* This idiom uses *heart* in the sense of "courage."

**take hold 1.** Grasp something with the hand, as in *Take hold of this end of the rope.* **2.** Become established, as in *The new plants quickly took hold,* or *This idea will never take hold with the voters.*

**take ill** see GET SICK.

**take in 1.** Admit someone, receive as a guest or an employee, as in *They offered to take in two of the orphaned children.* **2.** Reduce something in size, make smaller or shorter, as in *I've lost some weight, so I'll have to take in my clothes.* **3.** Include or constitute something, as in *This list takes in all the members, past and present.* **4.** Understand something, as in *I couldn't take in all that French dialogue in the movie.* **5.** Deceive someone, cheat, as in *That alleged fundraiser took me in completely.* **6.** Look at something thoroughly, as in *We want to take in all the sights.* **7.** Accept work to be done at home, as in *His grandmother took in washing to support her children.* **8.** Receive money as proceeds, as in *We had a good audience; how much did we take in?* Also see the following idioms beginning with TAKE IN.

**take in good part** see IN GOOD PART.

**take *something* in hand** Deal with someone, assume control of something, as in *He's going to take their debts in hand and see if they can pay their bills,* or *Once the new teacher takes them in hand, this class will do much better.* Also see IN HAND, def. 2.

**take *something* in stride** Accept an event as a matter of course, not allow something to interrupt or disturb one's routine. For example, *There were certain to be setbacks, but Jack took them in stride.* This idiom refers to a horse clearing an obstacle without checking its stride.

**take *something* into account** Also, **take account of** or **take *something* into consideration.** Bear something in mind, consider, allow for, as in *We have to take into account that ten of the musicians were absent,* or *It's important to take account of what the audience wants,* or *When you take into consideration the fact that they were founded only a year ago, they've done very well.* The antonyms, **leave out of account** and **take no account of,** mean "ignore, pay no attention to," as in *They've left the most important item out of account.*

T

**take *someone* into one's confidence** Trust someone with a secret, as in *She took me into her confidence and admitted that she was quitting next month.* This idiom uses *confidence* in the sense of "trust."

**take *something* into one's head** see GET SOMETHING INTO ONE'S HEAD.

**take *something* into one's own hands** see TAKE THE LAW INTO ONE'S HANDS.

**take issue with** Disagree with something, as in *I take issue with those figures; they don't include last month's sales.* This idiom comes from legal terminology, where it was originally put as **join issue,** meaning "take the opposite side of a case."

**take it 1.** Understand something, as in *I take it they won't accept your proposal.* **2.** Endure abuse, criticism, harsh treatment, or unpleasantness, as in *Tell me what you really think of me—I can take it.* This phrase is sometimes put as **take just so much,** meaning "endure only up to a point." For example, *I can take just so much of this nonsense before I lose patience.* Also see TAKE IT ON THE CHIN; TAKE SOMETHING LYING DOWN. **3.** Accept or believe something, as in *I'll take it on the doctor's say-so.* Also see the following idioms beginning with TAKE IT.

**take it as it comes** Pay attention to events as they happen instead of worrying about the future, as in *You never what will happen in the future, so you might as well take it as it comes.*

**take it easy 1.** Proceed at a comfortable pace, relax. For example, *Take it easy—we don't have to be there till noon,* or *Bruce decided to take it easy this weekend and put off working on the house.* **2.** Take good care of oneself, as in *I have to leave now—take it easy. You do the same.* This expression is often used as a command when saying goodbye to someone.

**take it from here** Also, **take it from there.** Continue from a certain point onward, as in *I've done what I could with correcting the most obvious errors; you'll have to take it from here.*

**take it from me** Also, **you can take it from me.** Rest assured, believe me, as in *You can take it from me, we've been working hard on it.*

**take it on the chin** Suffer hardship or defeat, as in *Paul really took it on the chin today when he got fired for missing a deadline.* This idiom refers to taking a physical blow on the chin.

**take it or leave it** Accept or reject something with no further discussion or negotiation, as in *I'm asking $1,000 for this computer—take it or leave it.* This term is used to indicate one's final offer.

**take it out of one** Exhaust or tire one, as in *This construction job really takes it out of me.* This idiom refers to using up one's energy.

**take it out on** Also, **take something out on.** Transfer one's frustration or anger to a person or an object. For example, *I know you're furious about your grades, but don't take it out on me,* or *He took his anger out on the dog.*

**take its toll** Also, **take a toll.** Be damaging or harmful, cause loss or destruction, as in *The civil war has taken its toll on both sides,* or *The heavy truck traffic has taken a toll on the highways.* This expression transfers the taking of a *toll,* a tribute or tax, to exacting other costs.

**take it upon oneself** Also, **take on oneself.** Assume the responsibility for something, as in *I took it upon myself to count the number of children in the audience,* or *She took it on herself to call him.*

**take just so much** see under TAKE IT, def. 2.

**take kindly to** Be friendly toward someone or pleased with, accept something, as in *He'll take kindly to the criticism if it's constructive,* or *Henry won't take kindly to your stepping on his newly planted grass.* This idiom uses *kindly* in the sense of "in a pleasant or agreeable manner."

**take leave of 1.** Also, **take one's leave of.** Depart from someone, say good-bye to. For example, *Sorry, but I have to take leave of you now,* or *After the movie we'll take our leave of you.* **2. take leave of one's senses.** Behave irrationally, act crazy, as in *Give them the keys to the house? Have you taken leave of your senses?* Also see COME TO ONE'S SENSES.

**take liberties 1.** Behave improperly or disrespectfully; also, make unwanted sexual advances. For example, *He doesn't allow staff members to take liberties such as calling clients by their first names,* or *She decided that if Jack tried to take liberties with her she would go straight home.* This idiom uses *liberties* in the sense of "an overstepping of propriety," and thus differs markedly from TAKE THE LIBERTY OF. **2.** Make a statement or take an action not warranted by the facts or circumstances, as in *Their book takes liberties with the historical record.*

**take *something* lying down** Submit to an insult, scolding, or other harsh treatment without resisting, as in *He won't take that criticism lying down.* This idiom uses *lying down* in the sense of "passively." Also see TAKE IT, def. 2.

**take no for an answer, not** Not accept a refusal, continue to demand something, as in *I want you to show me the memo, and I won't take no for an answer.*

**take no prisoners** Do whatever one must do to be successful without any concern for the feelings or well-being of other people. For example, *When she decides she wants something, she takes no prisoners.*

**take note** Also, **take notice.** Pay attention, as in *Take note, not one man here is wearing a tie,* or *The aide took notice of the boys throwing food and reported them.* An antonym is **take no notice of,** meaning "ignore," as in *Take no notice of them, and they'll stop teasing you.* Also see TAKE NOTES.

**take notes** Also, **make notes.** Record one's observations or what one hears in order to help recall them later. For example, *Jim never takes notes in class, and I think he'll regret it,* or *The decorator made notes of the window measurements and other dimensions.* Also see TAKE NOTE.

**taken with, be** Be attracted to someone or something, be charmed by, as in *I was quite taken with those paintings,* or *The composer seemed to be taken with the young soprano who performed his songs.*

**take off 1.** Remove something, as in *Take off your coat and stay for a while,* or *I took my foot off the brake.* **2.** Deduct something, decrease, as in *He took 20 percent off the original price,* or *I want you to trim my hair, but please don't take off too much.* **3.** Carry or take someone or something away, as in *The passengers were taken off the train one by one.* **4.** Also, **take oneself off.** Leave, go away, as in *I'm taking off now,* or *We take ourselves off for China next month,* or, as a command, *Take yourself off right now!* **5.** Also, **take off after.** Move forward quickly, as in *The dog took off after the car.* **6.** Become well known or popular, or achieve sudden growth, as in *That actor's career has really taken off,* or *Sales took off around the holidays.* **7.** Rise in flight, as in *The airplane took off on time.* **8.** Discontinue something, as in *The railroad took off the commuter special.* **9.** Imitate someone humorously or satirically, as in *He had a way of taking off the governor that made us howl with laughter.* **10.** Also, **take off from.** Not work or go to school, as in *I'm taking off from work today because of the funeral.*

**take offense** Feel resentment or emotional pain, as in *I didn't realize he would take offense when he wasn't invited.*

**take office** Assume an official position or employment, as in *The new chair takes office after the first of the year.*

**take off one's hands** see OFF ONE'S HANDS.

**take on 1.** Assume a role or begin to deal with something, as in *I took on new responsibilities,* or *She took on too much when she accepted both assignments.* **2.** Hire someone, engage, as in *We take on extra workers during the busy holiday season.* **3.** Oppose someone in competition, as in *This young wrestler was willing to take on all opponents.* **4.** Imitate someone or appear to be something else, as in *He took on the look of a prosperous banker.*

**take one back** see TAKE BACK, def. 2.

**take one's breath away** Astonish or shock one with pleasure, surprise, or some other emotion. For example, *That beautiful sunset just takes my breath away.* This idiom refers to the way one holds one's breath when overcome with sudden emotion.

**take one's chances** Accept the risks, resign oneself to whatever happens, as in *I've no idea whether this scheme will work; I'll just take my chances.*

**take one's cue from** Follow the lead of another, as in *I'm not sure what to bring, so I'll take my cue from you.* This expression refers to the cue giving an actor a signal to speak.

**take oneself off** see TAKE OFF, def. 4.

**take one's hat off to** Express one's admiration, as in *I take my hat off to you—you've done very well indeed.* Also see HATS OFF TO.

**take one's leave of** see TAKE LEAVE OF.

**take one's life in one's hands** Do something that is very dangerous, as in *Skydiving is one way to take your life in your hands.* This expression is also used humorously to exaggerate the danger of an action or a situation, as in *You're taking your life in your hands if you disagree with her.*

**take one's lumps** Be able to endure times of hardship or bad luck, as in *I know this decision isn't fair, but she'll have to take her lumps like the rest of us.*

**take one's medicine** Tolerate something unpleasant, learn one's lesson. For example, *After failing math, he had to take his medicine and go to summer school.* This idiom uses *medicine* in the sense of "a bitter-tasting remedy."

**take one's own life** see TAKE SOMEONE'S LIFE, def. 2.

**take one's time** Also, **take one's sweet time.** Act slowly or when one is ready, as in *You can take your time altering that dress; I don't need it right away,* or *You certainly took your sweet time about calling me back.*

**take one's word for** see TAKE SOMEONE AT HIS OR HER WORD.

**take on faith** see ON FAITH.

**take on oneself** see TAKE IT UPON ONESELF.

**take out** **1.** Extract something, remove, as in *He should take out that splinter.* **2.** Secure something by applying to an authority, as in *She took out a real estate license.* **3.** Escort someone on a date, as in *He's been taking out a different girl every night of the week.* **4.** Give vent to one's anger; see TAKE IT OUT ON. **5.** Carry something away for use elsewhere, as in *Can we get some pizza to take out?* This sense can also be used as a noun or an adjective. For example, *We've eaten takeout every night this week,* or *Where can I get the best takeout pizza?* **6.** Obtain something as an equivalent in different form, as in *We took out the money she owed us by having her baby-sit.* **7.** Leave, as in *Jan and Herb took out for the beach,* or *The police took out after the suspects.* **8.** Kill someone, destroy something, as in *Two snipers took out a whole platoon,* or *Flying low, the plane took out the enemy bunker in one pass.* **9.** Knock someone or something over by accident, as in *The dog took out two lamps as he ran to greet us.* Also see TAKE OUT OF.

**take out of** see TAKE A LEAF OUT OF SOMEONE'S BOOK; TAKE IT OUT OF ONE; TAKE THE BREAD OUT OF SOMEONE'S MOUTH; TAKE THE STARCH OUT OF; TAKE THE STING OUT OF; TAKE THE WIND OUT OF ONE'S SAILS; TAKE THE WORDS OUT OF SOMEONE'S MOUTH.

**take over** Assume control, management, or possession of something, as in *The pilot told his copilot to take over the controls,* or *There's a secret bid to take over our company.*

**take pains** see AT PAINS.

**take part** Play a role in something, share in, participate, as in *Will you be taking part in the wedding?* or *He did not take part in the discussion.* Also see TAKE SOMEONE'S PART.

**take pity on** Also, **have pity on.** Show compassion or mercy to someone, as in *Take pity on the cook and eat that last piece of cake.* This idiom may be used seriously or half-jokingly, as in the example.

**take place** **1.** Happen, as in *Let me know where the ceremony will take place.* **2. take the place of.** Substitute for something or someone, as in *These plastic cups will have to take the place of glasses,* or *Jane took her sister's place in line.*

**take potluck** Come to eat whatever happens to be served; also, take one's chances. For example, *You're welcome to join us for supper, but you'll have to take potluck,* or *When the flight was canceled, passengers had to take potluck on other airlines.* This idiom refers to accepting whatever happens to be available.

**take pride in** see PRIDE ONESELF ON.

**take root** Become established or fixed, as in *We're not sure how the movement took root, but it did so very rapidly.* This idiom transfers the establishment of a plant, whose roots settle into the earth, to other matters.

**take shape** Also, **shape up.** Turn out, develop, acquire a distinctive form, as in *Her reelection campaign is already taking shape, two years before the election,* or *Can you tell us how the book is shaping up?*

**take sick** see GET SICK.

**take sides** Also, **take someone's side.** Support or favor one party in a dispute, as in *Parents shouldn't take sides in their children's quarrels,* or *Thanks for taking my side concerning the agenda.* Also see TAKE SOMEONE'S PART.

**take some doing** see under TAKE DOING.

**take someone at his or her word** Also, **take someone's word for it.** Accept what someone says on trust, as in *Since he said he'd agree to any of my ideas, I'll take him at his word,* or *She said she wanted to help out, and I took her word for it.*

**take someone for a ride** **1.** Cheat or deliberately mislead someone, as in *Car salesmen* *will take you for a ride in more ways than one!* **2.** Murder someone, as in *The gang threatened to take him for a ride.* Both usages refer to taking a person for an automobile ride.

**take someone in** see TAKE IN, def. 5.

**take someone's life 1.** Kill someone, as in *They argued about invoking the death penalty for taking someone's life.* **2. take one's own life.** Commit suicide, as in *Most churches have long opposed taking one's own life.*

**take someone's measure** Also, **take the measure of.** Evaluate someone or something, as in *At their first meeting, heads of state generally try to take each other's measure,* or *The voters are taking the measure of the union's demands.*

**take someone's name in vain** Speak casually or idly of someone, as in *There he goes, taking my name in vain again.* This idiom originated as a translation from a Latin version of the Bible and for a time was used only to mean blasphemy and vulgarity. It later began to be used more loosely as well.

**take someone's part** Stand up for or support someone, as in *Thanks for taking my part against the supervisor.* This idiom uses *part* in the sense of "side in a dispute." Also see TAKE SIDES.

**take someone's point** Understand what someone is saying, agree that what someone said was true, as in *Am I taking your point correctly when you say you disagree but do not object?*

**take someone's side** see TAKE SIDES.

**take someone's word for it** see TAKE SOMEONE AT HIS OR HER WORD.

**take someone up on** see TAKE UP, def. 4.

**take something hard** Feel very bad about something unpleasant that has happened or that someone has done, as in *When Sue's cat was killed, she took the death very hard,* or *Don't take it so hard—there'll be other opportunities.*

**take something on faith** see ON FAITH.

**take something out on** see TAKE IT OUT ON.

**takes one to know one** see IT TAKES ONE TO KNOW ONE.

**take steps** Begin a course of action, as in *The town is taking steps to provide better streetlights,* or *They took steps to keep their plans secret.*

**take stock** Make an estimate or appraisal of something, as in *We have to take stock of our finances before we can undertake a new project,* or *The career counselor advised Mark to take stock before changing his plans.* This expression transfers making an inventory of goods (*stock*) to other kinds of appraisal.

**take stock in** Believe something, attach importance to, as in *He exaggerates so much that I don't take stock in anything he says.* This term uses *stock* in the sense of "capital."

**takes two** see IT TAKES TWO TO TANGO.

**take the bait** see SWALLOW THE BAIT.

**take the bit in one's mouth** Also, **take the bit between one's teeth.** Throw off restraints and proceed very quickly on a course, take control. For example, *My partner took the bit in his mouth and laid his cards on the table,* or *Jane took the bit between her teeth, and now there's no stopping her.* This idiom refers to a *bit,* the metal mouthpiece of a bridle that a rider uses to control a horse.

**take the bitter with the sweet** Accept difficulties as well as good fortune, as in *Although he got the job, he hadn't counted on having to work with Mike; he'll just have to take the bitter with the sweet.* This idiom uses *bitter* for "bad" and *sweet* for "good." For a synonym, see TAKE THE ROUGH WITH THE SMOOTH.

**take the bread out of someone's mouth** Take away someone's work or ability to survive, as in *Lowering wages is taking the bread out of the workers' mouths.*

**take the bull by the horns** Face a problem head-on, as in *We'll have to take the bull by the horns and tackle the civil rights question.* This term most likely refers to grasping a safely tethered bull, not one the matador is fighting in the ring.

**take the cake** Be the most outstanding in some respect, either the best or the worst. For example, *That advertising slogan really took the cake,* or *What a mess they made of the concert—that takes the cake!*

**take the edge off** Ease something, make less severe, as in *That snack took the edge off our hunger,* or *Her kind manner took the edge off her refusal.* This term refers to blunting the sharp edge of a cutting instrument.

**take the fall** Be blamed or harshly criticized for another's misdeeds, as in *She has taken the fall for you in terms of any political damage,* or *A senior official took the fall for the failed intelligence operation.* This expression originated as underworld slang and later began to be extended to less criminal kinds of blame. Also see TAKE A FALL, def. 2; TAKE THE RAP.

**take the field** Enter a competition, as in *The country's best spellers took the field in the national spelling bee.* This term originally meant "open a military campaign," with *field* referring to the field of battle.

**take the Fifth** Refuse to answer a question on the grounds that one may incriminate oneself, as in *He took the Fifth on so many of the prosecutor's questions that we're sure he's guilty.* This idiom refers to the Fifth Amendment to the U.S. Constitution, which states that no person shall be compelled to be a witness against himself or herself.

**take the floor** Rise to speak formally to an assembled group, as in *After that long introduction, the treasurer took the floor.* This idiom uses *floor* in the sense of "right to speak," which in turn came from *floor* as the part of the legislature from which members address the group.

**take the heat** Endure severe criticism, as in *He was known for being able to take the heat during a crisis.* This idiom uses *heat* in the sense of "intense pressure," as in IF YOU CAN'T STAND THE HEAT, GET OUT OF THE KITCHEN.

**take the helm** Take control of a group, a project, or a particular situation, as in *Business has really increased since she took the helm.* This idiom compares being at the helm and guiding a ship to being in control and guiding an enterprise.

**take the hint** see TAKE A HINT.

**take the initiative** Begin a task or plan of action, as in *The boss was on vacation when they ran out of supplies, so Julie took the initiative and ordered more.* This term uses *initiative* in the sense of "the power to originate something."

**take the law into one's hands** Also, **take the law into one's own hands.** Replace the established authority with one's own, as in *While the captain was on shore, the sailors took the law into their own hands and sneaked the prisoner off the ship.* This idiom generally indicates disapproval of a forbidden action. Also see TAKE THINGS INTO ONE'S HANDS.

**take the liberty of** Act on one's own authority without permission from another, as in *I took the liberty of forwarding the mail to his summer address.* It is also put as **take the liberty to,** as in *He took the liberty to address the governor by her first name.* This rather formal expression does not imply the disapproval evident in the similar-sounding TAKE LIBERTIES.

T

**take the load off** Also, **take the weight off.** Sit down, relax, as in *I wish you'd rest for a while and take the load off,* or *Come on in and take the weight off.* These expressions are short forms of **take the load off one's feet** and **take the weight off one's feet.** The first expression is sometimes put as **take a load off.**

**take the measure of** see TAKE SOMEONE'S MEASURE.

**take the plunge** Attempt something, commit oneself, as in *You've been living together for a year, so when are you going to take the plunge and get married?* It is also put as **make the plunge.** In both expressions *plunge* refers to diving into a body of water.

**take the pulse of** Also, **feel the pulse of.** Try to determine the intentions or feelings of a person or group, as in *They claim these exit polls take the pulse of the voters, but I don't think they're very meaningful.* Also see FEEL OUT.

**take the rap** Be punished or blamed for something, as in *I don't want to take the rap for Mary; she's the one who forgot to mail the check in time,* or *Steve is such a nice guy that he's always taking the rap for his colleagues.* This slang idiom originally used *rap* in the sense of "a criminal charge," a usage still current.

**take the rough with the smooth** Accept the bad along with the good, as in *You can't expect to make a lot of sales every week—you have to take the rough with the smooth.* Also see TAKE THE BITTER WITH THE SWEET.

**take the shine off** Make something less appealing, as in *That remark will take the shine off their relationship,* or *Wait until he has to earn his own money—that'll take the shine off.*

**take the starch out of** Ridicule someone, make someone feel less confident, as in *That practical joke at the office party really took the starch out of him.* This expression refers to the starch used to stiffen a shirt.

**take the sting out of** Lessen the severity or unpleasantness of something, as in *That senior citizen discount took the sting out of the new airfares.*

**take the trouble** see GO TO THE TROUBLE.

**take the weight off** Also, **take the weight off one's feet.** See TAKE THE LOAD OFF.

**take the wind out of one's sails** Suddenly make one feel less confident, put one at a disadvantage, as in *When they announced they were doing the same study as ours, it took the wind out of our sails,* or *The applause for the pianist took the wind out of the conductor's sails.* This expression refers to robbing another ship of wind for its sails.

**take the words out of someone's mouth** Know in advance what someone is about to say; also, completely agree with someone. For example, *When you mentioned her dislike of fish, you took the words right out of my mouth,* or *You took the words out of my mouth when you said he was stupid.*

**take *something* the wrong way** Also, **take *something* amiss.** Misunderstand something, misinterpret, especially so as to take offense. For example, *I don't want you to take this the wrong way, but you have to give others a chance to speak,* or *Please don't take their criticism amiss; they mean well.*

**take things into one's hands** Make the decision to control a person or a situation, as in *We're going to miss our deadline unless* *you take things into your own hands.* Also see TAKE THE LAW INTO ONE'S HANDS.

**take to** **1.** Go to, as in *They took to the woods.* **2.** Develop as a habit or steady practice, as in *He took to coming home later and later.* **3.** Like, readily adapt to, as in *I took to him immediately,* or *The first time she skied she took to it.* This expression is sometimes expanded to **take to it like a duck to water.** **4. take *something* to be.** Understand something, consider or assume, as in *I took it to be the right entrance.* Also see the following idioms beginning with TAKE TO.

**take *something* to heart** Be deeply moved, affected, or upset by something, as in *I know you'll take these comments about your story to heart,* or *She really took that college rejection to heart.*

**take to one's heels** Run away, as in *When the burglar alarm went off, they took to their heels.* This expression refers to the fact that the heels are all one sees of someone running away fast. Also see SHOW ONE'S HEELS.

**take *someone* to one side** see TAKE SOMEONE ASIDE.

**take *someone* to task** Scold someone, blame. For example, *The teacher took Doris to task for turning in such a sloppy report.* This term originally meant assigning or challenging someone to a task.

**take *someone* to the cleaners** **1.** Take or cheat someone out of all of his or her money or possessions, as in *Her divorce lawyer took him to the cleaners,* or *That broker has taken a number of clients to the cleaners.* **2.** Beat someone up, as in *He didn't just knock you down—he took you to the cleaners.*

**take turns** Alternate, as in *Since there is only one horse, Beth and Alice are taking turns riding,* or *Take turns reading the sentences.* This phrase uses *turn* in the sense of "one of a series of actions done in succession." Also see IN TURN.

**take umbrage** Feel resentment, take offense, as in *Her aunt is quick to take umbrage at any suggestion about how to do things differently.* This expression features one of the rare surviving uses of *umbrage,* which now means "resentment" but comes from the Latin *umbra,* for "shade," and may refer to the "shadow" of displeasure.

**take up** **1.** Raise something, lift, as in *We have to take up the old carpet and sand the floor.* **2.** Reduce something in size, shorten, tighten, as in *I have to take up the hem of this coat,* or *If you don't take up the slack in that line, you'll trip someone.* **3.** Assume a position, settle in, as in *We took up our positions at the front of the auditorium.* **4.** Accept an option, a wager, or a challenge, as in *No one wanted to take up that bet.* This usage is often expanded to **take someone up on,** as in *You're offering to clean the kitchen? I'll take you up on that.* **5.** Develop an interest in an activity, begin, as in *Jim took up gardening.* Also see GO INTO, def. 3. **6.** Use up or occupy something entirely, as in *The extra duties took up most of my time,* or *This desk takes up too much space in the office,* or *How much room will your car take up?* **7.** Begin something again, resume, as in *I'll take up the story where I left off.* **8.** Deal with an issue, as in *Let's take up these questions one at a time.* **9.** Absorb something, as in *These large trees are taking up all the water in the soil.* **10.** Support someone, adopt as a student, as in *She's always taking up one or another young singer.* Also see the following idioms beginning with TAKE UP.

**take up a collection** Request and gather donations, as in *They were taking up a collection for the church that burned down,* or *Every month the veterans' group takes up a collection of household goods and furniture.*

**take up arms** Become involved in a conflict, either physical or verbal, as in *The soldiers took up arms against the queen's enemies.*

**take up for** Support in an argument, as in *To our surprise her father took up for her fiancé.*

**take *someone* up on** see TAKE UP, def. 4.

**take up with** Begin to associate with someone, as in *She took up with the wrong people.* This idiom is often used in a negative way, as in the example.

**take wing** see TAKE FLIGHT.

**take *something* with a grain of salt** see WITH A GRAIN OF SALT.

**take years off one's life** Make someone appear to be much younger than he or she is, as in *Those trips abroad have taken years off my life.* For an antonym, also see PUT YEARS ON ONE'S LIFE.

**tale** see LIVE TO TELL THE TALE; OLD WIVES' TALE; TALL TALE; TELL TALES; THEREBY HANGS A TALE.

**talk** In addition to the idioms beginning with TALK, also see ALL TALK; DIRTY JOKE (TALK DIRTY); DOUBLE TALK; HEART TO HEART (TALK); KNOW WHAT ONE IS TALKING ABOUT; LOOK WHO'S TALKING; MONEY TALKS; NOW YOU'RE TALKING; SMALL TALK; STRAIGHT TALK; SWEET TALK; WALK THE WALK, TALK THE TALK.

**talk about** **1.** Very, as in *What a day it's been—talk about stressful!* **2.** Showing a great deal of a quality in someone or something, or emphasizing the truth of a statement. For example, *Talk about mean! I've never met anyone so mean,* or *You can't believe a word he says. Talk about a liar!* This expression is used for emphasis and is always put as a command.

**talk around** Persuade someone, as in *I talked him around to my point of view,* or *He had a hard time talking them around, but they finally agreed to cancel the tournament.* Also see TALK SOMEONE INTO.

**talk at** Speak to someone without regard for or interest in his or her reaction or response. For example, *She had a way of talking at us that was quite unpleasant.*

**talk back** Also, **answer back.** Reply rudely or imprudently to someone, as in *She was always in trouble for talking back,* or *The teacher won't allow anyone to answer back to her.* This idiom is often used to describe children speaking to adults in an inappropriate way.

**talk big** Brag, boast, as in *I don't believe he's ever shot anything, but he sure talks big about hunting.*

**talk dirty** see under DIRTY JOKE.

**talk down 1.** Make something seem less important or inferior, as in *They talked down the importance of the move.* **2.** Silence someone by speaking loudly and persistently, as in *They talked down whatever objections she brought up.* **3.** See TALK DOWN TO.

**talk down to** Address someone as though he or she is less important, patronize, as in *Just because she's editor in chief doesn't give her the right to talk down to her staff.*

**talked out** Weary from speaking, as in *I haven't another thing to say; I'm all talked out.* Also see TALK OUT.

**talking heads** People on television who work as newscasters, sportscasters, or commentators. For example, *I don't want any more opinions from those talking heads.* This expression refers to the fact that the camera only shows the heads and shoulders of these people.

**talk *someone* into** Persuade someone, as in *They talked me into going swimming with them.* The antonym is **talk *someone* out of,** meaning "dissuade," as in *They tried to talk me out of going alone.*

**talk of the town, the** A subject of considerable gossip, as in *Turning up drunk at a formal dinner party certainly made him the talk of the town.*

**talk one's way into** Speak so well and so intelligently that one can easily gain entrance to a group or situation, as in *My sister has the best seat in the theater—she can talk her way into anything.* The antonym is **talk one's way out of,** and the positive and negative versions often occur together. For example, *We don't know how he does it, but he can talk his way into or out of anything.*

**talk out 1.** Discuss a matter thoroughly, as in *We talked out our marital problems with the therapist.* Also see TALKED OUT. **2.** Resolve or settle something by discussion, as in *Karen felt that she and her father should talk out their differences.*

**talk *someone* out of** see under TALK SOMEONE INTO. Also see OUT OF TURN, def. 2.

**talk over 1.** Discuss a subject or an issue thoroughly, as in *Let's talk over the entire plan and see if we discover any flaws.* **2.** Win someone over by persuasion, as in *We talked them over to our point of view.* Also see TALK AROUND.

**talk sense** Speak in a reasonable and realistic way, as in *Shouting won't help; it's time we talked sense,* or *I wish you'd talk some sense into that son of yours.*

**talk shop** Discuss one's business or profession, as in *Whenever John and his dad get together, they talk shop.*

**talk someone's arm off** Also, **talk someone's ear** or **head** or **pants off; talk a blue streak; talk until one is blue in the face.** Talk so much as to tire the listener, as in *Whenever I run into her, she talks my arm off,* or *Louise was so excited that she talked a blue streak,* or *You can talk until you are blue in the face, but you still won't convince me.*

**talk through one's hat** Talk nonsense; also, talk at length about something one knows very little about. For example, *He was talking through his hat when he described the shipwreck,* or *Mother went on and on about various screwdrivers, but in fact she was talking through her hat.*

**talk to** Also, **give *someone* a talking to.** Scold someone, reprimand, as in *The teacher said he'd have to talk to Jeff after school,* or *Dad gave us both a good talking to.*

**talk to a brick wall** Saying anything to someone is useless, because he or she won't listen. For example, *Talking to you is like talking to a brick wall,* or *Have you ever talked to a brick wall? I have.* Also see WASTE ONE'S BREATH.

**talk tough** Try to scare someone by pretending to be very mean or aggressive, as in *He always talks tough, but he's really just a pussy cat.*

**talk turkey** Speak plainly, get to the point, as in *Don't call me until you're ready to talk turkey.*

**talk up** Speak in favor of someone or something, promote, as in *They were talking up their candidate all over the state,* or *We need to talk up the project.*

**tall** In addition to the idioms beginning with TALL, also see WALK TALL.

**tall order, a** A goal that is hard to fulfill or achieve, as in *Getting a thousand new subscribers is a tall order indeed.* This expression uses *tall* in the sense of "impressively great" or "difficult."

**tall tale** A fanciful or greatly exaggerated story, as in *Some youngsters love tall tales* *about creatures from outer space coming to earth.* This idiom uses *tall* in the sense of "exaggerated."

**tamper with** **1.** Interfere with something, especially in a harmful way. For example, *If you tamper with that lock, it's sure to break.* **2.** Engage in improper or secret dealings, as in *He was accused of tampering with the jury.*

**tangent** see ON A TANGENT.

**tank** In addition to the idiom beginning with TANK, also see THINK TANK.

**tank up** **1.** Fill a gas tank with fuel, as in *As soon as we tank up the car, we can leave.* **2.** Drink to the point of intoxication. For example, *He's so drunk he must have really tanked up before coming to the party.*

**tan someone's hide** Also, **have someone's hide.** Spank or beat someone, as in *Dad said he'd tan Billy's hide if he caught him smoking,* or *I'll have your hide if you take something without paying for it.* This term uses *hide* in the sense of "skin." The reference in the first expression is to a spanking that will change one's skin just as chemicals tan animal hide (convert it into leather).

**tantrum** see THROW A TANTRUM.

**tap** see ON TAP.

**tape** see RED TAPE.

**taper off** **1.** Become thinner or narrower at one end, as in *The road began to taper off until it was just a narrow path.* **2.** Become less gradually, end by degrees, as in *The storm finally tapered off.*

**tar** In addition to the idiom beginning with TAR, also see BEAT THE LIVING DAYLIGHTS (TAR) OUT OF.

**tar and feather** Criticize someone severely, punish, as in *The traditionalists often want to tar and feather those who don't conform.* This expression refers to a former brutal punishment in which a person was smeared with hot tar and then covered with feathers.

**target** see ON TARGET; SITTING DUCK (TARGET).

**tarred with the same brush** Having the same faults or bad qualities, as in *He may be lazy, but if you ask me, his friends are all tarred with the same brush.*

**task** see TAKE SOMEONE TO TASK.

**taste** see ACQUIRED TASTE; DOSE (TASTE) OF ONE'S OWN MEDICINE; LEAVE A BAD TASTE IN ONE'S MOUTH; NO ACCOUNTING FOR TASTES; POOR TASTE.

**tat** see TIT FOR TAT.

**tax** In addition to the idiom beginning with TAX, also see DEATH AND TAXES.

**tax with** Charge someone, accuse, as in *He was taxed with betraying his fellows.*

**tea** see CUP OF TEA; NOT FOR ALL THE TEA IN CHINA; TEMPEST IN A TEAPOT.

**teach *someone* a lesson** Punish someone or something in order to prevent a repetition of bad behavior. For example, *Timmy set the wastebasket on fire; that should teach him a lesson about playing with matches.* This term uses *lesson* in the sense of "a punishment or scolding." Also see LEARN ONE'S LESSON.

**teach an old dog new tricks** Change long-standing habits or ways, especially in an older person. For example, *He refuses to buy a computer—you can't teach an old dog new tricks.* This expression refers to the difficulty of changing one's ways.

**teacher's pet** A person who has gained favor with authority, as in *Al has managed to be teacher's pet in any job he has held.* This expression transfers the original sense of a teacher's favorite pupil to broader use.

**team up with** Beging to work with someone, as in *Our pediatrician is teaming up with specialists in such areas as orthopedics and cardiology.* This expression refers to the harnessing together of animals, such as oxen.

**teapot** see TEMPEST IN A TEAPOT.

**tear** In addition to the idioms beginning with TEAR, also see RIP (TEAR) INTO; WEAR AND TEAR. Also see under TEARS.

**tear apart** **1.** Upset or distress someone, as in *The parents' divorce tore apart the grandparents.* **2.** Criticize someone or something severely, as in *The professor tore her paper apart.* **3.** Search a place completely, as in *The police tore the house apart, looking for drugs.* **4.** Separate people, especially unwillingly, as in *The war tore many families apart.*

**tear around** Move about in an excited or angry hurry, as in *He tore around the house, searching for the dog.*

**tear at** **1.** Pull at or attack something violently, as in *Jane eagerly tore at the wrapping paper,* or *The dog tore at the meat.* **2.** Distress someone, as in *Their plight tore at his heart.*

**tear *oneself* away** Remove oneself unwillingly or reluctantly, as in *I couldn't tear myself away from that television series.*

**tear down** **1.** Destroy something, take apart, as in *They tore down the old buildings,* or *He loved to tear down old engines.* **2.** Talk badly about someone, discredit, as in *He's always tearing down his friends.*

**tear into** see RIP INTO.

**tear it** Ruin something, spoil one's chances, as in *She knew she'd torn it when she lost the address.* It is often put as **that tears it,** as in *He's a whole hour late—well, that tears it for our dinner reservation.*

**tear off** **1.** Produce something hurriedly and casually, as in *He tore off a poem a day for an entire month.* **2.** Leave in a hurry, as in *She tore off to the store because it was about to close.*

**tear one's hair** Also, **tear out one's hair.** Be greatly upset or distressed, as in *I'm tearing my hair over these errors.* This expression

T

literally refers to tearing out one's hair in a frenzy of grief or anger. Today it is generally used in an exaggerated way.

**tears** see BORE TO DEATH (TEARS); BURST INTO (TEARS); CROCODILE TEARS. Also see under TEAR.

**tear someone limb from limb** Also, **rip someone limb from limb.** Attack someone verbally or physically, as in *She'll tear me limb from limb when she finds out what I've done,* or *I swear, I'll rip you limb from limb if you tell anyone about this.* This idiom is often used to exaggerate the unpleasant results of what one has done or will do.

**tease out** Lure something out, obtain or extract with effort, as in *We had a hard time teasing the wedding date out of him,* or *I think I can tease the splinter out of your finger.* This term refers to the literal sense of *tease,* "untangle or release something with a pointed tool."

**tee off 1.** Start or begin something, as in *We teed off the fundraising drive with a banquet.* This expression comes from golf, where **tee off** means "start play by driving a golf ball from the tee." **2.** Make one angry or irritated, as in *That rude comment teed him off,* or *I was teed off because it rained all weekend.* Also see TICK ONE OFF.

**teeth** see ARMED TO THE TEETH; BY THE SKIN OF ONE'S TEETH; CUT ONE'S TEETH ON; FED UP (TO THE TEETH); FLY IN THE FACE (TEETH) OF; GIVE ONE'S EYETEETH; GNASH ONE'S TEETH; GRIT ONE'S TEETH; IN THE TEETH OF; KICK IN THE PANTS (TEETH); LIE THROUGH ONE'S TEETH; LIKE PULLING TEETH; SCARCE AS HEN'S TEETH; SET ONE'S TEETH ON EDGE; SINK ONE'S TEETH INTO; TO THE TEETH. Also see under TOOTH.

**tell** In addition to the idioms beginning with TELL, also see DO TELL; KISS AND TELL; LIVE TO TELL THE TALE; SEE (TELL) A MILE OFF; SHOW AND TELL; SOMETHING TELLS ME; THERE'S NO TELLING; TIME WILL TELL; (TELL) WHICH IS WHICH; YOU NEVER CAN TELL; YOU'RE TELLING ME. Also see under TOLD.

**tell a mile off** see SEE A MILE OFF.

**tell apart** Discern or distinguish things or people, as in *It's hard to tell the twins apart,* or *It's hard to tell apart the real paintings from the fake ones in this exhibit.*

**tell it like it is** Speak the truth, no matter how unpleasant. For example, *We must tell it like it is to the stockholders.*

**tell me** Also, **tell me about it.** I know, I agree with you, as in *Since the layoffs, I have been overloaded with work. Tell me!* or *We had a hard time finding the place. Tell me about it! It took me an hour.* This expression must be distinguished from a literal request to be told about something by the context and the speaker's tone.

**tell off** Scold someone severely, criticize harshly, as in *It's time someone told her off about her behavior.* There is also a synonymous expression, **tell someone where to get off,** as in *When he called back a third time, I told him where to get off.* Also see GET OFF, def. 7.

**tell on** Inform on someone, as in *Marjorie said she'd tell on her brother if he pulled her hair again.*

**tell someone where to get off** see TELL OFF.

**tell tales** Reveal secrets, as in *Don't trust him; he's apt to tell tales.* A variant, **tell tales out of school,** may originally have referred to schoolchildren gossiping but was soon broadened to revealing secret or private information.

**tell time** Keep track of the hours; also, know how to read a clock or watch. For example, *This old clock still tells time quite accurately,* or *He taught his niece to tell time.* This expression uses *tell* in the sense of "calculate."

**temper** see HOLD ONE'S TEMPER; LOSE ONE'S TEMPER; THROW A (TEMPER) TANTRUM.

**temperature** see RUN A FEVER (TEMPERATURE).

**tempest in a teapot, a** Also, **a tempest in a teacup.** A great disturbance or uproar over something of little or no importance. For example, *All that because a handful of the invited guests didn't show up? What a tempest in a teapot!* For a synonym, see MUCH ADO ABOUT NOTHING.

**tempt fate** Also, **tempt the fates.** Take a severe risk, as in *It's tempting fate to start climbing that mountain so late in the day,* or *Pat thought driving that old car was tempting the fates; it was sure to break down.* This expression uses *tempt* in the sense of "test in a way that involves risk or danger."

**ten** see COUNT TO TEN; NOT TOUCH WITH A TEN-FOOT POLE.

**tender** see LEAVE ONE TO SOMEONE'S TENDER MERCIES.

**tender age** A young age, as in *It's a great advantage to learn languages at a tender age,* or *They were married at the tender age of eighteen.*

**tender loving care** Also, **TLC.** Kind and thoughtful care, as in *These houseplants sure have had tender loving care,* or *Older house for sale, needs some renovation and TLC.* Originally used to describe the work of caregivers such as nurses, this term today is often used ironically or euphemistically.

**tender mercies** see LEAVE ONE TO SOMEONE'S TENDER MERCIES.

**tend to 1.** Apply one's attention to a task, as in *We should tend to our business, which is to teach youngsters.* This term uses *tend* in the sense of "attend." **2.** Be inclined to; usually, as in *We tend to believe whatever we are told.* This meaning is always followed by the base form of the verb, as in the example.

**tenterhooks** see ON TENTERHOOKS.

**terms** see BRING ONE TO TERMS; COME TO TERMS WITH; CONTRADICTION IN TERMS; IN GLOWING TERMS; IN NO UNCERTAIN TERMS; IN TERMS OF; ON GOOD TERMS; ON SPEAKING TERMS.

**territory** see COME WITH THE TERRITORY; COVER THE FIELD (TERRITORY).

**terror** see HOLY TERROR.

**test** In addition to the idioms beginning with TEST, also see ACID TEST; PUT SOMETHING TO THE TEST.

**test of time, the** Continued popularity, enjoyment, or usefulness over a long period of time. For example, *Only the test of time with show how well this car is made.* It is often put as **stand the test of time,** as in *Her poetry has stood the test of time and is still read by many people.*

**test the water** Also, **test the waters.** Find out whether an idea or a project will be accepted or successful before beginning to act, as in *If I were you, I'd test the water before I invested a lot of money in their proposal,* or *Let's test the waters before we make an offer.*

**tether** see END OF ONE'S ROPE (TETHER).

**than** see ACTIONS SPEAK LOUDER THAN WORDS; BARK IS WORSE THAN ONE'S BITE; BEFORE (QUICKER THAN) YOU CAN SAY JACK ROBINSON; BETTER LATE THAN NEVER; BETTER SAFE THAN SORRY; BETTER THAN; BITE OFF MORE THAN ONE CAN CHEW; BLOOD IS THICKER THAN WATER; EASIER SAID THAN DONE; EYES ARE BIGGER THAN ONE'S STOMACH; IN (LESS THAN) NO TIME; LESS THAN; MORE DEAD THAN ALIVE; MORE FUN THAN A BARREL OF MONKEYS; MORE OFTEN THAN NOT; MORE THAN MEETS THE EYE; MORE THAN ONE BARGAINED FOR; MORE THAN ONE CAN SHAKE A STICK AT; MORE THAN ONE WAY TO SKIN A CAT; NONE OTHER THAN; NO SOONER SAID THAN DONE; OTHER THAN; WEAR ANOTHER (MORE THAN ONE) HAT.

**thank** In addition to the idioms beginning with THANK, also see GIVE THANKS FOR SMALL BLESSINGS.

**thank God** Also, **thank goodness** or **thank heaven.** I'm grateful, as in *Thank God you arrived safely,* or *We didn't run out of food, thank goodness,* or *Thank heaven the book arrived on time.* These phrases originally expressed gratitude to a god but today tend to be used in a more casual way.

**thank one's lucky stars** Be grateful for good fortune, as in *I thank my lucky stars that I wasn't on the plane that crashed.* This phrase reflects the ancient belief in the influence of stars over human destinies. Today it is more a general expression of relief than of belief in the stars' protection. Also see THANK GOD.

**thanks to** On account of someone, because of, as in *Thanks to your help, we'll be done on time.* This phrase refers to gratitude being due to someone or something. It is also put negatively, **no thanks to,** meaning "without the benefit of help from," as in *We finally found your house, no thanks to the confusing map you drew.*

**that** In addition to the idioms beginning with THAT, also see ALL'S WELL THAT ENDS WELL; ALL THAT; ALL THAT GLITTERS IS NOT GOLD; AND ALL (THAT); AS FAR AS THAT GOES; AT THAT POINT; AT THIS (THAT) RATE; AT THIS (THAT) STAGE; BE THAT AS IT MAY; BITE THE HAND THAT FEEDS YOU; CROSS A (THAT) BRIDGE; FOR THAT MATTER; GAME THAT TWO CAN PLAY; HOW ABOUT THAT; HOW DOES THAT GRAB YOU; HOW'S THAT; IN ORDER (THAT); IN THAT; IS THAT A FACT; IT (THAT) FIGURES; IT'S THE THOUGHT THAT COUNTS; JUST LIKE THAT; JUST THE (THAT'S THE) TICKET; LAST STRAW (THAT BREAKS); LIKE THAT; LOOK LIKE THE CAT THAT ATE THE CANARY; NOT BUILT THAT WAY; NOW THAT; ON CONDITION THAT; ON THE CHANCE (THAT); POWERS THAT BE; PUT THAT IN YOUR PIPE; SEEING THAT; SHIPS THAT PASS IN THE NIGHT; SO THAT; SUFFICE IT TO SAY THAT; TEAR (THAT TEARS) IT; THIS AND THAT; TO THAT EFFECT; WHEN IT COMES TO (THAT); WOULD THAT; YOU CAN SAY THAT AGAIN.

**that ain't hay** That's a great deal, especially of money; also, that's important. For example, *He's making ten thousand a month, and that ain't hay.* Originally used to describe a sum of money that is large, this phrase was later extended to other circumstances, as in *She married a prince, and that ain't hay.*

**that does it** **1.** Also, **that does the trick.** The last requirement has been fulfilled; that accomplishes it. For example, *That does it; we're ready to send in the application now,* or *That last screw does the trick—it's fully assembled.* The *it* here may stand for *the trick.* Also see THAT'S THAT. **2.** That's enough, do not continue to behave in an annoying way or perform an undesirable activity. For example, *He's cheated on her for the last time. That does it—she's getting a divorce,* or *I've told you for the last time not to nag me, and that does it!*

**that figures** see IT FIGURES.

**that is** Also, **that is to say.** In order to explain more clearly, in other words, as in *It's on the first floor, that is, at street level,* or *We're coming next month, that is to say, in November.* Also see under THAT'S.

**that'll be the day** That will never happen, that's very unlikely, as in *You think I'll win the lottery? That'll be the day!* This phrase may be short for *that will be the day worth waiting for,* but it is nearly always used ironically, as in the example.

**that makes two of us** I agree, me too, as in *I'm sure it's going to rain. That makes two of us.*

**that's about it** **1.** One has finished a task or project; also, one can leave now, as in *I guess that's about it—let's pick up our tools,* or *It's five o'clock—that's about it for today.* **2.** That says all there is to say about something, as in *You're refusing to help me? That's about it.* Also see THAT'S ABOUT THE SIZE OF IT.

**that's about the size of it.** That sums up the situation; that's how things are. For example, *So he's going to resign next month? Yes, that's about the size of it,* or *Mary's applying to all those colleges? That's about the size of it.* Also see THAT'S ABOUT IT, def. 2.

**that's a good one** That's a very funny joke or comment, as in *That's a good one—can I use that joke in my speech?* This expression is also used ironically to show that one disagrees or dislikes what another person has said. For example, *You can't afford a new car? That's a good one! What about all that money in your bank account?*

**that's all** Also, **that's it. 1.** Someone is finished with a task or being removed from a game. For example, *I've wrapped all the presents—that's all for me,* or *That's it for you—you've made too many errors in this game.* **2.** I've put up with all I can tolerate; this is the end, as in *That's it! She's been late one too many times.*

**that's all she wrote** **1.** Something is over or finished. For example, *That's all she wrote, guys—let's head home.* **2.** Whatever happens next cannot be controlled, as in *If you refuse to let him go to the party, that's all she wrote. He'll find a way to get there.*

**that's a new one on me** see under THAT'S ONE ON ME.

**that's *someone or something* for you** This is the way someone or something is, as in *She's changed her mind again; that's Mary for you,* or *They came close to winning, but they lost; that's tennis for you.*

T

**that's how the ball bounces** Also, **that's the way the ball bounces** or **that's the way the cookie crumbles.** That is the way matters have worked out and nothing can be done about it. For example, *I'm sorry you got fired, but that's how the ball bounces,* or *They wanted a baby girl but got a third boy—that's the way the cookie crumbles.* These phrases refer to an odd bounce or a crumbled cookie that cannot be put back together. Also see THE BREAKS.

**that's it** see THAT'S ALL.

**that's more like it** Better than an earlier attempt or closer to what one wants, as in *You're beginning to understand what I'm telling you—that's more like it,* or *We can see the improvement in her attitude—that's more like it.*

**that's one on me** That's a joke at my expense, as in *And after all that discussion they didn't show up—that's one on me.* This phrase must be distinguished from **that's a new one on me,** which means "this is the first time I've heard of or seen that" (as in *A checkerboard rug—that's a new one on me* ). Both idioms can be used with other personal pronouns (for example, **that's one on you**).

**that's right** Yes; that's correct; I agree. For example, *Are you leaving early? That's right, I have to go now,* or *So you were classmates? That's right.*

**that's that** Also, **that takes care of that.** There's no more to be said or done; the matter is finished, the issue is settled. For example, *Dad's not buying you a television set, and that's that,* or *We've paid all we owe, and that takes care of that.* Also see THAT'S ABOUT IT; THAT'S ALL SHE WROTE.

**that's the beauty of** This is the most satisfactory feature of, as in *And our vacations fall at the same time; that's the beauty of working in this company.*

**that's the ticket** see JUST THE TICKET.

**that's what one calls *something or someone*** An excellent, pleasing, or interesting thing or person. For example, *Look at how hard he can throw a ball. Now that's what I call a pitcher,* or *I'm still hungry—is that what you call a meal?*

**that's what one thinks** A person is wrong, as in *I'm sure I left my keys on the table. That's what you think—I saw them in the car,* or *He says he's going to the party. That's what he thinks—he's not invited.*

**that's where one came in** Also, **which is where one came in.** The point or stage of a situation where one entered or became involved. For example, *He's filed again for divorce? That's where I came in,* or *They were threatening to arrest her, which is where we came in.*

**that's where someone or something comes in** Also, **that's where someone or something comes into it.** Someone or something has an important role to play in a task or a situation. For example, *Someone will have to buy the tickets. That's where she comes in—she has the money,* or *As soon as I give the signal, that's where you come into it.*

**that will do** That is enough of something, as in *Please don't give me more peas; that will do,* or *That will do, children! There's to be no running near the pool.*

**the beauty of** see THAT'S THE BEAUTY OF.

**the bigger they come** see BIGGER THEY COME.

**the breaks** Bits of luck, turns of events, as in *No matter how well he pitches, the team always makes fielding errors—that's the breaks, I guess,* or *There's not much you can do if the breaks are against you.* In the singular and modified forms, this term becomes **good break** or **bad break** or **lucky break,** as in *She got a bad break and lost her wallet.* In the plural form, only the context determines its favorable or unfavorable meaning. Also see TOUGH BREAK.

**the business** **1.** Verbal abuse, scolding, or teasing; also, a beating. For example, *At school new kids often get the business,* or *The boxer faked and then gave his opponent the business.* **2.** A harsh questioning, as in *The detectives gave each suspect the business.* **3.** Dismissal from work or rejection, as in *Once the new management takes over, I'm sure to get the business,* or *Dorothy gave him the business and married someone else.*

**the creeps** Also, **the willies.** A sensation of horror or disgust, as in *That weird man gives me the creeps,* or *I get the willies when I hear that kind of music.* The first of these terms refers to a sensation of something crawling on one's skin. It was originally applied to a physical ailment but soon began to be used to describe fear and loathing. The reference in the variant is unknown.

**the damage** The cost or price of something, as in *So what's the damage for this outfit?* This idiom uses *damage* to refer to the harm done to one's pocketbook.

**the good old days** An expression that suggests that things were better in the past. For example, *Those were the good old days—no responsibilities, no boss, no money.*

**the hell with** see TO HELL WITH.

**the horse's mouth** see FROM THE HORSE'S MOUTH.

**the idea** see WHAT'S THE IDEA.

**the in thing** see THE THING.

**the latest** Also, **the latest thing.** The most recent development, as in fashion or the news. For example, *Wearing straw hats to the beach is the latest thing,* or *Have you heard the latest about the royal family?* Also see THE THING.

**the likes of** see LIKES OF.

**the limit** The most extreme; someone or something that irritates, delights, or surprises the most. For example, *Hiring and firing someone the same day—that's the limit in employee relations!* or *That excuse of yours for missing the wedding, that's the limit,* or *He has done wonders before, but this last one is the limit.* This idiom uses *limit* in the sense of "the last possible point or boundary."

**the long and the short of it** see LONG AND SHORT OF IT.

**the lowdown on** The whole truth about something, as in *We're waiting to hear the lowdown on what happened after we left.* This term uses *lowdown* in the sense of "the basic or fundamental part."

**the masses** The body of common people, or people of low socioeconomic status, as in *TV sitcoms are designed to appeal to the masses.* This idiom is nearly always used in a snobbish context that puts down the taste, intelligence, or some other quality of the majority of people.

**the matter** see WHAT'S THE MATTER.

**the more the merrier** see MORE THE MERRIER.

**them's fighting words** see FIGHTING WORDS.

**then** In addition to the idioms beginning with THEN, also see AND THEN SOME; EVERY NOW AND THEN.

**then again** Also, **but then.** On the other hand, an opposite possibility. For example, *I think it'll arrive tomorrow; then again, it may not,* or *We think you'll like this restaurant, but then again, not everyone does,* or *The play was a bit dull, but then she's a great actress.*

**then and there** Also, **there and then.** At that exact time and place; on the spot. For example, *When the board questioned his judgment again, he resigned then and there.*

**the other day** see OTHER DAY.

**the other way round** see OTHER WAY ROUND.

**the picture** see IN THE PICTURE.

**the pits** The worst possible situation, as in *Spending your birthday working alone is the pits,* or *That job is the pits.*

**there** In addition to the idioms beginning with THERE, also see ALL THERE; GET THERE; HANG IN (THERE); HERE AND THERE; HERE, THERE, AND EVERYWHERE; IN THERE PITCHING; LIKE THERE'S NO TOMORROW; NEITHER HERE NOR THERE; NO SMOKE WITHOUT (WHERE THERE'S SMOKE THERE'S) FIRE; (THERE'S) NOTHING TO IT; SOMEBODY UP THERE LOVES ME; SO THERE; TAKE IT FROM HERE (THERE); THEN AND THERE; WHERE THERE'S A WILL; WHILE THERE'S LIFE THERE'S HOPE.

**there and then** see THEN AND THERE.

**there but for the grace of God goes one** Anyone else also could be in that terrible situation, as in *Seeing him with two flat tires on the highway, she said "There but for the grace of God go I."*

**thereby hangs a tale** That detail or incident reminds one of another story, as in *So he went without supper, but thereby hangs a tale.*

**there for, be** Be prepared to help or support one during a difficult time or terrible situation, as in *Maybe you don't like her, but she was there for me when I needed her.*

**there one goes again** Repeating an undesirable action, as in *There you go again,* *interrupting me while I'm talking,* or *There I go again, forgetting to buy milk.*

**there's a first time for everything** Also, **there's always a first time.** Something will happen that hasn't happened before. For example, *I told you she would be on time—there's a first time for everything,* or *Don't promise you'll never lie—there's always a first time.*

**there's always one** Also, **there's one in every crowd.** You can expect to find one person in a group who is stubborn, stupid, hostile, or somehow unpleasant. For example, *You can count on him to ask a stupid question—there's always one,* or *She really gave us a hard time—oh well, there's one in every crowd.*

**there's a sucker born every minute** Also, **there's a fool born every minute.** People who can easily be fooled or deceived at always available, as in *I told him that car wasn't a good buy, but there's a sucker born every minute,* or *Someone will buy this rundown house—there's a fool born every minute.* This expression, often attributed to P.T. Barnum (1810-1891), a cofounder of the Barnum & Bailey Circus, is so well know that *one* is often substituted for *a sucker* or *a fool.* For example, *My grandmother told me there's one born every minute, and now I know she's right.*

**there's no accounting for tastes** see NO ACCOUNTING FOR TASTES.

**there's no fool like an old fool** see NO FOOL LIKE AN OLD FOOL.

**there's no smoke without fire** see NO SMOKE WITHOUT FIRE.

**there's no telling** It's impossible to determine, as in *There's no telling how many children will come down with measles,* or *There's no telling what will happen in the next episode of that soap opera.* This idiom uses *telling* in the sense of "reckoning."

**there's no time like the present** see NO TIME LIKE THE PRESENT.

T

**there's one in every crowd** see THERE'S ALWAYS ONE.

**there you go** Also, **there you are; here you go** or **here you are.** A phrase used when someone gives something to another person, either as a favor or part of a business transaction. For example, *There you go. It's exactly the color you wanted,* or *Here you are, a new box of computer disks.*

**the ropes** see KNOW THE ROPES; ON THE ROPES.

**the rub** The difficulty or problem, as in *We'd love to come, but there's the rub—we can't get reservations.*

**the score** see KNOW THE SCORE.

**these** see ONE OF THESE DAYS.

**the soul of** see SOUL OF.

**the stake** see BURN AT THE STAKE.

**the thing** Also, **the in thing.** A fad, something in style, the latest trend. For example, *Wearing oversized clothes is the thing these days,* or *Sport utility vehicles have been the in thing for some time now.* The second term uses *in* in the sense of "popular." Also see THE LATEST.

**the thing is** The issue, main point, or problem is, as in *The thing is, we don't have enough money for the tickets.*

**the ticket** see JUST THE TICKET.

**the very idea** see WHAT'S THE IDEA.

**the willies** see THE CREEPS.

**the wiser** see NONE THE WISER.

**the works** **1.** Everything, the full range of possibilities, as in *He ordered a pizza with the works,* or *All right, tell me, give me the works on it.* This usage comes from *works* in the sense of "a complete set of parts for a machine or mechanism." **2.** A beating or other severe treatment. This usage is often put as **give someone the works,** as in *They took him outside and gave him the works.*

**they** see BIGGER THEY COME; LET THE CHIPS FALL WHERE THEY MAY.

**thick** In addition to the idioms beginning with THICK, also see BLOOD IS THICKER THAN WATER; IN THE THICK OF; LAY IT ON THICK; PLOT THICKENS; THROUGH THICK AND THIN.

**thick and fast** Rapidly crowding, coming so fast they run together, as in *The questions came at him thick and fast.* For a synonym, see FAST AND FURIOUS.

**thick and thin** see THROUGH THICK AND THIN.

**thick as thieves** Closely allied, as in *The sisters-in-law are thick as thieves.* This term uses *thick* in the sense of "intimate," a meaning that is no longer used except in this expression.

**thick skin** Insensitivity to criticism or insult, as in *You can tell him exactly what you think of his new piece; unlike most composers, he has a thick skin.* This term transfers a hard outer coating to mental or emotional toughness. The expression is also used as an adjective, as in *She has to be more thick-skinned if she wants to succeed.* For an antonym, see THIN SKIN.

**thick with** **1.** Very close friends, as in *Those people she's thick with will get her in trouble.* **2.** Full of or dense with someone or something. For example, *The streets are thick with police—one on every corner,* or *The sky was thick with hawks circling above us.*

**thief** see IT TAKES ONE TO KNOW ONE (A THIEF TO CATCH A THIEF); THICK AS THIEVES.

**thin** In addition to the idioms beginning with THIN, also see INTO THIN AIR; ON THIN ICE; SPREAD ONESELF TOO THIN; THROUGH THICK AND THIN; WEAR THIN.

**thin as a rail** Very slender, as in *I do not know why she's dieting; she's thin as a rail already.*

**thing** In addition to the idioms beginning with THING, also see ALL THE RAGE (THING); ALL THINGS BEING EQUAL; ALL THINGS CONSIDERED; ALL THINGS TO ALL MEN; AMOUNT TO THE SAME THING; DO ONE'S THING; FIRST THING; FIRST THINGS FIRST; FOR ONE (THING); GET (A THING) GOING; GET INTO THE SWING OF THINGS; GREATEST THING SINCE SLICED BREAD; HAVE A GOOD THING GOING; HAVE A THING ABOUT; JUST ONE OF THOSE THINGS; KNOW ALL THE ANSWERS (A THING OR TWO); LITTLE KNOWLEDGE IS A DANGEROUS THING; NEAR THING; NO SUCH THING; NOT KNOW BEANS (THE FIRST THING); OF ALL THINGS; OTHER THINGS BEING EQUAL; SCHEME OF THINGS; SEEING THINGS; SURE THING; TAKE THE LAW (THINGS) INTO ONE'S HANDS; THE LATEST (THING); THE THING; THE THING IS; TOO MUCH OF A GOOD THING.

**thing or two** Quite a lot, as in *You can count on Bob to tell you a thing or two about Iran.* This term is nearly always an understatement. Also see under KNOW ALL THE ANSWERS.

**things are looking up** Matters are improving; see under LOOK UP.

**things go from bad to worse** A situation that is already hard or unpleasant becomes worse, as in *Once he decided to help us, things went from bad to worse,* or *If you do that, things will go from bad to worse.*

**things that go bump in the night** Strange or scary noises that children believe are made by monsters who are out to get them. For example, *Don't worry—I'll protect you from things that go bump in the night.*

**think** In addition to the idioms beginning with THINK, also see COME TO THINK OF IT; HAVE ANOTHER GUESS (THINK) COMING; HEAR ONESELF THINK; JUST THINK; NOT THINK MUCH OF; PUT ON ONE'S THINKING CAP; TO THINK THAT; WHO DOES ONE THINK ONE IS; WISHFUL THINKING. Also see under THOUGHT.

**think again** **1.** Reconsider a decision and think about changing it, as in *Think again about what you're planning.* **2.** Be wrong about whether something will happen. For example, *If you think she'll let the insult pass, think again.* Also see THAT'S WHAT ONE THINKS.

**think a lot of** Also, **think highly of** or **think well of** or **think the world of.** Have a good opinion of someone or something, regard very favorably, as in *I think a lot of my mother-in-law,* or *He didn't think highly of this company,* or *Dean thought the world of his youngest.* These expressions use *think* in the sense of "regard" or "value." For antonyms, see NOT THINK MUCH OF; THINK LITTLE OF.

**think aloud** Speak one's thoughts out loud, as in *We need flour, sugar, butter—I'm just thinking aloud.*

**think back** Remember or reflect on an earlier event, as in *When I think back on my days as a child, I really had a good time,* or *As he thought back to his father, long dead, tears came to his eyes.*

**think better of** **1.** Reconsider a decision, change one's mind about, as in *I hope you'll think better of it before you quit your job.* Also see THINK AGAIN, def. 1; THINK TWICE, def. 1. **2.** Have a higher opinion of someone or something. For example, *She'll think better of you if you admit you lied,* or *Jean thought better of the school when she found out how highly rated it was.*

**think big** Think about something in grander terms, as in *There's no point in moving to a place the same size; we have to think big and plan for expansion.*

**think fit** see SEE FIT.

**think highly of** see THINK A LOT OF.

**thinking cap** see PUT ON ONE'S THINKING CAP.

**think little of** Have a poor opinion of someone or something, as in *I think little of moving to Florida since none of us likes heat or humidity.* This term uses *think* in the sense of "regard" or "value." Also see NOT THINK MUCH OF.

**think nothing of** **1.** Give little consideration to doing something, regard as routine, as in *He thinks nothing of driving 100 miles to see a new movie.* **2. think nothing of it.** It's not important, as in *Thanks for the lift. Think nothing of it.* This usage is a way of saying YOU'RE WELCOME.

**think one's shit doesn't stink** Also, **think one's shit doesn't smell.** Think of oneself as superior to other people, as in *He'll never admit that he was wrong—he thinks his shit doesn't smell.* [Vulgar slang]

**think on one's feet** React quickly, be mentally quick, as in *The reporters asked difficult questions, but Bill was very good at thinking on his feet.* This expression uses *on one's feet* in the sense of "wide awake, alertly."

**think out** see THINK THROUGH.

**think over** Consider an idea or plan carefully, reflect about, especially in order to make a decision. For example, *I'll have to think it over carefully before I can say yes or no.*

**think positive** Be optimistic, concentrate on the good rather than the bad, as in *It's true you were fired, but think positive—now you can look for a job you really like.*

**think straight** Think in a clear and orderly way, as in *I'm tired right and now and can't think straight.* This idiom is often used in the negative, as in the example.

**think tank** A group or an organization dedicated to problem-solving and research, especially in such areas as technology, social or political planning, and the military. For example, *The congressional leaders rely too heavily on that conservative think tank.*

**think the world of** see THINK A LOT OF.

**think the world owes one a living** Believe that one is such a wonderful or valuable person that society will give one everything needed to survive, without having to work for it. For example, *Some people seem to think the world owes them a living, and they wind up bums.*

**think the world revolves around one** Consider oneself the center of the universe, believe that everything that happens is somehow related to one. For example, *Many children think the world revolves around them, but they learn as they grow older that the world doesn't know they exist.*

**think through** Also, **think out.** Arrive at a thorough understanding of; create or discover. For example, *That answer doesn't work; I don't believe you've thought the problem through,* or *He thought out a far more efficient method.* Also see THINK UP.

**think twice 1.** Reconsider something, weigh something carefully, as in *I have to think twice before spending that much on a car.* Also see THINK AGAIN, def. 1; THINK BETTER OF, def. 1. **2. not think twice.** Take no notice, not worry about, as in *She didn't think twice about flying off to Europe with only a day's notice.*

**think up** Create or come up with an idea, as in *She's an expert at thinking up interesting programs.*

**think well of** see THINK A LOT OF.

**thin on top** Becoming bald, as in *I notice that he's getting a little thin on top.* The *top* in this expression refers to the top of the head.

**thin skin** Extreme sensitivity to remarks or criticism made by other people, as in *You have such a thin skin, the slightest criticism makes you angry.* This idiom is also used as an adjective, as in *He's very thin-skinned and can't take criticism.* For an antonym, see THICK SKIN.

**third degree** Thorough, hostile questioning or rough treatment used to obtain information or a confession, as in *The detectives gave him the third degree,* or *Her father gave her the third degree when she came home so late.*

**third rail** Something that is dangerous to tamper with, as in *Anything concerning veterans is a political third rail.* This term refers to the rail that supplies the high voltage powering an electric train. On the other hand, **grab hold of the third rail** means "become full of energy."

**third world** Those countries that do not have an economy based on industrialization, as in *The conditions in our poorest cities resemble those in the third world.* This expression originally referred to those countries in Asia and Africa that were not aligned with either the Communist nations or the non-Communist Western nations. Because they were for the most part poor and lacked industrialization, the term was transferred to all countries with those characteristics, and later still to poorer groups within a larger culture.

**this** In addition to the idioms beginning with THIS, also see AT THIS POINT; AT THIS RATE; AT THIS STAGE; IN THIS DAY AND AGE; OUT OF THIS WORLD; SHUFFLE OFF (THIS MORTAL COIL).

**this and that** Also, **this, that, and the other.** Various unrelated items, one thing and another, as in *He said this and that about the budget, but nothing new or of great substance,* or *We spent all evening chatting about this, that, and the other.*

**this side of** Short of, before, as in *I think she's still this side of forty,* or *I doubt that they'll arrive this side of noon.*

**thither** see HITHER AND YON (THITHER).

**Thomas** see DOUBTING THOMAS.

**thorn in one's side, a** A constant source of irritation, as in *Paul's complaining and whining are a thorn in my side.*

**those** see JUST ONE OF THOSE THINGS; ONE OF THOSE DAYS.

**though** see AS IF (THOUGH).

**thought** see FOOD FOR THOUGHT; HAVE SECOND THOUGHTS; IT'S THE THOUGHT THAT COUNTS; LOST IN THOUGHT; PENNY FOR YOUR THOUGHTS; PERISH THE THOUGHT; SCHOOL OF THOUGHT; TRAIN OF THOUGHT. Also see under THINK.

**thousand** see BAT A THOUSAND; BY THE DOZEN (THOUSAND); ONE IN A MILLION (THOUSAND); PICTURE IS WORTH A THOUSAND WORDS.

**thrash about** Also, **thrash around.** Move wildly or violently, as in *He thrashed about all night, unable to sleep,* or *The fish thrashed around on the dock, so Meg threw it back in the water.*

**thrash *something* out** Discuss a topic fully, especially to solve a problem, as in *We'll just have to thrash out our ideas about where to go on vacation.*

**thread** see HANG BY A THREAD; LOSE THE THREAD.

**threat** see TRIPLE THREAT.

**three cheers for** Good for someone, hurrah for, congratulations to, as in *Three cheers for our mayor! Hip, hip, hooray!* The term is also used to indicate that one is not sincere when one is not really offering congratulations, as in *So you finally passed; well, three cheers for you.*

**three-ring circus, a** A situation of complete confusion, as in *It was a three-ring circus, with the baby crying, the dog barking, both telephones ringing, and someone at the front door.* This term originally referred to a circus where three rings or arenas are featuring performances at the same time. Perhaps coined by show business producer P.T. Barnum, the term was later extended to other confused situations.

**three R's** The fundamentals of education, as in *It's a terrible school; the children are not even taught the three R's.*

**three's a crowd** Also, **two's company, three's a crowd.** A third person spoils the ideal combination of a couple, as in *No, I won't join you—three's a crowd.* This expression refers to a third person spoiling the privacy of a pair of lovers. For a synonym, see FIFTH WHEEL.

**three sheets to the wind** Also, **three sheets in the wind.** Drunk, intoxicated, as in *After six beers he's three sheets to the wind.*

**three square meals** The amount of food required to keep a person in good health, as in *That child looks as though she's never had three square meals.*

**thrills and spills** Also, **thrills and spills of.** Both the excitement of success and the sadness of failure experienced in something, especially a competitive sport. For example, *She's not one to seek thrills and spills,* or *He enjoys the thrills and spills of skiing.*

**thrill *someone* to pieces** Also, **thrill *someone* to death.** Give someone great pleasure, delight, as in *I was just thrilled to pieces with our new grandson,* or *He was thrilled to death when he first saw the Himalayas.* Both of these exaggerated expressions use *thrill* in the sense of "affect with sudden emotion," and are often used in the passive voice, as in the examples. Also see TICKLED PINK.

**throat** see AT EACH OTHER'S THROATS; CUT SOMEONE'S THROAT; FROG IN ONE'S THROAT; JUMP DOWN SOMEONE'S THROAT; LUMP IN ONE'S THROAT; RAM SOMETHING DOWN SOMEONE'S THROAT; STICK IN ONE'S CRAW (THROAT).

**throe** see IN THE THROES OF.

**throne** see POWER BEHIND THE THRONE.

**through** In addition to the idioms beginning with THROUGH, see BREAK THROUGH; CARRY THROUGH; COME THROUGH; COME UP (THROUGH); CROSS (PASS THROUGH) ONE'S MIND; FALL BETWEEN (THROUGH) THE CRACKS; FALL THROUGH; FOLLOW THROUGH; GET THROUGH; GET SOMETHING THROUGH ONE'S HEAD; GO THROUGH; GO THROUGH CHANNELS; GO THROUGH THE MOTIONS; GO THROUGH THE ROOF; JUMP THROUGH HOOPS; LEAF THROUGH; LET SLIP (THROUGH THE FINGERS); LIE THROUGH ONE'S TEETH; LIVE THROUGH; MUDDLE THROUGH; PAY THROUGH THE NOSE; PULL THROUGH; PUT THROUGH; PUT SOMEONE THROUGH HIS OR HER PACES; RISE THROUGH THE RANKS; RUN THROUGH; SAIL THROUGH; SEE THROUGH; SEE THROUGH ROSE-COLORED GLASSES; SINK THROUGH THE FLOOR; SIT OUT (THROUGH); SLEEP THROUGH; SQUEAK BY (THROUGH); SQUEEZE THROUGH; TALK THROUGH ONE'S HAT; THINK THROUGH; WORK ONE'S WAY INTO (THROUGH).

**through and through** In every part or aspect, completely. For example, *I was wet through and through,* or *He was a success through and through.* This idiom originally was used literally to indicate penetration, as by a sword.

**through one's hat** see TALK THROUGH ONE'S HAT.

**through one's head** see GET SOMETHING THROUGH ONE'S HEAD.

**through one's mind** see CROSS ONE'S MIND.

**through rose-colored glasses** see SEE THROUGH ROSE-COLORED GLASSES.

**through the mill** Enduring hardship or rough treatment, as in *They put him through the mill, making him work at every one of the machines,* or *Jane was exhausted; she felt she'd been through the mill.* This term refers to being ground down like grain in a mill.

**through the motions** see GO THROUGH THE MOTIONS.

**through thick and thin** Despite all obstacles or adversities, as in *She promised to stand by him through thick and thin.* This term refers to moving through a forest that has both thick and sparse undergrowth. Today it is nearly always used with the idea of supporting something or someone in all circumstances, as in the example.

**throw** In addition to the idioms beginning with THROW, also see CAST (THROW) ONE'S LOT WITH; CAST (THROW) THE FIRST STONE; HAVE (THROW) A FIT; (THROW) IN SOMEONE'S FACE; KNOCK (THROW) ONE FOR A LOOP; POUR (THROW) COLD WATER ON; SHED (THROW) LIGHT ON; STONE'S THROW.

**throw *someone* a curve** Surprise or outsmart someone, as in *They threw me a curve when they said that our department would be combined with yours.* This term comes from baseball, where a pitcher tries to fool the batter by using a *curve ball,* which is thrown with sufficient spin to make it change abruptly from its expected path. The term was later transferred to other kinds of surprise, not necessarily unpleasant ones.

**throw a fit** see HAVE A FIT.

**throw a monkey wrench into** Undermine or frustrate a project or plans, as in *The boss threw a monkey wrench into our plans for a picnic when he said we'd have to work Saturday.* This expression transfers industrial sabotage—that is, throwing a tool inside machinery—to other activities.

**throw a party** Put on or hold a social gathering, as in *They're throwing a party to introduce their nephew to the neighbors,* or *She threw a party last Saturday night.*

**throw a punch** Deliver a blow with the first, as in *He was furious enough to throw a punch at the other driver.* This term originated in boxing but has been extended to less formal fighting as well.

**throw a tantrum** Also, **throw a temper tantrum.** Become very angry and show it in a physical way, such as by thrashing one's arms, crying or scream very loudly, or flinging oneself to the ground. For example, *That child will throw a tantrum if he doesn't get his way,* or *I'm tired of you throwing temper tantrums.* This idiom also appears as a noun, as in *Does he always have such temper tantrums?*

**throw away 1.** Also, **throw out** or **toss out.** Dispose of something, discard, as in *This coat is too good to throw away,* or *Did you throw out the rest of the milk?* or *She tossed out all his old letters.* **2.** Waste something, fail to use, as in *She's thrown away her inheritance on all kinds of foolish enterprises,* or *He's thrown away his chances for an engineering job.* **3.** Also, **throw out.** Utter or perform something in a casual or seemingly careless way, as in *He threw away the news that their summer cottage had been broken into,* or *She threw out some suggestions.* The first and third senses of this expression can also be used as adjectives, as in *Throwaway diapers are very expensive,* or *We can ignore his throwaway comments.*

**throw back 1.** Stop the progress of someone or something, as in *His illness threw his schooling back a year,* or *The troops were thrown back by heavy gunfire.* **2.** Return to an earlier type or stage, as in *That dog throws back to his wolf ancestors.* This usage led to the noun **throwback,** a return to a former stage or type. **3. throw back on.** Cause to depend on someone or something, make reliant on, as in *When the violinist didn't show up, they were thrown back on the pianist.*

**throw caution to the winds** Also, **throw discretion to the winds.** Behave or speak without thinking about the possible results, as in *Throwing caution to the winds, he ran after the truck,* or *I'm afraid she's thrown discretion to the winds and told everyone about the divorce.*

T

**throw cold water on** see POUR COLD WATER ON.

**throw down the gauntlet** Declare or issue a challenge, as in *The senator threw down the gauntlet on the abortion issue.* This expression refers to the medieval practice of a knight throwing down his gauntlet, or metal glove, as a challenge to combat. A related but less frequently heard term is **take up the gauntlet,** meaning "accept a challenge."

**throw dust in someone's eyes** Mislead someone, as in *The governor's press aide threw dust in their eyes, talking about a flight at the airport when he was heading for the highway.* This expression refers to throwing dust or sand in the air to confuse a pursuing enemy.

**throw *one* for a loop** see KNOCK ONE FOR A LOOP.

**throw good money after bad** Spend even more money in hopes of making up for previous losses, as in *Hiring him to improve that software is throwing good money after bad; it's based on an older operating system and will soon be useless.*

**throw in 1.** Insert or introduce something into a conversation, interject, as in *He always threw in a few jokes to lighten the atmosphere.* **2.** Add something with no additional charge, as in *The car salesman said he'd throw in the air conditioning.* **3. throw in with.** Enter into association with, as in *His friends warned him against throwing in with that street gang.* Also see CAST ONE'S LOT and the following idioms beginning with THROW IN.

**throw in one's hand** Give something up, abandon, as in *I'm through trying to fix this; I'm throwing in my hand.* This expression comes from card games such as poker, where it is used when one leaves the game.

**throw in one's lot with** see CAST ONE'S LOT.

**throw *something* in someone's face** Confront or upbraid someone with something, as in *Dean keeps throwing her poor driving record in her face.*

**throw in the towel** Also, **throw in the sponge.** Give up, acknowledge defeat, as in *Bill decided to throw in the towel and resign from his job,* or *I can't move this rock; I'm throwing in the sponge.* This idiom comes from boxing, where formerly a fighter would acknowledge defeat by throwing the towel or sponge used to wipe his face into the ring.

**throw it up to** see THROW UP, def. 4.

**throw light on** see SHED LIGHT ON.

**throw off 1.** Cast something out, rid oneself of, as in *He threw off all unpleasant memories and went to the reunion.* **2.** Give something off, emit, as in *The garbage was throwing off an awful smell.* Also see THROW OUT, def. 1. **3.** Also, **put *someone* off the scent.** Distract someone, mislead, as in *A mistaken estimate threw off her calculations,* or *These clues were designed to throw the detective off the scent.* The variant comes from hunting, where the quarry may try to put pursuing hounds off the scent. Also see OFF THE TRACK. **4.** Perform an action in a quick, impulsive, or casual manner, as in *He threw off one sketch after another.*

**throw *one* off balance** see OFF BALANCE.

**throw *one* off the track** see OFF THE TRACK.

**throw one** Cause someone to be confused or puzzled, surprise someone, as in *We didn't let our worries throw us,* or *That unfavorable review really threw her.* Also see KNOCK ONE FOR A LOOP.

**throw oneself at** Go after someone one finds attractive in an eager, aggressive way, as in *As long as she throws herself at him, he'll ignore her.*

**throw oneself at someone's feet** Ask someone's forgiveness, mercy, or help in a humble way. For example, *All you can do now is throw yourself at his feet and beg for mercy.*

**throw oneself into** Begin or engage in a project or an activity with enthusiasm, as in *Nora threw herself into making the invitations.* This idiom uses *throw* in the sense of "toss impulsively."

**throw oneself on someone's mercy** Beg someone to be merciful, especially if one has done something wrong or made a bad mistake, as in *She didn't mean to run a red light, but she'll have to throw herself on the court's mercy.*

**throw one's hat in the ring** Also, **toss one's hat in the ring.** Announce one's willingness to enter a political campaign or a contest, as in *The governor was slow to throw his hat in the ring in the senatorial race.* This term comes from boxing, where throwing a hat in the ring formerly indicated a challenge; today the idiom nearly always refers to political candidacy.

**throw one's money around** Spend one's money in a wasteful, extravagant way. For example, *He thinks he can impress people by throwing his money around.*

**throw one's weight around** Act as though one has great power or authority, especially in an arrogant way. For example, *One doesn't make oneself popular by throwing one's weight around.*

**throw open** Make something more accessible, especially suddenly or dramatically, as in *His withdrawal threw open the nomination to all comers.*

**throw out** **1.** Give off something, emit, as in *That flashlight throws out a powerful beam.* Also see THROW OFF, def. 2. **2.** Reject something, as in *We threw out her proposal.* **3.** Get rid of something, discard; see THROW AWAY, def. 1. **4.** Offer a suggestion or plan, as in *The nominating committee threw out names for our consideration.* Also see THROW AWAY, def. 3. **5.** Forcibly eject someone, force the departure of, as in *The bartender threw out the drunk,* or *He was thrown out of the country club for failing to pay his dues.* **6.** Put something out of alignment, as in *I threw out my back when I lifted that sofa.* **7.** In baseball or cricket, put a player out by throwing the ball. In baseball, the throw is to a base before the batter reaches it; in cricket, the throw must hit the batsman's wicket.

**throw out the baby with the bath water** Discard something valuable along with something not wanted. For example, *I know you don't approve of that one item in the bill, but we shouldn't throw out the baby with the bath water by voting the bill down.*

**throw *someone* over** Reject someone, abandon, as in *They'd lived together for a year when she suddenly threw him over and moved out.* This idiom may refer to throwing something or someone overboard.

**throw the book at** Punish or scold harshly, as in *I just knew the professor would throw the book at me for being late with my paper.* This expression originally meant "sentence a convicted person to the maximum penalties allowed," the *book* being the record of relevant laws.

**throw together** **1.** Assemble something hurriedly, as in *I just threw together some salad and took it along.* **2.** Cause someone to associate, as in *Their parents were always throwing the young couple together, hoping they would like each other.*

**throw *someone* to the wolves** Also, **throw *someone* to the dogs** or **throw *someone* to the lions.** Send someone to a terrible fate; sacrifice someone, especially to save oneself. For example, *Leaving him with hostile reporters was throwing him to the wolves,* or *If Bob doesn't perform as they expect, they'll throw him to the lions.* All three exaggerated terms refer to the greedy appetite of these animals, which will probably devour the victim. The first term comes from Aesop's fable about a nurse who threatens to throw her charge to the wolves if the child does not behave.

**throw up** **1.** Vomit, as in *The new drug makes many patients throw up.* **2.** Abandon something, give up, as in *After the results of the poll came in, she threw up her campaign for the Senate.* **3.** Construct something hurriedly, as in *The builder threw up three houses in just a few months.* **4. throw *something* up to.** Criticize someone, remind of a past mistake, as in *Dad was always throwing it up to the boys that they were careless and messy.*

**throw up one's hands** Show or express complete hopelessness. For example, *Jim was getting nowhere, so he threw up his hands and abandoned the argument.* This idiom refers to a traditional gesture for giving up.

**throw *something* up to** see THROW UP, def. 4.

**thumb** In addition to the idioms beginning with THUMB, also see ALL THUMBS; RULE OF

THUMB; STICK OUT (LIKE A SORE THUMB); TWIDDLE ONE'S THUMBS; UNDER SOMEONE'S THUMB.

**thumb a ride** see HITCH A RIDE.

**thumbnail sketch, a** A brief outline or description, as in *Let me give you a thumbnail sketch of the situation.* This idiom refers to drawing a picture no larger than the size of a thumbnail.

**thumb one's nose at** Express scorn or ridicule. For example, *I'm sure the members of the school committee will thumb their noses at any suggestions we make.* This expression refers to a traditional gesture of contempt, that is, placing the thumb under the nose and wiggling the fingers.

**thumbs up** An expression of approval or hopefulness, as in *The town said thumbs up on building the assisted-care living facilities.* The antonym **thumbs down** indicates disapproval or rejection, as in *Mother gave us thumbs down on serving beer at our party.* These idioms refer to crowd signals used in Romans arenas to indicate whether someone was to live or die. In ancient times the meaning of the gestures was opposite that of today. Thumbs down indicated approval; thumbs up, rejection.

**thunder** see under STEAL SOMEONE'S THUNDER.

**thus far** see under SO FAR.

**tick** In addition to the idiom beginning with TICK, also see CLOCK IS TICKING; WHAT MAKES ONE TICK.

**ticket** see JUST THE TICKET; MEAL TICKET; SPLIT TICKET; STRAIGHT TICKET; WRITE ONE'S OWN TICKET.

**tickled pink** Also, **tickled to death.** Delighted, very happy, as in *I was tickled pink when I got his autograph,* or *His parents were tickled to death when he asked to marry her.* The first term refers to one's face turning pink with laughter when one is being tickled.

**tickle one's fancy** Appeal to one, be to one's liking, as in *That joke tickled my fancy.* This term uses *fancy* in the sense of "liking" or "taste."

**tickle the ivories** Play the piano, as in *He went on tickling the ivories until three in the morning.* This expression refers to a piano's white keys, traditionally made of ivory.

**tick *one* off** Infuriate one, make angry. For example, *That article ticked me off.* For a vulgar synonym, see PISS OFF, def. 1.

**tide** In addition to the idiom beginning with TIDE, also see STEM THE TIDE; SWIM AGAINST THE CURRENT (TIDE); SWIM WITH THE TIDE; TIME AND TIDE WAIT FOR NO MAN; TURN OF THE TIDE.

**tide *someone* over** Support someone through a difficult period, as in *I asked my brother for $100 to tide me over until payday.* This expression refers to the way the tide carries something.

**tie** In addition to the idioms beginning with TIE, also see FIT TO BE TIED; PUT (TIE) ON THE FEED BAG; WITH ONE ARM TIED BEHIND ONE'S BACK.

**tie *one* down** Constrain one, confine or limit, as in *As long as the children were small, she was too tied down to look for a job.*

**tied to someone's apron strings** Completely dependent on or controlled by a woman, especially one's mother. For example, *At 25, he was still too tied to her apron strings to get an apartment of his own.*

**tie in** Also, **tie in to** or **tie in with.** Relate something closely with something else, coordinate, as in *His story does not tie in with the facts,* or *They are trying to tie in the movie promotion with the book it is based on.*

**tie *one* into knots** Confuse someone or oneself, upset or bewilder, as in *He tied himself into knots when he tried to explain how the engine works,* or *Don't let the rumors about the merger tie you into knots.* This idiom transfers a knotted tangle to mental confusion.

**tie one on** Become intoxicated; go on a drinking spree. For example, *They went out and really tied one on.* The precise reference here—what it is one ties on—is unclear.

**tie one's hands** Prevent one from acting, as in *I can't help you this time; my hands are tied by the club's rules.* This term transfers being tied up physically to other kinds of restraint.

**tie the knot** Get married; also, perform a marriage ceremony. For example, *So when are you two going to tie the knot?* or *They asked their friend, who is a judge, to tie the knot.*

**tie up 1.** Fasten something securely; also, moor a ship. For example, *Can you help me tie up these bundles?* or *The forecast was terrible, so we decided to tie up at the dock and wait out the storm.* **2.** Stop the progress of something, block, as in *The accident tied up traffic for hours.* **3.** Keep someone occupied, engage, as in *She was tied up in a meeting all morning.* **4.** Make funds or property hard to convert to other uses, as in *Her cash is tied up in government bonds.*

**tiger by the tail** Something too difficult to manage or deal with, as in *You know nothing about the commodities market; you'll end up catching a tiger by the tail.* This colorful expression creates the image of grabbing a powerful but fierce animal by the tail, only to have it turn on one.

**tight** In addition to the idioms beginning with TIGHT, also see IN A BIND (TIGHT CORNER); SIT TIGHT.

**tight as a drum** Tightly stretched or close-fitting; also, watertight. For example, *That* *baby's eaten so much that the skin on his belly is tight as a drum,* or *You needn't worry about leaks; this tent is tight as a drum.* Originally this expression referred to the skin of a drumhead, which is tightly stretched. Later, however, it sometimes referred to a drum-shaped container, such as an oil drum, which had to be well sealed to prevent leaks, and the expression then meant "watertight."

**tighten one's belt** Spend less money, be more careful about spending money, as in *Business has been bad, so we'll have to tighten our belts.* This term refers to pulling in one's belt after losing weight from not having enough to eat.

**tighten the screws on** see under TURN UP THE HEAT ON.

**tight rein on, keep a** Maintain strict control over, as in *We told them to keep a tight rein on spending for the next year.* This expression refers to the narrow strap (rein) attached to a bit and used to control a horse's movements.

**tightrope** see WALK A TIGHTROPE.

**tight ship** A well-managed organization, as in *The camp director runs a tight ship.* This term refers to a ship in which the ropes are taut and by extension the ship is strictly managed. It often is put as **run a tight ship,** as in *Our new boss told us that she intends to run a tight ship.*

**tight spot** see under IN A BIND.

**tight squeeze, a** A difficulty caused by too little time or space, or too little credit or funds. For example, *It will be a tight squeeze to get there on time,* or *I don't know if the sofa will go through the door; it's a tight squeeze,* or *The company's in a tight squeeze because of poor cash flow.* This idiom uses *tight* in the sense of "too narrow or constricted."

**till** In addition to the idioms beginning with TILL, also see HAND IN THE TILL; UNTIL.

**till all hours** see ALL HOURS.

**till hell freezes over** Forever, as in *They said they'd go on searching till hell freezes over, but I'm sure they'll give up soon.* An antonym to this exaggerated expression is **not till hell freezes over,** meaning "never," as in *I'm not giving in, not till hell freezes over.*

**till now** Also, **up till now** or **up to now** or **up to this point** or **up until now.** Until the present time, previously, as in *We were good friends till now,* or *Up till now, she was sure she'd be promoted,* or *I was looking forward to camping up to now,* or *You had the right idea up to this point,* or *He was willing to loan us money up until now.* In the variants of this idiom, *up* is used for emphasis.

**till the cows come home** Also, **when the cows come home.** For a long time, as in *You can keep asking till the cows come home, but you still may not go bungee-jumping.* This term refers to when the cows return to the barn for milking.

**tilt** see FULL TILT.

**tilt at windmills** Engage in conflict with an imaginary opponent; also, pursue a vain goal. For example, *Trying to reform campaign financing in this legislature is tilting at windmills.* This expression refers to the hero of Miguel de Cervantes' *Don Quixote,* who rides with his lance at full tilt (poised to strike) against a row of windmills, which he mistakes for evil giants.

**time** In addition to the idioms beginning with TIME, also see ABOUT TIME; AGAINST THE CLOCK (TIME); AHEAD OF ONE'S TIME; AHEAD OF TIME; ALL THE TIME; ANY TIME; AT ALL TIMES; AT ONE TIME; AT ONE TIME OR ANOTHER; AT THE SAME TIME; AT THE TIME; AT THIS POINT (IN TIME); AT TIMES; BEAT TIME; BEFORE ONE'S TIME; BEHIND IN (TIME); BEHIND THE TIMES; BIDE ONE'S TIME; BIG TIME; BUY TIME; CALL ONE'S (TIME ONE'S) OWN; CHOW DOWN (TIME); CRUNCH TIME; DO TIME; EVERY TIME ONE TURNS AROUND; FOR THE MOMENT (TIME BEING); FROM TIME TO TIME; GOOD-TIME CHARLIE; HARD TIME; HAVE A GOOD TIME; HIGH TIME; IN BETWEEN TIMES; IN DUE COURSE (OF TIME); IN GOOD TIME; IN NO TIME; IN THE FULLNESS OF TIME; IN THE NICK OF TIME; IN THE RIGHT PLACE AT THE RIGHT TIME; IN TIME; KEEP TIME; KEEP UP (WITH THE TIMES); KILL TIME; LESS THAN (NO TIME); LONG TIME NO SEE; LOSE TIME; MAKE GOOD TIME; MAKE TIME; MAKE UP FOR (LOST TIME); MANY IS THE (TIME); MARK TIME; NOT GIVE SOMEONE THE TIME OF DAY; NO TIME FOR; NO TIME LIKE THE PRESENT; OF ONE'S LIFE, TIME; ON BORROWED TIME; ONCE UPON A TIME; ONE BY ONE (AT A TIME); ON ONE'S OWN TIME; ON TIME; PASS THE TIME; PLAY FOR TIME; POINT IN TIME; PRESSED FOR TIME; SERVE TIME; SHOW SOMEONE A GOOD TIME; SIGN OF THE TIMES; SMALL TIME; STITCH IN TIME; TAKE ONE'S TIME; TELL TIME; TEST OF TIME; THERE'S A FIRST TIME FOR EVERYTHING; WHALE OF A TIME.

**time after time** Also, **time and again** or **time and time again.** Repeatedly, again and again, as in *Time after time he was warned about the river rising,* or *We've been told time and time again that property taxes will go up next year.*

**time and a half** A rate of pay for overtime work that is one and one-half times higher than the regular hourly wage, as in *I don't mind working Sunday so long as I get time and a half.* This expression uses *time* in the sense of "the number of hours worked."

**time and tide wait for no man** One must not hesitate to do something or delay, as in *Let's get on with the voting; time and tide won't wait, you know.* This proverb refers to the fact that human events or concerns cannot stop the passage of time or the movement of the tides.

**time bomb, a** A situation that threatens to have terrible results at some future time, as in *That departmental dispute is a time bomb just waiting to go off.* This term refers to an explosive device that is set to go off at a specific time. It transfers the literal meaning to an explosive person or situation that will eventually be disastrous.

**time flies** Time passes quickly, as in *It's midnight already? Time flies when you're having fun,* or *I guess it's ten years since I last saw you—how time flies.*

**time hangs heavy** Also, **time hangs heavy on one's hands.** Time passes slowly, as in *While she waited for the doctor to call, time hung heavy on her hands.* This idiom compares the passage of time to a burdensome weight.

**time immemorial** Also, **time out of mind.** Long ago, beyond memory or recall, as in *These ruins have stood here since time immemorial,* or *His office has been on Madison Avenue for time out of mind.*

**time is money** One's time is a valuable resource, as in *I can't stay home and wait any longer; time is money, you know.* This proverb goes back to an earlier one, **time is precious,** in a discourse on very high interest rates for money that one lends.

**time is on one's side** Eventually one will get what one wants, as in *He figures he'll end up the boss sooner or later, because time is on his side.*

**time is ripe, the** This is the right moment for something, as in *The time is ripe for a revival of that play.*

**time is up** The period of time allowed for something is ended, as in *Turn in your papers, students; time is up.* This idiom uses *up* in the sense of "completed."

**time of day** The hour shown on a clock; also, a stage in any activity or period. For example, *What time of day is the repairman coming?* or *This is hardly the time of day to ask for another installment when he's just turned one in.* Also see NOT GIVE SOMEONE THE TIME OF DAY.

T

**time off** A break from one's work or school, as in *I need some time off from teaching to work on my book,* or *He took time off to make some phone calls.*

**time of one's life** An extremely pleasurable experience; see under OF ONE'S LIFE.

**time on one's hands** A period of time with nothing to do; see under ON ONE'S HANDS; TIME HANGS HEAVY.

**time out** **1.** A short break from work or play, as in *People rush around so much these days that I think everyone should take some time out now and then.* **2.** A punishment for misbehavior in young children by briefly separating them from the group, as in *We don't throw food, Brian; you need some time out to think about it.* This expression comes from **time-out,** used in a number of sports to mean an interruption in play where the officials stop the clock, for purposes of rest, making a substitution, or consultation. The phrase is also used as a command when the speaker wants to interrupt a conversation that could develop into an argument, as in *Time out! Yelling at each other won't make the situation any better.*

**time out of mind** see TIME IMMEMORIAL.

**time warp** A stoppage in the passage of time; also, a change of time whereby an event or person could supposedly move from one time period to another. For example, *Nothing in their lives has changed since the sixties; they're in a time warp,* or *Having a seventy-year-old actress portray a teenager—that was some time warp!* This term originated in science fiction, where it means "a supernatural movement from one era to another." It later began to be used more loosely.

**time was** Formerly, in the past, as in *Time was, the city streets were perfectly safe at night.*

**time will tell** Sooner or later something will become known or be revealed, as in *I don't know whether or not they'll like the gift; only time will tell.*

**tin god** A self-important, domineering, small-minded person who imposes his or her ideas, beliefs, and standards on other people. For example, *The officials in these small towns often act like tin gods.* The *tin* in this expression refers to the fact that tin is a base metal with relatively little value.

**tinker** In addition to the idiom beginning with TINKER, also see NOT WORTH A DAMN (TINKER'S DAMN).

**tinker with** Also, **tinker around.** Try to repair something; work aimlessly on something, such as a hobby, as in *He tinkered with the engine all day, but it still wouldn't start,* or *My father likes to tinker around.* This idiom refers to working as a tinker, that is, mending metal utensils.

**tip** In addition to the idioms beginning with TIP, also see FROM HEAD (TIP) TO TOE; ON THE TIP OF ONE'S TONGUE.

**tip off** Supply someone with secret or private information; also, warn or alert. For example, *The broker often tipped her off on stocks that were about to go down in price,* or *Somehow they were tipped off and left the country before the police could catch them.*

**tip of the iceberg, the** Only a little evidence of a much larger problem, as in *Laying* *off a hundred workers is only the tip of the iceberg.* This idiom refers to the structure of an iceberg, which has most of its bulk underwater.

**tip one's hand** Accidentally reveal one's real intentions, as in *He avoided any comments on birthdays for fear of tipping his hand about the surprise party.* This idiom probably refers to holding one's hand in such a way that others can see the cards one is holding.

**tip over** Knock something over or fall over, as in *The baby tipped over her juice again,* or *Don't move! The canoe will tip over.*

**tip the balance** Also, **tip the scales.** Make the balance uneven in a situation, thereby favoring one side or initiating an action. For example, *He felt that affirmative action had tipped the balance slightly in favor of minority groups,* or *New high-tech weapons definitely tipped the scales in the Gulf War.*

**tiptoe** see ON TIPTOE.

**tire** see SPARE TIRE.

**tired** In addition to the idiom beginning with TIRED, also see DEAD ON ONE'S FEET (TIRED); SICK AND TIRED.

**tired out** Also, **tired to death.** Exhausted, as in *She looked tired out after that trip,* or *He came home tired to death.* Also see SICK AND TIRED; TO DEATH.

**tit for tat** Repayment in kind, revenge, as in *If he won't help with the beach clean-up, I won't run a booth at the bake sale; that's tit for tat.* This term is believed to be a corruption of *tip for tap,* which meant "a blow for a blow."

**tizzy** see IN A DITHER (TIZZY).

**to a certain degree** Also, **to a degree** or **to an extent.** See TO SOME DEGREE.

**to advantage** see SHOW TO ADVANTAGE.

**to a fare-thee-well** To the most extreme degree, especially a condition of perfection. For example, *We've cleaned the house to a fare-thee-well,* or *He played the part of Scrooge to a fare-thee-well.* This term first appeared as **to a fare-you-well** and was later replaced by the more archaic-sounding present form.

**to a fault** Excessively, extremely, as in *He was generous to a fault.* This phrase always qualifies an adjective.

**to all intents and purposes** Also, **for all intents and purposes** or **for all practical purposes.** In every practical sense. For example, *For all intents and purposes the case is closed,* or *For all practical purposes the Vice President is the chief executive while the President is in the hospital.* The first phrase originated in English law, where it was put as *to all intents, constructions, and purposes.* A shorter synonym is IN EFFECT, def. 1.

**to a man** Also, **to a woman.** Unanimously, without exception, as in *The committee voted against the proposal to a man.* This expression uses *man* in the sense of "everyone." It continues to be so used despite its sexist tone. Its counterpart, **to a woman,** is rarely used. Also see AS ONE; WITH ONE VOICE.

**to and fro** Back and forth, as in *He was like a caged animal, pacing to and fro.* Strictly speaking, *to* means "toward" and *fro* "away from," but this idiom is used more vaguely in the sense of "moving alternately in different directions."

**toast** see WARM AS TOAST.

**to a T** Also, **to a turn.** Perfectly, exactly right, as in *The description fitted him to a T,* or *The roast was done to a turn.* The first expression may refer to a T-square, used for accurate drawing, but some think it refers to crossing one's T's. The variant refers to meat being turned on a spit until it is cooked to the proper degree.

**to beat the band** Also, **to beat all.** To the greatest possible degree. For example, *The baby was crying to beat the band,* or *The wind is blowing to beat the band,* or *John is dressed up to beat all.* This idiom uses *beat* in the sense of "do better than." The first term may, according to one theory, refer to a desire to arrive before the musicians who led a parade, in order to see the entire event. Another theory holds that it means "make more noise than (and thereby beat) a loud band."

**to begin with** see TO START WITH.

**to be sure** Without question, certainly, of course, as in *The coat is expensive, to be sure, but it's bound to last longer than a cheap one.*

**to blame, be** Be responsible for or guilty of something wrong or bad, as in *Obviously the teacher was to blame for the chaos in the classroom,* or *Mary was not to blame for these errors.*

**to boot** Besides, in addition. For example, *It rained every day, and it was cold to boot,* or *He said they'd lower the price of the car by $1,000 and throw in air conditioning to boot.* This expression has nothing to do with footwear. *Boot* here is an old noun meaning "advantage," and in the idiom has been broadened to include anything additional, good or bad.

**to burn** see MONEY TO BURN.

**to date** Up to now, until the present time, as in *To date we've received no word from them.*

**today** see HERE TODAY, GONE TOMORROW.

**to death** To an extreme or intolerable degree, as in *I am tired to death of these fundraising phone calls,* or *That movie just thrilled me to death.* This exaggerated phrase is used as an intensifier. Also see SICK AND TIRED; TIRED OUT.

**toe** In addition to the idiom beginning with TOE, also see DIP ONE'S TOES INTO; FROM HEAD TO TOE; ON ONE'S TOES; STEP ON SOMEONE'S TOES.

**to each one's own** One has a right to one's personal preferences, as in *I'd never pick that color, but to each his own,* or *I would never tolerate what she does, but to each her own.* Also see NO ACCOUNTING FOR TASTES.

**toe the line** Also, **toe the mark.** Meet a standard, follow the rules, as in *The new director will make us toe the line, I'm sure,* or *At daycare Tom has to toe the mark, but at home his mother's quite easygoing.* This idiom refers to runners in a race placing their toes on the starting line and not moving until the starting signal.

**together** In addition to the idiom beginning with TOGETHER, also see GET ONE'S ACT TOGETHER; GET TOGETHER; GO TOGETHER; HANG TOGETHER; KEEP BODY AND SOUL TOGETHER; KNOCK SOMETHING TOGETHER; LIVE TOGETHER; PIECE SOMETHING TOGETHER; PULL ONESELF TOGETHER; PULL SOMETHING TOGETHER; PUT OUR HEADS TOGETHER; PUT SOMETHING TOGETHER; PUT TWO AND TWO TOGETHER; SCARE SOMETHING UP (SCRAPE TOGETHER); STICK SOMETHING TOGETHER; STRING SOMETHING TOGETHER; THROW TOGETHER.

**together with** In the company of someone; also, in addition to. For example, *He arrived at the theater together with his girlfriend,* or *The lawyer found the will, together with other papers, in the murdered man's files.* For a synonym, see ALONG WITH.

**to good purpose** To effective use, as in *A donation to the homeless shelter will be put to good purpose.* Also see TO LITTLE PURPOSE.

**to hand 1.** Also, **at hand.** Nearby, readily available, as in *I don't have the right tools to hand, but I asked her to get them for me.* **2.** Also, **in hand.** In one's possession, as in *He had their letter to hand,* or *She had the money in hand.* Also see HAND TO HAND.

**to heel 1.** Close behind someone, as in *The dog started chasing the car, but Miriam called him to heel.* This expression is used almost solely in reference to dogs. The *heel* in this idiom is a person's heel. **2.** Under control or discipline, as in *By a series of surprise raids the police brought the gang members to heel.* This expression refers to controlling a dog by training it to follow at one's heels.

**to hell and gone** Also, **to hell and back.** Far away, forever, as in *I don't know where it is—to hell and gone,* or *I can keep talking to hell and back, but it won't do any good.*

**to hell with** Also, **the hell with.** I'm disgusted with someone or something; also, get rid of, as in *To hell with that plan; it's ridiculous,* or *The hell with that so-called genius; he's made a serious mistake in this report.*

**token** see BY THE SAME TOKEN; IN TOKEN OF.

**told** see ALL TOLD; I TOLD YOU SO; LITTLE BIRD TOLD ME. Also see under TELL.

**to little purpose** Also, **to no purpose.** Of little or no use, in vain, as in *Hiring a new lawyer will be to little purpose.* The related phrases are sometimes combined in **to little or no purpose** and used as a general indicator of uselessness. For a synonym, see TO NO AVAIL. Also see TO GOOD PURPOSE.

**toll** see TAKE ITS TOLL.

**Tom** see EVERY TOM, DICK, AND HARRY; PEEPING TOM.

**tomorrow** In addition to the idiom beginning with TOMORROW, also see HERE TODAY, GONE TOMORROW; LIKE THERE'S NO TOMORROW; PUT SOMETHING OFF (UNTIL TOMORROW).

**tomorrow is another day** One may not accomplish everything today but will have another chance. For example, *We've stuffed hundreds of envelopes and still aren't done, but tomorrow is another day.* This comforting saying was first put as *Tomorrow is a new day,* was widely repeated, and was later changed to its present form.

**to my mind** As I see it, in my opinion, as in *To my mind, we have enough money to start building now.*

**ton** see LIKE A TON OF BRICKS.

**tone** In addition to the idiom beginning with TONE, also see SET THE TONE FOR.

**tone down** Make something less colorful, harsh, or violent; moderate. For example, *That's a little too much eye shadow; I'd tone it down a bit,* or *Do you think I should tone down this letter of complaint?* This idiom uses *tone* in the sense of "adjust the tone or quality of something," as does the antonym, **tone up,** meaning "brighten or strengthen." For example, *These curtains will tone up the whole room,* or *This exercise is said to tone up the arm muscles.* This phrase is also use to mean "get into good condition," as in *I sit around all day, so I decided to tone up.*

**tong** see HAMMER AND TONGS.

**tongue** In addition to the idioms beginning with TONGUE, also see BITE ONE'S TONGUE; CAT GOT SOMEONE'S TONGUE; HOLD ONE'S TONGUE; KEEP A CIVIL TONGUE; LOOSEN ONE'S TONGUE; ON THE TIP OF ONE'S TONGUE; SLIP OF THE TONGUE; WATCH ONE'S TONGUE.

**tongue hangs out, one's** One is eagerly awaiting something, as in *Their tongues were hanging out at the thought of seeing the movie stars in person.* This expression refers to an animal's tongue hanging out of its mouth in anticipation of food.

**tongue in cheek, with** Ironically or as a joke, as in *Was he speaking with tongue in* *cheek when he said Sally should run for president?* This term may refer to the facial expression produced by poking one's tongue in one's cheek, perhaps to hold back a smile. It can also be used as an adjective, as in *Ignore his tongue-in-cheek comments.*

**tongues wag** People are gossiping. For example, *Tongues wagged when another police car was parked in front of their house,* or *Their arrival in a stretch limousine set the neighbors' tongues wagging.* This expression transfers the rapid movement of the tongue to idle or indiscreet chatter.

**to no avail** Also, **of little or no avail.** Of no use or advantage, ineffective, as in *All his shouting was to no avail; no one could hear him,* or *The life jacket was of little or no avail.* This idiom uses *avail* in the sense of "advantage" or "assistance." Also see TO LITTLE PURPOSE.

**to no purpose** see TO LITTLE PURPOSE.

**too** In addition to the idioms beginning with TOO, also see CARRY SOMETHING TOO FAR; (TOO) CLOSE TO HOME; EAT ONE'S CAKE AND HAVE IT, TOO; GO TOO FAR; IN (TOO) DEEP; IRONS IN THE FIRE, TOO MANY; LIFE IS TOO SHORT; NONE TOO; NOT (TOO) BAD; ONLY TOO; SPEAK TOO SOON; SPREAD ONESELF TOO THIN.

**too bad** That's unfortunate, as in *Too bad the shoes don't fit you,* or *It's too bad he can't come.*

**too big for one's britches** Also, **too big for one's boots.** Conceited, self-important, as in *Ever since he won that tournament, he's gotten too big for his britches,* or *There's no talking to Jill anymore—she's just too big for her boots.* This idiom refers to becoming so "swollen" with conceit that one's pants or boots no longer fit.

**too close for comfort** Also, **too close to home.** Dangerously nearby or accurate, as in *That car came too close for comfort,* or *Their attacks on the speaker hit too close to home, and he left angrily.*

**too close to call** Resulting in too narrow a margin to make a decision, as in *That ball didn't miss by much, but it was too close to call,* or *The election was too close to call, so they decided to have a runoff.* This expression comes from sports, where *call* means "a judgment." Later it began to be applied to preelection polls and then to the outcome of elections.

**too good to be true** So excellent that one cannot believe it, as in *She loves all her in-laws? That's too good to be true.* This term expresses the skeptical view that something so seemingly fine must have something wrong with it.

**too hot to handle** So controversial that anyone who tries to deal with it is likely to fail, as in *I warned her that that issue is too hot to handle.*

**too little, too late** Not enough as a remedy and not in time to be useful, as in *The effort to divert the stream into a corn field was too little too late—the houses were already flooded.* This term originated in the military, where it was applied to reinforcements that were insufficient and arrived too late to be of help.

**tools of the trade** Equipment or something else necessary to engage in a particular activity or occupation. For example, *Knowing how and when to lie are tools of the trade for a politician.*

**tool up 1.** Provide the equipment for a particular task, as in *Now that we're all tooled up, let's repair the boat.* This term originated in industry, where it is used for supplying a factory with machinery or other equipment for production. **2.** Arm oneself, as in *They tooled up for their encounter with the rival gang.*

**too many cooks spoil the broth** Also, **too many cooks spoil the soup.** Too many people involved in managing an activity can ruin it, as in *Without a conductor, every player had an idea for how the music should be played—too many cooks spoil the broth.* This expression refers to each of many cooks adding something to a soup, which finally tastes awful.

**too much of a good thing** Too large an amount of a beneficial or useful thing or activity can be harmful or useless. For example, *The indoor decorations are fine, but the outdoor Santa, sled, reindeer, lights—it's just too much of a good thing.*

**to oneself** see KEEP TO ONESELF.

**to one's face** Openly, directly, as in *I do not have the nerve to tell him to his face that he wasn't invited and shouldn't have come.* This idiom refers to a direct confrontation. Also see IN SOMEONE'S FACE.

**to one's feet** see GET TO ONE'S FEET.

**to one's heart's content** As much of an activity as one likes, without limitation, as in *I've been eating strawberries to my heart's content,* or *The youngsters played in the sand to their hearts' content.*

**to one's name** Owned by one, as in *He has not got a nickel to his name,* or *She has only one pair of shoes to her name.*

**to order** see MADE TO ORDER.

**tooth** In addition to the idiom beginning with TOOTH, also see FIGHT TOOTH AND NAIL; FINE-TOOTH COMB; LONG IN THE TOOTH; SWEET TOOTH. Also see under TEETH.

**tooth fairy** An imaginary giver of money, as in *So who will finance this venture—the tooth fairy?* This expression refers to the fairy who supposedly leaves money under a child's pillow in place of a baby tooth that has fallen out, a practice popular with U.S. parents.

**toot one's own horn** see BLOW ONE'S OWN HORN.

**top** In addition to the idioms beginning with TOP, also see AT THE TOP OF ONE'S LUNGS; BIG TOP; BLOW ONE'S TOP; BRASS HAT (TOP BRASS); FROM HEAD TO TOE (TOP TO BOTTOM); OFF THE TOP OF ONE'S HEAD; ON TOP; ON TOP OF; ON TOP OF THE WORLD; OVER THE TOP; THIN ON TOP.

**top banana** Also, **top dog.** The most powerful person in a group, an organization, or an undertaking, as in *His plan was to be top banana within ten years,* or *Now that she's top dog, you can't talk to her at all.* The first term comes from show business, where it refers to the leading comedian. It also led to **second banana,** for a supporting actor, usually a straight man. Both were later transferred to more general use. The variant, **top dog,** originated in sports and means the odds-on favorite or winner in a contest; it refers to the dog who wins (comes out on top) in a dogfight.

**top brass** see under BRASS HAT.

**top dog** see TOP BANANA.

**top dollar** The highest price, as in *They'll have to pay top dollar at that resort.*

**top drawer** Of the highest quality, importance, or rank, as in *The musicians in this orchestra are top drawer.* This expression probably refers to the uppermost drawer in a bureau or chest, where the most valuable objects (such as jewelry) are usually kept.

**to pieces** Into fragments, disorganized, or confused, as in *I tore his argument to pieces.* Also see GO TO PIECES; PICK SOMETHING APART (TO PIECES); THRILL SOMEONE TO PIECES.

**top it all off** Be the very final thing or the most extreme event, either good or bad. For example, *And, to top it all off, the dog ate my shoes,* or *The last song she sang really topped it all off for me.* The context in which this expression is used indicates whether it should be interpreted as positive or negative.

**top off** **1.** Fill a container, especially when it is almost full to begin with. For example, *I don't need much gas; just top off the tank, please.* **2.** Finish something, especially in a spectacular way, as in *They topped off their trip with a visit to the White House.* Also see TOP IT ALL OFF.

**top of the ladder** Also, **top of the heap.** At the highest point in a group, an organization, or a career, as in *She's reached the top of the ladder in her field.* For an antonym, see BOTTOM OF THE LADDER.

**top out** **1.** Complete the top portion of a building, as in *They were scheduled to top out the dome next week.* **2.** Fill up a ship or complete its cargo, as in *The ship was topped out with scrap iron.* **3.** Stop rising, as in *Interest rates topped out at 10 percent.* **4.** Retire just as one becomes very successful, as in *He decided that at 60 it was time to top out.*

**top secret** Too important or useful to someone else to reveal publicly, as in *We must keep our plans top secret.* Originally used as the highest government classification for military information, this phrase is now used in an exaggerated way to refer to any secret. It is also used as an adjective, as in *My briefcase contains top-secret plans.*

**top to bottom** see FROM HEAD TO TOE.

**torch** see CARRY A TORCH; PASS THE TORCH.

**to rights** see DEAD TO RIGHTS; SET TO RIGHTS.

**torn between, be** Have difficulty choosing between two conflicting choices, be in a dilemma, as in *I'm torn between going to the mountains or going to the seashore; each appeals to me.*

**to save one's life** Even if one's life depended on it, as in *I couldn't eat another bite to save my life,* or *Betty wouldn't climb a mountain to save her life.* This exaggerated expression nearly always follows a negative statement that one wouldn't or couldn't do something.

**to say nothing of** see under NOT TO MENTION.

**to say the least** Not to exaggerate, as in *When the diamond ring turned up in the lost and found, she was delighted, to say the least.*

**to some degree** Also, **to a certain degree; to some extent** or **to a certain extent; to a degree** or **to an extent.** Somewhat, in a way, as in *We'll have to compromise to some degree,* or *To an extent, it's a matter of adjusting to the colder climate.*

**to spare** In addition to what is needed, extra, leftover, as in *We paid our bills and still had money to spare.* This expression uses *spare* in the sense of "leftover" or "unused."

**to speak of** Worth mentioning; see NOTHING TO SPEAK OF; NOT TO MENTION.

**toss** In addition to the idioms beginning with TOSS, also see THROW AWAY (TOSS OUT); THROW (TOSS) ONE'S HAT IN THE RING.

**toss off** **1.** Do something easily or quickly, as in *Some writers are amazing, tossing off book after book.* **2.** Also, **toss down.** Consume something quickly, especially a drink. For example, *He tossed off the beer and headed for the door,* or *She tossed down one glass of wine after another.*

**toss one's cookies** Vomit, as in *A roller coaster ride may make her toss her cookies.*

**toss one's hat in the ring** see THROW ONE'S HAT IN THE RING.

**toss out** see THROW AWAY, def. 1.

**to start with** Also, **to begin with.** In the first place, initially, as in *We'll notify him by e-mail to start with,* or *To begin with, they haven't paid their taxes in years.* Also see FOR OPENERS.

**totem** see LOW MAN ON THE TOTEM POLE.

**to that effect** With that basic or general meaning, as in *He said he was very worried, or words to that effect.* This term is also put as **to the effect that** when introducing a clause, as in *She was a little vague but said something to the effect that she'd repay the loan very soon.*

**to the best of** To the greatest extent of, especially of one's ability, knowledge, or power. For example, *I'm sure he'll do it to the best of his ability,* or *To the best of my knowledge, they arrive tomorrow.*

**to the bitter end** see BITTER END.

**to the bone** see CHILLED TO THE BONE; CUT TO THE BONE; WORK ONE'S FINGERS TO THE BONE.

**to the contrary** To the opposite effect, in denial, as in *No matter what they say to the contrary, I am positive that he was present.* Also see ON THE CONTRARY.

**to the core** see ROTTEN TO THE CORE.

**to the effect that** see TO THAT EFFECT.

**to the ends of the earth** see ENDS OF THE EARTH.

**to the fore** Also, **to the forefront.** In, into, or toward a position of importance or greater visibility, as in *A new virtuoso pianist has come to the fore.*

**to the full** Also, **to the fullest.** To the greatest extent, completely, as in *He had always lived life to the full.*

**to the good** Also, **all to the good.** To an advantage or a profit, as in *We've got extra material, and that's all to the good, I think.*

**to the hilt** Also, **up to the hilt.** Completely, to the greatest degree, as in *The house was mortgaged up to the hilt.* This idiom refers to the handle (*hilt*) of a sword, the only portion that remains out when the weapon is plunged all the way in.

**to the last** To the end, especially to the end of one's life. For example, *The defenders held out to the last, but the bombs finished them.*

**to the letter** Precisely, as in *If you follow the directions to the letter, you can't go wrong.* The noun *letter* here refers to the exact terms of some statement.

**to the manner born** Accustomed from birth to a particular behavior or lifestyle, as in *At a high-society function she behaves as though to the manner born, but we know she came from a poor family.* The *manner* in this expression was later sometimes changed to *manor,* meaning "the main house of an estate," and the idiom's sense became equated with "highborn" (and therefore accustomed to luxury), a way in which the term is often used today.

**to the nines** To perfection, to the highest degree; see under DRESSED TO KILL.

**to the nth degree** To the greatest possible, as in *They'd decked out the house to the nth degree.* This expression comes from mathematics, where *to the nth* means "to any required power" (*n* standing for any number).

**to the point** **1.** Relevant, concerning the matter at hand, as in *Her remarks were brief and to the point,* or *He rambled on and on, never speaking to the point.* This usage is often put as **come to the point** or **get to the point,** meaning "address the important issue." For example, *Please come to the point; we haven't much time,* or *Do you suppose he'll ever get to the point of all this?* Also see BESIDE THE POINT. **2.** Concerning the important or essential issue, as in *More to the point, she hasn't any money.*

**to the teeth** **1.** Completely, fully, as in *Obviously new to skiing, they were equipped to the teeth with the latest gear.* Also see ARMED TO THE TEETH; FED UP (TO THE TEETH). **2.** Also, **up to the teeth** or **up to one's teeth.** Fully committed, as in *We're in this up to our teeth.* Both of these exaggerated idioms refer to being fully covered or immersed in something up to one's teeth. Also see UP TO ONE'S EARS.

**to the tune of** To the sum or extent of, as in *They had profits to the tune of about $20 million.* This idiom transfers *tune,* a sequence of musical tones, to a succession of figures.

**to the victor belong the spoils** The winner gets everything, as in *He not only won the tournament but also ended up with numerous profitable endorsements—to the victor belong the spoils.* This expression refers to the spoils system of U.S. politics, whereby the winner of an election gives desirable jobs to party supporters.

**to the wall** see BACK TO THE WALL; GO TO THE WALL.

**to think that** **1.** See JUST THINK. **2.** Be unable to believe that someone has behaved so badly or that something has turned out so badly. For example, *To think that I trusted her, and she's been lying to me the whole time,* or *It's pouring rain—to think that we might have gone on our picnic.*

**touch** In addition to the idioms beginning with TOUCH, also see COMMON TOUCH; FINISHING TOUCH; HIT (TOUCH) BOTTOM; IN TOUCH; LOSE ONE'S TOUCH; LOSE TOUCH; NOT TOUCH WITH A TEN-FOOT POLE; OUT OF TOUCH; PUT THE ARM (TOUCH) ON; SOFT TOUCH.

**touch and go** Extremely uncertain or risky, as in *It was touch and go after the surgery; we were not sure he would survive,* or *It was touch and go, but they finally gave me a seat on the plane.* This idiom implies that a simple touch may cause a disaster.

**touch base with** Make contact or renew communications with someone, as in *I'll try to touch base with you when I'm in Ohio,* or *The candidate touched base with every ethnic* *group in the city.* This idiom comes from baseball, where a runner must touch each base without being tagged before a run can be scored.

**touch bottom** Reach the lowest point, as in *During the recession the economists kept saying that we hadn't touched bottom yet.* This expression refers to reaching the ground under a body of water.

**touch down** Land on the ground, as in *The spacecraft touched down on schedule.*

**touched by, be** Also, **be touched with.** Be affected by some emotion, especially a tender feeling like gratitude, pity, or sympathy. For example, *She was very touched by his concern for her welfare.* This idiom refers to touching or reaching one's heart, regarded as the seat of emotions.

**touched in the head** Also, **touched.** A little bit crazy, somewhat irrational, as in *I think the war left him a little touched in the head.*

**touch off** Cause something to explode or fire; also, start something, trigger. For example, *The boys touched off a whole line of firecrackers,* or *These disclosures will touch off a public uproar.*

**touch on** Also, **touch upon. 1.** Mention something briefly or casually in passing, as in *He barely touched on the subject of immigration.* **2.** Approach something closely, be close to, as in *This madness touched on clinical insanity.*

**touch up** Make minor changes or improvements, as in *This wall needs some touching up but not complete repainting.*

**tough** In addition to the idioms beginning with TOUGH, also see GET TOUGH WITH; HANG TOUGH; HARD (TOUGH) ACT TO FOLLOW; HARD (TOUGH) NUT TO CRACK.

**tough break** Also, **tough luck.** A troublesome situation, bad luck, as in *He got a tough break when he was denied a raise,* or *Tough luck for the team last night.* This idiom uses *tough* in the sense of "difficult." The variant is also used as a sarcastic comment, as in *So you didn't make straight A's—tough luck!* Vulgar versions of this expression are **tough shit** and **tough titty.**

**tough customer** A person who is very stubborn or self-confident and hard to deal with or satisfy. For example, *She can be a tough customer when it comes to her children.*

**tough it out** Also, **gut it out.** Show courage and perseverance in the face of opposition or difficult. For example, *I know it's hard, but we'll just have to tough it out,* or *His leg hurts, but Joe is determined to gut it out.*

**tough nut** see HARD NUT TO CRACK.

**tough row to hoe, a** Also, **a hard row to hoe.** A difficult course, hard work to accomplish, as in *He knew he'd have a tough row to hoe by running against this popular candidate.*

**tough sledding** Difficult work or progress, as in *This bill faces tough sledding in the legislature.* This idiom transfers the route on which a sled can travel to other kinds of progress toward a goal. For an antonym, see EASY SLEDDING.

**tow** see IN TOW.

**to wake the dead, loud enough** Very loud, as in *That band is loud enough to wake the dead.*

**toward** see GO A LONG WAY TOWARD.

**towel** see CRYING TOWEL; THROW IN THE TOWEL.

**tower** In addition to the idiom beginning with TOWER, also see IVORY TOWER

**tower of strength** Also, **pillar of strength.** A dependable person on whom one can lean in time of trouble, as in *After Dad died, Grandma was a tower of strength for the whole family,* or *I always thought my father was a pillar of strength.*

**to whom it may concern** To the appropriate recipient for this message, as in *I didn't know who was responsible for these complaints, so I just addressed it* "*to whom it may concern.*" This phrase is used in letters and speeches when one does not know the name of the proper person to address.

**to wit** That is to say, namely, as in *There are three good reasons for not going, to wit, we don't want to, we don't have to, and we can't get a reservation.* This expression comes from the old verb *wit,* meaning "know or be aware of," which is no longer in use except in this phrase.

**town** see ALL OVER THE PLACE (TOWN); GHOST TOWN; GO TO TOWN; MAN ABOUT TOWN; ONE-HORSE TOWN; ONLY GAME IN TOWN; ON THE TOWN; OUT OF TOWN; PAINT THE TOWN RED; TALK OF THE TOWN.

**toy with 1.** Amuse oneself idly with something, trifle with, as in *I'm toying with the idea of writing a novel.* **2.** Treat someone casually or without seriousness, as in *He teased her, toying with her as a cat toys with a mouse.*

**track** In addition to the idioms beginning with TRACK, also see COVER ONE'S TRACKS; DROP IN ONE'S TRACKS; FOLLOW IN SOMEONE'S FOOTSTEPS (TRACKS); INSIDE TRACK; JUMP THE TRACK; KEEP (LOSE) TRACK; MAKE TRACKS; OFF THE BEATEN TRACK; OFF THE TRACK; ONE-TRACK MIND; ON THE FAST TRACK; ON THE RIGHT TACK (TRACK); RIGHT SIDE OF THE TRACKS; STOP COLD (IN ONE'S TRACKS); WRONG SIDE OF THE TRACKS.

**track down** Follow someone successfully, locate something, as in *I've been trying to track down that book but haven't had any luck.* This term refers to the literal use of *track,* "follow the footsteps of."

**track record** A record of actual performance or achievements, as in *This company has an excellent track record.*

**trade** In addition to the idioms beginning with TRADE, also see STOCK IN TRADE; TRICKS OF THE TRADE.

**trade down** see.

**trade in** Give or sell an old or used item and apply the value or amount received to a new item. For example, *Some people prefer to trade in their old car to the dealer, but we feel we'll do better by simply selling it.*

**trade off** Exchange one thing for another, especially as a compromise or for convenience. For example, *They were willing to trade off some vacation for the freedom to work flexible hours,* or *Can you trade off baby-sitting with me next week?* The first example of this idiom led to the noun **trade-off** for "an exchange."

**trade on** Profit by something, exploit, as in *The children of celebrities often trade on their family names.*

**trade secret** Something that a person is unwilling to share, such as knowledge of how something is done or accomplished. For example, *How she does so much work in so little time is a trade secret,* or *Mom's recipe for meat loaf remains a trade secret.*

**trade up** Make an exchange for something of higher value or price, as in *We traded up to a luxury car.* Similarly, **trade down** means "exchange for something of lower value or price," as in *They've moved into a smaller house, trading down in order to save money.*

**trail** see BLAZE A TRAIL.

**train of thought** A series of connected ideas, a path of reasoning, as in *You've interrupted my train of thought; now what was I saying?* This idiom uses *train* in the sense of "an orderly sequence."

**trap** see FALL INTO A TRAP; MIND LIKE A STEEL TRAP.

**travel light** Take little baggage; also, be relatively free of responsibilities or deep thoughts, as in *I can be ready in half an hour; I always travel light,* or *I don't want to buy a house and get tied down; I like to travel light.*

**tread** In addition to the idiom beginning with TREAD, also see FOOLS RUSH IN WHERE ANGELS FEAR TO TREAD; STEP (TREAD) ON ONE'S TOES.

**tread water** Maintain one's status but not make much progress toward a goal, as in *He was just treading water from paycheck to paycheck.* This idiom refers to the term's literal meaning, that is, "keep one's head above water by remaining upright and pumping the legs."

**treat** In addition to the idiom beginning with TREAT, also see DUTCH TREAT; TRICK OR TREAT.

**treat *someone* like dirt** Behave badly or show contempt toward someone, as in *Her boss treats all the secretaries like dirt.* This idiom uses *dirt* in the sense of "something worthless."

**treatment** see RED CARPET (TREATMENT).

**tree** see BARK UP THE WRONG TREE; CAN'T SEE THE FOREST FOR THE TREES; UP A TREE.

**trial** In addition to the idioms beginning with TRIAL, also see ON TRIAL.

**trial and error** An attempt to accomplish something by trying different means until one that works is found. For example, *The only way to solve this problem is by trial and error.* The *error* here refers to failed means or attempts, which are discarded until a right way is found.

**trial balloon** An idea or plan advanced tentatively to test public reaction, as in *Let's send up a trial balloon for this new program before we commit ourselves.* This expression refers to sending up balloons to test weather conditions.

**trial by fire** A test of one's abilities to perform well under pressure, as in *Finishing this huge list of chores in time for the wedding is really a trial by fire.* This expression refers to the medieval practice of determining a person's guilt by having them undergo an ordeal, such as walking barefoot through a fire.

**trial run** A first attempt to do something in order to find out whether it works properly. For example, *Let's go through a trial run of the whole play.*

**trials and tribulations** Tests of one's ability to endure something, as in *She went through the trials and tribulations of being admitted to law school only to find she couldn't afford to go.* This redundant expression—*trial* and *tribulation* here both mean the same thing—is also used semi-humorously, as in *Do you really want to hear about the trials and tribulations of my day at the office?*

**trick** In addition to the idioms beginning with TRICK, also see BAG OF TRICKS; CON GAME (CONFIDENCE TRICK); DIRTY TRICKS; DO THE TRICK; HAT TRICK; HOW'S TRICKS; NOT MISS A TRICK; TEACH AN OLD DOG NEW TRICKS; THAT DOES IT (THE TRICK); TURN A TRICK; UP TO ONE'S OLD TRICKS.

**trick or treat** A greeting used by children asking for treats on Halloween and threatening to play a trick on those who refuse to give them. For example, *The children went from house to house, shouting "Trick or treat!"*

**tricks of the trade** Clever ways of operating a business or performing a task or an activity, especially slightly dishonest or unfair ones. For example, *Marge knows all the tricks of the trade, cutting the fabric as close as possible,* or *The butcher weighs meat after it's wrapped; charging for the wrapping is one of the tricks of the trade.*

**tried and true** Tested and proved to be worthy or reliable, as in *Let me deal with it—my method is tried and true.*

**trigger** In addition to the idiom beginning with TRIGGER, also see QUICK ON THE DRAW (TRIGGER).

**trigger happy** Inclined to act violently at the slightest excuse, as in *They feared that the President was trigger happy and would send in troops too quickly.* This expression refers to being too eager to fire a gun.

**trim one's sails** Change one's position, adapt to circumstances, as in *His advisers told him to trim his sails before he alienated voters and bungled the election completely.* This expression refers to adjusting a ship's sails to take full advantage of prevailing winds.

**trip** In addition to the idiom beginning with TRIP, also see BAD TRIP; EGO TRIP; ROUND TRIP.

**triple threat** A person who is adept in three areas, as in *She's a triple threat on the editorial staff—she can edit, write, and design pages.* This term comes from football, where it refers to a player who is good at running, passing, and kicking.

**trip up** Make or cause someone to make a mistake, as in *The other finalist tripped up when he was asked to spell "trireme,"* or *They tripped him up with that difficult question.*

**trolley** see OFF ONE'S HEAD (TROLLEY).

**trooper** see SWEAR LIKE A TROOPER.

**trot** In addition to the idiom beginning with TROT, also see HOT TO TROT.

**trot out** Bring out and show something in a proud way, as in *He trotted out all his old war medals.* This expression refers to leading out a horse to show off its various paces, including the trot.

**trouble** In addition to the idioms beginning with TROUBLE, also see BORROW TROUBLE; FISH IN TROUBLED WATERS; GO TO THE TROUBLE; HALF THE TROUBLE; IN TROUBLE WITH; POUR OIL ON TROUBLED WATERS.

**troubled waters** A situation that is very confused or disturbed; see FISH IN TROUBLED WATERS; POUR OIL ON TROUBLED WATERS.

**trouble one's head with** Also, **trouble oneself about.** Bother or worry about something, as in *Don't trouble your head with these details; I'll take care of it,* or *It seems to me that teachers should trouble themselves more about teaching and less about manners.*

**trouble someone for** Politely ask someone for something, as in *May I trouble you for a drink of water?* This idiom uses *trouble* in the sense of "disturb."

**trowel** see under LAY IT ON THICK.

**truck** see HAVE NO TRUCK WITH.

**true** In addition to the idioms beginning with TRUE, also see COME TRUE; DREAM COME TRUE; HOLD GOOD (TRUE); RING FALSE (TRUE); RUN (TRUE) TO FORM; TOO GOOD TO BE TRUE; TRIED AND TRUE.

**true blue** Loyal, faithful, as in *You can count on her support; she's true blue.* This expression refers to the idea of blue being the color of loyalty, but the exact reference is unclear.

**true colors** see SHOW ONE'S TRUE COLORS.

**true to** **1.** Loyal or faithful to something or someone, as in *She knew he'd be true to his marriage vows.* **2.** Also, **true to type.** Conforming to or consistent with something, as in *The speech was true to the party platform,* or *True to type, he died while working at his desk.* **3. true to life.** Consistent with reality, realistically represented, as in *This painting is very true to life.* For **true to form,** see under RUN TO FORM.

**trump** In addition to the idioms beginning with TRUMP, also see HOLD ALL THE ACES (TRUMPS); TURN UP TRUMPS.

**trump card** A key resource to gain an advantage at the best time, as in *That surprise witness was the defense's trump card,* or *She played her trump card, announcing that the senator would speak.* This expression transfers the trump card of card games such as bridge, which can win over a card of another suit, to other kinds of advantage.

**trump up** Make up something that is untrue, as in *They trumped up a charge of conspiracy,* or *She had trumped up another excuse for not doing the work.* This expression uses *trump* in the sense of "devise falsely," a usage that is otherwise obsolete.

**trust** see BRAIN TRUST; IN TRUST.

**truth** In addition to the idioms beginning with TRUTH, also see GOSPEL TRUTH; MOMENT OF TRUTH; UNVARNISHED TRUTH.

**truth is stranger than fiction** Real life can be more surprising than made-up stories, as in *In our two-month trip around the world we ran into long-lost relatives on three separate occasions, proving that truth is stranger than fiction.*

**truth will out** The facts will be known, as in *She thought she could get away with it, but truth will out, and I'm sure she'll get caught.* Also see MURDER WILL OUT.

**try** In addition to the idioms beginning with TRY, also see OLD COLLEGE TRY.

**try on** Test the fit or look of a garment by putting it on, as in *Do you want to try on this dress?* This expression is also put as **try *something* on for size,** which is sometimes used figuratively, as in *The teacher wanted to try the new method on for size before agreeing to use it.*

**try one's hand** **1.** Attempt to do something for the first time, as in *I thought I'd try my hand at snorkeling.* This idiom uses *try* in the sense of "learn by experiment or effort." **2.** Also, **try one's luck.** Take a chance doing something, as in *We thought we'd try our luck at getting a hotel room at the last minute.*

**try one's patience** Put one's tolerance to a severe test, cause one to be annoyed, as in *Putting these parts together really tries my patience,* or *Her constant lateness tries our patience.* This idiom uses *try* in the sense of "test."

**try one's wings** see SPREAD ONE'S WINGS.

**try out** **1.** Undergo a qualifying test, as for an athletic team. For example, *I'm trying out for the basketball team.* **2.** Test or use something as an experiment, as in *They're trying out new cars,* or *We're trying out this new margarine.*

**tube** see BOOB TUBE; DOWN THE TUBES.

**tuck** In addition to the idioms beginning with TUCK, also see NIP AND TUCK.

**tuck away** **1.** Eat food heartily, as in *He tucked away an enormous steak.* **2.** Hide something, put in storage, as in *She had several hundred dollars tucked away.*

**tuckered out** Exhausted, very tired, as in *I was all tuckered out after that game.*

**tuck in** Put in the edge or end of something, such as bed linens or a shirt; also, make a child secure in bed by folding in the bedclothes. For example, *Tuck in your shirt; it looks awful hanging out of your pants,* or *Mother went upstairs to tuck in the children.*

**tug of war** A struggle for power, as in *There's a constant tug of war between those who favor giving more power to the states and those who want a strong federal government.*

**tumble** see ROUGH AND TUMBLE.

**tune** In addition to the idioms beginning with TUNE, also see CALL THE TUNE; CARRY A TUNE; CHANGE ONE'S TUNE; DANCE TO ANOTHER TUNE; IN TUNE; TO THE TUNE OF.

**tune in** **1.** Adjust a receiver to receive a particular program or signals at a particular frequency, as in *Tune in tomorrow, folks, for more up-to-date news.* **2.** Be aware or responsive, as in *She's really tuned in to teenagers.* For an antonym, see TUNE OUT.

**tune out** **1.** Adjust a receiver so as not to receive a signal, as in *Let's tune out all this interference.* **2.** Dissociate oneself from one's surroundings; also, disregard, ignore. For example, *The average reader, used to seeing lots of color images, tunes out when confronted with big blocks of text,* or *Some mothers are expert at tuning out the children's whining and quarreling.* For an antonym, see TUNE IN.

**tune up** Adjust machinery so it is in proper condition, as in *I took the car in to be tuned up.*

**tunnel** In addition to the idiom beginning with TUNNEL, also see LIGHT AT THE END OF THE TUNNEL.

**tunnel vision, have** Consider only one aspect of a problem or situation, be unable to look at something as a whole, as in *When it comes to sports, he has tunnel vision and only enjoys golf,* or *No politician can afford tunnel vision about the budget.*

**turkey** see COLD TURKEY; TALK TURKEY.

**turn** In addition to the idioms beginning with TURN, also see AT EVERY TURN; BY TURNS; EVERY TIME ONE TURNS AROUND; GOOD TURN; HEAR THE WHEELS TURNING; IN TURN; NOT KNOW WHERE TO TURN; ONE GOOD TURN DESERVES ANOTHER; OUT OF TURN; TAKE A TURN FOR THE BETTER; TAKE TURNS; TO A T (TURN); TWIST (TURN) SOMEONE AROUND ONE'S FINGER; TWIST (TURN) THE KNIFE; WHATEVER TURNS ONE ON; WHEN SOMEONE'S BACK IS TURNED.

**turn a blind eye** Overlook something on purpose, ignore, as in *She decided to turn a blind eye to her roommate's late hours,* or *You have to deal with the situation—you can't just turn a blind eye.* Also see TURN A DEAF EAR.

**turnabout is fair play** Taking alternate turns at doing something is just and equitable. For example, *Come on, I want to sit in the front seat now—turnabout is fair play.*

**turn a deaf ear** Refuse to listen to someone, as in *You can plead all day, but he's turning a deaf ear to everyone.* Also see FALL ON DEAF EARS.

**turn against** Cause someone to rebel or become hostile, as in *Adolescents often turn against their parents, but usually only temporarily,* or *She turned him against his colleagues by telling him they were spying on him.*

**turn around** Reverse the direction or improve the course of something or someone, as in *He has a way of turning around a failing business,* or *If someone doesn't turn him around, he's headed for trouble.*

**turn *one* around one's finger** see TWIST SOMEONE AROUND ONE'S FINGER.

**turn a trick** Engage in sex for pay, as in *A young prostitute may turn a dozen tricks in a few hours.* This idiom uses *trick* in the sense of "a sexual act." [Vulgar slang]

**turn away** **1.** Send someone away, dismiss, as in *They ran short and had to turn away many customers.* **2.** Repel someone, as in *The high prices turned away prospective buyers.* **3.** Divert something, deflect, as in *She managed to turn away all criticism.*

**turn back** **1.** Reverse one's direction, as in *We had to turn back earlier than expected.* **2.** Drive someone back or away, as in *They turned back anyone who didn't have an invitation,* or *Our forces soon turned back the enemy.* **3.** Fold something down, as in *Turn back the page you're on to keep your place in the magazine.* Also see TURN ONE'S BACK ON.

**turn down** **1.** Fold something down, as in *They always turn down your bed here,* or *Turn down your collar.* **2.** Invert something, as in *She turned down her cards,* or *They turn down the glasses in the cupboard.* **3.** Reject something, fail to accept someone, as in *They turned down his proposal,* or *Joe was turned* *down at four schools before he was finally accepted.* **4.** Decrease the volume, brightness, or speed of something. For example, *Please turn down the radio; it's too loud,* or *They turned down the lights and began to dance.*

**turn for the better** Also, **turn for the worse.** See under TAKE A TURN FOR THE BETTER.

**turn in 1.** Hand something in, give over, as in *I turned in my exam and left the room.* **2.** Surrender or inform on someone, especially to the police, as in *The shoplifter turned herself in.* **3.** Produce something, as in *He turned in a consistent performance every day.* **4.** Go to bed, as in *I turned in early last night.*

**turn in one's grave** Also **turn over in one's grave.** Be very upset. This idiom is used only of a dead person, who in all likelihood would have been upset by the developments in question, as in *If she knew you'd sold her jewelry, she'd turn over in her grave.*

**turn *something* inside out** Also, **turn *something* upside down.** Search a place for something thoroughly, often making a big mess in the process, as in *I've turned the drawers inside out but still can't find my keys,* or *We'll have to turn the house upside down for those concert tickets.*

**turn loose** see LET LOOSE.

**turn of events** An unexpected change in a situation, as in *Our team wouldn't have won the game but for a sudden turn of events.*

**turn off 1.** Stop the operation, activity, or flow of something; shut off, as in *Turn off the lights when you leave.* **2.** Affect someone with dislike, revulsion, or boredom; cause to lose interest. For example, *That vulgar comedian turned us off completely,* or *The movie was all right for an hour or so, but then I was turned off.* This sense can also be used as a noun, as in *That horror movie was such a turnoff.*

**turn of mind** A particular interest or a special ability, as in *My sister has a mathematical turn of mind.*

**turn of phrase** A particular way of saying something, as in *I'd never heard that turn of phrase before,* or *An idiom can be described as a turn of phrase.* This idiom refers to the turning or shaping of objects (as on a lathe).

**turn of the century** The beginning or end of a particular century, as in *That idiom dates from the turn of the last century, that is to say, about 1900.*

**turn of the tide** A change of fortune, as in *This last poll marked the turn of the tide, with our candidate gaining a sizable majority.* Similarly, **turn the tide** means "reverse a situation," as in *The arrival of reinforcements turned the tide in the battle.* This idiom transfers the ebb and flow of the ocean's tides to human concerns.

**turn on 1.** Cause to begin the operation, flow, or activity of something, as in *Turn on the lights, please,* or *Don't turn on the oven yet.* **2.** Begin to display or employ something, as in *He turned on the charm.* **3.** Also, **get high** or **get high on.** Take or cause to take a mind-altering drug, as in *The boys were caught turning on,* or *They tried to get her high.* **4.** Be or cause someone to become excited or interested, as in *His mother was the first to turn him on to classical music.* **5.** Be or become sexually aroused, as in *He blushed when she asked him what turned him on.* **6.** Also, **turn upon.** Depend on something, relate to, as in *The entire plot turns on mistaken identity.* These phrases use *turn* in the sense of "revolve on an axis or a hinge." **7.** Also, **turn upon.** Attack someone, become hostile toward, as in *Although normally friendly, the dog suddenly turned on everyone who came to the door.* Also see TURN AGAINST.

**turn one's back on** Deny something, reject; also abandon someone. For example, *I can't turn my back on my own daughter, no matter what she's done,* or *He simply turned his back on them and never gave it a second thought.* Also see WHEN ONE'S BACK IS TURNED.

**turn one's hand to** Also, **put one's hand to.** Apply oneself to a task or project, begin working at, as in *Next she turned her hand to starting her dissertation,* or *He was so lazy he wouldn't put his hand to anything.*

**turn one's head 1.** Cause one to become attracted, as in *The new teacher turned all the girls' heads.* **2.** Cause to become conceited, as in *Winning that prize has turned his head.*

**turn one's stomach** Nauseate one, disgust one, as in *That mess of spoiled food turns my stomach.* This idiom refers to being so nauseated that one vomits—that is, the stomach in effect turns around and brings up food.

**turn on one's heel** Leave abruptly, as in *When I inquired about his sister, he turned on his heel and walked away.* This idiom refers to making a sharp about-face similar to a military step but here usually implies a sudden departure.

**turn on the waterworks** Start to cry, as in *Whenever Dad refuses a request of hers, she turns on the waterworks.* This term implies that one begins to cry deliberately, as though switching on a system of pipes connected to a source of water.

**turn out 1.** Shut off something, as in *He turned out the light.* **2.** Arrive or assemble for an event, as in *A large number of voters turned out for the rally.* **3.** Produce something, as in *They turn out three thousand cars a month.* **4.** Be found to be in the end; also, end up, result, as in *The rookie turned out to be a fine fielder,* or *The cake didn't turn out* *very well.* Also see TURN OUT ALL RIGHT. **5.** Dress or outfit someone, as in *The bride was turned out beautifully.* **6.** Get out of bed, as in *Come on, children; time to turn out.* **7.** Evict someone, expel, as in *The landlord turned out his tenant.* **8.** Put animals in a pasture to graze, as in *The sheep have been turned out already.*

**turn out all right** Also, **work out all right.** Succeed, go well, as in *The new cover turned out all right,* or *We're hoping their vacation will work out all right.* The first term uses *turn out* in the sense of "result"; the variant uses *work out* in the sense of "proceed so as to produce a certain outcome." Also see PAN OUT; WORK OUT.

**turn *someone* out to pasture** see PUT SOMEONE OUT TO PASTURE.

**turn over 1.** Invert something, bring the bottom to the top, as in *Turn over the cup, please.* **2.** Shift position, as by rolling from side to side. For example, *This bed is so narrow I can barely turn over.* **3.** Rotate, cycle, as in *The engine turned over, but the car wouldn't start.* **4.** Think about something, consider, as in *She turned over the idea in her mind.* **5.** Transfer something to another, surrender, as in *I turned over the money to the children.* **6.** Do business to the extent or amount of, as in *We hoped the company would turn over a million dollars the first year.* **7.** Seem to roll or move convulsively, as in *The plane hit an air pocket, and my stomach turned over.* **8.** Replace or renew the parts or people, as in *Half of our staff turns over every few years.* Also see TURN OVER A NEW LEAF.

**turn over a new leaf** Make a fresh start, change one's conduct or attitude for the better, as in *He promised the teacher he would turn over a new leaf and behave himself in class.* This expression refers to turning the page of a book to a new page.

**turn over in one's grave** see TURN IN ONE'S GRAVE.

**turn tail** Run away, as in *When they heard the sirens, the boys turned tail.* This term refers to an animal turning its back in flight.

**turn the clock back** see SET BACK, def. 3.

**turn the corner** Pass a critical point, begin to recover. For example, *Experts say the economy has turned the corner and is in the midst of a recovery,* or *The doctor believes he's turned the corner and is on the mend.* This expression refers to passing around the corner in a race, particularly the last corner.

**turn the knife** see TWIST THE KNIFE.

**turn the other cheek** Respond without hostility to insult or injury. For example, *There's no point in arguing with that unreasonable supervisor; just turn the other cheek.*

**turn the tables** Reverse a situation and gain the upper hand, as in *Susan won their previous three matches, but today Mary turned the tables.* This expression refers to the former practice of reversing the table or board in games such as chess, thereby switching the opponents' positions.

**turn the tide** see TURN OF THE TIDE.

**turn the trick** see DO THE TRICK.

**turn to 1.** Begin work, apply oneself to a task, as in *Next he turned to chopping the onions.* **2.** Refer to something, consult, as in *She turned to the help-wanted ads.* **3.** Appeal to someone, apply to for help, as in *At a time like this one turns to one's closest friends,* or *We'll have to turn to the French consulate for more information.* **4.** Change from one state or condition to another, as in *Winter turned to spring,* or *The lake has turned to ice.* Also see TURN SOMETHING TO GOOD ACCOUNT.

**turn *something* to good account** Use something for one's benefit, as in *He turned the delay to good account, using the time to finish his correspondence.*

**turn turtle** Turn upside down, as in *When they collided, the car turned turtle.* This expression refers to the helplessness of a turtle turned on its back, where its shell can no longer protect it.

**turn up 1.** Increase the volume, speed, intensity, or flow of something, as in *Turn up the air conditioning; it's too hot in here.* **2.** Find something or be found, as in *She turned up the missing papers,* or *Your keys turned up in my pocket.* **3.** Appear, arrive, as in *His name turns up in the newspaper now and then,* or *Some old friends turned up unexpectedly.* This usage led to **turn up like a bad penny,** meaning that something unwanted constantly reappears, as in *Ken turns up like a bad penny whenever there's free food. Bad* here refers to a counterfeit coin. **4.** Fold something or be capable of being folded, as in *I'll just turn up the hem,* or *He preferred cuffs that turn up.* **5.** Happen unexpectedly, as in *Something turned up, so I couldn't go to the play.* Also see the following idioms beginning with TURN UP.

**turn upon** see TURN ON, def. 6 and 7.

**turn up one's nose** Regard with dislike or scorn, as in *She turned up her nose at the broccoli.*

**turn *something* upside down** see TURN SOMETHING INSIDE OUT.

**turn up the heat on** Also, **put the heat on** or **put the screws on** or **put the squeeze on; tighten the screws on.** Pressure someone, as in *The cops turned up the heat on drivers who show signs of drunkenness,* or *They said they'd tighten the screws on her if she didn't confess.* All of these slang terms refer to forms of physical force or torture.

**turn up trumps** End well, succeed, as in *Some brief courtships and hasty marriages turn up trumps.* This expression refers to card games in which trump cards are superior to cards of other suits.

**turtle** see TURN TURTLE.

**tweedledum and tweedledee** Two matters, persons, or groups that are very much alike, as in *Bob says he's not voting in this election because the candidates are tweedledum and tweedledee.* This term became popular after Lewis Carroll used it for two fat little men in *Through the Looking-Glass.* For a synonym, see SIX OF ONE, HALF DOZEN OF THE OTHER.

**twenty-twenty hindsight** Knowledge after the fact, as in *With twenty-twenty hindsight, I wouldn't have bought these tickets.* This idiom uses *twenty-twenty* in the eye doctor's sense, that is, "indicating normal vision," and *hindsight* in the sense of "looking back" or "reconsidering."

**twice** see CHEAP AT TWICE THE PRICE; LIGHTNING NEVER STRIKES TWICE; ONCE BITTEN, TWICE SHY; THINK TWICE.

**twiddle one's thumbs** Be bored or idle, as in *There I sat for three hours, twiddling my thumbs, while he made call after call.* This expression refers to the habit of idly turning one's thumbs about one another during a period of inactivity.

**twinkling** see IN THE TWINKLING OF AN EYE.

**twist** In addition to the idioms beginning with TWIST, also see LEAVE ONE TWISTING IN THE WIND.

**twist *someone* around one's finger** Also, **turn** or **wind** or **wrap *one* around one's finger.** Have complete control over someone, do as one likes with someone, as in *Gail could twist just about every man around her finger.*

**twist in the wind** see LEAVE ONE TWISTING IN THE WIND.

**twist someone's arm** Force or persuade someone to do something, as in *If you twist my arm, I'll stay for another drink,* or *She didn't really want to go to the theater, but he twisted her arm.* Originally referring to physical force, this term is now generally used more loosely and often jocularly.

T

**twist the knife** Also, **turn the knife.** Cause someone more pain after already having hurt him or her. For example, *First he flunked my essay, then he twisted the knife by making fun of it in front of the class.* This expression often follows another idiom, STICK THE KNIFE IN, because twisting the knife after stabbing someone causes great pain.

**two** In addition to the idioms beginning with TWO, also see FOR TWO CENTS; GAME THAT TWO CAN PLAY; GOODY-TWO-SHOES; IN TWO SHAKES; IT TAKES TWO TO TANGO; KILL TWO BIRDS WITH ONE STONE; KNOW ALL THE ANSWERS (A THING OR TWO); LESSER OF TWO EVILS; LIKE AS TWO PEAS IN A POD; NO TWO WAYS ABOUT IT; OF TWO MINDS; PUT TWO AND TWO TOGETHER; THAT MAKES TWO OF US; THING OR TWO; WEAR TWO HATS.

**two bits** see under FOR TWO CENTS.

**two can play at that game** see GAME THAT TWO CAN PLAY.

**two cents** see FOR TWO CENTS.

**two heads are better than one** Two people working on a problem together are more likely to arrive at a solution, as in *Why don't you work with me on the project? Two heads are always better than one.*

**two left feet, have** Be clumsy, as in *I'll never get the hang of this dance; I've got two left feet.* This expression uses an image of feet that are not coordinated, as left and right are, therefore causing imbalance or stumbling.

**two of a kind** Very similar individuals or things, as in *Patricia and John are two of a kind—they're true hiking enthusiasts.* This idiom uses *kind* in the sense of "a class with common characteristics."

**two's company** see THREE'S A CROWD.

**two shakes of a lamb's tail** see IN TWO SHAKES OF A LAMB'S TAIL.

**two strikes against** Strong factors in opposition, as in *There are two strikes against her possibility of a promotion.* This term comes from baseball, where a batter is allowed three strikes at a fairly pitched ball before being called out; thus, a batter with two strikes has but one more chance to hit a fair ball.

**two ways about it** see NO TWO WAYS ABOUT IT.

**two wrongs do not make a right** A second misdeed or mistake does not cancel the first, as in *Don't take his ball just because he took yours—two wrongs do not make a right.*

**typhoid Mary** A carrier or spreader of misfortune, as in *I swear he's a typhoid Mary; everything at the office has gone wrong since he was hired.* This expression refers to a real person, Mary Manson, who died in 1938. She transmitted typhoid fever to others and was referred to as "typhoid Mary." The term was later broadened to other carriers of disaster or misfortune.

# Uu

**ugly** In addition to the idioms beginning with UGLY, also see REAR ITS UGLY HEAD.

**ugly as sin** Physically or morally hideous, as in *I can't think why she likes that dog; it's ugly as sin.* This simile replaced the earlier *ugly as the devil.*

**ugly customer** An ill-natured or mean individual, as in *Watch out for Charlie when he's drinking; he can be an ugly customer.* This phrase uses *ugly* in the sense of "mean" or "dangerous."

**ugly duckling** A homely or unpromising individual who grows into an attractive or talented person, as in *She was the family ugly duckling but blossomed in her twenties.* This term refers to Hans Christian Andersen's fairy tale about a baby swan hatched with ducklings that is despised for its clumsiness until it grows up into a beautiful adult swan.

**umbrage** see TAKE UMBRAGE.

**unawares** see CATCH NAPPING; OFF GUARD.

**uncalled for** Not justified, undeserved, as in *That rude remark was uncalled for.* Also see CALL FOR, def. 3.

**uncertain** see IN NO UNCERTAIN TERMS.

**uncle** see CRY UNCLE; DUTCH UNCLE.

**under** In addition to the idioms beginning with UNDER, also see BELOW (UNDER) PAR; BORN UNDER A LUCKY STAR; BUCKLE UNDER; COME UNDER; CUT THE GROUND FROM UNDER; EVERYTHING BUT THE KITCHEN SINK (UNDER THE SUN); FALL UNDER; (SAILING UNDER) FALSE COLORS; GET UNDER SOMEONE'S SKIN; GO UNDER; HIDE ONE'S LIGHT UNDER A BUSHEL; HOT UNDER THE COLLAR; KEEP UNDER ONE'S HAT; KNOCK THE BOTTOM OUT (PROPS OUT FROM UNDER); KNUCKLE UNDER; LET THE GRASS GROW UNDER ONE'S FEET; LIGHT A FIRE UNDER; NOTHING NEW UNDER THE SUN; OF (UNDER) AGE; OUT FROM UNDER; PLOW UNDER; PULL THE RUG OUT FROM UNDER; PUT THE SKIDS UNDER; SIX FEET UNDER; SNOW UNDER; SWEEP UNDER THE RUG; WATER OVER THE DAM (UNDER THE BRIDGE).

**under a cloud** Under suspicion, in trouble, or out of favor, as in *Ever since his brother was accused of fraud, he's been under a cloud.* This expression calls up the image of a single black cloud hanging over an individual.

**under age** see under OF AGE.

**under any circumstances** Also, **under no circumstances.** See UNDER THE CIRCUMSTANCES.

**under arrest** In police custody, as in *They put him under arrest and charged him with stealing a car.*

**under consideration** Being thought about or discussed, as in *Your application is under consideration; we'll let you know next week.*

**under cover 1.** Protected by a shelter, as in *It began to rain, but fortunately we were under cover.* **2. under cover of.** Also, **under the cover of.** Hidden or protected by something, as in *They sneaked out under cover of darkness.*

**under false colors** see FALSE COLORS.

**under fire** Criticized or held responsible, as in *The landlord is under fire for not repairing the roof.* This expression originally referred to being within range of enemy guns.

**underground railroad** A secret network for moving and housing fugitives, as in *There's definitely an underground railroad helping women escape abusive husbands.* This term refers to the network that secretly transported runaway slaves through the northern states to Canada.

**under lock and key** Securely locked up, as in *He keeps the wine under lock and key.*

**under one's belt** Experienced or achieved, as in *Once a medical student has anatomy under her belt, she'll have much less to memorize.* This expression compares food that has been consumed to an experience that has been digested.

**under one's breath** Softly, in an undertone or whisper, as in *"I can't stand one more minute of that music," she muttered under her breath.* This idiom is probably an exaggeration referring to a sound that is softer than breathing.

**under one's feet** In one's path or annoyingly in one's way, as in *Come on, children, get out from under my feet.*

**under one's hat** see KEEP UNDER ONE'S HAT.

**under one's nose** Right there, in plain view, as in *Your keys are on the table, right under your nose.* This expression is generally a reminder that something one cannot find is actually there.

**under one's own steam** Independently, without help, as in *For two years I published the quarterly newsletter under my own steam.* This expression uses *steam* in the sense of "driving power," as in a steam engine.

**under one's skin** see GET UNDER ONE'S SKIN.

**under pain of** see ON PAIN OF.
**under par** see BELOW PAR.
**under someone's spell** Fascinated or influenced by someone, as in *I think he has our daughter under his spell.* This idiom derives from the literal meaning of *spell,* "a word or formula that has magical power."
**under someone's thumb** Controlled or dominated by someone, as in *He's been under his mother's thumb for years.* The reference in this idiom is unclear, that is, why a thumb rather than a fist or some other stronger part of the anatomy should symbolize control.
**under someone's wing** Guided or protected by someone, as in *The department head asked Bill to take Joe under his wing during his first few weeks with the company.* This term refers to a mother hen sheltering its chicks.
**understand** see GIVE SOMEONE TO UNDERSTAND.
**under the aegis of** Also, **under the auspices of.** Protected or sponsored by something or someone, as in *The fund drive for the new field is under the aegis of the city council,* or *He was admitted to the club under the auspices of Mr. Leonard.* The first term comes from Greek myth, where the *aegis* was the protective shield of Zeus.
**under the circumstances** Also, **in the circumstances.** Given these conditions, such being the case, as in *Under the circumstances we can't call Mary.* This idiom uses *circumstance* in the sense of "a particular situation." It may also be modified in various ways, such as **under any circumstances,** meaning "no matter what the situation," as in *We'll phone her under any circumstances;* **under no circumstances,** meaning "in no case, never," as in *Under no circumstances may you smoke here;* **under any other circumstances,** meaning "in a different situation," as in *I can't work under any other circumstances;* and **under the same circumstances,** meaning "given the same situation," as in *Under the same circumstances anyone would have done what I did.*
**under the counter** Secretly, especially, in an illegal way, as in *I'm sure they're selling liquor to minors under the counter.* This expression most often refers to an illegal transaction, the *counter* being a flat-surfaced table or other piece of furniture *over* which legal business is conducted. Also see UNDER THE TABLE.
**under the gun** Under pressure to solve a problem or meet a deadline, as in *The reporter was under the gun for that article on taxes.* This idiom refers to a gun being pointed at a person to force him or her to act.
**under the hammer** For sale, as in *These paintings and Oriental rugs must come under the hammer if we're to pay the bills.* This expression refers to an auctioneer's hammer, which is rapped to indicate a completed transaction.
**under the impression** Thinking, assuming, or believing something, as in *I was under the impression that they were coming today.* This idiom often suggests that the idea or belief one had is mistaken.
**under the influence** Unable to function normally as a result of consuming alcohol or a drug, as in *He was accused of driving under the influence.* This expression is legal jargon. Since it is nearly always applied to drivers suspected or so accused, it has given rise to the police acronyms **DUI,** for "driving under the influence," and **DWI,** for "driving while intoxicated."
**under the knife** Having surgery, as in *He was awake the entire time he was under the knife.* The phrase is often put as **go under the knife,** meaning "be operated on," as in *When do you go under the knife?*
**under the sun** see EVERYTHING BUT THE KITCHEN SINK (UNDER THE SUN); NOTHING NEW UNDER THE SUN.
**under the table** In secret, as in *They paid her under the table so as to avoid taxes.* This term refers to money being passed under a table in some illegal transaction, such as a bribe. Also see UNDER THE COUNTER.
**under the weather** Ailing, ill; also, suffering from a hangover. For example, *She said she was under the weather and couldn't make it to the meeting.* This expression may refer to the influence of the weather on one's health.
**under the wire** Barely, scarcely, just within the limit, as in *This book will be finished just under the wire.* This term comes from horseracing, where the wire marks the finish line. Also see DOWN TO THE WIRE.
**under way** **1.** In motion, as in *The ship got under way at noon.* **2.** Already started, in progress, as in *Plans are under way to expand.*
**under wraps** Concealed or secret, as in *The design for the new plant is under wraps.* This idiom frequently is put as **keep under wraps,** meaning "keep secret," as in *Let's keep this theory under wraps until we've tested it sufficiently.* It refers to covering something completely by wrapping it up.
**undivided attention** Concentration on one person or a single task, as in *Class, I want your undivided attention,* or *She's giving her undivided attention to the problem.*
**unglued** see under COME APART AT THE SEAMS.
**unheard of** Very unusual, extraordinary, as in *It's unheard of to have all one's money refunded two years after the purchase.* This expression refers to a circumstance so unusual that it has never been heard of.

U

**unkindest cut, the** The worst insult, ultimate betrayal, as in *And then, the unkindest cut of all—my partner walks out on me just when the deal is about to go through.*

**unknown quantity** An unpredictable person or thing, as in *We don't know how the new pitcher will do—he's an unknown quantity.* This expression comes from algebra, where it means an unknown numerical value.

**unlikely** see IN THE UNLIKELY EVENT.

**unseen** see SIGHT UNSEEN.

**unstuck** see under COME APART AT THE SEAMS.

**until** see PUT OFF UNTIL TOMORROW; TALK ONE'S ARM OFF (UNTIL BLUE IN THE FACE). Also see under TILL.

**untimely** see COME TO AN (UNTIMELY) END.

**unto** see DO UNTO OTHERS; LAW UNTO ONESELF.

**unturned** see LEAVE NO STONE UNTURNED.

**unvarnished truth, the** The plain facts without anything added, as in *Let's just have the unvarnished truth about the sale.*

**unwritten law** An accepted although informal rule of behavior, as in *It's an unwritten law that you lock the gate when you leave the swimming pool.*

**up** In addition to the idioms beginning with UP, also see ACT UP; ADD UP; ADD UP TO; ALL SHOOK UP; ANTE UP; BACK UP; BALL UP; BANG UP; BARK UP THE WRONG TREE; BEAR UP; BEAT UP; BEEF UP; BID UP; BLOW UP; BOB UP; BONE UP; BOOT UP; BOTTLE UP; BOUND UP IN; BRACE UP; BREAK UP; BRING ONE UP SHORT; BRING UP; BRING UP THE REAR; BRING UP TO DATE; BRUSH UP; BUCKLE UP; BUCK UP; BUDDY UP; BUILD UP; BUMP UP; BURN UP; BUTTER UP; BUTTON UP; BUY UP; CALL UP; CAMP IT UP; CARD UP ONE'S SLEEVE; CATCH UP; CHALK UP; CHARGE UP; CHAT UP; CHEER UP; CHOKE UP; CHOOSE UP; CLAM UP; CLEAN UP; CLEAR UP; CLOSE UP; CLOUD OVER (UP); COME (UP) FROM BEHIND; COME UP; COME UP AGAINST; COME UP WITH; COMING UP ROSES; COOK UP; COUGH UP; COVER UP; COZY UP; CRACKED UP; CRACK UP; CRANK UP; CRAP UP; CREEP UP (ON); CROP UP; CURL UP; CUT UP; DEAD FROM THE NECK UP; DIG UP; DOLL UP; DOUBLE UP; DO UP; DRAW UP; DREAM UP; DRESS UP; DRUM UP; DRY UP; EASE OFF (UP); EAT OUT (SOMEONE UP); EAT UP; END UP; FACE UP TO; FED UP; FEEL SOMEONE UP; FEEL UP TO; FIGURE UP; FIRE UP; FIT OUT (UP); FIX UP; FLARE UP; FOLD UP; FOLLOW UP; FOUL UP; FROM THE GROUND UP; GAME IS UP; GANG UP; GAS UP; GET SOMEONE'S BACK UP; GET UP; GET UP ON THE WRONG SIDE OF BED; GET UP STEAM; GIVE ONESELF UP; GIVE UP; GIVE UP THE GHOST; GO BELLY UP; GOOF UP; GO UP; GO UP IN FLAMES; GROW UP; GUM UP; HAM UP; HANDS UP; HANG UP; HARD UP; HAUL UP; HAVE HAD IT (UP TO HERE); HEADS UP; HEAD UP; HEAT UP; HIT UP; HOLD ONE'S END UP; HOLD ONE'S HEAD HIGH (UP); HOLD UP; HOLE UP; HOOK UP; HOPPED UP; HURRY UP AND WAIT; HUSH UP; JACK UP; JAZZ UP; JUICE UP; KEEP IT UP; KEEP ONE'S CHIN UP; KEEP (SOMEONE) UP; KEY UP; KICK UP; KICK UP A FUSS; KICK UP ONE'S HEELS; KISS AND MAKE UP; KNOCK UP; KNOW WHICH WAY IS UP; LAID UP; LAND IN (UP); LAP UP; LAUGH UP ONE'S SLEEVE; LAY IN (UP); LEAD DOWN (UP) THE GARDEN PATH; LEAD UP TO; LEG UP, GIVE ONE A; LET UP; LIGHTEN UP; LIGHT UP; LINE UP; LIVE IT UP; LIVE UP TO; LOCK UP; LOOK OVER (UP AND DOWN); LOOK UP; LOUSE UP; MAKE UP; MAKE UP FOR; MAKE UP ONE'S MIND; MAKE UP TO; MARK UP; MEASURE UP; MEET UP WITH; MESS UP; MIX IT UP; MIX UP; MOP UP; MOP UP THE FLOOR WITH; MOVE UP; MUCK UP; NOT ALL IT'S CRACKED UP TO BE; NUMBER IS UP; ONE UP; ON THE UP-AND-UP; OPEN UP; OWN UP; PAIR OFF (UP); PASS UP; PATCH UP; PAY UP; PEP SOMEONE UP; PERK UP; PICK UP; PICK UP ON; PILE UP; PIPE UP; PLAY UP; PLAY UP TO; PLUCK UP ONE'S COURAGE; POINT UP; PONY UP; POP UP; PRICK UP ONE'S EARS; PSYCH UP; PULL ONESELF UP BY THE BOOTSTRAPS; PULL UP; PULL UP STAKES; PUMP UP; PUSH UP DAISIES; PUT ONE'S FEET UP; PUT SOMEONE UP TO; PUT UP; PUT-UP JOB; PUT UP OR SHUT UP; PUT UP WITH; RACK UP; RAKE UP; RAISE (UP) THE ANTE; READ UP ON; REV UP; RIDE UP; RIGHT-SIDE UP; RIGHT UP ONE'S ALLEY; RING UP; ROLL UP; ROLL UP ONE'S SLEEVES; ROUGH UP; ROUND UP; RUN UP; RUN UP AGAINST; RUSTLE UP; SAVE UP; SCARE UP; SCREW UP; SCROUNGE AROUND (UP); SCRUB UP; SEAL OFF (UP); SEIZE UP; SEND UP; SERVE UP; SETTLE UP; SET UP; SET UP HOUSEKEEPING; SEW UP; SHACK UP; SHAKE UP; SHAPE UP; SHINE UP TO; SHOOT UP; SHORE UP; SHOT UP; SHOW UP; SHUT UP; SIGN UP; SIT UP; SIT UP; SIZE UP; SLIP UP; SLOW UP; SMELL UP; SNAP UP; SOAK UP; SOFTEN UP; SOMEBODY UP THERE LOVES ME; SPEAK OUT (UP); SPEED UP; SPIT UP; SPRUCE UP; SQUARE UP; STACK UP; STAND UP; STAND UP AND BE COUNTED; STAND UP FOR; STAND UP TO; START UP; STEAMED UP; STEP UP; STICK UP; STIR UP; STIR UP A HORNETS' NEST; STOP UP; STRAIGHTEN UP; STRAIGHT UP; STRING UP; SUCK UP TO; SUIT UP; SUM UP; TAKE UP; TAKE UP A COLLECTION; TAKE UP ARMS; TAKE UP FOR; TAKE UP ON; TAKE UP WITH; TALK UP; TANK UP; TEAM UP WITH; THINK UP; THROW UP; THROW UP ONE'S HANDS; THUMBS UP; TIE UP; TIME IS UP; TONE DOWN (UP); TOOL UP; (UP) TO THE HILT; TOUCH UP; TRADE DOWN (UP); TRIAL BALLOON, SEND UP A; TRIP UP; TRUMP UP; TUNE UP; TURN UP; TURN UP ONE'S NOSE; TURN UP THE HEAT ON; TURN UP TRUMPS; WAIT UP; WAKE-UP CALL; WARM UP; WASH UP; WHAT'S COOKING (UP); WHAT'S (UP) WITH; WHIP UP; WHOOP IT UP; WIND UP; WISE UP; WORKED UP; WORK ONE'S WAY (UP); WORK UP; WRAPPED UP; WRAP UP; WRITE UP. Also see under UPPER.

**up a creek** Also, **up shit creek** or **up the creek (without a paddle).** In trouble, in a serious predicament, as in *If the check doesn't arrive, today I'm up a creek,* or *The car wouldn't start, so I was up the creek without a paddle.* This slang idiom creates the image of a stranded canoeist with no way of moving (paddling) the canoe. The first variant is considered vulgar.

**up against** Contending or confronted with, as in *I'm up against a strong opponent in this election.* This idiom is also put as **up against it,** which means "in serious difficulty, especially in desperate financial straits." For example, *When the collection agency called again, we knew we were up against it.*

**up and about** Also, **up and around** or **up and doing.** Active again, especially after an illness or rest, as in *They had her up and about just one day after surgery,* or *I'm so glad you're up and around; we need your help,* or *It's time to be up and doing.*

**up and at 'em** Get going, get busy, as in *Up and at 'em—there's a lot of work to be done.* This colloquial idiom, often uttered as a command, uses *at 'em* (for "at them") in the general sense of tackling a project and not in reference to specific persons.

**up and down** **1.** Everywhere, as in *We've been up and down looking for the key.* **2.** Sometimes feeling well, sometimes feeling bad; from one extreme to the other, as in *Since she's had chemotherapy, she's been up and down,* or *He has his sudden changes of mood—one minute he's up, the next he's down.*

**up a tree** In a difficult situation, as in *They found the drugs in his suitcase, so he was up a tree.* This expression refers to an animal, such as a raccoon or squirrel, that climbs a tree to escape its attackers, which then surround the tree so it cannot come down.

**up for** Ready to do something, enthusiastic, as in *Are you up for a hike?*

**up for grabs** Available to anyone, as in *Now that he has resigned, his job is up for grabs.* This term refers to something being thrown in the air for anyone to grasp or catch.

**up front** **1.** In the forward section, as of an airplane or theater. For example, *We'd like two seats as far up front as possible.* **2.** Paid in advance, as in *We need at least half of the money for the production up front.* **3.** Honest, direct, as in *Now tell me straight up front what you think of this outfit.* In this sense, the idiom can also be used as an adjective, as in *He gave us an up-front answer to our question.*

**uphill battle, an** A difficult problem, as in *Winning the election will be an uphill battle.* It is often put as **face an uphill battle,** as in *He faces an uphill battle in his fight against cancer.*

**up in arms** Angry, rebellious, as in *The town was up in arms over the state's plan to allow commercial flights at the air base.*

**up in the air** Not settled, uncertain, as in *The proposal to build a golf course next to the airport is still up in the air.* This expression compares something floating in the air to an unsettled matter.

**upon** see ACT ON (UPON); CALL ON (UPON); CHANCE ON (UPON); COME ACROSS (UPON); COME ON (UPON); COUNT ON (UPON); DAWN ON (UPON); DWELL ON (UPON); ENTER ON (UPON); FALL BACK ON (UPON); FALL ON (UPON); GROW ON (UPON); HARD ON (UPON); HIT ON (UPON); INCUMBENT UPON; LIGHT ON (UPON); ONCE UPON A TIME; PLAY ON (UPON); PUT UPON; SEIZE ON (UPON); SET AT (UPON); TAKE IT UPON ONESELF; WAIT ON (UPON); WEIGH ON (UPON); WORK ON (UPON).

**up on *something,* be** Be well informed or up-to-date about something, as in *I'm not up on the latest models of cars.*

**up one's alley** see under RIGHT UP ONE'S ALLEY.

**up one's sleeve** see CARD UP ONE'S SLEEVE.

**upper** In addition to the idioms beginning with UPPER, also see KEEP A STIFF UPPER LIP.

**upper crust** The highest social class, as in *She wanted badly to be one of the upper crust, but it wasn't going to happen.* This term refers to the choicest part of a pie or loaf of bread.

**upper hand** Also, **whip hand.** A superior or controlling position, as in *Once you let Jeff get the upper hand, there'll be no stopping him,* or *When it comes to checkers, my son-in-law generally has the whip hand.*

**upright** see BOLT UPRIGHT.

**uproar** see MAKE A SCENE (AN UPROAR).

**ups and downs** Good times and bad times, successes and failures, as in *We've had our ups and downs, but things are going fairly well now.*

**upset the applecart** Spoil carefully laid plans, as in *Now, don't upset the applecart by revealing where we're going.*

**up shit creek** see UP A CREEK.

**upside** In addition to the idiom beginning with UPSIDE, also see TURN UPSIDE DOWN.

**upside the head** Against the side of someone's head, as in *Sometimes the police have to knock suspects upside the head with their nightsticks.*

**upstairs** see KICK ONE UPSTAIRS.

**uptake** see ON THE UPTAKE.

**up the ante** see RAISE THE ANTE.

**up the creek** see UP A CREEK.

**up the river** To or in prison, as in *They sent him up the river for five years.* This phrase originally referred to Sing Sing Prison, on the Hudson River about 30 miles north of New York City. It was later broadened to apply to any prison.

**up the wall** see under DRIVE SOMEONE CRAZY.

**up the wazoo** Also, **out the wazoo; up the ying-yang.** More of something, especially money, than can be told. For example, *That movie star has money up the wazoo,* or *He's got brains out the wazoo,* or *We have work up the ying-yang.* These expressions are considered vulgar by some people.

**up till now** Also, **up to now** or **up to this point** or **up until now.** See TILL NOW.

**up to 1.** As far as or approaching a certain point. For example, *The water was nearly up to the windowsill,* or *They allowed us up to two hours to finish the test,* or *This seed should yield up to 300 bushels per acre.* **2. be up to.** Be able to do or deal with, as in *When I got home, she asked if I was up to a walk on the beach.* This usage is often put negatively, that is, **not be up to something,** as in *He's not up to a long drive.* **3.** Occupied with, engaged in, as in *What have you been up to lately?* This usage can mean "devising" or "scheming," as in *We knew those two were up to something.* It also appears in **up to no good,** meaning "occupied with or devising something harmful," as in *I'm sure those kids are up to no good.* **4.** Dependent on, as in *The success of this project is up to us.* Also see the following idioms beginning with UP TO.

**up to a point** To some extent, somewhat, as in *I can work weekends up to a point, but after a month or so I get tired of it.* This phrase uses *point* in the sense of "a definite position."

**up to date** see BRING UP TO DATE.

**up to no good** see UP TO, def. 3.

**up to one's ears** Also, **up to one's eyes** or **eyeballs** or **neck** or **elbows.** Deeply involved; also, oversupplied, overwhelmed. For example, *I'm up to my ears in work,* or *He's in up to his eyes with the in-laws.* This exaggerated slang idiom implies that one is flooded with something up to the organs mentioned.

**up to one's old tricks** Behaving in one's usual deceitful or mischievous fashion, as in *She's up to her old tricks, telling her parents one thing and her teachers another,* or *He's up to his old tricks, teasing his sisters until they're in tears.*

**up to par** Also, **up to scratch** or **up to snuff** or **up to speed** or **up to the mark.** Satisfactory, up to a given standard, as in *She didn't feel up to par today, so she stayed home,* or *I'm sure he'll come up to scratch when the time comes,* or *She's up to snuff again.* Nearly all the versions of this idiom come from sports, *par* from golf, *scratch* and *mark* from boxing (after being knocked down a fighter has eight seconds to make his way to a mark scratched in the center of the ring), and *speed* from racing. However, the reference to *snuff* is unknown.

**upwards of** Also, **upward of.** More than, in excess of, as in *Upwards of 30,000 spectators filled the ballpark.*

**up with 1.** New or presently going on in someone's life, as in *So, what's up with you?* **2.** Wrong with someone or something. For example, *What's up with Mary? Isn't she feeling well?* or *Something is up with this door—I can't get it to close.*

**up yours** A vulgar exclamation of contempt or dismissal, as in *So you think you can beat me? Well, up yours!* This expression, a shortening of the even more vulgar **stick it up your ass,** is sometimes accompanied by an obscene gesture. [Vulgar slang] Also see GIVE SOMEONE THE FINGER.

**use** In addition to the idioms beginning with USE, also see HAVE NO USE FOR; MAKE USE OF; NO USE; PUT SOMETHING TO GOOD USE.

**use *someone* as a punching bag** Beat someone up in order to take out one's anger or frustration on a person who is not responsible for a difficult situation. For example, *The big kids use the little ones as punching bags,* or *I didn't invite him to your party, so don't use me as your punching bag.* This idiom refers to the heavy bag that boxers use to practice timing their punches.

**used** In addition to the idiom beginning with USED, also see IT TAKES GETTING USED TO.

**used to 1.** Accustomed or adapted to. This expression is often put as **be** or **get used to,** as in *I'm not used to driving a manual-shift car,* or *She can't get used to calling him Dad.* **2.** Formerly. This sense is used with a verb to indicate a past state, as in *I used to ride my bicycle to the post office,* or *This used to be the best restaurant in town.*

**use one's head** Think, have common sense, as in *Use your head, Michael. No one's coming out in this weather.* This idiom uses *head* in the sense of "brain" or "intellect."

**use up 1.** Consume something completely, as in *The kids used up all their money playing video games.* **2.** Exhaust one, tire out, as in *I'm totally used up from digging that hole.*

**usual** see AS USUAL; BUSINESS AS USUAL.

**utter a word** see under NOT OPEN ONE'S MOUTH.

# Vv

**vacuum** see IN A VACUUM.
**vain** see IN VAIN; TAKE SOMEONE'S NAME IN VAIN.
**valor** see DISCRETION IS THE BETTER PART OF VALOR.
**value** see AT FACE VALUE.
**vanish** see under INTO THIN AIR.
**variations on a theme** **1.** Ways of saying or doing something that are very similar to each other, as in *The questions on the history test were variations on a theme, in this case, World War I.* **2.** Information that is boring or not worth hearing, as in *His last few speeches have been variations on a theme—he has nothing new to say.*
**variety is the spice of life** Diversity makes life interesting, as in *Jim dates a different girl every week—variety is the spice of life, he claims.*
**variety store** A retail shop that carries a large selection of usually inexpensive merchandise, as in *What this town needs is a good variety store.*
**various and sundry** Of different kinds, miscellaneous, as in *Various and sundry items did not sell, so they'll probably hold another auction.* This expression is redundant; the two adjectives mean just about the same thing.
**veil** see DRAW A VEIL OVER.
**velvet** see under IRON HAND.
**vengeance** see WITH A VENGEANCE.
**vent** In addition to the idiom beginning with VENT, also see GIVE VENT TO.
**vent one's spleen** Express one's anger, as in *Some people see town council meetings as a place where they can vent their spleen.* This expression uses *vent* in the sense of "air" and *spleen* in the sense of "anger," referring to the fact that this organ was once thought to be the seat of ill humor and sadness.

**venture** see NOTHING VENTURED, NOTHING GAINED.
**verge** In addition to the idiom beginning with VERGE, also see ON THE VERGE OF.
**verge on** **1.** Approach something, come close to, as in *Her ability verges on genius.* **2.** Be on the edge or border of, as in *Our property verges on conservation land.*
**verse** see CHAPTER AND VERSE.
**very** In addition to the idioms beginning with VERY, also see ALL VERY WELL; WHAT'S THE IDEA (THE VERY IDEA).
**very thing, the** Exactly what is needed or wanted, as in *That hat's the very thing to complete the costume.* This idiom uses *very* to mean exact identity.
**very well** **1.** Exceedingly healthy, as in *How are you? Very well, thank you.* **2.** Extremely skillfully or properly, as in *He manages that sailboat very well.* **3.** All right, I agree to, as in *Will you take her hand? Very well, but only to cross the street.* Also see ALL VERY WELL.
**vested interest, a** A personal stake in something, as in *She has a vested interest in keeping the house in her name.* This term uses *vested* in the sense of "established" or "secured."
**vicious circle, a** A series of events in which each problem creates another and makes the original one worse. For example, *The fatter I get, the unhappier I am, so I eat to cheer myself up, which makes me fatter yet—it's a vicious circle.*
**victor** see TO THE VICTOR BELONG THE SPOILS.
**view** see BIRD'S EYE VIEW; IN (VIEW) LIGHT OF; IN VIEW; ON VIEW; POINT OF VIEW; TAKE A DIM VIEW; WITH A VIEW TO.
**vim and vigor** Great vitality and energy. It is often put as **full of vim and vigor,** as in *He was full of vim and vigor after that swim.* This redundant expression uses both *vim* and *vigor* in the sense of "energy" or "strength."
**vine** see CLINGING VINE; WITHER ON THE VINE.
**violet** see SHRINKING VIOLET.
**virtue** see BY VIRTUE OF; MAKE A VIRTUE OF NECESSITY.
**vision** see TUNNEL VISION.
**visit** see PAY A CALL (VISIT).
**voice** In addition to the idiom beginning with VOICE, also see AT THE TOP OF ONE'S LUNGS (VOICE); GIVE VOICE TO; HAVE A SAY (VOICE) IN; RAISE ONE'S VOICE; WITH ONE VOICE.
**voice crying in the wilderness, a** The only person trying to warn others of danger or protesting against an action or condition. For example, *Until recently, she was a voice crying in the wilderness about the coming crisis,* or *I feel as though I've been a voice crying in the wilderness about the way animals are treated.*
**void** see NULL AND VOID.
**volume** see SPEAK VOLUMES.
**vote down** Defeat a candidate or measure, as in *The new amendment was voted down by a narrow margin.*

**vote with one's feet** Show one's disapproval by walking out or leaving a place, as in *The service at that restaurant was so bad that we decided to vote with our feet,* or *Thousands of Hong Kong residents voted with their feet and left before the Chinese takeover.*

**voyage** see MAIDEN VOYAGE.

# Ww

**wade in** Also, **wade into.** Plunge into something, begin or attack energetically and with determination, as in *She waded into that pile of correspondence.* This idiom transfers entering water to beginning some action.

**wag** see TAIL WAGGING THE DOG; TONGUES WAG.

**wages of sin, the** The results or consequences of doing evil or something bad, as in *She ate all of the strawberries and ended up with a terrible stomachache—the wages of sin, no doubt.*

**wagon** see FIX SOMEONE'S WAGON; HITCH ONE'S WAGON; ON THE BANDWAGON; ON THE WAGON.

**wail like a banshee** Scream in a shrill voice, as in *Terrified, she wailed like a banshee.* In Irish folklore, a *banshee* is a spirit in the form of a wailing woman whose appearance is an omen that one member of a family will soon die.

**wait** In addition to the idioms beginning with WAIT, also see ACCIDENT WAITING TO HAPPEN; CAN'T WAIT; HURRY UP AND WAIT; IN WAITING; LIE IN WAIT; PLAY A WAITING GAME.

**wait a minute 1.** Stop, I want to say something, as in *Wait a minute—he wasn't there yesterday.* **2.** What a surprise, as in *Wait a minute! It was you who called the police?* For a similar phrase, see HOLD EVERYTHING.

**wait and see** Wait for events to run their course, as in *Do you think they'll raise taxes? We'll have to wait and see.*

**wait for the other shoe to drop** Await an event that is thought to be sure to happen, as in *Now that she has a good enough job to leave her husband, we're just waiting for the other shoe to drop.* This expression refers to a person who is awakened by a neighbor loudly dropping one shoe on the floor and is waiting for the second shoe to be dropped.

**waiting game** see PLAY A WAITING GAME.

**waiting in the wings** see IN THE WINGS.

**wait on 1.** Also, **wait upon.** Serve someone, minister to, especially for personal needs or in a store or restaurant. For example, *Guests at the motel should not expect to be waited on—they can make their own beds and get their own breakfast.* **2.** Also, **wait upon.** Await something, remain in readiness for, as in *We're waiting on their decision to close the school.* This usage is a synonym of **wait for.** Although it was criticized by many authorities in the past, it has now come into increasingly wider use and is again largely accepted.

W

**wait on *someone* hand and foot** Do everything for someone, serve someone's every need, as in *Her mother has always waited on her hand and foot.*

**wait out** Delay until the end of something, as in *They waited out the war in Paris.* This expression comes from baseball, where it refers to a batter not swinging at pitches in the hope of being walked (getting to first base on balls).

**wait table** Also, **wait on table.** Serve at a meal, as in *She got a summer job at a resort waiting table,* or *Waiting on table usually does not pay very well.* Also see WAIT ON.

**wait up 1.** Delay going to bed in anticipation of someone or something, as in *My parents always wait up until I get home, no matter how late it is.* **2.** Stop or pause so that another can catch up, as in *Let's wait up for the stragglers,* or *Don't walk so fast; wait up for me.*

**wake** In addition to the idiom beginning with WAKE, also see IN THE WAKE OF; TO WAKE THE DEAD.

**wake-up call 1.** A telephone call arranged in advance at a hotel to awaken a sleeper. For example, *I requested a 6:00 wake-up call.* **2.** An important event, report, or situation that brings an issue to immediate attention. For example, *The rise in unemployment has given a wake-up call to state governments,* or *The success of the online subscription is a wake-up call to publishers.*

**walk** In addition to the idioms beginning with WALK, also see HANDS DOWN (IN A WALK); WORSHIP THE GROUND SOMEONE WALKS ON.

**walk all over** Also, **walk over.** Treat someone without respect, be overbearing and rude to, as in *I don't know why she puts up with the way he walks all over her* or *Don't let those aggressive people in sales walk over you.* This idiom transfers physically treading on someone to trampling on one's feelings.

**walk a tightrope** Also, **be on a tightrope.** Take or be on a very risky course, as in *A university press must walk a tightrope to publish scholarly books and still make money,* or *The general was on a tightrope as to whether he should advance or retreat.* This idiom transfers the balancing act performed by tightrope or high-wire acrobats to other concerns.

**walk away from 1.** Survive an accident with little injury, as in *They were lucky to walk* *away from that collision.* **2.** Refuse to deal with someone or become involved, abandon, as in *No parent finds it easy to walk away from a child in trouble.* **3.** Outdo someone, outrun, or defeat with little difficulty, as in *The Eagles are walking away from the other teams in their division.* Also see WALK OVER.

**walk away with** see WALK OFF WITH.

**walking encyclopedia** Also, **walking dictionary.** A very knowledgeable person, as in *Ask Bob—he's a walking encyclopedia of military history.* The variant **walking dictionary** refers to someone who knows a lot about words, especially how they are spelled, and is often used to ask a sarcastic question, as in *What do you think I am? A walking dictionary?*

**walking papers** Notification that one has lost one's job, as in *They're downsizing, and I got my walking papers last week.* This slang expression originally referred to a written notice of dismissal.

**walk off with 1.** Also, **walk away with.** Win something easily, as in *Our team walked off with the pennant,* or *He expected a tough opponent, but to his surprise he walked away with first place.* **2.** Steal something, as in *Someone walked off with my suitcase.*

**walk of life** A trade, profession, or occupation, as in *He'll do well in whatever walk of life he chooses.* This expression uses *walk* in the sense of "line of work."

**walk on air** Feel happy or greatly joyful, as in *She was walking on air after she found out she'd won the teaching award.* This term compares feeling happy to floating.

**walk on eggs** Proceed very cautiously, as in *I knew I was walking on eggs when I asked about the department's involvement in the lawsuit.* This idiom transfers walking on fragile eggs to discussing or investigating a dangerous subject.

**walk out 1.** Go on strike, as in *The union threatened to walk out if management would not listen to its demands.* **2.** Leave suddenly, especially as a sign of disapproval. For example, *The play was so bad we walked out after the first act.* **3.** Also, **walk out on.** Desert someone, abandon, as in *He walked out on his wife and five children.*

**walk over 1.** See WALK ALL OVER. **2.** Defeat someone easily, as in *We walked over them in that practice game, but I don't know how we'll do in the tournament.*

**walk tall** Show pride and self-confidence, as in *The most important thing she taught us was to walk tall.*

**walk the floor** Pace up and down, as in *In former times expectant fathers walked the floor, but now they often are labor coaches,* or *The baby was sick, so she walked the floor with him all night.*

**walk the plank** Be forced to resign, as in *We were sure that Ted hadn't left of his own accord; he'd walked the plank.* This idiom refers to a form of execution used mainly by pirates, in which a victim was forced to walk off the end of a board placed on the edge of the ship's deck and thereby drown.

**walk the walk, talk the talk** Do and say what one has committed oneself to, as in *If you want to work with me again, you'll have to walk the walk, talk the talk.*

**walk through 1.** Perform something in a casual way, as in *She was just walking through her job, hoping to quit very soon.* This idiom originally referred to practicing parts in a play at an early rehearsal. Also see GO THROUGH THE MOTIONS. **2. walk someone through.** Instruct someone carefully, one step at a time, as in *He was very helpful, walking me through all the steps in this complex computer program.*

**wall** In addition to the idiom beginning with WALL, also see BACK TO THE WALL; BEAT ONE'S HEAD AGAINST THE WALL; BETWEEN YOU AND ME (AND FOUR WALLS); CLIMB THE WALLS; DRIVE SOMEONE CRAZY (UP THE WALL); FLY ON THE WALL; GO TO THE WALL; HANDWRITING ON THE WALL; HOLE IN THE WALL; OFF THE WALL; RUN INTO A STONE WALL.

**wallop** see PACK A PUNCH (WALLOP).

**walls have ears, the** What is being said can easily be overheard, someone is listening, as in *Be careful what you say; the walls have ears.*

**Walter Mitty** A person, generally a quite ordinary or inadequate one, who indulges in fantastic daydreams of personal triumphs. For example, *He's a Walter Mitty about riding in a rodeo but is actually afraid of horses.* This term comes from James Thurber's short story, "The Secret Life of Walter Mitty," describing just such a character.

**wane** see WAX AND WANE.

**want** In addition to the idioms beginning with WANT, also see WASTE NOT, WANT NOT.

**want for nothing** Not lack any necessities or comforts, as in *He saw to it that his mother wanted for nothing.* This term uses *want* in the sense of "lack."

**want in 1.** Desire to enter, as in *The cat wants in.* The antonym is **want out,** as in *The dog wants out.* **2.** Wish to join a business, project, or other undertaking, as in *Some investors want in but have not yet been admitted.* Again, the antonym is **want out,** as in *Many Quebec residents want out of Canada.*

**war** In addition to the idioms beginning with WAR, also see ALL'S FAIR IN LOVE AND WAR; AT WAR; DECLARE WAR ON; TUG OF WAR.

**ward off** **1.** Turn someone's attack aside, repel, as in *He tried to ward off her blows.* **2.** Try to prevent something, avoid, as in *She took vitamin C to ward off a cold.*

**war horse** Also, **old war horse.** A dependable, frequently performed attraction, as in *The opera company is doing nothing but old war horses this season, like,* Aïda *and* La Bohème. This term originally referred to a military charger that had been through many battles. It later began to be used for human veterans and then for popular productions, especially of musical works.

**warm** In addition to the idioms beginning with WARM, also see COLD HANDS, WARM HEART; LOOK LIKE DEATH (WARMED OVER).

**warm as toast** Comfortably warm, as in *It was freezing outside, but we were warm as toast in front of the fire.* Despite the British custom of serving toasted bread in a rack that rapidly cools it, this idiom originated in England, at first as *hot as toast.*

**warm body** Any person will serve the purpose, it does not matter who it is, as in *They're looking for warm bodies to help in the kitchen,* or *I'm nothing but a warm body in that class.*

**warm heart** see COLD HANDS, WARM HEART.

**warm the bench** Also, **ride the bench.** Be a secondary or substitute participant; wait one's turn to participate. For example, *I can't wait till the head of accounting retires; I've been warming the bench for years.* This expression comes from such sports as baseball and football, and their standard practice of having substitute players sit on a bench in case they are needed in a game.

**warm the cockles of one's heart** Gratify one, make one feel good, as in *It warms the cockles of my heart to see them getting along so well.* This expression uses a corruption of the Latin name for the heart's ventricles, *cochleae cordis.*

**warm up** **1.** Prepare for exercise or an athletic event by stretching or practicing beforehand, as in *It's important to warm up before you play any sport.* The idiom is also applied to musicians getting ready to perform. **2.** Make enthusiastic, excited, or animated, as in *He was good at warming up an audience for the main speaker.* **3.** Also, **warm up to.** Become friendlier or more receptive toward someone, as in *I had a hard time warming up to my new manager.* **4.** Reach a temperature high enough to work well, as in *I'll go out and warm up the car.* **5.** Reheat food, as in *If we warm up the leftovers, we'll have enough for everyone.* **6.** Approach a state of violence or confrontation, as in *Racial tension was rapidly warming up.* Also see HEAT UP.

**warm welcome, a** A hearty, hospitable reception or greeting, as in *We got a very warm welcome when we finally arrived.*

**war of nerves, a** A conflict characterized by psychological pressure, such as threats and rumors, aiming to destroy an enemy's confidence. For example, *Her lawyer said the university had waged a war of nerves to persuade his client to resign.* This expression refers to tactics used in World War II.

**warp** In addition to the idiom beginning with WARP, also see TIME WARP.

**warp and woof** The underlying structure or basis of something, as in *He foresaw great changes in the warp and woof of the nation's economy.* This expression refers to the threads that run lengthwise (*warp*) and crosswise (*woof*) in a woven fabric.

**warpath** see ON THE WARPATH.

**warrant** see SIGN ONE'S OWN DEATH WARRANT.

**warrior** see WEEKEND WARRIOR.

**warts and all** Including all blemishes, faults, and shortcomings, as in *Rather unwisely, they decided to buy the house, warts and all.*

**wash** In addition to the idioms beginning with WASH, also see COME OUT IN THE WASH; WON'T WASH.

**wash down** **1.** Clean something by washing it from top to bottom, as in *He always washes down the walls before painting.* **2.** Drink a liquid after eating food or taking medicine, as in *He washed down the pills with a glass of water.*

**washed out** Faded in color; also, lacking liveliness. For example, *This carpet is all washed out from the sun,* or *He looks all washed out.* Also see WASH OUT, def. 3.

**washed up** see under WASH UP, def. 3.

**wash one's dirty linen in public** Also, **air one's dirty linen** or **air one's dirty laundry.** Expose private matters to public view, especially embarrassing secrets. For example, *Reporters seem determined to persuade all of us to wash our dirty linen in public,* or *He's quite willing to air his dirty linen if it will make him the center of attention.*

**wash one's hands of** Refuse to accept responsibility for something; abandon or renounce something or someone. For example, *I've done all I can for him, and now I'm washing my hands of him.* This expression refers to Pontius Pilate washing his hands before having Jesus put to death.

**wash out** **1.** Remove or be removed by washing; also, cause to fade by laundering. For example, *Give it to me; I'll wash out that stain,* or *The bleach has really washed out that bright print.* **2.** Wear away or be worn away by the flow of water, as in *The river rose and washed out the dam,* or *The road has* *completely washed out.* **3.** Deplete or be depleted of energy, as in *Working on her feet all day just washed her out,* or *I just washed out after that long tennis match.* **4.** Eliminate or be eliminated as unsatisfactory, as in *He washed out of medical school after just one year,* or *After only two months as chairman I washed out.* **5.** Cancel something because of bad weather, as in *The picnic was washed out.* Also see WASHED OUT.

**wash up 1.** Wash one's hands and face, as in *It's time to wash up for dinner.* Also see CLEAN UP, def. 2. **2.** Clean the utensils after a meal, as in *I'll cook dinner if you promise to wash up.* Also see DO THE DISHES. **3.** Bring about the end or ruin of someone; finish. This usage is often used put in the passive, **be washed up,** as in *She's all washed up as a singer.*

**waste** In addition to the idioms beginning with WASTE, also see GO TO WASTE; HASTE MAKES WASTE; LAY WASTE.

**waste away** Lose energy and energy, become weak gradually, as in *She was wasting away before our eyes.*

**waste not, want not** Wise use of one's resources will keep one from being poor. For example, *I just hate to throw out good food—waste not, want not.*

**waste one's breath** Speak in vain (because no one agrees), as in *Don't waste your breath complaining to the supervisor—it won't help.* Also see SAVE ONE'S BREATH.

**watch** In addition to the idioms beginning with WATCH, also see KEEP WATCH; LOOK (WATCH) OUT; ON THE LOOKOUT (WATCH).

**watched pot never boils, a** Anxious waiting does not speed up matters, as in *Stop running downstairs for every mail delivery—a watched pot never boils, you know.* This exaggerated saying reflects the experience of anyone who has ever been in a hurry to bring water to a boil, which eventually happens but can seem to take forever.

**watch it** Also, **watch out.** Be careful, as in *Watch it as you go down that ladder,* or *Watch out, there are a lot of cars on this road.* Also see LOOK OUT.

**watch *someone* like a hawk** Observe someone very closely, as in *I was watching him like a hawk, but I never did see him take your wallet.* This simile refers to the hawk's exceptionally keen sight.

**watch my dust** Also, **watch my smoke; eat my dust.** See how fast I am, or how quickly I'll succeed. For example, *I'm going to turn that investment into my first million, just you watch my dust,* or *I'll make it, just watch my smoke.* The first and third terms refer to the dust raised by a galloping horse; the second refers to the smoke generated by an engine.

**watch one's step** Be careful, as in *You'd better watch your step talking to them about a merger.* Often put as a warning, this phrase transfers taking care in walking to other kinds of caution.

**watch one's tongue** Be careful what one says, when one says it, or where one says it, as in *Watch your tongue around the children.*

**watch out** see LOOK OUT; WATCH IT.

**watch over** Guard someone or something for protection or safekeeping, as in *There were only two aides watching over that large group of children,* or *They hired a new guard to watch over the property.*

**watch the world go by** Relax and do nothing while other people are busy with their lives, as in *When I retire, I'm going to sit and watch the world go by.*

**water** In addition to the idioms beginning with WATER, also see ABOVE WATER; BLOOD IS THICKER THAN WATER; BLOW ONE OUT (OF THE WATER); COME ON IN (THE WATER'S FINE); DEAD IN THE WATER; FISH IN TROUBLED WATERS; FISH OUT OF WATER; HEAD ABOVE WATER, KEEP ONE'S; HELL OR HIGH WATER; HIGH-WATER MARK; HOLD WATER; HOT WATER; IN DEEP (WATER); LIKE WATER OFF A DUCK'S BACK; MAKE ONE'S MOUTH WATER; MUDDY THE WATERS; POUR COLD WATER ON; POUR OIL ON TROUBLED WATERS; STILL WATERS RUN DEEP; TAKE TO (LIKE A DUCK TO WATER); THROW OUT THE BABY WITH THE BATH WATER; TREAD WATER; YOU CAN LEAD A HORSE TO WATER.

**water down** Make something weaker or less substantial, as in *He watered down that unfavorable report with feeble excuses.*

**waterfront** see COVER THE FIELD (WATERFRONT).

**Waterloo** see MEET ONE'S WATERLOO.

**water over the dam** Also, **water under the bridge.** Something that is over and done with, especially an unfortunate event. For example, *Last year's problems with delivery are water over the dam,* or *Never mind that old quarrel; that's water under the bridge.* These phrases refer to water that has flowed over a dam or under a bridge and thus is gone forever.

**waterworks** see TURN ON THE WATERWORKS.

**wave** see MAKE WAVES.

**wavelength** see ON THE SAME WAVELENGTH.

**wax** In addition to the idiom beginning with WAX, also see WHOLE BALL OF WAX.

**wax and wane** Increase and decrease, as in size, number, strength, or intensity, as in *Enrollments in these programs wax and wane from year to year.* This expression refers to the phases of the moon, with its periodic changes in size.

**way** In addition to the idioms beginning with WAY, also see ALL THE WAY; BY THE WAY; BY

WAY OF; CAN'T PUNCH ONE'S WAY OUT OF A PAPER BAG; COME SOMEONE'S WAY; CUT BOTH WAYS; DOWNHILL ALL THE WAY; EVERY WHICH WAY; FEEL ONE'S WAY; FIND ONE'S WAY; FROM WAY BACK; GET ONE'S WAY; GIVE WAY; GO ALL THE WAY; GO A LONG WAY TOWARD; GO ONE'S WAY; GO OUT OF ONE'S WAY; HARD WAY; HAVE A WAY WITH; HAVE IT BOTH WAYS; HAVE ONE'S WAY WITH; IN A BAD WAY; IN A BIG WAY; IN A WAY; IN ONE'S WAY; IN THE FAMILY WAY; IN THE WAY; IN THE WORST WAY; KNOW ALL THE ANSWERS (ONE'S WAY AROUND); KNOW WHICH WAY IS UP; LAUGH ALL THE WAY TO THE BANK; LEAD THE WAY; LEARN THE HARD WAY; LIE ONE'S WAY OUT OF; LOOK THE OTHER WAY; MAKE ONE'S WAY; MAKE WAY; MEND ONE'S WAYS; MORE THAN ONE WAY TO SKIN A CAT; NOT BUILT THAT WAY; NO TWO WAYS ABOUT IT; NO WAY; ONE WAY OR ANOTHER; ON ONE'S WAY; ON THE WAY; ON THE WAY OUT; OTHER WAY ROUND; OUT OF HARM'S WAY; OUT OF THE WAY; PARTING OF THE WAYS; PAVE THE WAY; PAY ONE'S WAY; PICK ONE'S WAY; PUT IN THE WAY OF; RIGHT OF WAY; RUB ONE THE WRONG WAY; SEE ONE'S WAY TO; SET IN ONE'S WAYS; SHOW THE WAY; SMOOTH OVER (THE WAY); SWING BOTH WAYS; TAKE THE WRONG WAY; THAT'S HOW (THE WAY) THE BALL BOUNCES; UNDER WAY; WEND ONE'S WAY; WORK ONE'S WAY.

**way of the world, the** What often happens in life, and there's nothing one can do about it, as in *Don't blame yourself—it's just the way of the world.* A variant of this idiom, **ways of the world,** refers to how people usually act, as in *He doesn't really know the ways of the world, but he will soon enough.*

**wayside** see FALL BY THE WAYSIDE.

**way the wind blows, which** Also, **how the wind blows.** How matters stand, as in *Let's see which way the wind blows before we decide,* or *He's going to find out how the wind blows concerning a promotion.*

**way to go!** Well done, as in *That was a great lecture—way to go!* This exclamation of approval and encouragement originated in sports, addressed to athletes who are performing well, and later began to be used for any kind of achievement.

**wazoo** see UP THE WAZOO.

**weak** In addition to the idioms beginning with WEAK, also see SPIRIT IS WILLING BUT THE FLESH IS WEAK.

**weak as a kitten** Feeble and delicate, as in *After that bout with flu she was weak as a kitten.* This simile has largely replaced the earlier **weak as a cat.**

**weak link** The least dependable member of a group, as in *The shipping department, slow in getting out orders, is our weak link in customer service,* or *They're all very capable designers except for Ron, who is clearly the weak link.* This expression refers to the fragile portion of a chain, where it is most likely to break.

**weak moment, in a** At a time of weakness or little resistance, as in *In a weak moment I agreed to let our son rent a truck.*

**weakness** see HAVE A WEAKNESS FOR.

**wear** In addition to the idioms beginning with WEAR, also see IF THE SHOE FITS, WEAR IT; NONE THE WORSE FOR (WEAR); WORSE FOR WEAR.

**wear and tear** Damage and decay that result from ordinary use and exposure, as in *This sofa shows a lot of wear and tear; we should replace it.*

**wear another hat** Also, **wear a different hat** or **wear two hats; wear more than one hat.** Have more than one role or position, as in *I'm wearing another hat today; yesterday I was a mother, today I'm an attorney,* or *I wear two hats—are you asking me as a member of the city council or as a storeowner?* This expression refers to headgear worn for different occupations.

**wear down** Lessen something, weaken or tire someone by continual pressure, as in *The heels of these shoes are quite worn down,* or *Her constant nagging about getting a new car wore down his resistance.*

**wear off** Decrease gradually, lose effectiveness, as in *We'll wait till the drug wears off,* or *It looks as though the excitement has worn off.*

**wear one's heart on one's sleeve** Also, **pin one's heart on one's sleeve.** Openly show one's feelings, especially loving ones. For example, *You can't help but see how he feels about her; he wears his heart on his sleeve.* This expression refers to the former custom of tying a woman's favor, such as a scarf, to her lover's sleeve, thereby announcing their relationship.

**wear out 1.** Become or cause something to become unusable through long or heavy use, as in *She wears out her shoes in no time,* or *The motor in this device has worn out.* **2.** Exhaust someone, tire, as in *I was worn out from packing all those books.* Also see TIRED OUT.

**wear out one's welcome** Visit for longer than one's host wants, as in *She wanted to stay another few days but feared she would wear out her welcome.* This expression uses *wear out* in the sense of "exhaust" or "use up."

**wear the pants** Exercise controlling authority in a household, as in *Grandma wears the pants at our house.* This idiom, generally applied to women and dating from a time when they wore only skirts, equates pants with an authoritative male role. Originally put as *wear the breeches,* it remains in use despite current fashions.

**wear thin 1.** Be weakened or diminished gradually, as in *My patience is wearing thin.* **2.** Become less convincing, acceptable, or popular, as in *His excuses are wearing thin.* Both usages transfer the thinning of a physical object, such as cloth, to nonmaterial characteristics.

**wear two hats** see WEAR ANOTHER HAT.

**wear well** Hold up under continual or hard use; also, withstand criticism or the test of time. For example, *These boots have worn well,* or *His poetry wears well.*

**weasel out** Back out of a situation or commitment, especially in a sneaky way. For example, *I'd love to weasel out of serving on the board,* or *You promised to help us move, so don't weasel out now.* This expression refers to the stealthy hunting and nesting habits of the weasel, a small, slender-bodied predator.

**weather** In addition to the idiom beginning with WEATHER, also see FAIR-WEATHER FRIEND; HEAVY GOING (WEATHER); UNDER THE WEATHER.

**weather the storm** Live through hardship or difficulties, as in *If she can just weather the storm of that contract violation, she'll be fine.* This expression refers to a ship coming safely through bad weather. Also see RIDE OUT.

**weave in and out** Move by twisting and turning or winding in and out, as in *The motorcycle wove in and out of traffic, leaving us far behind.* This expression is redundant, since *weave* literally means "intertwine strands of thread."

**wedding** see SHOTGUN WEDDING.

**wedge in** Insert something in a very small space, as in *We were able to wedge the chair in between the wall and the window,* or *The doctor can wedge you in between three and four o'clock.*

**wedlock** see OUT OF WEDLOCK.

**weed *someone* out** Eliminate someone as inferior, unsuited, or unwanted, as in *She was asked to weed out the unqualified applicants.* This expression transfers removing weeds from a garden to removing unwanted elements from other activities.

**wee hours** see SMALL HOURS.

**weekend warrior** A person who participates in athletic activities only on weekends, as in *Those weekend warriors are always complaining about how sore they are.*

**weep buckets** Cry a lot, as in *That sad tale of lost love always made her weep buckets.*

**weepers** see FINDERS KEEPERS, LOSERS WEEPERS.

**weigh down** Burden someone, oppress, as in *Their problems have weighed them down.* This expression transfers bowing under a physical weight to emotional burdens.

**weigh in 1.** Be weighed; also, having a particular weight. For example, *Because it was such a small plane, the passengers and their luggage had to weigh in before takeoff,* or *The fish weighed in at 18 pounds.* **2.** Give one's opinion about something, as in *The senator weighed in on the tax issue.*

**weigh on** Also, **weigh upon.** Depress or burden someone, as in *His criticism weighed on her,* or *The long silence began to weigh upon us.*

**weigh one's words** Speak or write with great thoughtfulness or care, as in *The doctor weighed his words as he explained her illness.*

**weight** see BY WEIGHT; CARRY WEIGHT; DEAD WEIGHT; PULL ONE'S WEIGHT; PUT ON WEIGHT; TAKE THE WEIGHT OFF; THROW ONE'S WEIGHT AROUND; WORTH ONE'S WEIGHT IN GOLD.

**welcome** see WARM WELCOME; WEAR OUT ONE'S WELCOME; YOU'RE WELCOME.

**welcome mat** A friendly welcome, as in *They put out the welcome mat for all new members.* This expression refers to a doormat with the word "Welcome" printed on it.

**welcome to, be** Be happily or freely allowed to, as in *You're most welcome to join us,* or *He's welcome to borrow my car whenever he likes.* Also see YOU'RE WELCOME.

**well** In addition to the idioms beginning with WELL, also see ALIVE AND KICKING (WELL); ALL'S WELL THAT ENDS WELL; ALL VERY WELL; AS WELL; AS WELL AS; BODE WELL FOR; DAMN WELL; DO WELL; FULL WELL; GET WELL; LEAVE WELL ENOUGH ALONE; ONLY TOO (WELL); PRETTY WELL; SIT WELL WITH; THINK A LOT (WELL) OF; TO A FARE-THEE-WELL; VERY WELL; WEAR WELL.

**well and good** Also, **all well and good.** Acceptable, all right, as in *If you can get a better discount elsewhere, well and good,* or *Whatever she decides is all well and good.* Both of these expressions can also be preceded by *that is* or the contraction *that's,* as in *If you want to delay your payment, that's well and good,* or *If he can't be here, that's all well and good.*

**well aware, be** Also, **know perfectly well.** Be fully aware of a situation, as in *She's well aware of my limitations,* or *We were well aware that you would be late,* or *You knew perfectly well the results of your refusal to work,* or *Didn't he know perfectly well that we were serious?*

**well off** In fortunate circumstances, especially wealthy or prosperous, as in *They're quite well off now.* This phrase may be a shortening of *come well off,* that is, "emerge in good circumstances."

**well out of, be** Be lucky not to be involved in something, as in *You're well out of that marriage; he was never right for you.* This expression is a shortening of *well to be out of.*

**well preserved** Still active and in good health, as in *I can't believe he's 65; he's certainly well preserved.*

**well's run dry, the** A supply or resource has been used up, as in *There's no more principal left; the well's run dry,* or *There's not another novel in her; the well's run dry.* This expression compares an underground water source to other plentiful sources.

**wend one's way** Proceed along a course, go, as in *It's getting late; we should wend our way home.*

**west** see GO WEST.

**wet** In addition to the idioms beginning with WET, also see ALL WET; GET ONE'S FEET WET; LIKE (WET AS) A DROWNED RAT; MAD AS A HORNET (WET HEN).

**wet behind the ears** Also, **not dry behind the ears.** Immature, inexperienced, as in *How can you take instructions from Tom? He's still wet behind the ears,* or *Jane's not dry behind the ears yet.* This term refers to the fact that the last place to dry in a newborn colt or calf is the indentation behind its ears.

**wet blanket** A person who discourages enjoyment or enthusiasm, as in *Don't be such a wet blanket—the carnival will be fun!* This expression refers to smothering a fire with a wet blanket.

**wet one's whistle** Have a drink, as in *I'm just going to wet my whistle before I go out on the tennis court.* This expression uses *whistle* in the sense of "mouth" and may refer to the fact that it is very hard to whistle with dry lips.

**we wuz robbed** Also, **we was robbed** or **we were robbed.** We were cheated out of a victory; we were tricked or outsmarted. For example, *That ball was inside the lines—we wuz robbed!* This expression, with its attempt to reproduce nonstandard speech, is used most often in a sports context.

**whack** In addition to the idiom beginning with WHACK, also see HAVE A CRACK (WHACK) AT; OUT OF KILTER (WHACK).

**whacked out** **1.** Tired, exhausted, as in *They were whacked out after that long flight.* **2.** Crazy, especially under the influence of drugs. For example, *She looked whacked out when the police picked her up.*

**whack off** **1.** Cut something off, as in *The cook whacked off the fish's head with one blow,* or *The barber whacked off more hair than I wanted him to.* **2.** Masturbate, as in *He went to his room and whacked off.* [Vulgar slang]

W

**whale away at** Attack physically or verbally, as in *Our boys whaled away at the enemy,* or *The talk-show host whaled away at the hostile critics.* The word *whale* here does not refer to the ocean mammal; rather, it means "flog" or "thrash."

**whale of a time, a** A very enjoyable experience, as in *We had a whale of a time in Puerto Rico.* This idiom refers to the largest mammal to describe something very large and impressive.

**wham, bam, thank you ma'am** **1.** Of a sexual encounter, a man's brief, quick dismissal of his partner. For example, *It was just wham, bam, thank you ma'am and he was gone.* **2.** Performed very quickly or suddenly, as in *The construction was done in a wham, bam, thank you ma'am way.*

**what** In addition to the idioms beginning with WHAT, also see COME WHAT MAY; FOR ALL ONE IS (WHAT IT'S) WORTH; GET WHAT'S COMING TO ONE; IT'S (WHAT) A ZOO; JUST WHAT THE DOCTOR ORDERED; KNOW THE SCORE (WHAT'S WHAT); LEFT HAND DOESN'T KNOW WHAT THE RIGHT HAND IS DOING; NO MATTER (WHAT); OR WHAT; PRACTICE WHAT ONE PREACHES; SAUCE FOR THE GOOSE IS SAUCE FOR THE GANDER, WHAT'S; SO WHAT; YOU KNOW SOMETHING (YOU KNOW WHAT).

**what about?** **1.** Would you like, as in *What about another beer?* or *What about a game of bridge?* **2.** What do you think of, as in *So what about renting that white house on the corner?* **3.** Why, concerning what, as in *I need your frank opinion. What about?* **4. what about it?** What should we do, what course of action should be taken? For example, *We're supposed to be there at noon and bring two sandwiches each—now what about it?* Also see HOW ABOUT.

**what do you know** What a surprise, as in *What do you know, our suitcases are the first off the plane.*

**what do you take me for?** What sort of person do you think I am? For example, *What do you take me for, an idiot?*

**whatever** In addition to the idiom beginning with WHATEVER, also see OR WHATEVER.

**whatever turns one on** Also, **whatever floats one's boat.** It's not important enough or not worth knowing what someone will enjoy. For example, *Stay home and miss the party—whatever turns you on,* or *He's planning to open another restaurant—whatever floats his boat.* The first idiom uses *turn on* in the sense of "excite," and the variant refers to the ability of a boat to remain upright in the water.

**what for** **1.** For what purpose or reason, why, as in *I know you're going to England, but what for?* **2.** A punishment or scolding, as in *You'll get what for from Mom if she catches you smoking,* or *The teacher really gave Jim what for.*

**what gives** see WHAT'S COOKING; WHAT'S WITH.

**what goes around comes around** A person's good (or bad) behavior or treatment of others will lead to good (or bad) luck or treatment in the future. For example, *After firing a* *dozen people, he was fired himself—what goes around comes around.*

**what have you, and** What remains and need not be mentioned; and the like. For example, *The display room is full of stereos, TVs, and what have you.* This expression uses an old form of putting a question (using *have you* instead of *do you have*) as a noun clause, and *what* in the sense of "anything that." A synonym is **and who knows what,** as in *When we cleaned out the tool shed, we found old grass seed, fertilizer, and who knows what other junk.* Also see OR WHATEVER.

**what if?** Suppose that, as in *What if the speaker doesn't get here in time?* This expression is in effect a shortening of **what would happen if.**

**what in the world** see under ON EARTH.

**what is more** Also, **what's more.** In addition, furthermore, as in *I never got there; what's more, I never really intended to go.*

**what it takes** The necessary skill or qualities, as in *She's got what it takes to make a good doctor,* or *Inherited wealth is what it takes to maintain that lifestyle.* This idiom uses *what* in the sense of "that which" and *take* in the sense of "require."

**what makes one tick** What makes one function characteristically, what motivates one, as in *We've never figured out what makes these chess players tick.* This expression refers to *tick* in the sense of "function as an operating mechanism, such as a clock."

**what of it?** Also, **what's it to you?** What does it matter? Also, how does it concern or interest you? For example, *I know I don't need another coat but what of it?—I like this one,* or *What's it to you how many hours I sleep at night?* The first term is a synonym of SO WHAT. The second is another way of saying "mind your own business."

**what price?** How much will one have to pay or endure in order to accomplish a goal, as in *I hear he worked 20 years before he could start his own business. What price success?*

**what's cooking** Also, **what's new (with you)** or **what's up** or **what gives.** What's going on, what is happening, as in *What's cooking at the office these days?* or *What's new at your house?* or *Why are all those cars honking their horns? What's up?* or *Are you really going to France next week? What gives?* Also see WHAT'S WITH.

**what's done is done** There is no changing something; it's finished or final. For example, *I forgot to include all my income in my tax return, but what's done is done—I've already mailed the form.* This expression uses *done* in the sense of "ended" or "settled."

**what's eating one** Also, **what's bugging one.** What is annoying or bothering one. For example, *I have no idea what's eating her now,* or *What's bugging me is how long we had to wait to be served* The first slang term may use *eat* in the sense of "consume"; the variant uses *bug* in the sense of "annoy." Also see WHAT'S WITH.

**what's it to you** see WHAT OF IT.

**what's more** see WHAT IS MORE.

**what's new** see WHAT'S COOKING.

**what's one's beef?** Why is someone complaining? For example, *What's your beef about the way I'm doing things?* Also see HAVE A BEEF.

**what's the good of?** Also, **what's the use?** What purpose or advantage is there in something, as in *What's the good of crying when you can't do anything about it?* or *What's the use? She's impossible to convince.*

**what's the idea** Also, **what's the big idea; the very idea.** What do you think you are doing? What foolishness do you have in mind? For example, *What's the idea of taking the car without permission?* or *You've invited yourself along? What's the big idea?* or *Take a two-year-old on vacation? The very idea!* These phrases, all indicating the speaker's disapproval, use *idea* in the sense of "what one has in mind."

**what's the matter?** What is the difficulty or problem? What troubles you or makes you sick? For example, *You look upset—what's the matter?* or *Can you tell me what's the matter with my car?* This idiom uses *matter* in the sense of "the essence of something," in this case a problem. Also see WHAT'S WITH.

**what's the use** see WHAT'S THE GOOD OF.

**what's up** see WHAT'S COOKING.

**what's what** see KNOW WHAT'S WHAT.

**what's with?** Also, **what's up with?** or **what gives with?** What is going on with; tell me about it or explain it. For example, *What's with all the food they're giving away?* or *What's up with Lee these days?* or *What gives with Jack? Why is he so sad?* This idiom is also sometimes used as a substitute for **how are you** or **what's wrong,** as in *Hi, Pam, what's with you?* or *What gives with you—where have you been?*

**what the hell 1.** It's not important, who cares, as in *It cost a lot more, but what the hell, we can afford it.* Also see WHAT OF IT. **2.** An intensifier of *what,* as in *What the hell do you think you're doing?* Also see ON EARTH.

**what with** Taking into consideration, because of, as in *What with all you have to carry, we should take a taxi.* This usage replaced the earlier *what for.*

**wheel** In addition to the idioms beginning with WHEEL, also see ASLEEP AT THE SWITCH (WHEEL); AT THE WHEEL; BIG CHEESE (WHEEL); COG IN THE WHEEL; FIFTH WHEEL; GREASE (OIL)

THE WHEELS; HEAR THE WHEELS TURNING; HELL ON WHEELS; PUT ONE'S SHOULDER TO THE WHEEL; REINVENT THE WHEEL; SET (WHEELS) IN MOTION; SPIN ONE'S WHEELS; SQUEAKY WHEEL GETS THE GREASE.

**wheel and deal** Use or manipulate other people for one's own interest, especially in an aggressive or unfair way. For example, *Eddie's wheeling and dealing has made him rich but not very popular.* This term comes from gambling in the American West, where a *wheeler-dealer* was a heavy bettor on the roulette wheel and at cards. A variant, **wheeling and dealing,** is used as a verb and as a noun, as in *She's been wheeling and dealing all day,* or *If you'd listen to someone and stop all your wheeling and dealing, you might be more successful.*

**wheels in motion** see under SET IN MOTION.

**wheels turning** see HEAR THE WHEELS TURNING.

**wheels within wheels** Complex interacting processes, agents, or motives, as in *It's difficult to find out just which government agency is responsible; there are wheels within wheels.* This term refers to the complex interaction of gears.

**when** In addition to the idioms beginning with WHEN, also see CROSS A BRIDGE WHEN ONE COMES TO IT; PUSH COMES TO SHOVE, WHEN.

**when all's said and done** Also, **after all is said and done.** In the end, nevertheless, as in *When all's said and done, the doctors did what they could for him, but he was too ill to survive.*

**when hell freezes over** see WHEN PIGS FLY.

**when in Rome do as the Romans do** Follow local custom, as in *Kate said they'd all be wearing shorts or blue jeans to the outdoor wedding, so we'll do the same—when in Rome.*

**when it comes to** Also, **if it comes right down to** or **when it comes right down to.** As regards, when the situation entails. For example, *When it comes to renting or buying, you'll spend about the same amount.* It is also put as **when it comes down to it** or **when it comes down to that,** as in *If it comes right down to it, they said you could visit any time you're able to,* or *When it comes to that, we can lend you the fare.* This idiom uses *come to* in the sense of "amount to" or "be equivalent to."

**when it rains, it pours** Also, **it never rains but it pours.** When something happens, it often does so to excess. For example, *First my aunt said she and my uncle were coming for the weekend, and then my sister and her children said they were coming too—when it rains, it pours,* or *For a month we had no work, and now we have more than we can handle—it never rains but it pours.*

**when least expected** When something is not awaited, as in *My brother always calls when least expected,* or *You might know that the furnace would break down when least expected—we just had it rebuilt.*

**when one's back is turned** When one is away or not looking, as in *You can count on the children to misbehave when the teacher's back is turned,* or *I don't dare go on vacation; he'll take my job when my back is turned.* Also see WHEN THE CAT'S AWAY, THE MICE WILL PLAY.

**when one's ship comes in** When one has made one's fortune, as in *When my ship comes in, I'll get an expensive car.* This term refers to ships returning from distant off places with a valuable cargo.

**when pigs fly** Also, **when hell freezes over.** Never, as in *Sure he'll pay for the drinks—when pigs fly.* This expression compares the flight of pigs to something impossible. The idiom is also put as **pigs may fly.**

**when the cat's away, the mice will play** Without anyone to watch them, people will do as they please, especially in ignoring or breaking rules. For example, *As soon as their parents left, the children invited all their friends over—when the cat's away, you know.* This expression is so well known that it is often shortened, as in the example.

**when the chips are down** When a situation is urgent or desperate, as in *When the chips were down, all the children came home to help their mother.* This expression comes from poker, where *chips* represent money being bet. When all the bets have been made and the chips put down on the table, the hand is over and the players turn up their cards to see who has won.

**when the dust has settled** Also, **after the dust settles** or **once the dust settles.** When matters have calmed down, as in *The merger is complete, and when the dust has settled, we can start on new projects.* This idiom uses *dust* in the sense of "turmoil" or "commotion."

**when the going gets tough, the tough get going** see under GET GOING, def. 2.

**when the shit hits the fan** see SHIT WILL HIT THE FAN.

**when the spirit moves one** At the time one is ready to do something, and not before, as in *I'll wash the car when the spirit moves me.* Also see GOOD AND.

**where** In addition to the idioms beginning with WHERE, also see CLOSE TO HOME (HIT WHERE ONE LIVES); FOOLS RUSH IN WHERE ANGELS FEAR TO TREAD; GIVE CREDIT (WHERE CREDIT IS DUE); KNOW WHERE ONE STANDS; LET THE CHIPS FALL WHERE THEY MAY; NOT KNOW WHERE TO TURN; PUT ONE'S MONEY WHERE

ONE'S MOUTH IS; TELL SOMEONE WHERE TO GET OFF.

**where does one get off** Exactly who does one think he or she is, usually asked after that person has said or done something perceived as insulting or arrogant, as in *We won't put up with such treatment. Where does she get off?* Also see WHO DOES ONE THINK ONE IS.

**where do we go from here?** Given the present situation, what should we do next? For example, *Unemployment's rising and numerous banks have failed; where do we go from here?* This phrase is most often applied to the political, economic, social, or moral state of a country, business, or something similar.

**wherefore** see WHYS AND WHEREFORES.

**where it's at** Also, **where the action is.** The center of activity; where important things are happening. For example, *He decided to set up his store here, convinced that this is where it's at,* or *I'm going into the brokerage business; that's where the action is these days.* The action or activity in this phrase can relate to just about anything—financial, political, social, or commercial.

**where one is coming from** What one means, from one's point of view, based on one's background or prior experience. For example, *I don't believe in capital punishment, but a pacifist knows where I'm coming from.*

**where one lives** see under CLOSE TO HOME.

**where's the fire?** What's the big hurry, as in *We've got to finish up. Why, where's the fire?* This phrase, generally addressed to someone in an unseemly rush (such as a speeding motorist pulled over by a police officer), refers to firemen hurrying to put out a fire.

**where there's a will, there's a way** If one really wants to do something, one can. For example, *Max has no idea of how to get the money to repair his boat, but where there's a will.* This proverb is so well known it is often shortened, as in the example.

**where there's life there's hope** see WHILE THERE'S LIFE THERE'S HOPE.

**where there's smoke** see NO SMOKE WITHOUT FIRE.

**whether or not** Also, **whether or no.** Regardless of something happening or being done, no matter if. For example, *Whether or not it rains, we're going to walk to the theater,* or *She plans to sing at the wedding, whether or no anyone asks her to.* The negative element in these constructions may also follow the subject and verb, as in *I have to attend, whether I want to or not.*

**whet one's appetite** Arouse one's interest or eagerness, as in *That first song whetted my appetite; I hope she sings some others.* This idiom transfers making one hungry for food to other kinds of eagerness.

**which** In addition to the idiom beginning with WHICH, also see EVERY WHICH WAY; KNOW WHICH SIDE OF ONE'S BREAD IS BUTTERED; KNOW WHICH WAY IS UP; WAY THE WIND BLOWS, WHICH.

**which is which** What particular one is what particular one, or what is the difference between different ones. For example, *These twins look so much alike I can't tell which is which,* or *Both our raincoats are tan; do you know which is which?*

**which way the wind blows** see WAY THE WIND BLOWS.

**while** In addition to the idioms beginning with WHILE, also see ALL THE TIME (WHILE); A WHILE BACK; EVERY NOW AND THEN (ONCE IN A WHILE); FIDDLE WHILE ROME BURNS; GET OUT WHILE THE GETTING IS GOOD; IN A WHILE; MAKE HAY WHILE THE SUN SHINES; ONCE IN A WHILE; QUIT WHILE YOU'RE AHEAD; STRIKE WHILE THE IRON'S HOT; WORTH ONE'S WHILE.

**while away** Spend time idly or pleasantly, as in *It was a beautiful day, and we whiled away the hours in the garden.* This expression is the only surviving use of the verb *while,* meaning "spend time."

**while back** see A WHILE BACK.

**while the going is good** At this time there is an opportunity to do something and it should be done immediately or the chance may be lost, as in *She's job-hunting now, while the going is good.*

**while there's life there's hope** Also, **where there's life there's hope.** So long as someone or something ailing is alive, there is hope for recovery. For example, *The company has survived previous recessions; while there's life there's hope.* This expression was originally used only to refer to dying individuals. Today it is also applied to inanimate entities.

**whip** In addition to the idiom beginning with WHIP, also see CRACK THE WHIP; LICK (WHIP) INTO SHAPE; SMART AS A WHIP; UPPER (WHIP) HAND.

**whipping boy** A person who is punished for something that he or she is not responsible for, a scapegoat, as in *This department's always been the whipping boy when things don't go well.* This expression refers to the former practice of keeping a boy to be whipped in place of a prince who was to be punished.

**whip up** **1.** Arouse something, excite, as in *The speaker whipped up the mob.* **2.** Prepare something quickly, as in *I can easily whip up some lunch.*

**whirl** see GIVE SOMETHING A WHIRL; IN A WHIRL.

**whisker** see BY A HAIR (WHISKER); WIN BY A NOSE (WHISKER).

**whisper** see STAGE WHISPER.

**whispering campaign** A deliberate spreading of negative rumors about a candidate, as in *That whispering campaign destroyed his chances for election.*

**whistle** In addition to the idioms beginning with WHISTLE, also see BLOW THE WHISTLE ON; CLEAN AS A WHISTLE; SLICK AS A WHISTLE; WET ONE'S WHISTLE.

**whistle Dixie** Engage in unrealistic, hopeful fantasizing, as in *If you think you can drive there in two hours, you're whistling Dixie.* This idiom refers to the song "Dixie" and the vain hope that the Confederacy, known as *Dixie,* would win the Civil War.

**whistle for** Ask for or expect something without any prospect of success, as in *If you want a cash refund for that camera, you can just whistle for it.*

**whistle in the dark** Gather one's courage in a frightening situation, make a show of bravery. For example, *They knew they were lost and were just whistling in the dark.* This expression refers to a literal attempt to keep up one's courage.

**white** In addition to the idioms beginning with WHITE, also see BLACK AND WHITE; BLEED SOMEONE WHITE; GREAT WHITE HOPE.

**white as a sheet** Also, **white as a ghost.** Very pale in the face, as in *She was white as a sheet after that near encounter,* or *He turned white as a ghost when he saw us come in.* The first expression survives despite the fact that bedsheets now come in all colors; the second may refer to the paleness attributed to the spirits of dead people.

**white elephant** An unwanted or useless item, as in *The cottage at the lake had become a real white elephant—too rundown to sell, yet costly to keep up,* or *Grandma's ornate silver is a white elephant; no one wants it but it's too valuable to discard.*

**white flag, show the** Also, **hang out the white flag** or **hoist the white flag.** Surrender, yield, as in *Our opponents held all the cards tonight, so we showed the white flag and left early.* This expression refers to the white flag indicating a surrender in battle, a custom apparently dating from Roman times and adopted as an international symbol of surrender or truce.

**white lie** An untruth told to spare feelings or from politeness, as in *She asked if I liked her dress, and of course I told a white lie.* This term uses *white* in the sense of "harmless."

**white sale** A special offering of towels, bed linens, and similar goods, not necessarily white-colored. For example, *The big stores always have white sales in January.*

**who does one think one is** How important does a person think he or she is. This expression is used to say that the speaker thinks the individual is not important. For example, *She deleted my files without asking me—who does she think she is?* or *No matter who you think you are, you have no right to call me so late.* Also see WHERE DOES ONE GET OFF.

**who knows what** see under WHAT HAVE YOU.

**whole** In addition to the idioms beginning with WHOLE, also see AS A WHOLE; GO WHOLE HOG; ON THE WHOLE; OUT OF WHOLE CLOTH.

**whole ball of wax, the** Also, **the whole enchilada** or **the whole shooting match** or **the whole shebang.** Everything, all the elements, the entire affair. For example, *The union demanded higher wages, a pension plan, job security—the whole ball of wax,* or *The contract includes paperback rights, film rights, electronic media rights—the whole enchilada,* or *She lost her job, her pension, her health-care coverage, the whole shooting match.* Also see WHOLE KIT AND CABOODLE; WHOLE MEGILLAH.

**whole hog** see GO WHOLE HOG.

**whole kit and caboodle, the** Everything, every part, as in *He packed up all his gear, the whole kit and caboodle, and walked out.* This expression is redundant. *Kit* here means "a collection or group" (though this meaning survives only in the full idiom today), and *caboodle* means the same thing. In fact, *caboodle* is thought to be a corruption of the phrase *kit and boodle,* another redundant phrase, since *boodle* also meant "a collection."

**whole megillah** Also, **whole schmeer.** Everything, every aspect or element, as in *The accountant went through the whole megillah all over again,* or *Her divorce lawyer took him for the house, the car, the whole schmeer.* The first term refers to the *Megillah,* five books of the Bible read on certain Jewish feast days and considered by some to be very long and tedious. *Schmeer* is Yiddish for "smear" or "smudge."

**whole new ball game, a** A completely altered situation, as in *It will take a year to reassign the staff, and by then some will have quit and we'll have a whole new ball game.* This expression comes from baseball, where it means a complete turn of events, as when the team that was ahead falls behind. Now it is also used in other sports, such as basketball and football.

**whole nine yards, the** Everything that is relevant; the whole thing. For example, *He decided to take everything to college—his books, his stereo, his computer, his skis, the whole nine yards.*

**whole shebang** Also, **whole shooting match.** See WHOLE BALL OF WAX.

**whoop it up** **1.** Celebrate noisily, as in *After exams they decided to whoop it up at their apartment,* or *Down in the basement the resi-*

*dents were making whoopee.* **2.** Arouse enthusiasm, especially politically, as in *The volunteers' job is to whoop it up for the candidate.*

**who shall remain nameless** Also, **who shall go nameless.** No identification of the person being talked about will be given, out of consideration or kindness, as in *The people who stole the money shall be nameless.* The variant is also used humorously to say that naming the person is not necessary because everyone knows who he or she is, especially if that person is present. For example, *A certain person, who shall go nameless, is always late.* Also see YOU KNOW WHO.

**who's who** The outstanding or best-known individuals of a group, as in *Tonight's concert features a who's who of musicians.* This expression comes from the name of a famous reference work, *Who's Who,* which contains biographical sketches of famous individuals and is regularly updated. Its name in turn was based on the phrase **who is who,** that is, the identity of each of a number of persons.

**whys and wherefores** All the underlying causes and reasons, as in *She went into the whys and wherefores of the adoption agency's rules and procedures.* This idiom today is redundant because *why* and *wherefore* mean the same thing. Formerly, however, *why* indicated the reason for something and *wherefore,* how it came to be.

**wide** In addition to the idioms beginning with WIDE, also see CUT A WIDE SWATH; FAR AND WIDE; GIVE A WIDE BERTH TO; LAY (ONESELF WIDE) OPEN; LEAVE SOMETHING (WIDE) OPEN; OFF (WIDE OF) THE MARK.

**wide awake** Fully awake; also, very alert. For example, *He lay there, wide awake, unable to sleep,* or *She was wide awake to all the possibilities.* The *wide* in this idiom refers to the eyes being wide open.

**wide open 1.** Unresolved, unsettled, as in *The fate of that former colony is still wide open.* **2.** Unprotected or vulnerable, as in *That remark about immigrants left him wide open to hostile criticism.* This expression originated in boxing, where it means being off one's guard and open to an opponent's punches. Also see LEAVE OPEN.

**wig** In addition to the idiom beginning with WIG, also see FLIP ONE'S LID (WIG).

**wig out** Become or make one wildly excited or irrational, as in *He'll wig out when he gets the bill for that party.* This idiom probably refers to the earlier *flip one's wig* (see under FLIP ONE'S LID). Also see FREAK OUT, def. 2.

**wild** In addition to the idioms beginning with WILD, also see GO HOG WILD; RUN AMOK (WILD); SOW ONE'S WILD OATS.

**wild about, be** Be highly excited or enthusiastic about someone or something, as in *She was just wild about that jazz band from New Orleans.* This usage replaced the slightly earlier *wild after.*

**wild card** An unpredictable person or event, as in *Don't count on his support—he's a wild card,* or *A traffic jam? That's a wild card we didn't expect.* This expression comes from card games, especially poker, where it refers to a card that can stand for any rank chosen by the player who holds it. The term was adopted in sports for an additional player or team chosen to take part in a contest after the regular places have been taken. It is also used in computer terminology for a symbol that stands for one or more characters in searches for files that share a common specification.

**wilderness** see VOICE CRYING IN THE WILDERNESS.

**wildfire** see SPREAD LIKE WILDFIRE.

**wild goose chase** A useless search or pursuit, as in *I think she sent us on a wild goose chase looking for their beach house.* This idiom originally referred to a form of horseracing requiring riders to follow a leader in a particular formation (probably resembling a flock of geese in flight).

**wild horses couldn't drag one** Nothing could persuade one, as in *Wild horses couldn't drag them to that nightclub.* This idiom, always in negative form, is believed to have replaced *wild horses couldn't draw it from one,* referring to the medieval torture of using horses to stretch a prisoner and thereby force a confession.

**wild oats** see SOW ONE'S WILD OATS.

**wild pitch** A careless statement or action, as in *Calling comic books great literature—that's a wild pitch.* This term comes from baseball, where it refers to a pitched ball so far off target that the catcher misses it and a base runner is able to advance.

**will** see AGAINST ONE'S WILL; AT WILL; BOYS WILL BE BOYS; HEADS (WILL) ROLL; MURDER WILL OUT; OF ONE'S OWN ACCORD (FREE WILL); SHIT WILL HIT THE FAN; THAT WILL DO; TIME WILL TELL; TRUTH WILL OUT; WHEN THE CAT'S AWAY, THE MICE WILL PLAY; WHERE THERE'S A WILL, THERE'S A WAY; WITH A WILL; WITH THE BEST WILL IN THE WORLD; WONDERS WILL NEVER CEASE.

**willies** see under THE CREEPS.

**willing** see READY, WILLING, AND ABLE; SPIRIT IS WILLING BUT THE FLESH IS WEAK.

**will not hear of** see NOT HAVE IT.

**win** In addition to the idioms beginning with WIN, also see (WIN) HANDS DOWN; NO-WIN SITUATION; SLOW BUT SURE (STEADY WINS THE RACE); YOU CAN'T WIN; YOU CAN'T WIN 'EM ALL.

**win by a nose** Also, **win by a whisker.** Just barely succeed, as in *Sally's political cartoon* *came in first in the contest, but I heard that she won by a nose.* This term comes from horseracing, where it refers to a finish so close that only a portion of the horse's nose reaches the finish line ahead of the second horse. A *whisker*—that is, a hair—is a narrower margin yet.

**wind** In addition to the idioms beginning with WIND, also see BREAK WIND; GET WIND OF; GONE WITH THE WIND; ILL WIND; IN THE WIND; LEAVE ONE TWISTING IN THE WIND; LIKE GREASED LIGHTNING (THE WIND); PISS INTO THE WIND; SECOND WIND; STRAW IN THE WIND; TAKE THE WIND OUT OF ONE'S SAILS; THREE SHEETS TO THE WIND; THROW CAUTION TO THE WINDS; WAY THE WIND BLOWS.

**wind down** **1.** End or close gradually, as in *By midnight the party had wound down.* Also see WIND UP. **2.** Relax, as in *Today was a hard day, and we need some time to wind down.*

**windmill** see TILT AT WINDMILLS.

**window** In addition to the idioms beginning with WINDOW, also see OUT OF THE WINDOW.

**window-dressing** An addition or effect that is superficial, as in *That painting in his office is just window-dressing—he knows nothing about art,* or *Her willingness to listen to other people's ideas is window-dressing—she's already made up her mind.*

**window of opportunity** A brief time to do something, a chance that does not happen often, as in *We should buy a house now; the low interest rates are a window of opportunity.*

**window on the world** A chance to learn about life and people in other areas, as in *Taking that course in world literature gave me a window on the world.*

**wind up** **1.** Come or bring something to a finish, as in *The party was winding up, so we decided to leave,* or *Let's wind up the meeting and get back to work.* Also see WIND DOWN. **2.** Put something in order, settle, as in *She had to wind up her financial affairs before she could move.* **3.** Arrive somewhere following a course of action, end up, as in *We got lost and wound up in another town altogether,* or *If you're careless with your bank account, you can wind up overdrawn.* **4. be wound up.** Also, **get wound up.** Be very tense or excited, as in *She was so wound up I thought she'd never relax,* or *Don't let the children get all wound up before bedtime.*

**wine and dine** Entertain someone or treat someone to a fine meal, as in *The company likes to wine and dine visiting scientists,* or *Businesspeople spend a lot of time wining and dining.*

**wing** In addition to the idiom beginning with WING, also see CLIP SOMEONE'S WINGS; IN THE WINGS; LEFT WING; ON THE WING; TAKE FLIGHT (WING); UNDER SOMEONE'S WING.

**wing it** Make something up without planning in advance what one will do, as in *The interviewer had not read the author's book; he was just winging it.* This expression comes from the theater, where it refers to an actor studying a part in the wings (the areas to either side of the stage) because he or she has been suddenly called on to replace another actor. It eventually was extended to other kinds of improvisation based on lack of preparation.

**win hands down** Also, **win in a walk** or **win in a breeze.** See under HANDS DOWN.

**wink** In addition to the idiom beginning with WINK, also see FORTY WINKS; QUICK AS A WINK; SLEEP A WINK.

**wink at** Deliberately ignore something because it is illegal or unimportant, pretend not to see, as in *Sometimes it's wise to wink at a friend's shortcomings,* or *The police just winked at the illegal drug activity.* This idiom uses *wink* in the sense of "close one's eyes."

**winning streak** An unbroken series of successes, a run of good luck, as in *Our son-in-law has been on a winning streak with his investments.* This expression comes from gambling.

**win on points** Succeed but barely, especially by a technicality. For example, *Both sides were forceful in that argument about the new tax, but I think the senator won on points.* This term comes from boxing, where in the absence of a knockout the winner is decided on the basis of points awarded for each round.

**win out** Succeed, be successful in the end, as in *She was sure she'd win out if she persisted.*

**win over** Persuade someone, gain someone's support, as in *It won't be easy to win him over to our point of view.*

**win some, lose some** It's not possible to win all the time, as in *The coach was philosophical about our being shut out, saying "Win some, lose some."* This expression, generally said about a loss, originated among gamblers who bet on sporting events. A variant, **win some, lose some, some rained out,** suggests that the idiom comes from baseball. Also see YOU CAN'T WIN 'EM ALL.

**win the day** End successfully, be victorious, as in *We didn't know until the very end if they would win the day,* or *It seems that hard work won the day.* This term originally referred to the outcome of a battle.

**wipe** In addition to the idioms beginning with WIPE, also see MOP UP (WIPE) THE FLOOR WITH; SETTLE (WIPE OUT) A SCORE.

**wipe *something* off the map** Also, **wipe *something* off the face of the earth.** Eliminate something completely, as in *Some day we hope to wipe malaria off the map.* This idiom uses *wipe* in the sense of "obliterate," and *map* and *face of the earth* in the sense of "everywhere."

**wipe out 1.** Destroy something, as in *The large chains are wiping out the independent bookstores.* **2.** Kill someone; also, murder. For example, *The entire crew was wiped out in the plane crash,* or *The gangsters threatened to wipe him and his family out.* **3.** Lose one's balance on a surfboard and fall into the water, as in *The sea is so rough she's wiped out three times.*

**wipe the slate clean** see under CLEAN SLATE.

**wipe the smile off one's face** Stop smiling because it is making another person irritated or angry. For example, *They couldn't help but be amused when he fell in the mud, and he was so frustrated that he told them to wipe the smiles off their faces.* In this idiom *wipe* is used in the sense of "remove something as if by rubbing."

**wire** see DOWN TO THE WIRE; GET ONE'S WIRES CROSSED; LIVE WIRE; PULL STRINGS (WIRES); UNDER THE WIRE.

**wise** In addition to the idioms beginning with WISE, also see GET WISE TO; NONE THE WISER; PENNY WISE AND POUND FOOLISH; SADDER BUT WISER; WORD TO THE WISE.

**wise guy** An offensive know-it-all, a person who makes sarcastic or annoying remarks, as in *the teacher was delighted that the worst wise guy in the class was moving out of town.* Also see SMART ALECK.

**wise up** Make someone aware or become aware, informed, or sophisticated, as in *It's time someone wised you up to Mary; she's an incorrigible flirt,* or *As soon as Tony wised up to what the company was doing, he quit,* or *When will you wise up and stop gambling?*

**wish** In addition to the idioms beginning with WISH, also see IF WISHES WERE HORSES; MAKE ONE'S WISHES KNOWN; YOUR WORD (WISH) IS MY COMMAND.

**wishful thinking** Interpreting matters as one would like them to be, as opposed to what they really are. For example, *Matthew wanted to be a basketball player, but he was so short it was wishful thinking.* This term comes from Freudian psychology.

**wish *something* on** Force or impose something on another, as in *I wouldn't wish this job on my worst enemy.* The complete idiom is **wish something on one's worst enemy,** as in the example.

**wish someone well** Wish someone good luck or success, as in *We talked briefly, then I wished them well and went on my way.* This expression also has a negative form, **wish one ill,** as in *As far as I know, she's never wished anyone ill.*

**wit** see AT ONE'S WIT'S END; HAVE ONE'S WITS ABOUT ONE; LIVE BY ONE'S WITS; SCARE OUT OF ONE'S WITS; TO WIT.

**witching hour** Midnight, as in *They arrived just at the witching hour.* This term refers to superstitions concerning the time for witchcraft and other supernatural events.

**with** In addition to the idioms beginning with WITH, also see ALIVE WITH; ALL OVER WITH; ALL RIGHT WITH; ALONG WITH; AT HOME (WITH); AT ODDS (WITH); AT ONE (WITH); BEAR WITH; BORN WITH A SILVER SPOON; BOTH BARRELS, WITH; BOUND UP IN (WITH); BREAK WITH; BURST WITH; CAN DO WITH; CAN'T DO ANYTHING WITH; CAST ONE'S LOT WITH; CAUGHT WITH ONE'S PANTS DOWN; CHARGE WITH; CLEAR WITH; COME DOWN WITH; COME OUT WITH; COME TO GRIPS WITH; COME TO TERMS (WITH); COME UP WITH; COME WITH THE TERRITORY; COOKING WITH GAS; DAMN WITH FAINT PRAISE; DEAL WITH; DIE WITH ONE'S BOOTS ON; DISPENSE WITH; DO AWAY WITH; DOWN WITH; FALL IN WITH; FENCE WITH; FIGHT FIRE WITH FIRE; FIT IN (WITH); GET ALONG (WITH); GET AN IN WITH; GET AWAY WITH; GET INVOLVED (WITH); GET IN WITH; GET ON (WITH IT); GET OVER (WITH); GET TOGETHER (WITH); GET TOUGH WITH; GO ALONG (WITH); GO HALVES (WITH); GO HARD WITH; GONE WITH THE WIND; GO OUT (WITH); GO THROUGH (WITH); GO TO BED WITH; GO WITH; GO WITH THE FLOW; GREEN WITH ENVY; HANDLE SOMEONE WITH GLOVES; HAVE A BRUSH WITH; HAVE A WAY WITH; HAVE A WORD WITH; HAVE DONE (WITH); HAVE NO TRUCK WITH; HAVE PULL WITH; HAVE TO DO WITH; HAVE WORDS WITH; HOLD WITH; IN BAD WITH; IN BED WITH; IN GOOD WITH; IN LEAGUE WITH; IN (WITH) REGARD TO; IN TROUBLE WITH; IN WITH; IT'S ALL OVER WITH; KEEP UP WITH; KILL SOMEONE WITH KINDNESS; LAUGH AND THE WORLD LAUGHS WITH YOU; LEAD WITH ONE'S CHIN; LEARN TO LIVE WITH; LEVEL WITH; LIE WITH; LIKE A CHICKEN WITH ITS HEAD CUT OFF; LISTEN WITH HALF AN EAR; OVER AND DONE WITH; OVER WITH; PAL AROUND WITH; PART WITH; PLAY BALL (WITH); PLAY WITH FIRE; PUT UP WITH; RECKON WITH; ROLL WITH THE PUNCHES; RUB ELBOWS WITH; RUN AROUND (WITH); RUN AWAY WITH; RUN OFF WITH; RUN WITH; SADDLE SOMEONE WITH; SEE WITH HALF AN EYE; SETTLE WITH; SHAKE HANDS WITH; SHAKE WITH LAUGHTER; SIDE WITH; SIGN ON (WITH); SIT WELL WITH; SLEEP WITH; SPAR WITH; SQUARE WITH; STAY WITH; STICK WITH; STUCK WITH; SWIM WITH THE SHARKS; SWIM WITH THE TIDE; TAKE ISSUE WITH; TAKEN WITH; TAKE THE BITTER WITH THE SWEET; TAKE THE ROUGH WITH THE SMOOTH; TAKE UP WITH; TAMPER WITH; TARRED WITH THE SAME BRUSH; TAX WITH; TEAM UP WITH; TINKER WITH; TOGETHER WITH; TO HELL WITH; TOP OFF (WITH); TO START

WITH; TOY WITH; TROUBLE ONE'S HEAD WITH; VOTE WITH ONE'S FEET; WALK OFF WITH; WHAT'S WITH; WHAT WITH; YOU CAN'T TAKE IT WITH YOU.

**with a grain of salt** Also, **with a pinch of salt.** With reservations. For example, *I always take Sandy's stories about illness with a grain of salt—she tends to exaggerate.* This expression is a translation of the Latin *cum grano salis.*

**with all due respect** Although I think highly of you, as in *With all due respect, you haven't really answered my question,* or *With all due respect, that account doesn't fit the facts.* This phrase always comes before a polite disagreement with what a person has said or brings up a controversial point.

**with all one's heart** With great willingness or pleasure; also, with the deepest feeling or devotion. For example, *I wish you well with all my heart.*

**with an eye to** see HAVE ONE'S EYE ON, def. 2.

**with a vengeance** With great violence or energy; also, to an extreme degree. For example, *The house was filthy, and Ruth began cleaning with a vengeance,* or *December has turned cold with a vengeance.* Also see WITH A WILL.

**with a view to** For the purpose of, aiming toward, as in *A-frame houses were designed with a view to avoiding heavy accumulations of snow.*

**with a will** Vigorously, energetically, as in *He started pruning the bushes with a will.* This term uses *will* in the sense of "determination."

**with bad grace** Reluctantly, rudely, as in *He finally agreed to share the cost, but with bad grace.* Also see WITH GOOD GRACE.

**with bated breath** Eagerly or anxiously, as in *We waited for the announcement of the winner with bated breath.* This expression literally means "holding one's breath" (*bate* means "restrain"). Today it is also used somewhat ironically, indicating one is not all that eager or anxious. Also see HOLD ONE'S BREATH, def. 2.

**with bells on** Ready to celebrate, eagerly, as in *Of course I'll come; I'll be there with bells on.* This expression refers to decorating oneself or one's clothing with little bells for some special performance or occasion.

W

**wither on the vine** Fail to happen or mature, as in *This building project will wither on the vine if they don't agree on a price.* This expression refers to grapes drying up because they were not picked when ripe.

**with flying colors, pass with** Also, **come through with flying colors.** Win, succeed, as in *She came through the bar exam with flying colors.* This expression refers to a victorious ship sailing with its flags high.

**with good grace** Willingly, pleasantly, as in *They had tried hard to win but accepted their loss with good grace.* Also see WITH BAD GRACE.

**with half a heart** see HALF A HEART.

**within** In addition to the idioms beginning with WITHIN, also see IN (WITHIN) REASON; IN (WITHIN) VIEW; LIVE WITHIN ONE'S MEANS; SPITTING DISTANCE, WITHIN; WHEELS WITHIN WHEELS.

**within an inch of** Very close to, within a narrow margin of, as in *We were within an inch of buying tickets for that concert.*

**within bounds** Reasonable and allowable, up to a certain point, as in *It's all right to play your stereo, but please keep the volume within bounds.* Like its antonym, OUT OF BOUNDS, this term originally referred to the boundaries of a playing area or field.

**within reach** see IN REACH.

**within reason** see IN REASON.

**with interest** With more than what one should receive, extra, and then some. For example, *Mary borrowed Jane's new dress without asking, but Jane paid her back with interest—she drove off in Mary's car.* This idiom refers to *interest* in the financial sense.

**within the orbit of** see IN THE ORBIT OF.

**with it, be** Also, **get with it. 1.** Be or become knowledgeable about the latest trends, fashions, or ideas, as in *She just turned 60, but she's still very much with it,* or *Get with it, Dad, that kind of razor hasn't been made for years.* **2.** Be able to work properly or think clearly, as in *I need to take a break—I'm just not with it today,* or *It's time you got with it and did what we pay you to do.* The variant **get with it** is also often used in the idiom **get with the program,** as in *You'll enjoy your classes more if you just get with the program.*

**with one, be 1.** Understand what another is saying, as in *I'm trying to be clear—are you with me?* **2.** Support another or agree with another's decision. For example, *I'm with you—let's get to work.* **3.** Join or help someone soon, as in *A client is on the other line—I'll be with you in a moment.*

**with one arm tied behind one's back** Also, **with one hand** or **with one's eyes closed.** Very easily, as in *I can assemble that chair with one arm tied behind my back,* or *I could make a better dinner with one hand,* or *He can do that puzzle with his eyes closed.* All these phrases are exaggerations. Also see DO BLINDFOLDED.

**with one's eyes open** Fully aware, as in *We started this project with our eyes open and are not surprised at the results.* Also see KEEP ONE'S EYES OPEN.

**with one's pants down** see CAUGHT WITH ONE'S PANTS DOWN.

**with one voice** Unanimously, in complete agreement, as in *The board rejected the proposal with one voice.* Also see AS ONE; TO A MAN.

**with open arms** Enthusiastically, warmly, as in *They received their new daughter-in-law with open arms.* This term refers to an embrace.

**without** In addition to the idioms beginning with WITHOUT, also see ABSENT WITHOUT LEAVE; DO WITHOUT; GET ALONG (WITHOUT); GOES WITHOUT SAYING; LOST WITHOUT; NO SMOKE WITHOUT FIRE.

**without a leg to stand on** With no chance of success, as in *He tried to get the town to change the streetlights, but because there was no money in the budget, he found himself without a leg to stand on.* A related idiom is **not have a leg to stand on,** as in *Once the detective exposed his false alibi, he didn't have a leg to stand on.* This idiom transfers lack of physical support to arguments or theories.

**without a stitch on** Naked, as in *They let their baby run around outside without a stitch on.* A related phrase is **not have a stitch on.** These expressions use *stitch* in the sense of "a piece of clothing."

**without batting an eye** Also, **without blinking an eye.** Showing no emotion, acting as though nothing were unusual. For example, *Richard ate the snails without batting an eye,* or *She watched the gang rob the store without blinking an eye.* Related phrases include **not bat an eye** or **not blink an eye,** as in *He didn't bat an eye when she told him he was being laid off.*

**without doubt** Also, **without a doubt.** See NO DOUBT.

**without fail** For certain, as in *That check will arrive tomorrow morning without fail.* This idiom today is used mainly to strengthen a statement.

**without further ado** Also, **without more ado.** Without more work, ceremony, or fuss. For example, *Without further ado they adjourned the meeting and went home,* or *And now, without more ado, here is our speaker of the day.* This idiom has one of the few surviving uses of the noun *ado,* meaning "what is being done." (Another is MUCH ADO ABOUT NOTHING.)

**without question** Certainly, undoubtedly, as in *Without question, he's the best editor we've ever had.*

**without so much as** With not even, as in *She stormed out without so much as a goodbye.* This expression is also put as **without so much as a by your leave,** meaning "without asking one's permission or agreement," as in *Without so much as a by your leave, he drove off in my car.*

**with reason** For a cause, justifiably, as in *He turned down their offer, but with reason—he didn't want to move his family to a big city.*

**with reference to** Also, **with regard to** or **with respect to.** See IN REGARD TO.

**with the best of them** As well as anyone, as in *Donna can pitch a ball with the best of them.*

**with the best will in the world** No matter how much one wants to or tries, as in *I couldn't eat another bite, not with the best will in the world.*

**with the exception of** see EXCEPT FOR.

**with the gloves off** With or ready to engage in rough treatment, as in *Prepared to oppose the council, the mayor marched into the meeting with the gloves off.* This idiom refers to the early days of boxing, when gloves were not used.

**wives** see OLD WIVES' TALE.

**wolf** In addition to the idioms beginning with WOLF, also see CRY WOLF; KEEP THE WOLF FROM THE DOOR; LONE WOLF; THROW SOMEONE TO THE WOLVES.

**wolf down one's food** Eat food as though one is very hungry, in a great rush, or lacking table manners. For example, *She knew the child was hungry by the way he wolfed down his food,* or *Stop wolfing your food down—the ball game will wait,* or *What a slob—look how he wolfs his food down.*

**wolf in sheep's clothing** An enemy disguised as a friend, as in *Dan was a wolf in sheep's clothing, pretending to help but all the while spying for our competitors.* This term comes from the ancient fable about a wolf that dresses up in the skin of a sheep and sneaks up on a flock.

**woman** see MARKED MAN (WOMAN); (WOMAN) OF FEW WORDS; OWN PERSON (WOMAN); RIGHT-HAND MAN (WOMAN); SCARLET WOMAN.

**wonder** In addition to the idiom beginning with WONDER, also see NO WONDER; WORK WONDERS.

**wonders will never cease** What a surprise, as in *He's on time—wonders will never cease.* This expression is generally used ironically.

**won't hear of** see under NOT HAVE IT.

**won't wash** Will not stand up to examination, is unconvincing, will not work, as in *That excuse about your sick aunt just won't wash.* This expression originally referred to a fabric that would not endure washing and was later used figuratively for other kinds of failure.

**wood** see BABE IN THE WOODS; CAN'T SEE THE FOREST (WOOD) FOR THE TREES; KNOCK ON WOOD; NECK OF THE WOODS; OUT OF THE WOODS.

**wool** see PULL THE WOOL OVER SOMEONE'S EYES.

**word** In addition to the idioms beginning with WORD, also see ACTIONS SPEAK LOUDER THAN WORDS; AT A LOSS (FOR WORDS); AT A WORD; BREAK ONE'S WORD; EAT ONE'S WORDS; FAMOUS LAST WORDS; FIGHTING WORDS; FOUR-LETTER WORD; FROM THE WORD GO; GET A WORD IN EDGEWISE; GIVE THE WORD; GO BACK ON (ONE'S WORD); GOOD AS ONE'S WORD; HANG ON SOMEONE'S WORDS; HAVE A WORD WITH; HAVE WORDS WITH; IN BRIEF (A WORD); IN OTHER WORDS; IN SO MANY WORDS; KEEP ONE'S WORD; LAST WORD; LEAVE WORD; MAN OF HIS WORD; MARK MY WORDS; MINCE MATTERS (WORDS); MUM'S THE WORD; NOT BREATHE A WORD; NOT OPEN ONE'S MOUTH (UTTER A WORD); OF FEW WORDS; PICTURE IS WORTH A THOUSAND WORDS; PLAY ON WORDS; PUT IN A GOOD WORD; PUT INTO WORDS; PUT WORDS IN SOMEONE'S MOUTH; SAY THE WORD; SOMEONE'S WORD IS LAW; SWALLOW ONE'S WORDS; TAKE ONE'S WORD FOR IT; TAKE SOMEONE AT HIS OR HER WORD; TAKE THE WORDS OUT OF SOMEONE'S MOUTH; TRUE TO (ONE'S WORD); WEIGH ONE'S WORDS; YOUR WORD IS MY COMMAND.

**word for word** Exactly as written or spoken, as in *That was the forecast, word for word.* This phrase is also used as an adjective, as in *I gave him a word-for-word translation of the letter.*

**word is that, the** Also, **word has it that.** A report about a person, an event, or a situation that is presented as a fact, as in *The word is that she's divorcing him,* or *Word has it that you've been promoted.*

**word of honor** A pledge of one's good faith, as in *On his word of honor he assured us that he was telling the truth.*

**word of mouth, by** Orally, by one person telling another, as in *They don't advertise; they get all their customers by word of mouth.*

**words fail me** I can't put my thoughts or feelings into words, especially because of surprise or shock, as in *When she showed up at the wedding with all three ex-husbands—well, words fail me.*

**words stick in one's throat** see STICK IN ONE'S THROAT.

**words to that effect** see TO THAT EFFECT.

**word to the wise, a** Here's good advice, as in *A word to the wise: don't walk alone here, because these streets are not safe at night.* This phrase is a shortening of *A word to the wise is enough.*

W

**work** In addition to the idioms beginning with WORK, also see ALL IN A DAY'S WORK; ALL WORK AND NO PLAY; AT WORK; BUSY WORK; DIRTY WORK; GET DOWN (TO WORK); GOOD WORKS; GUM UP (THE WORKS); HAVE ONE'S WORK CUT OUT; IN THE WORKS; IN WORKING ORDER; MAKE SHORT WORK OF; OUT OF WORK; SHOOT THE WORKS; THE WORKS; TURN (WORK) OUT ALL RIGHT.

**work both sides of the street** Pretend to be on the side of only one person or group but really work for both without either knowing it, as in *The real estate agent was known for working both sides of the street, advising first the buyer and then the seller.* This term transfers opposite sides of a street to opposite sides of a negotiation.

**worked up, be** Also, **get all worked up.** Be or become excited or upset, as in *She got all worked up about the idea of adopting a baby.* Also see WORK UP.

**work in 1.** Insert or introduce something, as in *As part of their presentation they worked in a request for funding the exhibit.* Similarly, **work into** means "insert or introduce something into something else," as in *She worked more flour into the mixture.* **2.** Make time for something in a schedule, as in *The dentist said he would try to work her in this morning.* Here, too, **work into** is sometimes used, as in *She had to work two emergency cases into her morning schedule.*

**working knowledge of, have a** Know enough about a particular subject, academic discipline, machine, or process that one can perform or respond in an adequate way, as in *She has a working knowledge of accounting—maybe she can help us with our taxes.*

**work it** Arrange or plan something, bring about, as in *We'll try to work it so that the board meets tomorrow.*

**work it out** Resolve an unpleasant situation or solve a problem. For example, *We disagree about what we should do next, but I think we can work it out,* or *If we have enough time to identify the problem, I'm sure we can work it out.*

**work like a beaver** Also, **work like a dog** or **work like a horse.** Work very energetically and hard, as in *She worked like a beaver to clean out all the closets,* or *I've been working like a dog weeding the garden,* or *He's very strong and works like a horse.* Also see WORK ONE'S FINGERS TO THE BONE.

**work like a charm** Function very well, have a good effect or outcome, as in *That knife sharpener works like a charm,* or *Her deferential manner worked like a charm; he agreed to everything they'd asked for.* This expression uses *charm* in the sense of "a magic spell." Also see WORK WONDERS.

**work like a dream** Perform or operate without any problems, as in *This new vacuum cleaner works like a dream.*

**work off** Get rid of something by work or effort, as in *They worked off that big dinner by running on the beach,* or *It'll take him* *months to work off that debt.* Also see WORK OUT, def. 4.

**work on** Also, **work upon.** Exercise influence on someone, persuade, as in *If you work on him, he might change his mind,* or *She always worked upon their feelings by pretending to be more ill than she really was.*

**work oneself to death** Work so hard and so long that one dies, as in *I won't work myself to death like my mother did.* This idiom is often used to exaggerate a situation. For example, *My boss is determined that we'll all work ourselves to death.*

**work one's fingers to the bone** Also, **work one's tail off** or **work one's butt off.** Exert oneself, labor very hard, as in *She's working her fingers to the bone to support her children,* or *I work my tail off, and then the government takes half my income in taxes.* The first exaggerated phrase calls up the image of working the skin and flesh off one's fingers.

**work one's way** Exert oneself to proceed in a particular direction; also, finance a project by working. For example, *The painters are working their way from the top floor to the basement,* or *I'm trying to work my way into the publishing world,* or *She's working her way through college.* A variant of this idiom, **work one's way up,** means "start a job in the lowest position and gradually be promoted to the top (of a business or organization)."

**work out 1.** Accomplish something by work or effort, as in *I think we can work out a solution to this problem.* For **work out all right,** see TURN OUT ALL RIGHT. **2.** Find a solution for a problem, solve, as in *They hoped to work out their personal differences,* or *Can you help me work out this equation?* Also see WORK IT OUT. **3.** Formulate or develop something, as in *We were told to work out a new plan,* or *He's very good at working out complicated plots.* **4.** Get rid of a debt by working instead of paying money, as in *She promised she'd work out the rest of the rent by babysitting for them.* Also see WORK OFF. **5.** Prove effective or successful, as in *I wonder if their marriage will work out.* **6.** Have a specific result, add up, as in *It worked out that she was able to go to the party after all,* or *The total works out to more than a million dollars.* **7.** Engage in energetic exercise for physical conditioning, as in *He works out with weights every other day.* **8.** Use up a resource, such as a source of ore, as in *This mine has been completely worked out.*

**work *someone* over** Beat someone up, as in *The secret police worked him over, and he's never been the same.*

**work up 1.** Also, **get all worked up.** Be or become very excited or annoyed. For example, *You were really worked up about something. What happened?* or *He got all worked up because we forgot to buy bread.* **2.** Increase one's skill, status, or responsibility through effort, as in *He worked up to 30 situps a day,* or *She worked up to bank manager.* Also see WORK ONE'S WAY. **3.** Intensify gradually, as in *The film worked up to a thrilling climax.* **4.** Develop or produce something by effort, as in *Swimming always works up an appetite.*

**work wonders** Also, **work miracles; do wonders.** Succeed, produce a good outcome, as in *The new coat of paint works wonders with this bedroom,* or *The physical therapy has worked miracles with these patients,* or *That vacation did wonders for you.* Also see WORK LIKE A CHARM.

**world** In addition to the idioms beginning with WORLD, also see ALL OVER THE PLACE (WORLD); BEST OF BOTH WORLDS; BRAVE NEW WORLD; BRING INTO THE WORLD; COME UP (IN THE WORLD); DEAD TO THE WORLD; FOR ALL THE WORLD; HAVE THE WORLD AT ONE'S FEET; IN ONE'S OWN WORLD; IT'S A SMALL WORLD; LAUGH AND THE WORLD LAUGHS WITH YOU; MAN OF THE WORLD; MOVE UP (IN THE WORLD); NOT FOR ALL THE TEA IN CHINA (FOR THE WORLD); NOT THE END OF THE WORLD; ON EARTH (IN THE WORLD); ON TOP OF THE WORLD; OUT OF THIS WORLD; SEE THE WORLD; SET THE WORLD ON FIRE; THINK A LOT (THE WORLD) OF; THINK THE WORLD OWES ONE A LIVING; THINK THE WORLD REVOLVES AROUND ONE; THIRD WORLD; WINDOW ON THE WORLD; WITH THE BEST WILL IN THE WORLD.

**world is one's oyster, the** Everything is going well, as in *I was younger then, and the world was my oyster.* In this term the oyster is something from which to extract great profit, such as a pearl.

**world of difference, there's a** Two or more people or things have little in common, as in *In spite of their physical likeness, there's a world of difference between the twins in their political views,* or *There's a world of difference between social drinking and alcoholism.*

**world of good, a** A great benefit, as in *A vacation will do you a world of good.* This expression uses *world* in the sense of "a great deal."

**worlds apart, be 1.** Be separated by a great distance, as in *Although they live worlds apart, the two sisters are very close.* **2.** Also, **poles apart.** Have very different approaches to life, political views, or activities. For example, *We're worlds apart on animal rights,* or *That couple is poles apart on how to raise children.* Also see WORLDS AWAY.

**worlds away, be 1.** Be mentally distant from a situation, daydream. For example, *I* *could tell she was worlds away when we tried to explain what had happened,* or *He misses most of what the teacher says because he's worlds away.* **2.** With very different views or approaches, as in *We're worlds away from each other on the issue of civil rights.*

**worm** In addition to the idioms beginning with WORM, also see CAN OF WORMS; EARLY BIRD CATCHES THE WORM.

**worm into** Insinuate oneself subtly or gradually, as in *He tried to worm into her confidence.* This idiom refers to the weaving path of a worm.

**worm out of** Get information or make one's way by artful or deceptive means. For example, *He tried to worm the answer out of her,* or *She can't worm out of this situation.* This expression refers to the steady passage of a worm.

**worm turns, the** Also, **the worm has turned.** Even a very tolerant person will one day lose patience. For example, *He bullied his assistant for years, but one day the worm turned, and she walked out without notice, taking along his best clients.* This expression comes from the proverb *Tread on a worm and it will turn.*

**worn out** see WEAR OUT.

**worn to a frazzle** In a state of nervous exhaustion, as in *The very idea of moving again has us worn to a frazzle.* This expression transfers *frazzle,* which means "a frayed edge," to one's feelings.

**worry** In addition to the idiom beginning with WORRY, also see NOT TO WORRY.

**worry *one* sick** Also, **worry *one* to death.** Be extremely anxious, as in *Her parents worry sick when she doesn't come home on time,* or *We worry to death about the drop in the stock market.* These are somewhat exaggerated phrases, since one might feel ill from worrying but would hardly die from it.

**worse** In addition to the idiom beginning with WORSE, also see ALL THE (WORSE); BARK IS WORSE THAN ONE'S BITE; FATE WORSE THAN DEATH; FOR BETTER OR FOR WORSE; FROM BAD TO WORSE; IF WORST (WORSE) COMES TO WORST; NONE THE WORSE FOR; TAKE A TURN FOR THE BETTER (WORSE). Also see under WORST.

**worse for wear** Also, **the worse for the wear.** In poor physical condition owing to long use; also, drunk. For example, *This television set is really worse for the wear; we'll have to replace it with a newer model,* or *He'd better not drive home; he's definitely the worse for the wear.* For an antonym, see NONE THE WORSE FOR.

**worship the ground someone walks on** Regard someone with awe, as in *Jim just worships the ground his father walks on.* This idiom exaggerates one's deep admiration or romantic feeling.

**worst** see AT WORST; GET (HAVE) THE WORST OF IT; IF WORST COMES TO WORST; IN THE WORST WAY. Also see under WORSE.

**worth** In addition to the idioms beginning with WORTH, also see BIRD IN THE HAND (IS WORTH TWO IN THE BUSH); FOR ALL ONE IS WORTH; FOR WHAT IT'S WORTH; GET ONE'S MONEY'S WORTH; NOT WORTH A DAMN; PICTURE IS WORTH A THOUSAND WORDS.

**worth one's keep, be** Work well enough to deserve what one earns, as in *He's not worth his keep as a team player.* Also see WORTH ONE'S SALT.

**worth one's salt, be** Perform a job or task in an excellent way, as in *If you were worth your salt, you'd do something about that problem.* This idiom is also often used in the negative, as in *That boy is not worth his salt.* Also see WORTH ONE'S KEEP.

**worth one's weight in gold** Also, **worth its weight in gold.** Very valuable, as in *John's been extremely helpful; he's worth his weight in gold,* or *That tractor's been worth its weight in gold.*

**worth one's while** Also, **worth it. 1.** Merit one's time or efforts, as in *It's hardly worth your while to count the sales; it can be done by computer,* or *Don't bother looking for the letter—it's not worth it.* **2. make something worth one's while.** Pay one for one's time or efforts, as in *If you take care of our yard while we're away, I'll make it worth your while,* or *If I have to do the dishes again, it had better be worth it.* Both expressions use *while* in the sense of "a period of time spent."

**worthy of the name** Deserving a name or description, as in *Any artist worthy of the name can draw better than that.* This expression uses *worthy of* in the sense of "deserving by reason of merit."

**would** In addition to the idioms beginning with WOULD, also see AS LUCK WOULD HAVE IT. Also see under WOULDN'T.

**wouldn't** In addition to the idiom beginning with WOULDN'T, also see BUTTER WOULDN'T MELT; CAUGHT DEAD, WOULDN'T BE; NOT (WOULDN'T) LIFT A FINGER. Also see under NOT.

**wouldn't dream of** Also, **not dream of.** Not occur to one, not consider, as in *Even if it were lying open on my desk, I wouldn't dream of reading another person's letter.* This expression uses *dream of* in the sense of "remotely think of."

**would rather** Prefer to, as in *We would rather eat dinner before the movie.*

**would that** I wish that, as in *Would that I could stop working and go hiking with you.* For a synonym, see IF ONLY.

**wound** see LICK ONE'S WOUNDS; RUB IN (SALT INTO A WOUND).

**wrack** see under RACK AND RUIN.

**wrap** In addition to the idiom beginning with WRAP, also see TWIST (WRAP) AROUND ONE'S FINGER; UNDER WRAPS.

**wrapped up in** Completely preoccupied by or absorbed in an activity or a person, as in *She is wrapped up in her studies.* Also see WRAP SOMETHING UP.

**wrap *something* up** **1.** Bring something to a conclusion, settle successfully, as in *As soon as we wrap up this deal, we can go on vacation.* Also see WIND UP. **2.** Summarize something, as in *To wrap up, the professor went over the three main categories.*

**wreak havoc** see PLAY HAVOC.

**wreck** see NERVOUS WRECK.

**wrench** see THROW A MONKEY WRENCH.

**wringer** see under PUT THROUGH (THE WRINGER).

**wrist** see SLAP ON THE WRIST.

**write** In addition to the idioms beginning with WRITE, also see NOTHING TO WRITE HOME ABOUT.

**write down** **1.** Put something in writing, record, as in *Please write down your new address and phone number.* **2.** Reduce something in rank, value, or price, as in *They've written down their assets.* **3.** Write in a simple style or with a superior attitude, as in *These science texts are written down for high school students.*

**write *something* in** **1.** Cast a vote by inserting a name not listed on the ballot, as in *He asked them to write in his name as a candidate.* **2.** Insert something in a text or document, as in *Please don't write in your corrections on the printed pages; list them separately on a blank piece of paper.* **3.** Communicate with an organization by mail, as in *Listeners are being asked to write in their requests.*

**write off** **1.** Reduce an asset's book value to zero because it is worthless, as in *The truck was wrecked completely, so we can write it off.* **2.** Cancel a debt from an account as a loss, as in *Since they'll never be able to pay back what they owe, let's just write off that debt.* Also see CHARGE OFF, def. 2. **3.** Regard something as a failure or worthless, as in *There was nothing to do but write off the first day of our trip because of the bad weather,* or *She resented their tendency to write her off as a mere housewife.* **4.** Amortize an asset, as in *We can write off the new computer network in two years or less.* Also see CHARGE OFF, def. 2.

**write one's own ticket** Set one's own conditions or course of action according to one's wishes or needs. For example, *This generous grant lets recipients write their own tickets.* This term uses *ticket* in the sense of "something entitling the holder to a privilege."

**write out** **1.** Express something in writing, especially in full form. For example, *Write out your request on this form,* or *No abbreviations allowed; you have to write everything out.* **2. write oneself out.** Exhaust one's energies or abilities by writing too much, as in *He's been doing a novel a year for ages, but now he's written himself out.*

**write up** **1.** Write a report or description, as for publication, as in *She's been writing up these local concerts for years.* **2.** Overvalue an asset, as in *That accountant is always writing up our equipment, forgetting depreciation.*

**writing on the wall** see HANDWRITING ON THE WALL.

**written all over one's face, be** Be obvious to everyone, as in *Guilt was written all over his face, so we knew he'd eaten all the cookies,* or *You can tell she's in love; it's written all over her face.*

**wrong** See BARK UP THE WRONG TREE; DO SOMEONE WRONG; GET SOMEONE WRONG; GET UP ON THE WRONG SIDE OF BED; GO WRONG; IN THE WRONG; ON THE RIGHT (WRONG) FOOT; ON THE RIGHT (WRONG) TACK (TRACK); RIGHT (WRONG) SIDE OF THE TRACKS; RUB ONE THE WRONG WAY; TAKE THE WRONG WAY; TWO WRONGS DO NOT MAKE A RIGHT.

**wrong end of the stick, the** **1.** A misunderstanding or distortion, as in *We ordered a full quart of rice, but the clerk got hold of the wrong end of the stick and sent us four quarts instead.* **2.** The worst or most unpleasant role in or result of a situation. For example, *Don't trust him—if you do, you'll end up on the wrong end of the stick.* This expression refers to a walking stick held upside down, which does not help a walker much. Also see SHORT END OF THE STICK.

**wrong-foot** Deceive by moving differently from what one expects, as in *He won quite a few points by wrong-footing his opponent.* This expression comes from tennis, where it means to hit the ball in the direction the opponent is moving away from.

**wrong scent, on the** On a false trail or track, as in *He managed to put the police on the wrong scent and got away.* This term refers to hunting with hounds.

**wrong side of** see under RIGHT SIDE, ON SOMEONE'S.

**wrong side of the tracks** A poor section of a town or city, as in *He didn't marry her because she was from the wrong side of the tracks.* The *tracks* here refer to railroad tracks. For an antonym, see RIGHT SIDE OF THE TRACKS.

**wrote the book on** Knows nearly everything about a particular subject, as in *Ask Dr. Lock; he wrote the book on pediatric cardiology,* or *I wrote the book on job-hunting; I've been looking for two years.* This expression is always put in the past tense.

# XxYyZz

**X marks the spot** This mark shows the location, as in *On the postcard, X marks the spot where we picked blueberries.*

**X-rated** So sexually explicit, vulgar, or obscene that one cannot repeat it, as in *His remarks on the quality of the food are X-rated.* This expression originally referred to a rating system established for motion pictures, in which films rated X could not be viewed by people under the age of 17.

**yadda, yadda, yadda** And so forth, because what is being reported is boring or already known or very predictable, as in *He told us all about his new job, his new car, his new this, yadda, yadda, yadda.*

**yank someone's chain** see PULL SOMEONE'S CHAIN.

**yard** see IN ONE'S OWN BACK YARD; WHOLE NINE YARDS.

**yarn** see SPIN A YARN.

**year** In addition to the idiom beginning with YEAR, also see ALL YEAR ROUND; ALONG IN YEARS; BY THE DAY (YEAR); PUT YEARS ON ONE'S LIFE; TAKE YEARS OFF ONE'S LIFE.

**year in, year out** Regularly, every year, as in *We've been going to the Cape, year in, year out, ever since we were children.*

**year round** see ALL YEAR ROUND.

**yellow streak, a** An element of cowardice, as in *His younger brother does seem to have a yellow streak.*

**yen** see HAVE A YEN FOR.

**yes and no** In some ways and not others, as in *Did you enjoy yourself? Yes and no, I liked the music itself but hated the conductor.* This idiom is always a reply to a question.

**yesterday** see NOT BORN YESTERDAY.

**yet** In addition to the idiom beginning with YET, also see AS YET.

**yet again** One more time, said of a behavior or situation of which one disapproves, as in *Yet again he's been arrested for drunk driving.*

**ying-yang** see UP THE WAZOO (YING-YANG).

**yon** see HITHER AND YON.

**you** In addition to the idioms beginning with YOU, also see ALL RIGHT FOR YOU; AS YOU PLEASE; BEFORE YOU CAN SAY JACK ROBINSON; BETTER SOMEONE THAN ONE; BETWEEN YOU AND ME; BITE THE HAND THAT FEEDS YOU; DO YOU READ ME; FOR SHAME (ON YOU); FUCK YOU; GOOD FOR (YOU); HOW DOES THAT GRAB YOU; HOW DO YOU DO; IF YOU CAN'T BEAT THEM, JOIN THEM; I'LL BE SEEING YOU; I TOLD YOU SO; LOOK BEFORE YOU LEAP; MY HEART BLEEDS FOR YOU; NO MATTER HOW YOU SLICE IT; NOT IF YOU PAID ME; NOW YOU'RE TALKING; PAY AS YOU GO; PRACTICE WHAT YOU PREACH; QUIT WHILE YOU'RE AHEAD; SAME TO YOU; SAYS WHO (YOU); SCREW YOU; THAT'S SOMEONE OR SOMETHING FOR YOU; WHAT DO YOU KNOW; WHAT DO YOU TAKE ME FOR; WHAT HAVE YOU; WHAT OF IT (WHAT'S IT TO YOU).

**you bet!** Also, **you bet your ass** or **you can bet your bottom** or **you can bet your bottom dollar** or **you can bet your (sweet) life.** You can be absolutely sure, definitely, as in *Are you coming? You bet I am,* or *You bet your ass I'll be there,* or *You can bet your sweet life that was Bill with another woman.* All these phrases in effect mean that one can be so sure of something that one's body or life or valuables can be wagered on it; *ass* is considered vulgar, and *bottom dollar* means "last dollar." In spoken English, this expression is usually pronounced "you betcha" and is very slangy.

**you better believe it** see YOU'D BETTER BELIEVE IT.

**you can lead a horse to water but you can't make it drink** Even favorable circumstances won't force one to do something one doesn't want to, as in *We've gotten all the college catalogs, but he still hasn't applied—you can lead a horse to water.* This expression is so well known that it is often shortened, as in the example.

**you can say that again!** Also, **you said it!** I totally agree with what you said, as in *What a relief that Ben didn't get hurt. You can say that again!* or *This is a huge house. You said it!*

**you can't take it with you** Enjoy material things while you're alive, as in *Go ahead and buy the fancier car; you can't take it with you.*

**you can't take someone anywhere** Also, **you just can't take some people anywhere.** A humorous way of saying that one has done something unacceptable or embarrassing in public. For example, *How sloppy—you've spilled coffee all over the table. I just can't take you anywhere,* or *Sorry I got in a fight with that bully—you can't take some people anywhere.*

**you can't win** Also, **you just can't win.** Whatever one does is wrong or not enough, as in *Every time I block one of the holes in the grass, I find another; you just can't win.* For a synonym, see DAMNED IF ONE DOES, DAMNED IF ONE DOESN'T.

**you can't win 'em all** Success is not guaranteed, as in *They published your article but not your rebuttal to the reviewer? Well, you can't win 'em all.* For a synonym, see WIN SOME, LOSE SOME.

**you could cut it with a knife** Something very thick, such as muggy air or a heavy accent; also, a very tense atmosphere. For example, *The smoke was so thick you could cut it with a knife,* or *When I walked in, they all stopped talking and you could cut the air with a knife.*

**you'd better believe it!** Also, **you better believe it!** You can be sure, as in *You walk ten miles every day? You'd better believe it!* This imperative is almost synonymous with YOU BET.

**you don't say!** How surprising, is that true? Also, I find that hard to believe. For example, *I've been working on this project for two years. You don't say,* or *The man who runs this soup kitchen is a real saint. You don't say!* This expression, a shortening of **you don't say so,** may be used literally or ironically.

**you get what you pay for** Cheap goods or services are likely to be inferior, as in *That vacuum cleaner fell apart in a year—I guess you get what you pay for,* or *The volunteers take three times as long with the mailing, but you get what you pay for.*

**you just can't take some people anywhere** see YOU CAN'T TAKE SOMEONE ANYWHERE.

**you just can't win** see YOU CAN'T WIN.

**you just don't get it** see under GET IT, def. 2.

**you know** You are aware, you see, do you remember, used to get a positive response from the person being addressed, as in *You know that old shirt I used to have?* or *She's very lonely, you know, so do go and visit,* or *You know, this exhibit ends tomorrow,* or *You know that black dog our neighbors had? She was run over a year ago.* As a question, it is also used to be sure that the person addressed has understood the message completely, as in *You know what I mean?* or *There are some things we can't tolerate, you know?* This expression is probably a shortened version of *Do you know what I mean?* The phrase is also quite often a conversational filler, equivalent to "um" and occasionally repeated over and over (as in *It's a fine day for, you know, the beach, and, you know, we could leave now*). This usage is more oral than written, and many consider its repeated use to be a sign of ignorance.

**you know something?** Also, **you know what?** Listen to what I'm going to tell you, as in *You know something? He's always hated spicy food,* or *You know what? They're not getting married after all.* These expressions are shortenings of *Do you know something?* or *Do you know what?* and are used to emphasize the following statement or to introduce a surprising fact or comment. The variant should not be confused with WHAT DO YOU KNOW or YOU KNOW.

**you know who** I do not need to refer to the person by name because you know as well as I do who I'm talking about. For example, *Did you invite you know who to the party?* or *You know who showed just as we were leaving.* Also see WHO SHALL REMAIN NAMELESS.

**you name it** Everything one can think of, as in *We've got a tent, sleeping bag, food—you name it.*

**you never can tell** Also, **you never know.** Perhaps, possibly, one can't be certain, as in *You never can tell, it might turn into a beautiful day,* or *You may yet win the lottery—you never know.* The first term uses *tell* in the sense of "discern."

**young at heart** Having a youthful outlook, especially in spite of one's age. For example, *She loves carnivals and fairs; she's a grandmother, but she's young at heart.*

**you're all set** A phrase used at the end of a transaction. For example, *The clerk handed me the change and said, "You're all set."*

**you're telling me** I'm well aware of that, as in *She's a terrific dancer. You're telling me! I taught her how,* or *You're telling me, the prices are very high here.*

**you're welcome** Also, **don't mention it.** No thanks are needed, I was glad to do it. For example, *Thanks for picking me up. You're welcome,* or *I appreciate what you did for Mother. Don't mention it.* Both phrases are polite formulas for responding to thanks. For synonyms, see FORGET IT; NO PROBLEM, def. 2. Also see WELCOME TO.

**your guess is as good as mine** I don't know any more than you do, as in *As for when he'll arrive, your guess is as good as mine.*

**yours** In addition to the idiom beginning with YOURS, also see UP YOURS.

**yours truly** **1.** A closing formula for a letter, as in *It was signed "Yours truly, Mary Smith."* **2.** I, me, myself, as in *Jane sends her love, as does yours truly.*

**your word is my command** Also, **your wish is my command.** I am willing to do whatever you tell me to do, as in *Is it time to walk the dog? Your word is my command,* or *Your wish is my command—should I leave now?* This expression is also used to hint that one finds a person arrogant, as in *Get you another beer? Your wish is my command.*

**you said it** In addition to the idiom beginning with YOU SAID IT, also see YOU CAN SAY THAT AGAIN.

**you said it, I didn't** Even though you made the remark about something, I agree with you but am not responsible for saying it. For example, *I don't know why I acted so nasty. You said it, I didn't,* or *He'll never get a promotion with his attitude. You said it, I didn't.*

**you scratch my back and I'll scratch yours** see SCRATCH ONE'S BACK.

**you've got me there** I have no idea, I'm completely confused, as in *How long will we have to wait in line? You've got me there.* This expression is also shortened to **got me,** as in *When did the dog run off? Got me!*

**you've lost me** I can't follow what you're saying, I'm puzzled or confused. For example, *Please explain it again; you've lost me.* This phrase transfers losing one's way to failing to understand something.

**Z** see CATCH SOME Z'S; FROM SOUP TO NUTS (A TO Z).

**zap out** Interrupt or delete unwanted parts of a television program or video, as in *We've taped the show, and now we can zap out all the commercials.*

**zero in on** **1.** Aim precisely at a target, as in *They zeroed in on the last snipers.* **2.** Direct one's attention to something, concentrate or focus on, as in *We must zero in on the exact combination of ingredients,* or *The whole class zeroed in on the new assignment.* This usage transfers aiming a firearm to directing one's attention. **3.** Come together at a point, close in on, as in *The children zeroed in on the electric train display.*

**zone out** Stop paying attention, remove oneself mentally from a situation; also, engage in a mindless activity. For example, *When Felicia starts talking about her ailments and her friends' ailments, I totally zone out.* This idiom also occurs in the passive, **be zoned out.** It originally referred to narcotic intoxication and then was broadened to other kinds of dissociation. For a synonym, see TUNE OUT, def. 2.

**zonk *one* out** **1.** Completely tire one, as in *Climbing that last cliff zonked me out.* **2.** Be or get very high on drugs, as in *Smoking all that marijuana really zonked him out.* Both usages of this expression can be used in the passive voice. For example, *I'm zonked out after working all day,* or *The last time we saw her she was zonked out on some drug.*

**zoo** see IT'S A ZOO.

**zoom in on** **1.** Obtain a close-up view of the subject with a camera, as in *The TV people zoomed in on the Olympic gold medalist.* **2.** Focus on something, examine closely, as in *The moderator got the panelists to zoom in on the health-care issue.*